PROPERTY
Land Ownership and Use

PROPERTY
Land Ownership and Use

Fourth Edition

CURTIS J. BERGER
Lawrence A. Wien Professor of Law
Columbia University

JOAN C. WILLIAMS
Professor of Law
American University College of Law

ASPEN LAW & BUSINESS
A Division of Aspen Publishers, Inc.

Permissions
Aspen Law & Business
A Division of Aspen Publishers, Inc.
1185 Avenue of the Americas
New York, NY 10036

2 3 4 5

To Viv

     —C.J.B.

To my father, Norman Williams (1915–1996),
who dedicated his life to these issues

     —J.C.W.

SUMMARY OF CONTENTS

CONTENTS

LIST OF FIGURES

PREFACE

This is at once both a fourth edition and an original manuscript. Users of the prior editions will see some familiar ground and friendly old faces. But they will also find much that is new. The changes reflect far more than the 14-year interval from the earlier edition. They also reflect the new partnership of authors and their melded views as to the scope and direction of the basic property course.

Professor Williams uses these materials in a year-long, five-hour, first-year course. Professor Berger excludes Chapter 12 (real estate transactions) in his four-hour, second-semester course. A brief summary of each chapter reveals our course design:

Chapter 1 introduces three visions of property — the feudal vision, the republican vision, and the liberal vision — and plays them against the intuitive image of property ownership that most students (and other laypersons) begin with. We see these visions in such varied settings as homeownership, wild animals, intellectual property, Native American property, and welfare benefits.

Chapter 2 presents the feudal core: estates in land and the law of wealth transmission. Here, students meet the common-law estates, as well as that bug-a-boo, the Rule against Perpetuities, and its less formalistic cousin, the Rule against Unreasonable Restraints on Alienation. Compared with the earlier editions, this chapter is somewhat expanded, with more attention, for example, to future interests. But to make the material also more user-friendly, the authors have added many examples and problems to guide students and test their grasp.

Chapter 3 moves through landlord and tenant law. The chapter stresses rental housing and examines who the tenants and the owners are and the economics of this demography. In many instances, the materials contain not only cases but also statutory and lease clauses to help inform the doctrine and strengthen the students' lawyering skills. One student's detailed account of her representation of an indigent tenant in an actual summary proceeding reveals how complex even a simple matter often becomes.

Chapter 4 deals with common ownership. It includes the common law concurrent estates, an extended section on marital property, and how equitable distribution has reshaped (or failed to reshape) the property rights of marriage partners.

Chapter 5 (Adverse Possession) and 6 (Eminent Domain) make an attractive package as they explore two settings in which an intuitive image of property — one should be free *not* to transfer ownership — is violated.

Chapter 7 (Easements, Covenants, and Servitudes) has been wholly revamped from the earlier edition. In presenting this material, we have borrowed heavily from the structure and content of the A.L.I. Restatement of Servitudes project, begun in the mid-1980s and now nearing its terminus. The new Restatement has sought to eliminate much of the mysticism and all of the confusion that has plagued this body of law. While we believe it necessary to inform students as to how the mess happened, we trust that, as lawyers trained in the new Restatement, they will be ready to clean the mess up.

Chapter 8 is a lengthy treatment of regulatory takings law, from *Pennsylvania Coal* through *Dolan* and beyond. The chapter makes clear, as it moves through this murky domain, that takings law is not an internally consistent area of doctrine, but rather opposing arguments, complete with different views of which cases are the "leading" cases, what cases mean, and what is at stake politically and financially.

Chapter 9 continues our look at land-use regulation, in part through the eyes of a planner, with discourse as to whether zoning and other controls do more mischief than good. The chapter examines Euclidian zoning, statewide planning acts, growth controls, developer exactions, and efforts to end exclusionary zoning. The chapter ends with procedural material, including the transcript of a variance hearing, and a section on nonconforming uses.

Chapter 10 is brand new. Its theme is discrimination, and it surveys the endless battle to end unreasonable discrimination, both private and public, in the sale, rental, service-providing, and regulation of housing. The chapter examines the law's current status for four protected groups: racial minorities, the physically or mentally impaired, nonmarried partners, and families with children.

Chapter 11, Commodification, is also new. The chapter asks whether whatever has possible commercial value can be the object of commerce. The answer, clearly, is no, vis., the Thirteenth Amendment or the sale of one's vote, but not every line is so well drawn. The material forces students to plumb their most basic beliefs as they examine the sale of bodily parts, the rental of a woman's womb, or the acquiring of Native American artifacts.

Chapter 12 introduces students to the basic real estate transaction through text, problems, and standard documents, as well as a sprinkling of cases. We have organized the chapter around the four stages of a transaction for the sale or purchase, including the financing, of a house: contract formation, the executory interval, the closing, and the postclosing. Much of this material is reprinted from Berger and Johnstone, Land Transfer and Finance (4th edition).

Students often begin their study of property prepared to find the subject static and dull. This may have once been true, but modern property, which this text has sought to portray, touches on some of life's most fundamental issues and, individually, on some of our deepest views on the role of government and the uses of wealth. The authors would be surprised if property does not become for most students one of their most intellectually challenging and rewarding experiences in the first year of law school.

Curtis Berger
Joan Williams

January 1997

ACKNOWLEDGMENTS

We would like to acknowledge the help of a supportive community of friends, colleagues, and support staff who gave up their time to help us work on this project. These include Evelyn Abavanel, Elizabeth Andrews, Ashley Barr, Susan Bennett, Barbara Bezdek, Donna Bradley, Taylor Branch, Dawn Browning, Barlow Burke, Amy Carpenter, Christopher Crean, Adrienne Davis, James X. Dempsey, Julie Dimmick, Johnna Dumler, Jackie Duobinis, Liz Finberg, Terry Fisher, Ilsa Flanagan, Terry Frazier, Swata Gandhi, Deborah Gardner, Elma Gates, Laura Geyer, Mary Ann Glendon, Nancy Griffitts, Jenifer Gundlack, Patricia Hammes, Chester Hartman, Ann Marie Hay, Frederick Hertz, Sharon Huie, Peter Jaszi, Reesha Kang, Kate Kendall, James Kloppenberg, Jodi Kraus, Megan Mahoney, Maureen Markwith, Jane Marquardt, Paul Melbostad, Frank Michelman, Binnie Miller, Jennifer Boughner Miller, Ronald Morales, Elizabeth Morgan, Laura Mozeleski, Elizabeth Nowicki, Karen Nowregrod, Arzoo Osanloo, Marc Poirier, Peggy Radin, Jaime Raskin, Gabriela Richeimer, Florence Roisman, Eleanor Sanchez, Scott Semer, Janice Simmons, Janet Spragens, Catherine Starakis, Glenn Sugamelli, George Thomas, Amanda Van Beuren, Burt Weschler, Cornel West, Mark Williams, Norman Williams, Judith Winston, James Witkin, and Sarah Wollman.

The authors acknowledge the permissions kindly granted to reproduce the materials indicated below.

Samuel Bassett Abbott, Housing Policy, Housing Codes, and Tenant Remedies: An Integration. Boston University Law Review. Reprinted with permission.

Bruce Ackerman, Regulating Slum Housing Markets on Behalf of the Poor: Of Housing Codes, Housing Subsidies and Income Distribution Policy. Reprinted by permission of The Yale Law Journal Company and Fred B. Rothman & Company from The Yale Law Journal, Vol. 80, pages 1093-1197.

Gregory Alexander, Dilemmas of Group Autonomy: Residential Associations and Community. Reprinted with permission of the Cornell Law Review, Vol. 75, no. 1 (1989).

Fran Ansley, Standing Rusty and Rolling Empty: Law, Poverty and America's Eroding Industrial Base. Reprinted with permission of the publisher, Georgetown Law Journal, © 1993 Georgetown University.

Lance Banning, Jeffersonian Ideology Revisited. Reprinted with permission of the William and Mary Quarterly, Vol. 43, no. 3, pages 11-12.

Curtis J. Berger, Hard Leases Make Bad Law. Columbia Law Review. Reprinted with permission.

Barbara Bezdek, Silence in the Court: Participation and Subordination of Poor Tenants' Voices in Legal Process. Hofstra Law Review. Reprinted with permission.

John G. Casagrande, Acquiring Property Through Forced Partitioning Sales: Abuses and Remedies. Boston College Law Review. Reprinted with permission.

Felix Cohen, Transcendental Nonsense and the Functional Approach. This article originally appeared at 35 Columbia Law Review 809 (1935). Reprinted by permission.

Arthur L. Corbin, Jural Relations and Their Classification. Reprinted by permission of The Yale Law Journal Company and Fred B. Rothman & Company from The Yale Law Journal, Vol. 30, pages 226-238.

Leo Cullum, drawing: "Some people say you can't put a price on a wife's twenty-seven years of loyalty . . ." Copyright © 1993 The New Yorker Magazine, Inc. Reprinted with permission.

D.C. Court General Sessions, Landlord and Tenant: Self-Help. Permission granted by The Daily Washington Law Reporter.

Harold Demsetz, Toward a Theory of Property Rights. American Economic Review. Reprinted with permission.

Faye Ellman Photography, photo: "Symphony Space in Manhattan." Reprinted with permission.

Carl W. Engleman, cartoon: "I hold the organ donors record." The National Review Magazine. Reprinted with permission.

Richard R. Epstein, Past and Future: The Temporal Dimension in the Law of Property. Washington Law Quarterly. Reprinted with permission.

Henry Fagin, Regulation the Timing of Urban Development. Copyright © 1955 Law and Contemporary Problems, Duke University School of Law. Reprinted with permission.

William W. Fisher III, The Law of the Land: An Intellectual History of American Property Doctrine, 1776-1880 (Ph.D. diss., Harvard University, 1991). Reprinted with permission.

Folger Shakespeare Library, Art File S528 h1 #114, Delacroix, Hamlet with Yorrick's skull. From the Art Collection of the Folger Shakespeare Library. Reprinted with permission.

Eric Foner, Reconstruction: America's Unfinished Revolution. Reprinted with permission.

Lawrence M. Friedman, Government and Slum Housing: A Century of Frustration. Reprinted with permission.

Wendy J. Gordon, A Property Right in Self-Expression: Equality and Individualism in the Natural Law of Intellectual Property. Reprinted by permission of The Yale Law Journal Company and Fred B. Rothman & Company from The Yale Law Journal, Vol.102, pages 1533-1609.

Thomas C. Grey, The Disintegration of Property. Reprinted with permission.

Cathy Guisewite, cartoon. Cathy © 1995 Cathy Guisewite. Reprinted with permission of Universal Press Syndicate. All rights reserved.

Bob Hallinen, photo: "Villagers unloading a carved house post in Klukwan, Alaska." Anchorage Daily News. Reprinted with permission.

Henry B. Hansmann, The Economics of Markets for Human Organs. Journal of Health and Pol., Policy and Law. Reprinted with permission.

Cheryl Harris, Whiteness as Property. Harvard Law Review. Copyright © 1993 by the Harvard Law Review Association. Reprinted with permission.

Thomas Haskell, Capitalism and the Origins of the Humanitarian Sensibility, Part I. American Historical Review. Reprinted with permission.

Wesley Newcomb Hohfeld, Some Fundamental Legal Conceptions as Applied in Judicial Reasoning. Reprinted by permission of The Yale Law Journal Company and Fred B. Rothman & Company from The Yale Law Journal, Vol. 23, pp. 16-59.

Oliver Wendell Holmes, The Path of the Law. Copyright © 1897 by the Harvard Law Review Association. Reprinted with permission.

Morton J. Horwitz, The History of the Public/Private Distinction. Copyright © 1982 University of Pennsylvania Law Review and Fred B. Rothman & Company. Reprinted with permission from 130 University of Pennsylvania Law Review, Vol. 130, page 1423.

Richard Huber, Creditor's Rights in Tenancies by the Entireties, 1 Boston College Industry and Com. Law Review 197. Reprinted with permission.

Karkkainen, A Reply to the Critics. Copyright © 1994 Journal of Land Use and Environmental Law. Reprinted with permission.

Stanley N. Katz, Thomas Jefferson and the Right to Property in Revolutionary America. Journal of Law and Economics. Reprinted with permission.

Duncan Kennedy, The Effect of the Warranty of Habitability of Low Income Housing: Milking and Class Violence. Copyright © 1987 Florida State University Law Review. Reprinted with permission.

King Features Syndicate, cartoon: "Curtis" (2/2/96). Reprinted with special permission of King Features Syndicate.

King Features Syndicate, cartoon: "Mutts" (8/27/95). Reprinted with special permission of King Features Syndicate.

Nancy Oliver Lesourd, A Case Study—Now Comes the Defendant, By and Through Counsel. Reprinted with permission.

New York Times, "Contract to share a lottery ticket, August 23, 1985." Copyright © 1985 by The New York Times Company. Reprinted with permission.

Georgia O'Keeffe, "Cow's Skull with Calico Roses." Copyright © 1995 The Art Institute of Chicago. Reprinted with permission.

Peabody Essex Museum, Embroidery, "Home Sweet Home," negative 30, 389. Reprinted courtesy of Peabody Essex Museum, Salem, Massachusetts.

Lisa Peattie, Reflections on Advocacy Planning, 34 J. Am. Inst. Planners 80 1968. Reprinted by permission of the Journal of the American Planning Association, (or Journal of the American Institute of Planners if applicable).

Constance Perin, Everything in Its Place. Copyright © 1977 by Princeton University Press. Reprinted by permission of Princeton University Press.

Richard A. Posner, Economic Analysis of Law. Reprinted with permission.

Anthony T. Kronman and Richard Posner, The Economics of Contract Law. Reprinted with permission.

J. Robert Pritchard, A Market for Babies. Reprinted with permission from 34 University of Toronto Law Journal 341 (1984).

Margaret Jane Radin, Reinterpreting Property. Stanford Law Review. Reprinted with permission.

Margaret Jane Radin, "Time, Possession and Alienation" from Reinterpreting Property (University of Chicago Press 1993). Reprinted with permission.

Margaret Jane Radin, "Justice and the Market Domain" from Market Rhetoric and Reality: Commodification in Words and the World (Harvard University Press 1995). Reprinted with permission.

Margaret Jane Radin, "Market Inalienability" from Market Rhetoric and Reality: Commodification in Words and the World (Harvard University Press 1995). Reprinted with permission.

Lois Raimondo, photo: "Beach house damage from storm on Long Island." NYT Pictures. Reprinted with permission.

Charles A. Reich, The New Property. Reprinted by permission of The Yale Law Journal Company and Fred B. Rothman & Company from The Yale Law Journal, Vol. 73, pages 733, 787.

Henry R. Richmond, From Sea to Shining Sea: Manifest Destiny and the National Land Use Dilemma, 13 Pace Law Review 327 (1993). Reprinted with permission.

Carol Rose, Property as Storytelling: Perspectives from Game Theory, Narrative Theory, Feminist Theory. Copyright © 1990 Yale Journal of Law and the Humanities. Reprinted with permission.

Saxon, drawing: "I feel I should warn you. They've taken down most of Boston. . . ." Copyright © 1969 The New Yorker Magazine, Inc. Reprinted with permission.

Schomburg Center for Research in Black Culture, image: Woodcut illustration of Harriet Tubman, c. 1863-68. Sc-CN-79-0274. The New York Public Library. Reprinted with permission.

Robert Schoshinkski, American Law of Landlord and Tenant. Reprinted with permission of the copyright holder, Clark Boardman Callaghan, a division of Thomson Legal Publishing.

Joseph William Singer, The Legal Rights Debate in Analytical Jurisprudence from Bentham to Hohfeld. Wisconsin Law Review. Reprinted with permission.

John G. Sprankling, An Environmental Critique of Adverse Possession. Cornell Law Review. Reprinted with permission.

Glenn P. Sugameli, Takings Issues in Light of Lucas v. South Carolina Coastal Council: A Decision Full of Sound and Fury Signifying Nothing. The Virginia Environmental Law Journal. Reprinted with permission.

E. M. W. Tillyard, The Elizabethan World Picture. Copyright © 1943 Alfred A. Knopf Inc. Reprinted with permission.

Harriet Tubman, Woodcut Illustration, c. 1863-68. Schomburg Center for Research in Black Culture, Photographs and Prints Division, New York Public Library, Astor, Lenox and Tilder Foundations.

James A Wickersham, The Quiet Revolution Continues: The Emerging New Model for State Growth Management Statutes. Harvard Environmental Law Review. Copyright © 1994 by the President and Fellows of Harvard College. Reprinted with permission.

Norman Williams Jr., Planning Law and Democratic Living. Law and Contemporary Problems. Reprinted with permission.

Patricia J. Williams, On Being the Object of Property. Signs: Journal of Women in Culture and Society. Reprinted with permission.

Patricia J. Williams, Spare Parts, Family Values, Old Children, Cheap. New England Law Review. Copyright © New England School of Law 1994. All rights reserved. Reprinted by permission.

Patty Wood, photo: "Zoning — Houston, Texas." Washington Post. Reprinted with permission.

Marlene Stein Wortman, Women in American Law. Holmes & Meier Publishers, Inc. Reprinted with permission.

Jeanie Wylie, Poletown, Community Betrayed. University of Illinois Press. Reprinted with permission.

Yale Alumni Magazine, The Yale Campaign advertisement. The Yale Campaign. Reprinted with permission.

Zillman and Deeny, Legal Aspects of Solar Energy Development, 1976 Arizona State Law Journal 25 (1976). Reprinted with permission.

A NOTE TO STUDENTS

Lawyering involves different kinds of skills. One important one, traditionally stressed in the Property course, is the ability to state a legal test, apply it to the facts at hand, and draw conclusions. Here's an example:

Rule: Finders keepers.[1]
Facts: A chimney sweep finds a jewel, which he brings to a jeweler for appraisal. Instead the jeweler keeps the jewel, on the grounds that he has as much right to it as has the sweep, who clearly was not the true owner. The sweep sues to recover the jewel.[2]
Apply the law/draw conclusions: The sweep is the finder, so he is entitled to the jewel. The sweep wins.

In this context, law tends to look like a neutral system of self-executing rules. The ability to state the test, apply the test, and draw conclusions are important skills, but limited ones. What if, for example, you represent a client in the following situation.

New facts: Your client A finds a jewel. While he is taking it for appraisal, it falls out of his pocket onto the sidewalk, where B finds it. A notices it is gone in half a block and returns to find B just pocketing the jewel.
Apply the law: Note that A's lawyer can argue "finders keepers," but so can B's lawyer. Instead of acting as if the law is merely "a

---

1. This is actually the law, although the "losers weepers" is not accurate: The true owner ordinarily can recover her lost property from a finder if she (a) can identify the finder and (b) takes action within the statute of limitations period. See Ray A. Brown, The Law of Personal Property 26 (Walter B. Raushenbush ed., 1975). Also, many states have lost property procedures that require the deposit of found property with the police, to be held for a statutory period, and returned to either the owner or, if no claimant proves ownership, the finder. N.Y. Pers. Prop. Law, §§252, 253 (McKinney 1992). Presumably the true owner is not crying because of her lack of a legal right, but because of the practical unlikelihood of recovery.
2. Armorie v. Delamirie. 93 Eng. Rep. 664 (1722). Actually, it was a goldsmith's apprentice who withheld the jewel from the sweep's "boy."

math problem with humans,"[3] each lawyer must give *reasons* why the judge should interpret the rule in favor of her client.[4]

The job of a litigator (a lawyer trying a case) is to apply the law in a creative way to argue that his client wins.[5] In this context, law looks less like a neutral system of self-executing rules than like a system of persuasion that calls not only on crystallized "rules" but also on legal culture and the larger political culture. Indeed, law looks like a system of persuasion every time lawyers (including judges) are involved in giving *reasons* for their decisions, to defend their application of the rules (or to argue that the rules should be changed).

This casebook is designed to help you state the test, apply the test, and draw conclusions: These are the bread and butter of the first-year property course.[6] Yet these materials also provide an introduction to property law as a system of persuasion. To understand what kinds of reasons lawyers and judges tend to give in property cases, you will need to become familiar with the different visions of property law that coexist in American law and politics. These visions will help in analyzing the rationales of the court opinions, in generating creative arguments, and in understanding the two key changes in American property law since 1950: the so-called revolution in landlord-tenant law,[7] discussed in Chapter 3, and the ongoing struggle over takings law, discussed in Chapter 8.

These materials also attempt to teach other legal skills not traditionally taught in first-year courses. Statutes play a central role in American law: In property law, the interplay between statutes and case law often forces real dilemmas—when is statutory, rather than common-law, change the better-suited vehicle for reform? As you will see, property law has become heavily

---

3. Carol Gilligan, In a Different Voice 26 (1982).

4. In fact, over time, the "finders keeper" rule has been generalized to include either finders or prior possessors, so that A would probably win, assuming that he could convince a court he actually gained possession of the jewel. See Clark v. Maloney, 3 Del. (3 Harr.) 68 (1840). But suppose that A had found the jewel lying in B's front yard, where it had been lost by B's house guest, C. On this version of the facts, B might well prevail against A. Cf. South Staffordshire Water Co. v. Sharman, 2 Q.B. 44 (1986) (P hired D, a workman, to clean out a pool on P's land. D found two gold rings in the mud at the bottom of the pool. The owner of the rings could not be found. Held: P entitled to recover rings).

5. Within bounds set by your own sense of propriety and by the American Bar Association's Model Rules of Professional Conduct (1983), which set out minimum ethical standards for lawyers and which most states have now enacted, often somewhat modified. ABA Model Rule 3.1 says in part that "a lawyer shall not bring or defend a proceeding, or assert or controvert an issue therein, unless there is a basis for doing so that is not frivolous, which includes a good faith argument for an extension, modification or reversal of existing law."

6. This skill tends to be emphasized in Property because of the prevalence of crystallized legal tests. See Carol Rose, Crystals and Mud in Property Law, 40 Stan. L. Rev. 577 (1988).

7. See Edward H. Rabin, The Revolution in Landlord/Tenant Law: Causes and Consequences, 69 Cornell L. Rev. 517 (1984) (crediting Samuel B. Abbott for calling the transformation of landlord/tenant law in the 1970s a revolution).

codified. This casebook, therefore, spends substantial time examining statutes and requiring statutory analysis.

Another skill required for the practice of property law is the ability to handle documents. When a client comes to a lawyer with a landlord-tenant problem or with a question about a real estate transaction, often the first step is to read the relevant documents. Now that you are in law school, you may well find relatives and friends consulting you about their mortgages, leases, and other real estate matters. You may believe that anyone with a college degree should be able to read a legal document, but to read a legal document as would a college graduate and to read a legal document as would a careful and informed lawyer are two tasks worlds apart. Most of the legal documents contained in this casebook are actual documents from real transactions. However, most of the names and other identifying information has been changed to protect the privacy of those involved. When you have completed this course, you will better understand the difference.

Good luck! Lawyering is a complex business, but it varies enough so that many different kinds of people, with different kinds of skills and interests, can succeed at it. These materials are meant, of course, to teach you property law. But they are also meant to spark your thoughts about what kind of lawyer you want to be.

MUTTS   *BY PATRICK M^{c}DONNELL*

PROPERTY
Land Ownership and Use

Chapter 1

Introduction: Different Visions of Property

§1.1   The Intuitive Image of Property

> Texans as a whole still pretty much have that little bit of pioneer spirit: I can do what I want with my property.[1]

> That is why the Englishmen's belief that his home is his castle and that the king cannot enter it, like the American's belief that he must be able to look any man in the eye and tell him to go to hell, are the very essence of the free man's way of life.[2]

We begin by asking ourselves, as representative Americans, what it means to own property. Take a minute to jot down at least five rights you have when you own property.

We will call this the intuitive image of ownership and will be testing it throughout the book to assess whether it accurately reflects the law and the institution of property in the United States at the cusp of a new century. Our study of property law suggests that Americans' beliefs are more complex than they suspect. We believe that various and quite different visions of property, each having its own historical and intellectual rationale, coexist in our tradition. We will examine each of these visions shortly. Before we do so, however, consider the following.

---

1. Laura E. Keeton & Dave Harmon, Officials Want More Authority to Regulate Rural Development, The Monitor (McAllen, Texas), May 5, 1994, at 7A (quoting a Rio Grande Valley lawyer).
2. Walter Lippman, The Method of Freedom 102 (1924).

1

THOMAS C. GREY, THE DISINTEGRATION OF PROPERTY

in Nomos XXII at 69, 69-70 (J. Roland Pennock & John W. Chapman eds., 1980)

I

In the English-speaking countries today, the conception of property held by the specialist (the lawyer or economist) is quite different from that held by the ordinary person. Most people, including most specialists in their unprofessional moments, conceive of property as *things* that are *owned by persons*. To own property is to have exclusive control of something — to be able to use it as one wishes, to sell it, give it away, leave it idle, or destroy it. Legal restraints on the free use of one's property are conceived as departures from an ideal conception of full ownership.

By contrast, the theory of property rights held by the modern specialist tends both to dissolve the notion of ownership and to eliminate any necessary connection between property rights and things. Consider ownership first. The specialist fragments the robust unitary conception of ownership into a more shadowy "bundle of rights." Thus, a thing can be owned by more than one person, in which case it becomes necessary to focus on the particular limited rights each of the co-owners has with respect to the thing. Further, the notion that full ownership includes rights to do as you wish with what you own suggests that you might sell off *particular aspects* of your control — rights to certain uses, to profits from the thing, and so on. Finally, rights of use, profit, and the like can be parcelled out along a temporal dimension as well — you might sell your control over your property for tomorrow to one person, for the next day to another, and so on.

Not only can ownership rights be subdivided, they can even be made to disappear as if by magic, if we postulate full freedom of disposition in the owner. Consider the convenient legal institution of the trust. Yesterday A owned Blackacre; among his rights of ownership was the legal power to leave the land idle, even though developing it would bring a good income. Today A puts Blackacre in trust, conveying it to B (the trustee) for the benefit of C (the beneficiary). Now no one any longer has the legal power to use the land uneconomically, or to leave it idle — that part of the rights of ownership is neither in A nor B nor C, but has disappeared.[3] As between B and C, who owns Blackacre? Lawyers say B has the legal and C the equitable ownership, but upon reflection the question seems meaningless: what is important is that we be able to specify what B and C can legally do with respect to the land.

---

3. No one has the right to leave Blackacre idle, since the legal owner has given over management of the trust to the trustee, who has a fiduciary duty to use the trust assets "productively" — ordinarily interpreted to mean that the trust assets must either increase in size, produce income, or both. — EDS.

The same point can be made with respect to fragmentation of owner-ship generally. When a full owner of a thing begins to sell off various of his rights over it — the right to use it for this purpose tomorrow, for that pur-pose next year, and so on — at what point does he cease to be the owner, and who then owns the thing? You can say that each one of many right holders owns it to the extent of the right, or you can say that no one owns it. Or you can say, as we still tend to do, in vestigial deference to the lay conception of property, that some conventionally designated rights consti-tute "ownership." The issue is seen as one of terminology; nothing signifi-cant turns on it.

NOTES AND QUESTIONS

1. **Blackstone and absoluteness.** "There is nothing which so gener-ally strikes the imagination, and engages the affections of mankind, as the right of property; or that sole and despotic dominion which one man claims and exercises over the external things of the world, in total exclusion of the right of any other individual in the universe." William Blackstone, Com-mentaries on the Laws of England in Four Books, book II, ch. 1, *2. Does this sound more like the specialist's or the ordinary person's view of prop-erty? According to one commentator, "Blackstone's sweeping definition of the right of property overstated the case; indeed, he devoted the succeed-ing 518 pages of [his *Commentaries*] . . . to qualifying and specifying the exceptions to his" absolutist definition of property.[4] Another author shows that conservative American lawyers took up Blackstone's image of absolute-ness to counter the spate of redistributive statutes passed by late eighteenth and early nineteenth century state legislatures. (Chief among these were debtor relief statutes, which forgave debts, thereby eliminating creditors' property rights.[5])

2. **Layperson to specialist.** We will call the image of property that Grey attributes to the ordinary person "the intuitive image of property." Your task is to compare the intuitive image with your own growing knowl-edge of property law, in order to watch (or resist) your transformation from a layperson into a specialist.

3. **Property as a "bundle of rights."** According to Grey, the "bundle of rights" conception of property first appears "in well-articulated form" in Wesley Newcomb Hohfeld, Some Fundamental Legal Conceptions as

4. Forrest McDonald, Novus Ordo Seclorum: The Intellectual Origins of the Constitu-tion 13 (1985). See also Robert P. Burns, Blackstone's Theory of the "Absolute" Rights of Property, 54 Cinn. L. Rev. 67 (1985) (emphasizing gap between Blackstone's image of abso-luteness and the law of property he describes).
5. See Stuart Bruchey, The Impact of Concern for the Security of Property Rights on the Legal System of the Early American Republic, 1980 Wis. L.R. 1135.

Applied in Judicial Reasoning, 23 Yale L.J. 16 (1913), excerpted in §1.2.b
infra.

The following case, which deals with whether the government has
regulated property to such a degree that it has in effect "taken" the property away from its owner, highlights the extent to which lawyers today agree
on the "bundle of rights" analysis. Note that the opinion was near unanimous on a court that included both liberals and conservatives.[6]

ANDRUS v. ALLARD

---

444 U.S. 51 (1979)

Mr. Justice Brennan delivered the opinion of the Court.

The Eagle Protection Act and the Migratory Bird Treaty Act are conservation statutes designed to prevent the destruction of certain species of
birds. Challenged in this case is the validity of regulations promulgated by
appellant Secretary of the Interior that prohibit commercial transactions in
parts of birds legally killed before the birds came under the protection of
the statutes. The regulations provide in pertinent part:

50 C.F.R. §21.2 (a)(1978)

Migratory birds, their parts, nests, or eggs, lawfully acquired prior to the effective date of Federal protection under the Migratory Bird Treaty Act . . . may
be possessed or transported without a Federal permit, but may not be imported, exported, purchased, sold, bartered, or offered for purchase, sale,
trade, or barter. . . .

50 C.F.R. §2.2 (a)(1978)

Bald eagles, alive or dead, or their parts, nests, or eggs lawfully acquired prior
to June 8, 1940, and golden eagles, alive or dead, or their parts, nests, or eggs
lawfully acquired prior to October 24, 1962, may be possessed, or transported
without a Federal permit, but may not be imported, exported, purchased,
sold, traded, bartered, or offered for purchase, sale, trade or barter. . . .

Appellees are engaged in the trade of Indian artifacts: several own
commercial enterprises, one is employed by such an enterprise, and one is
a professional appraiser. A number of the artifacts are partly composed of

---

6. Chief Justice Warren Burger agreed with the holding of the court but not, evidently,
with the reasoning of the opinion.

the feathers of currently protected birds, but these artifacts existed before the statutory protections came into force. After two of the appellees who had sold "pre-existing" artifacts were prosecuted for violations of the Eagle Protection Act and the Migratory Bird Treaty Act,[2] appellees brought this suit for declaratory and injunctive relief in the District Court for the District of Colorado. The complaint alleged that the statutes do not forbid the sale of appellees' artifacts insofar as the constituent birds' parts were obtained prior to the effective dates of the statutes. It further alleged that if the statutes and regulations do apply to such property, they [constitute a taking of private property in violation of] the Fifth Amendment. [The district court ruled in favor of the plaintiff Allard on both questions.] We reverse.

I

[The court ruled that the statutes did prohibit the sale of artifacts created prior to the passage of the statutes.]

II

We also disagree with the District Court's holding that, . . . the Eagle Protection and Migratory Bird Treaty Acts violate appellees' Fifth Amendment property rights because the prohibition wholly deprives them of the opportunity to earn a profit from those relics.

Penn Central Transportation Co. v. New York City, 438 U.S. 104, 123-128 (1978), is our most recent exposition on the Takings Clause.[7] That exposition need not be repeated at length here. Suffice it to say that government regulation — by definition — involves the adjustment of rights for the public good. Often this adjustment curtails some potential for the use or economic exploitation of private property. To require compensation in all such circumstances would effectively compel the government to regulate by *purchase*. "Government hardly could go on if to some extent values incident to property could not be diminished without paying for every such change in the general law." Pennsylvania Coal Co. v. Mahon, 260 U.S. 393, 413 (1922); see *Penn Central, supra*, at 124. . . .

The regulations challenged here do not compel the surrender of the artifacts, and there is no physical invasion or restraint upon them. Rather, a significant restriction has been imposed on one means of disposing of the

---

2. Appellee L. Douglas Allard was convicted and fined for violating the Eagle Protection Act, 16 U.S.C. §668(a), which establishes criminal penalties for unpermitted eagle sales. United States v. Allard, 397 F. Supp. 429 (D. Mont. 1975). Appellee Pierre Bovis was prosecuted under the Eagle Protection Act and under the Migratory Bird Treaty Act, 16 U.S.C. §707, which provides criminal penalties for the unlawful sale of migratory birds. United States v. Bovis, Nos. 75-CR-63 and 75-CR-66 (D. Colo. 1975).

7. *Penn Central* is no longer the most recent exposition of the Takings Clause. See Chapter 8 — EDS.

artifacts. But the denial of one traditional property right does not always amount to a taking. At least where an owner possesses a full "bundle" of property rights, the destruction of one "strand" of the bundle is not a taking, because the aggregate must be viewed in its entirety. . . . In this case, it is crucial that appellees retain the rights to possess and transport their property, and to donate or devise the protected birds.

It is, to be sure, undeniable that the regulations here prevent the most profitable use of appellees' property. Again, however, that is not dispositive. When we review regulation, a reduction in the value of property is not necessarily equated with a taking. Compare Goldblatt v. Hempstead, *supra,* at 594, and Hadacheck v. Sebastian, 239 U.S. 394 (1915), with Pennsylvania Coal Co. v. Mahon, *supra.*[22] In the instant case, it is not clear that appellees will be unable to derive economic benefit from the artifacts; for example, they might exhibit the artifacts for an admissions charge. At any rate, loss of future profits — unaccompanied by any physical property restriction — provides a slender reed upon which to rest a takings claim. Prediction of profitability is essentially a matter of reasoned speculation that courts are not especially competent to perform. Further, perhaps because of its very uncertainty, the interest in anticipated gains has traditionally been viewed as less compelling than other property-related interests. . . .

It is true that appellees must bear the costs of these regulations. But, within limits, that is a burden borne to secure "the advantage of living and doing business in a civilized community." Pennsylvania Coal Co. v. Mahon, *supra,* at 422 (Brandeis, J., dissenting). We hold that the simple prohibition of the sale of lawfully acquired property in this case does not effect a taking in violation of the Fifth Amendment.

Reversed.

NOTES AND QUESTIONS

1.   *Andrus* **and the intuitive image.** Does the Andrus v. Allard court project the image of property rights as absolute and unchanging? How does its image differ from the intuitive image of property?

2.   **Hodel v. Irving.** Compare Andrus v. Allard with Hodel v. Irving, 481 U.S. 704 (1987). In *Hodel,* the Court ruled unanimously that §207 of the Indian Land Conservation Act of 1983 effected a "taking" of property without just compensation.

Congress passed §207 to limit the fragmentation of title to Indian-owned lands. Under an earlier law, Congress had directed the division of the Great Reservation of the Sioux Nation, which had been communally

---

22. It should be emphasized that in *Pennsylvania Coal* the loss of profit opportunity was accompanied by a physical restriction against the removal of the coal.

owned, into 320-acre allotments for each male Sioux head of household and 160-acre allotments for most other individuals. "This legislation seems to have been in part animated by a desire to force Indians to abandon their nomadic ways in order to 'speed the Indians'' assimilation into American society, . . . and in part a result of pressure to free new lands for further white settlement." 481 U.S. at 706. The lands, however, were held in trust by the United States, and the beneficial owners (the Sioux Indians) were permitted to dispose of their interests only at their death, either by will or through intestacy.

Because of these arrangements, as successive generations came to hold the beneficial interests, ownership became fractionated, with some parcels having hundreds of beneficial owners. By the 1960s, according to congressional studies, more than 3 million acres were held by more than 6 heirs to the parcel. In one area, for example, the average tract had 196 owners.

Concern over this problem led to §207, which provided for the *escheat* to the tribe, at the death of the interest holder, of any beneficial interest representing 2 percent or less of the total acreage in a tract if the share had earned its owner less than $100 in the year preceding the owner's death. Congress provided no compensation to the putative owners (that is, heirs of the decedent) of the escheated interest.

In defending §207 against a takings claim, the United States relied partly on Andrus v. Allard, cleverly arguing that while the statute effectively abolished both descent and devise, it remained possible for the owners to control disposition upon death through complex inter vivos arrangements such as revocable trusts. Do you see how the *Andrus* opinion would support that argument? The Court, however, was unimpressed, and Justice O'Connor, writing for the Court, stated:

> But the character of the Government regulation here is extraordinary. In Kaiser Aetna v. United States, 444 U.S., at 176, 100 S. Ct., at 391, we emphasized that the regulation destroyed "one of the most essential sticks in the bundle of rights that are commonly characterized as property — the right to exclude others." Similarly, the regulation here amounts to virtually the abrogation of the right to pass on a certain type of property — the small undivided interest — to one's heirs. In one form or another, the right to pass on property — to one's family in particular — has been part of the Anglo-American legal system since feudal times. . . . Since . . . the availability of inter vivos transfer [does not] obviate the need for descent and devise, a total *abrogation* of these rights cannot be upheld.

481 U.S. at 716-717.

While *Hodel* was pending, Congress amended the escheat law, but the Supreme Court refused to consider the newer version, which did not apply to the land at issue. Under the amendment, the statute would permit landowners, in order to avoid escheat, to devise their (minimal) interest to any other owner of an undivided fractional interest, and would also permit tribes to adopt their own laws governing the disposition of escheatable interests. The amendment, too, has been deemed an unconstitutional taking, in that it continued to bar both the descent and devise of land to any heir who did not already own a share in the parcel. Youpee v. Babbitt, 67 F.3d 194 (9th Cir. 1995).

The Supreme Court had suggested that Congress might, to reduce fractionation, force owners to formally designate a single heir to avoid escheat. 481 U.S. at 718. Does this seem less objectionable? What if the measure applied to all owners, and not only to owners of miniscule interests?

3. **Property and expectations.** If the "intuitive" image of property stems from deeply felt expectations, what is the source of those expectations? Is property law simply a merry-go-round of circularity? Consider the following excerpt from Jeremy Bentham, whose eighteenth-century writings on property were very influential.

> The better to understand the advantages of law, let us endeavour to form a clear idea of *property*. We shall see that there is no such thing as natural property, and that it is entirely the work of law.
>
> Property is nothing but a basis of expectation; the expectation of deriving certain advantages from a thing, which we are said to possess, in consequence of the relation in which we stand towards it.
>
> There is no image, no painting, no visible trait, which can express the relation that constitutes property. It is not material, it is metaphysical; it is a mere conception of the mind.
>
> To have a thing in our hands; to keep it; to make it; to sell it; to work it up into something else; to use it; — none of these physical circumstances, nor all united, convey the idea of property. A piece of stuff which is actually in the Indies may belong to me, while the dress I wear may not. The ailment which is incorporated into my very body may belong to another, to whom I am bound to account for it.
>
> The idea of property consists in an established expectation; in the persuasion of being able to draw such or such an advantage from the thing possessed, according to the nature of the case. Now this expectation, this persuasion, can only be the work of law. I cannot count upon the enjoyment of that which guarantees it to me. It is law alone which permits me to forget my natural weakness. It is only through the protection of law, that I am able to enclose a field, and to give myself up to its cultivation, with the sure though distant hope of harvest.
>
> But it may be asked, what is it that serves as a basis to law, upon which to begin operations, when it adopts objects which under the name of property, it promises to protect? Have not men, in the primitive state, a *natural* expectation of enjoying certain things, — an expectation drawn from sources anterior to law?
>
> Yes. There have been from the beginning, and there always will be, circumstances, in which a man may secure himself by his own means, in the enjoyment of certain things. But the catalogue of these cases is very limited. The savage who has killed a deer, may hope to keep it for himself, so long as his

cave is undiscovered; so long as he watches to defend it, and is stronger than his rivals; but that is all. How miserable and precarious is such a possession! If we suppose the least agreement among savages to respect the acquisitions of each other, we see the introduction of a principle to which no name can be given, but that of law. A feeble and monetary expectation may result from time to time from circumstances purely physical; but a strong and permanent expectation can result, only from law. That which in the natural state was an almost invisible thread, in the social state, becomes a cable.

Property and law are born together, and die together. Before laws were made there was no property; take away laws, and property ceases.

Theory of Legislation: Principles of the Civil Code 111-113 (Hildreth ed. 1931).

4.   **Transcendental nonsense.** Felix S. Cohen wrote in the 1930s:

> . . . [I]n every field of law we should find the same habit of ignoring practical questions of value or of positive fact and taking refuge in "legal problems" which can always be answered by manipulating legal concepts in certain approved ways. In every field of law we should find peculiar concepts which are not defined either in terms of empirical fact or in terms of ethics but which are used to answer empirical and ethical questions alike, and thus bar the way to intelligent investigation of social fact and social policy. *Corporate entity, property rights, fair value,* and *due process* are such concepts. So too are *title, contracts,* . . . and all the rest of the magic "solving words" of traditional jurisprudence. Legal arguments couched in these terms are necessarily circular, since these terms are themselves creations of law, and such arguments add precisely as much to our knowledge as Moliere's physician's discovery that opium puts men to sleep because it contains a dormitive principle.

Transcendental Nonsense and the Functional Approach, 35 Colum. L. Rev. 809, 820, 826, 833, 840 (1935).

In place of "transcendental nonsense," Cohen recommends the "functional approach." "[I]nstead of assuming hidden causes or transcendental principles behind everything we see or do," Cohen recommends an approach based on experience.

> All concepts that cannot be defined in terms of the elements of actual experience are meaningless. . . . Creative legal thought will more and more look behind the pretty array of "correct" cases to the actual facts of judicial behavior, will make increasing use of statistical methods in the scientific description and prediction of judicial behavior, will more and more seek to map the hidden springs of judicial decision and to weigh the social forces which are represented on the bench. And on the critical side, I think that creative legal thought will more and more look behind the traditionally accepted principles of "justice"; and "reason" to appraise in ethical terms the social values at stake in any choice between two precedents.

Id. at 833. Cohen stressed not only the need to go outside the law to explain the patterns within it; he also stressed the ethical character of judicial decision making. "It is the great disservice of the classical conception of law that it hides from judicial eyes the ethical character of every judicial question, and thus serves to perpetuate class prejudices and uncritical moral assumptions that could not survive the sunlight of free ethical inquiry." Id. at 840.

5. **Talking persuasively about property.** If a clear rule exists that, when applied in a straightforward way, cuts for your client, your task as a lawyer is a relatively simple one. But what if the law suggests that your client should lose, whereas justice suggests that your client should win? What if there are two ways to apply the law, or two conflicting rules that potentially apply? How do you argue persuasively for your client's interest when your success turns on *giving persuasive reasons* why the client should win?

The standard law school formulation is that judges and other lawyers in these situations make "public policy" arguments. Think, for a moment, exactly what that means. Does it mean that law is politics by other means? If so, is it exactly like politics? (What kind of politics?) How is it similar to politics? How is it different?

The more you think about the "public policy" formulation, the less it seems to illuminate. What counts as "public policy"? When are "public policy" arguments appropriate? Conversely, when are they dismissed as "politics, not law"? What kinds of arguments are persuasive in what contexts?

In this book, we will attempt to go beyond the "public policy" formulation, to ask what arguments are considered persuasive (and suitably "legal") in what contexts. As we examine the rationales of judicial opinions and begin to formulate arguments of our own, we will note some established patterns of argumentation about property rights in the Anglo-American tradition. These patterns stem from the different visions of property explored below.

§1.2   Property as Social Glue: The Feudal Vision and Beyond

a.   The Feudal Vision

> The rich man in his castle,
> The poor man at his gate,
> God made them, high or lowly,
> And ordered their estate.[8]

As you read these materials, consider how the vision of property as social glue differs from the intuitive image of absolute "ownership."

8. Mrs. Cecil Frances Alexander, "All Things Bright and Beautiful," Hymns for Little Children, 1848.

The following excerpt describes an outlook it cites to a text written in the 1400s; in fact, the "great chain of being" is an outlook that lasted from feudal times into the eighteenth century.

E. M. W. TILLYARD, THE ELIZABETHAN WORLD PICTURE

25-27 (1943)

THE CHAIN OF BEING

. . . It would be easy to accumulate texts describing the chain of being. One of the finest short accounts is by Sir John Fortescue, the fifteenth-century jurist, in his Latin work on the law of nature:

In this order hot things are in harmony with cold, dry with moist, heavy with light, great with little, high with low. In this order angel is set over angel, rank upon rank in the kingdom of heaven; man is set over man, beast over beast, bird over bird, and fish over fish, on the earth, in the air and in the sea: so that there is no worm that crawls upon the ground, no bird that flies on high, no fish that swims in the depths, which the chain of this order does not bind in most harmonious concord. Hell alone, inhabited by none but sinners, asserts its claim to escape the embraces of this order. . . . God created as many different kinds of things as he did creatures, so that there is no creature which does not differ in some respect from all other creatures and by which it is in some respect superior or inferior to all the rest. So that from the highest angel down to the lowest of his kind there is absolutely not found an angel that has not a superior and inferior; nor from many down to the meanest worm is there any creature which is not in some respect superior to one creature and inferior to another. So that there is nothing which the bond of order does not embrace.

The most direct expressions of the feudal vision in contemporary property law are in the system of estates in land (discussed in Chapter 2), and in landlord-tenant law (discussed in Chapter 3). The so-called revolution in landlord-tenant law, accomplished in the 1960s and 1970s, is most often described as a shifting away from the feudal treatment of the lease, a theme we will examine in considerable depth. The system of estates in land — taught as the heart of the property course until very recently — dates directly back to the feudal era. There is, in addition, that remarkable invention of English law, the trust device, which evolved during the Middle Ages partly to avoid feudal strictures.

To understand the role of property in feudal society, keep in mind that when William the Conqueror ascended the English throne in 1066, he acquired a state that was unstable, chaotic, and dangerous; think of Beirut in the 1980s, with masses of hostile and heavily armed men laying waste to those engaged in ordinary life. The first force behind the feudal system was that overlords-in-the-making could not simply assemble and maintain the armies they needed to establish their power, for the simple reason that the feudal economy did not produce enough surplus to supply large armies. The result was that overlords obtained the services of the warriors necessary to keep themselves in power by offering conquered land in return for knight service. The knights thus became *tenants,* required to fight for the king for 40 days each year in return for their land grant. Almost all the land granted by William the Conqueror during his reign was granted in exchange for knight services. Thomas Bergin and Paul G. Haskell, Preface to Estates in Land and Future Interests 4 (1984).

From the overlords' perspective, the point of military tenures was to ensure a flow of military services. An outright, unconditional grant to the tenant in perpetuity would not accomplish this goal, for what if the grantee's heir was a weakling, or (God forbid) a woman? In early feudal times, therefore, the grants were conditional on continued service. Tenants pressed for more permanence. Gradually, the grants shifted from a temporary arrangement into a permanent grant for the life of the tenant. Still, though, land was not automatically inheritable, nor could it be sold.

Feudal society was organized in a hierarchical pyramid, with the king at the top, the tenants-in-chief below him, intermediate lords below them, all the way down to the serfs at the bottom of the pyramid. Military service played the central role at the top of the pyramid; at the bottom, the tenures involved not military, but agricultural services. Remember that Europe after the fall of Rome in 432 was poor and relatively empty, in sharp contrast with the flourishing and accomplished empires of Byzantium, China, and Arabia. Most peasants lived on grains, died before the age of thirty, and never traveled beyond five miles from the place they were born. Even lords with large land grants faced starvation if they could not obtain labor to work their land. And obtaining labor was difficult, given low population densities and the complete lack of transportation and communication systems and markets as we know them.

Imagine yourself as a peasant at this period. I come up and hit you, threatening to burn your crops and kill you. What would you do? Remember, police are a nineteenth-century invention.

Lords needed labor; peasants needed protection: thus emerged the bottom of the feudal pyramid. "Socage" tenure, the most common form of feudal tenure, involved the exchange of lordly protection for economic services ranging from 10 days' ploughing, to delivering a dish of mushrooms for the king's breakfast, to keeping a bridge in repair.

> So strong was the notion of tenure that, upon a grant, some service — even if symbolic — was thought to be due. A father granting land to a younger son might require yearly an arrow, feathered with eagle's feathers, or from a

daughter a red rose at midsummer. One Rowland is recorded as having held 110 acres for which on Christmas Day, every year, he was to perform before the king "altogether, and once, a leap, a puff [whistle], and a fart."

Thomas Blout, Ancient Tenures 60 (2d ed. 1784), quoted in Jesse Dukeminier and James E. Krier, Property 196 (3d ed. 1993).

Note first the literalness with which feudal law observed forms once they became established. This rigid insistence on observing the niceties of formal categories gives rise to the "crystals" of property law. As one insightful commentator has noted, property law entails an unusual combination of crystals and mud; we will study both, and ponder their relationship. See Carol Rose, Crystals and Mud in Property Law, 40 Stan. L. Rev. 577 (1988). Note, second, that the purpose of property in feudal society was to express and cement interdependent social relationships: The lord needed the peasants to work the land, or he would starve; the peasants needed the lords for protection, or their lands would be seized and they would starve.

In the early Middle Ages, these social relationships were not only conceptualized as temporary; they actually *were* temporary. Relatively soon, however, relationships initially conceived as temporary became more permanent. Gradually, the ordinary practice was for lords to pass on tenants' lands to their heirs automatically on the payment of a sum whose amount was a matter of tradition. History does not proceed smoothly in one direction, and lords periodically tried to reassert their formal right to grant feudal tenures to someone other than the sitting tenant, but property gradually became, in effect, inheritable by one's heirs according to preset rules; only much later (in 1540) were tenants given the right to devise their tenancies by will. Bergin and Haskell, Preface to Estates, *supra,* at 104. Property became salable by statute in the 13th century, when the great expansion of the rural population meant that demand for land rose, its value increased, and tenants were increasingly tempted to sell their land. In 1290, the complex Statute Quia Emptores gave lords some important rights in exchange for giving tenants the right to substitute a new tenant without permission of their lords. Bergin and Haskell, Preface to Estates, *supra,* at 16. In short, land became a salable commodity for the first time in the Anglo-American tradition.

The notion of property rights as expressing the interdependence of the community persisted long after the feudal period. "Absolute" ownership, a tradition inherited from Roman law, came to be seen as the norm by the early modern period, but the actual practice of Anglo-American property law retained many instances of simultaneous ownership rights in a single parcel. Legal historian Forrest McDonald points out that in the North American colonies many common rights still existed in "private" property, including rights of common grazing, wood gathering, hunting, passage, and water use. In southern colonies, common rights of grazing were so strong that the fencing of any land except arable land actually under cultivation was prohibited; an open-range system lasted until the twentieth century. Forrest McDonald, Novus Ordo Seclorum: The Intellectual Origins of the Constitution 30 (1985). In theory, these rights were limited by the prohibition against trespassing; in practice, the laws of trespass "contained so many exceptions as to be inconsequential except in regard lands or buildings actively in use for agricultural or residential purposes." Id. at 33.

NOTES AND QUESTIONS

1. **Mentality of legal participation.** How does the feudal "mentality of legal participation," described in the excerpt below, differ from the intuitive image of property?

diff by here R+S. are not viewed to be absolute but Community based

... [T]he word "ownership," as applied to landed property, would have been almost meaningless. . . . For nearly all land [was] burdened . . . with a multiplicity of obligations differing in their nature, but all apparently of equal importance. None implied that fixed proprietary exclusiveness. . . .The tenant who — from father to son, as a rule — ploughs the land and gathers in the crop; his immediate lord, to whom he pays dues and who, in certain circumstances, can resume possession of the land; the lord of the lord, and so on, right up the feudal scale — how many persons there are who can say, each with as much justification as the other, "That is my field!"

Marc Bloch, 1 Feudal Society 113-116 (L.A. Manyon trans., 1970).

2. **Canned history.** The classic, canned history is that property rights *used* to be absolute and recently have become less so. Is this description accurate? If not, why is it so prevalent? See §1.1 *infra.* they never were

3. **Compare attitudes towards hierarchy.** How did the attitude towards hierarchy in feudal times differ from our own? The high needed. the low to survive

4. **Autonomy or interdependence?** Did the feudal vision stress autonomy or interdependence? Which do we stress more? F=I W=A

5. **Stability or flexibility?** Did the feudal vision stress flexibility or stability in the design of legal categories and (other) social relationships? STAbility

b.   Modern Language of Property Rights as Defining Relationships among Persons: Hohfeld's Analysis

In a series of articles published between 1913 and 1917, Yale law professor Wesley Newcomb Hohfeld reformulated property theory to contest the intuitive image of property as defining absolute rights of people over things. Hohfeld returned to the feudal notion of property as establishing complex relationships among people. Hohfeld died shortly after completing the last of his articles, but his legacy, Hohfeldian analysis, remains part of the modern language lawyers use to describe property-based (and contract-based) relationships.

In one of his articles, Hohfeld focused on the difference between in personam and in rem rights.[9] This distinction, introduced by John Austin in 1832, was between rights against people (in personam) and rights against things (in rem). Hohfeld rejected this distinction by pointing out that all rights, in fact, are rights against people.

To illustrate Hohfeld's claim, let's return to finders law, see A Note to Students, *supra,* to the situation of A (a first finder) and B (a second finder). Who owns the jewel? Ownership is best described in terms of the complex relationships established by the legal rules amongst the various participants. A owns the jewel as against everyone but the true owner. B owns it as against everyone but A and the true owner. Still, it may not be the case that the true owner owns the jewel as against the whole world. If the true owner has abandoned the jewel, then his claim is extinguished; his claims also may be extinguished by adverse possession, discussed in Chapter 5.

In certain contexts, the rights of finders are subservient to the rights of the landowner on whose land the jewel is discovered. Compare South Staffordshire Water Co. v. Sharman, 2 Q.B. 44 (1896) (finder v. landowner; landowner wins); Favorite v. Miller, 407 A.2d 974 (Conn. 1978) (finder of pre-Revolutionary War statue v. landowner; landowner wins), with Bridges v. Hawkesworth, 21 L.J. (Q.B.) 75, 15 Jur. 1079 (finder v. landowner; finder wins); Hannah v. Peel, 1 K.B. 509 (1945) (finder v. landowner; finder wins).

Finders law is commonly held to show the *relativity of title,* a phrase designed to combat the intuitive image of absolute ownership, and to stress instead property law's role in expressing (and constituting) complex interrelationships among people. The excerpts that follow are summaries of Hohfeld from Hohfeld himself and from Arthur Corbin.

WESLEY NEWCOMB HOHFELD, FUNDAMENTAL LEGAL CONCEPTIONS AS APPLIED IN JUDICIAL REASONING

26 Yale L.J. 710, 746 (1917)

Suppose . . . that A is fee-simple owner of Blackacre. His "legal interest" or "property" relating to the tangible object that we call *land* consists of a complex aggregate of rights (or claims), privileges, powers, and immunities. *First:* A has . . . legal rights, or claims, that *others,* respectively, shall *not* enter on the land, that they shall not cause physical harm to the land, etc., such others being under respective correlative legal duties. *Second:* A has an indefinite number of legal privileges of entering on the land, using the land, harming the land, etc., that is, within limits fixed by law on

---

9. The standard law dictionary defines in rem as "a technical term used to designate proceedings or actions instituted *against the thing,* in contradistinction to personal actions, which are said to be in personam." Black's Law Dictionary 793 (6th ed. 1990). The distinction still exists in civil procedure.

grounds of social and economic policy, he has privileges of doing on or to the land what he pleases; and correlative to all such legal privileges are the respective legal no-rights of other persons. *Third:* A has the legal power to alienate his legal interest to another, i.e., to extinguish his complex aggregate of [legal] relations and create a new and similar aggregate in the other person . . . ; also the legal power to create a privilege of entrance in any other person by giving "leave and license"; and so on indefinitely. Correlative to all such legal powers are the legal liabilities in other persons, — this meaning that the latter are subject . . . to the changes of [legal] relations involved in the exercise of A's powers. *Fourth:* A has an indefinite number of legal immunities, using the term immunity in the very specific sense of non-liability or non-subjection to a power on the part of another person. Thus he has the immunity that no ordinary person can alienate A's legal interest or aggregate of [legal] relations to another person; the immunity that no ordinary person can extinguish A's own privileges of using the land; the immunity that no ordinary person can extinguish A's right that another person X shall not enter on the land or, in other words, create in X a privilege of entering on the land. Correlative to all these immunities are the respective legal disabilities of other persons in general.

In short, A has vested in himself, as regards Blackacre, . . . *in rem,* "right — duty" relations, . . . *in rem,* "privilege — no-right" relations, . . . *in rem,* "power — liability" relations, and . . . *in rem,* "immunity — disability" relations. It is important, in order to have an adequate analytical view of property, to see all these various elements in the aggregate. It is equally important, for many reasons, that the different classes of [legal] relations should not be loosely confused with one another. A's privileges, e.g., are strikingly independent of his rights or claims against any given person, and either might exist without the other. Thus A might, for $100 paid to him by B, agree in writing to keep off Blackacre. A would still have his rights or claims against B, that the latter should keep off, etc.; yet, as against B, A's own privileges of entering on Blackacre would be gone. On the other hand, with regard to X's land, Whiteacre, A has, as against B, the privilege of entering thereon; but, not having possession, he has no right, or claim, that B shall not enter on Whiteacre.

ARTHUR L. CORBIN, JURAL RELATIONS AND THEIR CLASSIFICATION

30 Yale L.J. 226, 226-229 (1921)

In determining what is the law in any given case, we are invariably interested in finding the answer to one question: what will our organized society, acting through its appointed agents, do? . . .

[T]here is no law and there can be no legal relations of any sort where there is no organized society. The fact that is essential is the existence of societal force; and the question that is of supreme interest is as to when and how that force will be applied. What will the community of citizens cause their agents to do? It is this multitude of busy little fellow citizens who constitute "society" or "the state," and it is their cumulative strength that constitutes the personified giant whose arm may be so powerful to aid or to destroy. In law, the ultimate question is, what will this giant do?

Now with respect to the little individual, who will be called A, in whose fortunes we may be interested, this giant either will or he will not act; there is no third possibility (although a wide variety is possible in the kind of act that he may do). And the little individual, A, himself, either can or he cannot do something that will stimulate the giant to act or not to act. The giant sleeps; can I wake him? He wakens; can I soothe him to inaction? From this it appears that we have four interesting possibilities: The giant will act so as to affect A, or he will not so act; A can influence the giant's conduct, or he cannot influence his conduct. Introduce a second little individual, B, and you at once double these interesting possibilities. The giant will act for A as against B, or he will not; he will act for B as against A, or he will not. A can influence the giant's action with respect to B, or he cannot; B can influence the giant's action with respect to A, or he cannot. Of course we are deeply interested in the particular sort of act the giant will do, and in the various ways in which A and B are able to affect the giant's conduct. . . . [However,] underneath [all legal relations] we have eight fundamental conceptions with respect to any two little individuals, A and B. The giant will aid A against B, or he will not; he will aid B against A, or he will not. A can stimulate the giant's conduct with respect to himself and B, or he cannot; B can so stimulate the giant's conduct, or he cannot. . . .

[Wesley Hohfeld chose words used in judicial reasoning to express these legal relations.] The concept that the giant will aid A by forcibly controlling B's conduct we express by saying that A has a *right*. If the giant will not so aid A, he has *no right*. If the giant will aid B by using force to control A's conduct, A has a *duty*. If he will not so aid B, and A is free from such constraint, this fact is expressed by saying that A has a *privilege*. If A can, by his voluntary act, influence the giant's conduct with respect to B, whether to act or not to act, and whether presently or contingently, A has a *power*. If A cannot do this, he has a *disability*. If B can, by his voluntary act, influence the giant's conduct with respect to A, A has a *liability*. If B cannot do this, A has an *immunity*. . . .

NOTES AND QUESTIONS

1. **Restatement of Property.** The Restatement of Property §§1-4 (1936) relied heavily on Hohfeld for several of its basic terms.[10]

10. The Restatements are produced by the American Law Institute, a group of established scholars, jurists, and practitioners. Whether the Restatements simply restate the existing

§1. *Right.*   A right, as the word is used in this Restatement, is a *legally enforceable claim of one person* against another, that the other shall do a given act or shall not do a given act.

Comment: a. Correlative duty.   The relation indicated by the word "right" may also be stated from the point of view of the person against whom that right exists. This person has *a duty,* that is, is under a legally enforceable obligation to do or not to do an act. The word "duty" is used in this Restatement with this meaning.

Illustration: 1. A is the owner of Blackacre. B is any other person. A normally has a right that B shall not walk across Blackacre. . . .

§2. *Privilege.*   A privilege, as the word is used in this Restatement, is *a legal freedom on the part of one person as against another* to do a given act or a legal freedom not to do a given act.

Comment: a. Correlative absence of right.   The relation indicated by the word "privilege" may also be stated from the point of view of the person against whom the privilege exists. From the point of view of this other person it may be said that there is no right on his part that the first person should not engage in the particular course of action or of nonaction in question.

Illustration: 1. A is the lessee of a farm. The lease contains a covenant with the landlord B that A will cultivate field one, and that he will not cultivate field two, and has no covenant as to field three. As between A and B, A has both the duty and privilege of cultivating field one; he has both the duty and the privilege of not cultivating field two; except so far as he is affected by the law of waste, he has the privilege of cultivating and the privilege of not cultivating field three.

§3. *Power.*   A power, as the word is used in this Restatement, is an ability *on the part of a person to produce a change in a given legal relation* by doing or not doing a given act.

Comment: a. Correlative liability.   The relation indicated by the word "power" may also be stated from the point of view of the person whose legal relation is thus liable to be changed. This subjection of the second person to having his legal relation affected by the conduct of the person having the power is a "liability" and the word is used in this Restatement with this meaning.

Illustrations: 1. A, the owner of Blackacre, gives B a power of attorney to transfer Blackacre to a purchaser. B has a power. A is under liability. . . .

3. B has the recorded title to Blackacre. He transfers the land to A. A does not record his deed. B makes a formally sufficient conveyance of the same land to C who buys in ignorance of the conveyance to A, and who pays full value for the land and records his deed. B in so conveying to C exercised a power to destroy A's interest and A was under a corresponding liability with regard to B. B has no privilege to do so and in doing so violates A's rights. . . .

§4. *Immunity.*   An immunity, as the word is used in this Restatement, is a *freedom on the part of one person against having a given legal relation altered* by a given act or omission to act on the part of another person.

Comment: a. Correlative disability.   The relation indicated by the word

---

law or try to influence its development is a matter of interpretation (and some dispute). (The emphasis here is ours.)

"immunity" may also be stated from the point of view of the person with respect to whom the immunity exists, that is, who has no ability so to alter the
given legal relation. This second person has, in this particular, a disability with
regard to the first person and the word "disability" is used in this Restatement
with this meaning. . . .

   Illustration: 1. A owns Blackacre in fee simple absolute. B is a judgment
creditor of A. B has a power with regard to Blackacre and A has a liability. A
discharges in full B's judgment debt. So far as B's powers as a judgment creditor are concerned, A now has an immunity and B has a disability with regard
to Blackacre.

   2.   **More on Hohfeld.** In addition to the 1917 Yale Law Journal article, *supra,* Hohfeld's influential series included:

   Some Fundamental Legal Conceptions as Applied in Judicial Rea-
      soning, 23 Yale L.J. 16 (1913)
   The Relations between Equity and Law, 11 Mich. L. Rev. 537 (1913)
   Supplemental Note on the Conflict of Equity and Law, 26 Yale L.J. 767
      (1917)
   Faulty Analysis in Easement and License Cases, 27 Yale L.J. 66 (1917)

   3.   **Hohfeld's defenders and critics.** Over the years, Hohfeld has had
both staunch defenders and vigorous assailants. Good examples of the latter include Isaac Husik, Hohfeld's Jurisprudence, 72 U. Pa. L. Rev. 263
(1924); Max Radin, A Restatement of Hohfeld, 51 Harv. L. Rev. 1141
(1938); Roy L. Stone, An Analysis of Hohfeld, 48 Minn. L. Rev. 313 (1963);
Jeanne Lorraine Schroeder, Virgin Territory: Margaret Radin's Imagery of
Personal Property as the Inviolate Feminine Body, 79 Minn. L. Rev. 55
(1994). The attack is met in Arthur L. Corbin, Jural Relations and Their
Classification, 30 Yale L. J. 226 (1921), and E. Adamson Hoebel, Fundamental Legal Concepts as Applied in the Study of Primitive Law, 51 Yale L. J. 951
(1942).

   4.   **Is Hohfeld's language predictive? Is it normative?** You should
quickly see that Hohfeldian analysis, while giving a clarifying language to
help describe property-based relationships, is neither predictive nor normative. Return to Andrus v. Allard and, speaking Hohfeldian, describe the
set of rights, privileges, powers, and so forth that emerge from the decision.
Does Hohfeld help you predict the Court's decision, or help you consider
whether the Court decided the case correctly?

   5.   **Circularity.** Recall Felix Cohen's argument that legal arguments
couched in terms like "property rights" "are necessarily circular, since
these terms are themselves creations of law, and such arguments add precisely as much to our knowledge as Moliere's physician's discovery that
opium puts men to sleep because it contains a dormitive principle." Cohen,
supra, at 820. To test Felix Cohen's observation: Did Andrus lose because he
had no property, or did Andrus have no property because he lost?

6.   **Two ways of looking at property.** This discussion suggests that Hohfeld was a central figure in the "disintegration" of property. As you proceed with your study of property law, try to formulate the various areas of law both in terms of people's rights over things and in terms of relationships among people. For example, does a landlord-tenant relationship involve an owner's (tenant's) rights with respect to a thing or an ongoing relationship between a landlord and a tenant?

c.   Native American Property: Use Rights v. Absolute Ownership

Virtually all of the land that was claimed by European settlers was settled prior to their arrival. See William W. Fisher III, The Law of the Land: An Intellectual History of American Property Doctrine, 1776-1880 (Ph.D. diss., Harvard Univ., 1991). The process by which Europeans claimed title to Native American lands was complex. European governments obtained some land through force; other land was transferred in transactions that settlers at times understood as transfers of property pursuant to a sale, while native inhabitants understood them as involving transfers of revokable use rights pursuant to a treaty.[11] William Cronon, Changes in the Land 66-69 (1983). In theory, representatives of European governments obtained title and then passed it on to the colonists. In practice, colonial governments and groups of settlers made deals with individual tribes. Sometimes the settlers' deals were ratified by the governments; sometimes they were not. Intense conflicts resulted between Native Americans and settlers as well as among settlers.

Most Native American property systems are closer to the participatory image of mutual sharing than to the intuitive image of absolute ownership. In Native American societies, as in medieval Europe, the concept of ownership typically did not play a central role; instead, the focus is interdependent relationships cemented through use rights.

The clash between Native American property systems and the intuitive image of absolute ownership can be seen in the following opinion.

TEE-HIT-TON INDIANS v. UNITED STATES

348 U.S. 272 (1955)

MR. JUSTICE REED delivered the opinion of the Court.

This case rests upon a claim under the Fifth Amendment by petitioner, an identifiable group of American Indians of between 60 and 70 individuals residing in Alaska, for compensation for a taking by the United

---

11. While some of the sales of Indian land were valid, others were negotiated by individual tribe members who did not in fact represent the tribe, involved sales by one tribe of another tribe's land, or involved chiefs who were bribed.

States of certain timber from Alaskan lands allegedly belonging to the group. The area claimed is said to contain over 350,000 acres of land and 150 square miles of water. The Tee-Hit-Tons, a clan of the Tlingit Tribe, brought this suit in the Court of Claims under 28 U.S.C. §1505. The compensation claimed does not arise from any statutory direction to pay. Payment, if it can be compelled, must be based upon a constitutional right of the Indians to recover.

. . . [The] petitioner claims a compensable interest [in land] located near and within the exterior lines of the Tongass National Forest. By Joint Resolution of August 8, 1947, 61 Stat. 920, the Secretary of Agriculture was authorized to contract for the sale of national forest timber located within this National Forest "notwithstanding any claim of possessory rights.[7]

. . . The Secretary of Agriculture, on August 20, 1951, pursuant to this authority contracted for sale to a private company of all merchantable timber in the area claimed by petitioner. This is the sale of timber which petitioner alleges constitutes a compensable taking by the United States of a portion of its proprietary interest in the land.

The problem presented is the nature of the petitioner's interest in the land, if any. Petitioner claims a "full proprietary ownership" of the land; or, in the alternative, at least a "recognized" right to unrestricted possession, occupation and use. Either ownership or recognized possession, petitioner asserts, is compensable. If it has a fee simple interest in the entire tract, it has an interest in the timber, and its sale is a partial taking of its right to "possess, use and dispose of it." United States v. General Motors Corp., 323 U.S. 373, 378. It is petitioner's contention that its tribal predecessors have continually claimed, occupied and used the land from time immemorial; that when Russia took Alaska, the Tlingits had a well-developed social order which included a concept of property ownership; that Russia, while it possessed Alaska, in no manner interfered with their claim to the land; that Congress has by subsequent acts confirmed and recognized petitioner's right to occupy the land permanently and therefore the sale of the timber off such lands constitutes a taking pro tanto of its asserted rights in the area.

The Government denies that petitioner has any compensable interest. It asserts that the Tee-Hit-Tons' property interest, if any, is merely that of the right to the use of the land at the Government's will; that *Congress has never recognized any legal interest of petitioner* in the land and therefore without such recognition no compensation is due the petitioner for any taking by the United States. . . .

II.   INDIAN TITLE

(a) . . . It is well settled that in all the States of the Union the tribes who inhabited the lands of the States held claim to such lands after the

---

7. Id., §1: "That 'possessory rights' as used in this resolution shall mean all rights, if any should exist, which are based upon aboriginal occupancy or title."

coming of the white man, under what is sometimes termed original Indian title or permission from the whites to occupy. That description means mere possession not specifically recognized as ownership by Congress. After conquest they were permitted to occupy portions of territory over which they had previously exercised "sovereignty," as we use that term. This is not a property right but amounts to a right of occupancy which the sovereign grants and protects against intrusion by third parties but which right of occupancy may be terminated and such lands fully disposed of by the sovereign itself without any legally enforceable obligation to compensate the Indians.

This position of the Indian has long been rationalized by the legal theory that discovery and conquest gave the conquerors sovereignty over and ownership of the lands thus obtained. 1 Wheaton's International Law, c. V. The great case of Johnson v. McIntosh, 8 Wheat. 543, denied the power of an Indian tribe to pass their right of occupancy to another. It confirmed the practice of two hundred years of American history "that discovery gave an exclusive right to extinguish the Indian title of occupancy, either by purchase or by conquest." 8 Wheat. at page 587. . . .

No case in this Court has ever held that taking of Indian title or use by Congress required compensation. The American people have compassion for the descendants of those Indians who were deprived of their homes and hunting grounds by the drive of civilization. They seek to have the Indians share the benefits of our society as citizens of this Nation. Generous provision has been willingly made to allow tribes to recover for wrongs, as a matter of grace, not because of legal liability. . . .

(c) What has been heretofore set out deals largely with the Indians of the Plains and east of the Mississippi. The Tee-Hit-Tons urge, however, that their stage of civilization and their concept of ownership of property takes them out of the rule applicable to the Indians of the States. They assert that Russia never took their lands in the sense that European nations seized the rest of America. The Court of Claims, however, saw no distinction between their use of the land and that of the Indians of the Eastern United States. That court had no evidence that the Russian handling of the Indian land problem differed from ours. The natives were left the use of the great part of their vast hunting and fishing territory but what Russia wanted for its use and that of its licensees, it took. The court's conclusion on this issue was based on strong evidence.

In considering the character of the Tee-Hit-Tons' use of the land, the Court of Claims had before it the testimony of a single witness who was offered by plaintiff. He stated that he was the chief of the Tee-Hit-Ton tribe. He qualified as an expert on the Tlingits, a group composed of numerous interconnected tribes including the Tee-Hit-Tons. His testimony showed that the Tee-Hit-Tons had become greatly reduced in numbers. Membership descends only through the female line. At the present time there are only a few women of childbearing age and a total membership of some 65.

The witness pointed out that their claim of ownership was based on possession and use. The use that was made of the controverted area was for the location in winter of villages in sheltered spots and in summer along fishing streams and/or bays. The ownership was not individual but tribal. As the witness stated, "Any member of the tribe may use any portion of the land that he wishes, and as long as he uses it . . . for his own enjoyment, and is not to be trespassed upon by anybody else, but the minute he stops using it then any other member of the tribe can come in and use that area."

When the Russians first came to the Tlingit territory, the most important of the chiefs moved the people to what is now the location of the town of Wrangell. Each tribe took a portion of Wrangell harbor and the chief gave permission to the Russians to build a house on the shore.

The witness learned the alleged boundaries of the Tee-Hit-Ton area from hunting and fishing with his uncle after his return from Carlisle Indian School about 1904. From the knowledge so obtained, he outlined in red on the map, which petitioner filed as an exhibit, the territory claimed by the Tee-Hit-Tons. Use by other tribal members is sketchily asserted. This is the same 350,000 acres claimed by the petition. On it he marked six places to show the Indians' use of the land: (1) his great uncle was buried here, (2) a town, (3) his uncle's house, (4) a town, (5) his mother's house, (6) smokehouse. He also pointed out the uses of this tract for fishing salmon and for hunting beaver, deer and mink. . . .

In addition to this verbal testimony, exhibits were introduced by both sides as to the land use. These exhibits are secondary authorities but they bear out the general proposition that land claims among the Tlingits, and likewise of their smaller group, the Tee-Hit-Tons, was wholly tribal. It was more a claim of sovereignty than of ownership. The articles presented to the Court of Claims by those who have studied and written of the tribal groups agree with the above testimony. There were scattered shelters and villages moved from place to place as game or fish became scarce. There was recognition of tribal rights to hunt and fish on certain general areas, with claims to that effect carved on totem poles. From all that was presented, the Court of Claims concluded, and we agree, that the Tee-Hit-Tons were in a hunting and fishing stage of civilization, with shelters fitted to their environment, and claims to rights to use identified territory for these activities as well as the gathering of wild products of the earth. We think this evidence introduced by both sides confirms the Court of Claims' conclusion that the petitioner's use of its lands was like the use of the nomadic tribes of the States Indians.

The line of cases adjudicating Indian rights on American soil leads to the conclusion that Indian occupancy, not specifically recognized as ownership by action authorized by Congress, may be extinguished by the Government without compensation.[21] Every American schoolboy knows that

21. The Department of Interior, Agriculture and Justice agree with this conclusion. See Committee Print No. 12, Supplemental Reports dated January 11, 1954, on H.R. 1921, 83d

the savage tribes of this continent were deprived of their ancestral ranges by force and that, even when the Indians ceded millions of acres by treaty in return for blankets, food and trinkets, it was not a sale but the conquerors' will that deprived them of their land.

[Given] the history of the Indian relations in this Nation, no other course would meet the problem of the growth of the United States except to make congressional contributions for Indian lands rather than to subject the Government to an obligation to pay the value when taken with interest to the date of payment. Our conclusion does not uphold harshness as against tenderness toward the Indians, but it leaves with Congress, where it belongs, the policy of Indian gratuities for the termination of Indian occupancy of Government-owned land rather than making compensation for its value a rigid constitutional principle.

Affirmed.

MR. JUSTICE DOUGLAS, with whom THE CHIEF JUSTICE WARREN and MR. JUSTICE FRANKFURTER concur, dissenting.

The first Organic Act for Alaska shows clearly that Congress in the 1884 Act recognized the claims of these Indians to their Alaskan lands. . . . Congress did the humane thing of saving to the Indians all rights claimed; it let them keep what they had prior to the new Act. . . . That purpose is wholly at war with the one now attributed to the Congress of reserving for some future day the question whether the Indians were to have any rights to the land.

There remains the question what kind of "title" the right of use and occupancy embraces. Some Indian rights concern fishing alone. See Tulee v. Washington, 315 U.S. 681. Others may include only hunting or grazing or other limited uses. Whether the rights recognized in 1884 embraced rights to timber, litigated here, has not been determined by the finders of fact. The case should be remanded for those findings. It is sufficient now only to determine that under the jurisdictional Act the Court of Claims is empowered to entertain the complaint by reason of the recognition afforded the Indian rights by the Act of 1884.

Cong., 2d Sess.

Department of Interior: "That the Indian right of occupancy is not a property right in the accepted legal sense was clearly indicated when United States v. Alcea Band of Tillamooks, 341 U.S. 48 (1951), was reargued. The Supreme Court stated, in a per curiam decision, that the taking of lands to which Indians had a right of occupancy was not a taking within the meaning of the fifth amendment entitling the dispossessed to just compensation.

"Since possessory rights based solely upon aboriginal occupancy or use are thus of an unusual nature, subject to the whim of the sovereign owner of the land who can give good title to third parties by extinguishing such rights, they cannot be regarded as clouds upon title in the ordinary sense of the word. . . ."

NOTES AND QUESTIONS

1. **Ownership versus "mere possession."** How did the Tee-Hit-Tons use the land? Why did that constitute "mere possession," not ownership? Would the court have drawn the same legal conclusion about the feudal system of use rights? *no blc they were working for & paying for their land*

2. **Different systems of use rights.** For a detailed description of Native American property rights in New England, see Eric T. Freyfogle, Land Use and the Study of Early American History, 94 Yale L.J. 717, 721-722 (1985) (book review) (citations omitted):

> In their use of property, the Indians clearly embraced a system of private ownership, although they carved up property rights [very] differently than the colonists did and retained more property rights for communal use. Indian families owned exclusively the land on which their wigwams or other dwellings stood. This exclusive right of use continued until the family abandoned the land. Village agricultural lands were divided up and owned by individual families, with each family's ownership rights in the farm lands continuing only so long as the family made actual use of the lands. . . . Ownership interests in all other Indian lands — "the clam banks, fishing ponds, berry-picking areas, hunting lands, the great bulk of a village's territory" — were even more clearly limited to usufruct rights. . . .

How did this description of the Indians' property system differ from that of the Tee-Hit-Tons'? Of the feudal system? See also William Cronin, Changes in the Land: Indians, Colonists, and the Ecology of New England (1983); Stephen Innis, Labor in a New Land: Economy and Society in Seventeenth-Century Springfield (1983).

3. **Tee-Hit-Tons' use of precedent.** Note the Court's reliance on Johnson v. M'Intosh, 21 U.S. (8 Wheat.) 543, 572-573, 587-588 (1823), an opinion written by Supreme Court Chief Justice John Marshall. Johnson v. M'Intosh involved two whites, one of whom traced his title back to Native Americans; the other traced title back to a grant from the U.S. government. Marshall held that the U.S. government had the exclusive right to sell land to Native Americans, in an opinion that appeared to give considerable deference to Native American rights in the land.

> As the right of society to prescribe those rules by which property may be acquired and preserved is not, and cannot be drawn into question; as the title to lands, especially, is and must be admitted to depend entirely on the law of the nation in which they lie; it will be necessary, in pursuing this inquiry, to examine, not singly those principles of abstract justice, which the Creator of all things had impressed on the mind of his creature man, and which are admitted to regulate, in a great degree, the rights of civilized nations . . . ; but those principles also which our own government has adopted in the particular case, and given us as the rule for our decision.

On the discovery of this immense continent, the great nations of Europe were eager to appropriate to themselves so much of it as they could respectively acquire. Its vast extent offered an ample field to the ambition and enterprise of all; and the character and religion of its inhabitants afforded an apology for considering them as a people over whom the superior genius of Europe might claim an ascendancy. The potentates of the old world found no difficulty in convincing themselves that they made ample compensation to the inhabitants of the new, by bestowing on them civilization and Christianity. . . .

The exclusion of all other Europeans, necessarily gave to the nation making the discovery the sole right of acquiring the soil from the natives, and establishing settlements upon it. It was a right with which no Europeans could interfere. It was a right which all asserted for themselves, and to the assertion of which, by others, all assented.

In the establishment of these relations, the rights of the original inhabitants were, in no instance, entirely disregarded; but were necessarily, to a considerable extent, impaired. They were admitted to be the rightful occupants of the soil, with a legal as well as just claim to retain possession of it, and use it according to their own discretion; but their rights to complete sovereignty, as independent nations, were necessarily diminished, and their power to dispose of the soil at their own will, to whomsoever they pleased, was denied by the original fundamental principle, that discovery gave exclusive title to those who made it.

The ceded territory was occupied by numerous and warlike tribes of Indians; but the exclusive right of the United States to extinguish their title, and to grant the soil, has never, we believe, been doubted. . . .

The United States, then, have unequivocally acceded to that great and broad rule by which its civilized inhabitants now hold this country. They hold, and assert in themselves, the title by which it was acquired. They maintain, as all others have maintained, that discovery gave an exclusive right to extinguish the Indian title of occupancy, either by purchase or by conquest; and gave also a right to such a degree of sovereignty, as the circumstances of the people would allow them to exercise.

The title by conquest is acquired and maintained by force. The conqueror prescribes its limits. Humanity, however, acting on public opinion, has established, as a general rule, that the conquered shall not be wantonly oppressed, and that their condition shall remain as eligible as is compatible with the objects of the conquest. Most usually, they are incorporated with the victorious nation, and become subjects or citizens of the government with which they are connected. The new and old members of the society mingle with each other; the distinction between them is gradually lost, and they make one people. Where this incorporation is practicable, humanity demands, and a wise policy requires, that the rights of the conquered to property should remain unimpaired; that the new subjects should be governed as equitably as the old, and that confidence in their security should gradually banish the painful sense of being separated from their ancient connexions, and united by force to strangers.

When the conquest is complete, and the conquered inhabitants can be blended with the conquerors, or safely governed as a distinct people, public opinion, which not even the conqueror can disregard, imposes these restraints upon him; and he cannot neglect them without injury to his fame, and hazard to his power.

However extravagant the pretension of converting the discovery of an inhabited country into conquest may appear; if the principle has been asserted in the first instance, and afterwards sustained; if a country has been acquired and held under it; if the property of the great mass of the community originates in it, it becomes the law of the land, and cannot be questioned. So, too, with respect to the concomitant principle, that the Indian inhabitants are to be considered merely as occupants, to be protected, indeed, while in peace, in the possession of their lands, but to be deemed incapable of transferring the absolute title to others. However this restriction may be opposed to natural right, and to the usages of civilized nations, yet, if it be indispensable to that system under which the country has been settled, and be adapted to the actual condition of the two people, it may, perhaps, be supported by reason, and certainly cannot be rejected by Courts of justice. . . .

Note Marshall's statement that the Indians "are admitted to be the rightful occupants of the soil, with a legal, as well as just claim to retain possession of it, and to use it according to their own discretion." One way of reading Johnson v. M'Intosh is as an attempt to protect Native Americans by making it impossible for whites to "buy" land in sales in which whites often took advantage of Indians, rather than as a statement of the limited nature of their property rights. Part of the holding of Johnson v. M'Intosh was that Indians could lose their land only by purchase *by the U.S. government* or by conquest. A later case, Worcester v. Georgia, 31 U.S. (6 Pet.) 515 (1832), appeared to limit situations in which title could be gained to Indian lands to just wars in which the Indians were the aggressors.

For what purpose did the *Tee-Hit-Ton* case cite Johnson v. M'Intosh? One commentator has argued that:

> The dicta in *Johnson* regarding extinguishment of Indian Title by conquest does not support Justice Reed's conclusion that all Indian land had been conquered. . . . [I]t is evident that *Johnson* did *not* establish that all Indian title has been extinguished by conquest, for *Johnson* itself, as well as its progeny, recognized that purchase was the primary method of extinguishment of Indian title. Had discovery itself extinguished Indian title to land, most of the decisions in [*Johnson* and subsequent cases] would have been unnecessary. In addition, Justice Reed's use of the term "conquest" is itself questionable. Both at the time of *Johnson* and today, conquest has been a narrow concept. . . . Finally, even if the federal government's actions in the forty-eight contiguous states could have been interpreted as examples of the "conqueror's will," the Alaskan natives had never fought a skirmish with either Russia or the United States, but instead welcomed the newcomers with open arms. To say that the Alaska natives were subjugated by conquest stretches the imagination too far. The only sovereign that can be said to have conquered the Alaska native was the *Tee-Hit-Ton* opinion itself.

Nell Jessup Newton, At the Whim of the Sovereign: Aboriginal Title Reconsidered, 31 Hastings L.J. 1215 (1980).

§1.3   Republican Visions of Property: Ownership Gives a Stable Stake in the Society[12]

Property is so important that everybody should have some of it.[13]

We have come to a clear realization of the fact that true individual freedom cannot exist without economic security and independence. "Necessitous men are not freemen."[14]

As you read the following materials, ask yourself what are the major differences between the feudal and the republican visions. Does the republican vision retain the attitude towards hierarchy expressed in feudalism? What is the individual's place in society under feudal and republican theory? How does property further that vision? The first excerpt, written by the prominent legal historian Stanley Katz, discusses Thomas Jefferson's views on property ownership. Why is the unequal distribution of property incompatible with republican virtue, according to Jefferson? How did Jefferson reconcile himself with the unequal distribution of property in his own day? Did he expect the inequality to continue?

a.   Thomas Jefferson's Republicanism

STANLEY N. KATZ, THOMAS JEFFERSON AND THE RIGHT TO PROPERTY IN REVOLUTIONARY AMERICA

19 J.L. & Econ. 467 (1976)

Thomas Jefferson died at the age of eighty-three on July 4, 1826. His dying words are reported to have been the inquiry, "Is it the Fourth?" Astonishingly, John Adams passed away during the same summer night, and it is recorded that his final utterance was, "Thomas Jefferson still survives." And indeed the great Virginian still survives, but in 1976 his image is so complex and so confused that it may be no idle task to reexamine even part of his contribution to our revolutionary era.

---

12. Note that we are not using "republicanism" in the sense that "Newt Gingrich is a Republican"; instead, we are using the term to refer to a long-standing intellectual tradition.
13. Jim Hightower, Former Texas Commissioner of Agriculture, now talk show host.
14. Franklin D. Roosevelt, 1944 State of the Union Address.

Jefferson, we must remember, was both a man of property and a prophet of the Enlightenment. He was born the son of an Albermarle County planter, Peter Jefferson, and, thanks to the rule of primogeniture,[2] inherited the right to two-thirds of his father's 7,500 acre estate when only fourteen years of age. Trained as a gentleman and a lawyer, Jefferson devoted himself to improving his patrimony and serving his country, Virginia. In 1767 he began the planting and planning for his magnificent house on the "little mountain," Monticello, into which he moved after his marriage to the wealthy widow Martha Wayles Skelton in 1772. Martha Jefferson's father died in 1773, leaving the young couple with an inheritance of 11,000 acres of land and 135 slaves. By 1776 Jefferson managed three large plantations and several smaller ones (together they came to more than 10,000 acres) and he owned about 180 slaves. He served in the Virginia legislature and the Continental Congress, and he had begun to display the artistic, scientific, and intellectual virtuosity which characterized his entire life: he "could calculate an eclipse, survey an estate, tie an artery, plan an edifice, try a cause, break a horse, dance a minuet, and play the violin." He was, as Kurt Vonnegut aptly remarks, "a slave owner who was also one of the world's greatest theoreticians on the subject of human liberty." How can one deal with such a man, such a mind, and such a revolution?

My strategy is to isolate one theme in Jefferson's thought in order to blaze a tenuous trail through the richness of his mind and life and, at the same time, to try to show one of the ways in which Jefferson helped to shape the legacy of 1776: that theme is the right to property.

As in other pre-modern revolutions, it was not the intention of the American patriots, the revolutionary party, to destroy property rights or systematically to redistribute property. For one thing, it was pretty clearly not in the interest of Jefferson or the other patricians who formed the core of revolutionary leadership to throw either their own property or the fundamental arrangements for social order into doubt. . . .

What one must stress is that the right to property was an unquestioned assumption of the American revolutionaries. To assert this is merely to assert that they were eighteenth-century men. But one must go on to say that they did not defend property as an end in itself but rather as one of the bases of republican government. It is the sense in which property had political value that it was most important to Thomas Jefferson. . . .

In June, 1776 Jefferson sketched out (in three separate drafts) a proposed constitution for his beloved state of Virginia. Several of its provisions dealt importantly with property. One conferred the franchise on adult males who had a freehold estate of a quarter of an acre of land in any town or twenty-five acres of land in the country, as well as to all persons "resident

---

2. "The superiority or exclusive right possessed by the eldest son, and particularly, his right to succeed to the estate of his ancestor, in right of his seniority by birth, to the exclusion of younger sons." Black's Law Dictionary 1191 (6th ed. 1990).

in the colony who shall have paid *scot* and *lot* to the government the last [two years]." He made clear his concern with the broad distribution of property in the society:

> Every person of full age neither owning nor having owned [50] acres of land, shall be entitled to an appropriation of [50] acres or to so much as shall make up what he owns or has owned [50] acres in full and absolute dominion, and no other person shall be capable of taking an appropriation . . .

Many of these ideas were not made into law for many years, and some were never enacted, but Jefferson pressed ahead with several of them in the course of spearheading a movement to reform the law of the state. The first of these was his bill abolishing entail, the ancient English legal device by which a testator could limit the capacity of his descendants to alienate his estate. Jefferson felt that entail, one of the legal buttresses of the massive property holdings of the ruling families of England, was socially and politically undesirable in Virginia, since it tended to create:

> a distinct set of families who, being privileged by law in the perpetuation of their wealth were thus formed into a patrician order. To annul this privilege, and instead of an aristocracy of wealth, of more harm and danger, than benefit, to society, to make an opening for the aristocracy of virtue and talent, which nature has wisely provided for the direction of the interests of society, & scattered with equal hand through all its conditions, was deemed essential to a well ordered republic. To effect it no violence was necessary, no deprivation of natural right, but rather an enlargement of it by a repeal of the law. For this would authorize the present holder to divide the property among his children equally, as his affections were divided, and would place them, by natural generation on the level of their fellow citizens.

Jefferson next turned to the abolition of primogeniture and formulated a bill which proclaimed that "when any person having title to any real estate of inheritance, shall die intestate as to such estate, it shall descend and pass in parcenary to his kindred male and female." Jefferson's colleague in the revision of the Virginia laws, Edmund Pendleton (to whom we shall be returning shortly) objected to this radical change in the traditional system (which, it is easy to recognize, also aided landed families in preventing the fragmentation of their landed estates) and argued that, as Jefferson recalled:

> [W]e should adopt the Hebrew principle, and give a double portion to the elder son. I observed that if the eldest son could eat twice as much, or do double work, it might be a natural evidence of his right to a double portion, but being on a par in his powers & wants, with his brothers and sisters, he should be on a par also in the partition of the patrimony, and such was the decision of the other members.

Jefferson was tremendously proud of the bills abolishing primogeniture and entail and he was later to claim that they formed:

> [A] system by which every fibre would be eradicated of ancient or future aristocracy, and a foundation laid for a government truly republican. The repeal of the laws of entail would prevent the accumulation and perpetuation of wealth in select families, and preserve the soil of the country from being daily more & more absorbed in Mortmain. The abolition of primogeniture, and equal partition of inheritances removed the feudal and unnatural distinctions which made one member of every family rich, and all the rest poor, substituting equal partition, the best of all Agrarian laws.

During 1776 and subsequently during his career, Jefferson defined and defended another fundamental attitude toward property — "that every emigrant to the West must be able to take up and hold securely the lands he needed." He argued that the Virginia legislature, rather than either the Crown or land speculators, held title to Virginia's land claims west of the mountains, that Virginia should extract minimal fees for the sale of this land, that it should be sold in small parcels, and that the western territories should be quickly organized on a republican basis. These will be recognized as the sentiments which lay behind the Northwest Ordinance of 1787 and also, less obviously, behind the Louisiana Purchase of 1803.

It seems fairly clear that several principles lay behind these legislative proposals. In the first place, Jefferson believed in the principle of equality where the state was compelled to allocate property — thus, equal shares among the heirs of intestates, the provision of a fifty-acre head right for each Virginia resident, and small land parcels for western frontiersmen. Secondly, and relatedly, he believed in the wide distribution of property. The law of descents, the abolition of entail, and the land distribution system all reflected this feeling. Thirdly, Jefferson was committed to the protection of existing property relationships. He was careful to defend the interests of the Church of England in its previously lawful property, he defended the right of heirs to inherit, and he supported the traditional western land claims of Virginia. I want to stress, however, that it was not only property rights in the abstract, but *land* which Jefferson thought critical for the development of this country. "Property," to Jefferson, meant "land."

The reason why is suggested in a famous passage in Jefferson's *Notes on the State of Virginia* (written in 1780 or 1781, but not published until 1785)....

> Those who labour in the earth are the chosen people of God, if ever he had a chosen people, whose breasts he has made his peculiar deposit for substantial and genuine virtue. It is the focus in which he keeps alive that sacred fire, which otherwise might escape from the face of the earth. Corruption of morals in the mass of cultivators is a phaenomenon of which no age nor na-

tion has furnished an example. It is the mark set on those, who not looking up to heaven, to their own soil and industry, as does the husbandman, for their subsistence, depend for it on the casualties and caprice of customers. Dependence begets subservience and venality, suffocates the germ of virtue, and prepares fit tools for the designs of ambition . . . It is the manners and spirit of a people which preserve a republic in vigour. A degeneracy in these is a canker which soon eats to the heart of its laws and constitution.

Here we have it. In the early stages of his career Jefferson was firmly wedded to the notion that land ownership and the tilling of one's own soil was not only good economics but good politics. It was only by independent labor (and in the mid-eighteenth century that was typically farming) that a man could divest himself of subordination to superiors and cultivate that inner strength upon which republicanism depended. . . . It was the virtue and judgment produced by such independent labor that rendered them capable of becoming republicans, and therefore rendered America capable of republican government.

Permit me to digress for a moment in order to point out that Jefferson's reasoning about property might have carried him much further than it did. While some of his reforms, such as the abolition of primogeniture and entail, would have the long range result of winnowing down the extent of the great landed estates, he did not propose anything which would immediately have a destructive impact on existing property holdings. His general sympathies, and his labor theory of property, might however, have carried him farther in the direction of redistribution, and so they did for a brief moment in his career. The occasion was his visit to France during the 1780's, when he for the first time experienced the impact of the property rules of the Old Regime on a society which lacked America's unsettled frontier. In a famous letter of October 1785 written from Fontainbleau, Jefferson mused on the inequality of the rated European division of property, which he thought "absolutely concentrated in a very few hands." He attributed European poverty to the fact that the nobility had enclosed great tracts of land and withdrawn them from production "mostly for sake of game."

> I am [he wrote] conscious that an equal division of property is impracticable. But the consequences of this enormous inequality producing so much misery to the bulk of mankind, legislators cannot invent too many devices for subdividing property, only taking care to let their subdivisions go hand in hand with the natural affections of the human mind.

He remarked that the abolition of primogeniture would be one way of moving toward this result, as would progressive taxation: "to exempt all from taxation below a certain point, and to tax the higher portions of property in geometrical progression as they rise." He concluded:

> Whenever there is in any country, uncultivated lands and unemployed poor, it is clear that the laws of property have been so far extended as to violate

natural right. The earth is given as a common stock for man to labour and live on. If, for the encouragement of industry we allow it to be appropriated, we must take care that other employment be furnished to those excluded from the appropriation. If we do not, the fundamental right to labour the earth returns to the unemployed. It is too soon yet in our country to say that every man who cannot find employment but who can find uncultivated land, shall be at liberty to cultivate it, paying a moderate rent. But it is not too soon to provide by every possible means that as few as possible shall be without a little portion of land. The small landholders are the most precious part of a state.

This was the same line of thought which later led Jefferson to try out on Madison the proposition which he supposed to be "self evident, *'that the earth belongs in usufruct to the living.'* " Staughton Lynd has pointed out that the radical potential for this line of thinking, but Jefferson never pursued the thought after his return to the United States in 1789.

There were probably two reasons why Jefferson did not espouse such a radical, redistributive line of thought. In the first place, it ran squarely athwart one of the cardinal principles of his political thinking, namely, that the state should exercise no more than the minimum powers necessary to maintain social order. Taxation, confiscation or any other broadly redistributive program would necessitate precisely the kind of governmental action which Jefferson was pledged to avoid. Second, and probably more important, Jefferson did not think that such radical surgery upon the body politic was necessary. For, in a country in which all men had land upon which they could labor and in which they participated freely in governmental process, redistribution was not necessary.

NOTES AND QUESTIONS

1. **Republicanism and feudalism.** Answering the questions posed before the Katz excerpt, compare the republican and the feudal visions.

2. **Republicanism as a reaction to feudalism.** The republican vision rejects feudalism. Consider the following excerpt from a major historian of republicanism:

> The function of property [in republicanism] is to guarantee the citizen his independence. The dependence from which it must save him is the political dependence upon others which constitutes corruption, and the modes of economic being which it is important to avoid are those in which property and political dependence go hand in hand. A feudal society in which the proprietor is someone's vassal is a case in point, and . . . the disappearance of [the feudal system was seen as] the restoration of civic virtue. . . .

J. G. A. Pocock, Civic Humanism and its Role in Anglo-American Thought, in Politics, Language and Time 80, 92 (1973).

3.   **Virtue, self-interest and the common good.** Independence was seen as enabling citizens to pursue the common good, instead of concentrating on their own self-interest. The republican tradition "emphasized . . . the ideal of a citizenry devoted less to private-gain than to political participation in pursuit of the public good. Property, on this view, was valued insofar as its distribution aided the citizenry in the free pursuit of that good." See Gregory S. Alexander, Time and Property in the American Republican Legal Culture, 66 N.Y.U. L. Rev. 273, 274 (1991). In the words of another author:

> At the center of republican thought lay a belief in a common good and a conception of society as an organic whole. The state's proper role consisted in large part of fostering virtue, of making the individual unselfishly devote himself to the common good. . . . "The sacrifice of individual interests to the greater good of the whole formed the essence of republicanism. . . ." (Citations omitted.)

William Michael Treanor, The Origins and Original Significance of the Just Compensation Clause of the Fifth Amendment, 94 Yale L.J. 694, 699 (1985). Treanor argues that in the days of the early republic, many states did not even compensate landowners for lands taken for use in building roads or other public purposes. He notes the republican roots of this practice — that the institution of property should be designed to achieve the public good — as well as "a powerful strand of English legal thought, a strand that had its origins in feudal notions of property and kingship [which] legitimized such redistributions. According to this theory, property was held from the state; the state could therefore limit the individual's ownership claims. . . ."[15] Id. at 697. These issues emerge strongly in contemporary takings cases, in which government regulations are challenged as takings of private property without compensation. See Chapter 8. Does Andrus v. Allard depend on notions of the common good?

b.   The Egalitarian and Elitist Strains of Republicanism

Many strains of republicanism are present in American history. For our purposes, we can divide the tradition into an elitist and an egalitarian strain. Both started from the premise that only citizens with sufficient property to be independent could be virtuous enough to pursue the common good.[16] The elitist strain (expressed in the widespread restrictions of the

---

15. Treanor's thesis has been challenged by William W. Fisher III, The Law of the Land: An Intellectual History of American Property Doctrine, 1776-1880 (Ph.D. diss., Harvard University, 1991).

16. If you think you spot parallels between republicanism and contemporary communitarianism, you are right. Communitarians such as William Galston, Liberal Purposes: Goods, Virtues, and Diversity in the Liberal State (1991), draw on the same Aristotelian tradition that

franchise to property owners after the Revolution) sought to limit civic participation to (white male) propertied voters[17] whose property gave them the independence necessary for virtuous pursuit of the common good. The egalitarian strain instead advocated widespread distribution of property, as a way of ensuring the independence, and therefore the virtue, of as broad a band of (white male) [18] citizens as possible.

Not only Thomas Jefferson, but also Thomas Paine, worked in the tradition of egalitarian republicanism. Both believed that land was the common stock of all and called for economic as well as political reforms to ensure widespread distribution of property. Jefferson called for public distribution of land to the landless. Allen David Haskin, Tenants and the American Dream: Ideology and the Tenant Movement 5 (1983). Paine proposed a direct redistribution of wealth, through an inheritance tax levied on land. The funds collected would be distributed to people reaching the age of majority, as a patrimony ensuring independence and therefore virtue, and to people when they reached 50 who were presumed to be unable to continue working. Thomas Paine, ed., Agrarian Justice, in The Complete Political Works of Thomas Paine (1922). Other voices went further and advocated the forced redistribution of property. Sean Wilentz, Chants Democratic (1984).

Nineteenth-century federal land policy became the key institutional expression of the egalitarian strain. See Irving Mark, The Homestead Idea and the Conservation of the Public Domain, 22 Am. J. Econ. & Soc. 263, 266-269 (1963) (associating the homestead idea with egalitarian republicanism); Paul Goodman, The Emergence of Homestead Exemption in the United States: Accommodation and Resistance to the Market Revolution, 1840-1880, 80 J. Am. Hist. 470 (1993). That policy showed that, the farther the classical republican "ideal receded from the dynamic reality of the nineteenth century [market] economy, the more Americans liked to think of themselves in its terms." [19] The purest expressions of that policy were the

---

informed republicanism. See also Robert Bellah, et al., The Habits of the Heart (1985) (research on the relationship between public and private life in the United States).

17. See Derrick Bell and Preeta Bansal, Symposium. The Republican Civic Tradition: The Republican Revival and Racial Politics, 97 Yale L.J. 1609, 1609-1610 (1988); Frank I. Michelman, The Supreme Court, 1985 Term: Foreword: Traces of Self-Government, 100 Harv. L. Rev. 4, 20 (1986); Cass R. Sunstein, Symposium, The Republican Civic Tradition, 97 Yale L.J. 1539 (1988).

18. Republicanism definitely envisioned a republic of men. See Hannah F. Pitkin, Fortune Is a Woman (1984); Linda K. Kerber, Symposium: The Republican Civic Tradition-Making Republicanism Useful, 97 Yale L.J. 1663, 1664, 1668 (1988). Before the Civil War, women's rights activists such as Elizabeth Cady Stanton and Susan B. Anthony, who had worked for the abolition of slavery, expected women to be granted the vote when black men were. They were bitterly disappointed when the Radical Republicans abandoned the cause of female suffrage, arguing, "this hour belongs to the negro." See Ellen C. DuBois, Feminism and Suffrage: The Emergence of an Independent Women's Movement in America 1848-1849, at 59 (1978).

19. Rowland Berthoff, Independence and Attachment, Virtue and Interest: From Republican Citizen to Free Enterpriser, 1787-1837, in Uprooted Americans 106 (Richard L. Bushman, et. al eds., 1978).

Homestead Act of 1862,[20] which distributed federal lands to individual settlers in small 100-acre parcels, and the homestead exemptions, passed in all
but a few states by the end of the nineteenth century, which typically exempted the family home and other assets from the claims of creditors.
These policies were driven by the sense that Americans had a natural right
"to live and to be upon this earth . . . to share of the products of the earth,
and hence a right to a portion of the earth,"[21] to quote one advocate for
homestead exemptions in 1846. Three developments limited the impact of
the Homestead Act. First, the amount of desirable land available for distribution was limited by the large parcels distributed to the railroads. See William W. Fisher III, The Law of the Land: An Intellectual History of
American Property Doctrine, 1776-1880 (Ph.D. diss., Harvard University,
1991). Second, large amounts of land ended up in the hands of speculators.
P. W. Gates, Landlords and Tenants on the Prairie Frontier 156 (1973).
Third, the distribution of federal lands meant their distribution largely to
white males. The 1866 Southern Homestead Act was designed specifically
to provide farms to freed slaves in five southwestern states. However, the
high filing costs prohibited most former slaves from participating, and hostile administrators granted only inferior land. Only 4,000 former slaves received land by the time the program ended in 1870. Ray Allen Billington,
Westward Expansion: A History of the American Frontier 606 (4th ed.
1974). The acts permitted single women to file claims, but only about 10
percent of homestead claims went to women. The title of married couples
was invariably held by the husband. See David Burner, et al., 1 An American
Portrait: A History of the United States 369 (2d ed. 1985).

After the Civil War, many freedmen assumed that southern plantations would be distributed as homesteads to give former slaves "forty acres
and a mule." Harriet Jacobs expresses this hope; the historian Eric Foner
traces its rise and fall.

HARRIET A. JACOBS, INCIDENTS IN THE LIFE OF A SLAVE GIRL: WRITTEN BY HERSELF

201 (1861; 1987)

I and my children are now free! We are as free from the power of
slaveholders as are the white people of the north; and though that, according to my idea, is not saying a great deal, it is a vast improvement in *my*
condition. The dream of my life is not yet realized. I do not sit with my
children in a home of my own. I still long for a hearthstone of my own,
however humble. I wish it for my children's sake far more than for my own.

---

20. 43 U.S.C. §§161-164 (repealed 1973).
21. Goodman, *supra* at 486 (quoting an editorial from the *Milwaukee Courier*).

HARRIET TUBMAN.

FIGURE 1-1
Harriet Tubman (1820?-1913), born into slavery, escaped,
then helped others to escape

FIGURE 1-2
Masthead of the *Working Man's Advocate,* c. 1840s

ERIC FONER, RECONSTRUCTION: AMERICA'S
UNFINISHED REVOLUTION

104-05 (1988)

The desire to escape from white supervision and establish a modicum
of economic independence profoundly shaped blacks' economic choices
during Reconstruction, leading them to prefer tenancy to wage labor and
leasing land for a fixed rent to sharecropping. Above all, it inspired the
quest for land of their own. Indeed, the same blacks arraigned for idleness
sacrificed and saved in the attempt to acquire land, and those who succeeded clung to it with amazing tenacity. "They will almost starve and go
naked before they will work for a white man," wrote a Georgia planter, "if
they can get a patch of ground to live on, and get from under his control."
Owning land, the freedmen believed, would "complete their independence." Without land, there could be no economic autonomy, for their
labor would continue to be subject to exploitation by their former owners.
"Gib us our own land and we take care ourselves," a Charleston black told
Northern correspondent Whitelaw Reid, "but widout land, de ole masses
can hire us or starve us, as dey please." . . .

For some blacks, moreover, land distribution seemed a logical consequence of emancipation. "If you had the right to take Master's niggers," one Virginia freedman told an army officer, "you had the right to take Master's land too." Others contended that "the land ought to belong to the man who (alone) could work it." Most often, however, blacks insisted that their past labor entitled them to at least a portion of their owners' estates. As an Alabama black convention put it: "The property which they hold was nearly all earned by the sweat of *our* brows."

Note that the freedmen associated small farms with independence in a manner reminiscent of Thomas Jefferson. Some of the Radical Republicans agreed. The Freedmen's Bureau began making land grants to former slaves, often in 40-acre tracts; by the end of 1865, some 40,000 freedmen had been settled in lands that had been abandoned or confiscated. Then, in a dramatic reversal of policy, President Andrew Johnson ordered the restoration of virtually all Confederate lands to their former owners. See Foner, *supra*, at 159-160.

The events of 1865 and 1866 kindled a deep sense of betrayal among freedmen throughout the South. Land enough existed, wrote former Mississippi slave Merrimon Howard, for every "man and woman to have as much as they could work." Yet blacks had been left with

> no *land*, no *house*, not so much as place to lay our head. . . . Despised by the world, hated by the country that gives us birth, denied of all our writs as a people, we were friends on the march, . . . brothers on the battlefield, but in the peaceful pursuits of life it seems that we are strangers.

Long after the end of slavery, the memory of this injustice lingered. "De slaves," a Mississippi black would recall, "spected a heap from freedom dey didn't git. . . . Dey promised us a mule an' forty acres o' lan'." "Yes sir," agreed a Tennessee freedman, "they should have give us part of Maser's land as us poor old slaves we made what our Masers had."

NOTES AND QUESTIONS

1. **Wealth distribution.** The egalitarian strain of republicanism places the current distribution of wealth at center stage. The richest 20 percent of U.S. households today own more than 80 percent of its wealth, making the United States the most economically stratified nation in the industrialized world. Michael Vermeulen, What People Earn, Parade Magazine, Wash. Post, June 18, 1995, at 4. "The 1980s ended with wage-and-salary earnings more unequally divided than at any time since 1939." Paul Starobin, Unequal Shares, Natl. J., Sept. 11, 1993, at 2176, 2176. Inequality is growing between more and less educated workers; the incomes of high

school educated men have been particularly affected. Men with high school educations, who could deliver a solid middle-class life to their families in the decades after World War II, today find it increasingly difficult to do so. One economist estimated that "the average guy with a high school diploma" earned $24,000 in today's dollars in the late 1970s, but today makes only $18,000.[22] Among 30-year-old men, college graduates earned about 20 percent more than high school graduates in the late 1970s; by 1989, the gap had risen to 47 percent.[23]

2.   **Race and ethnicity.** White households have ten times the median net wealth of black households and eight times that of Hispanic households. Charlotte V. Churaman, Financing of College Education by Minority and White Families, J. Consumer Aff., Dec. 22, 1992, at 324. Disparities of income (as opposed to wealth) are also substantial. While roughly 70 percent of white households are middle class or above, only 44 percent of black households are.[24] Andrew Hacker, Two Nations: Black and White, Separate, Hostile and Unequal 98 (1992). Although nearly twice as many whites as blacks are poor,[25] African Americans are overrepresented among the poor: They made up 12 percent of the U.S. population but 62 percent of the persistently poor.[26] To what extent are the disparities between African and European Americans the result of discrimination, and to what extent are they attributable to other factors? This is currently the topic of considerable debate. Under the republican vision of property, are the reasons for disparities of income determinative of whether such disparities should be allowed to persist?

3.   **Women and children.** Children are the poorest group in the United States: One-fifth of all children and one-half of African American children are poor.[27] Most of those who end up in poverty are single mothers and their children[28]: Such households are five times more likely to be

22. Frank Levy and R. C. Michel, The Economic Future of American Families: Income and Wealth Trends 28-29 (1991); Frank Levy, The Next Priority, Inc., May 1989, at 28. See also Frank Levy, Dollars and Dreams: The Changing American Income Distribution 49-60 (1987); Average White Male No Longer Leads the March to Prosperity, L.A. Times, Oct. 20, 1985, Business Sec., at 1, quoted in Kevin Phillips, The Politics of Rich and Poor 18 (1990) (median inflation-adjusted income of white males serving as family's only breadwinner fell 22 percent between 1976 and 1984).

23. Robert J. Samuelson, Casualties of the "Rising Tide," Wash. Post, Aug. 31, 1994. By 1993, the average high school graduate's hourly wage had fallen to $9.92 compared with $15.71 for the average college graduate. John Cassidy, Who Killed the Middle Class?, The New Yorker, Oct. 16, 1995, 113, 120.

24. We have defined middle class as anyone earning over $25,000 annually.

25. Mickey Kaus, The End of Equality 106 (1992).

26. Bruce W. Klein and Philip R. Rones, A Profile of the Working Poor, Monthly Labor Rev., Oct. 1, 1989, at 3.

27. National Commission on Children, Speaking of Kids: A National Survey of Children and Parents (Report on the National Opinion Research Project 1 (1991)).

28. Frank Levy and R. C. Michel, The Economic Future of American Families 38 (1991).

poor[29] and ten times more likely to stay poor than households with a male present.[30] The causes of poverty in woman-headed households are complex: the gender gap in wages plays an important role. Even if poor female heads of household worked full time earning a typical wage (for women of similar age and education), few would rise above poverty.[31] See also Ruth Sidel, Women and Children Last: The Plight of Poor Women in Affluent America (1986).

c. The "New" Property

Charles Reich's 1964 article "The New Property" is one of the most cited law review articles ever written.[32] It spawned several influential decisions in which the Supreme Court required that hearings be held before persons could be deprived of governmental benefits ranging from welfare payments, Goldberg v. Kelly, 397 U.S. 254 (1970), to drivers' licenses, Bell v. Burson, 402 U.S. 535 (1971), to "tenured" government jobs, Perry v. Sinderman, 408 U.S. 593 (1972).

Reich's theory, when he wrote it, was far-reaching and unprecedented. What made his argument so persuasive?

CHARLES REICH, THE NEW PROPERTY

73 Yale L.J. 733 (1964)

The institution called property guards the troubled boundary between individual man and the state. It is not the only guardian; many other institutions, laws, and practices serve as well. But in a society that chiefly values material well-being, the power to control a particular portion of that well-being is the very foundation of individuality.

One of the most important developments in the United States during the past decade has been the emergence of government as a major source of wealth. Government is a gigantic syphon. It draws in revenue and power, and pours forth wealth: money, benefits, services, contracts, franchises, and

---

29. Ruth Sidel, Women and Children Last: The Plight of Poor Women in Affluent America 3 (1986).

30. Diana Pearce, Welfare Is Not for Women, in Women, The State and Welfare 226 (Linda Gordon ed., 1990).

31. Bruce W. Klein and Phillip L. Rones, A Profile of the Working Poor, Monthly Lab. Rev. 1989, at 3, 8.

32. See Fred R. Shapiro, The Most-Cited Law Review Articles, 73 Cal. L. Rev. 1540, 1549 (1985) ("The New Property" is the fourth most-cited law review article).

licenses. Government has always had this function. But while in early times it was minor, today's distribution of largess is on a vast, imperial scale.

The valuables dispensed by government take many forms, but they all share one characteristic. They are steadily taking the place of traditional forms of wealth — forms which are held as private property. Social insurance substitutes for savings; a government contract replaces a businessman's customers and goodwill. The wealth of more and more Americans depends upon a relationship to government. Increasingly, Americans live on government largess — allocated by government on its own terms, and held by recipients subject to conditions which express "the public interest."

The growth of government largess, accompanied by a distinctive system of law, is having profound consequences. It affects the underpinnings of individualism and independence. It influences the workings of the Bill of Rights. It has an impact on the power of private interests, in their relation to each other and to government. It is helping to create a new society. . . .

I.   THE LARGESS OF GOVERNMENT

A.   THE FORMS OF GOVERNMENT-CREATED WEALTH

The valuables which derive from relationships to government are of many kinds. Some primarily concern individuals; others flow to businesses and organizations. Some are obvious forms of wealth, such as direct payments of money, while others, like licenses and franchises, are indirectly valuable.

Income and benefits. For a large number of people, government is a direct source of income although they hold no public job. Their eligibility arises from legal status. Examples are Social Security benefits, unemployment compensation, aid to dependent children, veterans benefits, and the whole scheme of state and local welfare. These represent a principal source of income to a substantial segment of the community. Total federal, state and local social welfare expenditures in 1961 were almost fifty-eight billion dollars.

Jobs. More than nine million persons receive income from public funds because they are directly employed by federal, state, or local government. The size of the publicly employed working force has increased steadily since the founding of the United States, and seems likely to keep on increasing. If the three to four million persons employed in defense industries, which exist mainly on government funds, are added to the nine million directly employed, it may be estimated that fifteen to twenty per cent of the labor force receives its primary income from government.

Occupational licenses. Licenses are required before one may engage in many kinds of work, from practicing medicine to guiding hunters through the woods. Even occupations which require little education or training, like that of longshoremen, often are subject to strict licensing. Such licenses, which are dispensed by government, make it possible for their holders to receive what is ordinarily their chief source of income.

Franchises. A franchise, which may be held by an individual or by a company, is a partial monopoly created and handed out by government. Its value depends largely upon governmental power; by limiting the number of franchises, government can make them extremely remunerative. A New York City taxi medallion, which costs very little when originally obtained from the city, can be sold for over twenty thousand dollars. The reason for this high price is that the city has not issued new transferable medallions despite the rise in population and traffic. A television channel, handed out free, can often be sold for many millions. Government distributes wealth when it dispenses route permits to truckers, charters to bus lines, routes to air carriers, certificates to oil and gas pipelines, licenses to liquor stores, allotments to growers of cotton or wheat, and concessions in national parks.

Contracts. Many individuals and many more businesses enjoy public generosity in the form of government contracts. Fifty billion dollars annually flows from the federal government in the form of defense spending. These contracts often resemble subsidies; it is virtually impossible to lose money on them. Businesses sometimes make the government their principal source of income, and many "free enterprises" are set up primarily to do business with the government.

Subsidies. Analogous to welfare payments for individuals who cannot manage independently in the economy are subsidies to business. Agriculture is subsidized to help it survive against better organized (and less competitive) sectors of the economy, and the shipping industry is given a dole because of its inability to compete with foreign lines. Local airlines are also on the dole. So are other major industries, notably housing. Still others, such as the railroads, are eagerly seeking help. Government also supports many nonbusiness activities, in such areas as scientific research, health, and education. Total federal subsidies for 1964 were expected to be just under eight and a half billion dollars.

Use of public resources. A very large part of the American economy is publicly owned. Government owns or controls hundreds of millions of acres of public lands valuable for mining, grazing, lumbering, and recreation; sources of energy such as the hydroelectric power of all major rivers, the tidelands reservoirs of oil, and the infant giant of nuclear power; routes of travel and commerce such as the airways, highways, and rivers; the radio-television spectrum which is the avenue for all broadcasting; hoards of surplus crops and materials, public buildings and facilities; and much more. These resources are available for utilization by private businesses and individuals; such use is often equivalent to a subsidy. The radio-television industry uses the scarce channels of the air, free of charge; electric companies use publicly-owned water power; stockmen graze sheep and cattle on public lands at nominal cost; ships and airplanes arrive and depart from publicly-owned docks and airports; the atomic energy industry uses government materials, facilities, and know-how, and all are entitled to make a profit.

Services. Like resources, government services are a source of wealth.
Some of these are plainly of commercial value; postal service for periodicals, newspapers, advertisers, and mail-order houses, insurance for home
builders and savings banks; technical information for agriculture. Other
services dispensed by government include sewage, sanitation, police and
fire protection, and public transportation. The Communications Satellite
represents an unusual type of subsidy through service: the turning over
of government research and know-how to a quasi-private organization.
The most important public service of all, education, is one of the greatest
sources of value to the individual. . . .

C.   LARGESS AND THE CHANGING FORMS OF WEALTH

The significance of government largess is increased by certain underlying changes in the forms of private wealth in the United States. Changes
in the forms of wealth are not remarkable in themselves; the forms are constantly changing and differ in every culture. But today more and more of
our wealth takes the form of rights or status rather than of tangible goods.
An individual's profession or occupation is a prime example. To many
others, a job with a particular employer is the principal form of wealth. A
profession or a job is frequently far more valuable than a house or bank
account, for a new house can be bought, and a new bank account created,
once a profession or job is secure. For the jobless, their status as governmentally assisted or insured persons may be the main source of subsistence.

The automobile dealer's chief wealth is his franchise from the manufacturer which gives him exclusive sales rights within a certain territory, for
it is his guarantee of income. His building, his stock of cars, his organization, and his goodwill may all be less valuable than his franchise. Franchises
represent the principal asset of many businesses: the gasoline station, chain
restaurant, motel or drug store, and many other retail suppliers. To the
large manufacturer, contracts, business arrangements, and organization
may be the most valuable assets. The steel company's relationships with coal
and iron producers and automobile manufacturers and construction companies may be worth more than all its plant and equipment.

The kinds of wealth dispensed by government consist almost entirely
of those forms which are in the ascendancy today. To the individual, these
new forms, such as a profession, job, or right to receive income, are the
basis of his various statuses in society, and may therefore be the most meaningful and distinctive wealth he possesses.

II.   THE EMERGING SYSTEM OF LAW

Wealth or value is created by culture and by society; it is culture that
makes a diamond valuable and a pebble worthless. Property, on the other

hand, is the creation of law. A man who has property has certain legal rights with respect to an item of wealth; property represents a relationship between wealth and its "owner." Government largess is plainly "wealth," but it is not necessarily "property."

Government largess has given rise to a distinctive system of law. This system can be viewed from at least three perspectives; the rights of holders of largess, the powers of government over largess, and the procedure by which holders' rights and governmental power are adjusted. At this point, analysis will not be aided by attempting to apply or to reject the label "property." What is important is to survey — without the use of labels — the unique legal system that is emerging.

A.   INDIVIDUAL RIGHTS IN LARGESS

As government largess has grown in importance, quite naturally there has been pressure for the protection of individual interests in it. The holder of a broadcast license or a motor carrier permit or a grazing permit for the public lands tends to consider this wealth his "own," and to seek legal protection against interference with his enjoyment. The development of individual interests has been substantial, but it has not come easily.

From the beginning, individual rights in largess have been greatly affected by several traditional legal concepts, each of which has had lasting significance:

Right vs. privilege. The early law is marked by courts' attempts to distinguish which forms of largess were "rights" and which were "privileges." Legal protection of the former was by far the greater. If the holder of a license had a "right," he might be entitled to a hearing before the license could be revoked; a "mere privilege" might be revoked without notice or hearing.

[Query: Is Professor Reich using the right-privilege dichotomy as did Hohfeld, §1.2 *supra?*]

The gratuity principle. Government largess has often been considered a "gratuity" furnished by the state. Hence it is said that the state can withhold, grant, or revoke the largess at its pleasure. Under this theory, government is considered to be in somewhat the same position as a private giver.

The whole and the parts. Related to the gratuity theory is the idea that, since government may completely withhold a benefit, it may grant it subject to any terms or conditions whatever. This theory is essentially an exercise in logic: the whole power must include all of its parts.

Internal management. Particularly in relation to its own contracts, government has been permitted extensive power on the theory that it should have control over its own housekeeping or internal management functions. Under this theory, government is treated like a private business. In its dealings with outsiders it is permitted much of the freedom to grant contracts and licenses that a private business would have. . . .

These sentiments are often voiced in the law of government largess, but individual interests have grown up nevertheless. The most common forms of protection are procedural, coupled with an insistence that government action be based on standards that are not "arbitrary" or unauthorized. Development has varied mainly according to the particular type of wealth involved. The courts have most readily granted protection to those types which are intimately bound up with the individual's freedom to earn a living. They have been reluctant to grant individual rights in those types of largess which seem to be exercises of the managerial functions of government, such as subsidies and government contracts. . . .

In all of the cases concerning individual rights in largess the exact nature of the government action which precipitates the controversy makes a great difference. A controversy over government largess may arise from such diverse situations as denial of the right to apply, denial of an application, attaching of conditions to a grant, modification of a grant already made, suspension or revocation of a grant, or some other sanction. In general, courts tend to afford the greatest measure of protection in revocation or suspension cases. The theory seems to be that here some sort of rights have "vested" which may not be taken away without proper procedure. On the other hand, an applicant for largess is thought to have less at stake, and is therefore entitled to less protection. The mere fact that a particular form of largess is protected in one context does not mean that it will be protected in all others.

While individual interests in largess have developed along the lines of procedural protection and restraint upon arbitrary official action, substantive rights to possess and use largess have remained very limited. In the first place, largess does not "vest" in a recipient; it almost always remains revocable. . . .

When the public interest demands that the government take over "property," the Constitution requires that just compensation be paid to the owner. But when largess is revoked in the public interest, the holder ordinarily receives no compensation. For example, if a television station's license were revoked, not for bad behavior on the part of the operator, but in order to provide a channel in another locality, or to provide an outlet for educational television, the holder would not be compensated for its loss. This principle applies to largess of all types.

In addition to being revocable without compensation, most forms of largess are subject to considerable limitations on their use. Social Security cannot be sold or transferred. A television license can be transferred only with FCC permission. The possessor of a grazing permit has no right to change, improve, or destroy the landscape. And use of most largess is limited to specified purposes. Some welfare grants, for example, must be applied to support dependent children. On the other hand, holders of government wealth usually do have a power to exclude others, and to realize income.

The most significant limitation on use is more subtle. To some extent, at least, the holder of government largess is expected to act as the agent of "the public interest" rather than solely in the service of his own self-interest. The theory of broadcast licensing is that the channels belong to the public and should be used for the public's benefit, but that a variety of private operators are likely to perform this function more successfully than government; the holder of a radio or television license is therefore expected to broadcast in "the public interest." The opportunity for private profit is intended to serve as a lure to make private operators serve the public. . . .

III.   THE PUBLIC INTEREST STATE

What are the consequences of the rise of government largess and its attendant legal system? What is the impact on the recipient, on constitutional guaranties of liberty, on the structure of power in the nation? It is important to try to picture the society that is emerging, and to seek its underlying philosophy. The dominant theme, as we have seen, is "the public interest," and out of it there grows the "public interest state." . . .

V.   TOWARD INDIVIDUAL STAKES IN THE COMMONWEALTH

Ahead there stretches — to the farthest horizon — the joyless landscape of the public interest state. The life it promises will be comfortable and comforting. It will be well planned — with suitable areas for work and play. But there will be no precincts sacred to the spirit of individual man.

There can be no retreat from the public interest state. It is the inevitable outgrowth of an interdependent world. An effort to return to an earlier economic order would merely transfer power to giant private governments which would rule not in the public interest, but in their own interest. If individualism and pluralism are to be preserved, this must be done not by marching backwards, but by building these values into today's society. If public and private are now blurred, it will be necessary to draw a new zone of privacy. If private property can no longer perform its protective functions, it will be necessary to establish institutions to carry on the work that private property once did but can no longer do.

In these efforts government largess must play a major role. As we move toward a welfare state, largess will be an ever more important form of wealth. And largess is a vital link in the relationship between the government and private sides of society. It is necessary, then, that largess begin to do the work of property.

The chief obstacle to the creation of private rights in largess has been the fact that it is originally public property, comes from the state, and may be withheld completely. But this need not be an obstacle. Traditional property also comes from the state, and in much the same way. Land, for example, traces back to grants from the sovereign. In the United States, some was the gift of the King of England, some that of the King of Spain. The sovereign extinguished Indian title by conquest, became the new owner, and then granted title to a private individual or group. Some land was the gift of the sovereign under laws such as the Homestead and Preemption Acts. Many other natural resources — water, minerals and timber — passed into private ownership under similar grants. In America, land and resources all were originally government largess. In a less obvious sense, personal property also stems from government. Personal property is created by law; it owes its origin and continuance to laws supported by the people as a whole. These laws "give" the property to one who performs certain actions. Even the man who catches a wild animal "owns" the animal only as a gift from the sovereign, having fulfilled the terms of an offer to transfer ownership.

Like largess, real and personal property were also originally dispensed on conditions, and were subject to forfeiture if the conditions failed. The conditions in the sovereign grants, such as colonization, were generally made explicit, and so was the forfeiture resulting from failure to fulfill them. In the case of the Preemption and Homestead Acts, there were also specific conditions. Even now land is subject to forfeiture for neglect; if it is unused it may be deemed abandoned to the state or forfeited to an adverse possessor. In a very similar way, personal property may be forfeited by abandonment or loss. Hence, all property might be described as government largess, given on condition and subject to loss.

If all property is government largess, why is it not regulated to the same degree as present-day largess? Regulation of property has been limited, not because society had no interest in property, but because it was in the interest of society that property be free. Once property is seen not as a natural right but as a construction designed to serve certain functions, then its origin ceases to be decisive in determining how much regulation should be imposed. The conditions that can be attached to receipt, ownership, and use depend not on where property came from, but on what job it should be expected to perform. Thus in the case of government largess, nothing turns on the fact that it originated in government. The real issue is how it functions and how it should function. . . .

D.   FROM LARGESS TO RIGHT

The proposals discussed above, however salutary, are by themselves far from adequate to assure the status of individual man with respect to largess. The problems go deeper. First, the growth of government power based on the dispensing of wealth must be kept within bounds. Second, there must be a zone of privacy for each individual beyond which neither government nor private power can push — a hiding place from the all-pervasive system of regulation and control. Finally, it must be recognized that we are becoming a society based upon relationship and status — status deriving primarily from source of livelihood. Status is so closely linked to personality that destruction of one may well destroy the other. Status must therefore be surrounded with the kind of safeguards once reserved for personality.

Eventually those forms of largess which are closely linked to status must be deemed to be held as of right. Like property, such largess could be governed by a system of regulation plus civil or criminal sanctions rather than a system based upon denial, suspension and revocation. As things now stand, violations lead to forfeitures — outright confiscation of wealth and status. But there is surely no need for these drastic results. Confiscation, if used at all, should be the ultimate, not the most common and convenient penalty. The presumption should be that the professional man will keep his license, and the welfare recipient his pension. These interests should be "vested." If revocation is necessary, not by reason of the fault of the individual holder, but by reason of overriding demands of public policy, perhaps payment of just compensation would be appropriate. The individual should not bear the entire loss for a remedy primarily intended to benefit the community.

The concept of right is most urgently needed with respect to benefits like unemployment compensation, public assistance, and old age insurance. These benefits are based upon a recognition that misfortune and deprivation are often caused by forces far beyond the control of the individual, such as technological change, variations in demands for goods, depressions, or wars. The aim of these benefits is to preserve the self-sufficiency of the individual, to rehabilitate him where necessary, and to allow him to be a valuable member of a family and a community; in theory they represent part of the individual's rightful share in the commonwealth. Only by making such benefits into rights can the welfare state achieve its goal of providing a secure minimum basis for individual well-being and dignity in a society where each man cannot be wholly the master of his own destiny.

Conclusion

The highly organized, scientifically planned society of the future, governed for the good of its inhabitants, promises the best life that men have ever known. In place of the misery and injustice of the past there can be prosperity, leisure, knowledge, and rich opportunity open to all. In the rush of accomplishment, however, not all values receive equal attention; some are temporarily forgotten while others are pushed ahead. We have made provision for nearly everything, but we have made no adequate provision for individual man.

This article is an attempt to offer perspective of the transformation of society as it bears on the economic basis of individualism. The effort has been to show relationships; to bring together drivers' licenses, unemployment insurance, membership in the bar, permits for using school auditoriums, and second class mail privileges, in order to see what we are becoming.

Government largess is only one small corner of a far vaster problem. There are many other new forms of wealth: franchises in private businesses, equities in corporations, the right to receive privately furnished utilities and services, status in private organizations. These too may need added safe-guards in the future. Similarly, there are many sources of expanded governmental power aside from largess. By themselves, proposals concerning government largess would be far from accomplishing any fundamental reforms. But, somehow, we must begin.

At the very least, it is time to reconsider the theories under which new forms of wealth are regulated, and by which governmental power over them is measured. It is time to recognize that "the public interest" is all too often a reassuring platitude that covers up sharp clashes of conflicting values, and hides fundamental choices. It is time to see that the "privilege" or "gratuity" concept, as applied to wealth dispensed by government, is not much different from the absolute right of ownership that private capital once invoked to justify arbitrary power over employees and the public.

Above all, the time has come for us to remember what the framers of the Constitutions knew so well — that "a power over a man's subsistence amounts to a power over his will." We cannot safely entrust our livelihoods and our rights to the discretion of authorities, examiners, boards of control, character committees, regents, or license commissioners. We cannot permit any official or agency to pretend to sole knowledge of the public good. We cannot put the independence of any man — least of all our Barskys and our Anastaplos — wholly in the power of other men.

If the individual is to survive in a collective society, he must have protection against its ruthless pressures. There must be sanctuaries or enclaves where no majority can reach. To shelter the solitary human spirit does not merely make possible the fulfillment of individuals; it also gives society the power to change, to grow, and to regenerate, and hence to endure. These were the objects which property sought to achieve, and can no longer achieve. The challenge of the future will be to construct, for the society that is coming, institutions and laws to carry on this work. Just as the Homestead Act was a deliberate effort to foster individual values at an earlier time, so we must try to build an economic basis for liberty today — a Homestead Act for rootless twentieth century man. We must create a new property.

NOTES AND QUESTIONS

1. **Republican elements of Reich's argument.** What elements of the republican vision underlie Reich's argument?

2. **Aspects of Reich's argument that are not republican.** What aspects of Reich's argument and rhetoric do not seem consonant with the republican vision?

3. **"Dependence begets subservience . . ."** Remember Thomas Jefferson's argument that property ownership enabled men to avoid subservience, enabling them to gain instead the independence necessary to preserve the republic by pursuing the common good. Note the parallels between this argument and Reich's use of the term "the public interest."

FIGURE 1-3
Phrase originating from women's role of providing "haven from the heartless world" of nineteenth-century capitalism

The latter is a term dating from the Progressive era at the turn of the twentieth century, yet it can fruitfully be viewed as a continuation of certain themes in the republican tradition.[33]

Reich's use of the republican vision to effect a sharp shift in the law illuminates several important linkages. The first is between "the law" and the larger realm of political discourse. In some contexts, we have noted, one can simply cite a settled rule in arguing for one's client, apply the rule in a straightforward way, and draw a favorable conclusion. But where the rule cuts against your client, where you have to defend your choice of one rule as opposed to another potentially damaging rule, and so forth, you cannot do your job by treating the law as a neutral system of self-executing rules. In these contexts, the key to good lawyering is the art of persuasion.

What arguments are persuasive in the realm of property? The Reich piece suggests that when lawyers search for *reasons* why the law should be changed, they often call on the different visions of property to make a persuasive argument. Consider the following case. It involves an attempt by a landlord to evict a tenant where both parties signed a binding lease that gave the landlord the right to evict the tenant upon 30 days' notice at any time for any reason. Yet the court holds that the landlord cannot exercise his contract right. Instead, to trump the landlord's "old property" rights, the court declares a "new property" right for Mrs. Joy. What reasons does the court give in support of the new property right? In what ways are these resonant of republican themes? What strains of republican thought are not stressed or adopted by the court?

---

33. This is not to say that no important differences exist between late-eighteenth-century republicanism and turn-of-the-twentieth-century progressivism. One difference is that whereas Jefferson's republicanism depends on moral character ("virtue") to lead men to the common good, the Progressives depended on "expertise" to achieve the public interest. See Joan C. Williams, Virtue, in Richard Wrightman Fox and James Kloppenberg, A Companion to American Thought (1994).

The case involves the Fifth Amendment of the U.S. Constitution, which states that "nor shall any person be . . . deprived of life, liberty or property without due process of law." The issue of whether the plaintiff has been deprived of property without due process ultimately focuses on whether she has "property" at all.

JOY v. DANIELS

479 F.2d 1236 (4th Cir. 1973)

CRAVEN, J. . . . [P]laintiff challenges, as violative of the fifth and fourteenth amendments, her threatened eviction from the Joseph Paul Apartments. The apartments are quasi-public, having been constructed and now being operated by defendant, Joseph Paul Apartments, Inc., under Section 221(d)(3) of the National Housing Act. The district court held that the plaintiff could properly be evicted since her tenancy had expired under the terms of the lease, and that no other cause need be assigned for the eviction. We reverse.

I

The plaintiff, Thelma Joy, is the head of her household and with her four minor children constitutes a "family" within the statutory scheme. Her effective monthly income[1] of $222.20 is a "low income" for purposes of the federal housing programs, and she thus qualifies for occupancy in the Joseph Paul Apartments. On September 2, 1970, plaintiff leased one of defendant's apartments. The standard form lease provided in relevant part:

> At the end of one year, lease is automatically renewed from month to month, rent to be payable in advance without demand on first day of each month. Either party may terminate lease at end of term or any successive term by giving 30 days' notice in advance to other party.

On September 11, 1971, the defendant gave plaintiff 30 days' notice to vacate, no cause being assigned.[2] It appears that the plaintiff has continued to occupy her apartment on a month-to-month basis, with her tenancy dependent on the outcome of this litigation.

---

1. It consists of a welfare benefit in the amount of $122.20, plus $126.00 worth of food stamps at a cost to her of $26.00.
2. In its answer to the complaint the defendant alleged that the plaintiff "maintained a slovenly and ill-kept apartment"; had destroyed window screens; failed to pay rent on time; and used excessive electricity. The district court found that it could be inferred that these were the reasons defendant sought eviction, but that such a finding was unnecessary to decision and thus no such inference was drawn.

Section 221(d)(3) of the National Housing Act, 12 U.S.C. §1715*l* (d)(3) (1971), is a statutory scheme for encouraging housing for low income families. To participate in this program, defendant was required to conform to a regulatory agreement with the Federal Housing Administration governing, inter alia, the construction, occupancy, and daily operations of the project. The FHA also grants defendant rent supplements for the plaintiff and other tenants under Section 101 of the Housing and Urban Development Act of 1965, 12 U.S.C. §1701s(b) (1971). Plaintiff, for example, enjoys occupancy of an apartment worth $157.00 per month at a cost to her of $48.00. FHA pays the difference, i.e., $109.00 per month, directly to defendant. As a prerequisite to participation in the rent supplement program, there must be local government approval. 24 C.F.R. §5.15(c) (1971). The County Council specifically approved rent supplements for Joseph Paul Apartments on August 6, 1968. . . .

III

The district court concluded that plaintiff had no right of occupancy upon expiration of the term of the lease. Plaintiff contends that despite expiration of the term she may be evicted only for "good cause" and is entitled to the protection of procedural due process in the determination of whether cause exists. Since procedural due process applies only to the deprivation of interest protected by the fourteenth amendment, i.e., liberty and property, we must first determine plaintiff's substantive rights. . . .

As stated in Board of Regents v. Roth:

> Certain attributes of "property" interests protected by procedural due process emerge from [the Court's] decisions. To have a property interest in a benefit, a person clearly must have more than desire for it. He must have more than a unilateral expectation of it. He must, instead, have a legitimate claim of entitlement to it. It is a purpose of the ancient institution of property to protect those claims upon which people rely in their daily lives, reliance that must not be arbitrarily undermined. It is a purpose of the constitutional right to a hearing to provide an opportunity for a person to vindicate those claims.
>
> Property interests, of course, are not created by the Constitution.[7] Rather, they are created and their dimensions are defined by existing rules or understandings that stem from an independent source such as state law —

---

7. Indeed, the Court has held with regard to eviction from private housing:

We do not denigrate the importance of decent, safe, and sanitary housing. But the Constitution does not provide judicial remedies for every social and economic ill. We are unable to perceive in that document any constitutional guarantee of access to dwellings of a particular quality or any recognition of the right of a tenant to occupy the real property of his [wholly private] landlord beyond the term of his lease, without the payment of rent or otherwise contrary to the terms of the relevant agreement.

Lindsey v. Normet, 405 U.S. 56, 75 (1972). [This is the case in which the Supreme Court held that no constitutional right to housing exists. — EDS.]

rules or understandings that secure certain benefits and that support claims
of entitlement to those benefits. . . .

408 U.S. at 577.

> A person's interest in a benefit is a "property" interest for due process
> purposes if there are such rules or mutually explicit understandings that sup-
> port his claim of entitlement to the benefit and that he may invoke at a
> hearing.

Perry v. Sinderman, 408 U.S. 593, 601 (1972). Thus we must now look to
applicable statutes, governmental regulations, and the custom and understandings of public landlords in the operation of their apartments to determine if a public tenant has a "property interest" in a tenancy beyond the
term of the lease except for cause.[8]

When Congress legislated with regard to mortgage insurance benefits
which defendant receives, it provided: "The Congress affirms the national
goal, as set forth in section 1441 of Title 42, of 'a decent home and suitable
living environment for every American family.'" 12 U.S.C. §1701t. This
policy of improving the "living environment of urban areas" was also the
policy of Congress in enacting the Housing and Urban Development Act of
1965. Pub. L. 89-117, 79 Stat. 451 (Aug. 10, 1965). "This [policy] includes
adequate, safe, and sanitary quarters. But it also implies an atmosphere of
stability, security, neighborliness, and social justice." [McQueen v. Drucker,
317 F. Supp. 1122, 1130 (D. Mass. 1970).] Cf., Trafficante v. Metropolitan
Life Ins. Co., 409 U.S. 205 (1972).

In addition to the policy statements contained in the relevant funding statutes, Congress has also expressed itself in part on how these programs should be run. "No person in the United States shall, on the ground
of race, color, or national origin, be excluded from participation in, be denied the benefits of, or be subjected to discrimination under any program
or activity receiving Federal financial assistance." 42 U.S.C. §2000d. The
policy of this statute, a person's right to be free of invidious discrimination
in federally assisted programs, is contained in many statutes, see, e.g., 42
U.S.C. §2000a. . . .

Not only the statutes, but also FHA regulations authorized under 12
U.S.C. §1701s(f), imply a right to be free from arbitrary and discriminatory
action. For example, 24 C.F.R. §221-536 (1971) provides that a landlord in
a §221(d)(3) apartment may not discriminate against any family because of
children.

The House Report dealing with the Housing and Urban Development
Act of 1965 said, with regard to the rent supplement program:

> If his income increases sufficiently so that he can pay the full economic rent
> with 25% of his income, rent supplement payments on his behalf would cease

---

8. [Footnote 8 consists of a long quotation from *The New Property*. — EDS.]

to be made. The tenant could, however, continue to live in the project and would not be required to pay more than the full economic rent.

H.R. Rep. No. 365, 89th Cong., 1st Sess. (1965), 1965 U.S. Code Cong. and Ad. News, pp.2614, 2618.

This suggests the Congress was contemplating more occupancy entitlement than limited leasehold terms. The tenant's expectation of some degree of permanency, seemingly shared by the Congress, if not by the landlord, is bolstered by "custom."[10] Just as there may be a "common law" of tenure at a college or university, there may be a common law of tenancy in public housing projects. See *Perry*, 408 U.S. at 602.

> The actual workings of the subsidized housing program must be examined to determine whether there is a reasonable basis for tenants to expect that in normal circumstances they will be permitted to remain in the housing indefinitely. And indeed one finds that the normal practice in subsidized housing, as in private housing, is to permit tenants to remain beyond the expiration of a lease unless a reason has arisen for eviction; termination is the exception, not the rule. Thus, tenants do have a reasonable expectation deserving of protection.

Note, Procedural Due Process in Government-Subsidized Housing, 86 Harv. L. Rev. 880, 905 (1973).

In view of the congressional policies of providing a decent home (with stability and security) for every American family, and of prohibiting arbitrary and discriminatory action, bolstered by the FHA regulations and custom, we find in the scheme of the National Housing Act and the Housing and Urban Development Act of 1965 a property right or entitlement to continue occupancy until there exists a cause to evict other than the mere expiration of the lease. We therefore hold that the lease provision purporting to give the landlord power to terminate without cause at the expiration of a fixed term is invalid. Accord, Rudder v. United States, 226 F.2d 51 (D.C. Cir. 1955); Brown v. Housing Auth., 340 F. Supp. 114 (E.D. Wis. 1972); *McQueen*, 317 F. Supp. at 1131.

In Caulder v. Durham Housing Auth., 433 F.2d 998 (4th Cir. 1970), *cert. denied*, 401 U.S. 1003 (1971), we stated:

> The "privilege" or the "right" to occupy publicly subsidized low-rent housing seems to us to be no less entitled to due process protection than entitlement to welfare benefits which were the subject of decision in *Goldberg* [v. Kelly, 397 U.S. 254 (1970)] or the other rights and privileges referred to in *Goldberg*.

---

10. Indeed, early common law provided that even an estate at will could be transformed into an estate similar to a life estate by continuous custom. "This custom, being suffered to grow up by the lord, is looked upon as the evidence and interpreter of his will: his will is no longer arbitrary and precarious: but fixed and ascertained." 2 Blackstone, Commentaries *147.

433 F.2d at 1003. The court then held tenants entitled to notice, confrontation of witnesses, counsel, and a decision by an impartial decision maker based on evidence adduced at a hearing. 433 F.2d at 1004. As stated by the court below, it could be inferred that the plaintiff here was to be evicted for cause. If so, she would be entitled to the same procedural safeguards set forth in *Caulder*. To allow a quasi public landlord to evict upon expiration of a fixed term is to enable secret and silent discrimination and would wholly emasculate the procedural safeguards of *Caulder*. . . .

[Discussion of "what process is due" is omitted.]

On remand the district court will enter its decree invalidating the lease expiration clause and enjoining the defendant from attempting to evict the plaintiff except for cause under the procedural and substantive law of South Carolina.

Reversed and remanded.

NOTES AND QUESTIONS

1. **Court's rationale.** What reasons does the court give for why Mrs. Joy should not be evicted except for cause? Do these reasons reflect the republican vision of property?

2. **Did the court create a property right or recognize a preexisting one?** The court argues that it is not creating a new property right; it is merely recognizing a right that Congress created. Are you convinced that the statutes, regulations, and other factors the court considers create the right not to be evicted except for "good cause"?

3. **Public housing tenants.** Earlier, the Department of Housing and Urban Development (HUD), which administers the nation's subsidized housing programs, had directed local (public housing) authorities to inform any tenant facing eviction of "the specific reason(s) for [the] notice to vacate"; thereupon, the tenant was to be "given an opportunity to make such reply or explanation as he may wish." Thorpe v. Housing Authority of the City of Durham, 393 U.S. 268, 273 (1969) (citing HUD circular of Feb. 7, 1967). Escalera v. New York City Hous. Auth., 425 F.2d 853 (2d Cir.), *cert. denied,* 400 U.S. 853 (1970), *motion granted,* 924 F. Supp. 1323 (S.D.N.Y. 1996), followed by requiring that public housing tenants, facing eviction for "non-desirability," receive additional procedural safeguards, including the right to confront and cross-examine persons who supplied information on which the charges of "non-desirability" were based. This led to a HUD circular on grievance procedures. The tenant, if she wishes, may compel a hearing before an impartial official or a hearing panel. If representatives of management are on the panel, tenants must be represented in equal numbers. A tenant is entitled to see the evidence against him, cross-examine witnesses, have the proceedings open or closed, and be represented by counsel. The final decision, in writing, must contain the reasons and the

evidence relied on. Renewal & Housing Management §§7465.8, 7465.9 (Feb. 22, 1971). Twenty-five years later, a federal court modified *Escalera* in the context of apartments used for drug trafficking. Noting that the quarter-century had seen a dramatic increase in drug activity and that *Escalera* meant that the Housing Authority could not "address swiftly the current epidemic of drug-trafficking in [its] apartments," the court allowed the authority to proceed directly against violators under the state's Bawdy House Law. 924 F. Supp. 1323 (S.D.N.Y. 1996).

Pursuant to President Clinton's March 28, 1996, announcement, suspected drug dealers and the households to which they belong could be evicted from public housing after the first drug-related crime. The one-strike policy was authorized in a 1988 federal law, but cities have not been required to enforce it until now. The guidelines provide for eviction by public housing officials once they have evidence of criminal activity; there is no need to wait for arrest or conviction. Tanya Jones, Clinton Gets Tough on Criminals in Public Housing, Baltimore Sun, Mar. 29, 1996, at 3A.

4. **What is a state instrumentality?** The court in Joy v. Daniels treats the privately owned, but federally aided, housing project as "governmental," thus subject to the Fifth (and Fourteenth) Amendments. Not all courts agreed. See, e.g., Grafton v. Brooklyn Law School, 478 F.2d 1137 (2d Cir. 1973); Weigand v. Afton View Apartments, 473 F.2d 545 (8th Cir. 1973) (§236 project); McGuane v. Chenango Court, 431 F.2d 1189 (2d Cir. 1970) (§221(d)(3) project), *cert denied,* 401 U.S. 994 (1971). See Note, Procedural Due Process in Government-Subsidized Housing, 86 Harv. L. Rev. 880 (1973).

5. **Comparing welfare and subsidized housing benefits.** The court's opinion mentions the due process protection given welfare benefits under Goldberg v. Kelly, 397 U.S. 254 (1970). Can it be argued that a public housing or other subsidized tenancy — in view of the urgent shortage of standard, low-rent units — should be safeguarded even more jealously than a welfare benefit? The loss of welfare frequently implies alternative income; but the loss of public housing (as a nondesirable) usually implies a return to squalor or unbearably higher rentals.

6. **Does *Joy* help or hurt tenants?** How would you argue that Joy v. Daniels might harm more low-income tenants (and prospective tenants) than the decision helps?

d.   The Mystique of Homeownership

Americans would sacrifice just about anything to own a home — it is one of their highest priorities in life.[34]

---

34. Fannie Mae. Fannie Mae National Housing Survey 8 (1992).

cathy®   **by Cathy Guisewite**

A special respect for individual liberty in the home has long been part of this Nation's culture and law.[35]

Why did the Supreme Court uphold zoning regulations[36] in an era when it was striking down other governmental regulations on private property? Why do homeowners receive a huge income tax subsidy through the deduction for home mortgage interest and local property taxes?[37] In these and many other contexts, we treat homeownership with a reverence that is difficult to fully understand without reference to republican notions linking property ownership with virtue and citizenship. The underlying assumptions are that homeowners add more to the community and that by protecting and promoting investment in one's owned home, we can enhance the common good.

CONSTANCE PERIN, EVERYTHING IN ITS PLACE

47, 64-64, 71-72 (1977)

. . . The family and the good citizenship that homeownership is believed to instill are equally idealized and, thereby, equated. A sacred quality endows both the family and its "home," sacred in the sense of being set apart from the mundane and having a distinctive aura. . . . [I]n the hierarchy of land uses all those below the apex partake of less of this sacred quality, but when one follows those "natural and orderly processes of progress,"

---

35. City of Ladue v. Gilleo, 512 U.S. 43 (1994).

36. See, e.g., Euclid v. Ambler Realty, 272 U.S. 365 (1926) (upholding zoning ordinance).

37. In 1994, the so-called tax expenditure resulting from these two deductions exceeded $70 billion. Kenneth R. Harney, The Nation's Housing — Budget Cutters Target Deductions on Interest, Taxes, Wash. Post, Nov. 12, 1994, at E1. As of 1990, about one-third of the subsidy goes to roughly 4 percent of taxpayers with incomes in excess of $100,000. Peter Drier and John Atlas, Stop Subsidized Housing for the Wealthy, *Valley News,* May 17, 1991.

if one engages in "competition" and "gets ahead," then one can achieve the ideal family existence, fulfilling the American Dream. . . . Any other residential dwelling . . . is a "compromise" with those ideals. . . .

> It is true that we in America more nearly approach the possibility of complete property in land. But even here . . . an undivided totality is not so common and the identification of anyone who may indisputably be called an "owner" is often more or less a game of blind man's bluff.

But no matter: ownership is a category so socially valuable that the many conditions fragmenting its totality do not affect its import. These fragmenting conditions [are, in part] legal — as in public laws of taxation, building codes, occupancy regulations, and the common law. Nevertheless: despite their chafing at "interferences" with their "rights" to "private property" (interferences not so different from those renters experience . . .), for Americans "to own" anything less than a single-family-detached house . . . is . . . a "compromise" with the American Dream. . . .

It is not a detour to explain why I put "owning" in quotation marks: paid-up mortgages constitute only about forty percent of all mortgages. The correct general term is homebuyer. . . . [Homebuying] is a lifelong process: only when "owners" are over sixty-five have eighty-five percent paid off the mortgage.

. . . The ideology of homeownership — its strong sentimental appeal — may account for the political decisions of these last forty years to buttress some consumers' ability to realize the dream. [These decisions include] improvements in the availability of mortgage credit, beginning during the Depression and lasting through 1950, [that] made home ownership possible for millions of families who would have had to defer or forgo ownership [without them]. Together, tax incentives and easier credit have created federal subsidies for private housing. . . .

Moreover, . . . the American ideal of homeownership is equally the ideal of perfected citizenship. Calvin Coolidge said: "No greater contribution could be made to the stability of the Nation, and the advancement of its ideals, than to make it a Nation of homeowning families." Franklin Roosevelt said: "A nation of home owners, of people who own a real share in their own land, is unconquerable." President Hoover's Conference on Home Building and Home Ownership in 1931, where many of today's selective incentives began, termed homeownership a "birthright" and an "epochal event" in a family's life. The awful alternative was to be condemned . . . "to die in a rented house." The Conference report concludes that "too much cannot be said about the value of stimulating home ownership because of its effect upon good citizenship and the strengthening of family ties." . . .

The U.S. homeownership rate is among the world's highest.[38] The central role of homeownership in American culture is linked with the massive subsidies for home ownership after World War II.[39] These subsidies, and a booming economy, made homeownership available to people of modest incomes until the 1970s. In 1973, the average American spent only about 20 percent of his income on housing,[40] and someone earning the median salary could afford to buy an average new house. This happy circumstance lasted only between roughly 1945 and 1975.[41] After about 1975, a combination of house price inflation and higher interest rates led to sharp increases in the cost of housing in relation to incomes, which have just begun to ameliorate.[42] During the 1980s, more than half of Americans could not afford to buy a median-priced house in their area,[43] and those who could typically paid up to half of their incomes on housing.[44] In addition, many Americans who grew up in single-family homes believed that they would never buy a house: This included not only the working poor and working-class families, but even many families who considered themselves to be solidly middle class.[45] The unattainability of homeownership for the middle class may have played an important role in creating the resentment and sense of disenfranchisement felt by many Americans as we entered the 1990s, particularly

---

38. The United States and United Kingdom have the highest rates of owner-occupation: 65 percent and 67 percent respectively. Rates in the remainder of Europe are much lower: 40 percent in the former West Germany, 44 percent in the Netherlands, 51 percent in France. Graham Hallett, National Similarities and Differences, in The New Housing Shortage: Housing Affordability in Europe and the USA 3 (1993). Note that each of the European countries has a significant segment of its population in rental housing provided by the government, from a high of 43 percent of housing in the Netherlands, to a low of 23 percent in France. In the United States, only 3 percent of housing is rented by the government. Id. at 3.

39. See Stephanie Coontz, The Way We Never Were 76-79 (1992) (documenting government subsidies to support suburban homeownership). In part as a result of these subsidies, between 1940 and 1980, a nation of renters was transformed into a nation of homeowners. George Sternlieb and James W. Hughes, Demographics and Housing in America, 4 Population Bulletin 2-34 (1986).

40. Frank Levy and Richard C. Michel, The Economic Future of American Families 64 (1991).

41. In 1975, the average-price, new single-family house cost $44,600, which would require a minimal annual income of $13,474, 2 percent below the nation's median family income that year. However, by 1981, the average-price, new single-family house cost $94,100, which would require a minimum annual income of $43,101 — nearly double the nation's median family income that year. Critical Perspectives on Housing xv (Rachel G. Bratt, et al. eds., 1986) (calculating from U.S. Bureau of Census, 1981c, 772 and U.S. Bureau of Census, 1981b, table 2).

42. See Leo Grebler and Frank Mittelbach, The Inflation of House Prices (1979). The year 1993 began a downward trend in housing prices which, because of lower mortgage interest rates and relative price stability, seems to have continued. In that year, for the first time since 1976, the cash burden of homeownership dropped below 30 percent of income for potential first-time buyers. BNA, HDR Current Developments, July 18, 1994, at 140; id., July 1, 1996, at 103.

43. Majority Can't Afford Homes, USA Today, June 14, 1991, at 2B.

44. Critical Perspectives on Housing xiv (Rachel G. Bratt, et al. eds., 1986).

45. Carol F. Steinbach, Housing the "Haves," Natl. J., June 22, 1991, at 1614-1619.

working-class men whose incomes would have allowed them to buy houses if they had lived 20 years earlier.[46]

Americans associate homeownership with financial security, and most believe that homeownership is a good investment. Traditionally, homeownership has been the primary way that working- and middle-class persons accumulate wealth. See Frank Levy and Richard C. Michel, The Economic Future of American Families 63 (1991). Yet the Fannie Mae National Housing survey, *supra,* stressed that nonfinancial reasons play a significant role as well. The survey notes that homeownership "is a metaphor for *personal and family* security" (emphasis in original). Id. at 6. "The sum total of the findings in this survey suggest that owning one's home is, in essence, an empowering act, giving people a stake in society and a sense of control over their own lives. Put differently, homeownership strengthens the social fabric." Id. at 10. This language very clearly echoes the republican vision.

Americans' imagination focuses not only on property ownership in general, but on ownership of a single-family house. Fully 80 percent of all Americans identify the traditional single-family house with a yard as the ideal place to live. Id. at 4. Is Americans' focus on the single-family house a carryover from the republican linkage of independence, virtue, and citizenship?

The continuing linkage between ownership and citizenship is striking. Homeowners had markedly higher rates of political participation: 73 percent of homeowners, but only 47 percent of renters said they voted in national elections; the proportions for local elections were 61 and 33. Id. at 3.

If the characteristically American fixation on the single-family house is resonant of assumptions derived from the republican linkage of property, stability, virtue, and citizenship, the comparatively low rate of homeownership among minority groups takes on an added political dimension. In the Fannie Mae survey, only 42 percent of blacks and 46 percent of hispanics surveyed owned their own homes, but 71 percent of whites did. Id. at 6. Only 59 percent of the nation's middle-class blacks own homes, compared with 74 percent of middle-class whites. *Money Magazine,* Dec. 1989, at 152. Even poor whites have a homeownership rate higher than all blacks, considered as a group.[47] Because of the central role homeownership plays in family wealth, the disparities in homeownership between blacks and whites help explain the dramatic racial differences in accumulated wealth.[48]

---

46. Cf. Levy and Michel, *supra* note 40, 90-91.

47. John O. Calmore, Spacial Equality and the Kerner Commission Report: A Back-to-the-Future Essay, 71 N.C. L. Rev. 1487, 1509-1510 (1993).

48. See Chapter 2 (median wealth of white household ten times greater than of black households). See Scott Minerbrook, Blacks Locked Out of the American Dream, Bus. & Socy. Rev., Sept. 22, 1993, at 26 ("In 1988, the U.S. Census Bureau concluded that white families had

Substantial literature documents the federal government's role in creating the disparities between homeownership rates of blacks and whites.[49] The story begins with the New Deal programs that led to widespread homeownership in the United States. Before these New Deal programs, homeownership was inaccessible to the middle class because banks offered only five- or ten-year loans with down payments of up to one-third of the total cost of the house.[50] After many homeowners defaulted on their loans during the Great Depression of the 1930s, the federal government created the Home Owners Loan Corporation (HOLC), which for the first time offered the low-interest, long-term loans still available to American home buyers.[51] HOLC was soon followed by the Federal Housing Administration (FHA), which offered federal guarantees to banks that gave loans to homeowners, thereby effectively eliminating the risk of default and giving banks a strong incentive to offer low-cost home loans.

Two federal policies ensured that racial minorities would have a much harder time securing home loans than would whites. The first was the HOLC neighborhood rating system, in which black neighborhoods were invariably given the lowest rating available, and virtually all of the lowest-rated neighborhoods were black.[52] Although HOLC did make loans to the lowest-rated neighborhoods, private banks, which often adopted the HOLC rating criteria, did not. Id. at 1258. The FHA also used explicit racial criteria in deciding which homeowners would receive federal housing benefits. The FHA refused to guarantee loans for homes in undesirable neighborhoods, and it defined the presence of minorities as undesirable, categorizing black neighbors as nuisances to be avoided (along with stables and pig pens).[53] The

---

ten times the wealth of blacks in America. Crucially, 40% of that difference was the lack of home equity between black and white families."), quoted in Richard T. Ford, The Boundaries of Race: Political Geography in Legal Analysis, 107 Harv. L. Rev. 1843, 1852 n.19 (1994); Robert Staples, The Urban Plantation: Racism and Colonialism in the Post Civil Rights Era 204-205 (1987) ("housing in a predominantly black neighborhood is devalued by thousands of dollars").

49. For examples of this literature, see the sources quoted in this discussion and John A. Calmore, To Make Wrong/Right: The Necessary of Proper Aspirations of Fair Housing, in The State of Black America 1989, at 77 (Janet Dewart ed., 1989). This legal literature draws on a nonlegal literature of racial geography. Some influential examples are Charles Abrams, Forbidden Neighbors: A Study of Prejudice in Housing (1955); Kenneth Jackson, Crabgrass Frontier: The Suburbanization of the United States (1985); Douglas S. Massey and Nancy A. Denton, American Apartheid: Segregation and the Making of the Underclass (1993); Robert Staples, The Urban Plantation: Racism and Colonialism in the Post Civil Rights Era (1987).

50. See Michael H. Schill and Susan M. Wachter, The Spacial Bias of Federal Housing Law and Policy: Concentrated Poverty in Urban America, 143 U. Pa. L. Rev. 1285, 1308 (1995).

51. These loans are called fixed-rate, self-amortizing loans. For more information about them, see Chapter 12.

52. See Martha Mahoney, Law and Racial Geography: Public Housing and the Economy in New Orleans, 42 Stan. L. Rev. 1251, 1257 (1990) (quoting Kenneth T. Jackson, Race, Ethnicity, and Real Estate Appraisal: The Home Owners Loan Corporation and the Federal Housing Administration, 6 Urb. Hist. 419-429 (1980)).

53. Richard T. Ford, The Boundaries of Race-Political Geography in Legal Analysis, 107 Harv. L. Rev. 1843, 1848 (1994). See also Calmore, Spacial Equality, *supra* note 47, at 1510

FHA advocated zoning and deed restrictions that forbade such nuisances. Id. at 1848. Indeed, the agency often *required* deed restrictions to bar residency by racial minorities. As a result, only 2 percent of FHA housing units were made available to minorities.[54] In addition, private builders adopted racially exclusionary deed restrictions so their property would be eligible for FHA insurance in the future.[55] Such zoning and deed restrictions are no longer legal in many states, but the racialized housing patterns they helped create remain in place.[56] "Race-neutral policies, set against an historical backdrop of state action in the service of racial segregation and thus against a contemporary background of racially identified space, . . . predictably reproduce and entrench racial segregation and the racial-caste system that accompanies it."[57]

Recent studies indicate that minorities still have more difficulty obtaining mortgage loans. A recent study by the Federal Reserve Bank of Boston concluded that minority applicants are about 60 percent more likely to be denied a mortgage loan than are whites.[58]

Attitudes toward homeownership varied by both race and income. "The farther down the income ladder one goes," the survey concluded, "the more acute is the desire to own a home." Fannie Mae National Housing Survey, *supra*, at 6. Nearly two-thirds of (nonhomeowning) respondents in the lowest-income brackets said owning a home was one of their most important goals, while only one-third of those in the highest income brackets felt the same way. African Americans were more willing than either whites or Hispanics to take a second job or put a young child in day care, if that was required to become a homeowner. Id. at 3.

Thus, housing is seen as more than just shelter. It is a "way . . . of structuring economic, social and political relationships."[59] This further evinces how the institution of property helps to achieve citizenship and participation in American society, and how "propertylessness" may lead to nonparticipation and a sense of disenfranchisement.

("Between 1934 and 1959, only two percent of the FHA units were made available to the nation's minorities, who comprised approximately fifteen percent of the overall population").

54. See Calmore, *supra* note 47, at 1509.

55. Mahoney, *supra* note 52, at 1258.

56. For examples of such deed restrictions, see Chapters 2 and 7; for examples of exclusionary zoning, see Chapter 9.

57. Ford, *supra* note 53, at 1845.

58. Alicia H. Munnell, Lynn E. Browne, James McEneaney, and Geoffrey M. B. Tootell, Mortgage Lending in Boston: Interpreting HMDA Data 2 (Federal Reserve Bank of Boston Working Paper No. 92-7, 1992), quoted in Anthony D. Taibi, Banking Finance, and Community Economic Empowerment: Structural Economic Theory, Procedural Civil Rights, and Substantive Racial Justice, 107 Harv. L. Rev. 1465, 1474 (1994).

59. Emily P. Achtenburg and Peter Marcuse, Towards the Decommodification of Housing: A Political Analysis and a Progressive Program, in America's Housing Crisis: What Is to Be Done? 202, 207 (Chester Hartman ed., 1983).

§1.4   Liberal Visions of Property[60]

a.   Economic Liberalism: Let a Thousand Deals Bloom

LANCE BANNING, JEFFERSON IDEOLOGY REVISITED: LIBERAL AND CLASSICAL IDEAS IN THE NEW AMERICAN REPUBLIC

43 Wm. & Mary Q. 3, 11-12 (1986)

Analytically, of course, modern liberalism and classic republicanism are distinguishable philosophies. *Liberalism* is a label most would use for a political philosophy that regards man as possessed of inherent individual rights and the state as existing to protect these rights, reviving its authority from consent. *Classical republicanism* is a term that scholars have employed to identify a mode of thinking about citizenship and the polity that may be traced from Aristotle through Machiavelli and Harrington to eighteenth-century Britain and her colonies. The two philosophies began with different assumptions about human nature and develop a variety of different ideas. Their incompatibility will seem much more pronounced if we expand our use of *liberalism* to encompass capitalism or imply a bourgeois attitude and set of values.

A full-blown, modern liberalism . . . posits a society of equal individuals who are motivated principally if not exclusively by their passions or self-interest; it identifies a proper government as one existing to protect these individuals' inherent rights and private pursuits. A fully classical republicanism . . . reasons from the diverse capacities and characteristics of different social groups, whose members are political by nature. No republicanism will still be "classical" if it is not concerned with the individual's participation with others in civic decisions where the needs and power of those others must be taken into account. Liberalism, thus defined, is comfortable with economic man, with the individual who is intent on maximizing private satisfactions and who needs to do no more in order to serve the general good. Classical republicanism regards this merely economic man as less than fully human. Assuming a certain tension between public good and private desires, it will identify the unrestrained pursuit of purely private interests as incompatible with preservation of commonwealth.

A key theorist of property in the liberal tradition is John Locke. As you read the following excerpts from his *The Second Treatise of Government,* written in the late seventeenth century, ask yourself how Locke's analysis reflects the tenets of liberal thought.

---

60. Note that we are not using "liberal" in the sense that "Teddy Kennedy is a Liberal," but as a description of a dominant way of thinking shared to a substantial extent by both liberals and conservatives.

JOHN LOCKE, TWO TREATISES OF GOVERNMENT

287, 304-307, 308-309, 314-315 (Peter Laslett ed., 1967; written c. 1679-1683)

4. To understand Political Power right, and derive from its Original, we must consider what State all Men are naturally in, and that is, a *State of perfect Freedom* to order their Actions, and dispose of their Possessions, and Persons as they think fit, within the bounds of the Law of Nature, without asking leave, or depending upon the Will of any other Man. . . .

26. God, who hath given the World to Men in common, hath also given them reason to make use of it to the best advantage of Life, and convenience. The Earth, and all that is therein, is given to Men for the Support and Comfort of their being. And though all the Fruits it naturally produces, and Beasts it feeds, belong to Mankind in common, as they are produced by the spontaneous hand of Nature; and no body has originally a private Dominion, exclusive of the rest of Mankind, in any of them, as they are in their natural state: yet being given for the use of Men, there must be a means *to appropriate* them some way or other before they can be of any use, or at all beneficial to any particular Man. . . .

27. Though the Earth, and all inferior Creatures be common to all Men, yet every Man has a *Property* in his own *Person*. This no Body has any Right to but himself. The *Labour* of his Body, and the *Work* of his Hands, we may say, are properly his. Whatsoever then he removes out of the State that Nature hath provided, and left it in, he hath mixed his *Labour* with, and joyned to it something that is his own, and thereby makes it his *Property*. It being by him removed from the common state Nature placed it in, it hath by this *labour* something annexed to it that excludes the common right of other Men. . . .

28. He that is nourished by the Acorns he pickt up under an Oak, or the Apples he gathered from the Trees in the Wood, has certainly appropriated them to himself. No Body can deny but the nourishment is his. I ask then, When did they begin to be his? When he digested? Or when he eat? Or when he boiled? Or when he brought them home? Or when he pickt them up? And 'tis plain, if the first gather made them not his, nothing else could. That *labour* put a distinction between them and common. That added something to them more than Nature, the common Mother of all, had done; and so they became his private right. And will any one say he had not right to those Acorns or Apples he thus appropriated, because he had not the consent of all Mankind to make them his? Was it a Robbery thus to assume to himself what belonged to all in Common? If such a consent as that was necessary, Man had starved, notwithstanding the Plenty God had given him. We see in *Commons,* which remain so by Compact, that 'tis the taking any part of what is common, and removing it out of the state Nature leaves it in, which *begins the Property;* without which the Common is of no use. And the taking of this or that part, does not depend on the express consent of all the Commoners. Thus the Grass my Horse has bit; the Turfs

my Servant has cut; and the Ore I have digg'd in any place where I have a right to them in common with others, become my *Property,* without the assignation or consent of any body. The *labour* that was mine, removing them out of that common state they were in, hath *fixed* my *Property* in them. . . .

32. But the *chief matter of Property* being now not the Fruits of the Earth, and the Beasts that subsist on it, but the *Earth it self;* as that which takes in and carries with it all the rest: I think it is plain, that *Property* in that too is acquired as the former. *As much Land* as a Man Tills, Plants, Improves, Cultivates, and can use the Product of, so must is his *Property.* He by his Labour does, as it were, inclose from the Common. Nor will it invalidate his right to say, Every body has an equal Title to it; and therefore he cannot appropriate, he cannot inclose, without the Consent of all his Fellow-Commoners, all Mankind. God, when he gave the World in common to all Mankind, commanded Man also to labour, and the penury of his Condition required it of him. God and his Reason commanded him to subdue the Earth, *i.e.* improve it for the benefit of Life, and therein lay out something upon it that was his own, his labour. He that in Obedience to this Command of God, subdued, tilled and sowed any part of it, thereby annexted to it something that was his *Property,* which had no Title to, nor could without injury take from him. . . .

40. Nor is it so strange, as perhaps before consideration it may appear, that the *Property of labour* should be able to over-ballance the Community of Land. For 'tis *Labour* indeed that *puts the difference of value* on everything; and let any one consider, what the difference is between an Acre of Land planted with Tobacco, or Sugar, sown with Wheat or Barley; and an Acre of the same Land lying in common, without any Husbandry upon it, and he will find, that the improvement of *labour makes* the far greater part of *the value.* I think it will be but a very modest Computation to say, that the *Products* of the Earth useful to the Life of Man 9/10 are the *effects of labour:* nay, if we will rightly estimate things as they come to our use, and cast up the several Expences about them, what in them is purely owing to *Nature,* and what to *labour,* we shall find, that in most of them 99/100 are wholly to be put on the account of *labour.*

41. There cannot be a clearer demonstration of any thing, than several Nations of the *Americans* are this, who are rich in Land, and poor in all the Comforts of Life; whom Nature having furnished as liberally as any other people, with the materials of Plenty, *i.e.* a fruitful of Soil, apt to produce in abundance, what might serve for food, rayment, and delight; yet for want of improving it by labour, have not one hundreth part of the Conveniences we enjoy: And a King of a large and fruitful Territory there feeds, lodges, and is clad worse than a day Labourer in *England.* . . .

NOTES AND QUESTIONS

1. **The intuitive image, revisited.** Note the links between the intuitive image of property and Locke's thought. The intuitive image incorporates

Locke's argument that property rights give men absolute dominion over things. We will see below that the intuitive image of property presents only one possible interpretation of Locke.

2.   **Which comes first, property or society?** Are property rights created by society or do they predate it, according to Locke? How does this differ from the republican vision?

3.   **The purpose of property.** Does Locke link the institution of property with citizenship and the pursuit of the common good through politics? Is the purpose of property to achieve political goals, as it is in the republican vision?

4.   **Property and narrative.** Note that Locke's political theory takes the form of a narrative. Why do Locke (and subsequent liberal theorists) formulate their political theory in the form of a mythic story of property's origins? Who cares about origins at this late date? Consider the following from Stanley Katz, Thomas Jefferson and the Right to Property in Revolutionary America, 19 J.L. & Econ. 467 (1976).

> For Englishmen in the years since the seventeenth-century civil war, the problem of reconciling revolution with the continuation of the traditional property system had taken a characteristic form, which has been analyzed in a doctoral dissertation by Professor Paul Lucas. The difficulty, Lucas argues, which first emerged in 1688 and is best expressed in the work of John Locke, was to destroy the monarchy without destroying the social system which was the legal and logical consequence of the royal system of government: the right to the crown was, legally, an hereditary property right, and if this most significant of all property rights could be abolished, how could one revolt without also destroying the right to property everywhere in the society? We must remember here that we are discussing a world which was only barely post-feudal. The solution as Locke defined it, was to separate the "two paths of descent," by arguing that the principles of inheritance of government were altogether separate from those of the inheritance of private property.
>
> Most commentators on Locke emphasize the idea that, if property is a natural right, landowners are to be protected from the depredations of the crown. It is well to remember, however, that military tenures, and certain other feudal inconveniences to landowners, had been abolished in 1679. Locke had, therefore, a more important purpose. By insisting that men had a natural right to the land on which they had first laboured; by proving that their legitimate title to the land did not require the explicit consent of others, but was permitted by the law of reason; Locke made private property antecedent to government and divorced society from government, thereby allowing for limited revolutions: an alteration in government need not alter the existing property structure, the dissolution of government did not dissolve society.[35]
>
> Locke accomplished this theoretical feat first by denying that public government was "a piece of divinely given and divinely transmitted property

---

35. Paul Lucas, Essays on the Margin of Blackstone's *Commentaries* 230-31 (unpublished PhD. dissertation, Princeton University, 1963).

following the private rule and indefeasible inheritance of the common land law," and secondly, by positing a "divine and natural basis for private property and its indefeasible inheritance." The result was Locke's provision for insuperable hereditary rights for the subject, but not for the government.

5.   **Creation versus distribution.** Note how Locke's nature narrative establishes a moral mandate for the current distribution of property, by setting up a mythic moment when ownership was "earned" by injecting labor into the common. What messages does Locke's nature narrative send about the moral legitimacy of property rights? Recall that republicanism has an explicit focus on how property should be distributed. Does Locke? How does his focus on the creation of property rights deflect attention from their current distribution? Note the implicit claim that the key determinative point was at the point at which property rights *originated.*

6.   **Locke and Marx.** Locke's labor theory of value was eventually developed (in a very different direction) by Karl Marx, who argued that labor is the source of all value, and that the capitalist's appropriation of the surplus value created by labor meant that "property is theft." See Karl Marx, Pre-Capitalist Economic Formations 114 (E.J. Hobsbawm ed., 1964).

The following excerpt explores the role of narrative at greater length and provides an introduction to economic liberalism, one important strain of the liberal tradition.

CAROL M. ROSE, PROPERTY AS STORYTELLING:
PERSPECTIVES FROM GAME THEORY, NARRATIVE
THEORY, FEMINIST THEORY

---

2 Yale J.L. & Human 37, 38-42 (1990)

Locke is undoubtedly the most influential of the classic property theorists, and Locke used this narrative approach in his famous discussion of property in the Second Treatise of Government. Although the parts are somewhat scattered, the Treatise clearly unfolds a story line, beginning in a plenteous state of nature, carrying through the growing individual appropriation of goods, then proceeding to the development of a trading money economy, and culminating in the creation of government to safeguard property. Indeed Locke's choice of a narrative mode is all the more striking because he appears to have been indifferent to the factual accuracy of the story as a genuine history.

Almost a century later, William Blackstone launched into a quite similar pseudo-history in explaining property as an institution with an origin and evolution: he too described human beings as beginning in a state of plenty, gradually accumulating personal and landed property, and finally creating government and laws to protect property. And in more recent days, the modern economist Harold Demsetz has chosen to illustrate his theory of property rights by reference to a narrative history of an evolving property regime among fur-hunting Indians on the American continent.

Why have these theorists turned to story-telling to discuss property? Why have they chosen a narrative explanatory mode, which often diverges from scientific/predictive modes, and instead envisions events as unfolding in ways that, at least arguably, are only understandable after the fact? . . . [W]hen we break down this very standard version of property, we find several critical points. The first point is that desire — that is, a desire for resources — is at the center of the whole institution of property.[17] The second point is that we need the capacity to shut out others from the resources that are the objects of our desire, at least when those objects become scarce. And the third point is that by allocating exclusive control of resources to individuals, a property regime winds up by satisfying even more desires, because it mediates conflicts between individuals and encourages everyone to work and trade instead of fighting, thus making possible an even greater satisfaction of desires.[18]

There is another element hidden in this analysis, though: it is the idea that we already know, at least roughly, how people are going to order their desires, or more technically, their *preferences* about themselves and others, and about their respective access to desired sources.

What is that understood ordering? Like many of our interesting ideas in this area, it comes to us from the seventeenth century, and most particularly from Hobbes first and later Locke. Hobbes' major point about human preferences is that individuals want to *live*. Our desire to stay alive is just *there*, omnipresent and undeniable; it needs no further explanation. When push comes to shove, Hobbes thought, we will prefer our own lives over other peoples', and by and large, we will also prefer our lives over highfalutin' causes, however noble. That is why in battle, for example, as Hobbes put it, "there is on one side, or both, a running away."

Locke's major addendum to this picture was to show the relevance of property to the desire to live. He pointed out that life depends on property, in a very primitive sense; if one cannot literally *appropriate* those berries and fruits, one will simply die.[22]

And so acquisitiveness, the desire to have property, is "just there" too,

---

17. To be sure, some resources are a burden, like that horrid lamp that your Aunt Tilly gave you. Still, *she* wanted you to have it. And besides, if you have any sense, you can sell the stupid thing and buy something else that you do want.

18. See Rose, *supra* note 6, at 427-429 (comparing non-propertied society to society with property regime; latter has more activity, goods).

22. Locke, 2d Treatise §28 (argues that if consent of all mankind were necessary for individual to propertize acorns or apples, "Man had starved, notwithstanding the Plenty God had given him").

also universal and omnipresent; thus one can always predict a human desire to have things for one's self, or as they say more lately, the human propensity to be a self-interested rational utility maximizer. The propensity is just a kind of fact of life, and the eighteenth century political economists took it for granted, rejecting as unrealistic the earlier condemnations of acquisitiveness. They attempted instead to carry forward the new science of political economy on the firm ground of irreducible self-interest, and indeed they toned down the language of "avarice" into that of the more benign "interest."

Indeed, if we do take these preferences for life and acquisitions as givens, then economics can make a bid to be a kind of logical science in politics and law. With these preferences understood, we can sensibly talk about how the law gives people incentives to do this thing and that, and we can manipulate future welfare by institutionalizing the proper ex-ante approaches.[25] Shifts of entitlements become predictable because we know how people order their preferences; with that knowledge, we can predict their responses and moves under different states of affairs.

NOTES AND QUESTIONS

1.   **Locke and economic liberalism.** Rose's essay is an example of law and economics, an influential school of contemporary American legal scholarship. It embeds a strain of liberalism we will call economic liberalism. Rose deftly shows the continuities between the thought of Locke and the modern, scientized language of economics. What are they? For an insightful discussion of the discontinuities, see James T. Kloppenberg, The Virtues of Liberalism, 74 J. Am. Hist. 9 (1987), discussed *infra*.

2.   **Self-interest.** Republicanism and liberalism project very different attitudes towards self-interest. Recall that in the republican tradition, the triumph of self-interest represented the downfall of the republic. Self-interest was viewed as inimical to pursuit of the common good; in sharp contrast, in the context of the economic strain of liberalism, self-interest is viewed as an inevitable part of human makeup, see, e.g., Richard A. Epstein, Utilitarian Foundations of Natural Law, 12 Harv. J.L. & Pub. Poly. 713, 720 (1989) ("Self-interest looks to be a well-nigh universal imperative that instructs all individuals how to manage their initial endowments, given variations in their external environment"). The view of self-interest as benign is an integral part of the economic image of man as a rational utility self-maximizer, which is pervasive in law and economics. See Richard A. Posner, Economic Analysis of Law 3 (4th ed. 1992) ("The task of economics, so

---

25. Alternatively, of course, we can collectively impoverish ourselves by giving people the wrong incentives. See, e.g., Frank H. Easterbrook, The Supreme Court 1983 Term: Forward: The Court and the Economic System, 98 Harv. L. Rev. 4. 10-13 (1984).

defined, is to explore the implications of assuming that man is a rational maximizer of his ends in life, his satisfaction — what we shall call his 'self-interest'").

3. **The purpose of property.** What is the purpose of property, according to Rose's rendering of economic liberalism?

4. **What motivates human beings?** A large literature exists, some of it written by scholars associated with law and economics, arguing that the economic model of human behavior is oversimplistic. See, e.g., Robert C. Ellickson, Bringing Culture and Human Frailty to Rational Actors: A Critique of Classical Law and Economics, 65 Chi.-Kent L. Rev. 23, 43-54 (1989); Jon Elster, Selfishness and Altruism, in Beyond Self-Interest 44 (Jane J. Mansbridge ed., 1990); Amitai Etzioni, The Moral Dimension: Towards a New Economics (1988); Arthur Leff, Economic Analysis of the Law: Some Realism about Nominalism, 60 Va. L. Rev. 451 (1974); Jane J. Mansbridge, On the Relation of Altruism and Self-Interest, in Beyond Self-Interest, *supra*, at 133; Amartya Sen, Rational Fools: A Critique of the Behavioral Foundations of Economic Theory, in Scientific Models and Man 1-25 (Henry Harris ed., 1979). Nonetheless, within much of law and economics, the model of the rational self-maximizer remains widely accepted.

The following is another example of property theory in the tradition of economic liberalism presented not as an objective description of human nature, but as a narration about history.

HAROLD DEMSETZ, TOWARD A THEORY OF PROPERTY RIGHTS

57 Am. Econ. Rev., Papers & Proceedings 347, 347-356 (1967)

THE CONCEPT AND ROLE OF PROPERTY RIGHTS

In the world of Robinson Crusoe property rights play no role. Property rights are an instrument of society and derive their significance from the fact that they help a man [from] those expectations which he can reasonably hold in his dealings with others. These expectations find expression in the laws, customs, and mores of society. An owner of property rights possesses the consent of fellow men to allow him to act in particular ways. An owner expects the community to prevent others from interfering with his actions, provided that these actions are not prohibited in the specifications of his rights.

It is important to note that property rights convey the right to benefit or harm oneself or others. Harming a competitor by producing superior products may be permitted, while shooting him may not. A man may be permitted to benefit himself by shooting an intruder but be prohibited from selling below a price floor. It is clear, then, that property rights specify how persons may be benefited and harmed, and, therefore, who must pay whom to modify the actions taken by persons. . . .

THE EMERGENCE OF PROPERTY RIGHTS . . .

It is my thesis in this part of the paper that . . . property rights develop to internalize externalities when the gains of internalization become larger than the cost of internalization. . . .

I do not mean to assert or deny that the adjustments in property rights which take place need be the result of a conscious endeavor to cope with new externality problems. These adjustments have arisen in Western societies largely as a result of gradual changes in social mores and in common law precedents. At each step of this adjustment process, it is unlikely that externalities per se were consciously related to the issue being resolved. These legal and moral experiments may be hit-and-miss procedures to some extent but in a society that weights the achievement of efficiency heavily, their viability in the long run will depend on how well they modify behavior to accommodate to the externalities associated with important changes in technology or market values.

A rigorous test of this assertion will require extensive and detailed empirical work. . . . In this part of the discussion, I shall present one group of such examples in some detail. They deal with the development of private property rights in land among American Indians. . . .

The question of private ownership of land among aboriginals has held a fascination for anthropologists. It has been one of the intellectual battlegrounds in the attempt to assess the "true nature" of man unconstrained by the "artificialities" of civilization. In the process of carrying on this debate, information has been uncovered that bears directly on the thesis with which we are now concerned. What appears to be accepted as a classic treatment and a high point of this debate is Eleanor Leacock's memoir on The Montagnes "Hunting Territory" and the Fur Trade. Leacock's research followed that of Frank G. Speck who had discovered that the Indians of the Labrador Peninsula had a long established tradition of property in land. This finding was at odds with what was known about the Indians of the American Southwest and it prompted Leacock's study of the Montagnes who inhabited large regions around Quebec.

Leacock clearly established the fact that a close relationship existed, both historically and geographically, between the development of private rights in land and the development of the commercial fur trade. The factual basis of the correlation has gone unchallenged. However, to my knowledge, no theory relating privacy of land to the fur trade has yet been articulated. The factual material uncovered by Speck and Leacock fits the thesis of this paper well, and in doing so, it reveals clearly the role played by property right adjustments in taking account of what economists have often cited as an example of an externality — the overhunting of game.

Because of the lack of control over hunting by others, it is in no person's interest to invest in increasing or maintaining the stock of game. Overly intensive hunting takes place. . . . Before the fur trade became established, hunting was carried on primarily for purposes of food and the relatively few furs that were required for the hunter's family. The externality was clearly present. Hunting could be practiced freely and was carried on without assessing its impact on other hunters. But these external effects were of such small significance that it did not pay for anyone to take them into account. . . .

We may safely surmise that the advent of the fur trade had two immediate consequences. First, the value of furs to the Indians was increased considerably. Second, and as a result, the scale of hunting activity rose sharply. Both consequences must have increased considerably the importance of the externalities associated with free hunting. The property right system began to change, and it changed specifically in the direction required to take account of the economic effects made important by the fur trade. The geographical or distributional evidence collected by Leacock indicates an unmistakable correlation between early centers of fur trade and the oldest and most complete development of the private hunting territory. . . . An anonymous account written in 1723 states that the "principle of the Indians is to mark off the hunting ground selected by them by blazing the trees with their crest so that they may never encroach on each other. . . . By the middle of the century these allotted territories were relatively stabilized."

The principle that associates property right changes with the emergence of new and reevaluation of old harmful and beneficial effects suggests in this instance that the fur trade made it economic to encourage the husbanding of fur-bearing animals. Husbanding requires the ability to prevent poaching and this, in turn, suggests that socioeconomic changes in property in hunting land will take place. The chain of reasoning is consistent with the evidence cited above. Is it inconsistent with the absence of similar rights in property among the southwestern Indians?

Two factors suggest that the thesis is consistent with the absence of similar rights among the Indians of the southwestern plains. The first of these is that there were no plains animals of commercial importance comparable to the fur-bearing animals of the forest, at least not until cattle arrived with Europeans. The second factor is that animals of the plains are primarily grazing species whose habit is to wander over wide tracts of land. The value of establishing boundaries to private hunting territories is thus reduced by the relatively high cost of preventing the animals from moving to adjacent parcels. Hence both the value and cost of establishing private hunting lands in the Southwest are such that we would expect little development along these lines. The externality was just not worth taking into account.

The lands of the Labrador Peninsula shelter forest animals whose habits are considerably different from those of the plains. Forest animals confine their territories to relatively small areas, so that the cost of internalizing the effects of husbanding these animals is considerably reduced. This reduced cost, together with the higher commercial value of fur-bearing forest animals, made it productive to establish private hunting lands. Frank G. Speck finds that family proprietorship among the Indians of the Peninsula included retaliation against trespass. Animal resources were husbanded. Sometimes conservation practices were carried on extensively. Family hunting territories were divided into quarters. Each year the family hunted in a different quarter in rotation, leaving a tract in the center as a sort of bank, not to be hunted over unless forced to do so by a shortage in the regular tract. . . .

THE COALESCENCE AND OWNERSHIP OF PROPERTY RIGHTS

I have argued that property rights arise when it becomes economic for those affected by externalities to internalize benefits and costs. But I have not yet examined the forces which will govern the particular form of right ownership. Several idealized forms of ownership must be distinguished at the outset. These are communal ownership, private ownership, and state ownership.

By communal ownership, I shall mean a right which can be exercised by all members of the community. Frequently the rights to till and to hunt the land have been communally owned. The right to walk a city sidewalk is communally owned. Communal ownership means that the community denies to the state or to individual citizens the right to interfere with any person's exercise of communally-owned rights. Private ownership implies that the community recognizes the right of the owner to exclude others from exercising the owner's private rights. State ownership implies that the state may exclude anyone from the use of a right as long as the state follows accepted political procedures for determining who may not use state-owned property. I shall not examine in detail the alternative of state ownership. The object of the analysis which follows is to discern some broad principles governing the development of property rights in communities oriented to private property.

It will be best to begin by considering a particularly useful example that focuses our attention on the problem of land ownership. Suppose that land is communally owned. Every person has the right to hunt, till, or mine the land. This form of ownership fails to concentrate the cost associated with any person's exercise of his communal right on that person. If a person seeks to maximize the value of his communal rights, he will tend to over-hunt and overwork the land because some of the costs of his doing so are borne by others. The stock of game and the richness of the soil will be diminished too quickly. It is conceivable that those who own these rights, i.e., every member of the community, can agree to curtail the rate at which they work the lands if negotiating and policing costs are zero. Each can agree to abridge his rights. It is obvious that the costs of reaching such an agreement will not be zero. What is not obvious is just how large these costs may be.

Negotiating costs will be large because it is difficult for many persons to reach a mutually satisfactory agreement, especially when each hold-out has the right to work the land as fast as he pleases. But, even if an agreement among all can be reached, we must yet take account of the costs of policing the agreement, and these may be large, also. After such an agreement is reached, no one will privately own the right to work the land; all can work the land but at an agreed upon shorter workweek. Negotiating costs are increased even further because it is not possible under this system to bring the full expected benefits and expected costs of future generations to bear on current users.

If a single person owns land, he will attempt to maximize its present value by taking into account alternative future time streams of benefits and costs and selecting that one which he believes will maximize the present value of his privately-owned land rights. We all know that this means that he will attempt to take into account the supply and demand conditions that he thinks will exist after his death. It is very difficult to see how the existing communal owners can reach an agreement that takes account of these costs.

In effect, an owner of a private right to use land acts as a broker whose wealth depends on how well he takes into account the competing claims of the present and the future. But with communal rights there is no broker, and the claims of the present generation will be given an uneconomically large weight in determining the intensity with which the land is worked. Future generations might desire to pay present generations enough to change the present intensity of land usage. But they have no living agent to place their claims on the market. Under a communal property system, should a living person pay others to reduce the rate at which they work the land, he would not gain anything of value for his efforts. Communal property means that future generations must speak for themselves. No one has yet estimated the costs of carrying on such a conversation.

The land ownership example confronts us immediately with a great disadvantage of communal property. The effects of a person's activities of his neighbors and on subsequent generations will not be taken into account fully. Communal property results in great externalities. The full costs of the activities of an owner of a communal property right are not borne directly by him, nor can they be called to his attention easily by the willingness of others to pay him an appropriate sum. . . .

The state, the courts, or the leaders of the community could attempt to internalize the external costs resulting from communal property by allowing private parcels owned by small groups with similar interests. The logical groups in terms of similar interests, are, of course, the family and the individual. Continuing with our use of the land ownership example, let us initially distribute private titles to land randomly among existing individuals and, further, let the extent of land included in each title be randomly determined.

The resulting private ownership of land will internalize many of the external costs associated with communal ownership, for now an owner, by virtue of his power to exclude others, can generally count on realizing the rewards associated with husbanding the game and increasing the fertility of his land. This concentration of benefits and costs on owners creates incentives to utilize resources more efficiently.

NOTES AND QUESTIONS

1. **The language of "externalities" embeds certain assumptions.** Demsetz argues that "a primary function" of property rights is to internalize costs that would otherwise exist as externalities. Costs will not always be internalized. Instead, they will only be internalized when the "gains of internalization [are greater] than the cost of internalization." Why is it a good thing to internalize externalities? Note the unstated assumptions: that the purpose of the property system is to produce wealth; and that the best society is the wealthiest society. These assumptions are embedded in Demsetz's specialized use of the word "efficiency." How does he use it? How do these assumptions about the good society and the goal of the property system differ from the republican vision?

2. **Wealth maximization.** Other law and economics scholars have been more explicit in their defense of wealth maximization as the ultimate goal. See, e.g., Richard Posner, The Economics of Justice 6 (1983) (equating efficiency with wealth maximization); Richard Posner, Utilitarianism, Economics and Legal Theory, 8 J. Legal Stud. 103 (1979) (proposing wealth maximization as a worthy norm for common law adjudication). See generally, Symposium on Efficiency as a Legal Concern, 8 Hofstra L. Rev. 485 (1980).

3. **Are property rights efficient?** Demsetz's conclusion that property rights are efficient has been contested in Duncan Kennedy and Frank Michelman, Are Property and Contract Efficient?, 8 Hofstra L. Rev. 711, 770 (1980) (concluding that "[i]nsofar as they have anything whatsoever to do with efficiency, private property and free contract are species of intervention").

4. **Are property rights presocial?** Does Demsetz accept Locke's definition of property rights as presocial?

5. **Bad history, bad sociology, bad economics?** Demsetz's treatment of the privatization of property, as evolving inevitably from the "tragedy" of

communal ownership,[61] has been critized as bad history, bad sociology, and bad economics. For a critique from the viewpoint of economics, see Richard A. Posner, Some Uses and Abuses of Economics in Law, 46 U. Chi. L. Rev. 281, 289 (1979) (criticizing Demsetz's "leap from assuming efficiency-maximizing behavior of individuals to assuming efficiency-maximizing behavior of a society"). For critiques from the viewpoint of history and sociology, see Frank I. Michelman, Ethics, Economics and the Law of Property, in Ethics, Economics, and the Law, Nomos XXIV, at 3, 31 (J. Roland Pennock and J. W. Chapman eds., 1982) (arguing that Demsetz ignores the existence of cooperation); Carol Rose, The Comedy of the Commons: Custom, Commerce, and Inherently Public Property, 53 U. Chi. L. Rev. 711 (1986) (tracing the role of custom in managing common resources); Susan J. Cox, No Tragedy of the Commons, 7 Envtl. Ethics 49 (1985) (documenting respect for, as well as abuses of, the commons in seventeenth-century England); William Cronin, Changes in the Land 184 n.7 (1983); Arthur Leff, Economic Analysis of the Law: Some Realism about Nominalism, 60 Va. L. Rev. 451, 473 n.61 (1974); Eric T. Freyfogle, Land Use and the Study of Early American History, 94 Yale L.J. 717, 740 n.73 (1985) (book review). Even in the face of so much criticism, Demsetz's article survives and thrives. Why does the thesis continue to persuade?

b.   Creating Intellectual Property

One context in which the initial assignment of property rights is of present concern is in intellectual property. Consider the following (dissenting) opinion. Does Judge Kozinski adopt the Lockian nature narrative? Does he share the Demsetz view of the commons as inevitably inefficient?

WHITE v. SAMSUNG ELECTRONICS AMERICA

989 F.2d 1512 (9th Cir. 1993)

KOZINSKI, J., with whom J. O'SCANNLAIN and KLEINFELD join, dissenting from the order rejecting the suggestion for rehearing en banc.

I

Saddam Hussein wants to keep advertisers from using his picture in unflattering contexts.[1] Clint Eastwood doesn't want tabloids to write about

---

61. See Garrett Hardin, The Tragedy of the Commons, 162 Science 1243 (1968), reprinted in Garrett Hardin and John Baden, Managing the Commons 16 (1977).

1. See Eben Shapiro, Rising Caution on Using Celebrity Images, N.Y. Times, Nov. 4, 1992, at D20 (Iraqi diplomat objects on right of publicity grounds to ad containing Hussein's

him. Rudolf Valentino's heirs want to control his film biography. The Girl Scouts don't want their image soiled by association with certain activities.[2] George Lucas wants to keep Strategic Defense Initiative fans from calling it "Star Wars." Pepsico doesn't want singers to use the word "Pepsi" in their songs.[6] Guy Lombardo wants an exclusive property right to ads that show big bands playing on New Year's Eve. Uri Geller thinks he should be paid for ads showing psychics bending metal through telekinesis. Paul Prud-homme, that household name, thinks the same about ads featuring corpu-lent bearded chefs. And scads of copyright holders see purple when their creations are made fun of.

Something very dangerous is going on here. Private property, includ-ing intellectual property, is essential to our way of life. It provides an incen-tive for investment and innovation; it stimulates the flourishing of our culture; it protects the moral entitlements of people to the fruits of their labors. But reducing too much to private property can be bad medicine. Private land, for instance, is far more useful if separated from other private land by public streets, roads and highways. Public parks, utility rights-of-way and sewers reduce the amount of land in private hands, but vastly enhance the value of the property that remains.

So too it is with intellectual property. Overprotecting intellectual property is as harmful as underprotecting it. Creativity is impossible without a rich public domain. Nothing today, likely nothing since we tamed fire, is genuinely new: Culture, like science and technology, grows by accretion, each new creator building on the works of those who came before. Over-protection stifles the very creative forces it's supposed to nurture.

The panel's opinion is a classic case of overprotection. Concerned

---

picture and caption "History has shown what happens when one source controls all the information").

2. Girl Scouts v. Personality Posters Mfg., 304 F. Supp. 1228 (S.D.N.Y. 1969) (poster of a pregnant girl in a Girl Scout uniform with the caption "Be Prepared").

6. Pepsico Inc. claimed the lyrics and packaging of grunge rocker Tad Doyle's "Jack Pepsi" song were "offensive to [it] and [are] likely to offend [its] customers," in part because they "associate [Pepsico] and its Pepsi marks with intoxication and drunk driving." Russell, Doyle Leaves Pepsi Thirsty for Compensation, Billboard, June 15, 1991, at 43. Conversely, the Hell's Angels recently sued Marvel Comics to keep it from publishing a comic book called "Hell's Angel," starring a character of the same name. Marvel settled by paying $35,000 to charity and promising never to use the name "Hell's Angel" again in connection with any of its publications. Marvel, Hell's Angels Settle Trademark Suit, L.A. Daily J., Feb. 2, 1993, §II, at 1.

Trademarks are often reflected in the mirror of our popular culture. See Truman Ca-pote, Breakfast at Tiffany's (1958); Kurt Vonnegut, Jr., Breakfast of Champions (1973); Tom Wolfe, The Electric Kool-Aid Acid Test (1968) (which, incidentally, includes a chapter on the Hell's Angels); Larry Niven, Man of Steel, Woman of Kleenex in All the Myriad Ways (1971); Looking for Mr. Goodbar (1977); The Coca-Cola Kid (1985) (using Coca-Cola as a metaphor for American commercialism); The Kentucky Fried Movie (1977); Harley Davidson and the Marlboro Man (1991); The Wonder Years (ABC 1988-present) ("Wonder Years" was a slogan of Wonder Bread); Tim Rice & Andrew Lloyd Webber, Joseph and the Amazing Technicolor Dream Coat (musical). . . .

The creators of some of these works have gotten permission from the trademark own-ers, though it's unlikely Kool-Aid relished being connected with LSD, Hershey with homicidal maniacs, Disney with armed robbers, or Coca-Cola with cultural imperialism. Certainly no free society can demand that artists get such permission.

about what it sees as a wrong done to Vanna White, the panel majority erects a property right of remarkable and dangerous breadth: Under the majority's opinion, it's a new tort for advertisers to remind the public of a celebrity. Not to use a celebrity's name, voice, signature or likeness; not to imply the celebrity endorses a product; but simply to evoke the celebrity's image in the public's mind. This Orwellian notion withdraws far more from the public domain than prudence and common sense allow. It conflicts with the Copyright Act and the Copyright Clause. It raises serious First Amendment problems. It's bad law, and it deserves a long, hard second look.

II

Samsung ran an ad campaign promoting its consumer electronics. Each ad depicted a Samsung product and a humorous prediction: One showed a raw steak with the caption "Revealed to be health food. 2010 A.D." Another showed Morton Downey, Jr. in front of an American flag with the caption "Presidential candidate. 2008 A.D."[12] The ads were meant to convey — humorously — that Samsung products would still be in use twenty years from now.

The ad that spawned this litigation starred a robot dressed in a wig, gown and jewelry reminiscent of Vanna White's hair and dress; the robot was posed next to a Wheel-of-Fortune-like game board. See Appendix. The caption read "Longest-running game show. 2012 A.D." The gag here, I take it, was that Samsung would still be around when White had been replaced by a robot.

Perhaps failing to see the humor, White sued, alleging Samsung infringed her right of publicity by "appropriating" her "identity." Under California law, White has the exclusive right to use her name, likeness, signature and voice for commercial purposes. Cal. Civ. Code §3344(a); Eastwood v. Superior Court, 149 Cal. App. 3d 409, 417, 198 Cal. Rptr. 342, 347 (1983). But Samsung didn't use her name, voice or signature, and it certainly didn't use her likeness. The ad just wouldn't have been funny had it depicted White or someone who resembled her — the whole joke was that the game show host(ess) was a robot, not a real person. No one seeing the ad could have thought this was supposed to be White in 2012.

The district judge quite reasonably held that, because Samsung didn't use White's name, likeness, voice or signature, it didn't violate her right of publicity. 971 F.2d at 1396-97. Not so, says the panel majority: The California right of publicity can't possibly be limited to name and likeness. If it were, the majority reasons, a "clever advertising strategist" could avoid using White's name or likeness but nevertheless remind people of her with impunity, "effectively eviscerating" her rights. To prevent this "evisceration," the panel majority holds that the right of publicity must extend beyond

---

12. I had never heard of Morton Downey, Jr., but I'm told he's sort of like Rush Limbaugh, but not as shy.

FIGURE 1-4
Vanna White

name and likeness, to any "appropriation" of White's "identity" — anything that "evokes" her personality. Id. at 1398-99.

III

But what does "evisceration" mean in intellectual property law? Intellectual property rights aren't like some constitutional rights, absolute guarantees protected against all kinds of interference, subtle as well as blatant. They cast no penumbras, emit no emanations: The very point of intellectual property laws is that they protect only against certain specific kinds of appropriation. I can't publish unauthorized copies of, say, *Presumed Innocent;* I

FIGURE 1-5
Ms. C3PO?

can't make a movie out of it. But I'm perfectly free to write a book about an idealistic young prosecutor on trial for a crime he didn't commit. So what if I got the idea from *Presumed Innocent*? So what if it reminds readers of the original? Have I "eviscerated" Scott Turow's intellectual property rights? Certainly not. All creators draw in part on the work of those who came before, referring to it, building on it, poking fun at it; we call this creativity, not piracy.[15]

15. In the words of Sir Isaac Newton, "if I have seen further it is by standing on [the shoulders] of Giants." Letter to Robert Hooke, Feb. 5, 1675/1676.
Newton himself may have borrowed this phrase from Bernard of Chartres, who said

The majority isn't, in fact, preventing the "evisceration" of Vanna White's existing rights; it is creating a new and much broader property right, a right unknown in California law. It's replacing the existing balance between the interests of the celebrity and those of the public by a different balance, one substantially more favorable to the celebrity. Instead of having an exclusive right in her name, likeness, signature or voice, every famous person now has an exclusive right to anything that reminds the viewer of her. After all, that's all Samsung did: It used an inanimate object to remind people of White, to "evoke [her identity]," 971 F.2d at 1399.

Consider how sweeping this new right is. What is it about the ad that makes people think of White? It's not the robot's wig, clothes or jewelry; there must be ten million blond women (many of them quasi-famous) who wear dresses and jewelry like White's. It's that the robot is posed near the "Wheel of Fortune" game board. Remove the game board from the ad, and no one would think of Vanna White. See Appendix. But once you include the game board, anybody standing beside it — a brunette woman, a man wearing women's clothes, a monkey in a wig and gown — would evoke White's image, precisely the way the robot did. It's the "Wheel of Fortune" set, not the robot's face or dress or jewelry that evokes White's image. The panel is giving White an exclusive right not in what she looks like or who she is, but in what she does for a living.[18]

This is entirely the wrong place to strike the balance. Intellectual property rights aren't free: They're imposed at the expense of future creators and of the public at large. Where would we be if Charles Lindbergh had an exclusive right in the concept of a heroic solo aviator? If Arthur Conan Doyle had gotten a copyright in the idea of the detective story, or Albert Einstein had patented the theory of relativity? If every author and celebrity had been given the right to keep people from mocking them or their work? Surely this would have made the world poorer, not richer, culturally as well as economically.

This is why intellectual property law is full of careful balances between what's set aside for the owner and what's left in the public domain for the rest of us: The relatively short life of patents; the longer, but finite, life of copyrights; copyright's idea-expression dichotomy; the fair use doctrine;

---

something similar in the early twelfth century. Bernard in turn may have snatched it from Priscian, a sixth century grammarian. See Lotus Dev. Corp. v. Paperback Software Int'l, 740 F. Supp. 37, 77 n.3 (D. Mass. 1990).

18. Once the right of publicity is extended beyond specific physical characteristics, this will become a recurring problem: Outside name, likeness and voice, the one thing that most reliably reminds the public of someone are the actions or roles they're famous for. A commercial with an astronaut setting foot on the moon would evoke the image of Neil Armstrong. Any masked man on horseback would remind people (over a certain age) of Clayton Moore. And any number of songs — "My Way," "Yellow Submarine," "Like a Virgin," "Beat It," "Michael, Row the Boat Ashore," to name only a few — instantly evoke an image of the person or group who made them famous, regardless of who is singing.

the prohibition on copyrighting facts; the compulsory license of television broadcasts and musical compositions; federal preemption of overbroad state intellectual property laws; the nominative use doctrine in trademark law; the right to make soundalike recordings. All of these diminish an intellectual property owner's rights. All let the public use something created by someone else. But all are necessary to maintain a free environment in which creative genius can flourish.

The intellectual property right created by the panel here has none of these essential limitations: No fair use exception; no right to parody; no idea-expression dichotomy. It impoverishes the public domain, to the detriment of future creators and the public at large. Instead of well-defined, limited characteristics such as name, likeness or voice, advertisers will now have to cope with vague claims of "appropriation of identity," claims often made by people with a wholly exaggerated sense of their own fame and significance. . . . Future Vanna Whites might not get the chance to create their personae, because their employers may fear some celebrity will claim the persona is too similar to her own.[21] The public will be robbed of parodies of celebrities, and our culture will be deprived of the valuable safety valve that parody and mockery create.

Moreover, consider the moral dimension, about which the panel majority seems to have gotten so exercised. Saying Samsung "appropriated" something of White's begs the question: Should White have the exclusive right to something as broad and amorphous as her "identity"? Samsung's ad didn't simply copy White's shtick — like all parody, it created something new. True, Samsung did it to make money, but White does whatever she does to make money, too; the majority talks of "the difference between fun and profit," 971 F.2d at 1401, but in the entertainment industry fun is profit. Why is Vanna White's right to exclusive for-profit use of her persona — a persona that might not even be her own creation, but that of a writer, director or producer — superior to Samsung's right to profit by creating its own inventions? Why should she have such absolute rights to control the conduct of others, unlimited by the idea-expression dichotomy or by the fair use of doctrine?

To paraphrase only slightly Feist Publications, Inc. v. Rural Telephone Service Co., 111 S. Ct. 1282, 1289-90 (1991), it may seem unfair that much of the fruit of a creator's labor may be used by others without compensa-

---

21. If Christian Slater, star of "Heathers," "Pump Up the Volume," "Kuffs," and "Untamed Heart" — and alleged Jack Nicholson clone — appears in a commercial, can Nicholson sue? Of 54 stories on LEXIS that talk about Christian Slater, 26 talk about Slater's alleged similarities to Nicholson. Apparently it's his nasal wisecracks and killer smiles, St. Petersburg Times, Jan. 10, 1992, at 13, his eyebrows, Ottawa Citizen, Jan. 10, 1992, at #2, his sneers, Boston Globe, July 26, 1991, at 37, his menacing presence, USA Today, June 26, 1991, at 1D, and his sing-song voice, Gannett News Service, Aug. 27, 1990 (or, some say, his insinuating drawl, L.A. Times, Aug. 22, 1990, at F5). That's a whole lot more than White and the robot had in common.

tion. But this is not some unforeseen byproduct of our intellectual property system; it is the system's very essence. Intellectual property law assures authors the right to their original expression, but encourages others to build freely on the ideas that underlie it. This result is neither unfair nor unfortunate: It is the means by which intellectual property law advances the progress of science and art. We give authors certain exclusive rights, but in exchange we get a richer public domain. The majority ignores this wise teaching, and all of us are the poorer for it.

[Section VI's discussion of copyright law is omitted.]

VII

For better or worse, we are the Court of Appeals for the Hollywood Circuit. Millions of people toil in the shadow of the law we make, and much of their livelihood is made possible by the existence of intellectual property rights. But much of their livelihood — and much of the vibrancy of our culture — also depends on the existence of other intangible rights: The right to draw ideas from a rich and varied public domain, and the right to mock, for profit as well as fun, the cultural icons of our time.

In the name of avoiding the "evisceration" of a celebrity's rights in her image, the majority diminishes the rights of copyright holders and the public at large. In the name of fostering creativity, the majority suppresses it. Vanna White and those like her have been given something they never had before, and they've been given it at our expense. I cannot agree.

NOTES AND QUESTIONS

1. **Case history.** The court's initial opinion, in which a Ninth Circuit panel held that an issue of material fact precluded summary judgment in favor of the defendant on plaintiff's claim for violation of her common-law right of publicity, appears at 971 F.2d 1395 (9th Cir. 1992). The three-judge panel divided 2 to 1. Judge Alarcon, in his dissent, concluded:

> The protection of intellectual property presents the courts with the necessity of balancing competing interests. On the one hand, we wish to protect and reward the work and investment of those who create intellectual property. In so doing, however, we must prevent the creation of a monopoly that would inhibit the creative expressions of others. We have traditionally balanced those interests by allowing the copying of an idea, but protecting a unique expression of it. . . .

Id. at 1408. The panel voted unanimously to deny the defendant's petition for rehearing. Judge Alarcon, however, voted to accept the defendant's "suggestion" for rehearing en banc, and a vote by the nonrecused Ninth

Circuit judges on whether to rehear the matter en banc led to a denial and Judge Kozinski's dissenting opinion. The U.S. Supreme Court denied certiorari; 508 U.S. 951 (1993).

2. **Vanna and economic liberalism.** In what ways does the dissenting opinion accept the assumptions of economic liberalism? In what ways does it reject them?

3. **Protection of intellectual property and the visions of property.** Drawing from the readings so far, how would you explain both the protection given original ideas and the limits placed on that protection?

c.   Wild Animals

PIERSON v. POST
_____

3 Cai. R. 175 (N.Y. 1805)

TOMPKINS, J. delivered the opinion of the court. This cause comes before us on a return to a certiorari directed to one of the justices of Queens county.

The question submitted by the counsel in this cause for our determination is, whether Lodowick Post, by the pursuit with his hounds in the manner alleged in his declaration, acquired such a right to, or property in, the fox as will sustain an action against Pierson for killing and taking him away?

The cause was argued with much ability by the counsel on both sides, and presents for our decision a novel and nice question. It is admitted that a fox is an animal *ferae naturae,* and that property in such animals is acquired by occupancy only. These admissions narrow the discussion to the simple question of what acts amount to occupancy, applied to acquiring right to wild animals.

If we have recourse to the ancient writers upon general principles of law, the judgment below is obviously erroneous. Justinians Institutes, lib. 2, tit. 1, s. 13, and Fleta, lib. 3, c. 2, p. 175, adopt the principle, that pursuit alone vests no property or right in the huntsman; and that even pursuit, accompanied with wounding, is equally ineffectual for that purpose, unless the animal be actually taken. The same principle is recognised by Bracton, lib. 2, c. 1, p. 8.

Puffendorf, lib. 4, c. 6, s. 2, and 10, defines occupancy of beasts *ferae naturae,* to be the actual corporal possession of them, and Bynkershock is cited as coinciding in this definition. It is indeed with hesitation that Puffendorf affirms that a wild beast mortally wounded, or greatly maimed, cannot be fairly intercepted by another, whilst the pursuit of the person inflicting the wound continues. The foregoing authorities are decisive to show that mere pursuit gave Post no legal right to the fox, but that he became the property of Pierson, who intercepted and killed him.

It therefore only remains to inquire whether there are any contrary principles, or authorities, to be found in other books, which ought to induce a different decision. Most of the cases which have occurred in England, relating to property in wild animals, have either been discussed and decided upon the principles of their positive statute regulations, or have arisen between the huntsman and the owner of the land upon which beasts *ferae naturae* have been apprehended; the former claiming them by title of occupancy, and the latter ratione soli. Little satisfactory aid can, therefore, be derived from the English reporters.

Barbeyrac, in his notes on Puffendorf, does not accede to the definition of occupancy by the latter, but on the contrary, affirms, that actual bodily seizure is not, in all cases, necessary to constitute possession of wild animals. He does not, however, describe the acts which, according to his ideas, will amount to an appropriation of such animals to private use, so as to exclude the claims of all other persons, by title of occupancy, to the same animals; and he is far from averring that pursuit alone is sufficient for that purpose. To a certain extent, and as far as Barbeyrac appears to me to go, his objections to Puffendorf's definition of occupancy are reasonable and correct. That is to say, that actual bodily seizure is not indispensable to acquire right to, or possession of, wild beasts; but that, on the contrary, the mortal wounding of such beasts, by one not abandoning his pursuit, may, with the utmost propriety, be deemed possession of him; since, thereby, the pursuer manifests an unequivocal intention of appropriating the animal to his individual use, has deprived him of his natural liberty, and brought him within his certain control. So also, encompassing and securing such animals with nets and toils, or otherwise intercepting them in such a manner as to deprive them of their natural liberty, and render escape impossible, may justly be deemed to give possession of them to those persons who, by their industry and labor, have used such means of apprehending them.

The case now under consideration is one of mere pursuit, and presents no circumstances or acts which can bring it within the definition of occupancy by Puffendorf, or Grotius, or the ideas of Barbeyrac upon that subject.

The case cited from 11 Mod. 74-130, I think clearly distinguishable from the present; inasmuch as there the action was for maliciously hindering and disturbing the plaintiff in the exercise and enjoyment of a private franchise; and in the report of the same case, (3 Salk. 9,) Holt, Ch. J., states, that the ducks were in the plaintiff's decoy pond, and so in his possession, from which it is obvious the court laid much stress in their opinion upon the plaintiff's possession of the ducks, ratione soli.

We are the more readily inclined to confine possession or occupancy of beasts *ferae naturae,* within the limits prescribed by the learned authors above cited, for the sake of certainty, and preserving peace and order in

Policy reasons

society. If the first seeing, starting, or pursuing such animals, without having so wounded, circumvented or ensnared them, so as to deprive them of their natural liberty, and subject them to the control of their pursuer, should afford the basis of actions against others for intercepting and killing them, it would prove a fertile source of quarrels and litigation.

However uncourteous or unkind the conduct of Pierson towards Post, in this instance, may have been, yet his act was productive of no injury or damage for which a legal remedy can be applied. We are of opinion the judgment below was erroneous, and ought to be reversed. *Didn't own it! need to have it*

LIVINGSTON, J. Whether a person who, with his own hounds, starts and hunts a fox on waste and uninhabited ground, and is on the point of seizing his prey, acquires such an interest in the animal, as to have a right of action against another, who in view of the huntsman and his dogs in full pursuit, and with knowledge of the chase, shall kill and carry him away?

This is a knotty point, and should have been submitted to the arbitration of sportsmen, without poring over Justinian, Fleta, Bracton, Puffendorf, Locke, Barbeyrac, or Blackstone, all of whom have been cited; they would have had no difficulty in coming to a prompt and correct conclusion. In a court thus constituted, the skin and carcass of poor reynard would have been properly disposed of, and a precedent set, interfering with no usage or custom which the experience of ages has sanctioned, and which must be so well known to every votary of Diana. But the parties have referred the question to our judgment, and we must dispose of it as well as we can, from the partial lights we possess, leaving to a higher tribunal, the correction of any mistake which we may be so unfortunate as to make. By the pleadings it is admitted that a fox is a "wild and noxious beast." Both parties have regarded him, as the law of nations does a pirate, "hostem humani generis," and although "de mortuis nil nisi bonum," be a maxim of our profession, the memory of the deceased has not been spared. His depredations on farmers and on barn yards, have not been forgotten; and to put him to death wherever found, is allowed to be meritorious, and of public benefit. Hence it follows, that our decision should have in view the greatest possible encouragement to the destruction of an animal, so cunning and ruthless in his career. But who would keep a pack of hounds; or what gentleman, at the sound of the horn, and at peep of day, would mount his steed, and for hours together, "sub jove frigido," or a vertical sun, pursue the windings of this wily quadruped, if, just as night came on, and his stratagems and strength were nearly exhausted, a saucy intruder, who had not shared in the honors or labors of the chase, were permitted to come in at the death, and bear away in triumph the object of pursuit? Whatever Justinian may have thought of the matter, it must be recollected that his code was compiled many hundred years ago, and it would be very hard indeed, at the distance of so many centuries, not to have a right to establish a rule for ourselves. In his day, we read of no order of men who made it a business, in the language of the declaration in this cause, "with hounds and dogs to find, start, pursue, hunt, and chase," these animals, and that, too, without any other motive than the preservation of Roman poultry; if this diversion had been then in fashion, the lawyers who composed his institutes, would have taken care not to pass it by, without suitable encouragement. If any thing, therefore, in the digests or pandects shall appear to militate against the defendant in error, who, on this occasion, was the fox hunter, we have only to say tempora mutantur; and if men themselves change with the times, why should not laws also undergo an alteration?

It may be expected, however, by the learned counsel, that more particular notice be taken of their authorities. I have examined them all, and feel great difficulty in determining, whether to acquire dominion over a thing, before in common, it be sufficient that we barely see it, or know where it is, or wish for it, or make a declaration of our will respecting it; or whether, in the case of wild beasts, setting a trap, or lying in wait, or starting, or pursuing, be enough; or if an actual wounding, or killing, or bodily tact and occupation be necessary. Writers on general law, who have favored us with their speculations on these points, differ on them all; but, great as is the diversity of sentiment among them, some conclusion must be adopted on the question immediately before us.

Now, as we are without any municipal regulations of our own, and the pursuit here, for aught that appears on the case, being with dogs and hounds of imperial stature, we are at liberty to adopt one of the provisions just cited, which comports also with the learned conclusion of Barbeyrac, that property in animals *ferae naturae* may be acquired without bodily touch or manucaption, provided the pursuer be within reach, or have a reasonable prospect (which certainly existed here) of taking, what he has thus discovered an intention of converting to his own use.

When we reflect also that the interest of our husbandmen, the most useful of men in any community, will be advanced by the destruction of a beast so pernicious and incorrigible, we cannot greatly err, in saying, that a pursuit like the present, through waste and unoccupied lands, and which must inevitably and speedily have terminated in corporal possession, or bodily seisin, confers such a right to the object of it, as to make any one a wrongdoer, who shall interfere and shoulder the spoil. The justice's judgment ought therefore, in my opinion, be affirmed.

Judgment of reversal.

Fox is his - opp of other decision

NOTES AND QUESTIONS

1. **Creation of property rights, again.** Note that many older property casebooks start out with cases on possession of wild animals and lost goods. This approach tracks the nature narrative's assumption that the key point in the design of a property system is the (utterly unknowable) point at

which property rights were first obtained. Note, in contrast, that neither of the other two property visions (that is, the feudal vision and the republican vision) focus on the origins of property rights and, in fact, as we have seen, writers in the republican tradition often argued that the institution of property should be designed with reference to the current — and the desirable — distribution of property. Is the point at which property rights were created determinative on the question of how to design the institution of property today? Robert Nozick is perhaps the most influential contemporary spokesman for the position that it is. Nozick argues that if an individual's property is acquired by consensual means from someone who originally was entitled to it, then coercive state appropriation of private property amounts to theft and is a violation of the owner's autonomy. See Robert Nozick, Anarchy, State and Utopia 149, 149-231 (1974). For example, if one's income is acquired by voluntarily trading away one's labor for money, then income taxation (at least for the purpose of redistributing income) is morally akin to forced labor. Id. at 169-172.

2.   **Who minds the children of the lonely hunter?** In Pierson v. Post, as in Locke, we have the lone hunters wresting food from the commons through the sweat of their brows. Note that this imagery leaves out the entire social and familial systems that support the hunters, all the way from the woman who minds the hunter's children while he hunts, to the organized industrial society that made his gun available. The nature narrative reads out of existence the kind of interdependence that the feudal and republican visions place at center stage.

3.   **Utilitarianism.** Notice how Judge Tompkins and Judge Livingston both make utilitarian arguments. What are they? Utilitarianism is often associated with Bentham, who crystallized the approach. See Daniel T. Rodgers, Contested Truths 17-44 (1987). The simplest statement of utilitarianism is that we should act in the way that promotes the best consequences. Utilitarians from Bentham on have struggled to define what are the consequences they desire to achieve. Bentham himself started out with General Utility; he subsequently suggested a string of alternatives, including "happiness," "public happiness," "the greatest possible happiness of the Community," and "the greatest good for the greatest number." Id. at 22. (Sometimes he even tried "pleasure," making himself, according to Rodgers, "simply a hedonist of a peculiarly mathematical sort." Id.)

4.   **Hunters and Hohfeld.** The traditional way to read Pierson v. Post is in terms of lonely hunters and rugged individualism. Yet it also fits well into the modern analysis of property rights as involving relationships among people. Spin out a Hohfeldian analysis of the case.

5.   **Modern application.** Wyoming's regulatory scheme for the taking of wildlife within the state opens certain private lands to the public during the hunting season. Landowners and ranch operators claimed that they owned the exclusive right to hunt animals on their land, and that state regulation had deprived them of property without compensation. In defeating

the claim, the federal court applied the capture doctrine: wild fish, birds, and animals are owned by no one; property rights in them are obtained by reducing them to possession. Without a property interest in the animals, plaintiffs had no takings claim. Clajon Production Corp. v. Petera, 854 F. Supp. 843 (D. Wyo. 1994), *aff'd,* 70 F.3d 1566 (10th Cir. 1995).

d.   The Liberal Dignity Strain: "Property Rights Serve Human Values"

We hold these truths to be self-evident, that all men are created equal, that they are endowed by their Creator with certain unalienable Rights, that among these are Life, Liberty, and the pursuit of Happiness.[62]

Economic liberalism is only one strain of the liberal tradition. Alternative strains share the vision of society as composed of individuals with rights making choices, but they do not share economic liberalism's serenity about self-interest. Indeed, historians recently have pointed out that John Locke himself was a very religious man and assumed that self-interest would be pursued within the bounds of "divinely established natural law, which encumbers the freedom of individuals at every turn with the powerful commands of duty." James T. Kloppenberg, The Virtues of Liberalism, 74 J. Am. Hist. 9, 16 (1987). See also John Dunn, Rethinking Modern Political Theory: Essays 1979-1983, at 21-26 (1985); Radoslav A. Tsanoff, The Moral Ideals of Our Civilization 227-232 (1942). Consider the following excerpts.

JOHN LOCKE, TWO TREATISES OF GOVERNMENT

287, 288, 298, 306, 308-309 (Peter Laslett ed., 1967; written c. 1679-1683)

4. . . . [All men are naturally in a state of perfect freedom.] A *State* also of *Equality,* . . . there being nothing more evident, than that Creatures of same species and rank promiscuously born to all the same advantages of Nature, and the use of the same faculties, should also be equal one amongst another without Subordination or Subjection, unless the Lord and Master of them all, should by any manifest Declaration of his Will set one above another. . . .

6. But though this be a *State of Liberty,* yet it is *not a State of Licence.* . . . The *State of Nature* has a Law of Nature to govern it, which obliges every one: And Reason, which is that Law, teaches all Mankind, who will but consult it, that being all equal and independent, no one ought to harm another in his Life, Health, Liberty, or Possessions. For men being all the Workmanship of

62. Thomas Jefferson, The Declaration of Independence, 1776, reprinted in Kermit L. Hall, William M. Wiecek, and Paul Finkelman, American Legal History: Cases and Materials 66 (1991).

one Omnipotent, and infinitely wise Maker, All the Servants of one Sovereign Master, sent into the World by his order and about his business, . . .
And being furnished with like Faculties, sharing all in one Community of
Nature, there cannot be supposed any such *Subordination* among us, that ⎞
may Authorize us to destroy one another, as if we were made for one anoth- ⎟
ers uses, as the inferior ranks of Creatures are for ours. . . . ⎠

19. . . . Men living together according to reason, without a common
Superior on Earth, with Authority to judge between them, is *properly the State
of Nature.* . . .

27. . . . [Men's] *[l]abour* being the unquestionable Property of the Labourer, no Man but he can have a right to what that is once joyned to, at
least where there is enough, and as good left incommon for others. . . .

31. It will perhaps be objected to this, That if gathering the Acorns, or
other Fruits of the Earth, *etc.* makes a right to them, then any one may *ingross* as much as he will. To which I Answer, Not so. The same Law of Nature,
that does by this means give us Property, does also *bound* that *Property* too.
God has given us all things richly, I Tim. Vi. 17. Is the Voice of Reason confirmed by Inspiration? But how has he given it us? *To enjoy.* As much as any ⎞
one can make use of to any advantage of life before it spoils; so much he ⎟
may by his labour fix a Property in. Whatever is beyond this, is more than ⎟
his share, and belongs to others. Nothing was made by God for Man to spoil ⎠
or destroy. . . .

32. But the *chief matter of Property* being now not the Fruits of the Earth,
and the Beasts that subsist on it, but the *Earth it self;* . . . I think it is plain,
that *Property* in that too is acquired [in land]. *As much Land* as a Man Tills,
Plants, Improves, Cultivates, and can use the Product of, so much is his
Property. . . . God and [his] Reason commanded him to subdue the Earth,
i.e. improve it for the benefit of Life. . . .

33. Nor was this *appropriation* of any parcel of *Land,* by improving it,
any prejudice to any other Man, since there was still enough and as good
left. . . .

In the following excerpt, Wendy Gordon uses Locke's proviso that
property rights only exist "where there is enough and as good left . . . for
others" to support an argument about intellectual property law.

WENDY J. GORDON, A PROPERTY RIGHT IN SELF-EXPRESSION: EQUALITY AND INDIVIDUALISM IN THE NATURAL LAW OF INTELLECTUAL PROPERTY

102 Yale L.J. 1533, 1562-1564 (1993)

Locke states the proviso thus: "Labour being the unquestionable
Property of the Labourer, no Man but he can have a right to what that is

once joyned [*sic*] to, *at least where there is enough and as good left in common for others.*"

With this proviso, Locke argues that one person's joining of her labor with resources that God gave mankind ("appropriation") should not give that individual a right to exclude others from the resulting product, unless the exclusion will leave these other people with as much opportunity to use the common as they otherwise would have had. A person who wants access is entitled to complain only if he is worse off (in regard to the common) when he is denied access then he would have been if the item had never come into existence. If the proviso is satisfied, others are no worse off if they are excluded from the resource the laborer has marked off as her own. . . .

The proviso that "enough and as good [be] left" lies at the center of this Article's thesis: that creators should have property in their original works, only provided that such grant of property does no harm to other persons' equal abilities to create or to draw upon the preexisting cultural matrix and scientific heritage. All persons are equal and have an equal right to the common.

If you never had it - you don't miss it

NOTES AND QUESTIONS

1. **Locke's proviso.** The two strains of liberalism reflect two different interpretations of the work of John Locke. Economic liberalism stresses Locke's general defense and justification of property rights; the liberal dignity strain focuses on Locke's proviso that property rights are limited by the requirement that "enough and as good" be left for others. Commentators are divided on the meaning of the proviso. Some believe that Locke's basic argument was that the proviso bound humanity only until money was introduced; thereafter, the proviso became inapplicable, since money (unlike food) did not spoil and (unlike land) contained no natural limitations on the amount one person could use fruitfully. See, e.g., C. B. MacPherson, The Political Theory of Possessive Individualism: Hobbes to Locke (10th ed. 1985). Other authors, like Wendy Gordon, place the proviso at the center of Locke's thought.

2. **Melding liberalism with republicanism.** Throughout the eighteenth century, according to the historian James Kloppenberg, most liberal thinkers assumed that self-interest would be pursued only within the bounds of virtue, as defined by religion, republicanism, or other traditions. See Kloppenberg, *supra.* Our evidence suggests that the pattern of melding liberal with republican precepts continues to this day: think back to Charles Reich's "The New Property," *supra.* Our initial analysis focused on the aspects of Reich's argument consonant with republican themes. But Reich's basic framework is a liberal one, particularly his notion that property "guards the troubled boundary between the individual man and the state." Charles A. Reich, The New Property, 73 Yale L.J. 733, 733 (1964).

Note how Reich's analysis is firmly set into the liberal tradition, projecting the image of an autonomous individual with rights making choices who is threatened by intrusive state power.

3.   **Religion, equality, and property.** Embedded in this passage of Locke is a potential clash between the new market ethic and older Christian and communitarian norms that "imposed moral constraints on acquisitiveness to protect the weak from the predatory, the strong from corruption, and the culture from secularist and materialist excess." See Paul Goodman, The Emergence of Homestead Exemption in the United States: Accommodation and Resistance to the Market Revolution, 1840-1880, 80 J. Am. Hist. 470, 474 (1993).

Note, in particular, the religious roots of the principle that later became the "self-evident truth" that "all men are created equal," see The Declaration of Independence para. 2. Locke derives the principle that all men are equal from the principle that they are all God's servants. "For Men being all the Workmanship of one Omnipotent, and infinitely wise Maker; All the Servants of one Sovereign Master, sent into the World by his order and about his business, . . . And being furnished with like Faculties, sharing all in one Community of Nature, there cannot be supposed any such *Subordination* among us. . . . Locke, Two Treatises of Government 289 (Peter Laslett ed., 1967).

The early nineteenth-century theorist Thomas Skidmore melded religion, republicanism, and liberalism into a theory of property that concluded that all existing property holdings were illegitimate. Skidmore reasoned from the self-evident principle "engraved on the heart of man" that each had an equal claim to the Creator's endowment. He asked:

> Is the work of creation to be let out on hire? And are the great mass of mankind to be hirelings to those who undertake to set up a claim, as government is now constructed, that the world was made for them? Why not sell the winds of heaven, that man might not breathe without price? . . .

Quoted in Sean Wilenz, Chants Democratic 185 (1984). As "the Creator has made all equal," read a Skidmore-inspired resolution in 1829, resolved that no man could give up his original right of the soil "without receiving a guaranty that reasonable toil shall enable him to live as comfortably as others." Id. at 191. Skidmore argued that private property — like slavery and the disenfranchisement of native Americans, black, women, and the unpropertied — violated the principle of God-given equality. He proposed that the "friends of equal rights," id. at 186, combine into a great mass movement to elect enough representatives to call and control state constitutional conventions that would enfranchise all adults and redistribute all property. Skidmore concluded that people of superior talent and diligence would accumulate greater wealth than others, but he proposed that inheritance be abolished, and that all property be redistributed upon death to persons who had just reached adulthood. Skidmore's is perhaps the most far-reaching theory of property that begins from the religious principle of equality and concludes that it requires a much more egalitarian property system.

The religious version of this principle of equality coexists in American political rhetoric to this day along with more secular formulations. Religion plays a particularly strong role in African American political rhetoric. Consider the following from a speech by Dr. Martin Luther King Jr.:

> In the final analysis, says the Christian ethic, every man must be respected because God loves him. The worth of an individual does not lie in the measure of his intellect, his racial origin, or his social position. Human worth lies in his relatedness to God. An individual has value because he has value to God. Whenever this is recognized, "whiteness" and "blackness" pass away as determinants in a relationship and "son" and "brother" are substituted.

See James Melvin Washington, A Testament of Hope — The Essential Writings of Martin Luther King Jr. 122 (1986). In a speech delivered in the year before his murder, Dr. King spun out the implications of this theme for property.

> I am aware that there are many who wince at a distinction between property and person — who hold both sacrosanct. My views are not so rigid. A life is sacred. Property is intended to serve life, and no matter how much we surround it with rights and respect, it has not personal being. It is part of the earth man walks on; it is not man.

Id. at 649.

4. **Persuasion.** "Most Americans . . . define life's ultimate moral questions in religious terms and in terms of virtue and personal moral responsibility. . . . For those of you who have yet to locate the gift of faith, I am not suggesting you have to return to your church or synagogue. I am suggesting that you cheat your client when you kid yourself about the moral language your jurors speak or refuse to learn it yourself. So go out and study a children's Bible or try to remember what your parents taught you as a kid. But meet the jury in the moral world it occupies." Prominent death penalty litigator Kevin Doyle, quoted in James Traub, The Life Preserver, The New Yorker, April 8, 1996, at 47, 50. What are some of the pitfalls of using religious language within the law? Of not using it?

5. **The golden rule, the categorical imperative, and the original position.** A central heuristic of Western thought is the proposal to model ethical thought around "putting yourself in someone else's shoes." The single most influential formulation in Western thought is the golden rule to "Love your neighbor as yourself." Mark 12:31.[63] Immanuel Kant reworked this

---

63. The inherent dignity of human beings is also an important theme in Judaism. See Michael J. Perry, Is the Idea of Human Rights Ineliminably Religious?, in Legal Rights: Histori-

heuristic in secular and analytic terms with his categorical imperative to "act only according to that maxim by which you can at the same time will that it should become a universal law" (i.e., to adopt rules that will treat your neighbor as yourself). Immanuel Kant, The Moral Law: Kant's Groundwork of the Metaphysics of Morals 84 (H. J. Paton trans., 1967). A still more recent formulation of the same heuristic is John Rawls's "original position," in which he proposes to generate a fair society by setting up the ground rule that no one will know where he or she will come out in the resulting society.[64] Rawls's assumption clearly is that if everyone were at risk of ending up at the bottom of the heap, each would design a society that treated their neighbors as themselves.

State v. Shack, which follows the excerpt from Blackstone, shows how the "golden rule" heuristic, in both its religious and its secular forms, functions to limit the supposed absoluteness of property rights.

BLACKSTONE, COMMENTARIES

575-576 (Ehrlich ed. 1959)

Trespass quare clausum fregit — But in the limited and confined sense, in which we are at present to consider it, it signifies no more than an entry on another man's ground without a lawful authority, and doing some damage, however inconsiderable, to his real property. For the right of meum and tuum (mine and thine) or property, in lands being once established, it follows, as a necessary consequence, that this right must be exclusive; that is, that the owner may retain to himself the sole use and occupation of his soil: every entry, therefore, thereon without the owner's leave, and especially if contrary to his express order, is a trespass or transgression.

The law of England has treated every entry upon another's lands (unless by the owner's leave, or in some very particular cases), as an injury or wrong, for satisfaction of which an action of trespass will lie; but determines the quantum of that satisfaction, by considering how far the offense was willful or inadvertent, and by estimating the value of the actual damages sustained.

---

cal and Philosophical Perspectives 217 (Austin Sarat and Thomas R. Kearns eds., 1996); Search of LEXIS, Nexis Library, People file (Aug. 12, 1991) (quoting Jewish scholar Hillel: "Do not unto others that which is hateful unto thee.").

64. John Rawls, A Theory of Justice 12-13 (1971).

STATE v. SHACK

58 N.J. 297, 277 A.2d 369 (1971)

The opinion of the Court was delivered by WEINTRAUB, C. J. Defendants entered upon private property to aid migrant farmworkers employed and housed there. Having refused to depart upon the demand of the owner, defendants were charged with violating N.J.S.A. 2A:170-31 which provides that "[a]ny person who trespasses on any lands . . . after being forbidden so to trespass by the owner . . . is a disorderly person and shall be punished by a fine of not more than $50." Defendants were convicted in the Municipal Court of Deerfield Township and again on appeal in the County Court of Cumberland County on a trial de novo. R. 3:23-8(a). We certified their further appeal before argument in the Appellate Division.

Before us, no one seeks to sustain these convictions. The complaints were prosecuted in the Municipal Court and in the County Court by counsel engaged by the complaining landowner, Tedesco. However Tedesco did not respond to this appeal, and the county prosecutor, while defending abstractly the constitutionality of the trespass statute, expressly disclaimed any position as to whether the statute reached the activity of these defendants.

Complainant, Tedesco, a farmer, employs migrant workers for his seasonal needs. As part of their compensation, these workers are housed at a camp on his property.

Defendant Tejeras is a field worker for the Farm Workers Division of the Southwest Citizens Organization for Poverty Elimination, known by the acronym SCOPE, a nonprofit corporation funded by the Office of Economic Opportunity pursuant to an act of Congress, 42 U.S.C.A. §§2861-2864. The role of SCOPE includes providing for the "health services of the migrant farm worker."

Defendant Shack is a staff attorney with the Farm Workers Division of Camden Regional Legal Services, Inc., known as "CRLS," also a nonprofit corporation funded by the Office of Economic Opportunity pursuant to an act of Congress, 42 U.S.C.A. §2809(a)(3). The mission of CRLS includes legal advice and representation for these workers.

Differences had developed between Tedesco and these defendants prior to the events which led to the trespass charges now before us. Hence when defendant Tejeras wanted to go upon Tedesco's farm to find a migrant worker who needed medical aid for the removal of 28 sutures, he called upon defendant Shack for his help with respect to the legalities involved. Shack, too, had a mission to perform on Tedesco's farm; he wanted to discuss a legal problem with another migrant worker there employed and housed. Defendants arranged to go to the farm together. Shack carried literature to inform the migrant farmworkers of the assistance available to

FIGURE 1-6
Migrant farm workers' housing in California desert

them under federal statutes, but no mention seems to have been made of that literature when Shack was later confronted by Tedesco.

Defendants entered upon Tedesco's property and as they neared the camp site where the farmworkers were housed, they were confronted by Tedesco who inquired of their purpose. Tejeras and Shack stated their missions. In response, Tedesco offered to find the injured worker, and as to the worker who needed legal advice, Tedesco also offered to locate the man but insisted that the consultation would have to take place in Tedesco's office and in his presence. Defendants declined, saying that they had the right to see the men in the privacy of their living quarters and without Tedesco's supervision. Tedesco thereupon summoned a State Trooper who, however, refused to remove defendants except upon Tedesco's written complaint. Tedesco then executed the formal complaints charging violations of the trespass statute.

I

The constitutionality of the trespass statute, as applied here, is challenged on several scores.

It is urged that the First Amendment rights of the defendants and of the migrant farmworkers were thereby offended. Reliance is placed on Marsh v. Alabama, 326 U.S. 501 (1946), where it was held that free speech was assured by the First Amendment in a company-owned town which was open to the public generally and was indistinguishable from any other town except for the fact that the title to property was vested in a private corporation. Hence a Jehovah's Witness who distributed literature on a sidewalk within the town could not be held as a trespasser. Later, on the strength of that case, it was held that there was a First Amendment right to picket peacefully in a privately owned shopping center which was found to be the functional equivalent of the business district of the company-owned town in *Marsh*. Amalgamated Food Employees Union Local 590 v. Logan Valley Plaza, Inc., 391 U.S. 308 (1968). See, to the same effect, the earlier case of Schwartz-Torrance Investment Corp. v. Bakery and Confectionery Workers' Union, 61 Cal. 2d 766, 40 Cal. Rptr. 233, 394 P.2d 921 (Sup. Ct. 1964), cert. denied, 380 U.S. 906 (1964). Those cases rest upon the fact that the property was in fact opened to the general public. There may be some migrant camps with the attributes of the company town in *Marsh* and of course they would come within its holding. But there is nothing of that character in the case before us, and hence there would have to be an extension of *Marsh* to embrace the immediate situation.

Defendants also maintain that the application of the trespass statute to them is barred by the Supremacy Clause of the United States Constitution, Art. VI, cl. 2, and this on the premise that the application of the trespass statute would defeat the purpose of the federal statutes, under which SCOPE and CRLS are funded, to reach and aid the migrant farmworker. The brief of the United States, amicus curiae, supports that approach. Here defendants rely upon cases construing the National Labor Relations Act, 29 U.S.C.A. §151 et seq., and holding that an employer may in some circumstances be guilty of an unfair labor practice in violation of that statute if the employer denies union organizers an opportunity to communicate with his employees at some suitable place upon the employer's premises. See NLRB v. Babcock and Wilcox Co., 351 U.S. 105 (1956), and annotation, 100 L. Ed. 984 (1956). The brief of New Jersey Office of Legal Services, amicus curiae, asserts the workers' Sixth Amendment right to counsel in criminal matters is involved and suggests also that a right to counsel in civil matters is a "penumbra" right emanating from the whole Bill of Rights under the thinking of Griswold v. Connecticut, 381 U.S. 479 (1965), or is a privilege of national citizenship protected by the privileges and immunities clause of the Fourteenth Amendment, or is a right "retained by the people" under the Ninth Amendment, citing a dictum in United Public Workers v. Mitchell, 330 U.S. 75, 94 (1947).

These constitutional claims are not established by any definitive holding. We think it unnecessary to explore their validity. The reason is that we are satisfied that under our State law the ownership of real property does not include the right to bar access to governmental services available to migrant workers and hence there was no trespass within the meaning of the penal statute. The policy considerations which underlie that conclusion may be much the same as those which would be weighed with respect to one or more of the constitutional challenges, but a decision in nonconstitutional terms is more satisfactory, because the interests of migrant workers are more expansively served in that way than they would be if they had no more freedom than these constitutional concepts could be found to mandate if indeed they apply at all.

II

Property rights serve human values. They are recognized to that end and are limited by it. Title to real property cannot include dominion over the destiny of persons the owner permits to come upon the premises. Their well-being must remain the paramount concern of a system of law. Indeed the needs of the occupants may be so imperative and their strength so weak, that the law will deny the occupants the power to contract away what is deemed essential to their health, welfare, or dignity.

Here we are concerned with a highly disadvantaged segment of our society. We are told that every year farmworkers and their families numbering more than one million leave their home areas to fill the seasonal demand for farm labor in the United States. The Migratory Farm Labor Problem in the United States (1969 Report of Subcommittee on Migratory Labor of the United States Senate Committee on Labor and Public Welfare), p. 1. The migrant farmworkers come to New Jersey in substantial numbers. The report just cited places at 55,700 the number of man-months of such employment in our State in 1968 (p. 7). The numbers of workers so employed here in that year are estimated at 1,300 in April; 6,500 in May; 9,800 in June; 10,600 in July; 12,000 in August; 9,600 in September; and 5,500 in October (p. 9).

The migrant farmworkers are a community within but apart from the local scene. They are rootless and isolated. Although the need for their labors is evident, they are unorganized and without economic or political power. It is their plight alone that summoned government to their aid. In response, Congress provided under Title III-B of the Economic Opportunity Act of 1964 (42 U.S.C.A. §2701 et seq.) for "assistance for migrant and other seasonally employed farmworkers and their families." Section 2861 states "the purpose of this part is to assist migrant and seasonal farmworkers and their families to improve their living conditions and develop skills necessary for a productive and self-sufficient life in an increasingly complex and technological society." Section 2862(b)(1) provides for funding of programs "to meet the immediate needs of migrant and seasonal farmworkers and their families, such as day care for children, education, health services, improved housing and sanitation (including the provision and maintenance of emergency and temporary housing and sanitation facilities), legal advice and representation, and consumer training and counseling." As we have said, SCOPE is engaged in a program funded under this section, and CRLS also pursues the objectives of this section although, we gather, it is funded under §2809(a)(3), which is not limited in its concern to the migrant and other seasonally employed farmworkers and seeks "to further the cause of justice among persons living in poverty by mobilizing the assistance of lawyers and legal institutions and by providing legal advice, legal representation, counseling, education, and other appropriate services."

These ends would not be gained if the intended beneficiaries could be insulated from efforts to reach them. It is in this framework that we must decide whether the camp operator's rights in his lands may stand between the migrant workers and those who would aid them. The key to that aid is communication. Since the migrant workers are outside the mainstream of the communities in which they are housed and are unaware of their rights and opportunities and of the services available to them, they can be reached only by positive efforts tailored to that end. The Report of the Governor's Task Force on Migrant Farm Labor (1968) noted that "One of the major problems related to seasonal farm labor is the lack of adequate direct information with regard to the availability of public services," and that "there is a dire need to provide the workers with basic educational and informational material in a language and style that can be readily understood by the migrant" (pp. 101-102). The report stressed the problem of access and deplored the notion that property rights may stand as a barrier, saying "In our judgment, 'no trespass' signs represent the last dying remnants of paternalistic behavior" (p. 63).

A man's right in his real property of course is not absolute. It was a maxim of the common law that one should so use his property as not to injure the rights of others. Broom, Legal Maxims (10 ed. Kersley 1939), p. 238; 39 Words and Phrases, "Sic Utere Tuo et Alienum Non Laedas," p. 335. Although hardly a precise solvent of actual controversies, the maxim does express the inevitable proposition that rights are relative and there must be an accommodation when they meet. Hence it has long been true that necessity, private or public, may justify entry upon the lands of another. For a catalogue of such situations, see Prosser, Torts (3d ed. 1964), §24, pp. 127-129; 6A American Law of Property (A. J. Casner ed. 1954) §28.10, p. 31; 52 Am. Jur., "Trespass," §§40-41, pp. 867-869. See also Restatement, Second, Torts (1965) §§197-211; Krauth v. Geller, 31 N.J. 270, 272-273 (1960).

The subject is not static. As pointed out in 5 Powell, Real Property (Rohan 1970) §745, pp. 493-494, while society will protect the owner in his permissible interests in land, yet

> such an owner must expect to find the absoluteness of his property rights curtailed by the organs of society, for the promotion of the best interests of others for whom these organs also operate as protective agencies. The necessity for such curtailments is greater in a modern industrialized and urbanized society than it was in the relatively simple American society of fifty, 100, or 200 years ago. The current balance between individualism and dominance of the social

interest depends not only upon political and social ideologies, but also upon the physical and social facts of the time and place under discussion.

Professor Powell added in §746, pp. 494-496:

> As one looks back along the historic road traversed by the law of land in England and in America, one sees a change from the viewpoint that he who owns may do as he pleases with what he owns, to a position which hesitatingly embodies an ingredient of stewardship; which grudgingly, but steadily, broadens the recognized scope of social interests in the utilization of things. . . .
>
> To one seeing history through the glasses of religion, these changes may seem to evidence increasing embodiments of the golden rule. To one thinking in terms of political and economic ideologies, they are likely to be labeled evidences of "social enlightenment," or of "creeping socialism" or even of "communistic infiltration," according to the individual's assumed definitions and retained or acquired prejudices. With slight attention to words or labels, time marches on toward new adjustments between individualism and the social interests.

This process involves not only the accommodation between the right of the owner and the interests of the general public in his use of his property, but involves also an accommodation between the right of the owner and the right of individuals who are parties with him in consensual transactions relating to the use of the property. Accordingly substantial alterations have been made as between a landlord and his tenant. See Reste Realty Corp. v. Cooper, 53 N.J. 444, 451-453 (1969); Marini v. Ireland, 56 N.J. 130, 141-143 (1970).

The argument in this case understandably included the question whether the migrant worker should be deemed to be a tenant and thus entitled to the tenant's right to receive visitors, Williams v. Lubbering, 73 N.J.L. 317, 319-320 (Sup. Ct. 1906), or whether his residence on the employer's property should be deemed to be merely incidental and in aid of his employment, and hence to involve no possessory interest in the realty. See Scottish Rite Co. v. Salkowitz, 119 N.J.L. 558 (E. & A. 1938); New Jersey Midland Ry. Co. v. Van Syckle, 37 N.J.L. 496, 506 (E. & A. 1874); Gray v. Reynolds, 67 N.J.L. 169 (Sup. Ct. 1901); McQuade v. Emmons, 38 N.J.L. 397 (Sup. Ct. 1876); Morris Canal & Banking Co. v. Mitchell, 31 N.J.L. 99 (Sup. Ct. 1864); Schuman v. Zurawell, 24 N.J. Misc. 180 (Cir. Ct. 1946). These cases did not reach employment situations at all comparable with the one before us. Nor did they involve the question whether an employee who is not a tenant may have visitors notwithstanding the employer's prohibition. Rather they were concerned with whether notice must be given to end the employee's right to remain upon the premises, with whether the employer may remove the discharged employee without court order, and with the availability of a particular judicial remedy to achieve his removal by process.

We of course are not concerned here with the right of a migrant worker to remain on the employer's property after the employment is ended.

We see no profit in trying to decide upon a conventional category and then forcing the present subject into it. That approach would be artificial and distorting. The quest is for a fair adjustment of the competing needs of the parties, in the light of the realities of the relationship between the migrant worker and the operator of the housing facility.

Thus approaching the case, we find it unthinkable that the farmer-employer can assert a right to isolate the migrant worker in any respect significant for the worker's well-being. The farmer, of course, is entitled to pursue his farming activities without interference, and this defendants readily concede. But we see no legitimate need for a right in the farmer to deny the worker the opportunity for aid available from federal, State, or local services, or from recognized charitable groups seeking to assist him. Hence representatives of these agencies and organizations may enter upon the premises to seek out the worker at his living quarters. So, too, the migrant must be allowed to receive visitors there of his own choice, so long as there is no behavior hurtful to others, and members of the press may not be denied reasonable access to workers who do not object to seeing them.

It is not our purpose to open the employer's premises to the general public if in fact the employer himself has not done so. We do not say, for example, that solicitors or peddlers of all kinds may enter on their own; we may assume for the present that the employer may regulate their entry or bar them, at least if the employer's purpose is not to gain a commercial advantage for himself or if the regulation does not deprive the migrant worker of practical access to things he needs.

And we are mindful of the employer's interest in his own and in his employees' security. Hence he may reasonably require a visitor to identify himself, and also to state his general purpose if the migrant worker has not already informed him that the visitor is expected. But the employer may not deny the worker his privacy or interfere with his opportunity to live with dignity and to enjoy associations customary among our citizens. These rights are too fundamental to be denied on the basis of an interest in real property and too fragile to be left to the unequal bargaining strength of the parties. See Henningsen v. Bloomfield Motors, Inc., 32 N.J. 358, 403-404 (1960); Ellsworth Dobbs, Inc. v. Johnson, 50 N.J. 528, 555 (1967).

It follows that defendants here invaded no possessory right of the farmer-employer. Their conduct was therefore beyond the reach of the trespass statute. The judgments are accordingly reversed and the matters remanded to the County Court with directions to enter judgments of acquittal.

For reversal and remandment — CHIEF JUSTICE WEINTRAUB and JUSTICES JACOBS, FRANCIS, PROCTOR, HALL and SCHETTINO — 6.

For affirmance — None.

NOTES AND QUESTIONS

1.   **Property and exclusivity.** The statement that exclusivity is a hall-mark of property is a common one. Black's Law Dictionary defines property as "[t]hat which is peculiar or proper to any person; that which belongs exclusively to one." Black's Law Dictionary 1216 (6th ed. 1990). See also International News Serv. v. Associated Press, 248 U.S. 215, 250 (1918) (stating that an essential component of property is the "right to exclude others from enjoying it"); Kaiser Aetna v. United States, 444 U.S. 164, 179 (1979) (the right to exclude traditionally has been treated as fundamental).

The excerpt from Blackstone, *supra,* while absolutist in tone, recognizes "some very particular cases" where an unauthorized entry on another's land would not be treated as an injury or wrong. Many of the exceptions stemmed from the system of interdependent property rights that originated in the feudal vision. Cf. Forrest McDonald, Novus Ordo Seclorum 33 (1985) ("The right of passage was explicitly recognized in the theory of natural law, and it was a well-established principle of English law that the ownership or right to use a particular area of land implicitly carried with it a right of passage . . . across such other lands as was necessary for access").

Under modern law, the Second Restatement of Torts contains more than twenty sections — exceptions to the law of trespass — enumerating "privileged" entries on land over the owner's objections. Restatement (Second) of Torts §§176-211 (1965). These include entry by a remainderman to view waste or make repairs, id. at §186; entry by a landlord to demand defaulted rent, id. at §187; entry because of private necessity, id. at §197.[65]

Consider also such statutorily privileged entries as those provided for in civil rights legislation: 42 U.S.C.A. §2000a (equal access to places of public accommodation); 42 U.S.C.A. §§3601-3617 (fair housing).

2.   **Human values.** "Property rights serve human values," State v. Shack, *supra.* Would you agree that a landowner's right to exclude, protected by criminal trespass statutes and civil trespass remedies, serves "human values?" If so, which human values?

Note, also, the court's reference to the golden rule: What rhetorical mechanisms does the court use to distance itself from this explicit reference to religion?

3.   **The right to exclude and economic liberalism.** Professor Richard Posner has written extensively about law and economics. Consider carefully the following excerpt from his writings, in defense of exclusivity. Is his

---

65. The notes to this section contain 15 illustrations of private necessity. These include the canoer A who lands on B's dock during a sudden storm, the aviator A who makes a forced landing on B's field, the visitor A who is overcome by illness while visiting at B's dwelling and is unable to leave, and the passerby A who enters B's dwelling after hearing screams from inside indicating distress. See id. comment b, illustrations 1, 3, 4; id. comment e, illustration 8.

argument necessary to your understanding of the right to exclude? Is it sufficient?

> To understand the economics of property rights, it is first necessary to grasp the economist's distinction between *static* and *dynamic* analysis. Static analysis suppresses the time dimension of economic activity: All adjustments to change are assumed to occur instantaneously. The assumption is unrealistic but often fruitful; the attentive reader of Chapter 1 will not be too disturbed by a lack of realism in assumptions.
>
> Dynamic analysis, in which the assumption of instantaneous adjustment to change is relaxed, is usually more complex than static analysis. So it is surprising that the economic basis of property rights was first perceived in dynamic terms. Imagine a society in which all property rights have been abolished. A farmer plants corn, fertilizes it, and erects scarecrows, but when the corn is ripe his neighbor reaps it and takes it away for his own use. The farmer has no legal remedy against his neighbor's conduct since he owns neither the land that he sowed nor the crop. Unless defensive measures are feasible (and let us assume for the moment that they are not), after a few such incidents the cultivation of land will be abandoned and society will shift to methods of subsistence (such as hunting) that involve less preparatory investment.
>
> As this example suggests, legal protection of property rights creates incentives to use resources efficiently. Although the value of the crop in our example, as measured by consumers' willingness to pay, may have greatly exceeded its cost in labor, materials, and forgone alternative uses of the land, without property rights there is no incentive to incur these costs because there is no reasonably assured reward for incurring them. The proper incentives are created by parceling out mutually exclusive rights to the use of particular resources among the members of society. If every piece of land is owned by someone — if there is always someone who can exclude all others from access to any given area — then individuals will endeavor by cultivation or other improvements to maximize the value of land. Of course, land is just an example. The principle applies to all valuable resources.
>
> All this has been well known for hundreds of years.[1] In contrast, the static analysis of property rights is little more than 50 years old.[2] Imagine that

---

1. See, e.g., 2 William Blackstone, Commentaries on the Laws of England 4, 7 (1766). And property-rights systems are prehistoric in their origins. Vernon L. Smith, The Primitive Hunter Culture, Pleistocene Extinction, and the Rise of Agriculture, 83 J. Pol. Econ. 727 (1975).

The proposition that enforcing property rights will lead to a greater output is questioned by Frank I. Michelman in Ethics, Economics, and the Law of Property, 24 Nomos 3, 25 (1982). He suggests that the farmer who knows that half his crop will be stolen may just plant twice as much. This suggestion overlooks

(1)   the added incentive to theft that will be created by planting a larger crop and the resulting likelihood that more than one-half of the larger crop will be stolen;

(2)   the unlikelihood that farming would be so much more profitable than substitute activities not entailing preparatory investment as to keep people in farming; and

(3)   the likelihood that the farmer, if he remained in farming, would divert some of his resources from growing crops to protecting them with walls, guards, etc.

2. See Frank H. Knight, Some Fallacies in the Interpretation of Social Cost, 38 Q.J. Econ. 582 (1924).

a number of farmers own a pasture in common; that is, none has the right to exclude any of the others and hence none can charge the others for the use of the pasture. We can abstract from the dynamic aspects of the problem by assuming that the pasture is a natural (uncultivated) one. Even so, pasturing additional cows will impose a cost on all the farmers. The cows will have to graze more in order to eat the same amount of grass, and this will reduce their weight. But because none of the farmers pays for the use of the pasture, none will take this cost into account in deciding how many additional cows to pasture, with the result that more cows will be pastured than would be efficient. (Can you see an analogy to highway congestion?)

The problem would disappear if someone owned the pasture and charged each farmer for its use (for purposes of this analysis, disregard the cost of levying such a charge). The charge to each farmer would include the cost he imposes on the other farmers by pasturing additional cows, because that cost reduces the value of the pasture to the other farmers and hence the price they are willing to pay the owner for the right to graze.

The creation of exclusive rights is a necessary rather than a sufficient condition for the efficient use of resources: The rights must be transferable. Suppose the farmer in our first example owns the land that he sows but is a bad farmer; his land would be more productive in someone else's hands. Efficiency requires a mechanism by which the farmer can be induced to transfer the property to someone who can work it more productively. A transferable property right is such a mechanism. Suppose Farmer A owns a piece of land that he anticipates will yield him $100 a year above his labor and other costs, indefinitely. Just as the price of a share of common stock is equal to the present value of the anticipated earnings to which the shareholder will be entitled, so the present value of a parcel of land that is expected to yield an annual net income of $100 can be calculated and is the minimum price that A will accept in exchange for his property rights. Suppose Farmer B believes that he can use A's land more productively than A. The present value of B's expected earnings stream will therefore exceed the present value calculated by A. Suppose the present value calculated by A is $1,000 and by B $1,500. Then at any price between $1,000 and $1,500 both A and B will be made better off by a sale. Thus there are strong incentives for a voluntary exchange of A's land for B's money.

This discussion implies that if every valuable (meaning scarce as well as desired) resource were owned by someone (the criterion of universality), ownership connoted the unqualified power to exclude everybody else from using the resource (exclusivity) as well as to use it oneself, and ownership rights were freely transferable, or as lawyers say alienable (transferability), value would be maximized. This leaves out of account, however, the costs of a property-rights system, both the obvious and the subtle ones. Those costs are a particular focus of this chapter.

An example will illustrate a subtle cost of exclusivity. Suppose our farmer estimates that he can raise a hog with a market value of $100 at a cost of only $50 in labor and materials and that no alternative use of the land would yield a greater net value — in the next best use, his income from the land would be only $20. He will want to raise the hog. But now suppose his property right is qualified in two respects: He has no right to prevent an adjacent railroad from accidentally emitting engine sparks that may set fire to the hog's pen, killing the hog prematurely; and a court may decide that his raising a hog on this land is a nuisance, in which event he will have to sell the hog at disadvantageous (why disadvantageous?) terms before it is grown. In light of these contingencies he must reevaluate the yield of his land: He must discount the $100 to reflect the probability that the yield may be much less, perhaps zero. Suppose that, after this discounting, the expected revenue from raising the hog (market value times the probability that it will reach the market) is only $60. He will not raise the hog. He will put the land to another use, which we said was less valuable;[4] the value of the land will fall.

But the analysis is incomplete. Removing the hog may increase the value of surrounding residential land by more than the fall in the value of the farmer's parcel; or the cost of preventing the emission of engine sparks may exceed the reduction in the value of the farmer's land when he switches from raising hogs to growing, say, fireproof radishes. But, the alert reader may interject, if the increase in value to others from a different use of the farmer's land exceeds the decrease to him, let them buy his right: The railroad can purchase an easement to emit sparks; the surrounding homeowners can purchase a covenant from the farmer not to raise hogs; there is no need to limit the farmer's property right. But as we shall see, the costs of effecting a transfer of rights — transaction costs — are often prohibitive, and when this is so, giving someone the exclusive right to a resource may reduce rather than increase efficiency.

We could, of course, preserve exclusivity in a purely notional sense by regarding the property right in a given thing as a bundle of distinct rights, each exclusive; that is in fact the legal position. The economic point however is that the nominal property owner will rarely have exclusive power over his property.

Richard Posner, Economic Analysis of Law 32-35 (4th ed. 1992).

4. **Constitutional or property law?** This case was argued on a constitutional law theory, but the court ultimately decided it was unnecessary to explore the constitutional issues because it could decide the case on the basis of property law.[66] Almost certainly, however, a decision grounded on the defendants' First Amendment right of entry would have been upset by the U.S. Supreme Court. See PruneYard Shopping Center v. Robins, 447 U.S. 74, 81 (1980); Hudgens v. NLRB, 424 U.S. 507 (1976); Lloyd Corp. v. Tanner, 407 U.S. 551 (1972) (First Amendment protection did not extend to persons engaged in antiwar protest in the interior mall area of a shopping center).

---

4. The anticipated profit from raising the hog is now only $10 (the farmer's costs are $50). The next best use, we said, would yield a profit of $20.

66. The general principle is that courts should avoid ruling on a constitutional ground if the court can reach the decision it wishes on either a statutory or common-law ground. See John E. Nowak and Ronald D. Rotunda, Constitutional Law 7 (4th ed. 1991).

Although the *PruneYard* decision cemented the Court's refusal to create a First Amendment right to enter private property over the owner's objection, the Court upheld a California state court decision barring a shopping center from denying reasonable access to individuals seeking signatures from center patrons to a pro-Zionist petition. The California court based its decision on the *state's* constitutional counterpart to the First Amendment. Accord New Jersey Coalition against War in the Middle East v. J.M.B. Realty Corp., 138 N.J. 326, 650 A. 2d 757 (1994); State v. Dameron, 101 Or. App. 237 (1990), *aff'd,* 316 Or. 448 (1993). Other courts, however, have refused to create a state-constitutional right of entry for speech purposes. See, e.g., Cologne v. WestFarm Assocs., 192 Conn. 48 (1984); SHAD Alliance v. Smith Haven Mall, 66 N.Y.2d 496 (1985).

Drawing from the analogy of State v. Shack, might state courts protect entry onto a shopping mall for speech purposes under property law? See Curtis J. Berger, *PruneYard* Revisited: Political Activity on Private Lands, 66 N.Y.U.L. Rev. 633 (1991).

5.   **The intuitive image of property.** The court explicitly takes on, and tries to discredit, the intuitive image of property as absolute. What kinds of arguments does it make? Note its use of the adage that one should use his property so as not to injure the property rights of another. This phrase has long been used to limit absolute property rights.[67]

6.   **Holding.** What is the holding of the case? Suppose a farmer employing migrant workers sought your legal advice in New Jersey and asked if he could deny access to a reporter writing an exposé of conditions of migrant farm workers. What would you advise? Does the court go further than is needed to address the facts of this particular case? Does the fact that this is the decision of a state supreme court affect your assessment of what parts of the decision to treat as holding, and what parts to treat as dicta?

7.   **Tort law.** Note the court's use of the products liability case of Henningsen v. Bloomfield Motors, Inc., 32 N.J. 358, 403-404 (1960) (purchaser of Plymouth automobile sued Chrysler Co. and dealer for injuries sustained by his wife based on theory of implied warranty of merchantability). How is *Henningsen Motors* relevant? For what purpose does the court cite it? This is the first of several examples we will see of property courts relying on products liability law.

---

67. See William J. Novak, Intellectual Origins of the State Police Power: The Common Law Vision of a Well-Regulated Society, Institute for Legal Studies, Legal History Program, Working Papers-Series 3, 84 (June 1989). Nineteenth-century theorists used the two maxims *salus populi suprema lex est* (the welfare of the people is the supreme law) and *sic utere tuo ut alienum non laedus* (use your property so as not to injure another) to limit absolute property rights. See §8.1(a) *infra.*

e.   Property and Personhood

MARGARET JANE RADIN, PROPERTY AND PERSONHOOD

34 Stan. L. Rev. 957, 959-960, 987-988, 990 (1982)

. . . Most people possess certain objects they feel are almost part of themselves. These objects are closely bound up with personhood because they are part of the way we constitute ourselves as continuing personal entities in the world. . . .

One may gauge the strength or significance of someone's relationship with an object by the kind of pain that would be occasioned by its loss. On this view, an object is closely related to one's personhood if its loss causes pain that cannot be relieved by the object's replacement.

The opposite of holding an object that has become a part of oneself is holding an object that is perfectly replaceable with other goods of equal market value. One holds such an object for purely instrumental reasons. The archetype of such a good is, of course, money, which is almost always held only to buy other things. . . . I shall call these theoretical opposites — property that is bound up with a person and property that is held purely instrumentally — personal property and fungible property respectively. . . .

Does it make sense to speak of two levels of property, personal and fungible? I think the answer is yes in many situations, no in many others. Since the personhood perspective depends partly on the subjective nature of the relationships between person and thing, it makes more sense to think of a continuum that ranges from a thing indispensable to someone's being to a thing wholly interchangeable with money. Many relationships between persons and things will fall somewhere in the middle of this continuum. Perhaps the entrepreneur factory owner has ownership of a particular factory and its machines bound up with her being to some degree. If a dichotomy telescoping this continuum to two end points is to be useful, it must be because within a given social context certain types of person-thing relationships are understood to fall close to one end or the other of the continuum, so that decisionmakers within that social context can use the dichotomy as a guide to determine which property is worthier of protection. For example, in our social context a house that is owned by someone who resides there is generally understood to be toward the personal end of the continuum. There is both a positive sense that people are bound up with their homes and a normative sense that this is not fetishistic. . . .

WELFARE RIGHTS AND A DICHOTOMY IN PROPERTY

. . . A welfare rights or minimal entitlement theory of just distribution might hold that a government that respects personhood must guarantee citizens all entitlements necessary for personhood. If the personhood dichotomy in property is taken as the source of a distributive mandate as part of such a general theory, it would suggest that government should make it possible for all citizens to have whatever property is necessary for personhood. But a welfare rights theory incorporating property for personhood would suggest not only that government distribute largess in order to make it possible for people to buy property in which to constitute themselves but would further suggest that government should rearrange property rights so that fungible property of some people does not overwhelm the opportunities of the rest to constitute themselves in property. That is, a welfare rights theory incorporating the right to personal property would tell the government to cease allowing one person to impinge on the personhood of another by means of her control over tangible resources, rather than simply tell the government to dole out resources. . . .

Residential Tenancy as Opportunity for Personhood

. . . The attempt to assure poor tenants of decent housing by imposing implied warranties of habitability may also be understood in light of the personhood perspective, although the argument is less direct. In an article [68] that defends imposing habitability obligations on landlords, Ackerman suggests that decent housing should become a right based upon the tenant's "dignity as a person." He argues further that it is fair to charge some of the costs to landlords rather than to tax society as a whole, because in a society in which wealth is unjustly distributed "it is fair to impose a requirement of decency upon those in the relatively privileged classes who engage in long-lasting relationships with the impoverished." [69] This may be a species of welfare right or "just wants" argument based on personhood, but it is not simply a conventional argument for wealth redistribution. Instead, it appears to be closer to the argument that private law should cease allowing some people's fungible property rights to deprive other people of important opportunities for personhood. While Ackerman did not elaborate this argument, considering residential tenancies as personal property helps complete the moral underpinning that he considered tentative and sketchy. The argument would justify charging habitability costs to landlords whenever landlords' fungible property rights are prohibiting tenants from establishing or maintaining the kind of personal relationship in the home that our culture considers the basis of individuality. . . .

---

68. Ackerman, Regulating Slum Housing Markets on Behalf of the Poor: Of Housing Codes, Housing Subsidies and Income Redistribution Policy, 80 Yale L.J. 1093 (1971). — Eds.
69. Id. at 1173. — Eds.

NOTES AND QUESTIONS

1. **Advertisement.** The following was posted in a university:

LOST

On March 4, 1995, in the first floor bathroom in
the women's dormitory between 8 and 11 pm.
I lost two pieces of jewelry:
— one was a white gold ring with a diamond
— the second was a gold and silver bracelet
If you have found these or know who has them please call me
or bring the items to public safety. The jewelry belonged
to my mother before she died.
Please, these are the only things I have of hers and
are very important to me.
Thanks
Sara
(phone number)

Does this provide evidence for Radin's theories? Note how the ad ties the emotional value of the jewelry to a sense of linkage to the past.

2. **Radin's "property as personhood" analysis as an expression of the liberal dignity strain.** In this early article, Radin links her analysis with the philosophy of Hegel, id. at 958. She distances herself from Hegel in her more recent work. See Margaret Jane Radin, Reinterpreting Property 7 (1993). Her basic goal is to explain certain "intuitions." Note the way she links the intuition that landlords should be liable for renting deteriorated housing to a sense that such housing is an affront to the tenant's "dignity as a person." This places Radin in the tradition represented by State v. Shack, in which courts limit the scope of absolute property rights to the extent they are felt to affront human dignity. See also discussion of the implied warranty of habitability, §3.9(c) *infra*.

3. **Personhood and homeownership.** Another "intuition" Radin identified with property and personhood is the American veneration of homeownership, which we have linked with the republican vision of property, *supra*. For an argument defending some forms of rent regulation that draws on Radin's personhood thesis, see Curtis J. Berger, Home Is Where the Hearth Is: A Reply to Professor Epstein, 54 Brooklyn L. Rev. 1239 (1989).

4. **Native American context.** The case of United States ex rel. Mariano v. Tsosie, No. CIV 92-1234 LH/DJS (D.N.M., Apr. 21, 1994), offers some insight into the application of the property and personhood analysis in the context of Native American property. The United States, on behalf of Reuben Mariano, brought action for trespass and ejectment of Grace Tsosie, a Navajo tribal member. Both Tsosie and Mariano claimed owner-

ship of the land in question. Mariano was given an allotment, which was approved in 1908-1910, but his trust patent (equivalent to a deed) was not granted until 1964. Tsosie claimed ownership of the land based on occupancy rights. She stated that her maternal ancestors had continuously occupied the land since 1868, her mother was born and raised on the land, and that her umbilical cord was buried there in 1901. She further asserted that Mariano's claim was not patented before 1917 and therefore was withdrawn under Executive Order 1901, which reserved such land from settlement and sale and "set apart for the use and occupancy of the Navajo and such other Indians as the Secretary of the Interior may see fit to settle thereon." Tsosie also stated that the the Secretary of the Interior settled her ancestors on the land and that the Superintendent of the Eastern Navajo Agency authorized and encouraged improvements on the land by her ancestors. The court found that the Bureau of Indian Affairs had made wholly inconsistent actions regarding ownership interest in the land. It required the exhaustion of tribal remedies and dismissed the case without prejudice.

5. **More on Native American property: property and community?** In 1978, a double pot sealed with limestone mortar was removed from White Rock Canyon in New Mexico. Daniel Ridlon, one of the two persons who found the pot, loaned it to the Los Alamos National Laboratory. Sometime between 1979 and 1985, the lab decided that the pot did not belong to Ridlon and requested that the New Mexico State Historic Preservation Office determine the rightful owner. The office was unable to decide whether Ridlon owned the pot or whether the county did. The pot is now being claimed by the San Ildefonso Pueblo, who claim ownership to the pot under the Native American Graves Protection and Repatriation Act. They believe that the pot has spiritual powers that could harm those who do not know how to handle it. A pueblo official stated that the pot was an object of ceremonial and spiritual importance, which the pueblo were to protect and respect to ensure the well-being of the pueblo and the world. Ridlon originally sued the museum and the county in 1987 and was on the verge of having the pot returned to him as abandoned property, when the county appealed and the pueblo intervened. The case is now pending before a federal district court. See Scott Sandlin, Man Continues Fight for Pot, Albuquerque J., Feb. 19, 1994; Scott Sandlin, Pueblo Demands Return of Sacred Pot, Albuquerque J., Dec. 28, 1993. Does this incident fit into Radin's property and personhood rubric? Does it highlight Radin's focus on the individual rather than the community?

Chapter 2

The Feudal Core: Estates in Land and the Law of Wealth Transmission

§2.1 Introduction

Should property be inheritable?

> The question . . . [w]hether one generation of men has a right to bind an-
> other, seems never to have been stated either on this or our side of the water.
> Yet it is a question of such consequences as not only to merit decision, but
> place also, among the fundamental principles of every government . . . I set
> out on this ground, which I suppose to be self evident, "that the earth belongs
> in usufruct to the living": that the dead have neither powers nor rights over it.
> The portion occupied by any individual ceases to be his when he himself
> ceases to be, and reverts to the society.

Letter from Thomas Jefferson to James Madison (Sept. 6, 1789), reprinted
in 7 The Writings of Thomas Jefferson 454 (Albert Ellery Bergh ed., 1904).

§2.2 The Estate-in-Land Concept

The estate-in-land concept brings us back to the feudal vision still embedded in modern property law. "Estates" in land are a form of legal short-
hand: They represent various bundles of property interests — that is, rights,
privileges, powers, and so forth, that one can enjoy with respect to land.
They also reflect a view of property that emerged from England's post-
Conquest feudal order. The word "estate" once denoted "station in life":
In feudal England, a person's social status generally depended on the extent

of his land holdings and, equally relevant, on the tenure by which he held.[1] In these arrangements we recognize the feudal vision of property as social glue to cement the social interdependencies in the "great chain of being."[2] One key element of this "chain" was the unchangeability (in theory, anyway) of one's "estate." Today we take for granted the desirability of social mobility, but that is a relatively recent development. Feudal theory asserted that one's place in the hierarchy was assigned by God; part of godliness was to preserve the fabric of society by acting in ways appropriate to one's station.

In the early feudal period, lords typically granted estates for the life of a tenant, with the provision that the estate would "escheat" (return) to the lord if the tenant failed to perform the requisite services. The grant of a life estate took the form "to A for life," and at the death of A, the land would revert to the lord, who was free to make whatever new arrangements he wished. Perhaps the lord *would* grant the parcel to the decedent's male heir, on his agreement to perform the services charged to his ancestor; but the lord was free to grant to others if the heir seemed unwilling or unable to shoulder his father's role.

As the feudal period advanced and the relationship between the lord and tenants became more impersonal, with money payments often substituted in place of tenant service, lords gave way to pressure from tenants and began to give advance consent to allow tenants to pass on their land to their heirs; grants "to A and his heirs" replaced grants "to A for life." Coupled with primogeniture — if there were male children, only the oldest son would inherit the family's entire estate — the use of the phrase "and his heirs" was significant; it denoted that succession was to continue indefinitely and not only for one generation. This estate in land would be known as "fee simple absolute." And in 1290, with the passage of the Statute Quia Emptores, the fee simple absolute could be transferred in the owner's lifetime (inter vivos) as well as at his death via inheritance.

Note that, in feudal times, land was not treated as a market commodity. Even after land became salable and inheritable, owners only had the right to pass it on to their heirs at law in a preset pattern of inheritance. The assumption that an owner should be able to leave property to whomever she wishes — an integral part of the liberal notion that society will function best if we let a thousand deals bloom — was not shared in medieval times. "Only God can make an heir," said the famous thirteenth-century lawyer Henry de Bracton, although the medieval conveyancers did the best they could with the legal categories available to them. Anne L. Spitzer, Joint Tenancy with Right of Survivorship: A Legacy from Thir-

---

1. A woman's estate also depended on her place in the hierarchy, but women had a different relationship with their land holdings because upon marriage their husbands ordinarily gained the right to manage their lands, as well as outright ownership of the profits therefrom. See §4.2.b *infra.*

2. The great chain of being is discussed in §1.2.a *supra.*

teenth Century England, 16 Texas Tech L. Rev. 629, 650 (1985). Not until
1540 did the Statute of Wills allow owners to ignore the preset inheritance
patterns. This signaled the last gasp of the feudal order and the move toward full commodification of land.

The contrasts between our own day and the feudal vision are worth
highlighting. The differences involved, first, self-image: Our society's self-
image is that every person has an equal chance to achieve wealth in his own
lifetime. The notion that social position is determined by inherited wealth
is anathema.[3] A second set of differences reflects the different roles of
wealth transmission in the two societies. In feudal society (and long afterwards), the law of wealth transmission, centered on land, formed the core
of the property system. Intergenerational wealth transmission no longer
plays the central economic and political role it did in earlier periods. Except for one's equity in a home, pensions, which end on the death of the
pension holder and/or spouse, form the chief asset of most Americans.[4]
Relatively few individuals leave large estates;[5] for most Americans, the chief
determinant of salary is what economists call "human capital": a "good
education" followed by "ambitious career development."[6]

Although the feudal system has long since vanished and new means
have appeared for acquiring wealth and status, the estate system has remained at the core of property law in the United States.[7] Some of its intri-
cacies, such as the Rule against Perpetuities, remain important today chiefly
in the practice of lawyers who write wills and create estate plans for the very
wealthy. But learning the language of estates in land is part of basic legal
literacy.

As you learn the highly formalistic system that lawyers use when discussing issues of wealth transmission, consider why this area of the law has
remained so full of formalistic thinking. Note that the effect of a formalistic

3. In fact, the chances of a poor person entering the ranks of the extremely wealthy are
relatively small. See Sylvia Nasar, Rich and Poor Likely to Remain So, N.Y. Times, May 18, 1992,
at D1, D5 ("[M]ost Americans do not move a great many rungs, up or down in a lifetime. The
changes tend to be one step forward or one step back, not from the lower half to the upper.").

4. See Gregory S. Alexander, Pensions and Passivity, 56 Law & Contemp. Probs. 111,
115 (1993); Frank S. Levy and Richard C. Michel, The Economic Future of American Families:
Income and Wealth Trends 63 (1991).

5. "[45,800] estates of decedents dying in 1986 filed returns reporting at least $500,000.
Combined, they reported assets of $66 billion." Mark L. Ascher, Curtailing Inherited Wealth,
89 Mich. L. Rev. 69, 91 n.120 (1990) (citing Johnson, Estate Tax Returns, 1986-1988, Statistics
of Income Bull., Spring 1990, at 27). The decedents who left these large estates represent about
2 percent of all deaths in the United States. See Vital Statistics of the United States 1986, Volume II — Mortality, Part A, Sec. 1, p.1, Table 1-1 (1988) (total number of U.S. deaths).

6. See §4.2.c infra. It is through transmission of human capital that family wealth is
passed on from generation to generation in our own day. See John H. Langbein, The Twentieth-
Century Revolution in Family Wealth Transmission, 86 Mich. L. Rev. 722, 723 (1988). Studies
show that the single most important determinant of what schools a student attends, and how
well the student performs, is the social status of her family. Id. at 733.

7. In England, significant parts of the traditional law were abolished by the Property
Act of 1925.

system is to focus attention on whether a given property transfer conforms to preexisting legal categories. Attention is steered away from "policy" questions, such as the question of whether property should be inheritable. Does this offer any insight into why "feudal" formalism has persisted so long in the law of wealth transmission?

The wealth boom of the 1980s was accompanied by a sharp increase in the concentration of wealth in the United States, such that the wealthiest 1 percent of Americans will inherit one-third of all wealth. The top 10 percent will inherit two-thirds of all wealth, leaving the remaining third to be divided among the remaining 90 percent of Americans.[8] As has been noted, race is also a strong factor in wealth accumulation: Whites as a group have ten times the wealth of blacks as a group.[9]

As you read the following materials, ask yourself whether the American law of intergenerational transfers strikes the optimal balance between the desire to allow wealth accumulation, so as to encourage capital formulation and achieve other goals, and the desire to limit wealth accumulation in the names of equality norms. Does your answer to these questions depend on your vision of property?

As you examine Table 2-1, note two distinctions basic to an understanding of estates in land. One is the distinction between *freehold* and *nonfreehold* estates. Freehold estates comprise what we today would call "ownership"; nonfreehold estates involve "rental" of property. This chapter will cover freehold estates; Chapter 3 will cover landlord-tenant estates.[10] Another basic distinction is between *present* and *future* interests. Present interests are interests that give their owner the right to immediate ("present") enjoyment of the property. Future interests give no right to present enjoyment; instead, they offer only the right to enjoyment of the property to begin at some point in the future. Ordinary ownership (which we shall soon see is called *fee simple* ownership) gives the owner both the right to present possession and the right to pass along possession to others in the future: either inter vivos, during the present holder's life, or by will (or without one), when the present holder dies. In sharp contrast, other estates in land are time limited. The most prominent example is the *life estate*, which gives its owner full ownership of the land for his life;[11] all rights to the land are extinguished by the death of the life tenant. The life estate

---

8. See Bob Ehlert, Boomers Set to Inherit Millions, St. Petersburg Times, July 20, 1992, at 2D. Note that more recent statistics tell us that the wealthiest 1 percent own nearly 40 percent of the nation's wealth and the top 20 percent hold more than 80 percent of the country's wealth. Keith Bradsher, Gap in Wealth in U.S. Called Widest in West, N.Y. Times, Apr. 17, 1995, at A1.

9. See Charlotte V. Churaman, Financing of College Education by Minority and White Families, J. Consumer Aff., Dec. 22, 1992, at 324.

10. In medieval times, anyone who did not own land was a serf, subject to a lord whose status as a free man was linked to his ownership of an estate in land.

11. As we shall see below, full rights of ownership of a life estate are less extensive than the full rights available to the owner of a fee simple. See §2.5.c *infra* (discussing the doctrine of waste).

TABLE 2-1

Present Interest	Future Interest	
	in grantor	*in third person*
FREEHOLD INTERESTS		
Fee simple absolute	None	None
Fee tail	Reversion	Vested remainder Contingent remainder* Executory interest*
Defeasible estates		
(a) Fee simple deter- minable (also called base fee, qualified fee, or fee on [special] limitation)	Possibility of reverter	Executory interest*
(b) Fee simple subject to a condition subsequent (also called fee on condition)	Power of termination (right of entry, right of reacquisition)	Executory interest*
Life estate	Reversion	Vested remainder‡ Contingent remainder* Executory interest*
NONFREEHOLD INTERESTS		
Term of years (estate for years)	Reversion	Vested remainder†
Tenancy at will (estate at will)		Executory interest†
Periodic tenancy		(Fee subject to term)†

*The contingent remainder and the executory interest both can follow the fee tail or the life estate. Although these two future interests stem from different sources, the unlikenesses between them are largely gone. Where dissimilarity remains, you will probably hear about it in a trusts and estates course. For now, simply be aware that both interests exist. Cf. O. Moynihan, Introduction to Real Property 205-207 (1962); Dukeminier, Contingent Remainders and Executory Interests: A Requiem for the Distinction, 43 Minn. L. Rev. 13 (1958).

Under common-law terminology, only an executory interest can follow a *defeasible* estate where the future interest is created *in third persons*. Under some statutes, however, remainder has displaced executory interest, as the proper usage, in all situations. See, e.g., N.Y. Est., Powers & Trusts L. 6-4.3 (McKinney 1992).

†These occur infrequently.

‡Vested remainders come in three styles: indefeasibly vested; vested subject to open; vested subject to complete defeasance. See, e.g., N.Y. Est., Powers & Trusts L. §§6-4.7-6-4.9 (McKinney 1992); §2-2-C notes 33 and 34, *infra*.

typically is followed by a future interest either in the original grantor or his heirs, called a *reversion,* or a future interest in a different grantee, called a *remainder.* These future interests give their owners no right to present possession. The only right they have is the right to full ownership after the death of the owner of the present interest. For now, the important point is that, when classifying an estate in land, *your first step will be to determine whether it is a present or a future interest.*

Here, as elsewhere, correct usage is essential: otherwise, classification will not serve even its minimum role of giving lawyers a common tongue. Therefore, do not say "remainder" when you mean "reversion." See Table 2-1.

a. The "Fee Simple Absolute" (O "to A and His Heirs")

The most extensive estate in land recognized at common law is the *fee simple,* also called the *fee simple absolute.* It is the crown jewel in the estate system and holds center stage in both the republican and the liberal visions of property, for it suggests independence unavailable to the holders of lesser estates. But as we shall see, there is little that is absolute in the fee simple absolute; moreover, the totality of property interests enjoyed by one owner in fee simple absolute may vary greatly from that of her neighbor who also owns in fee simple absolute. To give one example: A owns Lot 1 encumbered by a $100,000 first mortgage and a 10-year lease; B owns Lot 2 free and clear — no mortgage, no lease; yet both A and B own their respective parcels in fee simple absolute.

The *right to possession* is a focal point for estate analysis, although it is only one of the many possible rights we will consider. In the attention given the right to possession, the stress has been temporal, one devoted to *when* the right begins and to its *duration.* By analyzing possession along a plane of time, we can divide estates into *present interests,* entitling someone to possession now, and *future interests,* entitling someone to possession when (and if) the present estate ends. For example, if you occupy your apartment on a two-year lease, yours is a present interest, and your landlord's is a future interest.

What distinguishes the fee simple absolute from all other estates is the absence of anyone, other than the owner herself, from holding a future (possessory) interest. To put it differently: We say that the duration of a fee simple absolute is "potentially infinite." If we were to diagram a fee simple absolute, it would appear thus:

Historically, an ambiguous grant was construed as the grant of a life estate. Grantors had to be very explicit if their intention was to create a fee simple. In fact, grantors had to use the words "to A and his (or her) heirs." Thus "to A in fee simple absolute," or "to A," or any other form of words would create a life estate. Legal realists often decried this as "formalism" or

*[handwritten: * must say specifically to heirs or it will be only life estate]*

blind adherence to "mere technicality," but in fact the initial policy goals were clear: to protect lords' property from the results of an inept draftsman, courts construed all grants as life estates unless the intent was crystal clear. After all, if a lord had meant to create a fee simple, but had only created a life estate, he could always go back and alienate his future interest.[12]

This does not explain why, as late as 1957, a 12-year-old deed running "to B and assigns forever" failed to create a fee simple.[13] Most states have now shifted the assumption away from a life estate by means of statutes, of which the statute below is typical. *[handwritten: b/c could mean his doesn't say life pass on]*

> The use of terms of inheritance or succession are not necessary to create a fee simple estate, and every grant, conveyance, or mortgage of lands . . . shall convey or mortgage the entire interest which the grantor could lawfully grant, convey, or mortgage, unless it clearly appears by the deed, mortgage, or instrument that the grantor intended to convey or mortgage a lesser estate.[14]

PROBLEMS AND QUESTIONS

Describe the state of the title after the following devises, which appear in a will probated in 1995. Be careful to account for *all* the estates created and to account for the property from the moment of the devise for the rest of time.

1.   **"O to A and his heirs."** Do not be fooled by the use of "A and his heirs" into believing that A's heirs have any estate in the land. This grant does not give A's heirs any estate in land whatsoever, for an estate in land is the right to present protection of a present or future interest: They have no right to present possession of the property. Nor does anyone have any future interest, for "no one is the heir of the living": A is free to change his will up to the moment of his death, so that no rights vest in any person until the moment A dies. This thought is traditionally encapsulated in the assertion that "and his heirs" are *words of limitation*, not *words of purchase*.[15]

[handwritten: heirs, 0 interest]

---

12. The concept of merger in property law describes the common law rule that when lesser and future interests come into the hands of the same person, the interests will unite into the greater interest. For example, suppose that O grants "to A for life." Suppose furthermore that O then grants the reversion to A. A then holds both the life estate and the reversion in fee simple. Thus, by the common-law doctrine of merger, A has a fee simple — the life estate having been submerged in the fee — resulting from his holding both interests in the property. For another instance of the merger doctrine, see §7.7.a *infra*. *[handwritten: merger]*

13. Cole v. Steinlauf, 144 Conn. 629, 631-632 (1957). Four years later, the same court sharply questioned the earlier result. Dennen v. Searle, 149 Conn. 126, 137-138 (1961).

14. Ohio Rev. Code Ann. §5301.02 (Baldwin 1995).

15. What if a grant provides "To A for life, then to A's heirs"? According to English law originating with Abel's Case, Y.B. Edw. 2, f. 577 (1324), and crystallized in Shelley's Case, 1 Co. Rep. 93b (1581), this grant created a fee simple in A rather than giving any estate to A's heirs. We will not discuss this rule because it has been abolished in most American jurisdictions. See Lewis M. Simes and Allan F. Smith, The Law of Future Interests §1563 (2d ed. 1956 & Supp. 1991) (rule in Shelley's Case still in force only in Arkansas, Colorado, Delaware, and Indiana).

2.   "O to A." *[handwritten: Life / non free hold]*

3.   "O to A forever." *[handwritten: Fee simple]*

4.   Who has the present and who has the future interests in the following grants? *[handwritten: A present B future]*

   (a)   O grants "to A for her life, then to B and his heirs."

   (b)   O grants "to A so long as the land is farmed." (Hint: Who gets the land if it ceases to be farmed? If O fails to give away part of *[handwritten: non freehold]* this bundle of sticks, who owns the part never given away?) *[handwritten: O]*

5.   "O to A for life, then to B." Name the present and future interests created by this grant. *[handwritten: A present ; B—none yet as heir of A]*

b.   The Fee Tail (O to "A and the Heirs of his Body")

The heads of the high nobility in England wanted to make their family's lands inalienable, so that no single generation could dissipate dynastic wealth by selling off portions of the family estate. After one false start,[16] an answer arrived in 1285 when De Donis Conditionalibus (Statute of Westminster, 13 Edw., Ch. 1 (1285)) became law. This statute recognized the fee tail,[17] whereby a conveyance from O "to A and the heirs of his body" disabled A from granting more than an estate for his life;[18] nor would a creditor or the king (in case of forfeiture)[19] receive more. At A's death, the land descended to A's lineal heirs. If no heirs survived A, the land reverted to O (called a "reversion"). These successive life estates continued indefinitely, until the line of descent died out.[20]

The fee tail highlights the political consequences of property rules. The Statute De Donis (passed by a Parliament controlled by landed interests) confirmed the influence, and aided the further empowerment of the great barons of England, bent on overpowering the English monarchy. The

16. Grants "to A and the heirs of his body" first began to appear no later than the early thirteenth century to prevent A from transferring a fee simple absolute during his lifetime. But courts, responding to the demand of the present occupants for freer alienability, found a formula for undercutting the grantors' wishes. A was permitted to alienate a fee simple absolute as soon as he produced an heir of the designated class. All that was needed was a live birth (the heir might die minutes later), and A was free, at any time before his own death, to defeat the grantor's desire.

17. "Fee tail" derived from "tailler," an early French infinitive, meaning "to carve"; one could say that the grantor carved out an estate (fee) to fit his liking. Thus a grantor might carve out a fee tail estate "to A and the heirs female of his body," or "to A and the heirs of his body by his wife B," to give two further examples of this estate.

18. A's estate was called a tenancy in tail.

19. Landowners seeking to create a dynastic estate also had to worry about the risk of forfeiture for the present occupant's disloyalty or crime.

20. In creating the fee tail estate, O might also have placed the future interest in third parties, viz., "O to A and the heirs of his body, then to B and his heirs"; B would hold a vested remainder, *infra,* which a failure of descent would turn into a fee simple absolute.

struggle between the king and the landed aristocracy produced the War of the Roses. After the defeat of the opposing (Lancastrian) forces, the monarchy (Edward IV) sought to consolidate its power and corrode that of its opponents through the king's courts, which held in 1472 that a tenant in tail could "bar the entail" and pass on full ownership by means of a new type of lawsuit called a common recovery.[21] Taltarum's Case, Y.B. 12 Edw. IV, 19 (1472). This change in the law weakened the aristocracy's power base as the great landed estates began to break up through suits in common recovery.

Fee tail never became popular in the United States, partly because manorial holdings were uncommon beyond some areas in the South and along the Hudson River, and partly because the fee tail was already an ineffective dynastic device when American colonization began. Thomas Jefferson, who was acutely attuned to the link between the power of the landed aristocracy and their influence over government, led the Virginia fight for abolition of fee tail (and primogeniture), see §1.3.a *supra*. Where fee tail language appears — as it does rarely — in a deed[22] or will, most American jurisdictions now have laws that arrest its force. These measures either recognize the fee tail for one generation[23] or permit the tenant in tail to bar the entail by conveying a fee simple by deed.[24]

NOTES AND PROBLEMS

1.   **Problems.** On the assumption that the fee tail is still a valid estate in land, describe the state of the title after the following grants. Be careful to account for both the present and future interests created and to account for the property from the moment of the grant for the rest of time.

(a)   "O to A and the heirs of his body."

(b)   "O to A and the heirs male of his body."

(c)   "O to A and the heirs male of his body." A dies, leaving five daughters.

---

21.   Common recovery, and a companion procedure known as *fine,* were collusive lawsuits – fifteenth century legal charades. So widespread were the disentailing practices that they are mentioned by Hamlet in his musings on the skull of a lawyer (Act 5, scene 1); and a lawyer who dared criticize the common recovery was sharply reproved by the Chief Justice of the Common Pleas who referred to the device as a "legal pillar" and "founded upon great reason and authority." Mary Portington's Case, 10 Co. Rep. 35b, 40a, 77 Eng. Rep. 976, 984 (1614). So profitable were the disentailing schemes for solicitors, courts, and governmental offices that the *statutory* repeal of De Donis was not achieved until 1834, when fines and recoveries were abolished, and a simple conveyance by deed served to bar the entail.

22.   See, e.g., Morris v. Ulbright, 558 S.W.2d 660 (Mo. 1977) (construing a 1947 grant "to A and his bodily heirs").

23.   See, e.g., R.I. Gen. Laws §33-6-10 (1995).

24.   Id.

FIGURE 2-1
"Where be his quiddities [subtle arguments] and quillities [fine distinctions], his cases, his tenures, and his tricks?"

(d)   Think up a realistic hypothetical involving a grantor who grants a fee tail.[25] The hypothetical should be designed to explicate the peculiar features of the fee tail.

(e)   "O to A and the heirs of his body; then to B and his heirs."

---

25. Note that this is somewhat artificial because the fee tail has been abolished in most states. Yet it is helpful to ensuring that students understand the peculiarities involved in the fee tail.

2.   **Dreams of aristocratic grandeur.** The will of William Shakespeare illustrates the association of fees tail and primogeniture with the wealth of the landed aristocracy in England. Shakespeare evidently aspired to have his family join the landed class, as is evidenced by his will, which set up nine successive fees tail male.

Upon Shakespeare's death in 1616, his lands were devised to his elder daughter Susanna for life. Upon her death, the lands were devised to her first-born son in fee tail male. If the first-born son died without male issue, the lands went to her second-born son in fee tail male; if he died without male issue, to her third-, fourth-, fifth-, sixth-, and seventh-born sons in turn, all in fee tail male. If no sons produced male issue, the lands went to Susanna's older daughter in fee tail male; failing that, they went to her younger daughter in fee tail male. Only if all of the above grants failed to take effect — which they did — did the lands revert to Shakespeare's heirs (two granddaughters) in fee simple. See Jesse Dukeminier and James E. Krier, Property 215 (3d ed. 1993).

Did go to first born

3.   *Pride and Prejudice.* In Austen's Pride and Prejudice, the troubles of the Bennet family are partly due to the fact that Mr. Bennet's estate is held in fee tail male. "Mr. Bennet's property consisted almost entirely in an estate of two thousand a year, which, unfortunately for his daughters, was entailed, in default of heirs male, on a distant relation." Mrs. Bennet felt the injustice of it, and when her daughters "attempted to explain the nature of an entail," she "rail[ed] bitterly against the cruelty of settling an estate away from a family of five daughters, in favor of a man whom nobody cared anything about." Jane Austen, Pride and Prejudice (1813).

c.   Life Estates, Reversions, Remainders, and Executory Interests

As we have seen, in feudal times the life estate, which gave the tenant full rights to the land until his death, was the most common estate in land. Today, we are likely to meet life estates in three contexts: as a vestige of the common-law marital property system;[26] in *inter vivos* charitable donations;[27] and as an estate planning device.[28] The last use is by far the most important of the three. The advertisement on page 124 shows an example of estate planning and charitable contributions. Explain the grant Larry Hart gave to Yale.

Life estates are present interests; reversions, remainders, and executory interests are future interests, which confer rights to the enjoyment of

---

26. We refer to the widow's dower and the widower's curtesy interests. See §4.2.a *infra*.

27. For example, wealthy patrons may donate their art collections (or individual works of art) to a museum, reserving a life estate, for which the donor receives a charitable donation whose value is inversely related to the donor's expectancy.

28. For example, A, under her will, creates a trust, from which her surviving spouse receives income during his lifetime. At the spouse's death, all of the trust assets are then paid over to A's children.

Larry and Yale: Partners through Giving

"Making Money is Fun, But Giving it Away is Better"
Larry Hart, '36

"I never intend to retire. My economics major at Yale helped give me the confidence for a long career in business. Other Yale highlights were John Berdan's Daily Themes and playing water polo for Bob Kiphuth.

I've got a lot to be proud of. I attended a fine preparatory school and a wonderful University that just keeps getting better.

With pride comes responsibility. We have to give something back. Over the years I have written checks, given stock, and created a Charitable Trust. Yale's life-income options enabled me to contribute appreciated, low yielding stock and increase my income at no capital gains tax cost. And gave me a federal income tax charitable deduction to boot.

Most recently I gave Yale an interest in my Pebble Beach, California home. I can live in the house for my life, and I was entitled to a charitable deduction of about 60% of its appraised value. If I decid to move, Yale and I could sell my property and I would receive a por-tion of the prceeds.

I urge all alumni to explore gift options with Yale and to remember Old Eli generously- to educate the leaders of the next generation."

...and
for Yale

A $1.5 BILLION
INVESTMENT

For more information about giving options, please return the enclosed reply card or leave us a message.

The Yale Campaign
P.O. Box 2038
New Haven, CT 06521
(1-800-445-6086)

property to begin at some point in the future. For example, who will own the land subject to a life estate after the life tenant dies? If the estate will revert back to O (or her heirs), the future interest is called a *reversion*. Note that a reversion is created when the grant does not discuss what happens to the estate after the life tenant's death, on the (logical) theory that the owner retains whatever interests she has not given away. If the estate will go, after the termination of the prior estate, not back to the original grantor but to a third party (that is, someone other than the grantor and the life tenant), the future interest is called a *remainder*. A remainder is a future interest that waits around until the termination of the preceding estate(s), and then becomes possessory if it is then vested.

Example 1:   "O to A for life."

We can illustrate this grant as follows:

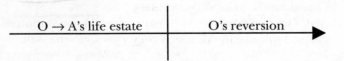

O → A's life estate | O's reversion

A has a life estate; O has a reversion. Note that the approved terminology does not indicate what estate O will get once her estate becomes possessory. This is sometimes expressed as the idea that "there is only one kind of reversion." On A's death, O will again have a fee simple absolute.

Example 2:   "O to A for life; then to B and his heirs." [29]

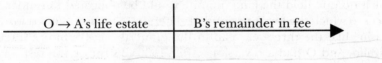

O → A's life estate | B's remainder in fee

A has a life estate; B has a remainder in fee simple. Note that the approved terminology for remainders requires identification not only of the remainder, but also of what estate B will get once his estate becomes possessory. In this case, B will get a fee simple. This is not always the case.

Example 3:   "O to A for life; then to B for life."

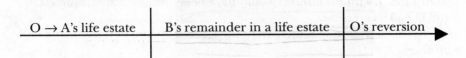

O → A's life estate | B's remainder in a life estate | O's reversion

A has a life estate; B has a remainder in a life estate; O has a reversion.

For a future interest in a third party to qualify as a remainder, it must follow two rules:

---

29. What if B dies without heirs while A is still living? In feudal times, if a person died intestate without any heirs, the person's real property *escheated* to the overlord. Today, such property escheats to the state in which it is located.

[handwritten: To have a remainder:]

Rule 1:   It is not permitted to take effect before the expiration of the preceding estate. Thus, it cannot cut short the life estate that preceded it.

Rule 2:   It is not permitted to take effect at a time subsequent to the expiration of the preceding estate. *[handwritten: must be R. on time]*

- As we shall see, a remainder may end up not becoming possessory (see *Contingent Remainder,* below), but any applicable condition must be ready to be tested (to see whether it has been met or not) by the time the prior estate expires.
- What if no heir whatsoever remains after the expiration of all prior estates? Typically, the property then *escheats* to the state.

Example 4:   "O to A for life, then three years after A's death, to B and her heirs."

B does not have a remainder because her future interest will not be ready to become possessory immediately upon the expiration of the prior estate. At common law until 1536 (Statute of Uses), B's future interest was invalid because it was essential under the feudal system that some identifiable person be entitled to possession (the technical term is had *seisin*) at all times, for if no one held the land, no one would be obligated to render the services to which the lord was entitled. Therefore, the law allowed no "gaps in seisin" like the three-year gap in the grant above: B's future interest was invalid, and O had a reversion. After 1536, B's future interest was recognized as valid, but it still was not classified as a remainder; this will be discussed shortly.

Example 5:   "O to A for life, but if B returns home from the Crusades, then to B immediately."

[handwritten: violate Rule #1]

B does not have a remainder because his future interest becomes possessory immediately upon B's arrival home; it could cut short the prior life estate. Until 1536, B's future interest would have been invalid: A had a life estate, and O had a reversion.

    Two kinds of remainders were recognized at common law: *vested* and *contingent.*[30]

Vested Remainder.   B has a vested remainder *if B's future interest qualifies as a remainder,* and

    (a)   B is a person born and ascertainable, and

---

30. Where an instrument is ambiguous, the courts construe a remainder as vested. In the words of Chief Justice Edward Coke, "the law delights in vesting of estates, and contingencies are odious in the law, and are the cause of troubles, and vesting and setling [*sic*] of estates, the cause of repose and certainty." Roberts v. Roberts, 2 Bulst. 123, 131, 80 Eng. Rep. 1002, 1009 (K.B. 1613).

[handwritten: FI = rem — person is born — no condition Subsequent = vested]

(b)   no condition must be met before B's interest becomes possessory other than the expiration of the prior estate.

Contingent Remainder.   B has a contingent remainder *if B's future interest qualifies as a remainder,* and

(a)   B is unborn or unascertained (sometimes called the "who" contingency), and/or

(b)   A condition exists that must be satisfied before B can come into possession (sometimes called the "if" contingency). (This is called a "condition precedent.") Since B's interest is a remainder, we know that we must be able to tell, at the time the preceding estate expires, whether or not the condition precedent has been met.   *[handwritten: FSCS = Contingent Rem]*

Example 6:   "O to A for life, then to B and his heirs."[31]

| O → A's life estate | B's vested remainder in fee |

A has a life estate; B's remainder is vested because there is no condition precedent he must meet to gain his remainder, nor is there an interval (a "gap in seisin") after A's death before B can acquire possession.

Example 7:   "O to A for life, then, if B survives A, to B and his heirs."

| O → A's life estate | B's contingent remainder in fee simple / O's reversion |

A has a life estate; B has a contingent remainder; O has a reversion. B's interest is a remainder because it is capable of taking effect immediately upon the expiration of the prior estate. It is contingent because there is a condition precedent to B's taking — he must survive A. Note that O will always have a reversion after a contingent remainder, which will become possessory in the event that the contingency does not take place and B's remainder never becomes possessory. (Note how the language encourages us to treat the legal categories as if they were something real and physical.)

---

31. You might be wondering what happens if B — or the owner of any vested remainder — does not survive the life tenant, A. Because B's survivorship of A was not made a condition precedent to his entitlement, if B predeceases A, B's remainder will pass to his heirs (or by intestate succession if he has no heirs).

Note that contingent remainders can be contingent upon more than one contingency. Here is an example.

Example 8:   "O to A for life, then to B's first-born daughter if she is living at the time of A's death, and her heirs." [B is childless at the time of the grant.]

```
                        |  contingent remainder in fee of B's
                        |  first-born daughter if alive at A's death
                        | ----------------------------------------->
  O → A's life estate   |                 O's reversion
                        | --------------------------------------------->
                        |
```

A has a life estate; O has a reversion; B's first-born daughter if still living at the time of A's death has a remainder because her interest is capable of taking effect immediately upon the expiration of A's life estate. Note that the remainder is contingent upon *both* her being born *and* upon her surviving A. The removal of the "who" contingency will still leave the owner with a contingent remainder because of the "if" contingency.

Example 9:   "O to A for life; then to the heirs of B (a living person)."

```
                        |  B's heirs' contingent remainder in fee simple
                        | ----------------------------------------->
  O → A's life estate   |                 O's reversion
                        | --------------------------------------------->
                        |
```

A has a life estate; B's heirs have a contingent remainder; O has a reversion. The remainder is contingent because no one is heir of the living. Even if B (the "testator") has written a will, she is allowed to change her will at any point up to the time of her death — so that no one can be sure that he or she will be an heir until death ends the testator's ability to change the will. And if B were to die without a will ("intestate"), we would not be able to identify her intestate successors until her death.[32]

___

32. You may be wondering why we called this interest a remainder, rather than "not a remainder," because it seems to fail one of our two remainder rules, *supra,* in that a remainder is not permitted to take effect after the expiration of the preceding (life) estate. Here, as we see, B may still be alive at the death of A, postponing until B's subsequent death the vesting of possession in the heirs of B.

The difference between this grant and that of Example 4 with its three-year gap is the certainty of the gap. Here, B may predecease A, in which case we will be able to identify B's heirs prior to the end of the life estate.

However, at common law, if there was a gap in seisin, because A, in fact, predeceased B, the remainder in B's heirs was destroyed under an arcane doctrine known as the "destructibility of contingent remainders." By contrast, prior to 1536 (the Statute of Uses), a future interest that was certain to follow a gap in seisin was void ab initio.

Example 10:   "O to A for life, then to the children of A."

A has children. A, of course, has a life estate. If A is childless, the children
of A have a contingent remainder, contingent upon being born. If A already
has children, those children have a vested remainder because they need
meet no condition precedent to take a share of the estate. But it is uncertain
what their percentage of the estate will be, because A may have more children. Their remainder is therefore a "vested remainder subject to partial
divestment"[33] (because subsequent children can partially divest existing
ones). Note that A cannot have children after his death, so that at the expiration of the preceding estate the children can ascertain what will be their
percentage of the estate. (Children in utero were considered alive at the
time of A's death.)

Example 11:   "O to A for life, then to the children of B."

B has no children. A has a life estate; the children of B have a contingent
remainder. Note, however, that B *may* have children after A's death. Does
this mean that the children's future interest is not a remainder? No: courts
again construed the grant so as to save it. They held that class of people who
took the contingent remainder consisted of all children of B alive at the
time of A's death. Gifts to someone's children or other groups are called
class gifts; one says that "the class closes when A dies."[34]

NOTES AND PROBLEMS

Here are some other examples to test your understanding. In analyzing the following problems, (1) classify the present interest, (2) determine
whether the future interests are in the grantor or a third party; (3) if the
future interests are in a third party, determine whether they qualify as remainders; (4) if they do not, they are executory interests (of which more
later); (5) if they do qualify as remainders, determine whether they are
vested or contingent; (6) after you have classified a remainder, determine
what estate its owner will have once it becomes possessory, to pinpoint what
kind of a vested or contingent remainder it is (for example, vested remainder in fee simple, contingent remainder in a life estate, and so forth). Be
careful to account for *all* the estates created and to account for the property
from the moment of the devise for the rest of time. It may be helpful to
diagram the grants to ensure that you have accounted for all the estates
created.

---

33. The interest may also be called a "vested remainder subject to open."
34. A final kind of remainder is a vested remainder subject to complete divestment. An
example: "O to A for life, remainder to B and her heirs, but if A ever serves liquor on the land,
then to C and his heirs." B's remainder is vested because it is not subject to any condition
precedent, but it may be divested (i.e., B may lose it) if A ever serves liquor on the land.

Describe the state of the title after the following grants, which are included in a will written in 1994. If a future interest in a third party is not a remainder, simply indicate that it is not a remainder until instructed otherwise.

1.   "O to A for life, then to B."

2.   "O to A for life, then to B for life."

3.   "O to A for life, but if B graduates from law school, to B and his heirs."

4.   "O to A for life, then to B and his heirs once B reaches the age of 21." B is two years old.

5.   "O to A for life, then to B and his heirs one year after A's death."

6.   "O to A for life, then to B and his heirs if B survives A."

7.   "O to A for life, then to B and his heirs, if B becomes a concert pianist."

8.   "O to A for life, then to the youngest child of Sally and Jim who is alive at A's death, and that person's heirs."

9.   "O to A for life, then to B for life, then to the heirs of C and their heirs."

   (a)   B is alive at the time of the grant.

   (b)   B died three years ago.

10.   "O to A for life, then to the children of B."

11.   "O to A for life, then to the children of B who have married."

   (a)   If B has five children at the time of the grant.

   (b)   If B is childless at the time of the grant.

12.   "O to A, then if B marries C, to B and his heirs."

13.   **Executory interests.** In 1536, the Statute of Uses, *infra,* recognized as valid a future interest that did not meet the requirements for a remainder (because it either cut short the prior interest or created a certain gap in seisin), but it still was not classified as a remainder. The statute invented a new category, an executory interest, which is a generic term for any future interest in a third person that does not qualify as a remainder.[35]

---

35. The difference between executory interests and contingent remainders is part of the structure of the estate system that remains in use today; manipulating the system is not possible without it. Do any differences result from this distinction? At common law, the distinction did make a difference. Contingent remainders, but not executory interests, were destroyed by a gap in seisin, and the rule in Shelley's Case, see *supra* note 15, applied to contingent remainders but not executory interests. These rules have been abolished in the overwhelming majority of jurisdictions; where they are abolished, there may be no significant differences between executory interests and remainders other than their role in structuring the taxonomy of estates. See Jesse Dukeminier and Stanley M. Johanson, Wills, Trusts, and Estates 754-758 (5th ed. 1995); J. J. Dukeminier Jr., Contingent Remainders and Executory Interests: A Requiem for the Distinction, 43 Minn. L. Rev. 13 (1958); John Makdisi, The Vesting of Executory Interests, 59 Tul. L. Rev. 366 (1984). Modern statutes often include executory

Two types of executory interests exist. Some "spring forth" from the grantor: These are called *springing executory interests*. Here is an example: "O to A for life, then two years after A's death, to the Lion's Club."

O → A's life estate	O's reversion	Lion's Club springing executory interest in fee

Other executory interests "shift the estate either from A to a third party (without a gap) or from one third party to another": these are called *shifting executory interests*. Here is an example: "O to A and his heirs, but if B runs for president, then to B and his heirs."

A's fee simple subject to O → an executory interest	B's shifting executory interest in fee

Go back to the examples above that involved future interests that are not remainders and determine what types of executory interests they involve.

Problems 15-19 involve thinking up a realistic hypothetical that involves each of the following grants.

15.   A life estate and vested remainder.

16.   A remainder contingent because of a condition precedent (an "if" contingency).   *Age + survivorship most common contingency*

17.   A remainder contingent because the recipient is an unascertained party (a "who" contingency).   *R in heirs of a living person*

18.   A future interest that is not a remainder because of a gap in seisin.   *1 day after provision*

19.   A future interest that is not a remainder because it cuts short the prior estate.   *#12 w/ F.S. not LE in P*

d.   Defeasible Estates

A defeasible estate is one that can be lost if certain conditions occur. Defeasible fees are most likely to appear as part of a donative transfer. Through the device, a donor may retain considerable control stretching for generations over the use of land. Although each of the defeasible fees punishes a violation of the restriction or condition with forfeiture of the present interest, the several estates have somewhat different rules on when a forfeiture occurs, the transferability of the future interest, and the impact of the Rule against Perpetuities.

---

interests in broad definitions of "remainder." See, e.g., N.Y. Est., Powers & Trusts Law §6-3.2 (McKinney 1992 & Supp. 1995).

Limit

Example 1:   "O to A and her heirs so long as no liquor is consumed on the premises."

A has a present interest called a *fee simple determinable*; it is followed by an (implied) future interest in O called a *possibility of reverter*. Note, when we give this language its natural reading, should A violate the limitation imposed on her fee simple determinable, she would lose the land *automatically*. Other ways to draft a fee simple determinable include "to A and her heirs until liquor is consumed on the premises" and "to A and her heirs while the land is farmed."

Limit w/
O
reentry

Example 2:   "O to A and her heirs; but if liquor is consumed on the premises, O or his heirs shall have the power to reenter the premises and to terminate A's estate."

A has a present interest called a *fee simple subject to a condition subsequent;* it is followed by an (express) future interest in O called a *power of termination* or a *right of reentry*. Note, when we give this language its natural reading, should A violate the condition placed upon her fee, she would lose the land only if O then elected to exercise his termination power. Other ways to draft a fee simple on a condition subsequent include "to A and her heirs, provided that . . ." or "on the condition that . . .".

Limit
& future
interest
other
than
O

Example 3:   "O to A and his heirs so long as no liquor is consumed on the premises; then to B and his heirs."

executory

When we compare this language with that in Examples 1 and 2, we see that the grantor has not retained the future interest for herself, but has given it to a third person. B's interest is called an *executory interest,* and as we shall see shortly, it may be invalid under the Rule against Perpetuities. A's interest is called a *fee simple subject to an executory interest.*

The following case illustrates the difficulty that modern courts still face in shaking off old usages. (Note that this court uses some unusual terminology. It calls fees simple determinable "determinable fees," and fees simple on a condition subsequent "defeasible fees" (that is, fees in which the grantor and his heirs have the right to reenter and take the fee away from the grantee).)

Diff b/w them is O's express Rt v. implied

CITY OF CARTHAGE, JASPER COUNTY v. UNITED MISSOURI BANK OF KANSAS CITY, N.A.

873 S.W.2d 610 (Mo. Ct. App. 1994)

The City of Carthage (City), Missouri, appeals from an amended judgment that declared the City "has a fee simple determinable interest" in certain real estate in Jasper County, Missouri. The judgment also declared (a) that Defendants United Missouri Bank of Kansas City, N.A., and Charles A. Parsons[1] hold an interest in the same real estate, (b) that Defendants' interest "is a possibility of reverter," and (c) that a possibility of reverter "is an interest in land that may be conveyed by deed or devised by will."

Summarized, the City argues on appeal that the trial court erred in finding that Defendants had an interest in the real estate at issue because (1) a possibility of reverter is inalienable, unassignable, and cannot be devised, and (2) any attempt to convey or devise a possibility of reverter destroys it.

In 1932, Edna Myers owned the property in question, a 159-acre tract of land. On December 23, 1932, she executed a warranty deed that conveyed the property in trust to the Carthage Chamber of Commerce, Inc. (Chamber). Pertinent provisions of the deed, which contained numerous trust terms and conditions, follow:

> 3. Said land shall be perpetually devoted only to municipal purposes such as airport, public park or agricultural purposes. . . .
>
> 5. Said land shall be known perpetually by a designation which shall include the name "Myers" therein. . . .
>
> 7. If at the date of the death of [Edna Myers] all the terms and conditions hereof shall have been faithfully and punctually kept and performed by the [Chamber], then the [Chamber] shall convey said land to the city of Carthage, a municipal corporation of Missouri, said conveyance to be made subject to paragraphs 3 and 5 above. . . .
>
> 9. Should any breach of the terms and conditions contained in paragraphs 3 and 5 occur after the death of [Edna Myers], then this conveyance shall be void, said property shall revert to and become a part of the estate of [Edna Myers] to be disposed of according to the terms and conditions of the last will of [Edna Myers] if she die testate, or to be disposed of according to the laws of descent if she die intestate.

Edna Myers died testate on March 16, 1933. Pursuant to the trust terms, the Chamber conveyed the property to the City on March 25, 1933. The deed to the City stated that "this conveyance is expressly made subject to paragraphs 3 and 5 of the [December 23, 1932] warranty deed. . . ."

Edna Myers' will was admitted to probate on March 23, 1933. It contained a residuary clause, which provided that the residue of her estate would pass to certain named individuals. Neither the City nor Defendants dispute that any interest Edna Myers retained in the 159 acres passed to those individuals by virtue of the residuary clause, if such an interest is devisable.

---

1. The declared interest of United Missouri Bank of Kansas City, N.A., arises by virtue of its being trustee of a trust created by the will of Gordon Parsons. Charles A. Parsons is the sole beneficiary of that trust.

On March 29, 1960, the residuary devisees executed a quitclaim deed*
to Gordon Parsons. In that document, the grantors conveyed "any and all
rights of reentry and/or forfeiture" they might later acquire due to a breach
of condition of the trust created by Edna Myers' December 23, 1932, deed
to the Chamber and incorporated in the March 25, 1933, deed to the City.
Gordon Parsons died testate on July 12, 1980. Under the terms of his will,
his interest in the subject real estate was distributed to the United Missouri
Bank of Carthage as trustee. Later, this bank conveyed the interest in question to the Defendant bank as trustee.

On May 7, 1991, the City filed a petition for declaratory judgment
against the Defendant bank, seeking a declaration that the City owns the
Myers property in fee simple absolute. The bank answered the City's petition and filed a counterclaim to quiet title to the property, requesting a
judgment that it holds "a valid and legally recognizable and protectable future interest" in the property and that this interest "was and is fully alienable, assignable, devisable, and descendible." Subsequently, Charles A.
Parsons, the sole trust beneficiary, intervened as a party defendant and
counterclaimant.

At trial, the only evidence came from various deeds and records of
probate proceedings, as well as a stipulation of certain facts by the parties.
One provision of the stipulation stated that from March 25, 1933, through
the date of trial, the City had devoted the subject property to municipal
purposes such as airport, public park or agricultural purposes and that, during that time, the property had been known by a designation that included
the name "Myers."

During the trial, the City took the position that the 1932 and 1933
deeds created a possibility of reverter in Edna Myers and her heirs. The City
contended that the 1960 quitclaim deed from the residuary devisees to Gordon Parsons destroyed the possibility of reverter, because such a future interest cannot be alienated, assigned, or devised. As a result, the City claimed
ownership of the subject property in fee simple absolute.

On appeal, the City makes those same arguments and also contends
that, by attempting to devise her possibility of reverter, Edna Myers destroyed that interest. We note that during oral argument the City said it had
no quarrel with the trial court's determination that the 1933 deed conveyed
a determinable fee simple estate to the City. Thus, the first essential question before us is whether a possibility of reverter is devisable and alienable.

We agree with the parties and the trial court that the conveyance to
the City created a fee simple determinable. Clearly, Edna Myers' entire estate was conveyed to the City, conditioned upon the use of the property for

---

* A quitclaim deed gives to the grantee whatever estate the grantor owns in the land.
In contrast to a warranty deed, which warrants that the grantor has marketable title, the quitclaim deed makes no representations as to whether or not the grantor has marketable title, or
as to the estate in the land the grantor owns. — Eds.

specified purposes; and, upon cessation of such use, the entire estate would revert to Edna Myers' heirs or devisees. The specific characteristics of a fee simple determinable are discussed infra.

Our review of this court-tried case is governed by Rule 73.01(c) and the principles enunciated in Murphy v. Carron, 536 S.W.2d 30 (Mo. banc 1976). We must affirm the judgment of the trial court unless there is no substantial evidence to support it, unless it is against the weight of the evidence, or unless it erroneously declares or applies the law. Id. at 32.

Resolving the City's first point requires an understanding of the type of estate created by the 1933 deed to the City. A determinable fee simple estate[3] automatically terminates upon the occurrence of a specified event or the cessation of use for a specified purpose. Donehue v. Nilges, 364 Mo. 705, 266 S.W.2d 553, 554-55 (1954). Upon the creation of this estate, the grantor retains an interest known as a "possibility of reverter." Id. Upon the happening of the event by which the determinable fee simple estate is limited, it will terminate and revert to the grantor without any entry or other act. Chouteau v. City of St. Louis, 331 Mo. 781, 55 S.W.2d 299, 301 (banc 1932).

The future interest following a determinable fee simple is different from the one following a defeasible fee simple.[4] The difference is well stated in *Chouteau*.

> The distinction between an estate upon condition, and the limitation by which an estate is determined upon the happening of some event, is that in the latter case the estate reverts to the grantor or passes to the person to whom it is granted by limitation over, upon the mere happening of the event upon which it is limited, without any entry or other act; while in the former the reservation can only be made to the grantor or his heirs, and an entry upon breach of the condition is requisite to revest the estate. The provision for re-entry is therefore the distinctive characteristic of an estate upon condition, and when it is found that by any form of expression the grantor has reserved the right, upon the happening of any event, to re-enter and thereby revest in himself his former estate, it may be construed as such. 2 Devlin: Deeds (3d Ed.) §974.

55 S.W.2d at 301.

The City relies on three cases to support its contention that a possibility of reverter is inalienable and not devisable. After a careful reading

---

3. A conveyance of real estate from A to B school "so long as used for school purposes" creates a determinable fee simple in the grantee. Willard L. Eckhardt and Paul M. Peterson, Possessory Estates, Future Interests and Conveyances in Missouri §11 (1952). Words used to create such an estate are "so long as," "while," "during," "until," and the like. Id.

4. A defeasible fee simple is created in the grantee when, for example, A conveys to B and his heirs, "provided that if liquor ever is sold on the premises A or his heirs may reenter and terminate the estate." The future interest that ordinarily follows this estate is a right of entry for condition broken. Eckhardt and Peterson, *supra* note 3, §13.

of those cases, we are convinced none of them supports the proposition advanced. . . .

Finally, the City points to Polette v. Williams, 456 S.W.2d 328 (Mo. 1970), the most recent Supreme Court decision to state that a possibility of reverter is inalienable and cannot be devised. Like the two previous cases, however, Polette did not involve a conveyance that created a determinable fee simple.

The deed at issue in Polette contained a clause requiring the grantee to provide grantors a suitable home and to provide proper care and support for the grantors during their lifetime. The clause concluded with the following language:

> In the event [grantee] fails to fully and faithfully comply with this provision and obligation, title to the above described premises shall revert to [grantors], and in such event [grantee] shall forfeit any and all payments made by him upon the purchase price of said real estate.

Id. at 329. The Supreme Court said, "We have no doubt that this provision constituted a condition subsequent; such a condition operates upon an estate already created and vested, and renders it liable to be defeated." Id. at 331.

By this language the Supreme Court decided the deed in Polette created a defeasible fee simple, which is followed by a right of entry for condition broken. As noted, a possibility of reverter does not follow a defeasible fee simple. Therefore, any discussion by the court concerning possibilities of reverter was dictum. . . .

In short, the City relies upon dicta from three cases to convince us that a possibility of reverter is not devisable or alienable. While no Missouri decision appears to have ruled squarely on this point, we believe the correct view is adverse to the City.

ALIENABILITY

At common law, the grantor of a determinable fee was not vested with any title or interest in the property (until the occurrence of the stated contingency) since the contingency might never occur. Until the happening of the stated contingency, the grantor held a possibility of reverter, but had nothing to convey or devise. 4A Thompson, supra note 7, §1978 at 382-83. As a consequence, various courts have said that at common law a possibility of reverter was not an estate and therefore, in the absence of an authorizing statute, was not alienable, assignable or devisable. Id.

The Defendants argue that §442.020[8] has abrogated any common law

---

8. Statutory references are to RSMo 1986, unless otherwise indicated.

restrictions on the alienability of possibilities of reverter. They find support for this assertion in Brown v. Weare, 348 Mo. 135, 152 S.W.2d 649 (1941). Defendants contend that Brown is the only Missouri Supreme Court decision that directly holds a possibility of reverter is alienable. They assert that the Supreme Court "found that a possibility of reverter is an 'estate or interest' in land, and thus freely alienable or transferable by virtue of Sec. 3401, RSMo 1939."[9]

In our view, Brown is not precedent for the proposition that Defendants seek to advance, because once more the court's statements on the matter were clearly dicta. . . . However, this does not mean the statements are meaningless. "Obiter dicta statements when supported by logic are persuasive, but they are not precedents." State ex rel. Dunlap v. Higbee, 43 S.W.2d 825, 831 (Mo. banc 1931).

We believe the statements concerning the possibility of reverter in Brown are supported by logic and are persuasive as we consider a proper determination of the instant case.

Since 1936, the Restatement of Property §159 has held the view that the owner of a possibility of reverter has the power to transfer that interest by inter vivos conveyance. A number of legal scholars share the Restatement's view and have concluded that, even in the absence of statutory provisions, the weight of authority is that possibilities of reverter are alienable.[10] Lewis M. Simes, Handbook of the Law of Future Interests §34 (2d ed. 1966).

Besides the Restatement, the Brown court also referred to the predecessor to §442.020, concluding that a possibility of reverter is clearly an "interest" in land within the meaning of that statute. Accordingly, the court suggested that this statute authorizes the conveyance of such an interest. While we find no Missouri case that so holds, we do find substantial authority that §442.020 authorizes the conveyance of contingent remainders. These cases are instructive as we consider possibilities of reverter.

In McNeal v. Bonnel, 412 S.W.2d 167, 169 (Mo. 1967), the court said that, without doubt, a contingent remainder is an interest in land within the meaning of §442.020. The court took that position after considering Grimes v. Rush, 355 Mo. 573, 197 S.W.2d 310 (1946), a case involving a deed that, at common law, would have created a fee tail. The Grimes court concluded that, by virtue of §3498, RSMo 1939 (the predecessor to §442.470), such an estate is deemed to vest a life estate in the grantee, a contingent remainder in the grantee's issue, and a reversion in the grantor. The remainder is contingent upon the grantee having issue and upon the issue surviving the grantee. Id. at 311.

---

9. This statute is identical to present day §442.020, which provides in part: "Conveyances of lands, or of any estate or interest therein, may be made by deed. . . ."

10. For a summary of cases that accord with this view, see [Lewis M. Simes and Allan F. Smith, The Law of Future Interests], §1860 at n.80 (2d ed. 1956 & Supp. 1993).

In discussing the effect of a quitclaim deed by the contingent remainderman, the *Grimes* court said:

> Contingent remainders of this class were considered merely a possibility of an estate at common law and, for that reason, not alienable inter vivos to strangers. The modern rule is that contingent remainders are ordinarily alienable. Based upon statutory enactment (Sec. 3401, R.S. 1939, Mo.R.S.A., authorizing the conveyance "of lands, or of any state or interest therein"), Missouri cases rule in broad terms that contingent remainders are alienable. Sufficient reasons, founded on statute and departures of modern life from that existing under the English Feudal system, are stated in Godman v. Simmons, 113 Mo. 122, 129, 20 S.W. 972, 973. Present day contingent remainders may not be defeated through the ancient method of fine or recovery. They constitute interests in land of far greater dignity and substance than existed when they were held inalienable at common law. The reasons for restraints on alienation under the feudal system no longer exist.

Id. (footnote omitted).

Because obvious similarities exist between a possibility of reverter and a contingent remainder, the rationale in Grimes provides a sound basis to treat them the same under §442.020. As noted in [4A George W. Thompson, Thompson on Real Property §1978 at 378 (John S. Grimes, 1979 Replacement], a "possibility of reverter is always contingent and corresponds to contingent remainders." Clearly, both interests are contingent upon the happening of some specified event and both can cut off an existing estate. While we recognize these two interests are not identical,[12] the common features between these interests in land compel a finding that no sound reason exists to treat them differently within the context of §442.020.

We hold that a possibility of reverter is an "interest" in land within the meaning of the statute and is therefore alienable. Accordingly, the trial court properly declared and applied the law.

DEVISABILITY

Under §474.310, "Any person of sound mind, eighteen years of age or older may by last will devise his real or personal property. . . ." This statute governed Gordon Parsons' devise of his real property upon his death in 1980.

The Missouri statute that governed the testamentary disposition of real property on the date of Edna Myers' death was §518, RSMo 1929. That section allowed any married or unmarried woman over the age of 21 years,

---

12. "The possibility of reverter differs from the remainder and from the executory interests in that it arises only in the transferor or his heirs, whereas such other interests are always created in persons other than the transferor." Simes and Smith, *supra* note [10], §282, at 330 (2d ed. 1956).

who was of sound mind, to "devise her land, tenements, or any descendible interest herein. . . ."

The only cases the City cites on this issue have been discussed earlier. None of them addresses a factual situation involving the devise of a possibility of reverter. Defendants contend that such an interest is devisable under the current statute and its predecessor.

In a scholarly discussion on this subject, Professor William F. Fratcher concludes that §442.020 and §474.310 "were designed to change the archaic rules of the medieval common law." Fratcher, Exorcise the Curse of Reversionary Possibilities, 28 J. Mo. Bar 34, 36 (1972). After noting that the Missouri Supreme Court has held that these two statutes establish that contingent remainders and executory interests are alienable by deed and devisable by will, the author states:

> A possibility of reverter differs from a shifting executory interest only in that one is created in a grantor, the other in a grantee. Each is a future interest which may cut off automatically an existing estate in fee simple upon the happening of a condition. What reason in logic or policy exists for holding these statutes applicable to contingent remainders and executory interests but not to possibilities of reverter?

We find no authority in Missouri holding that a possibility of reverter is or should be treated differently under the statutes than contingent remainders or executory interests. As already demonstrated, a possibility of reverter is an interest in land. Section 518, RSMo 1929, allowed Edna Myers to devise any of her descendible interest in land. In addition, an interest in land is real property, which is devisable under §474.310. If, as we have already determined, §442.020 allows the holder of a possibility of reverter to convey that interest, logic dictates that §474.310 (and §518, RSMo 1929) must be construed to allow a devise of that same interest. Otherwise, statutory abrogation of the common law rule only as to alienation would result in confusion and inconsistency.

As stated in Simes and Smith, *supra* note [10], §1903, "it is difficult to see why [possibilities of reverter] should not be devisable if, as is everywhere recognized, executory interests will pass by will." In §1903, the authors set forth statutes from a number of jurisdictions, which expressly provide that possibilities of reverter are devisable. They also collect cases from numerous jurisdictions that hold a possibility of reverter is devisable; some of these cases are based on statutes containing language similar to §474.310. In either case, it is obvious that the trend in most jurisdictions is to abrogate any common law restrictions on the devisability of a possibility of reverter.

Certainly, this is the view promulgated by the American Law Institute. The Restatement of Property §165 provides: "The owner of any future interest . . . has the power to make a testamentary disposition . . . of his interest . . . except to the extent that such disposition is precluded by facts other than the futurity characteristic of such interest." As to proper statutory construction in light of this principle, Comment f of the same section (which applies to possibilities of reverter and other interests) states: "When a statute declares broadly, that 'expectant estates,' or 'estates in reversion and remainder,' or 'lands or interests therein' are devisable, this provision is to be construed as stating the same rule as is stated in this Section."

Consistent with the Restatement view, we determine that the two statutes involved here allowed, first, Edna Myers and, later, Gordon Parsons to devise a possibility of reverter as an interest in the real property in question. For the sake of simplicity and consistency, §442.020 and §474.310 must be construed to allow a conveyance or devise of such an interest. The trial court committed no error.

In its second point, the City argues that an attempt to convey or devise a possibility of reverter destroys it and that the City now owns the property in question in fee simple absolute. In view of our holding under the first point, this claim has no merit.

Judgment affirmed.

NOTES AND QUESTIONS

1. **Determinable fee or fee simple subject to a condition subsequent?** This case is unusual in one respect: The parties and the trial court all agreed that the conveyance to the city created a fee simple determinable. Often the dispute centers on which defeasible estate it is. The examples can be multiplied, but here are several:

(a) The city of Long Beach quitclaimed some tidelands to the state of California. In the deed were these words: "This conveyance is made upon the express condition that the property conveyed hereby shall be used for a park . . . and should said property . . . be used for any other purpose, then, in that event, the property hereby conveyed shall immediately revert unto the grantor herein, its successors or assigns." A California court ruled that a fee simple subject to a condition subsequent had been created, and that the grantor had retained a "power of reentry" [*sic*]. People v. City of Long Beach, 200 Cal. App. 2d 609, 19 Cal. Rptr. 585 (1962).

(b) An 1868 deed to school trustees provided: "[This conveyance] is made and accepted subject to the following conditions and reservations, viz.: . . . and whenever the property hereby conveyed shall cease to be used for school and meeting purposes . . . then and in that case the same shall revert to and become the property of the first part[y]." A New York court decided that this language manifested the grantor's intent to create a fee simple subject to a condition subsequent. Fausett v. Guisewhite, 16 A.D.2d 82, 225 N.Y.S.2d 616 (1962). Cf. also United Methodist Church v. Kunz, 78 Misc. 2d 565, 357 N.Y.S.2d 637 (Sup. Ct. 1974).

(c) A railway acquired a 66-foot strip of land by a deed which read:

"Said second party hereby agrees to and with said first party that in case said Railway shall at any time be abandoned then the lands heretofore described shall revert to the grantors." In reversing the trial judge, a New York appellate court decided unanimously that this deed had conveyed a fee upon special limitation, and that the grantors had retained a possibility of reverter. Nichols v. Haehn, 8 A.D.2d 409, 187 N.Y.S.2d 773 (1959).

Where ambiguity is present, courts tend to favor the fee simple subject to a condition subsequent over the determinable fee. Why is that?

2.   **What of the negative pregnant — the nontransferability of the power of termination?** The court holds that the possibility of reverter may be transferred both inter vivos and at death. The negative pregnant, based on the earlier Missouri dicta, is that the power of termination is less alienable, and that any move to transfer that interest could destroy it.

The First Restatement of Property did treat the two interests differently. The possibility of reverter was said to be alienable (§159), devisable (§165), and descendable (§164). The power of termination, while devisable (§165) and descendable (§164), was said not to be capable of inter vivos transfer (§160) unless it supplemented a reversionary interest; for example, the landlord's interest in the fee (§161-c). (Two other exceptions to the rule also appear.) The Restatement also asserted (by a split decision of 41 to 35) that a power of termination would be destroyed by any attempt to make a "forbidden" transfer, §160, Comment c. On that issue, the Restatement later reversed itself. American Law Institute, Restatement of the Law 416 (1948 Supp.)

The nonalienability rule still survives in some jurisdictions, although England ended it more than 150 years ago. 7 Wm. 4 & 1 Vict., c. 26, §3 (1837) (applies to wills only); 7 & 8 Vict., 76, §5 (1844). An American trend to make powers of termination more freely alienable is now well underway. See, e.g., N.Y. Est., Powers & Trusts Law §6-5.1 (McKinney 1992 & Supp. 1995)

3.   **Problem.** In 1987, a prominent citizen, Dr. Fletcher Fairley, gave ten acres of land to his hometown of Mascon, Mississippi, by the deed in Figure 2-2. In 1992, the land reverted back to the grantor because the city had failed to meet the conditions enumerated in the deed. (The city's failure to grow the Tupelo Gum tree, a distinctive Mississippi tree native to cypress swamps, played a central role in this initial reverter.) Dr. Fletcher executed a second deed in January 1992, shown in Figure 2-3, with a slightly different set of development conditions. Keep in mind that the grantor is elderly and infirm; his children have stated publicly that they do not approve of the gift of land to the city under any circumstances. The land is worth approximately $20,000 per acre in its undeveloped state. The area nearby is being developed in upscale residential subdivisions, so it is likely that the value of the land will increase rapidly in the next few years. The grantor's children can be expected to be very strict about compliance with the conditions of the deed if they inherit the possibility of reverter.

BOOK 415 PAGE 509

DEED

FOR AND IN CONSIDERATION of the sum of Ten Dollars ($10.00), cash in hand paid, and other good and valuable considerations, the receipt and sufficiency of which are hereby acknowledged, the undersigned Fletcher M. Fairley and wife, Irma S. Fairley, Grantors, do hereby sell, convey, quitclaim and release unto the City of Mascon, Mississippi, Grantee, upon the conditions hereinafter stated, property located in the City of Mascon, Mascon County, Mississippi, and being more particularly described in Exhibit "A" attached hereto and incorporated herein.

This conveyance is made upon the condition that for a period of ninety-nine years from the date hereof, Grantee shall maintain said property as an arboretum and shall, within three (3) years of the date hereof, plant, and thereafter maintain, at least one variety of every tree which is native to the State of Mississippi, as well as sufficient number of other trees to constitute the said property as an arboretum, and to otherwise property maintain and develop said property as an arboretum. Grantee covenants and agrees to install and maintain a six to eight foot in width paved walking trail throughout the arboretum. Grantee covenants and agrees to install and maintain a parking lot of reasonable size to service the users of said arboretum; not to allow motorized vehicles or bicycles in said arboretum; and not to allow picnicking nor picnicking facilities therein.

The above described covenants shall run with the land and should Grantee breach any of said covenants during said ninety-nine year period or fail to comply with the conditions, then said property shall revert to Grantors, or their heirs, without the necessity of re-entry. Upon the expiration of ninety-nine years from the date of this conveyance, if title has not theretofore reverted to Grantors, or theirs heirs, and if the covenants have not been breached, title shall vest in fee simple to Grantee, the condition shall be discharged and the covenants shall terminate.

determinable OR K remedies b/c covenant

[signatures omitted]

DATE: Dec. 15, 1987

FIGURE 2-2
Deed No. 1

DEED

FOR AND IN CONSIDERATION of the sum of Ten Dollars ($10.00), cash in hand paid, and other good and valuable considerations, the receipt and sufficiency of which are hereby acknowledged, the undersigned Fletcher M. Fairley and wife, Irma S. Fairley, Grantors, do hereby sell, convey, quitclaim and release unto the City of Mascon, Mississippi, Grantee, upon the conditions hereinafter stated, property located in the City of Mascon, Mascon County, Mississippi, and being more particularly described in Exhibit "A" attached hereto and incorporated herein.

This conveyance is made upon the condition that for a period of ninety-nine years from the date hereof, Grantee shall maintain said property as an arboretum and shall, within five (5) years of the date hereof, plant, and thereafter maintain, at least two species of every variety of tree as possible which is native to the State of Mississippi, as well as a sufficient number of other trees to constitute the said property as an arboretum. Grantee covenants and agrees to install and maintain a walking trail (eventually to be hard surfaced) through the arboretum; to install and maintain a parking lot of reasonable size to service the users of said arboretum; to provide adequate water for irrigation purposes; not to allow motorized vehicles or bicycles in said arboretum; and not to allow picnicking nor picnicking facilities therein.

The above described covenants shall run with the land and should Grantee breach any of said covenants during said ninety-nine year period or fail to comply with the conditions, then said property shall revert to Grantors, or their heirs, without the necessity of re-entry. Upon expiration of ninety-nine years from the date of this conveyance, if title has not theretofore reverted to Grantors, or their heirs, and if the covenants have not been breached, title shall vest in fee simple in Grantee, the condition shall be discharged and the covenants shall terminate.

WITNESS OUR SIGNATURES, this 24 day of January, 1992.

Fletcher M. Fairley
Fletcher M. Fairley

Irma S. Fairley
Irma S. Fairley

FIGURE 2-3
Deed No. 2

FIGURE 2-4
Arboretum on which Problem 3 is based

What leverage will they have after Dr. Fletcher's death? How are the development conditions in the 1992 deed different from those in the 1987 deed? Are the development conditions in the second deed easier to meet than those in the first deed? Under the second deed, what kind of process should the city set up to decide what trees can feasibly be grown in the Arboretum? How should the city design such a process to stand up to future challenges by the grantor's children?

City officials are pessimistic about meeting even the conditions set out in the second deed. They are doubtful the city will pay for the (high) cost of paving the three miles of paths in the Arboretum and for other improvements such as bridges over various streams, although the city seems more open to paving the parking lot at city expense and bringing up a water line suitable for installing a drinking fountain (but not for irrigation).

You have volunteered to work pro bono with the Arboretum Committee, along with three others, all lawyers. The Committee's first recommendation was to go back and renegotiate a third time with Dr. Fletcher. If this approach were adopted, how would you redraft the development conditions yet again? Keep in mind that Dr. Fletcher does not seem receptive to donating funds to cover the expenses of developing the Arboretum. At any rate, the city seems to be reluctant to pursue this strategy. Can you think of

[handwritten marginalia: Sell part of land + use that money for meeting expenses — 2 Acres of land]

alternative strategies the city could use to secure the Fletcher Arboretum? In this counseling and negotiation problem, be sure you consider nonlegal as well as legal ways of achieving the Arboretum Committee goals. For more on counseling and negotiation, see David Binder, Paul Bergman, and Susan Price, Lawyers as Counsellors: A Client-Centered Approach (1991); Robert D. Dinerstein, Client-Centered Counseling: Reappraisal and Refinement, 32 Ariz. L. Rev. 501 (1990). Our thanks to Terry W. Frazier, Professor of Law, Mississippi College of Law, for help in developing this problem.

4. **Defeasible fees and suburbs.** When suburbanization in the United States began in earnest in the late nineteenth century, developers turned to a variety of legal mechanisms to control land use in residential areas. Defeasible fees were used for a number of purposes. First, they were used to forbid nuisances in residential areas or to forbid all uses except residential ones. Second, prohibitions against the sale or use of alcohol also became nigh-universal in some areas: "To A so long as no liquor is bought or sold on the premises." These prohibitions were related in part to the temperance movement (c. 1870-1920); they also represented an attempt to ban social and development patterns associated with immigrants from Italy, Ireland, and other areas, for whom the local pub or coffee-wine bar was an established part of settled life. Racial restrictions also became common in the late nineteenth century: "To A and his heirs, provided that the property shall be sold, leased, and occupied by Caucasians only; if it is not, O and his heirs reserve the right to reenter and retake the premises." Until the 1950s, courts uniformly enforced racial restrictions on occupancy, and many enforced restrictions on sale, holding that they violated neither public policy nor the Constitution. (See discussion of Shelley v. Kraemer below.) See Timothy Jost, The Defeasible Fee and the Birth of the Modern Residential Subdivision, 49 Mo. L. Rev. 695 (1984).

5. **Shelley v. Kraemer.** The U.S. Supreme Court in Shelley v. Kraemer, 334 U.S. 1 (1948), barred state courts from issuing injunctions enforcing privately created racially restrictive covenants. Several years later Barrows v. Jackson, 346 U.S. 249 (1953), denied courts the alternative power to award damages for a covenant violation. The Court held that judicial enforcement would be an exercise of state power in support of racial discrimination, which the Equal Protection Clause of the Fourteenth Amendment prohibited. This "state action" theory has been much criticized even by scholars sympathetic with the two decisions. See, e.g., Louis Henkin, *Shelley v. Kraemer:* Notes for a Revised Opinion, 110 U. Pa. L. Rev. 473 (1962).

6. **State action and judicial enforcement of racially restrictive defeasible estates.** The Court in the *Shelley* case refused to outlaw racially restrictive covenants and left open the avenue of voluntary compliance. Also uncertain after the *Shelley* decision was whether its principle would bar judicial enforcement of the forfeiture provisions of a racially restrictive defeasible estate.

Quite possibly the most cited case raising that issue, one relying on a key difference between the determinable fee and the fee simple subject to a condition subsequent, was Charlotte Park and Recreation Commission v. Barringer, 242 N.C. 311, 88 S.E.2d 114 (1955). The Barringer deed had granted land to the plaintiff for use as a public park (Revolution Park) and had provided that the park was to be "used and enjoyed by persons of the white race only." The deed further provided that if the park were not used by the white race only, "the lands hereby conveyed shall revert in fee simple to [Barringer, his heirs and assigns]."

Plaintiff, wishing to allow blacks to use the park golf course, sought a declaratory judgment that an effort by Barringer to regain possession of the park would offend Shelley v. Kraemer. In refusing the plaintiff, the North Carolina court (correctly) defined the plaintiff's estate as a determinable fee and continued:

> If negroes use the Bonnie Brae Golf Course, the determinable fee conveyed to plaintiff by Barringer, and his wife, automatically will cease and terminate by its own limitation expressed in the deed, and the estate granted automatically will revert to Barringer, by virtue of the limitation in the deed. . . . The operation of this reversion provision is not by any judicial enforcement by the State Courts of North Carolina, and Shelley v. Kraemer . . . has no application.

Charlotte Park and Recreation Commission v. Barringer, 242 N.C. 311, 322, 88 S.E.2d 114, 123.

Compare Capitol Fed. Sav. & Loan Assn. v. Smith, 136 Colo. 265, 316 P.2d 252 (1957), in which a Colorado court struck down the grant and awarded fee simple to the original grantee. The Colorado court explicitly rejected the argument that no state action existed because the estate at issue was a fee simple determinable.

> No matter by what . . . terms the [estate] under consideration may be classified by astute counsel, it is still a racial restriction in violation of the Fourteenth Amendment to the Federal Constitution. That this is so has been definitely settled by the decisions of the Supreme Court of the United States. High sounding phrases or outmoded common law terms cannot alter the effect of the agreement embraced in the instant case. While the hands may seem to be the hands of Esau to a blind Isaac, the voice is definitely Jacob's. We cannot give our judicial approval or blessing to [this].

316 P.2d at 255. Note the court's turn to biblical language in its refusal to let one of the thousand deals bloom because of its sense of the limits of ethical behavior. Isaac, who was blind, wanted to give his eldest son Esau the special blessing traditionally bestowed on the first-born son. Isaac's wife Rebecca wanted the blessing for their son Jacob, so when Isaac called for Esau to give his blessing, she disguised Jacob as Esau, putting sheep's skin on Jacob's hands and neck to make him hairy like Esau. Isaac noticed that the voice was Jacob's, so he asked him to come close. When he touched his

son he thought he recognized the hairy hands and neck of Esau, so he gave Esau's blessing to Jacob.[36] What analogy does the court draw between the stolen blessing and its decision?

7.   **Racial geography.** Would *Charlotte Park* be decided the same way today? Almost certainly not. Nor would any public corporation accept a gift wrapped with the Barringer strings. Today, formal barriers to equality have been largely eliminated. Nevertheless, we continue to live in a society in which racial divides have been translated into literal geography. "It really is quite remarkable: Blacks live with Blacks and whites live with whites."[37] Eighty percent of African Americans would have to move to achieve an integrated residential configuration.[38] Roughly one-fourth of all blacks live in ten hypersegregated metropolitan areas; no other ethnic or racial group experiences this pattern.[39] No significant decrease in the residential segregation of blacks occurs with increases in income: Blacks with incomes of over $50,000 are as segregated as blacks with incomes from $10,000 to $15,000.[40]

The current racialized patterns are creatures of the law in the sense that they stem from courts' past willingness to enforce racially discriminatory defeasible fees, covenants (see Chapter 7), and zoning (see Chapters 8 and 9), even if they do not do so today. What effect did the period when open discrimination was tolerated have on current housing conditions? Some have argued that the central discrimination issue is the perpetuation of past discrimination, which can occur without any conscious malice or intent to discriminate.[41] See Richard Thompson Ford, The Boundaries of Race: Political Geography in Legal Analysis, 107 Harv. L. Rev. 1843, 1845 (1994) ("[r]ace-neutral policies, set against an historical backdrop of state action in the service of racial discrimination . . . predictably reproduce and entrench racial segregation and the rac[e-]caste system that accompanies it"). Do you agree, or do you view the role of public policy at an end once formal, legal discrimination has been forbidden?

8.   **Other defeasible estates.** Although we are looking now at defeasible fees, defeasibility, as we have already hinted, may also extend to life estates; thus, "O to A for life, but if B graduates from law school, to B and

---

36. In fairness, one should note that Esau may have given up his birthright to Jacob in exchange for a "pottage of lentils." Gen. 25:31-34 (King James).

37. Alex M. Johnson Jr., How Race and Poverty Intersect to Prevent Integration: Destabilizing Race as a Vehicle to Integrate Neighborhoods, 143 U. Pa. L. Rev. 1595, 1636 (1995).

38. Douglas S. Massey and Nancy A. Denton, American Apartheid: Segregation and the Making of the Underclass 10, 61 (1993) (documenting the "hypersegregation" of "a chocolate city with vanilla suburbs").

39. John O. Calmore, Spacial Equality and the Kerner Commission Report: A Back-to-the-Future Essay, 71 N.C. L. Rev. 1487, 1504 (1993).

40. Id. at 1504. See also Martha Mahoney, Note, Law and Racial Geography: Public Housing and the Economy in New Orleans, 42 Stan. L. Rev. 1251, 1262 (1990) (showing income difference accounts for only 10 to 35 percent of existing racial segregation).

41. Eric Schnapper, Perpetuation of Past Discrimination, 96 Harv. L. Rev. 828 (1983).

his heirs" results in a defeasible life estate, one that will be cut short when (and if) B graduates from law school. B and his heirs hold an executory interest.

If you are a tenant, almost certainly you also have a defeasible estate, a one-year term, for example, that will be cut short if you do not pay the rent.

9. **Statutes cutting off rights of entry and possibilities of reverter.** Some states have statutes that cut off rights of entry and possibilities of reverter after a given period. Such statutes usually take one of two forms: the absolute cutoff of the future interest after a specified interval and the conditional cutoff, which happens unless the interest holder records notice of his intention to preserve it.

Illinois's Reverter Act of 1947, Ill. Rev. Stat. ch. 30, §37e (1969, Supp. 1978), represents the first genre. After 40 years, the future interests cease. The state court validated the statute even as to interests already in being. Trustees of Schools of T No. 1 v. Batdorf, 6 Ill. 2d 486, 130 N.E.2d 111 (1955). Compare Biltmore Village v. Royal, 71 So. 2d 727 (Fla. 1954) (21 year cutoff invalid as to existing interests).

A New York statute, N.Y. Real Prop. Law §345 (McKinney 1995), illustrates the second genre. This law requires persons to record a "declaration of intention to preserve" their future interest at the end of 30 years and to renew their declaration at 10-year intervals thereafter. At its adoption, the statute gave persons whose interests were already older than 30 years 3 years to comply. The court of appeals held the statute invalid as to outstanding interests but enforceable as to interests created after the statute's adoption. Board of Educ. v. Miles, 15 N.Y.2d 364, 207 N.E.2d 181 (1965). A similar Kentucky statute, creating a 5-year window of compliance for older outstanding interests, was upheld. Cline v. Johnson County Board of Educ., 548 S.W.2d 507 (Ky. 1977). Where, however, title had automatically reverted (fee simple determinable) to the future interest holder prior to the statute, even though the interest holder had taken no steps to regain possession, the Kentucky court refused to apply the statute. Caldwell v. Brown, 553 S.W.2d 692 (Ky. 1977). Why so?

If you were a donor's lawyer in New York, and your client was about to transfer land to a village on a defeasible estate, what steps would you recommend to your client to better the chances of compliance with §345 30 years later? Note that the declaration cannot be filed until 27 years have passed.

At least two other statutory modes exist to weaken the persistent grip of a long-standing possibility of reverter or power of termination.

(a) Conditions that "are nominal" and of no "substantial" benefit "to the party in whose favor they run are void and unenforceable." Mich. Comp. Laws Ann. §554.46 (1967); Wis. Stat. Ann. §700.15 (Supp. 1973); Ariz. Rev. Stat. §33-436 (1956). For a re-

view of cases construing these terms, see Hammond, *infra*, at
606-609.

(b)   After a fixed period, any possibility of reverter or power of termination shall be enforceable only by equitable remedies as
though it were a covenant or restriction. Fla. Stat. Ann. §689.18
(1969) (21 years).

ROBERT N. HAMMOND, LIMITATIONS UPON POSSIBILITIES OF REVERTER AND RIGHTS OF ENTRY: CURRENT TRENDS IN STATE LEGISLATION 1953-1954

589, 590-592 (1955)

In examining statutes which affect possibilities of reverter and rights
of entry, two basic policies of the law must be kept in mind because the use
of a possibility of reverter or a right of entry in a conveyance of land may
bring these policies into conflict. Any legislation in this field should seek to
resolve this conflict.

The first of the two policies concerned is that land should be freely
alienable; that is, land should be transferable by its owner with a minimum
of difficulty of any kind. This policy is believed to promote the fullest and
best economic use of land in the interests of society. There are two important elements in the free alienability of land. First, to be freely alienable, or
marketable, land must have a title that is free of defects and restrictions.
Defects in titles make purchase hazardous, and restrictions diminish the
potential usefulness of the land. Second, the state of title must be easily
discoverable so that prospective purchasers may know whether the title is
marketable. Such legislation as recording acts and marketable title acts are
attempts to make the title to real property readily discoverable and also, in
some instances, attempts to provide a basis for curing defects in title,
thereby effectuating the policy of free alienability of land.

The second important policy here involved is that owners should be
free to dispose of their land, imposing such limitations, conditions, and
restrictions as they choose. This policy is in accord with democratic political
ideas and free enterprise economic philosophy. It recognizes the right of
the individual to acquire property, to own property, and to dispose of property with a minimum of interference. . . .

The conflict between the policies of free alienability and of the right
to dispose of land as one chooses comes about as a result of the fact that
there is no limitation upon the length of time that possibilities of reverter
and rights of entry remain enforceable interests. Each interest remains a
part of the title to the land until the interest is in some way eliminated.
Thus, each interest may operate to cause a forfeiture or reverter at a remote

future time. Whenever such an interest appears in a title to land, account must be taken of it by a title examiner in approving his client's prospective purchase of the land. Because of the ever present possibility that the land will revert or be forfeited, many prospective purchasers hesitate to buy. Thus, the title is rendered partially unmarketable. In addition, if considerable time has elapsed since the creation of the interest, it may be difficult to secure a discharge of the interest. This may be because the owner cannot be found, because he demands unreasonable compensation for giving a discharge, or because there are numerous owners of the interest who either cannot all be found or who cannot all be persuaded to give discharges of their interests. Also, it may be difficult or impossible to determine whether circumstances may have occurred which render the interest unenforceable. The result is that it is often difficult to discover the true state of title where a possibility of reverter or right of entry appears in the title. This, combined with the restrictive effect of the limitation or condition itself, tends to hamper the free alienability of land.

PROBLEMS

Describe the state of the title after the following grants, which occur in 1996. Be careful to account for both the present and the future interests created and to account for the property from the moment of the grant for the rest of time.

1.   "O to A and her heirs so long as the land is farmed."

2.   "O to A, provided that the land is never developed; if it is developed, O and his heirs shall have the right to reenter and claim the land."

3.   "O to A and his heirs until the land shall no longer be used for church purposes, then to B and her heirs."

4.   "O to A and her heirs, but if the land is used for commercial purposes, then B shall have the right to reenter and retake the land."

5.   "O to A and his heirs, provided that no liquor is sold or consumed on the land; if it is, the land shall revert to O and her heirs."

6.   Think up a realistic hypothetical involving a grantor granting a fee simple determinable.

7.   Think up a realistic hypothetical involving a grantor granting a fee simple on a condition subsequent.

e.   Statute of Uses

The common-law system of estates in land involved a highly formalistic method of legal analysis, which set up predefined and mutually exclusive legal boxes and required the lawyer to fit the ever-changing patterns of life within the boxes. Under the common law, either a transaction fit within one of the recognized estates or was struck down as unenforceable.

A central force behind the construction of the accepted estates in land was the desire of the high aristocracy to build up powerful dynasties by accumulating large tracts of land and keeping them within the family. A second — and sometimes countervailing — force was that of the English crown, seeking to use the system of estates in land to contain the nobility's power.

The Statute of Uses was another famous installment in the struggle between the nobles and the crown. The English tax system, which benefited the crown, included a forerunner to the modern estate tax, a feudal incident called a *relief;* the tax was levied whenever land passed to a new tenant, as it would, for example, at the death of a life tenant and the succession by the remainderman. This tax could be avoided by means of a *use,* which was itself a forerunner — to the modern trust.[42] In 1536, when Henry VIII ran short of money, he crammed through Parliament the Statute of Uses, which recognized all uses as legal estates that triggered tax liability. This statute gave him and future kings a source of revenues independent of Parliamentary taxes and served the English monarchy well during the struggles that led up to the English Civil War. As one episode in those struggles, the nobles forced Charles I to abolish feudal incidents as a way of bringing his revenues under Parliamentary control. (After the Restoration in 1660, the crown was compensated for the loss of feudal incidents by a tax on beer and other beverages.) See A. W. B. Simpson, A History of the Land Law 173-207 (2d ed. 1986).

§2.3   Property, Politics, and Legal Formalism: The Issue of Dead Hand Control and the Rule against Perpetuities

a.   The Common-Law Rule against Perpetuities

As there was half a millennium ago, there remains today the direct linkage between the politics of wealth and the design of the system of wealth transmission. This focuses one of property's central policy issues: How much control should the present generation enjoy over the next generations' ownership and use of land-based resources? We refer, unflatteringly, to this issue as the legitimate extent of dead hand control.

The Statute of Uses, and the evisceration of fee tail, led to new devices seeking to tie up landed wealth for many generations. This new chapter in the power struggle between the landowning nobility on the one hand and

---

42. For a fuller description of a trust, see §2.5.a *infra.*

the crown (and various others, including ungrateful descendants) on the other hand culminated in the celebrated Duke of Norfolk's Case, 3 Ch. Cas. 1, 22 Eng. Rep. 931 (1681). There, the even more celebrated Lord Chancellor Nottingham coined a rule against "perpetuities," which — as the rule was fleshed out over the next 200 years — invalidated a wide array of contingent future interests.

The Duke of Norfolk had wanted to protect the family property from the consequences of the insanity of the Duke's eldest son; the Duke's lawyer drafted a complex legal structure that tied up rights in the land for terms of years with a devise over upon failure of issue within the lifetime of another person. The Lord Chancellor limited the time span over which a living grantor could control the disposition of assets, by reasoning that a grantor should be able to control disposition only to those persons whose capabilities he can judge when he makes the disposition.[43] Subsequent judges allowed grantors to extend their control beyond lives in being at the time of the grant, into the minority of the next generation.

The Rule against Perpetuities has had few rivals for the torment it can cause law students and the havoc it can occasionally wreak on badly drafted wills and other property transfers. Any attempt to master the Rule would take several weeks of effort, and because you are certain to meet the Rule again if you study trusts and estates — today, by far its most important application — you might defer your mastery until then. For present purposes, you will be well served to recognize a simple statement of the Rule, to work out a few untricky examples, to get a taste of its abominations, to understand the Rule's social policy, and to look at the principal reform efforts.

The nineteenth-century American lawyer John Chipman Gray has given us the classic statement of the Rule:

> No interest is good unless it must vest, if at all, not later than twenty-one years after some life in being at the creation of the interest.[44]

While simply stated, the Rule is sometimes treacherous to apply. Before you try a few examples, here are some "clarifying" guidelines.

(a) The Rule applies only to future interests. It does not apply to the fee simple absolute, the life estate, the fee simple determinable, or the fee simple subject to a condition subsequent, which are all present interests.

---

43. See Ashbel Gulliver, Future Interests 371-388 (1959), for a factual synopsis and edited opinion of the Duke of Norfolk's Case.

44. John Chipman Gray, The Rule against Perpetuities §201 (4th ed. 1942). The Rule would allow, according to one of its chief critics, "a man of property [to] provide for all of those in his family whom he personally knew and the first generation after them upon attaining majority." W. Barton Leach, 6 American Law of Property §24.16, at 51 (A. James Casner ed., 1952).

(b) The Rule applies only to future interests created in *third persons*. It does not apply to the reversion, the possibility of reverter, or the power of termination (right of reentry), which are all future interests that the grantor has reserved for himself and his heirs.

(c) The Rule applies only to *contingent* future interests. It applies to the contingent remainder and the executory interest, but it does not apply to the vested remainder. →Applies to vested R subject to open

(d) We refer to the "life in being" as the "measuring life." The measuring life is someone who is alive on the effective date of the instrument creating the contingent future interest. For inter vivos transfers (usually gifts), the effective date is when the deed or trust instrument is delivered; for wills, the effective date is when the testator dies. Thus, the perpetuities period (life in being plus 21 years) begins to run, in the case of a deed or trust instrument, on the delivery date, and in the case of a will, on the testator's death. We can also add relevant periods of gestation.

(e) We apply the common-law Rule *prospectively*. We ask whether the contingent future interest is certain to vest, if it vests at all, within the perpetuities period. An alternative way to put the question, and one that we believe simplifies analysis, is to ask: When will we be sure to learn whether the contingency is satisfied, or know that it cannot be satisfied? If that "determination date" falls within the perpetuities period, the future interest is valid; otherwise it is void ab initio. Because we look ahead when we ask the question, it makes no difference whether, as events later unfold, the future interest vests or fails within a life in being plus 21 years. Because we deal theoretically with the contingency, we sometimes call the common-law Rule the "what might happen" rule.

(f) One of the most puzzling aspects of the Rule is the choice of measuring lives. Remember that the purpose of a measuring life is to identify some living person about whom we can say that within 21 years after that person's death we will be sure to learn whether the contingency is satisfied. If no such person exists the interest is void.

Very often, an appropriate measuring life will be someone named in the instrument (example 1, *infra*). Sometimes, we must infer a measuring life.[45] But unless there is someone alive when the instrument becomes effective after whose death not more than 21 years will pass before the "determination" date, the interest must fail.

Now test your understanding of the Rule by working through the following examples. In each case you should ask a threshold question: whether there is a *contingent* future interest created in a *third person*. If so, then you should ask whether the interest must vest, if it vests at all, within the perpetuities period — that is, within 21 years after some life in being at the

---

45. One example: O leaves everything by will to "my first grandchild to reach the age of 21 years." (At O's death, O has one daughter, D, who is childless.) Daughter D would be the measuring life, even though the will does not name her.

creation of the interest. Once subject to the Rule, a future interest must either satisfy the Rule or be invalid.

Example 1: "O to A for life, remainder to B and his heirs if B survives A."

B holds a contingent remainder because of its condition of survivorship. This contingent future interest is subject to the Rule. We must therefore consider whether B's interest satisfies the Rule.

We suggest that you then ask when, at the latest, we will know whether the contingency is satisfied, that is, whether or not B's contingent interest will ever become vested.

If you answered when A dies, you have answered correctly. At A's death, B either will have survived (in which event, B's interest vests) or will not have survived (in which event, B's interest can never vest).

To go on: Does this "determination" date occur during the perpetuities period, that is, during a life in being (measuring life) plus 21 years? Once again, you should have answered yes, because A can serve as our measuring life.[46] We will thus know before the end of the common-law perpetuities period (A's life plus 21 years) whether B's interest will vest, if it vests at all. Because we can say yes absolutely as to the "determination" date, B's interest satisfies the Rule *even though B's interest may never become vested.*

Example 2:   O makes a gift "to the first child of A (who is alive and child-less at the date of the gift) to reach the age of 25 years."

O has created a contingent future interest in A's first child to reach age 25, since we cannot yet identify that person. Accordingly, the interest is subject to the Rule. Does it satisfy the Rule? No, it does not. Why not?

Again, we ask the "determination" question: When will we be sure to learn who, if anyone, satisfies the contingency? Will we be sure to learn during the perpetuities period (some life in being plus 21 years)? Not during A's life, since A can give birth to a child S who might reach 25 *more than 21* years after A's death. Nor can we name any other *living* person about whom we can surely say that within 21 years after that person dies we can identify A's first child to reach 25. Thus, this contingent future interest violates the Rule against Perpetuities and is void ab initio.

Example 3:   "O to A and his heirs, so long as no liquor is consumed on the premises; then to B and his heirs."

O has created a contingent future interest in B and his heirs because this executory interest cannot vest until liquor consumption — the limiting

---

46. So, too, can B.

event — occurs. Accordingly, the interest is subject to the Rule. Does it satisfy the Rule? Once again, the answer is no.

As before, we ask the "determination" question: When are we certain to find out whether liquor is ever consumed on the premises? Will we be sure to learn during the perpetuities period (some life in being plus 21 years)? No. Liquor consumption might occur sometime in the next 21 years, which is within the perpetuities period, but it might not occur for 50 years, or, indeed, not ever. Hence, B's interest is invalid under the Rule.

Remember, that the Rule is intent-defeating, given its presumed purpose to limit dead hand control. Thus, courts often have stretched the Rule to thwart rather than to abet the grantor's or testator's objectives.[47] This has spawned some famous characters: the unborn widow and the slothful executor.

The Unborn Widow.   While the grantor is alive, he grants "to A for life, remainder to his widow for life, remainder to A's surviving children." The grant to A's surviving children violates the Rule against Perpetuities because A could marry a woman who was born after the grantor's death: She is an "afterborn," that is, not a life in being when the gift was made. This afterborn-widow could die more than 21 years after A's death, in which case the contingent remainder in A's surviving children would vest more than 21 years after the death of A, the measuring life. Therefore the grant to the children violate the Rule.

The Slothful Executor.   Lucas v. Hamm, 56 Cal. 2d 583 (1961), is a well-known slothful executor case. Hamm, the attorney defendant in a malpractice suit, had prepared a complex will that involved several trusts that were to "cease and terminate at 12 o'clock noon on a day five years after the date upon which [the probate court signed a relevant order]." Id. at 586. This language led to a claim that the residuary clauses violated the Rule against Perpetuities, and the parties who were to have inherited under these clauses received, in settlement of the claim, $75,000 less than they otherwise would have.

Those beneficiaries then filed the malpractice suit. In holding for the defendant attorney, the California Supreme Court wrote:

> In view of the state of the law relating to perpetuities and restraints on alienation and the nature of the error, if any, assertedly made by defendant in preparing the [will], it would not be proper to hold that defendant failed to use such skill, prudence, and diligence as lawyers of ordinary skill and capacity commonly exercise. The provision of the will . . . that the trust was to terminate

47. For these and other lurid examples, as well as the classical treatment of the subject, see two articles by W. Barton Leach: Perpetuities in a Nutshell, 51 Harv. L. Rev. 638 (1938), and Perpetuities: The Nutshell Revisited, 78 Harv. L. Rev. 973 (1965).

five years after the order of the probate court distributing the property to the trustee, could cause the trust to be invalid only because of the remote possibility that the [court's] order of distribution would be delayed for a period longer than a life in being at the creation of the interest plus 16 years (the 21-year statutory period less the five years specified in the will). Although it has been held that a possibility of this type could result in invalidity of a bequest, the possible occurrence of such a delay was so remote and unlikely that an attorney of ordinary skill acting under the same circumstances might well have "fallen into the net which the Rule spreads for the unwary" and failed to recognize the danger. . . . [W]e have concluded that . . . an error of the type relied on by plaintiffs does not show negligence or breach of contract on the part of the defendant.

Id. at 592-593 (citations omitted).

NOTES AND QUESTIONS

1.   **Was it malpractice?** Was Lucas v. Hamm properly decided? Note that the slothful executor problem is commonly noted in hornbooks on property or on wills. What would be the reasonable course for an attorney consulted to draft a complex will who does not feel confident she has a full grasp of the Rule against Perpetuities?

2.   **Dead hand control.** The Rule is commonly justified as limiting "dead hand control"; to what extent should grantors be able to control the actions of their devisees? If one generation is given an entirely free hand, the options of future generations will be limited accordingly. The Rule against Perpetuities allows grantors to control disposition of their wealth for two generations. Is this an appropriate level of dead hand control in your view? Does your answer depend on your vision of property? In thinking through the implications of the republican vision of property, recall Thomas Jefferson's pride in abolishing the fee tail and primogeniture in Virginia, and the quotation with which this chapter began. In thinking through the implications of the liberal vision of property, note that the Rule against Perpetuities is an intent-defeating principle that addresses the issue of how to limit the 1,000 deals (or testamentary gifts) in balancing intergenerational claims.

3.   **Skits.** Develop a skit that shows how each of the following grants violates the Rule against Perpetuities, if it does, and what happens once the Rule has struck down the offending interest. Adopt the following pattern:

(i)   Name the estates at the time of the grant.
(ii)   Describe a scenario, if one exists, in which the Rule against Perpetuities is violated.
(iii) Describe who owns what (naming each of the estates) after the Rule against Perpetuities strikes down the original grant, if it does so.

    (iv)   Redraft the grant to avoid having it struck down as a violation of the Rule against Perpetuities. Note that this may entail creating a grant that differs from the original one.

    (a) O grants "to A and his heirs, so long as the land remains as farmland, then to B and her heirs."

    (b) O grants "to A and her heirs, so long as she farms the land, then to B and his heirs." *If A violated - goes to B* *A's death -*

    (c) O grants "to the first child of A to reach the age of 25 years." A is alive and childless.

    (d) O grants "to A for life, then to his widow for life, then to A's surviving children."

    4. **Savings clause.** When experienced lawyers draft documents creating future interests, they typically include a perpetuities savings clause. This clause is designed to ensure that the grants are not invalidated due to any potential violations of the Rule. The savings clause typically appears in documents that set up trusts, see *infra* Section 2.5.a, which are legal arrangements that provide for an amount of money to be held in trust, with the income to be paid out to the beneficiaries until the trust ends and the funds are distributed. A typical perpetuities savings provides that all trusts will be terminated and all assets distributed at the expiration of specified measuring lives plus 21 years, if the trust has not terminated earlier. This ensures that all the future (trust) interests will vest earlier than lives in being plus 21 years, thereby avoiding a Rule violation.

b. Reform Measures

1. Possibilities of Reverter and Powers of Termination

    Some states have statutorily extended the Rule against Perpetuities to include possibilities of reverter and powers of termination, or have otherwise limited their permissible duration. See, e.g., Illinois Reverter Act of 1947, Ill. Rev. Stat. ch. 30, para. 37e (Smith-Hurd 1969) (interests valid for 40 years); N.Y. Real Prop. Law §345 (McKinney 1989) (interest holders, after 30 years, must record declaration of intention to preserve at 10-year intervals); Robert N. Hammond, Limitations upon Possibilities of Reverter and Rights of Entry, in Current Trends in State Legislation 1953-1954, at 589, 590-592 (1954).

    England extended the common-law rule to the power of termination, a result confirmed by Law of Property Act of 1925, §4(3). Some years later, Parliament extended the Rule to the possibility of reverter within the Perpetuities and Accumulations Act 1964, §12, ending some confusion over whether the common-law rule already applied. See Ronald H. Maudsley, The Modern Law of Perpetuities 70-71 (1979).

2. Wait and See

At common law, a grant was invalid if there was even the remotest chance that a grant could vest later than lives in being plus 21 years. Many states today have adopted the so-called wait and see approach.[48] As formulated by the American Law Institute, in Restatement (Second) of Property: Donative Transfers, §1.4 (1981), one form of wait and see provides that "a donative transfer of an interest *in property* fails, if the interest *does not vest* within the period of the rule against perpetuities" (emphasis added). A somewhat different approach is that of the Uniform Statutory Rule against Perpetuities (USRAP), promulgated in 1986, which requires contingent interests to vest within 90 years. If any interest does not do so, the USRAP requires that the offending interest be reformulated by the court to approximate the donor's intent as closely as possible, so as to vest within 90 years.[49] The Restatement proposal contains a similar "cy pres" provision, id. at §1.5.[50]

c. Commercial Transactions

THE SYMPHONY SPACE, INC. v. PERGOLA PROPERTIES, INC.

669 N.E.2d 799 (N.Y. 1996)

KAYE, C.J.

This case presents the novel question whether options to purchase commercial property are exempt from the prohibition against remote vesting embodied in New York's Rule against Perpetuities (EPTL 9.1.1[b]). Because an exception for commercial options finds no support in our law, we decline to exempt all commercial option agreements from the statutory Rule against Perpetuities.

Here, we agree with the trial court and Appellate Division that the

---

48. If California had been a wait and see jurisdiction, any challenge to the will in Lucas v. Hamm would have been premature until it had become clear that the factual scenario would have violated the Rule.

49. For a discussion of USRAP, see Lawrence W. Waggoner, The Uniform Statutory Rule against Perpetuities: The Rationale of the 90-Year Waiting Period, 73 Cornell L. Rev. 157 (1988).

50. For a sampling of the extensive literature on this issue, see Jesse Dukeminier, Cleansing the Stables of Property: A River Found at Last, 65 Iowa L. Rev. 151, 157-164 (1979); Dukeminier, Perpetuities: The Measuring Lives, 85 Colum. L. Rev. 1648 (1985); Dukeminier, A Response by Professor Dukeminier, 85 Colum. L. Rev. 1730 (1985); Dukeminier, A Final Comment by Professor Dukeminier, 85 Colum. L. Rev. 1742 (1985); Lawrence W. Waggoner, Perpetuity Reform, 81 Mich. L. Rev. 1718 (1983); Waggoner, Perpetuities: A Perspective on Wait-and-See, 85 Colum. L. Rev. 1714 (1985); Waggoner, A Rejoinder by Professor Waggoner, 85 Colum. L. Rev. 1739 (1985); Waggoner, The Uniform Statutory Rule Against Perpetuities: The Rationale of the 90-Year Waiting Period, 73 Cornell L. Rev. 157 (1988).

option defendants seek to enforce violates the statutory prohibition against remote vesting and is therefore unenforceable.

I.   FACTS

The subject of this proceeding is a two-story building situated on the Broadway block between 94th and 95th Streets on Manhattan's Upper West Side. In 1978, Broadwest Realty Corporation owned this building, which housed a theatre and commercial space. . . . Plaintiff Symphony Space, Inc., a not-for-profit entity devoted to the arts, had previously rented the theatre for several one-night engagements. In 1978, Symphony and Broadwest engaged in a transaction whereby Broadwest sold the entire building to Symphony for the below-market price of $10,010 and leased back the income-producing commercial property, excluding the theatre, for $1 per year. . . . As a consideration of the sale, Symphony, for consideration of $10, also granted Broadwest an option to repurchase the entire building . . . on or before December 31, 2003 [for a price ranging from $15,000 to $28,000, which depended upon when Broadwest exercised the option]. . . . The purpose of this arrangement was to enable Symphony, as a not-for-profit corporation, to seek a property tax exemption for the entire building . . . predicated on its use of the theatre. The sale-and-leaseback would thereby reduce Broadwest's real estate taxes by $30,000 per year, while permitting

FIGURE 2-5
Building involved in *Symphony Space*

Broadwest to retain the rental income from the leased commercial space in the building. . . . Symphony, in turn, would have use of the theatre at minimal cost, once it received a tax exemption.

Thus, on December 1, 1978, Symphony and Broadwest — both sides represented by counsel — executed . . . several documents, each dated December 31, 1978: [These included] a deed for the property from Broadwest to Symphony; a lease from Symphony to Broadwest of the entire building except the theater for rent of $1 per year and for the term January 1, 1979 to May 31, 2003, unless terminated earlier; . . . and an option agreement by which Broadwest obtained from Symphony the exclusive right to repurchase all of the property, including the theatre.

It is the option agreement that is at the heart of the present dispute. Section 3 of that agreement provides that Broadwest may exercise its option to purchase the property during any of the following "Exercise Periods";

> (a) at any time after July 1, 1979, so long as the Notice of Election specified that the Closing is to occur during any of the calendar years 1987, 1993, 1998, and 2003. . . .

Symphony ultimately obtained a tax exemption for the theater. In the summer of 1981, Broadwest sold and assigned its interest under the lease [and] option agreement . . . to defendants' nominee. . . . The nominee contemporaneously transferred its rights under these agreements to [the defendants]. . . .

In March 1985, Symphony initiated this declaratory judgment action against defendants, arguing that the option agreement violated the New York statutory prohibition against remote vesting. In March 1987, [in the course of the litigation], Pergola served Symphony with a notice that it was exercising the option, with the closing scheduled for September 11, 1987. . . . The trial court granted Symphony's motion [for summary judgment]. In particular, the court concluded that the Rule against Perpetuities applied to the commercial option contained in the parties agreement, and that the option violated the Rule. . . . The trial court also dismissed defendants' counterclaim for rescission of the agreements underlying the transaction based on the parties' mutual mistake.

. . . The Appellate Division likewise determined that the commercial option was unenforceable under the Rule against Perpetuities and that recision was inappropriate. . . . We now affirm.

II.   STATUTORY BACKGROUND

The Rule against Perpetuities evolved from judicial efforts during the 17th century to limit control of title to real property by the dead hand of landowners reaching into future generations. Underlying both early and modern rules restricting future dispositions of property is the principle that

Policy for RoP

it is socially undesirable for property to be inalienable for an unreasonable period of time. These rules thus seek "to ensure the productive use and development of property by its current beneficial owners by simplifying ownership, facilitating exchange and freeing property from unknown or embarrassing impediments to alienability." MTA v. Bruken Realty Corp. 67 N.Y.2d 156, 161, *citing* De Peyster v. Michael, 6 N.Y. 467, 494.

New York's current statutory Rule against Perpetuities is found in EPTL 9-1.1. . . .The prohibition against remote vesting is contained in subdivision (b), which states that "[n]o estate in property shall be valid unless it must vest, if at all, not later than twenty-one years after one or more lives in being at the creation of the estate and any period of gestation involved."(EPTL 9-1.1[b]). This Court has described subdivision (b) as "a rigid formula that invalidates any interest that may not vest within the prescribed time period" and has "capricious consequences" (Wildenstein & Co. v. Wallis, 79 N.Y.2d 641, 647-648). Indeed, these rules are predicated upon the public policy of the State and constitute non-waivable, legal prohibitions (see MTA v. Bruken Realty Corp., 67 N.Y.2d at 161). . . .

Against this background, we consider the option agreement at issue.

III.   VALIDITY OF THE OPTION AGREEMENT

Defendants proffer three grounds for upholding the option: that the statutory prohibition against remote vesting does not apply to commercial options; that the option here cannot be exercised beyond the statutory period; and that this Court should adopt the "wait and see" approach to the Rule against Perpetuities. We consider each in turn.

A.   APPLICABILITY OF THE RULE TO COMMERCIAL OPTIONS

Under the common law, options to purchase land are subject to the rule against remote vesting. Such options are specifically enforceable and give the option holder a contingent, equitable interest in the land. This creates a disincentive for the landowner to develop the property and hinders its alienability, thereby defeating the policy objectives underlying the Rule against Perpetuities.

Typically, however, options to purchase are part of a commercial transaction. For this reason, subjecting them to the Rule against Perpetuities has been deemed "a step of doubtful wisdom." As one vocal critic, Professor W. Barton Leach, has explained

> [t]he Rule grew up as a limitation on family dispositions; and the period of lives in being plus twenty-one years is adapted to these gift transactions. The pressures which created the rule do not exist with reference to arms-length contractual transactions, and neither lives in being nor twenty-one years are periods which are relevant to business men and their affairs (Leach, Perpe-

tuities: New Absurdity, Judicial and Statutory Correctives, 73 Harvard L. Rev. 1318, 1321-1322).

Professor Leach, however, went on to acknowledge that, under common law, "due to an overemphasis on concepts derived from the nineteenth century, we are stuck with the application of the Rule to options to purchase," urging that "this should not be extended to other commercial transactions" (id. at 1322 . . .).

It is now settled in New York that, generally, EPTL 9-1.1(b) applies to options. In Buffalo Seminary v. McCarthy (86 A.D.2d 435), the Court held that an unlimited option in gross to purchase real property was void under the statutory rule against remote vesting. . . . In reaching its conclusion in *Buffalo Seminary,* the Court explained that, prior to 1965, New York's narrow statutory rule against remote vesting did not encompass options (86 A.D.2d at 443). A review of the history of the broad provision enacted in 1965, however, established that the Legislature specifically intended to incorporate the American common law rules governing perpetuities into the New York statute (id., at 441-442). . . . Inasmuch as the common law prohibition against remote vesting applies to both commercial and noncommercial options, it likewise follows that the Legislature intended EPTL 9-1.1(b) to apply to commercial purchase options as well.

Consequently, creation of a general exception to EPTL 9-1.1(b) for all purchase options that are commercial in nature, as advocated by defendants, would remove an entire class of contingent future interests that the Legislature intended the statute to cover. While defendants offer compelling policy reasons — echoing those voiced by Professor Leach — for refusing to apply the traditional rule against remote vesting to these commercial option contracts, such statutory reformation would require legislative action similar to that undertaken by numerous other state lawmakers [citing California, Florida, and Illinois statutes]. . . .

Here, the option agreement creates precisely the sort of control over future disposition of the property that we have previously associated with purchase options and that the common law rule against remote vesting — and thus EPTL 9-1.1(b) — seeks to prevent. As the Appellate Division explained, the option grants its holder absolute power to purchase the property at the holder's whim and at a token price set far below market value. This Sword of Damocles necessarily discourages the property owner from investing in improvements to the property. Furthermore, the option's existence significantly impedes the owner's ability to sell the property to a third party, as a practical matter rendering it inalienable. . . .

Generally, an option to purchase land that originates in one of the lease provisions, is not exercisable after the lease expiration, and is incapable of separation from the lease is valid even though the holder's interest may vest beyond the perpetuities period. Such options — known as options "appendant" or "appurtenant" to leases — encourage the pos-

sessory holder to invest in maintaining and developing the property by
guaranteeing the option holder the ultimate benefit of any such investment. Options appurtenant thus further the policy objectives underlying the rule against remote vesting and are not contemplated by EPTL
9-1.1(b)....

To be sure, the option here arose within a larger transaction that included a lease. Nevertheless, not all of the property subject to the purchase
option here is even occupied by defendant. The option encompasses the
entire building — both the commercial space and the theater — yet defendants are leasing only the commercial space. With regard to the theater space, a disincentive exists for Symphony to improve the property, since
it will eventually be claimed by the option holder at the predetermined
purchase price.

B. DURATION OF THE OPTION AGREEMENT

... Where, as here, the parties to a transaction are corporations and
no measuring lives are stated in the instruments, the perpetuities period
is simply 21 years (see MTA v. Bruken Realty Corp., 67 N.Y.2d at 161,
supra).... Even factoring in the requisite notice, then, the option could
potentially be exercised as late as July 2003 — more than 24 years after its
creation in December 1978....

Nor can EPTL 9-1.3 — the "saving statute" — be invoked to shorten
the duration of the exercise period under section 3(a) of the agreement.
That statute mandates that, "[u]nless a contrary intention appears," certain
rules of construction govern with respect to any matter affecting the rule
against perpetuities.... The specified canons of construction include that
"[]t shall be presumed that the creator intended the estate to be valid"...
and "[w]here the duration or vesting of an estate is contingent upon ...
the occurrence of any specified contingency, it shall be presumed that the
creator of such estate intended such contingency to occur, if at all, within
twenty-one years from the effective date of the instrument creating such
estate."...

The unambiguous language of the agreement here expresses the parties' intent that the option be exercisable "at any time" during a 24-year
period pursuant to section 3(a). The section thus does not permit a construction that the parties intended the option to last only 21 years.

Given the contrary intention manifested in the instrument itself, the
saving statute is simply inapplicable....

C. "WAIT AND SEE" APPROACH

Defendants next urge that we adopt the "wait and see" approach to
the Rule against Perpetuities: an interest is valid if it actually vests during
the perpetuities period, irrespective of what might have happened (see

Dukeminier, A Modern Guide to Perpetuities, 74 Calif. L. Rev. 1867, 1880).
The option here would survive under the "wait and see" approach since it
was exercised by 1987, well within the 21 year limitation.

This Court, however, has long refused to "wait and see" whether a
perpetuities violation in fact occurs. As explained in Matter of Fischer (307
N.Y. 149, 157), "[i]t is settled beyond dispute that . . . the courts will look to
what might have happened under the terms of the will rather than to what
has actually happened since the death of the testator" (see also, Matter of
Roe, 281 N.Y. 541, 547-548).

The very language of EPTL 9-1.1, moreover, precludes us from determining the validity of an interest based upon what actually occurs during
the perpetuities period. Under the statutory rule against remote vesting, an
interest is invalid "unless it *must* vest, if at all, not later than twenty-one years
after one or more lives in being" [emphasis added]. . . .

We note that the desirability of the "wait and see" doctrine has been
widely debated (see 5A Powell, Real Property, ¶¶827F[1][3]; see also Waggoner, Perpetuities Reform, 81 Mich. L. Rev. 1718 [describing "wait and
see" as "[t]he most controversial of the reform methods"]). Its incorporation into EPTL 9-1.1, in any event, must be accomplished by the Legislature,
not the courts.

IV.   REMEDY

As a final matter, defendants argue that, if the option fails, the contract of sale conveying the property from Broadwest to Symphony should
be rescinded due to the mutual mistake of the parties. We conclude that
rescission is inappropriate. . . .

A contract entered into under mutual mistake of fact is generally subject to rescission. CPLR 3005 provides that when relief against mistake is
sought, it shall not be denied merely because the mistake is one of law
rather than fact. Relying on this provision, defendants maintain that neither Symphony nor Broadwest realized that the option violated the Rule
against Perpetuities at the time they entered into the agreement and that
both parties intended the option to be enforceable. . . .

Defendants' plea that the unenforceability of the option is contrary to
the intent of the original parties ignores that the effect of the Rule against
Perpetuities — which is a statutory prohibition, not a rule of construction —
is always to defeat the intent of the parties who create a remotely vesting
interest. As explained by the Appellate Division, there is "an irreconcilable
conflict in applying a remedy which is designed to void a transaction because it fails to carry out the parties' true intent to a transaction in which
the mistake made by the parties was the application of the Rule against
Perpetuities, the purpose of which is to defeat the intent of the parties"
(214 A.D.2d 66, 80).

The Rule against Perpetuities reflects the public policy of the State.
Granting the relief requested by defendants would thus be contrary to pub-

lic policy, since it would lead to the same result as enforcing the option and tend to compel performance of contracts violative of the Rule. . . .

Accordingly, the order of the Appellate Divison should be affirmed. . . .

NOTES AND QUESTIONS

1.   **What was at stake?** The opinion indicates that as of August 1988, if defendants had been able to exercise the option (so as to complete an assemblage), the assembled property would be worth $27 million; if defendants could not acquire the parcel subject to the option, their assemblage would be worth only $5.5 million.

2.   **Malpractice?** Reconsider Lucas v. Hamm, *supra,* in the light of the outcome here. Has malpractice occurred? If so, whose? The attorneys for Broadwest? The attorneys for the defendants when they acquired the option? The Court of Appeals?

3.   **Purchase options and preemptive rights compared.** Preemptive rights, or rights of first refusal, require a property owner, when and if she decides to sell, to offer the property first to the person holding the preemptive right, either at a stipulated price, or more commonly, at a price (and on terms) a third-party purchaser would be willing to pay. An earlier Court of Appeals decision had exempted preemptive rights, in the context of governmental and commercial transactions, from the Rule's 21-year limit. MTA v. Bruken Realty Corp, 67 N.Y.2d 156 (1986). In refusing to extend the *Bruken* exemption to commercial purchase options, the court wrote:

> Enforcement of the preemptive right in the context of the governmental and commercial transaction . . . actually encourages the use and development of land . . . by insuring an opportunity to benefit from the improvements and to recapture any investment.

What if the purchase option price is set at appraised value: In that instance, to follow the court's logic, why should it matter whether the optionee has 21 or 25 years in which to exercise the option? What if the preemptive right is fixed at a price below appraised value: Again, why should it matter how long one holds the right? If the court is concerned that a 25-year purchase option, at a fixed price well below market, will chill the owner's readiness to develop the property, how does a 21-year option, presumably valid under the Rule, ease that concern? Shouldn't the court analyze the purchase option by asking whether it is an unreasonable restraint on alienation, *infra?* On that issue, compare Donzella v. New York Telephone Co., 218 A.D.2d 482 (N.Y. App. Div. 3d Dep't. 1996), decided a few months after *Symphony Space,* on very similar facts. The optionee in 1988 sought to exercise a fixed price purchase option exercisable "at any time after the expiration of the ten year original term [in 1970]." The appellate court refused to find either a statutory Rule against Perpetuities violation (the New York rule did not

cover options created prior to 1965) or an unreasonable restraint on alienation ("in view of the commercial motivation for the grant of the purchase
option and the fact that the [optioner] acquired title to the property as
part of the very same financial scheme as brought the option [given to the
lessee] into existence.").

4. **Public policy.** The court invokes "public policy" to explain why it
cannot grant plaintiff the relief it sought, reformation of the underlying
transaction to validate the option. In the arcane realm of the Rule against
Perpetuities, what is the public policy that informs the court's decision:
strict adherence to the common-law rule (which in its inception was not
directed at commercial transactions, and from which the court had already
carved out an exception); faithful adherence to the statute (whose "savings
clause" presumes "that the creator intended the estate to be valid"); pun-
ishing lawyers for sloppy or ignorant deal-making; something else?

5. **Judicial versus legislative reform.** The National Conference of
Commissioners on Uniform State Laws promulgated the Uniform Statutory
Rule against Perpetuities in 1986, and by 1993, 21 states (not including
New York) had enacted it. The Uniform Rule excludes all commercial transactions; id., at §4(1), including options in gross, preemptive rights, leases
to commence in the future, and options appurtenant to leasehold interests.
If a legislature has failed (but has not refused) to act, when a nationwide
tide seems inexorably to be moving in the direction of "reform," must the
highest state court feel unable to join the swim?

§2.4 Restraints on Alienation

The rule against direct restraints on alienation is much older than the
Rule against Perpetuities. Littleton wrote around 1475 that if a feoffment[51]
in fee simple (but not fee tail) were made on condition that the feoffee not
alienate to anyone, the condition would be void as "against reason"; not
so, however, a condition against alienating to a specific person. Littleton,
Tenures §§360-362 at 171-172 (1903). Lord Coke in his commentaries on
Littleton placed the earliest prohibition against such a restraint in the statute Quia Emptores (1290). Coke, Upon Littleton §§206b, 233a (1853).

As land has become fully commodified, the law has had to continue
to address the issue of whether to enforce the intent of grantors who exer-

---

51. Enfeoffment with livery of seisin was the ceremonial transfer of an estate in land
during the early centuries of the common law. The ceremony offers some insight into the
concreteness of the medieval imagination. It required the new tenant to go out to the land at
issue, where he was handed a clod or a twig, symbolizing his ownership of the land. Words
denoting the nature of the grant accompanied the ceremonial transfer.

cise their free choice to partially decommodify the land. The following case illustrates that tension.

MOUNTAIN BROW LODGE NO. 82 v. TOSCANO

257 Cal. App. 2d 22, 64 Cal. Rptr. 816 (1968)

GARGANO, J. This action was instituted by appellant, a non-profit corporation, to quiet its title to a parcel of real property which it acquired on April 6, 1950, by gift deed from James V. Toscano and Maria Toscano, both deceased. Respondents are the trustees and administrators of the estates of the deceased grantors and appellant sought to quiet its title as to their interest in the land arising from certain conditions contained in the gift deed.

The matter was submitted to the court on stipulated facts and the court rendered judgment in favor of respondents. However, it is not clear from the court's findings of fact and conclusions of law whether it determined that the conditions were not void and hence refused to quiet appellant's title for this reason, or whether it decided that appellant had not broken the conditions and then erroneously concluded that "neither party has a right to an anticipatory decree" until a violation occurs. Thus, to avoid prolonged litigation the parties have stipulated that when the trial court rendered judgment refusing to quiet appellant's title it simply decided that the conditions are not void and that its decision on this limited issue is the only question presented in this appeal. We shall limit our discussion accordingly.

The controversy between the parties centers on the language contained in the habendum clause of the deed of conveyance which reads as follows:

> Said property is restricted for the use and benefit of the second party, only; and in the event the same fails to be used by the second party or in the event of sale or transfer by the second party of all or any part of said lot, the same is to revert to the first parties herein, their successors, heirs or assigns.

Respondents maintain that the language creates a fee simple subject to a condition subsequent and is valid and enforceable. On the other hand, appellant contends that the restrictive language amounts to an absolute restraint on its power of alienation and is void. It apparently asserts that, since the purpose for which the land must be used is not precisely defined, it may be used by appellant for any purpose and hence the restriction is not on the land use but on who uses it. Thus, appellant concludes that it is clear that the reversionary clause was intended by grantors to take effect only if appellant sells or transfers the land.

Admittedly, the condition of the habendum clause which prohibits appellant from selling or transferring the land under penalty of forfeiture is an absolute restraint against alienation and is void. The common law rule prohibiting restraint against alienation is embodied in Civil Code section 711 which provides: "Conditions restraining alienation, when repugnant to the interest created, are void." However, this condition and the condition relating to the use of the land are in the disjunctive and are clearly severable. In other words, under the plain language of the deed the grantors, their successors or assigns may exercise their power of termination "if the land is not used by the second party" or "in the event of sale or transfer by second party." Thus, the invalid restraint against alienation does not necessarily affect or nullify the condition on land use (Los Angeles Investment Company v. Gary, 181 Cal. 680, 186 P. 596, 9 A.L.R. 115).

The remaining question, therefore, is whether the use condition created a defeasible fee as respondents maintain or whether it is also a restraint against alienation and nothing more as appellant alleges. Significantly, appellant is a non-profit corporation organized for lodge, fraternal and similar purposes. Moreover, decedent, James V. Toscano, was an active member of the lodge at the time of his death. In addition, the term "use" as applied to real property can be construed to mean a "right which a person has to sue or enjoy the property of another according to his necessities" (Mulford v. LeFranc (1864), 26 Cal. 88, 102). Under these circumstances it is reasonably clear that when the grantors stated that the land was conveyed in consideration of "love and affection" and added that it "is restricted for the *use* and benefit of the second party" they simply meant to say that the land was conveyed upon condition that it would be used for lodge, fraternal and other purposes for which the non-profit corporation was formed. Thus, we conclude that the portion of the habendum clause relating to the land use, when construed as a whole and in light of the surrounding circumstances, created a fee subject to a condition subsequent with title to revert to the grantors, their successors or assigns if the land ceases to be used for lodge, fraternal and similar purposes for which the appellant is formed.[2] No formal language is necessary to create a fee simple subject to a condition subsequent as long as the intent of the grantor is clear. It is the rule that the object in construing a deed is to ascertain the intention of the grantor from words which have been employed and from surrounding circumstances.

It is of course arguable, as appellant suggests, that the condition in appellant's deed is not a restriction on land use but on who uses it. Be this as it may, the distinction between a covenant which restrains the alienation of a fee simple absolute and a condition which restricts land use and creates a defeasible estate was long recognized at common law and is recognized in

---

2. It is arguable that the gift deed created a fee simple determinable. However, in doubtful cases the preferred construction is in favor of an estate subject to a condition subsequent (2 Witkin, Summary Calif. Law., Real Prop. §97, pp. 949-50).

this state.[3] Thus, conditions restricting land use have been upheld by the California courts on numerous occasions even though they hamper, and often completely impede, alienation. A few examples follow: Mitchell v. Cheney Slough Irrigation Co., 57 Cal. App. 2d 138, 134 P.2d 34 (irrigation ditch); Aller v. Berkeley Hall School Foundation, 40 Cal. App. 2d 31, 103 P.2d 1052 (exclusively private dwellings); Rosecrans v. Pacific Electric Railway Co., 21 Cal. 2d 602, 134 P.2d 245 (to maintain a train schedule); Schultz v. Beers, 111 Cal. App. 2d 820, 245 P.2d 334 (road purposes); Firth v. Marovich, 160 Cal. 257, 116 P. 729 (residence only).

Moreover, if appellant's suggestion is carried to its logical conclusion it would mean that real property could not be conveyed to a city to be used only for its own city purposes, or to a school district to be used only for its own school purposes, or to a church to be used only for its own church purposes. Such restrictions would also be restrictions upon who uses the land. And yet we do not understand this to be the rule of this state. For example, in Los Angeles Investment Company v. Gary, *supra*, 181 Cal. 680, 186 P. 596, land had been conveyed upon condition that it was not to be sold, leased, rented or occupied by persons other than those of Caucasian race. The court held that the condition against alienation of the land was void, but upheld the condition restricting the land use. Although a use restriction compelling racial discrimination is no longer consonant with constitutional principles under more recent decisions, the sharp distinction that the court drew between a restriction on land use and a restriction on alienation is still valid. For further example, in the leading and often cited case of Johnston v. City of Los Angeles, 176 Cal. 479, 168 P. 1047, the land was conveyed to the City of Los Angeles on the express condition that the city would use it for the erection and maintenance of a dam, the land to revert if the city ceased to use it for such purposes. The Supreme Court held that the condition created a defeasible estate, apparently even though it was by necessity a restriction on who could use the land. . . .

For the reasons herein stated, the first paragraph of the judgment below is amended and revised to read:

> 1. That at the time of the commencement of this action title to the parcel of real property situated in the City of Los Banos, County of Merced, State of California, being described as:
> Lot 20 Block 72 according to the Map of the Town of Los Banos was vested in the MOUNTAIN BROW LODGE NO. 82, INDEPENDENT ORDER

---

3. The distinction between defeasible estates and future interests that also curtail alienation was recognized at common law. In fact, the creation of future interests, through trusts and similar devises, whose vesting could be indefinitely postponed, resulted in the development of the rule against perpetuities. Significantly, the rule against perpetuities has no application to defeasible estates because reversions, possibilities of reverter and powers of termination are inherently vested in nature (Strong v. Shatto, 45 Cal. App. 29, 187 P. 159; Caffroy v. Fremlin, 198 Cal. App. 2d 176, 17 Cal. Rptr. 668).

OF ODD FELLOWS, subject to the condition that said property is restricted for the use and benefit of the second party only; and in the event the same fails to be used by the second party the same is to revert to the first parties herein, their successors, heirs or assigns.

As so modified the judgment is affirmed. Respondents to recover their costs on appeal.

The petition for rehearing is denied.

CONLEY, J., concurs.

STONE, J. I dissent. I believe the entire habendum clause which purports to restrict the fee simple conveyed is invalid as a restraint upon alienation within the ambit of Civil Code section 711. It reads: "Said property is restricted for the use and benefit of the second party, only; and in the event the same fails to be used by the second party or in the event of sale or transfer by the second party of all or any part of said lot the same is to revert to the first parties herein, their successors, heirs or assigns."

If the words "sale or transfer," which the majority find to be a restraint upon alienation, are expunged, still the property cannot be sold or transferred by the grantee because the property may be used by only the I.O.O.F. Lodge No. 82, upon pain of reverter. This use restriction prevents the grantee from conveying the property just as effectively as the condition against "sale or transfer . . . of all or any part of said lot." (Los Angeles Investment Co. v. Gary, 181 Cal. 680, 682, 186 P. 596; Property Restatement, §404 et seq.; 2 Witkin, Summary of Cal. Law, Real Property, p. 1004; Simes, Perpetuities in California since 1951; 18 Hastings L.J., p. 248.)

Certainly, if we are to have realism in the law, the effect of language must be judged according to what it does. When two different terms generate the same ultimate legal result, they should be treated alike in relation to that result.

Section 711 of the Civil Code expresses an ancient policy of English common law.* The wisdom of this proscription as applied to situations of

---

* The conceptual argument is that the law defines the exact nature of every estate in land, that each has certain incidents which are provided by law, and that one of the principal incidents of a fee is alienability. Manning, The Development of Restraints on Alienation Since Gray, 48 Harv. L. Rev. 373 (1935).

The first of the two reasons most often given for holding restraints void is that a restraint is repugnant to the nature of the fee. Murray v. Green, 64 Cal. 363, 28 P. 118 (1883); Eastman Marble Co. v. Vermont Marble Co., 236 Mass. 138, 128 N.E. 177 (1920); Andrews v. Hall, 156 Neb. 817, 58 N.W.2d 201 [42 A.L.R.2d 1239] (1963); 5 Tiffany, Real Property §1343 (3d ed. 1939); Manning, supra, at 401. However, Lord Coke believed that restraints were void, not only because they were repugnant to the fee, but because "it is absurd and repugnant to reason" that a tenant in fee simple should be restrained "of all his power to alien." Co. Litt. 223a.

The second and more practically oriented reason for holding restraints void is that a restraint, by taking land out of the flow of commerce, is detrimental to the economy. Gray, Restraints on Alienation §21 (2d ed. 1895); 6 Powell, Real Property 1 (1958); 5 Tiffany, op. cit. supra, §1343. Other reasons have been accepted on occasion by courts: to encourage improve-

this kind is manifest when we note that a number of fraternal, political and similar organizations of a century ago have disappeared, and others have ceased to function in individual communities. Should an organization holding property under a deed similar to the one before us be disbanded one hundred years or so after the conveyance is made, the result may well be a title fragmented into the interests of heirs of the grantors numbering in the hundreds and scattered to the four corners of the earth.

The majority opinion cites a number of cases holding use restrictions in deeds to be valid, but these restrictions impose limitations upon the manner in which the property may be used. The majority equates these cases with the restriction in the instant case to use *by* only Lodge No. 82. It seems to me that a restriction upon the use that may be made of land must be distinguished from a restriction upon *who* may use it. In the first place, a restriction upon the kind of use does not restrain alienation because the property may be conveyed to *anyone*, subject to the restriction. Moreover, as Professor Simes points out in his article, "Restricting Land Use in California by Rights of Entry and Possibility of Reverter," 13 Hastings Law Journal No. 3, page 293, where changed circumstances are shown a court of equity will free land from a property use restriction.

There is a judicially-created exception to public policy against restraint of alienation embodied in Civil Code section 711 which is broadly defined as "restraint on alienation when reasonable as to purpose." (Coast Bank v. Minderhout, . . . 61 Cal. 2d 311, 38 Cal. Rptr. 505, 392 P.2d 265.) In discussing this subject, a comment in 12 U.C.L.A. Law Review No. 3, says, in part, at pages 955-958:

> The alienability of realty has long been a jealously guarded incident of a fee simple estate. All jurisdictions invalidate absolute restraints on alienation, and *an overwhelming majority void restraints partial as to persons and temporary as to time.* California has codified the common law rule of restraints on alienation in Civil Code section 711. This provision not only voids restraints created by the grantor of an estate in a deed or conveyance but has been judicially interpreted to void restraints created by covenants executed separately from a deed. In mitigation of the harshness stemming from the rule invalidating restraints, both case law and statutory exceptions have been promulgated in most jurisdictions. In California, a restraint on the transfer of shares in a corporation has been upheld, as have the restraints created by the spendthrift thrust, a lease for a term of years, and a restraint on the alienability of a life

---

ment of property; hampering effective use of property if the buyer could put it to better use than the seller; removal from trade of increasing amounts of capital; not allowing an individual to appear more prosperous than he is, i.e., a borrower may appear to own property outright, thus able to sell it in payment of a debt, where in reality the property is restrained; balance of dead hand control, i.e., recognizing the right of the individual to control property after death, by the proposition that life is for the living and should be controlled by the living and not by the extended hand of the dead. Bernhard, The Minority Doctrine Concerning Direct Restraints on Alienation, 57 Mich. L. Rev. 1173, 1177 (1959). (12 U.C.L.A. Law Rev. No. 3, fn. p. 956.)

estate. The decision in *Minderhout* distinguished California as the first state not to invalidate a restraint on alienation when reasonable as to purpose. (Emphasis added.)

As I view the restraint in the instant case, it accomplishes no reasonable purpose within the rationale of Coast Bank v. Minderhout, *supra,* that would justify the indefinite suspension of alienation. . . .

NOTES AND QUESTIONS

1. **Alienation restraints and the liberal vision.** In your view, does the Rule against Restraints on Alienation further the liberal vision by letting 1,000 deals bloom, or does it do just the opposite, by limiting free choice as to the alienation of land? Why should (or shouldn't) a donor be able to attach strings to a gift of land, whether as to mode of use, identity of the user, or identity of the owner?

2. **Categories of restraint.** Restraints on alienation fall into three classes: disabling restraints, forfeiture restraints, and promissory restraints. Examples of each follow.

   (a)   O to A in fee simple absolute. A may not transfer without O's consent. (disabling restraint)
   (b)   O to A, provided, however that O shall have the power to terminate if A should transfer without O's consent. (forfeiture restraint)
   (c)   O to A in fee simple absolute. A convenants not to transfer without O's consent. (promissory restraint)

Looking at these several restraints abstractly, can you think of any reason for one to be more (or less) valid than another?

3. **Direct versus indirect restraints.** Compare the following grants.

   (a)   O to A so long as A owns and operates the property.
   (b)   O to A so long as A uses the property for a church.
   (c)   O to A so long as the property is used for a church.

Restraint (a) is direct, since it would result in the forfeiture of the property to O if A were to transfer it. A cannot sell the property to anyone else, nor — because A is required to operate the property — can A lease the property to anyone else.

Restraints (b) and (c) are indirect, since neither directly bars or penalizes an attempted transfer of the property. But in both cases, the restraint does narrow the universe of potential transferees because of the use restrictions. The Restatement (Second) of Property: Donative Transfers §3.4 (1981), has refused to treat generalized use restrictions (Example (c)) as restraints on alienation. "A restraint on the use that may be made of transferred property by the transferee is not a restraint on alienation, as that term is used in this Restatement."

4. **"Conditions repugnant to the interest created."** All the *Toscano* judges agreed that the prohibition against sale or transfer violated Civil Code §711: "Conditions restraining alienation, *when repugnant to the interest created,* are void." Stop and think about this, however. Is the prohibition invalid because it is "repugnant," or is the prohibition repugnant because it is invalid? Do you see the circularity that the judges seem to be blind to? Haven't they all assumed a legal conclusion without giving any reasons?

In this connection, does it (should it) make any difference whether the restraint appears in a fee simple absolute or in a defeasible estate? Is it at all persuasive that the fee simple absolute has potentially infinite duration, which implies broad, limitless powers of alienation, whereas a defeasible estate by its very nature can be cut short if the holder takes some disfavored action, and that alienation may well be the proscribed action? Or are we simply distinguishing between a disabling restraint and a forfeiture restraint (Note 2, *supra*)?

And looking ahead to the landlord-tenant estates, what do you think of a lease that bars the tenant, upon pain of forfeiture, from assigning his interest without landlord's consent? See §3.12, *infra*.

5. **The rule of reason.** The dissenting justice writes of restraints on alienation that are "reasonable as to purpose" and indicates that such restraints are valid, a judicially created exception, he states, to the public policy against restraints on alienation. In this instance, the exception has now overtaken the principle. Except for disabling restraints that would bar any transfer of the property, whether forever or for a shorter, fixed term, the Restatement (Second) of Property. Donative Transfers §4.2(3) has adopted the rule of reason as its test for deciding when a restraint is enforceable. What factors would you stress in weighing the reasonableness of a restraint: Its duration? Whether the transfer was for value? The continuing relationship, if any, between grantor and grantee? The purpose for which the restraint is sought? Any others?

6. **Restraints on personalty.** Restraint on the alienation of non-real estate assets must also be reasonable. Consider whether you believe courts should enforce the restraints on each of the following gifts:

  (a) O to my son S (O's wedding band), which he is not to sell or give away until his engagement.
  (b) O to my son S (O's wedding band), but if S marries X, whom I detest, then to my daughter D.
  (c) O to my son S (a Picasso painting), but if S marries outside his faith, then to the Museum of Modern Art.

Note that restraints (b) and (c) are indirect, since no direct restriction has been placed upon S's power to alienate the property, nor does alienation itself create a forfeiture or contract breach. But during S's lifetime, the marriage restrictions would either narrow the universe of potential buyers or reduce the price buyers would agree to pay for the property (unless the buyer received an indemnity against S's conduct).

§2.5   More on Life Estates

a.   Uses of Life Estates

As we have seen, the earliest conveyances of land in the common-law system created a life estate — one ending with the death of the transferee. Somewhat later, the fee tail, which created a life estate in the tenant in tail, became the instrument for limiting the present holder's autonomy over land. After the demise of the feudal system, life estates were often associated with women: The life estate enabled grantors to provide ongoing support without giving women full control over economic assets. This regime was attractive both for general cultural reasons — women were not thought to have the acumen to manage or devise property — and because of women's position at common law. Until the nineteenth (and in some contexts until the twentieth) century, the law ensured married women's dependence on their husbands[52] by providing that they lost control over their property when they married, see §4.2b *infra*. Thus in eighteenth- and nineteenth-century novels, we often encounter husbands who manipulate the laws of coverture to amass property. See, e.g., Emily Brontë, Wuthering Heights (1847) (Cathy Linton's father realized when Heathcliff forced her to marry Heathcliff's son, Linton, that "one of his enemy's purposes was to secure the personal property, as well as the estate, to his son, or rather to himself," and wanted to prevent it through the mechanism of a legal trust, following the practice of contemporary fathers who disapproved a daughter's marital choice. "[H]e felt that his will had better be altered: instead of leaving Catherine's fortune at her own disposal, he determined to put it into the hands of trustees, for her use during life; and for her children, if she had any, after her. By that means, it could not fall to Mr. Heathcliff should Linton die.").

Another major instance of the life estate were the common law spou-

---

52. This was the default rule that governed the property of most women. A few wealthy families protected property from their daughters' husbands through the legal mechanism of the "separate estate," an arrangement that most often gave legal control of the property not to the wife herself but to one of her male kin. On the right of women to devise property from a separate estate, see Lewis v. Hudson, 6 Ala. 463 (1844); Lamb v. Wragg, 8 Port. 73 (Ala. 1838); Jaques v. Methodist Episcopal Church, 17 Johns. 548 (N.Y. 1820). For an opposing rule, see Tarr v. Williams, 4 Md. 68 (1853). Generally, on separate estates, see Marylynn Salmon, Women and the Law of Property in Early America, chs. 5, 6 (1986).

sal interests. At the birth of live issue,[53] *curtesy* expanded the husband's interest in his wife's inheritable, freehold[54] lands. The husband would then
gain a life estate for his life which continued his control over his wife's property should she predecease him.[55] *Dower* was the married woman's counterpart. A widow was entitled, as a matter of law, to a life estate in *one-third* of
the inheritable, freehold lands of which her husband was seized during the
marriage. At the husband's death, the courts would decide which lands
should be set aside to meet the one-third requirement. In most states, curtesy and dower have little remaining importance. For a fuller discussion, see
§4.2.a, *infra*.

Today, the life estate serves a major role in estate planning — that is,
the donative transmission of wealth from one generation to the next. Thus,
a husband or wife may want at death to create a life estate in the surviving
spouse with a remainder over to third parties. Although the testator in this
case could devise the real estate directly to the survivor for his or her life
(a so-called *legal* life estate), this would seldom prove wise. The recipient
would be locked into the property in the sense that she could not sell a fee
simple absolute, or enter into a long-term lease, or obtain a mortgage.

To allow flexibility, most donors in this situation now use a trust, giving
the trustee "legal" title to the trust assets, in fee simple absolute, and creating an *equitable* life estate in the beneficiary. The trustee would (usually)
pay to the trust beneficiary the income generated by the trust assets, but the
trustee, having the power of sale, lease, or mortgage, could make investment and reinvestment decisions that best serve the interests of the beneficiary and the aims of the settlor. Thus, if the trustee thought it prudent to
exchange one parcel for a second, the trustee could readily do so. When
the trust terminates, for example, at the death of the income beneficiary,
the trust assets would then be distributed as the settlor has directed. The
trustee has fiduciary obligation to act in the best interests of the beneficiary
and can be sued for failure to fulfill these obligations.

b.   Life Estate pur Autre Vie

Suppose that a life tenant, A, before his death conveys his entire interest to B. What estate does B get? Since A cannot convey an estate greater
than his own, B's estate ends at A's death. Until then, B does enjoy a life

---

53. An infant's survival was often touch and go in an era of high infant mortality. Accordingly, the criteria for a live birth were in keeping with the hazards of childbirth. The
mother need not survive the child; and as for the child, it was enough for its heartbeat to have
been felt, or its cry to have been heard.

54. "Freehold" estates are those estates which at early common law were held by "free"
men — i.e., the various fee simples, fee tails, and life estates we have already considered. "Nonfreehold" estates were those held by villeins or serfs, the feudal ancestors of the modern leasehold estate.

55. A wife's predecease, given the hazards of childbirth, was not so uncommon as it
would be today.

estate, but the measuring life is one other than his own, thus, a *life estate pur autre vie* (the Gallic influence). It is as if the grantor, O, had created an estate "to B, for the life of A."

The life estate pur autre vie must be further analyzed when the life tenant dies before the end of the measuring life. In the example "O to B, for the life of A," what becomes of the land at B's death, if A is still alive? The grantor might have anticipated this event by designating a successor on B's predecease; also, if the grantor had not acted, B might himself have named a taker, either by inter vivos transfer, or by will. The designee would be known as the "special occupant."

But, suppose both have failed to name a special occupant. O is not entitled to regain the land quite yet, for he has deferred his right to possession until the death of A. Nor would the early common law let the land descend to B's heirs, for it regarded the life estate as noninheritable. To close this hiatus, the law simply allowed the first occupant — called a "general occupant" — to enjoy the remaining term. This crude device lasted until 1677 when it was abolished by statute (29 Car. 2, ch. 3, §12). Today, if a special occupant is not named, the remaining life term passes by intestacy to the tenant's heirs.

c.   Relationship between the Life Tenant and the Future Interest Holder

One troublesome aspect of the division of property into present and future estates is the potential conflict between those in possession and those awaiting possession who want the asset to reach them undiminished in value. This conflict can arise in several ways. For example, the municipality levies a special tax assessment for permanent improvements to the real estate. Who bears the cost: the life tenant or the remainderperson?[56] The following materials illustrate two other, recurring, sources of conflict.

1.   Waste

BROKAW v. FAIRCHILD

237 N.Y.S. 6 (Sup. Ct. 1929), aff'd, 245 N.Y.S. 402 (App. Div. 1930), aff'd, 177 N.E. 186 (N.Y. 1931)

HAMMER J. . . . In the year 1886 the late Isaac V. Brokaw bought for $199,000 a plot of ground in the borough of Manhattan, city of New York,

---

56. Cf. Robin C. Miller, Annotation, Duty as Between Life Tenant and Remainderman with Respect to Cost of Improvements or Repairs Made under Compulsion of Governmental Authority, 43 A.L.R.4th 1012 (1995); compare Gaugh v. Gatewood, 380 S.W.2d 84 (Ky. 1964) (apportionment), with Hamilton v. Kinnebrew, 161 Ga. 495, 131 S.E. 470 (1926) (life tenant), and Morrow v. Person, 195 Tenn. 370, 259 S.W.2d 665 (1953) (remainderman). How would you devise a formula for apportionment?

opposite Central Park, having a frontage of 102 feet 2 inches on the easterly side of Fifth avenue and a depth of 150 feet on the northerly side of Seventy-ninth street. Opposite there is an entrance to the park and Seventy-ninth street is a wide crosstown street running through the park. Upon the corner portion, a plot of ground 51 feet 2 inches on Fifth avenue and a depth of 110 feet on Seventy-fifth street, Mr. Brokaw erected in the year 1887, for his own occupancy, a residence known as No. 1 East Seventy-ninth street, at a cost of $300,000. That residence and corner plot is the subject-matter of this action. The residence, a three-story, mansard and basement granite front building, occupies the entire width of the lot. The mansard roof is of tile. On the first floor are two large drawing rooms on the Fifth avenue side and there are also a large hallway running through from south to north, a reception room, dining room and pantry. The dining room is paneled with carved wood. The hallway is in Italian marble and mosaic. There are murals and ceiling panels. There is a small elevator to the upper portion of the house. On the second floor are a large library, a large bedroom with bath on the Fifth avenue side and there are also four other bedrooms and baths. The third floor has bedrooms and baths. The fourth floor has servants' quarters, bath and storage rooms. The building has steam heat installed by the plaintiff, electric light and current, hardwood floors and all usual conveniences. It is an exceedingly fine house, in construction and general condition as fine as anything in New York. It is contended by plaintiff that the decorations are heavy, not of a type now required by similar residences, and did not appeal to the people to whom it was endeavored to rent the building.

Since 1913, the year of the death of Isaac V. Brokaw and the commencement of the life estate of plaintiff, there has been a change of circumstances and conditions in connection with Fifth avenue properties. Apartments were erected with great rapidity and the building of private residences has practically ceased. Forty-four apartments and only two private residences have been erected on Fifth avenue from Fifty-ninth street to One Hundred and Tenth street. There are to-day but eight of these fifty-one blocks devoted exclusively to private residences. (Exhibits 11 and 12.) Plaintiff's expert testified:

> It is not possible to get an adequate return on the value of that land by any type of improvement other than an apartment house. The structure proposed in the plans of plaintiff is proper and suitable for the site and show 172 rooms which would rent for $1,000 per room. There is an excellent demand for such apartments. . . . There is no corner in the City of New York as fine for an apartment house as that particular corner.

The plaintiff testified also that his expenses in operating the residence which is unproductive would be at least $70,542 greater than if he resided in an apartment. He claims such difference constitutes a loss and contends that the erected apartment house would change this loss into an income or profit of $30,000. Plaintiff claims that under the facts and changed conditions shown the demolition of the building and erection of the proposed apartment is for the best interests of himself as life tenant, the inheritance, and the remaindermen. The defendants deny these contentions and assert certain affirmative defenses. (1) That the proposed demolition of the residence is waste, which against the objection of the adult defendant remaindermen plaintiff cannot be permitted to accomplish. . . .

Coming, therefore, to plaintiff's claimed right to demolish the present residence and to erect in its place the proposed apartment, I am of the opinion that such demolition would result in such an injury to the inheritance as under the authorities would constitute waste. The life estate given to plaintiff under the terms of the will and codicil is not merely in the corner plot of ground with improvements thereon, but, without question, in the residence of the testator. Four times in the devising clause the testator used the words "my residence." This emphasis makes misunderstanding impossible. The identical building which was erected and occupied by the testator in his lifetime and the plot of ground upon which it was built constitute that residence. By no stretch of the imagination could "my residence" be in existence at the end of the life tenancy were the present building demolished and any other structure, even the proposed thirteen-story apartment, erected on the site.

It has been generally recognized that any act of the life tenant which does permanent injury to the inheritance is waste. The law intends that the life tenant shall enjoy his estate in such a reasonable manner that the land shall pass to the reversioner or remainderman as nearly as practicable unimpaired in its nature, character and improvements. The general rule in this country is that the life tenant may do whatever is required for the general use and enjoyment of his estate as he received it. The use of the estate he received is contemplated and not the exercise of an act of dominion or ownership. What the life tenant may do in the future in the way of improving or adding value to the estate is not the test of what constitutes waste. The act of the tenant in changing the estate, and whether or not such act is lawful or unlawful, i.e., whether the estate is so changed as to be an injury to the inheritance, is the sole question involved. The tenant has no right to exercise an act of ownership. In the instant case the inheritance was the residence of the testator — "my residence" — consisting of the present building on a plot of ground fifty-one feet two inches on Fifth avenue by one hundred and ten feet on Seventy-ninth street. "My residence" — such is what the plaintiff under the testator's will has the use of for life. He is entitled to use the building and plot reasonably for his own convenience or profit. To demolish that building and erect upon the land another building, even one such as the contemplated thirteen-story apartment house, would be the exercise of an act of ownership and dominion. It would change the inheritance or thing, the use of which was given to the plaintiff as tenant for life, so that the inheritance or thing could not be delivered to the remaindermen or reversioners at the end of the life estate. The receipt by them at the end of the life estate of a thirteen-story $900,000 apartment

FIGURE 2-6
Brokaw mansion

house might be more beneficial to them. Financially, the objecting adults may be unwise in not consenting to the proposed change. They may be selfish and unmindful that in the normal course of time and events they probably will not receive the fee. With motives and purposes the court is not concerned. . . .

[U]pon the present facts, circumstances and conditions as they exist and are shown in this case, regardless of the proposed security and the expressed purpose of erecting the proposed thirteen-story apartment, or any other structure, the plaintiff has no right and is not authorized to remove the present structures on or affecting the real estate in question. . . .

ENNIS, LANDMARK MANSION ON 79TH ST. TO BE RAZED

N.Y. Times, Sept. 17, 1964, at 1, cols. 2-5

A chateau at Fifth Avenue and 79th Street that had been designated by the city as a landmark is to be torn down along with two other mansions adjoining it to make way for a new commercial building. The City's Land-

FIGURE 2-7
Building that replaced Brokaw mansion

marks Preservation Commission said it would protest the move although it lacks the legal power to stop it.

The houses are on the property on the northeast corner of Fifth Avenue and 79th Street, at 984 Fifth Avenue, 1 East 79th Street, and 7 East 79th Street. The chateau-like structure at 1 East 79th Street, known as the

Brokaw mansion, has been designated by the Landmarks Commission as worthy of preservation.

James Grote Van Derpool, the Commission's executive director, when he was told of the plan yesterday, deplored it as "the threatened loss of still another example of New York in the Age of Elegance precisely at a time when new interest and understanding of that period is so strongly present."

"Architecture throws light on history," Mr. Van Derpool said, and added that "we need such structures in order to understand in a meaningful way how people lived at a time so very different from our own." . . .

The Fifth Avenue houses are under contract of sale to Anthony Campagna and his son John, builders of many apartment houses here. John Campagna said yesterday that he and his father planned a new building, but would give no further details.[57] The corner site, one of the city's choicest, consists of about 12,500 square feet of land, whose value is estimated at $2.5 million.

The property is being sold by the Institute of Electrical and Electronics Engineers through the Cross & Brown Company, real estate brokers. The institute has occupied the three houses for a number of years, and will move to the United Engineering Center, 345 East 47th Street at the United Nations Plaza, when the buyers take title to the Fifth Avenue property, probably next spring.

No expense was spared in constructing the palatial houses, and architects provided every conceivable luxury available at the time. The house at 1 East 79th Street, which was built for Isaac Vail Brokaw from 1887 to 1890, has huge, airy and well-lighted rooms.

Its grandiose entrance hall is of Italian marble and mosaic and huge murals line the walls. The ceilings are paneled in stone and wood and no two of them are alike. The library has a seven-foot-tall safe concealed behind a panel opened by pressing a hidden catch in a molding.

Mr. Brokaw, realty operator and head of Brokaw Brothers, men's clothing manufacturers, died in 1913. His youngest of three sons, George, occupied the mansion at the time of his marriage in 1923 to Clare Boothe, now Mrs. Henry Luce. Mrs. Luce, who divorced Mr. Brokaw in 1929, inherited a half interest in the house from her daughter, Ann Clare Brokaw, who was killed in an automobile accident. Mrs. Luce, who reportedly disliked the house, sold her share to Mr. Luce.

George Brokaw lived in the mansion until shortly before his death in 1935. He was said to have never liked the house because of its size and cost of its upkeep.

In 1926 he filed suit in the Supreme Court for permission to raze the mansion and erect an apartment house. He asked that his brothers Irving

---

57. The Brokaw site now has a new multistory stock cooperative, said to contain some of Manhattan's most expensive apartments. — EDS.

and Howard, who occupied adjoining houses and who opposed the demolition plans, be enjoined from interfering with the proposal for the new building.

George Brokaw won his suit and in November, 1926, filed plans for a 13-story building. However, the Supreme Court, on appeal, reversed its decision and the building plans were dropped.

He sued again in 1928 for permission to raze the mansion, but lost that suit on the ground that Isaac Brokaw's will would be violated. . . .

NOTES AND QUESTIONS

1. **Statutory aftermath.** Criticism of the decision appears in Irving I. Plotkin, Notes and Comment, 15 Cornell L.Q. 501 (1930); Recent Cases, 43 Harv. L. Rev. 490, 506 (1930); Recent Decisions, 7 N.Y.U. L. Rev. 750, 761 (1930); Comments, 30 Mich. L. Rev. 784 (1932).

Before the advent of recording acts and the use of metes and bounds description, property was described by its physical appearance with heavy reliance on natural landmarks. Thus, the ancient doctrine of waste was based not only on the reversioner's or remainderman's right to receive the property as it was conveyed to the tenant, but also on the quite understandable fear that if the property were significantly altered, even though improved, proof of title would be more difficult. What policies, if any, remain for putting some check on a life tenant's plans to improve (meliorate) the premises?

Following the *Brokaw* decision, the New York Legislature enacted a law "which release[d] whatever hold the English medieval law had on the New York law of waste." Recent Statute, 38 Colum. L. Rev. 532, 533 (1938). The New York law, N.Y. Real Prop. Acts. Law §803 (McKinney 1979), allows a tenant with an expectancy or unexpired term of at least five years to alter the premises without liability for waste if he fulfills the statutory conditions. Before looking, what conditions would you expect to find? Is it clear that the statute would have changed the *Brokaw* decisions?

2. **"Punishment for waste."** The English antecedents to the law of waste begin no later than the thirteenth century. The Statute of Marlborough, 52 Hen. 3, ch. 23 (1267), subjected life tenants and tenants for a term of years who "make waste" to the payment of full damages. The Statute of Gloucester, 6 Edw., ch. 5 (1278), upped the penalty to treble damages and forfeiture of the thing wasted.

"Punishment" for waste, although ended in Britain in the nineteenth century, has survived in many American states. A 1968 treatise lists 22 states and the District of Columbia as still having statutes permitting the recovery of multiple damages. Nearly as many states permit forfeiture. Richard R. Powell and Patrick J. Rohan, Powell on Real Property 698-699 (abr. ed. 1968).

Is there any present-day need to treat wasters more harshly than we treat most persons who break contracts?

3.   **Forms of waste.** The *Brokaw* case is an atypical waste dispute, in that the life tenant there was seeking to improve the premises. Allegations of waste are usually heard when the party in possession is stripping the land of its resources — for example, timber or minerals — or is failing to maintain the premises as the future interest holder would like.

Professors Powell and Rohan list five forms of waste (id. at 684).

1.   voluntary acts of commission that are *ameliorative* in effect (the *Brokaw* case)
2.   voluntary acts of commission that are destructive in effect (*active waste*)
3.   voluntary inactions that are injurious in effect (*permissive* waste)
4.   failures to prevent conduct of an outsider that is injurious in effect
5.   equitable waste

The authors criticize courts for allowing waste recoveries of the fourth type, where the holder of the future interest can sue the wrongdoing third party directly. Id. at 689; accord, Restatement of Property, Freehold Estates, §146 (1936).

So-called equitable waste traces its roots deep into sixteenth-century chancery. Before then, present-interest holders sometimes obtained their interests "without impeachment for waste," which the law courts saw as giving total freedom to the party in possession. At the plea of the future-interest holder, chancery stepped in to prevent willful and unconscionable plunder of the property. There has evolved, where someone holds "without impeachment for waste," a duty which chancery will enforce "[not] to strip the future interest owner of his asset with impunity." Powell, *supra,* at 689-690.

4.   **"Good husbandry" test.** In resolving waste disputes, American courts generally apply the "good husbandry" or "prudent owner" test. For a discussion of the underlying rationale and the difficulties in application, see 5 American Law of Property 75-93 (A. James Casner ed., 1952).

5.   **Mortgagor waste.** Mortgages create a security interest in real (or personal ("chattel") property that allows the lender (mortgagee) to satisfy its claim from the mortgaged property in the event of a default. Mortgages typically contain the borrower's (mortgagor's) covenant not to commit waste, upon pain of default. Might the criteria for waste depend on whether it is a mortgagee or some future interest holder who has complained? Consider, for example, whether a mortgagee holding a $10,000 mortgage may enjoin timber-cutting that would reduce the value of the mortgaged property from $50,000 to $25,000. Cf. Cal. Civ. Code §2929 (West 1993). May a remainderman?

2.   More Now or More Later?

BAKER v. WEEDON

262 So. 2d 641 (Miss. 1972)

Patterson, J. This is an appeal from a decree of the Chancery Court of Alcorn County. It directs a sale of land affected by a life estate and future interests with provision for the investment of the proceeds. The interest therefrom is to be paid to the life tenant for her maintenance. We reverse and remand.

John Harrison Weedon was born in High Point, North Carolina. He lived throughout the South and was married twice prior to establishing his final residence in Alcorn County. His first marriage to Lula Edwards resulted in two siblings, Mrs. Florence Weedon Baker and Mrs. Delette Weedon Jones. Mrs. Baker was the mother of her children, Henry Baker, Sarah Baker Lyman and Louise Virginia Baker Heck, the appellants herein. Mrs. Delette Weedon Jones adopted a daughter, Dorothy Jean Jones, who has not been heard from for a number of years and whose whereabouts are presently unknown.

John Weedon was next married to Ella Howell and to this union there was born one child, Rachel. Both Ella and Rachel are now deceased.

Subsequent to these marriages John Weedon bought Oakland Farm in 1905 and engaged himself in its operation. In 1915 John, who was then 55 years of age, married Anna Plaxco, 17 years of age. This marriage, though resulting no children, was a compatible relationship. John and Anna worked side by side in farming this 152.95-acre tract of land in Alcorn County. There can be no doubt that Anna's contribution to the development and existence of Oakland Farm was significant. The record discloses that during the monetarily difficult years following World War I she hoed, picked cotton and milked an average of fifteen cows per day to protect the farm from financial ruin.

While the relationship of John and Anna was close and amiable, that between John and his daughters of his first marriage was distant and strained. He had no contact with Florence, who was reared by Mr. Weedon's sister in North Carolina, during the seventeen years preceding his death. An even more unfortunate relationship existed between John and his second daughter, Delette Weedon Jones. She is portrayed by the record as being a nomadic person who only contacted her father for money, threatening on several occasions to bring suit against him.

With an obvious intent to exclude his daughters and provide for his wife Anna, John executed his last will and testament in 1925. It provided in part:

> Second; I give and bequeath to my beloved wife, Anna Plaxco Weedon
> all of my property both real, personal and mixed during her natural life and

upon her death to her children, if she has any, and in the event she dies without issue then at the death of my wife Anna Plaxco Weedon I give, bequeath and devise all of my property to my grandchildren, each grandchild sharing equally with the other.

Third; In this will I have not provided for my daughters, Mrs. Florence Baker and Mrs. Delette Weedon Jones, the reason is, I have given them their share of my property and they have not looked after and cared for me in the latter part of my life.

Subsequent to John Weedon's death in 1932 and the probate of his will, Anna continued to live on Oakland Farm. In 1933 Anna, who had been urged by John to remarry in the event of his death, wed J. E. Myers. This union lasted some twenty years and produced no offspring which might terminate the contingent remainder vested in Weedon's grandchildren by the will.

There was no contact between Anna and John Weedon's children or grandchildren from 1932 until 1964. Anna ceased to operate the farm in 1955 due to her age and it has been rented since that time. Anna's only income is $1000 annually from the farm rental, $300 per year from sign rental and $50 per month by way of social security payments. Without contradiction Anna's income is presently insufficient and places a severe burden upon her ability to live comfortably in view of her age and the infirmities therefrom.

In 1964 the growth of the city of Corinth was approaching Oakland Farm. A right-of-way through the property was sought by the Mississippi State Highway Department for the construction of U.S. Highway 45 bypass. The highway department located Florence Baker's three children, the contingent remaindermen by the will of John Weedon, to negotiate with them for the purchase of the right-of-way. Dorothy Jean Jones, the adopted daughter of Delette Weedon Jones, was not located and due to the long passage of years, is presumably dead. A decree pro confesso was entered against her.

Until the notice afforded by the highway department the grandchildren were unaware of their possible inheritance. Henry Baker, a native of New Jersey, journeyed to Mississippi to supervise their interests. He appears, as was true of the other grandchildren, to have been totally sympathetic to the conditions surrounding Anna's existence as a life tenant. A settlement of $20,000 was completed for the right-of-way bypass of which Anna received $7500 with which to construct a new home. It is significant that all legal and administrative fees were deducted from the shares of the three grandchildren and not taxed to the life tenant. A contract was executed in 1970 for the sale of soil from the property for $2500. Anna received $1000 of this sum which went toward completion of payments for the home.

There was substantial evidence introduced to indicate the value of the property is appreciating significantly with the nearing completion of U.S. Highway 45 bypass plus the growth of the city of Corinth. While the commercial value of the property is appreciating, it is notable that the rental value for agricultural purposes is not. It is apparent that the land can bring no more for agricultural rental purposes than the $1000 per year now received.

The value of the property for commercial purposes at the time of trial was $168,500. Its estimated value within the ensuing four years is placed at $336,000, reflecting the great influence of the interstate construction upon the land. Mr. Baker, for himself and other remaindermen, appears to have made numerous honest and sincere efforts to sell the property at a favorable price. However, his endeavors have been hindered by the slowness of the construction of the bypass.

Anna, the life tenant and appellee here, is 73 years of age and although now living in a new home, has brought this suit due to her economic distress. She prays that the property, less the house site, be sold by a commissioner and that the proceeds be invested to provide her with an adequate income resulting from interest on the trust investment. She prays also that the sale and investment management be under the direction of the chancery court.

The chancellor granted the relief prayed by Anna under the theory of economic waste. His opinion reflects:

> . . . [T]he change of the economy in this area, the change in farming conditions, the equipment required for farming, and the age of this complainant leaves the real estate where it is to all intents and purposes unproductive when viewed in light of its capacity and that a continuing use under the present conditions would result in economic waste.

The contingent remaindermen by the will, appellants here, were granted an interlocutory appeal to settle the issue of the propriety of the chancellor's decree in divesting the contingency title of the remaindermen by ordering a sale of the property.

The weight of authority reflects a tendency to afford a court of equity the power to order the sale of land in which there are future interests. Simes, Law of Future Interest, section 53 (2d ed. 1966), states:

> By the weight of authority, it is held that a court of equity has the power to order a judicial sale of land affected with a future interest and an investment of the proceeds, where this is necessary for the preservation of all interests in the land. When the power is exercised, the proceeds of the sale are held in a judicially created trust. The beneficiaries of the trust are the persons who held interests in the land, and the beneficial interests are of the same character as the legal interests which they formally held in the land.

See also Simes and Smith, The Law of Future Interest, §1941 (2d ed. 1956).

This Court has long recognized that chancery courts do have jurisdiction to order the sale of land for the prevention of waste. Kelly v. Neville,

136 Miss. 429, 101 So. 565 (1924). In Riley v. Norfleet, 167 Miss. 420, 436-437, 148 So. 777, 781 (1933), Justice Cook, speaking for the Court and citing *Kelly, supra,* stated:

> . . . The power of a court of equity on a plenary bill, with adversary interest properly represented, to sell contingent remainders in land, under some circumstances, though the contingent remaindermen are not then ascertained or in being, as, for instance, to preserve the estate from complete or partial destruction, is well established.

While Mississippi and most jurisdictions recognize the inherent power of a court of equity to direct a judicial sale of land which is subject to a future interest, nevertheless the scope of this power has not been clearly defined. It is difficult to determine the facts and circumstances which will merit such a sale.

It is apparent that there must be "necessity" before the chancery court can order a judicial sale. It is also beyond cavil that the power should be exercised with caution and only when the need is evident. Lambdin v. Lambdin, 209 Miss. 672, 48 So. 2d 341 (1950). These cases, *Kelly, Riley* and *Lambdin, supra,* are all illustrative of situations where the freehold estate was deteriorating and the income therefrom was insufficient to pay taxes and maintain the property. In each of these this Court approved a judicial sale to preserve and maintain the estate. The appellants argue, therefore, that since Oakland Farm is not deteriorating and since there is sufficient income from rental to pay taxes, a judicial sale by direction of the court was not proper.

The unusual circumstances of this case persuade us to the contrary. We are of the opinion that deteriorating and waste of the property is not the exclusive and ultimate test to be used in determining whether a sale of land affected by future interest is proper, but also that consideration should be given to the question of whether a sale is necessary for the best interest of all the parties, that is, the life tenant and the contingent remaindermen. This "necessary for the best interest of all parties" rule is gleaned from Rogers, Removal of Future Interest Encumbrances — Sale of the Fee Simple Estate, 17 Vanderbilt L. Rev. 1437 (1964); Simes, Law of Future Interest, *supra;* Simes and Smith, The Law of Future Interest, §1941 (1956); and appears to have the necessary flexibility to meet the requirements of unusual and unique situations which demand in justice an equitable solution.

Our decision to reverse the chancellor and remand the case for his further consideration is couched in our belief that the best interest of all the parties would not be served by a judicial sale of the entirety of the property at this time. While true that such a sale would provide immediate relief to the life tenant who is worthy of this aid in equity, admitted by the remaindermen, it would nevertheless under the circumstances before us cause great financial loss to the remaindermen.

We therefore reverse and remand this cause to the chancery court, which shall have continuing jurisdiction thereof, for determination upon motion of the life tenant, if she so desires, for relief by way of sale of a part of the burdened land sufficient to provide for her reasonable needs from interest derived from the investment of the proceeds. The sale, however, is to be made only in the event the parties cannot unite to hypothecate the land for sufficient funds for the life tenant's reasonable needs. By affording the options above we do not mean to suggest that other remedies suitable to the parties which will provide economic relief to the aging life tenant are not open to them if approved by the chancellor. It is our opinion, shared by the chancellor and acknowledged by the appellants, that the facts suggest an equitable remedy. However, it is our further opinion that this equity does not warrant the remedy of sale of all of the property since this would unjustly impinge upon the vested rights of the remaindermen.

Reversed and remanded.

NOTES AND QUESTIONS

1. **Feudal vision.** *Baker* and *Brokaw* dramatize the extent to which the feudal vision of a relatively static society retained some grip on American law centuries after feudalism had disappeared.

2. **Counterpoint.** Conner v. Shepherd, 15 Mass. 163 (1818), although nominally an assignment of dower case, provides an alternative, prodevelopment, (liberal?) vision of property management. At her husband's death, the plaintiff demanded that 200 acres of uncultivated timberland, which had belonged to her husband, be included in the property subject to her dower (life) estate. In refusing to make the assignment, Chief Justice Parker wrote:

> By the common law, the widow is dowable of all the real estate of which her husband was seised during the coverture, with the exception only of a castle erected for public defense, . . . and some other kinds of estate not known in this country. The question whether forests, parks, and other property of a similar nature, are also exceptions, seems never to have occurred; probably because there is no instance, in Great Britain, of any such property held separately and distinct from improved and cultivated estates.
>
> In this country, on the contrary, there are many large tracts of uncultivated territory owned by individuals who have no intention of reducing them to a state of improvement, but consider them rather as subjects of speculation and sale, or as a future fund for their prosperity, increasing in value with the population and improvement of the country. If dower could be assigned in estates of this nature, . . . in many instances the inheritance would be prejudiced, without any actual advantage to the widow to whom the dower might be assigned. For, according to the principles of common law, her estate would be forfeited if she were to cut down any of the trees valuable as timber. It would

seem, too, that the mere change of the property from wilderness to arable or pasture land, by cutting down the wood and clearing up the land, might be considered as waste; for the alteration of the property, even if it became thereby more valuable, would subject the estate in dower to forfeiture — the heir having a right to the inheritance in the same character as it was left by the ancestor.

It is no extravagant supposition that lands actually in a state of nature may, in a country fast increasing in its population, be more valuable than the same land would be with that sort of cultivation which a tenant for life would be likely to bestow upon it; and that the very clearing of the land, for the purpose of getting the greatest crops from the least labor, which is all that could be expected from a tenant in dower, would be actually, as well as technically, waste of the inheritance.

There would seem, then, to be no reason for allowing dower to the widow in property of this kind. If she did not improve the land, the dower would be wholly useless; if she did improve it she would be exposed to disputes with the heir, and to the forfeiture of her estate, after having expended her substance upon it.

d.   Valuation of Life Estates

Look over this!

We must sometimes value a life estate. In Baker v. Weedon, *supra,* if the property had been sold, some arrangement respecting the proceeds would clearly have been needed to reflect the divided interests. A similar situation arises if land subject to a life tenancy is condemned. One solution, mentioned in Baker v. Weedon, is to place the award in a court-supervised account; the life tenant would then receive the income until his death, when the remainderman would get the corpus. Although this procedure is sometimes used, courts shy away from unnecessary administration. The alternative solution, immediate valuation of the life estate, is usually preferred, and for some purposes, such as estate tax computation, immediate valuation is required.

Valuation of life estates is relatively simple, although it is based on two artificial conventions: that the duration of the life estate is measured by the tenant's projected life expectancy; that the earning power of the asset will equal a specified annual rate.

As to the life estate's duration, statutes usually prescribe which mortality table one should use in projecting a life expectancy. In New York the direction appears at N.Y. Real Prop. Acts. Law §403 (McKinney 1979 & Supp. 1996) [58] and specifies the Commissioners' Standard Ordinary Mortality Table compiled by the National Association of Insurance Commissioners in 1980. The importance of redating the statute to conform to ever-growing

---

58. This section refers to the mortality tables at N.Y. Ins. Law §4217(c)(2)(A) (McKinney 1985).

TABLE 2-2
Human Expectancy*

Age	Years of Expectancy	Age	Years of Expectancy
25	45.82	40	32.18
26	44.90	41	31.29
27	43.99	42	30.41
28	43.08	43	29.54
29	42.16	44	28.67
30	41.25	45	27.81
31	40.34	46	26.95
32	39.43	47	26.11
33	38.51	48	25.27
34	37.60	49	24.45
35	36.69		
36	35.78		
37	34.88		
38	33.97		
39	33.07		

*National Association of Insurance Commissioners, C.S.O. approved, 1958.
Source: Reeves, Handbook of Interest, Annuity and Related Fiscal Tables (1966).

human life expectancies was overlooked by the New York legislature for almost 100 years, which until 1966 had designated the American Experience Table compiled in 1868. You can see at once why remaindermen might yearn for the good old days.

As to the asset's earning power, this too is statutorily defined. The New York rate is 4 percent: N.Y. Real Prop. Acts. Law §402 (McKinney 1979). The federal rate for estate tax computation has been 10 percent since 1983:[59] 5 Fed. Tax. Reg. §20.2031-7(f), at 34-36 (1983). If the statutory rate is low (high) relative to current market conditions, who benefits: The life tenant? The remainderman? Does it depend on why the computation is made?

Let us try an example to see how the system works. Suppose that the value of Lot 1, located in New York, is $100,000; that B, age 30, has a life estate; that C and his heirs have the remainder. Consulting the prescribed table (partly reproduced, Table 2-2) we find that B enjoys (rounded off) a 41-year expectancy. Assuming a 4 percent rate, we must then calculate the sum of money which, if invested at this rate (compounded annually), will yield $4000 yearly (4% × $100,000) for 41 years and exhaust itself with the final payment — in short, an annuity. We consult a second table (partly re-

59. The rate had previously been 6 percent.

TABLE 2-3
Present Value of $1 Per Annum Receivable at Future Dates (N)
Discount Rate

N	4%	5%	6%	7%
31	17.588	15.592	13.929	12.531
32	17.873	15.802	14.084	12.646
33	18.147	16.002	14.230	12.753
34	18.411	16.192	14.368	12.854
35	18.664	16.374	14.498	12.947
36	18.908	16.546	14.620	13.035
37	19.142	16.711	14.736	13.117
38	19.367	16.867	14.846	13.193
39	19.584	17.017	14.949	13.264
40	19.792	17.159	15.046	13.331
41	19.993	17.294	15.138	13.394
42	20.185	17.423	15.224	13.452
43	20.370	17.545	15.306	13.506
44	20.548	17.662	15.383	13.557
45	20.720	17.774	15.455	13.605
46	20.884	17.880	15.524	13.650
47	21.042	17.981	15.589	13.691
48	21.195	18.077	15.650	13.730
49	21.341	18.168	15.707	13.766
50	21.482	18.255	15.761	13.800

Source: Reeves, Handbook of Interest, Annuity and Related Fiscal Tables (1966).

produced, Table 2-3), giving the present value of the right to receive $1.00 yearly for stated durations (N years), and we find this right valued at $19.99 where the annuity lasts 41 years. Since B is to receive $4000 yearly, the present value of his life estate is $79,960 (4000 × $19.99). Since the total value of Lot 1 is $100,000, C's remainder interest is worth only $20,040 ($100,000 − $79,960).

Lest you say, "Isn't this awful!" remember our assumptions. At the end of 41 years, C should have intact $100,000. This he will achieve if the $20,040 is invested for the entire term so as to yield 4 percent interest compounded annually. To confirm this, we consult yet another table (partly reproduced, Table 2-4) giving the accumulated value of $1.00 at the end of N years, if invested at specified rates. At 4 percent compound interest, $1.00 would increase to $4.9993 after 41 years. C's starting $20,040 would become $100,000 ($20,040 × $4.993).

Problems: Calculate the present value of B's life estate and C's remain-

TABLE 2-4
Accumulation of $1 at Compound Interest in N Years
Interest Rate

N	4%	5%	6%	7%
31	3.373	4.538	6.088	8.145
32	3.508	4.764	6.453	8.715
33	3.648	5.003	6.840	9.325
34	3.794	5.253	7.251	9.978
35	3.946	5.516	7.686	10.676
36	4.103	5.791	8.147	11.423
37	4.268	6.081	8.636	12.223
38	4.438	6.385	9.154	13.079
39	4.616	6.704	9.703	13.994
40	4.801	7.039	10.285	14.974
41	4.993	7.391	10.902	16.022
42	5.192	7.761	11.557	17.144
43	5.400	8.149	12.250	18.344
44	5.616	8.557	12.985	19.628
45	5.841	8.985	13.764	21.002
46	6.074	9.434	14.590	22.472
47	6.317	9.905	15.465	24.045
48	6.570	10.401	16.393	25.728
49	6.833	10.921	17.377	27.529
50	7.106	11.467	18.420	29.457

Source: Reeves, Handbook of Interest, Annuity and Related Fiscal Tables (1966).

der interest, making the following assumptions (round off life expectancies to whole years):

(1)   value of parcel $250,000, B's age 25, interest rate 5%.
(2)   value of parcel $175,000, B's age 28, interest rate 6%.
(3)   value of parcel $50,000, B's age 35, interest rate 7%.

Answers: (1) $223,500, $26,500
                    (2) $160,650, $14,350
                    (3) $ 45,920, $ 4,080

Query: At any given age, the life expectancies of a white male, white female, nonwhite male, and nonwhite female vary widely. Should the designated mortality tables embody these differences?[60]

60. Manufacturer's Hanover Trust Co. v. United States, 576 F. Supp. 837 (S.D.N.Y. 1983), *aff'd,* 775 F.2d 459 (2d Cir. 1985). In this case, the court held that "the IRS's use of

New York's Real Property Actions and Proceedings Law §404 provides: "In all valuations made under this article, no significance shall be given to the ancestry, health or habits of the person whose life is involved. Each valuation shall be based exclusively on the actuarial data." N.Y. Real Prop. Acts. Law §404 (McKinney 1979). (Section 401 specifies when this article shall be used.)

In the absence of a statutory mandate, courts prefer to consider such relevant matters as general health and habits. Thus, a New York court has held that "in view of the decedent's terminal illness immediately prior to his death, his life expectancy at that moment was practically nil and that the use of mortality tables to value his reversionary interest must give way to realism." In re Cushing, 49 Misc. 2d 454, 267 N.Y.S.2d 747 (Sur. Ct. 1966) (N.Y. estate tax proceeding). Accord, Hall v. United States, 353 F.2d 500 (7th Cir. 1965) (federal estate tax proceeding); Mercantile-Safe Deposit and Trust Co. v. United States, 368 F. Supp. 743 (D. Md. 1974) (federal estate tax proceeding); Rev. Rul. 66-307, 1966-2 Cum. Bull. 429.

§2.6   Review Problems: Doctrine

Describe the state of the title after the following grants, which are included in a will written in 1996. Be careful to account for *all* the estates created and to account for the property from the moment of the devise for the rest of time. Remember that the Rule against Perpetuities may apply.

1. "O to A for as long as no liquor is ever served on the premises; then to the Temperance Society if A or his assigns ever serves liquor."
2. "O to A for life, then to B and her heirs if B is still living."
3. "O to the Altmere School District, its assigns and successors, but if the land ever ceases to be used for school purposes, then Susanna and her heirs can reenter and retake the premises."
4. "O to A for life, then to B and his heirs until the land is no longer farmed."
5. "O to A for life, then to B and his heirs when B reaches the age of 21." B is five years old at the time of the grant.
6. "O to A for life, then to B when B reaches the age of 21." B was five years old at the time of the grant; it is now 20 years after the will in question was written.
7. "O to my daughter Mia, on condition that she or one of her chil-

---

gender-based mortality tables to value reversionary interests was substantially related to important governmental objectives . . . and did not violate equal protection."

Federal estate tax tables differentiate between male and female expectancies. 5 Fed. Tax. Reg. §20.2031-7(f), at 34-36 (1983).

dren shall occupy the house as his or her residence for 25 years; provided that, if they do not, the house shall revert to my other heirs." See Cast v. National Bank of Commerce Trust & Sav. Assn. of Lincoln, 186 Neb. 385, 183 N.W.2d 485 (1971).

8.   "O to my son for life, then to his children and their heirs."

(a)   The son is childless.
(b)   The son has two children.

9.   "O to A for life, then, ten years later, to B unless B has declared bankruptcy within that period."
10.   "O to A for life, then to whoever is president of the League of Women Voters."
11.   "O to A for life, then to B and his heirs if B survives A."

(a)   Name the estates created at the time of the grant.
(b)   B does not survive A; who owns what?

12.   "O to A for life, then to the children of A and their heirs who reach the age of 21." Name the estates after each of the following events.

(a)   At the time of the grant A has no children.
(b)   One child, B, is born to A.
(c)   A second child, C, is born to A. No other child is born to A.
(d)   C dies at age 2.
(e)   B reaches the age of 21.
(f)   A dies.

§2.7   Review Problem: Advocacy

In recent years, land reforms have given rise to the need for consultants to advise foreign governments on restructuring of property interests to effect (or partially undo) various land redistribution schemes. Your law firm represented a Central American rebel regime in the United States, doing lobbying, litigation, and other work, and has now been hired by the government to develop a property regime that will accomplish the following goals:

1.   to achieve economic stability and encourage agricultural production;

2. to encourage political stability, by balancing the rights of prior
    landowners with the need to avoid the dramatic concentrations
    of wealth that existed before the revolution;
3. to preserve and encourage a democratic system of government.

Here is some basic background. The country is a small, agrarian country in Central America. It is underdeveloped, has a small population, and
has large amounts of uncultivated arable land. In 1979 the rebel regime
successfully led a revolution that overthrew the central government. Before
the revolution, 1.4 percent of the total number of farms controlled 41.2
percent of the farmland while 50 percent of the farms (under 17 acres)
controlled 3.4 percent of the land;[61] because it is primarily an agricultural
country, wealth and power corresponded to land ownership in a system not
unlike English feudalism.

The new government significantly restructured the property regime.
After the revolution, three groups of landowners emerged: Some stayed on
their land and continued to farm it; some stayed on but let their land fall
idle; others fled and abandoned the country. The new regime acquired
much of the land of the latter two groups and redistributed it. Some was
redistributed to individuals to hold as collectives; some was distributed to
individuals to hold in cooperatives; some (arguably most) was retained by
the state for individual farmers to farm. About one-quarter of the arable
land was ultimately confiscated, as well as factories, stores, mines, and even
shopping malls.

The rebel forces were voted out of power in 1990; the current government's chief goals are to preserve the peace and to spur economic development. Immediately prior to the election, the government distributed
large amounts of state-owned land to individuals, to be held collectively,
cooperatively, and privately. This was done very quickly, without regularized
recordation or title transfers. The people to whom the land was transferred
now hold it in a variety of estates, while the previous owners — who held it
in fee simple absolute — now want it returned to them.

This history resulted in the current confused state of land title in the
Central American country, which has severe economic and political consequences. The president wants a design for a system of property rights that
will meet the goals articulated above. Your group should consider which
estates in land to recommend and should focus on how to handle alienabil-

61. David Kaimowitz and Joseph R. Thome, Nicaragua's Agrarian Reform: The First
Year (1979-1980), in Nicaragua in Revolution 225 (Thomas W. Walker ed., 1982) (discussing
Nicaragua's attempt at agrarian reform and the effects of such an undertaking); Larry Rohter,
U.S. Prods Nicaragua on Seized Land, N.Y. Times, July 25, 1995, at A7 (documenting claims
for compensation for property confiscated by Nicaraguan government; one-third of all claims
for compensation filed by associates of the Semoza family).

ity, inheritability, and restrictions on use and possession.[62] Adrienne Davis, Supplementary Materials on Property (1995).

For further background on land redistribution schemes, see Roy L. Prosterman and Jeffrey M. Riedinger, Land Reform and Democratic Development 12 (1987) (significant twentieth-century land reforms in Great Britain, Finland, Mexico, Bolivia, Ethiopia, Nicaragua, Russia, China, North Vietnam, Cuba, Egypt, Taiwan, South Vietnam, El Salvador, and others); Agrarian Reform and Grassroots Development: Ten Case Studies (Roy L. Prosterman et al. eds., 1990).

62. Our thanks to Adrienne Davis, Professor of Law, American University, who developed this problem.

Chapter 3

Landlord and Tenant Law

Landlord and tenant law is a particularly suitable topic for first-year students to study in depth for several reasons. First, law students generally have had more experience with landlord and tenant situations than with most other situations involving property law, so they can more readily relate "the law in the books" to "the law in action."[1] Second, the so-called revolution in landlord and tenant law in the 1970s allows students to ponder the process, scope, and limits of legal change. Moreover, the revolution is commonly described as a shift from a feudal to a liberal vision of property law, thus the law frames important questions about the several visions of property. Third, landlord and tenant law involves three quite different legal skills: case analysis, statutory analysis, and document analysis. While the first of these receives most attention in the traditional law school curriculum, the other skills are equally important. Moreover, they may well be more accessible to first-year students: Anyone who is willing to read precisely and rigorously can match the professor's skill in deciphering documents and statutes. Because most American law involves the interaction of statutes and case law (and document analysis is very commonly involved as well), approaching landlord and tenant law from this combined perspective helps students develop crucial skills too often ignored in the first-year curriculum.

NOTE: The statutory material included is for teaching purposes only. It may not be up to date by the time this volume reaches your hands. For research projects, go directly to the latest edition of the relevant code.

Note that the materials in this chapter conform to the following pattern: case law comes first, followed by lease provisions relevant to the same area of the law, followed by statutes from two different states. The two leases provided are closely parallel, yet contain important differences. One major difference is that one lease is written in "plain English," and so can help you understand the legalese present in the other lease. As part of your as-

---

1. This term was coined by Harvard Law School Dean Roscoe Pound, Law in the Books and Law in Action, 44 Amer. U. L. Rev. 12 (1910).

signment, you are expected not only to read the lease provisions, but to analyze them as well to discover how they are the same and how they are different. The materials also contain parallel statutory provisions, one from a state (Maryland) friendlier to tenants, one from a state (Virginia) friendlier to landlords. As a regular part of your assignment, you should closely analyze the statutes: Often they look more alike than they really are.

§3.1   Who Are the Homeowners and Who Are the Renters?

Figure 3-1 typifies one kind of document often produced by advocacy groups that often employ lawyers as well as nonlawyers. Note the presentation of carefully selected facts to send a vivid, easily graspable message. Who, do you suppose, is intended to receive this message, and for what purpose?

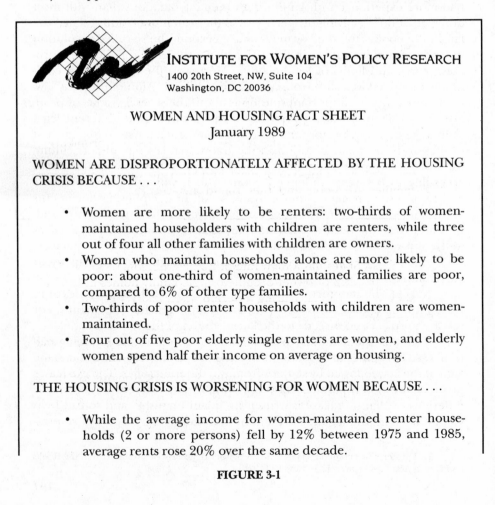

INSTITUTE FOR WOMEN'S POLICY RESEARCH
1400 20th Street, NW, Suite 104
Washington, DC 20036

WOMEN AND HOUSING FACT SHEET
January 1989

WOMEN ARE DISPROPORTIONATELY AFFECTED BY THE HOUSING CRISIS BECAUSE . . .

- Women are more likely to be renters: two-thirds of women-maintained householders with children are renters, while three out of four all other families with children are owners.
- Women who maintain households alone are more likely to be poor: about one-third of women-maintained families are poor, compared to 6% of other type families.
- Two-thirds of poor renter households with children are women-maintained.
- Four out of five poor elderly single renters are women, and elderly women spend half their income on average on housing.

THE HOUSING CRISIS IS WORSENING FOR WOMEN BECAUSE . . .

- While the average income for women-maintained renter households (2 or more persons) fell by 12% between 1975 and 1985, average rents rose 20% over the same decade.

FIGURE 3-1

- Rent burdens borne by single parent households increased from an average of 38% of their incomes in 1974 to an average of 58% of their incomes in 1987.
- Homeless families with children are the fastest growing group of the homeless.

THE HOUSING CRISIS IS MADE WORSE FOR WOMEN AND THEIR FAMILIES BECAUSE . . .

- The supply of low-cost housing is disappearing. In 1970, there were almost 15 million housing units that could be rented for the equivalent of 30% of a $5000 annual income. By 1985 there were only 1.8 million affordable units, which is only about one unit for every two low-income households.
- HUD subsidies are enough for only 4.3 million households, about one-third of the need.
- Cuts in the federal budget since 1980 for affordable housing have reduced spending by about 80% from 30 billion to 8 billion.
- Many face housing discrimination against families with children: in 1980, landlords excluded families with children altogether from one of every four rental units, and restricted the number, age, and so forth of children in another 50% of units. (Although now against the law, few believe this discrimination has or will disappear until there is vigorous enforcement of the law.)
- Racial and ethnic discrimination compounds the problems of women of color, especially those maintaining households alone with children. One-half of Black and Hispanic women-maintained families are poor, and they spend an average of 60% of their incomes on housing.

FIGURE 3-1 (continued)

The United States has a high rate of homeownership, resulting from a tremendous buildup of owner-occupied single family homes in the half-century after World War II. During a period when many Western nations were building apartments, the United States made tremendous investments in owner-occupied houses. Michael Harloe, Private Rented Housing in the United States and Europe 64 (1985). As a result, the proportion of Americans owning their own homes nearly doubled between 1940 and 1980.[2] Today, the United States is primarily a country of owners: Roughly two-thirds of American households occupied their own homes as of 1996.[3]

2. Albert Chaven, The Growth of Home Ownership: 1940-1980, 26 Demography 249 (1989).
3. Joint Center for Housing Studies of Harvard University, The State of the Nation's Housing 16 (1996). In contrast, only 37 percent of West Germans and 47 percent of French own their own homes. See Peter Saunders, A Nation of Homeowners 18 (1990).

The population that remains in rental housing consists of permanent and "life cycle" tenants. Life cycle tenants include young adults, the recently divorced, and elderly persons who rent after they sell the home in which they raised their families.[4] Life cycle tenants may or may not be poor, but permanent renters tend to be much poorer than homeowners — which is not surprising given the high priority most Americans place on owning a home. See §1.3.d *supra*. Thus, renters earn about half of homeowners' median income;[5] and almost twice as many renter households live in poverty as do homeowner households.[6]

Renters spend a higher proportion of their income on housing.[7] The average gross rent burden (that is, rent as a percentage of income) rose to over 30 percent in 1993, a 25-year record.[8] Incomes of renter households fell 8.6 percent from 1989 to 1992, exacerbating this high rent burden.[9] Thus, many poor renters are paying far more than they can afford for housing, and housing costs are rising as incomes decline. After adjustment for inflation, the median monthly gross rents paid by poor households rose from $258 in 1974 to $359 in 1991.[10]

Renters are more likely to be mother-headed families, many of which are poor. Although American families generally own their own homes, mother-headed families typically rent. Nearly three-quarters of all families maintained by women under age 45 are tenants compared with only one-third of same-age married couples.[11]

Race also affects the likelihood of being a renter rather than a homeowner. For example, only 59 percent of the nation's middle-class blacks own homes, compared with 74 percent of middle-class whites.[12]

---

4. George Sternlieb and James W. Hughes, Demographics and Housing in America, 41 Population Bull. 24 (1986).

5. In 1992, the median income of homeowning households was $38,088; for renters it was $20,731. 1994 Stat. Abst., Table 708.

6. Joint Center for Housing Studies of Harvard University, The State of the Nation's Housing 14 (1994). In 1992, 16.4 percent of homeowners had household incomes below $15,000; the corresponding rate for renters was 37.5 percent. 1994 Stat. Abst., Table 708.

7. Recent data show that homeowners spent 19 percent of their income on housing costs, compared to 28 percent paid by renters. About 43 percent of families with income under $10,000 spent at least half their income on rent, well above the federally suggested amount of 30 percent of income. Sara E. Rix, Women's Research and Education Institute, The American Woman 1990-1991, at 95 (1990).

8. The gross rent burden was 30.9 percent. Gross rent is rent plus the cost of utilities. Joint Center, *supra* note 6, at 3.

9. Joint Center for Housing Studies of Harvard University, The State of the Nation's Housing 13 (1993).

10. Joint Center, *supra* note 6, at 15.

11. Rix, *supra* note 7, at 94. The poverty rate for female-headed families who rent their housing approaches 50 percent. Id. at 101.

12. Walter E. Updegrave, Race and Money, *Money*, Dec. 1989, at 152.

§3.2 Classification of Landlord and Tenant Estates

a. Historical Introduction

Largely because of its function, the lease was not at once admitted into the family of estates. The lease had dubious origins: Moneylenders used it to evade the church's bar on usury. Upon receipt of the loan, the borrower would lease his lands to the lender, who would remain in possession for the lease term. In fixing the term, the parties would make it of sufficient duration to allow the lender to recoup, from the land's harvest, his original outlay together with the unlawful interest.[13] Because of his disreputable status, the lessee was originally denied the legal protection that the courts accorded "free" men — the essence of whose holdings was "the permanent and normal economic basis of the family."[14] Thus, a life tenant might seek a writ of right (recovery) if his possession were unlawfully disrupted, but not so the lessee. As against strangers, the lessee had no protection; his only recourse was a suit against the lessor for breach of covenant (for quiet enjoyment). Other, more trifling difficulties beset the leasehold interest.[15]

The early leases served one other important function. They were a form of agrarian contract wherein landowners arranged to have their lands farmed by the nonlandowning poor. Whereas husbandry leases grew steadily in importance, security leases were gradually replaced by other devices. By the early thirteenth century, as the lease gained respectability, the courts' prejudice against it began to weaken. But the courts, instead of letting the old remedies reach new parties, patched together a succession of new remedies, available only to lessees. Of these, the writ of *trespass de ejectione firmae* (ejectment) was most sweeping in the relief given, for it entitled the lessee to recover his lands from any person who had wrongfully supplanted him. Indeed, ejectment worked so efficiently compared with its freehold counterpart that the courts eventually sanctioned its use for all estates in land.[16] But, to this day, we still speak of leasehold estates as "nonfreehold" — a

---

13. The ways of man are such that even today hard-pressed borrowers and overreaching lenders use a similar device to avoid the appearance of usury. The borrower "sells" his land to the lender, who, upon getting the deed, delivers an option. This enables the seller to repurchase the land at the option price, set, as you would suppose, to equal the original sales price (the loan principal) plus the interest amount. By using this sham, the parties do not put in writing the interest rate. Also, if the borrower seeks later to invoke the usury statute, he must prove that the sale-and-option was a disguised usurious transaction. Sometimes, but not always, the borrower prevails. Compare Freedman v. Hendershott, 77 Idaho 213, 290 P.2d 738 (1955), and State v. Bosworth, 124 Vt. 3, 197 A.2d 477 (1963), with Sledge Lumber Corp. v. Southern Builders Equip. Co., 257 N.C. 435, 126 S.E.2d 97 (1962).

14. Theodore F. T. Plucknett, A Concise History of the Common Law 573 (5th ed. 1956).

15. Id. at 571.

16. Most important of all, ejectment also became a *landlord's* remedy.

gentle, quite harmless reminder that many of our property institutions are rooted deep in English soil.

For purposes of further classification, leasehold estates are arranged into several categories. These are: (1) term of years, (2) tenancy at will, (3) "occupancy" at sufferance, (4) periodic tenancy, (5) statutory tenancy, and (6) proprietary (cooperative) lease.

b.   Common-Law Classification System

1.   Term of Years (Estate for Years)

The Restatement (Second) of Property §1.4 defines this estate as having a "fixed or computable period of time." The term is fixed when both a beginning and termination date are specified. The term is computable when a specified formula will produce the two necessary dates. Regardless of the length of the term, usage refers to the tenancy as "terms of years." Thus, estates for one week, six months, or 999 years[17] all bear a generic likeness. Unless the parties validly agree otherwise, the term begins immediately after midnight on the starting date and ends just before midnight on the termination date.

A lease term may sometimes begin upon the happening of an event; e.g., L "to T, for twenty years, the term to begin when the improvements are erected and a certificate of occupancy is obtained." In that situation, the landlord-tenant relationship must await the stated occurrences. Also, because T holds a *contingent* future interest (the stipulated events are not certain to occur), the Rule against Perpetuities will apply.

Although the term of years must have a fixed (or computable) duration, the term may be defeasible; e.g., L "to T for fifty years, unless T shall die sooner," or, more commonplace, L "to T for two years, but if T does not pay the rent, etc., L may terminate the lease." Whether the defeasible event results in an automatic termination of the tenancy or an option to terminate is a matter for the parties' agreement; sometimes murkiness clouds that agreement.[18]

Ordinarily the estate for years ends automatically at the expiration of the fixed term. But sometimes the lease will provide that tenant must give advance notice (thirty, sixty, ninety, etc. days) of his intention to remove, and that the failure to give such requisite notice can — at landlord's elec-

---

17. A few states have placed statutory limits on a leasehold term. See, e.g., Calif. Civ. Code §717 (West Supp. 1981) (agricultural leases — 51 years); Ala. Code §35-4-6 (1991) (all leases — 99 years).

18. Compare Brause v. 2968 Third Avenue Inc., 41 Misc. 2d 348, 244 N.Y.S.2d 587 (Civ. Ct. 1963), with Remedco Corp. v. Bryn Mawr Hotel, 45 Misc. 2d 586, 257 N.Y.S.2d 525 (Civ. Ct. 1965).

tion — extend the original term, sometimes for an entire second term. Since tenant's forgetfulness, rather than his desire to remain, often leads to the failure to give notice, some states now require that landlord remind tenant of the notice provision if landlord plans to enforce it. See, e.g., N.Y. Gen. Oblig. Law §5-905 (McKinney 1989) (landlord must notify tenant in writing at least fifteen days and not more than thirty days before tenant's notice is due).

L L must Remind

The corollary to this situation is when the lease contains a tenant's option to renew, but requires tenant to give landlord advance notice of his election. Tenant's failure to serve timely notice can cost him his renewal privilege. In the absence of statutes requiring landlord to remind the tenant of the notice date, the neglectful tenant must rely, not always with success, upon the courts for relief from forfeiture.

Whether an estate for years *has* been created may be more than an academic quibble. Requirements as to writing, recordation, and notice of termination, as well as the lease's actual duration, may rest on the label.

2. Tenancy at Will (Estate at Will)

The Restatement (Second) of Property §1.6 defines a tenancy at will as one "created to endure only so long *as both* the landlord and the tenant desire." Such an estate, at common law, ended on the very day that a terminating notice from one of the parties was received by the other. You might ask when such an estate would arise in the normal dealings between landlord and tenant. After all, it would seem unusual for parties to enter into an arrangement that either party could end abruptly. For the landlord it might mean a sudden loss of income; for the tenant, an unplanned-for loss of shelter or investment in crops, good will, or fixtures.

As a rule, the tenancy at will is not the product of agreement, but instead is read into an arrangement *after the fact* — by a court to which the parties have carried a dispute. A few examples should suffice to suggest areas of possible controversy:

(1) While negotiating a lease (or a renewal of his term), T takes possession (or remains in possession) of the premises. The negotiations fail. Held: T is a tenant at will. Carteri v. Roberts, 140 Cal. 164, 73 P. 819 (1903).

(2) Because of a dangerous illness, T is unable to vacate the premises until fifteen days after the expiration of the term. Held: T is a tenant at will. Herter v. Mullen, 159 N.Y. 28, 53 N.E. 700 (1899). But see Mason v. Wierengo, 113 Mich. 151, 71 N.W. 489 (1897).

(3) T takes possession under a letting for an undefined period and there is no reservation of a periodic rent. Held: T is a tenant at will. Carruth v. Carruth, 77 Ga. App. 131, 48 S.E.2d 387 (1948).

(4) T takes possession under an oral lease in a jurisdiction requiring *all* leases to be written. T is a tenant at will. See, e.g., Mass Ann. Laws c. 183, §3 (1955).

Since a tenancy at will involves mutuality, what if the parties agree that either L or T, but not both, may terminate at will? Ignoring some contrary case law,[19] as well as the original Restatement,[20] the editors of the Restatement (Second) refused to convert such arrangements into a tenancy at will except where, under all the circumstances, an arrangement became unconscionable; in that instance, either party might terminate at will. Id. at §1.6, Comment g. Otherwise, a lease from L "to T for two years, unless L notifies T that the lease is terminated" would be seen as a determinable term of years.

The Restatement also asserts that the death of either party ends a tenancy at will, as does a transfer of either party's interest in the tenancy. Id. at §1.6, Comments c, d. Logically, why this result?

Statutes in many states have modified the common-law tenancy at will by requiring one or both parties to give notice of termination. Thus, in New York the landlord must give thirty days' notice (N.Y. Real Prop. Law §228) (McKinney 1989); in Georgia, the tenant must give thirty days' notice and the landlord sixty days' notice for an implied tenancy at will, but no notice, as at common law, for an express tenancy at will (Ga. Code Ann §44-7-7 (1991)). What are the various policy reasons for requiring notice, for treating the tenant more protectively than the landlord, or for distinguishing express from implied tenancies at will?

3.   Occupancy at Sufferance

Often confused with the tenancy at will is the estate, or more properly, the occupancy at sufferance. Quite simply, an occupant at sufferance is someone once having a valid tenancy[21] (or other possessory interest)[22] who has since lost the legal right to remain. A tenant will most often become an occupant at sufferance when he is ordered, after failing to pay the rent, to vacate the premises. At common law, the occupant at sufferance was subject to removal without further notice (causing the confusion with tenancy at will), and was not liable for rent during the sufferance period (distinguishing the tenancy at will).

Most states now give the landlord a statutory money claim against the occupant at sufferance, usually for the reasonable rental value; see, e.g.,

---

19. See, e.g., Foley v. Gamester, 271 Mass. 55, 57, 170 N.E. 799, 800 (1930).

20. Restatement of Property §21 drew a distinction between a lease terminable at the landlord's will and one terminable at the tenant's will. In the former case, the election to terminate was extended to the tenant, thereby creating a tenancy at will. In the latter case, the Restatement did not impose mutuality upon the parties, but regarded the landlord bound until the tenant terminated.

21. Ergo, a squatter is not an occupant at sufferance.

22. The occupant is sometimes a vendor who refuses to vacate after title passes, or a vendee in possession who refuses to vacate after the deal collapses.

Colo. Rev. Stat. §§13-40-104 and 13-40-110 (1987). See also Restatement (Second) of Property §14.5. But a few states measure this claim by the previous rent, see, e.g., Rogers v. Kolp, 272 S.W.2d 793 (Tex. Civ. App. 1954). The landlord may also have a claim for special damages reasonably foreseeable by the former tenant. Restatement (Second) of Property §14.6. During the holdover period, however, the Restatement (Second) would require the landlord to perform his regular leasehold duties. Id. at §14.7.

4.   Periodic Tenancy

Suppose that a tenant rents an apartment at a *fixed* monthly rental. Landlord and tenant agree that either party may end the arrangement by giving the other party thirty days' notice.

This arrangement, widely used by urban dwellers, would probably be construed as a periodic tenancy — one in which the estate continues automatically for successive periods unless either party acts, *through the giving of notice,* to terminate the estate. The periodic tenancy originated in the sixteenth century, as courts sought to ameliorate the hardship that the tenancy at will often occasioned. When a tenancy at will carried with it a periodic rent, courts began to read into the tenancy a requirement of notice should either landlord or tenant wish the estate to end. The length of required notice would vary with the period covered by a rent payment: six months' notice for a yearly rental;[23] one month's notice for a monthly rental; one week's notice for a weekly rental.[24] Moreover, the date stated in the notice for ending the tenancy had to coincide with the end of a period; otherwise the notice was defective. Thus, a landlord's notice dated October 15 terminating a month-to-month tenancy as of November 15 would be ineffectual if the tenant's rental term ran from the first to the 30th of each month. In addition, unless the landlord served a new notice, on or before November 1, terminating the tenancy as of November 30, the tenant would be privileged to remain after December 1. As pointed out, the duty of giving notice was reciprocal. Therefore, unless the tenant was also careful to have his notices conform to the common law requirement, he, too, might have leasehold duties for longer than he wanted. Statutes in some jurisdictions have now modified the notice requirements. See, e.g., Cal. Civ. Code §1946 (1985) (month-to-month tenancy terminable by thirty days' notice given *at any time*); N.Y. Real Prop. L. §232a (in New York City, only the landlord is required to give thirty days' notice to end month-to-month tenancy).

23. 28 Mott St. Co. v. Summit Import Corp., 64 Misc. 2d 860, 316 N.Y.S.2d 259 (Civ. Ct. 1970), illustrates how the 6 months' notice requirement can plague a landlord.

24. The rule for determining the time in which an act must be done is to exclude the first day and include the last. Thus, a 30-day notice, to be effective on October 31, must be served by October 1. Cf. Seminole Housing Corp. v. M & M Garages, Inc., 78 Misc. 2d 755, 359 N.Y.S.2d 711 (Civ. Ct. 1974).

c.   Must the Lease Be in Writing?

The English Statute of Frauds, 29 Car. 2, c. 3 (1677), required a writing for any lease longer than three years. American statutes have followed the English pattern, although many have reduced the permitted maximum for oral leases to one year; see, e.g., N.Y. Gen. Oblig. Law §5-703 (McKinney 1989). A few statutes have barred oral leases altogether; see, e.g., Mass. Ann. Laws c. 259, §1 (Law. Co-op. 1992). Should an oral term of years ever be permitted?

Suppose that on January 1 the parties agree to a lease for a one-year term to begin on February 1. Many statutes providing for written leases of *more* than one year also require a writing when a contract is "not to be performed within the space of one year from the making thereof." Is an agreement to lease a contract? If so, does the January 1 agreement come within this provision? Compare Ward v. Hasbrouck, 169 N.Y. 407, 62 N.E. 434 (1902) (a lease for one year to take effect in the future need not be in writing), with Crommelin v. Thiess, 31 Ala. 412 (1858) (contra). Restatement (Second) of Property adopts the New York rule. Id. at §2.1, Comment f.

When a writing is required, it must identify the parties, identify the premises, specify the duration of the lease, and state the rent to be paid. The writing must also be signed by the party to be charged, or by his lawful agent. Id. at §2.2. Some states go even further, however, and require in every instance for terms longer than 3 years that both parties sign the writing before either one may enforce its provisions against the other. See, e.g., Penn. Stat. Ann. tit. 68, §250.202 (1994).

Suppose that T takes possession under a two-year oral letting in a state requiring a writing for leases longer than one year. What is the nature of T's tenancy? See Restatement (Second) of Property §2.3.

NOTES AND QUESTIONS

1.   **Examine your own lease.** If you are a renter, what kind of lease do you have? Why did you choose to have a term tenancy as opposed to a month-to-month (or vice versa)? Did you choose? Did you know the difference when you signed your lease? What are the advantages of each from the viewpoint of a student enrolled in law school? The disadvantages?

2.   **Problem.** Jane Student signs a lease "from August 1, 1996, until July 31, 1997" and moves in. On July 31, she moves out without giving her landlord any notice. What recourse does the landlord have?

3.   **Problem.** Tom Student leases premises pursuant to a lease that provides that "Tenant's lease shall begin on August 1, 1996, and rent shall be paid to Landlord in advance at the rate of $650 monthly." No specific provisions concerning the type of tenancy are included in the lease. Tom

[handwritten margin notes: "Implied PT = He still pays rent till Tenancy terminates = Implied Notice next month"]

moves out on July 31, 1997, without giving the landlord any notice. What recourse does the landlord have?

4. **Lease in Joy v. Daniels.** Look back at the lease in Joy v. Daniels, §1.3.c *supra*. What kind of tenancy did Mrs. Joy have at the time she signed her lease? This is a very common leasehold arrangement (commonly called a *roll-over*).

5. **Lease versus license.** A final "box" available in some factual situations is the "license." A license is "a personal privilege to do some particular act or series of acts on land without possessing any estate or interest therein, and is ordinarily revocable at the will of the licensor and is not assignable.[25] Lehman v. Williamson, 35 Colo. App. 372, 533 P.2d 63, 65 (1975)." Black's Law Dictionary 919 (6th ed. 1990). Examples of common licenses are movie theater tickets, parking lot tickets, and the permission one receives to enter a restaurant or other establishment.

6. **Dormitory contracts.** If you are a student living in a dorm room, examine your contract carefully. Do you have a lease or a license? Consider the following problem: A law student lives in a dorm room pursuant to a "Dormitory Contract" that gives her a license to occupy a room at a given rate during the academic year from August 15 until June 15. It provides: "This license is revocable for any reason by the University upon forty-eight hours notice." During the school year, the student gets in a dispute with the university over the issue of an unauthorized roommate. Shortly before exams he receives a letter notifying him that he must vacate his dorm room within one week. He consults you for legal advice. What would you advise him? Would the student be in a better position under the Housing Agreement (lease) or the Dormitory License found below?

HOUSING AGREEMENT

The _____ University enters into this Agreement with Student ("Student") and any Co-signer ("Co-signer") effective as of the date specified at the end of this Agreement.

1. **GENERAL:** The purpose of this Agreement is to establish certain financial and other relationships between University and Student including lease of space in University Residence Halls. The relationship between University and Student shall be subject to the terms and conditions in this Agreement.

2. **LEASED SPACE:** Student has a right of occupancy in and access to a space shared with one or more fellow students; shared use of student common facilities in the Residence Hall in which the space is located; and use

---

25. "Assignable" in this context means transferable.

of bed, springs, mattress, desk, chair, drapes, and dresser, to be furnished by the University. The term will be the period of time covered by the Fall and Spring Semesters, subject to other terms of this Agreement.

3. **SPACE ASSIGNMENT: UNIVERSITY RESERVES ALL RIGHTS CONCERNING ASSIGNMENT, REASSIGNMENT AND ADJUSTMENTS, IN ACCOMMODATIONS IT MAY CONSIDER NECESSARY.** The University reserves the right to consolidate student spaces based on occupancy needs or other needs as the University sees fit. Consolidation refers to reassigning students without roommates together to create more space.

4. **CANCELLATION PRIOR TO OCCUPANCY:** Any Student who wishes to cancel his/her reservation must do so by written notice received by the University Housing Office not later than August 1. Prior to occupancy, if notice of cancellation is received after August 1 a charge of 25% of the semester's space fee will be assessed. [Other cancellation charges are also detailed.]

5. **WITHDRAWAL FROM HOUSING:**   [sets up penalties and schedules for withdrawal].

6. **TERMINATION:**   This Agreement may be terminated in the following manner:

A.   Should Student at any time cease to be duly enrolled as a student at University, this lease shall automatically be terminated without notice, such notice hereby being waived. In these cases, cancellation of space charges will be made in accordance with the provisions set forth in paragraph 5 of this agreement.

B.   If Student violates any of the terms and conditions of this lease, and in particular, those set forth in paragraphs 7 and 8, Student may be given written notice by University to quit and vacate leased premises pending a determination by Conduct Council.

C.   If Student exhibits behavior or mode of living by which, in the sole judgment of the Director of Residential Life and Housing Services, Dean of Students, or Vice Provost for Student Life (or designee of the foregoing), it would be in the best interest of the Student or other residents for the Student to leave the University Residence Halls, then this Agreement may be terminated unilaterally by University upon due notice, and a cancellation of space charges may be made.

D.   If Student fails to claim space by checking in prior to the first day of classes in each semester, this Agreement may be automatically terminated unless the Office of Housing has received written notice of Student's late arrival.

E.   If the Agreement is terminated as provided in A, B, C, or D above, student must vacate the space on the effective date of termination. Upon Student's failure to quit and vacate, University shall be entitled to immediate possession of the space and to take all summary action to secure possession without any other or further notice of any kind to Student under applicable law or otherwise, such notice being expressly waived. University may then, without notice to Student, enter, take possession of, and relet space. University is further irrevocably authorized on behalf of Student to remove and to store Student's belongings without any liability on the part of University for damage or loss. In that event, University will make no charge for the first three weeks storage; but thereafter storage charges shall accrue at the rate of $20.00 (twenty dollars) per week for the next five weeks; and at the end of this eight (8) week period University is irrevocably authorized on behalf of Student to dispose of these belongings in any manner which it shall see fit without any obligation to make payment of any kind to Student (or Co-signer) resulting from such disposition, damage or loss. In connection with disposition of such property by University, it is expressly agreed by Student (and Co-signer) with University as a condition of this Agreement that the value of Student's belongings is One Hundred Dollars ($100.00) or less.

7. CARE AND USE OF SPACE: Student shall use the space exclusively as Residence Hall lodging.

STUDENT SHALL:

A.   Take care of the space and surrender the same at the end of term of Agreement in good order and in as good condition as when received, reasonable wear and tear excepted.

B.   Conform and comply with all laws, regulations, and ordinances of the (state) and the United States of America.

C.   Abide by University policy entitled Rights, Responsibilities, and Code of Conduct for Students, and those regulations set forth in official University brochures and notices, including University regulations concerning Residence Hall alcohol and smoking policy; all of which are made a part of and specifically incorporated into this Agreement.

STUDENT SHALL NOT:

E.   Violate published rules governing University Residence Halls, nor use the space for any disorderly purpose, or in such a manner as to interfere with the rights of other students in their academic pursuits.

F.   Damage the space or furnishings (including common areas), aside from reasonable wear and tear. If such loss or damage does occur Student will be billed for repair or replacement costs.

8. **MOTOR VEHICLES:**   Resident freshmen, resident sophomores, and all other resident students whose names were not selected in the resident parking permit selection process are not permitted to park a motor vehicle (including a motorcycle) on campus or in the neighborhood areas contiguous to campus. This prohibition reflects strict conditions imposed on the University by (state) zoning requirements. Compliance with these zoning requirements is not only a legal requirement impressed on the University community, but also is an important factor in maintaining good neighbor relations and the residential character of the surrounding community. Violations of this provision may be referred to Conduct Council and may result in termination of this lease, among other sanctions.

LAW SCHOOL DORMITORY LICENSE

I, _____, the undersigned, hereby agree to accept a license as occupant of the quarters assigned for my own occupation in accordance with established laws, dormitory rules, and usages of the University, and to pay for such license for the entire academic year, subject to the following conditions:

The entire balance shall be due upon the first day of occupancy of the room, although payable in accordance with University rules. If the licensee fails to register with or return to the law school at the beginning of the academic year indicated on the application, this license shall be void. It is understood and agreed that the right of the student to reside in University housing terminates when he/she ceases to be a registered student.

The University retains the right, for any cause it deems reasonable, either to assign the student another room or terminate the license, making an appropriate refund.

The University shall not be liable directly or indirectly for any damage resulting from lack of heat, irregularity of electricity, or for the loss by theft or damage of any objects or belongings of the student, wherever situated, and retains the right to enter the student's room at any time for any reasonable purpose.

All students who accept a permanent room assignment must pay a NON-REFUNDABLE $100 DEPOSIT, which shall be deducted from the price of the room. THIS DEPOSIT IS NON-REFUNDABLE IN THE EVENT THIS LICENSE IS TERMINATED. Additional fees will be charged for the pre-term breach of contract depending on the date of the breach. A list of these fees is set forth in the dormitory policies and procedures.

It is understood that for purposes of residency, the _____
academic year commences on (date) and ends on (date).

Breach of the dormitory contract after the official dormitory opening date for reasons other than withdrawal, matriculation, or personal situations deemed by the Dean of Students and the Housing Office to be
uncontrollable shall result in a penalty fee, in addition to pro-rata rent, corresponding to the student's housing assignment.

Signature:
Date:

_____

The formalistic, box-like structure of landlord and tenant law reflects
the feudal vision of property relationships designed to channel (force?)
people into pre-set social relationships. Why do contemporary courts continue to enforce these feudal categories? The following case both provides
an instance of formalistic analysis and gives some hints as to why it has survived into the present day.

NITSCHKE v. DOGGETT

489 S.W.2d 335 (Tex. Civ. App. 1972), vacated on jurisdictional grounds, 498
S.W.2d 339, 16 Tex. Sup. J. 444 (1973)

SHANNON, J. The question is whether a lease for the balance of the life
of appellee, as lessee, created an estate for years or a tenancy at will. We
hold that the lease established a tenancy at will terminable at any time by
either the lessor or the lessee.

Appellants, James B. Nitschke and his sister, Mary Alice Nitschke Smith,
appeal from the judgment of the county court at law of Travis County in
favor of Appellee, D. A. Doggett, in the sum of $9,000.00. We will reverse
that judgment, and here render judgment that appellee take nothing and
that appellants recover that sum.

This appeal stems from a condemnation proceeding filed in 1967 by
the Board of Regents of the University of Texas System to acquire a lot
owned by appellants, who are the children of Mayme Lucile Nitschke and
Louis E. Nitschke. At the time of condemnation appellee was operating a
dry cleaning shop on the lot under an oral lease for the balance of his life
obtained from Mayme Lucile Nitschke.

The Regents deposited the award of the commissioners and took
possession by agreement the sum in controversy, representing the value of
appellee's leasehold interest determined on the basis of appellee's life ex-

pectancy of twenty-three years, was retained by the clerk of the court, and the balance of the award was withdrawn by appellants. The claim to that sum was severed from the condemnation proceeding[26] and tried separately before the court.

The facts pertaining to appellee's lease for the balance of his life are not complicated. Appellants' father built the shop on the lot in 1934, and appellee, either as a partner or employee of his brother, or as owner, was associated with the dry cleaning business there until the lot was condemned.

After the death of Mr. Nitschke in 1940, Mrs. Nitschke and appellants owned the lot until 1959 when appellants acquired her interest. After that time, Mrs. Nitschke continued to treat with appellee concerning the leasing of the lot and the payment of rents.

Before the oral lease appellee held the lot under a series of written leases. Concerning the origin of the oral lease appellee testified that in 1962 or 1963, after he had delivered a written lease form to her so that she might obtain the necessary signatures which she failed to do, Mrs. Nitschke told him on three occasions that he did not need a written lease, and that he could have the property for the balance of his life for a rental of $85.00 monthly. Appellee did not promise Mrs. Nitschke that he would remain on the lot for the balance of his life, or for any other period.

Appellee emphasizes his testimony that he agreed that he would pay $85.00 a month so long as he remained. In addition, he stresses his statement that up until the time of the taking, he had intended to remain a tenant under the oral lease for the rest of his life.

Although alive at the time of trial, Mrs. Nitschke did not testify for she was *non compos mentis*.[27]

Appellants bring four points of error. Under the first point they argue that the lease failed for want of consideration because it lacked mutuality since appellee did not promise to retain the lot for any specific period of time. Their argument is, in effect, that as appellee was not obligated to remain a tenant for any certain duration, the lease created only a tenancy at will terminable by either the lessor or the lessee at any time. Appellee replies that there was consideration in that he made improvements on the lot in reliance upon Mrs. Nitschke's offer and that, in addition, he paid the monthly rent until the time of taking.[2] Moreover, appellee maintains that the duration of the lease was for a time certain, his lifetime.

In the outset appellee attacks appellants' first point of error for the

26. The government is buying the premises through its power of eminent domain (also called condemnation): The issue is whether it has to compensate for the leasehold estate. Condemnation is when the government takes private property for public use, paying just compensation to the landowner. See Chapter 6. — EDS.

27. *Non compos mentis* means not in full possession of her faculties. — EDS.

2. Appellants' arguments, and appellee's rejoinder, couched largely in terms of contract illustrate the dual nature of the law of landlord and tenant which concept Thompson rather inelegantly describes as ". . . a hermaphrodite, a combination of property and contract." 3 Thompson on Real Property Section 1110, p.377 (1959 Replacement).

reason, he says, that is not supported by their trial pleadings. Appellee contends that the point of error complains of a "failure of consideration" and, accordingly, must be affirmatively pleaded pursuant to Rule 94, Texas Rules of Civil Procedure, and that appellants filed only a general denial. This argument is without merit. It is "lack of consideration," or "want of consideration," about which appellants complain. They claim that appellee has failed to meet the burden of showing a necessary element of the lease upon which he relies. "Want of consideration" in the case of an agreement not in writing, may be raised by a general denial. See Rules 92 and 93, Tex. R. of Civ. P.

The question to be decided is whether the oral lease created an estate for years or a tenancy at will. If he had an estate for years, appellee was entitled to the value of that estate. If, however, appellee were a tenant at will, he held the lot at the pleasure of the lessor and was not entitled to recover.

A lease for years must have a definite and certain time at which it begins and ends. 3 Thompson on Real Property, Section 1088, p. 309 (1959 Replacement). See also, Restatement of the Law of Property, Section 19, Comment b (1936). This was the rule at common law,[3] and, apparently, is still the law of this state. In those leases in which the duration of the term is uncertain, only a tenancy at will is created. Hill v. Hunter, *supra.*

Appellee claims that the lease under consideration is distinguishable from those in Hill v. Hunter and like cases, for the reason that the term of the lease was measured by his lifetime, and the inevitability of his death rendered the lease certain. This contention was apparently made and rejected as early as the fifteenth century; ". . . as if one makes a lease or so many yeares as he shall live, this is voide *in praesenti* for the uncertainty." Sir Edward Coke, Commentary Upon Littleton, p.45b (13 Ed. 1789). See also 1 Tiffany on Landlord and Tenant, p.61 (1910).

That we shall die, we know; only the hour of death's arrival is unknown. But, an event certain to occur, *but uncertain as to the time of its occurrence,* as the death of appellee, may not be used to mark the termination of a lease. See Stanmeyer v. Davis, 321 Ill. App. 227, 53 N.E.2d 22 (1944), National Bellas Hess Inc. v. Kalis, 191 F.2d 739 (8th Cir. 1951).

Emphasis upon the property aspect of the law of landlord and tenant has been roundly criticized in recent years. One writer has observed that, "The task of modern courts has been to divorce the law of leases from its medieval setting of real property law, and adapt it to present day conditions and necessities by means of contract principles, which were only emerging when the law of landlord and tenant first developed." University of Texas: Bennett, The Modern Lease, 16 Texas L. Rev. 47, 48 (1937).

We agree in general with Justice Holmes that "it is revolting to have

---

3. "For regularly in every lease for yeares the terme must have a certaine beginning and a certain end. . . .", Sir Edward Coke, Commentary Upon Littleton 45 (13th ed. 1789). . . .

no better reason for a rule of law than that it was laid down in the time of Henry IV." At the same time we are not unmindful of the cases in this state, beginning with Lea v. Hernandez, [10 Tex. 137 (1853)], which follow the common law rule with respect to the requirement of certainty in the creation of estates for years.

In view of our holding on appellants' point of error one, it is unnecessary to consider the other points. The judgment of the trial court is reversed, and here rendered that appellee take nothing, and that appellants recover the sum of $9,000.00.

Reversed and remanded.

NOTES AND QUESTIONS

1. **Court's rationale.** What reasoning and authorities does the court use to support its conclusion? This case gives a good picture of the continuing influence of the common law on American landlords and tenants.

2. **Common law boxes.** Note the court's focus on two common law boxes: the estate for years and the tenancy at will. Its focus is on trying to fit the lease in question into one or the other of these boxes. Why do courts still resolve landlord and tenant cases by placing them in the Procrustean bed?[28] How might this court's analysis differ from that of a court in a contracts case?

3. **"It is revolting . . ."** "It is revolting to have no better reason for a rule of law than that it was laid down in the time of Henry IV." The quote is originally from Oliver Wendell Holmes,[29] who served on the U.S. Supreme Court from 1902 to 1932, and who in many ways was a precursor of the legal realists in his ridicule of the formalism of traditional law (particularly traditional property law). The *Nitschke* court insults the common-law rules, yet it follows them. Why? The court's rationale highlights an important issue involved in any change of established property rules: Will change upset settled expectations? Does this concern mean that property law should remain static? That any change should be legislated rather than court-made? That any change should be prospective rather than apply to existing arrangements? In this context, consider the famous quote: A "person has no property, no vested interest, in any rule of common law," Munn v. Illinois, 94 U.S. 113, 134 (1876).

4. **Redraft the lease.** How would you draft a written lease that reflected the understanding between Mrs. Nitschke and Mr. Doggett, yet would be upheld?

---

28. Procrustes was a robber who, according to Greek legend, placed all those he captured on an iron bed. If they were longer than the bed, he cut off surplusage; if they were shorter, he stretched them to fit the bed. Brewer's Dictionary of Phrase and Fable 864 (Ivor H. Evans, rev. ed. 1970).

29. Oliver Wendell Holmes, The Path of the Law, 10 Harv. L. Rev. 457, 469 (1897).

d.   Lease Analysis

An attorney faced with a landlord and tenant question typically begins by looking at the applicable lease. Lease forms obviously differ, but familiarity with one lease will familiarize you with standard lease provisions. We will be comparing two lease forms that are closely parallel, but also contain important differences. See Figures 3-2 and 3-3. Both are variants of the so-called model apartment lease approved by the Association of the Bar of the City of New York.[30] Each time you read the provisions of the two leases, make sure you understand what the provisions mean, and list the differences between the two leases. This requires close reading; the leases need to be studied, not skimmed.

What types of tenancies do the leases in Figures 3-2 and 3-3 establish? Do any significant differences exist between the two leases?

	LEASE, made as of the ＿＿ day of ＿＿＿＿＿＿＿＿,
	19＿＿, between ＿＿＿＿＿＿＿＿＿＿＿＿＿＿＿＿,
	having an address at ＿＿＿＿＿＿＿, ＿＿＿＿＿＿＿
Parties;	(the "Landlord") and ＿＿＿＿＿＿＿＿＿＿＿,
Addresses	having an address at ＿＿＿＿＿＿＿＿＿＿＿＿
	(the "Tenant").
	WITNESSETH. The Landlord leases to the Tenant Apart-
Apartment	ment ＿＿＿＿＿＿ (the "Apartment") on the ＿＿＿＿＿
	floor of the building (the "Building") having the street
Use	address ＿＿＿＿＿＿＿＿＿＿＿＿＿＿＿＿＿＿,
	for use by the Tenant solely as a private residence.
Term of	The term of this lease shall commence on ＿＿＿＿＿,
Lease	19＿＿, and shall end on ＿＿＿＿＿＿＿＿＿＿＿,
	19＿＿, or earlier if this lease is terminated in accor-
Rent	dance with the provisions of Article 9. The annual rent
	shall be $＿＿＿＿＿, payable in equal monthly install-
	ments of $＿＿＿＿＿ each, in advance, on the first
	day of each calendar month during the term, except that,
	unless this lease is a renewal, the first monthly installment
	shall be paid on the signing of this lease. All other sums
	required to be paid by the Tenant under this lease shall
	be deemed additional rent.

FIGURE 3-2
Lease No. 1

---

30. The Association's Committee on Real Property approved the Model Lease in the 1960s to provide a more understandable and evenly balanced form than the unintelligible and

	This Lease is entered into on _____, 19_____, between _____ (will be called "Landlord") who owns the building known as _____ and _____ (will be called "Tenant") who wants to rent Apartment _____ in that Building. The words "Tenant's Guest" shall mean any person who uses or is in the Apartment.
Apartment	Landlord agrees that Tenant can use Apartment (the word "Apartment" also means the Equipment in it), from
Term	_____ to _____
Use	to live in with Tenant's family and relatives. The rent shall
Rent and	be _____ per month and shall be paid on the first
Payment	day of each month, except that Tenant shall pay the first month's rent when this Lease is signed unless Tenant now lives in the Apartment. Rent shall be paid by check or cash delivered to Landlord at _____ or at such other address as Landlord shall notify Tenant to use.

FIGURE 3-3
Lease No. 2

e.   Statutes

How do these statutes change the common law (if at all)? Consider also how the statutes blur the distinctions between the four types of common law tenancies.

Md. Code Ann., Real Prop. §8-208 (1994)

a) *Prohibited provisions.* — A lease may not contain any of the following provisions: . . .

(5) Any provision whereby the tenant agrees to a period required for landlord's notice to quit less than that provided by applicable law; provided, however, that neither party is prohibited from agreeing to a longer notice period than that required by applicable law.

---

wholly one-sided standard forms then widely used by New York City landlords. The tenant's "revolution" and the "plain English" movement would make the Association's 1960s "model" the legal equivalent of a model T, but plenty of nonmodel standard forms are still around, in New York and elsewhere.

Md. Code Ann., Real Prop. §8-402 (1994)

(b) *Notice to quit.* — (1) (i) Where any interest in property shall be leased for any definite term or at will, and the landlord shall desire to repossess the property after the expiration of the term for which it was leased and shall give notice in writing one month before the expiration of the term or determination of the will to the tenant or to the person actually in possession of the property to remove from the property at the end of the term, and if the tenant or person in actual possession shall refuse to comply, the landlord may make complaint in writing to the District Court of the county where the property is located. [Additional procedures are then detailed.]

Va. Code Ann. §55-222 (Michie 1994)

Notice to terminate a tenancy; on whom served; when necessary. — A tenancy from year to year may be terminated by either party giving three months' notice, in writing, prior to the end of any year of the tenancy, of his intention to terminate the same. A tenancy from month to month may be terminated by either party giving thirty days notice in writing, prior to the end of the month, of his intention to terminate the same. . . . When such notice is to the tenant it may be served upon him or upon anyone holding under him the leased premises, or any part thereof. When it is by the tenant it may be served upon anyone who, at the time, owns the premises in whole or in part, or the agent of such owner, or according to the common law. This section shall not apply when, by special agreement, no notice is to be given; nor shall notice be necessary from or to a tenant whose term is to end at a certain time.

Va. Code Ann. §55-248.37 (Michie 1994)

Periodic tenancy; holdover remedies. — The landlord or the tenant may terminate a week-to-week tenancy by serving a written notice on the other at least seven days prior to the next rent due date. The landlord or tenant may terminate a month-to-month tenancy by serving a written notice on the other at least thirty days prior to the next rent due date.

§3.3   Conveyance or Contract?

The idea of a lease as a conveyance fits well into the traditional agrarian context of English landlord and tenant law. Many English farmers had year-to-year leases. In theory, such leases were terminable upon six months' notice. In practice, such leases appear to have been renewed nigh-automatically as late as the nineteenth century. In Orley Farm, a novel by Anthony Trollope first published in 1861, Sir Peregrine Orme, who represents old-fashioned ways, disapproves of his young neighbor's decision to end a lease to shift to modern, scientific farming practices. "'Ah! he was wrong there,' said the baronet [Sir Peregrine], 'When a man has held land so long, it should not be taken away from him except under pressing circumstances; that is, if he pays his rent.'" [31]

In the course of the twentieth century, the lease moved to the cities. Between 1870 and 1920, 26 million immigrants entered the United States, and the great majority stayed in the cities.[32] Most worked in low-wage jobs and lived in rented tenement housing.[33] Moreover, commercial leases became increasingly common and often contained individually tailored clauses designed to the business specifications of the leasehold parties. In these contexts, the lease looked less and less like the conveyance of an interest in land, and more and more like a contract. Yet courts were inconsistent about treating the lease as a contract because contract law led to certain conclusions courts did not wish to reach, most notably that the landlord gave an implied warranty that rented premises were in habitable condition.[34]

Twentieth-century cases at times claim that the lease is now "really" a contract, but in fact the lease is "a hermaphrodite, a combination of property and contract," 3 Thompson on Real Property, §1110, at 377 (1959 Replacement). Courts characterize the lease as a contract or conveyance depending on the substantive conclusions they wish to reach and have done so since at least the eighteenth century.[35]

UNIVERSITY CLUB v. DEAKIN

265 Ill. 257, 106 N.E. 790 (1914)

Mr. Justice Cook delivered the opinion of the court. Defendant in error, the University Club of Chicago, brought suit in the municipal court of Chicago against Earl H. Deakin, the plaintiff in error, to recover rent alleged to be due under a lease. A trial was had before the court without a

---

31. Anthony Trollope, Orley Farm 39 (with introduction by Henry S. Drinker, 1950) (originally published in 1861).

32. Mary Beth Norton et al., A People and a Nation 317 (1988).

33. Id. at 178, 316 (working class earned too little to pay for trolley transportation to suburban houses), 317 (most immigrants stayed in cities). See also Richard Plunz, A History of Housing 36 (1990) (by 1890 immigrants comprised 42 percent of New York City's population; almost all lived in tenements).

34. See Michael Weinberg, From Contract to Conveyance: The Law of Landlord and Tenant, 1800-1920 (Part I), 1980 S. Ill. L.J. 29.

35. Id., passim.

jury and resulted in a judgment for $2007.66. Deakin prosecuted an appeal to the Appellate Court for the First District, where the judgment of the municipal court was affirmed. A writ of certiorari having been granted by this court, the record has been brought here for review.

On March 31, 1909, defendant in error leased to plaintiff in error, for a term of one year, a store room in its building at the corner of Michigan avenue and Monroe street, in the city of Chicago, at a rental of $5000 for the year. The lease provided that plaintiff in error should use the room for a jewelry and art shop and for no other purpose. It also contained the following clause, numbered 12: "Lessor hereby agrees during the term of this lease not to rent any other store in said University Club building to any tenant making a specialty of the sale of Japanese or Chinese goods or pearls." Shortly after this lease was made defendant in error leased to one Sandberg, for one year, a room in the University Club building, two doors from the corner, at a rental of $2500. The following provision was inserted in the Sandberg lease: "It is further distinctly understood and agreed by and between the parties hereto that at no time during the term of this lease will the lessee herein use the demised premises for a collateral loan or pawnshop or make a specialty therein of the sale of pearls." On May 1, 1909, being the first day of the term of the lease, plaintiff in error took possession of the premises and thereafter paid the rent, in monthly installments, for May and June. During the latter part of June plaintiff in error, through his attorney, sought to obtain from defendant in error a cancellation of his lease on the ground that by leasing a room in the University Club building to Sandberg and permitting him to display and sell pearls therein defendant in error had violated the provision of plaintiff in error's lease above quoted, and that for such violation plaintiff in error was entitled to terminate the lease. Defendant in error refused to cancel the lease, and on June 30 plaintiff in error vacated the premises, surrendered the keys and refused to pay any further installments of rent. This suit was brought to enforce payment of subsequent installments of rent accruing under the lease for the time the premises remained unoccupied after June 30.

The evidence offered by plaintiff in error tended to show that Sandberg had made a specialty of the sale of pearls in connection with the conduct of his general jewelry business ever since he took possession of the room leased to him, and that plaintiff in error vacated the premises and surrendered possession because of the failure of defendant in error to enforce the twelfth clause of his lease. The evidence offered by defendant in error tended to prove that Sandberg had not made a specialty of the sale of pearls, and that when plaintiff in error first made known his desire to assign or cancel his lease he gave as his only reason that his health was failing and that he had been advised by his physician to leave the city of Chicago.

Propositions were submitted to the court by both parties to be held as the law of the case. The court held, at the request of plaintiff in error, that the lease sued upon was a bi-lateral contract, and upon a breach of an es-

sential covenant thereof by the lessor the lessee had a right to refuse further
to be bound by its terms and to surrender possession of the premises, and
that a breach of the twelfth clause of the lease would be a good defense
to an action for rent if the tenant surrendered possession of the premises
within a reasonable time after discovery of the breach. The court refused to
hold as law propositions submitted by defendant in error stating the converse of the propositions so held at the request of plaintiff in error. The
court properly held that the lease in question was a bi-lateral contract. It
was executed by both parties and contained covenants to be performed by
each of them. The propositions so held with reference to the effect of a
breach of the twelfth clause of the lease correctly stated the law. By holding
these propositions the court properly construed the twelfth clause as a vital
provision of the lease and held that a breach of that provision by the lessor
would entitle the lessee to rescind. Where there is a failure to comply with
a particular provision of a contract and there is no agreement that the
breach of that term shall operate as a discharge, it is always a question for
the courts to determine whether or not the default is in a matter which is
vital to the contract. . . . While there was no provision in this contract that
plaintiff in error should have the option to terminate it if the terms of the
twelfth clause were not observed, it is apparent that it was the intention of
the parties to constitute this one of the vital provisions of the lease. It was
concerning a matter in reference to which the parties had a perfect right to
contract, and it will be presumed that plaintiff in error would not have entered into the contract if this clause had not been made a part of it. It is
such an essential provision of the contract that a breach of it would warrant
plaintiff in error in rescinding the contract and surrendering possession of
the premises. . . .

The following proposition was submitted by defendant in error and
held by the court as the law of the case: "The plaintiff performed all the
obligations imposed upon it by its covenant that it would not rent any other
store in its building to a tenant making a specialty of the sale of pearls, by
incorporating in its lease to the second tenant that said second tenant
should not make a specialty of the sale of pearls in the demised premises."

From a consideration of all the propositions of law held and refused,
it appears that the judgment of the trial court was reached from the application of the proposition just quoted to the facts in the case. The court
erred in holding this proposition as the law. By covenanting with plaintiff
in error not to rent any other store in this building, during the term of
plaintiff in error's lease, to any tenant making a specialty of the sale of
pearls, defendant in error assumed an obligation which could not be discharged by simply inserting in the contract with the second tenant a covenant that such tenant should not make a specialty of the sale of pearls. It
was incumbent upon it to do more than to insert this provision in the second lease. By the terms of its contract with plaintiff in error it agreed that
no other portion of its premises should be leased to any one engaged in the

prohibited line of business, and if it failed to prevent any subsequent tenant from engaging in the business of making a specialty of the sale of pearls, it did so at the risk of plaintiff in error terminating his lease and surrendering possession of the premises.

This precise question has never been passed upon by this court, so far as we are able to ascertain. Defendant in error cites and relies upon Lucente v. Davis, 101 Md. 526, which supports its theory. We cannot yield our assent to the doctrine there announced. Defendant in error cannot escape its obligation by the mere insertion of a clause in the lease with the second tenant prohibiting him from engaging in the line of business named. Plaintiff in error contracted for the exclusive right to engage in this particular business in that building. There was no privity between him and Sandberg, and he was powerless to enforce the provisions of the contract between defendant in error and Sandberg.[36] It is idle to say that an action for damages for a breach of contract would afford him ample remedy. He contracted with defendant in error for the sole right to engage in this specialty in its building, and if defendant in error saw fit to ignore that provision of the contract and suffer a breach of the same, plaintiff in error had the right to terminate his lease, surrender possession of the premises and refuse to further perform on his part the provisions of the contract.

For the errors indicated the judgment of the Appellate Court and the judgment of the municipal court are reversed and the cause is remanded to the municipal court for a new trial.

Reversed and remanded.

△ wins
Π Breached K

NOTES AND QUESTIONS

1. **Contract or conveyance?** Does the court treat the lease as a contract or a conveyance?

2. **Tenant's exclusive right to sell.** Retail tenants often obtain an exclusive right to sell, usually stated as a landlord's promise not to lease another store in the building or shopping mall to a merchant carrying a similar line of goods. Courts have regularly treated the landlord's covenant to bar competition as a vital part of the lease enabling tenant to rescind once she establishes breach. Cf. also Kulawitz v. Pacific Woodenware & Paper Co., 25 Cal. 664, 155 P.2d 24 (1944).[37] Courts have similarly regarded the covenant for quiet enjoyment. See §4.7 *infra*.

3. **Materiality of leasehold covenants.** By contrast, consider the quite recent case of Schulman v. Vera, 108 Cal. App. 3d 552, 166 Cal. Rptr. 620

---

36. For a discussion of privity of estate, see Note 6 *infra*. — EDS.
37. The Restatement (Second) of Property, Landlord and Tenant, §7.2 (1977), although it agrees that the landlord's failure to bar competition under a leasehold covenant places the landlord in default, notes also that some noncompetition promises are invalid as illegal restraints on trade. Id. at Comment a.

(1980). The *commercial* tenant had rented space on a ten-year lease. Included in the lease were a tenant's covenant to pay rent and a landlord's covenant to repair any damage to the roof or exterior walls of the building. When tenant failed to pay rent, landlord sued for possession; tenant pleaded as an affirmative defense the landlord's breach of the covenant to repair the roof. Landlord's motion to strike the affirmative defense was granted and the appellate court upheld the ruling:

> A covenant to repair on the part of the lessor and a covenant to pay rent on the part of the lessee are usually considered as independent covenants, and unless the covenant to repair is expressly or impliedly made a condition precedent to the covenant to pay rent, the breach of the former does not justify the refusal on the part of the lessee to perform the latter.

Id. at 558-559 (quoting Arnold v. Krigbaum, 169 Cal. 143, 145 (1915)).

Although language in the *Schulman* opinion, 108 Cal. App. 3d, at 562, 166 Cal. Rptr., at 626, intimates that the court might have decided differently if the landlord had been suing for the rent and not possession, the landlord's right to possession depended on an antecedent right to collect his rent in full despite his breach of the repair covenant.

Can you formulate any criteria for helping one to decide whether a landlord's covenant is vital? What about tenant's covenants? Suppose, in Schulman v. Vera, the premises were a dwelling unit that the landlord had failed to repair? Cf. Javins v. First National Realty Company, §3.9.c.1 *infra*. Suppose that the tenant promises to take good care of the premises and fails to do so?

4.   **Measurement of tenant's damages upon rescission.** If the tenant is entitled to terminate the lease because of the landlord's default, absent a valid agreement as to the measure of damages, damages may include one or more of the following items, wherever appropriate, so long as no double recovery is involved.

(a)   the fair market value (premium value) of the lease as of the termination date

(b)   the loss sustained by the tenant due to reasonable (and foreseeable) expenditures made by the tenant before the landlord's default

(c)   reasonable relocation costs

(d)   (in the case of business premises) loss of anticipated business profits proven to a reasonable degree of certainty

(e)   interest on the account recovered at the legal rate for the period appropriate under the circumstances

Restatement (Second) of Property §10.2 (1977).

The fair market value of the lease, (a) *supra,* is the present value of the difference between a higher fair rental value of the unit and the agreed-upon or bargained-for rental (reserved rental) over the unexpired term of the lease. The following discussion, appearing in Stanley L. McMichael and Paul T. O'Keefe, Leases: Percentage, Short and Long Term 118-119 (6th ed. 1974), elaborates the above rule:

> *In property where there is no capital investment made by the lessee, the leasehold has value only if the rent reserved in the lease is less than the true economic rental value.*[38] *The measure of leasehold value is the present-day discounted worth of the sum of the annual differentials for the remaining lease term.*
>
> The discount theory is based on the economic fact that present money, because of its earning potential, commands a premium over future money. $3312.12 invested today at 8 percent interest will pay an annuity of $1000 for four years at the end of which period the capital sum will have been exhausted. The difference between the $4000 in total annual payments and the $3312.12 is the discount. Obviously, the discount will vary as the assumed interest rate varies. . . .
>
> Anyone buying an annuity will discount it for interest as of the date of purchase. The lessee who holds a lease at less than the fair rental value has in effect an annuity (the differential between the fair rental value and the rent reserved in the lease) which stems from his leasehold interest. There is, of course, an assumption that this differential will be maintained during the remainder of the lease term.
>
> Translating the leasehold interest into value is the same as discounting the "annuities" for the balance of the lease. Take as an example the property with an assumed worth of $100,000 and a rental value of $8000 per annum net (8 percent of fee value). Let it be further assumed that the property is leased for a term of years, with 15 years remaining, at $6000 per annum.
>
> The differential between the rental value and the lease rental is $2000 per annum. This represents the lessee's "annuity" for 15 years. Discounted at 8 percent interest, the leasehold would be valued at $17,000.
>
> "In this same case, if the fee or lessor's interest were appraised, it would suffer a diminution in value because the lease is unfavorable from the lessor's or fee owner's point of view. The same mathematics would apply and a proper valuation of the fee interest would be $100,000 minus $17,000 or $83,000.
>
> "Similarly (although the value of the fee is not our primary concern), a lease to a *responsible* tenant at a rental in excess of true rental value might give property a value above the free and clear market value.
>
> "If we take the case above of the property valued at $100,000 with a fair rental value of $8000 and assume it to be rented for $10,000 per annum, it would give the lessor or fee owner an "annuity" of $2000 over and above the fair rental value predicated, of course, on the tenant's responsibility and ability to pay. In this case, the fee might be valued at $100,000 plus $17,000 or $117,000. The leasehold interest would be valueless. . . .

5.   **Measurement of tenant's damages absent rescission.** Where tenant does not rescind the lease after landlord's breach, through choice if the

---

38. This differential usually comes from a change in market conditions during the term of the lease. — EDS.

covenant is material, or because rescission is not permitted (if the covenant is either nonmaterial or "independent") tenant is entitled to recover damages to reflect any diminution in the value of the premises. Most courts measure tenant's damages as the difference in the leasehold's value with the landlord's covenant unbroken and with the same covenant broken. Where the tenant operates a business, courts allow tenant to introduce evidence of lost profits as indicating the difference in value. The Restatement (Second) of Property, Landlord and Tenant, §11.1 (1977), defines an alternative measure:

> If the tenant is entitled to an abatement of the rent, the rent is abated to the amount of that proportion of the rent which the fair rental value after the event giving the right to abate bears to the fair rental value before the event.

Compare the tenant's recovery under the prevailing and the Restatement methods (assuming that tenant has paid the reserved rental in advance) where the unexpired term is one year, the fair rental value of the premises before the event (covenant unbroken) is $50,000 yearly, the fair rental value of the premises after the event (covenant broken) is $30,000 yearly, and the reserved rental is $40,000 yearly. Suppose that the reserved rental were $50,000 yearly. Or $25,000 yearly. Which one of the two formulae do you prefer? Why?

6. **A first look at privity of estate.** Recall that the court in its *University Club* opinion stated that Deakin could not enforce the provisions of the lease between the landlord and the competing tenant Sandberg (in which Sandberg had covenanted not to compete) because "there was no privity between [Deakin] and Sandberg." Privity of estate in property law is a several-headed concept. In this context, it means that Deakin would have enjoyed the requisite privity only if he had acquired some interest from the landlord *after* Sandberg had made his promise. Cf. Restatement (First) of Property §547 (1944). However, under modern property law, Deakin can assert rights as the third-party beneficiary of Sandberg's promise. Deakin might also have had a claim against Sandberg derived from the covenant in Deakin's lease that landlord would not lease to a competitor. See Freedman v. Seidler, 233 Md. 39, 194 A.2d 778 (1963).

§3.4   Anatomy of a Residential Landlord and Tenant Case

The typical (that is to say, poor) residential tenant played a central role in the imagination of the courts that decided the leading cases of the 1970s "landlord and tenant revolution." For this reason, property casebooks typically focus on residential rather than commercial leases, a focus that is pedagogically suitable in view of the complexity of many commercial leases.

We focus here on one landlord and tenant case — of the millions of such cases every year — as a way of introducing one type of legal practice: that of legal services lawyers who represent clients too poor to pay for a private attorney. The Legal Services program began in the 1960s and was in full swing by 1971, by which time the number of lawyers representing poor people had risen by 650 percent to 2,500 lawyers.[39] Legal services lawyers had a substantial impact on many areas of the law: Note that Joy v. Daniels and State v. Shack both involved tenants represented by legal services lawyers. Funding for the program was cut back dramatically after the election of Ronald Reagan in 1980, yet legal services attorneys continue to serve clients around the country today.[40] Because the poor typically are renters, legal services programs (as well as many law school clinics) do a substantial amount of landlord and tenant law.

The classic pattern of a residential landlord and tenant case is as follows. First, the landlord terminates the tenant's tenancy and begins the eviction process. Then, the tenant raises any defenses she has, arguing that she should not be evicted. Finally, landlord evicts, raising issues of what eviction procedures must be followed.

The following is a student paper written for the District of Columbia Law Students in Court Landlord and Tenant Clinic. In it, a second-year student reports on her experiences handling the case of Johnson v. Management, Inc.[41] from start to finish. Note how little of her time is taken up with issues concerning legal doctrine — the standard fare in first-year law school. List, in order of descending importance, the lawyering tasks that take up her time. What do you find most surprising about the author's description of the practice of law? What kinds of skills seem most vital for effective lawyering in this context?

Note the process by which this tenant's problem gets translated into a legal case. What gets left out in that process? Name the central issues in the legal case. Do these issues reflect the landlord's basic concerns? The tenant's? To what extent in this case do the party's concerns and the legal issues diverge?

Note that, even when litigation becomes the focus of the case, a full-dress trial is not the form litigation takes. Instead — this is typical of many kinds of litigation — motion practice plays a far greater role. A motion you might already be familiar with is a motion to dismiss for lack of jurisdiction. Motion practice takes up the bulk of the court time of many practicing litigators.

39. Martha F. Davis, Brutal Need: Lawyers and the Welfare Rights Movement, 1960-1973, at 10 (1993). Before this period, a variety of privately funded programs had served the poor since the 1870s. Mark Kessler, Legal Services for the Poor 4-5 (1987).

40. But federal funding for legal services may be doomed. Congress in 1996 cut appropriations by nearly one-third, as part of a plan that, if implemented, would phase the program out in three years.

41. All the names other than those of the student attorney and her supervisors have been changed to protect the privacy of the client.

You will not fully understand the law involved in the *Johnson* case until we have completed our study of landlord and tenant law. Hence, your experience will be similar to that of a beginning attorney: You will have to "black box" what you don't understand in the process of analyzing what you do grasp. For now, two brief points of law will suffice. In the District of Columbia, as in most American jurisdictions, a tenant can be relieved of the obligation to pay part or all of the contract rent if the leasehold premises are in a deteriorated condition. See §3.9.c.3 *infra.* In D.C., however, a court-imposed requirement is that a tenant claiming he does not owe the full amount of rent to the landlord must nonetheless pay the contested rent into a court escrow[42] pursuant to a "protective order." See §3.9.c.4 *infra.*

This glimpse of trial practice also gives you a perspective from which to evaluate your own law school experience. How does this student attorney's relationship to the facts differ from your experience so far in law school? Note the way that landlord and tenant law, civil procedure, and ethical issues all are part of the picture: Remember that in the outside world, cases often involve issues from many areas of the law.

Make sure you make a time line so you can follow the progress of the case step by step. Come to class prepared to ask specific questions to clear up any aspects of the case you did not understand. This paper reminds us there are many different approaches to legal education. Clinics, normally offered to second- and third-year students, offer a very different perspective on the law than do the introductory classes of the first year.

NANCY OLIVER LESOURD, A CASE STUDY — NOW COMES THE DEFENDANT, BY AND THROUGH COUNSEL

Paper submitted in D.C. Law Students in Court Landlord/Tenant Clinic, June 1984.[43]

CAST OF CHARACTERS

Anne Marie, Rich, Evie, Dennis — clinic supervisors
Nancy — student attorney
Elma Johnson (a pseudonym) — tenant (and the defendant)
Management, Inc. (a pseudonym) — the company that managed the
     tenant's apartment (and the plaintiff)

---

42. Black's Law Dictionary defines escrow as follows: "A bank account generally held in the name of the depositor and an escrow agent, which is . . . paid to a third person on the fulfillment of escrow condition." Black's Law Dictionary 545 (6th ed. 1990). In simple terms, funds are placed with a third party with a contract to have them released subject to agreed-on conditions. In this case, the tenant will pay the court with the understanding that the court will release the funds to the landlord when certain conditions have been met. — EDS.

43. Our thanks to Anne Marie Hay for her help. This paper has been edited to clarify some passages. — EDS.

Tilman, Zuckerman & Hand (a pseudonym) — attorneys for the landlord

. . . By the third year of law school, students have learned how to fox-hole, balance difficult courses with guts, and cram fourteen weeks of material into two. Important as those skills may be to a third-year law student, they are exactly opposite the behavior one needs as a lawyer. Procrastination, a common law student characteristic, can greatly damage a case. The concept that the defendant[44] comes to the court, by and through counsel, by and through you, is both humbling and challenging.

THE CLIENT INTERVIEW

On September 12, 1983, I was Student of the Day and answered calls regarding our services. There was a call from a Ms. Elma Johnson whose ceiling had fallen in only minutes after she had sent her children out of the room. When she told me about all the other Housing Code violations, I thought perhaps this would be a case we could take. After conferring with [a supervisor], I called Ms. Johnson back to tell her to come to court prepared to pay a protective order.[45]

At our first court date, on September 19, 1983, we were able to get a two week continuance[46] to file responsive pleadings. This would give me two weeks to prepare an answer. We also agreed by mutual consent on the entrance of a protective order allowing Ms. Johnson to pay her rent of $299 into the court, rather than directly to the landlord. I then walked Ms. Johnson over to the L&T (landlord & tenant) office to show her how to pay a protective order. Since there are several steps involved, it was helpful for her (and me) to walk through the process. We then set up a client conference for Ms. Johnson to come to our offices.

It was at this court appearance that I had my first dealings with "the other side." Tilman, Zuckerman & Hand were the attorneys for the other side and it was this day that I met Ronald Hand. He is quite gruff and always seems a bit annoyed that he has to talk to a law student. It was also the first insight I had into their lawyering habits. For example, on the summons it noted that waiver of a notice to quit is usually a standard part of a lease. However, if they had checked the lease for the apartment for which they were seeking possession, they would have found that Ms. Johnson never signed the lease. [Because Ms. Johnson had never agreed in writing to waive

---

44. Ms. Johnson's landlord eventually filed to evict her for nonpayment of rent. Therefore, the landlord is the plaintiff and Ms. Johnson is the defendant. — Eds.

45. A protective order allows a tenant to pay her rent into an escrow account at the court instead of paying it to the landlord. District of Columbia law requires that a tenant who wants to withhold rent from a landlord must pay the rent into the court if the landlord so requests. See §3.9.c.4 *infra*. — Eds.

46. A continuance means an extension of a deadline. — Eds.

the notice to quit, the termination of her lease was invalid.] This was a substantial defect in their case that they did not deal with until long afterward
— in fact, until the day before trial. Moreover, the summons also stated that
the plaintiff sought a protective order "requiring all past due and future
accruing rents paid into the registry of the Court pendente lite."[47] Their
Latin won't save their law: as all clinic students know after orientation, protective orders are prospective only. The protective order would begin *that*
day and go forward.

On September 22, 1983 — Ms. Johnson came to our offices and we
spent four hours talking. She was confused and frightened about the whole
process. Her brother, who had cosigned the lease for her originally, wanted
her to try to handle this on her own. He had heard of our Clinic and gave
her the number. Ms. Johnson was very timid and shy during that meeting. I
found that I needed to ask a lot of very fact-oriented questions to help her
tell me her story. I think the reason that the interview took so long was not
only my lack of experience but my sense that this was the time to build
rapport with my client. I asked her a lot of questions about her kids. She
has six of them and they are very special to her. She really wants to do the
best she can for them. I picked that up very early in the conversation and I
asked her a lot of questions about each of her children. I knew this whole
process was strange and unnatural for her. Although I had the handout
from orientation regarding the important topical areas to cover during an
interview, I also sensed that I should try to go over these in as conversational
a manner as possible. I think that after two years of law school, where you
just get the facts as fast as possible, it was difficult for me to put aside that
drive to elicit information and to make primary the need to establish a relationship. I had only set aside two hours for the client interview because I
had class. It was difficult that first day not to speed things up to fit *my* needs.
That is a lesson I learned over and over in the Clinic.

I typed up my notes from the conference within two days. Because
information does not always come out in neat little categories and because
you often ask a question later about something a client stated at the beginning, it is most helpful to type up your notes in topical form as soon as
possible. I referred to these notes quite a bit during discovery, and when
checking on possible areas of weakness in our case. It helped immensely to
have the notes at hand and organized.

THE TWO-WEEK CONTINUANCE PERIOD

This is probably one of the busiest times of a case. You spend time
with the client, showing her how to pay a protective order and perhaps conducting a client interview if she has time. Then there is just a lot of running

---

47. "Pendente lite" means "for the duration of the litigation." — EDS.

around to do. You have to check with the Recorder of Deeds office to make sure there has been no change in ownership that affects the case. You must check the dockets to make sure the client has not been sued before and had a default judgment entered against her.

It is really important to see the apartment. Although you can see the pictures that an investigator takes, it really does help to actually see the condition of the apartment where your client lives. I think there may also be something positive communicated by your willingness to actually visit with your clients in their home and let them point out the things that are their greatest concerns. It is best to take pictures as quickly as possible after the case begins. There is an attempt on the part of many landlords to fix, albeit superficially, any problems that might raise substantial housing code violation concerns. For example, although Ms. Johnson had sent numerous written requests for painting after they had put up sheetrock to replace the ceiling in July, only two weeks after the case began they did actually come in to paint. Taking pictures of the apartment in the state of disrepair is so much more effective than trying to explain to court or the jury where the crack in the wall *was*.

Your greatest friends are the routine forms for answers, interrogatories, production of documents, trial memorandum, jury instructions, etc., which are all there just awaiting your "fill in the blank" ability. Two points that I learned the hard way: (1) Although it is "fill in the blank," it does not mean you can turn your mind off. Remember, you are stating the reasons why your client should not be liable. Having the Housing Code right there with you as you prepare the answer is critical. It may jog your memory as to other questions you should ask your client *before* you finish preparing your answer, which leads me to another suggestion. (2) Don't be so anxious to finish your document that if you do need to contact a client and thus need an extra day you are unable to do so without feeling put upon. Again, procrastination, the *sine qua non* of law students, is your greatest curse as counsel.

THE RETURN DATE

This is when fear sets in, my first time to talk to a judge. I had been Student of the Day my first court day, dealt with Ms. Johnson and Mr. Hand, opposing counsel, my second court day, and was in Small Claims my third court day. Now, the moment of truth was here. I was going to have to stand up in front of the judge and say something.

Ms. Johnson met me at the clinic at 8:45 A.M. to sign and have notarized the answer which we were to file with the court that morning. (An aside: Ms. Johnson was extremely punctual, thorough and conscientious. With other clients, however, you do not want the anxiety of wondering if they are going to show up to sign the answer when it's 9:10 and you know they're calling your case over in L&T. The panic is just not worth it. Have them come in the day before to sign the answer.) We walked over to the courthouse together and I explained to her what was going to happen that morning. I told Ms. Johnson about where we would stand and what I would say to the judge.

I hate to admit this but it is true: The one-line statement you make to the Court when filing an answer was written down on an index card and I had memorized it. Yes, Nancy Oliver, who had taught school for 5 years and lectured without notes for hours upon end was memorizing the one liner. When Anne Marie [a supervisor] told me what to say, I wrote it down and went over and over it. All the time, of course, reassuring Ms. Johnson what a simple process filing the answer was. I met Dennis [another supervisor] outside the court room and he asked me how I was. I replied, "Nervous." To which he replied, "Well, I'd be worried if you weren't." That reassurance did help but still, I have to admit it, that little index card with my one line on it was not far away from me at any moment.

The Clerk of the Court called the case: "Management, Inc. vs. Elma Johnson" and Ms. Johnson and I both walked to the front. "Good morning, your honor, my name is Nancy Oliver with D.C. Law Students in Court. We're here today to file our answer and to request that this case be certified to the civil division for placement on the jury calendar." That was it. Just one line. Just 20 seconds before the Court. Piece of cake. What was I worried about?

PROTECTIVE ORDERS

Not every case has an incident with protective orders, but a lot do. In Ms. Johnson's case, we had two separate problems with payment of the protective order.

My client was to pay $299.00 into the court registry by the 5th of each month. On the 24th of October, we received a copy of Plaintiff's Motion for Judgment for Possession for Failure to Comply with Protective Order. This motion was filed and a hearing requested for October 28th. All this occurred while I was in California on an interview trip. Because Ms. Johnson had paid her protective order, my supervisor was able to get the opposing counsel to withdraw his motion.

However, three days later, I received a phone call from Ms. Johnson. It was the third of November and she still had not received her public assistance check. It generally always arrives by the first of each month and had not been late once since she had been in D.C. (3 years). After conferring with a supervisor we decided to wait a few more days to see if it would come in. Several days later and still no check meant that we needed to make a timely motion to the court to request a delay in the payment of a protective order. I called the opposing counsel and at their request agreed to make the motion on November 14th, their regular court day. To cover myself, I prepared a statement to the effect that the Defendant had intended to come before the court on November 10th but upon request of Plaintiff, agreed to make the motion on November 14th.

If there ever was a day in this case that I can point to where I began to glimpse what it means to come before the Court on the behalf of the defendant, it was this day. No index cards. Not even a prepared written motion. It was an oral motion asking that the judge use his equitable powers to allow for a delay in payment of the protective order due to the lateness of my client's public assistance check. And it was against Ronald Hand, who was that morning quite belligerent. For example, I had approached him to ask him to sign the statement regarding our intention to come into court earlier and he had refused. Since Mr. Hand refused to sign this statement, I brought it up in court and he then orally stipulated[48] to it. I had also asked him if he would agree to mutual discovery, a device which saves both parties time. His response was that if I could beat him in court this morning then maybe he'd agree.

It was an interesting day. I was supposed to be at Dulles by 4:00 for my last interview trip to California. I had spent time in the library the night before to read Estelle Davis v. Rental Associates and various equitable action cases. My client was very worried they would evict her. I had spoken with her case worker several times to try to ascertain whether the check had been sent. No index cards, nothing to memorize, just a knowledge of the law and a concern for Elma.

To be honest, Hand's bellowing did scare me. He was so difficult to deal with. Also, I was somewhat concerned that the law was not heavily on our side and a lot would depend on the judge's willingness to exercise the equitable powers at his disposal. When they called the case and the parties introduced themselves, I made the request to the court for a delay in payment of the protective order, stating briefly the situation.

The Judge turned to Mr. Hand and asked him if he objected. Frankly, I was shocked. Hand began to go on for several minutes about how they had come into court the last month on this same case because Ms. Johnson had not paid her protective order and they were always having to accommodate us and that it just could not go on. Hand was lying. All I could do while he spoke was get a handle on my rising anger. So much for index cards, I knew exactly what I wanted to say to Judge Talieri.

Judge Talieri turned to me after Hand's diatribe and said, "Miss Oliver?" Although I was angry inside, I did not want to duplicate Hand's techniques. I very slowly said, "Your honor, I believe Mr. Hand has misrepresented the status of this case. If you look at the court jacket you will find that Mr. Hand had to withdraw his motion to strike the pleadings because he was in error about my client's payment of the protective order." I had more to say on the merits of the motion but Judge Talieri turned to Hand and asked if that was true. Hand attempted to dance out of it and Judge

---

48. "Stipulated" means that Mr. Hand agreed to the statement. — EDS.

Talieri just kept asking "Is that true?" "Did you or did you not have to with-draw your motion?" When it was clear that Hand had lied to the court, Judge Talieri then gave him a very strong reprimand and for ten minutes chastised him for his misrepresentation.

When Judge Talieri returned to the merits of the motion, he decided to take it under advisement during the lunch recess and asked me for the cite of *Estelle Davis,* a case I had mentioned during the argument. Another invaluable lesson: Do *not* leave key information in your briefcase if you are not going to remember to bring the briefcase with you to the defendant's table. Fortunately, for some amazing reason, I had memorized the citation. (Perhaps it was the one line-index card mentality at work.) Another key lesson: Expect the unexpected. I had thought it would be no problem get-ting out of there to catch my plane. Now, it would be 2:00 P.M. before the Judge resumed the bench. The supervisors were wonderful in saying they would handle it from there, but I really wanted to carry the motion through. Somehow it would be anticlimactic to hop on a plane to go talk about being a real lawyer when I had a chance to *be* a real lawyer. And besides, there was a sense of commitment to Elma which had been growing throughout the numerous conversations with her. She was so concerned about not being able to pay her protective order that I just could not leave at that point.

During lunch recess, while interviewing clients for other cases and continuing my court day responsibilities, I was also pouring over *Estelle Davis* one more time. When the case was called again I gave the factual reasons for why Ms. Johnson should be granted an extension of time in which to pay her November protective order: Ms. Johnson had paid on time thus far; Ms. Johnson had always paid her rent on time except for one month when she was in the hospital and the purposeful withholding of rent when her ceiling fell in; the numerous conversations Ms. Johnson has had with her case worker; my conversation with her caseworker. This was also Elma's first time to speak to the Judge. He asked her some questions about the public assistance check. Judge Talieri also asked me whether he had the power to grant what I was asking. At this point, I had a sense he was acting more professorial than anything. I knew he was inquiring about the court's equity powers and I was able to give several case citations for support. Judge Talieri granted our motion and we left the court room.

When we came out to the waiting area, Mr. Hand came up to me, slapped me on the back, and said, "You done good, kid." I took it as a compliment. However, as he was racing for the door, I stopped him with the document in hand (already filled out — another key lesson) and said, "Mr. Hand, you told me if I beat you in court, you'd agree to mutual discov-ery."[49] He signed it.

---

49. Mutual discovery is an agreement by each party to cooperate with the opposing party by handing over all information requested. Discovery can be ordered by a court, but often it is mutually agreed upon by parties, so that neither party need file a motion for discovery. Such agreements can also limit the scope of mutual discovery. — Eds.

Elma was ecstatic because her visions of being evicted proved false. Her November public assistance check arrived one week later and she was advised to go to the court and pay the protective order for November promptly even though, technically, the Judge had granted our request to delay payment until December 1. This would assist us should we ever need to go into court again on a similar matter. We would be able to point to her diligence and conscientious attitude toward payment of protective orders.

Sure enough, when December rolled around her public assistance check was late again. Ms. Johnson took her money order to pay the protective order as soon as she received the check. The court payment office would not accept it, however, because it was after the 5th. They said she would need to go into court to ask permission to pay it late. Ms. Johnson called me as soon as they told her that. It was 9:30 A.M. the morning of my afternoon Commercial Law exam. Again, an important lesson — Expect the unexpected and prepare for the worst. I jumped out of my sweats and into my suit and met Ms. Johnson at court. Since it was not a usual court day for Tilman, Zuckerman & Hand, I called their office to explain that I was going to go before the court to seek permission for late payment into the court registry, and to ask if they would be amenable to an agreement stating such. Perhaps it was the holiday cheer or good will in the air — whatever it was, I was not going to complain — they agreed to allow Ms. Johnson to make the late deposit of her rent money into the court registry. By 11:30, I was back in my sweats trying to make sense out of priorities in bankruptcy.

[Description of discovery omitted.]

TRIAL PREPARATION I

Because I received answers to interrogatories[50] so late in the midst of preparing for trial, I think I let slip by two very important facts which only later became critical. They had neglected to answer interrogatories about who was the owner of the building or about the period before Management, Inc. took over as managers of the property. Both later became crucial facts that led to a significant defect in our case.

Preparation for trial is not only that time where you are writing out your opening statement or preparing the direct and cross examinations. Preparation for trial is also a time of a lot of running around again. I think this was the biggest surprise of all — that so much running around was needed in order to get housing reports, deliver subpoenas, find out information about sheetrock, interview witnesses, and prepare them for testifying in court.

In this case, a lot of the testimony would surround the ceiling that

---

50. Interrogatories are written questions to the opposing side that are part of the discovery process. — EDS.

caved in and prompted Ms. Johnson to withhold her rent in order to get the landlord to take notice of her complaints. I was able to find an expert witness, Mr. Barnes, who had been in the dry wall and sheetrock business for over 30 years. We went out to Ms. Johnson's apartment because the crack in the bedroom which had begun when the adjacent living room ceiling fell in had gotten significantly worse. It was four days before trial but we were contemplating a temporary restraining order. The Housing Inspector had been extraordinarily helpful and stated that based on what Mr. Barnes found and his inspection, he would issue an emergency order for repair.

Mr. Barnes was particularly helpful in determining that the ceilings were not structurally sound and that the repair work had not been done in a workmanlike manner. I was especially appreciative of his willingness to come and testify for free since his expertise would greatly add to the case and he was a very likeable witness.

Two days before the trial we received what may be the strangest motion in history. The opposing counsel finally had realized the problem they were going to have with proving their prima facie case as they had never given Ms. Johnson a written notice to quit nor had they received a waiver of such notice. They decided to solve this by filing a Motion to Substitute Defendant. Essentially, they wanted to remove Ms. Johnson, the tenant who occupied the premises, and make Mr. Sandy, the brother who signed the lease on her behalf, the new defendant (and still have the trial begin the next day). Besides the obvious procedural and due process problems, the motion was also remarkable in its lack of points and authorities (Do you blame them? How could one ever find any authority for such a thing?).

I turned to Wright and Miller[51] to prove they couldn't do this. I wrote the Defendant's Opposition to Plaintiff's Motion to Substitute Defendant. (Another helpful hint: If you entitle your opposition to their motion as such and not as a motion in opposition, you save your client a $10 filing fee.) The morning of the hearing, I went to the judge's chambers to leave a courtesy copy of our opposition motion. I also made a copy for opposing counsel.

Again, that important lesson — expect the unexpected. That morning I received a call from Elma. She was on her way to D.C. General to seek emergency surgery. After talking with a supervisor, I realized we could try to seek a continuance from the Civil Assignment Court but that Judge Talieri was on the bench there and probably would not grant the continuance. Apparently, it might have been possible to begin the trial without Elma and just put her on at the end. So I went down to the court to deal with the strange motion and see if we could get a continuance.

For the first time, I met another attorney from Tilman, Zuckerman & Hand. Mr. Zuckerman recognized the absurdity of their motion and with-

---

51. A well-known treatise on a civil procedure. — EDS.

drew it. He also favored the continuance and so I went up to appear before Judge Talieri. I waited nearly an hour before the case was called. Judge Talieri denied every continuance request. But sometimes it helps to have made a dramatic appearance before a judge. Judge Talieri had been on the L&T bench the day Hand had lied to the court on this case. Although it was two months later, when I introduced myself to the court, Judge Talieri said, "Hello, Miss Oliver, I remember you. What is your request?" He granted our continuance and the trial was rescheduled for March 30th. Mr. Zuckerman suggested that this seemed like a good case for settlement and wondered if we would be open to settlement negotiations. I told him we would be glad to discuss settlement as long as the offer was reasonable in light of the facts of the case.

SETTLEMENT

In some ways this was the strangest period of the case. First of all, it was ridiculous how difficult it was to get in touch with Phil Zuckerman. Although I was working full-time and had my own direct line with rollover to my secretary, I never seemed to get the messages Mr. Zuckerman said he left. I called him sometimes 5 days in a row without any response. It was difficult because I did not want to appear too eager to settle the case; I just wanted to get in touch with opposing counsel.

There was $786 of money on the street;[52] $1,913 in the account held by the court and a tenant's counterclaim of over $8,000. Their offer was to forgive the money withheld. They rejected our settlement offer, which was admittedly high. Mr. Zuckerman also stated that his client did not have liability past June of 1982 when Management, Inc. took over management of the property. This tack was a complete surprise and prompted me to consider adding the owner as an additional party-plaintiff in order to cover ourselves and defeat their claim that because management changed, our counterclaim was cut short.[53]

They had cured their defect by sending Elma a written notice to quit the premises by March 31, 1984. However, it did not cure their defect for this particular case. They still were going to have to go to trial with a defect so blatant that they would not be able to prove their prima facie case. It became clear they would not settle; it was unclear why not, given the defect in their case.

52. "On the street" is a term used in a nonpayment case to refer to rent unpaid and owing. For example, if a tenant had not paid rent for two months and is sued in the third month, for which rent also remains unpaid, the amount of money "on the street" is three months' rent. — EDs.

53. The argument was that the counterclaim named the wrong party (i.e., Management, Inc.), instead of Stanford Rodgers Management, which (as it turned out) had managed the property for the period at issue).

TRIAL PREPARATION II

The second trial preparation was not as intense as the first. This was partially due to the fact that a lot of the preparation had already been done. I notified witnesses, got subpoenas ready and brushed up on the facts. The focus at this point was to prepare a motion to join Mr. George Howe, the owner of record since 1968, as an indispensable party-plaintiff.[54] Although the granting of that motion might delay the trial (since due process requirements would suggest that Mr. Hand have time to prepare Howe's case), it would protect us from the claim that our counterclaim was cut off because it was filed against the wrong party [i.e., against a management company that was not managing the building for the period in question].

I took another trip to the Recorder of Deeds office to check ownership records. Again, there was no change in the ownership. I requested official copies of those records for presentation to the court when arguing the motion. I was told they would be ready in 5 working days. I prepared the motion relying heavily on another clinic student's previous motion and a recent court order. The hearing date was scheduled for March 23, 1984, at 9:00 A.M.

On March 22, 1984, I received a phone call from the Recorder of Deeds office stating that it was urgent that I come to their office. Having already received a phone call telling me that the certificates were ready, I was surprised to receive this call of great urgency. I left work and went immediately to the Recorder of Deeds Office. They said that a most unusual thing had occurred the day before and they had new certificates of ownership for me. I then learned that a sale of the premises two years before to ABC Corporation had suddenly been recorded nine days before trial and two days before my motion to add the building owner as a party-plaintiff.[55]

Meanwhile, back at the ranch, we received in our offices on March 23, 1984, a copy of Plaintiff's Motion to Dismiss, which was based on the two facts that had eluded me when I failed to compel answers to interrogatories about the owner of the building and the period prior to which Management, Inc. had managed the building. The motion was based on the fact that Management, Inc. did not manage the building for the period covered by the counterclaim, and that Howe did not own it for the relevant period.

---

54. Adding the owner as a plaintiff would remedy the fact that Management, Inc. could not be liable on the tenant's counterclaim for the period when the building was still being managed by Stanford Rodgers Management, Inc., because the landlord would be liable for the entire period. — EDS.

55. As it turns out, Stanford Rodgers — who was the principal in Management, Inc.— was also the President, Treasurer, and member of the Board of Directors of ABC Corporation. It appears that the documents were signed effecting a sale to ABC Corporation but were not recorded. This procedure provided protection from liability for the landlord (Mr. Howe), who could record the sale if he was ever sued. Once recorded, the sale to ABC Corporation meant that he had ceased to own the building, as of some two years before this litigation. We will study recording acts in Chapter 12. — EDS.

I called Dennis [a supervisor] and discussed the motion to dismiss, which was problematic because it included a motion to dismiss our counterclaim. We talked about the various options. Maybe it was better to accept the settlement offer. Zuckerman was willing to release all funds in the court registry to my client. Elma would have nearly $2,000, and there would still be time for her to move out before they could serve her again. Perhaps they would never find her to serve her. On the other hand, maybe it would be better to have Elma waive the notice to quit and proceed with trial.

I expressed to Dennis my concern about Elma having all that money and then spending it, getting sued again, and really being in the hole. Dennis asked me if I wasn't being a bit maternalistic. I was really hit by that statement. I had become quite concerned for Elma's welfare throughout this year. But I also knew the truth of Dennis' statement. Elma is her own person, capable of making her own decisions, and facing the consequences.

I also took this time to run over to the Recorder of Deeds office to check the corporate records of the "new" owner, ABC Corporation. Remember the lesson "expect the unexpected?" I arrived at the Recorder of Deeds office only to discover that the corporate records had moved seven blocks away. After a quick run over there I asked to see the Certificate of Incorporation for ABC Realty Corporation, who had bought the building from Stanford Rodgers. What I discovered was a very cozy arrangement. The President, Treasurer, and member of Board of Directors was none other than Stanford Rodgers, the principal in both Management, Inc. and the company that succeeded it in managing Elma's building. Other Directors included Barbara Rodgers and Paula Rodgers. In fact, there was only one member of the Board who was not a Rodgers.

After several discussions with Rich and Dennis, and numerous phone calls to Elma, we decided to reschedule our motion [to join a party-plaintiff] for the same day as Plaintiff's motion [to dismiss our counterclaim], March 30th. It would give us some more time to think about strategy, find out about ABC, and it would give Elma some more time to consider her options regarding dismissal of the case.

Dennis reminded me that even though it was very late in the case, the court would most likely grant a plaintiff's motion to dismiss the case. We talked about ways we might try to preserve the counterclaim but we recognized that the likelihood of dismissal was great. In light of that, I spent a number of evenings over at Ms. Johnson's apartment meeting with her and her two brothers. There was obviously the practical problem of trying to find a place that would accept a woman with six kids. There was concern for the family — Elma wanted to do what was best for the kids.

After much thought it was finally agreed that the best course of action, since Zuckerman was so willing to release all funds in the court registry to Ms. Johnson, was to agree to their dismissal. Again, it was a running around game. First the agreement from our clinic with Dennis' signature, then over to Southwest D.C. for Elma's signature, and then out to Maryland to plaintiff's office for their signature. The case was dismissed; all money in the court registry to be released forthwith to the defendant.

THE AFTERMATH

Elma Johnson attempted to pay her April rent to the landlord and they refused it. On the 9th of April, Tilman, Zuckerman & Hand sent by mail to Ms. Williams a new summons. The return date was scheduled for April 27th.

I spoke with Elma when she returned from a visit home to see her parents. She had been required to appear before a court to testify as to whether or not she would agree to allowing her ex-husband to stay out of jail (child support) so that he could work to make up the back pay. She spoke lightheartedly because she had enjoyed the time with her parents. Her parents were trying to encourage her to return to the South.

Elma spoke quite freely about her courtroom experience there. A court-appointed lawyer had been assigned to advise her of her rights. After the judge finished speaking with her ex-husband, she spoke up and said, "May it please the Court . . . " She said the judge smiled and the court-appointed attorney looked up in surprise. I told her she had learned a lot through this whole experience. She said she felt encouraged because she felt like she could handle any legal problems now; that she'd learned how important it is to keep everything in writing; and that she wasn't afraid anymore.

An hour later, however, she called up despondent because she had opened her mail to discover the summons. The respite had been much too short.

The funds were released to her on April 19th and she decided to take the kids home to her parents over the Easter weekend and move out of her apartment. This mooted the second suit.

Where Elma will go from here is uncertain. She is a remarkable woman who through diligence and hard work earned herself a teaching position with a day care center. To leave this area is to leave the job she loves. She felt under a lot of pressure to get the kids out of the neighborhood. Sporadic fires, the lack of attention to her many notices of dangerous cracks, and her concern for the safety of her children had caused her to realize staying in that situation was not good. With this new suit hanging over her head, she had felt especially discouraged. She said several times, "I just wish the jury could have heard my story." She is going to take a month off and stay with her parents and her brothers are going to look for a place for her to live close to her teaching position. The supervisor of the school told her that her job would be waiting for her when she returned. This whole legal battle had its ups and downs for Elma emotionally. It was difficult for her to understand the blatant disregard for her family's well-being displayed by Management, Inc. It was hard to be at the mercy of court appearances, defects in cases, and the sense that it is just never finished, settled or over.

Yet, at the same time, Elma gained a certain sense of strength in her abilities to stand up to injustice. I myself saw her strength and confidence develop throughout the entire process. In fact, she was almost ecstatic with the way she had handled herself in her other court appearance. She told me very early on how important it was that she teach her kids that they can fight against wrongdoers. She said that even if she did decide to move back home, she knew she wasn't running away.

In anticipation of the second trial date, March 30th, the building's resident manager, Mr. Fishborn, approached Elma to ask when they could come in to make the repairs. It was two weeks before trial. Three of Elma's kids had contracted chicken pox. Elma told Mr. Fishborn that the repairmen were welcome to come at any time but they would have to do so at their own risk. She would notify them as soon as the kids were well, however. She then wrote a summary of their conversation in her notebook where she kept written records of all communication with the rental office; she confirmed in a letter to Mr. Fishborn that day why she was suggesting they come back later (she was convinced that at trial they would say she didn't let them in to do repairs); she requested her doctor to write a confirmation of the fact of the children's illnesses. She reported all this to me the day I called her about the possible dismissal of the case. She asked, "Did I do right?"

I shared this story with Dennis that day and remarked that Elma had become quite sophisticated through the whole process. Dennis replied simply, "You both have."

This paper was written in 1984. Today, its author is married, has two children, and is a partner in a Washington law firm, where she works part-time. She recently published a book about growing up in an alcoholic family entitled *No Longer the Hero*. She kept in touch with her client for many years, finally losing track of her when the client moved to South Carolina in 1990.

NOTES AND QUESTIONS

1. **Time line.** Make a time line of the events in the *Johnson* case.

2. **The practice of law.** What surprised you most about this description of the practice of law? What skills seem most vital for the effective practice of law?

3. **How attorneys spend their time.** List in descending order of effort the tasks the student attorney spent her time on.

4. **Lest you get the wrong idea.** Most poor residential tenants, notwithstanding the Legal Services Corporation, go unrepresented. By some

estimates, not more than one tenant in ten will have a lawyer at her side when she appears as a housing court defendant. See, e.g., Barbara Bezdek, Silence in the Court: Participation and Subordination of Poor Tenants' Voices in the Legal Process, 20 Hofstra L. Rev. 533 (1992). And given the caseload legal services lawyers typically carry, few clients can expect to receive the "hands on" attention the clinical student was able to give Ms. Johnson. It would be quite unusual, for example, for the attorney to visit the tenant's apartment for a first-hand look.

§3.5   Who Are the Residential Landlords?

In sharp contrast to the detailed information available on the tenant population, little detailed information exists on residential landlords, according to experts in the field. Set forth below are two contrasting images.

a.   The Slumlord

"You must pay the rent, you must pay the rent!"
"I can't pay the rent, I can't pay the rent!" [56]

The slumlord is a folk figure probably invented in the nineteenth century by muckraking journalists during the Industrial Revolution when Americans and recent immigrants were flooding into tenement housing in urban areas. The slumlord was someone who owned a large number of buildings and managed them ruthlessly, often engaging in sharp business practices, and putting families out onto the street without compunction. Keith Lehrer, The Landlord as Scapegoat 13-14 (1991). The slumlord is depicted as someone who makes huge profits off the backs of the poor and "milks" his buildings by pocketing a very high percentage of the building's cash flow and refusing to keep his housing stock in a suitable state of repair by reducing "maintenance below the level necessary to keep a building in existence as a residential unit." See, e.g., Duncan Kennedy, The Effect of the Warranty of Habitability on Low Income Housing: "Milking" and Class Violence, 15 Fla. St. U. L. Rev. 485, 489 (1987):

> [T]he milking landlord treats his property as a wasting rather than a renewable asset. He adopts a strategy of renting for what the market will bear as the building deteriorates, fully understanding that within some relatively short pe-

---

56. This vignette appears in a Mighty Mouse cartoon, but almost certainly originated earlier. In the classic rendition, we think of a single bow that serves as a bow-tie to identify the landlord, and a hair ribbon to identify the tenant, undoubtedly a stage (probably vaudeville) technique.

CURTIS
Landlord-as-Slumlord cartoon

riod of time he will be out of business. Either tenants will no longer pay him anything, or the authorities will close the building. At that point, he expects the building to have no market value. He will walk away from it, give it away, or lose it to tax foreclosure.

The landlord begins "milking" his property when the value of the property begins to decline as a result of external factors such as deteriorating market conditions or loss of affluent tenants.[56]

In the cases below, we will see vivid imagery of the slumlord. Slumlord imagery often emerges today where tenants are poor and particularly where tenants are immigrants, struggling to adapt to a new country. Lacking necessary language skills and economic stability, immigrants are forced to rent from landlords who refuse to maintain their properties. For three years, Miguel Zamora, a 39-year-old immigrant from Guadalajara, lived in a one-room studio apartment with his wife and four children. During this time, Zamora was forced to repair plumbing, install a water pump, and even change the locks of the apartment, all at his own expense. The landlord ignored all requests for repairs, choosing to demolish the property rather than face an 83-count criminal complaint for housing, health, and fire code violations. See Lee Romney, Beyond Repair?, L.A. Times, Nov. 19, 1992, at B1.

Note that tenants are often depicted as women — very vulnerable ones — and landlords are shown as men. That the tenants involved in the key cases of the "landlord-tenant revolution" are typically women see §3.9 *infra*. As you read the cases, consider whether this plays a role in the court's decisions.

Slumlord imagery implicitly asks whether ownership of property should give landlords overreaching power over people — a theme reminiscent of the republican apprehension about the linkage of ownership and power. Using arguments resonant of the liberal dignity strain, slumlord imagery also can suggest that the landlord is using his property in a way that constitutes an affront to the dignity of his tenants.

---

56. Id. at 490.

Legal services lawyers representing tenants generally believe that they are constantly dealing with slumlords. Recall Nancy Oliver Lesourd's experience: Does the landlord in Mrs. Johnson's case fit the "slumlord" image?

b.   The Honest, Struggling Entrepreneur

The opposing image is of the landlord as an honest, struggling entrepreneur. The core imagery is of a landlord who owns a small number of properties, often only one, and enters the rental business for self-support, retirement savings, and perhaps out of a genuine desire to help the poor. After investing in the rental property, the landlord soon discovers that the cost of maintaining the property exceeds the profit. He cannot raise rents to pay for his unexpected costs because rents are often limited by local rent controls or market conditions. In contrast to the "Scroogelike" slumlord, the honest, struggling entrepreneur is confronted by painful choices between maintaining the property at levels required by housing code and keeping rents affordable for tenants. This image of the honest landlord is often accompanied by the picture of the tenant as the deadbeat.

George Sternlieb's The Tenement Landlord[57] presents graphic images of the honest entrepreneur landlord struggling to break even while maintaining habitable housing for his tenants. He quotes one landlord as follows:

> "I would have to spend too much money to fix the parcel up and it takes too long to get the investment back. People don't pay rents so I have to evict them. I also have the problem of skips. This area is very bad and that keeps people away. Also, the tenants want central heat and have better properties for the same price."

The Tenement Landlord 172 (1966). Sternlieb also notes that property tax reassessments discourage the landlord from making improvements that will result in higher taxes:

> The owner presently has only two squatters in the house, but when he bought it some five years ago, he felt that he was immediately reassessed. He feels now that this was a penalty for bringing improvements to the property. His tax bill went up $200 because he admitted in court that he put in new plumbing fixtures, sinks, bathtubs, etc., rather than having bought the parcel with them.

Residential Abandonment-The Tenement Landlord Revisited 71 (1973). The economic hardships confronting Sternlieb's landlords of the

---

57. The Tenement Landlord (1966) and Residential Abandonment: The Tenement Landlord Revisited (1973) are sequels that study inner-city Newark, New Jersey, to uncover the causes of residential abandonment in troubled neighborhoods in deteriorating central cities.

1960s and 1970s persist in troubled big-city neighborhoods. The following article reports on a landlord who epitomizes the landlord-as-honest-entrepreneur theme.

DOUGLAS MARTIN, A LAMENT OF ONE LANDLORD: FROM RICHES TO RAGS

N.Y. Times, Oct. 26, 1992, at B3

It is a typical day at Equities Ltd., the 11 tenement buildings in East Harlem that Harley Brooke-Hitching so loftily named when she bought them.

A pregnant woman, homeless until now, sits with the office manager doing paperwork that will enable her to get city subsidies to live in one of Ms. Brooke-Hitching's 180 apartments. The woman is thrilled that she won't have to give birth in a shelter.

Ms. Brooke-Hitching pats her softly on the shoulder as she steps outside into the ceaseless salsa beat of the barrio. This slight, 40-something, redheaded woman seems an unlikely candidate for her chosen vocation: as a private landlord renting to poor and nearly poor New Yorkers in a troubled neighborhood, she is either a crucial provider of low-cost housing or a slumlord, depending on one's point of view. In either case, her risky real-estate speculation may yet prove her undoing.

Her father was a British aristocrat, her mother from Oklahoma, where she was born. She grew up on both sides of the Atlantic, was a high-school cheerleader in Oklahoma City and studied art at the Sorbonne. Early jobs included setting up an exclusive club for well-heeled visitors to London and opening an Amsterdam office for Sotheby's.

After a short marriage to an international banker, she stayed on in Bangkok and became a large and successful dealer in Asian art. She raised her son, Matthew, now 18, as a single mother, came to New York in 1980 and proceeded to make a killing on co-op conversions.

She is the founding chairwoman of City Harvest, a charity distributing surplus food to the needy. She carries a licensed handgun.

Ms. Brooke-Hitching, who lives in an airy Upper East Side apartment that opens into a 37 foot-long greenhouse, came north to Harlem in 1985 to profit from the soaring real-estate market. She reasoned that you could multiply your fun by buying more for less in a marginal neighborhood. She bought her buildings one by one, flipping a couple of early ones — industry jargon for immediately selling a newly purchased property — as if to prove her intuition.

Then things got tough. Part of it is the drugs and the crime that seem only to worsen. Mute testimony occupies a dish on her desk: it is full of spent shells she collected in and around her buildings.

The value of her 11 buildings rose by 1989 to $4.5 million from the $3.1 million she paid for them, but it has surely fallen since. Today, she says she would be very lucky to get back the purchase price.

A bigger problem looms. Costs have skyrocketed — from taxes to water and sewage fees to oil costs — and relief is nowhere in sight. And like many owners, she paid too much. Perhaps most ominously, she signed personally for a number of loans.

It is scant wonder Ms. Brooke-Hitching lies awake nights worrying that her entire $3.5 million investment — including $1.1 million in cash — will be lost. . . .

A WORRY FOR TENANTS, TOO

The stakes may be higher still for the more than 600 people she houses in apartments that fetch from $79 a month for a rent-controlled one-bedroom to $720 for a newly renovated three-bedroom.

Her little real-estate empire, with its cab drivers who sleep in shifts and aromas bespeaking faraway places, is made up of the kind of dwellings familiar to millions of New Yorkers.

She greets a hairdresser from the Ivory Coast who has lived in an Equities apartment for two years and is frequently frightened in this often cold city. She again unsuccessfully tries to persuade some tenants from Mexico, new arrivals, that they could sell more flowers if they arranged them more smartly.

She stops at the apartment of Ndao Daouda, who came to America from Senegal in 1984 with $47 and now peddles T-shirts and socks on East 116th Street. Mr. Daouda is the one who visits her when one of her many Senegalese tenants has a complaint or can't pay the rent on time. "When we talk together, we understand each other," said the man Ms. Brooke-Hitching calls "the diplomat." . . .

MAJOR SOURCE OF HOUSING

It is impossible to overstate the importance of this type of privately owned housing in New York City's struggling neighborhoods. Over the last decade, the million immigrants to this region have settled mainly in places like this. So will the million more expected this decade.

Of the million welfare recipients in New York City, many also end up in such housing. So, too, do the working poor. One of Ms. Brooke-Hitching's tenants is a Mexican man who commutes to Brooklyn to work 12 hours a day in a Korean grocery.

The Citizens Housing and Planning Council calculates that there are 350,000 units of private housing in areas of New York City with a poverty rate over 25 percent. At least twice as many people live in such private housing as in projects run by the Housing Authority.

The true number is obscured by the doubling and tripling up of families in apartments. This is a direct result of the impossible cost of living in New York City: the median rent of a two-bedroom apartment is $600 — about twice welfare's housing allowance for a family of three, and far beyond the reach of most immigrants.

"Literally half the people who live in this city don't earn what it takes to pay for housing here," said Kathryn Wylde, senior vice president of the New York City Housing Partnership.

So they make do. They combine welfare, jobs in the underground economy, whatever. And they find apartments like those offered by Ms. Brooke-Hitching.

NOT THE RITZ

To be sure, the accommodations in some such buildings are shameful. Repairs are infrequent, heat and hot water chancy at best. Some landlords physically threaten tenants and illegally enter their apartments, Ms. Brooke-Hitching said.

The problem is that poor New Yorkers desperately need somewhere to live, and landlords who cater to them claim to be an endangered species. Though it is the same complaint some have been making since time immemorial, the case is gathering weight.

"Private property owners have never faced the steepness of the hill they've got in front of them right now," said John Gilbert, president of the Rent Stabilization Association, composed of 25,000 landlords. Under the rent-stabilization process, the city and state regulate the rent of about 60 percent of the city's rental housing.

Mr. Gilbert said 16 percent of all apartment buildings in the city are so pressed they are a year or more behind in property taxes.

The rapidly rising cost of water and sewer fees — up 169 percent since 1987 — is generating the most pain. And water fees have increased ten-fold and more for some buildings where water meters have been installed, as they must be in all buildings by 1997. Under rent regulations, these charges cannot be automatically passed on to tenants.

The Citizens Housing and Planning Council, which analyzes housing issues from a public-interest perspective, warns that 50,000 units of private rent-regulated housing are in "immediate jeopardy of lapsing into abandonment or city ownership."

Joseph B. Rose, executive director of the council, said, "We're on the brink of a precipice."

MORE PROBLEMS LOOM

Ms. Brooke-Hitching feels she might already be falling off a cliff. To be sure, some would say she speculated and lost, and that's part of the game.

But whether or not the injury is deserved, Ms. Brooke-Hitching complains that it is accompanied by much insult. Her scars range from routinely losing on her many trips to Housing Court — a result, she says, of a pro-tenant bias there.

There is also the upcoming problem of stricter city standards on lead paint. Generations of paint cake the walls of the buildings and could be a huge expense to remove. Recycling garbage also proved difficult during a pilot program due to what Ms. Brooke-Hitching characterizes as tenant uncooperativeness. She paid many fines.

"Around here the environmental issue is not having your kid shot," she said.

On the plus side, Ms. Brooke-Hitching has paid for most major capital improvements, including new boilers, plumbing, windows and doors. Though it took two and a half years of waiting and a lawsuit against the city, she was allowed to raise rents 6 percent. The wait hurt her tenants perhaps as much as it did her: the rent increase was retroactive, leaving them owing large back-rent bills. What might have been another plus, lower interest rates, has not helped as much as it might have, as only 1 of her 11 mortgages is variable.

So the bills pile up. She owes $50,000 to an oil company and $60,000 in back taxes. The city has notified her that it will seize one building, the one more than a year behind in taxes, if she does not pay up.

She dimly remembers how she felt at the beginning, before a drug dealer gave her a black eye, before the girlfriend of a disheveled addict accused her of paying the man for sex. Before she risked losing her entire savings.

"I was so confident and optimistic," Harley Brooke-Hitching recalled. "I was fearless."

And now? "I feel like a rat in a cage."

c.   What's Wrong with This Picture?

Which picture of landlords is correct? Landlords no doubt fall into both categories: Some resemble the classic slumlords, ignoring complaints and necessary repairs, while others struggle to break even on their investments while continuing to accept low-income tenants. The proportion of each may well depend on conditions in the local housing market, as well as on other factors. We need to leave such studies to economists; more important for us is to recognize how effective lawyers utilize this cultural imagery to organize the available facts into a story line that makes judges or legislators *want* their clients to win. This story line is called the "theory of the case." Binny Miller, Give Them Back Their Lives: Recognizing Client Narrative in Case Theory, 93 Mich. L. Rev. 485 (1994). Judges, as well as advocates, need a theory of the case, for their job is to make a case for the winning party (or the losing party, in the case of a dissent). Commentators, too, need to utilize this cultural imagery in order to be persuasive, although often they do so in subtle ways, treating their characterizations as mere descriptions of the objective working of impersonal housing markets.

Note the assumption shared by the "slumlord" and "honest, struggling entrepreneur" story lines: Both focus on the landlord's character. An alternative analysis treats the problem of low-income housing as a structural problem. This alternative highlights the market's failure to provide an adequate supply of low-income housing. It points out that the incomes of the poor are too low to pay rents high enough to enable landlords to cover their expenses. In this light, the persistent problem of low-income housing emerges as a permanent feature of a society with very high standards of "adequate" housing and a large population of very poor people. Cf. E. Jay Howenstine, The New Housing Shortage, in The New Housing Shortage: Housing Affordability in Europe and the USA (Graham Hallett ed., 1993). As you read the following materials, ask yourself why lawyers tend to return time and again to the "slumlord" and "honest entrepreneur" stories, rather than to the structural analysis of the low-income housing problem.

In reading both the cases and the commentaries that follow, ask yourself what (often unstated) image of landlords and tenants underlie the courts' and commentators' conclusions.

§3.6   Termination of the Tenancy

a.   The Landlord's Right to Terminate at Common Law

Does the landlord have the right to terminate the tenancy if the tenant does not pay the rent? What would you assume? Can you translate that intuition into the language of contract law? Why would you expect the landlord to be able to terminate the tenancy when a tenant has not paid the rent?

It may come as a surprise that, at common law, if the lease was silent, a landlord could not evict a tenant who failed to pay the rent. Brown's Administrators v. Bragg, 22 Ind. 122 (1864). This conclusion reflected the theory that the lease was a conveyance of an interest in land; breaches of the lease, therefore, gave rise only to money actions — in this instance, an action for nonpayment of rent[58] — not to a right to rescind the lease. But,

---

58. The court in Brown's Administrators v. Bragg explained: As well might a man who sells a horse to be paid in the future, claim to recover him back on failure of the purchaser to pay according to his stipulation, as the lessor of real estate to recover it from his tenant because of his failure to pay rent, there being no stipulation that such failure should work a forfeiture. 22 Ind. at 123.

of course, landlords learned early — in written leases, anyway — to couple tenant's breach with a forfeiture of the estate. After all, in most instances, a landlord's judgment for unpaid rent, while the tenant was allowed to remain in possession until the end of the term, was an uninviting option. Most jurisdictions now have statutes that allow the landlord to terminate a tenancy for failure to abide by covenants, including the payment of rent. See Robert S. Shoshinski, American Law of Landlord and Tenant 377 (1980).

b.   Statutory Termination

Today every state has statutes that prescribe an expedited process ("summary proceeding"), rather than the (even more) painfully deliberate civil action known as ejectment. See also Robert Schoshinski, American Law of Landlord and Tenant §6:1, at 377 (1980). Consider how the following statutes from Maryland and Virginia set forth the landlord's termination power. Notice how each statute treats nonpayment of rent and other leasehold violations. Which statute is better from a landlord's point of view? From a tenant's?

Md. Code Ann., Real Prop.
§8-401 (1994)

Failure to pay rent.

(a) Right to repossession. — Whenever the tenant under any lease of property, express or implied, verbal or written, shall fail to pay the rent when due and payable, it shall be lawful for the landlord to have again and repossess the premises so rented. . . .

Md. Code Ann., Real Prop.
§8-402.1 (1994)

Breach of lease.

(a) When a lease provides that the landlord may repossess the premises if the tenant breaches the lease, and the landlord has given the tenant 1 month's written notice that the tenant is in violation of the lease and the landlord desires to repossess the premises, and if the tenant or person in actual possession refuses to comply, the landlord may make complaint in writing to the District Court of the county where the premises is located. [Description of additional procedures omitted.]

(b) If the court determines that the tenant breached the terms of the lease and that the breach was substantial and warrants an eviction, the court shall give judgment for the restitution of the possession of the premises and issue its warrant to the sheriff or a constable commanding him to deliver possession to the landlord. . . .

Va. Code Ann. §55-248.35 (Michie 1994)   LL

> *Remedy after termination.*
> If the rental agreement is terminated [pursuant to §55-248.31, which sets up certain minimum time periods for termination of the lease], the landlord may have a claim for possession and for rent and a separate claim for actual damages for breach of the rental agreement and reasonable attorney's fees. . . .

c. Lease Termination Provisions   "reentry Clause"

Despite the array of statutes giving landlords an eviction remedy, some statutes, even today, allow a landlord to reenter — for reasons other than rental nonpayment — only if he has a contractual right to do so. Every lease drafted by the landlord's lawyer should have a "reentry clause" allowing the landlord to evict for specified breaches of the lease.

A second reason lawyers draft reentry clauses is to set up a situation that gives the landlord maximum leverage when a problem arises. How do our leases' reentry provisions do that? Analyze the lease provisions in Figures 3-4 and 3-5, working through the exact sequence of events once a tenant has defaulted.

Tenant's Default	9 (a) If the Tenant refuses or fails to perform any of the Tenant's agreements or obligations under this lease, including the Tenant's obligation to pay rent and additional rent, the Landlord may give notice of such fact to the Tenant, and if such refusal or failure has not been cured within ten (10) days after the giving of such notice, then the Landlord may give the Tenant notice that the Landlord has elected to terminate this lease as of a date fixed by the Landlord (which shall not be less than five (5) days after the date of such notice), and on the date specified in the Landlord's notice.
Termination of Lease	This lease shall end, and the Tenant shall then surrender and deliver possession of the Apartment to the Landlord.
Landlord's Resumption of Possession	9 (b) If (i) the Tenant refuses or fails to pay rent or additional rent when due, or (ii) this lease has been terminated by the Landlord pursuant to subparagraph (a) of this Article 9, then and in either of such events the Land-

FIGURE 3-4
Lease No. 1

lord may at anytime thereafter reenter and take possession of the Apartment by any lawful means, and remove
the Tenant and other occupants and their effects, by dispossess proceedings, or otherwise, without being liable to
prosecution or damages. In any such case, the Landlord,
at the Landlord's option may relet the Apartment, and re-

Tenant to
Pay Damages

ceive the rent from the next tenant, applying the same
first to the payment of any expenses that the Landlord incurred in connection with said taking of possession and
reletting, including without limitation reasonable legal
fees and disbursements, brokerage fees, advertising costs,
the cost of cleaning, repairing and decorating the Apartment and its equipment and appliances, and then to the
payment of rent and the cost of performance of the other

this is mitigating but

Landlord Has
No Obligation
To Relet

agreements or obligations of the Tenant as provided in
this lease: and whether or not the Landlord has relet the
Apartment (it being agreed that the Landlord shall have
no obligation to relet the Apartment), the Tenant shall
pay the Landlord on the first day of each calendar month,

no ob to mitigate?

the rent and other sums for which the Tenant is responsible, less the proceeds of the reletting remaining after deduction of the amount of all of the aforementioned
expenses, if any, as ascertained from time to time.

Lease No. 1 (continued)

Default   p.   If Tenant does not comply with the terms of this Lease,
Landlord may give a notice to Tenant demanding that Ten-
ant must correct the default. If Tenant does not correct the
default within 5 days after the date the notice is mailed (or
within such longer period of time as may be reasonably required, if Tenant begins to correct the default in the 5-day
period and thereafter continues to act diligently) then
Landlord may give a second notice that this Lease shall end
on the date set forth in the second notice. The date set
forth in the second notice must be not less than 5 days nor
more than 10 days after the date the second notice is
mailed. On the date set forth in the second notice this
Lease shall end and Tenant shall deliver possession of the
Apartment to Landlord, but Tenant shall remain liable under this Lease.

FIGURE 3-5
Lease No. 2

Tenant Liable   q.   If this Lease has been ended as provided above, then
for Damages   Landlord may reenter and take possession of the Apartment
by any lawful means, and remove Tenant and Tenant's
Guests and their property, by dispossess proceedings, or
otherwise, without being liable in any way. Landlord may
rerent the Apartment and any rent received by Landlord
shall be used first to pay Landlord's expenses in getting
possession and rerenting the Apartment, including,
without being limited to, reasonable legal fees and costs,
fees of brokers, advertising costs and the cost of cleaning,
repairing and decorating the Apartment, and second to
pay any amounts Tenant owes under this Lease. Landlord
has no duty to rerent the Apartment. Tenant shall pay to
Landlord on the first day of each month any amounts
Tenant owes under this Lease, less, if Landlord rerents the
Apartment, any amounts received from the new tenant and
not used by Landlord to pay the expensees referred to
above.

[handwritten margin note: Mitigate?]

Lease No. 2 (continued)

d.   Notices to Cure Violation or Vacate

The statutes and lease clauses above all call for some notice to the
tenant that she is in default and must cure the default within a stated period
or face eviction. Figure 3-6 shows one example of such a notice.

e.   Acceptance of Rent Gives Rise to an Inference of Waiver

What if a month-to-month tenant consults you, a notice to quit in
hand? She wants to continue in her apartment. She did not pay last month's
rent, but now has the money to do so. What do you advise?   *[handwritten: Pay LL]*
If she sends the landlord a rent check, and he cashes it, his acceptance
of the rent gives rise to an inference that he has waived his right to evict and
has renewed her month-to-month tenancy. See Butterfield v. Duquesne
Mining Co., 182 P.2d 102 (Ariz. 1947); Duncan v. Malcomb, 351 S.W.2d 419
(Ark. 1961); Cottrell v. Gerson, 20 N.E.2d 74 (Ill. 1939); compare Johnson
v. Seaborg, 137 P. 191 (Or. 1913)

§3.7   General and Specific Antiwaiver Statutes

Suppose that the tenant agrees to waive a notice that the statute provides
for, or agrees to time periods shorter than those the statute prescribes, or
otherwise gives up some substantive or remedial rights. This leads us to the
important issue of antiwaiver statutes.

NOTICE TO CURE VIOLATION OF TENANCY OR VACATE

In accordance with the District of Columbia Rental Housing Act of 1885, D.C. Law 8-10, 45DC Code 2551(b) you are hereby given notice that you are violating the terms and conditions of your tenancy at: 6228 North Dakota Ave. N.W. #103 in the following manner:

TENANT WILL NOT USE NOR PERMIT ANY PART OF THE PREMISES TO BE USED FOR ANY UNLAWFUL OR DISORDERLY PURPOSE.
TENANT WILL NOT PERMIT ANY NUISANCE TO BE KEPT OR CONDUCTED ON OR ABOUT SAID PREMISES.

You are hereby given thirty days to cure the violation(s). The violation(s) may be cured as follows:

BY NOT ALLOWING EXCESSIVE TRAFFIC IN AND OUT OF YOUR APARTMENT AT ALL HOURS OF THE DAY AND NIGHT. YOUR GUEST ARE NOISY, LOITER IN AND AROUND THE PROPERTY, CAUSE LITTER IN AND AROUND THE PROPERTY AND ARE DISTURBING OTHER TENANTS IN THE PROPERTY BY THEIR ACTIONS.

YOU ARE VIOLATING TERMS OF YOUR LEASE BY UNDERMINING THE SECURITY IN THE BUILDING CAUSING DANGER TO OTHER TENANTS. YOUR GUESTS HAVE NUMEROUS KEYS TO THE PROPERTY WHICH ARE BEING DISTRIBUTED TO NUMEROUS PERSONS. YOU AND YOUR GUESTS ARE UNDERMINING THE SECURITY OF THE BUILDING BY LEAVING SECURITY DOORS PROPPED OPEN ALLOWING ANY PERSON ACCESS TO THE PROPERTY, CAUSING DANGER TO THE OTHER TENANTS.

Please be advised that if you fail to cure said violation(s) prior to the end of the thirty day period you are required to vacate the premises at the expiration of this notice. This notice will expire as of the expiration of your monthly tenancy which ends right after the expiration of the thirty days from the date this notice is served on you. This is the only notice you will receive. If you fail to so vacate the owner or agent will initiate an action for possession in the Landlord and Tenant Branch of the Superior Court of the District of Columbia. You will be required to pay rent while the tenancy continues and/or during the period of your occupancy.

RAD Reg. Required: Yes ___X___   No _____   By *Burgermeister Meisterburger*
Landlord Registration #:
Exemption Filed: _____

cc: D.C. Dept. of Consumer Reg. Affairs
       Rental Accommodations and Conversion Division
       614 H St., NW, Room 423, Phone 727-7315

CERTIFICATE OF SERVICE

I hereby certify that service of this notice was made at the above address on the _seventh_ day of _____ _March_, 19 _96_., as required by law as follows:

_____ (1)   By leaving a copy of the same with the tenant personally.
_____ (2)   By leaving a copy of the same with _____ a person above the age of sixteen years, residing in , or in possession of said premises, the tenant not to be found.
_____ (3)   By posting a copy of the same on the door of the above mentioned premises, where it can be conveniently read, the tenant not to be found, and no person above the age of sixteen years to be found in possession of, or residing in same premises after diligent effort having been made to obtain personal or substituted service.
_____ (4)   By mailing a copy to the tenant by regular mail, U.S. Postage prepaid.

Council Hall   *Burgermeister Meisterburger*
Washington, DC   _____
ADDRESS

FIGURE 3-6
Notice to Cure

States often refuse to enforce specified waivers. Examples would include the tenant's waiver of certain notices,[59] waiver of the right to jury trial,

59. For example, in the District of Columbia, tenants can waive their right to receive a notice to quit if termination of the tenancy is for nonpayment of rent but not if the termination

and waiver of the warranty of habitability.[60] Various other arrangements, all prejudicial to tenants, may also be unenforceable. Examples would include the tenant's confession of judgment, agreement to pay landlords' attorneys' fees (absent a reciprocal promise by landlord to pay the tenant's fees when the tenant prevails), agreement to pay a whopping late payment charge, agreement to accept notices to quit shorter than those set forth by statute, agreement to allow the landlord to use self-help, see §3.8.a *infra,* and agreement to allow landlord to seize the tenant's personal property when rent is overdue.[61]

Other states have enacted general antiwaiver provisions. Two examples follow. What do they prohibit? Which is broader? What remedies does each provide? If the following situation arose, as a tenant would you rather be in a jurisdiction with a general antiwaiver statute like Maryland's or Virginia's?

Md. Code Ann., Real Prop. §8-208 (1994)

(a) *Prohibited provisions.* — A lease may not contain any of the following provisions: . . .

(2) A provision whereby the tenant agrees to waive or to forego any right or remedy provided by applicable law.

(c) *Penalties for a violation.—*

(1) Any lease provision which is prohibited by terms of this section shall be unenforceable by the landlord.

(2) If the landlord includes in any lease a provision prohibited by this section or made unenforceable by §§8-105 [invalidating lease provisions which have the effect of indemnifying landlords] or 8-203 [regulating security deposits] of this title, at any time subsequent to July 1, 1975, and tenders a lease containing such a provision or attempts to enforce or makes known to the tenant an intent to enforce any such provision, the tenant may recover any actual damages incurred as a reason thereof, including reasonable attorney's fees.

Va. Code Ann. §55-248.9 (Michie 1994)

(A) A rental agreement shall not contain provisions that the tenant:

(1) Agrees to waive or forego rights or remedies under this chapter; . . .

(B) A provision prohibited by subsection (A) of this section included in a rental agreement is unenforceable. If a landlord brings an action to enforce any of said prohibited provisions, the tenant may recover actual damages sustained by him and reasonable attorney's fees. (1974, c. 680; 1977, c. 427.)

---

is for violation of another lease provision. See D.C. Code Ann. §45-2551(a) (1981). The theory is that tenants are bound to know it if they have not paid the rent, so that the landlord may proceed directly to the stage of issuing a summons to bring the tenant to court.

60. See, e.g., N.Y. Real Prop. L. §235-b (McKinney 1994).

61. The practice is called distraint.

PROBLEM

T signs a lease that allows L to terminate his tenancy upon two weeks' notice. (The applicable law requires one month.) L terminates, giving two weeks' notice; T requests more time. L refuses and threatens to bring an action if T does not vacate the premises. T leaves the apartment, but because of the short notice has to stay in a hotel for two weeks. He consults your law firm for advice.

§3.8   Landlord's Self-Help

a.   Recovery of Possession

Most judicial opinions in this and other casebooks are written by upper-level courts, usually by state or federal appeals or supreme courts. This opinion is different: it is a (relatively rare) opinion written by a judge in the local trial court in the District of Columbia. These opinions are not normally published in the standard case reporters. Instead, it was published in *The Daily Washingtonian Law Reporter,* which notes it is "A Daily Newspaper of Legal Intelligence Established 1871." Such publications often serve the local bar: the *Daily Washingtonian Law Reporter* is the only source of local trial court opinions in the District.

WHEELER v. THOMPSON

D.C. Gen. Sess. L. & T No. 103875-1 (December 9, 1969)

GREENE, C.J.: This is a petition for an order restoring defendant into premises she occupied before her forcible eviction by plaintiff and protecting her possession from further disturbance except through normal court processes.

I

Lula Thompson had been a resident in an apartment house owned by the plaintiff William Wheeler, trading as Sesso Real Estate Company, since October 1968. On November 10, 1969, plaintiff filed this action in the Landlord and Tenant Branch of this Court, requesting possession of the premises on the ground that rent in the amount of $249.00 was due for the period from October 1 to December 1, 1969. The matter was scheduled for trial for November 24, 1969. Defendant filed an answer, a set-off, and a jury demand, through her counsel, a staff attorney for Neighborhood Legal Services Program, raising various defenses.

On the day of the trial, Mrs. Thompson appeared in court with counsel. When her case was called shortly after 9:00 A.M., her attorney answered that he was ready for trial, whereupon plaintiff promptly dismissed the action. Immediately after the dismissal of the complaint, and while Mrs. Thompson was still at the court or on her way home, plaintiff proceeded to the Thompson apartment. He first attempted to gain entrance by having his janitor announce that he was there for some purpose connected with maintenance, but ultimately he had to cut a chain (and possibly a lock) to enter the premises. Mrs. Thompson was still not present at that time, but a friend was there, insisting that plaintiff could not enter in this manner. Eventually, an altercation ensued, and both plaintiff and Mrs. Thompson's friend were taken by police to the U.S. Attorney's Office — Mr. Wheeler on a charge of forcible entry, Mrs. Thompson's friend on a charge of assault. However, the United States Attorney did not prefer formal charges against either person.

Shortly after 10:00 A.M. defendant returned home, but when she arrived there, she found the door locked. The resident manager informed defendant that plaintiff had changed the lock on her door but permitted defendant to enter briefly. Then defendant left, and when she returned later in the afternoon, she again found the door locked. This time, the resident manager, upon instructions from Mr. Wheeler, refused to unlock the door. Plaintiff himself informed Mrs. Thompson that she could enter the apartment only if she paid him the rent he claimed was due or if she agreed to move by a certain date. However, according to Mr. Wheeler, "she said she wouldn't do anything until she talked to her attorney, and she just absolutely refused to cooperate."

Eventually, defendant's attorney contacted the Court, and a hearing was held about 8:00 P.M. that night to determine whether interim relief was appropriate. Plaintiff's attorney was present but plaintiff himself could not be located, and Mrs. Thompson, who has two small children, had to spend the night elsewhere. A hearing was held the following day on defendant's request to restore her to possession of the premises and for damages for the allegedly illegal eviction. Evidence was taken, and the Court entered an Order to restore her to such possession for a period of ten days pending determination of the appropriateness of more permanent relief. This Opinion explains the basis for that Order. . . .

III

In answer to defendant's request for relief, plaintiff relies upon the proposition that both at common law and in the District of Columbia he is not limited to court action to dispossess a tenant who, in his view, is no longer entitled to possession, but that he may use self help to evict such a person. Reliance is had in this connection upon the decision of the D.C. Court of Appeals in Snitman v. Goodman, 118 A.2d 394 (D.C. App. 1955), in which that court held that the common law right of self help survived the enactment of specific statutory remedies for reacquiring possession.

This Court is, of course, without authority to overrule or to deviate from a decision of the Court of Appeals. However, in deciding whether to enlarge such a decision beyond its specific facts or to consider it narrowly restricted to those facts, the Court may consider the historical background and the public policy underlying the ruling.

No doubt, at the early common law, a landlord had the right to enter premises and dispossess his tenant, if necessary by force. But even as early as 1381, this doctrine began to be eroded (Statute of Forcible Entry, 5 Richard II, ch. 2), and today most States have abandoned it. For there are at least three major defects in the self help doctrine as applied to the dispossession of tenants under modern conditions.

First, whenever there is resort to self help, violence and strife are close at hand. In this case, but a single assault occurred as a consequence of plaintiff's action in "taking the law into his own hands" by determining for himself, and without the benefit of a court order, his rights and obligations and those of his tenant. Any widespread use of self help by landlords in densely-settled urban areas is likely to have much more serious and lasting consequences. As noted in a recent annotation (3 A.L.R. 3rd 182), "public policy grounded on the consideration that to sanction the use of force would, in effect, sanction the use of violence, when this could be avoided by availing of statutory remedies for regaining possession, prompted the adoption, among a large number of states, of the rule that the landlord must, in all cases, resort to the courts to dispossess a tenant . . . "

Second, to sanction the validity of self help would be tantamount to denying the tenant the right to assert all those defenses that have become available to him as a result of numerous court decisions handed down after the *Snitman* case. Here, for example, the tenant's answer to the complaint recited that she was prepared to prove that such housing code violations as would under Brown v. Southall Realty, 237 A.2d 834 (D.C. App. 1968) defeat the landlord's claim for possession existed on the property. Plaintiff's extra-judicial eviction denied the defendant the opportunity to have a court pass upon the validity of that defense. Self help would also avoid, among others, the defense of retaliatory eviction (Edwards v. Habib, 397 F.2d 687 (C.A. D.C. 1968)) and the right to trial by jury (13 D.C. Code §1407).

The public interest and the due administration of justice are obviously not served by the nullification of rights and interests expressly declared by the Congress or the courts. Yet that is exactly what would occur if those against whom these rights run were permitted to defeat them by the simple expedient of proceeding by way of self help instead of by litigation. If this were the rule, tenants could insure the survival of their legally-recognized rights only by holding the landlord at bay pending a court adjudication. No more pernicious doctrine could be declared, for it would constitute an almost open invitation for landlord and tenant to fight for possession until the date of the court hearing.

Third, recognition of the self help doctrine is also undesirable on more general grounds of public policy. Those who, for one reason or an-

542-557 (1992). Landlords usually are not represented by attorneys either. Because tenants being evicted typically owe only one month's rent, the amounts at issue usually are too small to justify hiring an attorney; instead, 76 percent are represented by "landlord agents." "Landlord agents' specialization, experience, and familiarity with procedure and personnel, more than the limited law ever invoked, render them effective representatives for property owners." Id. at 555. Bezdek found that court personnel typically accommodate these agents, so that they can predict when their cases will be heard, whereas tenants had to wait for hours because court officials gave them no information in response to their requests to know when their cases would be heard.

2. **Wrongful eviction.** Ms. Thompson sought simply to recover possession of her apartment. But a wrongful eviction, or a forcible entry or detainer, *infra,* may also result in a money judgment, including exemplary damages, and awards for the tenant's mental anguish. See, e.g., Lopez v. City of New York, 78 Misc. 2d 575, 357 N.Y.S.2d 659 (N.Y. Civ. Ct. 1974) ($1,000 for mental anguish).

3. **Forcible entry and detainer.** Many states have forcible entry or detainer laws. Typical of such statutes are the following California provisions.

§1159. Every person is guilty of a forcible entry who either:

1. By breaking open doors, windows, or other parts of a house, or by any kind of violence or circumstance of terror enters upon or into any real property; or,

2. Who, after entering peaceably upon real property, turns out by force, threats, or menacing conduct, the party in possession.

§1160. Every person is guilty of a forcible detainer who either:

1. By force, or by menaces and threats of violence, unlawfully holds and keeps the possession of any real property, whether the same was acquired peaceably or otherwise; or

2. Who, in the night-time, or during the absence of the occupant of any lands, unlawfully enters upon real property, and who, after demand made for the surrender thereof, for the period of five days, refuses to surrender the same to such former occupant.

The occupant of real property, within the meaning of this subdivision, is one who, within five days preceding such unlawful entry, was in the peaceable and undisturbed possession of such lands.

Cal. Code of Civ. Proc., §§1159-1160 (West 1995).

Reexamine the facts in Wheeler v. Thompson. If a California-like statute had been in place in the District of Columbia, would the landlord have committed either a forcible entry or detainer?

4. **An historical note.** Forcible entry or detainer laws have an ancient lineage. The original forcible entry statute, 5 Rich. 2, c. 7 (1381), provided

that "none from henceforth [shall] make any Entry into any Lands and Tenements, but in case where Entry is given by the Law; and in such case not with strong Hand, nor with Multitude of People, but only in peaceable and easy Manner. And if any Man from henceforth do to the contrary, and thereof be duly convict, he shall be punished by Imprisonment of his Body and thereof ransomed at the King's Will."

Forcible detainer also was made a crime ten years later. 15 Rich. 2, c. 2 (1391). Then followed a civil remedy (treble damages) if a tenant was damaged by either act. 8 Henry 6, c. 9 (1429).

5.   **Restatement of Property.** The Restatement (Second) of Property, Landlord and Tenant, §§14.2-14.3 (1977), preserves the use of self-help where "controlling law permits." It would require, however, that recovery be accomplished

(1)   within a reasonable time after the lease terminates;
(2)   without causing physical harm, or the reasonable expectation of physical harm . . . ; and
(3)   by using reasonable care to avoid damage to the property of the tenant. . . .

6.   **Landlords' frustration.** One of the reasons the opinion in Wheeler v. Thompson is valuable is because the lower-level trial courts are far closer to the day-to-day impact of the law on landlords and tenants than are most appellate courts. The courts' final remarks about the inadequacies of the marshall's office and the "understandable" "exasperation of those aggrieved by these conditions" offer an intriguing picture of why some landlords will chance self-help despite potential legal exposure. Although Wheeler v. Thompson was decided 25 years ago, housing court conditions are often even worse today. See, e.g., Jan Hoffman, Chaos Presides in New York Housing Courts, N.Y. Times, Dec. 28, 1994, at A1.

7.   **How long does it take to evict a tenant?** In some states, it takes a long time to evict a tenant through the courts; in others, eviction can be very quick. In Maryland it can take a long time. No self-help is allowed; a landlord who wants to evict must give a tenant 30 days' notice, after which period the landlord files a complaint. The court's docket determines how much time will elapse before a hearing is granted; 3 weeks is the average waiting period. If either party fails to attend the hearing, the party (typically the tenant) who does not appear is given an additional 6 to 10 days to show up. A 10-day appeals period follows the disposition of the trial court; if the tenant files an appeal, another hearing is set for not less than 5 nor more than 15 days from the date on which the appeal is filed. If the landlord prevails upon appeal, the court issues a warrant to the sheriff authorizing him to evict. Eviction is not, however, immediate. It may take the sheriff anywhere from 3 weeks to several months to effect the eviction. Even after appeal, the tenant has one last resort if she alleges that title to the property has changed. In this situation, the court then summons this person and hearings begin anew. See Md. Code. Ann. §8-402 (Michie 1995). In general,

eviction in Maryland takes a minimum of 6 to 8 weeks and can take much longer.[62]

In Virginia, in sharp contrast, eviction can be very quick. A landlord must give the tenant 5 days' notice to quit or cure, after which he makes complaint to the court and the tenant is served with a summons. If the tenant contests, a hearing date is set; officials in Fairfax County noted that they usually try to set the hearing within a week.[63] If the landlord prevails (including if the tenant fails to appear), judgment is then entered against the tenant. To appeal, the tenant must post an appeal bond within 10 days. The judge determines the amount of the bond. Typically, this amount includes the full value of the judgment against the tenant, plus 30 to 60 days rent. Not surprisingly, appeals are rare. Once a warrant to evict is obtained, the sheriff calls the tenant within 2 or 3 days and sets up an eviction date. The eviction usually takes place within a week of this phone call. Thus, a landlord in Fairfax County typically can evict a tenant within a maximum of 6 to 8 weeks, and sometimes less.

Maryland allows no self-help; in Virginia, landlords may use self-help if the lease so provides. See Va. Code Ann. §55-79 (Michie 1995). However, Virginia landlords typically do not include such language in their form leases. Why?

b. Distraint and Statutory Lien

Some states will allow landlords to seize tenant's goods in lieu of unpaid rent. This common-law remedy of distraint may violate the tenant's due process, as appears in the following case.

HALL v. GARSON

468 F.2d 845 (5th Cir. 1972)

Before DYER, SIMPSON and MORGAN, J.J.

SIMPSON, J. Beginning May 23, 1967, plaintiff-appellant Hall was a tenant of the Cosmopolitan Apartments in Houston, Texas, which were operated by defendants-appellees Garson, Kaplan and Sud. On September 24, 1969, Hall was in arrears in her rent, although the amount of the arrearage was in dispute. Because of this due and unpaid rent, defendants-appellees' agent was sent to Hall's apartment and, on their instructions, entered Hall's

---

62. Telephone Interview with Clerk of Landlord Tenant Commission of Montgomery County, Maryland (May 29, 1996). These procedures do not apply in Baltimore, which has been given the authority to set up its own eviction procedures, which are much faster. See Barbara Bezdek, Silence in the Court: Participation and Subordination of Poor Tenants' Voices in Legal Process, 20 Hofstra L. Rev. 533 (1992).

63. Telephone Interview with Clerk of Fairfax County General District Court (May 29, 1996).

apartment and took therefrom a portable television set owned by Hall and delivered it to defendants-appelees. Neither the entry upon the premises nor the seizure of the television set was consented to by plaintiff-appellant Hall nor by any member of her household; nor was the entry or seizure authorized by any judicial or administrative officer.

Upon demand by Hall, defendant-appellee Garson or her agent, acting on behalf of all named defendants-appellees, refused to return the television set under authority of Vernon's Tex. Rev. Civ. Stat. Ann. Art. 5238a, which grants to the operator of any apartment a lien upon certain personal property found within the tenant's dwelling for all rents due and unpaid by the tenant thereof and grants to the operator the right to enforce that lien by peremptory seizure and retention of such property until the amount of unpaid rent is paid. Art. 5238a makes no provision for any kind of prior hearing.[2]

Subsequent to the taking of Hall's television set, defendants-appellees notified Hall that her television set was being held for the past due rent owed and that it would be returned upon her paying the arrearage. Appellant Hall has never paid nor tendered payment of the rent due and defendants-appellees have indicated they are ready and willing to return the television set to Hall at the time such payment is made.

Hall brought a class action under Rule 23, F.R. Civ. P. on behalf of herself and all other persons similarly situated, challenging the constitutionality of this statutory authority under the Due Process Clause of the Fourteenth Amendment of the U.S. Constitution and for appropriate injunctive relief against defendants-appellees. The district court dismissed the action as jurisdictionally premature, but we reversed and found that Title 28, U.S.C. Section 1343, provided the requisite jurisdiction and that plaintiffs-appellants stated a claim for which relief could be granted under

---

2. Tex. Rev. Civ. Stat. Ann. Art. 5238a:

> Art. 5238a. Baggage lien for rent
>
> Section 1. The operator of any residential house, apartment, duplex or other single or multi-family dwelling, shall have a lien upon all baggage and all other property found within the tenant's dwelling for all rents due and unpaid by the tenant thereof; and said operator shall have the right to take and retain possession of such baggage and other property until the amount of such unpaid rent is paid. . . .
>
> Sec. 2. In any sale to satisfy said lien, said operator shall be subject to the same duties and shall follow the same procedures as set out for proprietors of hotels, boarding houses, inns, tourist courts, and motels, in Article 4595, Revised Civil Statutes of Texas, 1925, as amended.
>
> Sec. 3. Notwithstanding any provisions to the contrary contained in Article 3840. Revised Civil Statutes of Texas, 1925, as amended, there shall be exempt from the lien set out in Section 1 of this Act, the following: (1) all wearing apparel and (2) all tools, apparatus and books belonging to any trade or profession. Additionally, the following shall be exempt from such lien when said house, duplex or apartment is occupied by a family, defined as a person and others whom he is under a legal or moral obligation to support: (1) one automobile and one truck, (2) family library and all family portraits and pictures, (3) household furniture to the extent of one couch, two living room chairs, dining table and chairs, all beds and bedding, and all kitchen furniture and utensils, (4) all agricultural implements, saddles, and bridles, and, (5) good subject to a recorded mortgage lien or financing agreement.

Title 42, U.S.C. Section 1983. Hall, et al. v. Garson, et al., 5 Cir. 1970, 430 F.2d 430. On remand, the district court denied the injunctive relief requested and dismissed the complaint by an unreported memorandum decision.

Fuentes v. Shevin, 1972, 407 U.S. 67, was decided by the Supreme Court subsequent to the instant appeal, but before oral argument. That case was a logical extension of the constitutional principles applied in Goldberg v. Kelly, 1970, 397 U.S. 254, and Sniadach v. Family Finance Corp., 1969, 395 U.S. 337. On the authority of *Fuentes* we hold that Tex. Rev. Stat. Ann. Art. 5238a works "a deprivation of property without due process of law insofar as [it denies] the right to a prior opportunity to be heard before chattels are taken from their possessor." 407 U.S. at 96.

In *Fuentes* the Supreme Court invalidated Florida and Pennsylvania statutes which provided for the summary seizure of goods in a person's possession under a writ of replevin to be issued upon the ex parte application of any other person who claimed a right to them and posted a security bond. The Court found the constitutional infirmity to be the complete absence of prior notice and opportunity to be heard to the party in possession of the property, and held that such violation of due process could be cured only by providing adequate safeguards at a meaningful time and in a meaningful manner so as to obviate the danger of an unfair or mistaken deprivation of property.

Here we have no such protections. Art. 5238a clothes the apartment operator with clear statutory authority to enter into another's home and seize property contained therein. This makes his actions those of the State. Screws v. United States, 1945, 325 U.S. 91, 110-111; United States v. Classic, 1941, 313 U.S. 299, 326; Ex parte Virginia, 1880, 100 U.S. 339, 346-347; Hall v. Garson, *supra,* 430 F.2d at 439-440. There is no requirement that the landlord first have the validity or the accuracy of his claim impartially determined, or that a need for immediate seizure be present. Those decisions are left to the operator himself to act upon with no prior opportunity for challenge by the possessor of the property. "The constitutional right to be heard is a basic aspect of the duty of government to follow a fair process of decisionmaking when it acts to deprive a person of his possessions." 407 U.S. at 80, 92 S. Ct. at 1994, 32 L. Ed. 2d at 570. And: "If the right to notice and a hearing is to serve its full purpose, then, it is clear that it must be granted at a time when the deprivation can still be prevented." 407 U.S. at 81, 92 S. Ct. at 1994, 32 L. Ed. 2d at 570.

We reverse the judgment of the district court and remand for further proceedings consistent with this opinion.

NOTES AND QUESTIONS

1. **Circuit split.** Accord: Culbertson v. Leland, 528 F.2d 426 (9th Cir. 1975). Contra: Davis v. Richmond, 512 F.2d 201 (1st Cir. 1975); Anastasia v.

Cosmopolitan National Bank of Chicago, 527 F.2d 150 (7th Cir. 1975). The Seventh Circuit, in dealing with the precedent of Hall v. Garson, wrote:

> Perhaps distinctions can be drawn between this case and *Hall,* but we do not think that they would be very satisfactory ones. For example, the Texas statute in *Hall* expressly granted landlords the right to enter a dwelling by authorizing them "to take and retain possession" of "property found within the dwelling." Id. at 432 n.1. Ch. 71, §2 does not contain the same language, cf. Calderon v. United Furniture Co., 505 F.2d 950 (5th Cir. 1974), but the right to enter a room may be implicit in the statute. Also, involved in this case is a hotel room, rather than an apartment or house. But there is no question that the plaintiffs in this case used the hotels as their principal long-term residences. Thus, the distinctions do not cut very deeply. Fundamentally, we simply disagree with the result in *Hall.* The historical accuracy of that case's assertion that the execution of liens was traditionally a state function has been questioned. Burke & Reber, State Action, Congressional Power and Creditors' Rights: An Essay on the Fourteenth Amendment, 47 S. Cal. L. Rev. 1, 50 (1973). And this assessment seems correct, except insofar as *Hall* may have relied on particular characteristics of prior Texas law. Plaintiffs freely acknowledge the hoary nature of the innkeepers' lien, and a landlord's right to seize property of a tenant whose rent is in arrears has common law roots as well. Thus, while the sheriff unquestionably is often the party who executes a lien, the function can hardly be said to be traditionally and exclusively that of the state. At most it is one that has been shared by the state with private persons. We see little similarity between this case and the public function cases decided by the Supreme Court and therefore find no basis for concluding that there is state action here.
>
> Because we hold that there is no state action, we have no occasion to consider whether the actions of the hotel proprietors would be violative of the Fourth or Fourteenth Amendment had state action been present. [Id. at 157-58]

Despite the split among the circuit courts, the Supreme Court has not yet dealt directly with the issue. The Supreme Court, however, has decided an analogous case adversely to the debtor. Flagg Bros., Inc. v. Brooks, 436 U.S. 149 (1978). At issue was the validity of New York's Uniform Commercial Code provision, which gave warehousemen the power to sell stored goods to satisfy unpaid charges. Ironically, the debtor in *Flagg Bros.* was a former tenant who had been evicted from her apartment for unpaid rent and whose household belongings had been placed in storage by the city marshall following the eviction.

2.   **Dilution of the *Fuentes* decision.** Since the decision in Hall v. Garson, the United States Supreme Court has watered down its holding in Fuentes v. Shevin, 407 U.S. 67 (1972), on which the *Hall* court partly relied. Mitchell v. W.T. Grant Co., 416 U.S. 600 (1974).

Consider also the related case of Jackson v. Metropolitan Edison Co., 419 U.S. 345 (1974). There the Supreme Court rejected the claim that a homeowner must receive a due process hearing before a regulated utility may cut off electrical service for alleged nonpayment.

3. **Restatement of Property.** Without taking a position on the validity of distraint, Restatement (Second) of Property (1977) lists twenty-four states that have no provision for or have expressly abolished restraint. Id. at §12.1 (statutory note 5(c)). U.R.L.T.A. §4.205 (1972) also abolishes the remedy.

4. **Related forms of landlord self-help.** What policies argue for allowing (or denying) landlords the remedy of distraint when tenants fail to pay rent or otherwise breach their leases? Do the arguments apply similarly to the forfeiture of a security deposit without a prior court hearing? to private repossessions when debtors fail to meet their installment obligations? to repossession of an apartment without a court warrant?

5. **Distraint and the homestead exemption.** Notice that the Texas statute in *Hall* exempted much of the tenant's personal belongings from distraint. State homestead laws (§4.1.a.5 *infra*), which extend their protection to tenants as well as homeowners, would similarly weaken the usefulness of distraint.

6. **Alternative *state* constitutional due process requirements.** Compare Sharrock v. Dell Buick-Cadillac, Inc., 45 N.Y.2d 152, 379 N.E.2d 1169, 408 N.Y.S.2d 39 (1978). New York gave garagemen a statutory lien on their customers' cars for repair and storage charges, and if the charges were unpaid, the power to conduct an ex parte sale of the bailed automobile. The court of appeals held that the statute failed to meet the procedural due process requirements of the *state* constitution by depriving the car owner of a significant property interest without a prior hearing.

> As noted, common law afforded the garageman only the right to possession; it was the State which authorized enforcement of the lien by means of ex parte sale of the vehicle without first affording its owner an opportunity to be heard (see L. 1909, ch. 38, as amd.). Thus, New York has done more than simply furnish its statutory imprimatur to purely private action. Rather, it has entwined itself into the debtor-creditor relationship arising out of otherwise regular consumer transactions. The enactment of substantive provisions of law which authorize the creditor to bypass the courts to carry out the foreclosure sale encourages him to adopt this procedure rather than to rely on more cumbersome methods which might comport with constitutional due process guarantees. Indeed, not only does the State encourage adoption of this patently unfair procedure, it insulates the garageman from civil or criminal liability arising out of the sale and requires one of its agencies, the Department of Motor Vehicles, to recognize and record the transfer of title (see Vehicle and Traffic Law, §401), thus enabling the garageman to transfer title to a vehicle he would not otherwise be deemed to own (Adams v. Department of Motor Vehicles, 11 Cal. 3d 146, 150-151; cf. Caesar v. Kiser, 387 F. Supp. 645; Barber v. Rader, 350 F. Supp. 183; Dielen v. Levine, 344 F. Supp. 823).
>
> Even more fundamentally, the underlying purpose of the sale provisions of the Lien Law — that of conflict resolution — has always been deemed one of the essential attributes of sovereignty. Absent consent of the debtor, the power to fashion the means to order legally binding surrenders of property has always been exclusively vested in the State. Implementation of dispute

settlement, irrespective of the strength of the competing interests of the parties, is the function of the judiciary, and is not dependent "on custom or the will of strategically placed individuals, but on the common-law model" (Boddie v. Connecticut, 401 U.S. 371, 375). But by permitting the possessory lienor to take those steps necessary to foreclose his lien in a nonjudicial setting where the power of sale is premised on possession alone, the State has permitted the garageman to arrogate to himself the exclusive power of the sovereign to resolve disputes. However strong the interest of the garageman in the vehicle may be, his power of foreclosure has no vitality until it is sanctioned by the State. It follows, then, that such a person vested by the State with the power to resolve unilaterally an otherwise judicially cognizable controversy, is nothing more than a delegate of an exclusively governmental function (cf. North Ga. Finishing v. Di-Chem, 419 U.S. 601, *supra;* Fuentes v. Shevin, 407 U.S. 67, 93, *supra*). For this reason, the debtor must be provided with that measure of due process as would be afforded in a court of law. [45 N.Y.2d at 161-162, 379 N.E.2d at 1174-1175, 408 N.Y.S.2d 45]

Keep in mind that state courts may read protections found in their own constitution more expansively than federal courts would construe parallel provisions in the United States Constitution.

7. **Disposition of the tenant's personal property.** Tenant vacates the apartment but fails to take all his personal belongings. What steps should a prudent landlord take as to the goods that tenant leaves behind? Cf. Boston Educational Research Co. v. American Machine & Foundry Co., 488 F.2d 344, 348-349 (1st Cir. 1973). Should a landlord exercise any greater (or lesser) care when, in the use of self-help to recover possession, she removes and stores the tenant's goods? When she (or, more likely, the marshal) executes a warrant of eviction? See, e.g., Stephenson v. Ridgewood Village Apts., 1994 U.S. Dist. LEXIS 16924 (W.D. Mich. 1994) (tenant's possessions removed from apartment, placed on street curb 200 yards from her apartment, and carried off or damaged).

8. **Virginia statute.** Virginia allows a landlord to effect a forcible entry for the purpose of attaching (confiscating) property for rent owed. If a tenant falls behind in the rent, the landlord makes a complaint in the local district court and can obtain a judgment against the tenant. This judgment is used to obtain a warrant that is then issued to the sheriff, authorizing him to break in to the tenant's dwelling and remove his personal property to satisfy the amount in arrears. See Va. Code Ann. §55-235 (Michie 1994).

§3.9   Tenants' Defenses to an Eviction or Unpaid Rent Proceeding

a.   Improper Termination of a Periodic Tenancy

Tenants' lawyers should consider, in the first instance, whether any "technical" defense is present that can send the landlord back to the drawing board. (Recall, for example, the nonexistent waiver of notice in the proceeding against Ms. Elma Johnson, see §3.4, *supra*). One such defense, available *only* to tenants with periodic tenancies, is the landlord's failure properly to terminate the tenancy. When this occurs, the court should dismiss the landlord's complaint. Upon dismissal of the complaint, what is the next step for the landlord's attorney?

While it is true that all that "technical" defenses give the tenant is more time, this delay is often important for several reasons. First, many poor tenants live very close to insolvency and find themselves without money to pay the rent if a public assistance check is late, or they are laid off, or if they spend the rent money because of a sudden emergency such as the sickness of a child. In these situations, a delay in eviction may help tenants get back on their feet financially.[64] A second reason delay can be important for tenants is that, even if they are resigned to leaving an apartment, alternative housing is often hard to find. Study after study has found the supply of low-income housing in the United States is not sufficient to meet demand.[65] And according to one 1986 study, 26 percent of the homeless in New York City became homeless when they were evicted.[66] A program specialist at the Children's Defense Fund asserts that

> The biggest cause of homelessness for *families* is the very dramatic and growing gap between families' incomes and the cost of housing. Poor families spend 70% or 80% of their income for housing. If your rent goes up a little bit or your income goes down a little bit — you have an uninsured medical emergency, your car breaks down, you need your car to get to work, you lose your job — any of those things can happen, and if you're living on the edge like that, you're going to become homeless.[67]

Keep in mind that the defense of improper termination of a periodic tenancy is available *only* to tenants with periodic tenancies. The following excerpt, from a standard property law treatise, explains why such tenancies are so common.

> [Periodic tenancies] include the arrangements under which a great many urban dwellers live. Persons in the lower income groups — even those in the lower middle-income groups — frequently do not occupy under written leases or have estates for years. They "rent" a space in which to live, agreeing to pay so

---

64. The way relatives step in to provide rent money in these kinds of situations is part of a larger pattern in which kinship networks in poor African American families provide mutual aid and support. See Carol Stack, All Our Kin 32 (1974).

65. See, e.g., Homelessness in the 1990's: Hearing before the Task Force on Urgent Fiscal Issues of the House Comm. on the Budget, 101st Cong., 1st Sess. 14 (Dec. 20, 1989), at 147; Sue Halpern, The Rise of the Homeless, The N.Y. Review of Books, Feb. 16, 1989, at 24; David C. Schwartz et al., A New Housing Policy for America: Recapturing the American Dream 24 (1988).

66. Sara Rimer, The Rent's Due and for Many It's Homelessness Knocking, N.Y. Times, Mar. 24, 1989, at A1.

67. Stacey L. Hawkins, Homeless Children: A National Tragedy, USA Today, July 30, 1991, at 9A.

much every week or every month, out of the periodically received pay check or pay envelope. Duration of the occupancy is undiscussed. The tenant's ability to pay is so dependent on the unpredictable regularity of earnings, and his desire to remain is so dependent upon possible changes in his place of employment, that an agreement obligating him to an estate for years is not commonly made. From the lessor's angle, no useful end is likely to be served by a more definitive arrangement. Few of these tenants have assets sufficient to make a judgment collectible. The uncertainties of life which beset our mobile industrial and white-collar population are suited by the fluidity of arrangement implicit in this type of nonfreehold estate. Two results flow from the foregoing. This type of estate is tremendously important sociologically in that occupancy thereunder conditions the home life of a very substantial fraction of the population. On the other hand, the financial smallness of the involved rights results in a great dearth of reported decisions from the courts concerning them. Their legal consequences are chiefly fixed in the "over the counter" mass handling of "landlord and tenant" cases of the local courts. So this type of estate, judged sociologically, is of great importance, but judged on the basis of its jurisprudential content, is almost negligible.

Powell on Real Property 177-178 (Richard R. Powell & Patrick J. Rohan eds., 1968).

In the words of one case that cites this discussion, "[t]he continuity factor in estates from period to period gives special importance to 'notice' as a means of ending the relationship." Thompson v. Gin, 27 Ariz. App. 463, 556 P.2d 17 (1976). The allegation that a periodic tenancy has been improperly terminated is often the single most effective tenant's defense because it is so easy to prove: all a tenant's attorney needs is in the notice to quit and the written lease (if there is a written one).

To determine whether a tenancy has been terminated properly, consider the following hypothetical. Say Tenant's rent is due on the first day of the month and that Landlord sends the notice to quit on March 7. What is the first day on which the tenancy can be properly terminated? Apply two rules:

1.   Statutes ordinarily require 30 days' notice to end a periodic tenancy: thirty days from March 7 is April 7;
2.   Under the common law, a periodic tenancy can only be terminated at the end of a period, so the first date when the tenancy can be ended is May 1.

PROBLEMS

1.   On January 10, 1996, Landlord serves Tenant with a notice stating that her tenancy will be terminated on February 1. Tenant has a month-to-month tenancy that began on August 1, 1987. The jurisdiction has a statute

even 30 days 15th
not 14th=
had notice

requiring 30 days' notice to terminate a periodic tenancy; otherwise it follows the common law. What are Landlord's rights when he sues to evict because the Tenant is still in the apartment on February 14?

2.   Same Tenant, same Landlord, same tenancy, except this time the Landlord sends a letter terminating Tenant's lease as of March 1, 1996. Landlord sues to evict on March 2. What are his rights? *— None*

3.   Kim Student leases premises pursuant to a lease that runs from August 1, 1995, until August 1, 1996, and further provides: "Should the Tenant continue in possession after the end of the term herein created with permission of the Landlord, it is agreed that the tenancy thus created can be terminated by either party giving to the other party not less than 30 days' written notice." On September 30, 1996, what kind of tenancy does Kim have? *PT - depending on Rent payments*

Although the extra time the technical defense makes available is often extremely important to a client, in the absence of other defenses, the technical defense is of limited value: A landlord whose case is dismissed on the grounds that the lease was not properly terminated can simply start the eviction process over by sending a new notice to quit that properly terminates the tenancy. In addition to the technical defense, a series of substantive tenants' defenses has arisen over the past century. The end result of these developments has been a substantial erosion of the doctrine of independent covenants. The law concerning tenants' defenses — the core of the so-called landlord-tenant revolution[68] — has come to influence many other areas of landlord-tenant law.

b.   Partial or Constructive Eviction

At the heart of every tenancy is the occupant's right to remain in possession of the entire premises until the lease term has come to an end. There are two formal legal sources for this intuitive truism, one grounded on the estate theory of leases — that is, the landlord has conveyed a nonfreehold estate that transfers the possessory right to the tenant, and one grounded on the implied covenant of quiet enjoyment, which the common law read into every lease, unless some express term of the lease negated the covenant.

Under the covenant, tenant is protected against any interference with her use of the demised premises caused by the landlord, or by someone having title paramount to that of the landlord, or by someone who derived authority for his acts from the landlord. Powell on Real Property 98-100 (Richard R. Powell & Patrick J. Rohan eds. 1968). Breach of the covenant

---

68.   Edward H. Rabin, The Revolution in Residential Landlord-Tenant Law: Causes and Consequences, 69 Cornell L. Rev. 517 (1984).

would follow routinely if landlord had previously rented the same premises to another tenant, if landlord's default on a mortgage caused tenant to lose her premises,[69] or if landlord without the right to do so were to lock tenant out of her apartment. Were any of these events to occur, tenant could — as one remedial option — rescind the lease and sue to recover her losses, which would include the premium value of the lease's unexpired term and consequential damages.

Total, actual eviction, as we have just illustrated it, happens quite often, but it is only one way — and less common than others — in which tenant's use and enjoyment of the premises suffers from conduct linked to the landlord. The materials that follow show other possibilities.

1.   Partial, Actual Eviction

SMITH v. McENANY

170 Mass. 26, 48 N.E. 781 (1897)

HOLMES, J. This is an action upon a lease for rent, and for breach of a covenant to repair. There is also a count on an account annexed, for use and occupation, etc., but nothing turns on it. The defense is an eviction. The land is a lot in the city of Boston, the part concerned being covered by a shed which was used by the defendant to store wagons. The eviction relied on was the building of a permanent brick wall for a building on adjoining land belonging to the plaintiff's husband, which encroached nine inches by the plaintiff's admission, or as his witness testified from measurements, thirteen and a half inches, or, as the defendant said, two feet, for thirty-four feet long the back of the shed. The wall was built with the plaintiff's assent, and with knowledge that it encroached on the demised premises. The judge ruled that the defendant had a right to treat this as an eviction determining the lease. The plaintiff asked to have the ruling so qualified as to make the question depend upon whether the wall made the premises "uninhabitable for the purpose for which they were hired, materially changing the character and beneficial enjoyment thereof." This was refused, and the plaintiff excepted. The bill of exceptions is unnecessarily complicated by the insertion of evidence of waiver and other matters; but the only question before us is the one stated, and we have stated all the facts which are necessary for its decision.

The refusal was right. It is settled in this State, in accordance with the law of England, that a wrongful eviction of the tenant by the landlord from a part of the premises suspends the rent under the lease. The main reason which is given for the decisions is, that the enjoyment of the whole con-

69. Or forced her to enter into a new lease with a new landlord (i.e., to attorn) as the price for remaining.

sideration is the foundation of the debt and the condition of the covenant and that the obligation to pay cannot be apportioned. . . . It also is said that the landlord shall not apportion his own wrong, following an expression in some of the older English books. . . . But this does not so much explain the rule as suggest the limitation that there may be an apportionment when the eviction is by title paramount, or when the lessor's entry is rightful. . . . It leaves open the question why the landlord may not show that his wrong extended only to a part of the premises. No doubt the question equally may be asked why the lease is construed to exclude apportionment, and it may be that this is partly due to the traditional doctrine that the rent issues out of the land, and that the whole rent is charged on every part of the land. . . . That land is hired as one whole. If by his own fault the landlord withdraws a part of it, he cannot recover either on the lease or outside of it for the occupation of the residue. . . .

It follows from the nature of the reason for the decisions which we have stated, that when the tenant proves a wrongful deforcement by the landlord from an appreciable part of the premises, no inquiry is open as to the greater or less importance of the parcel from which the tenant is deforced. Outside the rule de minimis, the degree of interference with the use and enjoyment of the premises is important only in the case of acts not physically excluding the tenant, but alleged to have an equally serious practical effect,[70] just as the intent is important only in the case of acts not necessarily amounting to an entry and deforcement of the tenant. Skally v. Shute, 132 Mass. 367. The inquiry is for the purpose of settling whether the landlord's acts had the alleged effect; that is, whether the tenant is evicted from any portion of the land. If that is admitted, the rent is suspended, because, by the terms of the instrument as construed, the tenant has made it an absolute condition that he should have the whole of the demised premises, at least as against willful interference on the landlord's part. . . .

We must repeat that we do not understand any question except the one which we have dealt with to be before us. An eviction like the present does not necessarily end the lease; Lieshman v. White, 1 Allen, 489, 490; or other obligations of the tenant under it, such as the covenant to repair. . . .

Exceptions overruled.

NOTES AND QUESTIONS

1. **The sword and the shield.** A leading New York case on partial, actual eviction is Fifth Avenue Building Co. v. Kernochan, 221 N.Y. 370, 117 N.E. 579 (1917). The landlord sued for rent. The leased premises included a vault beneath the sidewalk maintained under a license from the city of New York. The city revoked the license, thus excluding the tenant from part

---

70. See constructive eviction, *infra.* — EDS.

of his space. In denying the landlord full recovery, Judge Cardozo wrote for
the court:

> Eviction as a defense to a claim for rent does not depend upon a cove-
> nant for quiet enjoyment, either express or implied. It suspends the obligation
> of payment either in whole or in part, because it involves a failure of the con-
> sideration for which rent is paid [authorities cited]. We are dealing now with
> an eviction which is actual and not constructive. If such an eviction, though
> partial only, is the act of the landlord, it suspends the entire rent because the
> landlord is not permitted to apportion his own wrong. If the eviction is the
> act of a stranger by force of paramount title, the rent will be apportioned, and
> a recovery permitted for the value of the land retained. . . . A covenant for
> quiet enjoyment either express or implied, is essential where eviction by title
> paramount is the subject of a claim for damages. It is not essential where the
> tenant asserts a failure, either complete or partial, of the consideration for
> the rent. . . .

Do you understand the subtle distinction between failure of consideration (as a defense to a claim for rent) and breach of a covenant for quiet
enjoyment (as the subject of a claim for damages)? In the *Kernochan* case,
how would a court measure the landlord's recovery?

Consider the holding in Randall-Smith, Inc. v. 43rd St. Estates Corp.,
17 N.Y.2d 99, 215 N.E.2d 494, 268 N.Y.S.2d 306 (1966). There the landlord
forcibly ejected a tenant from 10 percent of the rented offices. In the tenant's suit for (treble) damages, the court declared that, for a partial eviction, the actual damages were the difference between the actual rental
value and the agreed-upon but unpaid rent. No note was taken of the fact
that the partial eviction was the act of the landlord. Is the holding consistent
with Smith v. McEnany?

2. **What happens next?** If a court suspends rent, is it likely that tenant
will be able to remain in possession for the remaining term rent-free? If you
were landlord's lawyer, what advice would you tender after the court has
dismissed your client's suit for rent? What will determine whether landlord
decides to remove the encroachment?

3. **Current status of the "suspension of rent" defense.** In a much
more recent case involving a luxury apartment, a lower New York court suspended a tenant's entire rent when the 11-room apartment agreed upon in
the lease was found to have only 10 rooms. Fifth Avenue Estates, Inc. v.
Scull, 42 Misc. 2d 1052, 249 N.Y.S.2d 774 (App. T. 1964). The Restatement
(Second) of Property, Landlord and Tenant (1976, main volume), however,
has rejected the "suspension of rent" defense. Id. at §6.2.

4. **No air-conditioning nights or weekends.** Landlord refuses to air-
condition offices after 6 P.M. and on weekends, making the offices unusable
during the summer. Partial actual eviction? See Barash v. Pennsylvania Terminal Real Estate Corp., 26 N.Y.2d 77, 256 N.E.2d 707, 308 N.Y.S.2d 649
(1970), *infra*.

2.   Constructive Eviction

DYETT v. PENDLETON

8 Cow. 727 (N.Y. 1826)

[The facts appear in the concurring opinion of Senator Crary.]

. . . The facts offered to be proved on the trial are, substantially, that in February, 1820, from time to time, and at sundry times, the plaintiff introduced into the house, (two rooms upon the second floor and two rooms upon the third floor whereof had been leased to the defendant,) divers lewd women or prostitutes, and kept and detained them in the said house all night, for the purpose of prostitution; that the said lewd women or prostitutes would frequently enter the said house in the day time, and after staying all night, would leave the same by daylight in the morning; that the plaintiff sometimes introduced other men into the said premises, who, together with him, kept company with the said lewd women or prostitutes during the night; that on such occasions, the plaintiff and the said lewd women or prostitutes, being in company in certain parts of the said house, not included in the lease to the defendant, but adjacent thereto, and in the occupation or use of the plaintiff, were accustomed to make a great deal of indecent noise and disturbance, the said women or prostitutes often screaming extravagantly, and so as to be heard throughout the house, and by the near neighbors, and frequently using obscene and vulgar language so loud as to be understood at a considerable distance; that such noise and riotous proceedings, being from time to time continued all night, greatly disturbed the rest of persons sleeping in other parts of the said house, and particularly in those parts thereof demised to the defendant; that the practices aforesaid were matters of conversation and reproach in the neighborhood, and were of a nature to draw, and did draw, odium and infamy upon the said house, as being a place of ill fame, so that it was no longer respectable for moral and decent persons to dwell or enter therein; that all the said immoral, indecent and unlawful practices and proceedings were by the procurement or with the permission and concurrence of the plaintiff; that the defendant, being a person of good and respectable character, was compelled, by the repetition of the said indecent practices and proceedings, to leave the said premises, and did, for that cause, leave the same on or about the beginning of March, 1820, after which he did not return thereto, &c.

This evidence, being objected to by the plaintiff's counsel, was rejected by the court, and is now to be considered as true. . . .

[The main opinion follows.]

SPENCER, SENATOR. It seems to be conceded that the only plea which could be interposed by the defendant below, to let in the defence which he offered, if any would answer that purpose, was, that the plaintiff had entered in and upon the demised premises, and ejected and put out the defendant. Such a plea was filed; and it is contended on the one side, that it must be literally proved, and an actual entry and expulsion established: while on the other side it is insisted, that a constructive entry and expulsion is sufficient, and that the facts which tended to prove it, should have been left to the jury. . . .

. . . The agreement set forth in the plea, contains a covenant that the defendant shall have "peaceable, quiet and indisputable possession" of the premises. This is in its nature, a condition precedent to the payment of rent, and whether the possession was peaceable and quiet, was clearly a question of fact for the jury. Such conduct of the lessor as was offered to be proved in this case, went directly to that point; and without saying at present, whether it was or was not sufficient to establish a legal disturbance, it is enough that it tended to that end, and should have been received, subject to such advice as the judge might give to the jury.

The opinion of the supreme court proceeds upon the ground that there must be an actual physical eviction, to bar the plaintiffs; and in most of the cases cited, such eviction was proved; and all of them show that such is the form of the plea. But the forms of pleading given, and the cases cited, do not establish the principle on which the recovery of rent is refused, but merely furnish illustrations of that principle, and exemplifications of its application. The principle itself is deeper and more extensive than the cases. It is thus stated by Baron Gilbert, in his essay on rents, p. 145:

> A rent is something given by way of retribution to the lessor, for the land demised by him to the tenant, and consequently the lessor's title to the rent is founded upon this: that the land demised, is enjoyed by the tenant during the term included in the contract; for the tenant can make no return for a thing he has not. If therefore the tenant be deprived of the thing letten, the obligation to pay the rent ceases, because such obligation has its force only from the consideration, which was the enjoyment of the thing demised.

And from this principle, the inference is drawn, that the lessor is not entitled to recover rent in the following cases: 1st. If the lands demised be recovered by a third person, by a superior title, the tenant is discharged from the payment of rent after eviction by such recovery. 2d. If a part only of the lands be recovered by a third person, such eviction is a discharge only of so much of the rent as is in proportion to the value of the land evicted. 3d. If the lessor expel the tenant from the premises, the rent ceases. 4th. If the lessor expel the tenant from a part only of the premises, the tenant is discharged from the payment of the whole rent; and the reason for the rule why there shall be no apportionment of the rent in this case as well as in that of an eviction by a stranger, is, that it is the wrongful act of the lessor himself, "that no man may be encouraged to injure or disturb his tenant in his possession, whom, by the policy of the feudal law, he ought to protect and defend."

This distinction, which is as perfectly well settled as any to be found in our books, establishes the great principle that a tenant shall not be required to pay rent, even for the part of the premises which he retains, if he has been evicted from the other part by the landlord. As to the part retained, this is deemed such a disturbance, such an injury to its beneficial enjoyment, such a diminution of the consideration upon which the contract is founded, that the law refuses its aid to coerce the payment of any rent. Here, then, is a case, where actual entry and physical eviction are not necessary to exonerate the tenant from the payment of rent; and if the principle be correct as applied to a part of the premises, why should not the same principle equally apply to the whole property demised, where there has been an obstruction to its beneficial enjoyment, and a diminution of the consideration of the contract, by the acts of the landlord, although those acts do not amount to a physical eviction? If physical eviction be not necessary in the one case, to discharge the rent of the part retained, why should it be essential in the other, to discharge the rent of the whole? If I have not deceived myself, the distinction referred to settles and recognizes the principle for which the plaintiff in error contends, that there may be a constructive eviction produced by the acts of the landlord. . . .

. . . Believing that [the tenant's testimony] tended to establish a constructive eviction and expulsion against the consent of the tenant; that it tended to prove a disturbance of his quiet possession, and a failure of the consideration on which only the tenant was obliged to pay rent, I am of opinion that it ought to have been received; and that therefore the judgment of the supreme court should be reversed, with directions to issue a venire denovo. . . .

[Then there is SENATOR CRARY's peroration:]

The whole science of law consists in the application of a few simple principles to the "affairs and bosoms of men." In Collins v. Blantern, (2 Wils. R. 350,) it is said by lord chief justice Wilmot, that "all writers upon our law agree in this: no polluted hand shall touch the pure fountains of justice." I should lay hold upon this principle, if there was no other, for the purpose of chastising vice and impudence, on the one hand, and protecting virtue and innocence, on the other. When the defendant is told that every right, when withheld, shall have its remedy, and every injury its proper redress, and that personal security, which includes reputation, is one of his absolute rights, and then told he must live in a brothel, against his will, or, at least, pay rent for it, he cannot but see the disparity between the text and the comment, and if the one is right, the other must be wrong.

If the evidence offered does not technically prove an eviction, yet, as there is no other plea under which the defence can be made, for the sake of giving effect to it, I should resort not to the statute law, nor to the common law, but to the great principles of morality, on which both are founded;

and if, in the long tract of ages which are past, I could find no case parallel with the present, I should decide against the plaintiff, satisfied that if the same case had ever existed, the principal actor in it had not aspired to immortality by publishing his own infamy.

[And finally there is the dissent:]

COLDEN, SENATOR. . . . It is conceded, on all hands, that to excuse the non-performance of a covenant to pay rent, an entry of the lessor and an eviction of the lessee must be pleaded. But the plaintiff in error contends that the evidence he offered, should have been received as proof of an entry and eviction. This doctrine appears to be entirely new, and no case was cited to show that it was not so. Indeed, the counsel of the plaintiff in error seemed to appeal to the moral, rather than to the municipal law. And if we were to decide this case according to the dictates of morality, we might be disposed to pronounce a judgment in his favor. It is true that the moral law and the law of the land should not be at variance; but if they be so, it is not for us, in our judicial capacity, to reconcile them. We are, in rendering our judgments, not to determine as we may think the law of our country should be, but as we find it established; and the question now presented for our decision is, whether a lessee, finding himself temporarily disturbed in the enjoyment of the demised premises by the misconduct or immoral practices of the lessor, may abandon the tenement for the whole term, and be exonerated from the payment of rent. If this question were to be answered in the affirmative, it would, in my opinion, introduce a new and very extensive chapter in the law of landlord and tenant; for if the encouragement or practice of lewdness, on premises under the same roof with the tenements leased, would warrant an abdication by the tenant, and release him from his covenant to pay rent, there is no reason why, if the landlord should by any other means render the occupation of the premises inconvenient or uncomfortable, the same consequences should not ensue. It would be so if the landlord were to maintain a house of ill fame adjoining or opposite to, or in the same street with the demised premises; if he were to set up a noisy or noxious manufactory near the tenements he had let; or if the landlord should happen to have the plague of a scolding wife under the same roof with his tenant, the tenant might feel himself authorized to leave the premises, and claim an exoneration from the payment of rent.

A decision that matters of this nature may be put in issue in an action of covenant for the non-payment of rent, would be to afford grounds for litigation on which there would be perpetual contentions. If the lessor illegally interferes with his lessee's enjoyment of the demised premises, otherwise than by an entry and eviction, the tenant has his remedy by civil suit or public prosecution . . . But merely because the tenant is interrupted or incommoded in the enjoyment of the demised premises, I am convinced the law does not allow him to redress himself by abandoning the tenement and withholding the rent. . . .

[But a majority were for reversal. For reversal, 16. For affirmance, 6.]

NOTES AND QUESTIONS

1. **Forms of the opinions.** Why does this case consist of a series of opinions by senators? In New York in the nineteenth century, a litigant's final appeal was to the upper house of the legislature. (In England, the final appeal is to the House of Lords to this day.)

2. **Style of argumentation.** This is one of the earliest cases that recognized the defense of constructive eviction. How does the style of legal argumentation differ from opinion to opinion? Which opinion(s) seem most modern in tone, and which the most old-fashioned? Note the explicitly moralistic language in Senator Crary's peroration. Does it signal different assumptions about the relationship between law and ethical judgments than we tend to have today? Perhaps the senator's tone is more "political" than "legal." Today's lawyers are much more likely to embed their ethical judgments ("policy arguments") in less emotive, more rationalistic terminology. Is this, in your opinion, a better approach?

3. **Traditional requirement that the tenant move out.** Why must abandonment precede the plea of constructive eviction? Abandonment must also be prompt. What if tenant cannot readily find another apartment? Or can only find a comparable apartment at a much higher rent? And who pays the tenant's moving expenses?

In this context, consider that the supply of low-income housing is stagnant or shrinking[71] as the demands grows with the spread of poverty. One study found three times as many poor renter households as low-cost housing units.[72] Another author summarizes the situation as follows:

> The supply of decent, moderately priced vacant units available to people living in substandard quarters does not exist in most areas — the overall vacancy rate is too low, the vacant units that exist do not match the need (by size, rent level, tenure, location) of those who need them and the prevalence of discrimination (on the basis of race, household size or composition, and source of income) keeps units out of the reach of needy households.[73]

---

71. Joint Center for Housing Studies of Harvard University, The State of the Nation's Housing 15 (1994) (the stock of low-cost and subsidized housing units has declined).

72. M. A. Turner & V. Reed, Housing America: Learning from the Past, Planning for the Future (1990), quoted in E. Jay Howenstine, The New Housing Shortage 14, in The New Housing Shortage: Housing Affordability in Europe and the USA (Graham Hallett ed., 1993).

73. Chester Hartman, Housing Policies under the Reagan Administration, in Critical Perspectives on Housing 362, 372 (Rachel G. Bratt et al. eds., 1986).

Furthermore, most families who are eligible for federal housing assistance do not receive it. In 1987, 30 percent of very low-income families received housing assistance. However, 60 percent of such families did *not* receive assistance but lived in structurally inadequate housing or paid excessive rent (defined as more than 30 percent of income).[74]

The demand for public housing far exceeds the supply. In 1988 Jonathan Kozol reported that in New York City, the average waiting period for an apartment in a housing project was 18 years.[75] In 1991 The Washington Post reported that Washington, D.C., had a public housing waiting list of 12,000 names for a total of 10,000 units (the great bulk of them currently occupied).[76] A 1986 survey of 64 cities found that 247,500 families were on waiting lists for vacancies in 374,150 units.[77] A 1985 study for the California legislature concluded that in California, there were 642,000 more low-income families than available low-income housing units.[78]

4. **General covenants of quiet enjoyment.** General covenants of quiet enjoyment are standard provisions in modern leases, but note that the court in *Dyett* did not require the existence of a written covenant of quiet enjoyment, nor is one necessary. However, many early cases (although not *Dyett*) set up a narrow and formalistic test for constructive eviction. To claim constructive eviction, a tenant had to be able to point to a *specific* covenant (promise) in the lease that had been violated — for example, the failure to provide heat. See, e.g., Keating v. Springer, 34 N.E. 805 (Ill. 1893) (no constructive eviction when landlord obstructs tenant's windows by building on adjacent property in the absence of a covenant forbidding him to do so).

5. **"Substantial" impairment of quiet enjoyment.** To prevail on a defense of constructive eviction, the tenant must prove a *substantial* impairment of his quiet enjoyment. Since the tenant must also abandon the premises to plead constructive eviction, the defense cannot be tested until the tenant has moved elsewhere. What exposure does tenant face if a court rules, after the fact, that the impairment was insubstantial? Does substantial mean "material?" (Do you see the analogy to contract rescission?)

6. **Modern trends in constructive eviction law.** In recent years, courts have interpreted certain requirements of the doctrine of constructive eviction more broadly. Robert Schoshinski, American Law of Landlord and

---

74. John C. Weicher, Comment on William Apgar's "Which Housing Policy is Best?," Housing Policy Debate, Vol. 1, No. 1, 1990, at 35.

75. Jonathan Kozol, The Homeless and Their Children, The New Yorker, Jan. 25, 1988, at 68.

76. Tracy Thompson, Turned Away: D.C. Has Scant Help to Offer Families with Nowhere to Go, Wash. Post, June 27, 1993, at A1, A16.

77. William E. Schmidt, Public Housing: For Workers or the Needy?, N.Y. Times, Apr. 17, 1990, at A1.

78. Donna Mascari, Homeless Families: Do They Have a Right to Integrity?, 35 UCLA L. Rev. 159, 182 (1987).

Tenant §3.5 (1980 & Supp. 1995). First, the duty breached by the landlord may arise from the lease itself, or it may come from statutes such as housing codes, or may be implied, like the warranty of habitability. Id. at 98-99. Second, there is currently a split in the courts over whether the tenant must actually move out to establish the defense. Some courts will allow the tenant to stay on, although in these cases, she may be required to leave the moment the court finds a constructive eviction. Id. at 100. In other courts, a finding of constructive eviction gives the tenant a claim for rent abatement in proportion to the diminishment in value caused by the breach, if the tenant does not leave. Id. (1995 Supp.) at 67; see, e.g., Jane Doe v. New Bedford Housing Auth., 417 Mass. 273, 630 N.E.2d 248 (1994). Finally, where the common-law rule was that the landlord is not responsible for the behavior of third parties, some courts will now allow a tenant to claim constructive eviction where the landlord knew of or authorized the conduct of the third party, or if it was within his power to abate it and he did nothing. Id. at 104.

7. **The disorderly neighbor.** A woman leases an apartment for a one-year term. The apartment immediately above is occupied by a young couple, who give noisy parties twice a week, operate a dishwasher at late hours, and often quarrel abusively with each other. Complaints to the landlord that she could not get proper sleep brought no relief, and the elderly woman vacated her apartment with seven months remaining on the lease. In landlord's action for rent, the trial court found for defendant, holding that there had been a constructive eviction. Colonial Court Apartments, Inc. v. Kern, 282 Minn. 533, 163 N.W.2d 770 (1968).

Notice how these facts differ from those in Dyett v. Pendleton, where the landlord was more actively involved in creating the disturbance. The Minnesota trial court concluded, however, that the landlord had failed to take such reasonable measures as were warranted under the circumstances.

Colonial Court Apartments expresses the now-current view, at least in states fairly sympathetic to tenants. See, e.g., Bocchini v. Gorn Management Company, 69 Md. App. 1, 515 A.2d 1179 (1986); Gottdiener v. Mailhot, 179 N.J. Super. 286, 431 A.2d 851 (1981). But this is a recent departure. Compare Stewart v. Lawson, 199 Mich. 497, 165 N.W. 716 (1917), where tenant unsuccessfully claimed a constructive eviction because of the "intolerably offensive" conduct and language of other tenants in the building:

> From the doctrine that the landlord is not responsible for the acts of strangers, it would follow that an act done by one tenant in a tenement house without the authority, consent, or connivance of the landlord cannot be treated as an eviction by other tenants. It is clear under this rule that no eviction took place which would bar a recovery of the rent, there being no evidence that the tenants causing the disturbance had any title interest in the premises or that [landlord] in any way encouraged it. The most that can be said is that [land-

lord] suffered it to continue. This would not be sufficient to bind her, unless she gave some active support or encouragement to the wrongful acts.

199 Mich. at 499, 165 N.W. at 717.

Stewart v. Lawson, when it was decided, had widespread support. Even though landlord might have sued to enjoin a tenant's offensive conduct or, alternatively, brought eviction proceedings, the landlord's failure to act was not seen as an implied authority for the tenant to create the disturbance. By contrast, however, courts would hold landlords responsible, so as to permit a complaining tenant to terminate his lease, where the disturbances emanated from the hallways and elevators — a "common nuisance, which the landlord had the complete power to abate." Phyfe v. Dale, 72 Misc. 383, 130 N.Y.S. 231 (App. T. 1911).

Restatement (Second) of Property, Landlord and Tenant, §6.1, Comment d (1976, main volume), imputes to the landlord the conduct of third parties if it takes place on property in which the landlord has an interest, provided that landlord can legally control the conduct.

8.   **Sexual harassment by the landlord.** A couple is evicted when a wife refuses to pose for nude photos or to have sex with the landlord. Shellhammer v. Lewallen, 770 F.2d 167 (6th Cir. 1985). A landlord threatens to raise a tenant's rent, or evict her, unless she complies with his sexual advances. Chomicki v. Wittekind, 128 Wis. 2d 188, 381 N.W.2d 561 (1985). A landlord asks tenant, in front of her young son, "how many times did you get laid this week?" Gnerre v. Massachusetts Commn. against Discrimination, 402 Mass. 504, 524 N.E.2d 84 (1988). Tenants facing sexual harassment by the landlord can claim discrimination under state or federal fair housing laws, which forbid discrimination on the basis of sex in the rental of housing.

PROBLEM

You represent a women's health clinic. Recently, they have been targeted by pro-life demonstrators, who have picketed, singing and chanting, in the building parking lot; spoken to patients in order to discourage them from entering the building; distributed literature; occupied the stairs leading to tenant's office; physically barred patients from the office by blocking the doorway; and had occasionally broken into the office waiting room. You have complained to the landlord, but he refuses to become involved. The Board has met to consider what its options are. It is thinking of moving out but is worried about its potential liability under its ten-year lease. Advise them. See Fidelity Mutual Life Ins. Co. v. Kaminsky, 768 S.W.2d 818 (Tex. App. 1989).

3.   Partial, Constructive Eviction

EAST HAVEN ASSOCIATES v. GURIAN

64 Misc. 2d 276, 313 N.Y.S.2d 927 (N.Y. Civ. Ct. 1970)

SANDLER, J. The most important of the several interesting issues presented by the proof in this case is whether or not the doctrine of constructive eviction is available to a residential tenant when a landlord is responsible for conditions that render part of the premises uninhabitable, and the tenant abandons that part but continues to reside in the rest of the premises. Put in another way, the question is whether New York law should recognize the doctrine of partial constructive eviction as a counterpart to partial actual eviction precisely as it has recognized for over a century constructive eviction as a counterpart to actual eviction. (See Dyett v. Pendleton, 8 Cow. 727.)

After a careful review of the authorities, I have concluded that the concept of partial constructive eviction is sound in principle, is supported by compelling considerations of social policy and fairness, and is in no way precluded by controlling precedent.

On May 26, 1963, the defendant entered into a lease with the then owner of 301 East 69 Street, with respect to apartment 18E under which the defendant agreed to pay rent for the apartment from December 1, 1963 to November 30, 1966 in the amount of $425 per month. The apartment in question had a terrace.

In April, 1966, the plaintiff acquired the building. At the end of July, 1966, the defendant and his family vacated the apartment and refused to pay rent for the months of August, September, October and November, 1966, the remaining period of the lease. Accordingly, plaintiff sued for the total of the four months rent, for the reasonable value of legal services, and for specific items of damages allegedly caused by the defendants. As to the last, I find the proof wholly deficient and these claims are accordingly dismissed.

The defense to the suit for rent rests upon the claim that the defendant was constructively evicted from the apartment as a result of the misconduct and neglect of the landlord, which allegedly rendered the terrace uninhabitable.

In addition, the defendant sues for damages to his furniture caused by the landlord's neglect, but this claim clearly must fail since the proof established that the damage complained of occurred before the plaintiff acquired the building. Finally, the defendant seeks return of his security in the amount of $425.

The central factual issue turns on the condition of the terrace and the factors causing that condition.

I find that from early 1965 the central air conditioner emitted quite steadily a green fluid and a stream of water overflow that fell in significant quantities on the terrace. I further find that the incinerator spewed forth particles of ash that were deposited in substantial part upon the terrace. The result was to render the terrace effectively unusable for its intended purposes, and the defendant and his family promptly abandoned the terrace, although it had been a prime factor in inducing them to enter the lease.

Nevertheless, I am unable to conclude that the departure of the defendant and his family from the apartment at the end of July, 1966 constituted their constructive eviction from the entire premises. The evidence clearly discloses that the terrace had become unusable no later than the early spring of 1965, and quite possibly earlier. The law is clear that the abandonment must occur with reasonable promptness after the conditions justifying it have developed. (See 1 Rasch, Landlord and Tenant, §877, and cases cited.)

Unquestionably, this rule should be given a flexible interpretation in light of the practical difficulties these days in finding satisfactory apartments. Moreover, tenants have a right to rely on assurances that the landlord will correct the objectionable conditions.

Although the question is troublesome, I have concluded that a delay of at least 17 months in moving, without any significant proof of an early sustained effort to find other apartments, cannot be reconciled with the current requirements of law.

Turning to the issue of partial eviction, the proof quite plainly established that the terrace had been promptly abandoned once the condition complained of had developed. I am satisfied that conforming the pleadings to the proof to permit consideration of the issue of partial eviction would serve the interests of justice. (CPLR 3025, subd. [c.].)

Although the matter is not clear, I am inclined to believe that the proof before me spelled out an actual partial eviction. It seems to me that the tangible and concrete physical character of the substances falling on the terrace provides a substantial basis for such a finding.

However, I do not rest my decision on that ground in view of the decision of the New York Court of Appeals in Barash v. Pennsylvania Term. Real Estate Corp. (26 N.Y.2d 77). Although the facts of the *Barash* case do not preclude such a finding, the wording of the opinion plainly suggests a disposition to define actual eviction rather narrowly. I therefore turn to consider the status of partial constructive eviction under New York law.

In his authoritative treatise, Rasch flatly asserted that constructive eviction requires "surrender of the entire possession by the tenant." (See 1 Rasch, Landlord and Tenant, §876.)

None of the cases he cites, however, supports that sweeping assertion. These cases, with many others, repeat the general formula that constructive eviction requires abandonment of the premises. None of the cases I have examined squarely address[es] the question here presented of the legal effect of abandonment of only that part of the premises rendered uninhabitable.

The doctrine of constructive eviction was developed by analogy to actual eviction on the basis of a very simple and obvious proposition. If a tenant is effectively forced out of leased premises as a result of misconduct by a landlord that substantially impairs enjoyment of the leased premises, the same legal consequences should follow as though the tenant were physically evicted.

In the eloquent landmark decision that firmly established constructive eviction in New York law, Dyett v. Pendleton (8 Cow. 727, *supra*) the following was said at page 734:

> Suppose the landlord had established a hospital for the small pox, the plague, or the yellow fever, in the remaining part of this house; suppose he had made a deposit of gunpowder, under the tenant, or had introduced some offensive and pestilential materials of the most dangerous nature; can there by any hesitation in saying that if, by such means, he had driven the tenant from his habitation, he should not recover for the use of that house, of which, by his own wrong, he had deprived his tenant? It would need nothing but common sense and common justice to decide it.

Why should a different test be applied where the tenant, through comparable means, is effectively deprived of the use of part of his residence and abandons that part? Ought not the same consequences to follow as would follow an "actual partial eviction"?

I am unable to see any basis in "common sense and common justice" for treating the two situations differently.

Support for this view appears in the careful phrasing of the first decision to establish the requirement of abandonment in constructive eviction cases (Edgerton v. Page, 20 N.Y. 281, 284, 285). The Court of Appeals squarely rested the requirement on the unfairness of suspending rent while the tenant continued to occupy the "entire premises." "I cannot see upon what principle the landlord should be absolutely barred from a recovery of rent, when his wrongful acts stop short of depriving the tenant of the possession of *any portion* of the premises. . . . The true rule, from all the authorities is, that while the tenant remains in possession of the *entire premises* demised, his obligation to payment continues."

While some later opinions have been less carefully worded, I know of none that requires a different result.

While the view here expressed seems to me inherent in "common sense and common justice" that gave rise originally to the doctrine of constructive eviction, the result is independently compelled by considerations of fairness and justice in the light of present realities.

It cannot be seriously disputed that a major shortage in residential housing has prevailed in our metropolitan area for several decades. The clear effect has been to undermine so drastically the bargaining power of tenants in relation to landlords that grave questions as to the fairness and relevance of some traditional concepts of landlord-tenant law are presented.

The very idea of requiring families to abandon their homes before they can defend against actions for rent is a baffling one in an era in which decent housing is so hard to get, particularly for those who are poor and without resources. It makes no sense at all to say that if part of an apartment has been rendered uninhabitable, a family must move from the entire dwelling before it can seek justice and fair dealing.

Accordingly, I hold that when the defendant and his family ceased to use the terrace, a partial constructive eviction occurred with the same legal consequences as attends a partial "actual" eviction.

These consequences were comprehensively defined in Peerless Candy Co. v. Halbreich (125 Misc. 889). It is clear that from the time of the partial eviction, the defendant had the right to stop paying rent. Accordingly, I find against the plaintiff on its action for rent and legal expenses, and for the defendant on his action to recover the security deposit of $425.

Judgment should be entered for the defendant for $425 with interest from August 1, 1966.

NOTES AND QUESTIONS

1. **Can you distinguish *Barash?*** The facts in Barash v. Pennsylvania Terminal Rental Real Estate Corp., 26 N.Y.2d 77, 256 N.E.2d 707, 308 N.Y.S.2d 649 (1970), were these: Tenant charged landlord with wrongful failure to air-condition his offices evenings and weekends, causing the offices to become "hot, stuffy, and unusable and uninhabitable" at those times. Claiming a partial actual eviction, tenant sought an order relieving him from payment of rent. Two lower courts refused to dismiss the tenant's complaint, but the court of appeals reversed.

> The tenant, who has not abandoned the premises, asserts that there has been an actual eviction, though partial only, thus permitting him to retain possession of the premises without liability for rent. To support this contention it is claimed that failure to supply fresh air constitutes actual eviction, if only, albeit, during the hours after 6:00 P.M. and on weekends. . . .
>
> All that tenant suffered was a substantial diminution in the extent to which he could beneficially enjoy the premises. Although possibly more pronounced, tenant's situation is analogous to cases where there is a persistent offensive odor, harmful to health, arising from a noxious gas, an open sewer . . . , or defective plumbing. . . . In all such cases there has been held to be only a constructive eviction. . . . Given these well-established rules, proper characterization of the instant failure to ventilate follows easily. . . . The tenant has neither been expelled nor excluded from the premises, nor has the landlord seized a portion of the premises for his own use or that of another. He

has, by his alleged wrongful failure to provide proper ventilation, substantially reduced the beneficial use of the premises. . . . Since the eviction, if any, is constructive and not actual, the tenant's failure to abandon the premises makes the first cause of action insufficient in law. . . .

2.   **Is *East Haven* sound law?** "The fallacy . . . is quite evident and manifest. Applying 'common sense and common justice,' a tenant deprived of the beneficial use and enjoyment of a portion of the demised premises cannot be placed in a better bargaining advantage than a tenant who is deprived of the beneficial use and enjoyment of the entire demised premises. For, if a tenant must abandon the demised premises to claim the benefit of a total constructive eviction, then, certainly, a tenant deprived of the beneficial use and enjoyment of a portion of the premises must either vacate the said premises or pay rent if he elects to remain in possession." Leonforte, J., in dismissing defense of partial constructive eviction where tenant unable to use the terrace of his fourth-floor apartment, but remained in possession. Zweighaft v. Remington, 66 Misc. 2d 261, 263, 320 N.Y.S.2d 151, 153 (Civ. Ct. 1971). Who has the better of the argument, Justice Sandler or his brother Leonforte?

3.   **New York follow-up.** Partial, constructive eviction seems to be alive and well in New York, and it has been especially useful for commercial tenants to whom the implied warranty of habitability, *infra,* does not apply. See, e.g., Manhattan Mansions v. Moe's Pizza, 149 Misc. 2d 43, 561 N.Y.S.2d (Civ. Ct. 1990) (operator of pizza and coffee shop forced to close repeatedly because of leak around grill area); Minjak Co. v. Randolph, 140 A.D.2d 245, 528 N.Y.S.2d 554 (1st Dept. 1988) (loft tenant unable to use two-thirds of space because of repeated water leaks from upstairs unit). Tenant, however, must physically vacate some part of the premises to establish the eviction.

c.   Breach of the Implied Warranty of Habitability

1.   From Tenement House Law to Modern Housing Codes[79]

Housing codes originated in New York City, where they stemmed from the conditions in tenement housing in the nineteenth century. New York City lots 25 feet wide by 100 feet long originally were designed for town houses, but "when the massive immigration in the nineteenth century bloated the demand for low-rent housing, developers responded by cramming the maximum number of rooms onto their land." New York City Planning Commission, Neighborhood Preservation in New York City 27 (1973) (John E. Zuccotti, chairman).

---

79. Thanks to Dr. Deborah Gardner for help in providing material for this section.

Overcrowding in such tenements was graphically described by Theodore Roosevelt, a state legislator in the 1890s, who noted small size of apartments, the ubiquitous presence of boarders, and the fact that tenement dwellers often did "homework" in their cramped apartments.

> In the overwhelming majority of cases . . . there were one, two, or three room apartments, and the work of manufacturing tobacco went on day and night in the eating, living, and sleeping rooms — sometimes in one room. I have always remembered . . . one room in which two families were living . . . [along with a] third adult male [who] was a boarder with one of the families. . . . The tobacco was stowed about everywhere, alongside the foul bedding, and in a corner where there were scraps of food. . . . [80]

In 1894, New York City had the greatest population density in the world: the Lower East Side, where many immigrants lived, had a population of 800.47 people per acre, which surpassed the highest known foreign density, of 759.66, in Bombay.[81] Figure 3-7 shows an overcrowded tenement, with a family living in a single room in which they lived, worked, and ate. Tenement apartments typically housed from 6 to 18 people in 3 tiny rooms whose floor area ranged from 300 to 450 square feet. An 1865 study found that of New York's population of 700,000, a total of 480,368 persons lived in tenements with substandard conditions.[82]

The Tenement House Acts of 1867 and 1879 resulted in "Old Law" tenements that covered no more than 80 percent coverage on a typical lot. Figure 3-8 shows the narrow air shafts that provided the only source of light and ventilation in Old Law tenements for all but the two rooms on the front of the building, and the two rooms facing the rear yard, typically filled with communal water taps in close conjunction with privies (outhouses).[83] A 1904 report found "Foul malodorous privy vaults, filled to the yard level and, in many cases, overflowing into the yards and draining into adjacent cellars, the floors and even the walls covered with an accumulation of fecal matter."[84] Figure 3-9 shows raw sewage in a New York tenement basement. The early tenement acts' requirement for one privy per 20 people was not enforced; one privy was often shared by 25 to 40 people. Requirements for metal fire escapes on the fronts of buildings were also widely ignored, and fire posed a severe hazard. By 1900, 2.3 million of New York's total population of 3.4 million lived in Old Law tenements or tenements built prior to passage of the Old Law.

80. Theodore Roosevelt, An Autobiography 82 (1914), quoted in Richard Plunz, A History of Housing in New York City 34 (1990).
81. Id. at 37 (citing an 1894 report).
82. Plunz, *supra* note 80, at 22.
83. As late as 1884, one study found that only 30.1 percent of tenements examined had any water closets at all, and almost none had running water above the first floor. Plunz, *supra* note 80, at 33.
84. Board of Tenement House Supervisors of New Jersey, First Report (Executive Document No. 26, 1904), at 35, quoted in Lawrence M. Friedman, Government and Slum Housing: A Century of Frustration 30 (1968).

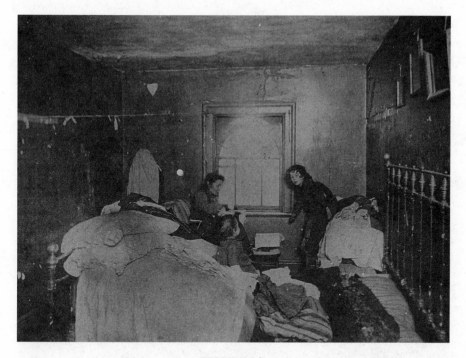

FIGURE 3-7

In these conditions, fire hazard was acute and disease flourished. Cholera and yellow fever flourished in poor New York City neighborhoods before the Civil War. One source calculated that 1 out of every 46 New Yorkers died annually in 1810; in 1859, eight years before the first Tenement House Act, that number had risen to 1 in 27.[85] By the late nineteenth century, tuberculosis was so widespread it was known as the "tenement house disease": overcrowded conditions contributed to its rapid spread among the poor. By the early twentieth century, polio was a major problem.

The link between housing type and disease was made as early as 1820.[86] Even in the height of nineteenth-century laissez-faire, the rapid spread of cholera and tuberculosis from slums to more affluent neighborhoods dramatized the interdependence of citizens in the body politic.

After the 1879 Act, further reforms were impeded by fears that regulations would be struck down as unconstitutional. Such fears were realized when the highest New York court invalidated a law limiting homework in tenements in 1885, on the grounds that it violated rights of "personal liberty and private property." The court concluded: "Such governmental interferences disturb the normal adjustments of the social fabric, and usually

---

85. Plunz, *supra* note 80, at xxxii (quoting a 1929 history of public health).
86. Id. at 3.

FIGURE 3-8

FIGURE 3-9

derange the delicate and complicated machinery of industry and cause a score of ills while attempting the removal of one." In re Jacobs, 98 N.Y. 98, 115 (1885).

Nonetheless, a new and comprehensive law passed in 1901 set the national standard for tenement legislation — and provided the prototype for future housing codes.[87] The floor plan in Figure 3-10 shows the resulting redesign of "New Law" tenements. A few large Eastern cities passed housing codes shortly afterwards; by 1954, some 56 housing codes had been enacted. Housing codes did not become commonplace until they were required as a prerequisite for participation in the urban redevelopment programs in the 1950s.[88]

> A housing code deals with the owner's and occupant's duty to keep existing housing in decent condition — to see to it that it is not occupied by more persons than are legally permitted for housing accommodations of that size; to keep it in proper repair; to maintain it in a sanitary condition; to see that it remains properly ventilated and lighted; to make sure that it has the required facilities for fire safety; that required machinery — elevators, boilers and heating plants, etc. — are kept in working order; and that required services — heat, hot and cold water — are provided in accordance with minimal requirements of law.

Roger A. Cunningham, The New Implied and Statutory Warranties of Habitability in Residential Leases: From Contract to Status, 16 Urb. L. Annual 3, 11-12 (1979) (quoting Frank Grad, Legal Remedies for Housing Code Violations (1968)).

2.   From Housing Codes to the Implied Warranty of Habitability

It was widely believed that housing codes created a cause of action only for the municipality if landlords failed to meet code requirements. But by the 1960s, legal services lawyers representing poor tenants began to assess how they could reform the law in ways that would help their poor clients. Housing was an obvious focus for legal services lawyers in urban areas. "Slum housing" had been a focus of efforts to help the poor for 100 years. In the District of Columbia, a small group of tremendously creative legal services lawyers coalesced. They included Patricia Wald, now a judge on the U.S. Court of Appeals for the District of Columbia, and Florence Roisman, currently a law professor.

Washington, D.C., was a particularly promising forum because it was the only jurisdiction in the country where landlord-tenant cases regularly were heard by federal courts. (D.C. was at that time a federal enclave with no home rule.) Federal courts had proven a receptive forum for legal change

---

87. Id. at 47.
88. Judith Gribetz and Frank P. Grad, Housing Code Enforcement: Sanctions and Remedies, 66 Colum. L. Rev. 1254, 1259-1260 (1966).

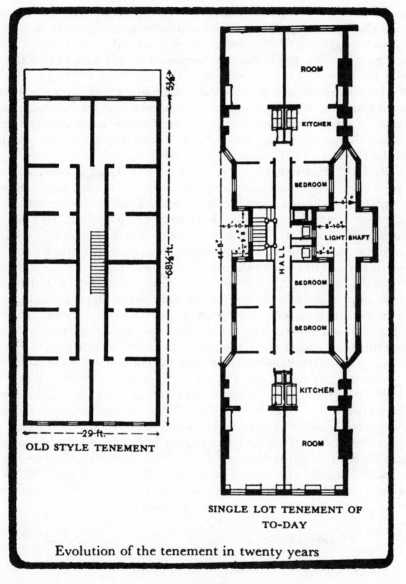

OLD STYLE TENEMENT

SINGLE LOT TENEMENT OF
TO-DAY

Evolution of the tenement in twenty years

FIGURE 3-10

in D.C.: They had used housing codes to impose liability on landlords in tort cases involving personal injury to tenants. Under then-traditional tort principles, a landlord ordinarily was liable to a tenant injured on the lease-hold premises only if the injury was caused by a hidden defect and in certain limited other circumstances.[89] In the 1960s, the federal courts in D.C. had

_____

89. Robert Schoschinski, American Law of Landlord and Tenant §4.3, at 188-189 (1980).

greatly widened the scope of landlords' liability by holding landlords liable for injuries incurred by tenants if those injuries were caused by defects in the leasehold premises that constituted violations of the local housing code. See, e.g., Whetzel v. Jess Fisher Management Co., 282 F.2d 943 (D.C. Cir. 1960). By the end of the decade, the D.C. courts were holding landlords liable even when the defect that caused the injury in question was not an explicit provision of the housing code, on the basis of the housing code's promise of housing maintained in a reasonably safe condition. See, e.g., Kanelos v. Kettler, 406 F.2d 951 (D.C. Cir. 1968); Clarke v. O'Conner, 435 F.2d 104 (D.C. Cir. 1970).

By 1968, legal services lawyers in D.C. were trying to overcome the severe limitations of existing tenants' defenses. As Florence Roisman now remembers it, "we tried every theory we could think of." [90] One argument was that constructive eviction should be extended to include deteriorated premises, and that the traditional requirement that the tenant move out be eliminated. But the arguments that ultimately worked were drawn not from property law, but from tort and contract law. One major victory was Brown v. Southall Realty Co., 237 A.2d 834 (D.C. 1968), which held that the lease of a premises in violation of the housing code was an illegal contract, such that the tenant could remain in the premises but would not owe rent until the housing code violations were remedied. The one problem with *Brown,* whose theory has never been adopted in any other jurisdiction, is that its rationale required the tenant to prove that the housing defects at issue were in existence at the start of the tenancy — often a difficult task. (Why?) Finally, in 1970, the tenants' lawyers persuaded the court to adopt quite a different theory, one that still relied heavily on contract language, but also drew on slightly earlier (and equally dramatic) developments in tort law. As you read the case, focus on the court's rationale. Remember that the court's theory was a radical departure from the doctrine of independent covenants, the traditional core of landlord-tenant law. What reasons does the court give for its decision? Does it focus on the continuities between its decision and the prior law, or the discontinuities (or both)?

3. Case Law

JAVINS v. FIRST NATIONAL REALTY CORP.

428 F.2d 1071 (D.C. Cir. 1970)

J. SKELLY WRIGHT, J.[91] These cases present the question whether housing code violations which arise during the term of a lease have any effect

---

90. Interview of Florence Roisman by Joan Williams (June 1993).

91. Amicus curiae briefs were filed by Neighborhood Legal Services, the National Housing Law Project, and the Washington Planning and Housing Association.

upon the tenant's obligation to pay rent. . . . We . . . hold that a warranty of habitability, measured by the standards set out in the Housing Regulations for the District of Columbia, is implied by operation of law into leases of urban dwelling units covered by those Regulations and that breach of this warranty gives rise to the usual remedies for breach of contract.

The facts revealed by the record are simple. By separate written leases, each of the appellants rented an apartment in a three-building apartment complex in Northwest Washington known as Clifton Terrace. The landlord, First National Realty Corporation, filed separate actions in the Landlord and Tenant Branch of the Court of General Sessions on April 8, 1966, seeking possession on the ground that each of the appellants had defaulted in the payment of rent due for the month of April. The tenants, appellants here, admitted that they had not paid the landlord any rent for April. However, they alleged numerous violations of the Housing Regulations as "an equitable defense or [a] claim by way of recoupment or set-off in an amount equal to the rent claim," as provided in the rules of the Court of General Sessions. They offered to prove

> [t]hat there are approximately 1500 violations of the Housing Regulations of the District of Columbia in the building at Clifton Terrace, where Defendant resides some affecting the premises of this Defendant directly, others indirectly, and all tending to establish a course of conduct of violation of the Housing Regulations to the damage of Defendants. . . .

Since, in traditional analysis, a lease was the conveyance of an interest in land, courts have usually utilized the special rules governing real property transactions to resolve controversies involving leases. However, as the Supreme Court has noted in another context "the body of private property law . . . , more than almost any other branch of law, has been shaped by distinctions whose validity is largely historical." Courts have a duty to reappraise old doctrines in light of the facts and values of contemporary life — particularly old common law doctrines which the courts themselves created and developed. As we have said before, "[T]he continued vitality of the common law . . . depends upon its ability to reflect contemporary community values and ethics."

The assumption of landlord-tenant law, derived from feudal property law, that a lease primarily conveyed to the tenant an interest in land may have been reasonable in a rural, agrarian society; it may continue to be reasonable in some leases involving farming or commercial land. In these cases, the value of the lease to the tenant is the land itself. But in the case of the modern apartment dweller, the value of the lease is that it gives him a place to live. The city dweller who seeks to lease an apartment on the third floor of a tenement has little interest in the land 30 or 40 feet below, or even in the bare right to possession within the four walls of his apartment. When American city dwellers, both rich and poor, seek "shelter" today, they seek a well known package of goods and services[9] — a package which includes not merely walls and ceilings, but also adequate heat, light and ventilation, serviceable plumbing facilities, secure windows and doors, proper sanitation, and proper maintenance.

Professor Powell summarizes the present state of the law:

> The complexities of city life, and the proliferated problems of modern society in general, have created new problems for lessors and lessees and these have been commonly handled by specific clauses inserted in leases. This growth in the number and detail of specific lease covenants has reintroduced into the law of estates for years a predominantly contractual ingredient. In practice, the law today concerning estates for years consists chiefly of rules determining the construction and effect of lease covenants. . . .

Ironically, however, the rules governing the construction and interpretation of "predominantly contractual" obligations in leases have too often remained rooted in old property law.

Some courts have realized that certain of the old rules of property law governing leases are inappropriate for today's transactions. In order to reach results more in accord with the legitimate expectations of the parties and the standards of the community, courts have been gradually introducing more modern precepts of contract law in interpreting leases. Proceeding piecemeal has, however, led to confusion where "decisions are frequently conflicting, not because of a healthy disagreement on social policy, but because of the lingering impact of rules whose policies are long since dead."

In our judgment the trend toward treating leases as contracts is wise and well considered. Our holding in this case reflects a belief that leases of urban dwelling units should be interpreted and construed like any other contract.[13] . . .

[In our judgment, the old no-repair rule cannot] coexist with the obligations imposed on the landlord by a typical modern housing code, and must be abandoned in favor of an implied warranty of habitability. In the District of Columbia, the standards of this warranty are set out in the Housing Regulations.

In our judgment the common law itself must recognize the landlord's obligation to keep his premises in a habitable condition. This conclusion is compelled by three separate considerations. First, we believe that the old

---

9. See e.g., National Commission on Urban Problems, Building the American City 9 (1968). The extensive standards set out in the Housing Regulations provide a good guide to community expectations.

13. We intend no alteration of statutory or case law definitions of the term "real property" for purposes of statutes or decisions on recordation, descent, conveyancing, creditors's rights, etc. We contemplate only that contract law is to determine the rights and obligations of the parties to the lease agreement, as between themselves. The civil law has always viewed the lease as a contract, and in our judgment that perspective has proved superior to that of the common law.

rule was based on certain factual assumptions which are no longer true; on its own terms, it can no longer be justified. Second, we believe that [recent] consumer protection cases . . . require that the old rule be abandoned in order to bring residential landlord-tenant law into harmony with the principles on which those cases rest. Third, we think that the nature of today's urban housing market also dictates abandonment of the old rule.

The common law rule absolving the lessor of all obligation to repair originated in the early Middle Ages.[30] Such a rule was perhaps well suited to an agrarian economy; the land was more important[31] than whatever small living structure was included in the leasehold, and the tenant farmer was fully capable of making repairs himself.[32] These historical facts were the basis on which the common law constructed its rule; they also provided the necessary prerequisites for its application.[33]

Court decisions in the late 1800's began to recognize that the factual assumptions of the common law were no longer accurate in some cases. For example, the common law, since it assumed that the land was the most important part of the leasehold, required a tenant to pay rent even if any building on the land was destroyed. Faced with such a rule and the ludicrous results it produced, in 1863 the New York Court of Appeals declined to hold that an upper story tenant was obliged to continue paying rent after his apartment building burned down. The court simply pointed out that the urban tenant had no interest in the land, only in the attached building.

Another line of cases created an exception to the no-repair rule for short term leases of furnished dwellings. The Massachusetts Supreme Judicial Court, a court not known for its willingness to depart from the common law, supported this exception, pointing out:

> [A] different rule should apply to one who hires a furnished room, or a furnished house, for a few days, or a few weeks or months. Its fitness for immediate use of a particular kind, as indicated by its appointments, is a far more important element entering into the contract than when there is a mere lease

---

30. The rule was "settled" by 1485. . . .

31. The land was so central to the original common law conception of a leasehold that rent was viewed as "issuing" from the land: "[T]he governing idea is that the land is bound to pay the rent. . . . We may almost go to the length of saying that the land pays it through [the tenant's] hand." 2 F. Pollock & F. Maitland, The History of English Law 131 (2d ed. 1923).

32. Many later judicial opinions have added another justification of the old common law rule. They have invoked the time-worn cry of *caveat emptor* and argued that a lessee has the opportunity to inspect the premises. On the basis of his inspection, the tenant must then take the premises "as is," according to this reasoning. As an historical matter, the opportunity to inspect was not thought important when the rule was first devised. See Note 30 *supra*. . . .

33. Even the old common law courts responded with a different rule for a landlord-tenant relationship which did not conform to the model of the usual agrarian lease. Much more substantial obligations were placed upon the keepers of inns (the only multiple dwelling houses known to the common law). Their guests were interested solely in shelter and could not be expected to make their own repairs. "The modern apartment dweller more closely resembles the guest in an inn than he resembles an agrarian tenant, but the law has not generally recognized the similarity." J. Levi, P. Hablutzel, L. Rosenberg & J. White, Model Residential Landlord-Tenant Code 6-7 (Tent. Draft 1969).

of real estate. One who lets for a short term a house provided with all furnishings and appointments for immediate residence may be supposed to contract in reference to a well-understood purpose of the hirer to use it as a
habitation. . . . It would be unreasonable to hold, under such circumstances,
that the landlord does not impliedly agree that what he is letting is a house
suitable for occupation in its condition at the time. . . .[37]

These as well as other similar cases[38] demonstrate that some courts began some time ago to question the common law's assumptions that the land
was the most important feature of a leasehold and that the tenant could feasibly make any necessary repairs himself. Where those assumptions no longer
reflect contemporary housing patterns, the courts have created exceptions to
the general rule that landlords have no duty to keep their premises in repair.

It is overdue for courts to admit that these assumptions are no longer
true with regard to all urban housing. Today's urban tenants, the vast majority
of whom live in multiple dwelling houses, are interested, not in the land, but
solely in "a house suitable for occupation." Furthermore, today's city dweller
usually has a single, specialized skill unrelated to maintenance work; he is unable to make repairs like the "jack-of-all-trades" farmer who was the common
law's model of the lessee. Further, unlike his agrarian predecessor who often
remained on one piece of land for his entire life, urban tenants today are
more mobile than ever before. A tenant's tenure in a specific apartment will
often not be sufficient to justify efforts at repairs. In addition, the increasing
complexity of today's dwellings renders them much more difficult to repair
than the structures of earlier times. In a multiple dwelling repair may require
access to equipment and areas in the control of the landlord. Low and middle
income tenants, even if they were interested in making repairs, would be unable to obtain any financing for major repairs since they have no long-term
interest in the property.

Our approach to the common law of landlord and tenant ought to be
aided by principles derived from . . . consumer protection cases. . . . In a lease
contract, a tenant seeks to purchase from his landlord shelter for a specified
period of time. The landlord sells housing as a commercial businessman and
has much greater opportunity, incentive and capacity to inspect and maintain the condition of his building. Moreover, the tenant must rely upon the
skill and bona fides of his landlord at least as much as a car buyer must rely
upon the car manufacturer. In dealing with major problems, such as heating,
plumbing, electrical or structural defects, the tenant's position corresponds
precisely with "the ordinary consumer who cannot be expected to have the
knowledge or capacity or even the opportunity to make adequate inspection
of mechanical instrumentalities, like automobiles, and to decide for himself
whether they are reasonably fit for the designed purpose." Henningsen v.
Bloomfield Motors, Inc., 32 N.J. 358, 375, 161 A.2d 69, 78 (1960).[42]

---

37. Ingalls v. Hobbs, 156 Mass. 348, 31 N.E. 286 (1892).
38. [Citing constructive eviction cases.]
42. Nor should the average tenant be thought capable of "inspecting" plaster, floor-
boards, roofing, kitchen appliances, etc. To the extent, however, that some defects are obvious,
the law must take note of the present housing shortage. Tenants may have no real alternative
but to accept such housing with the expectation that the landlord will make necessary repairs.
Where this is so, *caveat emptor* must of necessity be rejected.

Since a lease contract specifies a particular period of time during which the tenant has a right to use his apartment for shelter, he may legitimately expect that the apartment will be fit for habitation for the time period for which it is rented. We point out that in the present cases there is no allegation that appellant's apartments were in poor condition or in violation of the housing code at the commencement of the leases.[43] Since the lessees continue to pay the same rent, they were entitled to expect that the landlord would continue to keep the premises in their beginning condition during the lease term. It is precisely such expectations that the law now recognizes as deserving of formal, legal protection.

Even beyond the rationale of traditional products liability law, the relationship of landlord and tenant suggests further compelling reasons for the law's protection of the tenants' legitimate expectations of quality. The inequality in bargaining power between landlord and tenant has been well documented.[44] Tenants have very little leverage to enforce demands for better housing. Various impediments to competition in the rental housing market, such as racial and class discrimination[45] and standardized form leases, mean that landlords place tenants in a take it or leave it situation. The increasingly severe shortage[47] of adequate housing further increases the landlord's bargaining power and escalates the need for maintaining and improving the existing stock. Finally, the findings by various studies of the social impact of bad housing has led to the realization that poor housing is detrimental to the whole society, not merely to the unlucky ones who must suffer the daily indignity of living in a slum.[48]

Thus we are led by our inspection of the relevant legal principles and precedents to the conclusion that the old common rule imposing an obligation upon the lessee to repair during the lease term was really never intended to apply to residential urban leaseholds. Contract principles established in other areas of the law provide a more rational framework for the apportionment of landlord-tenant responsibilities; they strongly suggest that a warranty of habitability be implied into all contracts for urban dwellings.

We believe, in any event, that the District's housing code requires that a warranty of habitability be implied in the leases of all housing that it covers. The housing code — formally designated the Housing Regulations of the District of Columbia — was established and authorized by the Commissioners of the District of Columbia on August 11, 1955. Since that time, the code has been updated by numerous orders of the Commissioners. The 75 pages of the Regulations provide a comprehensive regulatory scheme setting forth in some detail: (a) the standards which housing in the District of Columbia must meet;

43. In Brown v. Southall Realty Co., 237 A.2d 834 (1968), the District of Columbia Court of Appeals held that unsafe and unsanitary conditions existing at the beginning of the tenancy and known to the landlord any lease of those premises illegal and void.

44. *See* Edwards v. Habib, 130 U.S. App. D.C. 126, 140, 397 F.2d 687, 701 (1968); 2 R. Powell [on Real Estate ¶ 221[1] (1991 & Supp.)], ¶ 221 [1] at 183; President's Committee on Urban Housing. A Decent Home 96 (1968).

45. President's Committee, *supra* Note 44, at 96: National Commission, *supra* Note 9, at 18-19; G. Sternlieb, The Tenement Landlord 71 (1966).

47. See generally President's Committee, *supra* Note 44.

48. A. Schorr, Slums and Insecurity (1963); J. Levi et al., *supra* Note 33, at 7-8.

(b) which party, the lessor or the lessee, must meet each standard; and (c) a system of inspections, notifications and criminal penalties. The Regulations themselves are silent on the question of private remedies.

Two previous decisions of this court, however, have held that the Housing Regulations create legal rights and duties enforceable in tort by private parties. [Discusses *Whetzel* and Brown v. Southall Realty.] . . . The duties imposed by the Housing Regulations may not be waived or shifted by agreement if the Regulations specifically place the duty upon the lessor.

We therefore hold that the Housing Regulations imply a warranty of habitability, measured by the standards which they set out, into leases of all housing that they cover.

In the present cases, the landlord sued for possession for nonpayment of rent. Under contract principles,[61] however, the tenant's obligation to pay rent is dependent upon the landlord's performance of his obligations, including his warranty to maintain the premises in habitable condition. In order to determine whether any rent is owed to the landlord, the tenants must be given an opportunity to prove the housing code violations alleged as breach of the landlord's warranty.[62]

At trial, the finder of fact must make two findings: (1) whether the alleged violations[63] existed during the period for which past due rent is claimed, and (2) what portion, if any or all, of the tenant's obligation to pay rent was suspended by the landlord's breach. If no part of the tenant's rental obligation is found to have been suspended, then a judgment for possession may issue forthwith. On the other hand, if the jury determines that the entire rental obligation has been extinguished by the landlord's total breach, then the action for possession on the ground of nonpayment must fail.[64]

The jury may find that part of the tenant's rental obligation has been suspended but that part of the unpaid back rent is indeed owed to the landlord. In these circumstances, no judgment for possession should issue if the tenant agrees to pay the partial rent found to be due. If the tenant refuses to pay the partial amount, a judgment for possession may then be entered.

The judgment of the District of Columbia Court of Appeals is reversed and the cases are remanded for further proceedings consistent with this opinion.[67]

So ordered.

61. In extending all contract remedies for breach to the parties to a lease, we include an action for specific performance of the landlord's implied warranty of habitability.

62. To be relevant, of course, the violations must affect the tenant's apartment or common areas which the tenant uses. Moreover, the contract principle that no one may benefit from his own wrong will allow the landlord to defend by proving the damage was caused by the tenant's wrongful action. However, violations resulting from inadequate repairs or materials which disintegrate under normal use would not be assignable to the tenant. Also we agree with the District of Columbia Court of Appeals that the tenant's private rights do not depend on official inspection or official finding of violation by the city government. Diamond Housing Corp. v. Robinson, 257 A.2d 492, 494 (1969).

63. The jury should be instructed that one or two minor violations standing alone which do not affect habitability are de minimis and would not entitle the tenant to a reduction in rent.

64. As soon as the landlord made the necessary repairs rent would again become due. Our holding, of course, affects only eviction for nonpayment of rent. The landlord is free to seek eviction at the termination of the lease or on any other legal ground.

67. Appellants in the present cases offered to pay rent into the registry of the court during the present action. We think this is an excellent protective procedure. If the tenant

NOTES AND QUESTIONS

1.   **Clifton Terrace.** Clifton Terrace came to the attention of the local legal services program, which defended the *Javins* suit, because it had its offices there. Some years later, after repeated efforts to get the landlord to make needed repairs, the U.S. Department of Housing and Urban Development (HUD) took over the complex on a mortgage default.

2.   **Landmark case.** This opinion is very consciously written as a landmark case that entails a sharp change in the existing law. The court itself notes that the common law allocating the duty to repair upon the tenant rather than the landlord was settled by 1485, 428 F.2d at 1077, n.30, and "many courts have been unwilling to imply warranties of quality, specifically a warranty of habitability, into leases of apartments." 428 F.2d at 1076. The court therefore spends a lot of time *giving reasons* for its decision. Other courts found its opinion so persuasive that they cited portions of it again and again. See, e.g., Green v. Superior Court of San Francisco, 517 P.2d 1168 (Cal. 1974); Spring v. Little, 280 N.E.2d 208 (Ill. 1972); Old Town Development Co. v. Langford, 349 N.E.2d 744 (Ind. Ct. App. 1976); Mease v. Fox, 200 N.W.2d 791 (Iowa 1972); Boston Housing Authority v. Hemingway, 293 N.E.2d 831 (Mass. 1973).

3.   **Cultural lag argument.** The court in its opinion develops a cultural lag argument that suggests that landlord and tenant law had passed down little changed from feudal times. By the eighteenth century, however, the lease-as-contract theory was well established, and for 200 years, courts have used the lease-as-conveyance and lease-as-contract theories interchangeably, depending on which theory helps them reach the conclusion they wanted. See Michael Weinberg, From Contract to Conveyance: The Law of Landlord and Tenant, 1800-1920 (Part I), 1980 S. Ill. L.J. 29. An important factor constraining nineteenth- and twentieth-century courts' adoption of the lease-as-contract theory was their desire to avoid applying implied warranties to landlord and tenant contracts. Ibid.

4.   **Court's use of contract language.** "[L]eases of urban dwelling units should be interpreted and construed like any other contract," *supra.* Does the court adopt the core contract idea that the courts' role is simply to enforce the parties' intent, thus to give effect to one of the "thousand deals"? Is the court enforcing the actual intent of both parties? Of one party? Consider the following footnote from *Javins*:

> As a general proposition, it is undoubtedly true that parties to a contract intend that applicable law will be complied with by both sides. We recognize, however, that reading statutory provisions into private contracts may have

---

defends against an action for possession on the basis of breach of the landlord's warranty of habitability, the trial court may require the tenant to make future rent payments into the registry of the court as they become due; such a procedure would be appropriate only while the tenant remains in possession. . . .

little factual support in the intentions of the particular parties now before us. But, for reasons of public policy, warranties are often implied into contracts by operation of law in order to meet generally prevailing standards of honesty and fair dealing. When the public policy has been enacted into law like the housing code, that policy will usually have deep roots in the expectations and intentions of most people. See Costigan, Implied-in-Fact Contracts and Mutual Assent, 33 Harv. L. Rev. 376, 383-385 (1920).

428 F.2d at 1081 n.56. How does this footnote attempt to diffuse the potential conflict between intent and implied warranties?

The central contract imagery of letting a thousand deals bloom, with courts only enforcing intent, dates from the nineteenth century, a translation into law of the economic liberalism. In the twentieth century, contract theory has moved away from merely enforcing the intent of the parties, towards an explicit appeal to normative values (most often referred to as the norms of "fair dealing"). See Grant Gilmore, The Death of Contract (1974). Gilmore documented this shift after he helped create it: he played a central role in drafting the Uniform Commercial Code, from which the *Javins* court drew the notion of an implied contractual warranty.

5. **Court's use of tort law.** Note that in overruling long-established property rules, the court turns not only to contract law but also to the law of torts. It relies heavily on the then-recent revolution in tort law, in which state courts eroded the doctrine of *caveat emptor* (buyer beware) and held manufacturers potentially liable for defects in consumer products. These tort decisions argued that manufacturers were better able than consumers to detect product defects. How does the *Javins* court use the tort decisions?

The tort decisions also argued that allocating the risk of accident to the manufacturer made sense from an economic standpoint, since that allocation would serve to spread the cost of the plaintiff's accident onto all of the product's buyers (as manufacturers raised prices to cover costs of paying out product liability judgments). Does *Javins* adopt this argument as well? Does the *Javins* court use any economic analysis to support its holding?

6. **Procrustes again: a warning.** *Javins*'s reliance on tort and contract law reminds us that the little packages in which topics come to you in first-year law school often meld together and overlap in practice. Do not, like Procrustes, insist on cutting off your client's head or feet to fit her problem into one box — say, the property box — when the tort, civil procedure, or contract boxes could provide useful resources. In practice, the sharp distinctions nineteenth-century lawyers saw between the common law subjects of tort, contract, and property law have blurred in significant ways. For famous studies, see Grant Gilmore, The Death of Contract 87 (1974) (convergence of contract and tort); Guido Calabresi and A. Douglas Melamed, Property Rules, Liability Rules, and Inalienability: One View of the Cathedral, 85 Harv. L. Rev. 1089 (1972) (discussing relationship of tort and property).

7.   **Community values and ethics.** "The continued vitality of the common law . . . depends upon its ability to reflect contemporary community values and ethics," *supra.* Compare Senator Crary's opinion in Dyett v. Pendleton. Is it appropriate for courts to change the law based on its sense of community values? Does your answer to this question depend on your vision of property? What visions of property does the *Javins* court mobilize in its opinion? Do you find the opinion persuasive?

8.   **Visions.** The high emotions surrounding the implied warranty of habitability suggest its importance. It taps into deep conflicts over what property ownership does and should mean in this society. The only other recent fight over property doctrine that has been as prolonged and bitter is the current fight over takings law, which we will examine in depth in Chapter 8. These two fights will be covered in some depth because they offer important insights into legal change and into the assumptions and patterns of argumentation in American property law. As you read through these materials, ask yourself why the implied warranty proved such an emotional issue. Did the fight over the implied warranty involve the clash between different visions of property rights?

9.   **Do judges make law? Should they?** Consider the following quotes. The first is in a letter from Felix Frankfurter to Hugo Black (two U.S. Supreme Court justices):

> Judges cannot escape the responsibility of filling in gaps which the finitude of even the most imaginative legislation renders inevitable. So the problem is not whether the judges makes the law, but when and how much. . . . I used to say to my students that legislatures made law wholesale, judges retail. In other words, they cannot decide things by invoking a new major premise out of whole cloth; they must make the law that they do make out of the existing materials with due deference to the presuppositions of the legal system of which they have been made a part. . . .

James Simon, Independent Journey: The Life of William O. Douglas 202 (1980). The second is from one of the most famous Supreme Court justices, Oliver Wendell Holmes, The Common Law 1 (1881):

> The life of the law has not been logic: it has been experience. The felt necessities of the time, the prevalent moral and political theories, intuitions of public policy, avowed or unconscious, even the prejudices which judges share with their fellow-men, have had a good deal more to do than the syllogism in determining the rules by which men should be governed.

10.   **Restatement of Property.** Proponents of the implied warranty generally won in the courts, but the doctrine's opponents were able to weaken the warranty when it came before the American Law Institute, the group of eminent lawyers that sponsors the Restatements of the Law. Restatement (Second) of Property, Landlord and Tenant, §5.5 (1977) reads:

(1) Except to the extent the parties to a lease validly agree otherwise, the
     landlord, under a lease of property for residential use, is obligated to the
     tenant to keep the leased property in a condition that meets the require-
     ments of governing health, safety, and housing codes, unless the failure
     to meet those requirements is the fault of the tenant or is the conse-
     quence of a sudden non-manmade force or the conduct of third parties.
(2) Except to the extent the parties to a lease validly agree otherwise, the
     landlord is obligated to the tenant to keep safe and in repair the areas
     remaining under his control that are maintained for the use and benefit
     of his tenants. . . .

Notice the qualifications:

a.   "except to the extent the parties to a lease validly agree
     otherwise"

The Restatement (Second) of Property §5.6 (1977) would allow the
parties to a lease to increase or decrease what would otherwise be the obligations of the landlord with respect to the condition of the leased property
[and similarly with respect to the tenant's remedies] unless the agreement
is "unconscionable or significantly against public policy." Many states which
have created a statutory warranty of habitability bar any contrary agreement, see, e.g., N.Y. Real Prop. L. §235-b (McKinney 1989); Ohio Rev. Code
Ann. §§5321.04, 5321.06 and 5321.07 (Baldwin 1995), or permit only limited change, see, e.g., Michigan Comp. Laws Ann. §554.139 (West 1988)
(contrary agreement allowed only for leases longer than one year); Virginia Code Ann. §§55-248.13 and 55-248.31 (Michie 1995) (contrary agreement allowed only when landlord's purpose is not to evade his primary
obligations).
     Under what circumstances might a residential tenant knowingly agree
to relinquish some of her rights to habitability?

b.   "a lease of property for residential use"

What are the arguments for and against extending the warranty of
habitability to nonresidential premises? See Note, Commercial Leases: Behind the *Green* Door, 12 Pacific L.J. 1067, 1091-1097 (1981); Restatement
(Second) of Property §5.1, Rep. Note 2 (1977) ("The present state of the
statutory development and judicial development does not warrant taking a
position one way or the other as to non-residential property . . . The Reporter is of the opinion that the rule of this section should be extended to
non-residential property. The small commercial tenant particularly needs
its protection.")
     If you believe that some, but not all, nonresidential tenants deserve
the protection of an implied warranty of habitability, how would you cast a
statute (or draft a common-law rule) that would separate the two classes?

To date, state courts have been reluctant to extend the implied warranty into the nonresidential area. Cf. Yuan Kane Ing v. Levy, 26 Ill. App. 3d 889, 892, 326 N.E.2d 51, 54 (1975); Van Ness Indus. v. Claremont Painting & Decorating Co., 129 N.J. Super. 507, 324 A.2d 102 (1974). But cf. Four Seas Investment Corp. v. International Hotel Tenant's Assn., 81 Cal. App. 3d 604, 613, 146 Cal. Rptr. 531, 535 (1978) (dicta).

    c.   "in a condition that meets the requirements of governing health, safety, and housing codes"

Some communities remain without housing codes, and many housing codes exempt one-family dwellings or owner-occupied two-family units. Does any justification exist for curtailing the warranty in such instances? Cf. Graham v. Wisenburn, 39 A.D.2d 334, 334 N.Y.S.2d 81 (1972) (pre-statutory decision: court refuses to extend implied warranty to tenant-occupied one-family house).

    d.   "unless the failure to meet those requirements . . . is the consequence of a sudden non-manmade force or the conduct of third parties"

The Restatement neither cites any supporting authority nor gives any explanation. Except with respect to matters of notice and reasonable opportunity to make the repairs, should the warranty of habitability be so qualified?

11. **Why do people continue to rent deteriorated housing?** Deteriorated housing is often the only option for people with low incomes. Only about one-sixth of the poor receive housing subsidies.[92] Without them, low-income households face a difficult trade-off. Either they can pay a high proportion of their income in rent (nearly 50 percent of low-income renters pay rents equal to *more than half* of their incomes), or they can rent very cheap — and probably deteriorated — housing.[93] In some housing markets, very low-income renters have to do both. One study found that 16 percent of very low-income tenants live in structurally inadequate housing, and roughly 12 percent of low-income tenants do.[94]

Javins was an early implied warranty opinion; we will now turn to one of the more recent. As you read *Hilder,* note how its focus differs from *Jav-*

---

92. Joint Center for Housing Studies of Harvard University, The State of the Nation's Housing (1994).

93. E. Jay Howenstine, The New Housing Shortage 16, in The New Housing Shortage: Housing Affordability in Europe and the USA (Graham Hallett ed., 1993).

94. Joint Center, *supra* note 92, at 31 (16 percent of households earning 25 to 50 percent of median income live in structurally inadequate housing; 11.8 percent of those earning 50 to 80 percent of median income do).

ins's. The *Javins* court spent most of the opinion explaining why it had adopted the then-novel theory. By the time *Hilder* was decided, that reasoning was well-entrenched in the law of many states. Consequently, *Hilder*'s focus extends beyond the court's rationale, as the court absorbs the mass of litigation and law review commentary on the implied warranty in the decade before. Note the court's focus on designing an implied warranty that would be most useful to tenants in litigation. The opinion is written by a long-term trial lawyer, who returned to the trial courts (as a federal district judge) after his tenure on the Vermont Supreme Court. Justice Billings clearly understands and relishes the trial process, and his opinion shows it. How does his opinion illustrate the persuasive skills of a good litigator? What role does his description of the condition of the premises play in communicating his vision of property? How does he use his knowledge of the economics and dynamics of litigation to design an implied warranty that is relatively cheap and easy to use? How does he use his knowledge of trial court judges to foreclose some rulings that would impose burdens on tenants? Last but not least, note the level of attention and detail he lavishes upon his discussion of remedies.

HILDER v. ST. PETER[95]

478 A.2d 202 (Vt. 1984)

BILLINGS, C.J. Defendants appeal from a judgment rendered by the Rutland Superior Court. The court ordered defendants to pay plaintiff damages in the amount of $4,945.00, which represented "reimbursement of all rent paid and additional compensatory damages" for the rental of a residential apartment over a fourteen month period in defendants' Rutland apartment building. Defendants filed a motion for reconsideration on the issue of the amount of damages awarded to the plaintiff, and plaintiff filed a cross-motion for reconsideration of the court's denial of an award of punitive damages. The court denied both motions. On appeal, defendants raise [two] issues for our consideration: first, whether the court correctly calculated the amount of damages awarded the plaintiff; secondly, whether the court's award to plaintiff of the entire amount of rent paid to defendants was proper since the plaintiff remained in possession of the apartment for the entire fourteen month period. . . .

The facts are uncontested. In October, 1974, plaintiff began occupying an apartment at defendants' 10-12 Church Street apartment building in Rutland with her three children and new-born grandson.[1] Plaintiff orally

---

95. Attorneys for the tenants were from Vermont Legal Aid, Inc. — EDS.

1. Between October, 1974, and December, 1976, plaintiff rented apartment number 1 for $140.00 monthly for 18 months, and apartment number 50 for $125.00 monthly for 7 months.

agreed to pay defendant Stuart S. Peter $140 a month and a damage deposit of $50; plaintiff paid defendant the first month's rent and the damage deposit prior to moving in. Plaintiff has paid all rent due under her tenancy. Because the previous tenants had left behind garbage and items of personal belongings, defendant offered to refund plaintiff's damage deposit if she would clean the apartment herself prior to taking possession. Plaintiff did clean the apartment, but never received her deposit back because the defendant denied ever receiving it. Upon moving into the apartment, plaintiff discovered a broken kitchen window. Defendant promised to repair it, but after waiting a week and fearing that her two year old child might cut herself on the shards of glass, plaintiff repaired the window at her own expense. Although defendant promised to provide a front door key, he never did. For a period of time, whenever plaintiff left the apartment, a member of her family would remain behind for security reasons. Eventually, plaintiff purchased and installed a padlock, again at her own expense. After moving in, plaintiff discovered that the bathroom toilet was clogged with paper and feces and would flush only by dumping pails of water into it. Although plaintiff repeatedly complained about the toilet, and defendant promised to have it repaired, the toilet remained clogged and mechanically inoperable throughout the period of plaintiff's tenancy. In addition, the bathroom light and wall outlet were inoperable. Again, the defendant agreed to repair the fixtures, but never did. In order to have light in the bathroom, plaintiff attached a fixture to the wall and connected it to an extension cord that was plugged into an adjoining room. Plaintiff also discovered that water leaked from the water pipes of the upstairs apartment down the ceilings and walls of both her kitchen and back bedroom. Again, defendant promised to fix the leakage, but never did. As a result of this leakage, a large section of plaster fell from the back bedroom ceiling onto her bed and her grandson's crib. Other sections of plaster remained dangling from the ceiling. This condition was brought to the attention of the defendant, but he never corrected it. Fearing that the remaining plaster might fall when the room was occupied, plaintiff moved her and her grandson's bedroom furniture into the living room and ceased using the back bedroom. During the summer months an odor of raw sewage permeated plaintiff's apartment. The odor was so strong that the plaintiff was ashamed to have company in her apartment. Responding to plaintiff's complaints, Rutland City workers unearthed a broken sewage pipe in the basement of defendants' building. Raw sewage littered the floor of the basement, but defendant failed to clean it up. Plaintiff also discovered that the electric service for her furnace was attached to her breaker box, although defendant had agreed, at the commencement of the plaintiff's tenancy, to furnish heat.

In its conclusions of law, the court held that the state of disrepair of plaintiff's apartment, which was known to the defendants, substantially reduced the value of the leasehold from the agreed rental value, thus constituting a breach of the implied warranty of habitability. The court based its award of damages on the breach of this warranty and on breach of an express contract. Defendant argues that the court misapplied the law of Vermont relating to habitability because the plaintiff never abandoned the demised premises and, therefore, it was error to award her the full amount of rent paid. Plaintiff counters that, while never expressly recognized by this Court, the trial court was correct in applying an implied warranty of habitability and that under this warranty, abandonment of the premises is not required. Plaintiff urges this Court to affirmatively adopt the implied warranty of habitability.

Historically, relations between landlords and tenants have been defined by the law of property. Under these traditional common law property concepts, a lease was viewed as a conveyance of real property. See Note, Judicial Expansion of Tenants' Private Law Rights: Implied Warranties of Habitability and Safety in Residential Urban Leases, 56 Cornell L.Q. 489, 489-90 (1971) (hereinafter cited as Expansion of Tenants' Rights). The relationship between landlord and tenant was controlled by the doctrine of caveat lessee; that is, the tenant took possession of the demised premises irrespective of their state of disrepair. Love, Landlord's Liability for Defective Premises: Caveat Lessee, Negligence, or Strict Liability?, 1975 Wis. L. Rev. 19, 27-28. The landlord's only covenant was to deliver possession to the tenant. The tenant's obligation to pay rent existed independently of the landlord's duty to deliver possession, so that as long as possession remained in the tenant, the tenant remained liable for payment of rent. The landlord was under no duty to render the premises habitable unless there was an express covenant to repair in the written lease. Expansion of Tenants' Rights, supra, at 490. The land, not the dwelling, was regarded as the essence of the conveyance.

An exception to the rule of caveat lessee was the doctrine of constructive eviction. Lemle v. Breeden, 51 Haw. 426, 430, 462 P.2d 470, 473 (1969). Here, if the landlord wrongfully interfered with the tenant's enjoyment of the demised premises, or failed to render a duty to the tenant as expressly required under the terms of the lease, the tenant could abandon the premises and cease paying rent. Legier v. Deveneau, 98 Vt. 188, 190, 126 A. 392, 393 (1924).

Beginning in the 1960's, American courts began recognizing that this approach to landlord tenant relations, which had originated during the Middle Ages, had become an anachronism in twentieth century, urban society. Today's tenant enters into lease agreements, not to obtain arable land, but to obtain safe, sanitary and comfortable housing.

> [T]hey seek a well known package of goods and services — a package which includes not merely walls and ceilings, but also adequate heat, light and ventilation, serviceable plumbing facilities, secure windows and doors, proper sanitation, and proper maintenance.

Javins v. First National Realty Corp., 428 F.2d 1071, 1074 (D.C.Cir.), *cert. denied*, 400 U.S. 925 (1970).

Not only has the subject matter of today's lease changed, but the characteristics of today's tenant have similarly evolved. The tenant of the Middle Ages was a farmer, capable of making whatever repairs were necessary to his primitive dwelling. Green v. Superior Court, 10 Cal. 3d 616, 622, 517 P.2d 1168, 1172, 111 Cal. Rptr. 704, 708 (1974). Additionally, "the common law courts assumed that an equal bargaining position existed between landlord and tenant. . . ." Note, The Implied Warranty of Habitability: A Dream Deferred, 48 UMKC L. Rev. 237, 238 (1980) (hereinafter cited as *A Dream Deferred*).

In sharp contrast, today's residential tenant, most commonly a city dweller, is not experienced in performing maintenance work on urban, complex living units. Green v. Superior Court, supra, 10 Cal. 3d at 624, 517 P.2d at 1173, 111 Cal. Rptr. at 707-08. The landlord is more familiar with the dwelling unit and mechanical equipment attached to that unit, and is more financially able to "discover and cure" any faults and breakdowns. Id. at 624, 517 P.2d at 1173, 111 Cal. Rptr. at 708. Confronted with a recognized shortage of safe, decent housing, see 24 V.S.A. §4001(1), today's tenant is in an inferior bargaining position compared to that of the landlord. Park West Management Corp. v. Mitchell, 47 N.Y.2d 316, 324-25, 391 N.E.2d 1288, 1292, 418 N.Y.S.2d 310, 314, *cert. denied*, 444 U.S. 992 (1979). Tenants vying for this limited housing are "virtually powerless to compel the performance of essential services." Id. at 325, 391 N.E.2d at 1292, 418 N.Y.S.2d at 314.

In light of these changes in the relationship between tenants and landlords, it would be wrong for the law to continue to impose the doctrine of caveat lessee on residential leases.

> The modern view favors a new approach which recognizes that a lease is essentially a contract between the landlord and the tenant wherein the landlord promises to deliver and maintain the demised premises in habitable condition and the tenant promises to pay rent for such habitable premises. These promises constitute interdependent and mutual considerations. Thus, the tenant's obligation to pay rent is predicated on the landlord's obligation to deliver and maintain the premises in habitable condition.

Boston Housing Authority v. Hemingway, 363 Mass., 184, 198, 293 N.E.2d 831, 842 (1973). . . .

Therefore, we now hold expressly that in the rental of any residential dwelling unit an implied warranty exists in the lease, whether oral or written, that the landlord will deliver over and maintain, throughout the period of the tenancy, premises that are safe, clean and fit for human habitation. This warranty of habitability is implied in tenancies for a specific period or at will. Boston Housing Authority v. Hemingway, *supra*, 363 Mass. at 199, 293 N.E.2d at 843. Additionally, the implied warranty of habitability covers all latent and patent defects in the essential facilities of the residential unit.[2] Id. Essential facilities are "facilities vital to the use of the premises for residential purposes. . . ." Kline v. Burns, 111 N.H. 87, 92, 276 A.2d 248, 252 (1971). This means that a tenant who enters into a lease agreement with knowledge of any defect in the essential facilities cannot be said to have assumed the risk, thereby losing the protection of the warranty. Nor can this implied warranty of habitability be waived by any written provision in the lease or by oral agreement.

In determining whether there has been a breach of the implied warranty of habitability, the courts may first look to any relevant local or municipal housing code; they may also make reference to the minimum housing code standards enunciated in 24 V.S.A. §5003(c) (1)-5003(c)(5). A substantial violation of an applicable housing code shall constitute prima facie evidence that there has been a breach of the warranty of habitability. "[O]ne or two minor violations standing alone which do not affect" the health or safety of the tenant, shall be considered de minimus and not a breach of the warranty. Javins v. First National Realty Corp., *supra*, 428 F.2d at 1082, n.63; Mease v. Fox, 200 N.W.2d 791, 796 (Iowa 1972); King v. Moorehead, *supra*, 495 S.W.2d at 76. In addition, the landlord will not be liable for defects caused by the tenant. Javins v. First National Realty Corp., *supra*, 428 F.2d at 1082, n.62.

However, these codes and standards merely provide a starting point in determining whether there has been a breach. Not all towns and municipalities have housing codes; where there are codes, the particular problem complained of may not be addressed. Park West Management Corp. v. Mitchell, *supra*, 47 N.Y.2d at 328, 391 N.E.2d at 1294, 418 N.Y.S.2d at 316. In determining whether there has been a breach of the implied warranty of habitability, courts should inquire whether the claimed defect has an impact on the safety or health of the tenant. Id.

In order to bring a cause of action for breach of the implied warranty of habitability, the tenant must first show that he or she notified the landlord "of the deficiency or defect not known to the landlord and [allowed] a reasonable time for its correction." King v. Moorehead, *supra*, 495 S.W.2d at 76.

Because we hold that the lease of a residential dwelling creates a contractual relationship between the landlord and tenant, the standard contract remedies of rescission, reformation and damages are available to the tenant when suing for breach of the implied warranty of habitability. Lemle v. Breeden, *supra*, 51 Haw. at 436, 462 P.2d at 475. The measure of damages

---

2. The warranty also covers those facilities located in the common areas of an apartment building or duplex that may affect the health or safety of a tenant, such as common stairways, or porches. Javins v. First National Realty Corp., *supra* 428 F.2d at 1082, n.62; King v. Moorehead, 495 S.W.2d 65, 76 (Mo. Ct. App. 1973).

shall be the difference between the value of the dwelling as warranted and the value of the dwelling as it exists in its defective condition. Birkenhead v. Coombs, *supra,* 143 Vt. at 172, 465 A.2d at 246. In determining the fair rental value of the dwelling as warranted, the court may look to the agreed upon rent as evidence on this issue. *Id.* "[I]n residential lease disputes involving a breach of the implied warranty of habitability, public policy militates against requiring expert testimony" concerning the value of the defect. Id. at 173, 465 A.2d at 247. The tenant will be liable only for "the reasonable rental value [if any] of the property in its imperfect condition during his period of occupancy." Berzito v. Gambino, 63 N.J. 460, 469, 308 A.2d 17, 22 (1973).

We also find persuasive the reasoning of some commentators that damages should be allowed for a tenant's discomfort and annoyance arising from the landlord's breach of the implied warranty of habitability. See Moskovitz, The Implied Warranty of Habitability: A New Doctrine Raising New Issues, 62 Calif. L. Rev. 1444, 1470-73 (1974) (hereinafter cited as *A New Doctrine; A Dream Deferred, supra,* at 250-51. Damages for annoyance and discomfort are reasonable in light of the fact that

> the residential tenant who has suffered a breach of the warranty . . . cannot bathe as frequently as he would like or at all if there is inadequate hot water; he must worry about rodents harassing his children or spreading disease if the premises are infested; or he must avoid certain rooms or worry about catching a cold if there is inadequate weather protection or heat. Thus, discomfort and annoyance are the common injuries caused by each breach and hence the true nature of the general damages the tenant is claiming.

Moskovitz, *A New Doctrine, supra,* at 1470-71. Damages for discomfort and annoyance may be difficult to compute; however, "[t]he trier [of fact] is not to be deterred from this duty by the fact that the damages are not susceptible of reduction to an exact money standard." Vermont Electric Supply Co. v. Andrus, 132 Vt. 195, 200, 315 A.2d 456, 459 (1974).

Another remedy available to the tenant when there has been a breach of the implied warranty of habitability is to withhold the payment of future rent. King v. Moorehead, *supra,* 495 S.W.2d at 77. The burden and expense of bringing suit will then be on the landlord who can better afford to bring the action. In an action for ejectment for nonpayment of rent, 12 V.S.A. §4773, "[t]he trier of fact, upon evaluating the seriousness of the breach and the ramification of the defect upon the health and safety of the tenant, will abate the rent at the landlord's expense in accordance with its findings." *A Dream Deferred, supra,* at 248. The tenant must show that: (1) the landlord had notice of the previously unknown defect and failed, within a reasonable time, to repair it; and (2) the defect, affecting habitability, existed during the time for which rent was withheld. See *A Dream Deferred, supra,* at 248-50. Whether a portion, all or none of the rent will be awarded

to the landlord will depend on the findings relative to the extent and duration of the breach.[4] Javins v. First National Realty Corp., supra, 428 F.2d
at 1082-83. Of course, once the landlord corrects the defect, the tenant's
obligation to pay rent becomes due again. Id. at 1083 n.64.

Additionally, we hold that when the landlord is notified of the defect
but fails to repair it within a reasonable amount of time, and the tenant
subsequently repairs the defect, the tenant may deduct the expense of the
repair from future rent. 11 Williston on Contracts §1404 (3d ed. W. Jaeger
1968); Marini v. Ireland, 56 N.J. 130, 146, 265 A.2d 526, 535 (1970).

In addition to general damages, we hold that punitive damages may
be available to a tenant in the appropriate case. Although punitive damages
are generally not recoverable in actions for breach of contract, there are
cases in which the breach is of such a willful and wanton or fraudulent nature as to make appropriate award of exemplary damages. Clarendon Mobile Home Sales, Inc. v. Fitzgerald, *supra*, 135 Vt. at 596, 381 A.2d at 1065.
A willful and wanton or fraudulent breach may be shown "by conduct manifesting personal ill will, or carried out under circumstances of insult or oppression, or even by conduct manifesting . . . a reckless or wanton disregard
of [one's] rights. . . ." Sparrow v. Vermont Savings Bank, 95 Vt. 29, 33, 112
A. 205, 207 (1921). When a landlord, after receiving notice of a defect, fails
to repair the facility that is essential to the health and safety of his or her
tenant, an award of punitive damages is proper. 111 East 88th Partners v.
Simon, 106 Misc. 2d 693, 434 N.Y.S.2d 886, 889 (N.Y. Civ. Ct. 1980).

> The purpose of punitive damages . . . is to punish conduct which is
> morally culpable. . . . Such an award serves to deter a wrongdoer . . . from
> repetitions of the same or similar actions. And it tends to encourage prosecu-
> tion of a claim by a victim who might not otherwise incur the expense or in-
> convenience of a private action. . . . The public benefit and a display of ethical
> indignation are among the ends of the policy to grant punitive damages.

Davis v. Williams, 92 Misc. 2d 1051, 402 N.Y.S.2d 92, 94 (N.Y. Civ. Ct.
1977). . . .

In its conclusions of law the trial court stated that the defendants'
failure to make repairs was compensable by damages to the extent of reimbursement of all rent paid and additional compensatory damages. The
court awarded plaintiff a total of $4,945.00; $3,445.00 represents the entire
amount of rent plaintiff paid, plus the $50.00 deposit. This appears to leave
$1,500.00 as the "additional compensatory damages." However, although

---

4. Some courts suggest that, during the period rent is withheld, the tenant should pay
the rent, as it becomes due, into legal custody. See, e.g., Javins v. First National Realty Corp.,
supra, 428 F.2d at 1083 n.67, see also King v. Moorehead, *supra*, 495 S.W.2d at 77 (*King* requires
the deposit of the rent into legal custody pending the litigation). Such a procedure assures the
availability of that portion, if any, of the rent which the court determines is due to the landlord.
King v. Moorehead, *supra*, 495 S.W.2d at 77; see *A Dream Deferred, supra*, at 248-50.

the court made findings which clearly demonstrate the appropriateness of an award of compensatory damages, there is no indication as to how the court reached a figure of $1500.00. It is "crucial that this Court and the parties be able to determine what was decided and how the decision was reached." Fox v. McLain, 142 Vt. 11, 16, 451 A.2d 1122, 1124 (1982).

Additionally, the court denied an award to plaintiff of punitive damages on the ground that the evidence failed to support a finding of willful and wanton or fraudulent conduct. See Clarendon Mobile Home Sales, Inc. v. Fitzgerald, supra, 135 Vt. at 596, 381 A.2d at 1065. The facts in this case, which defendants do not context, evince a pattern of intentional conduct on the part of defendants for which the term "slumlord" surely was coined. Defendants' conduct was culpable and demeaning to plaintiff and clearly expressive of wanton disregard of plaintiff's rights. The trial court found that defendants were aware of defects in the essential facilities of plaintiff's apartment, promised plaintiff that repairs would be made, but never fulfilled those promises. The court also found that plaintiff continued, throughout her tenancy, to pay her rent, often in the face of verbal threats made by defendant Stuart St. Peter. These findings point to the "bad spirit and wrong intention" of the defendants, Glidden v. Skinner, 142 Vt. 644, 648; 458 A.2d 1142, 1144 (1983), and would support a finding of willful and wanton or fraudulent conduct, contrary to the conclusions of law and judgment of the trial judge. However, the plaintiff did not appeal the court's denial of punitive damages, and issues not appealed and briefed are waived. R. Brown & Sons, Inc. v. International Harvester Corp., 142 Vt. 140, 142, 453 A.2d 83, 84 (1982).

Affirmed in part; reversed in part and remanded for hearing on additional compensable damages, consistent with the views herein.

NOTES AND QUESTIONS

1.   **Persuasive strategies.** The persuasive strategy of *Hilder* is very different from that in *Javins.*

(a) How would you describe the differences? Which approach do you find more convincing? Why does the opinion describe the conditions in the apartment in such loving detail? (Why does the *Javins* court provide almost no information on the housing code violations at issue?) What does the *Hilder* court try to convince us is at stake?

(b) What picture does the *Hilder* court supply of the landlord of the premises at issue? Of landlords in general? Compare the *Javins* decision: What pictures, if any, does it project of the Clifton Terrace landlord or of landlords in general? What role does the picture of landlords (or the specific landlord) play in each decision?

(c) What picture (if any) does the *Hilder* court project of Mrs. Hilder? Of tenants in general? What picture does *Javins* project of the tenants of

Clifton Terrace, or of tenants in general? Is the key issue one of individual bad actors, or of societal systems, according to *Javins? Hilder?* A substantial literature exists showing that, in many local housing markets, tenants' incomes are simply too low, and landlords' expenses are simply too high, for low-income housing to be economically viable. Do *Javins* and *Hilder* present the problems of low-income tenants as resulting from a *structural* problem (that our economy cannot provide enough low-income housing without outside subsidies), or a *personal* problem (involving character defects of individual landlords and tenants)? Why?

(d) Let us return to the question of whether *Javins* and *Hilder* are really turning to contract law. Consider the following excerpt, from Samuel Bassett Abbott, Housing Policy, Housing Codes and Tenant Remedies: An Integration, 56 B.U. L. Rev. 1, 12-14, 40 (1976):

> The warranty of habitability is an implied promise by the landlord that the demised premises are fit for human occupation at the inception of the tenancy and that they will remain so throughout the lease term. Much has been written about the warranty since its adoption began. However, little attention has been paid to several curious features whose collective impact upon the rationale of the warranty has not been sufficiently explored. Its name suggests that the warranty of habitability is a special application of the general warranty of merchantability implied for the sale of goods. If that were correct, several conclusions should follow. The warranty of habitability would apply to any premises used or occupied by human beings, whether for residential, commercial, or charitable purposes. In addition, acceptance of premises clearly uninhabitable or assent by the tenant to a lease provision describing the premises as conveyed "as is" would usually constitute a waiver of the warranty. The landlord's duty under the warranty would be discharged by delivering and maintaining rental premises of "fair average quality" fit for the ordinary purposes for which such premises are used. Ascertainment of damages for beach would be designed to compensate for and generally would approximate the loss to the tenant of his bargain. Yet, a study of the implied warranty cases and statutes suggests that none of these conclusions is substantially correct. . . .
>
> The warranty's limitation to residential premises, its mandatory nature, the measurement of the landlord's duty by code compliance and the civil fine aspect of damage ascertainment, all confirm that more effective housing code enforcement was the real justification and purpose underlying its adoption.

Does the *Hilder* court's willingness to award punitive damages fit with the "shifting to contract law" rationale for the implied warranty?

2. **Standard for breach.** The standard for breach differs from state to state. Abbott divides states in four groups, in ascending order to strictness:

(a) States where the implied warranty requires only substantial compliance with the housing code. In these states, only a substantial breach of the housing code constitutes breach of the implied warranty.

(b) States where any breach of the housing code is a breach of the implied warranty.

    (c)   States where compliance with the housing code is compelling but not conclusive evidence of compliance with the implied warranty. Courts adopting this test could require less than substantial code compliance, but, in practice, the test is most often used to require higher standards of fitness than those mandated under the housing code. New Jersey courts, for example, require an "adequate standard of habitability"; a breach occurs whenever the premises are "uninhabitable in the eyes of a reasonable person," although violation of a code provision is a "relevant factor." Berzito v. Gambino, 63 N.J. 460, 469-70, 308 A.2d 17, 21-22 (1973). In Massachusetts, the standard is fitness for human habitation; proof of a violation of the housing code usually would constitute proof of uninhabitability. Boston Housing Authority v. Hemingway, 363 Mass. 184, 201, 293 N.E.2d 831, 844 (1973).

    (d)   States where the standard for breach of the implied warranty is independent of the housing code, e.g., where premises must be "fit for human habitation" in order to comply with the implied warranty.

Id. at 17-20. Which of these four types of implied warranties is articulated in *Javins*? *Hilder*?

    3. **Prior notice to the landlord.** Note that the *Hilder* court requires the tenant to notify the landlord before claiming the implied warranty, as does the Restatement of Property (Second), Landlord and Tenant, §10.1, (1977). Does *Javins*? If you were a judge, would you impose this requirement?

    4. **Use of expert testimony.** In what ways is the *Hilder* opinion expressly designed to make the implied warranty easy and relatively cheap for tenants to use? Think back to Nancy Oliver Lesourd's experience (§3.4 *supra*). How did she go about proving a breach of the implied warranty? Would her job be easier in Vermont?

    5. **Remedies for breach of the implied warranty.** *Hilder* goes about as far as any implied warranty opinion in providing a wide range of remedies to tenants. How do *Hilder* and *Javins* differ with respect to remedies available to the tenant? List all the remedies available under each decision, and describe the situation(s) in which each would be useful to tenant-clients.

    a. *Total breach. Javins* and *Hilder* both state that under some conditions (total breach), tenants may remain in possession rent-free. Doesn't every apartment have some rental value? Suppose that someone buys a new automobile that has a top speed of only 17 miles an hour. Can he keep the automobile, use it as best he can, and refuse all payment? Cf. U.C.C. §2-602(2)(a)(1994). Is the analogy persuasive?

    b. *Damages for discomfort and annoyance.* Note that the court cited the remedy for discomfort and annoyance to a law review article, not to prior cases.

    c. *Punitive damages.* The punitive damage remedy also is unusual in the implied warranty context. Is the test for punitive damages that the court sets up identical to the traditional punitive damages test? Is the test harder or easier for tenants to meet?

6.   **Remedies problems.** The following problems will help you think through the remedies issues.

(a) Think back to Ms. Johnson (§3.4 *supra*). Explain the remedies the implied warranty offered her. Did *Javins* give her attorneys what they needed to achieve her goals? (Limit your answer to the four corners of the *Javins* decision; ignore the rest of the D.C. law as reflected in the Lesourd excerpt.) How, if at all, would the *Hilder* implied warranty have changed the options available to Ms. Johnson?

(b) Your client comes to you because her apartment has no heat; she has been using her gas stove to heat the apartment, but fears for the safety of her baby, who has just learned to crawl. She does not want to move out of the apartment; she just wants the heat fixed. What options are available under a constructive eviction theory?

7.   **Impact of the implied warranty on the defense of constructive eviction.** The *Hilder* case states that its implied warranty of habitability holding makes constructive eviction obsolete in Vermont. In fact, in most states, constructive eviction now coexists with the implied warranty, and, where it fits the tenant's needs, may at times be the wiser defense for a tenant to use. When may this be?

8.   **Why don't they just move?** Why don't tenants just move out of deteriorated housing? Consider the story of Bridge Ward, a 32-year-old black mother of two who moved from the mostly black and Hispanic section of North Philadelphia into a rented house in the white working-class neighborhood of Bridensburg. As she moved in, her next-door neighbor told her she did not belong in the neighborhood because of her race; later that evening she heard racist chants outside her window; the following morning, she found racial epithets on her windows, doors, and front porch; ketchup, looking like blood, was splattered on both front and back porches; a neighbor flew a Confederate flag. City officials stationed a police guard outside her house and began driving her children to school, after which things improved. But then she received a letter, which officials took seriously, threatening the safety of her family and referring to an unsolved hate crime. She moved out. See Michael A. Fletcher, A Neighborhood Slams the Door: Racist Acts Drive Philadelphia Family Out of White Area, Wash. Post, May 18, 1996, at A1. A study by the Urban Institute showed that 53 percent of black renters and 46 percent of Hispanic renters encounter at least one incident of racial discrimination during a housing search. Michael H. Schill and Susan M. Wachter, Housing Market Constraints and Spacial Stratification by Income and Race, 6 Housing Pol. Debate 141, 153 (1995). For an insightful study of the motivations that fuel this common dynamic, see Jonathan Ridder, Canarsie: The Jews and Italians of Brooklyn against Liberalism (1985).

9.   **Different strokes for different folks?** Consider two tenants: the first occupies a squalid one-bedroom apartment in a poor neighborhood; her monthly rent is $400; the second lives in a fashionable neighborhood and spends $3,000 monthly for a two-bedroom unit in a modern building.

Does "habitability" require a heightened warranty standard for the more expensive apartment?

Solow v. Wellner, 86 N.Y.2d 582, 658 N.E.2d 1005 (1995) involved a rent strike by 65 present and former tenants of a luxury building. Their complaints included "worn" hallway carpets, the occasional presence of roaches, inefficient "package room" service, and missing bathroom soap trays and interior doorknobs. After a 15-week hearing, the trial judge awarded tenants a rental offset for the landlord's breach of the statutory implied warranty of habitability, adopting the tenants' theory that higher rents justified increased expectations of a "well-run impeccably clean building of consistent and reliable services."

The Court of Appeals saw it differently and, except for elevator service problems, refused to extend the warranty to the landlord's other failures. In the court's words: "[T]he implied warranty protects only against conditions that materially affect the health and safety of tenants or deficiencies that in the eyes of a reasonable person deprive the tenant of those essential functions which a residence is expected to provide." 86 N.Y.2d at 588.

What lesson should a tenant's lawyer draw from this decision?

10.   **Law review literature.** The implied warranty spawned a huge law review literature between 1970 and the early 1980s; since then, relatively little has been written on the subject. Some especially useful articles are Samuel Bassett Abbott, Housing Policy, Housing Codes and Tenant Remedies: An Integration, 56 B.U. L. Rev. 1 (1976); Roger A. Cunningham, The New Implied and Statutory Warranties of Habitability in Residential Leases: From Contract to Status, 16 Urb. L. Ann. 3 (1979); Edward H. Rabin, Symposium: The Revolution in Landlord-Tenant Law: Causes and Consequences, 69 Cornell L. Rev. 517 (1984); Charles J. Meyers, The Covenant of Habitability and the American Law Institute, 27 Stan. L. Rev. 879 (1975) (criticism of implied warranty).

4.   Statutes

Implied habitability statutes are often long and complex. Typically they cut back on the landlord's duties, by limiting the types of conditions that breach the implied warranty, by imposing pre-conditions upon tenants (such as that they must not have defaulted on their rent more than a given number of times within the past year), and, most important, by stating that a tenant cannot withhold rent without first setting up an escrow account with the local court and paying the full rent due, on time, into that account. This last requirement finally allows you to fully understand the "protective orders" discussed in the Lesourd piece. Those orders are in effect judicially imposed escrow requirements. In Bell v. Tsintolas, 430 F.2d 474 (D.C. Cir. 1970), the D.C. Court of Appeals held that a tenant faced with a landlord's suit for possession who uses the implied warranty defense is required to deposit into the escrow the full amount of the contract rent (absent a "very

strong showing" that the premises violates the housing code). This requirement means that a tenant who does not pay her protective order (or statutorily mandated escrow account) will lose, even if a court would have held
on the merits that she did not own the full amount of her contract rent.
The escrow requirement protects landlords from tenants who might claim
the implied warranty because they have no money to pay their rent; it also
eliminates the usefulness of the implied warranty in the very typical situation where an attorney first learns of housing code violations when a tenant arrives in his law office with a notice to quit due to nonpayment of rent.
The following excerpts are from the Virginia statute. Describe ways in which
the implied warranty of habitability they set up is narrower than that established by *Hilder.*

Va. Code Ann. §55-248.27 (Michie 1994)

Rent escrow

The tenant may assert that there exists upon the leased premises, a condition or conditions which constitute a material noncompliance by the landlord with the rental agreement or with provisions of law, or which if not
promptly corrected, will constitute a fire hazard or serious threat to the life,
health or safety of occupants thereof, including but not limited to, a lack of
heat or hot or cold running water is the direct result of the tenant's failure to
pay the utility charge; or of light, electricity or adequate sewage disposal facilities; or an infestation of rodents, except if the property is a one-family dwelling; or of the existence of paint containing lead pigment on surfaces within
the dwelling, provided that the landlord has notice of such paint. The tenant
may file such an assertion in a general district court wherein the premises are
located by a declaration setting forth such assertion and asking for one or
more forms of relief as provided for in [the Virginia implied warranty of habitability statute].

5.   Leases

Compare the following lease provisions in Figures 3-11 and 3-12. Are
any of the provisions in violation of the law? In this context, consider the
following New York case. (Recall that these are New York leases.) In Park
West Management Corp. v. Mitchell, 47 N.Y.2d 316, 391 N.E. 2d 1288, 418
N.Y.S. 2d 310, cert. denied, 444 U.S. 992 (1979), the landlord owned an
apartment building in New York City. Each tenant had signed landlord's
form lease, in which landlord promised to keep the building in good repair
and to provide elevator, garbage collection, and other services, but in which
landlord was excused from rendering services for reasons beyond its control due to acts of God, strikes, etc. Then the landlord's maintenance and
janitorial staff went on strike for 17 days. Incinerators were wired shut; tenants had to take their garbage out to the sidewalk in paper bags provided
by the landlord. Eventually, the garbage piled up as high as the first-story

The parties further agree as follows:

Payment of Rent

1. The Tenant (a) will pay the rent to the Landlord, without deduction, at the Landlord's address set forth above or at such other address as the Landlord may designate by notice given to the Tenant, and (b) will not withhold rent for any reason.

Services by Landlord

(Unless this is a sublease, the Landlord shall provide: elevator service if applicable, reasonable quantities of hot and cold water, heat, air conditioning in the summer without the responsibility of cleaning or replacing air filters, and electricity for lights, small appliances and air-conditioning equipment or units in the apartment which are owned by the landlord.)

Landlord Not Liable for Interruption or Curtailment of Service

Interruption or curtailment of any or all such services, if caused by strikes, mechanical difficulties or any other cause reasonably beyond the Landlord's control, shall not entitle the Tenant to make any claim against the Landlord or to withhold or reduce any installment of rent;

No Representations or Agreements by Landlord

16. The tenant has inspected the Building and the Apartment and is thoroughly acquainted with their condition, and agrees to accept them "as is" except that, on or about the date on which the term of this lease commences, the Landlord agrees to do the following work:

The Tenant acknowledges that the taking of possession of the Apartment by the Tenant shall be conclusive evidence that the Apartment and the Building were in good and satisfactory condition at the time such possession was so taken, except as to latent defects. The Landlord agrees that the Apartment and all areas used in conjunction therewith in common with other tenants will be fit for human habitation and for the uses set forth in this lease and that, except to the extent such condition has been caused by the Tenant or any occupant of, or person permitted by the Tenant to use, the Apartment, the Tenant shall not be subjected to any conditions which would be dangerous, hazardous or detrimental to the Tenant's life, health or safety. The Landlord has not made any other representations or agreements except as contained in this lease.

FIGURE 3-11
Lease No. 1

Services By Landlord	(The landlord shall provide: elevator service if applicable, reasonable quantities of hot and cold water, heat, air conditioning in the summer without the responsibility of cleaning and replacing filters, and electricity for lights, small appliances and air-conditioning equipment or units in the Apartment which are owned by the Landlord.)
	If any services are reduced or discontinued because of matters beyond the control of Landlord, Tenant may not withhold or reduce rent unless permitted by law.
	2. Tenant agrees that:
	a. Tenant will pay the rent without any deductions, unless permitted by law.

FIGURE 3-12
Lease No. 2

windows, "causing it to fester and exude noxious odors." Vermin, roaches, and rodents flourished; the health department called a health emergency. Held: Tenants entitled to a 10% reduction in rent owed due to a breach of the implied warranty, notwithstanding the lease clause excusing the landlord from rendering services for reasons beyond his control.

d.   Retaliatory Eviction

Ordinarily, a landlord can terminate a periodic tenancy or refuse to renew a term of years tenancy for any reason or no reason, except where the tenancy is protected under either antidiscrimination or "secure tenancy" laws. Yet what if a landlord refuses to renew the lease of a tenant in retaliation for reporting housing code violations or claiming a breach of the implied warranty of habitability. Once courts began to adopt the implied warranty, it rapidly became apparent that the doctrine would be a dead letter if a landlord could simply terminate the tenancy of a tenant complaining about deteriorated conditions. An early, influential case was Edwards v. Habib, 397 F.2d 687 (D.C. Cir. 1968), decided by the District of Columbia Circuit two years before *Javins*. In *Habib*, a landlord terminated the tenancy of a month-to-month tenant after her complaints led to a housing inspection in which more than 40 violations were discovered.

> In reaching its decision [for the landlord, the court below] . . . relied on a series of its earlier decisions holding that a private landlord was not required . . . to give a reason for evicting a month-to-month tenant and was free to do so for any reason or no reason at all. . . . We hold that the promulgation of the

housing code by the District of Columbia Commissioners at the direction of Congress impliedly effected just such a change in the relative rights of landlords and tenants and that proof of a retaliatory motive does constitute a defense to an action of eviction. . . . [W]hile the landlord may evict for any legal reason or for no reason at all, he is not, we hold, free to evict in retaliation for his tenant's report of housing code violations to the authorities. As a matter of statutory construction [i.e., of the D.C. housing code] and for reasons of public policy, such an eviction cannot be permitted. . . .

In light of the appalling condition and shortage of housing in Washington, the expense of moving, the inequality of bargaining power between tenant and landlord, and the social and economic importance of assuring at least minimum standards in housing conditions, we do not hesitate to declare that retaliatory eviction cannot be tolerated. There can be no doubt that the slum dweller . . . will pause long before he complains of [housing code violations] if he fears eviction as a consequence.

397 F.2d at 689-690, 699, 701.

Most jurisdictions today forbid retaliatory eviction. See generally Restatement (Second) of Property, Landlord and Tenant, §§14.8-14.9 and Comments (1977). *Habib* held that after a claim of retaliation, a landlord could evict once the illegal retaliatory purpose was "dissipated," 397 F.2d at 702. A common statutory approach is to create a rebuttable presumption of retaliatory purpose if the landlord seeks to terminate a tenancy, increase rent, or decrease services within a 90- to 180-day period after a report of housing code violations or other action based on the condition of the premises. For retaliatory acts beyond the stated period, the tenant ordinarily bears the burden of proof.

Should the defense of retaliatory eviction extend to other situations, such as (1) the tenant has organized or become a member of a tenant's union or similar organization; (2) the tenant has complained to landlord of an impairment of the tenant's quiet enjoyment; (3) the tenant has sued landlord for a physical injury in the common areas; (4) the tenant has signed a petition opposing landlord's request for a zoning variance on the adjoining parcel, which landlord also owns? Might the answer partly depend on whether the landlord is a private individual or public body? Should the defense of retaliatory eviction be available to commercial tenants as well as residential ones? See, e.g., Espenschied v. Mallick, 633 A.2d 388 (D.C. 1993) (defense not available for commercial tenants).

e.   Secure Tenancies

The rule that landlords are entitled to terminate a tenancy for any or no reason has never been absolute. In fact, many tenancies are "secure tenancies," in which the landlord cannot terminate unless she provides adequate reasons, "good cause" or "just cause." Recall Sir Peregrine Orme's sense that a landlord should not terminate the lease of a long-term tenant "except under pressing circumstances." This sense of entitlement presumably underlay Britain's system, in which (as of 1980), sitting tenants could be evicted only for a limited number of reasons. See Trevor Aldridge, Rent Control and Leasehold Entitlement (8th ed. 1980).[96]

We have already seen one type of secure tenancy in the United States: Tenants in certain subsidized housing cannot be evicted without "good cause" because to do so would deprive them of property without due process in violation of the Fourteenth Amendment, Joy v. Daniels, which we read as an example of the republic vision of property, is part of a long (but not unbroken) line of cases holding that subsidized tenants cannot be evicted without good cause. These cases have been undermined to some extent by Department of Housing and Urban Development (HUD) regulations.[97]

Secure tenures are also common in jurisdictions, notably New York City and many California communities, that have rent control laws. See, e.g., N.Y. Admin. Code §26-408 (1986) (rent control statute requiring that landlord have "just cause" to evict). Secure tenures in this context prevent landlords from raising rents by the simple expedient of evicting their tenants. Secure tenancies also are becoming quite common in the context of mobile homes. Mobile homes play an extremely important role in the housing market today; about 1 in 16 American households lives in a mobile home. Dirk Johnson, Life in a Trailer Park: On the Edge, But Hoping, N.Y. Times, July 4, 1992, at 1.[98] Yet due to zoning and other restrictions, the amount of space available for mobile home parks is severely limited. Consequently, if a mobile homeowner is evicted from the "pad" on which her unit is located, she often faces severe difficulty in finding an alternative site: in effect, eviction often means that the mobile homeowner has no alternative but to junk the mobile home altogether, since there is no place to locate it. An increasing number of statutes limit owners of mobile home parks from evicting mobile homeowners from their "pads." One example is the California Mobilehome Residency Law, which prohibits a park owner from evicting a homeowner except for nonpayment of rent or where the park owner wants to change the use of his land. The law also provides that the park owner may not require removal of a mobile home when it is sold, and may neither disapprove of the buyer, nor charge a transfer fee. See Yee v. City of Escondido, 503 U.S. 819 (1992) (holding that the interaction of the California Mobilehome Residency Law and the City of Escondido rent control ordinance was not a taking).

---

96. This system was changed considerably during Margaret Thatcher's administration.
97. 24 C.F.R. §247.3. C.F.R. is the Code of Federal Regulations, in which are published the regulations of federal agencies.
98. Mobile homes are a key source of inexpensive housing in rural areas, particularly in the South and West. In Wyoming and South Carolina, for example, about 1 in 6 housing units is a mobile home or trailer. Mobile homes were the fastest-growing type of housing in the 1980s. According to the Census Bureau, half of mobile home residents earn less than $20,000 a year, and more than three-fourths earn less than $30,000 a year. Ibid.

By far the most far-reaching secure tenancy regime in the United States is the following New Jersey statute. For what reasons can a New Jersey landlord evict a sitting tenant?

N.J. Stat. Ann. §2A:18-61.1 (West 1994)

Removal of Residential Tenants; Grounds

No lessee or tenant or the assigns, under-tenants or legal representations of such lessee or tenant may be removed by the Superior Court from any house, building, mobile home or land in a mobile home park or tenement leased for residential purposes, other than (1) owner-occupied premises with not more than two rental units or a hotel, motel or other guest house or part thereof rented to a transient guest or seasonal tenant; (2) a dwelling unit which is held in trust on behalf of a member of the immediate family of the person or persons establishing the trust, provided that the member of the immediate family on whose behalf the trust is established permanently occupies the unit; and (3) a dwelling unit which is permanently occupied by a member of the immediate family of the owner of that unit, provided, however, that exception (2) or (3) shall apply only in cases in which the member of the immediate family has a developmental disability, except upon establishment of one of the following grounds as good cause:

a. The person fails to pay rent due and owing under the lease whether the same be oral or written;

b. The person has continued to be, after written notice to cease, so disorderly as to destroy the peace and quiet of the occupants or other tenants living in said house or neighborhood;

c. The person has willfully or by reason of gross negligence caused or allowed destruction, damage or injury to the premises;

d. The person has continued, after written notice to cease, to substantially violate or breach any of the landlord's rules and regulations governing said premises, provided such rules and regulations are reasonable and have been accepted in writing by the tenant or made a part of the lease at the beginning of the lease term;

e. The person has continued, after written notice to cease, to substantially violate or breach any of the covenants or agreements contained in the lease for the premises where a right of reentry is reserved to the landlord in the lease for a violation of such covenant or agreement, provided that such covenant or agreement is reasonable and was contained in the lease at the beginning of the lease term;

f. The person has failed to pay rent after a valid notice to quit and notice of increase of said rent, provided the increase in rent is not unconscionable and complies with any and all other laws or municipal ordinances governing rent increases;

g. The landlord or owner (1) seeks to permanently board up or demolish the premises because he has been cited by local or State housing inspectors for substantial violations affecting the health and safety of tenants and it is economically unfeasible for the owner to eliminate the violations; (2) seeks to comply with local or State housing inspectors who have cited him for substantial violations affecting the health and safety of tenants and it is unfeasible to so comply without removing the tenant; . . .

i. The landlord or owner proposes, at the termination of a lease, reasonable changes of substance in the terms and conditions of the lease, including specifically any change in the term thereof, which the tenant, after written notice, refuses to accept; provided that in cases where a tenant has received a notice of termination pursuant to subsection g of section 3 of P.L. 1974, c. 49 (C. 2A:18-61.2), or has a protected tenancy status pursuant to section 9 of the "Senior Citizens and Disabled Protected Tenancy Act," P.L. 1981, c. 226 (C. 2A:18-61.130 et al.), or pursuant to the "Tenant Protection Act of 1992," P.L. 1991, c. 509 (C. 2A:18-61.40 et al.), the landlord or owner shall have the burden of proving that any change in the terms and conditions of the lease, rental or regulations both is reasonable and does not substantially reduce the rights and privileges to which the tenant was entitled prior to the conversion;

j. The person, after written notice to cease, has habitually and without legal justification failed to pay rent which is due and owing; [Omitted are sections discussing evictions when the landowner is converting a building or mobile home park to condominium ownership and evictions of persons with drug offenses and offenses concerning threats to the landlord and his family. Note also that New Jersey has separate legislation that gives secure tenure to senior citizens.]

m. The landlord or owner conditioned the tenancy upon and in consideration for the tenant's employment by the landlord or owner as superintendent, janitor or in some other capacity and such employment is being terminated. . . .

PROBLEM

Say you are defending, or attacking, this statute when it is challenged as the unconstitutional taking of private property. Under what vision of property is it unjustifiable? What vision of property could you draw upon to justify it? Does the overriding concern for security have overtones of the republican focus on stable entitlements to ensure citizens a stake in their communities? Of the liberal dignitary?

§3.10   Landlord's Tort Liability

Traditional law held landlords liable for injuries resulting from defective and dangerous conditions in the premises if the injury was attributable to hidden defects and in a limited number of other contexts, including where the premises were leased for public use, where parts of the premises were retained under the landlord's control, such as common stairways, or where the premises were negligently repaired by the landlord. See Sargent v. Ross, 113 N.H. 388 (1973) (describing exceptions carved out of rule that landlords were generally exempted from tort liability). Courts, however, have expanded landlord liability as part of the revolution in landlord-tenant law. The court in Stoiber v. Smith Realty, 101 Cal. App. 3d 903, 162 Cal. Rptr. 194 (1980), for example, found that the lower court erred in ruling that the action against the landlord for breach of implied warranty of habitability was the tenant's only cause of action for the damages suffered from the "dilapidation and unsafe condition of the premises." The court explained that "[u]nder the law in California today, a tenant, by pleading the proper facts, may state a cause of action in tort against his landlord for failure to keep the premises in a lawful state of habitability."

The implied warranty has greatly widened the scope of landlords' potential tort liability, not only for physical conditions in the leasehold premises, but also in some circumstances for the actions of third parties. In Kline v. 1500 Massachusetts Ave., 439 F.2d 477 (D.C. Cir. 1970), the court held a landlord liable for foreseeable acts committed by a third party. In this case the tenant, Sarah Kline, was assaulted and robbed in the common hallway of the apartment building. The court cited *Javins* in describing the change in the nature of the landlord-tenant relationship and explained that "there is implied in the contract between landlord and tenant an obligation on the landlord to provide those protective measures which are within his reasonable capacity." Id. at 485. While as a general tort rule, a private person does not have a duty to protect a stranger from attack, this implied contractual agreement was found to create a special relationship between the landlord and the tenant. The Supreme Court of New Jersey in Trentacost v. Brussel, 82 N.J. 214 (1980) also held a rental landlord liable when he failed to provide adequate security for common areas. The Court explained that:

> There is no doubt that New Jersey has been faced with a chronic, desperate need for rental housing. Increasing urbanization, population growth and inflated construction costs have contributed to this shortage, thereby creating an "inequality of bargaining power between the landlord and tenant." As a result, the prevailing understanding regarding the nature of a residential lease has not found expression in explicit contractual terms. Because lease agreements are frequently from contracts of adhesion, they cannot be relied upon to represent a genuine "meeting of the minds" with respect to the landlord's responsibilities. The tenant therefore cannot realize his legitimate present-day demands for fair treatment in the economic forum.
>
> It is undisputed that maintaining minimum conditions of habitability, including security, is beyond an individual tenant's control. Where the task involves common areas of a multiple-dwelling building, tenants' efforts are entirely precluded. Nor in this highly mobile society should tenants be re-

quired to invest substantial sums in improvements that might outlast their tenancy. The landlord, however, can spread the cost of maintenance over an
extended period of time among all the residents enjoying its benefits. . . .
[W]ithout a minimum of security, their well-being is as precarious as if they
had no heat or sanitation. . . . Under modern living conditions, an apartment
is clearly not habitable unless it provides a reasonable measure of security
from risk of criminal intrusion.

Id. at 225-227. *Trentacost* was cited by the California Court of Appeals in
Kwaitkowski v. Superior Trading Co., 123 Cal. App. 3d 324 (1981), which
held the landlord liable when the tenant was "raped, assaulted and robbed
in the dimly lit lobby of a building with a defective front door lock in a high
crime area, after the landlords had notice of similar and other crimes committed on another tenant in a common hallway." The court in *Kwaitkowski*
premised liability on the special relationship between the landlord and tenant, the foreseeability of criminal attack, and the warranty of habitability
implicit in the lease contract. In Holley v. Mt. Zion Terrace Apts., Inc., 382
So. 2d 98 (Fla. Dist. Ct. App. 1980), the court held that the landlord was
liable in an action for wrongful death after the tenant was raped and murdered in the common area of an apartment complex. The action against
the landlord "was predicated on the landlord's negligent failure to provide
reasonable security measures in the building's common areas." The courts
in these cases focused on the implied contractual duty that the landlord
owed the tenant, the relationship between the modern landlord and tenant, and the foreseeability of the crime. These last two ideas are fundamental concepts in tort law and, thus, here we again see the crossover between
areas of the law that are traditionally taught as distinct and separate.

§3.11   Implications of the Reforms

The reforms of landlord and tenant law have been controversial from the
first. The much watered-down version of the implied warranty appearing in
the Restatement (Second) of Property was agreed upon only after a stormy
debate on the floor of the usually sedate American Law Institute. Opponents of the implied warranty argued that it was (a) not yet fully supported
by court decisions, (b) likely to be wholly ineffectual, and (c) certain to
reduce the supply, as well as raising the cost, of affordable housing for
lower-income tenants. These criticisms, elaborated by Charles J. Meyers,
The Covenant of Habitability and the American Law Institute, 27 Stan. L.
Rev. 879 (1975), came to dominate the law review literature on the implied
warranty. This debate is further sketched out in the excerpts below.

a.   Law and Economics

RICHARD POSNER, ECONOMIC ANALYSIS OF LAW

(4th ed. 1992)

Both public housing and rent supplements involve the taxing and spending branches of government rather than the courts. But there is a method of (purportedly) helping the poor to meet their housing needs that centrally involve the courts: the enforcement of housing codes. These codes specify minimum standards of housing — although whether in order to ensure a decent minimum level of safety and sanitation or to subsidize the building trades is a matter of debate. Legal scholarship has been imaginative in suggesting devices by which the violators of housing codes could be subjected to sanctions that would greatly reduce the incidence of violation. To deal with the problem of substandard housing by legal sanction has the additional attraction of enabling, or seeming to enable, a principal manifestation of poverty to be eliminated without any public expenditure.

The effects of housing code enforcement are depicted in Figure 3-13. D_1 is the market demand curve for low-income housing before enforcement. It slopes downward because not all tenants would leave if rentals rose as a result of an increase in the landlords' marginal costs. MC_1 is the landlords' pre-enforcement marginal cost curve and is positively sloped to reflect the fact that the creation of low-income rental housing involves the use of some specialized resources — in particular, land — that would be worth less in any other use.

Enforcing the housing code has two main effects on the market de-

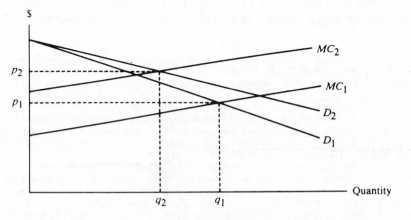

FIGURE 3-13

picted in Figure 3-13.[2] By improving the quality of the housing units it increases the demand for them. And by increasing the landlords' maintenance costs, which are marginal costs because they vary with the number of housing units provided, it shifts the marginal cost curve upward. The shift shown in Figure 3-13 is large relative to the shift in the demand curve, on the plausible assumption that if quantity demanded were highly responsive to an increase in the quality of the housing provided, the landlords would upgrade quality voluntarily and there would be no need to enforce a housing code. Both demand and supply in Figure 3-13 are depicted as being quite elastic, on the (again plausible) assumptions that slum dwellers lack the resources to pay substantially higher rentals and that slum rentals are already so depressed in relation to costs that a further reduction in those rentals would cause many landlords to withdraw from the low-income housing market (for example, by abandoning their property to the city).

Given these assumptions, housing code enforcement leads to a substantial reduction in the supply of low-income housing (from q_1 to q_2) coupled with a substantial rise in the price of the remaining supply (from p_1 to p_2). . . . Admittedly, the magnitude of the effects shown in Figure 3.13 depends on the (arbitrary) location of the curves. It has even been suggested that demand might be perfectly elastic in the relevant region (implying no price effect of housing code enforcement[5]) because the slightest increase would cause many tenants to double up.[6] But since doubling up is costly (it involves forgoing the value of the greater space and privacy of single family occupancy), tenants would surely be willing to pay something to avoid being forced to double up, the something being a somewhat higher rental. This implies a less than perfectly elastic demand. Empirical evidence suggests that Figure 3.13 provides a closer approximation to the actual conditions of the slum housing market than a model which assumes perfect elasticity of demand.[7]

Another suggestion is that the enforcement of a housing code would increase the supply of housing to the poor if enforcers focused their efforts

---

2. A third effect is a reduction in the rent of land received by the landlords (assuming they are the owners of the land). The irony here is that these "rentiers" include a number of almost-poor people for whom ownership of slum property represents the first stage in the escape from poverty. There would still be a quantity effect: show this graphically.

5. There would still be a quantity effect: show this graphically.

6. Bruce Ackerman, Regulating Slum Housing Markets on behalf of the Poor: Of Housing Codes, Housing Subsidies and Income Redistribution Policy, 80 Yale L.J. 1093 (1971), criticized in Neil K. Komesar, Return to Slumville: A Critique of the Ackerman Analysis of Housing Code Enforcement and the Poor, 82 Yale L.J. 1175 (1973).

One court has suggested that landlords might be forbidden, on a theory of retaliatory eviction, to abandon buildings as an alternative to code compliance if they were "able" to comply. Robinson v. Diamond Housing Corp., 463 F.2d 853, 869 (D.C. Cir. 1972). Would such a prohibition increase or decrease the long-run supply of housing to the poor?

7. Werner Z. Hirsch, Law and Economics: An Introductory Analysis 43-58 (1979); Hirsch, Effects of Habitability and Anti-Speedy Eviction Laws on Black and Aged Indigent Tenant Groups: An Economic Analysis, 3 Int'l Rev. Law & Econ. 121 (1983).

on buildings that landlords were "milking."[8] Milking refers to the practice of maintaining a building at a lower standard than would be appropriate if the landlord intended to keep the building in operation indefinitely. He might have figured for example that because of a changing neighborhood or rising fuel costs he would probably have to abandon the building in five years willy-nilly — by that time his variable costs will exceed his rental income. It may make sense for him, once he has made this calculation, to reduce his expenditures on maintenance at once, since any long-term effects of those expenditures in preserving the building would be of little or no value to him. . . . By reducing those expenditures, he will reduce the quality of the housing, and his rental income will fall, but maybe by less than his expenditures on maintenance fall. An incidental effect may be that he abandons the building even sooner (though this will end his income stream sooner), since those expenditures would have kept the building going a little longer. If the enforcement of the local housing code prevents him from economizing in this manner, maybe he will delay abandonment, since the expenditures he is forced to make may well have some, as it were inadvertent, effect in preserving the building.

All this is terribly "iffy." Even though milking is, doubtless, sometimes rational in the real estate market when all costs and benefits are taken into account, attempting to counteract it through housing code enforcement is as likely to accelerate as to delay abandonment. The costs of compliance with the code are variable costs, which means that, as a first approximation at least, declining rental income and rising variable costs will intersect sooner, leading to earlier abandonment. It is doubtful that a court or legislature could identify those buildings where enforcement of the housing code would delay abandonment through its effect in counteracting milking rather than accelerate it through its effect in making the continued ownership of the building more expensive.

A number of cities have enacted ordinances designed to protect tenants by giving them more procedural rights in the event the landlord tries to evict them, by entitling tenants to withhold rent if landlords fail to make repairs required by the lease, by requiring landlords to pay interest on security deposits, and so forth. The effects are much like those of housing code enforcement: They raise landlords' costs and therefore increase rentals and reduce the supply of housing (especially rental housing, since such laws encourage conversion to cooperatives and condominiums). From the standpoint of protecting poor people, the provisions regarding procedural rights and rent withholding are particularly pernicious. They are rights more likely to be invoked by the poor than by the rich. They therefore give landlords an added incentive to substitute toward more affluent

8. Duncan Kennedy, The Effect of the Warranty of Habitability on Low Income Housing: "Milking" and Class Violence, 15 Fla. State U. L. Rev. 485 (1986).

tenants, who are less likely to be late with the rent or to abuse the right to withhold rent.

BRUCE ACKERMAN, REGULATING SLUM HOUSING MARKETS ON BEHALF OF THE POOR: OF HOUSING CODES, HOUSING SUBSIDIES AND INCOME REDISTRIBUTION POLICY

80 Yale L.J. 1093, 1102-1106 (1971)

Imagine a city called Athens whose slums are concentrated in one geographic area that we shall call Slumville. While the residents of Slumville are extremely mobile within the confines of the slum district, Athenians living outside Slumville are extremely reluctant to move into the area even if there is a significant improvement in housing quality. Of course, if there is an enormous change in the character of the neighborhood, the city's residents may change their view of Slumville. But a moderate change will not lead them to discard their fears about the quality of life, as well as the quality of housing, enjoyed by the area's inhabitants.

While the middle-class Athenian's substantial reluctance to live in Slumville is fundamental to much of the argument that follows, several additional assumptions will be altered at subsequent stages of this essay. For purposes of the present discussion, then, assume (1) both landlords and tenants act rationally in their self-interest; (2) no landlord or group of landlords has successfully established a monopoly or oligopoly position in the rental market; (3) tenants are aware of the range of prices and quality levels of accommodations offered for rent in Slumville and experience no significant cost in moving from one part of Slumville to another; (4) all of Slumville's accommodations are not only slums, but are *equally* slummy; (5) similarly, all of Slumville's tenants inflict *equal* damage upon the physical structures of the houses in which they reside; (6) a significant number of poor provincials are not entering Athens from the outlands nor are Slumvillites emigrating to the hinterlands; (7) *each* and *every* landlord in Slumville earns a rate of return on his investment which substantially exceeds the return available when the property is used for other purposes; indeed (8) even if the landlords are forced to bring their residential properties up to code, their rate of return would still exceed that available for any other use of the property; and (9) no landlord will find it more profitable to abandon his building entirely when faced with the necessity of investing substantial sums to bring his tenement up to code. . . .

We are now in a position to trace the economic consequences of a code enforcement program in Slumville. Given the model which has been developed, it follows that when the costs of code improvements are imposed upon Slumville's landlords *none* of them will have an incentive to remove their properties from the rental housing market. For we have stipulated that even after code costs are taken into account, the return on slum investment still exceeds the rate of return available when the land is used for other purposes or not used at all. Since the imposition of code costs upon the landlords does not induce a fall in the supply of housing, rent levels will be determined by the effect of code enforcement upon the demand for housing.

Two different demand responses can be anticipated, depending upon the extent to which the housing code is enforced. First, assume that the code is enforced strictly only in one part (Area X) of Slumville and that the rest of Slumville (Area Y) is entirely ignored by the housing code inspectorate. In this case, one would expect that some of the residents of Y will find X a more attractive place than formerly and will bid the rents up in Area X. Those residents of X who find the new rent levels too steep for their taste will of course move to Y, where apartments have been vacated by those moving into the newly improved housing in X. Consequently, a program of selective housing code enforcement in Slumville will, in fact, partially fulfill the expectations of those administrators who doubt the desirability of code enforcement: rents will increase in the target area and tenants who cannot "afford" the higher rents will leave the area to find new abodes in the now slummier sections of Slumville.

If, however, one assumes that the housing code is enforced strictly in all of Slumville, the same result will not follow. Since we have assumed that before the code was enforced, houses in Areas X and Y were equally dilapidated, the comprehensive enforcement of the code throughout Areas X and Y will raise the quality of housing in all parts of Slumville to an equal degree, thereby providing no special incentive for a resident of Area Y to want to move to Area X. Thus, rents will not rise because of competition *among* Slumville residents as occurred in the case of partial code enforcement just discussed.

Indeed rents will not rise *at all* in Slumville if only a single further condition is met. Paradoxically, code enforcement will have "zero rent impact" if and only if there exists a class of Slumville tenants who do *not* believe that code enforcement will significantly improve their lives. A simple mathematical example will make this clear. Assume that, before the code is enforced, two types of families live in Slumville's 100,000 rental units: 90,000 families (the "homelovers") would be willing to pay a significant amount of money for code housing; in contrast, 10,000 families (the "lukewarm" families) would not be willing to pay extra rent for improved housing. This is not to say that even the lukewarm do not recognize that they will benefit from code enforcement — the improvement is simply not significant enough in their minds to warrant allocation of any more of their scarce funds to purchase it.

Now imagine that all of Slumville's landlords seek to pass their code costs on to tenants by raising rents by $25. While the 90,000 homelovers initially respond by paying the premium, the 10,000 lukewarm families act differently. Rather than paying the higher rent, they choose to pair up and share apartments instead, thus leaving 5000 units vacant. The lukewarm families will take this course since they believe that half an apartment at a lower rent is a better deal than a whole apartment at the inflated rental.

When the 10,000 lukewarm families decide to double-up, however, the owners of the 5000 vacant apartments are faced with a serious problem. Since no new residents have (under our assumptions) been attracted to Slumville as a result of code enforcement, there is no reason to expect that they will successfully fill their apartments if they persist in demanding the $25 premium. Rather, a landlord can rent his units in only one of two ways: (a) by inducing one of the homelovers to move by cutting the premium below the $25 level or (b) by cutting the rent sufficiently to induce one of the lukewarm families to prefer an entire apartment to its more crowded quarters. It should be apparent that if a given landlord fills a vacant apartment by offering one of the homelovers a better deal than his present landlord, the competitive dynamic will continue, for the owner of the newly vacated apartment will find himself in the same bleak position as his now successful competitor once occupied. It is only when prices are set low enough to induce the lukewarm families to resume their former habits and live in individual apartments that the economic situation will regain equilibrium. But if a significant number of lukewarm families are willing to spend no additional money for the code improvements, equilibrium will not be attained until the competing landlords absorb all of the code costs and rent all of their units at the pre-code price. Q.E.D. . . .

NOTES AND QUESTIONS

1. **Assumptions.** What assumptions does Posner make about the workings of the housing market? What assumptions does Ackerman make? Is the analysis of either author based on the characteristics of specific housing markets? If not, what are the analyses based on?

2. **Images of landlords.** What image of landlords underlies the analysis of each author?

3. **Visions of property.** What vision of property underlies each analysis?

4. **Commercial leases.** For an a priori discussion as to the effect of an implied warranty in the commercial area, see Note, An Economic Analysis of Implied Warranties of Fitness in Commercial Leases, 94 Colum. L. Rev. 658 (1994).

b.   Empirical Studies

A variety of studies over the past 25 years have found that few tenants have claimed the implied warranty and that it has had little impact on the housing market. See Roger Cunningham, The New Implied and Statutory Warranties of Habitability in Residential Leases: From Contract to Status, 16 Urb. L. Ann. 8 (1979). A 1968 study of the Pennsylvania Rent Withholding Act found that, two years after it was passed, only 1,340 out of 28,000 substandard housing units had been certified as eligible for rent withholding, and only 100 units had been brought into compliance with the housing code. Norman Krumholz, Rent Withholding as an Aid to Housing Code Enforcement, 25 J. Housing 242 (1968). A later study seemed to confirm these findings. Joseph R. Buckley and Gary N. Conley, Comment, Housing Market Operation and the Pennsylvania Rent Withholding Act — An Economic Analysis, 17 Vill. L. Rev. 886 (1972). A 1974 study of the rent withholding statute passed in Massachusetts in 1965 found that only 40 percent of summary process cases involved tenants represented by counsel; the rent abatement defense was raised in less than 15 percent of those cases. Yet, in contested cases where the rent abatement was raised, landlords won less often and settled more often. A 1970-1971 study of the 1968 Michigan tenants' rights legislation found that tenants raised no defenses at all in 90 percent of all landlord-tenant cases, and the new rent withholding and retaliation defenses were raised in only 3 percent of the cases. Marilyn Miller Mosier and Richard A. Soble, Modern Legislation, Metropolitan Court, Miniscule Results: A Study of Detroit's Landlord-Tenant Court, 7 U. Mich. J.L. Ref. 8 (1973). Another, slightly later study found that, although the implied warranty defense was being raised slightly more, the actual outcome of litigation was "almost exclusively pro-landlord." J. I. Rose & M. A. Scott, "Street Talk" summonses in Detroit's Landlord-Tenant Court: A Small Step for Urban Tenants, 52 J. Urb. L. 967 (1975). A 1976 study of the implied warranty adopted in California in 1974 found that it was not being extensively used. "Simply stated, the problem is that few low income tenants receive the legal advice necessary to make use of this innovation." Note, The Great Green Hope: The Implied Warranty in Practice, 28 Stan. L. Rev. 37 (1978).

A much more recent study of Baltimore Rent Court seemed to confirm the findings of earlier studies that the implied warranty was not making much of an impact. Barbara Bezdek, Silence in the Court: Participation and Subordination of Poor Tenants' Voices in Legal Process, 20 Hofstra L. Rev. 533 (1992). Like earlier studies, the Bezdek study found that few tenants were represented by counsel, and that landlords won the overwhelming number (84.7 percent) of landlord-tenant cases by default. Tenants win in roughly 3.5 percent of the cases; rent abatement or damages were imposed on landlords in only 1.75 percent of all cases.

Not surprisingly, more than one interpretation exists for why the implied warranty has been so little used. One analysis by Professor Charles Meyers suggested that tenants knew the implied warranty was available, but failed to claim it because they saw that the result of raising their landlords' maintenance costs was either abandonment of low-income buildings or raising low-income tenants' rent; and neither of those two options appealed to

them. Charles Meyers, The Covenant of Habitability and the American Law
Institute, 27 Stan. L. Rev. 879, 896 (1975). Bezdek, who runs a clinic representing low-income tenants in Baltimore, also found that many tenants
knew about the existence of the implied warranty. She gave a different explanation for why it so rarely was used effectively against landlords.

BARBARA BEZDEK, SILENCE IN THE COURT: PARTICIPATION AND SUBORDINATION OF POOR TENANTS' VOICES IN LEGAL PROCESS

20 Hofstra L. Rev. 533 (1992)

Cases in which both landlord and tenant appear typically take no
more than two minutes. The dullingly standard script proceeds as follows:

Judge: "Landlord claims rent due of $297. Is that amount due?"
Tenant: "Yes."
Judge: "Is there anything else? Judgment for landlord for possession
            showing $297 due and unpaid."

In a frequent minor variation on this script, the judge may add to the
tenant, "Would you like a slip for DSS? See the bailiff." Ordinarily the tenant's response is a nod, no other response seeming necessary. Whether this
is the tenant's self-identified need or purpose, or just acquiescence to the
judge's evident expectation, is not possible to observe.

This typical transcript illustrates *twin barriers to tenant's* [emphasis has
been added throughout] voicing of claims and the court granting a hearing
to tenants. These are the dysfunctional premises embedded in legal culture,
and the failure of the legal process to mediate the subtle, and not so subtle,
intrusions of the larger culture's calculus of social and material status.

A tenant asserting her claim of rent-impairing defects must satisfy the
judge on two levels of communication not likely to be familiar to her. These
are the formal requirements for claiming within the official legal culture
and the information gleaned from the tenant's presentation of herself and
her claim, which the judge uses to interpret the tenant before him. This
interpretation encompasses attributions as to race and social class. In the
elusive moment in which the tenant must state her claim or not, the tenant
faces hurdles both of *official legal culture* and of the *larger culture* for which
a lower court is scarcely a successful filter. As we shall see, both of these
hurdles silence most tenants.

The formal paradigm for rent court is the conceptual model of the
ordinary civil law suit, in which one believing himself aggrieved can bring a
claim in the court having the power to adjudicate the matter. The offending
party is given notice and an opportunity to be heard by an impartial court,

which acts only on a parties' initiative, and which will render a decision based on formal decisional rules and evidence presented. If they choose, parties may have the assistance of a lawyer, chiefly by paying for it. Most lawsuits settle, and — the paradigm presumes — settlements out of court reflect the parties' assessment of the relative strengths of their positions without the headaches and costs of litigation. In short, the civil-action paradigm provides that the parties participate in the process, either by appearing or negotiating.

But this paradigm is flawed to the extent that it masks the *systematic exclusion* by the operation of the law of litigants who are members of *socially subordinated* groups. As Kristin Bumiller has recently observed, the model of legal protection contains within its conception of claims an obligation of rights assertion, that is, the idea that the individual who fails to insist upon her rights in the legal process is herself at fault for the failure of the law to cloak her with its protection.

A similar cultural premise pervades the operation of rent court. The central normative function of the rent court is to ask of the tenant, *"Did you pay the money claimed or not?"* It implies a statement of the individual tenant's *unmitigable fault* for the failure to make out her own case of legitimate complaint against the landlord.

The social subtext of implied warranties of habitability, if they function, is very different. The tenants' statutory entitlement that their landlords maintain the premises to minimum standards of habitability recasts the social relationship of landlord and tenant. The experience of claiming rent and possession in rent court *potentially recasts the social relationship* as well, by providing a channel in which the tenant can counter the landlord's declaration with her own experience. In a jurisdiction with a functioning warranty of habitability, the subtext in tenant-claiming cases would be: it is the landlord who has done wrong by failing to fulfill societally recognized obligations. In Baltimore, however, the formal allocation of responsibilities between landlord and tenant is effectively overwritten by the "tenant as deadbeat" subtext which is reiterated by the court on behalf of the class of landlord litigants.

Like all conversations between people of unequal power, the typical script has perhaps several subtexts. Commonly, the subtext to the foregoing script is:

Judge: "Landlord claims rent due of $297. Is that amount due?" [The issue here is whether you paid. Have you paid? If you haven't paid the man, then you lose.]

Tenant: "Yes" [There are numerous subtexts for this one-word reply: Yes, I haven't paid; Yes, that is what he claims; and, Yes, you are the powerful one here.]

Judge: "Judgment for landlord for possession." [Pay the landlord this amount or plan to move.] . . .

In a surprising number of cases, the landlord says nothing. He hardly needs to since the merits of a nonpayment case are extraordinarily simple and the judge conducts the landlord's case anyway. Has the tenant paid the rent? If not, the tenant has ceased to pay for the right to possess, thus the landlord is entitled to have this tenant removed. Formally, the dispute is one of possession and the landlord's remedy is regaining possession. In reality, however, the scene is one of debt collection.

Formal legal rights do not modify this essential transaction because of the barriers to tenants' assertions of such rights. The way the rent court operates, the familiar formal allocation among the parties of the burdens of presentation and proof, are in fact turned on their heads. This is explained in part by the summary nature of the proceeding for repossession. It is strongly reinforced by the phenomenon, all too ordinary in rent court, of the judge trying the landlord's case.

At least in the first instance, I read this as a tale of *institutional exclusion rather than judicial bias.* Directed by the complaint form as well as by the sitting judge, scarcely a question is required of or put to the landlord, whose prima facie case is stated by filling in the blanks. As practiced in Baltimore's rent court, a person appearing at the landlord's table is virtually never asked to prove any element of his case, including the amount of rent allegedly unpaid, a lease basis for other claimed charges, authority to collect rent, or title.

With perhaps 2,500 cases on the day's docket and the legislative injunction of a summary process, the institution can scarcely address the caseload and require every landlord to prove every element of the claim. But Maryland taxpayers can infer the institution's central function from the form of the court, which is a collection agency at public expense. To view the dysfunction of this court merely as a conundrum of administrative pressures, rather than as defects in the substance or process of the law, is dangerous and destructive of essential principles of adjudication. . . .

The interplay of legal culture and class may be illustrated by the procedural hurdle of notice requirements most often employed to bar tenants from successfully claiming redress for defective conditions in the rented residences. Typically the judge requires that the tenant give written notice to the landlord more than thirty days before the tenant makes her claim to the court. Clearly "notice" to the landlord of the tenant's claim of defect and nonrepair is an essential element of the tenant's case. By law, the tenant is entitled to make her claim as an answer and defense to the landlord's suit for repossession which, as a summary proceeding, is scheduled for hearing within a week of the landlord's filing. Baltimore local law recognizes "actual notice" and notices issued by government inspectors as valid forms of notice. But it has been the practice of several rent court judges to prefer the statute's most stringent version of "notice" of defects — a tenant's certified letter to the landlord, of which the tenant has kept a copy and the returned receipt.

The cultural barrier is the judges' evident belief that it is "no big deal" for tenants to write letters or otherwise create paper trails for what they know. This may be both an unconscious projection of official legal culture or of a world view that one pilots one's own life, grounded in the social and economic status accompanying judges' professional station. Nevertheless, two points suggest that for many tenants, the letter requirement is clearly a significant hurdle to the hearing of real disputes by this court.

The first is Baltimore's legendary illiteracy rate — it has the least literate population of the nation's fifteen largest cities. *One-third* of the city's people above the age of sixteen are functionally illiterate, that is, unable to read bus and street signs or medicine bottles, much less the compound, complex "instructions" on the back of a tattered summons.

Second, the judges themselves have tended to raise the hurdle unreasonably high through their interpretation of simple letters which are submitted by some tenants. In one case the tenant's letter read:

> To whom it may concern, I am written you this letter to as you fix these thing in the house i rent from.

> 1.   Bathroom, toilet
> 2.   all window needs to be fix
> 3.   seil [ceiling] going up to the third floor. . . .

At trial, the judge rejected the letter as adequate notice, expressing concern that the letter did not sufficiently apprise the landlord that there was a defect in the toilet for which the landlord would be responsible. The landlord took the judge's cue that she did not "know" there was anything about the enumerated items to repair.

Ordinarily, a tenant learns of the requirement for written notice (or any other matter of procedure, practice, or proof) on the day she answers her landlord's claim for rent in court. During the period 1989-91, the sitting judge read a statement at the start of the morning docket which was intended as instructions to all the tenants. Despite the statutory provisions, judges routinely instruct tenants that "you must send the landlord a certified letter listing the repairs that are needed, and keep a copy of the letter and the returned receipt of delivery" if they wish to make an issue of the condition of their rental. Tenants who arrived late or could not hear the judge from their seats will hear the gist of this instruction in the other tenants' cases while they wait for their own case to be called. The dialogue concerning notice often proceeds as follows:

Judge: "Did you tell your landlord?"
Tenant: "Yes sir, I told him every time he came to get the rent" [or, "I told his workmen"].
Judge: "When was that? . . . Mr. Landlord?"
Landlord: "I didn't get the message."

Judge: "Did you send your landlord a letter?"
Tenant: "No, but I . . . "
Judge: "I understand ma'am, but the landlord is entitled to 30 days
              notice. Now, he has to fix it if it is defective. If he hasn't fixed it
              in a reasonable time, then come back here next month and tell
              me you were here today. Judgment for the landlord for the
              amount of rent claimed due, $xyz. Thank you."

The judge's preference for the most onerous of the three forms of notice
permitted by statute thus becomes an operational imperative.

Tenant education in the rent court consists of a set of direct and powerful instructions. Informed by the judge's formal instructions at the start
of docket, tenants are told that they cannot raise conditions issues if they
did not have the foresight to write a letter, mail it certified, and keep a copy.
Tenants see the judge try the landlords' cases. Tenants observe that few tenants participate or have much to say. The few tenants who do attempt to
gain the judge's ear are not assisted in making their claims in ways parallel
to the assistance afforded landlords. Tenants are placed under a different
burden of protection, presentation, and persuasion. The court makes no
reference to tenants' rights and no admonishment to landlords at the start
of docket in order to honor tenants' entitlements. . . .

NOTES AND QUESTIONS

1. **Competing explanations.** How does Bezdek's explanation for the
reason why few tenants claim the implied warranty differ from Meyer's explanation that tenants ignore the implied warranty because of the risk that
landlords will either raise rents or abandon buildings?

2. **Systemic failure.** Does the tenants' experience with the implied
warranty, in your view, merely dramatize the need for more lawyers, or does
it suggest some deeper limitations of law reform efforts?

3. **Bench-top computers.** Every judge in New York City's Housing
Courts, which handle more than one million cases yearly, has a bench-top
computer giving direct access to Housing Department records that show,
for each rental unit in the city, all outstanding code violations. In any nonpayment suit where the tenant does not default, the judge must first view
his terminal to determine whether the premises are violation-free. If violations exist that impair the tenant's habitability, the court may not grant the
landlord an eviction warrant based on the full rental. N.Y. Mult. Dwell. Law
§328(3) (McKinney 1994).

We now proceed to landlord and tenant law outside the bounds of the
paradigm urban apartment rental. Note that outside this paradigm, we

more often encounter commercial leases. Yet we will continue to encounter familiar themes, notably the use of contract language to access values from the republican vision and the liberal dignity strain.

§3.12   Assignments and Subleases

a.   The Basics: Case Law

Problem: A law student, X, signs a year-long lease that runs from September 1 to August 31. He moves to a different city to take a summer clerkship, and "subleases" his apartment to Y from June 1 until August 31. Y moves out after three and a half weeks and fails to pay any rent beyond the first month's rent, which he paid when he took possession of the apartment. Who can sue whom for the last two months' rent? Whom can the landlord sue, if X does not pay? Can X sue Y?

The law governing this (common!) problem takes us back to the formalistic approach characteristic of feudal law. The legal relationship of X and Y must be placed in one of two mutually exclusive legal boxes: It can be an assignment or a sublease. It is an assignment, at common law, if X signed over everything he owned to Y. If X retained any reversion, it is a sublease.

Instead of introducing the common law through an individual case, the following is a legal treatise of the sort often consulted by practicing attorneys to orient themselves in a new area of the law. Robert Schoshinski, American Law of Landlord and Tenant §8.11-8.13, at 555-575 (1980 & Supp. 1994).[99]

§8.11 Assignment and sublease distinguished

As has been pointed out, the traditional test to determine whether the lessee's transfer is an assignment or a sublease is whether he has retained a reversion — if he has, the transfer is sublease, if not, it is an assignment. The distinction is important because diverse legal consequences and relationships result from the two transactions. If the transfer is an assignment, privity of estate arises between the main lessor and the assignee, and the privity of estate that had existed prior to the assignment between the main lessor and the original tenant-assignor ends. If the transfer is a sublease, a new landlord-tenant relationship, privity of estate, is created between the original tenant-sublessor and his transferee, the sublessee; no privity of estate exists, however, between the original lessor and the sublessee, and the privity of estate that existed prior to the transfer between the original lessor and lessee continues.

---

99. Note that treatises contain lots of case citations in the footnotes, to enable the practitioner easy access to a case in her jurisdiction. For our purposes, the footnotes have been edited out.

Parties who are in privity of estate have the benefit and the burden of those covenants in the lease which "run with the land."

The common law, then, required the retention of a reversion for the transfer to be considered a sublease. Under traditional doctrine, a reversion is an absolute right of possession in the lessee, after the expiration of the transferee's interest, for a period of time, however short. Merely retaining a contingent right or possibility of possession — for instance, a right of reentry or power of termination upon failure to pay rent or upon breach of other conditions of the lease — does not constitute a reversion for purposes of the traditional test. However, in some states it has been held that retention of a right of reentry is a sufficient reversionary interest to constitute the transfer of a sublease.

The traditional distinction between assignment and sublease based on whether a term, however short, is reversed by the transferor was founded on certain concepts of the feudal system of land tenures which have no place in modern landlord-tenant law. Strict adherence to this test may in many cases thwart the intention of the parties to the transfer. . . . The test ought to be: did the parties to the transfer intend to establish a landlord-tenant relationship, a tenurial relationship between themselves. Under this test, the intent of the parties is to be gleaned from all the factors involved and circumstances surrounding the transfer, not just one factor, such as reservation of a right of possession for a particular period or reservation of a right of reentry. The totality of factors and circumstances should be determinative. . . .

§8.12 Effect of assignment

Upon the lessee's assignment of his leasehold, the privity of estate between lessor and lessee is destroyed and a new privity of estate is created between the lessor and the assignee. The lessor and lessee are still in privity of contract, however, and although the lessee is no longer subject to liabilities founded on the relationship of privity of estate, he still remains liable upon all the terms of his contract. As a practical matter, then, the liabilities of the lessee to the lessor are unaffected by an assignment by the lessee.

By reason of the assignment, the assignee comes into privity of estate with the lessor, and as a consequence, he assumes the burden and accedes to the benefit of all real covenants. The rights and liabilities of the assignee, absent an agreement to assume the contractual obligations of the lease, depend solely on the privity of estate relationship, and hence, when this relationship ceases to exist, the assignee cannot be held liable for subsequent breaches. As a result, the assignee's liability ends upon an assignment of his estate. Although he remains liable for breaches occurring prior to the transfer, the assignee, by reassigning, may escape further liability even though the transfer is made to a financially irresponsible person for the express purpose of escaping liability, notwithstanding that the lease purports to bind assigns.

Where the assignee agrees to assume the lessee's covenants and obligations, privity of contract arises between the lessor and the assignee. Such an assumption of the lease covenants must be clear and unambiguous, however, and some courts have gone so far as to indicate that such an assumption can never be implied. Indeed, there is a conflict of opinion as to whether an assignment "subject to the covenants and conditions" of the lease operates as an assumption of lease covenants that will create privity of contract between lessor and assignee. Where an assignee assumes by contract the obligations of the lease, the lessor, as third party beneficiary of that contract, thereby comes into privity of contract with the assignee, and may enforce all of the terms of the lease contract against him. As the assignee's liability in this situation is not based on privity of estate, it survives his subsequent assignment of the lease. The lessee-assignor cannot subsequently release the assignee from his assumed liability to the lessor, rather it has been held that such release can only be effected upon a clear showing that it was accepted by the lessor.

Although it is generally held that assignees of undivided interests in the lease are liable for only a proportionate share of the rent, there is authority that as to other lease covenants, particularly agreements to repair or surrender possession, they are jointly and severally liable. This seems a fair rule, especially in the common case where one tenant in common is in full possession and the other cannot be located; in such a case it seems more just to place the burden of finding and bringing suit against the absent co-tenant upon his co-assignee, rather than on the lessor.

§8.13 Effect of sublease

A sublease has no effect on the privity of estate or privity of contract relationship arising from the main lease. Thus, as between the main lessor and the main lessee, liability on the lease covenants remains the same, and the lessee can be held for breaches thereof, though occasioned by the sublessee.

As between the main lessor and the sublessee, since there is neither privity of estate nor privity of contract, neither has an action at law to enforce the lease covenants against the other. . . .

NOTES AND QUESTIONS

1. **Privity of estate.** This term is one of those circular terms Felix Cohen, see page 9, *supra*, found so tiresome. The term "privity of estate" can best be understood — when used in the present context — as a fancy name for the legal conclusion that a new landlord and tenant relationship has been established, resting on the new tenant's status rather than on any promises he may have given (privity of contract).

2. **Real covenants**. Later on in your study of property law, Chapter 7, you will be ready to struggle with the requirements for an enforceable real covenant. You should assume, however, that a covenant to pay rent is such a covenant and, where the Restatement, below, uses the term, "touches and concerns" the transferred interest.

3. **Restatement of Property**. The full text of Restatement (Second) of Property, Landlord and Tenant, §16.1 (1977) provides:

§16.1 Obligation Created by an Express Promise — Burden of Performance After Transfer

(1) A transferor of interest in leased property, who immediately before the transfer is obligated to perform an express promise contained in the lease that touches and concerns the transferred interest, continues to be obligated after the transfer if:

(a)   the obligation rests on privity of contract, and he is not relieved of the obligation by the person entitled to enforce it; or

(b)   the obligation rests solely on privity of estate and the transfer does not terminate his privity of estate with the person entitled to enforce the obligation, and that person does not relieve him of the obligation.

(2) A transferee of an interest in leased property is obligated to perform an express promise contained in the lease if:

(a)   the promise creates a burden that touches and concerns the transferred interest;

(b)   the promisor and promisee intend that the burden is to run with the transferred interest;

(c)   the transferee is not relieved of the obligation by the person entitled to enforce it; and

(d)   the transfer brings the transferee into privity of estate with the person entitled to enforce the promise.

(3) The transferee will not be liable for any breach of the promise which occurred before the transfer to him.

(4) If the transferee promises to perform an express promise contained in the lease, the transferee's liability rests on privity of contract and his liability after a subsequent transfer is governed by subsection (1)(a).

4.   **Problem.** In the light of the Restatement provision, consider the following: On January 1, 1994, L leased offices to T for three years ending December 31, 1996. The annual rental was $60,000. The lease did not restrict assignment or subletting. Thereafter, the following occurred:

(a)   On January 1, 1995, T signed over his lease to X. The agreement contained this clause: "X covenants to perform the terms and conditions [of the original lease]."

(b)   On July 1, 1995, X signed over the premises to Y for three months ending September 30, 1995. The subletting agreement contained this clause: "Y covenants to pay $5,000 monthly for the use of the premises."

(c)   On October 1, 1995, the AAA Corporation acquired X's leasehold interest at a judgment execution sale.

(d)   On January 1, 1996, the AAA Corporation signed over the lease

to Z. The assignment agreement contained this clause: "Z covenants to perform the terms and conditions [of the original
lease].

L, having received no rent for the years 1994, 1995, and 1996, finally
decides to sue. Discuss the potential liability of T, X, Y, Z, and the AAA Corp.

Note that a landlord can sue any tenant first, so long as he has a cause
of action based on privity of contract or privity of estate. See Robert Schoshinski, American Law of Landlord and Tenant §8.13, at 555-575 (1980 &
Supp. 1994). If Landlord in this problem sues a tenant other than Z, that
tenant (through a legal theory called subrogation) can step into Landlord's
shoes and sue any other tenant against whom Landlord himself had a cause
of action.

Suppose that L agreed, on January 1, 1996, to excuse X from any rent
he might owe. Would this in any way change L's rights against T? Cf. Gerber
v. Pecht, 15 N.J. 29, 104 A.2d 41 (1954) (after assignment, relationship between landlord and original tenant comparable to that of principal and
surety); Restatement (Second) of Property, Landlord and Tenant, §16.1,
Comment e (1977).

b.   Restraints on Alienation

1.   Case Law

KENDALL v. ERNEST PESTANA, INC.[100]

40 Cal. 3d 488, 709 P.2d 837, 220 Cal. Rptr. 818 (1985)

BROUSSARD, J. This case concerns the effect of a provision in commercial lease[1] that the lessee may not assign the lease or sublet the premises
without the lessor's prior written consent. The question we address is
whether, in the absence of a provision that such consent will not be unreasonably withheld, a lessor may unreasonably and arbitrarily withhold his or
her consent to an assignment.[2] This is a question of first impression in this
court.

---

100. Note that Pestana is referred to interchangeably throughout the opinion as both
a lessor and a lessee. This is because when Pestana acquired the Perlitchs' interest, he became
Bixler's landlord; yet, he remained the Perlitchs' tenant. — EDS.

1. We are presented only with a commercial lease and therefore do not address the
question whether residential leases are controlled by the principles articulated in this opinion.

2. Since the present case involves an assignment rather than a sublease, we will speak
primarily in terms of assignments. However, our holding applies equally to subleases. . . .

I

. . . The allegations of the complaint may be summarized as follows. The lease at issue is for 14,400 square feet of hangar space at the San Jose Municipal Airport. The City of San Jose, as owner of the property, leased it to Irving and Janice Perlitch, who in turn assigned their interest to respondent Ernest Pestana, Inc. Prior to assigning their interest to respondent, the Perlitches entered into a 25-year sublease with one Robert Bixler commencing on January 1, 1970. The sublease covered an original five-year term plus four 5-year options to renew. The rental rate was to be increased every 10 years in the same proportion as rents increased on the master lease from the City of San Jose. The premises were to be used by Bixler for the purpose of conducting an airplane maintenance business.

Bixler conducted such a business under the name "Flight Services" until, in 1981, he agreed to sell the business to appellants Jack Kendall, Grady O'Hara and Vicki O'Hara. The proposed sale included the business and the equipment, inventory and improvements on the property, together with the existing lease. The proposed assignees had a stronger financial statement and greater net worth than the current lessee, Bixler, and they were willing to be bound by the terms of the lease.

The lease provided that written consent of the lessor was required before the lessee could assign his interest, and that failure to obtain such consent rendered the lease voidable at the option of the lessor. Accordingly, Bixler requested consent from the Perlitches' successor-in-interest, respondent Ernest Pestana, Inc. Respondent refused to consent to the assignment and maintained that it had an absolute right arbitrarily to refuse any such request. The complaint recites that respondent demanded "increased rent and other more onerous terms" as a condition of consenting to Bixler's transfer of interest.

The proposed assignees brought suit for declaratory and injunctive relief and damages seeking, inter alia, a declaration "that the refusal of ERNEST PESTANA, INC. to consent to the assignment of the lease is unreasonable and is unlawful restraint on the freedom of alienation. . . ." The trial court sustained a demurrer to the complaint without leave to amend and this appeal followed.

II

The law generally favors free alienability of property, and California follows the common law rule that a leasehold interest is freely alienable. Contractual restrictions on the alienability of leasehold interest are, however, permitted. "Such restrictions are justified as reasonable protection of the interests of the lessor as to who shall possess and manage property in which he has a reversionary interest and from which he is deriving income."

(Schoshinksi, American Law of Landlord and Tenant (1980) §8:15, at
pp. 578-579. . . .)

The common law's hostility toward restraints on alienation has caused
such restraints on leasehold interests to be strictly construed against the
lessor. . . . This is particularly true where the restraint in question is a "forfeiture restraint," under which the lessor has the option to terminate the
lease if an assignment is made without his or her consent. . . .

Nevertheless, a majority of jurisdictions have long adhered to the rule
that where a lease contains an approval clause (a clause stating that the
lease cannot be assigned without the prior consent of the lessor), the lessor
may arbitrarily refuse to approve a proposed assignee no matter how suitable the assignee appears to be and no matter how unreasonable the lessor's objection. . . . The harsh consequences of this rule have often been
avoided through application of the doctrines of waiver and estoppel, under
which the lessor may be found to have waived (or be estopped from asserting) the right to refuse consent to assignment.

The traditional majority rule has come under steady attack in recent
years. A growing minority of jurisdictions now hold that where a lease provides for assignment only with the prior consent of the lessor, such consent
may be withheld *only where the lessor has a commercially reasonable objection to the
assignment,* even in the absence of a provision in the lease stating that consent to assignment will not be unreasonably withheld. (See Rest. 2d Property, §15.2(2) (1977); 21 A.L.R.4th 188 (1983).)

For the reasons discussed below, we conclude that the minority rule is
the preferable position. . . .

III

The impetus for change in the majority rule has come from two directions, reflecting the dual nature of a lease as a conveyance of a leasehold
interest and a contract. (See Medico-Dental etc. Co. v. Horton & Converse
(1942) 21 Cal. 2d 411, 418, 132 P.2d 457.) The policy against restraints on
alienation pertains to leases in their nature as *conveyances.* Numerous courts
and commentators have recognized that "[i]n recent times the necessity of
permitting reasonable alienation of commercial space has become paramount in our increasingly urban society." (Schweiso v. Williams [(1984)
150 Cal. App. 3d 883, 887, 198 Cal. Rptr. 238.)] . . .

Civil Code section 711 provides: "Conditions restraining alienation,
when repugnant to the interest created, are void." It is well settled that this
rule is not absolute in its application, but forbids only *unreasonable* restraints
on alienation . . . Reasonableness is determined by comparing the justification for a particular restraint on alienation with the quantum of restraint
that results from enforcement." (Wellenkamp v. Bank of America, *supra,* 21
Cal. 3d at p.949, 148 Cal. Rptr. 379, 582 P.2d 970.) In Cohen v. Ratinoff

[(1983) 147 Cal. App. 3d 321, 195 Cal. Rptr. 84], the court examined the reasonableness of the restraint created by an approval clause in lease:

> Because the lessor has an interest in the character of the proposed commercial assignee, we cannot say that an assignment provision requiring the lessor's consent to an assignment is inherently repugnant to the leasehold interest created. We do conclude, however, that *if such an assignment provision is implemented in such a manner that its underlying purpose is perverted by the arbitrary or unreasonable withholding of consent, an unreasonable restraint on alienation is established.* . . .

One commentator explains as follows:

> The common-law hostility to restraints on alienation had a large exception with respect to estates for years. A lessor could prohibit the lessee from transferring the estate for years to whatever extent he might desire. It was believed that the objectives served by allowing such restraints outweighed the social evils implicit in the restraints, in that they gave to the lessor a needed control over the person entrusted with the lessor's property and to whom he must look for the performance of the covenants contained in the lease. Whether this reasoning retains full validity can well be doubted. Relationships between lessor and lessee have tended to become more and more impersonal. Courts have considerably lessened the effectiveness of restraint clauses by strict construction and liberal applications of the doctrine of waiver. With the shortage of housing and, in many places, of commercial space as well, the allowance of lease clauses forbidding assignments and subleases is beginning to be curtailed by statutes. [2 Powell, *supra*, ¶246[1], at pp.372.97-372.98, fns. omitted.]

The Restatement Second of Property adopts the minority rule on the validity of approval clauses in leases: "A restraint on alienation without the consent of the landlord of tenant's interest in leased property is valid, *but the landlord's consent to an alienation by the tenant cannot be withheld unreasonably,* unless a freely negotiated provision in the lease gives the landlord an absolute right to withhold consent." (Rest. 2d Property, §15.2(2) (1977), italics added.) [14] A comment to the section explains:

> The landlord may have an understandable concern about certain personal qualities of a tenant, particularly his reputation for meeting his financial obligations. The preservation of the values that go into the personal selection of the tenant justifies upholding a provision in the lease that curtails the right of the tenant to put anyone else in his place by transferring his interest, but this justification does not go to the point of allowing the landlord arbitrarily and without reason to refuse to allow the tenant to transfer an interest in leased property. [Id., com. a.]

---

14. This case does not represent the question of the validity of a clause absolutely prohibiting assignment, or granting absolute discretion over assignment to the lessor. We note that under the Restatement rule such a provision would be valid if freely negotiated.

Under the Restatement rule, the lessor's interest in the character of his or her tenant is protected by the lessor's right to object to a proposed assignee on reasonable commercial grounds. (See id., reporter's note 7 at pp. 112-113.) The lessor's interests are also protected by the fact that the original lessee remains liable to the lessor as surety even if the lessor consents to the assignment and the assignee expressly assumes the obligations of the lease. . . .

The second impetus for change in the majority rule comes from the nature of a lease as a contract. As the Court of Appeal observed . . . "there has been an increased recognition of and emphasis on the duty of good faith and fair dealing inherent in every contract." (Id., 147 Cal. App. 3d at p. 329, 195 Cal. Rptr. 84.) . . . "[W]here a contract confers on one party a discretionary power affecting the rights of the other, a duty is imposed to exercise that discretion in good faith and in accordance with fair dealing." (Cal. P.2d 785. See also, Larwin-Southern California, Inc. v. J.G.B. Inv. Co. (1979) 101 Cal. App. 3d 626, 640, 162 Cal. Rptr. 52.) Here the lessor retains the discretionary power to approve or disapprove an assignee proposed by the other party to the contract; this discretionary power should therefore be exercised in accordance with commercially reasonable standards. "Where a lessee is entitled to sublet under common law, but has agreed to limit that right by first acquiring the consent of the landlord, we believe the lessee has a right to expect that consent will not be unreasonably withheld." (Fernandez v. Vasquez (Fla. App. 1981) 397 So. 2d 1171, 1174.)[1]

Under the minority rule, the determination whether a lessor's refusal to consent was reasonable is a question of fact. Some of the factors that the trier of fact may properly consider in applying the standards of good faith and commercial reasonableness are: financial responsibility of the proposed assignee; suitability of the use for the particular property; legality of the proposed use; need for alteration of the premises; and nature of the occupance, i.e., office, factory, clinic, etc.

Denying consent solely on the basis of personal taste, convenience or sensibility is not commercial reasonable. Nor is it reasonable to deny consent "in order that the landlord may charge a higher rent than originally contracted for." (Schweiso v. Williams, supra, 150 Cal. App. 3d at p.886, 198 Cal. Rptr. 238.) This is because the lessor's desire for a better bargain than contracted for has nothing to do with the permissible purposes of the restraint on alienation — to protect the lessor's interest in the preservation of the property and the performance of the lease covenants. " '[T]he clause is

---

1. Some commentators have drawn an analogy between this situation and the duties of good faith and reasonableness implied in all transactions under the Uniform Commercial Code. (U. Com. Code §§1-203, 2-103(b); see also U. Com. Code §1-102, com. 1 [permitting application of the U. Com. Code to matters not expressly within its scope].) See Comment, The Approval Clause in a Lease: Toward a Standard of Reasonableness 17 U.S.F.L. Rev. 681, 695 (1983); see also Levin, Withholding Consent to Assignment: The Changing Rights of the Commercial Landlord 30 DePaul L. Rev. 109, 136 (1980).

for the protection of the landlord *in its ownership and operation of a particular property* — not for its general economic protection.'"

In contrast to the policy reasons advanced in favor of the minority rule, the majority rule has traditionally been justified on three grounds. Respondent raises a fourth argument in its favor as well. None of these do we find compelling.

First, it is said that a lease is a conveyance of an interest in real property, and that the lessor, having exercised a personal choice in the selection of a tenant and provided that no substitute shall be acceptable without prior consent, is under no obligation to look to anyone but the lessee for the rent. This argument is based on traditional rules of conveyancing and on concepts of freedom of ownership and control over one's property.

A lessor's freedom at common law to look to no one but the lessee for the rent has, however, bene undermined by the adoption in California of a rule that lessors — like all other contracting parties — have a duty to mitigate damages upon the lessee's abandonment of the property by seeking a substitute lessee. (See Civ. Code, §1951.2.) Furthermore, the values that go into the personal selection of a lessee are preserved under the minority rule in the lessor's right to refuse consent to assignment on any commercially reasonable grounds. Such grounds include not only the obvious objections to an assignee's financial stability or proposed use of the premises, but a variety of other commercially reasonable objections as well. . . .

The second justification advanced in support of the majority rule is that an approval clause is an unambiguous reservation of absolute discretion in the lessor over assignments of the lease. The lessee could have bargained for the addition of a reasonableness clause to the lease (i.e., "consent to assignment will not be unreasonably withheld"). The lessee having failed to do so, the law should not rewrite the parties' contract for them. . . .

Numerous authorities have taken a different view of the meaning and effect of an approval clause in a lease. . . . "It would seem to be the better law that when a lease restricts a lessee's rights by requiring consent before these rights can be exercised, *it must have been in the contemplation of the parties that the lessor be required to give some reasons for withholding consent.*" . . . The same view was expressed by commentators in the 1950s. . . . Again in 1963, the court in Gamble v. New Orleans Housing Mart, Inc. (La. App. 1963) 154 So. 2d 625, stated: "Here the lessee is simply not permitted to sublet without the written consent of the lessor. This does not *prohibit* or *interdict* subleasing. To the contrary, it permits subleasing provided only that the lessee first obtain the written consent of the lessor. *It suggests or connotes that, when the lessee obtains a subtenant acceptable or satisfactory to the lessor, he may sublet.* . . . Otherwise the provision simply would prohibit subleasing." (Id., at p.627, final italics added.)

In light of the interpretations given to approval clauses in the cases cited above, and in light of the increasing number of jurisdictions that have adopted the minority rule in the last 15 years, the assertion that an approval clause "clearly and unambiguously" grants the lessor absolute discretion over assignments is untenable. It is not a rewriting of a contract, as respondent suggests, to recognize the obligations imposed by the duty of good faith and fair dealing, which duty is implied by law in every contract.

The third justification advanced in support of the majority rule is essentially based on the doctrine of stare decisis. It is argued that the courts should not depart from the common law majority rule because "many leases now in effect covering a substantial amount of real property and creating valuable property rights were carefully prepared by competent counsel in reliance upon the majority viewpoint." (Gruman v. Investors Diversified Services [(1956) 247 Minn. 502, 78 N.W.2d 377, 381.] . . .) As pointed out above, however, the majority viewpoint has been far from universally held and has never been adopted by this court. Moreover, the trend in favor of the minority rule should come as no surprise to observers of the changing state of real property law in the 20th century. The minority rule is part of an increasing recognition of the contractual nature of leases and the implications in terms of contractual duties that flow therefrom. We would be remiss in our duty if we declined to question a view held by the majority of jurisdictions simply because it is held by a majority. . . .

A final argument in favor of the majority rule is advanced by respondent and stated as follows: "Both tradition and sound public policy dictate that the lessor has a right, under circumstances such as these, to realize the increased value of his property." Respondent essentially argues that any increase in the market value of real property during the term of a lease properly belongs to the lessor, not the lessee. We reject this assertion. One California commentator has written:

> [W]hen the lessee executed the lease he acquired the contractual right for the exclusive use of the premises, and all of the benefits and detriment attendant to possession, for the term of the contract. He took the downside risk that he would be paying too much rent if there should be a depression in the rental market. . . . Why should he be deprived of the contractual benefits of the lease because of the fortuitous inflation in the marketplace[?] By reaping the benefits he does not deprive the landlord of anything to which the landlord was otherwise entitled. The landlord agreed to dispose of possession for the limited term and he could not reasonably anticipate any more than what was given to him by the terms of the lease. His reversionary estate will benefit from the increased value from the inflation in any event, at least upon expiration of the lease. [Miller & Starr, Current Law of Cal. Real Estate (1977) 1984 Supp., §27:92 at p. 321.]

Respondent here is trying to get *more* than it bargained for in the lease. A lessor is free to build periodic rent increases into a lease, as the lessor did here. . . . Any increased value of the property beyond this "belongs" to the lessor only in the sense, as explained above, that the lessor's reversionary estate will benefit from it upon the expiration of the lease. We must therefore reject respondent's argument in this regard.[17] . . .

IV

In conclusion, both the policy against restraints on alienation and the implied contractual duty of good faith and fair dealing militate in favor of adoption of the rule that where a commercial lease provides for assignment only with prior consent of the lessor, such consent may be withheld only where the lessor has a commercially reasonable objection to the assignee or the proposed use. Under this rule, appellants have stated a cause of action against respondent Ernest Pestana, Inc.

The order sustaining the demurrer to the complaint, which we have deemed to incorporate a judgment of dismissal, is reversed.

MALCOLM M. LUCAS, J., dissenting. I respectfully dissent. In my view we should follow the weight of authority which, as acknowledged by the majority herein, allows the commercial lessor to withhold his consent to an assignment or sublease arbitrarily or without reasonable cause. The majority's contrary ruling, requiring a "commercially reasonable objection" to the assignment, can only result in a proliferation of unnecessary litigation.

The correct analysis is contained in the opinion of Justice Carl Anderson for the Court of Appeal in this case. I adopt the following portion of his opinion as my dissent: . . . .

> The plain language of the lease provides that the lessee shall not assign the lease "without written consent of Lessor first had and obtained. . . . Any such assignment or subletting without this consent shall be void, and shall, at the option of Lessor, terminate this lease." The lease does not require that "the lessor may refuse consent only where he has a good faith reasonable objection to the assignment." Neither have the parties so contracted, nor has the Legislature so required. Absent such legislative direction, the parties should be free to contract as they see fit.

Appellant urges this court to rewrite the contract by adding a limitation on the lessor's withholding of consent — "that such consent may not be unreasonably withheld." He urges that such must be implied in the term "without written consent of lessor first had and obtained"; and he places the burden on the lessor to add language to negate that, if such be his

---

17. Amicus Pillsbury, Madison & Sutro request that we make clear that, "whatever principle governs in the absence of express lease provisions, nothing bars the parties to commercial lease transactions from making their own arrangements respecting the allocation of appreciated rentals if there is a transfer of the leasehold." This principle we affirm; we merely hold that the clause in the instant lease established no such arrangement.

intent — language such as "such consent may be arbitrarily, capriciously and/or unreasonably withheld."

However, it is obvious that the attorney for the lessor agreeing to such a term was entitled to rely upon the state of the law then existing in California. And at such time (Dec. 12, 1969), it is clear that California followed the "weight of authority" in these United States and allowed such consent to be arbitrarily or unreasonably withheld absent a provision to the contrary. . . .

To rewrite this contract (as appellant would have us do) for the benefit of one who was not an original party thereto, and to the detriment of one who stands in privity with one who was, and to hold that there is a triable issue of fact concerning whether respondents unreasonably withheld their consent when they had already contracted for that right, creates only mischief by breeding further uncertainty in the interpretation of otherwise unambiguously written contracts. To so hold only encourages needless future litigation.

We respectfully suggest that if California is to adopt the minority rule and reject the majority rule which recognizes the current proviso as valid, unambiguous and enforceable, that it do so by clear affirmative legislative action. To so defer to the legislative branch, protects not only this contract but those tens of thousands of landlords, tenants and lawyers who have relied on our unbroken line of judicial precedent. . . .

NOTES AND QUESTIONS

1. *Carma Developers.* The California Supreme Court distinguished Kendall v. Pestana in 1992 when it decided Carma Developers, Inc. v. Marathon Development California, Inc., 826 P.2d 710 (Cal. 1992). The court held that a lessor might terminate a commercial lease and recapture the leasehold, rather than consent to a proposed sublease, where parties had *expressly* contracted to restrict alienation of the lessee's interest. In so ruling, the court noted that neither *Kendall* nor its precedents concerned a situation in which the lease in question contained such an express provision. Furthermore, the court held that enforcement of such a lease provision was authorized by new California legislation specifically protecting the rights of parties to contract in restriction of alienation. See Cal. Civ. Code §§1995.010 et seq.

2. **Contract law.** What principles of contract law does the *Kendall* majority call upon to support its decision?

3. **Restatement of Property.** Restatement (Second) of Property, Landlord and Tenant, §15.2(2)(1977), would also qualify the landlord's absolute power over alienation. It reads:

A restraint on alienation without the consent of the landlord of the tenant's interest in the leased property is valid, but the landlord's consent to an alien-

ation by the tenant cannot be withheld unreasonably, unless a freely negotiated provision in the lease gives the landlord an absolute right to withhold
consent.

The Reporter acknowledges that the rule is contrary to the established
common-law. Id., Reporter's Note 7.

The Restatement fails to amplify "freely negotiated provision," an exception that would give landlord the absolute right to withhold consent.
Presumably, this would not cover the typical situation in which an apartment tenant signs a boiler-plate lease. Suppose, however, that the prospective apartment tenant asks that the "no assignment" clause be deleted or
modified, and the landlord flatly refuses. Has there been free negotiation?

3. **Trend toward reasonableness requirement.** Courts appear to be
tending towards implying a reasonableness requirement in landlord consent clauses. See Julian v. Christopher, 575 A.2d 735, 736, n.1 (Md. 1990)
(roughly 13 states have adopted minority rule, most of them in the 1980s).

4. **What is "reasonable?"** Assume that either case law or the lease
itself requires landlord not unreasonably to withhold his consent to a proposed assignment. In each of the following instances, would you think a
landlord unreasonable should she withhold consent?

(a)   The landlord wishes to sell the building and believes that a va-
      cant unit (should the tenant move out) betters his prospects of
      sale. Compare Wohl v. Yelen, 22 Ill. App. 2d 455, 161 N.E.2d
      339 (1959).

(b)   The unit has become more valuable, and the landlord wishes to
      relet the unit himself at a higher rental. Compare Equity Fund-
      ing Corp. v. Carol Management Corp., 66 Misc. 2d 1020, 322
      N.Y.S.2d 965 (Sup. Ct. 1972).

(c)   There are several vacancies in the building. The landlord would
      rather have the proposed assignee move into one of the vacant
      units.

(d)   The proposed assignee is in the same business as another ten-
      ant. Although he has no legal obligation to do so, the landlord
      wants to protect his present tenant against competition.

(e)   The landlord wishes the apartment for his personal use. Com-
      pare Matter of Cedarhurst Park Apartments, Inc. v. Milgrim, 55
      Misc. 2d 118, 284 N.Y.S.2d 330 (Dist. Ct. 1967).

(f)   The proposed assignee is a law student. The landlord dislikes
      law student tenants because they insist on the letter of their
      rights — and then some. Compare Kramarsky v. Stahl Manage-
      ment, 92 Misc. 2d 1030, 42 N.Y.S.2d 943 (Sup. Ct. 1977).

(g)   The landlord, a religious organization, objects to the activity of
      the proposed assignee, a family planning organization. Compare

American Books Co. v. Yeshiva University Development Foundation, Inc., 59 Misc. 2d 31, 297 N.Y.S.2d 156 (Sup. Ct. 1969).

6. **Strict construction.** Despite their validity, clauses limiting the tenant's power to alienate are construed with great strictness. Thus, a bar against assignment will not usually prevent a subletting or a mortgaging of the term. See 2 Powell, Real Property ¶246[1] (Rohan ed. 1973).

7. **Rule in Dumpor's Case.** A curiosity of the common law is the Rule in Dumpor's Case, 4 Coke 119b, 76 Eng. Rep. 1110 (K.B. 1603). Under the rule, once a landlord approves an assignment of the lease, he relinquishes his power to restrict future assignments. The rule does not apply to approved sublettings. This is one more instance of the courts' attempt to weaken, yet not repudiate, a questionable doctrine — the power of a landlord to restrain alienation. Burby, Real Property 200-201 (2d ed. 1953). The rule may yet linger in a few states. See Powell, Real Property 163 n. 16 (Powell & Rohan abr. ed. 1968).

2.   Statutes

How does the Virginia statute change the common law?

Va. Code Ann. §55-248.7 (Michie 1994)

Terms and conditions of rental agreement; copy for tenant.

A. A landlord and tenant may include in a rental agreement, terms and conditions not prohibited by this chapter or other rule of law, including rent, charges for late payment of rent, term of the agreement and other provisions governing the rights and obligations of the parties.

B. In the absence of agreement, the tenant shall pay as rent the fair rental value for the use and occupancy of the dwelling unit.

C. Rent shall be payable without demand or notice at the time and place agreed upon by the parties. Unless otherwise agreed, rent is payable at the place designated by the landlord and periodic rent is payable at the beginning of any term of one month or less and otherwise in equal installments at the beginning of each month.

D. Unless the rental agreement fixes a definite term, the tenancy shall be week to week in case of a roomer who pays weekly rent, and in all other cases month to month.

E. If the agreement contains any provision whereby the landlord may approve or disapprove a sublessee or assignee of the tenant, the landlord shall within ten business days of receipt by him of the written application of the prospective sublessee or assignee on a form to be provided by the landlord, approve or disapprove the sublessee or assignee. Failure of the landlord to act within ten business days shall be deemed evidence of his approval.

F. A copy of any written rental agreement signed by both the tenant and the landlord shall be provided to the tenant within one month of the effective date of the written rental agreement. The failure of the landlord to deliver such a rental agreement shall not affect the validity of the agreement.

3. Leases

Where the lease fails to restrain alienation, the tenant may freely assign or mortgage the lease and sublet the premises. Exceptions to this general rule of free alienability involve a tenancy at will and the lease that "requires significant personal services from either party, and a transfer of the party's interest would substantially impair the other party's chances of obtaining those services." Restatement (Second) of Property, Landlord and Tenant, §15.1 (1977).

Examine the leases in Figures 3-14 and 3-15. Which is the more pro-landlord?

No Assignment or Subletting By Tenant	10. Except as otherwise provided in Sections 226-b and 236 of the New York Real Property Law (which permit subleases or the termination of leases in certain circumstances), the Tenant shall neither assign this lease nor sublease the Apartment or any part thereof without the Landlord's prior consent. If this lease is assigned by the Tenant, or if the Apartment is subleased or occupied by anyone other than the Tenant, the Landlord may collect rent from the assignee, subtenant or occupant and apply the net amount collected to the rent and additional rent payable under the terms of this lease, and no such collection shall be deemed a waiver of these restrictions against assignment and subleasing or the acceptance of such assignee, subtenant or occupant as the tenant under this lease, or a release of the Tenant from further performance of the covenants contained in this lease.
Landlord May Accept Rent from Others	
Successors and Assigns	18. The provisions of this lease shall bind and endure to the benefit of the Landlord and the Tenant, and their respective successors, legal representatives and assigns. From and after each conveyance and transfer of Landlord's interest in the Building and the land on which the Building stands, the Landlord shall be released from and the Landlord's grantee shall become liable for, all unfulfilled obligations of the Landlord under this lease.
Landlord Released on Assignment	

FIGURE 3-14
Lease No. 1

Successor and Assigns	f. The provision of this Lease shall run in favor of and be for the benefit of Landlord and Tenant and anybody who succeeds to their respective interests in this Lease.
No Assignment or Subletting	m. Tenant shall not assign this Lease or enter into a sublease unless it is allowed by a law of the State of New York. If Tenant makes an assignment or sublease, with or without the consent of Landlord, Landlord may collect rent from the new tenant and deduct it from any money Tenant owes under this Lease. If Landlord collects rent from the new tenant it does not mean that Landlord consents to the assignment or sublease. Tenant shall remain liable under this Lease after a sublease or assignment, unless released by Landlord or unless otherwise provided by law.

FIGURE 3-15
Lease No. 2

§3.13 Tenant Abandonment of the Leasehold Premises

Suppose that tenant wants to break his lease before the term ends. He may find that landlord is happy to let him do so. The premises have become more valuable; the landlord wants to use the premises himself; the landlord can readily relet the premises to a "better" tenant. When landlord and tenant wish the same end, landlord will usually agree to release tenant from his unmatured duties under the lease. We say then that tenant has surrendered his unexpired term and that landlord has accepted the surrender. Upon surrender, landlord's recovery is limited to the rent accrued at the time of surrender. An express surrender[101] is subject to the Statute of Frauds. Whether the statute applies depends on the term remaining at the time of surrender. See, e.g., N.Y. Gen. Oblig. Law §5-703 (McKinney 1994) (writing required if unexpired term more than one year).

Suppose, however, that landlord is unwilling to release tenant, but that tenant abandons the premises anyway. What then are the options left to landlord?

---

101. Shortly you will see surrender by operation of law, §3.13.b *infra*.

a.   Mitigation

1.   Case Law

SOMMER v. KRIDEL

74 N.J. 446, 378 A.2d 767 (1977)

PASHMAN, J. We granted certification in these cases to consider whether a landlord seeking damages from a defaulting tenant is under a duty to mitigate damages by making reasonable efforts to re-let an apartment wrongfully vacated by the tenant. Separate parts of the Appellate Division held that, in accordance with their respective leases, the landlords in both cases could recover rents due under the leases regardless of whether they had attempted to re-let the vacated apartments. Although they were of different minds as to the fairness of this result, both parts agreed that it was dictated by Joyce v. Bauman, 113 N.J.L. 438, 174 A. 693 (E. & A. 1934), a decision by the former Court of Errors and Appeals. We now reverse and hold that a landlord does have an obligation to make a reasonable effort to mitigate damages in such a situation. We therefore overrule Joyce v. Bauman to the extent that it is inconsistent with our decision today.

I

A.   SOMMER V. KRIDEL

This case was tried on stipulated facts. On March 10, 1972 the defendant, James Kridel, entered into a lease with the plaintiff, Abraham Sommer, owner of the "Pierre Apartments" in Hackensack, to rent apartment 6-L in that building.[1] The term of the lease was from May 1, 1972 until April 30, 1974, with a rent concession for the first six weeks, so that the first month's rent was not due until June 15, 1972.

One week after signing the agreement, Kridel paid Sommer $690. Half of that sum was used to satisfy the first month's rent. The remainder was paid under the lease provision requiring a security deposit of $345. Although defendant had expected to begin occupancy around May 1, his plans were changed. He wrote to Sommer on May 19, 1972, explaining

> .I was to be married on June 3, 1972. Unhappily the engagement was broken and the wedding plans cancelled. Both parents were to assume re-

---

1. Among other provisions, the lease prohibited the tenant from assigning or transferring the lease without the consent of the landlord. If the tenant defaulted, the lease gave the landlord the option of re-entering or re-letting, but stipulated that failure to re-let or to recover the full rental would not discharge the tenant's liability for rent.

sponsibility for the rent after our marriage. I was discharged from the U.S. Army in October 1971 and am now a student. I have no funds of my own, and am supported by my stepfather.

In view of the above, I cannot take possession of the apartment and am surrendering all rights to it. Never having received a key, I cannot return same to you.

I beg your understanding and compassion in releasing me from the lease, and will of course, in consideration thereof, forfeit the 2 month's rent already paid.

Please notify me at your earliest convenience.

Plaintiff did not answer the letter.

Subsequently, a third party went to the apartment house and inquired about renting apartment 6-L. Although the parties agreed that she was ready, willing and able to rent the apartment, the person in charge told her that the apartment was not being shown since it was already rented to Kridel. In fact, the landlord did not re-enter the apartment or exhibit it to anyone until August 1, 1973. At that time it was rented to a new tenant for a term beginning on September 1, 1973. The new rental was for $345 per month with a six week concession similar to that granted Kridel.

Prior to re-letting the new premises, plaintiff sued Kridel in August 1972, demanding $7,590, the total amount due for the full two-year term of the lease. Following a mistrial, plaintiff filed an amended complaint asking for $5,865, the amount due between May 1, 1972 and September 1, 1973. The amended complaint included no reduction in the claim to reflect the six week concession provided for in the lease or the $690 payment made to plaintiff after signing the agreement. Defendant filed an amended answer to the complaint, alleging that plaintiff breached the contract, failed to mitigate damages and accepted defendant's surrender of the premises. He also counterclaimed to demand repayment of the $345 paid as a security deposit.

The trial judge ruled in favor of defendant. Despite his conclusion that the lease had been drawn to reflect "the 'settled law' of this state," he found that "justice and fair dealing" imposed upon the landlord the duty to attempt to re-let the premises and thereby mitigate damages. He also held that plaintiff's failure to make any response to defendant's unequivocal offer of surrender was tantamount to an acceptance, thereby terminating the tenancy and any obligation to pay rent. As a result, he dismissed both the complaint and the counterclaim. The Appellate Division reversed in a per curiam opinion, 153 N.J. Super. 1 (1976), and we granted certification. 69 N.J. 395, 354 A.2d 323 (1976).

B.   RIVERVIEW REALTY CO. V. PEROSIO

This controversy arose in a similar manner. On December 27, 1972, Carlos Perosio entered into a written lease with plaintiff Riverview Realty

Co. The agreement covered the rental of apartment 5-G in a building owned by the realty company at 2175 Hudson Terrace in Fort Lee. As in the companion case, the lease prohibited the tenant from subletting or assigning the apartment without the consent of the landlord. It was to run for a two-year term, from February 1, 1973 until January 31, 1975, and provided for a monthly rental of $450. The defendant took possession of the apartment and occupied it until February 1974. At that time he vacated the premises, after having paid the rent through January 31, 1974.

The landlord filed a complaint on October 31, 1974, demanding $4,500 in payment for the monthly rental from February 1, 1974 through October 31, 1974. Defendant answered the complaint by alleging that there had been a valid surrender of the premises and that plaintiff failed to mitigate damages. The trial court granted the landlord's motion for summary judgment against the defendant, fixing the damages at $4,050 plus $182.25 interest.[2]

The Appellate Division affirmed the trial court, holding that it was bound by prior precedents, including Joyce v. Bauman, *supra.* 138 N.J. Super. 270, 350 A.2d 517 (App. Div. 1976). Nevertheless, it freely criticized the rule which it found itself obliged to follow:

> There appears to be no reason in equity or justice to perpetuate such an unrealistic and uneconomic rule of law which encourages an owner to let valuable rented space lie fallow because he is assured of full recovery from a defaulting tenant. Since courts in New Jersey and elsewhere have abandoned ancient real property concepts and applied ordinary contract principles in other conflicts between landlord and tenant there is no sound reason for continuation of a special real property rule to the issue of mitigation. . . . [138 N.J. Super. at 273-74, 350 A.2d at 519; citations omitted]

We granted certification. 70 N.J. 145, 358 A.2d 191 (1976).

II

As the lower courts in both appeals found, the weight of authority in this State supports the rule that a landlord is under no duty to mitigate damages caused by a defaulting tenant. This rule has been followed in a majority of states, Annot. 21 A.L.R.3d 534, §2[a] at 541 (1968), and has been tentatively adopted in the American Law Institute's Restatement of Property. Restatement (Second) of Property, §11.1(3) (Tent. Draft No. 3, 1975).

Nevertheless, while there is still a split of authority over this question,

---

2. The trial court noted that damages had been erroneously calculated in the complaint to reflect ten months rent. As to the interest awarded to plaintiff, the parties have not raised this issue before this Court. Since we hold that the landlord had a duty to attempt to mitigate damages, we need not reach this question.

the trend among recent cases appears to be in favor of a mitigation requirement. The majority rule is based on principles of property law which equate
a lease with a transfer of a property interest in the owner's estate. Under this
rationale the lease conveys to a tenant an interest in the property which
forecloses any control by the landlord; thus, it would be anomalous to require the landlord to concern himself with the tenant's abandonment of his
own property. Wright v. Baumann, 239 Or. 410, 398 P.2d 119, 120-21, 21
A.L.R.3d 527 (1965).

For instance, in Muller v. Beck, 94 N.J.L. 311, 110 A. 831 (1920), where
essentially the same issue was posed, the court clearly treated the lease as
governed by property, as opposed to contract, precepts.[3] The court there
observed that the "tenant had an estate for years, but it was an estate qualified by this right of the landlord to prevent its transfer," 94 N.J.L. at 313,
110 A. at 832, and that "the tenant has an estate with which the landlord
may not interfere." Id. at 314, 110 A. at 832. . . .

Yet the distinction between a lease for ordinary residential purposes
and an ordinary contract can no longer be considered viable. As Professor
Powell observed, evolving "social factors have exerted increasing influence
on the law of estates for years." 2 Powell on Real Property (1977 ed.),
§221[1] at 180-81. The result has been that

> [t]he complexities of city life, and the proliferated problems of modern soci-
> ety in general, have created new problems for lessors and lessees and these
> have been commonly handled by specific clauses in leases. This growth in the
> number and detail of specific lease covenants has reintroduced into the law of
> estates for years a predominantly contractual ingredient. [Id. at 181.]

Thus in 6 Williston on Contracts (3 ed. 1962), §890A at 592, it is stated:
There is a clearly discernible tendency on the part of courts to cast aside
technicalities in the interpretation of leases and to concentrate their attention, as in the case of other contracts, on the intention of the parties. . . .

Application of the contract rule requiring mitigation of damages to a
residential lease may be justified as a matter of basic fairness.[4] Professor
McCormick first commented upon the inequity under the majority rule
when he predicted in 1925 that eventually

---

3. It is well settled that a party claiming damages for a breach of contract has a duty to
mitigate his loss. See Frank Stamato & Co. v. Borough of Lodi, 4 N.J. 14, 71 A.2d 336 (1950);
Sandler v. Lawn-A-Mat Chem. & Equip. Corp., 141 N.J. Super. 437, 455, 358 A.2d 805 (App.
Div. 1976); Wolf v. Marlton Corp., 57 N.J. Super. 278, 154 A.2d 625 (App. Div. 1956); 5 Corbin
on Contracts (1964 ed.), §1039 at 241 et seq.; McCormick, Damages, §33 at 127 (1935). See
also N.J.S.A. 12A:2-708.

4. We see no distinction between the leases involved in the instant appeals and those
which might arise in other types of residential housing. However, we reserve for another day
the question of whether a landlord must mitigate damages in a commercial setting. Cf. Kruvant
v. Sunrise Market, Inc., 58 N.J. 452, 456, 279 A.2d 104 (1971), modified on other grounds, 59
N.J. 330, 282 A.2d 746 (1971).

> the logic, inescapable according to the standards of a "jurisprudence of conceptions" which permits the landlord to stand idly by the vacant, abandoned premises and treat them as the property of the tenant to recover full rent, [will] yield to the more realistic notions of social advantage which in other fields of the law have forbidden recovery for damages which the plaintiff by reasonable efforts could have avoided. [McCormick, "The Rights of the Landlord Upon Abandonment of the Premises by the Tenant," 23 Mich. L. Rev. 211, 221-22 (1925)]

Various courts have adopted this position.

The pre-existing rule cannot be predicated upon the possibility that a landlord may lose the opportunity to rent another empty apartment because he must first rent the apartment vacated by the defaulting tenant. Even where the breach occurs in a multi-dwelling building, each apartment may have unique qualities which make it attractive to certain individuals. Significantly, in Sommer v. Kridel, there was a specific request to rent the apartment vacated by the defendant; there is no reason to believe that absent this vacancy the landlord could have succeeded in renting a different apartment to this individual.

We therefore hold that antiquated real property concepts which served as the basis for the pre-existing rule, shall no longer be controlling where there is a claim for damages under a residential lease. Such claims must be governed by more modern notions of fairness and equity. A landlord has a duty to mitigate damages where he seeks to recover rents due from a defaulting tenant.

If the landlord has other vacant apartments besides the one which the tenant has abandoned, the landlord's duty to mitigate consists of making reasonable efforts to re-let the apartment. In such cases he must treat the apartment in question as if it was one of his vacant stock.

As part of his cause of action, the landlord shall be required to carry the burden of proving that he used reasonable diligence in attempting to re-let the premises. We note that there has been a divergence of opinion concerning the allocation of the burden of proof on this issue. See Annot., 21 A.L.R.3d 534, §12 at 577 (1968). While generally in contract actions the breaching party has the burden or proving that damages are capable of mitigation, see Sandler v. Lawn-A-Mat Chem. & Equip. Corp., 141 N.J. Super. 437, 455, 358 A.2d 805 (App. Div. 1976); McCormick, Damages, §33 at 130 (1935), here the landlord will be in a better position to demonstrate whether he exercised reasonable diligence in attempting to re-let the premises. Cf. Kulm v. Coast to Coast Stores Central Org., 248 Or. 436, 432 P.2d 1006 (1967) (burden on lessor in contract to renew a lease).

III

The Sommer v. Kridel case presents a classic example of the unfairness which occurs when a landlord has no responsibility to minimize damages.

Sommer waited 15 months and allowed $4658.50 in damages to accrue before attempting to re-let the apartment. Despite the availability of a tenant who was ready, willing and able to rent the apartment, the landlord needlessly increased the damages by turning her away. While a tenant will not necessarily be excused from his obligations under a lease simply by finding another person who is willing to rent the vacated premises, see, e.g., Reget v. Dempsey-Tegler & Co., 70 Ill. App. 2d 32, 216 N.E.2d 500 (Ill. App. 1966) (new tenant insisted on leasing the premises under different terms); Edmands v. Rust & Richardson Drug Co., 191 Mass. 123, 77 N.E. 713 (1906) (landlord need not accept insolvent tenant), here there has been no showing that the new tenant would not have been suitable. We therefore find that plaintiff could have avoided the damages which eventually accrued, and that the defendant was relieved of his duty to continue paying rent. Ordinarily we would require the tenant to bear the cost of any reasonable expenses incurred by a landlord in attempting to re-let the premises, see Ross v. Smigelski, *supra,* 166 N.W.2d at 248-49; 22 Am. Jur. 2d, Damages, §169 at 238, but no such expenses were incurred in this case.[5]

In Riverview Realty Co. v. Perosio, no factual determination was made regarding the landlord's efforts to mitigate damages, and defendant contends that plaintiff never answered his interrogatories. Consequently, the judgment is reversed and the case remanded for a new trial. Upon remand and after discovery has been completed, R. 4:17 et seq., the trial court shall determine whether plaintiff attempted to mitigate damages with reasonable diligence, see Wilson v. Ruhl, *supra,* 356 A.2d at 546, and if so, the extent of damages remaining and assessable to the tenant. As we have held above, the burden of proving that reasonable diligence was used to re-let the premises shall be upon the plaintiff. See Annot., *supra,* §11 at 575.

In assessing whether the landlord has satisfactorily carried his burden, the trial court shall consider, among other factors, whether the landlord, either personally or through an agency, offered or showed the apartment to any prospective tenants, or advertised it in local newspapers. Additionally, the tenant may attempt to rebut such evidence by showing that he proffered suitable tenants who were rejected. However, there is no standard formula for measuring whether the landlord has utilized satisfactory efforts in attempting to mitigate damages, and each case must be judged upon its own facts. Compare Hershorin v. La Vista, Inc., 110 Ga. App. 435, 138 S.E.2d 703 (App. 1964) ("reasonable effort" of landlord by showing the apartment to all prospective tenants); Carpenter v. Wisniewski, 139 Ind. App. 325, 215 N.E.2d 882 (App. 1966) (duty satisfied where landlord advertised the premises through a newspaper, placed a sign in the window, and

---

5. As to defendant's counterclaim for $345, representing the amount deposited with the landlord as a security deposit, we note that this issue has not been briefed or argued before this Court, and apparently has been abandoned. Because we hold that plaintiff breached his duty to attempt to mitigate damages, we do not address defendant's argument that the landlord accepted a surrender of the premises.

employed a realtor); Re Garment Center Capitol, Inc., 93 F.2d 667, 115 A.L.R. 202 (2 Cir. 1938) (landlord's duty not breached where higher rental was asked since it was known that this was merely a basis for negotiations); Foggia v. Dix, 265 Or. 315, 509 P.2d 412, 414 (1973) (in mitigating damages, landlord need not accept less than fair market value or "substantially alter his obligations as established in the pre-existing lease"); with Anderson v. Andy Darling Pontiac, Inc., 257 Wis. 371, 43 N.W.2d 362 (1950) (reasonable diligence not established where newspaper advertisement placed in one issue of local paper by a broker); Scheinfeld v. Muntz T. V., Inc., 67 Ill. App. 2d 8, 214 N.E.2d 506 (Ill. App. 1966) (duty breached where landlord refused to accept suitable subtenant); Consolidated Sun Ray, Inc. v. Oppenstein, 335 F.2d 801, 811 (8 Cir. 1964) (dictum) (demand for rent which is "far greater than the provisions of the lease called for" negates landlord's assertion that he acted in good faith in seeking a new tenant).

IV

The judgment in Sommer v. Kridel is reversed. In Riverview Realty Co. v. Perosio, the judgment is reversed and the case is remanded to the trial court for proceedings in accordance with this opinion.

NOTES AND QUESTIONS

1. **The time-honored view.** Gruman v. Investors Diversified Services, Inc., 247 Minn. 502, 78 N.W.2d 377 (1956), typified the prevailing view of mitigation in the landlord and tenant context when the New Jersey Supreme Court decided Sommer v. Kridel. In the *Gruman* case, defendant had rented commercial premises for a 7-year term. The lease barred any assignment or subletting without the landlord's consent. With 14 months remaining on the term, defendant vacated the premises, but tendered for landlord's consent a subtenant, the United States postmaster general, who would use the space for a regional office. Although landlord conceded the government's suitability as a subtenant, he refused his consent. Defendant vacated the premises and landlord brought suit for the full rentals due under the unexpired term of the lease.

In holding for the landlord, the court wrote:

> In foreign jurisdictions, where the question has been presented, a majority of the courts have held that in a lease such as this the lessor does not have the duty of mitigating damages; may arbitrarily refuse to accept a subtenant suitable and otherwise responsible; and may recover from the lessee the full rentals due under the lease as and when they become due. [Citations from 22 jurisdictions omitted.]

The reasons expressed in support of this rule are that, since the lessor has exercised a personal choice in the selection of a tenant for a definite term and has expressly provided that no substitute shall be acceptable without his written consent, no obligation rests upon him to look to anyone but the lessee for his rent, Stern v. Thayer, 56 Minn. 93, 57 N.W. 329; White v. Huber Drug Co., 190 Mich. 212, 157 N.W. 60; that a lease is a conveyance of an interest in real property and, when a lessor has delivered the premises to his lessee, the latter is bound to him by privity of estate as well as by privity of contract, Davidson v. Minnesota Loan & Trust Co., 158 Minn. 411, 197 N.W. 833, 32 A.L.R. 1418; cf. W. C. Hines Co. v. Angell, 188 Minn. 387, 247 N.W. 387; that a lessor's right to reenter the premises upon lessee's default or abandonment thereof is at the lessor's option and not the lessee's, Kulawitz v. Pacific Woodenware & Paper Co., 25 Cal.(2d) 664, 155 P.(2d) 24; Rau v. Baker, 118 Ill. App. 150; and that a lessee's unilateral action in abandoning leased premises, *unless accepted by his lessor*, does not terminate the lease or forfeit the estate conveyed thereby, no the lessee's right to use and possess the leased premises and, by the same token, his obligation to pay the rent due therefor. Haycock v. Johnston, 81 Minn. 49, 83 N.W. 494, 1118; id. 97 Minn. 289, 106 N.W. 304. . . .

A number of writers have advanced the theory that a more modern and just viewpoint should be applied in situations such as the present; that the rule applicable in ordinary breach of contract cases, requiring efforts to mitigate damages after breach, should be applied to leases; and in furtherance of this view that a lessor should be obligated to accept a suitable subtenant offered by the lessee. See 2 Powell, Real Property, par. 229, note 79; McCormick, Rights of Landlord upon Abandonment, 23 Mich. L. Rev. 211, 222; 44 Harv. L. Rev. 993; 34 Harv. L. Rev. 217. Defendant also cites decisions from the Supreme Courts of Iowa, Kansas and Wisconsin as giving support to this viewpoint.

We feel that we must adhere to the majority rule. In reaching this conclusion we are motivated by the fact that the language of the assignment provision is clear and unambiguous and that many leases now in effect covering a substantial amount of real property and creating valuable property rights were carefully prepared by competent counsel in reliance upon the majority viewpoint. It would seem clear from the language adopted in all such cases that the lessors therein are entitled to place full reliance upon the responsibility of their respective lessees for the rentals they have contracted to pay. Should a lessee desire the right to assign or sublet to a suitable tenant, a clause might readily be inserted in the lease similar to those now included in many leases to the effect that the lessor's written consent to the assignment or subletting of the leased premises should not be unreasonably withheld. There being no clause in the present lease to such effect, we are compelled to give its terms their full force and effect as have the courts of a majority of other jurisdictions.

2. **The time-honored view revisited 40 years later.** Not all state courts are as path-breaking as the New Jersey Supreme Court, and certainly not the New York Court of Appeals. Thus, in Holy Properties Limited, L.P. v. Kenneth Cole Prod., Inc., 87 N.Y.2d 130, 661 N.E.2d 694 (1995), the New York court clung to the common-law view that a landlord had no duty to

mitigate damages after tenant's abandonment. It explained its decision, flatly rejecting contrary law from other states, as follows:

> The law imposes upon a party subjected to injury from breach of contract, the duty of making reasonable exertions to minimize the injury. . . . Leases are not subject to this general rule, however, for, unlike executory contracts, leases have been historically recognized as a present transfer of an estate in real property. . . . Defendant urges us to reject this settled law and adopt the contract rationale recognized by some courts in this State and elsewhere. We decline to do so. Parties who engage in transactions based on prevailing law must be able to rely on the stability of such precedents. In business transactions, particularly, the certainty of settled rules is often more important than whether the established rule is better than another or even whether it is the "correct" rule. . . . This is perhaps true in real property more than any other area of the law, where established precedents are not lightly to be set aside. 87 N.Y.2d at 133, 134.

3.   **Designing a law reform case.** What makes the *Sommer* case an attractive law reform vehicle? What techniques does the court use to seek persuasiveness? What images of the landlord and the tenant does the case project? Note in particular the court's use of narrative: Why does the appellate opinion quote Kridel's letter in full? (Is the appellate court's role to sift through evidence?)

4.   **Contract law.** When the court turns to contract law, does it turn to the core contract principles of enforcing the intentions of free-standing individuals with rights-making choices? We don't usually think of the contract law mitigation requirement as a normative rule, but in fact the non-breaching party's duty to mitigate is one of the normative, background rules set up within contract law. What changes does the court make to the contract rule concerning mitigation? Why?

5.   **Restatement of Property.** The Restatement of Property (Second), Landlord and Tenant, §12.1 (1977) dug in its heels in support of the non-mitigation view. The Restatement, at Comment i, explained:

> If the tenant has abandoned the leased property and the landlord stands by and does nothing, the lease is not terminated. A tenant who abandons leased property is not entitled to insist on action by the landlord to mitigate the damages, absent an agreement otherwise. Abandonment of property is an invitation to vandalism, and the law should not encourage such conduct by putting a duty of mitigation of damages on the landlord.

Convincing?

6.   **Acceleration of all unpaid rent.** Suppose that the lease in a non-mitigation jurisdiction were to provide: "In default of the payment of the rent in monthly installments, as herein provided, the whole of the rent remaining unpaid for the balance of the leasehold term shall at once become due and payable." Would this form of acceleration clause be enforceable?

Compare Fifty States Management Corp. v. Pioneer Auto Parks, Inc., 46 N.Y.2d 573, 389 N.E.2d 113, 415 N.Y.S.2d 800 (1979) (acceleration clause valid by analogy with similar provisions in mortgage bonds), with Ricker v. Rombough, 120 Cal. App. 2d Supp. 912, 261 P.2d 328 (1953) (acceleration clause invalid as being either a penalty or an agreement for liquidated damages when the damages are readily ascertainable). Also compare Fifty States Management Corp. v. Pioneer Auto Parks, Inc., *supra,* with Seidlitz v. Auerbach, 230 N.Y. 167, 129 N.E. 461 (1920) (acceleration clause invalid as penalty where landlord sought to accelerate $7,500 in rental after tenant failed to pay $17 insurance premium).

Even if the landlord may accelerate the unpaid rental installments, should his claim be limited to the present value of those installments?

7. **The tenant changes her mind.** Suppose, after tenant has vacated (or failed to take possession of) the premises, she changes her mind, and the premises have remained empty. Is she entitled to regain (or enter) possession?

8. **Interplay with the tenant's privilege to assign or sublet.** Notice carefully the interplay between the absence of the landlord's duty to mitigate, where this remains the law, and restrictions on the tenant's privilege to assign her lease or sublet the premises.

2.   Statutes

Md. Code Ann., Real Prop. §8-207 (1994)

> *Duty of aggrieved party to mitigate damage on breach of lease; secondary liability of tenant for rent.*
>
> (a) *Duty to mitigate damages.* — The aggrieved party in a breach of a lease has a duty to mitigate damages if the damages result from the landlord's or tenant's:
>
> (1) Failure to supply possession of the dwelling unit;
>
> (2) Failure or refusal to take possession at the beginning of the term; or
>
> (3) Termination of occupancy before the end of the term.
>
> (b) *No obligation to lease vacated unit in preference to others.* — The provisions of subsection (a) do not impose an obligation to show or lease the vacated dwelling unit in preference to other available units.
>
> (c) *Sublease of unit where tenant does not take possession or vacates.* — If a tenant wrongly fails or refuses to take possession of or vacates the dwelling unit before the end of his term, the landlord may sublet the dwelling unit without prior notice to the tenant in default. The tenant in default is secondarily liable for rent for the term of his original agreement in addition to his liability for consequential damages resulting from his breach, if the landlord gives him prompt notice of any default by the sublessee.
>
> (d) *Waiver prohibited.* — No provision in this section may be waived in any lease.

Va. Code Ann. §55-248.35 (Michie 1994)

> *Remedy after termination.*
> If the rental agreement is terminated, the landlord may have a claim for possession and for rent and a separate claim for actual damages for breach of the rental agreement and reasonable attorney's fees as provided in §55-248.31 [providing remedies for noncompliance with rental agreements], which claims may be enforced, without limitation, by the institution of an action for unlawful entry or detainer. Actual damages for breach of the rental agreement may include a claim for such rent as would have accrued until the expiration of the term thereof or until a tenancy pursuant to a new rental agreement commences, whichever first occurs; provided that nothing herein contained shall diminish the duty of the landlord to mitigate actual damages for breach of the rental agreement. In obtaining post-possession judgments for actual damages as defined herein, the landlord shall not be required to seek a judgment for accelerated rent through the end of the term of the tenancy.
> In any unlawful detainer action brought by the landlord, the section shall not be construed to prevent the landlord from being granted by the court a simultaneous judgment for money due and for possession of the premises without a credit for any security deposit. Upon the tenant vacating the premises either voluntarily or by a writ of possession, security deposits shall be credited to the tenants' account by the landlord in accordance with the requirements of §55-248.11.

QUESTIONS

1. **Comparing case law with statute.** How is the Maryland statute similar to Sommer v. Kridel? How is it different?

2. **Abandonment provision.** Most of the Virginia statute does not concern the situation where tenant abandons. What provision does address tenant abandonment?

3.   Leases

If tenant abandons and refuses or fails to pay present or future rent, he has breached the lease. Landlord's remedies are set forth in the lease default provisions, see §3.6.c *supra.*

b.   Reletting for the Tenant's Account

As we have noted, an express surrender — where both parties agree that the landlord may resume beneficial use and enjoyment of the premises — ends the lease and the tenant's future rental obligations. But troublesome questions may arise as to whether there has been a surrender when the lessor's action is something less than a complete beneficial repossession. The usual setting for a dispute over surrender is when landlord adopts the tenant's account theory of damages.

Under this theory, upon the tenant's abandonment, landlord seeks to relet the premises, not for his own use or gain, and not to discharge his duty to mitigate, but rather to establish his damages for the unexpired term of the lease.[102] The measure of damages in this instance becomes the excess of the reserved rental for the unexpired term over the rents collected less the expenses insured on reletting. Restatement (Second) of Property, Landlord and Tenant, §12.1(3)(b)(1977). For example, if the tenant abandoned the premises with four years remaining on the lease, annual rental $10,000, and landlord netted $33,000 after expenses from replacement tenants, landlord's recovery would be $7,000.

What creates ambiguity when landlord proceeds on a tenant's account theory is that, quite often, landlord will have to make repairs, or take steps to protect and care for the premises, in order to find a replacement tenant. Unless landlord makes clear in advance that he is taking possession for these limited purposes, some court — after the fact[103] — may decide that landlord's dominion over the premises has gone too far and amounts to an implied surrender or surrender by operation of law. Such a holding would deprive landlord of any rental claim for the unexpired term.

Adding to the uncertainty in this area are state law variations, as well as the many kinds of landlord conduct that may give rise to a tenant's claim of implied surrender. For example, at least one court has held that reletting for a term longer than that of the original lease resulted in a surrender, while another court rejected the tenant's account theory where landlord failed first to obtain the tenant's consent. But, in general, courts will use an "all the facts and circumstances" test to determine whether the lessor's action supports the tenant's account theory or an implied surrender. And a well-advised landlord should signal, as clearly as he can, what his intentions are.

---

102. Although the practical differences are slight, a conceptual difference remains between mitigation — where landlord regards the lease and tenant's continuing duty thereunder as unextinguished — and reletting for the tenant's account. Two practical differences are (1) in the first instance, tenant, upon tendering rent, would be absolutely entitled to gain possession if the unit were still unrented: under a tenant's account theory, landlord could reject the original tenant while continuing to seek a replacement tenant whom landlord preferred; (2) in the first instance, landlord would not be forced to rent the abandoned unit ahead of other comparable vacant units: under a tenant's account theory, landlord must make reasonable efforts to find the replacement tenant even though landlord might have comparable vacant units that he would prefer to rent first.

103. The claim arises, ordinarily, only after the landlord sues for his loss of rental. By then, it is too late for the landlord to retrace his steps, either to make his conduct less vulnerable to the tenant's claim or to manage the premises differently so as to minimize the rental loss.

NOTES AND QUESTIONS

1. **When may the landlord sue for his rental losses?** In Hermitage Co. v. Levine, 248 N.Y. 333, 162 N.E. 97 (1928), the facts were these: Plaintiff leased to defendant a seven-story building for a term of twenty-one years and two months, commencing August 1, 1924, and ending October 1, 1945. Defendant paid rent for only a few months and was dispossessed in summary proceedings on December 31, 1924. By August 1, 1925, plaintiff had relet the entire building in three separate leases: three-and-a-half floors were relet for 15 years; two-and-a-half, for ten years; and one, for three years. The plaintiff sued in March 1926 for the rental deficiencies computed to that time. Held: the action is premature; ascertainment of plaintiff's damages will be impossible until October 1, 1945.

> No doubt, a damage clause can be drawn in such a way as to make a tenant responsible for monthly deficits after the re-entry of his landlord, and this without charging the landlord with a duty to account for a surplus in other seasons. Such a clause will be found in McCready v. Lindenborn (172 N.Y. 400), where the lease was to the effect that the tenant would pay the difference in rent "in equal monthly payments as the amount of such difference shall from time to time be ascertained." A clause similar in effect, though more uncertain in its terms, will be found in Mann v. Munch Brewery (225 N.Y. 189), where the tenant was to "continue liable for the payment of the rent and the performance of all the other conditions herein contained." None the less, in the absence of a provision that points with reasonable clearness to a different construction, a liability for damages resulting from a reletting is single and entire, not multiple and several. The deficiency is to be ascertained when the term is at an end. . . .
>
> We do not overlook the hardship to the landlord in postponing the cause of action until October, 1945. The hardship is so great as to give force to the argument that postponement to a date so distant may not reasonably be held to have been intended by the parties. There is no reason to suppose, however, that the landlord was expectant of so early a default or so heavy a deficiency. It had in its possession a deposit of cash security in the sum of $30,000. Very likely this was supposed to be enough to make default improbable and the risk of loss remote. If the damage clause as drawn gives inadequate protection, the fault is with the draftsman. The courts are not at liberty to supply its omissions at the expense of a tenant whose liability for the future ended with the cancellation of the lease except in so far as he bound himself by covenant to liability thereafter. [248 N.Y. 333, 337-339, 162 N.E. 97, 98]

As landlord's attorney, draft a lease clause that avoids the rule of Hermitage Co. v. Levine. See, e.g., Bedford Myrtle Corp. v. Martin, 28 Misc. 2d 33, 209 N.Y.S.2d 201 (Sup. Ct. 1960).

2. **Who bears the risk of the replacement tenant's default?** Tenant abandons the premises. Landlord proceeds on a tenant's account theory. Landlord finds a replacement tenant who enters into a lease for a higher

rental and longer term than the original lease provided. However, the replacement tenant soon defaults. Who bears the risk of any uncollected rental under the original lease, the original tenant or the landlord? Cf. U.S. Natl. Bank of Oregon v. Homeland, Inc., 291 Or. 374, 631 P.2d 761 (1981) (the original tenant similar to one who assigns a lease, yet remains responsible for the rent if the assignee fails to pay).

3.   **Who gains the benefit of reletting surplus?** If in reletting the premises on a tenant's account theory a landlord collects more than the reserved rental, is tenant entitled to the surplus? Cf. A & J Realty Corp. v. Kent Dry Cleaners, Inc., 61 Misc. 2d 887, 307 N.Y.S.2d 99 (Dist. Ct. 1969).

c.   Anticipatory Breach

The landlord, in most states, has one more option when tenant abandons the premises. On the theory that when tenant makes clear his intention to repudiate the lease he has caused an anticipatory breach, landlord may recover his damages at once. Damages are measured by the present value of the excess of the reserved rental over the rental value of the premises.[104] For example, if four years remained on the lease, the yearly reserved rental was $50,000, and the yearly rental value was $35,000, landlord could obtain a judgment for the present value of the right to receive $15,000 yearly for four years. Having recovered the judgment, landlord may then relet the premises for whatever he can get, leave the premises idle, or use the premises himself. If the rental value were suddenly to rise, landlord would profit[105]; by contrast, if the rental value were to decline further, and — in the above example — landlord failed to find a tenant who would pay $35,000 yearly, landlord would be forced to swallow the added loss.

§3.14   Other Issues

In this section, we will work quickly through some areas of the law we have not yet studied.

a.   The Holdover Tenant

On August 1, L rents T an apartment for two years to start on September 1. X, the present occupant, has a lease expiring on August 31. X holds

104. If the rental value were greater than reserved rental, the tenant's breach, ordinarily, would not cause landlord damage, and landlord, likely, would treat tenant's breach as a surrender of the premises.

105. This assumes the judgment was collectible.

over, and does not vacate the premises when his lease ends. What are land-lord's remedies?

Landlord has two options. She can move to evict (and sue for dam-ages), or she can bind the holdover tenant to a new term. In most jurisdic-tions, holding over gives rise to a periodic tenancy; otherwise, a term tenancy is created. The length of the term or period for the new tenancy varies. The two most common alternatives are that the new tenancy lasts for the term or period for which rent was reserved in the old tenancy (that is, for one month if rent was paid once a month), or for the term or period of the old tenancy. In either case, a holdover tenancy can last no longer than one year. See 1 American Law of Property §3.35, at 244-246 (1952 & Supp. 1977).

Many states have passed statutes dealing with holdovers. Some specify the length of the holdover tenancy. Robert Schoshinski, American Law of Landlord and Tenant §2.23 nn.73-77, at 75-76 (1980 & Supp. 1994). A few statutes basically abolish the holdover doctrine by turning holdover tenan-cies into tenancies at will. Id. at §2.17 n. 88. And Arkansas may uniquely treat as a crime a tenant's willful refusal to vacate premises upon ten days' notice after the term expires; Ark. Stat. Ann. §18-16-101 (1987).

b.   Delivery of Possession

1.   Case Law

On August 1, L rents T an apartment for two years to start Septem-ber 1. X, the present occupant, holds a lease expiring August 31. That day L phones T to say that X cannot leave until October 1 (when X's new house will be finished). In the meantime, T's present apartment has been rented as of September 10. What are T's rights and remedies vis-à-vis L? Robert Schoshinski, American Law of Landlord and Tenant §§3.1-3.2, at 86-4 (1980 & Supp. 1994).

Under English common law, landlord was not required to place the incoming tenant in possession. If the landlord enjoyed good title and had not already rented the premises to someone else, his duties ended, and the incoming tenant was required the pay the agreed-upon rental and wage his cause against the holdover or wrongful occupant. The law explained this counter-intuitive result on the ground that the incoming tenant, having the legal right to possession, was the only party with standing to evict the wrong-ful occupant.

Most American states, at first, adopted this rule. Ironically, many states have clung to this rule even after England reversed itself and required, un-less the lease provided otherwise, that the landlord place the incoming tenant in actual possession. The ultimate irony is that we now refer to the original as the *American* rule, and the more modern version as the *English* rule.

What arguments support each of the two rules?

2.   Statutes

The following statutes look similar, but in fact are quite different: One offers far more protection to tenants than the other does. To help you analyze the statutes, answer the following questions:

1.   What options does T have if L "willfully" fails to deliver possession?
2.   What options does T have if L's failure to deliver possession is not "willful?"
3.   Will L's failure to deliver possession be "willful" in most instances?

Va. Ann. Code §55-248.22 (Michie 1994)

Failure to deliver possession.

If the landlord willfully fails to deliver possession of the dwelling unit to the tenant, rent abates until possession is delivered and the tenant may: terminate the rental agreement upon at least five days' written notice to the landlord and upon termination, the landlord shall return all prepaid rent and security; or demand performance of the rental agreement by the landlord and, if the tenant elects, maintain an action for possession of the dwelling unit against the landlord or any person wrongfully in possession and recover the damages sustained by him. If a person's failure to deliver possession is willful and not in good faith, an aggrieved person may recover from that person the actual damages sustained by him and reasonable attorney's fees.

Md. Code Ann., Real Prop. §8-204 (1994)

Covenant of quiet enjoyment.

(a) *Applicability of section.* — This section is applicable only to single or multi-family dwelling units.

(b) *Covenant of quiet enjoyment required.* — A landlord shall assure his tenant that the tenant, peaceably and quietly, may enter on the leased premises at the beginning of the term of any lease.

(c) *Abatement of rent for failure to deliver.* — If the landlord fails to provide the tenant with possession of the dwelling unit at the beginning of the term of any lease, the rent payable under the lease shall abate until possession is delivered. The tenant, on written notice to the landlord before possession is delivered, may terminate, cancel, and rescind the lease.

(d) *Liability of landlord.* — On termination of the lease under this section, the landlord is liable to the tenant for all money or property given as prepaid rent, deposit, or security.

(e) *Consequential damages.* — If the landlord fails to provide the tenant with possession of the dwelling unit at the beginning of the term of any lease, whether or not the lease is terminated under this section, the landlord is liable to the tenant for consequential damages actually suffered by him subsequent to the tenant's giving notice to the landlord of his inability to enter on the leased premises.

(f) *Eviction of tenant holding over.* — The landlord may bring an action of eviction and damages against any tenant holding over after the end of his term even though the landlord has entered into a lease with another tenant, and he may join the new tenant as a party to the action.

3.   Leases

Compare the lease provisions in Figures 3-16 and 3-17. Would they be enforceable in Maryland or Virginia?

Landlord Not Responsible for Failure to Deliver Apartment on Time: Rent Abatement	2. The Tenant waives the provision of Section 223-a of the New York Real Property Law (which would otherwise permit the Tenant to cancel this lease and hold the Landlord responsible for damages) in the event that the Landlord is unable or fails to deliver possession of the Apartment to the Tenant on the commencement of the term of this lease, but the Tenant shall not be required to pay rent until the Apartment is no longer leased to, or occupied by, anyone else. The term of this lease shall end on the date set forth above regardless of the date on which possession of the Apartment is delivered to the Tenant or the date on which the Tenant first occupies the Apartment.

FIGURE 3-16
Lease No. 1

2. (a)   Tenant waives the right it has under the law to cancel this Lease and collect damages if Landlord does not deliver possession of the Apartment to Tenant on the date the term of this Lease is supposed to start. However, Tenant does not have to pay rent until the date it does get possession.

FIGURE 3-17
Lease No. 2

c. Damage or Destruction of the Premises

1. Case Law

At common law, destruction of leased buildings did not end the tenant's duty to pay rent. This was explained on the theory that the lease had received an estate in *land*; fire, flood, or acts of war might ravish the structures, but the land itself would remain relatively intact. In a rural economy, when farm buildings were easily replaced and were seldom the central factor in a lease, this seemingly harsh rule may have worked little mischief. Unless he had negligently caused building damage, the tenant was under no duty to restore, and one might even suppose that he took greater pains to avoid destruction than he otherwise would. See Note, 24 Geo. L.J. 197 (1935).

As the lease moved into the city, where apartment tenancies became widespread, courts began to reform the law. In an early New York case, the Court of Appeals discharged an upper-story tenant from further rent after the building burned; its theory: the tenant had no interest in the land, only in the attached building. Graves v. Berdan, 26 N.Y. 498 (1863). Other courts have used contract analysis to reverse the common law, arguing that a destroyed premises gives rise to impossibility of performance. See, e.g., Albert M. Greenfield & Co., Inc. v. Kolea, 475 Pa. 351, 380 A.2d 758 (1977).

2. Statutes

How do the following statutes change the law?

Va. Ann. Code §55-226 (Michie 1994)

> *Buildings destroyed or lessee deprived of possession; covenant to pay rent or repair; reduction of rent.*
>
> No covenant or promise by a lessee to pay the rent, or that he will keep or leave the premises in good repair, shall have the effect, if the buildings thereon be destroyed by fire or otherwise, in whole or in part, without fault or negligence on his part, of if he be deprived of the possession of the premises by the public enemy, of binding him to make such payment or repair or erect such buildings again, unless there be other words showing it to be the intent of the parties that he should be so bound. But in case of such destruction there shall be a reasonable reduction of the rent for such time as may elapse until there be again upon the premises buildings of as much value to the tenant for his purposes as what may have been so destroyed; and, in case of such deprivation of possession, a like reduction until possession of the premises be restored to him.

Md. Code Ann., Real Prop. §8-112 (1994)

Termination of tenancy for fire or unavoidable accident.

If the improvements on property rented for a term of not more than seven years become untenantable by reason of fire or unavoidable accident, the tenancy terminates, and all liability for rent ceases on payment proportionately to the day of fire or unavoidable accident.

3. Leases

Compare the lease provisions in Figures 3-18 and 3-19. How do they change the common law? How do the "deals" struck here differ from the background common law rules?

Damage by Fire	7. If the Building, the Apartment or means of access there to is damaged or destroyed by fire or other casualty and the Landlord shall decide not to repair, restore or rebuild it, this lease shall terminate and the rent shall be apportioned as of the date on which the damage shall have occurred. If this lease is not so terminated, the Landlord shall repair the damage to the Apartment and means of access thereto as soon as practicable, and if the damage has made the Apartment untenantable, in whole or in part, there shall be an apportionment of the rent until the damage has been repaired (unless such damage was caused by the Tenant). The Landlord and the Tenant agree that the foregoing provisions of this Article are an express agreement made in lieu of the provisions of Section 227 of the New York Real Property Law which provide that a tenant may terminate a lease if an apartment is rendered untenantable. Neither the Landlord's decision not to repair, restore or rebuild, nor its obligation to repair damage shall be deemed to release the Tenant from any liability to the Landlord arising out of the Tenant's acts or omissions and any resulting damage from fire or other casualty.
Tenant to Rely First on Insurance and to Make No Claims Against Landlord For Insured Loss	The Tenant shall look first to any insurance which it carries before making any claim against the Landlord for recovery for loss or Against damage resulting from fire or other casualty not caused by the Tenant's acts or omissions, shall name the Landlord as an additional insured under any casualty policy held by the Tenant, and

FIGURE 3-18
Lease No. 1

Tenant to Name Landlord as Additional Insured on Tenant's Policy

to the extent that such insurance is in force and collectible and to the extent permitted by law, the Tenant releases, and waives all right of recovery against the Landlord for any such law. The Tenant understands that the Landlord will not carry insurance on the Tenant's alterations, furniture, furnishings, equipment, appliances, decorations and personal effects, and agrees that the Landlord will not be obligated to repair any damage to or to replace the same.

Lease No. 1 (continued)

3.   Landlord and Tenant agree as follows:

a.   If there is a fire or other casualty in the Building and Landlord advises Tenant within 10 days thereafter that it has decided not to repair the damage, this Lease shall end as of the date of the fire and any rent paid by Tenant for a period after that date shall be refunded to Tenant. If Landlord does repair the damage, it shall be done as soon as practical and if the Apartment cannot be used, no rent shall be payable from the date of the damage until the date it can be used. Tenant hereby gives up the right to end the Lease when the Apartment in unusable except in a case where there is less than 6 months left in the term of this Lease. Each party hereby gives up any right of recovery against the other party for any loss in connection with any fire damage.

FIGURE 3-19
Lease No. 2

d.   Security Deposits

Landlords typically require tenants to provide a security deposit of one month's rent upon the signing of a lease. This provides the landlord with cash in hand in the event the tenant does not pay rent or damages the apartment. Security deposits are often a source of contention between landlord and tenants, with tenants claiming that landlords withhold repayment of their security deposits with inadequate justification.

Typical security deposit statutes limit the amount of the security deposit to one or two months' rent, give the tenant the right to be present when the landlord inspects the premises for damages or require the landlord to make a public record of all damages charged to a tenant, require the landlord to inform the tenant of any damage to the apartment in writing within a limited time period after the lease is terminated, require landlords to pay interest for the period for which the security deposit is in their possession, provides for penalties (sometimes triple the amount of the security deposit) if the landlord requires more than the allowable security deposit.

§3.15   Consider the Lease as a Whole

We are now in a position to consider leases as a whole. If you have your own lease, examine it closely. Is it generally even-handed, or more pro-landlord or pro-tenant? Does it conform to the "Berger" doctrine of "contract integrity?" List places where it does not.

CURTIS J. BERGER, HARD LEASES MAKE BAD LAW

74 Colum. L. Rev. 791, 814-815 (1974)

While this may be so, a larger issue remains that the present system fails to moot. It is the issue of "contract integrity" — the integrity of the paper that seals the bargain. Here I use "integrity" in a dual sense. I refer both to the honesty or fairness of the contract and to its even-handed completeness.

In the context of the lease, let me illustrate what I mean. A and B make a lease. What they negotiate, however, is far less detailed than the instrument they sign. The negotiated oral transaction seldom goes beyond the monthly rental and the duration of the lease. These terms often are flexible, and the final bargain responds to the urgency with which each party needs to obtain or get rid of the space. Thus, even during an apartment shortage, some owners may readily make a rent concession if their buildings are renting poorly. Conversely, some tenants will pay dearly for apartments they badly want even during a market glut. Thus, as to the *negotiated* bargain, chronic disparity between landlord and tenant would be hard to prove.

If the negotiated bargain were the entire transaction, the written lease would be one paragraph long. But, of course, the landlord-tenant relation is far more complex, and the non-bargained part of the transaction occupies most of the written form. This is where the principle of contract integrity enters. It would require:

1. That the lease fairly describe all the unspoken expectations of the parties. For example, if the tenant expects to receive and the landlord expects to furnish heat, hot and cold running water, trash removal, a minimum level of security, or janitorial service, these rights and duties should be set forth.

2. That the lease fairly describe all basic statutory and common-law rights of the parties. For example, where statute requires landlord to hold the tenant's security deposit in an interest-bearing account, interest payable annually to the tenant, the lease should say so.

3. That the lease describe the tenant's remedies with the same completeness and detail that it describes the landlord's remedies. Thus, tenants would read in their lese of rent-withholding, repair-and-offset, or rescission, where these remedies were available.

4. That the lease distinguish *fairly* between major ("substantial") and minor ("insubstantial") duties, and indicate what penalties follow the breach of each.

5. That the lease not contain any surprises. A tenant who expected to get delivery of the apartment on April 1 should not discover, if the previous tenant unlawfully holds over, that the landlord may recover rent even though the apartment is not ready. If the landlord wants to bargain for such a surprising right, he must *ask* for it during the oral negotiations.

6. That the lease be written for a layman's understanding.

Contract integrity and contract unconscionability occupy the opposing ends of a spectrum. Between them lie many shades of tolerated agreement. Since unconscionability is a doctrine of last resort, virtually any contract that does not shock the conscience is presumptively valid. But I suggest that the legal system should espouse a higher norm, one that contract integrity can help fulfill. Each party who signs an agreement should sense its truth and essential fairness and should believe that the paper fully states his rights and remedies, that it captures both parties' understanding, that it conceals no hookers, and that it is understandable. Uninformed or misinformed parties to a contract are easily terrorized or disarmed into forgoing their rights and remedies, and contract integrity would help prevent that. I also believe, and have tried to show, that hard leases often make bad law, and while no reform can root out the defects of intellect or of fairness among our judges, contract integrity would allow courts to apply their powers of reason and their spirit of impartiality to a dispute far more readily than does today's standard form lease.

Chapter 4

Ownership in Common: Concurrent Estates and Marital Property

Part of the intuitive image of property is that it is owned by individuals. In fact, many — perhaps most — assets in the United States are group-owned. Notable are two forms of ownership not traditionally covered in property courses: partnerships and corporations. We will not discuss these in depth, but they are worth remembering as we start a unit in which we begin to test the intuitive image's assumption of individual ownership. The corporate and partnership forms remind us that groups, not individuals, own most commercial and industrial assets.

But many personal assets are also non-individually owned. Studies have shown that married couples tend to own both their real property (notably their house) and their personal property (notably their bank accounts, securities, and cars) in common: "to hold property in the name of only one spouse is the exception rather than the rule." Regis W. Campfield, Estate Planning for Joint Tenancies, 1974 Duke L.J. 669, 670.

The Lockean tradition assumes that property is "naturally" focused on individuals — so the idea that most property in the United States is owned by groups seems a bit startling: Recall Pierson v. Post's imagery of a lone hunter conceptualized apart from his system of societal and family supports. As you read these materials, ask yourself how the law of concurrent ownership reflects the intuitive image that property is "naturally" owned by individuals.

This section focuses on the two contexts involving common ownership that the traditional property course usually covers: concurrent estates and marital property.

§4.1   Concurrent Estates

Co-ownership arises in a wide range of situations. In commercial real estate transactions, co-ownership investment groups are common. Rights to
natural resources, notably water rights and oil and gas operating interests,
usually involve co-ownership. Nearly as widespread is the co-ownership of
intellectual property.

Co-ownership also plays a major role in the family. Typically, the
spouses, jointly, will own the family home and the principal checking account. Because the co-ownership of family assets is so central to household
wealth, this will be the focus of the discussion of co-ownership that follows.

a.   Common-Law Categories

We divide concurrent estates into common-law categories that date
back to the feudal era. See, e.g., Anne L. Spitzer, Joint Tenancy with Right
of Survivorship: A Legacy from Thirteenth Century England, 16 Tex. Tech.
L. Rev. 629 (1985). Thus, we again meet cases in which courts feel the need
to squash oddball examples of the "thousand deals" into rigid categories
that reflect the feudal vision of property as an institution designed to cement a limited number of preset social relationships.

There are three basic categories of concurrent estates: *tenancy in common, joint tenancy,* and *tenancy by the entirety.* All three tenancies give tenants
"unity of possession," that is, each tenant has the privilege of taking possession and enjoying the entire parcel. In addition, most of the legal rules that
govern relations among cotenants (see §4.1.b, *infra*) apply to each type of
concurrent estate. The major exception is that, while the joint tenancy and
tenancy in common can be divided ("partitioned") into individually owned
parcels (or sold at public auction and the proceeds divided) at the option
of any one cotenant, the tenancy by the entirety cannot, see §4.1.a.3, *infra*.
We first discuss the distinction between the joint tenancy and the tenancy
in common, and then turn to the tenancy by the entirety.

1.   Joint Tenancy and Tenancy in Common

The crucial distinction between these two basic concurrent estates
concerns not current use but wealth transmission. Whereas the interest of
a tenant in common passes onto his heirs, the interest of a joint tenant does
not. If A and B are tenants in common and A dies first, A's interest passes
onto his heirs (or if A dies testate, to persons named in the will). In contrast,
if A and B are joint tenants and A dies first, B takes A's interest automatically, as the survivor by operation of law, so that B now owns the entire parcel *in severalty,* that is, in individual ownership. A's interest does not pass to
his heirs and is unaffected by his will.

In typical feudal fashion, the explanation was metaphysical. Joint ~~ants~~ held *per my et per tout* (by the share, or moiety and by the whole). T~~h~~ old law Latin[1] means that the tenants inherited from each other becaus~~e~~ they were one legal entity: When one joint tenant died, the legal entity contained one fewer member but otherwise remained unchanged. A 1921 Iowa case explained the feudal theory:

> In a legal sense, [a cotenant's] death does not transfer the rights that he possessed in the property to the surviving tenants. Death does not enlarge or change the estate. Death terminates his interest in the estate. It is rather a falling away of the tenant from the estate than the passing of the estate to others.

Fleming v. Fleming, 194 Iowa 71, 88-89, 174 N.W. 946, 953 (1919). Note again how medieval (and twentieth-century!) lawyers treated the legal categories as preset entities with an internal logic that worked without human intervention.

Given the stress in English medieval law on keeping lands in large parcels instead of dividing them up,[2] the preferred estate at common law was the joint tenancy. Nathaniel Sterling, Joint Tenancy and Community Property in California, 14 Pac. L.J. 927, 931 (1983). Thus, if a grant was ambiguous and could create either a tenancy in common or a joint tenancy, common-law courts presumed a joint tenancy. A joint tenancy could only be created, however, if the *four unities* of time, title, interest, and possession were observed.[3]

Time — Each tenant's interest must be acquired or vest at the same time.

Title — All joint tenants must acquire title by the same document or by simultaneous adverse possession (see §5.1). A joint tenancy could never arise by intestate succession (automatic inheritance, in the absence of a will) or otherwise by operation of law.

Interest — All tenants must have equal shares and must hold the same estate in the land (i.e., fees simple, life estates, etc.)

Possession — Each tenant has the legal right to possess the whole.

During the Middle Ages, the joint tenancy served a variety of estate planning purposes. Individuals used it to set up trusts that enabled grantees

---

1. In the medieval era, Latin was the language of official business, including the law. Even as late as 100 years ago, Latin phrases were still common in the law. We will see more of them later. See Chapter 7.

2. A notable example of this stress was primogeniture. See §4.1.a.3 *infra.* In the joint tenancy context, the desire to avoid fragmentation of title was related to the desire of lords to thwart tenants' desire to avoid the payment of the taxes (called "feudal incidents") due on the tenant's death. See N. William Hines, Real Property Joint Tenancies: Law, Fact, and Fancy, 51 Iowa L. Rev. 582, 585 (1966).

3. In many states, these unities are still required to create a joint tenancy, but quite simple sleight-of-hand conveyancing can finesse some of them.

to avoid the payment of feudal taxes ("incidents") and to circumvent the prohibition (before the Statute of Wills) against devising property away from one's heirs at law. Some have called the joint tenancy the "darling of the property law." N. William Hines, Real Property Joint Tenancies: Law, Fact, and Fancy, 51 Iowa L. Rev. 582, 585 (1966).

All that had changed by the eighteenth century, and the joint tenancy came to be regarded as an "odious thing" that precluded all but the heirs of the last surviving joint tenant from inheriting. Id.; see also Nunn v. Keith, 289 Ala. 518, 268 So. 2d 792, 794 (1972). Gradually, through decision and statute, the common-law presumption in favor of the joint tenancy shifted, displaced by the modern presumption in favor of the tenancy in common. (There is one exception: An ambiguous grant to a *husband and wife* may create a joint tenancy — or even a tenancy by the entirety.) [4]

Many states have required (and some still do) that a conveyance, in order to create a joint tenancy, must follow precise wording patterns. Litigation may well attend grant language that "deviates from the prescribed text." See, Overheiser v. Lackey, 207 N.Y. 229, 100 N.E. 738 (1913); Montgomery v. Clarkson, 585 S.W.2d 483 (Mo. 1979). Cf. Note, Muddy Waters: Concurrent Ownership with Right of Survivorship in Alabama after *Durant v. Hamrick,* 34 Ala. L. Rev. 147 (1983). Note once again the existence of intent-defeating categories and presumptions designed not to let a thousand deals bloom but to channel property arrangements into tight-fitting niches.

The *tenancy in common* is the default category: any cotenancy arrangement that is neither a joint tenancy nor a tenancy by the entirety is regarded as a tenancy in common. Also, if a joint tenancy does exist, but one of the four unities is subsequently broken, the survivorship right is destroyed and a tenancy in common results. For example, if A and B are joint tenants, and A sells his interest to C, B and C become tenants in common, and there does not exist, as between B and C, any right of survivorship. Thus either A or B unilaterally (indeed, secretly) can turn a joint tenant into a tenancy in common by selling his interest to a third party.[5] Which unity does the sale break? *Title*

<hr>

4. In a recent count, 29 jurisdictions had a statutory presumption of a tenancy in common, 17 had statutes, and 3 states had judicial decisions that severely curtailed or abolished the right of survivorship. Anne L. Spitzer, Joint Tenancy with Right of Survivorship: A Legacy from Thirteenth Century England, 16 Tex. Tech. L. Rev. 629, 632 n.10 (1985).

5. Cases generally agree that a mortgage and an executory sales contract will affect a severance; but see American Natl. Bank & Trust Co. of Shawnee v. McGinnis, 571 P.2d 1198, 1200 (Okla. 1977) (a mortgage, a "mere lien," does not destroy joint tenancy unity). The effect of a lease given by one cotenant to a third party is somewhat unsettled. The English rule supports a conversion to a tenancy in common; the American rule does not. See, e.g., Tennet v. Boswell, 18 Cal. 3d 150, 554 P.2d 330, 133 Cal. Rptr. 10 (1976). Can you think of any reason why the giving of a deed and a lease should not produce the same result? See Annot., 64 A.L.R.2d 919 (1959) (exhaustive case presentation); Robert W. Swenson and Ronan E. Degnan, Severance of Joint Tenancies, 38 Minn. L. Rev. 466 (1954).

Note that a key difference between the joint tenancy and the tenancy in common is that the latter allows tenants to have unequal shares. Thus if A, B, and C are joint tenants, each must have a one-third undivided interest; if they are tenants in common, A and B may each have one-fourth, while C has one-half — and any other equal or unequal fractional allocation would be possible. Thus the effect of the common-law categories is to link two characteristics that are logically independent: the existence of equal shares and the right of survivorship. What if a grantor wants to create a cotenancy with unequal shares and the right of survivorship? Probably the best alternative is to create two concurrent (unequal) life estates with a contingent remainder to the survivor, for example, O to A, an undivided one-third, and B, an undivided two-thirds, for the joint lives of A and B, with a remainder to the survivor of A and B. Note the persistent influence of the common-law categories (and also, the relative ease with which a clever drafter may find a way to carry out her client's unusual wishes). Cf., Hass v. Hass, page 394, *infra.*

GAGNON v. PRONOVOST

96 N.H. 154, 71 A.2d 747 (1949), aff'd on rehearing,
96 N.H. 158, 71 A.2d 750 (1950)

Bill in equity, to remove a cloud on the title to real estate claimed to be owned by the plaintiff. The dispute involves the construction of a warranty deed under seal from Anthony Grady to Jules Letourneau and Georgiana Turgeon which read in part as follows:

> Know All Men By These Presents
> That I, Anthony Grady of Manchester, in the County of Hillsborough and State of New Hampshire, for and in consideration of the sum of One Dollar and other valuable consideration, to me in hand, before the delivery hereof, well and truly paid by Jules Letourneau and Georgiana Turgeon *and to the survivors of them,* the receipt whereof I do thereby acknowledge, have given granted, bargained, sold, and by these presents do give, grant, bargain, sell, alien, enfeoff, convey and confirm unto the grantees, their heirs and assigns forever.

The italicized words do not appear elsewhere in the body of the deed.

The plaintiff, as the successor in interest of Georgiana Turgeon, who survived Jules Letourneau, claims the deed created a joint tenancy and that she has the title to the whole. The defendants, as the heirs of Jules Letourneau, claim the deed created a tenancy in common and that they have title to an undivided one-half interest therein.

The Presiding Justice decreed the plaintiff to be the owner of the premises described in the deed. . . . The defendant's exceptions to the decree were reserved and transferred by Goodnow, C.J.

LAMPRON, J. This bill in equity to remove a cloud on title presents the question whether a joint tenancy or a tenancy in common was created by the deed. If the former, the plaintiff prevails and the appeal is dismissed; if the latter, the defendants prevail to the extent of an undivided one-half interest in common and the appeal is granted. The controlling statute, R.L. c. 259, §17, provides:

> Tenants in Common. Every conveyance or devise of real estate made to two or more persons shall be construed to create an estate in common and not in joint tenancy, unless it shall be expressed therein that the estate is to be holden by the grantees or devises as joint tenants, or to them and the survivor of them, or unless other words are used clearly expressing an intention to create a joint tenancy.

The purpose of the statute was to require that the intention to create a joint tenancy should be clearly expressed. Laws ed. 1830, p. 110; Stilphen v. Stilphen, 65 N.H. 126, 138, 23 A. 79. The use of the phrase "and to the survivors of them" in the clause of the deed which recites the consideration and names the grantees is too sketchy and speculative to comply with the statutory requirement of a clear expression to create a joint tenancy. In no other clause of the deed are there words which suggest any estate other than a tenancy in common. It is difficult to believe that the quoted phrase can qualify as an expression that the estate is "to be holden . . . (to the grantees) and the survivor of them." At most it was an obscure and inaccurate use of the statutory language and consequently insufficient to come within the statute.

While we are not bound by technical common law rules of construction, . . . we are not committed to a rule that may discourage the use of accurate and clear expressions in legal instruments. The phrase used in this case and its location in the deed is more indicative of lack of comprehension on the part of the draftsman as to the effect of the words used than it is indicative of an intent and purpose to create a joint tenancy. The deed created a tenancy in common . . .

Exceptions sustained.

JOHNSTON, C.J., and KENISON, J., dissented; the others concurred.

KENISON, J. (dissenting). The quoted statute as construed in this state is not a legislative expression of hostility to the creation of joint tenancies for "the purpose of the statute is not to forbid or prevent the creation of estates in joint tenancy, but to make certain that effect is given to the intention of the grantor." . . . If a joint tenancy is intended, it will be so construed even though it is contrary to common law rules of construction. . . . "It has been many years since the technicalities of real estate conveyancing have been much regarded here." Newmarket Mfg. Co. v. Nottingham, 86 N.H. 321, 324, 168 A. 892, 895.

Upon analysis it appears that the statute provides three ways to create a joint tenancy. The first method is an express statement in the deed that the grantees shall take as joint tenant. The second method calls for express statement of the grantees "and the survivor of them." The third method is the use of any other words "clearly expressing an intention to create a joint tenancy." The deed in question is not within the first and third methods enumerated above. The question remains whether it is a substantial compliance with the second.

There is considerable authority for the proposition that the use of the word "survivor" or "survivors" in deeds and wills is sufficient to negative the statutory presumption of a tenancy in common. . . . "There is no substantial difference between deeding or devising land to two persons, and the survivor of them, and deeding or devising land to two persons to be held in joint tenancy." 4 Thompson, Real Property, Perm. Ed. §1790. In Massachusetts, which has a statute similar to ours, it appears that words of survivorship in the singular or the plural will create a joint tenancy in the absence of other limiting or qualifying phrases. . . .

It may be conceded that the deed in dispute is not a model form to create a joint tenancy and that the notary public who prepared it was not a model draftsman. That is not fatal, however, if it can be fairly said that the intent was expressed in reasonably clear terms. "If the intent to create a right of survivorship is expressed, it is to be given effect." Burns v. Nolette, 83 N.H. 489, 496, 144 A. 848, 852, 67 A.L.R. 1051. The defendants argue that there can be no "survivors" of two grantees and that this is not the singular use of the word provided by the statute. We are content with the construction placed upon the word by the Trial Court as a substantial compliance with the statutes. "The law has outgrown its primitive stage of formalism when the principal word was the sovereign talisman, and every slip was fatal." Cardozo, J., Wood v. Lucy Lady Duff-Gordon, 222 N.Y. 88, 118, N.E. 214. It is a well established rule in this state in considering written instruments and pleadings that their expressed intent will be enforced even though inarticulately worded. . . .

Objection is made that the words of survivorship do not appear in other parts of the deed and are therefore ineffective. The relative weight to be given words appearing in different sections of the deed as developed at common law has never been followed in this jurisdiction. The intent of the grantor is to be gathered from all parts of the deed without resorting to presumption of law in determining their effect. It is finally suggested that the construction placed upon this deed discourages clearness of expression and the better forms of conveying. This argument has been considered many times in the last half a century but it has not been considered as important as the principle of carrying out of the expressed intent of written documents regardless of the method of their expression. Lawyers and judges sometimes have difficulty when they attempt to make a fortress out of the dictionary and we should impose no higher standards upon the layman. . . .

JOHNSTON, C.J., concurs in this opinion. . . .

NOTES AND QUESTIONS

1.   **Purpose of the statute.** Do Justices Lampron and Kenison view differently the statute's purpose? If so, is conflict between them unavoidable?

2.   **Advantages of joint tenancies.** One commentator summarized the advantages of the joint tenancy as follows:

> a. *Jointly held property oftentimes enjoys preferential treatment for state death tax purposes.* . . . [Some statutes exempt property held in joint tenancy by a husband and wife; others exempt property held by tenancy by the entirety.] . . .
>
> b. *Jointly held property is free from the claims of creditors of either spouse.* . . .[6]
>
> c. *Joint property expresses the idea of partnership in a marriage and reinforces family security and harmony.* This kind of argument is hard to combat, and it cannot be dismissed as trivial.[7] . . .
>
> d. *Joint property reduces administrative costs.* This is true in the sense that the estate's administrator cannot include joint property in the base he uses in computing his fee. It is, however, included in computing the attorney's fee, albeit at a lower percentage.
>
> e. *Joint property avoids probate delays.* Ordinarily probate cannot be distributed for at least six months after administration is commenced. . . . A substantial proportion, *but generally not all*, of the jointly held property is available to the survivor immediately after death.
>
> f. *Joint property avoids publicity.* It is common in some communities for the newspapers regularly to publish the contents of a decedent's estate as reported to the court having jurisdiction over estates. The joint property will appear only on tax returns which are, theoretically, confidential. . . .
>
> h. *Joint property avoids fragmentation of ownership.*[8] Intestate distribution of a decedent's property [the distribution that occurs pursuant to default rules that operate in the absence of a will] usually fragments ownership. The survivorship feature of a joint tenancy avoids that result. . . .

Regis W. Campfield, Estate Planning for Joint Tenancies, 1974 Duke L.J. 669, 671-673.

3.   **How to create a joint tenancy in view of the modern presumption against it.** "O grants to A and B jointly." See Montgomery v. Clarkson, 585

---

6. This applies only to tenancies by the entirety. See pages §4.1.a.3. *infra.*—EDS.

7. Note this very practical lawyer's respect for the symbolic function of the law.— EDS.

8. Note that lawyers have used the joint tenancy to accomplish this goal since the Middle Ages. See *supra.* — EDS.

S.W.2d 483 (Mo. 1979). This case highlights the lengths a court will go to construe a grant as a tenancy in common rather than a joint tenancy. "To James E. Stewart and Nancy E. Stewart jointly" was held to create a tenancy in common because the jurisdiction had a statute calling for "express declaration" of intent to create a joint tenancy and the use of the word "joint" was held "equivocal." The best way to ensure the creation of a joint tenancy is the following: "To A and B as joint tenants with right of survivorship, and not as tenants in common."

Know!

4. **When one joint tenant murders another.** When one joint tenant murders the other, courts have taken a variety of approaches with disparate outcomes. In Bierbrauer v. Moran, 279 N.Y.S. 176 (App. Div. 1935), H murders W in their home by beating her, strangling her, and leaving her in the bathroom to die after a final blow to the head using the heel of her shoe. He then places a pillowcase over his head and proceeds to inhale noxious gas through a tube. Held: Where there is no proof of survivorship (that is, it is not known who died first), a tenancy in common is created and the property is distributed as though both deaths occurred simultaneously; see Note 7, *infra*. However, public policy demands that where one of the deaths is the result of the willful act of the other, the murdering cotenant is barred from profiting from his crime. Therefore, the husband's estate cannot benefit from the murder, and the property is denied his heirs in favor of the heirs of the murdered cotenant.

All

In Bradley v. Fox, 7 Ill. 2d 106, 129 N.E.2d 699 (1955), H murders W, then conveys 100 percent of his property interest to his defense attorney. W's heirs sue alleging that H is not entitled to their mother's interest in the property. Held: The murder severs the joint tenancy by destroying the unity of possession. Tenancy in common is thus created between wife's heirs and murderous husband. He is thus entitled to a one-half undivided interest.

half

In Welsh v. Jones, 408 Ill. 18, 95 N.E.2d 872 (1950), H murders W in family home. Held: H has not profited by his wife's murder since, as joint tenants, each had full possessory interest to begin with. Public policy demands that the state constitution be upheld and "no conviction shall work corruption of blood or forfeiture of estate." *Bierbrauer*, 279 N.Y.S. at 875.

half

Which do you think is the correct approach? Note that these cases, while they seem far-fetched, may not be. Recall that most joint tenancies are held by married couples; "FBI statistics showed that husbands or boyfriends killed forty percent of all female homicide victims." Victoria M. Mather, The Skeleton in the Closet: The Battered Woman Syndrome, Self-Defense, and Expert Testimony, 39 Mercer L. Rev. 545, 548 (1988).

5. **Problems**. In each of the following instances, indicate whether the grantor has created a joint tenancy or a tenancy in common. All problems occur in 1996.

(a)   O grants "to A and B as joint tenants with right of survivorship and not as tenants in common."

JT

TC →

(b) O grants "to A, a one-third undivided interest, and B, a two-thirds undivided interest, as joint tenants."

TC

(c) A and B are tenants in common with equal shares. A dies intestate, leaving equal (one third) shares to X, Y, and Z.

TC-T

(d) "O grants to A and B jointly."

6. **Fractional interests.** A, B, and C are joint tenants. A conveys his interest to X. A dies intestate, leaving an heir, AH. How is title now held?

(a) X then dies intestate, leaving an heir, XH. How is title now held?
(b) B then dies intestate, leaving an heir, BH. How is title now held?
(c) C then dies intestate, leaving an heir, CH. How is title now held?

Cf. Giles v. Sheridan, 179 Neb. 257, 137 N.W.2d 828 (1965).

7. **Uniform Simultaneous Death Act.** A and B are joint tenants. A and B die together in an airplane crash. Each leaves an heir, AH and BH. How is title now held? See In re Strong's Will, 171 Misc. 445, 12 N.Y.S.2d 544 (Sur. Ct. 1939). The Uniform Simultaneous Death Act, which has been widely adopted, provides:

> Where there is no sufficient evidence that two joint tenants or tenants by the entirety have died otherwise than simultaneously the property so held shall be distributed one half as if one had survived and one half as if the other had survived. . . . If there are more than two joint tenants and all of them have so died the property thus distributed shall be in the proportion that one bears to the whole number of joint tenants.

Unif. Simultaneous Death Act §3 (1940). See also David Shapiro et al., Note, Estate Planning for the Common Disaster, 38 B.U. L. Rev. 257 (1958).

8. **"We are joint together."** On August 21, 1985, 21 factory workers won the largest Lotto jackpot in the history of the United States up to the time, $41 million. The workers, largely immigrants from countries in Latin America, Eastern Europe and Asia, worked in a factory that makes printing presses. In buying the ticket, they each pitched in $1, picked two combinations of six numbers, and entrusted their cards to Peter Lee, a 38-year-old Yonkers resident who bought the tickets. "We're like a big family here," said Mr. Lee. "We thought that by pooling our efforts, we would increase our luck — and we were right." The men, who earned between $25,000 and $35,000, agreed to share their winnings if any one of them won. What kind of tenancy does their agreement (reproduced in Figure 4-1) create?

9. **When does the equal-shares rule in joint tenancies turn into merely a presumption?** In general, as noted above, joint tenants necessarily have equal shares. An interesting exception is the case of Jezo v. Jezo, 23 Wisc. 2d 399, 127 N.W.2d 246 (1964). Martin and Stella Jezo both worked in a real estate business they built together. From 1921 to 1933, their home was used as an office; all real estate and assets were held jointly; when the business incorporated in 1934, a single certificate of stock was issued to

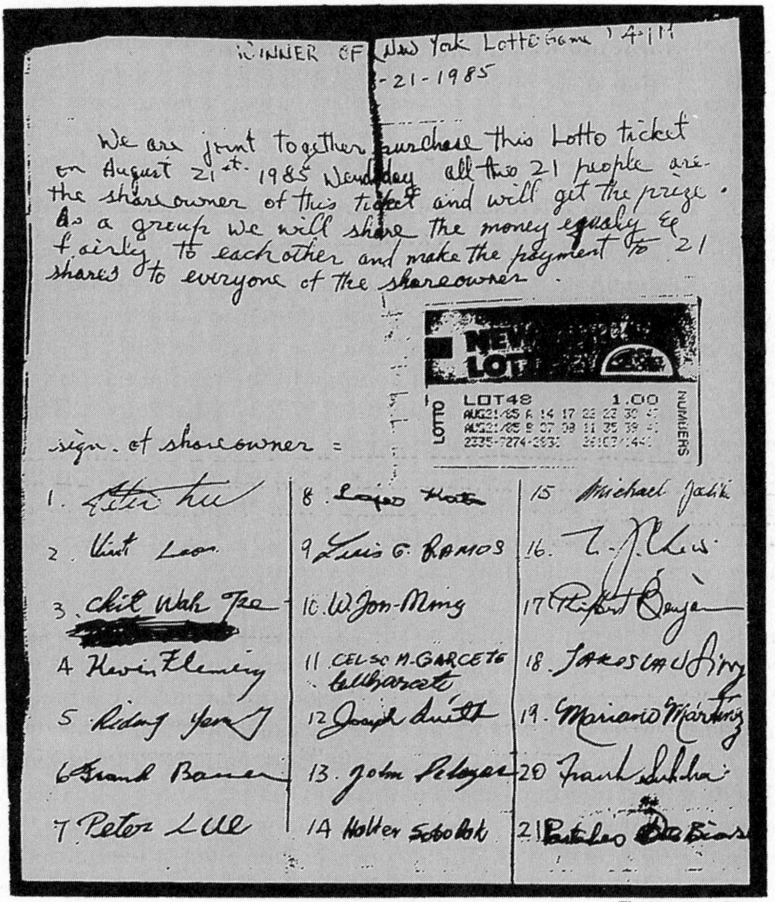
WINNER OF New York Lotto Game 8-21-1985

We are joint together purchase this Lotto ticket on August 21st 1985 Wendsday all the 21 people are the shareowner of this ticket and will get the prize. As a group we will share the money equaly & fairly to each other and make the payment to 21 shares to everyone of the shareowner.

sign. of shareowner =

9 Luis G. Ramos

11 CELSO M. GARCETE

The New York Times

FIGURE 4-1
Lotto Ticket Contract

"We are joint together purchase this Lotto ticket on August 21st 1985 Wednesday all the 21 people are the shareowner of this ticket and will get the prize," reads the agreement the men signed. "As a group we will share the money equally and fairly to each other and make the payment to 21 shares to everyone of the shareowner."

them jointly. Stella was an officer and director of the corporation from 1934 until 1957, and (to quote the court) "from 1934 to 1953, she did some office work for the business, for which she received a salary and bonuses." Id. at 403, 127 N.W. 2d at 248. All of the business's bank accounts were held in joint tenancy until Martin bought Stella out in 1957. He subsequently divorced her and won a claim that the business should not simply be divided up 50/50.

> The only issue . . . is whether, in an action for partition, where it is determined that one of the two joint owners made a larger contribution than the other

for jointly-owned assets, the division should be made on an equal basis, or whether there are other factors relating to the respective contributions made by each joint owner which should be taken into consideration. . . . In the instant action, the trial court found that Martin's monetary contributions to the jointly-held property "were substantially in excess" of those made by Stella, although no finding was made as to the precise amount of each party's contributions . . .

Id. at 405, 127 N.W. 2d at 250. Note that the court admitted that some uncertainty existed about the accuracy of Martin's figures. Why did the court focus on monetary contributions? It also refused to consider work within the home: "In the case of a joint tenancy between the husband and wife, however, the duties and services incidental to the marital relation are not considered in this respect." Id. at 406 n.1, 127 N.W. 2d at 250 n.1. The court held that the rule of equal shares in a joint tenancy was only a presumption and remanded to the trial court for a finding as to the relative contributions of the two spouses. Why did the court diverge from the (traditionally invariable) rule of equal division? Did assumptions about whose contributions were more valuable drive the court's decision?

10. **Straw men.** Mr. and Mrs. Burke are joint tenants. Mrs. Burke wants to sever the joint tenancy so she can pass her one-half interest on to her two sons by a previous marriage. At common law, she needed to use a "straw man."[9] This requirement went back to the medieval method of transferring ownership of land, a ceremony called foeffment with livery of seisin. Both parties typically went onto the land, and the grantor handed a clod of dirt, twig, or other symbol of the land to the grantee. The theory was that one could not enfeoff oneself, hence the need for a straw man.

In the *Burke* case, Mrs. Burke conveyed her interest to an associate at her lawyer's law firm, who conveyed the interest back to her the following day. She stated that she took this course of action because her husband had indicated that he would dispose of the property upon her death as he saw fit, if she should die first. The court noted: "While the actions of the wife, from the standpoint of a theoretically perfect marriage, are subject to ethical criticism, and her stealthy approach to the solution of the problems facing her is not to be acclaimed, the question before the court is not what should have been done ideally in a perfect marriage, but whether the decedent and her attorneys acted in a legally permissible manner." Burke v. Stevens, 264 Cal. App. 2d 30, 34, 70 Cal. Rptr. 87, 91 (1968).[10]

In some jurisdictions, a straw man is still necessary to turn a joint ten-

---

9. The term originates from the medieval period, when people advertised their availability to play this type of role (for a fee) by standing around the courthouse with straw in their shoes.

10. The court probably was not very sympathetic with the plaintiff-husband because he had represented to his wife's sons that he had only a one-half interest in the property, with a contingent life estate in the other half. The sons then contributed over $15,000 to pay back taxes and, that done, the husband brought suit to quiet title, claiming ownership of the whole as the surviving joint tenant.

ancy between A and B into a tenancy in common between A and B. See, e.g., Krause v. Crossley, 202 Neb. 806, 277 N.W. 2d 242 (1979). In California, courts eliminated the need for a straw man only in 1980. See Riddle v. Harmon, 102 Cal. App. 3d 524, 162 Cal. Rptr. 530 (1980). Again the question: Why has the medieval law survived?

In choosing a straw man, what precautions must the landowner take? For what other purposes might a straw man be used today? See Cook, Straw Men in Real Estate Transactions, 25 Wash. U. L.Q. 232 (1940); Note, The Use of Straw Men in Massachusetts Real Estate Transactions, 44 B.U. L. Rev. 187 (1964).

Many states have legislated away the need for a straw man, see, e.g., N.Y. Real Prop. Law §240-b (McKinney 1989); Ill. Rev. Stat. ch. 76, ¶2.1 (1966), while in other states courts on their own have rejected the straw man anachronism. See, e.g., Miller v. Riegler, 243 Ark. 251, 419 S.W.2d 599 (1967); Switzer v. Pratt, 237 Iowa 788, 23 N.W.2d 837 (1946).

11.   **Judicial v. legislative competence.** When should the courts discard a shopworn common-law principle rather than await legislative action? The opposing views are sharply stated in the following extracts:

> It is essential that titles and estates in land be definite and certain. It is not a field in which the court should undertake to establish that it is liberal and modernistic in keeping pace with changing conditions. The creation of hybrid estates unknown to the common law is to be deplored. It can only bring about uncertainty, confusion and want of stability in estates and their attributes. Carried to an absurd conclusion, there would eventually be as many different kinds of estates as there are tracts of land. The plan duty of this court is in the opposite direction. Many states have made changes by legislative action and this is entirely proper. Other states have made such changes by judicial fiat which have resulted in all the varied and conflicting decisions cited in the dissent. I submit that it is the obligation of this court to adhere to the landmarks of the common law [requirements of four unities] on this subject until we are directed by competent authority to diviate therefrom.

Stuehm v. Mikulski, 139 Neb. 374, 409-410, 297 N.W. 595, 603 (1941) (concurring opinion).

> In the absence of a contrary public policy or prohibitory legislation express or implied, it is the rule in this State that the expressed intention of the grantor will override, whenever possible, purely formalistic objections to real estate conveyancing based on shadowy, subtle and arbitrary distinctions and niceties of the feudal common law. . . . "It is revolting to have no better reason for a rule of law than that so it was laid down in the time of Henry IV. It is still revolting if the grounds upon which it was laid down have vanished long since, and the rule simply persists from blind imitation of the past." Holmes, Collected Legal Papers (1920) 187.

Therrien v. Therrien, 94 N.H. 66, 67, 46 A.2d 538, 539 (1946).

What if the legislature has considered the "nicety" and has failed to act?

Where a statute purports to overturn the existing case law, how would it affect a prior grant from A "to A and B, as joint tenants?" See, e.g., Anson v. Murphy, 149 Neb. 716, 32 N.W.2d 271 (1948); Moe v. Krupke, 255 Wis. 33, 37 N.W.2d 865 (1949).

12. **Secret severance.** For an argument that the law should be changed to preclude joint tenants from unilaterally (and at times secretly) defeating the right of survivorship, see Samuel M. Fetters, An Invitation to Commit Fraud: Secret Destruction of Joint Tenant Survivorship Rights, 55 Fordham L. Rev. 173, 177-178 n.19 (1986):

> [m]ost couples who own their family residence property as joint tenants prob-ably would describe the situation as follows: "We own our home as joint tenants so that if one of us, God forbid, should die tomorrow, the house would not be tied up in probate. The survivor would own it outright." My experience of teaching property law for over a quarter of a century is that . . . most law students resist understanding that, by severing the joint tenancy and turning it into a tenancy in common, the survivorship right is thereby destroyed. Once the meaning of "severance" is understood as a destruction of survivorship rights, and that either joint tenant may accomplish such destruction by his own unilateral act, students find the law as hard to swallow as chopped hay.

If this is an accurate description of what most people *think* they own when they own a joint tenancy, do you agree with Fetters that the law should be changed? Note that this is another instance of divergence between the law and the intuitive or popular image of property rights. This issue is further discussed below.

13. **Joint tenancy and the dissolution of gay and lesbian couples' rela-tionships.** In some states, notably California, entitlements can arise in a "quasi-marital relationship," gay or straight. In this context, the form of title in which property is held creates a rebuttable presumption that the couple intended the property to be owned in the way defined by the title document. However, the presumption can be overcome by both oral and implied agreements between the partners, who are held to have a fiduciary relationship to each other.[11] Therefore, a partner who can prove an oral or implied contract or a breach of fiduciary relationship can overcome the presumption. Estrada v. Garcia, 132 Cal. App. 2d 545, 282 P.2d 547 (1955). Consider the following situation:

Tom and Burt have lived together for 17 years and now are breaking up. Their chief asset is a 100-acre farm, which they hold in joint tenancy. Tom says he put up 80 percent of the money they used to buy the farm. You are advising him, in California, on matters relating to the dissolution of his relationship with Burt. He asks you whether Burt owns half of the farm, given that "I paid for virtually all of it." What do you advise? What kind of

---

11. A fiduciary relationship is "[o]ne founded on trust or confidence reposed by one person in the integrity and fidelity of another" and that can be "legal, social, domestic, or merely personal." Black's Law Dictionary (6th ed. 1990), at 626.

documentation would you ask for from Tom and what facts would you need to support Tom's claim? What if Tom kept track of every contribution, but Burt did not? What if Burt worked full-time on the farm, while Tom held a paying job and kept all his income separate? What if three-fourths of the farm income went to Tom, while only one-fourth went to Burt? What if Tom did most of the work on the farm?

14. **Joint tenancy and the testamentary dispositions to gay and lesbian partners.** Gay and lesbian couples have traditionally been advised that the surest way to leave assets to their partners upon their deaths is to put the property in joint tenancy. This is an effective mechanism because this takes the property out of their estates, so that even if their wills leaving property to their partners are contested by their families of origin, the partner will retain the property held in joint tenancy. In some recent cases, however, parents or other relatives of deceased gay or lesbian partners have successfully defeated the joint tenancy claims of the partners of their deceased children, especially if the will is silent about the joint tenancy assets. Say you are a lawyer counseling a lesbian couple who wants to make sure that, whichever dies first, the survivor will inherit her assets. Discuss at least two different legal structures that will ensure that this goal is accomplished.

15. **Malpractice?** Defendant lawyer prepared a will whereunder the testator left to plaintiff all his real property. A principal asset was held in joint tenancy, which passed to the testator's spouse upon his death. Plaintiff sued defendant, alleging negligence in failing to advise testator to terminate the joint tenancy. Judgment? Cf. Milboer v. Mottolese, 1996 WL 57022 (Conn. Super. Jan. 24, 1996).

PROBLEM

[handwritten: she broke their / J + D'S Joint tenancy]

[handwritten: Donald wins?]

Alma Soul, a widow, told her children Donald and Jane that she would leave half her assets to each. Last year, Alma became very ill and relations became strained between Donald and Jane. During this period, Donald managed her mother's affairs. Upon her death, the children learned that their mother had indeed left each half of her estate. When Jane asserted a one-half ownership interest in Alma's chief asset, a property in Cochise County, Arizona, Donald produced the documents shown in Figures 4-2 and 4-3 on pages 392–394 (which are duly recorded in the relevant county records). Who owns what?

A client visits you. She wants to leave her farm to her two unmarried sons who have been working the farm together, with the survivor to own the farm outright. She is worried, however, about the debts of one of the sons, and the possibility that this son's creditors might try to destroy the other son's right of survivorship. Do you suggest a joint tenancy? Is there any way to use life estates and remainders to better achieve the client's goals? Consider the following case.

at the request of Pioneer Title Agency, Inc.

when recorded mail to:

SIERRA VISTA, AZ. 85635
305402 FMM

FEE # 940821595
OFFICIAL RECORDS
COCHISE COUNTY
DATE   HOUR
8/04/94   8
REQUEST   OF
PIONEER TITLE AGENCY
CHRISTINE RHODES-RECORDER
FEE :   9.00   PAGES :   1

Warranty Deed

For the consideration of Ten Dollars, and other valuable considerations, I or we,

ALMA RUTH SOUL, A WIDOW

do hereby convey to

DEBBIE BROWN, AN UNMARRIED WOMAN

to the following real property situated in COCHISE   ,County, Arizona:

Lot 32, MISSION SHADOWS, according to Book 12 of Maps, pages 48 and 48A, and
as amended by Scrivener's Error in Document No. 8804-07150, records of
Cochise County, Arizona;

EXCEPT all coal, gas and other minerals and except all water and water rights
as reserved in Deeds recorded in Docket 932, page 271, and in Document No.
8608-17013 and Document No. 8702-04416, records of Cochise County, Arizona.

AFFIDAVIT EXEMPT FROM FILING PER ARS 42-1614, B-9

SUBJECT TO: Current taxes and other assessments,reservations in patents and all easements,rights of way,
encumbrances, liens,covenants,conditions,restrictions,obligations,and liabilities as may appear of record.

And I or we do warrant the title against all persons whomsoever,subject to the matters set forth.

Dated this 29 Day of July   , 1994

Alma Ruth Soul
ALMA RUTH SOUL

STATE OF ARIZONA   )
) ss
County of COCHISE)

OFFICIAL SEAL
FRANCISCA MILIANTA
PIMA COUNTY
NOTARY PUBLIC - STATE OF ARIZONA
My Commss. Expires July 8, 1996

This instrument was acknowledged before me
this 29 day of July   , 1994 by

ALMA RUTH SOUL

Francisca Milianta
                                Notary Public

My commission will expire 7-8-96
This instrument was acknowledged before me
this_____ day of_____, 19___ by

STATE OF   )
) ss
County of   )

_____
                                Notary Public
My commission will expire

E-31C

940821595

FIGURE 4-2
Seller Owns Title "Against all persons whomsoever, subject to the matters set forth"

FEE # 940821596
OFFICIAL RECORD
COCHISE COUNTY
DATE   HOUR
8/04/94   8
REQUEST   OF
PIONEER TITLE AGENCY
CHRISTINE RHODES-RECORDER
FEE :   10.00   PAGES :   2

at the request of Pioneer Title Agency, Inc.

when recorded mail to:

ALMA RUTH SOUL

SIERRA VISTA, AZ. 85635

305402 FMM

Joint Tenancy Deed

For the consideration of Ten Dollars, and other valuable considerations, I or we,

DEBBIE BROWN, AN UNMARRIED WOMAN

does hereby convey to

ALMA RUTH SOUL, A WIDOW AND DONALD A. SOUL AND VIRGINIA M. SOUL, HUSBAND AND WIFE

not as tenants in common and not as community property estate, but as joint tenants with right of survivorship, the following described property in the County of COCHISE   ,State of Arizona.
See Exhibit "A" attached hereto and made a part hereof

AFFIDAVIT EXEMPT FROM FILING PER ARS 42-1614, B-3

SUBJECT TO: Current taxes and other assessments,reservations in patents and all easements,rights of way, encumbrances, liens,covenants,conditions,restrictions,obligations,and liabilities as may appear of record.
  And I or we do warrant the title against all persons whomsoever,subject to the matters above set forth.

  The Grantees by signing the acceptance below evidence their intention to acquire said premises as joint tenants with the right of survivorship,and not as community property nor as tenants in common.

Dated this 29 day of July   , 19 94

Accepted and approved:

Donald A. Soul

DONALD A. SOUL

Virginia M. Soul

VIRGINIA M. SOUL

Alma Ruth Soul

ALMA RUTH SOUL

Debbie Brown

DEBBIE BROWN

                              Grantees   Grantors

STATE OF ARIZONA)
) ss
County of COCHISE)

OFFICIAL SEAL
FRANCISCA MILIANTA
PIMA COUNTY
NOTARY PUBLIC - STATE OF ARIZONA
My Commes. Expires July 0, 1996

This instrument was acknowledged before me
this 29 day of July , 19 94 by

DEBBIE BROWN

Francisca Milianta
                                Notary Public

My commission will expire 7-8-96

STATE OF ARIZONA)
) ss
County of COCHISE)

OFFICIAL SEAL
FRANCISCA MILIANTA
PIMA COUNTY
NOTARY PUBLIC - STATE OF ARIZONA
My Commes. Expires July 8, 1996

This instrument was acknowledged before me
this 1 day of August , 19 94 by

DONALD A. SOUL and VIRGINIA M. SOUL
and ALMA RUTH SOUL

Francisca Milianta
                                Notary Public

E-86C

My commission will expire 7-8-96

940821596

FIGURE 4-3
Joint Tenancy Deed

393

```
Escrow No. 305402
                                   EXHIBIT "A"

Lot 32, MISSION SHADOWS, according to Book 12 of Maps, pages 48 and 48A, and
as amended by Scrivener's Error in Document No. 8804-07150, records of
Cochise County, Arizona;

EXCEPT all coal, gas and other minerals and except all water and water rights
as reserved in Deeds recorded in Docket 932, page 271, and in Document No.
8608-17013 and Document No. 8702-04416, records of Cochise County, Arizona.
```

FIGURE 4-3 (continued)

HASS v. HASS

248 Wis. 212, 21 N.W.2d 398 (1946)

[This action was commenced on January 25, 1945, by Walter H. Hass, administrator of the estate of Bertha Hass, deceased, Walter H. Hass, Erna Haehlke, and Lavine Hass Krause and Gerald Hass, minors, by Leona Saeger, their guardian ad litem, plaintiffs, against Herbert W. Hass, Julius Hass, and Arnold Hass, defendants, to set aside a deed given by Bertha Hass to herself and Herbert W. Hass, dated February 8, 1944, and for a construction thereof. The court dismissed the first cause of action on the merits and rendered judgment construing the deed which was entered July 6, 1945. The defendant, Herbert W. Hass, appeals from that part of the judgment construing the deed. Other facts will be stated in the opinion.]

ROSENBERRY, C.J. The facts may be briefly stated as follows: On February 8, 1944, Bertha Hass, an elderly widow, was the owner of a one-hundred-twenty-acre farm and the personal property thereon. Her son, Herbert, was about thirty-seven years of age and had lived and worked on the farm all his life. Mrs. Hass had previously made a will bequeathing and devising the property to Herbert. During the winter of 1943-1944 she was in poor health and fearful that the son Walter might cause trouble, she asked her son Arnold to procure someone to draw a deed so that she could deed the farm to Herbert in such a way that it would be his after her death but would be hers in case Herbert should predecease her. After the execution of the deed in question the will was destroyed.

The deed was prepared on a printed form bearing across its top the label "Warranty Deed To Husband and Wife as Joint Tenants." The scrivener who drafted the instrument had been an abstractor and real-estate broker for more than twenty-five years but was not an attorney at law. The appropriate blanks, the description, the names of the parties to the instrument, and the recitation thereon below the description were all written in longhand by the scrivener in pen and ink. In the deed Bertha Hass, widow, was described as the party of the first part. The parties of the second part were described as — "Bertha Hass and Herbert W. Hass of Marathon county, mother and son, and the survivor of them in his or her own right."

The granting clause provided that the said party of the first part for a consideration, gives, grants, etc., — "unto the said parties of the second part, a life estate as joint tenants during their joint lives and an absolute fee forever in the remainder to the survivor of them, his or her heirs and assigns, in and to the following-described real estate [description]."

After the description is the following:

"The purpose of this conveyance is to vest the title to the above-described property in the grantees herein named as joint tenants and none other." . . .

The law relating to the creation of joint tenancies was modified by sec. 230.45 (2) and (3), Stats., ch. 437, Laws of 1933, which provides:

> (2) Any deed from husband to wife or from wife to husband which conveys an interest in the grantor's lands and by its terms evinces an intent on the part of the grantor to create a joint tenancy between grantor and grantee shall be held and construed to create such joint tenancy, and any husband and wife who are grantor and grantee in any such deed heretofore given shall hold the premises described in such deed as joint tenants.
>
> (3) Any deed to two or more grantees which, by the method of describing such grantees or by the language of the granting or habendum clause therein evinces an intent to create a joint tenancy in grantees shall be held and construed to create such joint tenancy. *4 unities?*

The trial court was of the view that if the deed in question had been given by a husband to his wife or by a wife to her husband, it would have created a joint tenancy in the husband and wife, but this only because of the express language contained in sub. (2), but that the parties to this deed not being husband and wife, only sub. (3) applies.

The court was further of the view that if the language of sub. (3) was broad enough to include a deed from an owner to himself and another as joint tenants, sub. (2) would be meaningless. The court further said:

> I do not think that it was the intent of this deed to create a mere life estate [in the grantor], as we think of the creating of a life estate.[12] It is true that they used language in here which is language that is customarily used, or at least is properly used, in creating a joint tenancy, but I don't think it was the intent of this instrument, "Exhibit A," to reserve a life estate merely, to the grantor, Bertha Hass. I think it was her clear intent that she should get this property in the event her son should die ahead of her. The express language written in pen and ink is as follows. "The purpose of this conveyance is to vest title to the above-described property in the grantees herein as joint tenants and none other." . . .

We agree with the trial court that sub. (3) does not apply but that does not dispose of the case. We have set out the material parts of the conveyance and while no doubt it was the intent of the scrivener to draft an instrument

---

12. Query: Who made this argument, and why? — Eds.

which would create a joint tenancy as between the mother and her son, the fact that the instrument as drawn did not accomplish that purpose does not make it void and the trial court so held. In the granting clause the following language is employed: The mother granted — "unto the said parties of the second part, a life estate as joint tenants during their joint lives and an absolute fee forever in the remainder to the survivor of them, his or her heirs and assigns, in and to the following-described real estate [description]."

Inasmuch as the conveyance was not effective to convey any interest or estate from the grantor to herself, the effective part of the conveyance is that which relates to the grant to the son. We can reach no other conclusion from the language employed than that the instrument created in the parties a tenancy in common for their joint lives and conveyed an estate in fee to the son if he survived his mother. If he predeceased his mother, his death terminated his interest in the estate. In that event the condition upon which the remainder was to pass to him could not happen and the entire title to the property would be in the grantor.

It is clear from the language of the deed that the conveyance was intended to create a tenancy for the joint lives of the parties with the remainder in the survivor. That it created a tenancy in common rather than a joint tenancy is also beyond question. We see no reason why this type of survivorship may not be created by deed. It has one advantage over the right of survivorship incident to joint tenancy, it cannot be destroyed by the act of one of the parties. A conveyance by one joint tenant of his interest in the property destroys the right of survivorship. . . .

In this case a joint tenancy was not created during the joint lives for the reason that the unities of time and title were absent. The result was there was a tenancy in common during their joint lives with the survivor to take the remainder in fee. . . .

By the Court. That part of the judgment appealed from is reversed on the defendant's appeal . . . with directions to the lower court to enter judgment adjudging the defendant to be the sole owner of real property in fee and the owner of the personal property described in the deed. . . .

Rosenberry, C.J. (on motion for rehearing). The defendants [*sic*][13] have made a motion for rehearing in this case which appears to be based upon a misconception of what the court decided. Counsel say:

> We feel that the court has created a legal oddity and has so unsettled the rules of tenancies as known by the bar in this state that the decision, if allowed to stand, will produce much unnecessary litigation. It, therefore, seems important not only to our clients but also to the court, the bar in general, and

---

13. Even Chief Judges err! The plaintiffs sought the rehearing, according to the motion papers on file with the clerk of the court. — Eds.

the public at large, that the court again examine into this matter before letting this decision become final. . . .

The court has created a tenancy in common with right of survivorship, although the court found the intent was to create a joint tenancy, and even though this court has always been committed to the doctrine that the only estate having the right of survivorship is a joint tenancy.

The term "survivorship" is used mainly in three classes of cases: (1) Those involving joint tenancy, an incident of which is the right of survivorship, where the instrument creating the joint tenancy "evinces an intention to create a joint tenancy in the grantees." In this class of cases survivorship is dependent upon the nature of the tenancy.

(2) Estates by the entirety which are abolished by the laws of this state. In this class of cases survivorship is dependent upon the status of the parties as it can exist only where the grantees are husband and wife. [Cf. §7.2, *infra.*]

(3) Cases where a surviving tenant in common by virtue of the express terms of the instrument creating the tenancy takes the remainder. This species of survivorship is referred to in the opinion as a type. Perhaps it would be more accurate to say that such an instrument creates an indestructible remainder rather than a type of survivorship. In this class the right of the survivor to take the remainder does not depend upon the nature of the tenancies or the status of the parties, but upon the express provisions of the instrument creating the remainder. The case under consideration falls in the third class.

With this explanation it ought to be perfectly clear that the court has done no violence to existing law.

By the Court. Motion denied with $25 costs.

NOTES AND QUESTIONS

1.   **Accord.** See also Holbrook v. Holbrook, 240 Or. 567, 403 P.2d 12 (1965) (concurrent life estates with contingent remainders in the life tenants, the remainder to vest in the survivor, will result from attempt to create joint tenancy after statute abolishes it). The *Hass* case is commented upon in Notes: 1947 Wis. L. Rev. 117 (best of the lot), 30 Marq. L. Rev. 182 (1946), 44 Mich. L. Rev. 1144 (1946), 23 Notre Dame Law. 103 (1947).

2. **Legislative aftermath.** The Wisconsin legislature acted promptly after the *Hass* decision to amend §230.45(3) to read:

> Any deed to two or more grantees, including any deed in which the grantor is also one of the grantees, which by the method of describing such grantees or by the language of the granting or habendum clause herein evinces an intent to create a joint tenancy in grantees shall be held and construed to create such joint tenancy.

Wis. Stat. Ann. §230.45(3) (1957); current version at Wis. Stat. Ann. §700.18 (1995).

— Done away w/ unities

Having amended §230.45(3), should the legislature also have repealed §230.45(2)? For the possibility that §230.45(2) may have an unexpected force of its own, suppose that A now makes a conveyance to B "as joint tenant with A." What is the nature of the estate created? *JT?*

Q ⎰ If the legislature has acted to remove a common-law anachronism, should the courts read the curative statute narrowly, or construe it liberally so as to advance the legislature's apparent goal?

3. **Drafting problem.** What language would you, as a draftsman, use to create an indestructible survivorship right in a cotenancy? If a grantor wants to create a cotenancy with right of survivorship, what factors should she weigh in choosing between a destructible and indestructible right? Should courts indiscriminately allow parties to create an indestructible right of survivorship?

4. **Judicial aftermath.** The Wisconsin Supreme Court faced a similar case three years after its decision in Hass v. Hass. In 1942, Emil A. Moe executed a deed to his 168-acre farm naming as joint tenants himself and his sister, Emma Moe. Emma predeceased her brother and, before long, Emil and his sister's heirs were disputing ownership of the farm. Relying heavily on the *Hass* decision, Emil argued for a survivorship interest even if the 1942 conveyance failed to create a common-law joint tenancy. The trial court, also relying on *Hass*, agreed. In reversing the judgment, the supreme court excoriated the court below:

HASS Reversed

> The trial court made a so-called first alternative conclusion that if the deed did not create a joint tenancy it created a tenancy in common during the lives of Emil A. Moe and Emma Moe, and that under such deed Emil A. Moe succeeded to the entire title in fee simple upon the death of Emma Moe. Just how the trial court arrived at this conclusion we are not informed. It appears to be a tour de force to make a survivorship an incident to a tenancy in common. It is considered that the court had no such power. [Moe v. Krupke, 255 Wis. 33, 40-41, 37 N.W.2d 865, 868 (1949)]

The author of the opinion? Rosenberry, C.J.

To distinguish its earlier decision, the court stressed that the Hass deed had contained the words "and an absolute fee forever in the remainder to the survivor, etc.," while no such words appeared in the Moe deed. But, how is this phrase relevant except as further evidence that the grantor intended to create a survivorship interest? Having stated this intention once by describing the grantees as "joint tenants," why should Moe's case collapse because he did not say it again?

Emma Moe was not exactly a gratuitous grantee. In consideration for the cotenancy interest, Emma had released a $10,000 mortgage that she held against her brother's farm. The court noted that Emma's rights as

Concurrent life Estate
w/ Remainder to Survivor
moe did not do this

mortgagee were more valuable than her rights as a tenant in common. On what theory might this evidence be admissible?

5. **Tax implications.** In estate planning situations like the one in the *Hass* case, tax considerations are often a crucial factor in deciding what to give to whom, and when, in families with substantial estates. Say that Bertha Hass is a wealthy woman. She could lower her federal estate tax by transferring some of her assets $10,000 yearly tax-free to each child during her life. Since they would not be in her estate, this would lower the size of her estate and therefore her estate tax liability. Although this option is desirable from an estate tax viewpoint, many people hesitate to give their property to their children during their lifetimes, because — after all — then they are dependent upon their children's generosity for their support. But sophisticated planning can help both to reduce that dependency and avoid taxes. This gives you a taste of the complex work of a tax lawyer.

2.   Law in Action: Who Has Concurrent Estates?

Based on the available empirical evidence, it appears that joint tenancies were very unusual for much of American history. After World War II, however, one study of land records in Iowa documented a "phenomenal rise" in the amount of property held by joint tenancy. N. William Hines, Real Property Joint Tenancies: Law, Fact, and Fancy, 51 Iowa L. Rev. 582, 586-591, 607-617 (1966). For several generations, bank personnel and real estate brokers have routinely advised married couples — in states not recognizing the tenancy by the entirety, *infra* — to take title to real property as joint tenants and in all states to take title to personal property. Regis W. Campfield, Estate Planning for Joint Tenancies, 1974 Duke L.J. 669, 671; Yale B. Griffith, Community Property in Joint Tenancy Form, 14 Stan. L. Rev. 87, 91 (1961). The result is that joint tenancies (or, where permitted, tenancies by the entirety) are now the norm for property held by married couples. In California, for example, where tenancy by the entirety no longer exists, 85 percent of recorded deeds to husbands and wives are in joint tenancy. Nathaniel Sterling, Joint Tenancy and Community Property in California, 14 Pac. L.J. 927, 928 (1983). See also William W. Stuart, Joint Ownership before and after the Tax Reform Act, 21 Ariz. L. Rev. 659 (1979). Dean Hines's 1970 Iowa study found astoundingly high levels of joint ownership: about 89 percent of checking accounts, 81 percent of savings accounts and time certificates, 55 percent of stock, 72 percent of bonds, 39 percent of first cars, and 20 percent of second cars. N. William Hines, Personal Property Joint Tenancies: More Law, Fact, and Fancy, 54 Minn. L. Rev. 509, 574 (1970).[14]

---

14. Hines's study was of a relatively small number of households. See N. William Hines, 54 Minn. L. Rev. 509, 510-511 (1970).

The popularity of the marital joint tenancy, while partly reflecting the spouses' emotional unity, rests largely on the tenancy's ability to function as the "poor man's will" without the need for probate or administration.[15] Because lawyers and court costs are involved, these proceedings are often costly and may take months or even years. See Charles Dickens, Bleak House (Norman Page ed., 1853) (probate of a large estate left the beneficiaries penniless). Property held in joint tenancy avoids probate or administration because of the legal fiction that no interest passes upon the death of one joint tenant. Consequently, the surviving joint tenant(s) take automatically: Usually all they need to do to clear their title to the property is to provide evidence of the death of the other co-owner(s).

3.   Tenancy by the Entirety

In roughly half the states and the District of Columbia,[16] a husband and wife may jointly acquire property as "tenants by the entirety." The tenancy by the entirety is like the joint tenancy in that it also features a right of survivorship (in the decedent's spouse) and, in many states, the four unities are necessary for its creation. A fifth requirement is that the cotenants must be married to each other at the time of the grant. (Thus unmarried couples cannot hold by the entirety,[17] and divorce automatically terminates a tenancy by the entirety; absent some agreement to the contrary, the parties usually become tenants in common.[18]) As in the case of the joint tenancy,

---

15. Probate or administration is the judicial supervision of the estate of the deceased person. Probate is the formal term for the proceeding where the deceased person has left a will and administration is the term where there is no will. Typically, the court appoints an executor (named in the will) or administrator to collect assets, pay debts and taxes, and distribute property to the beneficiaries.

For well-to-do individuals, however, joint ownership may not be the best way to own property where the spouses together own more than $600,000 in combined assets. By retaining up to $600,000 in assets in his or her own name, a spouse can bequeath this amount at death, to a "credit shelter" or a "bypass" trust that will not be subject to federal estate tax on the death of either the first or the second spouse, even though the second spouse is the trust beneficiary. See G. Warren Whitaker, Tenancy by the Entirety, N.Y.L.J., Aug. 30, 1995, at 5.

16. A recent survey of the current status of the tenancy by the entirety concluded that the estate was recognized in no fewer than 25 states and possibly as many as 37 states, and in the District of Columbia. See Samuel M. Fetters, An Invitation to Commit Fraud: Secret Destruction of Joint Tenant Survivorship Rights, 55 Fordham L. Rev. 173, 174 n.1 (1986) (discussing 4A Powell, Real Property ¶620, at 52-4–52-13 (Patrick Rohan ed., 1986)). Other estimates are a little lower. Id.

17. The grantees must be husband and wife when the entirety estate is created, and even if they subsequently intermarry, an entirety will not arise nunc pro tunc. Hiles v. Fisher, 144 N.Y. 306, 39 N.E. 337 (1895). The deed need not recite that the grantees are husband and wife so long as the intent to create an entirety is clear. Parol evidence is later admissible to establish the parties' intermarriage at the time of the conveyance. Dowling v. Salliotte, 83 Mich. 131, 47 N.W. 225 (1890). Parol evidence is equally admissible to rebut a statement of intermarriage appearing in the deed. Kent v. O'Neil, 53 So. 2d 779 (Fla. 1951).

18. See Millar v. Millar, 200 Md. 14, 87 A.2d 838 (1952); Bernatavicius v. Bernatavicius, 259 Mass. 486, 156 N.E. 685 (1927); Corder v. Corder, 546 S.W.2d 798 (Mo. Ct. App. 1977).

The District of Columbia, by statute, recognizes an entirety in property even after divorce if the divorced couple held the property by the entirety during marriage and agreed

the tenants constitute one legal entity.[19] Consequently, if one tenant by the entirety dies, the other inherits the whole automatically — so the tenancy by the entirety, like the joint tenancy, requires neither probate nor administration (but the property is subject to federal estate taxes).

The tenancy by the entirety is far more durable than the two other types of common-law cotenancy. Whereas any tenant can destroy a joint tenancy or tenancy in common by a unilateral request for partition,[20] the tenancy by the entirety can only be destroyed by the spouses' combined action or the marriage's end. Moreover, neither spouse may terminate the other spouse's survivorship right. The medieval explanation was that, unlike joint tenants, who held by the share and by the whole, tenants by the entirety held *per tout et non per my*, by the whole and not by the share. The underlying rationale apparently was to protect the wife from the actions of the husband, who had the sole right to manage the estate during his lifetime. See §4.1.a.4, *infra*.

At common law, a conveyance to a married couple was presumed to be a tenancy by the entirety, because the husband and the wife were "but one person in the law." Littleton, Tenures §291 (Eugene Wambaugh ed., 1903). Although this theoretical basis is gone, this presumption remains in most states that recognize the entirety. Hoag v. Hoag, 213 Mass. 50, 99 N.E. 521 (1912), is an extreme example: "To H and W, . . . as joint tenants in joint tenancy"; held: tenancy by the entirety created. Why do you suppose the presumption persists? What societal values, if any, does the entirety serve?

NOTES AND QUESTIONS

1. **Nonmarriage and the attempt to create a tenancy by the entirety.** A troublesome issue has been the treatment of an attempted entirety where the prerequisite marriage did not exist. Most courts have treated the parties as tenants in common, see, e.g., Collins v. Norris, 314 Mich. 145, 22 N.W.2d 249 (1946), yet the result ignores the parties' implied or stated preference for a survivorship right. Since the issue usually arises after one party has died, the survivor loses a half interest in favor of the decedent's creditors or heirs, the deserved fruit, some might say, of having pretended to be what one was not. Alternatively, the same court has sometimes found a joint tenancy. See, e.g., Jackson City Bank & Trust Co. v. Frederick, 271 Mich. 538, 260 N.W. 908 (1935). See also Donald Kepner, The Effect of Attempted

---

prior to divorce to continue this form of ownership afterwards. Cf. Benson v. United States, 442 F.2d 1221 (D.C. Cir. 1971).

19. The wife lost her legal identity upon marriage at common law and became one with the husband. See §4.2.b *infra*.

20. Partition is discussed at §4.1.b.1, *infra*. The cotenants may agree, however, not to partition unilaterally, and such agreements, of reasonable duration, are usually enforceable.

Creation of an Estate by the Entirety in Unmarried Grantees, 6 Rutgers L. Rev. 550 (1952).

2. **Effect of separation upon a tenancy by the entirety.** Many lawyers can recall instances of de facto separations involving a couple who would not cooperate in the management of the entirety parcel. Neither could sell or mortgage the premises without the other's consent; sometimes the other was nowhere to be found. Yet partition seemed technically impossible as long as the marriage continued. In this instance, should not an equity court exercise its power to order partition? Compare Tendrick v. Tendrick, 193 F.2d 368 (D.C. Cir. 1951) (partition embodied in a decree of separation).

3. **Does the entirety continue after the property is sold or destroyed?** H and W are tenants by the entirety. The real estate is sold and the sales proceeds are placed in a joint bank account. Does the entirety continue? Compare Hawthorne v. Hawthorne, 13 N.Y.2d 82, 192 N.E.2d 20 (1963) (no entirety in fire insurance proceeds after entirety property destroyed), with In re Siegel's Estate, 350 So. 2d 89 (Fla. Dist. Ct. App. 1977) (entirety in purchase money mortgage held by sellers after entirety property sold).

4. **Is the blameworthiness of one spouse imputed to the other?** H and W are tenants by the entirety. H deliberately sets fire to the real estate. W is an innocent party. The insurance company refuses to pay either spouse; it argues that the fraudulent acts of the husband are imputed to the wife as if they were "one entity." Convincing? Compare Rockingham Mutual Ins. Co. v. Hummel, 219 Va. 803, 250 S.E.2d 774 (1979) (spouse denied recovery), with Steigler v. Insurance Co. of No. Am., 384 A.2d 398 (Del. 1978) (spouse granted recovery).

4.   Relative Stability of the Tenancy by the Entirety:
       Creditors' Rights

Traditionally, the tenancy by the entirety functioned to protect the family home from the creditors of either spouse (typically, the husband's). In effect, the entirety represented a refusal fully to commodify the family home, much as the secure tenancy represented the refusal fully to commodify the tenant's interest in her rental apartment. Should the family home held by the entirety be treated like any other asset? Consider the following case.

KING v. GREENE

30 N.J. 395, 153 A.2d 49 (1959)

BURLING, J. This is an action seeking possession of lands, damages for mesne profits[21] and a declaration that a mortgage encumbrance held by defendant Margaretta P. W. Harrison is a nullity and directing its discharge

---

21. The rental value, i.e., the value of the use and occupation of land. — EDS.

of record. The Superior Court, Law Division, hearing the matter on stipulated facts, granted plaintiff's motion for summary judgment. Defendants appealed, and while pending and prior to argument in the Appellate Division, we certified the cause on our motion. After argument in this court, we directed that the cause be reargued and requested that the New Jersey Title Insurance Association appear as amicus curiae.

The following facts are stipulated: In 1913 plaintiff, Marie King, acquired the title to three lots on Patterson Avenue in the Borough of Shrewsbury, New Jersey. In 1931 her husband, Philip King, brought an action against her in the Court of Chancery which resulted in a decree being entered that plaintiff owed him $1225. It was further ordered that plaintiff execute a conveyance of the three lots to herself and her husband as tenants by the entirety. While the conveyance was never made, the decree was recorded, the self-operative effect which was to make Marie and Philip King become seized of the premises as tenants by the entirety. R.S. 2:29-61 (now N.J.S. 2a: 16-7, N.J.S.A.).

In 1932 execution was issued to satisfy the 1931 money judgment and a sheriff's deed was made to John V. Crowell of all plaintiff's right, title and interest in the property. In 1933 Philip King conveyed his right, title and interest in the three lots to Martin Van Buren Smock. John V. Crowell and his wife joined in the deed to Smock, conveying their interest acquired by virtue of the sheriff's deed. Philip King died in 1938. In 1946 Smock conveyed his interest to defendants Joseph and Mabel Greene.

In 1957 plaintiff, as surviving spouse of Philip King, instituted the present action for possession, contending that she is the sole owner of the property and that the 1932 sheriff's deed conveyed only one-half the rents, issues and profits of the property during the joint lives of the spouses and did not convey her right of survivorship. She alleges that when her husband died in 1938 the life estate for the joint lives of the spouses terminated and she became entitled to the fee. Defendants' contention is that the sheriff's deed conveyed plaintiff's right of survivorship as well as a life interest.

The trial court concluded that the sheriff's deed did not include the right of survivorship and entered a summary judgment for plaintiff which declared that she is the present holder of a fee simple in the premises; that a mortgage upon the premises held by defendant Margaretta Harrison and given by the defendants Joseph and Mabel Greene is discharged; that defendants John and Elaine Cusick, the Greenes' tenants, must vacate the premises and the plaintiff is entitled to mesne profits for six years prior to the commencement of this action.

The question at issue is whether the purchaser at an execution sale under a judgment entered against the wife in a tenancy by the entirety acquires the wife's right of survivorship. . . .

Involved are two fundamental problems: (A) the nature of an estate by the entirety at common law, and (B) the effect upon the estate by the entirety of the Married Women's Act (L. 1852, p. 407, now R.S. 37:2-12 et seq., N.J.S.A.)

A — Estates by the Entirety at Common Law

At the outset we note that the industry of counsel and our own independent research have failed to reveal any English case decided prior to 1776, touching upon the question of whether a voluntary or involuntary conveyance of a husband's interest in a tenancy by the entirety carries with it his right of survivorship.

The unique form of concurrent ownership at common law, labeled estates by the entirety, may be traced into antiquity at least as far back as the 14th and 15th Centuries. 3 Holdsworth, History of the English Law (3d ed. 1923), 128; Kepner, "The Effect of an Attempted Creation of an Estate by the Entirety in Unmarried Grantees," 6 Rutgers L. Rev. 550 (1952). The estate was unique because of the common-law concept of unity of husband and wife and the positing of that unity in the person of the husband during coverture. Putnam, "The Theory of Estates by the Entirety," 4 Southern L. Rev. 91 (1879). A husband and wife cannot hold by moieties or in severalty, said Littleton, "and the cause is, for that the husband and wife are but one person in law. . . ." Coke on Littleton, sec. 29. Blackstone, in his judicial capacity noted: "This estate [entirety] differs from joint-tenancy, because joint-tenants take by moieties, and are each seised of an undivided moiety of the whole, per my et per tout, which draws after it the incident of survivorship or jus accrescendi, unless either party chooses in his life-time to sever the jointure. But husband and wife, being considered in law as one person, they cannot, during the coverture take separate estates; and therefore upon a purchase made by them both, they cannot be seised by moieties, but both and each has the entirety. . . . They are seised per tout and not per my." Green v. King, 2 Wm. Blackstone 1211, 1214, 96 Eng. Rep. 713, 714 (C.P. 1777). To the same effect see the opinion of Chancellor Kent in Rogers v. Benson, 5 Johns. Ch. 431 (N.Y. 1821).

The unity of the spouses theory was early recognized in New Jersey as the foundation upon which estates by the entirety rested. Den ex dem. Hardenbergh v. Hardenbergh, 10 N.J.L. 42 (Sup. Ct. 1828).

By virtue of the jus mariti and jure uxoris[22] the husband was the dominant figure in the marital unity. Thus, in an estate by the entirety the husband had absolute dominion and control over the property during the joint lives. The husband was entitled to the rents, issues and profits during the joint lives of himself and his wife, with the right to use and alienate the property as he desired, and the property was subject to execution for his debts. Washburn v. Burns, 34 N.J.L. 18 (Sup. Ct. 1869) (it should be noted that although *Washburn* was decided after the Married Women's Act, the court overlooked the effect of the act and decided the case on common-law principles); Freeman, Co-Tenancy and Partition (2d ed. 1888) 140; 2 American Law of Property, §6.6 p. 28 (1952); Phipps, "Tenancy by Entire-

---

22. See §4.1.a.1 *infra.* — Eds.

ties," 25 Temple L.Q. 24, 25 (1951). As stated by the court in Washburn v. Burns, *supra*:

> . . . [T]he husband has an interest which does not flow from the unity of the estate, and in which the wife has no concern. He is entitled to the use and possession of the property during the joint lives of himself and wife. During this period the wife has no interest in or control over the property. It is no invasion of her rights, therefore, for him to dispose of it at his pleasure. The limit of this right of the husband is, that he cannot do any act to the prejudice of the ulterior rights of his wife. (34 N.J.L. at page 20.)

The remaining question is, could the husband unilaterally alienate his right of survivorship at common law? Our study of the authorities convinces us that he could. The entire thrust of the authorities on the common law, with one notable exception, is to the effect that the only distinction between a joint tenancy and a tenancy by the entirety at common law was that survivorship could not be affected by unilateral action in the latter estate.

It was settled in England as early as the 14th Century that the husband could not defeat the wife's right of survivorship. In that case, reported in 2 Coke on Littleton, sec. 291, William Ocle was found guilty of treason (he murdered Edward II) and his estate was forfeited. Edward III granted the forfeited lands (owned jointly with his wife) to someone else. It was held that the husband's act of treason could not deprive the wife of her right of survivorship. Back v. Andrew, 2 Vern. 120 (1690), stands for the same proposition. But to say that the husband cannot by his voluntary or involuntary act defeat the wife's right of survivorship is not to say that his own right of survivorship, subject to his wife's right of survivorship, should he predecease her, cannot be alienated. . . .

No prejudice would result to the wife's interest at common law by the husband's alienation of his right of survivorship. If he predeceased her, she would take a fee. If she predeceased him, her interests were cut off anyway. During his lifetime she had no interest in the estate. . . .

Most courts and commentators have taken the position that at common law the husband's right of survivorship was alienable, so that the purchaser or grantee would take the entire fee in the event the wife predeceased the husband and the interest was subject to execution for his debts. [Citations omitted.]

It is our view [also] that the husband could, at common law, alienate his right of survivorship, or, more properly, his fee simple subject to defeasance. . . .

B — EFFECT OF THE MARRIED WOMEN'S ACT OF 1852 (L. 1852, P. 407, NOW R.S. 37:2-12 ET SEQ., N.H.S.A.) UPON ESTATES BY THE ENTIRETY

R.S. 37:2-12, N.J.S.A. provides:

"The real and personal property of a woman which she owns at the time of her marriage, and the real and personal property, and rents, issues and profits thereof, of a married woman, which she receives or obtains in any manner whatsoever after her marriage, shall be her separate property as if she were a feme sole."

At least nine jurisdictions took the view that the Married Women's Act, having destroyed the spousal unity, destroyed the foundation upon which estates by the entirety rested, and therefore such concurrent ownership could no longer arise. Phipps, *supra*, 25 Temple L.Q., at pp. 28-29. This was the view originally taken in New Jersey, Kip v. Kip, 33 N.J. Eq. 213 (Ch. 1880), and was the view taken by the lower court in Rosenblath v. Buttlar, 7 N.J.L.J. 143 (Ch. 1884). It might be noted that presently tenancy by the entirety does not exist in 29 states. Phipps, *supra*, 25 Temple L.Q., at p. 32. In the absence of legislation abolishing or altering estates by the entirety, our role, in light of the settled precedent that they do exist in New Jersey, is merely to define their incidents.

The Court of Errors and Appeals in Buttlar v. Rosenblath, 42 N.J. Eq. 651, 9 A. 695 (E. & A. 1887), settled the question of the effect of the Married Women's Act upon estates by the entirety. After holding that the act does not destroy the estate, it was held that the effect and purpose of the act was to put the wife on a par with the husband. It was held:

> There is nothing in the married woman's act which indicates an intention to exclude this estate wholly from its operation. I think, therefore, that the just construction of this legislation, and the one in harmony with its spirit and general purpose, is that the wife is endowed with the capacity, during the joint lives, to hold in her possession, as a single female, one-half of the estate in common with her husband, and that the right of survivorship still exists as at common law. (42 N.J. Eq., at page 657, 9 A at page 698.)

Subsequent decisions have confirmed that presently husband and wife, by virtue of the Married Women's Act, hold as tenants in common for their joint lives; that survivorship exists as at common law and is indestructible by unilateral action; and that the rights of each spouse in the estate are alienable, voluntarily or involuntarily, the purchaser becoming a tenant in common with the remaining spouse for the joint lives of the husband and wife.

It is clear that the Married Women's Act created an equality between the spouses in New Jersey, insofar as tenancies by the entirety are concerned. If, as we have previously concluded, the husband could alienate his right of survivorship at common law, the wife, by virtue of the act, can alienate her right of survivorship. And it follows, that if the wife takes equal rights with the husband in the estate, she must take equal disabilities. Such are the dictates of complete equality. Thus, the judgment creditors of either spouse may levy and execute upon their separate rights of survivorship. . . .

It might be argued that the involuntary sale of right of survivorship will not bring a fair price. However, the creditor [under a prior decision] can receive a one-half interest in the life estate for the joint lives. It seems to us that if this interest were coupled with the debtor-spouse's right of survivorship the whole would command a substantially higher price and the creditor may thereby realize some present satisfaction out of the debtor-spouse's assets.

Moreover, to hold that a sheriff's deed does not pass the debtor-spouse's right of survivorship compels the creditor to maintain a constant vigilance over the estate. This is particularly true where the purchaser at execution sale of the debtor-spouse's life interest is someone other than the judgment creditor.[23] There is, in short, no compelling policy reason why a judgment creditor should be inordinately delayed, or, in some instances completely deprived of his right to satisfaction out of the debtor-spouse's assets.

The judgment appealed from is reversed and the cause is remanded for the entry of a judgment in accordance with the views expressed in this opinion.

For reversal: JUSTICES BURLING, JACOBS, FRANCIS, PROCTOR, AND SCHETTINO — 5.

For affirmance: CHIEF JUSTICE WEINTRAUB and JUSTICE HALL — 2.

WEINTRAUB, C.J. (dissenting). The estate by the entirety is a remnant of other times. It rests upon the fiction of a oneness of husband and wife. Neither owns a separate, distinct interest in the fee; rather each and both as an entity own the entire interest. Neither takes anything by survivorship; there is nothing to pass because the survivor always had the entirety. To me the conception is quite incomprehensible. The inherent incongruity permeates the problem before use.

Presumably the estate by the entirety was designed to serve a social purpose favorable to the parties to the marriage. We are asked to recognize incidents more compatible with present thinking. Specifically, we are asked to subject a spouse's interest in the *fee* to execution sale. I am not sure that I can identify just what is being sold. In theory there is no right of survivorship; nothing accrues on death. And during coverture neither spouse has a separate interest in the fee. Whatever the nature of the "fee" interest a purchaser receives, he can do nothing with it except wait and hope. What he buys is the chance that the non-debtor spouse will expire before the judgment debtor.

I do not seriously urge such academic difficulties; indeed, one cannot confidently make deductions from a premise that is fictional. My objection is a practical one, to wit, that so long as we adhere to the concept of an estate by the entirety, an execution sale will result in the sacrifice of economic interests. Since the purchaser at the sale does not acquire a one-half interest in the fee with a right to partition the fee, the execution sale can be but a gambling event, yielding virtually nothing to the debtor, or for that

23. Why is that? — EDS.

matter to the creditor either unless he is the successful wagerer at the sale and in the waiting game to follow.

I concede that earlier decisions recognizing a right to sell the *life interest* of the debtor presented the same problem in theory, but the practical consequences were negligible. I think it has been the general experience of the bar that judgments obtained against a spouse have not been followed by execution sales of the life interest. And in bankruptcy proceedings the interest of the debtor regularly has been sold for a nominal sum to the other spouse or a representative of both. The general assumption, I believe, has been that the fee was not involved; and the life interest for one reason or another was not regarded by outsiders as sufficiently attractive. But if the purchaser at an execution or bankruptcy sale may one day reap the harvest of a full title, there will be an invitation to speculators.

If public policy demands that a creditor's interest be respected (I have no quarrel with the thought), the basis should be just to both the creditor and the debtor. It cannot be unless what is offered for sale is a non-contingent, non-speculative one-half interest which would support a partition suit. In that setting, bidders would know what is being sold and the sale could yield a fair price. An equitable solution can be achieved only by a statute abolishing the estate by the entirety in favor of a joint tenancy, or at least entitling the purchaser at an involuntary sale to have partition. In my judgment, a half-way approach will prove unjust. It will appreciably turn against the husband and wife a fictional concept that doubtless was originated for their benefit. . . .

The impact upon the free movement of property in the market-place may also be noted. In effect, the purchaser at the involuntary sale becomes a member of the entity for title purposes. In the hands of a husband and wife, property will be sold when the common economic interests of the family will be furthered. But when the power to alienate the whole is divided between a spouse and a stranger with unrelated economic motivations, property will not be moved unless those diverse interests can come to terms. Neither can compel a sale. In practical effect, there is a new restraint upon alienability to the disservice of the public interest.

I accordingly vote to affirm.

HALL, J. (dissenting). . . .

NOTES AND QUESTIONS

1. **Majority.** From whose perspective(s) does the majority opinion view the case? What attitude towards full commodification of the property does this perspective reflect?

2. **Dissent.** From whose perspective(s) does the dissenting opinion view the case? What attitude towards full commodification of the property does this perspective reflect?

3.   **Rationale.** The original rationale for the tenancy by the entirety (that the husband and the wife were one) is outdated. Is there a more modern rationale for the tenancy by the entirety?

4.   **The general rule: tenancy by the entirety interests are not alienable.** Nowhere is the law in wilder disarray than in the handling of creditors' claims against entirety assets. The New Jersey rule is followed in Alaska, Arkansas, New York, and Oregon. Its disadvantages are well stated by Chief Justice Weintraub's dissenting opinion in King v. Greene.

In Massachusetts prior to 1980, the Married Women's Property Act had left the tenancy by the entirety essentially untouched. Courts there had ruled consistently that a statute protective of the *separate* rights of married women did not alter the spousal "unity" of the estate by the entirety. Translated, this view created quite a disparity between the creditors of husband and wife. A husband's creditor could levy execution against the entire property for the duration of the marriage, and if the husband survived, the purchaser at the execution sale would acquire absolute title.[24] Raptes v. Pappas, 259 Mass. 37, 155 N.E. 787 (1927). By contrast, the wife's creditor could not, during the marriage, subject any interest in the property to attachment, levy, and sale. Licker v. Gluskin, 256 Mass. 403, 164 N.E. 613 (1929).

No other state in recent years followed the "Massachusetts rule," which lost much of its force statutorily in 1979. Mass. Ann. Laws, ch. 209. §1 (L 1994). The Bay State, as to the *principal residence*[25] of the nondebtor spouse, now takes the majority lead, next paragraph *infra*.

Most states do not permit the separate creditor of husband or wife to reach any part of the entirety during coverture. The underlying rationale is that neither spouse has a divisible interest in the property (it is owned by the marital unity), and that because of the Married Women's Property Acts neither spouse alone can receive the income and profits of, nor alone transfer any interest in, the property. To permit the creditor of the debtor-spouse to reach his/her interest would interfere with the right of the other spouse to full enjoyment.

This majority rule sets forth a logical interaction between the common-law tenancy by the entirety and the Married Women's Property Acts. Note that the rule, in effect, decommodifies the individual interests of the husband and wife. While it is protective of husband and wife, it effectively deprives their separate creditors of potential assets.[26] This logic carried be-

---

24. One writer had likened the husband's interest to a determinable fee simple. Richard G. Huber, Creditors' Rights in Tenancies by the Entireties, 1 B.C. Ind. & Com. L. Rev. 197, 200 (1960).

25. It remains uncertain whether the husband-wife dichotomy continues to govern other forms of real property. If so, is this impermissible, gender-based discrimination? Who would have standing to raise this issue: the wife's creditors, the wife, or the husband? Cf. Friedman v. Harold, 638 F.2d 262 (1st Cir. 1981).

26. The recent Massachusetts statute excepts "debts incurred on account of necessaries furnished to either spouse or to a member of either family." With respect to such debts, the

yond its ultimate conclusion has denied creditors not only access to income and principal but also power to levy execution against the debtor's right of survivorship. Thus (except for Tennessee and Kentucky among this group of majority states), the debtor and spouse may join in a conveyance of entirety assets completely free of the creditor's lien. For an elaborate state-by-state comparison, see Oval A. Phipps, Tenancy by Entireties, 25 Temple L.Q. 24, 46-57 (1951).

Do you think that creditors should be able to reach entirety interests during coverture? Why or why not?

5.   **Problem.** To test your understanding of the several rules, consider the following: H and W own as tenants by the entirety a two-family dwelling worth $100,000. They occupy one unit and rent out the other unit for $500 monthly. (The units are of equal value.) X obtains a judgment against H for $20,000, and levies execution against H's interest in the real estate. What price might P bid at the execution sale if the combined expectancy of H and W is 10 years and if H has a 40 percent chance of surviving W? In Florida (majority rule)? In New Jersey? In Tennessee? Should P consider whether H and W are happily married?

6.   **Should there be limits on the use of the tenancy by the entirety?** After reviewing the present situation, one author concluded:

> The retention of the tenancy by the entirety has resulted, except in a few states, in a partial or nearly total exemption of the property from the claims of creditors. Is this a desirable social and legal result? The only apparent direct benefit is that the marital community is assured of some available resources for support. The state is thus pro tanto free of the obligation to support an indigent family. This may be particularly important to the wife who thus has an assured amount of property on her husband's death. In a broader sense, the exemption reflects a policy favoring the preservation of property interests over commercial use of property as a base for credit or as an article of commerce itself. But even if it is granted that these policies are sound, does the exemption of the tenancy from the claims of creditors accomplish the desired results? It is believed not. Any amount of property may be put into this form of holding, free from creditors' claims although its value well exceeds any reasonable amount necessary for support. While, of course, many persons may be aware of the benefit of this type of ownership and act accordingly, many others having a greater need for protection will not be so guided. Thus there can be no assurance of equality of treatment since much depends upon whether the spouses were sufficiently foresighted to take property in this form. As to the elimination of property so held as a base for commercial credit, the general effect of many such ownerships in a state will be to reduce credit and hence limit commercial activity.
>
>   Are there means readily available by which the valid portion of the policies favoring restrictions on creditors' rights in property held by a marital

---

creditor of either spouse may levy against all of the entirety property. Mass. Ann. Laws, ch. 209, §1 (Law. Co-op. 1994).

community may be effectuated while avoiding excessive restrictions on their rights? . . . Those state retaining the tenancy by the entirety but permitting creditors of each spouse to reach his half possessory interest and his right of survivorship have at least partly solved the problem. There the non-debtor-spouse's interest is protected while the debtor-spouse is still able to use his interest in the estate as a base for credit. But the rule of these states is unsatisfactory in other respects: the non-debtor-spouse's exempt interest is not limited in amount or value; the application of the exemption depends upon the accident of the form of ownership rather than upon any direct social policy of preserving some exempt marital assets; the debtor-spouse is not protected at all if he is the survivor and as such the one who requires some protection from the claims of his creditors.

The social policy favoring protection of the marital community from creditors can best be obtained by the use of devices other than the tenancy by the entirety. The tenancy no longer serves a useful social function and the legal consequences of its use are, in many cases, difficult to justify. It should be abolished. Protection of the marital community could be more readily assured by other existing although presently somewhat inadequate devices. Homestead and personal property exemption statutes, modernized as to content and values, should provide protection for the marital community during its existence. Upon its termination by death, the widow and possibly the widower should be given priority over creditors in the assets of the estate, up to a reasonable support value determined in part by other assets available to the survivor, the number of dependents, and the earning capacity of the survivors. . . . It is believed that with appropriate legislation drawn with particular attention to these and other special problems better protection could be afforded the surviving members of the family of the decedent without undue prejudice to the just claims of creditors and the needs of the commercial community.

Richard G. Huber, Creditors' Rights in Tenancies by the Entireties, 1 B.C. Ind. & Com. L. Rev. 197, 205-207 (1960).

5.   The Homestead Exemption: Further Protection for the Family Home

"The time must come, sooner or later, . . . when the Home *shall* be secure — when the cabin of the poor man shall really be his castle." [27] Homestead Acts, which shield the family home and sometimes other assets as well from the claims of creditors, are another expression of the republican view that property rights should be designed to protect the independence of small landholders and to secure the widespread distribution of property. The exemptions aimed "to cherish and support in the bosoms of individuals, those feelings of sublime independence which are essential to the

---

27. Paul Goodman, The Emergence of Homestead Exemption in the United States: Accommodation and Resistance to the Market Revolution, 1840-1880, 80 J. Am. Hist. 470, 470 (1993).

FIGURE 4-4
First Homestead in the U.S.

maintenance of free institutions." [28] They represented the desire to provide a measure of security for ordinary people in a volatile economy: The
succession of panics and depressions throughout the nineteenth century
wiped out many families in an era before such debtors' protections as bankruptcy laws and stay and insolvency laws.

Homestead Acts, which had been passed in all but a few states by the
end of the nineteenth century, represented different political forces in different parts of the country. They began in Texas in 1839,[29] with an Act that
melded Spanish and Mexican traditions with republican impulses to yield a
generous exemption designed to attract settlers to that underpopulated
state. They spread throughout the South as southern states competed for
settlers. The exemptions spread throughout New England and the Midwest
at mid-century. Particularly in New England, homestead exemptions drew
support from Jacksonian Democrats: The father of the Massachusetts act
reported it out in 1951 arguing, "Banks, userers, and capitalists" were gaining a monopoly of the earth; the homestead exemptions would defeat their
designs.[30] The exemptions also were defended with domestic rhetoric asso-

28. Id. at 487 (quoting a Texas judge in 1857).
29. Note that Texas had offered free land in the 1836 constitution. Goodman, *supra*
note 27, at 477.
30. Quoted in Goodman, *supra* note 27, at 486.

ciating them with the sacredness of the home, in sharp contrast with pre-
exemption law that allowed creditors to "drive a family from the sacred
spot."[31] Opponents of the homestead exemptions used the kind of rhetoric
common today when the efficacy of unrestricted markets is being defended:
They argued that the exemptions would discourage investment, weaken
respect for property rights, and would hurt the very people they were designed to help, by crippling people's ability to borrow using their homes as
security.[32]

The exemption seeks "to assure a permanent common home to members of a family by setting apart property and immunizing it from the claims
of general creditors and the misfortunes or improvidence of the head of
the family." 2A Powell, Real Property ¶263[1] (Rohan ed., 1991). Underlying the exemption was the lawmakers' attitude "that an economy containing a debtor living and working and a creditor partly unpaid was more
satisfactory than one harbouring the destitute beggar and the complacent
banker." Milner, Homestead Act for England? 22 Modern L. Rev. 458,
462 (1959).

To protect the family home against creditors, the states have usually
chosen either to exempt the value of the property up to a certain fixed
amount or to limit the exemption to a defined quantum of land. (Some
laws do both.) Where the exemption is stated solely in terms of dollar value,
there is no uniform pattern of protection. For example, Maryland grants a
$100 exemption which may be claimed in real property; Maine allows a
$3,000 exemption; and California permits a $15,000 exemption.

The inadequacy of the fixed-sum approach, especially when the limits
remain unchanged for years, has occasioned much criticism.

> In step with current economic and social realizations, the exemption
> laws should insofar as possible be flexible in nature so that with economic
> changes the same real exemtions will continue to be available to debtors. The
> old crystallized exemption provisions which become outmoded in a few short
> years should, as far as possible, be abandoned. The risk of fluid exemption
> laws to creditors seeking a future certainty is recognized. A more extensive
> use of some intermediate type of exemption law which gives fluidity in the
> changing economic picture and still gives the creditor reasonable grounds for
> forecasting available assets is the present need. Escalator and percentage ex-
> emption provisions should be more extensively utilized and experimentation
> with current, reliable indices to which exemption values could be tied is
> advisable.

G. Stanley Joslin, Debtor's Exemption Laws: Time for Modernization, 34
Ind. L.J. 355, 375-376 (1959).

---

31. Id. at 487. The movement in favor of homestead exemptions was associated with
the movement to protect women from their husbands' creditors through the Married Women's
Property Acts. See *infra.*
32. See §3.9.c and Chapter 8.

In states such as Kansas and Minnesota the homestead is limited only by area, but a distinction is made between urban and rural land, with a larger allowance for the latter. Other jurisdictions, including Arkansas, Mississippi, and North Dakota, establish both a dollar and an area limitation on the homestead exemption. Virginia permits the family debtor who does not hold an interest in land protected by the homestead statute to apply the exemption to personal property.

A head of a family need not own a fee simple interest in his land to avail himself of the homestead exemption. Nor must the homestead property be used exclusively for residential purposes; states may allow a homestead exemption even where the property is primarily used for the operation of a business. See, e.g., Phelps v. Loop, 64 Cal. App. 2d 332, 148 P.2d 674 (1944) (owner of 18-unit apartment house allowed a homestead exemption on the entire property although he occupied only one unit).

Generally, debts incurred for the acquisition of the homestead or for repairs and improvements to the homestead property do not fall within the homestead exemption. The rationale for these exceptions is clear — a "debtor should not be able to acquire a free home by means of the exemption." [33]

Some states require a formal declaration in order to establish a homestead, and a few of these states apply the homestead exemption only to liabilities incurred after declaration. Although this type of statute does serve to protect creditors against fraud, ignorance of the requirement by homeowners or their lawyers may deprive many families of the exemption's benefit. In other states the homestead exemption takes effect automatically upon acquisition of the property, or may apply even to antecedent liabilities.

Because of the relatively small dollar exemption allowed in many states, often a residence will be considerably more valuable than the maximum exemption permitted. In such cases the excess value can usually be reached by creditors of the record owners, either through partition in kind, if practicable, or by sale of the entire property with the proceeds of the sale above the exemption amount available to the creditor.

The homestead laws also serve the goal of family protection by vesting

---

33. Other "preferred" obligations include taxes and assessments. Some jurisdictions distinguish between obligations founded on contract and those arising from tort or criminal fine, the latter being free of the exemption. Where property is held by cotenants, one cotenant may not set up the homestead exemption to restrict the interest of the other. See Banner v. Welch, 115 Kan. 868, 225 P. 98 (1924).

Under the Bankruptcy Act, the bankrupt is entitled to the "exemptions which are prescribed by . . . the State laws in force at the time of the filing of the petition. . . ." 30 Stat. 548 (1898), as amended, 11 U.S.C. §24 (1964). Thus state homestead laws are applicable in bankruptcy proceedings. This is particularly important because of the frequency of petitions in bankruptcy. For example, in fiscal 1963 there were 27,608 bankruptcies filed in California alone. Rifkind, Archaic Exemption Laws, 39 Cal. St. B.J. 370 (1964).

some interest in the homestead property in the surviving spouse and minor children.[34] While most states limit the power of a spouse to devise the homestead, some require a surviving spouse to elect between the homestead and the provisions of the decedent's will.

Similar to homestead exemption laws are the constitutional and statutory provisions protecting certain personal property from execution. These laws also vary widely among the states, and may exempt specific property ranging from a spinning wheel to a television set,[35] or property necessary for a particular trade or profession, or a percentage of wages.

---

34. See George L. Haskins, Homestead Rights of a Surviving Spouse, 37 Iowa L. Rev. 36, 37-38 (1951):

> The degree of protection to which the surviving spouse is entitled under the homestead statutes varies considerably from state to state. The property interest may take the form of a right to rents and profits, a right of occupancy, a life estate, or an interest in fee. Its continuance is sometimes conditioned upon occupancy or widowhood. Its extent may depend upon such factors as the existence of children or upon the ownership of property in which the homestead during coverture was established. Generally, the survivor's interest is subject to the same limitations in value as those imposed upon the homestead during coverture, so that the excess is not within the exemption and may be reached by creditors, but it has occasionally been held that the survivor may hold the entire homestead exempt even when it exceeds the specified value.

35. See, e.g., Va. Code Ann. §34.26 (Michie 1996):

> *§34-26. Exempt articles enumerated.* — In addition to the estate, not exceeding in value five thousand dollars, which every householder residing in this State shall be entitled to hold exempt, as provided in chapter 2 (§34-4 et seq.) of this title, he shall also be entitled to hold exempt from levy or distress the following articles or so much or so many thereof as he may have, to be selected by him or his agents:
> (1)   The family Bible.
> (1a) Wedding and engagement rings.
> (2)   Family pictures, schoolbooks and library for the use of the family.
> (3)   A lot in a burial ground.
> (4)   All necessary wearing apparel of the debtor and his family, all beds, bedsteads and bedding necessary for the use of such family, two dressers or two dressing tables, wardrobes, chifforobes or chests of drawers or a dresser and a dressing table; carpets, rugs, linoleum or other floor covering; and all stoves and appendages put up and kept for the use of the family not exceeding three.
> (5)   All cats, dogs, birds, squirrels, rabbits and other pets not kept or raised for sale; one cow and her calf until one year old, one horse, six chairs, six plates, one table, twelve knives, twelve forks, two dozen spoons, twelve dishes, or if the family consists of more than twelve, then a plate, knife, fork and two spoons and a dish for each member thereof; two basins, one pot, one oven, six pieces of wooden or earthenware; one dining room table, one buffet, china press, one icebox, freezer or refrigerator of any construction, one washing machine, one clothes dryer not to exceed one hundred fifty dollars in value, one loom and its appurtenances, one kitchen safe or one kitchen cabinet or press, one spinning wheel, one pair of cards, one axe and provisions other than those hereinafter set out of the value of fifty dollars; two hoes; fifty bushels of shelled corn, or, in lieu thereof, twenty-five bushels of rye or buckwheat; five bushels of wheat, or one barrel of flour; twenty bushels of potatoes, two hundred pounds of bacon or pork, three

The Florida homestead exemption is $5,000 for nonresident owners and $25,000 for resident owners of dwellings in the state. Upon bankruptcy, the property remains exempt from the claims of creditors provided that the homeowner does not transfer nonexempt assets to the home in an effort to avoid the claims of creditors.[36] The Florida exemption is both generous and broad. It applies to single-family houses as well as to mobile homes, motor homes, and houseboats. Should pleasure boats or other recreational vehicles qualify for the exemption? See Miami Country Day School v. Bakst, 641 So. 2d 467 (Fla. D. Ct. App. 1994).

NOTES AND QUESTIONS

1. **Republican vision revisited.** The Homestead Exemption is an expression of the refusal fully to commodify the family home. See Chapter 2. Behind this refusal lies the republican sense that property rights should not be designed exclusively to create wealth but should also preserve the independence of small landowners. See Irving Mark, The Homestead Ideal and the Conservation of the Public Domain, 22 Am. J. Econ. & Soc. 263, 266-269 (1963); Paul Goodman, The Emergence of Homestead Exemption in the United States: Accommodation and Resistance to the Market Revolution, 1840-1880, 80 J. Am. Hist. 470 (1993).

2. **"A man's home is his castle."** Think back to King v. Greene. Does the homestead exemption also rest on a set of images about the nuclear family? What are they? Note that in the original republican vision the focus was on men's independence as they ruled over households of women and children ("Each man's home is his castle"). How has this image changed?

Split ♀ + ♂

---

hogs, fowl not exceeding in value twenty-five dollars, all canned and frozen goods, canned fruits, preserved fruits or home-prepared food put up and prepared for use and consumption of the family, twenty-five dollars in value of forage or hay, one cooking stove and utensils for cooking therewith, one sewing machine, and in case of a mechanic, the tools and utensils of his trade, and in case of an oysterman or fisherman his boat and tackle, not exceeding one thousand five hundred dollars in value; if the boat and tackle exceed fifteen hundred dollars in value the same shall be sold, and out of the proceeds the oysterman or fisherman shall first receive one thousand five hundred dollars in lieu of such boat and tackle.

No officer or other person shall levy or distrain upon, or attach, such articles, or otherwise seek to subject such articles to any lien or process. (Code 1919, §6552; 1934, p. 371; 1936, p. 322; 1956, c. 637; 1970, c. 428; 1975, c. 466; 1976, c. 150; 1977, cc. 253, 496.)

36. For example, if the debtor uses proceeds from sale of automobile to pay down mortgage only days before filing for bankruptcy.

b.   Relations Among Co-Owners

1.   Partition

Suppose that cotenants A and B have a falling-out and can no longer agree as to the use or management of the common property. They might agree to disagree and voluntarily divide the assets so that each thereafter owns his share in severalty. Alternatively, but less likely, they might themselves sell the assets and divide the sales proceeds. But if they cannot dissolve their cotenancy by joint action, either cotenant may sue for partition and obtain a decree ending the cotenancy.

The device of partition dates from the thirteenth century, originating in disputes among coparceners.[37] By 1539, the remedy was extended to joint tenants and tenants in common[38] but to this day, partition remains unavailable to tenants by the entirety. In the United States, every state has a partition statute that sets out the procedure for obtaining this remedy. See, e.g., Cal. Civ. Proc. Code §§872.810 et seq. (West 1980); N.Y. Real Prop. Acts. Law §§901 et seq. (McKinney 1979 & Supp.).

The court may order either division in kind or a public sale and division of the sales proceeds. Division in kind was at one time the only mode of partition; thus if A and B owned 100 acres of farmland as cotenants, the court would divide the farm into two parts, each representing the value of A and B's cotenancy interest. To this day, partition in kind is said to be preferred over partition by sale, and statutes regularly pay lip service to that preference. But the realities of real estate development in a nonrural society often make it unfeasible to divide improved property in kind, so that forced sale usually results from a partition suit. 4A Powell on Real Property ¶607 (Lori A. Hauser ed., 1991).

Partition can almost always be forced on joint tenants and tenants in common whenever any concurrent owner wants to split the parcel up into ownership in severalty (or force a partition sale), even in a situation where the other owner or owners want to continue the concurrent ownership. "The convenience or inconvenience of the parties is not to be considered." Wolford v. Wolford, 65 Nev. 710, 716, 200 P.2d 988, 991 (1948), quoting 4 Thompson on Real Property 493 (1981).

Cotenants by agreement, however, may restrict their right to partition, and if the restraint is not perpetual or unreasonably long, courts generally will allow the restraint. See Wade R. Habeeb, Contractual Provisions as Affecting Right to Judicial Partition, Annot., 37 A.L.R.3d 962 (1971). But a re-

---

37. Coparceners were two or more sisters who, in the absence of male heirs, acquired property via intestacy from their parents.

38. Anne L. Spitzer, Joint Tenancy with Right of Survivorship: A Legacy from Thirteenth Century England, 16 Tex. Tech. L. Rev. 629, 636 (1985).

straint otherwise valid may be set aside when circumstances between the parties have so changed as to make enforcement unduly harsh. See, e.g., Michalski v. Michalski, 50 N.J. Super. 454, 142 A.2d 645 (App. Div. 1958) (suit for partition between estranged husband and wife, tenants in common).

Equity has occasionally (but rarely) refused to allow partition so as to avoid "prejudice," or "in the interest of justice." [39] These cases usually involve the family home. Consider the following materials.

HARRIS v. CROWDER

174 W. Va. 83, 322 S.E.2d 854 (1984)

NEELEY, J. Our task today, for the first time in West Virginia decisional law, is to determine whether creditors can execute upon a husband's undivided interest in property held jointly with his wife. In the case before us the ineluctable logic of received property law strains in one direction while common humanity and sound public policy strain in the other.

Marvin C. Crowder and Mary Ann Crowder, his wife, bought their family house from Mitchell and Anna Clay, giving the Clays a first deed of trust to secure the purchase money note. Initially both Mr. and Mrs. Crowder lived on the purchased premises, but at the time the creditors' suit that is the subject of this appeal was brought they had separated and Mr. Crowder was living elsewhere. In the circuit court Jeff Harris, the plaintiff below, tried to enforce his March, 1982 judgment against Mr. Crowder for $9,241. Mr. Harris asked that the circuit court refer the case to a commissioner to take and state an account showing the nature, amount and order of priority of all valid and subsisting liens against Mr. Crowder's real estate and to force a sale of Mr. Crowder's property to discharge the plaintiff's lien. The case was referred to a commissioner who reported that the plaintiff had an eleventh priority lien against the defendant's property. The record before us indicates that Mr. Crowder had a small army of creditors.[1]

In February, 1984 the Circuit Court of Kanawha County denied Mrs. Crowder's motion to exclude from execution the property that she and her husband held as joint tenants with the right of survivorship and appointed a special commissioner to sell the jointly held property and retain the proceeds until further order of the court. The court then certified on his own motion the following question to this Court:

---

39. See, e.g., Newman v. Chase, 70 N.J. 254, 359 A.2d 474 (1976).
1. The creditors who had reduced their claims to judgment included the State of West Virginia for taxes, Hardman Supply Company, Young's, Inc., the United States government for federal taxes, Kerstein Engineering Co. Inc., Toledo Gardener's Cooperative, Huber Peat Co., Dorothy Jackson, and finally the Sarah and Pauline Maier Scholarships Foundation, Inc..

（handwritten: Wife wants to keep hers free from his debt even though joint owners = Possessory Interest）

Where Husband and Wife are joint owners of a parcel of land and the only encumbrance against Wife's undivided one-half interest is a recorded deed of trust securing a note signed by she [sic] and Husband, but where there are numerous judgment and tax liens filed against Husband solely, in addition to the deed of trust, should the Circuit Court grant Wife's Motion to Dismiss, where one of Husband's judgment lien creditors files suit seeking a judicial sale of both Husband and Wife's interest in the said parcel; or, simply put: Can a judgment lien creditor maintain a creditor's action to sell jointly-owned property where his judgment is against only one of the joint property owners? *(handwritten: ISSUE)*

Unfortunately, the answer to this certified question is neither a simple "yes" or "no." Each case of this type must be processed individually with due attention to considerations that we shall illuminate below.

I

In Anglo-American law there have been two methods by which a husband and wife can hold property and more or less protect that property from the judgment creditors of one of them alone. The first of these methods is the tenancy by the entireties that survives in twenty-two common law states and the second is the joint tenancy. We held in Wartenburg v. Wartenburg, 143 W. Va. 141, 100 S.E.2d 562 (1957), that tenancies by the entireties have been abolished in West Virginia by statute. Under W. Va. Code, 36-1-20 [1981], however, joint tenancies continue to flourish here.

There is no question in this jurisdiction that one joint tenant can unilaterally destroy the right of survivorship of the other joint tenant by *voluntarily* conveying his interest to a third party. Recently we held in syl. pt. 4 of Herring v. Carroll, W. Va., 300 S.E.2d 629 (1983) that:

> A joint tenant may convey his undivided interest in real property to a third person. When one of two joint tenants conveys his undivided interest to a third person the right of survivorship is destroyed. Such third party and the remaining joint tenant hold the property as tenants in common. . . . In our own *W. Va. Code,* 87-4-3 [1957] . . . the *Code* says: ". . . in any case in which partition cannot be conveniently made, if the interests of one or more of those who are entitled to the subject, or its proceeds, will be promoted by a sale of the entire subject, or allotment of part and sale of the residue, *and the interest of the other person or persons so entitled will not be prejudiced thereby,* the court . . . may order such sale." [Emphasis supplied by court.] *(handwritten: W.Va. Code)*

It is well established, therefore, that a joint tenant may bring an action to partition, and that the court will partition the property in kind or by sale, but only if no prejudice will result to the other joint tenant. "Prejudice," of course, is an extraordinarily difficult word to define: in this context, at least, the term has a certain inherent elasticity.

Land w/ LA — guaranteed
RO Su Risk

The appellant, Mr. Crowder, argues that his rights in the property are subject to his wife's survivorship interest and that, therefore, the creditor can sell only that which the debtor owns. But, as Herring v. Carroll, *supra,* holds, the debtor "owns" the right to destroy the survivorship interest by a voluntary conveyance during his lifetime. Under syl. pt. 4 of *Herring, supra,* whenever a joint tenant conveys his interest in the tenancy to a third party there is a rupture of the four unities necessary for a joint tenancy and the owners thereupon become tenants in common. The initial question, then, that must be answered in the case before us is whether a creditor can stand in the shoes of his debtor and do what the debtor could do himself, namely (1) partition the joint tenancy, (2) convert the joint tenancy into a tenancy in common, and (3) destroy the survivorship interest of the other joint tenant. . . .

Throughout the United States there appears to be widespread reluctance to allow the creditors of *one* spouse to sell the family house to satisfy debts. Some states approach the problem exclusively through the use of homestead exemptions,[4] but as we pointed out above, twenty-two states make it difficult, if not impossible, for a creditor to reach one spouse's interest in real property by preserving the ancient, common law tenancy by the entireties. When we observe that many of the states that do not recognize tenancies by the entireties are French- or Spanish-tradition community property states, the widespread preservation of tenancies by the entireties becomes pervasive evidence of a nationwide public policy of protecting wives and children in the use of the family house.

It is hardly productive here to recount the long and interesting history of tenancies by the entireties; however, let it suffice to point out that before the passage of the Married Women's Property Acts and other modern legislation giving social and economic equality to women, the tenancy by the entireties was a device that allowed the husband to manage and control all property owned jointly with his wife. Almost all of the attributes of the ancient tenancy by the entireties known to the common law have now been eliminated in the United States either by statute or by court decision. Indeed, it would appear that in all of the states that still recognize tenancies

---

4. The West Virginia homestead exemption found in W. Va. Const., art. VI, §48 is miserly. It amounts to a mere five thousand dollars. Under the authority of the Bankruptcy Reform Act of 1978, 11 U.S.C. §101 et seq. (Supp. IV 1980). West Virginia has "opted-out" of the federal exemptions and provides its bankrupts with a mandatory set of state legislated bankruptcy exemptions. Currently W. Va. Code, 38-10-4 [1981] permits the debtor in a bankruptcy proceeding to exempt real property of the estate, used as a residence, to a value of $7,500. This section, setting forth West Virginia's bankruptcy exemptions, mirrors the federal bankruptcy exemptions almost entirely. 11 U.S.C. §522(d). The one significant distinction is that a West Virginia debtor may exempt personal property up to only one thousand dollars although the federal act, in the absence of a state enactment, would permit the debtor to claim limitless personal exemptions as long as each claimed item does not exceed two hundred dollars in value. 11 U.S.C. §522(d)(3).

by the entireties, those tenancies are distinguished from joint tenancies by
only one palpable characteristic: the right of survivorship either cannot
be destroyed involuntarily by a creditor, or can be destroyed only with
great difficulty. In other words, the archaic fiction of a tenancy by the entireties is preserved *only* because it makes it almost impossible for creditors
to reach a debtor's family house. This is not, however, to say that creditors
do not try with some regularity to do so, and occasionally even with some
success.

In many of the states that recognize tenancies by the entireties, when
a husband's interest in the estate is sold at an execution sale, the purchaser
takes subject to the wife's right of survivorship and, in some cases, the purchaser's only benefit is a right to share the house with the debtor's terma-
gant wife, a dubious benefit at best.[7] In some states courts allow such a
purchaser to bring an action for partition, but the purchaser's resulting
moiety is itself subject to survivorship in the non-debtor spouse.[8] It all gets
terribly complicated and the whole subject provides a field day for law
school professors and law review editors. But, as is so often the case in the
law, the point is that complication is what humane public policy has strived
for: the more complicated the better. In the wake of complication come
uncertainty and exorbitant legal fees that chill the exercise of creditors'
rights against family homes! . . .

III

Under the free enterprise system our economy is regulated through recurring cycles of human suffering. Successful competitors take the markets
from unsuccessful competitors; new products are born and older products
die; plants and even whole industries migrate in response to opportunities
to achieve lower costs; and, people who have spent lifetimes learning crafts
find themselves confronted by new technology that make their hard-won
skills redundant. In the United States, then, low costs, high productivity,
and steady growth are achieved through the unrelenting discipline of competition and its attendant misery.

There is little question that the free enterprise system has produced a
higher rate of economic growth, a faster pace of job creation, and a substantially higher standard of living for the average person in the United States

---

7. Berlin v. Herbert, 48 Misc. 2d 393, 265 N.Y.S.2d 25 (1965). The essential point in
these cases remains the inseverability of a tenancy by the entirety; neither husband nor wife,
without the other's acquiescence, can alienate the estate and so affect the other's survivorship
rights. Moore v. Denson, 167 Ark. 134, 268 S.W. 609 (1924). In jurisdictions where the purchaser of the husband's interest is not entitled to shared physical possession of the premises,
the purchaser is entitled to an accounting based on the imputed rental value of the tenancy.
Newman v. Chase, 70 N.J. 254, 359 A.2d 474 (1976); In re Weiss, 4 B.R. 327 (Bkrtcy. 1980).

8. See, e.g., Newman v. Chase, 70 N.J. 254, 359 A.2d 474 (1976).

than any alternative available elsewhere.[10] But it is important to recognize that the inability to pay debts in a free enterprise economy is randomly distributed as an inherent part of a market mechanism that controls resource allocation. Although some debtors are besieged by their creditors because of conduct that is morally blameworthy, the great majority are not. One of the functions of law is to distribute the costs of operating this society in an equitable way: when loss is inevitable, it should fall on the strong and not upon the weak. St. Matthew 25:40.

We are not disposed, therefore, to allow the inexorable logic of property law to be entirely dispositive of the issue before us. When a creditor seeks to sell a family's home to satisfy the debts of one spouse alone, a whole new dimension is given to the equitable provision in our partition statute that excludes partition when prejudice occurs to another tenant. When, for example, a modest, jointly-owned house has an unassignable $75,000 mortgage at 8 percent and would sell on today's market for $100,000, how is the wife to be compensated for the loss of her contract right to a low interest mortgage? Under such circumstances partition of the family home would be like partition of a table: when we partition a table we do not emerge with two small tables; we emerge with two useless pieces of junk!

Nonetheless, we hold that creditors of one joint tenant may reach that joint tenant's interest and force partition either in kind or by sale, but only if "the interest of the other person or persons so entitled will not be prejudiced thereby." W. Va. Code, 37-4-3 [1957]; See also Consolidated Gas Supply Corp. v. Riley, 161 W. Va. 782, 247 S.E.2d 712 (1978). Obviously, the interest of a non-debtor spouse in jointly-held property can never be reached by the creditors of the other spouse. . . .

Since the enactment of the Married Woman's Property Acts, a wife's property is not liable for her husband's individual debts. See 4A Thompson, Real Property §1904. The interest of Mary Ann Crowder in the subject property cannot be reached to satisfy her husband's individual debts, but that does not mean that the property in question cannot be sold and the part of the proceeds attributable to her husband's interest attached to satisfy the judgment against him. Morris v. Baird, 72 W. Va. 1, 78 S.E. 371 (1913).

The equitable considerations that should instruct a circuit court's determination of when forced partition of a joint tenancy is equitable are too varied to be addressed in the abstract here. Certainly, however, the favored treatment that sound public policy would extend to family houses need not necessarily be extended to jointly owned business property. There should be a fairly strong presumption that business property may be reached in a creditor's suit. Similarly, both the size and the nature of joint holdings must be taken into consideration. Finally, it is an ancient maxim of equity that

10. See P. F. Ducher, "Why America's Got So Many Jobs," The Wall Street Journal, 24 January 1984.

those who seek equity must be willing to do equity. Of course, there is a limit to this obligation: creditors cannot demand the life's blood of an innocent spouse. . . .

NOTES AND QUESTIONS

1.   **King v. Greene sequel.** Recall King v. Greene, *supra*, in which the New Jersey Supreme Court held that one spouse in a tenancy by the entirety could, unilaterally, convey his or her interest to a third party, and that the transferee would receive a tenancy in common with the other spouse for the life of the marriage as well as the transferor's survivorship right. Newman v. Chase, 70 N.J. 254, 359 A.2d 474 (1976), was the inevitable sequel. The Chases owned their family home as tenants by the entirety. Plaintiff Newman acquired the husband's interest in the home as a result of the husband's bankruptcy. When, as a tenant in common with Mrs. Chase for the spouses' joint lives, he sought partition, plaintiff was unsuccessful.

In denying plaintiff relief, the court wrote:

> We do not go so far as to hold that a purchaser at an execution sale or from a receiver or trustee in bankruptcy may never be entitled to partition. There is no limit to the value of real property which can be held by husband and wife as tenants by the entirety. Were partition to be automatically denied, there might well be situations in which a debtor would thus be afforded "opportunity to sequester substantial assets from just liabilities." Way v. Root, 174 Mich. 418, 140 N.W. 577, 579 (1913). But where, as in the present case, a bankrupt husband lives with his young family in a modest home, we hold that it is within the equitable discretion of the court to deny partition to a purchaser of the husband's interest, leaving the creditor to resort to some other remedy.

70 N.J. 254, 266, 359 A.2d 474, 480.

The "other remedy" in this case was an accounting by Mrs. Chase for one-half the imputed rental value of the house after first deducting Newman's share of the property-related expenses. Suppose that Newman recovers a judgment that Mrs. Chase fails to pay: May Newman then levy execution against her entirety interest?

2.   **Rhetorical style.** Compare King v. Greene, *supra*, with Harris v. Crowder. How does the courts' reasoning differ? Do the two courts have different styles? Justice Neely of the West Virginia Supreme Court is famous for his flamboyant style. What makes his style flamboyant? The New Jersey Supreme Court's style is more measured and cerebral.

3.   **Free partition in the context of black family farms.** Free partition seems to have been used abusively throughout the South as a vehicle for dislodging independent black family farmers from the soil. Consider the following.

FIGURE 4-5
Black Extended Family

JOHN G. CASAGRANDE JR., NOTE, ACQUIRING PROPERTY THROUGH FORCED PARTITIONING SALES: ABUSES AND REMEDIES

27 B.C. L. Rev. 755-758, 775-779 (1986)

Tom Banks worked and lived on a ninety-acre family farm in Alabama since he was a child.[1] He and his two brothers, who assisted him on the farm, each owned a fifteen percent interest in the property. Other more distant relatives owned various fractional interests in the property ranging

---

1. Although the following facts are fictitious, they are similar to those in actual partitioning sale cases throughout the South. Telephone interviews with Henry Sanders, Esq, of Chestnut, Sanders, Sanders, Turner & Williams, P.C. (Aug. 27, 1986), and Michael A. Figures, Esq., of Figures, Ludgood & Figures (Sept. 15, 1986). Mr. Sanders and Mr. Figures have represented many cotenants seeking to protect their property interests from partitioning sale actions throughout Alabama.

from 1/10 to 5/1053. Many of these co-owners had disappeared or were unaware of their ownership.

In 1983, Mr. Banks received notice that a co-owner had petitioned a local court to sell the farm and divide the proceeds of the sale among the ascertainable owners. The petitioner, a local real estate agent, recently had purchased a 1/37 interest in the property from a distant relative of Mr. Banks for $500. That agent now was petitioning the court to sever his interest in the property from the remaining interests. The agent argued, however, that because the farm could not be divided conveniently, including into a 1/37 portion, it would have to be sold. Tom Banks testified at the hearing that he wished to continue farming the land, and that he would be willing to buy the agent's interest or divide the property to the latter's advantage and satisfaction. The court concluded, however, that the property had to be sold to the highest bidder. When put up for sale, the sole and highest bidder was the real estate agent because Tom Banks and his brothers did not have the financial resources necessary to purchase the land. As a result, the Bankses lost their farm, receiving in its place a sum of money worth less than either its actual or replacement value.

Although the preceding facts are fictitious, the scenario is a common one in rural areas throughout the southern United States.[2] One organization providing assistance to such property owners has monitored literally hundreds of similar actions over the past fifteen years. Many of these actions result in litigation, where more often than not those parties seeking to retain their property end up losing it in a court-ordered sale.

The United States Commission on Civil Rights recently reported that from 1920 to 1978, the number of farms operated by blacks in the United States diminished from 925,710 to 57,271, a loss of 93.8%. By comparison, farms operated by whites diminished during this same period from 5,499,707 to 2,398,726, a loss of 56.4%. Moreover, the divergence between these rates of loss has been increasing. Between 1969 and 1978 the rate of loss of black-operated farms was two and one half times that of white-operated farms. This dramatic drop in black ownership of land, termed "the largest single equity resource in minority hands in the South," is estimated to have been the result of partitioning sales in over half the recent cases.

Anglo-American law always recognized the ability of two or more persons to own undivided interests in the same property simultaneously. In the United States, co-ownership by cotenants generally takes the form of a ten-

---

2. Telephone interview with Edward Pennick, Federation of Southern Cooperatives/Land Assistance Fund (formerly the Emergency Land Fund) (Nov. 1, 1985) [hereinafter Pennick interview]. A private, nonprofit organization founded in 1971, the Emergency Land Fund ("ELF") addressed the problems of black land loss by providing outreach, technical assistance, and legal support to black farmers. In the late 1970's, the ELF contracted with the United States Department of Agriculture to study the impact of heir property on black ownership of land. U.S. Comm'n on Civil Rights, the Decline of Black Farming in America 66 (1982) [hereinafter Black Farming].

ancy in common, a joint tenancy, or a tenancy by the entirety. Courts also recognized the right of cotenants to separate their interests by partition, either voluntarily or by suit. Partitioning is the physical division, or the forced sale and division of the proceeds, of property jointly owned by cotenants. While partitioning by division in kind vests each cotenant with his or her property interest, partitioning sales typically result in the sale of those property interests to a third party. Throughout the southern United States, both cotenants and third parties have used partitioning sale actions to acquire private cotenancy property not otherwise for sale.

The prevalence of black farm cotenancies in southern states has resulted in the ownership of many properties by cotenants representing several generations. Land values throughout the South have increased dramatically since the Second World War.[20] These conditions provide a fertile environment for partitioning actions.[21] Typically, an outsider to the cotenancy purchases one cotenant's interest, intending to force the sale of the entire cotenancy. Or, a cotenant, sometimes at the urging of a land speculator, will petition the court for a sale. In either situation, the court may order a sale of the entire estate on the basis that the property is indivisible among the cotenants. The property consequently is put up for sale, where it is purchased more often than not by local white lawyers or relatives of local officials. The economic inability of many black cotenants to purchase all the real estate provides speculators with an easy bidding market.[26] Furthermore, these partitioning sale actions are sometimes instigated by lawyers to collect fees, and by judges who personally benefit by purchasing the properties.

This note traces the historical development of partitioning actions in law and equity and the influence of that development on modern partitioning statutes. It examines the changing use of partitioning sale actions in Alabama during the nineteenth and twentieth centuries. This note then demonstrates that early interpretations of partitioning sale statutes, and equity limitations thereon, are still relevant to partitioning actions today.

While the judiciary traditionally favored the use of partitioning in kind, the routine trend in Alabama and other jurisdictions is for courts to order

---

20. Telephone interview with Henry Sanders, Esq., of Chestnut, Sanders, Sanders, Turner & Williams, P.C. (Dec. 27, 1985) [hereinafter Sanders Interview]. See also Black Farming, *supra* note 2, at 4 ("The frequent pattern is for land to remain in minority hands only so long as it is economically marginal, and then to be acquired by whites when its value begins to increase.") (quoting U.S. Dept. of Commerce, Land and Minority Enterprise: The Crisis and the Opportunity ii, prepared by Dr. Lester M. Salamon for the Office of Minority Business Enterprise (1976)).

21. Black Farming, *supra* note 2, at 66-67. A sample survey found that 27% of the black-owned land in the Southeast consists of heir property. Such estates are owned by an average of eight cotenants, with an average of five residing outside of the Southeast. Id. at 66. This survey found that most such owners mistakenly believed that cotenants could not sell their interests without the consent of the others and that those who possessed the estate had greater rights to the property than those who did not. Id. at 69.

26. Id.

sales of property. The frequent use of judicial sales violates the purpose and original use of statutes preferring equitable partitioning by divisions in kind. Furthermore, this judicial preference for sales ignores the remedies in equity which courts traditionally used in partitioning actions. The same property interests once favored and protected by the preferred divisions in kind equally are in need of protection today. It is the province and duty of the courts to prevent partitioning sale actions from being used as a tool to acquire property otherwise unavailable. This is particularly true where minority interests, such as those of southern black cotenant farmers, are vulnerable to powerful marketplace pressures. . . .

II

A

2.A   Equity Limitations on Partitioning Sales

The historical preference for partitioning by division in kind over sale in Alabama and elsewhere is supported not only by the contemporary statutory interpretation and use of the partitioning sale legislation, but also by the equitable principles upon which partitioning actions are based. Most jurisdictions recognize that in addition to statutory authority, jurisdiction to partition lies in equity. In Alabama, courts recognize that equity jurisdiction to partition rests "on the inadequacy of remedies at law, and the capacity of the court to grant more complete relief, adjusting the equities of the parties, and meeting exigencies or necessities which may be peculiar to the particular [partitioning] case."

Courts construe legislation which interferes with traditional property rights narrowly because equity seeks to protect such fundamental individual rights. The Supreme Court of Mississippi recognized this principle in a 1944 partitioning sale action in Wight v. Ingram-Day Lumber Co. In *Wight*, the court reasoned:

> A particular piece of real estate cannot be replaced by any sum of money, however large; and one who wants a particular estate for a specific use, if deprived of his rights, cannot be said to receive an exact equivalent or complete indemnity by the payment of a sum of money. A title to real estate, therefore, will be protected in a court of equity by a decree which will preserve to the owner the property itself, instead of a sum of money which represents its value.

Thus, partitioning sale statutes should be construed narrowly and used sparingly because they interfere with property rights.

The ease with which equity courts assumed jurisdiction to partition by division in kind and the refusal of equity to sell in lieu of partitioning prior to the statutes suggest that equity courts recognized the unfair nature of such forced sales. Consequently, partitioning sales are "not a matter of unconditional right." Rather, they are contingent upon a clear showing by a party that the property cannot be divided in kind. Even if division is impossible, equity remedies might still preclude or limit the use of partitioning sales. Thus, the claim that judicial sales are an "absolute right," relied upon by so many courts, is misleading and probably erroneous.

A court of equity cannot order a partitioning sale unless a party proves its necessity by showing that a physical division in kind would be inequitable and unfair. In 1890, the Supreme Court of Alabama interpreted this equity burden of proof to mean that sales are justified only where division in kind cannot be made or where it would result "in a *total loss or destruction* of the property." This standard contradicts the current Alabama practice of justifying partitioning sales based on the topographical diversity of properties or the economic disadvantages of divisions in kind. Particularly with large parcels of land, some inconvenience or disincentive to partitioning by division in kind probably always exists. This problem would seem to be an integral part of co-ownership. . . .

B.   TOWARD A CLARIFIED BALANCE
OF EQUITIES

According to Justice Story, equity seeks to accomplish what courts of law cannot; namely, to "vary, qualify, restrain, and model the remedy, so as to suit it to mutual and adverse claims, controlling equities, and the real and substantial rights of all the parties." Wherever a petitioner submits a claim to equity jurisdiction, he or she submits it for consideration of *all* the equities involved in the action. Furthermore, a court exercising equity jurisdiction *must* consider all the equities involved; equity is not discretionary except where its use would be counterproductive to its principles.

Wherever land in partitioning actions cannot be divided fairly, equity courts protect the property interests of cotenants through a variety of remedies, such as owelty and allotment. Owelty is the payment of money between cotenants to equalize the division of unequal shares. Allotment allows cotenants desiring to retain their interests to set apart or allot their portions from the property prior to the remainder being sold. Both remedies were established and used early in Alabama, and both are codified in Alabama partitioning law. Nonetheless, both have been restricted severely by courts.

The use of owelty, for example, has been judicially limited in Alabama to situations where the property is divisible in kind. This precondition is inappropriate because properties divisible in kind by modern judicial standards are by definition divisible equally and consequently have no need of adjustment. In addition, the owelty statute on which this judicial opinion is based expressly allows owelty to be used "*to secure* an equal partition in kind." Most importantly, equity provides for owelty irrespective of any cumulative statute or restrictions. Courts, therefore, should use owelty to adjust any unequal divisions to fulfill their statutory and equitable duties to favor partitioning in kind.

NOTES AND QUESTIONS

1.   **Free partition in the context of black family farms (continued).**
See also Chris Kelley, Stemming the Loss of Black Owned Farmland through
Partition Actions — A Partial Solution, 1985 Ark. L. Notes.

For an in-depth study of intergenerational, black southern families,
see Herbert G. Gutman, The Black Family in Slavery and Freedom, 1750-
1925 (1976). Gutman traces the development of kinship structures in which
care, support, and emotional ties are distributed over a kinship network
that includes not only the nuclear family (parents and children), but also
grandparents, cousins, aunts and uncles, and other relatives. This analysis
suggests that when family farms are partitioned in this kind of context,
family members may lose not only a home and a means of support (usually
a farm); their entire network of relationships may also be destabilized. See
also Carol B. Stack, All Our Kin: Strategies for Survival in a Black Community (1974) (documenting that similar kinship system supported urban
black single mothers during the 1970s). Courts often appear unwilling to
adapt common-law rules in ways that might help preserve non-nuclear
family structures. See, e.g., Watson v. Durr, 379 So. 2d 1243 (Ala. 1980)
(court refuses co-owners' request that partitioned land be sold to family
members); McNeely v. Bone, 698 S.W.2d 512 (Ark. 1985) (court refuses to
order land partitioned in kind rather than partitioned through sale).

2.   **Personhood or fungible property?** The free partition rules are
commonly rationalized as being required by the need for efficient use of
property: If co-owners cannot get along, the best solution is for them to split
up the land. Yet consider once again that co-ownership may often arise precisely where people have emotional ties to a piece of property that may
make it inappropriate to treat that property as a fungible asset. In this context, consider Radin's property and personhood analysis, §1.4.e *supra*. Is co-
owned property more likely to be towards the personhood or the fungible
end of the continuum Radin describes? See also the Hines's discussion of
Iowa family farms, §4.1.a.2, *supra*.

2.   Possession and the Duty to Account

The unity of possession entitles each cotenant to occupy and enjoy
the common property. The rule at common law would allow A to enjoy the
property free of any duty to account for its value to cotenant B, unless B
objected to A's sole possession and wished also to use the property, that is,
unless B suffered an ouster. In an agrarian society, this rule made good
sense because it encouraged the productive use of land (which might otherwise be damaged by neglect); furthermore, disputes over use or management could readily be resolved by partition in kind. In today's urbanized
society, this rationale seems less persuasive, especially where the cotenancy
property, like a family home or business, is one that, in some circumstances,
cannot physically be readily shared with a cotenant "outsider." Thus, more

and more, courts have required the cotenant in possession to account for the property's rental value, even when no formal ouster has taken place.

The materials that follow flesh out the various accounting rules and test your ability to apply them.

NOTES AND QUESTIONS

1. **Rents received from third parties.** Since passage of the Statute of Anne, 4 & 5 Anne, c. 16, §27 (1705), it is settled law that with respect to rents paid by third parties collected by one cotenant, the other cotenants are entitled to an accounting.[40]

2. **Ouster.** "If one tenant in common occupies the whole estate, claiming it as his own, it is an ouster of his co-tenant, who must first establish his right at law, and thus recover his mesne profits (share of rental value). . . ." Izard v. Bodine, 11 N.J. Eq. 403, 404 (1857).

There is universal agreement as to the statement of this rule, but considerable confusion in the cases as to two of its aspects: (1) What is an "ouster"? (2) Is the aggrieved cotenant ever entitled to more than mesne profits (rental value)?

Because one does not usually eject a cotenant bodily, most claims of ouster do not involve assaults or even physical barriers to entry. Suppose instead that cotenant A, in possession, ignores cotenant B's letter asking to use the premises. Or suppose that because of her husband's verbal abuse, cotenant wife moves out. Or suppose that cotenant A expressly refuses to pay cotenant B any share of the rental value? Has an ouster occurred in each of these cases? See, e.g., Spiller v. Mackereth, 334 So. 2d 859 (Ala. 1976) (unanswered letter from nonresident cotenant demanding that resident cotenant either vacate or pay one-half the fair rental value held not an ouster); In re Estate of Holt, 14 Misc. 2d 971, 177 N.Y.S.2d 192 (Sur. Ct. 1958) (A's express refusal to pay rental value held an ouster); contra, Utah Oil Refining Co. v. Leigh, 98 Utah 149, 96 P.2d 1100 (1939).

As to the "ousted" cotenant's measure of damages, consider the following case: A and B are cotenants of a rental building with an annual rental value of $200,000. A "ousts" B and establishes a laundry in the building. At the end of the year A shows a net profit of $500,000 before deduction for rent. How much can B recover from A? $100,000? $150,000? $350,000? Compare Simkin v. New York Cent. R.R., 138 Ind. App. 668, 214 N.E.2d 661 (1966), with White v. Smyth, 147 Tex. 272, 214 S.W.2d 967 (1948).

Ordinarily, the courts distinguish between mesne profits (the prop-

---

40. Each cotenant may lease out his *interest* in the cotenancy premises to a lessee who obtains only those rights that his lessor has. The text addresses the different situation where one cotenant leases out to a third party the right to possess the whole, for example, making the representation that the lessee has the right to exclusive possession. See 2 American Law of Property §6.11, at 48-50 (1952).

erty's rental value), as to which the ousted cotenant may obtain an accounting, and entrepreneurial profits, that is, the gains that result from the business venture, which the entrepreneurial cotenant may keep for himself. But on occasion, as in White v. Smyth, *supra*, where the cotenancy property consists of a wasting asset, such as timber or mineral lands, and the entrepreneurial cotenant has shown bad faith, the court may force disgorgement of some of the business profits as well.

3.   **Problem.** H beats W. She obtains a restraining order. H is now barred from coming within 1,000 feet of their jointly owned family home. Has an ouster occurred? If so, does W owe H money? How much? How else might a court view this action?

4.   **Must an occupying cotenant pay rent to a nonoccupying one?** Suppose A and B own property as tenants in common or as joint tenants. A lives on the premises; B does not. Does A owe rent to B? Under the common law, A owed no rent (absent an ouster), on the theory that she was only exercising her right as a cotenant to occupy every square foot of the premises. Some jurisdictions have abandoned this rule and hold that B does owe rent to A. Compare Seesholts v. Beers, 270 So. 434 (Fla. Dist. Ct. App. 1972) (resident cotenant need not account to nonresident cotenant) *with* Cohen v. Cohen, 157 Ohio St. 503 (1952) (resident cotenant can be made to account for reasonable rental value).

5.   **Carrying charges such as taxes and mortgage payments.** A cotenant who pays more than her share of carrying charges, such as property taxes, debt service on a preexisting mortgage, or casualty insurance, ordinarily is entitled to contribution from the other cotenants, in proportion to their interest in the property. The principle at work is that each cotenant has an interest in preventing the loss of the property by a tax or foreclosure sale and therefore has a duty to contribute her proportionate share of the carrying charges. If a cotenant does not petition for immediate contribution, she can later receive a credit for excess carrying charges at partition.

6.   **Repairs and improvements.** A cotenant in possession is *not* entitled to contribution for repairs, even those necessary to preserve the premises, except where the cotenant is required to account for the premise's rental value. This rule presumably dates back to the feudal vision of property as land, with improvements relatively unimportant to its overall value. (Compare the common-law rule concerning tenant's continuing liability for rent in the event the leasehold premises burn down, see §3.14.c, *supra*.)

Today the general rule regarding improvements paid for by one of the cotenants is that the improver's outlay will be protected, even if the other cotenant was not consulted in advance or refused to give his consent. The protection is qualified, however. For example, the nonconsenting cotenant will not be required to contribute to the cost prior to partition.[41] If the

---

41. If the improved premises are then leased to a third party and the improvements are reflected in a higher rent, the improver should be entitled to some upward adjustment in his share of the rents until such time as he has recovered his outlay for the improvement.

premises are physically partitioned, the improver often will be awarded the improved portion of the premises. If the partition is by sale, however, the improver will gain a credit only for the amount the improvement added onto the value of the property. See Graham v. Inlow, 302 Ark. 414, 790 S.W.2d 428 (1990) (improvements must be made in good faith and confer benefit on the premises).

Law-and-economics scholars have been quick to point out that the rule that improvers are entitled to be reimbursed only to the extent their improvements add value to the premises promotes efficient (wealth-producing) investment. (Suppose a cotenant paved the roof in pink shells: no credit regardless of the amount he paid to do so, assuming the value of the premises was not enhanced.) For a discussion of concurrent ownership rules from the standpoint of law and economics, see Lawrence Berger, An Analysis of the Economic Relations between Cotenants, 21 Ariz. L. Rev. 1015 (1979), who proposes a redesign of these rules to achieve maximum economic efficiency.

7. **Problem.** A and B own a two-family house as equal cotenants. A resided in the lower-floor apartment rent-free through 1995. This apartment had a $2,000 monthly rental value. A leased out the upper-floor apartment, and in 1995 collected $24,000 — the agreed-upon rental — from the tenant. For the year 1995, A spent the following sums attributable to the property:

Real estate taxes*	$6,400
Fire insurance*	1,600
Fuel*	4,000
Utilities*	4,800
Mortgage interest*	12,000
Reduction of mortgage principal*	2,400
Repair of downstairs toilet	500

* These items cover both units. Assume an equal allocation.

(a) The court orders A to account for the year 1995 but does not require him to include the rental value of his unit. What does A owe B? (Suggested answer: B owes A $1,400.)

(b) Recompute this debt if A must account for his use and occupancy. (Suggested answer: A owes B $8,150.)

8. **Problem.** In 1920, Al Smith bought an old Vermont dairy farm near his home in Woodstock, Vermont. He used the farm as a country retreat, leasing out some land to local farmers, but letting most of the property (about 300 acres) return to its wild state. When Al died in 1959, he left the farm to his son (Al, Jr.) and his daughter (Edna), with the proviso that his ashes should be scattered over the hills behind the farmhouse. The terms of the will were carried out.

Al and Edna continued to own the farm jointly until 1980, when (after a fight with Al) Edna turned over her portion to her four sons. Throughout the period after their father's death, Al used the farm far more than Edna did. He never lived there (he had a house in town), but he had a garden up there every year and built a swimming hole that he used daily during the summer. One summer, his college-aged daughter lived there; another summer, his son lived there with his wife and their baby. In 1985, his youngest daughter married an artist, who started to live and work at the farm roughly five months a year, while his wife commuted from New York City. Before the fight with Edna, Al had tried to get Edna to share the expenses and upkeep of the property, with moderate success. When Edna passed the property on to her sons, Al more or less gave up and paid for all the upkeep and maintenance of the house himself. These included paying for a new roof that cost $10,000.

It is now 1992. Edna's son Burt has decided "he wants to take his portion of the farm out in cash." His uncle Al is dead set against selling the hills where his father's ashes were scattered. Advise Al of his rights under the law and formulate a strategy that will achieve his goals, if possible.

3.   The Cotenant as a Double-Dealer

Should the bare fact that A and B are cotenants invest them with any fiduciary duties relating to the property's use or potential value? Consider this question when you read the next case and the problems that follow it.

WHITE v. SMYTH

147 Tex. 272, 214 S.W.2d 967 (1948)

[The Smyth ranch contained 30,000 acres of land valuable for its rock asphalt deposits. On the death of J. G. Smyth, the ranch passed in undivided interests to his nine children, one of whom was the wife of the defendant, R. L. White. In 1923, the cotenants leased the ranch to the defendant for mining the rock asphalt, White agreeing to pay royalties of 25 cents (and lesser amounts) per ton of rock asphalt taken. The lease term was 99 years but was terminable at the defendant's option on payment of $14,222.22. White operated under the lease until 1941, when he exercised his power to terminate and advised that he would vacate the property shortly. Before leaving, however, White acquired his wife's one-ninth interest. The defendant then wrote to his newly acquired cotenants (and former lessors) that he would "now want to take out such part of my share of the rock as is practical before I move my machinery." Over his cotenants' objections, White continued mining. After several years, the cotenants sued White for a partition of the rock asphalt and also for an accounting for rock asphalt removed by him without their consent. The trial court found (a) that the rock asphalt was incapable of division in kind; (b) that the defendant had not mined more than one-ninth of the value of the rock asphalt still unmined when his cotenancy began; (c) that the value of the rock asphalt in the ground which was mined during the dispute was $99,334.53; and (d) that the net profit realized was $250,180.56. The trial court decreed that the property be sold and the proceeds distributed among the common owners and awarded plaintiffs a judgment against White for $222,382.72 (eight-ninths of his net profit). White appealed. (In preparing this summary of the facts, the editors have tampered with them slightly, but not significantly, in the hope that they has made the controversy more understandable.)]

MR. JUSTICE SMEDLEY delivered the opinion of the court. . . .

The application for writ of error presents under several points three principal contentions: First, the petitioner White owes no duty to account to respondents, because he has not taken more than his fair share of the rock asphalt in place, has not excluded respondents from the premises, and in mining has made merely normal use of the property, it having already been devoted to the mining of rock asphalt at the time petitioner acquired his undivided interest therein; second, that if he owes a duty to account, he is liable only for eight-ninths of the value in the ground of the rock asphalt he has mined and not for profits which he has realized; and third, that the jury's findings that the rock asphalt in certain surveys in the ranch and in all of the property outside of certain surveys cannot be equitably partitioned in kind are without evidence to support them. We consider first the points pertaining to partition, since the question whether the property is or is not capable of partition in kind has an important bearing upon the other questions.

The record contains many pages of testimony as to the nature, location, quantity and quality of the rock asphalt in the lands. [After summarizing this testimony, the court rules it sufficient to support the finding below that the mineral deposits were not susceptible of fair division by metes and bounds, and upholds the trial court's direction that the lands be sold and the proceeds be distributed.]

The amount of the trial court's judgment in favor of respondents against petitioner represents eight-ninths of the net profits realized by petitioner from mining, processing and selling 397,381.11 tons of rock asphalt taken from the land during the period from October 29, 1942, to September 30, 1945. This amount of net profits was found by the jury after deducting from the gross proceeds all expenses incurred by petitioner, together with a reasonable compensation for his personal services and the reasonable value of the use of his plant and other property in the operation of the mine. . . .

It seems that there are no decisions in this state as to the duty of a co-owner who takes solid minerals from the property to account to his cotenant. It is held, however, as in most of the other states that one who takes oil without the consent of his cotenants must account to them for their share of the proceeds of the oil less the necessary and reasonable cost of producing and marketing it. . . .

Petitioner contends that the rule above stated does not apply to this case, and that he need not account to his cotenants, because he has mined no more than his fair share of the rock asphalt in place and has not excluded them from the premises. He relies primarily upon Kirby Lumber Co. v. Temple Lumber Co., 125 Texas 284, 83 S.W. (2d) 638. . . .

In the *Kirby Lumber Company* case the Temple Company owned an undivided two-thirds interest and the Kirby Company owned an undivided one-third interest in a 640 acre tract of land on which there was valuable standing timber. The Temple Company, believing that it owned the entire title to a specific 427 acres of the land, cut all of the timber standing on that tract, amounting to ten million feet, and manufactured it into lumber. There remained uncut on the 640 acres, 2,783,325 feet of timber. The court's opinion states that the 640 acres was generally of uniform value as to timber and otherwise. The Kirby Company sued the Temple Company to recover the manufactured value of one-third of the timber that had been cut. The trial court found that the total amount of timber standing on the land before the cutting was 12,783,325 feet, of which the Kirby Company's one-third amounted to 4,261,108 feet, and that the amount left standing was 2,783,325 feet, which was treated as belonging to the Kirby Company, and that thus the Temple Company had cut 1,477,783 feet more than its share. Its judgment awarded to the Kirby Company $43,372.93, being the manufactured value of the 1,477,783 feet. The Court of Civil Appeals reversed and rendered the trial court's judgment, after holding that the Kirby Company was charged with notice that its predecessor in title had cut timber from part of the land. 42 S.W. (2) 1070. The Supreme Court reversed the judgments of the two lower courts and rendered judgment in favor of the Kirby Company against the Temple Company for the stumpage value, $5.00 per thousand feet, of the 1,477,783 feet of excess timber cut by the Temple Company. Most of the Court's opinion is devoted to a discussion of the question whether the Kirby Company should be charged with notice that timber had been cut by its predecessor in title and of the question as to the amount of the recovery, that is whether stumpage value or manufactured value. Little is said in the approval of that part of the trial court's judgment which charged the Temple Company with only the amount of the timber cut in excess of its share. The authorities there cited relate to timber and to the question whether stumpage value or manufacture value may be recovered.

The important distinction between the *Kirby Lumber Company* case and the instant case, in respect to the ruling that the Temple Company need not account for the timber cut not in excess of its two-thirds share, is that in that case, as shown by the Court's statement that "the 640 acres was generally of uniform value as to timber and otherwise," the timber was fairly subject to partition in kind, whereas in the instant case the rock asphalt is not. The Temple Company's action in cutting the timber up to its share and the Court's approval of that action by the judgment rendered worked in effect a partition of the timber. Here there has not been, and there could not be consistently with the finding that the rock asphalt is not capable of partition in kind, an approval by the court of White's action in taking for himself and disposing of a part of the rock asphalt. The ownership of all of the cotenants extends to all of the rock asphalt, and White was not authorized to make partition of it. . . .

The facts of this case attest the obvious soundness of the rule that a cotenant cannot select and take for himself part of the property jointly owned and thus make partition. While he was lessee under the lease that covered the entire ranch, White selected the site for and developed the present pit, making extensive improvements, including the construction of roads, excavations and grading for private tracks, other excavations and grading, all at great cost and of very substantial value. The location of the plant site was favorable and valuable. . . .

When White exercised the right to terminate the lease . . . he had no further right or interest in the rock asphalt in the lands, the mine or the mine site, except that he was given by the lease the right to remove his machinery, tools, houses and implements. The rock asphalt estate in all of the lands belonged to all of the cotenants, as did also the added advantages and values to the entire mineral estate created and existing by reason of the developed pit and mine site; but White, taking advantage for himself of the added values, after acquiring the one-ninth interest of his wife [and his wife's sister] mined from the pit about four hundred thousand tons of the rich, valuable and readily accessible rock asphalt. . . .

Kirby Lumber Co. v. Temple Lumber Co. [supra] is cited by petitioner to sustain his assignment of error that if he owes respondents the duty to account, he must account only for the value in the ground of the rock asphalt mined by him. That case is not an authority for this point. The plaintiff did not ask for an accounting for profits. There were no allegations as to profits and no issue as to profits was submitted. There is nothing to show that any profits were made. The question before the court was whether the defendant should be required to pay for the stumpage value of the timber cut or for its value after having been manufactured into lumber and without deduction for expenditures. The court held that the former, that is stumpage value, was the measure of recovery because the defendant had acted in good faith, believing that it owned all of the timber that it had cut. A fundamental difference between the facts of the Kirby case and the instant case, which has been noted herein, has an important bearing here. It is that in the Kirby case the standing timber was of uniform value and could readily be partitioned in kind, whereas in this case the rock asphalt cannot be fairly and equitably partitioned in kind.

Three cases are cited by petitioner in which the cotenant who had taken minerals was charged with their value in place: Appeal of Fulmer, 128 Pa. 24, 18 Atl. 49, 15 Am. St. Rep. 662; McGowan v. Bailey, 179 Pa. 470, 36 Atl. 325; and Clowser v. Joplin (W.D. Mo.) 4 Dill. 469n, Fed. Cas. No. 2908a. While the opinions in the two Pennsylvania cases contain reasoning to justify the use of that measure, they also indicate that it was deemed just and equitable under the peculiar facts, and that it might not be applicable to all cases. In the Federal case a memorandum opinion adopts the measure of liability stated in the two Pennsylvania cases as appropriate under the Missouri statute. The three cases depart from the majority rule, supported by the authorities cited and discussed herein, which majority rule is stated in American Jurisprudence as follows:

> Since any co-owner of a mine or mineral property is at liberty to work it, some courts have intimated that a co-owner who does not choose to avail himself of this right should have no claim upon the production of one who has elected to do so. But this view seems to be contrary to the weight of authority, and the prevailing rule appears to be that the producer must account to his cotenant for all profits made to the extent of his interest in the property. (14 Am. Jur., p. 104, §36.) . . .

It is argued by petitioner that his receipts have been from sales of a manufactured product, and that respondents should not be permitted, by sharing in the profits, to obtain the benefits of his personal skill and industry and of the flux oil and water used and the machinery, apparatus and equipment belonging to petitioner. We believe that the preparation of the rock asphalt for market, as described by petitioner's testimony and by that of other witnesses, is a processing rather than a manufacturing. The rock asphalt is rock asphalt in the ground, that is, limestone rock impregnated with asphalt. To make it ready for the market and for use in the building of roads it is mixed and crushed, and oil is mixed with it to give the small particles of rock a film of oil, and water is put in the mixture so that it will not become solid in transit. It is rock asphalt when it is sold and when it is used on the roads. The producing tenant is required to account to his cotenants for net profits realized from mining, smelting, crushing, processing or marketing solid minerals taken from the land. . . .

The judgments of the district court and the Court of Civil Appeals are affirmed. . . .

MR. JUSTICE SIMPSON, with whom JUSTICES SHARP, BREWSTER and FOLLEY concur, dissenting.

It is respectfully submitted that the measure of recovery allowed the respondents by the majority ruling is wrong, and is contrary to the applicable precedents under the established facts. It results in what is earnestly urged to be an unjust exaction of the petitioner White, who should have been required to account for $99,334.53, the value in place of the rock asphalt taken, and not $222,382.72, its net manufactured value.

Petitioner White had spent practically a lifetime in the rock asphalt business. He worked the asphalt deposits on the Smyth ranch from 1923 until 1941 under a contract with the landowners, which he then terminated, as he had the right to do. He had acquired one-ninth . . . of the rock asphalt under some 30,000 acres of the Smyth ranch, and continued working the deposits after the contract with his cotenants ended. He notified them what he was doing. He had a complete legal and moral right to be on the land and to mine the rock.

This rock, after mining, has to be manufactured into paving material before it is of any practicable use. It is blasted from its beds in large pieces, which are broken up by further blasting. It is then scooped onto trucks by steam shovels and hauled to and further pulverized by a crushing machine. It is then taken to a storage bin where the rock with high asphaltic content is placed at one end, that with a low content at the other. This bin is equipped with vibrating feeders which drop the rock in proper portions on a conveyor belt which takes it to other grinders for further processing. After the final crushing, the rock, by means of a screen, is separated into three bins according to the size of the particles into which it has been crushed. Then the rock, sizes kept separate, is weighed, dropped into a mixer known as a "pug mill" and oil is introduced into the product under pressures running from 75 to 100 pounds. Powerful paddles churn the material so the oil is thoroughly fused into it. . . . Suitable quantities of water are added and milled into the product. The resulting mixture is a manufactured paving material which petitioner has been selling under the registered name of "Valdemix."

The plant and equipment investment of the petitioner exceeded $500,000.00.

The asphalt business is highly competitive. So competitive in fact that petitioner's Uvalde Mines and Uvalde Asphalt Company are the only survivors among all who have tried. One adequately capitalized concern, for instance, abandoned the business after losing at least $1,000,000.00.

In addition to the manufacturing of crude rock asphalt into a finished paving product, petitioner employed his skill and experience in selling it. He would agree in advance with contractors bidding on road work that if the contractor should be the successful bidder he would deliver "Valdemix" in given quantities and at certain prices and times. His lifetime of experience in the business enabled him to succeed where others had failed. He knew how to mine, how to manufacture, and how to sell.

What the complaining cotenants are entitled to get is the value of that which was taken, that is, crude rock asphalt. Any higher figure would no longer be compensatory but punitive. . . .

NOTES AND QUESTIONS

1. **Criticism.** This decision is discussed critically in Donald R. Kee, Recent Decisions, 1 Baylor L. Rev. 364 (1949), and Herman I. Morris, Recent Cases, 27 Tex. L. Rev. 863 (1949).

2. **More criticism.** Having held that White took only his fair share of the rock asphalt in place, should not the trial court have regarded his activity as partition in kind? Although the opinion speaks of White's mined rock asphalt as being "rich, valuable and readily accessible," these are the very factors which, together with volume, must be applied to the unmined rock to determine its value. Whatever the superior advantages of White's rock, the court's initial finding as to the value of remaining rock carries with it an estimate that at least eight-ninths of the potential extraction profits were yet to be realized.

3. **Conventional wisdom.** It is hornbook law that *absent a special relationship* cotenants do not owe each other a fiduciary duty with respect to their dealing with common property. Scott v. Scruggs, 836 S.W.2d 278, 282 (Tex. Ct. App. 1992); William E. Burby, Handbook on the Law of Real Property §99 (3d ed. 1965). Even in the absence of a special relationship, however, there is an obligation to act in a manner that is not detrimental to the other cotenant's ownership and enjoyment of the property. There may also be a contract-like duty among cotenants of good faith and fair dealing. Several factors make this a murky legal area: the indeterminancy of the term "special relationship"; the ever-evolving content of "good faith and fair dealing"; the factual kinship of a business cotenancy with a formal partnership, whose members may not self-deal at their partners' expense, without the partners' prior consent. Meinhard v. Salmon, 249 N.Y. 458 (1928); Unif. Partnership Act §21, 6 U.L.A. 608 (1995 & Supp. 1996) (Partner Accountable as a Fiduciary).

4. **More applications.** (a)   A, B, and C are heirs of D, a life tenant who has the power to encroach upon the corpus. Upon D's death, they are to become cotenants of whatever property D has not transferred. Nine days before she dies, D executes a forty-year coal-mining lease to A. Is the lease valid? If so, do the operating profits from the lease inure to B and C as well? See Givens v. Givens, 387 S.W.2d 851 (Ky. 1965).

(b)   A and B are tenants in common. The property is sold for unpaid taxes. May A acquire the property for his own account? Cf. Gavin v. Hosey, 230 So. 2d 570 (Miss. 1970) (purchase of tax title by cotenant inures to the benefit of other cotenants). May A wait until after the redemption period has expired and then acquire the property from a stranger who purchased the property at the tax foreclosure sale? Compare Spencer v. Spencer, 160 Fla. 749, 36 So. 2d 424 (1948), with Pease v. Snyder, 169 Kan. 628, 220 P.2d 151 (1950). May A acquire the property for his own account at a partition sale? See 59A Am. Jur. 2d §90 (1987).

c.   The Condominium — The Modern Co-ownership Hybrid

The condominium arrived in the United States in the early 1960s[42] and within a decade became firmly rooted in American soil. Launched as a form of apartment ownership — better in many ways than the much older stock-cooperative — the condominium today also thrives in residential subdivisions and in commercial and industrial parks. Wherever one finds a community of property owners, it is quite possible that a condominium is involved.

Let us illustrate the condominium's legal structure through an apartment building, each of whose residents enjoys exclusive ownership of an individual unit. Unit ownership of an apartment takes the form of a fee simple absolute in the apartment's "four corners." But each unit owner owns more than "title" to his apartment; we must also account for the structure's common areas — the land, the hallways, the heating plant, and so forth.

As to these common areas — the project's "infrastructure" — co-ownership is created, whereby each unit owner becomes a tenant in common, joining every other unit owner in the cotenancy. Each owner's undivided share of the cotenancy, the percentage fixed when the condominium is formed, usually depends on his apartment's size or initial value, relative to that of the project's other units.[43] Importantly, this percentage determines the unit owner's pro rata share of the common expenses; the same percentage may also measure his voting interest in project affairs.[44] When he buys a unit, the purchaser receives a deed that describes both the exclusive interest in the apartment and the cotenancy interest in the common areas.

Every state has an enabling law; this becomes the legal roadmap to form a condominium. The two key documents, which the founder must record, are the *declaration* and the *operating bylaws*. The declaration contains a legal description of the underlying land, a description of the building, the common areas, the apartment units, and each unit's percentage interest in the common areas. The declaration also identifies the body, usually a condominium board, that is to govern the project. The bylaws flesh out the governance rules and deal with such matters as budget, collection of the common-area expenses, capital outlays and reserves, and the regulation of unit sales and rentals.

To preserve the project's legal integrity, the unit owners must (the

---

42. See Curtis Berger, Condominium: Shelter on a Statutory Foundation, 63 Colum. L. Rev. 987 (1963).

43. For example, if an apartment building had twenty units, equal in size and value, each unit owner would have a 5 percent undivided interest in the common areas.

44. Some condominiums are more egalitarian and, regardless of apartment size or value, accord each unit owner the same voting rights.

enabling laws require it) "suffer" two restraints upon their freedom to alienate. They may not separate ownership of the unit from ownership of the undivided interest in the common areas (do you see why?); nor may they seek to partition[45] the common areas while the structure remains intact and subject to the condominium regime.

Like the one-family house, the condominium unit and its undivided share of the common areas, is a legally discrete interest for purposes of mortgage financing and property taxation. Thus the unit owner can decide whether he wants a small or large mortgage, or any mortgage at all, and the unit bears its own tax assessment, the tax bill paid directly by the unit owner. This provides some advantage over the stock-cooperative, whose real estate taxes and mortgage debt are a blanket lien that all cooperators must carry; this may lead to somewhat greater financial risk during hard times.

§4.2   Marital Property

Under the current definition of marital property rights, women and the children who depend on them tend to end up among the ranks of the poor. Sixty percent of all people in poverty[46] and two-thirds of the elderly poor are women.[47] Female-headed households are five times more likely to be poor[48] and up to ten times more likely to stay poor than are families with a male present.[49] Single mothers and their children have become the paradigm poor[50] at a time when their numbers are increasing: 19 percent of all families[51] and 50 percent of African American families[52] are headed by women.

45. See pages §4.1.b.1 *infra.*

46. Zillah R. Eisenstein, The Sexist Politics of the New Right: Understanding the "Crisis of Liberalism" for the 1980's, in Feminist Theory 91 (Nannerl O. Keohane, Michelle Z. Rosaldo, and Barbara C. Gelpi eds., 1982).

47. Id.

48. Ruth Sidel, Women and Children Last 16 (1986).

49. Diane Pearce, Welfare Is Not for Women: Why the War on Poverty Cannot Conquer the Feminization of Poverty, in Women, the State and Welfare 266 (Linda Gordon ed., 1990).

50. See Frank Levy and Richard Michel, The Economic Future of American Families: Income and Wealth Trends 39 (1991) (noting a "swap in which elderly families moved from the bottom of the income distribution to the lower middle, while their vacated places at the bottom were fallen into by new female-headed families with children").

51. Irwin Garfinkel, Sara McLanahan, and Dorothy Watson, Divorce, Female Headship and Child Support, in Women's Life Cycle and Economic Insecurity 101 (Martha H. Ozawa, 1989). Estimates are that 45 percent of white children and 84 percent of African American children born in the late 1970s will live with a single mother at some time before they reach the age of 18. Id. at 102.

52. See R. Sidel, *supra* note 48, at 18.

Children are the poorest group in the United States.[53] Nearly one-fourth of all children[54] and one-half of African American children[55] are poor; three-fourths of children living in female-headed households will experience poverty before they reach 18.[56]

The social arrangements that leave many U.S. children poorer than those in any other industrialized country[57] stem in part from the way marital property rights are defined. This section discusses marital property rights, beginning with the common-law marital estates, proceeding to the common-law definition of married women's property rights, and concluding with an examination of the property rights of married women today.

a. Categories of Common-Law Marital Estates

Early in the feudal era, the common law gave each of the parties to a marriage vital interests in the lands owned by the other. In part, this was born of solicitude: for the guardianship of children after a mother's untimely death (viz., curtesy); for economic well-being of a surviving widow after her husband's death (viz., dower). In part, this was built upon notions of male primacy: when she became a spouse, the married woman lost more than her maidenhood; in the law's eyes (and who but men made the law), she also lost her legal competency — a state of affairs that gave her parity with infants, idiots, and felons, although she could end this disability by outlasting her husband (or the marriage).

The common-law marital estates have little present-day standing, and even this is disappearing. Yet, they have continuing interest for law students for several principal reasons: (1) as examples of legal life estates — that is, life estates created by operation of law; (2) as forerunners of the modern law of marital property; (3) as potential title problems in states where they once existed, or may still exist; (4) as further examples of the law's response to changing social attitudes and economic needs.

---

53. National Commission on Children, Speaking of Kids: A National Survey of Children and Parents 1 (1991)

54. See R. Sidel, *supra* note 48, at 3.

55. See Joan Williams, Gender Wars: Selfless Women in the Republic of Choice, 66 N.Y.U. L. Rev. 1559 (1991) (citing Delores Kong, Funding, Political Will, Crucial to Saving Babies' Lives, Boston Globe, Sept. 13, 1990, at 1).

56. See Gender Wars, *supra* note 55, at 1604 (citing Sara E. Rix, The American Woman 1990-91, at 5 (1990)).

57. National Commission on Children, Beyond Rhetoric — A New American Agenda for Children and Families 15 (1991). One study of six industrial countries found that the "United States, which is the wealthiest country of the six studied, had the highest poverty rate among children and the second highest among families with children." See also Timothy M. Smeeding and Barbara Boyld Torrey, Poor Children in Rich Countries, 242 Science 873 (1988).

1.   Estate by the Marital Right (*Jure Uxoris*)

At the moment of marriage, the husband acquired immediate control over his wife's property. He was entitled to the rents and profits of her freehold estates.[58] He could enjoy them without an accounting, transfer them as he wished, and permit his creditors to reach them by execution. The wife was powerless to protest. Except as it was transformed by curtesy, this utter dominion ended with the end of the marriage. Thus, the husband actually received a life estate (measured by the joint lives of husband and wife *qua* husband and wife), and this was all that his transferees would be allowed to take. Chancery steadily weakened the husband's unilateral control, and the Married Women's Acts of the nineteenth century brought it gradually to an end.

2.   Curtesy

At the birth of live issue[59] who were qualified to inherit their mother's estate,[60] the husband's jure uxoris was expanded to a life estate *for his life*[61] in *all of* his wife's inheritable, freehold lands. This newly formed estate, called *curtesy initiate,* was said to be granted "by the curtesy of England," [62] since it treated the husband more generously than did an earlier civil law prototype. If a man's wife predeceased him, his estate was renamed *curtesy consummate,* but its attributes were left unchanged. Both before and after his wife's death, the husband continued his plenary control over the rents and profits that had been his to enjoy under jure uxoris. So tenuous did the law regard the wife's status in her own lands that adverse possession *could not* begin to run against the married woman during his husband's lifetime. Can you explain this?

3.   Dower

The best known and the most enduring of the legal life estates is the dower interest of a wife in the lands of her husband. Its sources are Teu-

58. Personalty and nonfreehold estates also were subject to this dominion. As to these interests, the husband might dissipate or transfer not only the income but also the corpus.

59. An infant's survival was often touch and go in an era of high infant mortality. Accordingly, the criteria for a live birth were in keeping with the hazards of childbirth. The mother need not survive the child; and as for the child, it was enough for its heartbeat to have been felt or its cry to have been heard.

60. Thus, if the wife's estate was an estate tail female, the birth of a male child would not suffice.

61. A life estate that would still be cut short, however, by divorce.

62. Curtesy, perhaps, but courtesy, no! Neither a husband's adultery, nor his desertion, nor the two in combination, would bar curtesy.

tonic; the groom by custom promised the family of his bride to leave her an endowment should she survive him. In England, provision for a widow became a legal incident of marriage; a widow was entitled, as a matter of law, to a life estate in *one third* of the inheritable, freehold lands of which her husband was seized[63] during coverture. Before the husband's death, the wife's interest was *dower inchoate;* at his death, the widow's interest became *dower prior to assignment* until the courts decided which lands should be set aside to meet the one-third requirement. In the lands assigned to her, the widow then had *dower consummate,* a life estate ending with her death. In an era when land was the chief form of wealth, dower gave a measure of security both to the widow and to those of her children who, because of primogeniture and male preference, received no interest in their father's lands.

Whatever his feelings for his wife, the husband could not, without the wife's cooperation, strip her of dower. Any transfer or mortgage of his lands, or any levy of execution by his creditors, was subject to his wife's inchoate interest, unless the mortgage was given in a purchase money transaction or the creditor's claim preceded the husband's marriage. The wife might join, however, in the transfer or mortgage — for the sole purpose of relinquishing her dower interest.[64] And she might agree, before marriage, to accept some substitute for dower; as might be expected, such agreements were closely scrutinized for their essential fairness.[65]

For many reasons, including those advanced in the following opinion, dower and curtesy have been either whittled down or eliminated in most states. The Massachusetts statute, *infra,* typifies this process, and raises anew the pervasive issues of "due process" whenever property institutions get "reformed."

OPINION OF THE JUSTICES

337 Mass. 786, 151 N.E.2d 475 (1958)

On June 27, 1958, the Justices submitted the following answers to questions propounded to them by the Senate.

To the Honorable the Senate of the Commonwealth of Massachusetts:

The undersigned Justices of the Supreme Judicial Court respectfully submit these answers to the questions set forth in an order of the Senate dated June 18, 1958, and transmitted to us on June 20. The order refers to

---

63. What "seisin" is within the context of dower has caused endless controversy. For a discussion and citation of cases, see 2 Powell, Real Property ¶209[1] (Rohan ed. 1991).

64. Courts will sometimes transfer inchoate dower to the proceeds of sale when a wife refuses to join in her husband's transfer. In such event, either the entire sum realized or, more properly, the discounted value of the wife's expectancy interest is deposited into court. Id. ¶209[2], at 154.

65. Id. ¶212[3], at 170.8-170.9.

a pending bill, Senate No. 388, entitled "An Act to restrict dower and curtesy claims to land owned at the death of the claimant's spouse."

The bill has three sections. Section 1 seeks to amend by striking out
G.L. (Ter. Ed.) c. 189, §1, and substituting the following: "A husband shall
upon the death of his wife hold for his life one third of all land owned by
her at the time of her death. Such estate shall be known as his tenancy by
curtesy, and the law relative to dower shall be applicable to curtesy. A wife
shall, upon the death of her husband, hold her dower at common law in
land owned by him at the time of his death. Such estate shall be known as
her tenancy by dower. Any encumbrances on land at the time of the owner's
death shall have precedence over curtesy or dower. To be entitled to such
curtesy or dower the surviving husband or wife shall file in his or her election and claim therefor in the registry of probate within six months after
the date of the approval of the bond of the executor or administrator of the
deceased, and shall thereupon hold instead of the interest in real property
given in section one in chapter one hundred and ninety,[66] curtesy or dower,
respectively, otherwise such estate shall be held to be waived.[67] Such curtesy
and dower may be assigned by the probate court in the same manner as
dower is now assigned, and the tenant by curtesy or dower shall be entitled
to the possession and profits of one undivided third of the real estate of
the deceased from her or his death until the assignment of curtesy or
dower. . . . Except as preserved herein, dower and curtesy are abolished."

Section 2 reads: "If it should be held that this act cannot constitutionally apply to rights of dower or curtesy as they existed prior to the effective
date of this act, it shall nevertheless be fully effective except as to such
rights." Section 3 provides that the act shall take effect on January 1, 1959.

The questions are as follows:

"1. Can said pending bill, if enacted into law, constitutionally apply
to inchoate rights of dower or curtesy as they existed prior to the effective
date thereof under Article X of the Declaration of Rights of the Constitution of Massachusetts, section 10 of Article I of the Constitution of the
United States in so far as said section forbids any state to make any law
impairing the obligation of contracts, or the Fourteenth Amendment to the
Constitution of the United States?

"2. Can said pending bill, if enacted into law, constitutionally empower a person after the effective date thereof to deprive his spouse of such
inchoate rights of dower or curtesy of such spouse as were in existence prior
to said effective date under Article X of the Declaration of Rights of the

---

66. Chapter 190 is part of the state's law of intestate succession. After the decedent's
debts and funeral expenses are all paid, the surviving spouse will receive: (a) where the decedent leaves kindred but no issue, $25,000 and one-half of the remaining estate; (b) where the
decedent leaves issue, one-third of the estate; (c) where the decedent leaves no kindred and
no issue, the entire estate. — EDS.

67. If the husband dies intestate, under what conditions will the wife elect dower rather
than waive it? — EDS.

Constitution of Massachusetts, section 10 of Article I of the Constitution of the United States in so far as said section forbids any state to make any law impairing the obligation of contracts, or the Fourteenth Amendment to the Constitution of the United States?"[68]

The order recites that a substantially identical bill, Senate No. 274 of 1956, was referred to the Judicial Council by c. 10 of the Resolves of 1956; and that a majority of the Judicial Council in its thirty-second report in 1956, at pages 24-28, recommended passage but suggested the possibility of an advisory opinion of the Justices. In that report we read that the purpose of the bill "is to reduce the title problems affecting the marketability of land whether by sale or mortgage" (page 25). We there are told that these problems have two chief causes: (1) The omission of a husband or wife to declare an existing marriage and to obtain the signature of the spouse to a deed. (2) The ever growing number of migratory divorces with the attendant doubt as to their validity and the consequent uncertainty as to the legality of remarriage. The result might be described as a conveyancer's nightmare.

Under §1 as now in effect, curtesy is a life estate of a surviving husband in one third of all land owned by his wife during marriage unless he had joined in a deed of conveyance or "otherwise" released his right to claim curtesy; and dower is a similar life estate of a surviving wife in one third of land owned by the husband. And see G.L. (Ter. Ed.) c. 189, §1A. Either curtesy or dower may be "otherwise" released by a deed subsequent to the deed of conveyance executed either separately or jointly with the spouse. G.L. (Ter. Ed.). c. 189, §5. Of course, neither can exist without a valid marriage. By statute neither survives divorce. G.L. c. 208, §7 (as amended through St. 1949, c. 76, §2). This, of course, means a valid divorce. During marriage the right to claim curtesy or dower is said to be inchoate. (At common law the phrase was curtesy initiate.) Upon the death of the spouse, or, at any rate, after the later assignment of a specified one third of the land, it is said to be consummate. Curtesy and dower, under §1 in its present form, are superior to the rights of creditors. It should be noted that nothing like curtesy or dower exists as to personal property, which a husband or wife may dispose of freely without the consent of the spouse. . . .

That the bill would violate no provision of the Federal Constitution is settled by decisions of the Supreme Court of the United States. In Randall v. Kreiger, 23 Wall. 137, decided in 1874, it was said, at page 148: "During the life of the husband the right [of dower] is a mere expectancy or possibility. In that condition of things, the lawmaking power may deal with it as may be deemed proper. It is not a natural right. It is wholly given by law, and the power that gave it may increase, diminish, or otherwise alter it, or wholly take it away. It is upon the same footing with the expectancy of heirs, apparent or presumptive, before the death of the ancestor. Until that event

68. How are the questions different? — EDS.

occurs the law of descent and distribution may be moulded according to the will of the legislature." In Ferry v. Spokane, Portland & Seattle Ry., 258 U.S. 314, decided in 1922, the court upheld a decision of the Circuit Court of Appeals for the Ninth Circuit, 268 Fed. 117, to the effect that an Oregon statute limiting the right of dower of a nonresident to land of which the husband died seised was not unconstitutional. In the *Ferry* case the Supreme Court of the United States said, at pages 318-319: "Dower is not a privilege or immunity of citizenship, either state or federal, within the meaning of the provisions relied on [§2 of art. 4 and the Fourteenth Amendment]. At most it is a right which, while it exists, is attached to the marital contract or relation; and it always has been deemed subject to regulation by each State as respects property within its limits. Conner v. Elliott, 18 How. 491. . . . The cases recognize that the limitation of the dower right is to remove an impediment to the transfer of real estate and to assure titles against absent and probably unknown wives."

Turning to art. 10 of the Declaration of Rights of the Constitution of the Commonwealth, we observe in the thirty-second report of the Judicial Council that the doubt as to the validity of the bill springs from statements in several earlier decisions of the Supreme Judicial Court, in none of which, however, was the question before us presented. The question here is whether the bill if enacted would amount to a taking of property without due process of law. . . .

Dower and curtesy are of much less importance than formerly. This diminution in value is due to the great increase in the amount of personal property and in the superior alternative rights in the estate of a deceased husband or wife accorded by statute to a surviving spouse. The thirty-second report of the Judicial Council points to St. 1854, c. 406, as a source of such rights. These rights have been gradually increased by legislation. . . .

According to the thirty-second report of the Judicial Council claims of dower or curtesy in this Commonwealth have almost ceased to be made; and, in fact, a claim of neither is advisable except under two special circumstances: "(1) if the deceased owned real estate, but died insolvent or so nearly so that the bulk of the real estate must be sold to pay the debts and expenses; and (2) if the deceased during his or her lifetime conveyed a considerable amount of real estate without procuring a release of curtesy or dower in the deed." Newhall, Settlement of Estates (4th ed.) §213. It may be noted that statutory changes in dower as a common law incident of marriage have been made in this Commonwealth without making an exception of existing marriages. See 40 Mass. L.Q. No. 4, p. 36.

We are not surprised to learn that dower and curtesy either no longer exist or are of little practical importance in more than half the States. Powell, Real Property, §§217-218. . . .

In the light of the shrinking significance of curtesy or dower as alternatives which must be elected by a surviving husband or wife in the estate of a deceased spouse, we cannot regard the statements quoted from our cases as precluding inchoate curtesy and inchoate dower from being viewed in this Commonwealth in the same way as in a majority of the States. We are of opinion that as a matter of public policy the Legislature can restrict them in the manner proposed. Let it be conceded that each is a valuable interest and more than a possibility. Yet each is only a contingency — a contingency of waning value — which in the usual estate today is of slight importance. We think that inchoate curtesy and inchoate dower, as contingencies before the death of the predeceasing spouse, are subject to action by the Legislature, which may make an evaluation in the public interest, and determine that any slight advantage in their retention in a relatively few cases is outweighed by the far greater benefit to the general good accruing from their restriction.

To question 1, we answer, "Yes."

Believing that this answer covers all that is intended to be asked by question 2, we respectfully request that we be excused from making a separate answer to question 2.

NOTES AND QUESTIONS

1. **Before and after.** How did Senate No. 388 change the prior dower and curtesy statute? How did the prior statute change the common law?

2. **What is a "mere expectancy"?** The Massachusetts legislature passes a bill converting all fees on special limitation and fees on condition into fee simple absolutes. The accompanying report states that the bill's purposes are to reduce title problems and restrict dead-hand control. Your client is the present holder of a possibility of reverter. Can you distinguish the decision above?

3. **Title questions.** Contrast the Massachusetts bill with the New York statute that abolished curtesy outright, but retained dower as to real estate owned by a husband prior to the statute's effective date — September 1, 1930. Another law now sets a two-year limitation (after husband's death) for an action to assign dower. N.Y. Real Prop. Law. §§189, 190 (McKinney 1989); N.Y. Real Prop. Acts Law §1001 (McKinney 1979). When must a New York title examiner worry about dower?

4. **Current count.** At latest count, dower survives in its pristine form in nine or ten jurisdictions, curtesy in two. See 2 Powell, Real Property ¶213[1] at 15.122-15.123, ¶213[2] at 15.125-15.126 (Rohan ed. 1991). In the eight community property states, *infra*, the common-law marital estates never were recognized.

5. **Statutory substitutes.** The statutory substitutes for dower or curtesy are extremely varied. They include:

(a)   The surviving wife (husband) receives a share, not restricted to a life estate, in all of the assets owned by the husband (wife) at death.

(b)   The surviving wife (husband) receives a share, not restricted to a life estate, in all of the land owned by the husband (wife) during coverture.

(c)   The surviving wife (husband) is given an election, as against common-law dower (curtesy), to receive an intestate share in the husband's (wife's) estate.

6.   **Dower and power.** Historians have noted that the practice of giving widows the *use* rather than the *ownership* of land ensured that women remained in a subordinate economic status. In a book explaining why New England witchcraft accusations were overwhelmingly made against women, Carol Karlsen linked such accusations with the unsettled state of gender relations in seventeenth-century New England. In particular, she noted that prior to 1650 roughly half of male decedents left their widows the ownership, rather than the use of property — and that widows were less likely to remarry than widowers. These practices created a group of women whose economic independence may well have been perceived as threatening to the customs mandating the submission of women. See Carol F. Karlsen, The Devil in the Shape of a Woman 209 (1987).

7.   **Bibliography.** Several articles by Professor Haskins provide us with a rich lode on the common-law marital interests: Curtesy at Common Law, 29 B.U. L. Rev. 228 (1949); The Development of Common Law Dower, 62 Harv. L. Rev. 42 (1948); Curtesy in the United States, 100 U. Pa. L. Rev. 196 (1951); The Estate by Marital Right, 97 U. Pa. L. Rev. 345 (1949).

b.   Coverture — The Married Woman's Disability at Common Law

The common law enforced the traditional bargain of husbands' support in return for wives' services by making it legally impossible for wives to own property.

MARLENE STEIN WORTMAN, WOMEN IN AMERICAN LAW

vol. 1, at 27-28, 31-33, 38 (1985)

THE LAWES RESOLUTIONS OF WOMEN'S RIGHTS (1632)[69]

In this consolidation which we call wedlock is a locking together. It is true that man and wife are one person; but understand in what manner. When a small brooke or little river incorporateth with Rhodanus, Humber,

69.   From The Lawes Resolutions of Women's Rights: Or, the Laws Provision for Women (London, 1632). From Women's Life and Work in the Southern Colonies, by Julia Cherry Spruill *Laws or Lawes?* (1983).

or the Thames, the poor rivulet looseth her name; . . . it possesseth nothing during coverture. . . . A woman, as soon as she is married, is called *covert:* . . . she hath lost her streame. I may more truly . . . say to a married woman, Her new self is her superior; her companion, her master . . . Eve, because she had helped to seduce her husband, had inflicted upon her a special bane. See here the reason of that which I touched before — that women have no voice in Parliament. They make no laws, they consent to none, they abrogate none. All of them [women] are understood [as] either married, or to be married, and their desires are to their husbands. . . . The common laws here shaketh hand with divinitye.

WILLIAM BLACKSTONE, COMMENTARIES ON THE LAWS OF ENGLAND

430 (1765) (facsimile of 1st ed., vol. 1, 1979)

ON THE PRINCIPLE OF THE UNITY OF HUSBAND AND WIFE

By marriage, the husband and wife are one person in law: that is, the very being or legal existence of the woman is suspended during the marriage, or at least is incorporated and consolidated into that of the husband, under whose wing, protection, and *cover,* she performs every thing; and is therefore called in our law-French a *feme-covert* . . . or under the protection and influence of her husband, her *baron* or lord; and her condition during her marriage is called her *coverture.* . . . For this reason, a man cannot grant any thing to his wife, or enter into covenant [except through the intervention of a trustee] with her, for the grant would be to suppose her separate existence; and to covenant with her would be only to covenant with himself: and therefore it is also generally true, that all compacts made between husband and wife, when single, are voided by the intermarriage. A woman indeed may be attorney for her husband; for that implies no separation from, but is rather a representation of, her lord. And a husband may also bequeath any thing to his wife by will; for that cannot take effect till the coverture is determined by his death. The husband is bound to provide his wife with necessaries by law, as much as himself; and if she contracts debts for them, he is obliged to pay them: but any thing besides necessaries, he is not chargeable. Although if a wife elopes, and lives with another man, the husband is not chargeable even for necessaries; at least if the person who furnishes them is sufficiently apprised for her elopement. If the wife be indebted before marriage, the husband is bound afterwards to pay the debt; for he has adopted her and her circumstances together. If the wife be injured in her person or her property, she can bring no action for redress without her husband's concurrence, and in his name, as well as her own:

neither can she be sued, without making the husband a defendant. There is indeed one case where the wife shall sue and be sued as a feme sole, *viz.* where the husband has abjured the realm, or is banished: for then he is dead in law; and, the husband being thus disabled to sue for or defend the wife, it would be unreasonable if she had no remedy, or could make no defence at all. . . .

BUT, although our law in general considers man and wife as one person, yet there are some instances in which she is separately considered; as inferior to him, and acting by his compulsion. And therefore all deeds executed, and acts done, by her, during her coverture, are void, or at least voidable; except it be a fine, or the like manner of record, in which case she must be solely and secretly examined, to learn if her act be voluntary. She cannot by will devise lands to her husband, unless under special circumstances; for at the time of making it she is supposed to be under his coercion. . . .

THESE are the chief legal effects of marriage during the coverture; upon which we may observe, that even the disabilities which the wife lies under are for the most part intended for her protection and benefit. So great a favourite is the female sex of the laws of England.

TAPPING REEVE, THE LAW OF BARON AND FEME, OF PARENT AND CHILD, OF GUARDIAN AND WARD, OF MASTER AND SERVANT, AND OF THE POWERS OF COURTS OF CHANCERY

98 (New Haven, 1816)

ON THE CONCEPT OF "PARAPHERNALIA"

We will now inquire what advantages the wife may gain, eventually by marriage, in point of property, during the coverture. She gains nothing during his life; but upon the death of her husband intestate, she is entitled to one third of his personal property, which remains after paying the debts due from the estate of the husband, if he left any issue; but if he left no issue, she is entitled to one half of the residuum of the personal estate, after the debts are paid, but the husband, if he had chosen to do so, might have devised such estate from her [willed it to another]. . . .

There is one species of personal property in which she acquires a different interest from that which she may acquire in his other property, which is termed *paraphernalia*. This is of two kinds: the first consists of her beds and clothing, suitable to her condition in life; the second consists of her ornaments and trinkets, such as her bracelets, jewels, her watch, rich laces, and the like. As to the former, they cannot, with propriety, be considered as his estate, for they are not liable, upon the principles of the common law, without any aid from any statute, to the payment of his debts, and never ought to be inventoried as part of his estate; neither can they be devised from her by will.

As to the second kind, these cannot be devised from her by the husband, though he may take them from her, and dispose of them during the coverture. On the death of the husband, they vest in the wife, liable, indeed, to be taken by the executor of the husband, for the payment of his debts, provided that there are not sufficient assets beside to discharge his debts, but the whole of the personal estate must be exhausted before any resort can be had to them by the executor. Her right must yield to that of creditors; but in no instance to that of volunteers, for her *paraphernalia* can never be taken to pay legacies. . . .

She is often viewed as a creditor to her husband's estate, in respect of her *paraphernalia:* as when the husband, in his lifetime, being under the necessity of raising money, pledges her jewels, etc., and dies, leaving personal property more than sufficient to pay his debts, she shall have aid of this personal estate to redeem her *paraphernalia* thus pledged. So too, where real estate is devised for the payment of debts, and the executor takes the *paraphernalia,* on account of a deficiency of assets in the personal funds to pay the debts, she shall have the same right against this estate so devised for the payment of debts, to refund to her the real value of her *paraphernalia,* as a creditor can have, who is not paid for his debt for the want of assets. Where a real estate is given in trust (whether by deed or will) for the payment of debts, if her *paraphernalia* be taken by the executor, she shall be considered as a creditor the value of her *paraphernalia.* . . .

DIBBLE V. HUTTON

1 Day (Conn.) 221 (1802)

[Mary Hutton, widow of Samuel Hutton, petitioned the Chancery Court to order the executor of her deceased husband's will to pay her money she felt was due her. She claimed that during her marriage she and her husband jointly owned fifty-five acres of land. Samuel had owned three-quarters of the land and Mary one-quarter. Samuel wanted to sell the land but could not do so unless Mary agreed to sell her portion. In order to convince her to do so, Samuel promised to give Mary one-quarter of the proceeds of the sale for her private use. As a result of his promise, the land was sold to Caleb Comstock and Benoni St. John on January 6, 1798. Samuel received notes in the amount of 192 pounds, 10 shillings in return for the land, and he immediately gave Mary part of the notes. She kept the notes until Samuel died on 16 September 1799.

In May 1792, Samuel had made a will giving Mary nothing more than that part of his real estate to which she was entitled under dower rights. He appointed Nehemiah Dibble as executor of the will. After Samuel's death, Mary claimed that she was owed one-quarter of the 192 pounds, 10 shillings, but Dibble disagreed. He demanded the notes and threatened Mary with a lawsuit if she did not relinquish them so that he could include them in the inventory of Samuel's estate. Mary gave him the notes but refused to give up her claim to them. Dibble has since received the money from the notes but has not given Mary what she believes is due her.[70]]

BY THE COURT. The petitioner's claim . . . rests on the ground of the husband and wife's contract, or a combined view of the facts contained in the bill. Hence, the questions made relate to the competency of a husband and wife to contract with each other; the competency of the wife to have an estate for her separate use; and the equity of the particular case.

By the common law, the husband and wife are considered as one person in law, the existence of the wife being merged in that of the husband, or suspended during the coverture. As a consequence of this union of persons, . . . husband and wife cannot contract with each other, nor the husband make a grant or gift to the wife, nor the wife have personal estate, to her sole and separate use.

If these principles are to be received and applied . . . to this claim, they, at once, determine all the questions that arise in considering the case. They preclude the idea of the husband's and wife's competency to contract with each other, and the wife's competency to have, during *coverture*, personal estate to her separate use; And these being precluded, no equity arises out of the facts in the case, which, consistently with those principles of the common law, can be recognized by a court of chancery. Nor, indeed, is any equity perceived to exist in this case, to distinguish it from the ordinary transaction of the wife's estate being sold and the avails thereof coming, in personal estate, to the husband.

It is, however, insisted that those principles of the common law have been qualified, and modified, in the courts of chancery, in England, in such manner, as to recognize the wife's right and competency to have personal estate to her separate use, and the validity of certain contracts between husband and wife; and that those qualifications and modifications which have taken place in the English courts of chancery, ought to be adopted in ours. . . .

In tracing the history of the English chancery on this subject, it is found, that the doctrine of the wife's separate personal estate, a little more than a century past, since the emigration of our ancestors into this country, first insinuated itself into practice. It was not received without difficulty; but has gradually gained ground, and soon introduced the principle of contract between husband and wife. . . . It owes its rise to that state of manners and society which it has followed and accommodated.

---

70. These first two paragraphs are a summary written by Marlene Stein Wortman. — EDS.

the marriage. When death terminated the civilian community, the survivor succeeded to one-half of the community property, and the other half passed by devise or descent along with the decedent's separate property.

4.   **Community property and gay couples.** Gay couples, because they lack the legal ability to marry, are not covered by community property laws. In contexts where married couples automatically own equal shares of community property (typically real estate) acquired during marriage regardless of the form of title in which the property is held, property acquired by gay (and other unmarried) couples typically follows formal title. If the property is held in joint tenancy, each party typically will be awarded 50 percent if the relationship breaks up. But what if, as is sometimes done for tax reasons, the property is in the name of one party only? See Ireland v. Flanagan, 627 P.2d 496 (Or. Ct. App. 1981) (court upholds oral contract between lesbians to share property despite the fact that the property was held in the sole name of one partner). Absent an explicit agreement, gay or other unmarried partners must rely on an implied contract theory, see, e.g., Boland v. Catalano, 521 A.2d 142 (Conn. 1987) (court found implied contract to share assets where unmarried heterosexual cohabitants pooled assets, despite the fact that the realty was in the separate name of one party and the couple kept separate bank accounts); on implied partnership theory, see, e.g., Carroll v. Lee, 712 P.2d 923 (Ariz. 1986) (court found "implied partnership or joint enterprise agreement" where unmarried heterosexual cohabitants held property "acquired through joint common effort and for a common purpose"; the court made it clear that this type of property is distinct from "community property," which is reserved only to married couples); unjust enrichment, see, e.g., Watts v. Watts, 405 N.W.2d 303 (Wis. 1987); quantum meruit, Poe v. Levy, 411 So. 2d 253 (Fla. App. 1982); or various trust theories, see Watts v. Watts, 405 N.W.2d 303, (Wis. 1987) (constructive trust); Slocum v. Hammond, 346 N.W.2d 485 (Iowa 1984).

Would you suspect that cases based on these theories are easy or hard to win? Should gay couples be granted the same economic rights upon break-up as married couples?

c.   Is Coverture Dead? Unpaid Services in Exchange for Support

The Married Women's Property Acts (discussed in §4.1.a.4 *supra*) made wives eligible to own property at common law. Yet wives still were left with little property to own. Marriage was considered an exchange: The wife traded (unpaid) domestic labor in return for support. Thus the law continued to define the husband's wage as his sole property, absent clear and convincing evidence of a "gift" to the wife. Nor was this mindset wholly absent in the community property states when at issue was a husband's promise to leave his separate property to his wife in exchange for her services.

BORELLI v. BRUSSEAU

12 Cal. App. 4th 647, 16 Cal. Rptr. 2d 16 (1993)

Plaintiff and appellant Hildegard L. Borelli (appellant) appeals from a judgment of dismissal after a demurrer was sustained . . . to her complaint against defendant Grace G. Brusseau, as executor of the estate of Michael J. Borelli (respondent). The complaint sought specific performance of a promise by appellant's deceased husband Michael J. Borelli (decedent), to transfer certain property to her in return for her promise to care for him at home after he had suffered a stroke.

Appellant contends that the trial court erred [when it ruled that] the "alleged agreement . . . [was] without consideration and . . . void as against public policy." We conclude that the contention lacks merit.

FACTS

On April 24, 1980, appellant and decedent entered into an antenuptial contract. On April 25, 1980, they were married. Appellant remained married to decedent until the death of the latter on January 25, 1989.

In March 1983, February 1984, and January 1987, decedent was admitted to a hospital due to heart problems. As a result, "decedent became concerned and frightened about his health and longevity." He discussed these fears and concerns with appellant and told her that he intended to "leave" the following property to her.

1. "An interest" in a lot in Sacramento, California.
2. A life estate for the use of a condominium in Hawaii.
3. A 25 percent interest in Borelli Meat Co.
4. All cash remaining in all existing bank accounts at the time of his death.
5. The costs of educating decedent's stepdaughter, Monique Lee.
6. Decedent's entire interest in a residence in Kensington, California.
7. All furniture located in the residence.
8. Decedent's interest in a partnership.
9. Health insurance for appellant and Monique Lee.

In August 1988, decedent suffered a stroke while in the hospital. Throughout the decedent's August 1988 hospital stay and subsequent treatment at a rehabilitation center, he repeatedly told [appellant] that he was uncomfortable in the hospital and that he disliked being away from home. The decedent repeatedly told [appellant] that he did not want to be admitted to a nursing home, even though it meant he would need round-the-clock care, and rehabilitative modification to the house, in order for him to live at home.

In or about October, 1988, [appellant] and the decedent entered an oral agreement whereby the decedent promised to leave to [appellant] the property listed [above], including a one hundred percent interest in the Sacramento property. . . . In exchange for the decedent's promise to leave her the property . . . [appellant] agreed to care for the decedent in his home, for the duration of his illness, thereby avoiding the need for him to move to a rest home or convalescent hospital as his doctors recommended. The agreement was based on the confidential relationship that existed between [appellant] and the decedent.

Appellant performed her promise but the decedent did not perform his. Instead his will bequeathed her the sum of $100,000 and his interest in the residence they owned as joint tenants. The bulk of decedent's estate passed to respondent, who is decedent's daughter.

Discussion

"It is fundamental that a marriage contract differs from other contractual relations in that there exists a definite and vital public interest in reference to the marriage relation. . . ." "The laws relating to marriage and divorce . . . have been enacted because of the profound concern of our organized society for the dignity and stability of the marriage relationship. This concern relates primarily to the status of the parties as husband and wife. The concern of society as to the property rights of the parties is secondary and incidental to its concern as to their status." (Sapp v. Superior Court (1953) 119 Cal. App. 2d 645, 650 [260 P.2d 119].) . . .

In accordance with these concerns the following pertinent legislation has been enacted: Civil Code section 242 — "Every individual shall support his or her spouse . . ." Civil Code section 4802 — "[A] husband and wife cannot, by any contract with each other, alter their legal relations, except as to property . . ." Civil Code section 5100 — "Husband and wife contract toward each other obligations of mutual respect, fidelity, and support." Civil Code section 5102 — "[E]ither husband or wife may enter into any transaction with the other . . . respecting property, which either might if unmarried." Civil Code section 5132 — "[A] married person shall support the person's spouse while they are living together . . ."

The courts have stringently enforced and explained the statutory language. "Although most of the cases, both in California and elsewhere, deal with a wife's right to support from the husband, in this state a wife also has certain obligations to support the husband."

"Indeed, husband and wife assume mutual obligations of support upon marriage. These obligations are not conditioned on the existence of community property or income." (See v. See (1966) 64 Cal. 2d 778, 784.) "In entering the marital state, by which a contract is created, it must be assumed that the parties voluntarily entered therein with knowledge that they have the moral and legal obligation to support the other." (Department of Mental Hygiene v. Kolts (1966) 247 Cal. App. 2d 154, 165.)

Moreover, interspousal mutual obligations have been broadly defined. "[Husband's] duties and obligations to [wife] included more than mere cohabitation with her. It was his duty to offer [wife] his sympathy, confidence, and fidelity." (In re Marriage of Rabie (1974) 40 Cal. App. 3d 917, 922.) When necessary, spouses must "provide uncompensated protective supervision services for" each other. (Miller v. Woods (1983) 148 Cal. App. 3d 862, 877.)

Estate of Sonnicksen (1937) 23 Cal. App. 2d 475, 479 and Brooks v. Brooks (1941) 48 Cal. App. 2d 347, 349-350, each hold that under the above statutes and accordance with the above policy a wife is obligated by the marriage contract to provide nursing-type care to an ill husband. Therefore, contracts whereby the wife is to receive compensation for providing such services are void as against public policy; and there is no consideration for the husband's promise.

Appellant argues that *Sonnicksen* and *Brooks* are no longer valid precedents because they are based on outdated views of the role of women and marriage. She further argues that the rule of those cases denies her equal protection because husbands only have a financial obligation toward their wives, while wives have to provide actual nursing services for free. We disagree. The rule and policy of *Sonnicksen* and *Brooks* have been applied to both spouses in several recent cases arising in different areas of the law. . . .

These cases indicate that the marital duty of support under Civil Code sections 242, 5100, and 5232 includes caring for a spouse who is ill. They also establish that support in a marriage means more than the physical care someone could be hired to provide. Such support also encompasses sympathy, . . . love, companionship and affection. . . . Thus, the duty of support can no more be "delegated" to that third party than the statutory duties of fidelity and mutual respect (Civ. Code, §5100). Marital duties are owed by the spouses personally. This is implicit in the definition of marriage as "a personal relation arising out of a civil contract between a man and a woman." (Civ. Code, §4100.)

We therefore adhere to the long-standing rule that a spouse is not entitled to compensation for support, apart from rights to community property and the like that arise from the marital relation itself. Personal performance of a personal duty created by the contract of marriage does not constitute a new consideration supporting the indebtedness alleged in this case.

We agree with the dissent that no rule of law becomes sacrosanct by virtue of its duration, but we are not persuaded that the well-established rule that governs this case deserves to be discarded. If the rule denying compensation for support originated from considerations peculiar to women, this has no bearing on the rule's gender-neutral application today. There is as much potential for fraud today as ever, and allegations like appellant's could be made every time any personal care is rendered. This concern may not entirely justify the rule, but it cannot be said that all rationales for the rule are outdated.

Speculating that appellant might have left her husband but for the agreement she alleges, the dissent alleges that marriages will break up if such agreements are not enforced. While we do not believe that marriages would be fostered by a rule that encouraged sickbed bargaining, the question is not whether such negotiations may be more useful than unseemly. The issue is whether such negotiations are antithetical to the institution of marriage as the Legislature has defined it. We believe that they are.

The dissent maintains that mores have changed to the point that spouses can be treated just like any other parties haggling at arm's length. Whether or not the modern marriage has become like a business, and regardless of whatever else it may have become, it continues to be defined by statute as a personal relationship of mutual support. Thus, even if few things are left that cannot command a price, marital support remains one of them.

The judgment is affirmed. Costs to respondents.

POCHÉ, Associate Justice, dissenting: A very ill person wishes to be cared for at home personally by his spouse rather than by nurses at a health care facility. The ill person offers to pay his spouse for such personal care by transferring property to her. The offer is accepted, the services are rendered and the ill spouse dies. Affirming a judgment of dismissal rendered after a general demurrer was sustained, this court holds that the contract was not enforceable because — as a matter of law — the spouse who rendered services gave no consideration. Apparently, in the majority's view she had a preexisting or precontract nondelegable duty to clean the bedpans herself. Because I do not believe she did, I respectfully dissent.

The majority correctly read Estate of Sonnicksen (1937) 23 Cal. App. 2d 475 and Brooks v. Brooks (1941) 48 Cal. App. 2d 347 as holding that a wife cannot enter into a binding contract with her husband to provide "nursing-type care" for compensation. It reasons that the wife, by reason of the marital relationship, already has a duty to provide such care, thus she offers no new consideration to support an independent contract to the same effect. The logic of these decisions is ripe for reexamination.

Sonnicksen and Brooks are the California Court of Appeal versions of a national theme. Excerpts from several of these decisions reveal the ethos and mores of the era which produced them.

"It would operate disastrously upon domestic life and breed discord and mischief if the wife could contract with her husband for the payment of services to be rendered for him in his home; if she could exact compensation for services, disagreeable or otherwise, rendered to members of his family; if she could sue him upon such contracts and establish them upon the disputed and conflicting testimony of the members of the household.

To allow such contracts would degrade the wife by making her a menial and servant in the home where she should discharge marital duties in loving and devoted ministrations, and frauds upon creditors would be greatly facilitated, as the wife could frequently absorb all her husband's property in the payment of her services, rendered under such secret, unknown contracts."

"A man cannot be entitled to the services of his wife for nothing, by virtue of a uniform and unchangeable marriage contract, and at the same time be under obligation to pay her for those services. . . . She cannot be his wife and his hired servant at the same time. . . . That would be inconsistent with the marriage relation, and disturb the reciprocal duties of the parties." (In re Callister's Estate (1897) 153 N.Y. 294.) . . .

Statements in these cases to the effect that a husband has an entitlement to his wife's "services" smack of the common law doctrine of coverture which treat a wife as scarcely more than an appendage to her husband. According to the United States Supreme Court, "At the common law the husband and wife were regarded as one. The legal existence of the wife during coverture was merged in that of the husband, and, generally speaking, the wife was incapable of making contracts, of acquiring property or disposing of the same without her husband's consent. They could not enter into contracts with each other, nor were they liable for torts committed by one against the other." The same court subsequently denounced coverture as "peculiar and obsolete", "a completely discredited . . . archaic remnant of a primitive caste system" founded upon "medieval views" which are at present "offensive to the ethos of our society." (United States v. Dege (1960) 364 U.S. 51, 52-53.) One of the characteristics of coverture was that it deemed the wife economically helpless and governed by an implicit exchange: " 'The husband, as head of the family, is charged with its support and maintenance in return for which he is entitled to the wife's services in all those domestic affairs which pertain to the comfort, care, and well-being of the family. Her labors are her contribution to the family support and care.' " But coverture has been discarded in California where both husband and wife owe each other the duty of support. (Civ. Code, §242, 5100, 5132.)

Not only has this doctrinal base for the authority underpinning the majority opinion been discarded long ago, but modern attitudes toward marriage have changed almost as rapidly as the economic realities of modern society. The assumption that only the rare wife can make a financial contribution to her family has become badly outdated in this age in which many married women have paying employment outside the home. A two-income family can no longer be dismissed as a statistically insignificant aberration. Moreover today husbands are increasingly involved in the domestic chores that make a house a home. Insofar as marital duties and property rights are not governed by positive law, they may be the result of informal accommodation or formal agreement. (See Civ. Code, §5200 et seq.) If spouses cannot work things out, there is always the no longer infrequently used option of divorce. For better or worse, we have to a great extent left behind the comfortable and familiar gender-based roles evoked by Norman Rockwell paintings. No longer can the marital relationship be regarded as "uniform and unchangeable."

Fear that a contract struck between spouses "degrades" the spouse providing service, making him or her not better than a "hired servant" justifies the result in several cases. Such fears did not prevent California from enacting a statute specifying that "either husband or wife may enter into any transaction with the other, or with any other person, respecting property, which either might if unmarried." (Civ. Code, §5103, subd. (a), 4802.) This is but one instance of "the utmost freedom of contract [that] exists in California between husband and wife. . . ."

Reduced to its essence, the alleged contract issue here was an agreement to transmute Mr. Borelli's separate property into the separate property of his wife. Had there been no marriage and had they been total strangers, there is no doubt Mr. Borelli could have validly contracted to receive her services in exchange for certain of his property. The mere existence of a marriage certificate should not deprive competent adults of the "utmost freedom of contract" they would otherwise possess.

No one doubts that spouses owe each other a duty of support or that this encompasses "the obligation to provide medical care." (Hawkins v. Superior Court (1979) 89 Cal. App. 3d 413, 418-419). There is nothing found in *Sonnicksen* and *Brooks,* or cited by the majority, which requires that this obligation be personally discharged by a spouse except the decisions themselves. However, at the time *Sonnicksen* and *Brooks* were decided — before World War II — it made sense for those courts to say that a wife could perform her duty of care only by doing so personally. That was an accurate reflection of the real world for women years before the exigency of war produced substantial employment opportunities for them. For most women at that time there was no other way to take care of a sick husband except personally. So to the extent those decisions hold that a contract to pay a wife for caring personally for her husband is without consideration they are correct only because at the time they were decided there were no other ways she could meet her obligation of care. Since that was the universal reality, she was giving up nothing of value by agreeing to perform a duty that had one and only one way of being performed.

However the real world has changed in the 56 years since *Sonnicksen* was decided. Just a few years later with the advent of World War II Rosie the Riveter became not only a war jingle but a salute to hundreds of thousands of women working on the war effort outside the home. We know what happened there after. Presumably, in the present day husbands and wives who work outside the home have alternative methods of meeting this duty of care to an ill spouse. Among the choices would be: (1) paying for professional help; (2) paying for nonprofessional assistance; (3) seeking help from relatives or friends; and (4) quitting one's job and doing the work personally.

A fair reading of the complaint indicates that Mrs. Borelli initially chose the first of these options, and that this was not acceptable to Mr. Borelli, who then offered compensation if Mrs. Borelli would agree to personally care for him at home. To contend in 1993 that such a contract is without consideration means that if Mrs. Clinton becomes ill, President Clinton must drop everything and personally care for her.

According to the majority, Mrs. Borelli had nothing to bargain with so long as she remained in the marriage. This assumes that an intrinsic component of the marital relationship is the personal services of the spouse, an obligation that cannot be delegated or performed by others. The preceding discussion has attempted to demonstrate many ways in which what the majority terms "nursing-type care" can be provided without either husband or wife being required to empty a single bedpan. It follows that, because Mrs. Borelli agreed to supply this personal involvement, she was providing something over and above what would fully satisfy her duty of support. That personal something — precisely because it was something she was not required to do — qualifies as valid consideration sufficient to make enforceable Mr. Borelli's reciprocal promise to convey certain of his separate property.

Not only does the majority's position substantially impinge upon a couple's freedom to come to a working arrangement of marital responsibilities, it may also foster the very opposite result of that intended. For example, nothing compelled Mr. Borelli and plaintiff to continue living together after his physical afflictions became known. Moral considerations notwithstanding, no legal force could hvae stopped plaintiff from leaving her husband in his hour of need. Had she done so, and Mr. Borelli promised to give her some of his separate property should she come back, a valid contract would have arisen upon her return. Deeming them contracts promoting reconciliation and the resumption of marital relations, California courts have long enforced such agreements as supported by consideration. Here so far as we can tell from the face of the complaint, Mr. Borelli and plaintiff reached largely the same result without having to endure a separation.[3] There is no sound reason why their contract, which clearly facilitated continuation of their marriage, should be any less valid. It makes no sense to say that spouses have greater bargaining rights when separated than they do during an unruptured marriage.

What, then, justifies the ban on interspousal agreements of the type refused enforcement by *Sonnicksen, Brooks,* and the majority? At root it appears to be the undeniable allure of the thought that, for married persons, "to attend, nurse, and care for each other . . . should be natural prompting of that love and affection which should always exist between husband and

---

3. Plaintiff's allegation in her complaint that she forewent the opportunity "to live an independent life in consideration of her agreement" with Mr. Borelli carries the clear implication that she would have separated from him but for the agreement.

wife." All married persons would like to believe that their spouses would cleave unto them through thick and thin, in sickness and in health. Without question, there is something profoundly unsettling about an illness becoming the subject of interspousal negotiations conducted over a hospital sickbed. Yet sentiment cannot substitute for common sense and modern day reality. Interspousal litigation may be unseemly, but it is no longer a novelty. The majority preserves intact an anomalous rule which gives married persons less than the utmost freedom of contract they are supposed to possess. The majority's rule leaves married people with contracting powers which are more limited than those enjoyed by unmarried persons or than is justified by legitimate public policy. In this context public policy should not be equated with coerced altruism. Mr. Borelli was a grown man who, having amassed a sizeable amount of property, should be treated — at least on demurrer — as competent to make the agreement alleged by plaintiff. The public policy of California will not be outraged by affording plaintiff the opportunity to try to enforce that agreement. . . .

A petition for a rehearing was denied February 17, 1993, and appellant's petition for review by the Supreme Court was denied April 1, 1993. KENNARD, J., was of the opinion that the petition should be granted.

NOTES AND QUESTIONS

1. **Nature narrative.** Think back to Locke's nature narrative, §1.4.a, and the notion that each person gains property through labor. The *Borelli* case suggests that certain types of labor create property rights, while others do not. Think back to Pierson v. Post, §1.4.c, and the way the imagery of the nature narrative elides over the support provided to the hunter by social and familial systems.

2. **Who owns what?** Why, according to the majority, was there no consideration for the contract between Mr. and Mrs. Borelli? Is the dissent correct in its claim that the assumptions about who owned what reflect a continuation of coverture?

3. **Commodification again.** What role does commodification anxiety play in the majority's decision? Do you agree that the alternative to invalidating the contract is a reduction of marriage to "arm's length haggling?"

4. **Marital regimes and gay, lesbian, and other unmarried couples.** Because gay and lesbian relationships are not legally recognized in any state, they are cut off from the manifold advantages marriage offers to married couples. These include a number of rights related to property. See William B. Rubenstein, Lesbians, Gay Men, and the Law (1993). Unmarried heterosexual couples may be similarly disadvantaged.

Tax benefits. Substantial tax benefits are available to married couples, including the right to avoid estate tax to the extent one's estate is willed to one's spouse; the right to exclude money given to one's spouse from gift taxes; and various income tax benefits given to spouses, notably the right to file a joint return, deduction for dependents, the right to deduct alimony payments and marital property settlements, and the right to certain tax exemptions given on the sale of a primary residence by persons 55 years or older.

Procedural advantages. Marital couples also have access to a number of procedural advantages. Divorcing couples have access to family courts, complete with quicker hearings, form complaints, mediation, as well as certain presumptions concerning possession of property during divorce proceedings. In contrast, gay and lesbian couples' dissolutions are treated, for procedural purposes, as the dissolutions of business partnerships.

Family law. Finally, family law doctrines concerning divorce do not apply directly to gay and lesbian partners. In contexts where marital couples can rely on either community property, see *supra* pages 454 (which automatically give a 50 percent ownership interest in all property acquired during marriage to each spouse) or equitable distribution, nonmarital couples must rely on a variety of alternative theories. Where a party has sufficient proof, ownership rights in assets accumulated during a nonmarital relationship can be acquired by: express contract (written or oral), implied contract, various quasi contract theories, implied partnership, or various theories stemming from courts holding that the parties are in a fiduciary relationship. See Ireland v. Flanagan, 627 P.2d 496 (Or. Ct. App. 1981) (court upholds express (oral) contract between lesbians to share property despite the fact that the property was held in the sole name of one partner); Boland v. Catalano, 521 A.2d 142 (Conn. 1987) (court found implied contract to share assets where unmarried heterosexual cohabitants pooled assets, despite the fact that the realty was in the separate name of one party and the couple kept separate bank accounts); Watts v. Watts, 405 N.W.2d 303 (Wis. 1987) (unjust enrichment); Poe v. Levy, 411 So. 2d 253 (Fla. App. 1982) (quantum meruit); Carroll v. Lee, 712 P.2d 923 (Ariz. 1986) (court found "implied partnership or joint enterprise agreement" where unmarried heterosexual cohabitants held property "acquired through joint common effort and for a common purpose;" the court made it clear that this type of property is distinct from community property, which is reserved only to married couples.); Watts v. Watts, 405 N.W.2d 303 (Wis. 1987) (constructive trust); Slocum v. Hammond, 346 N.W.2d 485 (Iowa 1984). In one recent California case, the long-term girlfriend of the inventor of the "Maglight" flashlight, who had lived with him for 25 years and worked in his company, was awarded over $50 million on the theory that her boyfriend had breached his fiduciary duty by giving her an annual salary of $300,000 instead of stock in the company. Claire Maglica v. Anthony Maglica, No. G016463, pending, Court of Appeal, State of California.[73]

Would you suspect that cases based on these theories are easier or

73. Our thanks to Frederick C. Hertz, Esq. for bringing this case to our attention.

harder to win than cases argued on community property or equitable distribution theories? Should gay and lesbian couples be granted the same economic rights on breakup as married couples?

d. "Equitable" Distribution of Property

In an era when nearly one marriage in two will end in divorce and two-thirds of all wives hold a job, the common-law treatment of property acquired during the marriage can often work quite an injustice on one of the spouses. When a marriage ends in death, common-law states (through dower, curtesy, intestacy, right of election[74]) have to some degree recognized that marriage itself creates mutual interests in property acquired during the marriage, even though legal title is held only by one partner. However, if the marriage ends in divorce, the emphasis on legal title generally has meant, for example, that if one spouse (usually the husband) has taken title to real estate or corporate stock in his own name, what he holds remains with him after the divorce unless the other spouse can show that she (he) helped pay for the asset. The community law recognition that marriage was an economic partnership, even when only one of the spouses was a breadwinner, was absent at common law.

All that has changed dramatically since the 1970s. Today, all common-law states have provided for the "equitable distribution" of property in the event a marriage dissolves. Stated simply, this requires that property accumulated during the marriage be distributed so as to reflect the individual needs and circumstances of the parties rather than the formal ownership of the asset. Paralleling the community property sytem, equitable distribution laws distinguish between separate[75] and marital property. As to marital property, courts must distribute it "equitably" between the parties. The New York statute typifies the factors that judges are expected to consider in the name of equity:

> (1) the income and property of each party at the time of marriage, and at the time of the commencement of the action;
> (2) the duration of the marriage and the age and health of both parties;

---

74. "Right of election," created by statute, enables a surviving spouse, who would have received a greater share of the decedent's estate had the decedent died intestate than the survivor received under the terms of the decedent's will, to elect to take an intestate share rather than the legacy.

75. A common situation involves the marital property that the spouses bought originally with separate assets, often making unequal contributions; years later, when the marriage dissolves, the property has become far more valuable. Courts will generally give each spouse dollar-for-dollar credit for their initial contributions. See, e.g., Butler v. Butler, 171 A.D.2d 89, 574 N.Y.S. 2d 387 (1991).

(3)   the need of a custodial parent to occupy or own the marital residence and to use or own its household effects;

(4)   the loss of inheritance and pension rights upon dissolution of the marriage as of the date of dissolution;

(5)   any award of maintenance under subdivision six of this part;

(6)   any equitable claim to, interest in, or direct or indirect contribution made to the acquisition of such marital property by the party not having title, including joint efforts or expenditures and contributions and services as a spouse, parent, wage earner and homemaker, and to the career or career potential of the other party;

(7)   the liquid or non-liquid character of all marital property;

(8)   the probable future financial circumstances of each party;

(9)   the impossibility or difficulty of evaluating any component asset or any interest in a business, corporation or profession, and the economic desirability of retaining such asset or interest intact and free from any claim or interference by the other party;

(10)   the tax consequences to each party;

(11)   the wasteful dissipation of assets by either spouse;

(12)   any transfer or encumbrance made in contemplation of a matrimonial action without fair consideration;

(13)   any other factor which the court shall expressly find to be just and proper.

N.Y. Dom. Rel. Law §236(B)(5)(d) (McKinney 1986).

Still in its adolescence, equitable distribution has provoked much litigation, commentary, and statutory change. And, as the following matter shows, it has forced lawyers and judges to reexamine conventional views as to how to define property in order to apply equitable distribution laws.

1.   Allocation of Human Capital

The noted legal scholar and historian John Langbein has argued that, although traditionally "wealth transmission from parents to children tended to center upon major items of patrimony such as the family farm or the family firm, today for the broad middle classes, wealth transmission centers on a radically different kind of asset: *the investment in skills.*" [76] This concept cuts close to home: You are attending law school to build up your human capital. According to the calculation of one law-and-economics scholar, human capital constitutes roughly three-fourths of wealth in contemporary America.[77]

---

76. John H. Langbein, The Twentieth-Century Revolution in Family Wealth Transmission, 86 Mich. L. Rev. 722, 723 (1988) (emphasis added).

77. Robert C. Ellickson, The Untenable Case for an Unconditional Right to Shelter, 15 Harv. J.L. & Pub. Poly. 17, 30 (1992) (compensation of employees made up 73 percent of total national income).

This investment in human capital, as opposed to tangible assets, becomes important in the context of divorce. Because most families invest in human capital rather than tangible assets, few divorcing families have accumulated substantial tangible assets. A 1990 study found that even the accumulated wealth of relatively wealthy families came to only slightly more than one year's income.[78] Instead, human capital is the chief form of family wealth. Marriage as an institution typically corrodes the human capital of women and enhances the human capital of men. This is another way of saying that husbands' careers are typically favored within families, so that husbands typically end up with much higher salaries than their wives. In the typical white middle-class family, the husband earns roughly 70 percent of the income.[79]

The law defines the husband's human capital as his personal property. More often assumed than stated, this "he who earns it, owns it" rule emerges clearly in Rasmussen v. Oshkosh Sav. & Loan Assn., 151 N.W.2d 730 (Wis. 1967). In that case, a wife set aside certain sums of money from her husband's paycheck to pay for their sons' education. When she died, the husband, who had since remarried, claimed the amounts as his own. The husband won. The money was his, the court found; the wife's estate could win only if it could provide clear and convincing evidence of his intention to gift the money to her.

Divorce courts start from this premise[80] and then have the power to redistribute money from husband to his wife and children in the form of child support, alimony, and allocations of tangible assets.

Tangible assets. As has been noted, few families have substantial assets: The key to future standard of living is the allocation of the parents' income after divorce.

Child support. Child support payments in the United States average 12 percent of fathers' incomes. Andrea H. Beller and John W. Graham, Small Change: The Economics of Child Support 34 Table 2.7 (1993) (1985 figures). One 1979 study found that fathers typically paid more for their car payments than their child support.[81]

Alimony. Only between 9 and 18 percent of women are awarded ali-

---

78. Marsha Garrison, Good Intentions Gone Awry: The Impact of New York's Equitable Distribution Law on Divorce Outcomes, 57 Brooklyn L. Rev. 621, 658, 662 (1990).

79. The proportion of income earned by black middle-income men is lower since among black families, earnings of husbands and wives are more likely to be equal. Andrew Hacker, Two Nations: Black and White, Separate, Hostile, Unequal 94-95 (1992). According to Hacker, in a black middle-class family the husband is likely to be a bus driver and earn $32,000, while his wife is likely to be a teacher or a nurse and earn $28,000. Id. at 98-99.

80. This is true in both community property states and equitable distribution states: For purposes of the allocation of human capital after divorce, no meaningful distinction exists between the two types of family law systems.

81. Lucy M. Yee, What Really Happens in Child Support Cases: An Empirical Study of Establishment and Enforcement of Child Support Orders in the Denver District Court, 57 Denv. U. L. Rev. 21, 36 (1979).

mony. See Mary E. O'Connell, Alimony after No-Fault: A Practice in Search of a Theory, 23 New Eng. L. Rev. 437, 437 n.1 (1988). Historical studies suggest that the percentage of women awarded alimony always has been low. Lenore J. Weitzman, The Divorce Revolution 144 (1985). The big difference is that most alimony awards used to be permanent, whereas now most are temporary awards of less than two years. Id. at 165.

The end result is that divorced women and their children typically are cut off from the bulk of husbands' human capital accumulated during the marriage. Consequently, divorce is a key path to poverty in the United States. Studies show that not only are women with poor and modest incomes impoverished by divorce, so are many middle-class women. Fully 40 percent of divorced women with children live in poverty.[82] Numerous studies document that women's and children's standard of living falls sharply, while men's rises substantially, upon divorce. For an extensive listing, see Joan Williams, Is Coverture Dead? Beyond a New Theory of Alimony, 82 Geo. L.J. 2227 (1994). One recent study found fathers' living standards rising by 34 percent, while women's and children's fell by 26 percent.[83]

In a narrow range of cases, principally involving educational degrees as property and goodwill, courts have considered alternative allocations of human capital upon divorce. Cases involving the allocation of human capital follow.

ELKUS v. ELKUS

169 A.D.2d 134, 572 N.Y.S.2d 901 (App. Div., 1st Dept. 1991)

ROSENBERGER, J. . . . In this matrimonial action, the plaintiff, Frederica von Stade Elkus, moved for an order determining, prior to trial, whether her career and/or celebrity status constituted marital property subject to equitable distribution. The parties have already stipulated to mutual judgments of divorce terminating their seventeen-year marriage and to joint custody of their two minor children. The trial on the remaining economic issues has been stayed pending the outcome of this appeal from the order of the Supreme Court, which had determined that the enhanced value of the plaintiff's career and/or celebrity status was not marital property subject to equitable distribution. Contrary to the conclusion reached by the Supreme Court, we find that to the extent the defendant's contributions and efforts led to an increase in the value of the plaintiff's career, this appreciation was a product of the marital partnership, and, therefore, marital property subject to equitable distribution.

---

82. Demie Kurz, For Richer, For Poorer 3 (1995).
83. G. Diane Dodson, Children's Standard of Living under Child Support Guidelines: Women's Legal Defense Fund Report Card, in U.S. Department of Health and Human Services, Child Support Guidelines 98 (1994).

At the time of her marriage to the defendant on February 9, 1973, the plaintiff had just embarked on her career, performing minor roles with the Metropolitan Opera Company. During the course of the marriage, the plaintiff's career succeeded dramatically and her income rose accordingly. In the first year of the marriage, she earned $2,250. In 1989, she earned $621,878. She is now a celebrated artist with the Metropolitan Opera, as well as an international recording artist, concert and television performer. She has garnered numerous awards, and has performed for the President of the United States.

During the marriage, the defendant travelled with the plaintiff throughout the world, attending and critiquing her performances and rehearsals, and photographed her for album covers and magazine articles. The defendant was also the plaintiff's voice coach and teacher for ten years of the marriage. He states that he sacrificed his own career as a singer and teacher to devote himself to the plaintiff's career and to the lives of their young children, and that his efforts enabled the plaintiff to become one of the most celebrated opera singers in the world. Since the plaintiff's career and/or celebrity status increased in value during the marriage due in part to his contributions, the defendant contends that he is entitled to equitable distribution of this marital property.

The Supreme Court disagreed, refusing to extend the holding in O'Brien v. O'Brien, 66 N.Y.2d 576, 498 N.Y.S.2d 743, 489 N.E.2d 712, in which the Court of Appeals determined that a medical license constituted marital property subject to equitable distribution, to the plaintiff's career as an opera singer. The court found that since the defendant enjoyed a substantial life style during the marriage and since he would be sufficiently compensated through distribution of the parties' other assets, the plaintiff's career was not marital property.

There is a paucity of case law and no appellate authority in New York governing the issue of whether a career as a performing artist, and its accompanying celebrity status, constitute marital property subject to equitable distribution. The plaintiff maintains that since her career and celebrity status are not licensed, are not entities which are owned like a business, nor are protected interests which are subject to due process of law, they are not marital property. In our view, neither the Domestic Relations Law, nor the relevant case law, allows for such a limited interpretation of the term marital property.

Domestic Relations Law §236[B][1][c] broadly defines marital property as property acquired during the marriage "regardless of the form in which title is held." In enacting the Equitable Distribution Law (L.1980, ch. 281, §9), the Legislature created a radical change in the traditional method of distributing property upon the dissolution of a marriage (Price v. Price, 69 N.Y.2d 8, 14, 511 N.Y.S.2d 219, 508 N.E.2d 684). By broadly defining the term "marital property," it intended to give effect to the "economic partnership" concept of the marriage relationship. . . . It then left it to the courts to determine what interests constitute marital property.

Things of value acquired during marriage are marital property even though they may fall outside the scope of traditional property concepts (O'Brien v. O'Brien, *supra;* Florescue, "Market Value," Professional Licenses and Marital Property: A Dilemma in Search of a Horn, 1982 N.Y. St. Bar Assn. Fam. L. Rev. 13 [Dec.]). The statutory definition of marital property does not mandate that it be an asset with an exchange value or be salable, assignable or transferable. The property may be tangible or intangible. (Id.)

Medical licenses have been held to enhance the earning capacity of their holders, so as to enable the other spouse who made direct or indirect contributions to their acquisition, to share their value as part of equitable distribution (O'Brien v. O'Brien, *supra*). A Medical Board Certification (Savasta v. Savasta, 146 Misc. 2d 101, 549 N.Y.S.2d 544 (Sup. Ct. Nassau Co.), a law degree (Cronin v. Cronin, 131 Misc. 2d 879, 502 N.Y.S.2d 368 (Sup. Ct. Nassau Co.), an accounting degree (Vanasco v. Vanasco, 132 Misc. 2d 227, 503 N.Y.S.2d 480 (Sup. Ct. Nassau Co.), a podiatry practice (Morton v. Morton, 130 A.D.2d 558, 515 N.Y.S.2d 499), the licensing and certification of a physician's assistant (Morimando v. Morimando, 145 A.D.2d 609, 536 N.Y.S.2d 701), a Masters degree in teaching (McGowan v. McGowan, 142 A.D.2d 355, 535 N.Y.S.2d 990) and a fellowship in the Society of Actuaries (McAlpine v. McAlpine, 143 Misc. 2d 30, 539 N.Y.S.2d 680 (Sup. Ct. Suffolk Co.) have also been held to constitute marital property.

Although the plaintiff's career, unlike that of the husband in *O'Brien,* is not licensed, the *O'Brien* court did not restrict its holding to professions requiring a license or degree. In reaching its conclusion that a medical license constitutes marital property, The *O'Brien* court referred to the language contained in Domestic Relations Law §236 which provides that in making an equitable distribution of marital property, "the court shall consider: . . . any equitable claim to, interest in, or direct or indirect contribution made to the acquisition of such marital property by the party not having title, including joint efforts or expenditures and contributions and services as a spouse, parent, wage earner and homemaker, and *to the career or career potential* of the other party [and] . . . the impossibility or difficulty of evaluating any component asset or any interest in a business, corporation or profession" (Domestic Relations Law §236[B][5][d][6], [9] (emphasis added). The court also cited §236[B][5][e] which provides that where equitable distribution of marital property is appropriate, but "the distribution of an interest in a business, corporation or profession would be contrary to law," the court shall make a distributive award in lieu of an actual distribution of the property (O'Brien v. O'Brien, *supra,* 66 N.Y.2d at 584, 498 N.Y.S.2d 743, 489 N.E.2d 712).

The Court of Appeals' analysis of the statute is equally applicable here. "The words mean exactly what they say: that an interest in a profession or professional career potential is marital property which may be represented by direct or indirect contributions of the non-title-holding spouse, including financial contributions made by caring for the home and family" (O'Brien v. O'Brien, *supra,* 66 N.Y.2d at 576, 584, 498 N.Y.S.2d 743, 489 N.E.2d 712). Nothing in the statute or the *O'Brien* decision supports the plaintiff's contention that her career and/or celebrity status are not marital property. The purpose behind the enactment of the legislation was to prevent inequities which previously occurred upon the dissolution of a marriage. Any attempt to limit marital property to professions which are licensed would only serve to discriminate against the spouses of those engaged in other areas of employment. Such a distinction would fail to carry out the premise upon which equitable distribution is based, i.e., to which both parties contribute, as spouse, parent, wage earner or homemaker. . . .

In Golub v. Golub, 139 Misc. 2d 440, 527 N.Y.S.2d 946 (Sup. Ct. New York Co.), the Supreme Court agreed with the defendant husband that the increase in value in the acting and modeling career of his wife, Marisa Berenson, was marital property subject to equitable distribution as a result of his contributions thereto. Like Ms. von Stade, Ms. Berenson claimed that since her celebrity status was neither "professional" nor a "license," and, since her show business career was subject to substantial fluctuation, it should not be considered "marital property."

The court disagreed, concluding at 139 Misc.2d 447, 527 N.Y.S.2d 946, that "the skills of an artisan, actor, professional athlete or any person whose expertise in his or her career has enabled him or her to become an exceptional wage earner should be valued as marital property subject to equitable distribution." As the *Golub* court found, it is the enhanced earning capacity that a medical license affords its holder that the *O'Brien* court deemed valuable, not the document itself. There is no rational basis upon which to distinguish between a degree, a license, or any other special skill that generates substantial income.

As further noted by the *Golub* court, there is tremendous potential for financial gain from the commercial exploitation of famous personalities. While the plaintiff insists that she will never be asked to endorse a product, this is simply speculation. More and more opportunities have presented themselves to her as her fame increased. They will continue to present themselves to her as she continues to advance in her career. The career of the plaintiff is unique, in that she has risen to the top in a field where success is rarely achieved.

Like the parties here, after Joe Piscopo and his wife married in 1973, they focused on one goal — the facilitation of his rise to stardom (Piscopo v. Piscopo, 231 N.J. Super. 576, 555 A.2d 1190, *aff'd,* 232 N.J. Super. 559, 557 A.2d 1040, *certification denied,* 117 N.J. 156, 564 A.2d 875). The defendant wife claimed that her husband's celebrity goodwill was a distributable asset and that she was entitled to a share in his excess earning capacity to which she contributed as homemaker, caretaker of their child, and sounding board for his artistic ideas.

Rejecting Mr. Piscopo's argument that celebrity goodwill is distinguishable from professional goodwill since professional goodwill has educational and regulatory requirements while celebrity goodwill requires ineffable talent, the court held that "it is the person with particular and uncommon aptitude for some specialized discipline whether law, medicine or entertainment that transforms the average professional or entertainer into one with measurable goodwill" (Piscopo v. Piscopo, *supra,* 231 N.J. Super., at 580-581, 555 A.2d, at 1191). We agree with the courts that have considered the issue, that the enhanced skills of an artist such as the plaintiff, albeit growing from an innate talent, which have enabled her to become an exceptional earner, may be valued as marital property subject to equitable distribution.

The plaintiff additionally contends that her career is not marital property because she had already become successful prior to her marriage to the defendant. As noted, *supra,* during the first year of marriage, the plaintiff earned $2,250. By 1989, her earnings had increased more than 275 fold. Further, in Price v. Price, *supra,* 69 N.Y.2d at 11, 511 N.Y.S2d 219, 503 N.E.2d 684, the Court of Appeals held that "under the Equitable Distribution Law an increase in the value of separate property of one spouse, occurring during the marriage and prior to the commencement of matrimonial proceedings, which is due in part to the indirect contributions or efforts of the other spouse as homemaker and parent, should be considered marital property (Domestic Relations Law §236[B][1][d][3])." In this case, it cannot be overlooked that the defendant's contributions to plaintiff's career were direct and concrete, going far beyond child care and the like, which he also provided.

While it is true that the plaintiff was born with talent, and while she had already been hired by the Metropolitan Opera at the time of her marriage to the defendant, her career, at this time, was only in the initial stages of development. During the course of the marriage, the defendant's active involvement in the plaintiff's career, in teaching, coaching, and critiquing her, as well as in caring for their children, clearly contributed to the increase in its value. Accordingly, to the extent the appreciation in the plaintiff's career was due to the defendant's efforts and contributions, this appreciation constitutes marital property.

In sum, we find that is the nature and extent of the contribution by the spouse seeking equitable distribution, rather than the nature of the career, whether licensed or otherwise, that should determine the status of the enterprise as marital property. . . .

Accordingly, the order of the Supreme Court, New York County (Walter M. Schackman, J.), entered September 26, 1990, which determined that the plaintiff's career and/or celebrity status was not "marital property" sub-

"Some people say you can't put a price on a wife's twenty-seven years of loyalty and devotion. They're wrong."

FIGURE 4-6
Does Wives' Work Give Rise to Legal Entitlements? Should It?

ject to equitable distribution [it is hereby] . . . unanimously reversed, on the law, without costs, and the matter remitted to the Supreme Court for further proceedings.

MARTINEZ v. MARTINEZ

169 Utah Adv. Rep. 29, 818 P.2d 538 (Utah 1991)

STEWART, J. This case is here on a writ of certiorari to the Utah Court of Appeals to review the single issue of whether that court erred in fashioning a new remedy in divorce cases which it called equitable restitution and which may be awarded in addition to alimony, child support, and property. See Martinez v. Martinez, 754 P.2d 69 (Utah Ct. App. 1988).

I. FACTS

Karen and Jess Martinez were married in 1968, while Mr. Martinez was serving in the United States Army. Both had high school educations. Mr. Martinez began his college education in 1970. Three children were born to the marriage between 1970 and 1975. While an undergraduate student, Mr. Martinez decided to attend medical school, a decision Mrs. Martinez did not agree with because she thought that medical school would be financially draining and would limit her husband's ability to spend time with the family. Nevertheless, Mr. Martinez entered medical school in 1977 and graduated in 1981. He obtained financial support for his education primarily from his own earnings, student loans, the G.I. Bill, and a bequest from his mother's estate. Mrs. Martinez did not contribute financially to her husband's medical education.

Karen Martinez filed a complaint for divorce in 1983, and a decree of divorce was entered in 1985. The trial court found that Dr. Martinez's gross annual income as a resident was $100,000 and that "[d]uring fourteen years that the parties lived together, [Mrs. Martinez] assisted extensively in [Dr. Martinez's] obtaining a college education, medical degree and internship. In addition, [she] made substantial sacrifices in order to facilitate the completion of [his] medical schooling and internship." Mrs. Martinez also earned a very minor amount of income for a short period which was used for family expenses.

The trial court awarded Mrs. Martinez the house the couple had acquired during the marriage and required her to make the mortgage payments of $309 per month. Dr. Martinez was awarded a lien on that property in the amount of $17,678, which represented half the equity in the home. The court also awarded Mrs. Martinez child support of $300 per month per child, and $400 per month alimony for a period of five years, with the condition that the alimony terminate after three years if she remarried. Dr. Martinez was ordered to provide health, accident, and dental insurance for the children and to maintain a life insurance policy on himself for the benefit of the children. He was also awarded the federal tax exemptions for two of the children. The personal property acquired during the marriage was divided equally. Debts in the amount of approximately $19,000 for student loans were assigned to Dr. Martinez. Finally, the court awarded Mrs. Martinez attorney fees in the amount of $2,500. The trial court ruled that Dr. Martinez's medical degree and training were not a marital asset subject to distribution, but considered his right to practice medicine as it affected his income and ability to pay alimony and child support.

On appeal to the Court of Appeals, Mrs. Martinez contended, *inter alia*, that the child support, alimony, and attorney fees awarded by the trial court were so inadequate as to constitute an abuse of discretion and that the tax exemptions should not have been awarded to Dr. Martinez. That court awarded the tax exemptions to Mrs. Martinez, increased the child support award to $600 per month per child, and awarded permanent alimony of $750 per month. The court affirmed the trial court's award of only a portion of Mrs. Martinez's attorney fees. Martinez v. Martinez, 754 P.2d 69, 72-75 (Utah Ct. App. 1988). Relying on its own prior decisions, the Court of Appeals also held that Dr. Martinez's medical degree was not marital property subject to division. . . .

The court concluded, however, that a means should be devised to compensate Mrs. Martinez for the contribution she had made to the family. The court stated that Mrs. Martinez "has earned an award of some permanent financial benefit, in her own right, that will allow her to share in the economic benefits achieved through their joint efforts" and that Dr. Martinez's earning capacity "must be recognized in fashioning those 'legal equitable remedies' necessary to assist plaintiff to readjust her life." 754 P.2d at 75, 76. Accordingly, the court created a new type of property interest which it called "equitable restitution," to be awarded to Mrs. Martinez in addition to her interest in the home, alimony, and child support.[1] Judge Jackson, in dissent concluded that although Mrs. Martinez was entitled to a "generous but fair distribution of property and award of alimony," the concept of "equitable restitution" was not supportable. 754 P.2d at 82 (Jackson, J., dissenting).

The Court of Appeals listed five factors for trial courts to consider in determining when an award of "equitable restitution" should be made. Those factors are (1) the length of the marriage, (2) financial contributions and personal development sacrifices made by the spouse requesting equitable restitution, (3) the duration of the contributions and sacrifices during the marriage, (4) the disparity in earning capacity between the spouses, and (5) the amount of property accumulated during the marriage. 754 P.2d at 78. Although the court failed to indicate what weight those factors should be accorded or just how equitable restitution should be computed, it remanded the case to the trial court to determine what the amount of equitable restitution should be.

Dr. Martinez filed a petition for a writ of certiorari to this Court. We granted the petition solely on the issue of whether the Court of Appeals erred in devising "equitable restitution" as a new form of property in divorce cases.

Mrs. Martinez argues that the concept of equitable restitution is justified on the ground that the remedies available under current law for the distribution of property and the support of a former spouse are inadequate to provide a fair and equitable result. She contends, in essence, that a new form of property must be recognized by the courts to provide for a just and equitable distribution of the increased earning power which one spouse realizes from an advanced education acquired during the marriage. The "investment" referred to by Mrs. Martinez is whatever effort, support, and sacrifice that is made by the nonadvantaged spouse. (Hereinafter, we refer

---

1. The Court of Appeals purported to rely on this Court's opinion in Gardner v. Gardner, 748 P.2d 1076 (Utah 1988), as the starting point to devise the property interest it called "equitable restitution." In *Gardner*, this Court sidestepped the issue of whether an advanced degree could be valued as a marital asset and made subject to distribution in a property award. We observed that there were sufficient marital assets in that case to distinguish it "from others in which equity and fairness required another solution." 748 P.2d at 1081. That statement, however, did not contemplate any such thing as "equitable restitution."

to the spouse receiving the education as the advantaged spouse and the other spouse as the nonadvantaged spouse.)

The very idea of marriage contemplates mutual effort and mutual sacrifice. Yet, in this case, Mrs. Martinez would value only her contribution to the marriage and not his. In any event, the spouses' contributions cannot be reduced to a common denominator that allows for a valid comparison in monetary terms. Indeed, the very attempt to do so would interfere with the trial court's ability to achieve an equitable result based on the needs of the spouses in light of the monetary resources available. For example, if a spouse avoids his or her marital responsibilities, the partnership theory might result in denying that spouse any award of support or property at divorce, irrespective of his or her need and the other spouse's ability to pay. That is not the law.

Second, an award of equitable restitution would be extraordinarily speculative. Although the Court of Appeals' opinion is somewhat unclear as to what kind of economic interest it intended to create or just how it should be computed, it did state, "An award of equitable restitution will not terminate upon plaintiff's remarriage, and may be payable in lump sum or periodically over time depending on the circumstances of each case." 754 P.2d at 78-79. Clearly, the Court of Appeals contemplated a substantial award.[2] Mrs. Martinez asserts that equitable restitution should be based on the discounted value of Dr. Martinez's earnings as a physician over his remaining working life to age 65, less the amount a high school graduate would have earned over the same time. Based on those calculations, Mrs. Martinez values Dr. Martinez's medical education at $1,555,000.[3]

Although the Court of Appeals did not specifically adopt this formula for calculating the amount of equitable restitution, neither did it reject it or refer to any formula by which the amount of equitable restitution could be calculated. In any event, any formula which accomplished that court's purpose would necessarily be inherently and highly speculative. If, for example, a court awarded a lump-sum payment, the award would be based upon a wholly false assumption if the payor spouse's working life were cut short by death, illness, change of profession, or early retirement or if the working life were interrupted for any other reason. Furthermore, whether

---

2. The Court of Appeals stated that on remand the trial court might, for example, extinguish Dr. Martinez's lien on the family home and credit that amount against the overall award of equitable restitution. The court stated that this amount, $17,428, "would probably be only a fraction of the total amount of equitable restitution awarded." 754 P.2d at 79 n.12.

3. Dr. W. Chris Lewis was the expert used by Mrs. Martinez to place a value on the increased "income stream" that Dr. Martinez would have for the remainder of his career. Dr. Lewis had not previously valued a medical degree or medical practice. He calculated the present value of the lifetime earnings of a healthy 38-year-old currently earning $100,000 per year to be $2,482,500. He then deducted what he thought an average high school graduate would earn over the same period of time, or $926,000, and concluded that the value of Dr. Martinez's "medical education and training" based on his increased earning capacity was $1,555,000. On the basis of that amount, Mrs. Martinez would be awarded a substantial sum.

a court awarded a lump sum or periodic payments, the receiving spouse would be given what is tantamount to a lifetime estate in the paying spouse's earnings that have no necessary relationship to the receiving spouse's actual contribution to the enhanced earning power or to that spouse's needs, however broadly defined.

Third, although the Court of Appeals stated that it rejected the proposition that Dr. Martinez's medical degree should be valued as property interest and Mrs. Martinez given an interest in it, that court's concept of equitable restitution is essentially indistinguishable.

The recipient of an advanced degree obtains that degree on the basis of his or her innate personal talents, capabilities, and acquired skills and knowledge. Such a degree is highly personal to the recipient and has none of the traditional characteristics of property. "It does not have an exchange value or any objective transferable value on an open market. It is personal to the holder. It terminates on death of the holder and is not inheritable. It cannot be assigned, sold, transferred, conveyed, or pledged." In re Marriage of Graham, 194 Colo. 429, 432, 574 P.2d 75, 77 (1978). The time has long since passed when a person's personal attributes and talents were thought to be subject to monetary valuation for commercial purposes. In short, we do not recognize a property interest in personal characteristics of another person such as intelligence, skill, judgment, and temperament, however characterized.

The law accepted in other jurisdictions almost unanimously is that professional degrees are not marital property and are not subject to equitable distribution. Of twenty-four jurisdictions that have considered the issue, all but two have held that a professional degree or license is not marital property subject to equitable distribution. See Archer v. Archer, 303 Md. 347, 493 A.2d 1074, 1077 (1985); see also, In re Marriage of Graham, 194 Colo. 429, 574 P.2d 75 (1978); Grosskopf v. Grosskopf, 677 P.2d 814 (Wyo. 1984). See generally Annotation, Spouse's Professional Degree or License as Marital Property for Purposes of Alimony, Support, or Property Settlement, 4 A.L.R.4th 1294 (1981 & Supp. 1990). See contra O'Brien v. O'Brien, 114 Misc. 2d 233, 452 N.Y.S.2d 801 (N.Y. Sup. Ct. 1982), aff'd as modified, 66 N.Y.2d 576, 489 N.E.2d 712, 498 N.Y.S.2d 743 (1985) (holding that a professional degree is a marital asset based on a New York statute unlike Utah's).

Mrs. Martinez's contention that the remedies provided by Utah Code Ann. §30-3-5 are insufficient is without merit. Those remedies are adequate to fashion an appropriate award that meets the standards to be applied in determining awards of alimony. An alimony award should be determined by the receiving spouse's earning capacity, financial condition, and needs and by the ability of the other spouse to provide support. See Jones, 700 P.2d at 1075.

Usually the needs of the spouses are assessed in light of the standard of living they had during marriage. Gardner v. Gardner, 748 P.2d 1076, 1081 (Utah 1988); Jones, 700 P.2d at 1075. In some circumstances, it may be appropriate to try to equalize the spouses' respective standards of living. *Gardner,* 748 P.2d at 1081; see also Olson v. Olson, 704 P.2d 564, 566 (Utah 1985); Higley v. Higley, 676 P.2d 379, 381 (Utah 1983). When a marriage of long duration dissolves on the threshold of a major change in the income of one of the spouses due to the collective efforts of both, that change, unless unrelated to the efforts put forward by the spouses during marriage, should be given some weight in fashioning the support award. Cf. Savage v. Savage, 658 P.2d 1201, 1205 (Utah 1983). Thus, if one spouse's earning capacity has been greatly enhanced through the efforts of both spouses during the marriage, it may be appropriate for the trial court to make a compensating adjustment in dividing the marital property and awarding alimony. See, e.g., Kerr v. Kerr, 610 P.2d 1380 (Utah 1980); Tremayne v. Tremayne, 116 Utah 483, 211 P.2d 452 (1949).

Here, the trial court found that the parties would have enjoyed a higher family income because of Dr. Martinez's increased income, which was due to some extent to the efforts of both spouses during the marriage. Although Dr. Martinez earned $100,000 a year before the parties divorced, Mrs. Martinez had not enjoyed a higher standard of living as a result of that increased income. The trial court awarded Mrs. Martinez alimony in the amount of $400 per month for a period of five years. That amount was nonterminable for a period of three years even if Mrs. Martinez remarried. The Court of Appeals, relying upon Jones v. Jones, 700 P.2d 1072 (Utah 1985), modified that award by increasing it to $750 per month subject to the provisions of Utah Code Ann. §30-3-5 (1987), which provides for the termination of a permanent alimony award in certain circumstances. That and other modifications made by the Court of Appeals in favor of Mrs. Martinez have not been challenged by either party in this Court.

We granted certiorari solely on the issue of equitable restitution and denied certiorari on all other issues. We therefore express no opinion on the appropriateness of the other modifications made by the Court of Appeals in the divorce decree.

The Court of Appeals' direction to the trial court to devise an award of equitable restitution is reversed, and the case is remanded to the trial court for further proceedings in light of this opinion and the opinion of the Court of Appeals. . . .

ZIMMERMAN, J. (concurring and dissenting). I join Justice Stewart's opinion in its rejection of the equitable restitution doctrine created by the court of appeals. As he states, the trial court has ample power to make alimony and property division awards which will ensure that equity is done to a spouse who is denied an increase in standard of living because a divorce occurs on the threshold of an event that is economically advantageous to the other spouse. There is no reason to create a new and conceptually ill-defined property concept to meet this need.

Justice Durham's dissent deserves some comment. She suggests that we should affirm the court of appeals' adoption of an equitable restitution doctrine because our existing case law on property division and alimony is insufficiently flexible to allow for the fashioning of a remedy for situations of the type presented here. She then suggests that if we are going to rely upon property division and alimony law to deal with these problems, we need to articulate guidelines for the trial courts in dealing with this area.

I disagree with Justice Durham's premise that our cases do not permit the use of alimony and property division to produce a fair result in these cases. It may be that our prior cases have not addressed the issue, but the opinion Justice Stewart has authored today does. The majority specifically states:

> When a marriage of long duration dissolves on the threshold of a major change in the income of one of the spouses due to the collective efforts of both, that change, unless unrelated to the efforts put forward by the spouses during marriage, should be given some weight in fashioning the support award.

At 542.

The majority opinion also makes it clear that the trial court can make such compensating adjustments to both the property division and the alimony award as it deems necessary to make the ultimate decision equitable:

> [I]f one spouse's earning capacity has been greatly enhanced through the efforts of both spouses during the marriage, it may be appropriate for the trial court to make a compensating adjustment in dividing the marital property and awarding alimony.

At 542.

In light of this language, joined in by four members of the court, there can be no doubt that trial judges are empowered and enjoined to take circumstances like those presented here into account in making alimony and property division awards. To the extent that Justice Durham's opinion suggests the contrary, it misstates the law.

As for what appears to be Justice Durham's larger concern — that we have given the trial courts insufficient guidance as to how to make the required adjustments in awards — I agree that over time, we will have to give further shape to the rules governing the division of property and the award of alimony to be sure that both parties in cases like this one are dealt with fairly. However, there seems little need to opt for one theoretical framework now. In this area, law development on a case-by-case basis may be the best approach.

On a separate issue, I dissent from the majority's remand of this matter to the trial court. The court of appeals found that the trial court abused its discretion and attempted to modify the decree to make it sufficiently

equitable to pass appellate muster. In doing so, the court of appeals modified the alimony award and the child support award and ordered equitable
restitution. We granted certiorari to consider only the equitable restitution
portion of that modification of the divorce decree, and we have now said
that in making that specific modification, the court of appeals overreached.
We have not said that the decree was equitable without some adjustment
that would address the problem which motivated the creation of the equitable restitution doctrine. We have only said that the equitable result sought
by the court of appeals cannot be achieved that way. In fact, the opinion of
Justice Stewart recognizes that the trial court had the power to effect a
remedy for the underlying problem.

Under these circumstances, we should remand the matter to the court
of appeals for further proceedings. It should be allowed to again address
the propriety of the trial court's decree in light of our explication of the law.
There is no occasion for us to send this matter back to the trial court. If the
court of appeals thinks it needs more information from the trial court,
there will be time enough for such a remand.

DURHAM, J., dissenting. The majority opinion holds that professional
degrees are not marital property and rejects the principle of equitable restitution fashioned by the court of appeals, on the theory that currently recognized rights to alimony, child support, and property distribution are
sufficient to solve the complex problems posed by cases like this. I disagree
and would argue that if we are going to prohibit the use of the principles
relied on by the court of appeals, then we must fashion a new and more
flexible theory of alimony.

First, there is insufficient tangible property to compensate the spouse
who has been "investing" time, labor, earnings, and postponed improvements in standard of living for the long-term benefit of the marital community when the marriage ends before the investment has "paid off."
Second, child support protects the rights of the children of divorcing
spouses to share in present and future benefits of earning capacity; it may
not legitimately be used to compensate a former spouse for the value of
what she has "invested" without return (or lost) as a result of the termination of the marriage. Finally, alimony as currently understood in our law is
theoretically inadequate to perform the compensation function that the
court of appeals identified as necessary in this case. One need only examine
the alimony decisions cited by the majority opinion to ascertain that alimony in this state has depended on (1) the financial conditions and needs
of the recipient spouse, (2) the ability of the recipient spouse to produce
sufficient income for self-support, and (3) the ability of the payor spouse to
provide support. See, e.g., Jones v. Jones, 700 P.2d 1072, 1075 (Utah 1985).
To those fundamental principles, we have added the consideration that
"[a]n alimony award should, in as far as possible, equalize the parties' respective standards of living and maintain them at a level as close as possible

to the standard of living enjoyed *during the marriage.*" Higley v. Higley, 676 P.2d 379, 382 (Utah 1983) (emphasis added).

I submit that none of the foregoing principles address the specific problem posed by termination of a marriage in which one or both spouses have sacrificed in tangible and intangible ways, foregoing income, accumulation of property, an enhanced standard of living, and the educational and career-development opportunities of one so that the other might acquire a valuable and prestigious professional degree. When the marriage ends before the marital community has enjoyed the benefits expected from that sacrifice, the nonholder of the degree suffers a very real loss. Whether we adopt a doctrine of "equitable restitution" or rethink the theory and function of alimony, we must address the requirements of equity and justice to compensate in some fashion for that loss. As David S. Dolowitz recently noted in the Utah Bar Journal, equitable restitution is a form of alimony "paid to produce an equitable balancing of property and income *that cannot be otherwise effected*" by the traditional forms of support alimony and rehabilitative alimony. Dolowitz, The Impact of Tax Laws on Divorce, Utah B.J., at 8, 9 (August/September 1991) (emphasis added).

Other commentators have recently devoted a great deal of scholarly attention to the problems of compensating spouses for losses they suffer because of decisions to further the marital enterprise by enhancing the education or career of one spouse at cost to both. In a recent article discussing the question Should "The Theory of Alimony" Include Nonfinancial Losses and Motivations?, 1991 B.Y.U. L. Rev. 259, law professor Ira Ellman (author of The Theory of Alimony, 77 Calif. L. Rev. 1 (1989)) observes:

> [T]he purpose of alimony under "The Theory" is to eliminate the financial disincentives for marital sharing behavior that would be present in the absence of a remedy, rather than to provide positive incentives. . . . The principle is actually rather modest in scope. The policy upon which it is based would seem, at least at first, to be broadly acceptable: spouses otherwise inclined to conduct themselves during the marriage in a manner that benefits the marital community ought not be discouraged from acting that way for fear that, if the marriage were to dissolve, they would be left with all of the financial loss arising from their decision. This is especially true when, for example, the wife has a loss while her husband has no loss, or even reaps a gain (as would be the case where the wife gives up her employment to advance her husband's).

B.Y.U. L. Rev. at 265.

This approach is connected to an assessment of *loss*, not one of need, as has traditionally been the case in the theory of alimony. It requires the courts to discover or create means by which a spouse may recover after divorce the value of what he or she lost by reason of investment in the marital enterprise, where that investment has resulted in a net gain to the other spouse.

Once the spouses' gain or loss from the marriage has been measured, they can be compared against one another to determine if one spouse has a loss that should be reallocated to the other. Clearly all losses cannot be compensable, for the simple reason that the claim is against the other spouse, and both spouses may have suffered a loss from their marriage. A loss is compensable, in whole or part, only if the other spouse's loss is smaller, or if the other spouse has achieved a gain.

Id. at 271. Professor Ellman goes on to describe this as a "reliance measure" of loss, as opposed to the traditional contract damage measure of expectation, and explains its justification at some length. He also suggests several important limitations on his theory of alimony: for example, (1) only residual post-marriage losses are compensable, not inequities in the exchange during marriage; (2) only financial losses are compensable; and (3) only losses arising from marital "sharing behavior" are compensable.

I do not propose that we adopt Professor Ellman's theory wholesale; I only cite it as one example of a thoughtful effort to solve the problems posed by the common circumstances illustrated in this case. My criticism of the majority opinion is that it makes no effort to guide the trial courts in fashioning a realistic remedy for what is a realistic loss. It rejects the effort of the court of appeals to do precisely that and offers no alternative. The legal status quo is unacceptable, in my view, and I hope that the majority will be willing in the future to make good on its representation that the concept of alimony (or property distribution when there is any property) can be accommodated to the need for equity. Unless and until that happens, any woman (or man, for that matter) who sacrifices her own education, earning capacity, or career development so that a spouse may advance and the marriage may prosper as a joint venture will inevitably suffer the full cost of that decision at divorce, while the advantaged spouse will continue to walk away from the marriage with all of the major financial gain. That is unfair, and in this area at least, the responsibility of the law is to seek fairness.

NOTES AND QUESTIONS

1. **Degree cases.** Courts generally have taken one of three tacks in degree cases. A small minority of courts, New York among them, have held that a degree is property, subject to equitable distribution. See Stewart E. Sterk, Restraints on Alienation of Human Capital, 79 Va. L. Rev. 383, 433 (1993) (courts have generally rejected arguments that "increased earning capacity" is property). The leading New York case, cited in *Elkus*, is O'Brien v. O'Brien, 66 N.Y.2d 576, 498 N.Y.S.2d 743, 489 N.E.2d 712 (1985); see also McSparron v. McSparron, 87 N.Y.2d 275, 662 N.E.2d 745 (1995) (*O'Brien* reaffirmed: license or degree does not merge with the career or ever lose

its character as a separate distributable asset). Many more states hold that the contributing spouse is entitled to share in the value of the benefitted spouse's license or degree, but limit the contributing spouse's interest to restitution for "out-of-pocket" contributions made to the education of the other spouse. Thus money contributed towards tuition would be reimbursed, but supporting the family and doing the housework and child care would not, nor would career opportunities foregone by the contributing spouse. A third group of states refuses both reimbursement and treatment of the license or degree as property. See, e.g., In re Marriage of McNamara, 272 Ind. 483, 399 N.E.2d 371 (1980). Such states may take into account the efforts of the contributing spouse in some situations. For example, if the spouses had been able to acquire traditional property during the marriage, the contributing spouse might receive a larger share of the property to reflect her financial and homemaking contributions toward the degree.

Which of these three approaches do you think is most appropriate? Explain why.

2. **The mythology of property.** Consider the following excerpt, which "explains" why a professional (or other advanced) degree cannot be property:

> The recipient of an advanced degree obtains that degree on the basis of his or her innate personal talents, capabilities, and acquired skills and knowledge. Such a degree is highly personal to the recipient and has none of the traditional characteristics of property. "It does not have an exchange value or any objective transferable value on an open market. It is personal to the holder. It terminates on death of the holder and is not inheritable. It cannot be assigned, sold, transferred, conveyed, or pledged." In re Marriage of Graham, 194 Colo. 429, 432, 574 P.2d 75, 77 (1978). The time has long since passed when a person's personal attributes and talents were thought to be subject to monetary valuation for commercial purposes. In short, we do not recognize a property interest in personal characteristics of another person such as intelligence, skill, judgment, and temperament, however characterized.

Martinez v. Martinez, 169 Utah 29, 818 P.2d 538 (1991). Is this persuasive? Accurate?

3. *Martinez* **below.** From the lower court decision, Martinez v. Martinez, 80 Utah Adv. Rep. 35, 754 P.2d 69 (1988), it appears that the couple relocated from Utah to Pennsylvania to enable the husband to accept an internship there. The move evidently was a stressful one; within a few months the husband admits to having an affair with another woman. See also Sorenson v. Sorenson, 769 P.2d 820 (Utah Ct. App. 1989).

4. **Crux of the disagreement.** What was the disagreement between the majority opinion and that of Justice Zimmerman?

5. **Commodification anxiety.** Does the *Martinez* court exhibit anxiety over what it might mean to commodify "twenty-seven years of loyalty and devotion?" See Chapter 11. Courts in degree cases often use anticommodi-

fication rhetoric to argue against recognizing any interest in the wife. A 1980 Wisconsin court asserted that awarding a claim to the wife "treats the parties as though they were strictly business partners, one of whom has made a calculated investment in the commodity of the other's professional training, expecting a dollar for dollar return. We do not think that most marital planning is so coldly undertaken." DeWitt v. DeWitt, 296 N.W.2d 761, 767 (Wis. Ct. App. 1980). A 1988 West Virginia court stated that "characterizing spousal contributions as an investment in each other as human assets demeans the concept of marriage. . . . Marriage is not a business arrangement, and this Court would be loathe to promote any more tallying of respective debts and credits than already occurs in the average household." Hoak v. Hoak, 370 S.E.2d 473, 476, 478 (W. Va. 1988). Does a refusal to commodify the husband's human capital eliminate property rights in his earning power, or only eliminate such property rights for his former wife? Have courts in other contexts shied away from awarding remedies that involve commodification of intimate relationships? Consider recovery in tort for loss of consortium. See W. Page Keeton et al., Prosser and Keeton on the Law of Torts, §125 at 931-933 (5th ed. 1984).

6. **Family home.** One effect of equitable restitution as applied by the trial court of appeals was to give Mrs. Martinez title to the family home. Until about 1980, the common practice was to allow the mother and children to continue to live in the family home. Mothers still are awarded physical custody in roughly 90 percent of divorces, see Lenore Weitzman, The Divorce Revolution 257 (1985), but today divorce courts often order the family home sold, with the husband and wife each awarded 50 percent of the assets. The result often is that the mother and children have to move to a new neighborhood (and often a less affluent one), see Lenore Weitzman, The Divorce Revolution 104 (1985).

7. **Equitable restitution.** It appears that no court has ever adopted the equitable restitution theory (at least by that name).

8. **Disproportionate attention to degree cases?** The allocation of human capital upon divorce has been decided primarily in the context of cases involving professional degrees. Note that only 1.4 percent of Americans have professional degrees. U.S. Census Bureau, Education Attainment in the United States, March 1992 & 1993, cited in Considering the Top 5%, EPM Communicator, Inc., Affluent Markets Alert, November 1992. In this context, the importance of the degree cases, which have received enormous attention, has probably been overestimated. See Lesli F. Burns and Gregg A. Grauer, Human Capital as Marital Property, 19 Hofstra L. Rev. 499 (1990).

9. **Alimony awards.** The amount of alimony and child support awarded by the *Martinez* trial court was typical of the award levels found in the report of the Maryland Joint Committee, Gender Bias in the Courts 55-59, 62-69, 72-74 (May 1989). The trial court found that the husband's income was $100,000; it set alimony (to terminate after five years) at $4,800;

child support was set at $3,600 per child. This would give the mother and
children a peak annual income of $15,600,[84] while the father retained
$84,200 of his salary. What assumptions about ownership do these awards
reflect? Are they in compliance with the relevant statute (cited in the case),
in your view? These numbers show why roughly 40 percent of divorced
women with children live in poverty.[85]

10. **Valuation of the professional degree.** The *Martinez* court was
clearly troubled about placing a value on a professional degree. Mrs. Martinez had asserted that equitable restitution should be based on the discounted value of Dr. Martinez's earnings as a physician over his remaining
working life to age 65, less the amount a high school graduate would have
earned over the same time. The present value of the lifetime earnings of a
healthy 38-year-old then earning $100,000 per year was nearly $2.5 million.
The average high school graduate would earn over the same period about
$925,000. Thus, the value of Dr. Martinez's medical school education, she
calculated, would be more then $1.5 million, and would entitle her, she
argued, to a "substantial sum."

The present value of the right to receive, let us say, $20,000 yearly for
38 years, using a 6 percent discount factor, would come to $297,000. With
this amount in mind, can you argue that Mrs. Martinez, had she prevailed
at that level, would have gained, through her contribution to her husband's
education, a cotenancy interest in the medical license?

11. **What kind of labor gives rise to property?** Which of the services
provided by Peter Elkus gave rise to his property claim? Note the court's
focus on the fact that he sacrificed his own career. Studies suggest that the
sacrifice of one spouse's career to advance the other is common, but that
the economically disadvantaged spouse is usually the wife. See Norma A.
Heckman et al., Problems of Professional Couples: A Content Analysis, 39
J. Marriage & Family 323, 329 (1977) (finding that women are expected to
place their careers secondary to the needs of their children and the needs
of their husband's careers); Jeylan Mortimer et al., Husbands' Occupational
Attitudes as Constraints on Wives' Employment, 5 Soc. Work & Occupations
285 (1978) (suggesting that attributes of husband's work limit sharing of
family work and put pressure on wife to support husband's career to the
detriment of her own work participation and attainment). In addition,
families often move to accommodate husbands' careers, but much more
rarely move to accommodate wives' careers. See Joan C. Williams, Gender
Wars: Selfless Women in the Republic of Choice, 66 N.Y.U. L. Rev. 1559,
1616-1617 (1991). Professional women who are mothers typically have
career paths different from their husbands'. Whereas fathers' careers tend

---

84. This income would fall after alimony ended five years after the divorce and as child
support ended as the children reached the age of majority.
85. Fourteen and one-half percent of the general population lives in poverty. Committee on Ways & Means, 103d Cong., 2d Sess., Green Book 1154 (Comm. Print 1994).

to follow the traditional upward trajectory, mothers' did not. Wives' career progress was generally much slower than husbands' because the families placed a higher priority on the demands of children and of husbands' careers than on wives' career development. See Margaret Poloma, Reconsidering the Dual Career Marriage — A Longitudinal Approach, in Two Paychecks 188-189 (Joan Aldous ed., 1982).

These career patterns have affected women's progress in the law, a field known for very long hours. An American Bar Association Commission concluded in 1988 that "although women have made significant advancements in gaining access to the practice of law, . . . opportunities in the legal profession remain less available to women, at all levels, than to their male colleagues." ABA Commission on Women in the Profession, Report to the House of Delegates 2 (approved Aug. 10, 1988). Numerous articles document women lawyers dropping out of the profession or working part-time (which, in large Washington or New York firms, often means a nine-to-five schedule); in most firms, attorneys who work part-time are immediately taken off the partnership track, with no guarantee that they will be allowed back onto it. See Joan C. Williams, Sameness Feminism and the Work/ Family Conflict, 35 N.Y.L. Sch. L. Rev. 347, 349-350 n.19 (1990); Richard Connelly, Ten Years Later: Class of '81, Tex. Law., Apr. 29, 1991, at S-1 (considering University of Texas class roster showing that most of the women lawyers from the class of '81 were not on partnership track). One commentator expressed concern that law firms will evolve into institutions "topheavy with men and childless women, supported by a pink-collar ghetto of mommy-lawyers," often with permanent associate status. Mary C. Hickey, The Dilemma of Having It All, Wash. Law., May-June 1988, at 38, 39.

12.   **Contracts by gay, lesbian, or unmarried couples to make a will or to share assets upon divorce.** Gay or lesbian partners have to set up individual contracts or wills to gain the financial benefits family law and the law of wills give automatically to married people.[86] See Frederick C. Hertz, For Better or for Worse: Fostering the Good Gay Marriage, Avoiding the Ugly Gay Divorce (manuscript) (detailing advantages the law of wills gives to spouses and exploring the implications of the law for gay couples); Legal Guide for Lesbian and Gay Couples (Hayden Curry, Denis Clifford, and Robin Leonard 8th ed. 1994). Following the well-known "palimony" case of Marvin v. Marvin, 557 P.2d 106 (Cal. 1976), such contracts will be upheld if they do not depend on "illicit meretricious consideration," that is, sexual services. A lawyer drafting such an agreement is well advised not to mention the sexual element of such a relationship and to stress instead the companionship and domestic work involved. What if the contract mentions both the sexual and the other aspects of the relationship? Sometimes courts will

---

86. If no express contract exists, gay partners can argue on the basis of a variety of equitable and other doctrines. See *supra* at page 456.

refuse to uphold it on the grounds that the "meretricious" cannot be separated from the other consideration, see, e.g., Jones v. Daly, 176 Cal. Rptr. 130 (Cal. Ct. App. 1981) (court refused to uphold contract to render services as "lover, companion, homemaker, traveling companion, housekeeper and cook"); Thomas v. LaRosa, 400 S.E.2d 809 (W. Va. 1990) (court refused to enforce contract between unmarried, heterosexual partners where one party was still married to someone else). Sometimes courts enforce such contracts on the grounds that the sexual services can be severed from the other services, see, e.g., Crooke v. Gilden, 414 S.E.2d 645 (Ga. 1992) (written contract of lesbian couple to split residential property upon breakup enforced); Whorton v. Dillingham, 248 Cal. Rptr. 405 (Cal. Ct. App. 1988) (contract enforced; sexual services severable from other consideration); Small v. Harper, 638 S.W.2d 24 (Tex. Ct. App. 1982) (contract of lesbian partners to split property not void on public policy grounds). See also Harry G. Prince, Public Policy Limitations on Cohabitation Agreements: Unruly Horse or Circus Pony?, 70 Minn. L. Rev. 163 (1985).

2.   Allocation of Goodwill

Another context in which courts have wrestled with the issue of a spouse's human capital is in the allocation of goodwill from a business or professional practice. (The term "goodwill" is defined in the case.) Courts have been much more willing to find that human capital constitutes property in contexts involving goodwill than in other contexts. The following case provides a thorough review of the law.

PRAHINSKI v. PRAHINSKI

321 Md. 227, 582 A.2d 784 (1990)

COLE, J. In this case we must determine whether the goodwill of a solo law practice is a value includable as marital property for purposes of calculating a monetary award upon divorce.

The facts are neither complicated nor in dispute. Margaret and Leo F. X. Prahinski were married on March 20, 1965. Margaret discontinued her education after her freshman year in college in order to maintain the family home. Leo continued his formal education and eventually obtained a law degree. In 1971, Leo started his own law practice. Margaret became his secretary, and as the law practice grew, so did Margaret's responsibilities in the office. Gradually, the focus of the practice shifted to real estate and settlements and Margaret's position evolved into that of office manager.

Leo became involved with another woman in 1983. The parties separated thereafter, and Margaret filed for divorce on November 14, 1986. The

Circuit Court for Prince George's County granted an absolute divorce, and on July 10, 1987, the court filed a written order determining what was marital property, providing for distribution of marital assets, and granting both a monetary award and indefinite alimony. Included in the monetary award was one-half of the value of the law practice.

Leo appealed to the Court of Special Appeals claiming that the trial court erred in considering his law practice to be marital property consisting totally of goodwill and dividing the value thereof equally between the parties. Leo also questioned the propriety of setting the amount of alimony at a time far in advance of when the alimony payments were to commence.

The Court of Special Appeals, 75 Md. App. 113,540 A.2d 883 (1988), held that the value of the practice consisted entirely of the reputation of Leo F. X. Prahinski, Attorney-at-Law, and was therefore personal to him. As such, the value of the practice was not marital property and could not be subject to distribution as part of the monetary award. The intermediate appellate court left open the possibility that goodwill in a solo practice could be marital property if it could be shown that the goodwill was severable from the reputation of the practitioner. Additionally, the Court of Special Appeals held that it was improper for alimony to be set now when the payments were not to begin until some future time because it would be impossible to predict the economic circumstances of the parties on the date when alimony was to begin. Furthermore, that court held that alimony should take into consideration the monetary award. Since that award must be recalculated, that court declared the previous alimony calculation was invalid. The intermediate appellate court, therefore, remanded the case to the trial court for proper calculation of both the monetary award and alimony. Margaret petitioned this Court for certiorari which we granted in order to address the important issue involved. . . .

Margaret argues that the value of the practice should be considered marital property, and therefore subject to a monetary award to compensate her for her contribution thereto. She insists that the majority of the work handled by the practice did not require an attorney, and that she contributed to the overwhelming majority of the time and effort which made the practice successful. To deny her an equitable share of the goodwill inherent in the practice, she claims, would frustrate the purpose of the monetary award statue, which seeks to adjust the rights of the parties based upon their contributions during the marriage.

Specifically, Margaret contends that goodwill is a form of property which the practice acquired during the marriage; hence it fits the defintiion of marital property, no matter whose name is on the business. She further urges this Court to adopt the position that the professional goodwill of a sole proprietorship is valuable property to be included in the marital estate.

Leo maintains that his vocation has always been a solo law practice. As such, any intangible value assigned to the business is a result of his personal reputation as an attorney. The only way that goodwill could be considered marital property, he argues, is if the goodwill had a value independent of the continued presence or reputation of the sole practitioner. He contends that he is the only person who can practice under the name "Leo F. X. Prahinski, Attorney-at-Law." He claims that he could not sell his practice and its intangible assets to anyone; therefore, he concludes that the goodwill is personal to him and should not be considered marital property.

The characterization of goodwill and its relationship to a business is crucial to the determination of this issue. . . . [We have before had the occasion to quote] Lord Eldon's definition of goodwill as "the probability that the old customers will resort to the old place."

In Brown v. Benzinger, 118 Md. 29, 84 A.79 (1912) the Court was confronted with a sale of a "business conducted by [the vendor] as surgeon chiropodist." 118 Md. at 31, 84 A. at 79. That opinion makes clear that as long ago as 1912, this Court considered the goodwill involved in a profession to be different from other jurisdictions, the *Brown* court noted that in the context of a non-competition agreement in the sale of a business, the goodwill of a professional practice had been held to be personal to the practitioner. The Court specifically observed that there was a distinction

> between the sale of the good will of a trade or business of a commercial character where the location is an important feature of the business, and the sale of an established practice and good will of a person engaged in a profession or calling where the income therefrom is the immediate or direct result of his labor and skill and where integrity, skill, ability and other desirable personal qualities follow the person and not the place.

Id. at 36, 84 A. at 81 and cases cited therein.

Having recognized the existence of goodwill in the above situations, we must now determine whether goodwill can exist in the particular circumstances of the instant case. Although the trial court found that the business was predominantly a title company and treated it as such, both parties' arguments to this Court are based on the Court of Special Appeals' holding that the business was a sole proprietorship, and in particular a solo law practice. It should be noted that neither party is contesting the status of the license to practice law.[1] What is being contested is the existence of goodwill in a practice established once the professional license has been obtained.

Because the question of whether professional goodwill is marital property is one of first impression in Maryland, we found it beneficial to review the decisions of the courts of other states which have addressed the issue. This review revealed three positions. The view most often followed treats

---

1. As we held in Archer v. Archer, 303 Md. 357, 493 A.2d 1074 (1985), "a professional degree or license does not possess any of the basic characteristics of property within the ambit of marital property." Id. at 357, 493 A.2d at 1079.

goodwill as marital property in all cases.[1] The next largest group considers goodwill to be personal to the practitioner, and therefore not marital property.[2] Finally, a small group of states requires a case-by-case examination to determine how goodwill should be treated.[3] . . .

The view that the goodwill of a solo practice should be considered as marital property was early on set forth in the California decisions of Mueller v. Mueller, 144 Cal. App. 2d 245, 301 P.2d 90 (1956) and Golden v. Golden, 270 Cal. App. 2d 401, 75 Cal. Rptr. 735 (1969).

In *Mueller*, the husband was the sole owner of a dental laboratory, which employed six people. The wife sought to have the value of the business divided at the time of the divorce. The husband argued that the goodwill of the business was wholly dependent upon his personal skill and ability. The court examined the business and concluded that the business was too old and too large to be dependent solely upon the owner for its goodwill, 144 Cal. App. 2d at 251, 301 P.2d at 95, and held that the value of this business was to be divided between the parties. Furthermore, the *Mueller* court examined the argument that goodwill cannot arise in a professional business depending upon the personal skill and ability of a particular person. Even though unnecessary to its decision, the court stated that this argument was based on the definition of goodwill set forth by Lord Eldon, and the better, more modern, view is that the skill and learning acquired by a professional has intangible value which may be transferred. Id. at 251, 301 P.2d at 94-95. This left open the possibility that professional goodwill could also be divided upon divorce.

The court in *Golden* used the opening left by *Mueller* to hold that professional goodwill was marital property. The husband in *Golden* was a sole practicing physician. The wife sought a division of the value of the practice when the couple was divorced. The court, looking to *Mueller*, 270 Cal. App. 2d at 405, 75 Cal. Rptr at 737, set forth the holding that "the better rule is that, in a divorce case, the good will of the husband's professional practice as a sole practitioner should be taken into consideration in determining the award to the wife." Id. . . .

> Although the California court used community property law to give the wife credit for the increase in the goodwill value during the marriage, the nonmonetary contribution aspect of equitable distribution principles tends to accomplish the same result. Note, Treating Professional Goodwill as Marital Property in Equitable Distribution States, 58 N.Y.U.L. Rev. 554, 558 (1983)

The New Jersey Case of Dugan v. Dugan, 92 N.J. 423, 457 A.2d 1 (1983) presents a situation which is quite similar to the instant case, but in

---

1. [Citing cases from 19 states. Footnote number is that used in original opinion. — EDS.]

2. [Citing cases from 7 states. — EDS.]

3. [Citing cases from 7 states. — EDS.]

that case the court held that the goodwill of a solo law practice was marital property. The husband was an attorney who operated his practice as a wholly-owned professional corporation. New Jersey and Maryland both place the following limitations on the practice of law: (1) sole practitioners cannot sell their law practices, id. at 436, 457 A.2d at 8, (2) restrictive covenants prohibiting competition by the transferor of the practice are not allowed, and (3) clients may not be sold between practices. Regarding domestic relations law, both Maryland and New Jersey are equitable distribution states, and neither treats a professional degree or license to practice as property. See Lynn v. Lynn, 91 N.J. 510, 453 A.2d 539 (1982). The New Jersey court began its analysis by looking at the various definitions of goodwill used in other states. Its conclusion was that goodwill exists and is a legally protected interest. 92 N.J. at 429, 457 A.2d at 4. Next the court examined the relationship between goodwill and "going concern value." Goodwill was found to be closely related to reputation, and the definition settled on by New Jersey court was that goodwill "is equivalent to the excess of actual earnings over expected earnings based on a normal rate of return on investment." Id. at 431, 457 A.2d at 5.

Examining the relationship between goodwill and earning capacity (as that relates to a medical degree), the court found a difference between the two:

> Future earning capacity per se is not goodwill. However, when that future earning capacity has been enhanced because reputation leads to probable future patronage from existing and potential clients, goodwill may exist and have value. When that occurs the resulting good will is property subject to equitable distribution.

Id. at 433, 457 A.2d at 6.

Having distinguished goodwill from earning capacity and having found goodwill subject to equitable distribution, the court went on to state its rationale for the decision:

> After divorce, the law practice will continue to benefit from that goodwill as it had during the marriage. Much of the economic value produced during an attorney's marriage will inhere to the goodwill of the law practice. *It would be inequitable to ignore the contribution of the non-attorney spouse to the development of that economic resource.* An individual practitioner's inability to sell a law practice does not eliminate existence of goodwill and its value as an asset to be considered in equitable distribution. Obviously, equitable distribution does not require conveyance or transfer of any particular asset. The other spouse, in this case the wife, is entitled to have that asset considered as any other property acquired during the marriage partnership.

Id. at 434, 457 A.2d at 6 (emphasis added).

The view that professional goodwill is personal to the practitioner and is not marital property is articulated by the Texas court in Nail v. Nail, 486

S.W.2d 761 (Tex. 1972). Despite the fact that Texas, like California, is a community property state, the *Nail* court held that the goodwill built up by a medical practice was personal to the husband doctor. The court determined that the goodwill was based on the husband's personal skill, experience, and reputation. Because the goodwill was not an asset separate and apart from the doctor, it would be extinguished if he died, retired, or became disabled. Because of the personal nature of this asset, it was not considered by the court as an earned or vested property right at the time of the divorce, and did not qualify as property subject to division in a divorce proceeding. Id. at 764

Taylor v. Taylor, 222 Neb. 721, 386 N.W.2d 851 (1986), sets forth the middle ground between the two extremes. The trial court found that the husband's professional medical corporation contained no goodwill which was subject to distribution upon divorce. On appeal, the Nebraska Supreme Court affirmed that finding. In so doing, however, the appellate court noted that in proper circumstances, professional goodwill might exist as a salable or marketable business asset. Id. at 732, 386 N.W.2d at 858-59. Whether such a situated existed would be a question of fact. If the goodwill was found to be saleable or marketable, the court could divide that goodwill as a marital asset. The court stated that the essential factor which would determine the goodwill to be personal would be its dependence upon the continued presence of the individual. Id. at 731, 386 N.W.2d at 858.

Taylor, therefore, provides for a case-by-case analysis to determine whether goodwill in a particular situation should be considered marital property. Unlike the Texas court, *Taylor* does not rule out the possibility that a professional solo practice might contain such goodwill. And unlike the California cases, it allows for distinctions between those situations where goodwill is truly personal and where it is indeed marital property. It was this rationale which the Court of Special Appeals found persuasive. 75 Md. App. at 133, 540 A.2d at 843.

After reviewing these three alternatives and the rationale of their respective supporting cases, we are of the opinion that the goodwill of a solo law practice is personal to the individual practitioner. Goodwill in such circumstances is not severable from the reputation of the sole practitioner regardless of the contributions made to the practice by the spouse or employees. In order for goodwill to be marital property, it must be an asset having a separate value from the reputation of the practitioner.

We are not convinced that the goodwill of a solo practice can be separated from the reputation of the attorney. It is the attorney whose name, whether on the door or stationery, is the embodiment of the practice. We are cognizant that in this computer age many law practices, and in Leo's practice in particular, much of the research and "form" work is done by nonlawyers. In the final analysis, however, it is the attorney alone who is responsible for the work that comes out of the office. Rule of Professional Conduct 5.3(c). In the instant case, the responsibility is solely Leo's, and no amount of work done by Margaret will shift the responsibility to her. The attorney's signature or affidavit places his seal of approval on the work being done and makes the attorney liable for its accuracy and authenticity. This professional assurance is what might have convinced some clients to use Leo F. X. Prahinski, Attorney-at-Law, instead of going to a title company to have their settlements completed. The assurance would end should Leo somehow remove himself from the practice. Therefore, the goodwill generated by the attorney is personal to him and is not the kind of asset which can be divided as marital property.

Because the instant case involved the practice of law, special considerations arise which might not be present in other professional practices. . . . The ABA/BNA Lawyer's Manual on Professional Conduct §91:801 states:

> because of [the] ethical proscriptions, authorities have generally prohibited a lawyer's sale of his or her goodwill.

Since a lawyer's goodwill is not a saleable asset, it has no commercial value. The methods for valuing the marketable goodwill of a profession or business would not be applicable to an attorney's nonmarketable goodwill. The fact that a lawyer's goodwill cannot be sold by the lawyer is another factor in our determination that it is not marital property.

Of equal importance is the fact that Maryland lawyers are governed by the Rules of Professional Conduct [Rule 5.4], which . . . clearly prohibits Leo from making Margaret a partner in his law practice. In fact, the practice was set up as "Leo F. X. Prahinski, Attorney-at-Law" and there is no indication that Rule 5.4(d) was not followed. Because Margaret cannot be a partner in the practice, she cannot claim a partner's interest in the practice upon her divorce from her lawyer husband.

Under these circumstances the non-lawyer spouse has no interest in the lawyer-spouse's practice and therefore the goodwill of the practice may not be included as marital property. We hold that a non-lawyer spouse cannot be a partner (silent or otherwise) in the practice of law in Maryland.

We have noted, as did the Court of Special Appeals, that the circuit court included the value of the goodwill of the legal practice of Leo F. X. Prahinski as a part of the marital property. The alimony and the monetary award were both calculated with the value being a factor. This was error. Therefore, the entitlements of the spouse must be recalculated.

Judgment of the Court of Special Appeals Affirmed. Petitioner to Pay the Costs.

RODOWSKY, J., dissenting. I respectfully dissent. By mixing the Marital Property Act, Family Law Article §§8-201 through 8-205, with the Rules of Professional Conduct, . . . without giving effect to the purpose of either ingredient, the Court has produced an inequitable result. Although the spouse of a person engaged as a sole proprietor in a trade or business may receive an equitable award in the value of the goodwill of that proprietorship, and although the spouse of a person engaged as a sole practitioner in a profession, other than law, may receive an equitable award in the value of the goodwill of that professional practice, the Court holds that the spouse of a person engaged as a sole practitioner in the legal profession cannot even be considered for an equitable award in the value of the goodwill of that law practice because, solely in the latter instance, goodwill is not marital property.

Archer v. Archer, 303 Md. 347, 493 A.2d 1074 (1985), held that there is no marital property in a license to practice medicine. But there this Court said:

> "Our cases have generally construed the word 'property' broadly, defining it as a term of wide and comprehensive signification embracing ' "everything which has exchangeable value or goes to make up a man's wealth — every interest or estate which the law regards of sufficient value for judicial recognition." ' . . . In Bouse v. Hutzler, 180 Md. 682, 686, 26 A.2d 767 (1942), we said that the word 'property,' when used without express or implied qualifications, 'may reasonably be construed to involve obligations, rights and other intangibles as well as physical things.' 'Goodwill,' for example, has been characterized as a legally protected valuable property right. Schill v. Remington Putnam Co., 179 Md. 83, 88-89, 17 A.2d 175 (1941)."

303 Md. at 356, 493 A.2d at 1079.

Indeed, the majority opinion acknowledges that "[t]he view most often followed treats goodwill as marital property in all cases." Opinion at 787 (footnote omitted). Thus, if a brain surgeon or a house painter were to divorce, most courts would permit the spouse to show both goodwill in the solo practice or sole proprietorship and the value thereof. This is consistent with the policy of Maryland's Marital Property Act

> "that nonmonetary contributions within a marriage should be recognized in the event that marriage is dissolved; that a spouse whose activities do not include the production of income may nevertheless have contributed toward the acquisition of property by either or both spouses during the marriage; that when a marriage is dissolved, the property interests of the spouses should be adjusted fairly and equitably, with careful consideration given to both monetary and nonmonetary contributions made by the respective spouses; and that the accomplishment of these objectives necessitates that there be a departure from the inequity inherent in Maryland's old 'title' system of dealing with the marital property of divorcing spouses."

Archer v. Archer, 303 Md. at 351-52, 493 A.2d at 1076-77.

The Court nevertheless holds that the majority rule in this country does not apply here because "the goodwill of a solo law practice is personal to the individual practitioner. . . . In order for goodwill to be marital property, it must be an asset having separate value from the reputation of the practitioner." Opinion at 790. Because the instant case involves the practice of law, special considerations arise which might not be present in other professional practices." Opinion at 790.

Although today's holding is clearly limited to solo legal practitioners, there seems to rest, at least in part, on equating goodwill with professional reputation and then denying marital property in a professional reputation. In my view that does not distinguish attorneys and brain surgeons from house painters for marital property purposes. Where services involved a reputation, competently rendering the particular service is a component of goodwill whether we deal with a trade, business or a profession. The non-monetary support rendered by the spouse while the service provider was expending time and effort required for quality performance, and thereby was building the reputation, is precisely the type of contribution within a marriage which the General Assembly intended to be recognized under the Marital Property Act.

If, on the other hand, both the rationale and the holding of the majority opinion are limited to solo legal practitioners, then it seems to be principally because, under the majority's reasoning, "an attorney, as distinguished from other professionals, may not covenant to abstain from the practice of law, and therefore, may not sell his or her goodwill." Opinion at 790. Rule 5.6 entitled "Restrictions on Right to Practice," subsection (a), prohibits a lawyer from participating in offering or making "[a] partnership or employment agreement that restricts the rights of a lawyer to practice after termination of the relationship, except an agreement concerning benefits upon retirement[.]" The rationale underlying the prohibition "is that such covenants impinge upon the right of future clients to free choice of counsel." G. Hazard, Jr. & W. Hodes, The Law of Lawyering: A Handbook on the Model Rules of Professional Conduct 486 (1985). The freedom of choice of future clients is in no way diminshed by recognizing a spouse's marital property interest in the goodwill of a solo practice.

The only effect of the Rules of Professional Conduct on the problem before us is to complicate valuation. Because a solo law practice, unlike a medical practice or accounting practice, cannot be sold directly, valuation of a law practice might require comparisons to be drawn to other professions, particularly if a multiplier of some part of the net earnings of the law practice must be used. See Dugan v. Dugan, 92 N.J. 423, 439-40, 457 A.2d 1, 9-10 (1983) (multiplier to be applied to excess of average annual net income from practice over annual salary available in same general locale to attorney of comparable experience, expertise, education and age).

Finally, it is at least interesting to note that experienced counsel for the respondent did not even urge the majority holding. Recognizing the inequity of denying marital property in the goodwill of a professional practice while allowing marital property in the goodwill of sole proprietorships, trades and businesses, counsel urged that goodwill which ultimately rested on personal reputation not be included in marital property in the case of any trade, business or profession.

Chief Judge MURPHY and Judge ELDRIDGE authorize me to state that they join in the views expressed in this dissenting opinion.

NOTES AND QUESTIONS

1.   **Who did the work?** A lower court opinion gives some of the background of the *Prahinski* case. Prahinski v. Prahinski, 75 Md. App. 113, 540 A.2d 833 (1988). The couple met in college. They were married after the wife's freshman year, and she dropped out of college "to maintain the family home and, eventually, to raise the parties' two children." 540 A.2d at 836. The husband completed college and law school, and started his own law practice. The wife worked in the practice as a legal secretary, office manager, paralegal, and (in her husband's words) "Gal Friday, doing anything and everything necessary. She was very helpful." Id. By the time of the trial, the husband's practice was 95 to 97 percent real estate settlements, a type of practice that involves a lot of paperwork and filings, a significant percentage of which is often handled by paralegals. A Guide for Legal Assistants (Michele C. Gowen ed., 2d ed. 1986) How does the court of appeals opinion handle the wife's contributions to the husband's practice?

2.   **No-fault.** In 1983, after 21 years of marriage, the husband became involved with another woman. Current "no-fault" divorce law generally does not take fault into account in dividing assets upon divorce. See Lenore J. Weitzman, The Divorce Revolution 16 (1985). Do you think this is the right approach?

3.   **Goodwill.** The cases cited in *Prahinski* show that courts have been much more willing to treat human capital as property in cases where the human capital can be treated as goodwill. Why would courts be more willing to treat human capital as property in the cases involving goodwill than in other cases?

4.   **Goodwill in a legal practice.** Do you agree with the *Prahinski* court that goodwill in a legal practice is different from goodwill in other kinds of professional practices?

5.   **Who is working for whom?** Note that at common law, under coverture, any wife working in a family business was assumed to be working for her husband. See Reva B. Siegel, Home as Work: The First Women's Rights Claims Concerning Wives' Household Labor, 1850-1880, 103 Yale L.J. 1073, 1085 (1994).

6.   **How broad is *Prahinski*?** Note how the dissent tries to limit the holding of the case by stating that it is "clearly limited to solo legal practitioners." Do you agree?

7.   **Pensions and goodwill.** Courts are beginning to systematically award economically disadvantaged spouses a property interest in their

spouse's pensions. See Mary A. Throne, Note, Pension Awards in Divorce and Bankruptcy, 88 Colum. L. Rev. 194 (1988). Do you find the majority's distinction between pensions and goodwill convincing? Pensions, degrees, and goodwill all are forms of deferred compensation. Should they be treated the same? Why or why not? How should they be treated?

Chapter 5

Adverse Possession and the Doctrine of Agreed Boundaries

In the last section, we focused on one dimension of the intuitive image of property: its assumption of individual ownership. In the next two chapters we will reexamine the assumption of an owner's free will as to whether to transfer ownership or not.

This chapter will focus primarily on adverse possession, an ancient doctrine that, in certain circumstances, transfers title in land from A to B over A's objection. We are familiar with courts reallocating part of the bundle of sticks between A and B (think of landlord-tenant law), but adverse possession goes much further, for it transfers *all* of the bundle of sticks from one owner to another.[1]

The next chapter will discuss another ancient doctrine, eminent domain. Eminent domain describes the state power to take land through a forced sale as, for example, when a local government unit wants to assemble parcels of land to build a road. In this case as well, title to land is transferred from A to B by operation of law.

As to both adverse possession and eminent domain, you should consider why these doctrines developed to cloud the intuitive vision of property.

§5.1 Introduction to Adverse Possession: Use It or Lose It

Take the following case. A owns a parcel of land. Neighbor B builds a fence that encroaches onto A's land. A may sue to enjoin the fence and recover

---

1. Related instances of an involuntary transfer of ownership from A to B are (1) judgment execution sales; (2) mortgage foreclosure sales; (3) statutory distraint.

possession of his entire parcel. A's suit to recover possession, like legal remedies generally, must begin before the governing statute of limitations has run. A's penalty for delaying his suit may be loss of title, *by adverse possession,* of the strip B occupies.

Adverse possession dates back as far as 1275. Statute of Westminster I, 3 Edw. I, c. (1275); 3 American Law of Property §15.1 at 755 (A. James Casner ed., 1954 & Supp. 1977) (adverse possession began with the Statute of Westminster) The 20-year statute of limitations, still in force in some jurisdictions today, appears in 21 Jac. 1, c. 16 §§1, 2 (1623). Significantly, this statute did more than bar the remedy; its expressed goals were the "avoiding of Suits" *and* the "quieting of Man's Estates." Thus, once the action was barred, the original owner could not recover title simply by regaining possession.

Most American jurisdictions first adopted the English model of a 20-year statute of limitations. But the trend is towards shorter limitations periods. Why should this be?[2]

Not every occupancy gives rise to a cause of action. In fact, most do not. A complex multipart test has to be met for an occupant to gain title by adverse possession. This is one of a large number of such tests in property law. One commentator has referred to such formalized tests as "crystals." See Carol M. Rose, Crystals and Mud in Property Law, 40 Stan. L. Rev. 577 (1988). Other examples of property law crystals are the system of estates in land (Chapter 2) and the common law of landlord-tenant (Chapter 3), concurrent interests (Chapter 4), and servitudes (Chapter 7). Why does property law contain so many "crystals"? In what contexts do they tend to appear?

§5.2   Why? Theories of Adverse Possession

One traditional rationale for adverse possession is that it eliminates stale claims to land. 7 Powell on Real Property (1990) ¶1012(3). This rationale derives from the 1623 statute of limitations for "quieting of men's estates,

---

2. In a 1995 computer survey, only three states were found to have a statute of limitations over 20 years: Mississippi (25 years), Ohio and Pennsylvania (21 years). Fourteen states had a statute of 20 years (Alabama, Delaware, Georgia, Hawaii, Illinois, Maine, Maryland, Massachusetts, New Hampshire, New Jersey, North Carolina, North Dakota, South Dakota, and Wisconsin), 1 had a statute of 18 years (Colorado), 9 had a statute for 15 years (Connecticut, District of Columbia, Kansas, Kentucky, Michigan, Minnesota, Oklahoma, Vermont, and Virginia), 16 had a statute for 10 years (Arizona, Indiana, Iowa, Louisiana, Missouri, Montana, Nebraska, New Mexico, New York, Oregon, Rhode Island, South Carolina, Texas, Washington, West Virginia, and Wyoming), 5 had a statute for 7 years (Alaska, Arkansas, Florida, Tennessee, and Utah) and 3 have a statute for 5 years (California, Idaho, and Nevada).

and avoiding of suits," 21 Jam. I, c. 16 (1623); it is translated into the language of economics by Richard A. Epstein, Past and Future: The Temporal Dimension in the Law of Property, 64 Wash. U. L.Q. 667, 674-680 (1986) (key value of adverse possession is in preventing dubious cases from being filed, thereby decreasing litigation costs).

The excerpts below suggest other rationales for adverse possession.

MARGARET JANE RADIN, TIME, POSSESSION, AND ALIENATION

64 Wash. U. L. Q. 739, 739-742 (1986)

There are three traditional strains in liberal property theory: the Lockean labor-desert theory; the Benthamite utilitarian (and economic) theory; and the Hegelian personality theory. In the Lockean theory, the temporal or dynamic dimension of human affairs seems to be irrelevant, but it plays an important role in the other two.

A.   LOCKEAN ENTITLEMENT

. . . Entitlements come into being through mixing one's labor with an unowned object, or, in Epstein's version, through occupancy or first possession of an unowned object, and thereby are fixed forever. Thus, one moment in time is relevant to entitlement, the moment when non-property becomes property; but the temporal dimension of human affairs, our situation in an ongoing stream of time, is irrelevant. . . .

B.   UTILITARIANISM

Utilitarian theory is more directly time-bound. In act-utilitarianism the preferred or justified course of action is to maximize welfare (or utility, or whatever is the maximand) right now. But human interactions and our environment are dynamic, so as time moves on the preferred or justified course of action changes. Furthermore, in determining the preferred course of action the future is what governs. To judge an act by its consequences for utility is, from the standpoint of the time of making the decision, to rest rightness on prediction.

In rule-utilitarianism, the preferred or justified course of action is to maximize welfare (or whatever) in "the long run" in contradistinction to right now. Hence, the dynamic nature of human affairs is more directly implicated in the preferred course of action. One consequence of this is that in rule-utilitarianism we are always cognizant of systemic concerns: How will any given choice affect the entire system of entitlements and expectations as it produces and maintains welfare over time? Thus, time is embedded at the heart of rule-utilitarianism. Indeed, its temporal heart harbors its deepest puzzles. How long is the long run? Does it include future generations? If so, how do we attribute utility (or whatever) to them, and how do we compare it with the utility of people alive today? Is the utility of people who are not alive today but were alive yesterday of any relevance? If so, at what point does the utility of the dead cease to count? In order to maximize utility, should we (in light of the principle of decreasing marginal utility) maximize population until everyone is at bare subsistence level? And so forth.

C.   Property and Personhood

Time is also at the heart of the personality theory, but in a different way. In the Hegelian theory, ownership is accomplished by placing one's will into an object. A modern extrapolation of this idea suggests that the claim to an owned object grows stronger as, over time, the holder becomes bound up with the object. Conversely, the claim to an object grows weaker as the will (or personhood) is withdrawn. In other words, in personality theory the strength of property claims is itself dynamic because over time the bond between persons and objects can wax and wane.

Because personality theory concerns individual rights and not general welfare, it does not harbor the same temporal puzzles as rule-utilitarianism. Since it places entitlement in the present state of the relationship between person and object and not in some aboriginal appropriation, it also avoids the major problem of the Lockean individual rights theory. Personality theory must struggle instead with how to construe the notion of personhood and the notion of relationships between persons and objects. In coherence and contextualist philosophical views, these central notions themselves are developing through history; that is, they have a temporal dimension. . . .

Consider the following three excerpts and see if they fit into any of Radin's three boxes. Which justification for adverse possession do you find most compelling? Utility (for society or individual)? First in time, first in right (in perpetuity)? Property as an expression of and necessity for personhood?

OLIVER WENDELL HOLMES, THE PATH OF THE LAW

10 Harv. L Rev. 457, 476-477 (1897)

Let me now give an example to show the practical importance, for the decision of actual cases, of understanding the reasons of the law, by taking an example from rules which, so far as I know, never have been explained or theorized about in any adequate way. I refer to statutes of limitation and the law of prescription. The end of such rules is obvious, but what is the justification for depriving a man of his rights, a pure evil as far as it goes, in consequence of the lapse of time? Sometimes the loss of evidence is referred to, but that is a secondary matter. Sometimes the desirability of peace, but why is peace more desirable after twenty years than before? It is increasingly likely to come without the aid of legislation. Sometimes it is said that, if a man neglects to enforce his rights, he cannot complain if, after a while, the law follows his example. . . .

I should suggest that the foundation of the acquisition of rights by lapse of time is to be looked for in the position of the person who gains them, not in that of the loser. Sir Henry Maine has made it fashionable to connect the archaic notion of property with prescription. But the connection is further back than the first recorded history. It is in the nature of man's mind. A thing which you have enjoyed and used as your own for a long time, whether property or an opinion, takes root in your being and cannot be torn away without your resenting the act and trying to defend yourself, however you came by it. The law can ask no better justification than the deepest instincts of man. It is only by way of reply to the suggestion that you are disappointing the former owner, that you refer to his neglect having allowed the gradual dissociation between himself and what he claims, and the gradual association of it with another. If he knows that another is doing acts which on their face show that he is on the way toward establishing such an association, I should argue that in justice to that other he was bound at his peril to find out whether the other was acting under his permission, to see that he was warned, and, if necessary, stopped.

RICHARD A. POSNER, ECONOMIC ANALYSIS OF LAW 79

(4th ed. 1992)

If for a given period of years (which is different in different states, but seven is a common number) you hold property adversely to the real owner (i.e., not as tenant, agent, etc.), claiming it as your own, and he does not bring suit to assert his right, the property becomes yours. Oliver Wendell Holmes long ago suggested an economic explanation for adverse possession. Over time, a person becomes attached to property that he regards as his own, and the deprivation of the property would be wrenching. Over the same time, a person loses attachment to property that he regards as no longer his own, and the restoration of the property would cause only moderate pleasure. This is a point about diminishing marginal utility of income. The adverse possessor would experience the deprivation of the property as a diminution in his wealth; the original owner would experience the restoration of the property as an increase in *his* [emphasis in original] wealth. If they have the same wealth, then probably their combined utility will be greater if the adverse possessor is allowed to keep the property.

RICHARD A. EPSTEIN, PAST AND FUTURE: THE TEMPORAL DIMENSION IN THE LAW OF PROPERTY

64 Wash. U. L.Q. 667, 669-670 (1986)

Every one knows and follows the rule of ordinary life that applies to such prosaic matters as waiting in line for theater tickets or in a cafeteria: "first come, first served." The rule of first possession at common law converts that intuition into the analytical foundation for the entire system of private property: the party who takes first possession of a thing is entitled to exclude the rest of the world from it, forever. The element of time is part of the priority rule and of the definition of the property interest acquired.

The rationales for this rule are many and complex. Often the rule has been regarded as something akin to a self-evident truth. But the rule also has clear political and utilitarian virtues that account for its lofty status. These deserve to be mentioned briefly. The first possession rule promotes a system of decentralized ownership: private actions by private parties shape the individual entitlements in ways that do not involve the active role of the state, whose job, as umpire, is neatly restricted to protecting entitlements previously acquired by private means. The rule thus allows one to organize a system of rights that is not dependent upon the whim of the sovereign, and makes it possible to oppose on normative grounds the all too frequent historical truth that ownership rights rest upon successful conquest, nothing more and nothing less. It is not surprising therefore that a variant of the first possession rule exerted so large an influence in the writing of John Locke, whose political mission was to defend a theory of representative government against the power of the Crown.

The first possession rule also has more direct economic virtues for it yields a consistent and exhaustive set of property rights, whereby everything has in principle one, and only one, owner. Vesting ownership in the first possessor makes it highly likely that a person who owns the land will use it efficiently and protect it diligently. At every stage the rule reduces transaction costs. There is no need for a routine lawsuit for the true owner, however identified, to pry property away from the party in wrongful possession. The uniqueness of owners means that development and sale can take place at relatively low cost. The first possession rule does give rise to serious problems in the case of common-pool assets, such as oil, gas and fish. Yet even here it furnishes a baseline of entitlements which permits the state to organize forced exchanges that on average work to the long-term advantage of persons with interests in the pool. . . .

NOTES AND QUESTIONS

1. **Application of theories.** Which of the theories Radin enumerates describe each of these excerpts?

2. **Is adverse possession efficient?** In the United States today, a comprehensive system exists for recording land titles (see Chapter 12). In this context, wouldn't it be more efficient to simply rely on that recording system, rather than allowing potentially expensive adverse possession litigation? In fact, doesn't adverse possession undercut the usefulness of the recording system, since it means that the holder of record title may not, in fact, own the land described in the deed (if an occupant has gained title through adverse possession)?

3. **Does adverse possession avoid litigation?** Very often, the adverse party claiming title sues *after* the original owner's suit is barred. Does the doctrine avoid lawsuits, or does it simply switch the parties?

4. **When should land be taken from its owner and given to someone who will use it more productively?** If the purpose of adverse possession is to take unproductive land and give it to someone who is using it more productively, should all unproductive land be taken from its owners and given to other, more productive users? What would become of the stability of property rights?

5. **What is "productive" use?** John G. Sprankling, An Environmental Critique of Adverse Possession, 79 Cornell L. Rev. 816 (1994), argues that American courts shifted in the nineteenth century from the original English model of adverse possession to a "developmental model" designed to encourage settlement and productive economic use of wild lands.

> By 1803 more than ninety percent of the nation consisted of sparsely populated, publicly owned wild lands. The broad federal policy toward these wild lands was to transfer them into private ownership, initially through sale. Because the government had never been able to enforce its theoretical ban against squatting on these lands, sales often resulted in conflicts between new absentee owners holding legal title and actual settlers who had already placed the land in productive use.

Id. at 843. Sprankling points out that the development model, which made adverse possession freely available to anyone who developed the land, favored settlers (who worked the land) over land speculators in the nineteenth century (who may never have entered the parcel in dispute). Today, he argues, the development model effect quite different results:

> In a broad sense, the owner of wild lands never holds absolute title. Rather his title is always subject to what might be considered a condition subsequent of exploitation. The owner may be vulnerable to adverse possession if he fails to devote the land to an appropriate economic use.

Id. at 853.

Sprankling points out the widespread assumption in the nineteenth century that development of land served utilitarian goals. Justice Story expressed this sentiment in an 1829 Supreme Court decision: "The country was a wilderness; and the universal policy was to procure its cultivation and improvement." Van Ness v. Pacard, 27 U.S. (2 Pet.) 137, 145 (1829). Compare this use of utilitarianism with Posner's. How are they similar? Different?

6. **Holmes offers a different explanation.** How does Holmes's explanation for adverse possession differ from that given by Posner? Note how Margaret Jane Radin translates this reasoning into her "property and personhood" terminology.

7. **Another slippery slope?** If adverse possession allows land to be taken away from A so long as B's being has become bound up with the land, does this introduce a new instability into the ownership of all fungible (as opposed to personhood) property? Robert Ellickson has called adverse possession a "dent" in the "libertarian" image of property as absolute and unchanging. Ellickson finds that in a libertarian utopia, the state would give each landowner the maximum degree of freedom to use the land, granting total freedom of alienation, constrained only by the law of nuisance and other doctrines which speak to external harms. "Libertarians . . . are therefore suspicious of any 'efficiency' justifications for legal rules that allow forced exchanges for compensation, must less rules that legitimize uncompensated expropriations." Robert C. Ellickson, Adverse Possession and Perpetuities Law: Two Dents in the Libertarian Model of Property Rights, 64 Wash. U. L.Q. 723, 724 (1986).

The following excerpt explores how adverse possession has functioned in U.S. property law.

WILLIAM W. FISHER III, THE LAW OF THE LAND: AN INTELLECTUAL HISTORY OF AMERICAN PROPERTY DOCTRINES 1776-1880

(Ph.D. diss., Harvard University, 1991)

One of the odd features of Anglo-American property law is that if an intruder can contrive to remain in possession of someone else's land long enough, he becomes entitled to remain there indefinitely. Until a certain moment, the intruder is deemed a trespasser and, as such, not only is subject to eviction but also is liable both for any damages done to the premises and for the fair rental value of the land during the period in which he has been in wrongful possession. After that magic moment, he is immune to suit and may claim that land as his own. . . .

The English courts interpreted [the statutes applicable to adverse possession] purely as statutes of limitation. Their sole purpose effect the courts asserted, was to cut off a title-holder's remedies if he failed to assert them within the prescribed periods. This view of the statutes had a number of practical implications. Most importantly, it prompted the courts to ignore, when applying the provisions, what was happening on the land while the rightful owner was out of possession. Once he had been disseised, the clock began running. The disseisor might, if he wished, leave the premises for substantial periods. He might even be ousted himself by another disseisor. In the courts' opinion, none of this mattered. When the time prescribed by the statute had elapsed, the title-holder was forever barred from asserting his rights.

Another practical implication of the English judges' interpretive approach was that the state of mind of the intruder was equally irrelevant. . . . [T]he attitude of the intruder had no legal significance. . . . Once the clock had run, he had the equivalent of a fee simple interest in the property. . . .

The law of adverse possession puzzled and troubled antebellum [i.e., pre-Civil War] judges — just at it puzzles and troubles contemporary law students. Different judges reached different conclusions, but over time they developed a common language for discussing adverse possession claims — a language markedly different from the discourse of the English courts.

The earliest American adverse-possession decisions contain only casual references to the foundations of the doctrine. Insofar as general theories can be teased out of the language, they fit one of two patterns. The first was derived, not surprisingly, from the English doctrine. The propositions on which it rested was that someone would be able to exercise notorious dominion for a long time over a piece of land which he did not own only if the title-holder were negligent in some respect — either by not keeping track of his property or by failing to assert his rights when he knew someone was infringing them. The possessor having relied (to his probable disadvantage, were he ousted after a long tenure) upon the title-holder's laxity, the latter "deserved" to be deprived of his legal rights.

The second of two early theories emphasized, not the neglect or "laches" of the plaintiff, but rather the evidentiary implications of long-term occupancy of land by the defendant. According to this view, the fact that the defendant's claim to the land had gone unchallenged for many years is reliable evidence that he is indeed the rightful owner. The documentation for his title may have been lost through lapse of time, but it is highly unlikely that he would have been permitted to enjoy the estate for so long had he (or his predecessor) not at one time been granted the land — either by the state or by the predecessor in interest of the person now seeking to displace him.

Beginning in the 1820's, judges and commentators began to diversify and integrate their conceptions of the rationale for [adverse possession]. A seminal decision in this regard was Ricard v. Williams, decided by the United States Supreme Court in 1822. The principal issue in the case was whether the Connecticut statute of limitations would be interpreted to prevent a group of creditors from reaching the real estate formerly owned by a deceased debtor in a situation in which the debtor's son had been in possession for longer that the statutory period but in which, because of an unexplained delay in the administration of the debtor's estate, the creditors' causes of actions technically had only recently accrued. Justice Story ruled that the statute was not, by its terms, applicable to the dispute, then turned to an analysis of the policies underlying it to decide whether to extend its provision "by analogy." Relying heavily upon the argument of Daniel Webster, who represented the son, Story determined that the true basis of the law was a combination of the neglect of the title-holder and the "convenience of mankind." Persons who slept on their rights deserved to lose them. And there was an important "public policy" interest in "protecting innocent purchasers, and the repose of title honestly acquired." Concluding that both of these principles clearly applied to the case at bar, Story held that the creditors' rights had been lost and that the son could keep the property.

In two respects, Story's opinion in *Ricard* set the tone for the rationales of adverse possession that would be used to shape or buttress judicial decisions for the next thirty years. First, it introduced "public policy" as a major justification of the operation of statutes of limitations. Between 1822 and mid-century, the "convenience of mankind" would gradually assume ever greater importance in the minds of judges until it came to dominate their opinions. Second, Story developed "policy" arguments in ways that portrayed them as consistent with the two rationales that had underlain earlier decision — the laches and evidentiary theories. The implicit message of his opinion (occasionally made explicit in the decisions that succeeded it) was that the perfection of a statutory bar to the recovery of real property did not entail the sacrifice of equity, justice in the particular case, to the public welfare. Rather, the demandant, who had sat on his rights, and the possessor, who had innocently been making productive use of the premises, got their just deserts, and (best of all) the resultant "security of title" and favorable climate for investment redounded to the benefit of the community.

Accompanying and facilitating the emergence of this new, composite theory was a shift in . . . the images of the standard prototypal adverse-possession dispute. . . . The two, sharply different vignettes that informed the early cases — the image of the present occupant as knowing wrongdoer, resisting a legitimate owner who has neglected to assert his rights in a timely fashion and the image of the present occupant as a beleaguered rightful owner, who has unfortunately lost the documentation for his title, being harassed by an opportunistic plaintiff — gradually gave way to third. In the new image of the standard dispute, either the plaintiff or his predecessor originally had a valid claim to the land, but either never entered upon and exercised dominion over it or long ago abandoned it. The present occupant (or his predecessor) found the premises unoccupied and undeveloped, assumed (erroneously) that he himself had title to it or, at a minimum, that no one did, and began to improve, cultivate and live upon the land. Now, many years later, the title-holder has discovered what has happened and is seeking to cast out the possessor. The crucial features of this model are that, though the present tenants lacks paper title, he came into possession more or less innocently, and he has made productive use of the premises during this tenure. By 1830, this new scenario had large displaced it predecessors. . . .

The emergence . . . of a coherent theory of adverse possession can be traced in [two] areas of doctrine. The first is the development of the distinctively American "state of mind" required . . . Led by the courts of New York, the American judiciary early and firmly established the principle that only a possessor who, at the time of his entrance, asserts a "claim of right" to the premises in question is entitled to the benefit of the statutes of limitations. Moreover, in the period between 1815 and 1840, the courts in most American jurisdictions interpreted "claim of right" to mean, not only an intention to make the land one's own, but an honest belief that one owns it already. There was some ambiguity (as late nineteenth-century commentators hostile to the requirement were fond of pointing out) in almost all of the opinions instituting such a "good faith belief" requirement. But there is no denying that most judges recognized, as a significant factor in an occupant's favor, the fact that, when he entered into possession, he honestly believed he already had title to the premises.

This amorphous but crucial "state of mind" requirement . . . nicely reconciled two competing "public policy" considerations: it promoted "security" and productivity by guaranteeing that possessors who claimed a right to the land they occupied could, after the prescribed period of time, confidently labor and invest knowing they would not be displaced and, at the same time, served the interest of those who wished to use real estate for "commercial" purposes by providing that occupancy of their lands by "mere squatters" would not result in the invalidation of disruption of mortgages and conveyances. [The state of mind requirement also] led to the equitable resolution of individual controversies by ensuring that, while well-meaning "finders and improvers" were given invulnerable titles after the requisite number of years, those who deliberately ousted rightful owners would at any time be deprived of their ill-gotten gains.

The second doctrinal manifestation of the courts' assumptions and theories is the establishment of the equally distinctively American privity requirement for "tacking" successive adverse possessions. Repudiating the English rule — that what happened on the land after the ouster of the title-holder did not affect the running of the statute — the American courts, again led by those of New York, insisted that, if neither of two successive adverse occupants had been in possession of the land for the statutory period, neither could claim the benefit of the statute unless there were some kind of "privity of estate" between them. . . .

In sum, American courts in the early nineteenth century reconceived the doctrine of adverse possession and modified accordingly several of the particular rules that comprised the doctrine. Some of the sources of the reform they adopted should by now be apparent. As was true of their handling during the period of other aspects of the law pertaining to intruders, the courts drew heavily, when reshaping adverse possession, on utilitarian theories of the origin and purpose of property rights. In addition, one can see many manifestations in their opinions of the Grand Style of legal reasoning — in particular, the aspiration simultaneously to promote the welfare of the community and do justice in particular cases.

But why, exactly, did antebellum judges find arguments of these sorts congenial? The concluding section of the previous chapter suggested that judges' choices of rules and styles of reasoning can be traced at least in part of the phenomenon of cultural hegemony — the tendency (only partially purposeful) by the members of a dominant social class to develop and disseminate a world-view that helps to make sense (both to themselves and to members of less advantaged groups) of the extant social and political order. We are now in a position to explore that contention in more detail.

Recall that, during the first two-thirds of the nineteenth century, social critics, most of them associated with the Jeffersonian and then the Jacksonian parties — denounced ever more vehemently the growing concentration of landholding in the United States. Two related principles underlay most of their attacks. First, every man has a natural right to occupy, own, and cultivate as much land as is necessary to support himself and his family. Second, the engrossing of land by persons or organizations not intending to put it to productive use is illegitimate. Assertions of the propositions were common in the prolonged debates over the policy the federal government should be pursuing in the disposition of the public lands. But the two principles were also advanced effectively on behalf of "squatters" — settlers who had occupied and cultivated land belonging to others and now wished to claim it for their own.

In view of the currency of such arguments in antebellum political discourse, it is striking that the judges, when reforming the law of adverse possession, made no mention of them. The relevance of two principles must have been obvious. The notion that every person deserved an opportunity to cultivate and own a portion of the earth plainly strengthens the position of adverse occupants, while the notion that the acquisition of land for speculative purposes is immoral, weakens the position of many title holders. The absence from the courts' opinions of any discussion of the moral implication of productive *versus* nonproductive uses of property is thus difficult to dismiss as an accident. It seems much more likely that the judges felt that such arguments (like the natural-law critique of slavery) were too dangerous, too threatening to the existing distribution of wealth and power to be incorporated in their deliberations.

But the judges did not simply ignore the claims of the Jacksonians. Their (unconscious) strategy was more subtle. Instead of seeking to avoid engagement in moral arguments, they displaced the radical critics' moral contentions with moral contentions of their own. As indicated above, the antebellum judges and treatise writers defended their doctrinal reforms on the grounds that they simultaneously promoted economic development and secured justice. But the "justice" the new rules purportedly advanced was highly individual. If a particular adverse occupant was innocent — i.e., was unaware that the land he developed was owned by someone else — he was rewarded with title to the tract; if he was a "deliberate wrong-doer," he was punished with a denial of the title and with liability in trespass. The effect of framing the issue in this way was that the attention of all participants in adverse possession controversies was effectively deflected from the overriding, systemic questions: Was the background allocations of entitlement to land just? Does the act of putting land to productive use — regardless of the state of mind of the actor — give the actor a moral claim to the land itself? . . .

NOTES AND QUESTIONS

1. **Does adverse possession challenge the intuitive image of property?** Why did antebellum judges find adverse possession so troubling, according to Fisher? How did they formulate the law to diffuse the clash between the intuitive image and adverse possession doctrine?

2. **Good faith?** Why were antebellum judges so eager to find "good faith," according to Fisher?

3. **Utilitarianism.** Did utilitarianism influence antebellum judges?

4. **Republican vision?** Do the social critics discussed by Fisher reflect the republican vision of property? How? Why did judges shy away from adopting this rhetoric in adverse possession cases?

§5.3   The Mechanics of Adverse Possession

Adverse possession cases are common: A computer search of state cases between 1980 and 1990 generated more than 1,000 cases involving questions of adverse possession. Most modern cases involve either "wild land or disputed border strips in developed areas." John G. Sprankling, An Environmental Critique of Adverse Possession, 79 Cornell L. Rev. 816, 826 (1994). Each standard element of the adverse possession test has been litigated. In some states, moreover, other elements are added or variations of adverse possession have been created by statute or case law. A lawyer handling an adverse possession case must check carefully to determine what are the specific elements of the relevant test for adverse possession in the particular jurisdiction.

a.   The Basic Test

Under the standard test, an adverse possessor must meet the following four elements, and then sustain qualifying possession for the relevant statute of limitations:

1. Actual and exclusive possession;
2. Open and notorious possession;
3. "Adverse" continuous possession;
4. Continuous possession for the statutory period.

Of course, the test for adverse possession in a given jurisdiction may vary from this standard test. One standard variation sets forth a shorter statute of limitations where the adverse possessor's claim is pursuant to "color of title" — an invalid deed (or a deed that describes only part of the land claimed). The Illinois statute, for one, requires only a 7-year occupancy under color of title as against 20 years for other occupancies. Ill. Ann. Stat. ch. 735, ¶5, §13-101 at nn.79, 87 (Smith-Hurd 1992 & Supp. 1996). In some western states, an adverse possessor may have to prove that she paid property taxes during the occupancy period. Examples are Cal. Civ. Proc. Code §325, ¶62 (West 1995) or West's Ann. Cal. C.C.P. §325 (1995); Idaho Code §5-210 (1995) (making payment of state, local, and municipal taxes an additional requirement for establishing adverse possession); Mont. Code Ann. §70-19-411 (1995); N.M. Stat. Ann. §37-1-22 (Michie 1994); Utah Code Ann. §78-12-12 (1994); Wash. Rev. Code §7.28.070 (1992) (requiring a showing that all legally assessed taxes have been paid by the adverse possessor during the statutory period). In addition, statutes in some states set forth statutory definitions of some of the elements of adverse possession. See Civ. Prac. Act §34, 38, 39 (1948) or N.Y. Civ. Prac. L. & R. §212(a) (McKinney 1995) (repealed).

When you read the cases below, consider whether the jurisdiction introduces any variations on the standard list of elements of adverse possession and identify the evidence introduced to establish that each element of the relevant test is met.

NOME 2000 v. FAGERSTROM

799 P.2d 304 (Alaska 1990)

MATTHEWS, C.J. This appeal involves a dispute over a tract of land measuring approximately seven and one-half acres, overlooking the Nome River (hereinafter the disputed parcel). Record title to a tract of land known as mineral survey 1161, which includes the disputed parcel, is held by Nome 2000.

On July 24, 1987, Nome 2000 filed suit to eject Charles and Peggy Fagerstrom from the disputed parcel. The Fagerstroms counterclaimed that through their use of the parcel they had acquired title by adverse possession.

A jury trial ensued and, at the close of the Fagerstroms' case, Nome 2000 moved for a directed verdict on two grounds. First, it maintained that the Fagerstroms' evidence of use of the disputed parcel did not meet the requirements of the doctrine of adverse possession. Alternatively, Nome 2000 maintained that the requirements for adverse possession were met only as to the northerly section of the parcel and, therefore, the Fagerstroms could not have acquired title to the remainder. The trial court denied the motion. After Nome 2000 presented its case, the jury found that the Fagerstroms had adversely possessed the entire parcel. The court then entered judgment in favor of the Fagerstroms.

On appeal, Nome 2000 contests the trial court's denial of its motion for a directed verdict and the sufficiency of the evidence in support of the jury verdict. . . .

I.   FACTUAL BACKGROUND

The disputed parcel is located in a rural area known as Osborn. During the warmer seasons, property in Osborn is suitable for homesites and subsistence and recreational activities. During the colder seasons, little or no use is made of Osborn property.

Charles Fagerstrom's earliest recollection of the disputed parcel is his family's use of it around 1944 or 1945. At that time, his family used an abandoned boy scout cabin present on the parcel as a subsistence base camp during summer months. Around 1947 or 1948, they moved their summer campsite to an area south of the disputed parcel. However, Charles and his family continued to make seasonal use of the disputed parcel for subsistence and recreation.

In 1963, Charles and Peggy Fagerstrom were married and, in 1966, they brought a small quantity of building materials to the north end of the disputed parcel. They intended to build a cabin.

In 1970 or 1971, the Fagerstroms used four cornerposts to stake off a twelve acre, rectangular parcel for purposes of a Native Allotment application.[3] The northeast and southeast stakes were located on or very near min-

---

3. Federal law authorizes the Secretary of the Interior to allot certain non-mineral lands to Native Alaskans. See Act of May 17, 1906, 34 Stat. 197, as amended, Act of August 2, 1956, 70 Stat. 954; repealed by the Alaska Native Claims Settlement Act, 18, with a savings clause for applications pending on December 18, 1971, 43 U.S.C. §1617(a) (1982); modified by the Alaska National Interest Lands Conservation Act, 43 U.S.C. §1634 (1982). As a result of her application, Peggy was awarded two lots (lots 3 and 12) which border the disputed parcel along its western boundary.

eral survey 1161. The northwest and southwest stakes were located well to the west of mineral survey 1161. The overlap constitutes the disputed parcel. The southeast stake disappeared at an unknown time.

Also around 1970, the Fagerstroms built a picnic area on the north end of the disputed parcel. The area included a gravel pit, beachwood blocks as chairs, firewood and a 50-gallon barrel for use as a stove.

About mid-July 1974, the Fagerstroms placed a camper trailer on the north end of the disputed parcel. The trailer was leveled on blocks and remained in place through late September. Thereafter, until 1978, the Fagerstroms parked their camper trailer on the north end of the disputed parcel from early June through September. The camper was equipped with food, bedding, a stove and other household items.

About the same time that the Fagerstroms began parking the trailer on the disputed parcel, they built an outhouse and a fish rack on the north end of the parcel. Both fixtures remained through the time of trial in their original locations. The Fagerstroms also planted some spruce trees, not indigenous to the Osborn area, in 1975-76.

During the summer of 1977, the Fagerstroms built a reindeer shelter on the north end of the disputed parcel. The shelter was about 8x8 feet wide, and tall enough for Charles Fagerstrom to stand in. Around the shelter, the Fagerstroms constructed a pen which was 75 feet in diameter and 5 feet high. The shelter and pen housed a reindeer for about six weeks and the pen remained in place until the summer of 1978.

During their testimony, the Fagerstroms estimated that they were personally present on the disputed parcel from 1974 through 1978, "every other weekend or so" and "[a] couple times during the week . . . if the weather was good." When present they used the north end of the parcel as a base camp while using the entire parcel for subsistence and recreational purposes. Their activities included gathering berries, catching and drying fish and picnicking. Their children played on the parcel. The Fagerstroms also kept the property clean, picking up litter left by others.

While so using the disputed parcel, the Fagerstroms walked along various paths which traverse the entire parcel. The paths were present prior to the Fagerstroms' use of the parcel and, according to Peggy Fagerstrom, were free for use by others in connection with picking berries and fishing. On one occasion, however, Charles Fagerstrom excluded campers from the land. They were burning the Fagerstroms' firewood.

Nome 2000 placed into evidence the deposition testimony of Dr. Steven McNabb, an expert in anthropology, who stated that the Fagerstroms' use of the disputed parcel was consistent with the traditional Native Alaskan system of land use. According to McNabb, unlike the non-Native system, the traditional Native system does not recognize exclusive ownership of land. Instead, customary use of land, such as the Fagerstroms' use of the disputed parcel, establishes only a first priority claim to the land's resources. The claim is not exclusive and is not a matter of ownership, but is more in the nature of a stewardship. That is, other members of the claimant's social group may share in the resources of the land without obtaining permission, so long as the resources are not abused or destroyed. McNabb explained that Charles' exclusion of the campers from the land was a response to the campers' use of the Fagerstroms' personal property (their firewood), not a response to an invasion of a perceived real property interest.[5]

Nevertheless, several persons from the community testified that the Fagerstroms' use of the property from 1974 through 1977 was consistent with that of an owner of the property. For example, one Nome resident testified that since 1974 "[the Fagerstroms] cared for [the disputed parcel] as if they owned it. They made improvements on it as if they owned it. It was my belief that they did own it."

During the summer of 1978, the Fagerstroms put a cabin on the north end of the disputed parcel. Nome 2000 admits that from the time that the cabin was so placed until the time that Nome 2000 filed this suit, the Fagerstroms adversely possessed the north end of the disputed parcel. Nome 2000 filed its complaint on July 24, 1987.

II.   Discussion

A

The Fagerstroms' claim of title by adverse possession is governed by AS 09.10.030, which provides for a ten-year limitations period for actions to recover real property.[6] Thus, if the Fagerstroms adversely possessed the disputed parcel, or any portion thereof, for ten consecutive years, then they have acquired title to that property. See Hubbard v. Curtiss, 684 P.2d 842, 849 (Alaska 1984) ("Title automatically vests in the adverse possessor at the end of the statutory period."). Because the Fagerstroms' use of the parcel increased over the years, and because Nome 2000 filed its complaint on July 24, 1987, the relevant period is July 24, 1977 through July 24, 1987.

We recently described the elements of adverse possession as follows: "In order to acquire title by adverse possession, the claimant must prove, by clear and convincing evidence, . . . that for the statutory period 'his use of the land was continuous, open and notorious, exclusive and hostile to the true owner.'" Smith v. Krebs, 768 P.2d 124, 125 (Alaska 1989). The first three conditions — continuity, notoriety and exclusivity — describe

---

5. However, Charles Fagerstrom testified that when he excluded the campers he felt that they were "on our property." He also testified that during the mid to late 70's he would have "frowned" upon people camping on "my property."

6. A seven-year period is provided for by AS 09.25.050 when possession is under "color and claim of title." The Fagerstroms do not maintain that their possession was under color of title.

the physical requirements of the doctrine. See R. Cunningham, W. Stoe-buck and D. Whitman, The Law of Property §11.7 at 758-60, 762-63 (1984). The fourth condition, hostility, is often imprecisely described as the "intent" requirement. Id. at 761.

On appeal, Nome 2000 argues that as a matter of law the physical requirements are not met absent "significant physical improvements" or "substantial activity" on the land. Thus, according to Nome 2000, only when the Fagerstroms placed a cabin on the disputed parcel in the summer of 1978 did their possession become adverse. For the prior year, so the argument goes, the Fagerstroms' physical use of the property was insufficient because they did not construct "significant structures" and their use was only seasonal. Nome 2000 also argues that the Fagerstroms' use of the disputed parcel was not exclusive because "others were free to pick the berries, use the paths and fish in the area." We reject these arguments.

Whether a claimant's physical acts upon the land are sufficiently continuous, notorious and exclusive does not necessarily depend on the existence of significant improvements, substantial activity or absolute exclusivity. Indeed, this area of law is not susceptible to fixed standards because the quality and quantity of acts required for adverse possession depend on the *character* of the land in question. Thus, the conditions of continuity and exclusivity require only that the land be used for the statutory period as an average owner of similar property would use it. . . .

The character of the land in question is also relevant to the notoriety requirement. Use consistent with ownership which gives visible evidence of the claimant's possession, such that the reasonably diligent owner "could see that a hostile flag was being flown over his property," is sufficient. Shilts v. Young, 567 P.2d 769, 776 (Alaska 1977). Where physical visibility is established, community repute is also relevant evidence that the true owner was put on notice.[7] Id.

Applying the foregoing principles to this case, we hold that the jury could reasonably conclude that the Fagerstroms established, by clear and convincing evidence, continuous, notorious and exclusive possession for ten years prior to the date Nome 2000 filed suit. We point out that we are concerned only with the first year, the summer of 1977 through the summer of 1978, as Nome 2000 admits that the requirements of adverse possession were met from the summer of 1978 through the summer of 1987.

The disputed parcel is located in a rural area suitable as a seasonal homesite for subsistence and recreational activities. This is exactly how the Fagerstroms used it during the year in question. On the premises through-

---

7. The function of the notoriety requirement is to afford the true owner an opportunity for notice. However, actual notice is not required; the true owner is charged with knowing what a reasonably diligent owner would have known. [Alaska National Bank v. Linck], 559 P.2d at 1053 [(Alaska 1977)].

out the entire year were an outhouse, a fish rack, a large reindeer pen (which, for six weeks, housed a reindeer), a picnic area, a small quantity of building materials and some trees not indigenous to the area. During the warmer season, for about 1-3 weeks, the Fagerstroms also placed a camper trailer on blocks on the disputed parcel. The Fagerstroms and their children visited the property several times during the warmer season to fish, gather berries, clean the premises, and play. In total, their conduct and improvements went well beyond "mere casual and occasional trespasses" and instead "evinced a purpose to exercise exclusive dominion over the property." See [Peters v. Juneau-Douglas Girl Scout Council, 519 P.2d 826, 830 (Alaska 1974)]. That others were free to pick berries and fish is consistent with the conduct of a hospitable landowner, and undermines neither the continuity nor exclusivity of their possession. See id. at 831 (claimant "merely acting as any other hospitable landowner might" in allowing strangers to come on land to dig clams).

With respect to the notoriety requirement, a quick investigation of the premises, especially during the season which it was best suited for use, would have been sufficient to place a reasonably diligent landowner on notice that someone may have been exercising dominion and control over at least the northern portion of the property. Upon such notice, further inquiry would indicate that members of the community regarded the Fagerstroms as the owners. Continuous, exclusive, and notorious possession were thus established.

Nome 2000 also argues that the Fagerstroms did not establish hostility. It claims that "the Fagerstroms were required to prove that they intended to claim the property as their own." According to Nome 2000, this intent was lacking as the Fagerstroms thought of themselves not as owners but as stewards pursuant to the traditional system of Native Alaskan land usage. We reject this argument and hold that all of the elements of adverse possession were met.

What the Fagerstroms believed or intended has nothing to do with the question whether their possession was hostile. See *Peters*, 519 P.2d at 832 (with respect to the requirement of hostility, the possessor's "beliefs as to the true legal ownership of the land, his good faith or bad faith in entering into possession . . . are all irrelevant."); The Law of Property at 761 (citing, inter alia, *Peters* for the view "of most decisions and of nearly all scholars, that what the possessor believes or intends should have nothing to do with [hostility]"). Hostility is instead determined by application of an objective test which simply asks whether the possessor "acted toward the land as if he owned it," without the permission of one with legal authority to give possession. *Hubbard*, 684 P.2d at 848 (citing *Peters*, 519 P.2d at 832). As indicated, the Fagerstroms' actions toward the property were consistent with ownership of it, and Nome 2000 offers no proof that the Fagerstroms so acted with anyone's permission. That the Fagerstroms' objective manifestations of ownership may have been accompanied by what was described as a traditional Native Alaskan mind-set is irrelevant. To hold otherwise would be inconsistent with precedent and patently unfair.

Having concluded that the Fagerstroms established the elements of adverse possession, we turn to the question whether they were entitled to the entire disputed parcel. Specifically, the question presented is whether the jury could reasonably conclude that the Fagerstroms adversely possessed the southerly portion of the disputed parcel.

Absent color of title,[10] only property actually possessed may be acquired by adverse possession. Bentley Family Trust v. Lynx Enterprises, Inc., 658 P.2d 761, 768 (Alaska 1983) and Alaska National Bank v. Linck, 559 P.2d at 1049, 1052-53 n.8 (Alaska 1977). See also *Krebs,* 768 P.2d at 126 and n.7 (recognizing the possibility that the requirements of adverse possession may be met only as to a portion of a disputed parcel). Here, from the summer of 1977 through the summer of 1978, the Fagerstroms' only activity on the southerly portion of the land included use of the pre-existing trails in connection with subsistence and recreational activities, and picking up litter. They claim that these activities, together with their placement of the cornerposts, constituted actual possession of the southerly portion of the parcel. Nome 2000 argues that this activity did not constitute actual possession and, at most, entitled the Fagerstroms to an easement by prescription across the southerly portion of the disputed parcel.

Nome 2000 is correct. The Fagerstroms' use of the trails and picking up of litter, although perhaps indicative of adverse use, would not provide the reasonably diligent owner with visible evidence of another's exercise of dominion and control. To this, the cornerposts add virtually nothing. Two of the four posts are located well to the west of the disputed parcel. Of the two that were allegedly placed on the parcel in 1970, the one located on the southerly portion of the parcel disappeared at an unknown time. The Fagerstroms maintain that because the disappearing stake was securely in place in 1970, we should infer that it remained for a "significant period." Even if we draw this inference, we fail to see how two posts on a rectangular parcel of property can, as the Fagerstroms put it, constitute "the objective act of taking physical possession" of the parcel. The two posts simply do not serve to mark off the boundaries of the disputed parcel and, therefore, do not evince an exercise of dominion and control over the entire parcel. Thus, we conclude that the superior court erred in its denial of Nome 2000's motion for a directed verdict as to the southerly portion. This case is

---

10. "Color of title exists only by virtue of a written instrument which purports to pass title to the claimant, but which is ineffective because of a defect in the means of conveyance or because the grantor did not actually own the land he sought to convey." *Hubbard,* 684 P.2d at 847. As noted above, see n.6, the Fagerstroms do not claim the disputed parcel by virtue of a written instrument.

remanded to the trial court, with instructions to determine the extent of
the Fagerstroms' acquisition in a manner consistent with this opinion.

NOTES AND QUESTIONS

1.   **State the test.** What is the test for adverse possession set forth in
the *Nome 2000* case?

2.   **Apply the test.** Upon what evidence does the court base its conclusions concerning whether each element of the test is met? In applying the
test, which element(s) of the test does the court focus upon? Why? What
years does the court focus upon? Why?

3.   **Actual and exclusive possession.** *Actual possession:* The general
rule is that an adverse possessor must use land as an ordinary true owner
would use it. Most courts require a lesser showing in the context of undeveloped lands: "wild and undeveloped land that is not readily susceptible
to habitation, cultivation, or improvement does not require the same quality of possession as residential or arable land, since the usual acts of ownership are impossible or unreasonable." 7 Richard R. Powell and Patrick J.
Rohan, Powell on Real Property ¶1012[2] at 91-98 (16th ed. 1993).

> Wild, undeveloped lands so situated and of such character that they cannot
> be readily improved, cultivated or resided upon involve a very different de-
> gree of control evidenced by much less actual exercise of ownership . . . [as]
> making improvements, cultivation of the soil and residing on it are impossible
> or unreasonable.

3 American Law of Property §15.3 at 766-767 (A. James Casner ed., 1952 &
Supp. 1977). One commentator had argued that this test makes owners of
wild lands too vulnerable to adverse possession, pointing to cases where
owners lost land on which adverse possessors' acts did not give true owners
effective notice. John G. Sprankling, An Environmental Critique of Adverse
Possession, 79 Cornell L. Rev. 816, 827 (1994). See, e.g., Butler v. Lindsey,
361 S.E.2d 621, 623-624 (S.C. Ct. App. 1987) (court implies that docking
boats and hunting are sufficient to establish adverse possession); Barnard
v. Elmer, 515 A.2d 1209 (N.H. 1986) (occasional timbering and cutting
Christmas trees sufficient to establish adverse possession); Quarles v. Ar-
cega, 841 P.2d 550 (N.M. Ct. App. 1992), *cert. denied,* 841 P.2d 1149 (N.M.
1992) (seasonal grazing sustains a claim for adverse possession of range
land); Stowell v. Swift, 576 A.2d 204 (Me. 1990) (adverse possession of large
forest tract established by gathering firewood, removing gravel, hunting
and picnicking). See generally, Sprankling, *supra,* at 829-834, 836 ("Not surprisingly, owners in wild lands cases who did visit their land during the statutory period commonly testify in later proceedings that they saw no traces of
the activities upon which the adverse possessors rely").

Exclusive possession: Cases hold that the claimant's possession must be exclusive and that a "scrambled" possession is not enough. But the cases rather scramble the doctrine. One thing that "exclusive" will mean is that A's occupancy must be to the exclusion of O, the original owner — not entirely self-evident even when A claims adversely to O. (Why should an occasional *use* by O interrupt A's claim?) But "exclusive" seems (usually) not to mean that only one person at a time may acquire an adverse interest. For example, if A and B together occupy O's parcel and are acting in concert, they may obtain a cotenancy interest. (Different result if A and B are acting adversely to each other, as well as to O.) Nor will A's occupancy be nullified if he overlooks an occasional trespass by strangers or gives a permissive use to others, so long as his occupancy remains consistent with a claim of ownership.

4. **Open and notorious possession.** The key to open and notorious possession, as *Nome 2000* indicates, is notice to the true owner. The focus generally is not on *actual notice,* but on whether a reasonable true owner would have been placed on notice under the circumstances. See Roger Cunningham et al., The Law of Property §11.7 at 810-811 (2d ed. 1993) (notice is "seeing what reasonable inspection would disclose"). Consider the following:

a. Construction of a 16-story apartment building began in 1960. While excavating for the foundation, the plaintiff discovered that the Sixth Avenue subway had been encroaching (30 feet beneath the surface) since its construction 21 years before. In a suit for trespass, the plaintiff denied any knowledge of the encroachment prior to 1960. Has the defendant acquired an interest by operation of law? 509 Sixth Avenue Corp. v. New York City Transit Auth., 203 N.E.2d 486 (N.Y. 1964) (claim is not barred because subterranean encroachment was a continuous trespass giving rise to successive causes of action, plaintiff not limited by three-year statute of limitations for injury to property).

b. Plaintiff and defendant were adjoining landowners. In 1883 a cave opening was discovered on defendant's land, and almost at once Marengo's Cave, as it was called, became a popular attraction. The plaintiff learned only in 1932, 25 years after he had acquired title, that part of the cave extended beneath his land, yet he was well acquainted with the cave throughout this period. Plaintiff sues to quiet title. Result? Marengo Cave Co. v. Ross, 10 N.E.2d 917 (Ind. 1937) (use of land beneath plaintiff's property was trespass and was under such circumstances that the owner did not know or by the exercise of reasonable care, could not know of the secret occupancy. Such trespass, even in excess of 20 years, does not give fee-simple title against the holder of legal title because the possession was not open, notorious, or exclusive as required by law of adverse possession).

Many modern property scholars think that *Marengo Cave* was incorrectly decided, according to Professor A. Dan Tarlock, Bill of Particulars, Winter 1977-78, at 7.

5. **"Adverse" or "hostile" possession.** The requirement of adversity or hostility is the most confused area of adverse possession law; the Fisher excerpt, *supra* §5.2, suggests why.[3] To mute adverse possession's redistributive spin, some U.S. courts limit adverse possession to situations where the adverse possessor mistakenly thought he owned the land. See, e.g., Halpern v. Lacy Inv. Corp., 379 S.E.2d 519 (Ga. 1989):

> We hold that the correct rule is that one must enter upon the land claiming in good faith the right to do so. To enter upon the land without any honest claim of right to do so is but a trespass and can never ripen into prescriptive title. . . . Here there was evidence that the Halperns knew the parcel of land was owned by another yet they simply took possession when their offer to purchase was declined.

Good faith adverse possession usually involves mistaken boundaries. See, e.g. Lewis v. Moorehead, 522 N.W.2d 1 (S.D. 1994). One commentator has argued that, even though most states reject the *good-faith test,* they in fact award adverse possession only to good faith possessors by manipulating the other requirements. Richard Helmholz, Adverse Possession and Subjective Intent, 61 Wash. U. L.Q. 331 (1983). A reply claimed that the cases do not support his conclusion. Roger A. Cunningham, Adverse Possession and Subjective Intent: A Reply to Professor Helmholz, 64 Wash. U. L.Q. 1 (1986). Helmholz responded that Cunningham had misinterpreted the case law. Richard Helmholz, More on Subjective Intent: A Response to Professor Cunningham, 64 Wash. U. L.Q. 65 (1986). Commentators agree that most modern courts do not explicitly apply the good faith test for adverse possession. See Grantland M. Clapacs, "When in Nome . . .": Custom, Culture and the Objective Standard in Alaskan Adverse Possession Law, 11 Alaska L. Rev. 301 (1994) (citing Peters v. Juneau-Douglas Girl Scout Council, 519 P.2d 826, 832 (Alaska 1974): "his good faith or bad faith in entering into possession . . . are irrelevant" and Per C. Olsen, Adverse Possession in Oregon: The Belief-in-Ownership Requirement, 23 Envtl. L. 1297, 1298 (1993) (stating that the majority of states find a good faith belief in ownership to be irrelevant to policies of adverse possession)).

While some courts require adverse possessors to prove good faith, others require exactly the opposite subjective intent: that the adverse possessor must be aware that the land in question is owned by someone else and intend to take it anyway. Under this *intent to dispossess test,* possession by someone who mistakenly thinks she owns the land in question does not give rise to adverse possession. See, e.g., Ellis v. Jansing, 620 S.W.2d 569 (Tex. 1981) (holding no adverse possession because the adverse possessor

---

3. Note that "hostility" for purposes of adverse possession does not entail ill will. "While the word 'hostile' has been held not to mean ill will or hostility, it does imply the intent to hold title against the record title holder." Vlachos v. Witherow, 118 A.2d 174, 177 (Pa. 1955).

"never claimed or intended to claim any property other than that described in his deed . . . and he never intended to claim any property owned by the abutting property owners"). The origin of this test is obscure; few courts or commentators endorse it. But the existence of a test that openly challenges the norm of enforcing existing property owners' expectations remains intriguing.

By far the majority of modern courts use an *objective test* for assessing whether the adversity requirement has been met. 3 American Law of Property §15.4 (A. J. Casner ed., 1952 & Supp. 1977). In other words, most American courts have adopted the English approach, which does not focus on the adverse possessor's intent: The statute of limitations begins to run as soon as the true owner is dispossessed by someone who takes possession inconsistent with his own. Chaplin v. Sanders, 100 Wash. 2d 853, 861, 676 P.2d 431, 436 (1984) (adverse possessor's "subjective belief regarding his true interest in the land and his intent to dispossess or not dispossess another is irrelevant"); Smith v. Tippett, 569 A.2d 1186 (D.C. 1990).

Still other courts handle adversity through presumptions. Two opposing presumptions exist: some courts rely on a *presumption of permission,* in which case the adverse possessor will lose absent evidence that the use was nonpermissive; or courts use a *presumption of hostility,* in which case the adverse possessor will win absent evidence that the use was permissive. In the ordinary case, where no direct evidence exists regarding intent, the presumption will determine who wins the case.

Most courts use the presumption of hostility. Roger Cunningham et al., The Law of Property §11.7, at 760-761 (1984). This means that the adverse possessor need only show that he possessed a piece of land to satisfy the hostility requirement — in effect, the hostility requirement adds nothing beyond the requirement for actual possession.

Jurisdictions that use a presumption of hostility do not apply the presumption in situations where use typically is permissive. Thus, possession by a co-owner, as where siblings own land jointly, is exempted from the presumption of hostility. See Y A Bar Livestock Co. v. Harkness, 887 P.2d 1211 (Mont. 1994), and Le Vasseur v. Roullman, 20 P.2d 250 (Mont. 1933).

6. **Continuity.** Continuous means something less than unbroken physical presence for every instant of the limitations period. For example, where the premises were vacant for various intervals between tenancies, a court wrote:

> While no principle of law of adverse possession is more firmly settled in Kentucky than that requiring continuous and uninterrupted possession for the full statutory period in order to ripen an adverse claim into a legal title, an exception to the rule is just as well recognized; that a temporary break or interruption, not of unreasonable duration, does not destroy the continuity of the adverse possession and where the periods of vacancy are occasioned by change of possession or by the substitution and possession of one tenant for another which are not of longer duration than is reasonable in view of the

character of the land and the uses to which it is adopted and devoted, they do not constitute interruption of possession destroying its continuity in legal contemplation where there is no intention to abandon.

Gillis v. Curd, 117 F.2d 705, 710 (6th Cir. 1941). Note that the test for continuity (use expected of an owner) is the same as the test for actual possession quoted above. See Ray v. Beacon Hudson Management Corp., 88 N.Y.2d 154 (1996) (occupation of summer cottage for one month each summer coupled with regular efforts to secure and improve premises sufficient to establish adverse possession. In fact, the continuity requirement is often subsumed into courts' discussion of "actual possession." See John G. Sprankling, An Environmental Critique of Adverse Possession, 79 Cornell L. Rev. 816 (1994).

7.   **If an adverse possessor proves ownership, how much does he own?** Once the *Nome 2000* court concludes its discussion of whether the test for adverse possession has been met for any part of the land, it turns to the issue of *how much* land the adverse possessor possessed. The latter issue is called the issue of constructive adverse possession. What test does this court use to resolve this issue? How is the issue resolved? Compare the test in *Nome 2000* with that discussed, *infra,* when the occupant claims that she has "color of title."

8.   **Doctrinal problem.** A and B are neighbors. A constructs a fence on what she incorrectly believes to be the boundary line between her land and B's. In fact, the fence is five feet over the boundary, on B's land. A uses the land as an ordinary owner would for the statutory period; B then learns the truth and sues to eject A. Who will win? (Be sure to answer the question in all possible types of jurisdictions.)

9.   **Advocacy problem.** You represent an environmental group dissatisfied with your state's adverse possession statute. Your initial proposal to your allies in the legislature is to redraft the statute to exempt privately owned wild land from adverse possession, but you have been informed that that approach stands no chance in the current legislature. Propose an alternative solution that achieves (as much as possible of) your goals.

10.   **Claim for rental value.** In many jurisdictions, the limitations period for an action in contract (or quasi contract) is six years. If A's possession ripens into title in 1996, may the original owner, D, still recover the rental value of the premises for A's occupancy between 1990 and 1996? Cf. Counce v. Yount-Lee Oil Co., 87 F.2d 572 (5th Cir. 1937), *cert. denied sub nom.* G. B. Wilkinson Estate, Inc. v. Yount-Lee Oil Co., 302 U.S. 693 (1937); Breuer v. Covert, 614 P.2d 1169 (Or. 1980).

11.   **Does the adverse possessor take free of judgments and other nonpossessory interests?** X is a judgment creditor of the original owner, D. If A's adverse possession of D's land ripens into title, does A take free of X's judgment lien? Cf. American Employers Ins. Co. v. Davis, 153 S.W.2d 501 (Tex. Civ. App. 1941). Does A take subject to outstanding mortgages, ease-

ments, and tract restrictions? Cf. 6 Powell, Powell on Real Property ¶1025 at 762.9 (Rohan ed. 1973).

12. **Improvements by adverse possessors.** What happens when a would-be adverse possessor makes improvements or additions to a property but fails to gain title through adverse possession? At common law, improvements and additions made without right became the property of the owner. The modern trend has been to grant market value compensation to the occupant or allow for the removal of fixtures or other improvements upon repossession by the true owner. See Kelvin H. Dickinson, Mistaken Improvers of Real Estate, 64 N.C. L. Rev. 37 (1985).

b.   Occupancy under Color of Title

Many states give favored treatment to an occupancy that begins under "color of title" — that is, under a writing (deed, mortgage, decree, etc.) professing to pass title, but not doing so, usually because of a procedural defect or a defect in the grantor's title. While color of title is rarely a necessary element of adverse possession, the claimant having a semblance of title often enjoys two statutory benefits: (1) a shorter limitations period; (2) use of the doctrine of "constructive possession." The Illinois statute, for one, requires only a 7-year occupancy under color of title against 20 years for other occupancies. Ill. Stat. Ann. ch. 735, ¶5, §13-101 n.n.79, 87 (Smith-Hurd 1992 & Supp. 1996); see also In re Tobin, 531 N.E. 2d. 440, 444 (Ill. App. Ct. 1989) (explaining that the statutory period is shortened when the person claiming has paid property taxes under color of title and has met the good faith requirement).[4]

Constructive possession permits the occupant to gain title to the entire parcel described in the written instrument, even though his occupancy extends only to some of the parcel. Thus, the New York statute provides:

> For the purpose of constituting an adverse possession by a person claiming a title founded upon a written instrument or a judgment or decree, . . . [w]here a known farm or a single lot has been partly improved, the portion of the farm or lot that has been left not cleared or not inclosed, according to the usual course and custom of the adjoining country, is deemed to have been occupied for the same length of time as the part improved and cultivated.

N.Y. Real Prop. Act. Law §512 (McKinney 1979). Lawmakers invented the doctrine of constructive possession to address the problem of poor title records that plagued the westward movement. Settlers would invest their

---

4. Most color of title statutes require the occupant to pay real estate taxes during the occupancy period on the parcel claimed. California imposes a tax-paying requirement on all claims of adverse possession. Cal. Civ. Proc. Code §325 (West 1995).

energies in clearing land, then learn they had faulty title. Conventional adverse possession doctrine would have secured title only to the land actually worked.

As courts have fleshed out the doctrine, they have generally refused to extend title to a noncontiguous parcel, to a contiguous parcel separately owned, or even, in some cases, to a contiguous parcel held by the same original owner.

PROBLEMS

1. Manticore Corp. owns three contiguous lots, #1-#3. In 1985, shortly before the company treasurer absconds with $2 million of corporate funds, he conveys all three to A. The sale is invalid because the treasurer does not have authority under the corporate charter to authorize sales without the signature of the CEO of the company. A moves onto lot #1 and builds a modest farming operation, much like other such operations in the area. Later that year, B moves onto lot #2 without any deed whatsoever. The corporation sues to eject both A and B in 1995. The relevant statutes of limitations are seven years for adverse possession generally and five years for adverse possession under color of title. Who will win? What if the tract had not been divided into lots? See 3 American Law of Property §15.11 at 819-820 (A. J. Casner ed., 1952 & Supp. 1977):

> Where entry is made under an invalid deed or other written instrument which purports to transfer title to the possessor, actual possession of a small portion of the parcel described in the record of such instrument gives constructive possession of the rest of the parcel included within the description described in the deed without proof of such acts of the user of the unoccupied part and without proof of fences or other visible boundaries. . . . This is called constructive possession under "color of title" of such part not actually occupied. . . . If part of the parcel is in the actual possession of the owner, his prior constructive possession prevents any constructive possession in a trespasser who actually takes possession of a small part of the property involved under color of title and his adverse possession is limited to the land actually occupied by him.

See also Pepper v. O'Dowd, 39 Wis. 538 (1876) (holding that when one enters into and holds continual possession of part of the premises included under color of title, he shall be deemed to hold adversely all the premises included in it); Perpignani v. Vonasek, 408 N.W.2d 1 (Wis. 1987) (citing Pepper v. O'Dowd); Apo v. Dillingham Inv. Corp., 549 P.2d 740 (Haw. 1976), *review denied*, 57 Haw. 672 (1976) (finding that ownership extends to whole parcel when there is proof of possession of a portion of the parcel); Arrien v. Levanger, 502 P.2d 573 (Or. 1972) (title of whole parcel can be acquired through actual possession of only a part, if possessor has color of title).

2.   A owns a 250-acre farm. B occupies and improves the back 100 acres pursuant to an invalid deed from C. A sues to quiet title to the entire 250 acres. Will he win? See, e.g., Harrison v. Beaty, 137 S.W.2d 946 (Tenn. App. 1939); Moore v. Brannan, 304 S.W.2d 660, 667 (Tenn. App. 1957) ("Evidence of adverse possession is strictly construed, every presumption being in favor of the holder of legal title."); Goen v. Sansbury, 149 A.2d 17, 21 (Md. 1959); Culpepper v. Weaver Bros. Lumber Corp. 195 So. 349 (La. 1940). (Do you need additional information?)

3.   Lot #1 is owned by Mr. Gyme, who lives in a different state; lot #2 is owned by another absentee owner, Mr. Starr. Mr. Scam sells both lots to a gentleman farmer, Avery Post, who lives in the farmhouse on lot #1 for the period set by the statute of limitations but does not farm the land on lot #2 because it has reverted to forest. Once Mr. Post finds out that his deed from Mr. Scam was invalid, he sues to quiet title to both lots. Will he win? What if Mr. Post has grazed cattle on lot #2?

c.   Tacking

The term "tacking," well known to sailors, tailors, and carpet layers, also has its meaning for the property lawyer. Suppose that A enters Blackacre and remains in possession, adversely and continuously for 19 of the statutory 20 years. A dies, and his heir, AH, replaces him in possession. Must AH complete a 20-year term in his own right or may he avail himself of the ancestor's prior occupancy? Although Blackacre's owner has a theoretical argument for insisting that the statute should run anew, the courts have allowed the two periods of occupancy to be joined or *tacked* together. Can you explain why?

Tacking occurs whenever the successive occupiers are said to be in "privity of estate." Privity of estate is a term that recurs often and, to the dismay of law students, is not always blessed with quite the same content. Here, however, privity would be satisfied if the first and second occupiers had one of five relationships: grantor-grantee; landlord-tenant; testator-devisee; decedent-heir; mortgagor-mortgagee. In each instance, either a consensual or a legally formed nexus exists to join the two occupiers. See Howard v. Kunto, 477 P.2d 210, 215 (Wash. 1970), *overruled on other grounds,* Chaplin v. Sanders, 676 P.2d 431 (Wash. 1984) ("[W]e believe the requirement of 'privity' is no more than judicial recognition of the need for some reasonable connection between successive occupants of real property"). If A is forcibly ousted by B, no privity exists. See, e.g., Doe ex dem. Harlan v. Brown, 4 Ind. 143, 145 (1853). What policy goals does the privity requirement serve? See the Fisher excerpt, *supra* §5.2.

Suppose that the adverse claim depends on the tacking between A and B, grantor-grantee, but that A's deed to B fails to describe the parcel claimed. Has tacking occurred? Compare Berryhill v. Moore, 881 P.2d 1182

(Ariz. 1994) (holding that adverse possessors could "tack" time of previous landowners' tenants' use of disputed property for purposes of establishing adverse possession since tenants' use inured to benefit of previous landowners); Smith v. Ritchie, 1988 WL 87680 (Tenn. App. Aug. 26, 1988) (refusing to allow grantee to tack time of possession onto that of grantor because no evidence exists to show that grantor undertook to transfer possessory right in disputed area to grantee); King Ranch Properties Ltd. Partnership v. Smith, 762 P.2d 558 (Ariz. 1988) (holding that evidence that tenant actually possessed and farmed subject property during his entire lease period pursuant to lease was sufficient to establish privity so as to permit tacking).

PROBLEMS

Assume that all problems take place in a jurisdiction with a ten-year statute of limitations.

1. Fox buys a tract of land from Turtle. In 1980 Rabbit begins to adversely possess this land but is thrown off the land by Deer in 1987. Who owns the land in 1990? Can anyone eject Deer? See 3 American Law of Property §15.10 at 816-817 (A. J. Casner ed., 1952 & Supp. 1977) ("When the adverse possessor is ousted by a third party without right his possession cannot be tacked to the prior possession because of lack of privity. . . .[T]he owner has a new right of action in ejectment against the third party which arises when he ousts the original adverse possessor.).

What if Rabbit leaves in 1987 but reenters five weeks later? If Fox remains inactive, will Rabbit own the land in 1990? If not then, when? See 3 American Law of Property §15.10 at 818 (A. J. Casner ed., 1952 & Supp. 1977) ("[P]ossessory title is ended by . . . abandonment and (adverse possessor's) subsequent re-entry establishes a new possessory title and the statute starts to run anew").

What if Rabbit abandoned the property in 1987 and Deer immediately begins his adverse possession. When will Deer own the land? See 3 American Law of Property §15.10 at 815-816 (A. J. Casner ed., 1952 & Supp. 1977) ("[T]he two possessions may be tacked . . . only where the succeeding possessor holds as successor to the possessory title . . . either as . . . heir, devisee, or grantee").

2. Rabbit begins to adversely possess land in 1970 and dies in 1977, bequeathing the land to Deer for life and remainder to Fox. Deer takes control of the land and dies in 1993. Who owns the land? See 3 American Law of Property §15.4 at 778-785, §15.10 (A. J. Casner ed., 1952 & Supp. 1977). ("The adverse possession is . . . continued in the grantee or devisee for life or for years, so that his possessory estate for life or for years so transferred to him becomes absolute when the true owner's action in ejectment is barred by the statute, as does the remainder created at the same time").

d.   Disability

One other factor must be present before the statute of limitations can begin to run: The claimant must have capacity to sue. If the aggrieved person is disabled when the cause of action accrues, the statute is tolled. The 1623 statute, *supra,* set an early pattern for listing the conditions of disability and their relationship to the limitations period:

> II. Provided nevertheless, That if any Person or Persons . . . entitled to such Writ . . . or (having) such Right . . . of Entry . . . shall be at the Time . . . the said Right . . . first . . . accrued . . . within the Age of one and twenty years, Feme Covert, Non Compos Mentis, imprisoned or beyond the Seas, that then such Person and Persons . . . shall or may, notwithstanding the said twenty Years be expired, bring his Action, or make his Entry, as he might have done before this Act; (2) so as such Person and Persons . . . shall within ten Years next after his and their full Age, Discoverture, coming of sound Mind, Enlargement out of Prison, or coming into this Realm, or Death, take Benefit of and sue forth the same, and at no time after the said ten Years.

Foreign travel or a woman's equally venturesome journey into marriage are no longer legally disabling events, nor is imprisonment in most jurisdictions. But infancy and, less often, mental incapacity remain so.

To understand their effect in states having adopted the English model, work through the following problems:

(a)   A enters Blackacre in 1970 and remains in possession, adversely and continuously thereafter. In 1970, the Blackacre owner, O, is five years old. When does the statute of limitations expire?

(b)   A enters Blackacre in 1970 and remains in possession, adversely and continuously thereafter. In 1970, Blackacre's owner, O, is legally incompetent. O dies in 1985. When does the statute of limitations expire?

(c)   A enters Blackacre in 1970 and remains in possession, adversely and continuously thereafter. In 1970, Blackacre's owner, O, is 15 years old and also legally incompetent. In 1980, O is declared legally competent. When does the statute of limitations expire?

(d)   A enters Blackacre in 1970 and remains in possession, adversely and continuously thereafter. In 1975, Blackacre's owner, O, is declared legally incompetent. O dies in 1985. When does the statute of limitations expire?

(e)   A enters Blackacre in 1970 and remains in possession, adversely and continuously thereafter. In 1970, Blackacre is owned by O and P, as tenants in common. O is legally incompetent. In 1986, O is declared legally competent. When does the statute of limitations expire?

In some states, the limitations period runs for its full term after the disability ends. In a few others, the statute expires after a given interval even if the disability remains.

Of the three statutory approaches to disability, which one do you prefer? Is there any policy justification for retaining the disability feature?

In its relation to adverse possession, disability may appear in a rather distinctive form. Suppose that the ownership of Blackacre is divided into present and future interests when the adverse occupancy begins. Does possession ripen into title at one time against both sets of interest holders? Remember that the cited statute speaks of persons "entitled" to the writ of entry. Take these examples:

(f)   A enters Blackacre in 1970 and remains in possession, adversely and continuously thereafter. In 1970, Blackacre is owned by O, for life, remainder in P. O dies in 1980. Given a 20-year limitations period, who owns Blackacre in 1995? What if O were still alive? 6 Powell, Real Property ¶1014 (Rohan ed. 1991); 3 American Law of Property §15.8 at 804 (A. J. Casner ed., 1952 & Supp. 1977). ("[The owner's] right of action is what passes to his transferees, so that when held by a life tenant followed by a remainder, these succeeding owners take it subject to the running of the statute which accrued before the transfer").

(g)   A enters Blackacre in 1970 and remains in possession, adversely and continuously thereafter. In 1970, Blackacre is owned by O, for life, remainder in those persons whom O shall appoint by will. Given a 20-year limitations period, who owns Blackacre in 1990?

(h)   A enters Blackacre in 1970 and remains in possession, adversely and continuously thereafter. In 1960, Blackacre was leased to O for a term of 99 years, reversion in P. Given a 20-year limitations period, who owns Blackacre in 1990?

(i)   A enters Blackacre in 1970 and remains in possession, adversely and continuously thereafter. In 1969, O transfers Blackacre to P, for life, remainder to Q. Given a 20-year limitations period, who owns Blackacre in 1980?

If these were cases of first impression, what factors might the court consider in reaching its decision?

§5.4   Adverse Possession, Squatting, and Homesteading

Property rights are often interpreted in the eyes of the beholder. One person's "adverse possessor" is another person's "squatter." In fact, until the statute of limitation has run against the legal owner, anyone else in possession of the property without permission could be called a squatter.[5]

Squatting is no doubt as old as the concept of real property ownership rights; however, it has a unique place in recent urban history.[6] Most American cities have seen a rise in abandoned housing (titles to which cities frequently claim for nonpayment of taxes) as well as a demand for affordable housing. For many reasons, the properties abandoned are just that type of housing.

Could urban residents use adverse possession to acquire title to abandoned properties? Consider the following: How did the doctrine of adverse possession make Ms. Lee and Mr. Donaldson vulnerable?

DAMON DARLIN, URBAN PIONEERS: DETROITERS WHO SQUAT IN ABANDONED HOUSES FIND RISKS, REWARDS

Wall St. J., Sept. 5, 1985, at 1

DETROIT — Denise Lee and her fiancé, Glenn Donaldson, hacked through chest-high weeds, gnarled bushes and grapevines as thick as ships' cable to get to the house of their dreams last spring.

Once inside, they started shoveling out the rotting garbage that was piled more than a foot deep in each room and even filled the bathtub. Ms. Lee scrubbed dried human waste off the living-room floor with ammonia, while Mr. Donaldson, his eyes watering because of the fumes, installed a toilet to replace the one that had been stolen. "If we weren't fixing it up, it would be burned down," said an exhausted Ms. Lee during a break. "This will be the best-looking house on the street. It will be ours."

Ms. Lee and Mr. Donaldson aren't yuppies gentrifying a neighborhood. They are squatters. And the northwest Detroit bungalow they worked on is one at least 10,000 abandoned or vacant homes here. If caught by the city, the couple and Ms. Lee's four children could have been evicted. "What they were doing is illegal," says Albert Thomas, the administrative assistant

---

5. A British judge defined a squatter as "one who, without any colour of rights, enters on an unoccupied house or land, intending to stay there as long as he can. He may seek to justify or excuse his conduct. He may say he was homeless and that this house or land was standing empty. But this plea is of no avail in law." McPhail v. Persons Unknown, 1 Ch. 447, 456 B (1973) (Denning, J.)

6. It is not only in U.S. cities that squatting is growing. In Mexico and other Latin American countries, governments are encouraging the approach to low-income housing that squatters take. In Mexico, the government offers assistance to squatters by expropriating squatted land and selling it to residents for a price well below market value. See Jane E. Larson, Free Markets Deep in the Heart of Texas, 84 Geo. L.J. 179 (1995). See also David Collier, Squatters and Oligarchs: Authoritarian Rule and Policy Change in Peru (1976) (Peru); Janice E. Perlman, The Myth of Marginality: Urban Poverty and Politics in Rio de Janeiro (1976) (Brazil).

for Detroit's Building and Safety Department. "It's called violating property rights." It is also risky, as the couple would eventually find out.

Some Supporters

Not everyone thinks that squatting is bad. Some people believe that squatters are Detroit's best hope of rebuilding inner-city neighborhoods. "Some houses are getting fixed up, people are getting houses," says Mary-ann Mahaffey, a city council member who supports Detroit's scores of squatters. "Neighbors don't have to worry about their kids doing drugs or being raped in the abandoned homes."

Two years ago, Detroit's city council unanimously passed an ordinance allowing homeless families to take over abandoned houses. But [the Mayor] won't implement the law. He is afraid that homeowners will return and sue the city for "letting squatters take their property" forcing the squatters back out on the street, despite all the hard work.

The city has its own low-income housing programs and a lottery to sell about 300 abandoned homes each year to poor people. But while the city erects colorful billboards urging people to move back into Detroit, it tears down some 2,000 abandoned homes a year at a cost of $6 million, or about $3,000 a home.

That would go a long way toward fixing up a house, squatters say. "If the mayors keep tearing down houses in the neighborhoods, there won't be anyone to come to the downtown that he's been fixing up," adds Grant Williams, the former executive director of the Detroit chapter of the Association of Community Organizations for Reform Now, or ACORN.[7] The group advises squatters, most of whom are poor and black, and it is suing the mayor in state court to make him enforce the ordinance.

One Explanation

Henry Murphy, who isn't a squatter but lives in a neighborhood filled with abandoned homes, puts it simply: "The whole system is all hooched up."

Abandoned homes aren't found only in Detroit. New York City, St. Louis and Philadelphia grappled with huge abandonment problems. The problem also isn't confined to the old industrial cities of the Northeast and Midwest. Indeed, if it weren't for cactuses in the front yards, the graffiti-covered, boarded-up and fire-scorched bungalows in North Las Vegas, Nev., would look just like northwestern Detroit.

---

7. ACORN began as a grass-roots organization in Philadelphia that placed 200 squatters into single-family houses owned by the federal Department of Housing and Urban Development. ACORN spread ultimately to ten states. — Eds.

But Detroit has more abandoned homes than most — more than 12 miles, according to conservative estimates, and even more counting vacant lots. In the city's east-side slums abandoned houses outnumber inhabited ones on many streets. Even on the northwest side, which is historically the first step for Detroiters into the middle class, few streets — black, white or integrated — don't have at least one. It is such a big problem says a top city official, that "we truly don't know what to do about it."

POPULATION LOSSES

The root of the problem is clear: the exodus from Detroit. It started after the 1967 riots and continued through several auto-industry recessions. In 1983 and 1984, the city lost a total of 51,000 people — 70 people a day.

Sometimes a home is abandoned because its owner is laid off and can't make the mortgage payments. In other instances, the owner discovers that the resale value has dropped substantially below the purchase price or that there aren't any buyers. Unscrupulous absentee landlords rent properties until they are too dilapidated to be profitable and then walk away, leaving tax bills unpaid. Sometimes, an elderly resident dies and the heirs, if there are any, don't want to deal with an aging inner-city house.

But the city is caught in a bind. Because of an old Michigan law passed to protect the state's farmers, only after county taxes are delinquent for three years does the deed revert to the state, which gives it to the city to dispose of. And three years is a long time.

Within weeks after a home is abandoned, scavengers strip the vacant house of pipes, wiring and fixtures, even of exterior bricks. Young vandals playing in the houses cover them with graffiti. (In Detroit, houses marked "Pony" are hangouts for the Pony Boys rings, juvenile drug dealers who take their name from the high-top basketball shoes they favor.) In recent years police have also contended with a rash of rapes in which young schoolgirls have been dragged into abandoned homes. And many houses are eventually set on fire, sometimes, police say, by frustrated neighbors.

Indeed, the homes can start a chain reaction of rising crime and declining property values breeding more abandonment. That angers those left behind.

Viola Jenison lives next to a two-story abandoned house on Lauder Street in northwestern Detroit. The house, which is hidden behind a wall of weeds, used to be grand. But now the windows are broken and the front porch is an obstacle course of spongy rotting wood. Inside, the plaster walls have gaping holes and the oak floors are scorched by small campfires. "Nothing has happened yet, but the way it is going, something will," Mrs. Jenison says. "There are kids in there at night making noise." She wants the frame house torn down.

The squatters see themselves as urban pioneers who can slow a neighborhoods' decline. "I hate the word squatter," says Ms. Lee, who occupied the northwest Detroit bungalow. "It sounds like a dirty word, like scab. A lot of people think we are freeloaders."

"A Better Life"

In a sense they are. But this may be the only way Ms. Lee, an unemployed medical technician on welfare, and Mr. Donaldson who finds work where he can as a handyman, will ever own a house. For many squatters, home ownership and the stability it symbolizes are the real motivation. "I want my kids to have a better life," says Ms. Lee, age 27, whose four girls range in age from a preteen to a young baby. "Maybe in a few years we can sell the house and move into the suburbs," she says.

Last winter, Ms. Lee and Mr. Donaldson drove around the northwest side of Detroit in a borrowed car making a list of abandoned homes. "Most of them needed to be torn down," she says. ACORN showed her how to go to city hall to find out which houses belonged to the federal government — off limits because marshals would immediately evict squatters — and which were scheduled for demolition by the city because they posed such a hazard to the neighborhood. Those on the city list are choice. Their inclusion usually means that the real owners don't want the property and when city inspectors are informed that a house is no longer a hazard, they will remove it from the list.

Ms. Lee and Mr. Donaldson finally found a house on Grandmont Street. "It was near church and Glenn's folks," says Ms. Lee. "Best of all, it was only a block from an elementary school."

When spring came, they went to work. Friends from ACORN, armed with shovels, brooms and lawn clippers, cut down the bushes and dragged out more than 50 garbage bags groaning with trash. Among the items found: an 1801 Indian-head penny and a photograph from the 1930's of a woman and a boy on a pony in front of the house. Ms. Lee guessed that the woman was the homeowner, who neighbors said was dead.

There was a lot to be done on the house, which had been scheduled for demolition within weeks. But the first thing Mr. Donaldson did was hook up the doorbell. "That made it seem like a real home," he says.

Stolen Window Frames

Then came the real work. A fire in the basement had damaged the furnace, and firefighters had cut a gaping hole in the roof. Water pipes had burst during the cold winter. "They took the window frames, can you beat that?" Mr. Donaldson asks. Then, noting that the gas meter was stolen and gas was leaking, he adds, "Just one match and the block would have gone up like a bomb."

But Ms. Lee and Mr. Donaldson kept their spirits up. For several weeks, they spent every day — the electricity wasn't connected so they had to quit work at dusk — washing walls, painting and repairing. Driven by a friend, they scoured junkyards for window frames, kitchen counters and a toilet.

Finally, after the holes had been patched, the walls had been painted a pastel blue, green or yellow, and the electricity and the water — though not the gas — had been connected, Ms. Lee, Mr. Donaldson and the four children moved in.

Neighbors lent their support. Several let the squatters use their showers or cook meals. Some even came over to help shovel out the mess or to lend a ladder. "I'm happy as a lark somebody's doing something about that place," said a neighbor. "Now if we can only get to the place down that away."

Some squatters don't tell their new neighbors that they are squatting. Lorraine Griffin is one of them. She wanted to live in a house, but she couldn't accumulate $3,000 for a down payment. When a minister suggested squatting, she said to her two boys, "C'mon we're going to find us a house."

The house they found in November 1983 had been severely damaged by a kitchen fire. Only a single board remained in the kitchen floor. Plaster walls had been destroyed by the firefighters who extinguished the blaze. A burned couch and chair sat in the water-damaged living room, leading her to believe that the owners had just packed up and left after the fire.

"Boy, it was a mess in here" says her son Omar, age four.

But Mrs. Griffin still worries that after all her work, the owner will come back and she will lose the house. "I just pray, 'Please Lord, work everything out,'" she says, "As days go by, you get more comfortable. If they wanted the house, they would have come back by now."

That happened to Ms. Lee and Mr. Donaldson. The little boy on the pony grew up and was living in Canada. His lawyer contacted the couple out of the blue and one day offered to sell them the house for $5,000.

Ms. Lee never knew how they were discovered, but she knew she didn't have $5,000 and neither did her fiancé.

So, they packed their possessions, removed their toilet and left to find another house. . . .

Two major obstacles normally preclude squatters from using adverse possession: (1) title to these properties are frequently claimed by local governments, against whom adverse possession does not run (see *infra* §5.5), and (2) the length of the statutes of limitations is too long to guarantee possessors any security of tenure. In other words, potential squatters quite realistically fear that the absent owners will return and evict them, taking advantage of improvements made to the property.

ACORN (Association of Community Organizers for Reform Now) and other activists in several cities have successfully lobbied for statutes that offer qualified low-income people title to abandoned dwellings in exchange for their labor to fix up the properties. This process is called "urban homesteading," recalling the federal homestead program that settled much of the west in the nineteenth century.

NOTES AND PROBLEMS

1. **Problem.** You have been asked by ACORN to redraft the state's adverse possession statute to make squatting less risky for squatters, while maintaining fairness to owners. What features would you provide?

2. **Nineteenth-century "squatting": the homestead movement.** Seth Borgos, Low-Income Homeownership and the ACORN Squatters Campaign, in Critical Perspectives on Housing 429-431 (Rachel G. Bratt, Chester Hartman, Ann Meyerson eds., 1986):

> . . . To squat is to occupy property without permission of its owner. It is the time-hallowed response of the landless to the contradiction between their own impoverishment and a surfeit of unutilized property.
>
> In nineteenth-century America, with its vast expanses of wilderness, squatting was a common way of life. Though widely sanctioned on the frontier, its extension to settled and urbanizing areas was more problematic. . . . A[] common response is to "tame" squatting by licensing it within a restricted context. In the United States this has gone under the name of "homesteading."
>
> The first national homesteading legislation . . . provided free grants of federal land to applicants who would improve the land for agriculture and reside there for at least five years.
>
> The Homestead Act was the product of a 20-year debate over the disposition of public land on the frontier. Supporters of homesteading contended that it would encourage owner occupancy of land and accelerate settlement; they also saw homesteading as an "escape valve for the urban poor and a way of avoiding downward pressure on wages." Opponents of homesteading argued that "giving away land would lower property values of remaining land and create an injustice to those who had paid for the property." . . .
>
> The initial homesteading proposals reflected the radical view of their sponsors: Grants were to be limited to the poor, and the sale of government land was to be curtailed. But . . . , as finally enacted, the Homestead Act of 1862 contained no eligibility restrictions on income or assets. And the federal government continued to sell prime land to speculators and award large tracts to railroad companies. . . .

3. **Amsterdam.** In the 1960s, squatting became a Netherlands political movement headed by intellectuals, artists, and students. Squatting, at first, resulted from a shortage of available housing. But this soon led to a

protest against developers and property speculators. Organized squatters set up their own alternative government having its own bureaucracy and radio and television stations, and for a time, the *kraker movement,* as it was called, had some political influence. It championed a 1980 law that barred speculation on vacant properties.

In 1983, a pitched battle between squatters and the Amsterdam police lasted two days and ended only after the city agreed to renovate an abandoned building for its illegal tenants. In May 1990, squatters caused a riot in Groningen, a town in northeastern Holland, as they defended three homes from demolition. One hundred thirty-seven persons were arrested after two days of fighting and looting, but the buildings came down. This seems to have been the death rattle of Holland's squatter era. Richard Reeves, The Permissive Dutch, N.Y. Times, Oct. 20, 1985, at §6, 28; Tim Kelsey, Last Ditch Battle for a Return to Bronze Age Values; The Era of the Dutch Squatter Has Come to a Violent End, The Independent, July 22, 1990, at 15.

4.   **New York City's Tompkins Square Park.** In the summer of 1988, New York City's Tompkins Square Park was a "base for nearly 150 homeless people, a playground, sometimes a drug market. It [was] also a gathering place for young and sometimes drunk rock fans . . ." In an attempt to discourage loud congregating in the park at night, a curfew was instituted. In the enforcement of this curfew, "about 100 police officers evicted the park's occupants, *except for the homeless."* The homeless were confined to a quadrant of the park in the hours after the curfew. Several weeks after the initiation of the curfew, a riot erupted when protesters, describing the curfew as an attempt to take the park from the public, engaged in violent conflict with over 100 police officers. Todd S. Purdum, Melee in Tompkins Sq. Park: Violence and Its Provocation, N.Y. Times, Aug. 14, 1988, at 1 (emphasis added).

In June 1991, after months of pressure from neighbors and local officials, police officers demolished an encampment that had been set up by homeless people in the park. Sam Roberts, What Led to Crackdown on Homeless, N.Y. Times, Oct. 28, 1991, at B1.

Nearly five years later, Tompkins Square Park again became the scene of an ugly confrontation, when city police arrested 23 persons protesting the eviction of squatters from three city-owned buildings on the Lower East Side. The squatters had been left alone in these buildings for more than a decade, until the summer of 1994, when the city decided that it wanted to renovate the structures for low-income families. In the litigation that preceded the eviction, a trial court judge granted the squatters a preliminary injunction, holding that they had demonstrated a reasonable chance of prevailing in their claim of ownership by adverse possession. The Appellate Division reversed, and eviction followed shortly. N.Y. Times, Aug. 15, 1996, at B1.

The squatters had rebuilt burnt-out roofs and had replaced electrical and plumbing systems stripped by scavengers. They claimed that but for these improvements, the city would not have had buildings worth renovating. N.Y. Times, Oct. 27, 1995, at B3.

§5.5   Adverse Possession against Government-Owned Lands

HINKLEY v. STATE OF NEW YORK

234 N.Y. 309, 137 N.E. 599 (N.Y. 1992)

CRANE, J. Chapter 555 of the Laws of 1918 provides for the construction of a barge canal terminal at Poughkeepsie, New York, and for the entry upon and acquisition of land needed for the site. The title states the purpose to be "with a view of improving the commerce of the state, and making an appropriation therefor."

Part of the land selected has been the subject of this litigation before the Court of Claims. It consists of property purchased on the water front of the Hudson river in 1818 by Matthew Vassar. Part of the land is upland, and the rest, as it exists today, is filled-in land. For the land under water, with the exception of that known as parcel T 192 (appropriation map), patents were granted by the state. Parcel T 192, which is in question, consist of land bulkheaded and filled in, about 0.615 acres. How early this land, for which there was no patent, was filled in is not definitely known, but it must have been done shortly after the acquisition of the property by Vassar. It appears as filled-in land, docked and bulkheaded, on a map of the incorporated village of Poughkeepsie, dated September, 1834.

Vassar was a brewer, and on this filled-in land was erected a malt house and other buildings. To the north and to the south of parcel T 192 the land under water has been filled in under grants from the state to the respective upland owners. The water front along all of his property has been well bulkheaded and presents a straight and even frontage. The entire land appropriated, therefore, consists of upland and filled-inland, one parcel on the water front having been filled in without authority from the state, other than that which the law may give to riparian owners. For this parcel in question there could be found no grant or patent.

The property which the state has sought to appropriate for the barge canal terminal, including the parcel in question, T 192, was owned or claimed at the time of this proceeding by Etheline H. Hinkley, who received it through mesne conveyances from Matthew Vassar.

The state and the owner entered into negotiations for the purchase of this property, the state offering for the whole tract the sum of $35,000. On examination of the title it was for the first time discovered by the parties that no water grant for parcel T 192 could be found. This, as before stated, was land under water filled in level with the upland. Negotiations were entered into between the state, the city of Poughkeepsie and Mrs. Hinkley, which need not here be referred to at length, and which resulted in Mrs. Hinkley transferring to the state of New York all the upland which she owned at this point, together with the filled-in land for which there had been patents granted, reserving under stipulation parcel T 192, appropriation map, for submission to the Court of Claims. Mrs. Hinkley claimed the fee of this parcel by reason of adverse possession for a period of seventy or eighty years. The state claimed that she had no title, and that, in the interest of navigation, the state could take it without compensation for the barge canal terminal.

In accordance with the stipulation Mrs. Hinkley submitted her claim known as claim No. 16,427 to the Court of Claims on the 15th day of October, 1920, in which she stated her rights to be as follows: "The claimant was at the time of the appropriation the sole owner in fee of the premises appropriated. The plaintiff claims a good and sufficient title to the lands appropriated by and through an uninterrupted adverse possession of the same by her and her preceding grantors for over fifty years before the date of said appropriation and before the filing of her said claim in this court. The plaintiff further claims and alleges that neither the said claimant herein or her preceding grantors, during a period of at least fifty years before said appropriation, or at any time prior thereto, paid any rentals or profits for the use or occupation of the premises so appropriated to the state of New York or to any of its officers or authorities."

By the stipulation of submission previously signed by Mrs. Hinkley it was expressly understood that for the parcel in question she would receive a sum not to exceed $5000 as the value of her right, interest or estate in the property.

The Court of Claims found for the claimant in the sum of $5000, holding that she had established her title by adverse possession. The Appellate Division reversed this award and dismissed the case. The finding of fact that the possession of Mrs. Hinkley and her predecessors in title had been exclusive and adverse to any claim of title on the part of the people of the state of New York was set aside. It is necessary for us, therefore, to determine from the record whether there be any evidence of adverse possession tending to establish title as against the state.

The situation presented is this: An upland owner has certain riparian rights in the Hudson river. In the exercise of those rights he bulkheads and fills in the land under water using the made land as a dock and for the erection of buildings thereon. This possession and use continues for nearly seventy-five years without any interference or claim of authority by the state. No grant or patent has been given to the upland owner for the lands under water which he has filled in. What are the rights of the respective parties?

Section 31 of the Civil Practice Act (L. 1920, ch. 925), formerly section 362 of the Code of Civil Procedure, provides:

§31. When the people will not sue. The people of the state will not sue a person for or with respect to real property, or the issues or profits thereof, by reason of the right or title of the people to the same, unless either:

1. The cause of action accrued within forty years before the action is commenced; or

2. The people, or those from whom they claim, have received the rents and profits of the real property or of some part thereof, within the same period of time.

It may be that there is a distinction in the class of property owned by the state, and that there can be no adverse possession whatever as against the property which the state holds in trust for the public, as distinguished from such property as it may hold in a private or proprietary character. No time, for instance, can run against the state as to property which it could not grant to private individuals, such as forest lands set aside for a park (People v. Baldwin, 197 App. Div. 285; *affd.*, 233 N.Y. 672), or as to canal property, . . . (Donahue v. State of New York, 112 N.Y. 145). . . .

Whether title can be gained by adverse possession as to lands under water which the state could have granted by patent we need not now decide as in our opinion the evidence does not justify the conclusion that the possession of Mrs. Hinkley and her predecessors back to Matthew Vassar has been adverse.

Adverse possession must be exclusive, under no permission or license or favor upon the part of the owner; the claim must be under color of independent title, exclusive of any right derived from the actual owner. . . .

When the entry upon land has been by permission or under some right or authority derived from the owner, adverse possession does not commence until such permission or authority has been repudiated and renounced and the possessor thereafter has assumed the attitude of hostility to any right in the real owner.

Occupation must not only be hostile in its *inception,* but it must continue hostile, and at all times, during the required period of twenty years, challenge the right of the true owner in order to found title by adverse possession upon it. The *entry* must be strictly adverse to the title of the rightful owner, *for if the first possession is by permission it is presumed to so continue until the contrary appears.* If the occupation begins with the recognition of the real owner's estate it is presumed to be subservient, and that the one making the entry intends to hold honestly and not tortiously. The character of the possession depends on the intention with which entry is made and occupation continued. There is no disseisin until there is occupation with intention to claim title, and the fact of entry and the quo animo fix the character of the possession. The burden of proving all the facts necessary to constitute adverse possession is upon the one who asserts it, for in the absence of such proof possession is presumed to be in subordination to the true title. (Lewis v. New York & Harlem R.R. Co., 162 N.Y. 202, 220.)

STAT

She → Hostile to the state?

Excessive use or violation of the right or privilege granted by the owner cannot create adverse possession until it amounts to a claim openly distinct from any claim of ownership on the part of the original proprietor.

"The object of the statute defining the acts essential to constitute an adverse possession is that the real owner may, by unequivocal acts of the usurper, have notice of the hostile claim and be thereby called upon to assert his legal title." (Monnot v. Murphy, 207 N.Y. 240, 245.) See, also, Culver v. Rhodes, 87 N.Y. 348; Flora v. Carbean, 38 N.Y. 111.

Matthew Vassar as riparian owner had certain rights which involved the land under water. These were given to him by law and may be considered as a permission or license from the people of the state of New York. The right of a riparian owner was fully considered in Town of Brookhaven v. Smith (188 N.Y. 74, 84) and in Thousand Island Steamboat Co. v. Visger (179 N.Y. 206). He has the right of access to the channel or the navigable part of the river for navigation, fishing and such other uses as commonly belong to riparian ownership, the right to make a landing wharf or pier, for his own use, or for that of the public, with the right of passage to and from the same with reasonable safety and convenience. A pier may be constructed without a grant from the state of the land under water upon which it rests. In this country it has generally been held that the upland owner has the right of constructing a proper pier, or landing, for the use of himself and the public, subject to the general regulations prescribed by the state or the United States. What form or shape or size the pier may take varies with use and necessity. The upland owner has no right to fill in the land under water for purposes foreign to commerce and navigation. (Barnes v. Midland R.R. Terminal Co., 193 N.Y. 378.)

Vassar, the upland owner, in 1835 and thereafter, as well as his successors in title, had the right to wharf or pier out to the navigable part of the Hudson river. They could build piers which would rest upon the land under water, or they could build wharves and erect bulkheads. They also could fill in marshy ground and erect a substantial wharf for use of navigation and commerce connected with their business. (People v. Mould, 37 App. Div. 35.) All these things could be done under the implied permission of the people of the state of New York by reason of the law pertaining to upland owners, i.e., the law of riparian rights. When Vassar built his pier or bulkheaded and erected his wharf he did not act adversely to the interests or title of the people of the state of New York, but acted under a right given to him by the people through the law. His use may have been excessive. It may be that he had no right to fill in this land and build thereon a malt house or manufacturing plant, as distinguished from structures connected with navigation, but this abuse of his privilege could not of itself make the use adverse. What was the state to do? There are many miles of water front upon the waterways of the state of New York. The upland owners have, as above stated, the right to build wharves and piers for use in navigation. Such use is not adverse. Must the state keep a body of paid employees to constantly inspect all its waterways to see that riparian rights are not pushed beyond lawful limitations and the occupation ripen into adverse possession? Such a demand upon the resources of the state would be unreasonable. "Who is to watch," said the court in Jersey City v. Hall (79 N.J.L. 559, 574), "so as to detect within a certain period all encroachments upon the innumerable public highways in the state, or who is to keep similar guard over all parts of its extensive harbors and navigable rivers?" . . .

There may be circumstances which would justify the running of the Statute of Limitations against the state, and we refrain from holding that in no instance can title be acquired by adverse possession where the state in the first instance could have made a grant of the land to private individuals. (Matter of City of New York, 217 N.Y. 1, 13; 2 Corpus Juris, p.214, note 38B.) The cases referred to by Judge Cullen in Fulton Light, H. & P. Co. v. State of New York (200 N.Y. 400, 422) are cases where the state had no right at any time to make a grant of the property or privilege claimed. We leave that question open. We do hold, however, that where, as in this case, an upland owner enters upon the land under water for the purpose of erecting piers, wharves or filling in for bulkhead and wharf purposes, his use does not become adverse merely by the erection of a building thereon. Something more must have been done or claimed to make this lawful entry adverse as against the state. . . .

The judgment appealed from should be affirmed, with costs.

HOGAN, CARDOZO, POUND and McLAUGHLIN, J., concur; ANDREWS, J., concurs in result; HISCOCK, CH. J., not voting.

Judgment affirmed.

NOTES AND QUESTIONS

1. **Time does not run against the king.** At common law the Latin epigram *nullum tempus occurrit regi* (time does not run against the king) said it succinctly: Adverse possession could not defeat the state's title. Even today, many states have retained the tradition, relying on rationales such as the state is "trustee" for all its citizens (a trustee's power to alienate is often circumscribed), or, state lands that have been made inalienable or whose mode of conveyance has been prescribed by constitution or statute cannot be transferred by operation of law. Often, the bar against adverse possession has been formalized by statute. See, e.g., N.H. Rev. Stat. Ann. §§477.34 (1992), 539.6 (1974).

In several states, the contrary doctrine has gained an insecure toehold. Thus, as in New York, statutes have opened up state-owned lands to the claim of adverse possession, although the limitations period tends to exceed that for privately held lands. Several courts (and statutes) have embraced a distinction between "public lands," which are not subject to adverse possession, and "private or proprietary lands," which are. See, e.g., Brown v. Trustees of Schools, 224 Ill. 184, 79 N.E. 579 (1906); Herndon v. Board of Commrs., 158 Okla. 14, 11 P.2d 939 (1932). Occasionally, the doctrine of estoppel has been brought to the aid of a private claimant. See, e.g., Bridges v. Grand View, 158 Iowa 402, 139 N.W. 917 (1913).

But, in general, the courts have yielded the state's dominion reluctantly, even when a statute has freed them to do so. In this respect, the *Hinkley* case is quite typical. Moreover, if one can sense a trend, legislators are themselves becoming more jealous of the state's resources. In Delaware, for example, a century-old statute allowing adverse possession was repealed in 1953, 49 Del. Laws, ch. 386 (1953). Other states also have re-established the earlier common-law immunity. See, e.g., Mich. Comp. Laws Ann. §317.294 (1995) (swamp lands along Great Lakes, etc.); Or. Rev. Stat. §12.250 (1994) (removes impediment to county's ability to defend its record title to real property).

Looking behind the easy generalizations, do you see any basis for giving state-owned lands an immunity that is not available to lands privately held? Should it make a difference whether the lands in question are the boundaries of a schoolyard, tidal lands that have been farmed and grazed by upland owners, a highway right-of-way that has been only partly used, or a state forest? Does it matter that "The people of the United States are the nation's largest landowner, holding about 730 million acres of land, rich in natural resources"? See Majority Staff Report of the Subcommittee on Natural Resources of the U.S. House of Representatives, 103d Cong., 2d Sess., Taking from the Taxpayer: Public Subsidies for Natural Resource Development (Comm. Prints 1994).

2. **Congressional action.** Congress has carved some exceptions from the immunity from adverse possession that federal lands once enjoyed. U.S.C.A. tit. 43, §1068 (1986), is the most inclusive, directing the Secretary of the Interior to issue patents for up to 160 acres of public land, where the claimant can show:

(a) peaceful, adverse possession
(b) under claim or color of title,
(c) in good faith
(d) for more than twenty years, and
(e) improvements or partial cultivation

The secretary must charge for the patent not less than $1.25 per acre.

This section also gives the secretary *discretionary* power to issue a patent where the claimant's possession dates from 1901 or before, and the claimant has paid state or local taxes levied against the parcel; under this provision, the claimant need not have built improvements or have cultivated the soil. Id.

The Mining Claim Occupancy Act, 30 U.S.C.A. §§701-709 (West 1986), authorizes federal patents in limited situations to parties lacking valid title.

Unless a claimant can bring himself within one of these statutory exceptions, he cannot assert title by adverse possession or prescription against the United States. See United States v. 1,629.6 Acres of Land, 503 F.2d 764, 767 (3d Cir. 1974).

The Public Land Law Review Commission recommended to the president and the Congress an expanded doctrine of adverse possession operating against the government. Report, One Third of the Nation's Land 15,260-15,262 (1970). At least one commentator has angrily attacked the proposal. Elmer M. Million, Adverse Possession against the United States — A Treasure for Trespassers, 26 Ark. L. Rev. 467 (1973).

3. **England.** One might note that in England, adverse possession is now available against state-owned lands. Thirty years of occupancy is required generally, 60 years for shorelands. Limitations Act, 1939, 2 & 3 Geo. 6, ch. 21, §4(1).

§5.6   The Doctrine of Agreed Boundaries

The "agreed boundaries" doctrine often arises in the same context as a dispute over title by adverse possession. Sometimes a claimant, unable to prove the necessary elements for adverse possession, may turn to an agreed boundaries theory in an effort to establish title. Consider the use of agreed boundaries in the following case.

JOAQUIN v. SHILOH ORCHARDS

84 Cal. App. 3d 192, 145 Cal. Rptr. 495 (1978)

FRANSON, J. The fundamental question presented by this quiet title action is the extent of the trial court's obligation to fix the location of an agreed boundary between contiguous owners of land where the monument fixing the line (a fence) has been removed without a survey or other marking to identify its precise location. As we shall explain, the trial court is required to fix the location of the agreed boundary according to the evidence presented at trial if it is reasonably possible to do so. Thus, in the present case the court erred in refusing to determine the location of the agreed boundary and in quieting title in respondents according to their complaint.

Prior to 1942 the Bank of America was the common owner of the adjoining parcels of real property now owned by appellant and respondents, the boundary line of which is the subject of this controversy. On April 6, 1942, the bank sold one parcel to the respondents' predecessors in interest and on March 1, 1943, sold the other parcel to the appellant's predecessor in interest. The deed to both parcels described their common boundary as the quarter section line separating the southwest quarter section from the northwest quarter section of section 19, in township 4 south, range 8 east, Mount Diablo base and Meridian, in the County of Stanislaus. There is a 5-inch diameter concrete monument located in Shiloh Road marking the western quarter section corner, which the federal government established in 1854. The monument set at the easterly corner of the section line in 1854 has never been located, but a surveyor established this point in 1974 for a survey of nearby property.

At sometime prior to 1944, a fence was constructed which divided one portion of the property from the other, and the two portions were separately farmed and utilized up to the fence. In addition, the separate farming practices of the adjoining owners over the years created a line demarcating the differing cultural practices, evidenced by a change in elevation or "bench" between the two farms at the fence line, ranging from 12 to 36 inches in height. The fence was located at the top of this bench. The area between the fence line and the quarter section line is approximately 2.4 acres.

Respondents acquired their parcel on September 5, 1967, and appellant acquired its parcel on December 28, 1973. At the date of appellant's acquisition, appellant and its predecessors in interest accepted and understood the fence to be the boundary between the respective parcels. Appellant entered into possession of its parcel to the fence and dealt with the property as if the fence constituted the boundary, cultivating and improving its parcel, including the now disputed piece.

In 1974 appellant removed the fence to establish an almond orchard on the property, which it accomplished in 1975. The fence line was removed to help control weeds that had grown along the fence. Appellant used a disc to control the weeds on the old fence line. The effect of the discing was to "round" the bench somewhat, but not enough to extinguish the original line. Appellant leveled the property, installed a sprinkler system, and planted an almond orchard, at the cost of approximately $2,100 per acre . . .

In the course of constructing a power line project, respondents began to suspect that the former fence line might not be the boundary described in the deeds to the respective parcels. Respondents commissioned a land survey, which indicated that the boundary described in the deeds was some distance to the north of the newly planted almond orchard, leaving ownership of a portion of the orchard in dispute and leading to this action.

The trial court found that although a fence had been in existence for many years south of the quarter section line, and the parties and their predecessors had each farmed the land to the fence, causing the formation of an embankment of soil along the fence line, the removal of the fence without a survey or other methods of marking its exact location resulted in a loss of appellant's title in the land to the fence. In support of this conclusion, the court found that appellant had disced and broadened the bank after the fence had been removed; that neither the top nor the bottom of the bank as it existed prior to 1974 had been established; and that no remnants of the fence post remaining below ground had been shown. From these findings the court concluded that "[t]he only ascertainable boundary which can be defined in words and which can be translated into monuments on the ground is the common quarter section line as used and described in the recorded deed of each property." It then quieted title in respondents according to the prayer of their complaint.

The doctrine of acquiescence to a boundary line is referred to in California as the doctrine of title by agreed boundary. (See Ernie v. Trinity Lutheran Church (1959) 51 Cal. 2d 702, 707, 336 P.2d 525.) It is a mixture of implied agreement and estoppel. (Miller and Starr, Current Law of California Real Estate (1977) §21:27, pp. 552-559.) The elements of the doctrine are an uncertainty as to the true boundary line, an agreement between the adjacent owners establishing the line, and acceptance and acquiescence in that line. (Ernie v. Trinity Lutheran Church, *supra;* Duncan v. Peterson (1970) 3 Cal. App. 3d 607, 611, 83 Cal. Rptr. 744.)

The doctrine clearly applies to this case. The inability to locate the eastern quarter section monument demonstrates the requisite uncertainty. The evidence shows that the owners had accepted the fence as the boundary line. "A longstanding acceptance of a fence as a boundary line gives rise to an inference that there was, in fact, a boundary agreement between the coterminous owners resulting from an uncertainty or dispute as to the location of the true line." (Current Law of California Real Estate, *supra*, 51 Cal. 2d 702, 708, 336 P.2d 525.)

The trial court apparently misunderstood the full legal consequences of the agreed boundary.

> . . . [W]hen such owners, being uncertain of the true position of the boundaries so described, agree upon its true location, mark it upon the ground, or build up to it, occupy on each side up to the place thus fixed, and acquiesce in such location for a period equal to the statute of limitations, or under such circumstances that substantial loss would be caused by a change of its position, *such line becomes, in law, the true line called for by the respective descriptions, regardless of the accuracy of the agreed location, as it may appear by subsequent measurements.* [Emphasis added. Young v. Blakeman (1908) 153 Cal. 477, 481, 95 P. 888,889; Duncan v. Peterson, *supra*, 3 Cal. App. 3d 607, 611, 83 Cal. Rptr. 744.]

Once an agreement between parties over an uncertain boundary line is established according to law, the agreement is conclusive as to the correctness of the boundary. (Martin v. Lopes (1946) 28 Cal. 2d 618, 622, 170 P.2d 881; 2 Cal. Jur. 3d, Adjoining Landowners, §93, p.146.) The agreement establishes the true boundary line which the parties are estopped to deny. If more land is given to one than the description of his deed actually requires,

he holds the excess by legal and not merely equitable title. (Sneed v. Osborn (1864) 25 Cal. 619, 631; 2 Cal. Jur. 3d, *supra,* §93, p.146.) Thus, once
appellant proved by uncontradicted evidence that the fence line was the
agreed boundary separating the two properties, respondents lost their right
to quiet title to the quarter section line.

The decree quieting title in respondents to the real property described in their complaint is reversed. The matter is remanded to the trial
court with directions to receive such additional evidence as either party
shall desire to produce and determine the location of the agreed line according to the evidence available.

NOTES AND QUESTIONS

1. **Intent?** The theory behind the doctrine of agreed boundaries is
that the court is merely enforcing the preexisting intent of the two neighboring landowners. Does the way this court applies the doctrine belie the
court's claim to be enforcing intent? If so, why does the doctrine continue
to claim to be enforcing intent?

2. **Why not claim adverse possession?** The defendant had not
pressed a claim to the disputed 2.4 acres based on title by adverse possession. Were any of the elements for such a claim missing?

3. **Real estate taxes.** California requires a successful claimant in adverse possession to have paid the real estate taxes on a disputed parcel for
a five-year period (the statute of limitations term). In practice, on the facts
given, to whom would the 2.4 acre parcel have been assessed? If the defendant had tried to pay taxes on the disputed parcel, what problems would he
have faced? As an element of adverse possession, does the tax-paying requirement serve any valid purpose? See Moira Ford, Comment, The Payment of Taxes Requirement in Adverse Possession Statutes, 37 Cal. L. Rev.
477, 478-481 (1949). The Comment listed 17 states as then having some tax-
paying requirement, id. at 482-483, although 9 of the states also had an
alternative mode of adverse possession not requiring tax payment, id. at
484. Frequently the tax-paying requirement seems to be coupled with a
shorter limitations periods or with adverse possession claims based on color
of title.

4. **Policy goals.** Does the agreed boundaries doctrine serve any of
the same policy goals as those of the adverse possession doctrine? Cf. Bryant
v. Blevins, 9 Cal. 4th 47, 55, 884 P.2d 1034, 1039 (1994).

5. **Problem.** A and B are adjoining landowners. They agree orally to
relocate their boundary line; they then build a fence marking the new line.
Each cultivates up to the fence on his side. Some years later A and B have a
dispute and seek to rescind their agreement. Are they bound?

6. **Liberal application?** Having formulated the agreed boundaries
doctrine, should the courts liberally apply it? Discretion centers on two key

elements: whether there was both "uncertainty" and "agreement" as to the boundary line. The court in Minson v. Aviation Finance, 113 Cal. Rptr. 223, 226, 38 Cal. App. 489, 493 (Ct. App. 1974), found the key elements in the 1883 decision of two neighbors to ask the county to build a road between their parcels and to accept the county survey, which located the road, as fixing the boundary.

§5.7   Adverse Possession of Chattels[8]

Is it possible to gain title of personal property by adverse possession? While reading the following case, recall the Lockean entitlement, utilitarianism, and property as personhood theories. How would each apply in the context of adverse possession of chattels?

O'KEEFFE v. SNYDER

83 N.J. 478, 416 A.2d 862 (1980)

POLLOCK, J. [In omitted material, the court reverses Appellate Division's award of summary judgment to O'Keeffe and remands to trial court.]

I

The record, limited to pleadings, affidavits, answers to interrogatories, and depositions, is fraught with factual conflict. Apart from the creation of the paintings by O'Keeffe and their discovery in Snyder's gallery in 1976, the parties agree on little else.

O'Keeffe contended the paintings were stolen in 1946 from a gallery, An American Place. The gallery was operated by her late husband, the famous photographer Alfred Stieglitz.

An American Place was a cooperative undertaking of O'Keeffe and some other American artists identified by her as Marin, Hardin, Dove, Andema, and Stevens. In 1946, Stieglitz arranged an exhibit which included an O'Keeffe painting, identified as Cliffs. According to O'Keeffe, one day in March, 1946, she and Stieglitz discovered Cliffs was missing from the wall

---

8. "An article of personal property. . . . It may refer to animate as well as inanimate property." Black's Law Dictionary (6th ed. (1990)). "Since only domestic animals were ever the primary personal properties of value, [cattle] could be used to mean chattel in general (which is from the same linguistic root as "cattle")." Arthur Allen Leff, The Leff Dictionary of Law: A Fragment, 94 Yale L.J. 1855, 2110 (1985).

of the exhibit. O'Keeffe estimates the value of the painting at the time of the alleged theft to have been about $150.

About two weeks later, O'Keeffe noticed that two other paintings, Seaweed and Fragments, were missing from a storage room at An American Place. She did not tell anyone, even Stieglitz, about the missing paintings, since she did not want to upset him.

Before the date when O'Keeffe discovered the disappearance of Seaweed, she had already sold it (apparently for a string of amber beads) to a Mrs. Weiner, now deceased. Following the grant of the motion for summary judgment by the trial court in favor of Snyder, O'Keeffe submitted a release from the legatees of Mrs. Weiner purportedly assigning to O'Keeffe their interest in the sale.

O'Keeffe testified on depositions that at about the same time as the disappearance of her paintings, 12 or 13 miniature paintings by Marin also were stolen from An American Place. According to O' Keeffe, a man named Estrick took the Marin paintings and "maybe a few other things." Estrick distributed the Marin paintings to members of the theater world who, when confronted by Stieglitz, returned them. However, neither Stieglitz nor O'Keeffe confronted Estrick with the loss of any of the O'Keeffe paintings.

There was no evidence of a break and entry at An American Place on the dates when O'Keeffe discovered the disappearance of her paintings. Neither Stieglitz nor O'Keeffe reported them missing to the New York Police Department or any other law enforcement agency. Apparently the paintings were uninsured, and O'Keeffe did not seek reimbursement from an insurance company. Similarly, neither O'Keeffe nor Stieglitz advertised the loss of the paintings in Art News or any other publication. Nonetheless, they discussed it with associates in the art world and later O'Keeffe mentioned the loss to the director of the Art Institute of Chicago, but she did not ask him to do anything because "it wouldn't have been my way." O'Keeffe does not contend that Frank or Snyder had actual knowledge of the alleged theft.

Stieglitz died in the summer of 1946, and O'Keeffe explains she did not pursue her efforts to locate the paintings because she was settling his estate. In 1947, she retained the services of Doris Bry to help settle the estate. Bry urged O'Keeffe to report the loss of the paintings, but O'Keeffe declined because "they never got anything back by reporting it." Finally, in 1972, O'Keeffe authorized Bry to report the theft to the Art Dealers Association of America, Inc., which maintains for its members a registry of stolen paintings. The record does not indicate whether such a registry existed at the time the paintings disappeared.

In September, 1975, O'Keeffe learned that the paintings were in the Andrew Crispo Gallery in New York on consignment from Bernard Danenberg Galleries. On February 11, 1976, O'Keeffe discovered that Ulrich A. Frank had sold the paintings to Barry Snyder, d/b/a Princeton Gallery of

Fine Art.[9] She demanded their return and, following Snyder's refusal, instituted this action for replevin.

Frank traces his possession of the paintings to his father, Dr. Frank,
who died in 1968. He claims there is a family relationship by marriage between his family and the Stieglitz family, a contention that O'Keeffe disputes. Frank does not know how his father acquired the paintings, but he
recalls seeing them in his father's apartment in New Hampshire as early as
1941-1943, a period that precedes the alleged theft. Consequently, Frank's
factual contentions are inconsistent with O'Keeffe's allegation of theft. Until 1965, Dr. Frank occasionally lent the paintings to Ulrich Frank. In 1965,
Dr. and Mrs. Frank formally gave the paintings to Ulrich Frank, who kept
them in his residences in Yardley, Pennsylvania and Princeton, New Jersey.
In 1968, he exhibited anonymously Cliffs and Fragments in a one day art
show in the Jewish Community Center in Trenton. All of these events precede O'Keeffe's listing of the paintings as stolen with the Art Dealers Association of America, Inc. in 1972.

Frank claims continuous possession of the paintings through his father for over thirty years and admits selling the paintings to Snyder. Snyder
and Frank do not trace their provenance, or history of possession of the
paintings, back to O'Keeffe.

As indicated, Snyder moved for summary judgment on the theory that
O'Keeffe's action was barred by the statute of limitations and title had
vested in Frank by adverse possession. For purposes of his motion, Snyder
conceded that the paintings had been stolen. On her cross motion,
O'Keeffe urged that the paintings were stolen, the statute of limitations had
not run, and title to the paintings remained in her. . . .

III

On the limited record before us, we cannot determine now who has
title to the paintings. That determination will depend on the evidence adduced at trial. Nonetheless, we believe it may aid the trial court and the
parties to resolve questions of law that may become relevant at trial.

Our decision begins with the principle that, generally speaking, if the
paintings were stolen, the thief acquired no title and could not transfer
good title to others regardless of their good faith and ignorance of the theft.
Proof of theft would advance O'Keeffe's right to possession of the paintings
absent other considerations such as expiration of the statute of limitations.

Another issue that may become relevant at trial is whether Frank
or his father acquired a "voidable title" to the paintings under N.J.S.A.

---

9. The defendant Snyder paid the impleaded third-party defendant Frank $35,000 for
the paintings. — EDS.

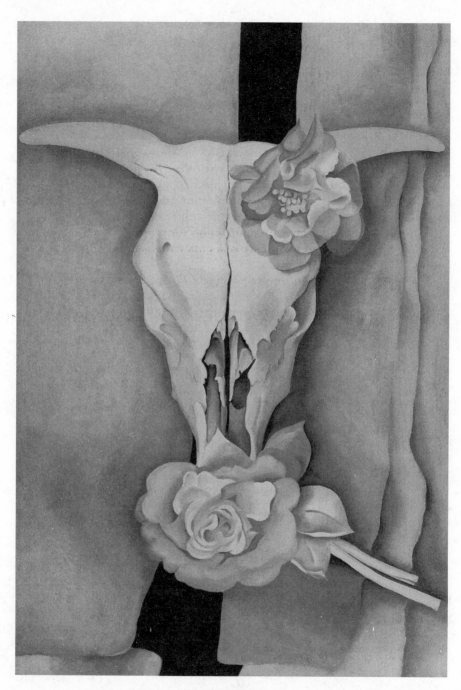

FIGURE 5-1
Cow's Skull with Calico Roses

12A:2-403(1). That section, part of the Uniform Commercial Code (U.C.C.),[10] does not change the basic principle that a mere possessor cannot transfer good title. Nonetheless, the U.C.C. permits a person with voidable title to transfer good title to a good faith purchaser for value in certain circumstances. N.J.S.A. 12A:2-403(1). If the facts developed at trial merit application of that section, then Frank may have transferred good title to Snyder, thereby providing a defense to O'Keeffe's action. No party on this appeal has urged factual or legal contentions concerning the applicability of the U.C.C. Consequently, a more complete discussion of the U.C.C. would be premature, particularly in light of our decision to remand the matter for trial.

On this appeal, the critical legal question is when O'Keeffe's cause of action accrued. The fulcrum on which the outcome turns is the statute of limitations . . . which provides that an action for replevin of goods or chattels must be commenced within six years after the accrual of the cause of action.

The trial court found that O'Keeffe's cause of action accrued on the date of the alleged theft, March, 1946, and concluded that her action was barred. The Appellate Division found that an action might have accrued more than six years before the date of suit if possession by the defendant or his predecessors satisfied the elements of adverse possession. As indicated, the Appellate Division concluded that Snyder had not established those elements and that the O'Keeffe action was not barred by the statute of limitations. . . .

---

10. Uniform Commercial Code §2-403 provides:

§2-403. *Power to Transfer; Good Faith Purchase of Goods; "Entrusting."*
   (1) A purchaser of goods acquires all title which his transferor had or had power to transfer except that a purchaser of a limited interest acquires rights only to the extent of the interest purchased. A person with voidable title has power to transfer a good title to a good faith purchaser for value. When goods have been delivered under a transaction of purchase the purchaser has such power even though
      (a) the transferor was deceived as to the identity of the purchaser, or
      (b) the delivery was in exchange for a check which was later dishonored, or
      (c) it was agreed that the transaction was to be a "cash sale," or
      (d) the delivery was procured through fraud punishable as larcenous under the criminal law.
   (2) Any entrusting of possession of goods to a merchant who deals in goods of that kind gives him power to transfer all rights of the entruster to a buyer in the ordinary course of business.
   (3) "Entrusting" includes any delivery and any acquiescence in retention of possession regardless of any condition expressed between the parties to the delivery or acquiescence and regardless of whether the procurement of the entrusting or the possessor's deposition of the goods have been such as to be larcenous under the criminal law. — Eds.

IV

The purpose of a statute of limitations is to "stimulate to activity and punish negligence" and "promote repose by giving security and stability to human affairs." Wood v. Carpenter, 101 U.S. 135, 139 (1879); Tevis v. Tevis, 79 N.J. 422, 430-431 (1979) . . . A statute of limitations achieves those purposes by barring a cause of action after the statutory period. In certain instances, this Court has ruled that the literal language of a statute of limitations should yield to other considerations.

To avoid harsh result from the mechanical application of the statute, the courts have developed a concept known as the discovery rule. Lopez v. Swyer, 62 N.J. 267, 273-275 (1973); Prosser, The Law of Torts (4 ed. 1971), §30 at 144-145; 51 Am. Jur. 2d, Limitation of Actions, §146 at 716. The discovery rule provides that, in an appropriate case, a cause of action will not accrue until the injured party discovers, or by exercise of reasonable diligence and intelligence should have discovered, facts which form the basis of a cause of action. The rule is essentially a principle of equity, the purpose of which is to mitigate unjust results that otherwise might flow from strict adherence to a rule of law.

This Court first announced the discovery rule in Fernandi [v. Strully, 35 N.J. 434, 434 (1961)]. In Fernandi, a wing nut was left in a patient's abdomen following surgery and was not discovered for three years. Id. at 450-451. The majority held that fairness and justice mandated that the statute of limitations should not have commenced running until the plaintiff knew or had reason to know of the presence of the foreign object in her body.

Increasing acceptance of the principle of the discovery rule has extended the doctrine to contexts unrelated to medical malpractice. . . .

We conclude that the discovery rule applies to an action for replevin of a painting under N.J.S.A. 2A:14-1. O'Keeffe's cause of action accrued when she first knew, or reasonably should have known through the exercise of due diligence, of the cause of action, including the identity of the possessor of the paintings. . . .

In determining whether O'Keeffe is entitled to the benefit of the discovery rule, the trial court should consider, among others, the following issues: (1) whether O'Keeffe used due diligence to recover the paintings at the time of the alleged theft and thereafter; (2) whether at the time of the alleged theft there was an effective method, other than talking to her colleagues, for O'Keeffe to alert the art world; and (3) whether registering paintings with the Art Dealers Association of America, Inc. or any other organization would put a reasonably prudent purchaser of art on constructive notice that someone other than the possessor was the true owner.

V

The acquisition of title to real and personal property by adverse possession is based on the expiration of a statute of limitations. . . .

To establish title by adverse possession to chattels, the rule of law has been that the possession must be hostile, actual, visible, exclusive, and continuous. Redmond v. New Jersey Historical Society, 132 N.J. Eq. 464, 474 (E. & A. 1942); 54 C.J.S. Limitations of Actions §119 at 23. *Redmond* involved a portrait of Captain James Lawrence by Gilbert Stuart, which was bequeathed by its owner to her son with a provision that if he should die leaving no descendants, it should go to the New Jersey Historical Society. The owner died in 1887, when her son was 14, and her executors delivered the painting to the Historical Society. The painting remained in the possession of the Historical Society for over 50 years, until 1938, when the son died and his children, the legatees under his will, demanded its return. The Historical Society refused, and the legatees instituted a replevin action.

The Historical Society argued that the applicable statute of limitations, the predecessor of N.J.S.A. 2A:14-1, had run and that plaintiffs' action was barred. The Court of Errors and Appeals held that the doctrine of adverse possession applied to chattels as well as to real property, *Redmond, supra,* 132 N.J. Eq. at 473, and that the statute of limitations would not begin to run against the true owner until possession became adverse. Id. at 475. The Court found that the Historical Society had done nothing inconsistent with the theory that the painting was a "voluntary bailment or gratuitous loan" and had "utterly failed to prove that its possession of the portrait was 'adversary,' 'hostile.'" Id. at 474-475. The Court found further that the Historical Society had not asserted ownership until 1938, when it refused to deliver the painting to plaintiff, and that the statute did not begin to run until that date. Consequently, the Court ordered the painting to be returned to plaintiffs.

The only other New Jersey case applying adverse possession to chattels is Joseph v. Lesnevich, 56 N.J. Super. 340 (App. Div. 1949). In *Lesnevich,* several negotiable bearer bonds were stolen from plaintiff in 1951. In October, 1951, Lesnevich received an envelope containing the bonds. On October 21, 1951, Lesnevich and his business partner pledged the bonds with a credit company. They failed to pay the loan secured by the bonds and requested the credit company to sell the bonds to pay the loan. On August 1, 1952, the president of the credit company purchased the bonds and sold them to his son. In 1958, within one day of the expiration of six years from the date of the purchase, the owner of the bonds sued the credit company and its president, among others, for conversion of the bonds. The Appellate Division found that the credit company and its president held the bonds "as openly and notoriously as the nature of the property would permit." *Lesnevich, supra,* 56 N.J. Super. at 355. The pledge of the bonds with the credit company was considered to be open possession.

As *Lesnevich* demonstrates, there is an inherent problem with many kinds of personal property that will raise questions whether their possession has been open, visible, and notorious. In Lesnevich, the court strained to conclude that in holding bonds as collateral, a credit company satisfied the requirement of open, visible, and notorious possession.

Other problems with the requirement of visible, open, and notorious possession readily come to mind. For example, if jewelry is stolen from a municipality in one county in New Jersey, it is unlikely that the owner would learn that someone is openly wearing that jewelry in another county or even in the same municipality. Open and visible possession of personal property, such as jewelry, may not be sufficient to put the original owner on actual or constructive notice of the identity of the possessor.

The problem is even more acute with works of art. Like many kinds of personal property, works of art are readily moved and easily concealed. O'Keeffe argues that nothing short of public display should be sufficient to alert the true owner and start the statute running. Although there is merit in that contention from the perspective of the original owner, the effect is to impose a heavy burden on the purchasers of paintings who wish to enjoy the paintings in the privacy of their homes.

In the present case, the trial court and Appellate Division concluded that the paintings, which allegedly had been kept in the private residences of the Frank family, had not been held visibly, openly, and notoriously. Notwithstanding that conclusion, the trial court ruled that the statute of limitations began to run at the time of the theft and had expired before the commencement of suit. The Appellate Division determined it was bound by the rules in Redmond and reversed the trial court on the theory that the defenses of adverse possession and expiration of the statute of limitations were identical. Nonetheless, for different reasons, the majority and dissenting judges in the Appellate Division acknowledged deficiencies in identifying the statute of limitations with adverse possession. The majority stated that, as a practical matter, requiring compliance with adverse possession would preclude barring stale claims and acquiring title to personal property. *O'Keeffe, supra,* 170 N.J. Super. at 86. The dissenting judge feared that identifying the statutes of limitations with adverse possession would lead to a "handbook for larceny." Id. at 96. The divergent conclusions of the lower courts suggest that the doctrine of adverse possession no longer provides a fair and reasonable means of resolving this kind of dispute.

The problem is serious. According to an affidavit submitted in this matter by the president of the International Foundation for Art Research, there has been an "explosion in art thefts" and there is a "worldwide phenomenon of art theft which has reached epidemic proportions."

The limited record before us provides a brief glimpse into the arcane world of sales of art, where paintings worth vast sums of money sometimes are bought without inquiry about their provenance. There does not appear to be a reasonably available method for an owner of art to record the ownership or theft of paintings. Similarly, there are no reasonable means readily available to a purchaser to ascertain the provenance of a painting. It may be time for the art world to establish a means by which a good faith purchaser may reasonably obtain the provenance of a painting. An efficient registry of original works of art might better serve the interests of artists, owners of art, and bona fide purchasers than the law of adverse possession with all of its uncertainties. L. DuBoff, The Deskbook of Art Law at 470-472 (Fed. Pub. Inc. 1977). Although we cannot mandate the initiation of a registration system, we can develop a rule for the commencement and running of the statute of limitations that is more responsive to the needs of the art world than the doctrine of adverse possession.

We are persuaded that the introduction of equitable considerations through the discovery rule provides a more satisfactory response than the doctrine of adverse possession. The discovery rule shifts the emphasis from the conduct of the possessor to the conduct of the owner. The focus of the inquiry will no longer be whether the possessor has met the tests of adverse possession, but whether the owner has acted with due diligence in pursuing his or her personal property.

For example, under the discovery rule, if an artist diligently seeks the recovery of a lost or stolen painting, but cannot find it or discover the identity of the possessor, the statute of limitations will not begin to run. The rule permits an artist who uses reasonable efforts to report, investigate, and recover a painting to preserve the rights of title and possession.

Properly interpreted, the discovery rule becomes a vehicle for transporting equitable considerations into the statute of limitations for replevin. . . . It is consistent also with the law of replevin as it has developed apart from the discovery rule. In an action for replevin, the period of limitations ordinarily will run against the owner of lost or stolen property from the time of the wrongful taking, absent fraud or concealment. Where the chattel is fraudulently concealed, the general rule is that the statute is tolled. . . .

A purchaser from a private party would be well-advised to inquire whether a work of art has been reported as lost or stolen. However, a bona fide purchaser who purchases in the ordinary course of business a painting entrusted to an art dealer should be able to acquire good title against the true owner. Under the U.C.C. entrusting possession of goods to a merchant who deals in that kind of goods gives the merchant the power to transfer all the rights of the entrusted to a buyer in the ordinary course of business. N.J.S.A. 12A:2-403(2). In a transaction under that statute, a merchant may vest good title in the buyer as against the original owner. See *Anderson, supra,* §2-403:17 et seq. The interplay between the statute of limitations as modified by the discovery rule and the U.C.C. should encourage good faith purchases from legitimate art dealers and discourage trafficking in stolen art without frustrating an artist's ability to recover stolen art works.

The discovery rule will fulfill the purposes of a statute of limitations and accord greater protection to the innocent owner of personal property whose goods are lost or stolen. Accordingly, we overrule *Redmond v. New Jersey Historical Society, supra,* and *Joseph v. Lesnevich, supra,* to the extent that they hold that the doctrine of adverse possession applies to chattels.

By diligently pursuing their goods, owners may prevent the statute of limitations from running. The meaning of due diligence will vary with the facts of each case, including the nature and value of the personal property. For example, with respect to jewelry of moderate value, it may be sufficient if the owner reports the theft to the police. With respect to art work of greater value, it may be reasonable to expect an owner to do more. In practice, our ruling should contribute to more careful practices concerning the purchase of art.

The considerations are different with real estate, and there is no reason to disturb the application of the doctrine of adverse possession to real estate. Real estate is fixed and cannot be moved or concealed. The owner of real property knows or should know where his property is located and reasonably can be expected to be aware of open, notorious, visible, hostile, continuous acts of possession on it.

Our ruling not only changes the requirements for acquiring title to personal property after an alleged unlawful taking, but also shifts the burden of proof at trial. Under the doctrine of adverse possession, the burden is on the possessor to prove the elements of adverse possession. Under the discovery rule, the burden is on the owner as the one seeking the benefit of the rule to establish facts that would justify deferring the beginning of the period of limitations.

VI

Read literally, the effect of the expiration of the statute of limitations . . . is to bar an action such as replevin. The statute does not speak of divesting the original owner of title. By its terms the statute cuts off the remedy, but not the right of title. Nonetheless, the effect of the expiration of the statute of limitations, albeit on the theory of adverse possession, has been not only to bar an action for possession, but also to vest title in the possessor. There is no reason to change that result although the discovery rule has replaced adverse possession. History, reason, and common sense support the conclusion that the expiration of the statute of limitations bars the remedy to recover possession and also vests title in the possessor.

Before the expiration of the statute, the possessor has both the chattel and the right to keep it except as against the true owner. The only imperfection in the possessor's right to retain the chattel is the original owner's right to repossess it. Once that imperfection is removed, the possessor should have good title for all purposes. Ames, The Disseisin of Chattels, 3 Harv. L. Rev. 313, 321 (1890) (Ames).

Recognizing a metaphysical notion of title in the owner would be of little benefit to him or her and would create potential problems for the possessor and third parties. The expiration of the six-year period of N.J.S.A. 2A:14-1 should vest title as effectively under the discovery rule as under the doctrine of adverse possession.

VII

We next consider the effect of transfers of a chattel from one posses-sor to another during the period of limitation under the discovery rule. Under the discovery rule, the statute of limitations on an action for replevin begins to run when the owner knows or reasonably should know of his cause of action and the identity of the possessor of the chattel. Subsequent trans-fers of the chattel are part of the continuous dispossession of the chattel from the original owner. The important point is not that there has been a substitution of possessors, but that there has been a continuous disposses-sion of the former owner.

For the purpose of evaluating the due diligence of an owner, the dis-possession of his chattel is a continuum not susceptible to separation into distinct acts. Nonetheless, subsequent transfers of the chattel may affect the degree of difficulty encountered by a diligent owner seeking to recover his goods. To that extent, subsequent transfers and their potential for frustrat-ing diligence are relevant in applying the discovery rule. An owner who diligently seeks his chattel should be entitled to the benefit of the discovery rule although it may have passed through many hands. Conversely, an owner who sleeps on his rights may be denied the benefit of the discovery rule although the chattel may have been possessed by only one person.

We reject the alternative of treating subsequent transfers of a chattel as separate acts of conversion that would start the statute of limitations run-ning anew. At common law, apart from the statute of limitations, a subse-quent transfer of a converted chattel was considered to be a separate act of conversion. . . . Adoption of that alternative would tend to undermine the purpose of the statute in quieting titles and protecting against state claims.

The majority and better view is to permit tacking, the accumulation of consecutive periods of possession by parties in privity with each other. *Lesnevich, supra,* 56 N.J. Super. at 357. . . .

O'Keeffe is a distinguished American artist, now 92 years old and liv-ing in New Mexico. In this proceeding, she has been deposed in her attor-ney's office in New York City. At oral argument, we were informed that she had visited New York recently for reasons unrelated to the litigation. None-theless, if, because of her age, O'Keeffe is unable to travel to New Jersey for trial, an appropriate application may be made to the trial court to perpetu-ate her testimony. Furthermore, we direct the trial court to expedite both discovery proceedings and the trial.

We reverse the judgment of the Appellate Division in favor of O'Keeffe and remand the matter for trial in accordance with this opinion. . . .

HANDLER, J., dissenting.

The Court today rules that if a work of art has been stolen from an artist, the artist's right to recover his or her work from a subsequent possessor would be barred by the statute of limitations if the action were not brought within six years after the original theft. This can happen even though the artist may have been totally innocent and wholly ignorant of the identity of the thief or of any intervening receivers or possessors of the stolen art. The Court would grudgingly grant some measure of relief from this horrendous result and allow the artist to bring suit provided he or she can sustain the burden of proving "due diligence" in earlier attempting to retrieve the stolen artwork. No similar duty of diligence or vigilance, however, is placed upon the subsequent receiver or possessor, who, innocently or not, has actually trafficked in the stolen art. Despite ritualistic disavowals, the Court's holding does little to discourage art thievery. Rather, by making it relatively more easy for the receiver or possessor of an artwork with a "checkered background" to gain security and title than for the artist or true owner to reacquire it, it seems as though the Court surely will stimulate and legitimatize art thievery.

I believe that there is a much sounder approach in this sort of case than one that requires the parties to become enmeshed in duplicate or cumulative hearings that focus on the essentially collateral issues of the statute of limitations and its possible tolling by an extended application of the discovery doctrine. The better approach, I would suggest, is one that enables the parties to get to the merits of the controversy. It would recognize an artist's or owner's right to assert a claim against a newly-revealed receiver or possessor of stolen art as well as the correlative right of such a possessor to assert all equitable and legal defenses. This would enable the parties to concentrate directly upon entitlement to the artwork rather than entitlement to bring a lawsuit. By dealing with the merits of the claims instead of the right to sue, such an approach would be more conducive to reconciling the demands for individual justice with societal needs to discourage art thievery. In addition, such a rule would comport more closely with traditional common law values emphasizing the paramountcy of the rights of a true owner of chattels as against others whose possession is derived from theft. Simultaneously, it would acknowledge that the claims of the true owner as against subsequent converters may in appropriate circumstances be counterbalanced by equitable considerations. . . .

Equitable considerations have special pertinency in the instant proceedings. They appropriately require the fullest exposure of all facets of the controversy: the uniqueness of the chattels — paintings created by a renowned artist whose artworks have in general grown greatly in value; the theft or mysterious disappearance of these paintings several decades ago; the subsequent possession and enjoyment of the paintings by the Frank family; Frank's subsequent attempts to sell the paintings, and their eventual acquisition by Snyder; the experience and status of Snyder in the art world, and whether he sufficiently investigated the provenance of the O'Keeffe paintings and acted with commensurate due care and reasonable prudence when he purchased them. The difficulties caused by the lengthy interim between the original disappearance of the paintings and their ultimate surfacing in Snyder's gallery also has a definite bearing upon the equities in this case. These considerations, I believe, should be given at most, as required by the majority opinion, oblique application as an aspect of the discovery rule relevant only as to whether O'Keeffe is entitled to assert a claim for the stolen paintings.

I therefore dissent.

PROBLEMS

Analyze the following hypotheticals under the U.C.C.:

1. I steal something from its true owner. I sell it to you. Can the true owner get it back from you? *NO if you are a merchant*

2. Finder sells an object she has found. Can the true owner get it back? *—NO -good faith*

3. Wholesaler buys an Apple from manufacturer, paying with a bad check. Wholesaler sells to retailer. Manufacturer tries to cash wholesaler's check, realizes it's bad, wants his Apple back. Can manufacturer get Apple back from retailer? *—NO* Could manufacturer recover from wholesaler if wholesaler still had the computer? *yes or value of*

4. I buy an Apple from you, giving you a bad check. Then I give the Apple to a business acquaintance, to "cement a deal." Can the true owner (you) get the Apple back from my business acquaintance? *NO*

5. X brings a watch in for repairs to a shop that both repairs watches and sells new ones. The shopkeeper sells X's watch to me. Can the watch's true owner recover from me? *NO - merchant = GFP*

NOTES AND QUESTIONS

1. **Subsequent case history.** O'Keeffe and Snyder ultimately settled before retrial. O'Keeffe took "Seaweed," Snyder took another painting, and a third was sold at auction to pay attorneys' fees.

2. **Two sharply different versions of the facts.** Tell the story of what happened from O'Keeffe's point of view, and then from Snyder's. Is this a proper case for a summary judgment?

3. **"The critical legal issue."** What is the critical legal issue from this court's standpoint? From that of the Appellate Division?

4. **Legal realism, revisited.** Note that this is the same court that decided State v. Shack, *supra* §1.4.d., and Sommer v. Kridel, *supra* §3.13.a. Do all three of these opinions illustrate a similar approach to judicial decision making?

5. **What law applies?** How many different legal rules are potentially relevant to this case? How is a court to decide which to use?

6.   **Tort law.** Note how the court turns to recent innovations in tort law as a way of changing property law. Compare *Javins, supra* §3.9.c. Why does tort law play this role?

7.   **New York.** Art theft is a significant and growing problem world-wide. In financial terms this theft is comparable to the international drug "trade." Lynn Macritchie, Survey of Lloyd's of London in World Insurance, The Financial Times (London), Mar. 30, 1992, at VII. Estimates place the annual toll of stolen, smuggled, and looted art at $4.5 billion to $6 billion. N.Y. Times, Nov. 20, 1995, at C11-12. See also Renee Graham, Art Stolen from Gardner Museum was Uninsured, Boston Globe, Mar. 20, 1990, at 1 (increasing number of reported art thefts is linked to increasing value of fine art).

New York, probably the most important art center in the United States, considered and rejected a discovery rule for actions to recover stolen art objects. This bill would have provided that once an institution gave notice of its possession of an art object, the Statute of Limitations would start to run.

A demand and refusal rule is in effect that provides greater protection for true owners of artwork in cases of theft. See Solomon R. Guggenheim Found. v. Lubell, 77 N.Y.2d 311, 320, 569 N.E.2d 426, 431 (1991) ("To place the burden of locating stolen artwork on the true owner would . . . encourage illicit trafficking in stolen art. Three years after the theft, any purchaser . . . would be able to hold onto stolen artwork unless the true owner was able to establish . . . a reasonable search.").

Chapter 6

Eminent Domain

> Nobody can tell me . . . how much that house is worth. To me it is worth a
> million dollars.[1]

Traditionally, eminent domain is considered part of "public law,"
whereas adverse possession and the doctrine of agreed boundaries are considered part of "private law." Yet, to the extent that owners lose personhood
property,[2] the government's eminent domain power — which enables it to
force a landowner to sell his property to the state at fair market value —
parallels adverse possession in undermining the intuitive image of property
as absolute and unchanging over time.

Eminent domain is the power of the government to force a sale of
land "to answer the necessities of the State."[3] It does not even appear
among Congress's enumerated powers, so clearly established was this basic
power of sovereignty.[4] The only question was whether compensation had to
be paid. Before the American Revolution, some colonies allowed property
to be taken for public purposes without compensation, pursuant to the republican vision of property:

> The principle that the state necessarily owes compensation when it takes
> private property was not generally accepted in either colonial or revolutionary
> America. Uncompensated takings were frequent, and found justification first
> in appeals to the Crown, and later in republicanism. . . . At the center of re-

---

1. John Saber, Poletown resident, quoted by Ron Brownstein of the Center for Study of
Responsive Law, June 5, 1981, in Jeanie Wylie, Poletown: Community Betrayed 63 (1989).

2. See *supra* §1.4.e.

3. Puffendorf, The Law of Nature and Nations, Book VIII, ch. 5, §7 (circa 1650). The
term "dominium eminens" first appears in the writings of Grotius (circa 1625) and was
roundly criticized by contemporary scholars who thought "imperium eminens" a more accurate phrase. "Dominium" is a civil-law property term that denotes proprietorship.

4. Cf. United States v. Jones, 109 U.S. 513 (1883). Strangely, Kohl v. United States,
91 U.S. 367 (1875), is the earliest Supreme Court decision to validate the power. One commentator notes that federal officials prior to the *Kohl* decision seemed uncertain if a federal
condemnation power actually existed, so that they would ask state officials to condemn land
for federal purposes. William B. Stoebuck, A General Theory of Eminent Domain, 47 Wash.
L. Rev. 553, 559 (1972).

publican thought lay a belief in a common good and a conception of society as an organic whole; [compensation was not required if land was taken for the common good because] "[t]he sacrifice of individual interests to the greater good of the whole formed the essence of republicanism. . . ."[5] Drawing on these premises, a major strand of republican thought held that the state could abridge the property right in order to promote common interests.

William Michael Treanor, The Origins and Original Significance of the Just Compensation Clause of the Fifth Amendment, 94 Yale L.J. 694, 694, 699-700 (1984).

Even if this was the practice in some areas before the Constitution was adopted, compensation clearly was required after the Fifth Amendment included these words: "Nor shall private property be taken for public use without just compensation."[6] State constitutions tend to repeat the federal pattern of implying the power by expressing the limitation. See, e.g., N.Y. Const. art. 1, §7; even if they do not, the Fifth Amendment now binds states via incorporation into the Fourteenth Amendment. Fallbrook Irrigation Dist. v. Bradley, 164 U.S. 112 (1896).[7]

Through the nineteenth century, the eminent domain power was used sparingly for several reasons: Much of the nation's land was publicly held and could be devoted — or donated as in the case of the railways or land-grant universities — for essential purposes; the nature of the role of government was far more circumscribed than it is today; the automobile was not yet invented. Today, government at all levels spends many billions yearly on condemnation; the annual land acquisition cost of just one program, urban renewal, has run in the hundreds of millions, and the federal highway program is one of the most extensive public works projects in history. As we shall see, the power to condemn is not held by government alone. The legal limitation that the land be condemned only for public purposes opens up for analysis the distinction between what is public and what is private. This chapter will examine both that distinction and the two major issues with which the law of eminent domain has been concerned. First, when (for what purposes) may the power be exercised? Second, what constitutes "just compensation"?

NOTE

South Africa. A significant number of blacks owned land in South Africa in areas subsequently designated for whites. Roughly 3.5 million

---

5. G. Wood, The Creation of the American Republic, 1776-1787, at 53 (1969).

6. One finds a more florid statement in the French Declaration of the Rights of Man, Aug. 26, 1789, art. 17: "The right to property being inviolable and sacred, no one shall be deprived of it, except in cases of evident public necessity, legally ascertained, and on condition of a previous just indemnity."

7. For an early state case where private property was permitted to be taken without payment, see Patrick v. Commissioners of Cross Roads, 4 McCord 541 (S.C. 1828).

blacks were evicted from their homes and relocated to "homelands" often located hundreds of miles away, according to a recent survey by the South African Institute of Race Relations, quoted in Michael Robertson, Land Reform: South African Options, 21 Colum. Hum. Rts. L. Rev. 193, 193 n.2 (1990). See also Colin Bundy, Land, Law and Power: Forced Removals in Historical Context, in No Place to Rest: Forced Removals and the Law in South Africa 8 (Christina Murray & Catherine O'Regan eds., 1990). In the homelands, blacks lived under a system of private property law different from that available to whites. While whites enjoyed the traditional rights to sell, lease, mortgage, and devise their land to heirs, the state owned most land available to blacks, who obtained only use rights subject to extensive government regulation. This regulation allowed the state to extinguish the holder's rights to the land in a wide variety of circumstances (including if its use was changed); did not allow the land to be passed on to heirs; required government approval of all sales and mortgages; retained mineral rights in government hands. See Sherry Soanes-Spencer, The Future of Land Reform in a Post-Apartheid South Africa (1995) (unpublished manuscript, on file at the library of the Washington College of Law, American University).

On May 8, 1996, South Africa's Constitutional Assembly voted 421 to 2, with ten abstentions, to approve a new democratic constitution. However, the difficult issue of full compensation to white property owners who had acquired black-owned lands during Apartheid seems to have been verbally finessed, shy of a guarantee that current owners would be fully compensated if the government seized land for redistribution. The constitution permits people or groups to seek restitution for land seized under "past racially discriminatory laws or practices" and bars any measures that would impede government efforts "to achieve land reform or equitable access to natural resources." Facts on File World News Digest, May 9, 1996, at 309 A1.

§6.1   Poletown and Other State Law Cases: What Is a "Public Use"?

ELLEN FRANKEL PAUL, PROPERTY RIGHTS AND EMINENT DOMAIN

28-29 (1987)

THE EMINENT DOMAIN POWER: HOW INNOCUOUS IS IT?

The power of eminent domain may seem innocuous to some, but its use can cause serious psychological and economic damage to property owners. Perhaps, the reason that most citizens unaffected by its use find it noncontroversial is that for most of its history it was used in a very limited way.

Few people would quibble over a power used to provide land for post offices or even highways. Today, however, its reach has been greatly extended, and many landowners have been severely affected. This damage has become worse in recent times as courts have emasculated one of the principal constraints upon the exercise of eminent domain: the "public use" proviso, which used to mean that property could not be taken merely to transfer it to another private owner. Eminent domain — the "power of the sovereign to take property for public use without the owner's consent" — is a potentially tyrannical power if it is released from the bounds of strict accountability. One such limiting notion is provided by the requirement that courts examine the necessity for any taking. But with the Supreme Court's sanction for the taking of a nondilapidated building that happened to lie within a blighted area destined for urban renewal (in Berman v. Parker in 1954), courts throughout the country have been encouraged to find a public use in a variety of imaginative takings by the states. These takings have only a tenuous connection to public necessity or public purpose, and they often simply transfer property from one private owner to another.

MORTON J. HORWITZ, THE HISTORY OF
THE PUBLIC/PRIVATE DISTINCTION

130 U. Pa. L. Rev. 1423, 1423-1426 (1982)

Taxation provides a fascinating example of the emergence of the public/private distinction. As late as the sixteenth century, English judges still analyzed taxation, not as an exaction by the state but as a private gift from the donor — the taxpayer. Parliament was thought to have simply arranged this consensual private transaction. Only with the development of theories of sovereignty in the seventeenth century did taxation begin to be understood as part of public law.

Another set of issues illustrates the same point, highlighting how recently it was that a distinctively public realm came to be a generally understood part of political and legal consciousness. Until the nineteenth century, lawsuits involving the removal of a public official from office were analyzed more frequently than not as questions of property. The officeholder often successfully claimed a property interest in the office from which he could not be divested.

So we see, on one side, that it was only gradually that English and American law came to recognize a public realm distinct from medieval conceptions of property. And equally gradually legal doctrines developed the idea of a separate private realm free from public power.

Although one can find the origins of the idea of a distinctively private realm in the natural-rights liberalism of Locke and his successors, only in the nineteenth century was the public/private distinction brought to the center of the stage in American legal and political theory. Before this could occur, it was necessary to undermine an earlier tradition of republican thought that had closely identified private virtue and public interest.

The emergence of the market as a central legitimating institution brought the public/private distinction into the core of legal discourse during the nineteenth century. Although, as we have seen, there were earlier anticipations of a distinction between public law and private law, only the nineteenth century produced a fundamental conceptual and architectural division in the way we understand the law. . . .

Let me offer some illustrations. Among the most famous is the entirely novel separation between public and private corporations in the *Dartmouth College Case*,[9] decided in 1819. Its purpose — certainly the purpose of Justice Story's famous concurring opinion — was to free the newly emerging business corporation from the regulatory public law premises that had dominated the prior law of corporations, whether municipal or trading corporations, both of which were regarded as arms of the state. . . .

What were the concerns that created a virtual obsession with separating public and private law, both conceptually and practically, during the nineteenth century? Above all was the effort of orthodox judges and jurists to create a legal science that would sharply separate law from politics. By creating a neutral and apolitical system of legal doctrine and legal reasoning free from what was thought to be the dangerous and unstable redistributive tendencies of democratic politics, legal thinkers hoped to temper the problem of "tyranny of the majority." Just as nineteenth-century political economy elevated the market to the status of the paramount institution for distributing rewards on a supposedly neutral and apolitical basis, so too private law came to be understood as a neutral system for facilitating voluntary market transactions and vindicating injuries to private rights. The hostility to statutes expressed by nineteenth-century judges and legal thinkers reflected the view that state regulation of private relations was a dangerous and unnatural public intrusion into a system based on private rights.

JEANNE WYLIE, POLETOWN: COMMUNITY BETRAYED

48-52 (1989)

GM's proposed Detroit plant would cost the corporation $500 million and would represent a substantial chunk of its $40 billion plan. In addition, Michigan officials were well aware that GM had, just a few months earlier, broken ground for a nearly identical plant in suburban Pontiac. To some it

---

9. Trustees of Dartmouth College v. Woodward, 17 U.S. (4 Wheat.) 518, 559, 669-783 (1819).

appeared that GM's new corporate investment plan might restore Michigan to its former affluence, putting Michigan's workers back on line.

GM's announcement that it would build in Detroit was greeted with banner headlines and a spirit of festivity downtown. This factory, and the one under construction in suburban Pontiac, were, after all, the first auto plants to be built in Michigan since the 1950's. They appeared to be a promise on GM's part that it would not allow the area's industrial infrastructure to become obsolete. The Poletown plant was projected to provide 6,000 union jobs and tens of thousands of spin-off jobs for parts suppliers and service stores.

Detroit officials were delighted, even though they would have to evict 4,200 people from Poletown homes and businesses, to provide the "greenfield site" General Motors wanted. They had been trying to sell the city to corporate investors for some time. So when GM made its announcement, city officials speculated that the corporation's decision to locate a new multimillion-dollar facility in Detroit would lure other companies to do the same.

City officials boasted that GM's investment would improve the city's tax revenue both by yielding property taxes and by employing workers whose wages, whether they lived in the city or the suburbs, would be subject to a city income tax. Detroit's Community and Economic Development officials vowed to accommodate GM as thoroughly and quickly as possible. They viewed GM's construction in Detroit as a sort of test case, which they hoped they could use to illustrate to other companies that Detroit knew how to do business.

It was fortunate Detroit officials were eager to cooperate quickly with GM, because the corporation gave the city just 10 months to clear the 465-acre site. General Motors executives made it clear that if the city of Detroit could not clear the neighborhood off the site by May 1, 1981, they would locate the plant elsewhere. . . .

To accommodate GM, Detroit officials would have to obtain title to Poletown's 1,400 homes, 144 businesses, and 16 churches which lay north of I-94 between Chene and Mount Elliott. Taking these parcels, under the auspices of the state's eminent domain law, would require the most massive and rapid relocation of citizens for a private development project in U.S. history. The city of Detroit would have to pay the property owners market value plus relocation costs, bulldoze the buildings, remove any toxic wastes found in the site area, fill in all basement areas and sewage and utility tunnels, and remove all asphalt and concrete. In addition, GM demanded a twelve-year, 50-percent property tax abatement, all necessary air, water, and waste permits, rezoning of the land, city expenditures to provide the plant with adequate access to rail lines, highways, water, utilities, and sewage removal, and city-funded upgrading of the ingress and egress roads to the plant, including more street lights, in order to provide "adequate security."

Initially, observers estimated that the city of Detroit was going to have to invest $240 million to satisfy GM's demands. In time, that estimate was increased to over $300 million. The burden was considerable. When the Department of Housing and Urban Development (HUD) wrote guidelines for public-private projects, it indicated a preference for projects where the private interest invested $4 for every $1 invested by the public. In the Poletown case the starting ratio was two corporate dollars for every single dollar. As time went on, the ratio was likely to come closer to a dollar-for-dollar investment.

LARRY TELL, DETROIT'S FRAY: PROGRESS v. PROPERTY

Natl. L.J., June 1, 1981, at 1

Like an inmate on Death Row, Detroit's Poletown neighborhood is clinging to the last thread of hope that it can avert the final decree.

Poletown's remaining residents have mounted some last-ditch legal maneuvers as part of their strategy to stop the city's death sentence, which would clear the community for a new General Motors Corp. automotive assembly plant.

Legal battles between a community and the wrecker's ball are not new. Although Poletown's fate seems sealed by a long line of judicial precedents from around the country, the community's looming demise has been seized upon as a symbol by both ends of the political spectrum — conservatives who see it as a new threat to the sanctity of private property and those on the left who see it as a triumph of corporate and political power over a helpless neighborhood. Critics from both camps say Poletown could spark a renewed debate over similar protests across the nation.

The underlying issue in Michigan is survival, for Poletown and for Detroit. When GM threatened last year to move some important facilities out of the Detroit area, it gave the city a take-it-or-leave-it offer for the new plant on the 465-acre Poletown site.

The economically strapped city had no choice. It decided to take the GM offer — and to "take" by eminent domain more than 1,100 homes in one of the city's oldest, still-thriving ethnic neighborhoods, as well as the beautiful Church of the Immaculate Conception and the historic former Dodge "Main" assembly plant. . . .

With unemployment in Detroit at 18 percent and the city's economic mainstay, the auto industry, facing record losses, Mayor Coleman Young thinks that Detroit is getting a good deal from GM.

"I believe this program is beyond a doubt the most important single program that has been undertaken since I became mayor," he said at the first state court trial.

The project's supporters — who probably represent every powerful political, economic and social interest in the state — blast the Poletown resi-

FIGURE 6-1
Poletown Protests

dents and their lawyers as obstructionists who will bring the city to its knees. In their last-ditch effort to stop the project, they have "no hope of prevailing," said Mr. Christopher, the city's lawyer.

"They're not doing Detroit any good, they're not doing the neighborhood any good," he says.

Attorneys who are fighting the plant give different reasons for their persistence. Some say they object to the procedural short-cuts taken to push the project through at GM's behest. Others see it as a struggle between well-heeled corporate power and the individual citizen, outgunned by high-priced legal talent and GM's pressure tactics with the city.

But none deny that Detroit desperately needs the plant.

POLETOWN NEIGHBORHOOD COUNCIL v. CITY OF DETROIT

410 Mich. 616, 304 N.W.2d 455 (1981)

PER CURIAM. This case arises out of a plan by the Detroit Economic Development Corporation to acquire, by condemnation if necessary, a large tract of land to be conveyed to General Motors Corporation as a site for construction of an assembly plant. The plaintiffs, a neighborhood association and several individual residents of the affected area, brought suit in Wayne Circuit Court to challenge the project on a number of grounds, not all of which have been argued to this Court. Defendants' motions for summary judgment were denied pending trial on a single question of fact: whether, under 1980 PA 87; MCL §213.51 et seq.; MSA §8.265(1) et seq., the city abused its discretion in determining that condemnation of plaintiffs' property was necessary to complete the project.

The trial lasted 10 days and resulted in a judgment for defendants and an order on December 9, 1980, dismissing plaintiffs' complaint. The plaintiffs filed a claim of appeal with the Court of Appeals on December 12, 1980, and an application for bypass with this Court on December 15, 1980.

We granted a motion for immediate consideration and an application for leave to appeal prior to decision by the Court of Appeals to consider the following questions:

> Does the use of eminent domain in this case constitute a taking of private property for private use and, therefore, contravene Const., art. 10, §2?
>
> Did the court below err in ruling that cultural, social and historical institutions were not protected by the Michigan Environmental Protection Act?

We conclude that these questions must be answered in the negative and affirm the trial court's decision.

I

This case raises a question of paramount importance to the future welfare of this state and its residents: Can a municipality use the power of eminent domain granted to it by the Economic Development Corporations Act, MCL §125.1601 et seq., MSA §5.3520(1) et seq., to condemn property for transfer to a private corporation to build a plant to promote industry and commerce, thereby adding jobs and taxes to the economic base of the municipality and state?

Michigan Const. Art. 10, §2, states in pertinent part that "[p]rivate property shall not be taken for public use without just compensation therefore being first made or secured in a manner prescribed by law." Art. 10, §2 has been interpreted as requiring that the power of eminent domain not be invoked except to further a public use or purpose. Plaintiffs-appellants urge us to distinguish between the terms "use" and "purpose," asserting they are not synonymous and have been distinguished in the law of eminent domain. We are persuaded the terms have been used interchangeably in Michigan statutes and decisions in an effort to describe the protean concept of public benefit. The term "public use" has not received a narrow or inelastic definition by this Court in prior cases. Indeed, this Court has stated that "'[a] public use changes with changing conditions of society'" and that "'[t]he right of the public to receive and enjoy the benefit of the use determines whether the use is public or private.'"

The Economic Development Corporations Act is a part of the comprehensive legislation dealing with planning, housing and zoning whereby the State of Michigan is attempting to provide for the general health, safety, and welfare through alleviating unemployment, providing economic assistance to industry, assisting the rehabilitation of blighted areas, and fostering urban redevelopment.

Section 2 of the act provides:

> There exists in this state the continuing need for programs to alleviate and prevent conditions of unemployment, and that it is accordingly necessary to assist and retain local industries and commercial enterprises to strengthen and revitalize the economy of this state and its municipalities; that accordingly it is necessary to provide means and methods for the encouragement and assistance of industrial and commercial enterprises in locating, purchasing, constructing, reconstructing, modernizing, improving, maintaining, repairing, furnishing, equipping, and expanding in this state and in its municipalities; and that it is also necessary to encourage the location and expansion of commercial enterprises to more conveniently provide needed services and facilities of the commercial enterprises to municipalities and the residents thereof. *Therefore, the powers granted in this act constitute the performance of essential public purposes and functions for this state and its municipalities.*

MCL §125.1602; MSA §5.3520(2). (Emphasis added.)

To further the objectives of this act, the Legislature has authorized municipalities to acquire property by condemnation in order to provide

heightened scrutiny the claim that the public interest is the predominant interest being advanced. Such public benefit cannot be speculative or marginal but must be clear and significant if it is to be within the legitimate purpose as stated by the Legislature. We hold this project is warranted on the basis that its significance for the people of Detroit and the state has been demonstrated.

Plaintiffs' complaint also alleged that the proposed project violates the Michigan Environmental Protection Act (MEPA), MCL §691.1201 et seq.; MSA §14.528(201) et seq., *because it "will have a major adverse impact on the adjoining social and cultural environment which is referred to as Poletown." The trial court dismissed this claim, stating that "'social and cultural environments' are matters not within the purview of the MEPA and outside its legislative intent."* We agree.

MCL §691.1202(1); MSA §14.528(202)(1) permits maintenance of an action for declaratory and equitable relief against the state, its political subdivisions, or private entities, "for the protection of the air, water and other natural resources and the public trust therein from pollution, impairment or destruction." (Emphasis supplied.) The reference to "air, water and other natural resources" is also made in other sections of the act and in its title. Given its plain meaning, the term "natural resources" does not encompass a "social and cultural environment." Moreover, under the principle of ejusdem generis, where a statute contains a general term supplementing a more specific enumeration, the general term will not be construed to refer to objects not of like kind with those enumerated. 2A Sutherland, Statutory Construction (4th ed.), §§47.18-47.19, pp.109-114.

The decision of the trial court is affirmed.

No costs, a public question being involved.

FITZGERALD, J. (dissenting). This Court today decides that the power of eminent domain permits the taking of private property with the object of transferring it to another private party for the purpose of constructing and operating a factory, on the ground that the employment and other economic benefits of this privately operated industrial facility are such as to satisfy the "public use" requirement for the exercise of eminent domain power. Because I believe the proposed condemnation clearly exceeds the government's authority to take private property through the power of eminent domain, I dissent.

I

In the spring of 1980, General Motors Corporation informed the City of Detroit that it would close its Cadillac and Fisher Body plants located within the city in 1983. General Motors offered to build an assembly complex in the city, if a suitable site could be found. General Motors set four criteria for the approval of a site: an area of between 450 and 500 acres; a rectangular shape (¾ mile by 1 mile); access to a long-haul railroad line; and access to the freeway system. The city evaluated a number of potential sites and eventually made an in-depth study of nine sites. Eight of the sites were found not to be feasible, [1] and the ninth, with which we are concerned, was recommended. It occupies approximately 465 acres in the cities of Detroit and Hamtramck. [2] A plan was developed to acquire the site, labeled the Central Industrial Park, under the Economic Development Corporations Act, 1974 PA 338. As authorized by the statute, the project plan contemplated the use of condemnation to acquire at least some of the property within the site. . . . I concur with the discussion of the environmental protection act issue, but disagree with the analysis of the eminent domain question.

II

The city attaches great importance to the explicit legislative findings in the Economic Development Corporations Act that unemployment is a serious problem and that it is necessary to encourage industry in order to revitalize the economy of this state, and to the legislative declaration that the use of eminent domain power pursuant to a project under the act, "shall be considered necessary for public purposes and for the benefit of the public." It is undeniable that such legislative pronouncements are entitled to great deference. However, determination whether a taking is for a public or a private use is ultimately a judicial question. E.g., Lakehead Pipe Line Co. v. Dehn, 340 Mich. 25, 39-40, 64 N.W.2d 903 (1954); Cleveland v. City of Detroit, 322 Mich. 172, 179, 33 N.W.2d 747 (1948). Through the years this Court has not hesitated to declare takings authorized by statute not to be for public use in appropriate cases. E.g., Shizas v. City of Detroit, 333 Mich. 44, 52 N.W.2d 589 (1952); Berrien Springs Water-Power Co. v. Berrien Circuit Judge, 133 Mich. 48, 94 N.W. 379 (1903). This is as it must be, since if a legislative declaration on the question of public use were conclusive, citizens could be subjected to the most outrageous confiscation of property for the benefit of other private interests without redress. Thus, while mindful of the expression of the legislative view of the appropriateness of using the eminent domain power in the circumstances of this case, this Court has the responsibility to determine whether the authorization is lawful.

Our role was well stated by Justice Cooley in "A Treatise on the Constitutional Limitations." Writing subsequent to the Court's decision in People ex rel. Detroit and Howell R. Co. v. Salem Township Board, 20 Mich.

---

1. Indeed, according to the Draft Environmental Impact Statement prepared by the city, none of the other eight sites studied met even the four basic criteria specified by General Motors.

2. Although approximately 145 of the 465 acres of the project lie within the city of Hamtramck, this case involves only the portion of the project located in Detroit.

452 (1870), he noted: "The question what is a public use is always one of law. Deference will be paid to the legislative judgment, as expressed in enactments providing for an appropriation of property, but it will not be conclusive." 2 Cooley, Constitutional Limitations (8th ed.), p.1141.

III

Our approval of the use of eminent domain power in this case takes this state into a new realm of takings of private property; there is simply no precedent for this decision in previous Michigan cases. . . .

[I]n the present case the transfer of the property to General Motors after the condemnation cannot be considered incidental to the taking. It is only through the acquisition and use of the property by General Motors that the "public purpose" of promoting employment can be achieved. Thus, it is the economic benefits of the project that are incidental to the private use of the property.

The city also points to decisions that have found the objective of economic development to be a sufficient "public purpose" to support the expenditure of public funds in aid of industry. Advisory Opinion on Constitutionality of 1975 PA 301, 400 Mich. 270, 254 N.W.2d 528 (1977); City of Gaylord v. Gaylord City Clerk, 378 Mich. 273, 144 N.W.2d 460 (1966). What constitutes a public purpose in a context of governmental taxing and spending power cannot be equated with the use of that term in connection with eminent domain powers. The potential risk of abuse in the use of eminent domain power is clear. Condemnation places the burden of aiding industry on the few, who are likely to have limited power to protect themselves from the excesses of legislative enthusiasm for the promotion of industry. The burden of taxation is distributed on the great majority of the population, leading to a more effective check on improvident use of public funds. . . .

V

The majority relies on the principle that the concept of public use is an evolving one; however, I cannot believe that this evolution has eroded our historic protection against the taking of private property for private use to the degree sanctioned by this Court's decision today. The decision that the prospect of increased employment, tax revenue, and general economic stimulation makes a taking of private property for transfer to another private party sufficiently "public" to authorize the use of the power of eminent domain means that there is virtually no limit to the use of condemnation to aid private businesses. Any business enterprise produces benefits to society at large. Now that we have authorized local legislative bodies to decide that a different commercial or industrial use of property will produce greater public benefits than its present use, no homeowner's, merchant's or manufacturer's property, however productive or valuable to its owner, is immune from condemnation for the benefit of other private interests that will put it to a "higher" use.[15] As one prominent commentator has written:

> It often happens that the erection of a large factory will be of more benefit to the whole community in which it is planned to build it than any strictly public improvement which the inhabitants of the place could possibly undertake; but even if the plan was blocked by the refusal of the selfish owner of a small but necessary parcel of land to part with it at any price, the public mind would instinctively revolt at any attempt to take such land by eminent domain.

2A Nichols, Eminent Domain §7.1[1] (rev. 3d ed.).

The condemnation contemplated in the present action goes beyond the scope of the power of eminent domain in that it takes private property for private use. I would reverse the judgment of the circuit court.

RYAN, J. (dissenting). This is an extraordinary case. The reverberating clang of its economic, sociological, political, and jurisprudential impact is likely to be heard and felt for generations. By its decision, the Court has altered the law of eminent domain in this state in a most significant way and, in my view, seriously jeopardized the security of all private property ownership.

The evidence, then, is that what General Motors wanted, General Motors got. The corporation conceived the project, determined the cost, allocated the financial burdens, selected the site, established the mode of financing, imposed specific deadlines for clearance of the property and taking title, and even demanded 12 years of tax concessions.[9]

From the beginning, construction of the new assembly plant in Detroit was characterized by the city administration as a do or die propo-

---

15. It would be easy to sustain the proposed project because of its large size and the extent of the claimed benefits to flow from it. The estimate is that approximately 6150 persons would be employed in the factory itself, with the generation of substantial other employment, business activity, and tax revenue as a result. However, it must be remembered that the dislocations and other costs of the project are also massive. The project plan indicates that a total of 3438 persons will be displaced by the project, that it will require the destruction of 1176 structures, and that the cost of the project to the public sector will be nearly $200,000,000.

9. What is reported here is not meant to denigrate either the role or the good faith of General Motors Corporation. It is a private, profit-making enterprise. Its managers are answerable to a demanding board of directors who, in turn, have a fiduciary obligation to the corporation's shareholders. It is struggling to compete worldwide in a depressed economy. It is a corporation having a history, especially in recent years, of a responsible, even admirable, "social conscience." In fact, this project may well entail compromises of sound business dictates and concomitant financial sacrifices to avoid the worsening unemployment and economic depression which would result if General Motors were to move from the state of Michigan as other major employers have. The point here is not to criticize General Motors, but to relate accurately the facts which attended the city's decision to condemn private property to enable General Motors to build a new plant in Detroit and to "set the scene" in which, as will be seen hereafter, broad-based support for the project was orchestrated in the state, fostering a sense of inevitability and dire consequence if the plan was not approved by all concerned. General Motors is not the villain of the piece.

sition. Accordingly, the city, aided by the Michigan "quick-take" statute, marshalled and applied its resources and power to insure that CIP was a fait accompli before meaningful objection could be registered or informed opposition organized. Faced with the unacceptable prospect of losing two automotive plants and the jobs that go with them, the city chose to march in fast lock-step with General Motors to carve a "green field" out of an urban setting which ultimately required sweeping away a tightly-knit residential enclave of first- and second-generation Americans, for many of whom their home was their single most valuable and cherished asset and their stable ethnic neighborhood the unchanging symbol of the security and quality of their lives. . . .

The judiciary, cognizant of General Motors' May 1 deadline for the city's taking title to all of the property, moved at flank speed. The circuit court conducted a trial on defendants' motion to dismiss plaintiffs' complaint from November 17 to December 2, 1980, and the decision to dismiss the complaint was made on December 9, 1980. Application for leave to appeal prior to decision by the Court of Appeals was received in this Court on December 15, 1980. However, the trial transcript was not received by us until January 5, 1981. We promptly convened, conferred, and granted leave to appeal on January 29, 1981. The case was argued on March 3, 1981.

In less than two weeks, the lead opinions were filed by this Court and released. It is in such circumstances that we were asked to decide, and did decide, an important constitutional issue having towering implications both for the individual plaintiff property owners and for the City of Detroit and the state alike, to say nothing of the impact upon our jurisprudence.

I now turn to set down separately my understanding of the law which governs this case and the outcome it ought to have dictated. My disagreement with my colleagues in the majority, while vigorous, is nonetheless respectful. Vigorous, because I think the unintended jurisprudential mischief which has been done, if not soon rectified, will have echoing effects far beyond this case, and respectful because the crushing burden of litigation which this Court must address daily did not afford adequate time for sufficient consideration of the complex constitutional issues involved within the two-week deadline the Court set for itself for submission, consideration, and decision of the case.

NOTES AND QUESTIONS

1.   **Poletown.** Like many other urban neighborhoods, Poletown's heyday was past by 1981. According to John J. Bukowczyk, The Decline and Fall of a Detroit Neighborhood: Poletown vs. G.M. & The City of Detroit, 41 Wash. & Lee L. Rev. 49, 51-62 (1984), Polish settlement in the area began in the 1860s, reached 22,000 in 1885, and 48,000 by 1900. Immigrants found jobs in the iron and steel industries, railroad car manufacturers, cigar

FIGURE 6-2
Poletown, Before and After

factories, and later, in the automotive industry. At the beginning of World War II, 60,000 people worked in Poletown. Bukowczyk cites deindustrialization, the exodus to the suburbs, and freeway construction that chopped up the neighborhood as factors that left Poletown "visibly blighted" by the 1970s. Over the years as well, the Polish character of the neighborhood was tempered by the settlement of immigrants from other countries as well as poor white and black Americans attracted by the low cost of housing. In 1980, the plans for the 465-acre GM plant displaced 1,176 buildings, 143 businesses and other institutions (including sixteen churches, two schools, and one hospital) 1,362 households, and 3,438 people. An estimated 40 to 60 percent of the population was black, 30 to 50 percent was Polish, and the rest included ethnic Albanians, Yemeni, Ukrainians, Filipinos and southern whites. The question is, what level of population and economic activity makes a neighborhood viable?

2.   **Urban flight and unemployment.** In Detroit in 1980, unemployment was 15 percent. Large industries had laid off over 100,000 employees and closed or relocated to the suburbs. Minority unemployment was over 26 percent. GM, Ford, and Chrysler reported record losses. Between 1954 and 1977, Detroit lost 59,706 jobs in retail stores while the suburbs gained 76,760. Between 1970 and 1980, Detroit's property tax base shrank from $5.3 billion to $5.2 billion. In suburban Oakland county, the property tax base increased by 500 percent to $14 billion. Jeanie Wylie, Poletown: Community Betrayed 29-31 (1989). How do these statistics relate to the "public purpose" of providing jobs for city residents and improving the tax base?

3.   **Update.** A news article from 1989 updates the Poletown story. The $700 million General Motor Corp.'s plant has not lived up to its expectations. The expected 5,300 to 5,400 jobs for which the city spent $300 million came into fruition only briefly in the fall of 1985. But by 1989, only 3,000 hourly workers were being employed for a single shift. Land acquisition costs reached more than twice the expected total, and after the first four years of production, the plant had returned no taxes to the city. The promise of new business also never transpired. The plant is self-contained and has brought more pain to a community that was already suffering. About 4,300 people were moved to accommodate the plant but the dreams of new development were shattered. "People thought that the plant would be their salvation. It wasn't." Jack A. Seamonds, Poletown Hasn't Matched Promise, Detroit Free Press, May 31, 1989, at 17A. Is any of this data relevant to your assessment of whether Poletown was taken for a valid "public" use?

4.   **World Trade Center.** Twenty years before Poletown, the New York courts had faced a similarly heated controversy involving the condemnation that led to erection of the World Trade Center, twin 1,360-foot towers containing 10 million square feet of office space. The developer, a public authority, proposed to gather together as its tenants businesses relating to international trade, in order to strengthen the city's harbor activity. Opponents included merchants and landowners within the 13-block area

whose parcels faced condemnation and private real estate investors whose office-building holdings faced competition. All legal attacks were finally beaten off. Courtesy Sandwich Shop v. Port of New York Authority, 12 N.Y.2d 379, 190 N.E.2d 402, 240 N.Y.S.2d 1 (1963), *app. dismissed*, 375 U.S. 78 (1963) (concept of World Trade Center fulfills public purpose); Port of New York Auth. v. 62 Cortlandt St. Realty Co., 18 N.Y.2d 250, 219 N.E.2d 797, 273 N.Y.S. 337 (1966) (developer entitled to proceed with condemnation despite allegations that of 372 proposed tenants not over 103 would have real relation to World Trade functions).

5. **Blight?** In both the Poletown and World Trade Center situations, the project area was neither slum nor blighted. Would the controversy over the proposed reuse be without legal bearing if the legislature had declared (with appropriate factual findings) that the reuse area was physically substandard? Compare Yonkers Community Dev. Agency v. Morris, 37 N.Y.2d 478, 335 N.E.2d 327 (1975) ("substandard" land condemned to provide for expansion of Otis Elevator Company, one of the city's leading industrial employers; held: condemnation valid), and Miller v. City of Tacoma, 61 Wash. 2d 374, 378 P.2d 464 (1963) ("blighted area" condemned as part of comprehensive urban renewal plan; held: condemnation valid), with Hogue v. Port of Seattle, Note 6(b), *infra* (held: condemnation invalid).

6. **Requiem?** Comment, The Public Use Limitation on Eminent Domain: An Advance Requiem, 58 Yale L.J. 599, 614 (1949):

> Legal doctrines usually die quietly, if slowly. Their demise is generally accompanied by no more than soft sighs of relief at the courts' final acknowledgment of decay. But the theory of "public use" as a limitation on eminent domain — the notion that there are only certain limited "public purposes" for which private property may be expropriated — bulked so large in its prime and has taken so long in dying that, at the risk of disturbing the deathwatch, a few final words may be in order. . . . Doubtless the doctrine will continue to be evoked nostalgically in dicta and may even be employed authoritatively in rare, atypical situations. Kinder hands, however, would accord it the permanent interment in the digests that is so long overdue.

Consider, in the light of the following decisions, whether the words above are entirely prophetic.

(a) *Oakland Raiders.* In City of Oakland v. Oakland Raiders, 646 P.2d 835 (Cal. 1982), the California Supreme Court considered the legality of the city's attempt to condemn the professional football franchise and acquire it under eminent domain when the Raiders decided to move the team to Los Angeles. The city based its condemnation on the public use theory, and the court agreed that operating a professional football franchise could qualify as a public purpose. The court acknowledged that the definition of "public use" is not restricted "to matters of mere business necessity and ordinary convenience, but may extend to matters of public health, recreation and enjoyment." Id. at 841. The court cited several cities that own and operate municipal stadiums that are home to professional sports teams, and stated that from the evidence presented, it could make no significant distinction between owning the stadium and owning the team that plays in the stadium. Id. at 842.

> From the foregoing we conclude only that the acquisition and, indeed, the operation of a sports franchise may be an appropriate municipal function. . . . We caution that we are not concerned with the economic or governmental wisdom of City's acquisition or management of the Raiders' franchise, but only with the legal propriety of the condemnation action. In this period of fiscal constraints, if the city fathers of Oakland in their collective wisdom elect to seek the ownership of a professional football franchise are we to say to them nay? And, if so, on what legal ground? Constitutional? Both federal and state Constitutions permit condemnation requiring only compensation and public use. Statutory? The applicable statutes authorize a city to take "any property," real or personal to carry out appropriate municipal functions. Decisional? Courts have consistently expanded the eminent domain remedy permitting property to be taken for recreational purposes.

Id. at 843. The court ordered the case back to the trial court, where it originally received summary judgment for the Raiders, for a full trial.

(b) *Boeing.* Civic leaders in the Seattle area had become concerned with the imbalance of industrial employment: One company, Boeing, engaged more than half the area's industrial workforce. Believing that the lack of suitable plant sites was a major deterrent to a broadened industrial base, the leaders obtained a state law that enabled the Port of Seattle (a public body) to condemn so-called marginal land — fully developed agricultural and residential acreage — for resale as industrial sites.

The Supreme Court of Washington did not find a lawful public purpose. Hogue v. Port of Seattle, 54 Wash. 2d 799, 838-839, 341 P.2d 171, 193 (1959).

> [T]he property owner is assured that, until our state constitution is amended, he may continue to own, possess, and use his property (for any lawful purpose) regardless of whether the state or any subdivision thereof may devise a plan for putting the property to a higher or better economic use than that to which the owner is currently devoting it. Unless the state or its subdivision can prove to the satisfaction of a court that it seeks to acquire the property for a "really public" use (and also pays just compensation for it), the owner may not be deprived of it without his consent.

Accord: Merrill v. City of Manchester, 127 N.H. 234, 499 A.2d 21b (1985) (26 acres of forest land condemned for private industrial park; held: condemnation invalid). But see Cannata v. City of New York, 11 N.Y.2d 210, 182 N.E.2d 395, 227 N.Y.S.2d 903 (1962) (95 acres of predominantly vacant residential tract condemned for industrial park; held: condemnation valid); but see People ex rel. City of Salem v. McMackin, 53 Ill. 2d 347, 291 N.E.2d 807 (1972) (state's Industrial Project Revenue Bond Act, which would stimulate private enterprise, held valid). Cf. also David E. Pinsky, State Constitutional Limitations on Public Industrial Financing: An Historical and Economic Approach, 111 U. Pa. L. Rev. 265 (1963); Comment, State Constitutional Provisions Prohibiting the Loaning of Credit to Private Enterprise — A Suggested Analysis, 41 U. Colo. L. Rev. 135 (1969).

(c) *Charleston convention center complex.* The City of Charleston proposed a joint venture with a private concern whereby the city would condemn several parcels that would be leased to the concern for the construction and operation of a 500-car parking garage and convention center. On an adjoining two-acre parcel, which would be acquired privately, the concern would build a hotel, major department store, and restaurant. The convention center-hotel complex was intended to help revitalize downtown Charleston.

The South Carolina Supreme Court denied the city its power of eminent domain. The court concluded that the proposed undertaking failed constitutionally because it envisioned a taking of private property that would not be devoted to a public use. "However attractive the proposed complex, however desirable the project from a municipal planning viewpoint, the use of the power of eminent domain for such purposes runs squarely into the right of an individual to own property and use it as he pleases." Karesh v. City Council of City of Charleston, 271 S.C. 339, 247 S.E.2d 342 (1978).

(d) *Massachusetts housing.* A bill pending in the Massachusetts legislature would have created a state agency to help finance mixed projects of low and moderate rental housing. The agency would make the mortgage loans to limited profit developers, but the precondition to a loan was an acceptable tenant selection plan. Tenants were to be selected so as "to avoid undue economic homogeneity." To help achieve this goal, the agency — through rent supplements — would additionally subsidize at least one quarter of the units in each project. The housing could be located anywhere, for the bill was not specifically directed to slum or blight removal.

The Supreme Judicial Court was asked to render an advisory opinion as to the legality of the proposed measure. At issue was whether the commonwealth's tax power, which, like eminent domain, must be used for a public purpose, could validly underwrite the program described above. Although the court implicitly endorsed the use of tax money to help clear slums or furnish low-income rental housing, it boggled at a program that would encourage the building of "moderate" rental housing, for which no need had been asserted, in order to bring about mixtures of low- and middle-income families within a single project. Opinion of the Justices, 351 Mass. 716, 219 N.E.2d 18 (Mass. 1966). Cf. also Russin v. Town of Union, 113 A.D.2d 1014, 521 N.Y.S.2d 160 (3d Dept. 1987) (construction and sale of 19 two-family homes for low-income elderly persons not "public use").

7.   **Defining a "public use."** Lawrence Berger, The Public Use Requirement in Eminent Domain, 57 Or. L. Rev. 203, 205, 209 (1978):

> The conventional statement of the historical case development holds that there are two basic opposing views of the meaning of "public use": (1) that the term means advantage or benefit to the public (the so-called broad view); and (2) that it means actual use or right to use of the condemned property by the public (the so-called narrow view). . . .
>
> While the narrow view of public use held considerable sway, especially in the latter half of the nineteenth century, it never completely took over the field. The two doctrines competed, leaving the commentators in hopeless confusion as to what the "true rule" (for in those days they believed in such things) was. . . . Thus the narrow use by the public rule would have allowed condemnation for the purpose of erecting a privately owned theater or hotel, something which no one then (or perhaps even now) would seriously advocate. And the broad public advantage test would have allowed a toy manufacturer who provided substantial employment in a vicinity to condemn land for the construction of a plant, likewise then unthinkable. . . .

8.   **Should there be a public use requirement?** Do you believe there *should* be a "public use" limitation on how the legislature may spend its money for land acquisition via eminent domain, if the lawmakers have spoken and the city is ready to pay fair value? Consider this question in the light of the following situations:

(a)   City A acquires a privately owned parcel for resale to a developer of luxury housing as part of a program to keep wealthy residents within the city.

(b)   City B acquires a privately owned business building for resale to a minority owned bank as part of a program to stimulate minority enterprise.

(c)   City C acquires some privately owned apartment houses for resale to an investment syndicate that will use the site for a professional sports arena and convention center.

(d)   City D acquires some privately owned "holdout" properties for resale to an office developer who needs the sites to complete his land assemblage. This is done to promote efficient and aesthetic office development.

Would your views be any different if the cities instead were to give various other subsidies to promote the several goals indicated?

In this connection, do you agree or disagree with the following?

> The conclusion is that there is no sufficient reason to limit the exercise of eminent domain any more than of other powers of government. All exercises, including regulations and taxations, are intrusions upon individual liberty,

but they are necessary to prevent greater human losses in an interdependent society. Eminent domain poses no special threat to the individual that would require special limitations on the occasions of its exercise. It is not black magic, but merely one of the powers of government, to be used along with the other powers as long as some ordinary purpose of government is served.

William B. Stoebuck, A General Theory of Eminent Domain, 47 Wash. L. Rev. 553, 597 (1972).

9. **Eminent domain v. police power.** Do the "general welfare" limitation on police power and the "public purpose" limitation on eminent domain mean the same thing? Professor Stoebuck argues above that eminent domain should not suffer any greater restraint on the scope of its exercise than does the police power. Turn the statement around. Should the police power suffer any greater restraint on the *scope* of its exercise than does eminent domain?

10. **Use of eminent domain by municipalities.** One author has examined whether municipalities can use the power of eminent domain to keep factories from moving away from rustbelt areas.

> In some instances the present owners of a plant are not interested in selling to the workers or their friends, or to any competitor. This attitude on the part of U.S. Steel in Youngstown gave impetus to the efforts of people there, and later in Pittsburgh, to explore the use of eminent domain as a tool to take over productive capacity in cases in which an owner was unwilling to sell at a fair price or unwilling to sell period.

Fran Ansley, Standing Rusty and Rolling Empty: Law, Poverty, and America's Eroding Industrial Base, 81 Geo. L.J. 1757 (1993). Exploration of the eminent domain power in the Pittsburgh area took place after sustained grassroots organizing efforts that grew out of the dismantling of the steel industry. Plant closing opponents, cooperating under the banner of the Tri-State Conference on Steel, succeeded in establishing the Steel Valley Authority (SVA). The Authority is a quasi-public agency formed by the joint action of ten cities and boroughs in and around Pittsburgh, under Pennsylvania's Municipal Authorities Act of 1945.

> The SVA has not yet actually exercised its eminent domain power, but it has seriously investigated that option on a number of occasions. Sometimes the credible threat of such an exercise can alter outcomes. For instance, the Nabisco company altered plans to close its bakery in Pittsburgh when a plausible threat of eminent domain arose, especially in light of the public promise by a local official that Pittsburgh would learn "how to make its own oreos." [299]
>
> The use of eminent domain is not greeted with equal confidence or

---

299. Telephone interview with Jim Benn, Director of the Federation for Industrial Renewal and Retention (Feb. 4, 1993).

enthusiasm, however, by all public officials. While some see it as an admirable way to protect the community against the forced destruction of accumulated human and social capital, others see it as an unprecedented and dangerous intrusion on free enterprise, or at any rate, a risky venture. And whichever way a local official sees such an exercise of governmental authority, she is likely to be worried about the "business climate."

. . . The use of eminent domain to preserve industrial capacity may face another constitutional obstacle. In the 1980's the City of Oakland, California took steps to take the Oakland Raiders football team by eminent domain in order to prevent it from moving out of town. The California Supreme Court upheld the constitutionality of such action in the face of a challenge that the taking lacked a public purpose.[305] On remand, however, the court of appeals ruled that the city's action was contrary to the commerce clause of the federal constitution, in that it violated the dormant prohibition of state regulation of interstate commerce.[306]

. . . Despite obstacles and hesitancies, some state or local government in the future is likely to attempt to use the eminent domain power to preserve local industrial capacity. Governments will be drawn into such activities by the logic of the economic transformation going on around them and by the mobilized pain and anger of their constituents.

Fran Ansley, Standing Rusty and Rolling Empty: Law, Poverty and America's Eroding Industrial Base, 81 Geo. L.J. 1757, 1833-1837 (1993).

11. **Who may exercise the power of eminent domain?** In the United States, a long tradition exists of allowing certain regulated industries — for example, railroads and public utilities — to meet their land needs through eminent domain. More recently, nonprofit institutions — for example, universities and hospitals — and limited-profit companies formed to build below-market rental or sales housing, have been given the power to condemn. But when may the power be validly delegated to private landowners who are not rendering a "public service"?

Consider the Utah statute before the Supreme Court in Clark v. Nash, 198 U.S. 361 (1905), which permitted persons to condemn privately held land to obtain water for farming or mining. An individual, owning arid farmland, sought to run an irrigation ditch across his neighbor's land that would connect with the Fort Canyon Creek. Against the claim that the taking was for a private use, the U.S. Supreme Court, through Justice Peckham, wrote (at 367-368):

In some States, probably in most of them, the proposition contended for by the plaintiffs in error would be sound. But whether a statute of a State

305. City of Oakland v. Oakland Raiders, 646 P.2d 835 (Cal. 1982).
306. City of Oakland v. Oakland Raiders, 220 Cal. Rptr. 153, 156-158 (Ct. App. 1986); see also Edward P. Lazarus, The Commerce Clause Limitation on the Power to Condemn a Relocation, 96 Yale L.J. 1343 (1987) (arguing that use of the eminent domain power by local governments to prevent business from relocating violates the Commerce Clause).

permitting condemnation by an individual for the purpose of obtaining water for his land or for mining should be held to be a condemnation for a public use, and, therefore, a valid enactment, may depend upon a number of considerations relating to the situation of a State and its possibilities for land cultivation. . . . It is not alone the fact that the land is arid and that it will bear crops if irrigated, or that the water is necessary for the purpose of working a mine, that is material; other facts might exist which are also material, such as the particular manner in which the irrigation is carried on or proposed, or how the mining is to be done in a particular place where water is needed for that purpose. The general situation and amount of the arid land, or of the mines themselves, might also be material, and what proportion of the water each owner should be entitled to; also the extent of the population living in the surrounding country, and whether each owner of land or mines could be, in fact, furnished with the necessary water in any other way than by condemnation in his own behalf, and not by a company, for his use and that of others.

Helped by findings that the condemnor had no alternative source of water supply, that his land would not produce without artificial irrigation, and that the condemnee's own water supply would not be impaired, the Court approved both the statute and its application.

The condemnee's damages, it should be noted, were only $40. Might the landowner have acquired the interest he sought, even against his unwilling neighbor, without benefit of eminent domain? Compare Berkeley Dev. Corp. v. Hutzler, *supra*. Might an inverted nuisance argument also be made? The refusal to permit a right-of-way essential for irrigation can be as damaging to the adjoining land as many of the forms of positive activity that courts would enjoin as a nuisance.

For further instance of the "private" exercise of eminent domain, see Strickley v. Highland Boy Gold Mining Co., 200 U.S. 527 (1906) (Court approved mining concern's use of the Utah statute to erect an aerial bucket line over privately owned lands to carry ore down to a railway station 1200 feet below the mines); Linggi v. Garovotti, 45 Cal. 2d 20, 286 P.2d 15 (1955) (landowner may be permitted to lay a private sewer line across an adjoining lot to connect with the public system).

12. **Motives.** Where the proposed reuse is one that is clearly "public" — a park or playground, for example — may a court look into the condemnor's motives to see if they are pure?

In several instances condemnation appears to have been used to thwart black or interracial housing from entering white neighborhoods. The most litigated attempt concerned the village of Deerfield, Illinois, a Chicago suburb. There, after approving two new subdivisions, the village learned of the builder's plan for an interracial development. Within days, the village park board voted to acquire the subdivision sites for park use, although the parcels had not previously been considered in discussions over park expansion. Condemnation was begun in the state court, which the developer then sought to block in the federal court. Both suits enjoyed a lively time of it as they stepped from trial to appellate stage and back again, but the outcome turned on the state court decision. There, in Deerfield Park Dist. v. Progress Development Corp., 26 Ill. 2d 296, 186 N.E.2d 360 (1962), the Illinois Supreme Court refused to forestall the taking unless "its sole and exclusive purpose" was racially inspired. If the village could establish, as it ultimately did, both a need for parks and the suitability of the land in question, the condemnation was valid despite the accompanying motive. The U.S. Supreme Court denied certiorari, 372 U.S. 968 (1963). For a stirring account of the goings-on in Deerfield before the lawsuits began, see H. Rosen and D. Rosen, But Not Next Door (1962).

Similar occurrences have been reported around the country.

(a)   Creve Coeur, Missouri: A black physician was unable to complete his house when his land (and that of two other families) was taken for a park and playground. Although conceding the questionability of improper motive, the court declared that "the motive which actuates and induces the legislative body to enact legislation is wholly the responsibility of that body, and courts have no jurisdiction to intervene in that area." City of Creve Coeur v. Weinstein, 329 S.W.2d 399 (Mo. Ct. App. 1959) (injunction denied).

(b)   Western Springs, Illinois: After a black surgeon had purchased a homesite, the park district moved to condemn his lot.

(c)   Rutledge, Pennsylvania: The borough selected the home of an NAACP official "for use as a site for a municipal building and other municipal purposes."

(d)   Richland, Oregon: A water district voted to condemn the lot of a homebuilding black couple "to preserve sufficient land for future development and sanitation control."

In the last three instances injunctions to bar condemnation were reportedly issued.

Cf. also Blankner v. City of Chicago, 504 F.2d 1037, 1040-1041 (7th Cir. 1974), citing Green Street Assn. v. Daley, 373 F.2d 1, 6 (7th Cir.), cert. denied, 387 U.S. 932 (1967) (if the area were in fact slum and blighted, the defendants' motives in designating it for renewal would be irrelevant).

13.   **The necessity for the public use.**

(a)   "The property of no person shall be taken for public use without just compensation." Conn. Const. art. 1, §11. This language, typical of that found in most state constitutions, was at issue in a 1965 statewide referendum. By a sharply divided vote, a constitutional convention had proposed an amendment to §11, reading: "No property shall be taken for public use unless the taking be necessary for such use, and then, only upon the payment of just compensation."

Consider the implications of this proposed change. Its chief drafter defended it by saying that "constitutional protection of property rights against greatly increased governmental agency land taking is of prime importance." New Haven Register, Oct. 14, 1954. Opponents spoke of the added expense and delay. Some called the change "meaningless." Id.

After a bitter campaign, in which the Connecticut Urban Renewal Association spent large sums to fight the change, the electorate voted to leave the constitution as it was.

(b)   "In all cases where land is required for public use, . . . it must be located in the manner which will be most compatible with the greatest public good and the least private injury. . . ." Mont. Code Ann. §70-30-110 (1995).

Without considering seriously whether it would be feasible to improve an existing right of way, the State Highway Commission decided to build a 14.2-mile parallel route that would cut across fertile farmland. On the "benefit" side, both the new and the old routes were of equal merit. Relying on the above statute, the court refused to allow condemnation if a detailed study, which the commission was directed to make, failed to show that the proposed route would cause "less private injury" than improvement of the existing route. State Highway Commn. v. Danielsen, 146 Mont. 539, 409 P.2d 443 (1965). Should every state have such a statute? How is "private injury" fixed? Is it simply computing what it will cost to acquire the right of way?

14.   **Excess condemnation.** The state plans to widen an existing roadway from 60 feet to 100 feet. May it condemn a 190-foot strip — 150 feet more than is now needed — to serve any of the following purposes?

(a)   Should further widening become necessary, the state will have already acquired the needed frontage — at present-day prices.

(b)   Since increased traffic is expected to cause a sharp rise in the value of abutting lands, the state can capture this value by selling off to private developers what it does not need; see, e.g., City of Cincinnati v. Vester, 33 F.2d 242 (6th Cir. 1929).

(c)   The additional frontage will produce a less expensive source of landfill than could be purchased commercially; cf. United States v. Certain Parcels of Land, 233 F. Supp. 544 (W.D. Mich. 1964).

(d)   The additional frontage will help to protect the scenic view along the highway.

(e)   The additional frontage, inter alia, will make it unlikely that the state will be forced to pay excess severance damages to abutting owners; cf. People ex rel. Dept. of Pub. Works v. Superior Court, 68 Cal. 2d 206, 436 P.2d 342, 65 Cal. Rptr. 342 (1968).

See generally 2A Nichols, Eminent Domain §7.06[7][a] (rev. 3d ed. 1996); Michael J. Matheson, Excess Condemnation in California; Proposals for Statutory and Constitutional Change, 42 S. Cal. L. Rev. 421 (1969).

15.   **Extraterritorial condemnation.** When may community A accommodate its needs by acquiring land in community B? Must the state legislature first give approval? If approval is given, will (should) the courts intervene to protect the "interests" of community B? Consider the following examples:

(a)   A downstate city acquires an upstate watershed for water supply.

(b)   A city acquires farmland in an unincorporated township (incorporated village) for a jetport.

(c)   A city acquires woodland (a public golf course) in an unincorporated township (incorporated village) for a recreational center for city residents.

(d)   A city housing authority acquires a 100-acre parcel in an unincorporated township (incorporated village) for a low-income housing project that will help to relocate the city's urban renewal site occupants.

See generally 2A Nichols, Eminent Domain §2.24 (rev. 3d ed. 1996).

16.   **How broad?** How broad should be the scope of a "public" use? Does your answer depend on your vision of property?

§6.2   The Supreme Court Enters the Field

HAWAII HOUSING AUTHORITY v. MIDKIFF

467 U.S. 229 (1984)

O'CONNOR, J.

The Fifth Amendment of the United States Constitution provides, in pertinent part, that "private property [shall not] be taken for public use, without just compensation." These cases present the question whether the Public Use Clause of that Amendment, made applicable to the States through the Fourteenth Amendment, prohibits the State of Hawaii from taking, with just compensation, title in real property from lessors and transferring it to lessees in order to reduce the concentration of ownership of fees simple in the State. We conclude that it does not. . . .

The Hawaiian Islands were originally settled by Polynesian immigrants from the western Pacific. These settlers developed an economy around a feudal land tenure system in which one island high chief, the ali'i nui, controlled the land and assigned it for development to certain subchiefs. The subchiefs would then reassign the land to other lower ranking chiefs, who would administer the land and govern the farmers and other tenants working it. All land was held at the will of the ali'i nui and eventually had to be returned to his trust. There was no private ownership of land. . . .

Beginning in the early 1800's, Hawaiian leaders and American settlers repeatedly attempted to divide the lands of the kingdom among the crown, the chiefs, and the common people. These efforts proved largely unsuccessful, however, and the land remained in the hands of a few. In the mid-1960's, after extensive hearings, the Hawaii Legislature discovered that, while the State and Federal Governments owned almost 49% of the State's land, another 47% was in the hands of only 72 private landowners. . . . The legislature further found that 18 landholders, with tracts of 21,000 acres or more, owned more than 40% of this land and that on Oahu, the most urbanized of the islands, 22 landowners owned 72.5% of the fee simple titles. Id., at 32-33. The legislature concluded that concentrated land ownership was responsible for skewing the State's residential fee simple market, inflating land prices, and injuring the public tranquility and welfare.

To redress these problems, the legislature decided to compel the large landowners to break up their estates. The legislature considered requiring large landowners to sell lands which they were leasing to homeowners. However, the landowners strongly resisted this scheme, pointing out the significant federal tax liabilities they would incur. Indeed, the landowners claimed that the federal tax laws were the primary reason they previously had chosen to lease, and not sell, their lands. Therefore, to accommodate the needs of both lessors and lessees, the Hawaii Legislature enacted the Land Reform Act of 1967 (Act), Haw. Rev. Stat., Ch. 516, which created a mechanism for condemning residential tracts and for transferring ownership of the condemned fees simple to existing lessees. By condemning the land in question, the Hawaii Legislature intended to make the land sales involuntary, thereby making the federal tax consequences less severe while still facilitating the redistribution of fees simple.

Under the Act's condemnation scheme, tenants living on single-family residential lots within developmental tracts at least five acres in size are entitled to ask the Hawaii Housing Authority (HHA) to condemn the property on which they live. Haw. Rev. Stat. §§516-1(2), (11), 516-22 (1977). When 25 eligible tenants,[1] or tenants on half the lots in the tract, whichever is less, file appropriate applications, the Act authorizes HHA to hold a public hearing to determine whether acquisition by the State of all or part of the tract will "effectuate the public purposes" of the Act. §5166-22. If HHA finds that these public purposes will be served, it is authorized to designate some or all of the lots in the tract for acquisition. It then acquires, at prices set either by condemnation trial or by negotiation between lessors and lessees,[2] the former fee owners' full "right, title, and interest" in the land. §516-25.

---

1. An eligible tenant is one who, among other things, owns a house on the lot, has a bona fide intent to live on the lot or be a resident of the State, shows proof of ability to pay for a fee interest in it, and does not own residential land elsewhere nearby.

2. In either case, compensation must equal the fair market value of the owner's leased fee interest. §516-1(14). The adequacy of compensation is not before us.

After compensation has been set, HHA may sell the land titles to tenants who have applied for fee simple ownership. HHA is authorized to lend these tenants up to 90% of the purchase price, and it may condition final transfer on a right of first refusal for the first 10 years following sale. §§516-30, 516-34, 516-35. If HHA does not sell the lot to the tenant residing there, it may lease the lot or sell it to someone else, provided that HHA may not sell to any one purchaser, or lease to any one tenant, more than one lot, and it may not operate for profit. §§516-28, 516-32. In practice, funds to satisfy the condemnation awards have been supplied entirely by lessees. See App. 164. While the Act authorizes HHA to issue bonds and appropriate funds for acquisition, no bonds have issued and HHA has not supplied any funds for condemned lots.

In April 1977, HHA held a public hearing concerning the proposed acquisition of some of appellees' lands. HHA made the statutorily required finding that acquisition of appellees' lands would effectuate the public purposes of the Act. Then, in October 1978, it directed appellees to negotiate with certain lessees concerning the sale of the designated properties. Those negotiations failed, and HHA subsequently ordered appellees to submit to compulsory arbitration.

Rather than comply with the compulsory arbitration order, appellees file suit, in February 1979, in United States District Court, asking that the Act be declared unconstitutional and that its enforcement be enjoined. The District Court temporarily restrained the State from proceeding against appellees' estates. Three months later, while declaring the compulsory arbitration and compensation formulae provisions of the Act unconstitutional, the District Court refused preliminarily to enjoin appellants from conducting the statutory designation and condemnation proceedings. Finally, in December 1979, it granted partial summary judgment to appellants, holding the remaining portion of the Act constitutional under the Public Use Clause. See 483 F. Supp. 62 (Haw. 1979). The District Court found that the Act's goals were within the bounds of the State's police powers and that the means the legislature had chosen to serve those goals were not arbitrary, capricious, or selected in bad faith.

The Court of Appeals for the Ninth Circuit reversed. 702 F.2d 788 (1983). . . . [T]he Court of Appeals determined that the Act could not pass the requisite judicial scrutiny of the Public Use Clause. It found that the transfers contemplated by the Act were unlike those of takings previously held to constitute "public uses" by this Court. The court further determined that the public purposes offered by the Hawaii Legislature were not deserving of judicial deference. The court concluded that the Act was simply "a naked attempt on the part of the state of Hawaii to take the private property of A and transfer it to B solely for B's private use and benefit." Id., at 798. One judge dissented.

On applications of HHA and certain private appellants who had intervened below, this Court noted probable jurisdiction. . . . We now reverse. . . .

The starting point for our analysis of the Act's constitutionality is the Court's decision in Berman v. Parker, 348 U.S. 26 (1954). In *Berman*, the Court held constitutional the District of Columbia Redevelopment Act of 1945. That Act provided both for the comprehensive use of the eminent domain power to redevelop slum areas and for the possible sale or lease of the condemned lands to private interests. In discussing whether the takings authorized by that Act were for a "public use," id., at 31, the Court stated:

> We deal, in other words, with what traditionally has been known as the police power. An attempt to define its reach or trace its outer limits is fruitless, for each case must turn on its own facts. The definition is essentially the product of legislative determinations addressed to the purposes of government, purposes neither abstractly nor historically capable of complete definition. Subject to specific constitutional limitations, when the legislature has spoken, the public interest has been declared in terms well-nigh conclusive. In such cases the legislature, not the judiciary, is the main guardian of the public needs to be served by social legislation, whether it be Congress legislating concerning the District of Columbia . . . or the States legislating concerning local affairs. . . . This principle admits of no exception merely because the power of eminent domain is involved. . . .

Id., at 32 (citations omitted). The Court explicitly recognized the breadth of the principle it was announcing, noting:

> Once the object is within the authority of Congress, the right to realize it through the exercise of eminent domain is clear. For the power of eminent domain is merely the means to the end. . . . Once the object is within the authority of Congress, the means by which it will be attained is also for Congress to determine. Here one of the means chosen is the use of private enterprise for redevelopment of the area. Appellants argue that this makes the project a taking from one businessman for the benefit of another businessman. But the means of executing the project are for Congress and Congress alone to determine, once the public purpose has been established.

Id., at 33. The "public use" requirement is thus coterminous with the scope of a sovereign's police powers.

There is, of course, a role for courts to play in reviewing a legislature's judgment of what constitutes a public use, even when the eminent domain power is equated with the police power. But the Court in *Berman* made clear that it is "an extremely narrow" one. Id., at 32. The Court in *Berman* cited with approval the Court's decision in Old Dominion Co. v. United States, 269 U.S. 55, 66 (1925), which held that deference to the legislature's "public use" determination is required "until it is shown to involve an impossibility." The *Berman* Court also cited to United States ex rel. TVA v. Welch, 327 U.S. 546, 552 (1946), which emphasized that "[any] departure from this judicial restraint would result in courts deciding on what is and is not a governmental function and in their invalidating legislation on the basis of their view on that question at the moment of decision, a practice which has proved impracticable in other fields." In short, the Court has made clear that it will not substitute its judgment for a legislature's judgment as to what constitutes a public use "unless the use be palpably without reasonable foundation." United States v. Gettysburg Electric R. Co., 160 U.S. 668, 680 (1896).

To be sure, the Court's cases have repeatedly stated that "one person's property may not be taken for the benefit of another private person without a justifying public purpose, even though compensation be paid." Thompson v. Consolidated Gas Corp., 300 U.S. 55, 80 (1937). See, e.g., Cincinnati v. Vester, 281 U.S. 439, 447 (1930); Madisonville Traction Co. v. St. Bernard Mining Co., 196 U.S. 239, 251-252 (1905); Fallbrook Irrigation District v. Bradley, 164 U.S. 112, 159 (1896). Thus, in Missouri Pacific R. Co. v. Nebraska, 164 U.S. 403 (1896), where the "order in question was not, *and was not claimed to be,* . . . a taking of private property for a public use under the right of eminent domain," id., at 416 (emphasis added), the Court invalidated a compensated taking of property for lack of a justifying public purpose. But where the exercise of the eminent domain power is rationally related to a conceivable public purpose, the Court has never held a compensated taking to be proscribed by the Public Use Clause. See Berman v. Parker, *supra*; Rindge Co. v. Los Angeles, 262 U.S. 700 (1923); Block v. Hirsh, 256 U.S. 135 (1921); cf. Thompson v. Consolidated Gas Corp., *supra* (invalidating an uncompensated taking).

On this basis, we have no trouble concluding that the Hawaii Act is constitutional. The people of Hawaii have attempted, much as the settlers of the original 13 Colonies did, to reduce the perceived social and economic evils of a land oligopoly traceable to their monarchs. The land oligopoly has, according to the Hawaii Legislature, created artificial deterrents to the normal functioning of the State's residential land market and forced thousands of individual homeowners to lease, rather than buy, the land underneath their homes. Regulating oligopoly and the evils associated with it is a classic exercise of a State's police powers. See Exxon Corp. v. Governor of Maryland, 437 U.S. 117 (1978); Block v. Hirsh, *supra*; see also People of Puerto Rico v. Eastern Sugar Associates, 156 F.2d 316 (1st Cir. 1946), *cert. denied,* 329 U.S. 772 (1946). We cannot disapprove of Hawaii's exercise of this power.

Nor can we condemn as irrational the Act's approach to correcting the land oligopoly problem. The Act presumes that when a sufficiently large number of persons declare that they are willing but unable to buy lots at fair prices the land market is malfunctioning. When such a malfunction is signalled, the Act authorizes HHA to condemn lots in the relevant tract. The Act limits the number of lots any one tenant can purchase and authorizes HHA to use public funds to ensure that the market dilution goals will be achieved. This is a comprehensive and rational approach to identifying and correcting market failure.

Of course, this Act, like any other, may not be successful in achieving its intended goals. But "whether *in fact* the provision will accomplish its objectives is not the question: the [constitutional requirement] is satisfied if . . . the . . . [state] Legislature *rationally could have believed* that the [Act] would promote its objective." Western & Southern Life Ins. Co. v. State Bd. of Equalization, 451 U.S. 648, 671-672 (1981); see also Minnesota v. Clover Leaf Creamery Co., 449 U.S. 456, 466 (1981); Vance v. Bradley, 440 U.S. 93, 112 (1979). When the legislature's purpose is legitimate and its means are not irrational, our cases make clear that empirical debates over the wisdom of takings — no less than debates over the wisdom of other kinds of socio-economic legislation — are not to be carried out in the federal courts. Redistribution of fees simple to correct deficiencies in the market determined by the state legislature to be attributable to land oligopoly is a rational exercise of the eminent domain power. Therefore, the Hawaii statute must pass the scrutiny of the Public Use Clause.

The State of Hawaii has never denied that the Constitution forbids even a compensated taking of property when executed for no reason other than to confer a private benefit on a particular private party. A purely private taking could not withstand the scrutiny of the public use requirement; it would serve no legitimate purpose of government and would thus be void. But no purely private taking is involved in these cases. The Hawaii Legislature enacted its Land Reform Act not to benefit a particular class of identifiable individuals but to attack certain perceived evils of concentrated property ownership in Hawaii — a legitimate public purpose. Use of the condemnation power to achieve this purpose is not irrational. Since we assume for purposes of these appeals that the weighty demand of just compensation has been met, the requirements of the Fifth and Fourteenth Amendments have been satisfied. Accordingly, we reverse the judgment of the Court of Appeals, and remand these cases for further proceedings in conformity with this opinion.

NOTE

Historic context. While on the facts presented in the case, *Midkiff* appears to be a victory for the land-poor masses over the wealthy landlords, the "landlord" in this particular case was a trust that benefits native Hawaiians. Frank E. Midkiff was a trustee of the Bishop Estate, a tax-exempt charitable trust worth about $1.5 billion in 1983. The trust owned 9 percent of all land in the state and collected rents on land it leased to homeowners. The following account explains what was at stake.

LEE CATTERALL, LAND OWNERSHIP ENTERS NEW ERA
IN HAWAII

Natl. L.J., June 18, 1984

The U.S. Supreme Court's recent decision upholding Hawaii's Land Reform Act has residents here reeling over what some are calling the second Great Mahele.

The term refers to King Kamehameha III's decision in 1848 that, contrary to custom, people could own land. Under Kamehameha's decree, about 250 Hawaiian chiefs became owners of more than one-third of the land in Hawaii, another third went to the government and remainder was kept by the king as crown land. Fewer than 30,000 of the islands' 4 million acres went to commoners.

Much of the ownership soon changed hands. In the four decades that followed, Caucasians — "haoles," as they are called here — had bought two-thirds of the government land, much of the land that had been given to chiefs and commoners and even some of the crown land.

Mainly, the haole buyers were the families of missionaries, who — it is said — came to Hawaii to do good and did very well. Others obtaining large landholdings were adventurous entrepreneurs like James Campbell (sugar), John Parker (cattle), Charles Brewer (sugar) and Charles Reed Bishop, the most fortunate of all.

Mr. Bishop married into much of the land ownership, being wed four years after his arrival in 1846 to Princess Bernice Pauahi Paki, the last descendant of the Kamehameha line.

The Campbell Estate, Parker Ranch, C. Brewer & Co. and the Bishop Estate remain among the state's biggest landowners.

Today, more than 80 percent of the private land in Hawaii is in the hands of fewer than 40 landowners. On Oahu, as Justice O'Connor pointed out, 22 landowners own nearly three-fourths of the land.

Understandably, aboriginal Hawaiians harbor bad feelings about the Great Mahele. But they do not necessarily welcome a second mahele to break it up. A number of giant estates are associated with philanthropies designed to aid native Hawaiians in such domains as public health and education.

The clear leader in such philanthropies is the Bishop Estate, the largest private landowner with more than 340,000 acres, overseen by a group of trustees appointed by the state Supreme Court and each paid $250,000 a year out of the estate revenues.

The estate's beneficiary is the system of Kamehameha Schools, which serve 2,850 full-time and 33,000 off-campus students of Hawaiian blood. Estate trustee Myron Thompson told reporters that the Supreme Court's decision is a "ripoff" that will greatly reduce the estate's further income.

Mr. O'Connor, of Barlow & O'Connor here, suggested that the decision could lead to the redistribution of other lands, including land now belonging to the giant agricultural companies that run the state's sugar and pineapple industries.

Is the land owned by the Bishop's Estate already used for a public purpose? Is "regulating oligopoly" a more important public purpose than education? How should a legislature make that determination?

§6.3   Just Compensation

a.   Highest and Best Use

STATE OF NEW JERSEY v. CAOILI

135 N.J. 252, 639 A.2d 275 (1994)

HANDLER, J.

This is a condemnation case in which the dispute centers on the fair market value of property taken by the State of New Jersey under its eminent domain powers. The main issue posed by the case relates to the standard of proof applicable to evidence of a potential zoning change affecting the use of the condemned property. Also at issue is the type of valuation methodology that may be followed in determining the fair market value of condemned property when the record contains sufficient evidence of a prospective zoning change affecting the use of the property.

At the trial, the property owners introduced evidence of potential zoning and subdivision changes affecting the land's future use. Based on that evidence, the jury returned a verdict awarding compensation to the owners. The State appealed and the Appellate Division, in a reported decision, affirmed the judgment, 262 N.J. Super. 591, 621 A.2d 546 (1993). The State sought certification, which this Court granted, 134 N.J. 477, 634 A.2d 525 (1993).

I

Estrella and Frederico Caoilo owned nearly an acre of land located near a highway in Dover Township. On July 15, 1989, the State of New Jersey, Commissioner of Transportation, filed a complaint to condemn the property for the purpose of constructing a "jug-handle" turn for a nearby highway. At that time the property was zoned for residential use. Although there was some dispute as to whether the property was subdivided into two lots at the time of taking, two single-family homes were located on the property. A 262-foot border of the property ran along a highway on which were located a number of nearby commercial establishments, including a gas station, bank, and bus garage. Another portion of the property fronted on a residential street that led into a large residential development.

The State determined that $232,500 was just compensation for the property and it deposited that amount with the Clerk of the Superior Court. Because the owner disputed the State's determination of just compensation, a panel of commissioners was appointed to appraise the property. The commissioners determined that the "highest and best use" of the property was to subdivide it into three residential lots and they valued the property accordingly, finding a fair market value at the time of the taking of $278,000. The commissioners specifically declined to take into account the possibility that a use variance might have been obtained for the property because they found that obtaining such a variance was improbable and "too speculative."

The State appealed from the commissioners' finding, and a jury trial was held to determine the fair market value of the property at the time of the taking.

At trial, the State moved to exclude the appraisal report of the owners' experts, Jon Brody and William Steinhart (the "Brody/Steinhart Report"), on the ground that the evidence was insufficient to support their conclusion that a reasonable probability existed that the property would receive a zoning variance for commercial development. In their report, Brody and Steinhart valued the property at $445,000. They arrived at that figure by comparing the property to allegedly similar properties and estimating the value of the property based on the recent sale prices of those properties. The properties used for comparison in the Brody/Steinhart Report were all zoned for commercial use at the time of their sale. Brody and Steinhart justified the use of commercially-zoned property in their appraisal by claiming that a reasonable probability existed that the property would receive a use variance, which would allow the property to be used for a specific non-residential purpose. In valuing the property, the experts discounted the sale prices of the comparison properties by ten percent to account for the fact that the property had not yet obtained a zoning variance. The State also objected to the introduction of the appraisal report on the ground that the valuation methodology used by Brody and Steinhart was improper.

In denying the State's motion to exclude the Brody/Steinhart Report, the trial court found that

> there [are] . . . sufficient facts and circumstances spread upon the record which would justify the prospective purchaser as of the date of taking in concluding there may be a zoning change, and further that the price . . . that prospective purchaser would be willing to pay and the price that prospective seller would be willing to accept would be reflective of that circumstance.

At trial, Brody testified that "based on analyzing and looking at close to fifteen years worth of variances that had taken place in Dover Township," the property had a "very strong probability of obtaining a variance to utilize that parcel of land for something other than what it's presently zoned for."

One of the state's three witnesses, William Burke, testified that in his opinion the property had a fair market value at the time of the taking of $232,500. Burke arrived at that figure by comparing the property to allegedly similar properties, but the comparison properties used in Burke's appraisal were residential properties because he believed that a reasonable probability existed that the zoning for the property would remain residential.

The State's next witness, Joseph Layton, testified that in his opinion the property could not meet all the requirements that an applicant must satisfy before a variance will be granted and therefore no reasonable probability existed that the property owner could obtain a variance. James Henbest, a Deputy Zoning Officer and Assistant Planner for Dover Township, testified for the State that he had previously told Layton that it was unlikely that the property would receive a variance.

The possible subdivision of the property into three lots was also the subject of testimony. The court decided to admit that testimony so long as the jury found that it was reasonably probable that the property could be subdivided into three lots. It gave the jury a cautionary instruction to that effect.

On cross-examination, Burke, over the State's objection, testified that although he had not considered the possibility of a subdivision when making his appraisal, the property could be subdivided into three lots consistent with the physical requirements of the relevant zoning ordinance. Burke further testified, however, that no reasonable probability existed that an owner of the property could get approval to subdivide because subdividing would harm the residential integrity of the area. Henbest also testified, on cross-examination, that it was possible to subdivide the property into a third lot which bordered the highway. He stated, however, that if the property were subdivided in that manner a "better than 50/50 chance" existed that a variance would be granted for that third lot.

The court instructed the jury that zoning regulations may restrict the types of uses that may be considered in determining the highest and best use of the property. With respect to the potential variance, the court said:

> But suppose there were signs that the law regulating the property's use might change so as to permit a use in the future which would make the property more valuable or less valuable.
>
> Parties negotiating a price for the sale of the property would not ignore these signs, nor should you.
>
> It is for you to determine what effect, if any, any indications of a zoning change or planning change would have on the market value. You may con-

sider that the change then appeared so speculative that there would have
been no effect on the property's value.

You may consider the change so likely that the value of the property
would fully reflect the change. You may consider that change would have appeared uncertain but would have some effect on the property.

With respect to the potential subdivision, the trial court, as already
mentioned, had provided a cautionary instruction when it admitted testimony, namely that the jury could consider the potential subdivision only if
it found that the subdivision was reasonably probable. In submitting that
issue to the jury, the court gave the following instruction:

> Now if you do consider this [potential subdivision], you must find —
> and in all cases you must use this standard: Is it reasonably probable that the
> governmental body is going to allow this? And [if] it could be subdivided.
>
> There are certain standards that have to be met, and they were . . . gone
> into detail during the attorneys' summations but nonetheless, you have to find
> that it is likely that it would be allowed.

The jury awarded the owners $351,000. The jury responded affirma-
tively to the following special interrogatory: "In arriving at your decision as
to just compensation, did you include in your calculation a potential subdivision of the property to utilize part thereof for commercial use?"

On appeal, the Appellate Division determined that the trial court's
disposition of the evidence relating to potential zoning and subdivision
changes and the valuation methodology were correct, and affirmed the
judgment.

II

When the State exercises its power to take private property under the
Eminent Domain Act, N.J.S.A. 20:3-1 to -50, the State must pay the property
owner just compensation for the property taken. N.J. Const. art. I ¶20. Just
compensation is "the fair market value of the property as of the date of the
taking, determined by what a willing buyer and a willing seller would agree
to, neither being under any compulsion to act." State v. Silver 92 N.J. 507,
513, 457 A.2d 463 (1983). It is the "value that would be assigned to the
acquired property by knowledgeable parties freely negotiating for its sale
under normal market conditions based on all surrounding circumstances
at the time of the taking." Id. at 514, 457 A.2d 463.

In a condemnation proceeding, all reasonable uses of the property
bear on its fair market value. However, most relevant in ascertaining fair
market value is the property's highest and best use. 4 Nicholas on Eminent
Domain §12.02[1], at 12-75 (1993) (hereinafter Eminent Domain). The
reasonableness of a use of condemned property, including its highest and

best use, must be considered in light of any zoning restrictions that apply to the property. Hence, the zoning restrictions that govern the use of the property are material factors in determining its fair market value. Because the inquiry into the uses of property is usually wide-ranging, "courts in this state have shown considerable liberality in admitting evidence of market value, particularly in terms of the highest and best use of the subject property." *Silver, supra,* 92 N.J. at 515, 457 A.2d 463. That evidence encompasses all "relevant facts at the time of the taking[, which] may include those that have a bearing on an available future use of the property." Ibid.

This Court in State v. Gorga, 26 N.J. 113, 138 A.2d 833 (1958), addressed the standard for judging the sufficiency of evidence of potential zoning changes affecting the future use of condemned property in considering its highest and best use as a basis for determining its fair market value. There, as in this case, the condemned residentially-zoned property was located on a highway. State v. Gorga, 45 N.J. Super. 417, 419, 133 A.2d 349 (App. Div. 1957), *aff'd,* 26 N.J. 113, 138 A.2d 833 (1958). Almost all the other property along the highway was zoned for business use, ibid., and a real estate expert testified that a "reasonable chance" existed that the property owner could get the property rezoned for business use. The defendants sought to admit evidence of a zoning ordinance adopted ten months after the taking of the property that had changed the zoning of the condemned property from residential to commercial use. Ibid. The trial court excluded the evidence and the Appellate Division reversed on the ground that the subsequently enacted ordinance was relevant evidence because it demonstrated that at the time of the taking a zoning amendment was a reasonable probability.

The Court acknowledged that both "probable" and "remotely possible" zoning amendments could affect the price agreed on by hypothetical reasonable buyers and sellers. It reasoned, however, that allowing consideration of all zoning changes that were merely possible could lead to "unbridled speculation" regarding the fair market value of such property. Ibid. The Court therefore imposed, in effect, a two-step standard governing the consideration of evidence of zoning changes affecting the future use of property. It established one standard for the admissibility and another for the substantive consideration of such evidence. It stated: "if as of the date of taking there is a reasonable probability of a change in the zoning ordinance in the near future, the influence of that circumstance upon the market value as of that date may be shown," but that before allowing a jury to consider the issue, the trial court should first decide whether the record contains sufficient evidence of a probability of a zoning change to warrant consideration by the jury.

Lower courts interpreting *Gorga* generally have applied a standard of probability at least with respect to the admissibility of evidence of an available future use of condemned property.

A number of jurisdictions have also used a standard of probability as a basis for admissibility of evidence of future use of condemned property. Federal courts have likewise followed the approach taken by *Gorga:*

> The federal rule is that in a condemnation case, it is the responsibility of the trial judge to screen proper potential uses and exclude from jury consideration those which have not been demonstrated to be practicable and reasonably probable uses. Thus, the trial judge should first screen evidence concerning potential uses, and then decide whether the landowner has produced credible evidence that a potential use is reasonably practicable and reasonably probable within the near future. If credible evidence of a potential use is produced, the jury is to decide whether the property's suitability for such use enhances its market value and, if so, by how much.

Eminent Domain, *supra,* §12B.14[1], at 12B-158 ("Potential Subdivisions").

That two-step approach was expressed in United States v. 341.45 Acres of Land, 633 F.2d 108 (8th Cir. 1980), *cert. denied sub nom.* Bassett v. United States, 451 U.S. 938 (1981):

> First, the trial judge should screen the evidence concerning potential uses. Then, the trial judge should decide whether "the landowner has produced credible evidence that a potential use is reasonably practicable and reasonably probable within the near future. . . ." If credible evidence of the potential use is produced, the jury then decides "whether the property's suitability for this use enhances its market value, and if so, by how much."

633 F.2d at 111 (quoting United States v. 320.0 Acres of Land, 605 F.2d 762, 817 (5th Cir. 1979).

The Appellate Division here did not construe *Gorga* as imposing a threshold requirement for the admissibility of such evidence, namely, that the evidence must demonstrate a reasonable probability that such a zoning change would occur. It interpreted "reasonable probability of a change" as used in *Gorga* to require only "that a reasonable buyer and seller would consider the likelihood of a change to be a factor affecting the price, though the change is not more likely than not." 262 N.J. Super. at 596, 621 A.2d 546.

In dispensing with any requirement that there must be a judicial finding of reasonable probability of a zoning change before such evidence may be considered by the jury, the Appellate Division relied to a great extent on the following passage from *Gorga:* "in short if the parties to a voluntary transaction would as of the date of taking give recognition of the probability of a zoning amendment in agreeing upon the value, the law will recognize the truth." 26 N.J. at 117, 138 A.2d 833. That observation, however, was based on the premise that the trial court would have made an antecedent, threshold determination of a probability of a zoning change.

We remain convinced, as was the *Gorga* Court, that allowing a factfinder to consider evidence of a zoning change that indicates at most that a change was not probable or only possible could lead to "unbridled speculation" regarding the fair market value of such property. The risk of unsound and speculative determinations concerning fair market value is real when that determination is based on evidence of a future change that is inherently vague or tenuous because it suggests no more than the possibility of change. That risk can be reduced substantially if the determination of fair market value is based on more cogent evidence indicating beyond a mere possibility that a change of use is likely and, further, that such a change would be an important factor in the valuation of the property. The court can accomplish that reduction in risk by performing, in effect, a gatekeeping function by screening out potentially unreliable evidence and admitting only evidence that would warrant or support a finding that zoning change is probable.

The jury, however, need not be required to find that the zoning change is probable. We agree with the Appellate Division that in the jury's consideration of evidence of a zoning change, the critical inquiry is the reasonable belief by a buyer and seller engaged in voluntary negotiations over the fair market value of property that a change may occur and will have an impact on the value of the property regardless of the degree of probability. As stated by the Appellate division, "even though the parties to a voluntary transaction may not believe that a zoning change is more likely than not, their belief that there may be a change should be taken into account if that belief is reasonable and it affects their assessment of the property's value." 262 N.J. Super. at 596-97, 621 A.2d 546.

In conclusion, we now hold, consistent with our decision in *Gorga*, that in determining the fair market value of condemned property as a basis for just compensation, the jury may consider a potential zoning change affecting the use of the property provided the court is satisfied that the evidence is sufficient to warrant a determination that such a change is reasonably probable. If evidence meets that level of proof, it may be considered in fixing just compensation in light of the weight and effect that reasonable buyers and sellers would give to such evidence in their determination of the fair market value of the property.

The further question is whether prejudicial error occurred in this case with respect to the disposition of the evidence relating to the potential zoning changes in light of the applicable standard of proof. We conclude that it did not.

The trial court, in denying the State's motion to exclude the report of the owners' experts, did not make an express determination that the evidence would warrant a determination that the potential zoning variance was reasonably probable. The trial court found that a prospective purchaser would believe that use variance might be granted and that that possibility would affect the price at which the purchaser would buy the property.

Nevertheless, that the trial court understood that such evidence of probability was present and that it would warrant jury consideration is fairly inferable. The only evidence that formed the basis for the court's finding consisted of the Brody/Steinhart Report, which expressed the experts' opinion that the zoning variance was reasonably probable. Thus, although the jury should not have been allowed to consider a potential variance without an express antecedent finding that sufficient evidence existed to show that the variance was reasonably probable, such a finding is implicit in the trial court's admissibility ruling when measured against the evidence that was actually presented. We may assume the admissibility ruling would have been the same if the court had consciously attempted to conform and express its finding on admissibility under the correct standard.

The court instructed the jury that it must "determine what effect, if any, any indications of a zoning change or planning change would have on the market value." In so doing, the trial court used language that mirrors that of the model civil jury instructions regarding potential zoning changes. See Model Civil Jury Instructions Manual §10.02(B) (1978). Thus, as long as the evidence actually considered by the jury enabled it to conclude that a zoning change was reasonably probable, the effect of that evidence in light of the weight that a buyer and seller would give that factor in determining the fair market value of the property was for the jury to assess.

Moreover, any possible error with respect to the admissibility of the evidence relating to the potential variance was somewhat mitigated by the disposition of the evidence relating to the potential subdivision. The court instructed the jury to consider that evidence so long as the jury found it reasonably probable that the property could be subdivided into three lots. Guided by that instruction, the jury responded affirmatively to the following special interrogatory: "in arriving at your decision as to just compensation, did you include in your calculation a potential subdivision of the property to utilize part thereof for commercial use?" In the context of the evidence, the reference in the special interrogatory to the use of the property for "commercial purposes" could relate only to a change of use by variance from residential to commercial. To answer that question affirmatively, as the jury did, it must have concluded that the variance change for commercial use was reasonably probable. That interpretation of the jury's determination is consistent with and supported by the testimony of the State's expert, Henbest, who testified that if the subdivision were granted, a "better than 50/50 chance [existed] that a variance would also be granted."

The trial court's determination of admissibility and its instruction concerning the evidence of a potential zoning change do not appear to have confused or misled the jury to the prejudice of the State. . . .

IV

The State also disputes the valuation methodology used by the owners' experts and considered by the jury.

Three valuation methodologies may be used in appraising condemned property with a reasonable probability of a zoning change: the reproduction cost, the capitalization cost, and the comparable value. American Institute of Real Estate Appraisers, The Appraisal of Real Estate 51-53 (1983); see Eminent Domain, *supra*, §12C.01[3][a]-[c], at 12C-24 to -38. Our courts have consistently refrained from mandating that a specific methodology be used in appraising condemned property. For example, in State v. Mehlman, 118 N.J. Super. at 587, 289 A.2d 539, the court declined to designate which method of appraisal should have been used, stating that an appellate court should determine only whether the method used at trial was reasonable. Id. at 591, 289 A.2d 539; see County of Middlesex v. Clearwater Village, Inc., 163 N.J. Super. 166, 173, 394 A.2d 390 (App. Div. 1978). "[T]here is no precise and inflexible rule for the assessment of just compensation. The Constitution does not contain any fixed standard of fairness by which it must be measured. Courts have been careful not to reduce the concept to a formula." Jersey City Redevelopment Agency v. Kugler, 58 N.J. 374, 387-89, 277 A.2d 873 (1971).

Plaintiffs' experts used the comparable sales approach in their appraisal of the owners' property. State v. Township of S. Hackensack, 65 N.J. 377, 382, 322 A.2d 818 (1974) (noting that where appropriate, evidence of comparable sales is "most satisfactory proof" of value). They first valued the property as if it had obtained the variance, and then discounted that amount ten percent to account for the fact that the variance remained a probability.

In *Gorga,* this Court approved the method of valuation urged by the State:

> The important caveat is that the true issue is not the value of the property for the use which would be permitted if the amendment were adopted. . . . No matter how probable an amendment may seem, an element of uncertainty remains and has its impact upon the selling price. At most a buyer would pay a premium for that probability in addition to what the property is worth under the restriction of the existing ordinance.
>
> In support of his opinion of the then market value, an expert may advert to the value the property would have if rezoned, but only by way of explaining his opinion of the existing market value.

25 N.J. at 117-18, 138 A.2d 833.

The purpose of any methodology is to arrive at an appraisal that reflects the current value of the property and not the value of the property at a future date. Thus, so long as the method used yields a current value rather than a future value, whether the appraiser starts with the value as currently zoned and adjusts upward, assigning a "premium" to reflect the likelihood of a zoning change, or starts with the value of the property as it is likely to be zoned in the future, assigning a "discount" of that value to account for the likelihood of such a zoning change, would not appear significant.

Under the comparable-use methodology, the value of the condemned property can be reached either by valuing the land as if the proposed change were in place and then discounting that value to reflect the likelihood of the change, or the value can be ascertained by valuing the land under the existing land-use restrictions and then adding some value to reflect that likelihood. Although "courts appear to favor the practice of using comparable sales with zoning the same as the existing zoning on the property being appraised, rather than using higher-zoned sale properties and discounting them, . . . the ultimate decision is generally left to the judgment of the appraiser." James D. Eaton, Real Estate Valuation in Litigation 95-96 (1982). ("If there is little doubt that the property will be rezoned, and the discount applicable to the higher-zoned sales will be comparatively minimal, it may be advisable to use sales of higher zoned property.") Therefore, "it has been held that an award may be made on the basis of an impending rezoning (as an accomplished fact), minus a discount factor to allow for the uncertainty." Eminent Domain, *supra,* §12C.03[2], at 12C-89; see also William B. Knipe, Valuing the Probability of Rezoning, 56 Appraisal J. 217, 220 (1988) ("[T]he parties can be expected to bargain toward a price that can be viewed as the value of the property with the more valuable zoning classification, discounted by some amount.").

We view *Gorga* as expressing a preference that condemned property be valued under the existing ordinance and then some value be added to reflect the likelihood of the proposed zoning change. That approach most clearly identifies the "premium" of the likelihood of a zoning change that should be reflected in the fair market value of the condemned property. Perhaps that "premium" approach more effectively assures that the current fair market value of the condemned property is not the value of the property as though the proposed change were a fait accompli. 26 N.J. at 117-18, 138 A.2d 833. We do not, however, read or apply the observations in *Gorga* to mandate that in the valuation process experts must use addition instead of subtraction. E.g., State v. Speare, 86 N.J. Super. 565, 575, 207 A.2d 552 (App. Div. 1965) (involving condemned property zoned residential and fronting on highway, with respect to which both commercially- and residentially-zoned comparison properties were used in valuing residentially-zoned property; ruling that weight to be accorded allegedly comparable sales is for jury to decide, but not mandating only "premium" comparable sales approach).

We are satisfied that the methodology used by the owners' experts was reasonable. As noted, other courts and commentators have explicitly endorsed that methodology. Accordingly, we reject the State's contention that the owners' evidence should have been excluded because it used commercially-zoned properties as comparable sales in arriving at an initial value of the property and then discounted that valuation in accordance with their estimation of the likelihood of such a variance to arrive at the property's fair market value on the date of taking.

V

The judgment below is affirmed.

NOTES AND QUESTIONS

1. **"Speculative" value.** Land buyers whose plans depend on zoning change approval are very likely to condition their purchase on the requisite approval: no change, no purchase.

Suppose that land, zoned for R-1 use, has a $200,000 market value, but X agrees, if he can get the zoning change within 90 days, to purchase the parcel for $350,000. Suppose, further, that the likelihood of change is only 40 percent. What is the parcel's value: $350,000? $260,000? $200,000? Should the compensation system assume that a buyer who is willing to pay $260,000 unconditionally does exist?

2. **The "reasonable probability" standard.** At what percentage does zoning change become reasonably probable? Anything more than 40 percent? 50 percent? 75 percent? What evidence would bear on the percentage determination?

b.   Loss of Goodwill and Business Advantage

CITY OF DETROIT v. MICHAEL'S PRESCRIPTIONS

143 Mich. App. 808; 373 N.W.2d 219 (1985)

KELLY, J. The City of Detroit appeals as of right from a jury verdict of $275,000 in this condemnation action arising out of the Central Industrial Park Project, more commonly known as the *"Poletown* Project." See generally, Poletown Neighborhood Council v. Detroit, 410 Mich. 616, 304 N.W.2d 455 (1981). The condemned property in this case was a neighborhood pharmacy known for over 40 years as "Michael's Prescriptions," a sole proprietorship owned and operated since 1971 by pharmacist Harry Kablak and located on East Grand Boulevard in Detroit. The issue on appeal is whether respondent may be compensated for the going concern value of the business.[1]

---

1. Prior to entering proofs, the petitioner moved for a directed verdict on the ground that the respondent's proofs did not meet the standards under Michigan law allowing compensation for going-concern value. Petitioner also moved to strike the testimony of respondent's expert witnesses on this issue.

We are presented in this case with an issue that is common to several other *Poletown* cases presently before this Court. After the Supreme Court expeditiously decided, in *Poletown Neighborhood Council, supra,* that the condemnation of *Poletown* was for a public purpose, the city pursued a plethora of condemnation petitions in circuit court in which the sole issue was valuation of the property taken. Apparently, these cases were heard by two specially assigned judges who diverged on allowing recovery for the going concern value of businesses. Because of this "split" at the trial level a careful review of this issue is in order.

The law of eminent domain is governed in Michigan by the Constitution and by statute. Const. 1963, art. 10, §2 obligates the condemnor of private property to render just compensation to the property owner: "Private property shall not be taken for public use without just compensation therefor being first made or secured in a manner prescribed by law. Compensation shall be determined in proceedings in a court of record." . . . Just compensation should, however, place the owner of the property in as good a position as was occupied before the taking.

This Court's review of condemnation awards is limited. Absent an abuse of discretion with regard to evidentiary matters, we will generally affirm the award if it is within the range of the valuation testimony produced at trial. State Highway Comm'r v. Schultz, 370 Mich. 78, 84-85; 120 N.W.2d 733 (1963); Fenton v. Lutz, 73 Mich. App. 117, 124; 250 N.W.2d 579 (1977). A controversy over the going concern value of a business will usually be presented on appeal as an evidentiary issue with this Court deciding whether evidence of the going concern value of a business was properly admitted or excluded at trial. In this case, the city argues that the trial court abused its discretion in admitting such evidence.

The general rule of law is that, unless a business is taken for use as a going concern, the owner of the business located on a condemned parcel of realty will not be compensated for the good will or going concern value of the business. In re Jeffries Homes Housing Project, 306 Mich. 638, 651; 11 N.W.2d 272 (1943); In re Lansing Urban Renewal (Lansing v. Wery), 68 Mich. App. 158, 163; 242 N.W.2d 51 (1976), *leave to appeal denied,* 397 Mich. 828 (1976). See also 58 A.L.R.3d 566, §2, p.568; 81 A.L.R.3d 198, §2, p.202, and 17 A.L.R.4th 337, §17, p.437 ff. The justification for this general rule is that the owner of a successful business may generally transfer that business to another location. Where the government does not appropriate the business for its value as a going concern, the owner of that interest need not be compensated since nothing is taken. See Community Redevelopment Agency of the City of Los Angeles v. Abrams, 15 Cal. 3d 813; 126 Cal. Rptr. 473; 543 P.2d 905; 81 A.L.R.3d 174 (1975), *cert. den.* 429 U.S. 869; (1976).

As with most general principles of law, however, the rule prohibiting recovery is not without exception. As far back as 1888, in Grand Rapids & Indiana R.R. Co. v. Weiden, 70 Mich. 390; 38 N.W. 294 (1888), the Michigan Supreme Court considered with favor the claims of two business owners

seeking compensation for businesses located on condemned parcels of realty. The Court held:

> Both of the appellants were using their property in lucrative business,
> in which the locality and its surroundings had some bearing on its value. Apart
> from the money value of the property itself, they were entitled to be compen-
> sated so as to lose nothing by the interruption of their business and its damage
> by the change. A business stand is of some value to the owner of the business,
> whether he owns the fee of the land or not, and a diminution of business
> facilities may lead to serious results. There may be cases when the loss of a
> particular location may destroy business altogether, for want of access to any
> other that is suitable for it. Whatever damage is suffered, must be compen-
> sated. Appellants are not legally bound to suffer for petitioner's benefit. Peti-
> tioner can only be authorized to oust them from their possessions by making
> up to them the whole of their losses.

70 Mich. 395.

. . . [This case convinces] us that Supreme Court precedent exists for
allowing recovery of the going concern value of a business lost through condemnation, although the circumstances under which such recovery may be
had have not yet been articulated by that Court. We arrive at our conclusion
despite the Supreme Court's seemingly inconsistent holding in *Jeffries Homes
Housing Project, supra,* where the Court summarily stated:

> Each of the appealing defendants makes special objections. One claims that
> he was allowed nothing for the loss of good will in the sale of a plumbing
> business which he conducted from his home. The loss of good will is not an
> element of compensation where the business is not taken for use as a going
> concern. . . . A good plumber should be able to continue his business in almost
> any location and do as well as he formerly did in a neighborhood where in
> many homes there was a lack of adequate plumbing facilities.

306 Mich. 651. While the pronouncement of the general rule in *Jeffries
Homes Housing Project* is unequivocal, the Court did not go so far as to
overrule *Weiden.* We attribute summary treatment of the issue in *Jeffries* to
the weakness of the defendant plumber's claim. As the Court noted, the
evidence did not suggest that defendant's home-based plumbing business
could not be transferred.

While the Supreme Court has approved the principle of compensation for the going concern value of businesses lost to condemnation, the
task of applying and developing this principle of recovery has, in recent
years, been left to this Court. In a series of decisions spanning a 10-year
period, this Court has developed what we believe to be a workable framework for analyzing going concern recovery in the *Poletown* cases. In 1971,
Justice Levin, as judge of the Court of Appeals, authored State Highway
Comm. v. L & L Concession Co., 31 Mich. App. 222; 187 N.W.2d 465 (1971).
In that case, the State Highway Commission, under MCL 213.171 et seq.;

MSA 8.171 et seq., condemned a parcel of realty in Grand Rapids improved by an automobile racetrack and grandstands. Defendant was the owner of a leasehold interest in the property by which it had the exclusive grandstand concession rights for a specified period of time. At trial, L & L was denied the opportunity to present evidence regarding the value of its leasehold interest and the highway commissioners returned a judgment in favor of the realty owner only. L & L appealed, alleging error in the exclusion of evidence as to the going concern value of the concession business, and this Court agreed.

While recognizing that the good will or going concern value of a business is generally not recoverable in condemnation proceedings, this Court in *L & L* nevertheless observed:

> In a large number of cases owners and lessees have recovered going-concern value where the condemned property could not be realistically valued apart from the business there conducted, or, as it is sometimes said, the business for which the property is best "adapted."

31 Mich. App. 232. The panel went on to identify some of the factors which must be considered in determining whether the condemned property and the business could be separately valued.

> The going-concern value of L & L's business is not related to customers L & L cultivated but to the patronage of the racetrack; the concession gives L & L a monopoly on food and souvenir sales at the Speedrome. The value of the concession flows from locational advantage and L & L's monopoly position at that location, not conventional customer good will. The value flows from an "adaptation" of the grandstand to a use for which it is suited. Viewed from that perspective, allowing compensation for the value of the concession is consistent with the case law which recognizes that in valuing real estate for condemnation purposes it is proper to include value attributable to a use for which the real estate is adapted.

31 Mich. App. 232-233. The case was remanded for a hearing to determine as a separate element of damages the amount recoverable by L & L for its leasehold interest in the condemned realty.

Five years later, this Court decided In re Lansing Urban Renewal (Lansing v. Wery), *supra*, involving the condemnation of a parcel of property upon which was located the Kewpee Hamburger Shoppe. The trial court described the business as:

> "a unique 'hamburger shop,' which had a wide reputation for both the quality of its product and quickness of service. The 'Kewpee' was a 'downtown institution' lying on the fringe of the central business district within easy walking distance from the State Capitol, the commercial center of Lansing, and the ever-growing Lansing Community College. Its drive-in window operation also provided a facility for those who wanted a 'good hamburger' to drive in throughout the day and evening hours.

"The basic costs of this business were excellent. They reflected good controls, careful pricing and competent management. The restaurant had produced substantial profit during the period when other operations were suffering from competition from the new wave of fast-food franchises."

68 Mich. App. 160. Defendants' attempts to relocate were unsuccessful primarily because of restrictions imposed by the various branches of the city government. The trial court compensated defendant for the loss of the going concern value of the business and this Court affirmed, stating:

> As the trial court in the instant case specifically found, the Kewpee Hamburger Shoppe was a unique operation in a unique location. It depended greatly on that location, and any significant move would so greatly impair its business as to nearly destroy it. The trial court found, further, that "[the] premises were adapted for a particular highly productive use *no way dependent on ownership by these particular defendants.*" (Emphasis in original.) The importance of Kewpee's business location is underscored by the fact that, notwithstanding numerous attempts, the parties could not obtain a location remotely comparable to the one condemned.

68 Mich. App. 165. This Court in *Wery* relied heavily on the analysis set forth in *L & L* but did not find it dispositive.

Contrasted to these two cases are Detroit v. Whalings, Inc, 43 Mich. App. 1; 202 N.W.2d 816, *leave to appeal denied,* 388 Mich. 813 (1972), and State Highway Comm. v. Gaffield, 108 Mich. App. 88; 310 N.W. 2d 281 (1981), in which this Court applied the principles announced in *L & L*, and relied upon in *Wery*, but concluded that the business owners could not recover the going concern value of their businesses. In *Whalings*, a men's clothing store, located for over 100 years on Woodward Avenue in downtown Detroit, was closed as a result of the city's condemnation of the parcel of land on which it was located. Defendant's attempts to relocate were unsuccessful due to the unavailability of business space in the immediate area. The trial court excluded evidence of the going concern value of the defendant's business and this Court affirmed, holding:

> Whalings' going-concern value does not derive primarily from its location; it does not enjoy a monopoly, and its customers are not a captive audience. In an affidavit offered to prove that Whalings' present location is crucial, a customer begins by attributing his patronage to Whalings' "fine quality clothing," and only secondarily mentions the convenience of its location. While the convenience of its present location is no doubt a factor in attracting the patronage of the professional persons working in the surrounding area, the quality of its merchandise must certainly be of at least equal concern to those patrons.
>
> Second, the possibility of finding a suitable location nearby with the same or nearly the same convenience factors is not foreclosed by reason of the condemnation herein. In the *L & L* case, a "suitable location nearby" could only be within the racetrack grounds. The possibility of such relocation was

foreclosed by reason of the condemnation of the entire racetrack. For this case to come within the facts of *L & L*, the entire downtown area would have to be included in the condemnation order.

43 Mich. App. 9-10.

In *Gaffield*, this Court was presented with a claim for going-concern value similar to the one pursued by the plumber in In re Jeffries Homes Housing Project, *supra*. Respondents in *Gaffield* owned and operated a photography studio in Plymouth and used the backyard of their private residence as an outdoor set. In proceedings initiated by the highway commission for the condemnation of their residential property, respondents sought and were denied the going concern value of their backyard. This Court affirmed:

> In the instant case no competent testimony going to the merits which may have changed the result was excluded. Those factors cited in *L & L* and *In re Lansing Urban Renewal* justifying an award of going-concern value were not present in the instant case. Respondents did not lose their entire business because of the condemnation of their residential property. The location of their residential property was not crucial to the conduct of their downtown photography business. Their business did not consist solely of environmental photography. Respondents drew customers because of Mr. Gaffield's acclaim as a photographer, not because he took, on some occasions, outdoor photographs. Relocation was possible, though admittedly difficult, as is evidenced by the fact that respondents have subsequently purchased comparable property for their residence. Nor did respondents have a monopoly on environmental photography, much less the photography business as a whole, in Plymouth, as was the situation in *L & L*. Also, the going-concern value of respondents' photographic business did not derive primarily from the location of their residence. Unlike *L & L*, respondents' customers were not a captive audience. Finally, unlike the restaurant in Lansing, respondents' move did not "so greatly impair its business as to nearly destroy it." Also, unlike the restaurant, ownership of the photography studio by respondents in the instant case is vital. The instant case does not involve a situation where "the premises were adapted for a particular highly productive use." In re Lansing Urban Renewal, *supra*, 165.

108 Mich. App. 94.

Despite the different results reached in these four cases, it is clear that recovery of the going-concern value of a business lost to condemnation will depend on the transferability of that business to another location. If the business can be transferred, nothing is taken and compensation is therefore not required.[2] Whether a business is transferable will be decided on a

---

2. We note, however, that where a business is transferable, the business owner may recover for certain business interruption expenses. See In re Park Site on Private Claim 16, 247 Mich. 1; 225 N.W. 498 (1929). It should be clear that recovery for business interruption damages and recovery for going concern value are mutually exclusive since one assumes the continuation of the business and the other assumes its loss. This distinction was not always made by respondents below.

case by case basis inasmuch as a specific factual analysis is required. Generally, however, recovery will be allowed where the business derives its success from a location not easily duplicated or where relocation is foreclosed for reasons relating to the entire condemnation project. In large scale condemnation projects such as *Poletown*, involving the elimination of an entire segment of the residential and business community, transferability of neighborhood businesses is often foreclosed.

Michael's Prescriptions was located directly across the street from the entrance to St. Joseph Mercy Hospital. The Samaritan Medical Clinic was located one block away and at some point during the condemnation project occupied the same building that housed Michael's Prescriptions. Also in the same building were two physicians' offices. Michael's Prescriptions sold only pharmaceuticals, measured 20 feet by 28 feet, and was operated by Mr. Kablak, whose severe hearing impairment necessitated both amplified telephones and his son's assistance in filling prescriptions.

Respondent's accountant testified that due to the unique location of the pharmacy and monopolization of the prescription business of St. Joseph Mercy Hospital's emergency room, Michael's Prescriptions generated phenomenal gross sales of pharmaceuticals. Testimony established that when Michael's Prescriptions and St. Joseph Mercy Hospital were the only businesses operating in the condemned area, Michael's Prescriptions still generated its highest sales and most profitable year. The accountant classified the condemned property as a neighborhood pharmacy but considered it unique because of its location, operation and high income in comparison to eight other prescription pharmacies that he represented.

Evidence presented at trial regarding relocation efforts suggest that Michael's Prescriptions was nontransferable. Mr. Kablak and a professional realtor were unsuccessful in their attempts to find a location with a similar traffic pattern. While the business did relocate 12 blocks away from its original vantage point, sales and profits have already declined and evidence introduced at trial established that the trend would continue.

In our view, a significant factor in the inability of Michael's Prescriptions to relocate as a going concern is the nature of the condemnation project itself. As Justice Ryan pointed out in his dissenting opinion in *Poletown Neighborhood Council, supra,* the Poletown project swept away an entire community, "a tightly-knit residential enclave of first- and second-generation Americans." 410 Mich. 658. The *Poletown* condemnations entailed "intangible losses, such as severance of personal attachments to one's domicile and neighborhood and the destruction of an organic community of a most unique and irreplaceable character." 410 Mich. 682-683. The success of Michael's Prescriptions was attributable in part to the locational advantage of being so near a hospital, an emergency room, a clinic, and two physicians' offices. Its success also derived in no small part from the character of the neighborhood as described above and the good will of its established customers. Because of the condemnation of the entire surrounding neighborhood, the relocation of Michael's Prescriptions and other similar neighborhood businesses was realistically foreclosed by the scattering of established customers throughout the metropolitan area and by the elimination of other "business-generating businesses." This situation was recognized in Community Redevelopment Agency of the City of Los Angeles v. Abrams, *supra*, pp. 825-826, where the court rejected a claim similar to the one submitted in the instant case but nevertheless stated:

> We judicially notice the following as facts 'of generalized knowledge that are so universally known that they cannot reasonably be the subject of dispute' . . . : The conditions of modern American life, including the increased concentration of people in urban centers and the need for increased governmental activity in the areas of transportation and urban redevelopment, have resulted in the disruption and displacement of increased numbers of people and businesses by government projects. Moreover, the peculiar nature of urban redevelopment programs, which act upon large areas of contiguous property, often involves the uprooting of entire neighborhoods and the consequent dispersal of their business and residential occupants to other areas. . . .
>
> While the effects of this process are severe in both a personal and social sense for the residential occupants of areas subjected to redevelopment, its effects upon business occupants may be even more serious. One such effect relates to the business goodwill which such a businessman has built up in the location of which he is deprived by condemnation. In some cases, as for example in the case of a mail order business whose clientele is not rooted in the area affected by redevelopment, business goodwill may be transferred with relative ease to a new location outside the redevelopment area. At the other end of the spectrum, however, are businesses which depend on a clientele within the redevelopment area. In many such cases business goodwill is based almost wholly upon the businessman's personal acquaintance with his customers and his knowledge of their particular needs. Such goodwill is by its nature not freely transferable within the context of wholesale condemnation pursuant to urban redevelopment, for the inevitable effect of such condemnation is to disperse the businessman's clientele throughout the urban area, with the result that any new location chosen by him will be unable to continue to profitably serve a significant portion of them.

15 Cal. 3d 825-826.

In the instant case, Michael's Prescriptions lost its leasehold interest in the underlying realty, its established customers and the prescription market generated by the neighborhood hospital, clinic and physicians' offices. Unlike *Whalings, supra,* and *Gaffield, supra,* this respondent did not provide the type of specialized product that would encourage its established customers to continue patronage at a new and more distant location. As this Court recognized in rejecting the claim for going concern value in *Whalings, supra,* "[for] this case to come within the facts of *L & L,* the entire downtown area would have to be included in the condemnation order." The *Poletown* project fits this requirement hand and glove.

We conclude that the trial court did not err in allowing the introduction of evidence as to the going concern value of Michael's Prescriptions. Since the verdict was within the range of the valuation testimony offered at trial, we decline to disturb it on appeal. Moreover, we find that the method of valuation used in determining the going concern value of Michael's Prescriptions was proper under In re Park Site on Private Claim 16, 247 Mich. 1; 225 N.W. 498 (1929), and that the jury's award reflects the value of the leasehold interest. Wery, 68 Mich. App. 163.

Affirmed.

NOTES AND QUESTIONS

1. **Precedent.** Does the Michigan Supreme Court follow the precedent it cites?

2. **Merits.** Does the *Michael's Prescriptions* case reach the right conclusion, in your view? Under it, would most businesses in Poletown be compensated for their going concerned value?

3. **No compensation for goodwill is the general rule.** Most American state courts refuse to compensate for loss of goodwill. See Banner Milling Co. v. State of New York, 240 N.Y. 533, 148 N.E. 668 (1925); 4 Nichols, Eminent Domain §13.13 (1996). But a few courts, even while stating the rule, seem to have fudged. See, for example, Housing Authority of Bridgeport v. Lustig, 139 Conn. 73, 90 A.2d 169 (1952) (poultry slaughterer awarded $16,500 for loss of building valued at $6,500 qua building; higher award based on building's location and "suitability" for business); State v. Williams, 65 N.J. Super. 518, 168 A.2d 233 (1961) (gas station owner awarded $60,000 after testifying to business losses as evidence of the suitability of the site for a gas station).

Can it be argued that the value of land necessarily includes the "quasi monopoly" advantage of the site that should be capitalized — based on business income — in the same way that a site bearing an office building or apartment house is valued?

The courts of Britain and Canada have long required compensation for loss of goodwill. See, e.g., White v. Commissioners, 22 L.T.R. (n.s.) 591 (Ex. 1870); Re McCauley and City of Toronto, 18 Ont. 416 (ch. 1889).

4. **Statutes.** Also, occasional American statutes require compensation for loss of goodwill. See also Fla. Stat. Ann. §73.071(3) (1979 & Supp. 1995) (business of more than five years' standing); 19 Vt. Stat. Ann. §221(2) (1968); New York City Admn. Code §§K51-44.0 (acquisition in upstate New York for expansion of New York City water supply). The latter statute, which dates from 1906, was imposed on the city by a none-too-friendly state legislature. Under its terms, a businessperson may also recover for the loss of customers forced to leave their homes even though the businessperson's site has not been condemned. Matter of Huie, 18 A.D.2d 270, 239 N.Y.S.2d 178 (3d Dept. 1963).

Might a New York City condemnee, for whom the loss of goodwill is usually noncompensable, claim a denial of equal protection in view of the statute cited above?

5. **Two types of goodwill.** One author distinguishes two forms of goodwill: the increment attributable to trade advantage that may derive from a strategic location (quasi monopoly), and the increment attributable to the personality or business acumen of the proprietor (a laundry route, for example). One indication of the second is that a prospective buyer would demand either a management contract with the seller or his promise not to compete for a specified time.

Those who would not compensate for goodwill damages argue that the businessperson is a risk-taker, and that the prospect of an uncompensated taking is simply another risk to be shouldered along with those of increased competition, technological change, population movement, and so on. In reply, one might ask whether businesspersons do, in fact, account for this risk; if so, might they not overcompensate and become chary of new investment? Finally, is not the risk often borne by the small operator who is already insecurely financed?

Also opposed to compensation is the argument that the loss of a quasi monopoly should not entitle one to be made whole. Yet, competitors (if there are any) will benefit from the removal — and they are *not* assessed; the cost of public improvement is partly concealed and, more important, unevenly distributed. See generally Note, An Inquiry into the Nature of Goodwill, 53 Colum. L. Rev. 660 (1953).

6. **Direct or consequential damages.** During World War I, the federal government acquired a large tract of land in Maryland for the Aberdeen Proving Ground. One parcel, consisting of 440 acres, was used by plaintiffs in the business of growing and canning whole-grain shoe-peg corn, a special grade for which their lands were especially adapted. In the condemnation proceeding, plaintiffs were paid for their land and buildings, but denied compensation for the loss of business that could not be reestablished elsewhere. The Supreme Court upheld the judgment for the defendant. Mitchell v. United States, 267 U.S. 341 (1925).

Justice Brandeis wrote the opinion:

> The special value of land due to its adaptability for use in a particular business is an element which the owner of land is entitled, under the Fifth Amendment, to have considered in determining the amount to be paid as the just compensation upon a taking by eminent domain. . . . Doubtless such special value of the plaintiffs' land was duly considered by the President in fixing the amount to be paid therefor. The settled rules of law, however, precluded his considering in that determination consequential damages for losses to their business, or for its destruction. . . . No recovery therefor can be had now as for a taking of the business. There is no finding as a fact that the Government took the business, or that what it did was intended as a taking. . . . There can be no recovery . . . if the intention to take is lacking.

267 U.S. at 344-345.

7.   **When is a business "taken"?** When does a "taking" of a business occur? Consider, by contrast, Kimball Laundry v. United States, 338 U.S. 1 (1949). Here, the War Department condemned claimant's laundry plant for successive one-year terms from 1942 to 1946, and used the plant facilities for army personnel. Having no other means of servicing its own customers, the laundry suspended business. With four justices dissenting, the Court fixed the measure of damage to include the value of claimant's trade routes during the period of army occupancy. Justice Frankfurter, who wrote for the Court, spoke approvingly of *Mitchell* but was able to distinguish it. Can you see how? Justice Douglas's dissent read in part (id. at 23-24):

> The truth of the matter is that the United States is being forced to pay not for what it gets but for what the owner loses. The value of trade-routes represents the patronage of the customers of the laundry. Petitioner, I assume, lost some of them as a result of the government's temporary taking of the laundry. But the government did not take them. There was indeed no possible way in which it could have used them. Hence the doctrine that makes the United States pay for them is new and startling. It promises swollen awards which Congress in its generosity might permit but which it has never been assumed the Constitution compels.

Which is the more valid measure of compensation — value to the condemner or loss to the condemnee?

If government acquires (nationalizes?) a going business and continues its operation, it must pay for the "going-concern" value of the business. See, e.g., Omaha v. Omaha Water Co., 218 U.S. 180 (1910); In re Fifth Ave. Coach Lines, Inc., 18 N.Y.2d 212, 219 N.E.2d 410, 273 N.Y.S.2d 52 (1966).

8.   **Moving and start-up expenses.** Other noncompensable expenses, in the absence of statute, may include the removal cost of business equipment and inventory, moving expenses, and "starting-up" expenses at a new location. See generally 4A Nichols, Eminent Domain §14A.02 (1996). For a statutory attempt to mitigate these losses in urban renewal and other federally aided acquisitions, see 42 U.S.C.A. §§4601 et seq. (West 1995).

Chapter 7

Easements, Covenants, and Servitudes

This chapter, and those on takings (Chapter 8) and land use (Chapter 9), all concern the use of land. The traditional view is that covenants are *private* land use restrictions, whereas land use regulation sets out *public* land use restrictions (although, as we shall see, the sharp division between public and private obfuscates as much as it clarifies).

The notion that easements, covenants, and zoning constitute *regulations* rests on the intuitive image of property as absolute. In fact, as has been noted, ownership has often been far from absolute. "Blackstone's sweeping definition of property overstated the case: indeed, he devoted the succeeding 518 pages . . . of his Commentaries . . . to qualifying and specifying the exceptions to his definition."[1] Limitations on the owner's "sole and despotic dominion" included many rights that belonged to the sovereign, such as the right to all swans, whales, and tall timbers.[2] The public also retained extensive rights over "private" land, rights that today would be understood as easements (the right to use land owned by another), including rights to graze, gather wood, hunt, pass over, and use the water on "private" property.[3]

Today easements are common; covenants (promises relating to land) are even more important. Covenants played an important role in this country's division into racially segregated inner cities and suburbs. See Douglas S. Massey and Nancy A. Denton, American Apartheid: Segregation and the Making of the Underclass 10, 61 (1993) (documenting the hypersegregation of blacks into central cities). A 1928 study of early luxury suburban neighborhoods found that their "high class," purely residential character was set by complex systems of covenants that prohibited business activities, limited housing to single-family houses, required approval of individuals'

1. Forrest McDonald, Novus Ordo Seclorum: The Intellectual Origins of the Constitution 13 (1985).
2. Id. at 19.
3. Id. at 29.

building plans, prescribed minimum costs of buildings, prohibited nuisances such as livestock, signs, saloons,[4] signs, and factories. The 1928 study also found that nearly half of the subdivisions studied also excluded racial or ethnic minorities: "Africans, Mongolians prohibited," "Caucasians only," "Negroes barred," "White race only," "Asiatics and Negroes barred," "Mongolians and Africans barred," and "Caucasians only, except business."[5]

Residential segregation really took hold, as noted in Chapter 1, *supra* page 62, with the boom in suburban homebuilding after World War II. During that period, Federal Housing Administration (FHA) loan insurance made cheap, very long-term loans available to qualified buyers. The FHA, which "had a more pervasive and powerful impact on the American people over the past half-century" than any other agency of the U.S. government,[6] opposed racial mixing. It enforced this by refusing to guarantee mortgages in racially mixed neighborhoods and requiring banks to include exclusionary racial covenants in their loans in order to be eligible for federal loan guarantees. The 1938 Underwriting Manual noted the need to guard against "adverse influences":

> Areas surrounding a location are investigated to determine whether incompatible racial and social groups are present, for the purpose of making a prediction regarding the probability of being invaded by such groups. If a neighborhood is to retain stability, it is necessary to be occupied by the same social and racial classes. A change in social or racial occupancy generally contributes to instability and a decline in values.[7]

The FHA strongly recommended that racially restrictive covenants be placed in the deeds of houses to qualify them for FHA loan insurance.[8]

By the late 1940s, racially restrictive covenants were very widespread. A 1947 Chicago study undertaken in connection with litigation found that "over half the residential area not occupied by Negroes is covenanted against colored people."[9] A 1947 study of 300 New York subdivisions found

4. Prohibitions against saloons often operated to exclude ethnic groups, notably from Italy and Ireland, who expected to have a local bar or pub in their neighborhoods. See Timothy Jost, The Defeasible Fee and the Birth of the Modern Residential Subdivision, 49 Mo. L. Rev. 695 (1984.)

5. By 1947, a standard drafting was "No race other than the Caucasian race shall use or occupy any building or lot, except that this restriction shall not prevent occupancy by domestic servants of a different race employed by an owner or tenant." See Evan McKensie, Privatopia: Homeowner Associations and the Rise of Residential Private Government 70 (1994). One of the author's fathers, arriving in Washington, D.C., in the 1930s, had a difficult time finding an apartment to rent because his roommate was Jewish, and most properties prohibited occupation by Jews. Interview, Norman Williams Jr., May 1994.

6. Kenneth Jackson, Crabgrass Frontier: The Suburbanization of the United States 203-204 (1985).

7. As quoted in Evan McKensie, Privatopia: Homeowner Associations and the Rise of Residential Private Government 65 (1994).

8. Id. at 65-67.

9. Id. at 69.

"*A Beautiful Dream*
COME TRUE"

THE KINNARD CLUB HOUSE

THE developers of Kinnard had a vision of an Ideal Suburban Community and planned it on 240 acres of gently rolling fields and virgin woodland almost within the shadow of the Nation's Capital.

To date scores of distinctive homes have been built and more than 3 miles of roadways are planted with over 2000 Japanese Cherry Trees. Every Spring in excess of 100,000 visitors come to drink in the beauty of Kinnard's floral display.

The Cherry Blossoms are only one of the unique features that have made this community nationally famous — the choice of discriminating people.

Kinnard has its own country club with a fine 18-hole golf course, an outdoor swimming pool, second to none around Washington, and splendid tennis courts.

Rigid restrictions assure home owners security of their investment, beautiful surroundings, the right sort of neighbors. In short "A Beautiful Dream Come True".

Homes and Homesites Sold Only To Approved Purchasers.

LIVE WHERE YOU WALK TO PLAY

To reach Kinnard: North on either Connecticut or Wisconsin Avenue to Bradley Lane, turn left to Kinnard Entrance.

Kinnard Champaigne Development Company
50 KINNARD DRIVE
KINNARD, CHEVY CHASE, MARYLAND

The basic substance of the above advertisement was taken from a well-known magazine, but names have been altered.

FIGURE 7-1
"The Right Sort of Neighbors," Achieved by Selling to "Approved Purchasers" under "Rigid Conditions"

DEED—SHORT FORM D. C.

Law Reporter Blank No. 222
518 FIFTH ST. N.W., WASHINGTON, D.C.

BOOK 9289 PAGE 102

37103

Sep 6 11 44 AM '50

This Deed

Made this TWENTY-EIGHTH *day of* JULY *in the year one thousand nine hundred and* FIFTY, *by and between* JAMES E. DISMUKE AND IRMA A. DISMUKE, HIS WIFE

parties of the first part, and

FRED A. SMITH COMPANY a corporation organized under the Laws of the State of Delaware,

party of the second part:

Witnesseth, *that in consideration of* TEN ($10.00) *Dollars the parties of the first part do hereby grant unto the party of the second part, in fee simple, all* that *piece or parcel of land, together with the improvements, rights, privileges and appurtenances to the same belonging, situate in the District of Columbia, described as follows, to wit:* Lot numbered Eighty-five (85) in Square numbered Thirty-nine hundred and seventy-five (3975) in the subdivision made by George W. Young as per plat recorded in the Office of the Surveyor for the District of Columbia in Liber 108 at folio 178; subject to the building restriction line as shown on said plat, and to the provisions of the Act of Congress of May 31st, 1900 regulating the use of the land within said building restriction line; subject to the covenants that said land and premises shall not be leased, rented, sold, demised, transferred or conveyed unto or in trust for or permitted to be used or occupied by any negro or colored person or person of negro blood or extraction and that no dwelling house shall be erected costing less than $5,000.00; these covenants to run with the land; subject to the further covenants that no apartment house or apartment houses shall be erected on said property or any part thereof.

And *the said parties of the first part covenant that* they *will warrant specially the property hereby conveyed; and that* they *will execute such further assurances of said land as may be requisite.*

Witness their *hands and seals the day and year hereinbefore written.*

IN PRESENCE OF—

William F. McIntosh — James E. Dismuke [SEAL]

Irma A. Dismuke [SEAL]

FIGURE 7-2
Deed Showing Racial Covenant

BOOK 9289 PAGE 103

District of Columbia, to wit:

I, _____, a Notary Public in and for the District aforesaid,

HEREBY CERTIFY that James E. Dismuke and Irma A. Dismuke

who are personally well known to me as the grantor s in, and the person s who executed the aforegoing and annexed deed, dated July 28th , A. D. 19 50 personally appeared before me in the said District and acknowledged the said deed to be their act and deed.

Given under my hand and seal this 28th day of July 19 50

_____
Notary Public

JAMES E. DISMUKE
ET UX
IRMA A. DISMUKE
TO
FRED A. SMITH COMPANY

SEP 6 11 44 AM '50

RECEIVED FOR RECORD on the _____ day of _____, A. D. 19____ at _____ o'clock ____M, and recorded in Liber No. 9289 at Folio 102, one of the Land Records for the District of Columbia, and examined by _____

Recorder.

SEP 6 11 44 AM '50

37103 360005

Deed 1/3

SEP-650 159562 A 37105 A

1.60

PLEASE MAIL TO: Fred A. Smith
1113-17th St. N.W.
Washington, D.C.

FIGURE 7-2
(continued)

621

that "no less than 56% of all homes checked were forbidden to Negroes,"[10] and that 85 percent of large subdivisions were restricted to whites. After Shelley v. Kraemer, 334 U.S. 1 (1948), barred state courts from enforcing racial covenants, various plans for evading the prohibition were developed. A 1948 article in the U.S. News and World Report helpfully listed a variety of evasions:

> Plans that have the effect of restricting neighborhoods and that apparently are within the law, under the ruling of the Supreme Court, already are in use here and there. . . . Any of these plans that prove practical as well as legally valid are expected to come into more general use. . . . Self-enforcement of a covenant that limits property ownership in a neighborhood to the members of a racial or religious group is one such plan. . . .[11] Requiring membership in a club or a co-operative as a condition for owning or occupying property is a second plan, already in use, by which the sale of property is restricted to certain groups.[12]

In the second half of the twentieth century, measures explicitly to exclude specific racial groups gradually disappeared. But the pattern of all or predominantly white suburbs, especially in newer neighborhoods, continued, in part due to the difficulties other racial groups experienced when they tried to rent or buy housing, see *infra* at Chapter 10, outside traditionally minority areas. Today controversy exists over the proper response to past discrimination. Some argue that what is past is past; others argue that "[r]ace-neutral policies, set against an historical backdrop of state action in the service of racial discrimination . . . predictably reproduce and entrench racial segregation and the race-caste system that accompanies it." Richard Thompson Ford, The Boundaries of Race: Political Geography in Legal Analysis, 107 Harv. L. Rev. 1841, 1845 (1994).

Another major use of covenants has been to ensure that all inhabitants have a certain level of affluence. Earlier in the century, this was accomplished by covenants limiting the number of persons per room and preventing conversions that could allow owners to rent out rooms at a time when many less affluent families took in boarders.[13] More recently, many subdivisions impose elaborate design restrictions or require review by an Architectural Control Board. These covenants underlie the distinctive homogeneity of the American suburbs, a trend reinforced by exclusionary zoning, see *infra* at Chapter 9.

The law of covenants not only is dramatic from the standpoint of social policy; it is also notoriously complex. Said one commentator: "The law is an unspeakable quagmire. The intrepid soul who ventures into this formi-

---

10. Id.
11. Because *Shelley* forbade only the involvement of state actors, voluntary enforcement by private parties without state involvement was not precluded by the decision.
12. As quoted in McKensie, *supra* note 5, at 75-76.
13. Id. at 77-78.

FIGURE 7-3
Washington, D.C., Deed Book, with Stamp Saying Covenants Are Unenforceable

dable wilderness never emerges unscarred. Some, the smarter ones, quickly turn back and take up something easier, like astrophysics."[14] Luckily, the new Restatement of Servitudes promises to simplify the law of covenants. The presentation of law in this chapter will often track the Restatement, although it introduces the traditional law as well.

This chapter begins with a brief examination of two phenomena that define the outer limits of easement law: irrevocable licenses and the use of nuisance law in solar energy cases. It then proceeds to discuss easements and covenants.[15]

§7.1   Coming to Terms with Easements, Covenants, and Servitudes

You have already met the easement once or twice along the way, but we will now examine this interest and its various siblings with more than passing

---

14. Edward Rabin, Fundamentals of Modern Real Property Law 447 (3d ed. 1992).
15. Note that even the terminology in this area is confused, for the words "servitude" and "covenants" are each used in the names of particular legal categories and as generic terms.

concern, because this family has long offered, and still provides, a principal technique for realizing private wishes about the use of land.

Here, as elsewhere in this course, vocabulary is important, and since there is much to assimilate, we will first illustrate and discuss the most widely used terms.

Affirmative easement. Maintaining a shaky distinction between possession and use, the first Restatement of Property describes an easement as an interest in land that is in the possession of another, permitting a "limited use or enjoyment of the land in which the interest exists." Restatement of Property §450.[16] A owns Lot 1, B owns adjoining Lot 2; a paved driveway straddles the two lots. The two neighbors agree that each is to have "perpetual" use of the driveway for getting to or from the garages on their respective lots. The interest that each one has in the other's land is called an *affirmative* easement, which, in Hohfeldian terms, privileges A (B) to enter and make affirmative use of B's (A's) land, and bars B (A) from interfering with that use. Most easements are affirmative, generally occurring as rights-of-way, public utility easements (for example, telephone poles and wires), and drainage easements.[17]

Profit a prendre. This is a form of affirmative easement that privileges its holder to enter another's land to remove something of value. Early forms of profit, prevalent in a rural society, included "turbary" (the right to cut turf for fuel), "estover" (the right to cut timber for fuel), "piscary" (the right to take fish), and the right of pasture. More recently, profits have sometimes been given for the extraction of minerals, such as coal, iron, oil, and gas. 3 Powell, Real Property ¶405 (Rohan ed., 1979).

Negative easement and negative covenant. Consider, for example, the following: Neighbors A and B reach an agreement wherein A agrees, in order to protect B's view, not to build any structure higher than two stories. This agreement is said to create a *negative easement.* In Hohfeldian terms, the easement entitles B to enjoy the view and bars A from interfering with that view — a privilege that A as a landowner would otherwise have. Unlike the holder of an affirmative easement, the holder of a negative easement receives an advantage that does not permit physical entry upon another's land.

"Servitude" is now favored as a generic term that includes both easements and covenants; it also is part of the common law name of easements that run at equity: equitable servitudes. The term "covenants" is often used as a generic name for both covenants running at law and in equity; it also is part of the common-law name of covenants that run at law ("covenants at law").

16. The Restatement emphasizes that an easement is not terminable at the will of the possessor of the land, thus distinguishing it from the "revocable" license.

17. An easement might also be described as affirmative when it privileges its holder to create what might otherwise be a nuisance. For example, A might agree to let A operate a rubbish dump whose stench limits B's enjoyment of his own land, and, had he never consented, B might seek to enjoin the odors as a nuisance. In this instance, A holds an affirmative easement; see, e.g., Waldrop v. Town of Brevard, 233 N.C. 26, 62 S.E.2d 512 (1950).

Because the usual form of B's agreement is a covenant not to sue A for causing a nuisance, one might also classify this arrangement as a negative covenant, *infra.*

Common-law courts recognized only a few negative easements, chiefly those that clearly benefited the easement holder's land. These included negative easements for light, air, or view, and for greater lateral support[18] or water from a riparian stream than the easement holder would otherwise be entitled to.[19]

With the advent of the industrial age, landowners began to restrict their holdings so as to avoid overrun by the grimier aspects of urban life. For example, residential neighbors A and B might mutually agree not to conduct business on their land. In Hohfeldian terms, this arrangement seems no different from a negative easement, that is, it would entitle A (B) to bar B (A) from opening a retail shop — a privilege each landowner would otherwise have. The law courts, however, refused to regard this arrangement as a negative easement, because it did not fit neatly into one of the five existing doctrinal boxes.

We often refer to these negative easement-like arrangements as *negative covenants* or *restrictive covenants*. In the nineteenth century, courts of equity began to enforce these covenants much as they would negative easements, giving injunctive relief to the covenant holder to prevent a covenant breach.[20] This became a pivotal step in advancing private control over land use, because the negative covenant is so often at the heart of private land

---

18. Each landowner enjoys the right that, in its natural state, her land not subside because of excavation that takes place next door. Thus, if X and Y are neighboring owners, X would be deemed to have a (negative) easement in Y's land, which would bar Y from any soil removal on his land that would impair the integrity of X's soil. We call this the right to lateral support. And, of course, Y would have corresponding rights against X.

Because the common-law doctrine of lateral support protects only land in its natural state — adequate for a rural setting — more refinement has been added when the supported land contains a structure. When the excavator acts negligently, for example, by departing from accepted methods of excavation, the injured party may recover for damage both to the land and building, unless injury would have resulted, due to the building's location and weight, even without negligence. When damage results from nonnegligent excavation, however, two lines of authority have emerged. Under the American rule, the injured owner recovers nothing for structural damage to his building, cf. Moellering v. Evans, 121 Ind. 195, 22 N.E. 989 (1889) ("The owner of the house is without remedy. It was his own folly to put it there."). The English rule, increasingly popular in the United States, provides recovery, cf. Prete v. Cray, 49 R.I. 209, 141 A. 609 (1928).

Many states have legislated procedural safe harbors, for example, 30 days' notice to one's neighbor that excavation is to occur below a stated depth, which, if followed, would absolve the excavator of liability for nonnegligent work. See, e.g., Cal. Civ. Code §832 (West 1992). The parties, by contract, can agree to modify their baseline rights against the other.

19. A negative easement for light and air may restrict the servient estate in one of several respects: as to building location, building height, or percentage of lot coverage. Such restrictions also serve an additional purpose in the high-density areas of Manhattan and other commercial centers where zoning laws limit a building's floor space to a specified multiple of the lot area. See Chapter 8. A developer can obtain the equivalent of more land (thus permitting a bulkier building) if his neighbor will agree to underuse his lot. The developer then applies for a building permit based on the combined floor area limits for his lot and the unused capacity of the servient lot. See Hotel Taft Assoc. v. Summer, 34 Misc. 2d 367, 374, 226 N.Y.S.2d 155 (Sup. Ct. 1962), *aff'd mem.*, 18 A.D.2d 796, 236 N.Y.S.2d 939 (N.Y. 1963).

20. Tulk v. Moxhay, 2 Ph. 774, 41 Eng. Rep. 1143 (Ch. 1848); Trustees of Columbia College v. Lynch, 70 N.Y. 440 (1877).

use agreements. In time, the law courts followed suit (weak pun intended!); thus, we have all but forgotten the historical difference between negative easements and covenants, and lawyers may use the terms interchangeably.

Affirmative covenant. Suppose that in the common driveway agreement between A and B, each promises to pay one-half of the driveway's upkeep costs. Notice A's (B's) promise. Although it concerns land, it is analytically different from A's earlier agreement permitting B the use of that part of the driveway located on A's land. That agreement, though fixing a duty on A (not to interfere with B's access), requires no affirmative action; A could perform his duty doing nothing. We sometimes refer metaphorically to such a duty as a "rocking chair" duty. As to the upkeep agreement, however, A has a duty to spend money and B has a correlative right that A do so. We call A's promise an *affirmative covenant,* or, more vividly, a "cash register" duty.

This definitional difference between affirmative easements and covenants may seem labored to you, but it has caused, as you will learn shortly, an enormously confusing body of law, which we are still seeking both to clarify and simplify.

Servitude. The Restatement of Servitudes[21] defines a servitude "as a burden on land . . . that automatically binds successors to the land, regardless of their consent, unless they are entitled to protection under the recording act."[22] The term "servitude" stems from "equitable servitude," a phrase often given to the negative (and, later, some affirmative) covenants that were enforced equitably, even when the law courts might turn their backs on the covenant because it was technically flawed. The Restatement's approach is to develop a common set of rules to reflect the "modern analytical perception that all the servitude devices [affirmative easements, profits, negative easements and covenants, affirmative covenants] are functionally similar, and that for the most part they are, or should be, governed by the same rules. Only in the relatively few instances where there are real differences among the servitude devices are different rules justifiable."[23]

In this text, therefore, we will use both the modern generic "servitude," and where it seems sensible to do so, because legal usage changes slowly, retain some of the common-law specifics.

Servient estate. The land that is subject to, or burdened by, any servitude is called the *servient estate.* As to the above driveway agreement between A and B, Lot 1 is the servient estate vis-à-vis B's affirmative easement and covenant, and, reciprocally, Lot 2 is the servient estate vis-à-vis A's.

Dominant estate. Suppose that A were now to sell Lot 1 to A', and A'

21. The Restatement of Servitudes, launched by the American Law Institute in 1988, is designed "to restate the law of servitudes for the future, rather than to document the past." Restatement of the Law Third, Property (Servitudes), Introduction to Tentative Draft No. 1, of six (1989). This is a multiyear project, unlikely to be finished much before the year 2000.

22. Id. at xxi.

23. Id. at xxiii.

continued to use the common driveway. Is she privileged to do so? The answer requires us to examine the original agreement between A and B and possibly, depending on what we find, the conveyance from A to A'.

It is almost certain, in this instance, that A bargained for an interest that would benefit not only himself but would continue to benefit Lot 1 regardless of who became its owner (or occupant). If so, then the servitude is said to be *appurtenant* to Lot 1, that is, its benefit becomes an incident to the ownership of Lot 1 and passes automatically from one owner to the next.[24] The deed from A to A' need not even mention the driveway agreement for A' to enjoy its benefit. The benefited land, Lot 1, is called the *dominant* estate, and A', now the lot's new owner, may continue using the common driveway. (We would make the same analysis of B's interest in that part of the driveway lying on Lot 1; thus, in a common driveway agreement, both lots are servient, and quite probably dominant.)

Servitude in gross.[25] An *"in gross"* servitude is intended to benefit a person (or business) rather than to add to the value of the easement holder's land.[26] A public utility easement is a good example, since the easement would allow its holder, a water or electric company, to run lines through servient estates as an incident to the company's business; there is no dominant estate. Today, the holder of an in gross servitude, unless the servitude is "personal," *infra,* or unless the parties creating the servitude intended otherwise, may transfer its benefit freely.[27] For example, holders of a public utility easement are able to assign the servitude to a successor water or electric company.

"Personal" servitudes, by contrast, benefit only the original holder and may not be transferred, although, in some instances, the benefit may be shared with family, friends, and invitees. The benefit may be held in gross or, on occasion, only while the servitude holder owns or occupies specific land. We can usually tell that the servitude is personal from the relationship of the parties, and the (absence of) consideration.[28]

---

24. A not-so-recent case held that if A were to sell the dominant estate and try to keep the appurtenant easement for himself, the easement would be extinguished; see Cadwalader v. Bailey, 17 R.I. 495, 23 A. 20 (1891).

25. The Restatement of Servitudes recognizes the possibility, although fairly uncommon, of an in gross burden. For example, a water company might covenant to supply water for domestic use to each lot in a residential subdivision. See, e.g., Eagle Enter. v. Gross, 39 N.Y.2d 505 (1976).

26. Restatement, Servitudes (T.D. 4, 1994).

27. Restatement, Servitudes (T.D. 4, 1994), §4.6.

28. Id. at §4.6. The Restatement gives the following illustration:

O, who owned a summer home on a lakefront parcel, enjoyed a close relationship with his nephew, A, who spent his childhood summers with O at the lake. When A graduated from college, O granted A an easement over the property for access to the lake, together with the right to build a dock and moor a boat. A did not own any land in the area and paid nothing for the easement. The lack of consideration, the fact that the easement is in gross, and the relationship of the parties should lead to the conclusion that A's easement is personal and not transferable. (Illus. 2.)

The nature of the servitude and the circumstances of its creation will usually tell us whether the benefit was intended to be appurtenant or in gross. If it appears that the benefit is more useful to the next holder of a parcel of land than to the original beneficiary once she has transferred the land, this strongly implies an appurtenant servitude.[29] In a close case, the law presumes that the parties intended to create an appurtenant servitude.[30] This makes it easier to identify the servitude holder, through land and tax records. It also makes it easier to negotiate servitude changes or releases.

Appurtenant trumps Gross

NOTES AND QUESTIONS

1. **Can easements be sold?** The early common law was unrelenting about all easements in gross: They could not be assigned. Underlying this attitude was a weighing of the relative inutility of easements in gross against their potential for title-clogging if assignability were freely allowed. But the balance began to shift as in gross grants became the vehicle for railroad and public utility rights-of-way. The first Restatement of Property, reacting to this development, divided easements in gross into "commercial" and "non-commercial" types, making assignable only those easements that "result primarily in economic benefit rather than personal satisfaction." Id. §489, Comment c. The Restatement of Servitudes, by treating personal servitudes as a subset of in gross burdens, draws a somewhat different line.

2. **Conservation easements.** Conservation organizations often obtain conservation easements from owners of historic properties as a way of preserving the properties for future generations. The following is the standard preservation restriction agreement the Society for the Preservation of New England Antiquities (SPNEA) now uses; SPNEA now has restrictions on 50 properties. Some tax benefits are available to owners who donate easements to SPNEA, but the primary motivation is the desire to preserve the historic properties for future generations. Note how carefully the document identifies the features to be preserved. Note also that it calls itself a "preservation restriction agreement"; nowhere is the word "easement" used. Why not? What technical problems does a conservation easement present at common law? How does the Restatement solve the problem?

---

29. Restatement Servitudes (T.D. 4, 1994), §4.5. The Restatement gives the following illustration:

> O, the owner of Blackacre and Whiteacre, conveyed Whiteacre to A, subject to a servitude requirement that no structure or vegetation on Whiteacre be permitted to exceed 30 feet above the level of the street abutting Whiteacre. Blackacre was located across the street and enjoyed a view across Whiteacre. Because protection of the view across Whiteacre would be more useful to a successor to Blackacre than to O after transferring Blackacre, the conclusion would be justified that the benefit is appurtenant to Blackacre. Id. at Illus. 1.

30. Id. at Comment d. Profits are an exception to the usual presumption, since most profits are held in gross.

PRESERVATION RESTRICTION AGREEMENT

SOCIETY FOR THE PRESERVATION
OF NEW ENGLAND ANTIQUITIES

The Parties to this Preservation Restriction Agreement (this "Agreement") are the **SOCIETY FOR THE PRESERVATION OF NEW ENGLAND ANTIQUITIES,** a Massachusetts charitable corporation having an address at Harrison Gray Otis House, 141 Cambridge Street, Boston, Massachusetts 02114 (hereafter "SPNEA") and _____ having an address at _____ (herein together with their heirs, successors and assigns called "Owner").

PRELIMINARY STATEMENT

Owner is the owner in fee simple of certain property located at _____ Main Street in the Town of _____, County of _____, and Commonwealth of Massachusetts, free of mortgage or other encumbrance which includes certain premises (the "Premises") consisting of approximately 3.35 acres of land with four buildings hereon known as the _____ House, the Shop, the Hen House and Garage being more particularly described in Exhibit A attached hereto and made a part hereof and in that certain deed (the "Deed"), recorded with the _____ County Registry of Deeds (the "Registry") at Book _____, Page _____. The Premises are also shown in the photographs and diagrams attached as Exhibits B, C, and D hereto and incorporated herein by reference. The buildings located on the Premises which are protected by this Agreement consist of the _____ House, the Shop, the Hen House and the Garage as more particularly shown in Exhibits B, C, and D.

SPNEA is a charitable corporation incorporated in 1910 and exempt from income taxation under Section 501(c)(3) of the Internal Revenue Code. SPNEA is authorized to create, impose, accept and enforce preservation restrictions to protect sites and structures historically significant for their architecture, archaeology, or other associations.

The _____ House and its surrounding outbuildings are listed in the National Register of Historic Places. The house, its outbuildings and setting are historically significant and worthy of preservation. Constructed initially for _____ in 1764, the house preserves its eighteenth-century floorplan, central chimney and the majority of its decorative finishes. In the early 1840s, the house underwent alteration and enlargement by _____ whose journals and account books (1824-1889) record changes made to the house under his ownership.

This written record of the house's development combined with the continued existence of many of the features described in _____'s
account books gives the building a unique significance that warrants protecting and conserving the building in its present condition as an important
example of vernacular architecture in the Connecticut River Valley and the
Commonwealth of Massachusetts.

In addition to the _____ House, the Premises contain
two nineteenth-century outbuildings which add to the significance of the
property and preserve important evidence of its agrarian past. The Shop is
a one-storey, timber-frame structure that stands southeast of the House. Occupied as a workshop and containing the remains of a boiler for preparing
livestock feed, the Shop is a rare survivor from the property's past use as a
farm. Similarly, the Hen House is a low timber-frame shed which preserves
important evidence of the property's agricultural past. The Shop, Hen
House and large open lot which comprises the Premises preserve an open
setting that complements the historic structures on the Premises, thereby
endowing the _____ House the scenic, natural, and aesthetic value and significance.

Massachusetts General Laws, Chapter 184, Sections 31-33, authorizes
the creation and enforcement of preservation restrictions appropriate to
the preservation of a site or structure for its historical significance and for
its natural scenic and open condition.

Owner and SPNEA recognize the historic, architectural, cultural, scenic and aesthetic value and significance of the Premises and have the
common purpose of conserving and preserving the aforesaid value and significance of the Premises. To that end, Owner desires to grant to SPNEA,
and SPNEA desires to accept, the Preservation Restrictions set forth in this
Agreement, pursuant to Massachusetts General Laws, Chapter 184, Sections 31-33.

NOW, THEREFORE, for good and valuable consideration, receipt of
which is hereby acknowledged, Owner does hereby grant, release and convey to SPNEA, its successors and assigns a Preservation Restriction Agreement in perpetuity in and to the Premises.

In delineation and furtherance of this Preservation Restriction Agreement, SPNEA imposes and Owner accepts the following preservation
restrictions:

1.   **EXTERIOR RESTRICTIONS.** Owner agrees that, without the
prior written permission of SPNEA, no construction, alteration or any other
activity shall be undertaken which will alter or adversely affect the appear-

ance, workmanship or structural stability of certain exterior portions of the
_____ House, the Shop or the Hen House as they exist as
of the date of this Agreement. For convenience of reference the street facade of the house, facing Main Street, shall be called the west elevation, and
the rear elevation of the house shall be called the east elevation. The house
is composed of three sections, namely, a two-storey main block called "the
main house," a one-storey addition on the south side of the main house
called the "one-storey south addition," and a two-storey rear ell called the
"old garage ell." Such exterior portions, documented in a set of ten [10]
photographs attached hereto as part of Exhibit B and incorporated herein
by this reference, are as follows:
_____ House

(a)-(e)   [detail various facades, roof lines and features, chimneys,
foundations, and doors referring to photographs]. [Provi-
sions protecting the Shop and Hen House are substantially
similar.]

2.   **INTERIOR RESTRICTIONS.** Owner agrees that, without the
prior written permission of SPNEA, no construction, alteration or any other
activity shall be undertaken which will alter or adversely affect the appearance, workmanship or structural stability of certain interior portions of the
_____ House, the Shop or the Hen House as they exist as
of the date of this Agreement. Such interior portions, documented in a set
of forty-three [43] photographs attached hereto as part of Exhibit B, and
incorporated herein by this reference are as follows:
_____ House

(a)-(i)   [detail structural members, existing space configuration,
floors, plaster ceilings and walls, woodwork, fireplaces, built-
in cupboards, house date inscribed in a purlin, etc.]. [Similar
provisions protect interior features of the Shop and Hen
House.]

3.   **EXCEPTIONS.** For the purposes of these restrictions, redecorating or refurbishing work identified below shall not constitute construction,
alteration or remodeling requiring the prior written permission of SPNEA
subject to the following limitations:

(a)-(h)   [interior wall papering and plastering (sheet rock is "expressly forbidden"), interior and exterior painting, new
plumbing, screens, glass, storm windows, and insulation are
allowed "provided that such replacement shall not dislodge,
damage or destroy protected woodwork, paint & plaster as
identified in paragraphs . . . [specific paragraphs enumer-
ated] above . . ."]

Any and all redecorating or refurbishing work which may dislodge, damage or destroy protected woodwork, paint & plaster as identified in paragraphs 1(a) to (k) and 2(a) to (n) above shall require the prior written permission of SPNEA.

4. **DEMOLITION.** Owner shall not permit or allow to occur, either through its positive action, omission or neglect, demolition of part or all of the _____ House, the Shop or the Hen House.

5. **RELOCATION.** No portion of the _____ House, the Shop, the Hen House or Garage shall be moved from its present location unless such moving is required by a taking by eminent domain.

6. **CONDEMNATION.** If the Premises, or any substantial portion thereof, including without limitation the _____ House, the Shop, Hen House or Garage shall be taken by eminent domain, SPNEA shall immediately be given notice of the proceedings by Owner and shall have the right to enter its name as an additional party in eminent domain proceedings, pursuant to Massachusetts General Laws, Chapter 79, Section 5A.

7. **ADDITIONS.** No exterior additions to the _____ House, the Shop, the Hen House or Garage shall be erected without prior written permission and design approval from SPNEA.

8. **ADDITIONAL STRUCTURES.** No building or structure not on the Premises as of the date of this Agreement shall be erected or placed on the Premises hereafter without prior written permission and design approval from SPNEA except for temporary scaffolding needed to assist workers in performing permitted activities.

9. **FIRE EXITS.** No additional avenues of egress out of the _____ House, the Shop or the Hen House shall be constructed unless such is required to comply with applicable fire codes. No construction shall be undertaken without the prior written permission of SPNEA.

§7.2 Defining the Boundaries: Irrevocable Licenses and the "Nuisance" in Solar Energy Cases

a. Irrevocable License [31]

Suppose that A, the owner of Lot 1, *orally* grants a drainage easement across Lot 1 to B, the owner of adjoining Lot 2. B then installs the drain on

---

31. The Restatement calls the irrevocable license a servitude created by estoppel. Restatement, Servitudes (T.D. 1, 1989).

A's lot.[32] Or suppose that A gives B a written "license"[33] to drill a well on Lot 1, knowing that B has not found water on Lot 2. In reliance upon A's permission, B spends many thousands to drill a well, install a pump, and run water lines to B's house on Lot 2.[34] Although in both cases, were A now to terminate B's privilege — he would have a technical right to do so (violation of the Statute of Frauds;[35] revocable license) — most courts would hesitate to give A such relief. In the first case, B's installation serves the evidentiary role of the Statute of Frauds, and the change in B's position, reasonable reliance on A's grant of the affirmative easement, provides the grounds for cementing B's privilege.[36] In the second case, since A should have reasonably foreseen that B would only make so large an investment in the (mistaken) belief that A's permission would continue, A is estopped to deny the presence of a servitude upon his land.[37]

CALABRESI AND MELAMED, PROPERTY RULES, LIABILITY RULES, AND INALIENABILITY

85 Harv. L. Rev. 1089-1093, 1115-1124 (1972)

I.   INTRODUCTION

Only rarely are Property and Torts approached from a unified perspective. Recent writings by lawyers concerned with economics and by economists concerned with law suggest, however, that an attempt at integrating the various legal relationships treated by these subjects would be useful both for the beginning student and the sophisticated scholar. By articulating a concept of "entitlements" which are protected by property, liability, or inalienability rules, we present one framework for such an approach. We then analyze aspects of the pollution problem to demonstrate

---

32. Id. at §2.9 (T.D. 1, 1989), Illus. 4.

33. Licenses, in the real property realm, are terminable at the will of the licensor (or at his death). Revocable licenses, therefore, cannot be servitudes, which we have defined "as a burden on land . . . that automatically binds successors to the land. . . ." Restatement, Servitudes (T.D. 1, 1989), Intro., at xxi.

34. Id. at §2.10 (T.D. 1, 1989), Illus. 3.

35. The Statute of Frauds requires that interests in land be transferred by means of a writing. See Restatement (Second) Contracts §125 (Comment a) (1979).

36. Id. at §2.9 (T.D. 1, 1989), at 99-112. The Restatement admits an exception to the Statute of Frauds "if the beneficiary of the servitude, in reasonable reliance upon the existence of the servitude, has so changed position that injustice can be avoided only by giving effect to the parties' intent to create a servitude."

37. Id. at §2.10 (Creation by Estoppel), (T.D. 1, 1989), at 112-123. Although the Restatement treats "Exception to the Statute of Frauds" separately from "Creation by Estoppel," courts tend not to draw the distinction; see, e.g., Remilong v. Crolla, 576 P.2d 461 (Wyo. 1979) (vendor's oral promise that trailers would never be permitted on his remaining land enforced on the basis of estoppel); Pinkston v. Hartley, 511 So.2d 168 (Ala. 1987) (relocation of the field lines for a septic tank, pursuant to an oral agreement with neighbors, gave rise to an easement by estoppel).

how the model enables us to perceive relationships which have been ignored by writers in those fields.

The first issue which must be faced by any legal system is one we call the problem of "entitlement." Whenever a state is presented with the conflicting interests of two or more people, or two or more groups of people, it must decide which side to favor. Absent such a decision, access to goods, services, and life itself will be decided on the basis of "might makes right" — whoever is stronger or shrewder will win. Hence the fundamental thing that law does is to decide which of the conflicting parties will be entitled to prevail. The entitlement to make noise versus the entitlement to have silence, the entitlement to pollute versus the entitlement to breathe clean air, the entitlement to have children versus the entitlement to forbid them — these are the first order of legal decisions.

Having made its initial choice, society must enforce that choice. Simply setting the entitlement does not avoid the problem of "might makes right"; a minimum of state intervention is always necessary. Our conventional notions make this easy to comprehend with respect to private property. If Taney owns a cabbage patch and Marshall, who is bigger, wants a cabbage, he will get it unless the state intervenes. But it is not so obvious that the state must also intervene if it chooses the opposite entitlement, communal property. If large Marshall has grown some communal cabbages and chooses to deny them to small Taney, it will take state action to enforce Taney's entitlement to the communal cabbages. The same symmetry applies with respect to bodily integrity. Consider the plight of the unwilling ninety-eight pound weakling in a state which nominally entitles him to bodily integrity but will not intervene to enforce the entitlement against a lustful Juno. Consider then the plight — absent state intervention — of the ninety-eight pounder who desires an unwilling Juno in a state which nominally entitles everyone to use everyone else's body. The need for intervention applies in a slightly more complicated way to injuries. When a loss is left where it falls in an auto accident, it is not because God so ordained it. Rather it is because the state has granted the injurer an entitlement to be free of liability and will intervene to prevent the victim's friends, if they are stronger, from taking compensation from the injurer. The loss is shifted in other cases because the state has granted an entitlement to compensation and will intervene to prevent the stronger injurer from rebuffing the victim's request for compensation.

The state not only has to decide when to entitle, but it must also simultaneously make a series of equally difficult second order decisions. These decisions go to the manner in which entitlements are protected and to whether an individual is allowed to sell or trade the entitlement. In any given dispute, for example, the state must decide not only which side wins but also the kind of protection to grant. It is with the latter decisions, decisions which shape the subsequent relationship between the winner and the loser, that this article is primarily concerned. We shall consider three types of entitlements — entitlements protected by property rules, entitlements protected by liability rules, and inalienable entitlements. The categories are not, of course, absolutely distinct; but the categorization is useful since it reveals some of the reasons which lead us to protect certain entitlements in certain ways.

An entitlement is protected by a property rule to the extent that someone who wishes to remove the entitlement from its holder must buy it from him in a voluntary transaction in which the value of the entitlement is agreed upon by the seller. It is the form of entitlement which gives rise to the least amount of state intervention: once the original entitlement is decided upon, the state does not try to decide its value. It lets each of the parties say how much the entitlement is worth to him, and gives the seller a veto if the buyer does not offer enough. Property rules involve a collective decision as to who is to be given an initial entitlement but not as to the value of the entitlement.

Whenever someone may destroy the initial entitlement if he is willing to pay an objectively determined value for it, an entitlement is protected by a liability rule. This value may be what it is thought the original holder of the entitlement would have sold it for. But the holder's complaint that he would have demanded more will not avail him once the objectively determined value is set. Obviously, liability rules involve an additional stage intervention: not only are entitlements protected, but their transfer or destruction is allowed on the basis of a value determined by some organ of the state rather than by the parties themselves.

An entitlement is inalienable to the extent that its transfer is not permitted between a willing buyer and a willing seller. The state intervenes not only to determine who is initially entitled and to determine the compensation that must be paid if the entitlement is taken or destroyed, but also to forbid its sale under some or all circumstances. Inalienability rules are thus quite different from property and liability rules. Unlike those rules, rules of inalienability do not "protect" the entitlement; they may also be viewed as limiting or regulating the grant of the entitlement itself.

It should be clear that most entitlements to most goods are mixed. Taney's house may be protected by a property rule in situations where Marshall wishes to purchase it, by a liability rule where the government decides to take it by eminent domain, and by a rule of inalienability in situations where Taney is drunk or incompetent. This article will explore two primary questions: (1) In what circumstances should we grant a particular entitlement? and (2) In what circumstances should we decide to protect that entitlement by using a property, liability, or inalienability rule? . . .

IV. THE FRAMEWORK AND POLLUTION CONTROL RULES

Nuisance or pollution is one of the most interesting areas where the question of who will be given an entitlement, and how it will be protected, is in frequent issue. Traditionally, and very ably in the recent article by Professor Michelman, the nuisance-pollution problem is viewed in terms of three rules.[6] First, Taney may not pollute unless his neighbor (his only neighbor let us assume), Marshall, allows it (Marshall may enjoin Taney's nuisance). Second, Taney may pollute but must compensate Marshall for damages caused (nuisance is found but the remedy is limited to damages). Third, Taney may pollute at will and can only be stopped by Marshall if Marshall pays him off (Taney's pollution is not held to be a nuisance to Marshall). In our terminology rules one and two (nuisance with injunction, and with damages only) are entitlements to Marshall. The first is an entitlement to be free from pollution and is protected by a property rule; the second is also an entitlement to be free from pollution but is protected only by a liability rule. Rule three (no nuisance) is instead an entitlement to Taney protected by a property rule, for only by buying Taney out at Taney's price can Marshall end the pollution.

The very statement of these rules in the context of our framework suggests that something is missing. Missing is a fourth rule representing an entitlement in Taney to pollute, but an entitlement which is protected only by a liability rule. The fourth rule, really a kind of partial eminent domain coupled with a benefits tax, can be stated as follows: Marshall may stop Taney from polluting, but if he does he must compensate Taney.

As a practical matter it will be easy to see why even legal writers as astute as Professor Michelman have ignored this rule. Unlike the first three it does not often lend itself to judicial imposition for a number of good legal process reasons. For example, even if Taney's injuries could practicably be measured, apportionment of the duty of compensation among many Marshalls would present problems for which courts are not well suited. If only those Marshalls who voluntarily asserted the right to enjoin Taney's pollution were required to pay the compensation, there would be insuperable freeloader problems. If, on the other hand, the liability rule entitled one of the Marshalls alone to enjoin the pollution and required all the benefited Marshalls to pay their share of the compensation, the courts would be faced with the immensely difficult task of determining who was benefited how much and imposing a benefits tax accordingly, all the while observing procedural limits within which courts are expected to function.

The fourth rule is thus not part of the cases legal scholars read when they study nuisance law, and is therefore easily ignored by them. But it is available, and may sometimes make more sense than any of the three competing approaches. Indeed, in one form or another, it may well be the most frequent device employed. To appreciate the utility of the fourth rule and to compare it with the other three rules, we will examine why we might choose any of the given rules.

6. Michelman, Pollution as a Tort: A Non-Accidental Perspective on Calabresi's Costs, 80 Yale L. J. 647 (1971).

We would employ rule one (entitlement to be free from pollution protected by a property rule) from an economic efficiency point of view if we believed that the polluter, Taney, could avoid or reduce the costs of pollution more cheaply than the pollutee, Marshall. Or to put it another way, Taney would be enjoinable if he were in a better position to balance the costs of polluting against the costs of not polluting. We would employ rule three (entitlement to pollute protected by a property rule) again solely from an economic efficiency standpoint, if we made the converse judgment on who could best balance the harm of pollution against its avoidance costs. If we were wrong in our judgments and if transactions between Marshall and Taney were costless or even very cheap, the entitlement under rules one or three would be traded and an economically efficient result would occur in either case. If we entitled Taney to pollute and Marshall valued clean air more than Taney valued the pollution, Marshall would pay Taney to stop polluting even though no nuisance was found. If we entitled Marshall to enjoin the pollution and the right to pollute was worth more to Taney than freedom from pollution was to Marshall, Taney would pay Marshall not to seek an injunction or would buy Marshall's land and sell it to someone who would agree not to seek an injunction. As we have assumed no one else was hurt by the pollution, Taney could now pollute even though the initial entitlement, based on a wrong guess of who was the cheapest avoider of the costs involved, allowed the pollution to be enjoined. Wherever transactions between Taney and Marshall are easy, and wherever economic efficiency is our goal, we could employ entitlements protected by property rules even though we would not be sure that the entitlement chosen was the right one. Transactions as described above would cure the error. While the entitlement might have important distributional effects, it would not substantially undercut economic efficiency.

The moment we assume, however, that transactions are not cheap, the situation changes dramatically. Assume we enjoin Taney and there are 10,000 injured Marshalls. Now *even* if the right to pollute is worth more to Taney than the right to be free from pollution is to the sum of the Marshalls, the injunction will probably stand. The cost of buying out all the Marshalls, given holdout problems, is likely to be too great, and an equivalent of eminent domain in Taney would be needed to alter the initial injunction. Conversely, if we denied a nuisance remedy, the 10,000 Marshalls could only with enormous difficulty, given freeloader problems, get together to buy out even one Taney and prevent the pollution. This would be so even if the pollution harm was greater than the value to Taney of the right to pollute.

If, however, transaction costs are not symmetrical, we may still be able to use the property rule. Assume that Taney can buy the Marshalls' entitlements easily because holdouts are for some reason absent, but that the Marshalls have great freeloader problems in buying out Taney. In this situation the entitlement should be granted to the Marshalls unless we are sure the Marshalls are the cheapest avoiders of pollution costs. Where we do not know the identity of the cheapest cost avoider it is better to entitle the Marshalls to be free of pollution because, even if we are wrong in our initial placement of the entitlement, that is, even if the Marshalls are the cheapest cost avoiders, Taney will buy out the Marshalls and economic efficiency will be achieved. Had we chosen the converse entitlement and been wrong, the Marshalls could not have bought out Taney. Unfortunately, transaction costs are often high on both sides and an initial entitlement, though incorrect in terms of economic efficiency, will not be altered in the market place.

Under these circumstances — and they are normal ones in the pollution area — we are likely to turn to liability rules whenever we are uncertain whether the polluter or the pollutees can most cheaply avoid the cost of pollution. We are only likely to use liability rules when we are uncertain because, if we are certain, the costs of liability rules — essentially the costs of collectively valuing the damages to all concerned plus the cost in coercion to those who would not sell at the collectively determined figure — are unnecessary. They are unnecessary because transaction costs and bargaining barriers become irrelevant when we are certain who is the cheapest cost avoider; economic efficiency will be attained without transactions by making the correct initial entitlement.

As a practical matter we often are uncertain who the cheapest cost avoider is. In such cases, traditional legal doctrine tends to find a nuisance but imposes only damages on Taney payable to the Marshalls. This way, if the amount of damages Taney is made to pay is close to the injury caused, economic efficiency will have had its due; if he cannot make a go of it, the nuisance was not worth its costs. The entitlement to the Marshalls to be free from pollution unless compensated, however, will have been given *not* because it was thought that polluting was probably worth less to Taney than freedom from pollution was worth to the Marshalls, not even because on some distributional basis we preferred to charge the cost to Taney rather than to the Marshalls. It was so placed *simply because we did not know* whether Taney desired to pollute more than the Marshalls desired to be free from pollution, and the only way we thought we could test out the value of the pollution was by the only liability rule we thought we had. This was rule two, the imposition of nuisance damages on Taney. At least this would be the position of a court concerned with economic efficiency which believed itself limited to rules one, two, and three.

Rule four gives at least the possibility that the opposite entitlement may also lead to economic efficiency in a situation of uncertainty. Suppose for the moment that a mechanism exists for collectively assessing the damage resulting to Taney from being stopped from polluting by the Marshalls, and a mechanism also exists for collectively assessing the benefit to each of the Marshalls from such cessation. Then — assuming the same degree of accuracy in collective valuation as exists in rule two (the nuisance damage rule) — the Marshalls would stop the pollution if it harmed them more than it benefited Taney. If this is possible, then even if we thought it necessary to use a liability rule, we would still be free to give the entitlement to Taney or Marshall for whatever reasons, efficiency or distributional, we desired.

Actually, the issue is still somewhat more complicated. For just as transaction costs are not necessarily symmetrical under the two converse property rule entitlements, so also the liability rule equivalents of transaction costs — the cost of valuing collectively and of coercing compliance with that valuation — may not be symmetrical under the two converse liability rules. Nuisance damages may be very hard to value, and the costs of informing all the injured of their rights and getting them into court may be prohibitive. Instead, the assessment of the objective damage to Taney from foregoing his pollution may be cheap and so might the assessment of the relative benefits to all Marshalls of such freedom from pollution. But the opposite may also be the case. As a result, just as the choice of which property entitlements may be based on the asymmetry of transaction costs and hence on the greater amenability of one property entitlement to market corrections, so might the choice between liability entitlements be based on the asymmetry of the costs of collective determination.

The introduction of distributional considerations makes the existence of the fourth possibility even more significant. One does not need to go into all the permutations of the possible tradeoffs between efficiency and distributional goals under the four rules to show this. A simple example should suffice. Assume a factory which, by using cheap coal, pollutes a very wealthy section of town and employs many low income workers to produce a product purchased primarily by the poor; assume also a distributional goal that favors equality of wealth. Rule one — enjoin the nuisance — would possibly have desirable economic efficiency results (if the pollution hurt the homeowners more than it saved the factory in coal costs), but it would have disastrous distribution effects. It would also have undesirable efficiency effects if the initial judgment on costs of avoidance had been wrong and transaction costs were high. Rule two — nuisance damages — would allow a testing of the economic efficiency of eliminating the pollution, even in the presence of high transaction costs, but would quite possibly put the factory out of business or diminish output and thus have the same income distribution effects as rule one. Rule three — no nuisance — would have favorable distributional effects since it might protect the income of the workers. But if the pollution harm was greater to the homeowners than the cost of avoiding it by using a better coal, and if transaction costs — holdout problems — were such that homeowners could not unite to pay the factory to use better coal, rule three would have unsatisfactory efficiency effects. Rule four — payment of damages to the factory after allowing the homeowners to compel it to use better coal, and assessment of the cost of these damages to the homeowners — would be the only one which would accomplish both the distributional and efficiency goals.

An equally good hypothetical for any of the rules can be constructed.

Moreover, the problems of coercion may as a practical matter be extremely severe under rule four. How do the homeowners decide to stop the factory's use of low grade coal? How do we assess the damages and their proportional allocation in terms of benefits to the homeowner? But equivalent problems may often be as great for rule two. How do we value the damages to each of the many homeowners? How do we inform the homeowners of their rights to damages? How do we evaluate and limit the administrative expenses of the court actions this solution implies?

The seriousness of the problem depends under each of the liability rules on the number of people whose "benefits" or "damages" one is assessing and the expense and likelihood of error in such assessment. A judgment on these questions is necessary to an evaluation of the possible economic efficiency benefits of employing one rule rather than another. The relative ease of making such assessments through different institutions may explain why we often employ the courts for rule two and get to rule four — when we do get there — only through political bodies which may, for example, prohibit pollution, or "take" the entitlement to build a supersonic plane by a kind of eminent domain, paying compensation to those injured by these decisions. But all this does not, in any sense, diminish the importance of the fact that an awareness of the possibility of an entitlement to pollute, but one protected only by a liability rule, may in some instances allow us best to combine our distributional and efficiency goals.

We have said that we would say little about justice, and so we shall. But it should be clear that if rule four might enable us best to combine efficiency goals with distributional goals, it might also enable us best to combine those same efficiency goals with other goals that are often described in justice language. For example, assume that the factory in our hypothetical was using cheap coal *before* any of the wealthy homes were built. In these circumstances, rule four will not only achieve the desirable efficiency and distributional results mentioned above, but it will also accord with any "justice" significance which is attached to being there first. And this is so whether we view this justice significance as part of a distributional goal, as part of a long run efficiency goal based on protecting expectancies, or as part of an independent concept of justice.

Thus far in this section we have ignored the possibility of employing rules of inalienability to solve pollution problems. A general policy of barring pollution does seem unrealistic. But rules of inalienability can appropriately be used to limit the levels of pollution and to control the levels of activities which cause pollution.

One argument for inalienability may be the widespread existence of moralisms against pollution. Thus it may hurt the Marshalls — gentlemen farmers — to see Taney, a smoke-choked city dweller, sell his entitlement to be free of pollution. A different kind of externality or moralism may be even more important. The Marshalls may be hurt by the expectation that, while the present generation might withstand present pollution levels with no serious health damages, future generations may well face a despoiled, haz-ardous environmental condition which they are powerless to reverse. And this ground for inalienability might be strengthened if a similar conclusion were reached on grounds of self-paternalism. Finally, society might restrict alienability on paternalistic grounds. The Marshalls might feel that although Taney himself does not know it, Taney will be better off if he really can see the stars at night, or if he can breathe smogless air.

Whatever the grounds for inalienability, we should reemphasize that distributional effects should be carefully evaluated in making the choice for or against inalienability. Thus the citizens of a town may be granted an en-titlement to be free of water pollution caused by the waste discharges of a chemical factory; and the entitlement might be made inalienable on the grounds that the town's citizens really would be better off in the long run to have access to clean beaches. But the entitlement might also be made in-alienable to assure the maintenance of a beautiful resort area for the very wealthy, at the same time putting the town's citizens out of work.

b.   Solar Energy Cases

Cases involving claims by landowners that they have an "easement" that prevents their neighbors from blocking their sunlight help define the relationship between the law of servitudes and that of nuisance. Note that the landowners plead a negative easement, but that courts typically reject this claim because of the universal rejection in this country of the English doctrine of "ancient lights." For a fuller discussion of "ancient lights," see Note 4, page 673 *infra*.

FONTAINEBLEAU HOTEL CORP. v. FORTY-FIVE TWENTY-FIVE, INC.

---

114 So. 2d 357 (Fla. Dist. Ct. App. 1959)

PER CURIAM. This is an interlocutory appeal from an order tempo-rarily enjoining the appellants from continuing with the construction of a fourteen-story addition to the Fontainebleau Hotel, owned and operated by the appellants. Appellee, plaintiff below, owns the Eden Roc Hotel, which was constructed in 1955, about a year after the Fontainebleau, and adjoins the Fontainebleau on the north. Both are luxury hotels, facing the Atlantic Ocean. The proposed addition to the Fontainebleau is being constructed twenty feet from its north property line, 130 feet from the mean high water mark of the Atlantic Ocean, and 76 feet 8 inches from the ocean bulkhead line. The 14-story tower will extend 160 feet above grade in height and is 416 feet long from east to west. During the winter months, from around two o'clock in the afternoon for the remainder of the day, the shadow of the

FIGURE 7-4
Fountainebleau Hotel Tower and Eden Roc Hotel

addition will extend over the cabana, swimming pool, and sunbathing areas of the Eden Roc, which are located in the southern portion of its property.

In this action, plaintiff-appellee sought to enjoin the defendants-appellants from proceeding with the construction of the addition to the Fontainebleau (it appears to have been roughly eight stories high at the time suit was filed), alleging that the construction would interfere with the light and air on the beach in front of the Eden Roc and cast a shadow of such size as to render the beach wholly unfitted for the use and enjoyment of its guests, to the irreparable injury of the plaintiff; further, that the construction of such addition on the north side of defendants' property, rather than the south side, was actuated by malice and ill will on the part of the defendants' president toward the plaintiff's president; and that the construction was in violation of a building ordinance requiring a 100-foot setback from the ocean. It was also alleged that the construction would interfere with the easements of light and air enjoyed by plaintiff and its predecessors in title for more than twenty years and "impliedly granted by virtue of the acts of the plaintiff's predecessors in title, as well as under the common law and the express recognition of such rights by virtue of Chapter 9837, Laws of Florida 1923. . . ." Some attempt was also made to allege an easement by implication in favor of the plaintiff's property, as the dominant, and against the defendants' property, as the servient, tenement.

The defendants' answer denied the material allegations of the complaint, pleaded laches and estoppel by judgment.

The chancellor heard considerable testimony on the issues made by the complaint and the answer and, as noted, entered a temporary injunction restraining the defendants from continuing with the construction of the addition. His reason for so doing was stated by him, in a memorandum opinion, as follows:

> In granting the temporary injunction in this case the Court wishes to make several things very clear. The ruling is not based on any alleged presumptive title nor prescriptive right of the plaintiff to light and air nor is it based on any deed restrictions nor recorded plats in the title of the plaintiff nor of the defendant nor of any plat of record. It is not based on any zoning ordinance nor on any provision of the building code of the City of Miami Beach nor on the decision of any court, nisi prius or appellate. It is based solely on the proposition that no one has a right to use his property to the injury of another. In this case it is clear from the evidence that the proposed use by the Fontainebleau will materially damage the Eden Roc. There is evidence indicating that the construction of the proposed annex by the Fontainebleau is malicious or deliberate for the purpose of injuring the Eden Roc, but it is scarcely sufficient, standing alone, to afford a basis for equitable relief.

This is indeed a novel application of the maxim *sic utere tuo ut alienum non laedas*. This maxim does not mean that one must never use his own property in such a way as to do any injury to his neighbor. Beckman v. Marshall, Fla. 1956, 85 So. 2d 552. It means only that one must use his property so as not to injure the lawful *rights* of another. Cason v. Florida Power Co., 74 Fla. 1, 76 So. 535, L.R.A. 1918A, 1034. In Reaver v. Martin Theatres, Fla. 1951, 52 So. 2d 682, 683, 25 A.L.R.2d 1451, under this maxim, it was stated that "it is well settled that a property owner may put his own property to any reasonable and lawful use, so long as he does not thereby deprive the adjoining landowner of any right of enjoyment of his property *which is recognized and protected by law, and so long as his use is not such a one as the law will pronounce a nuisance*." [Emphasis supplied.]

No American decision has been cited, and independent research has revealed none, in which it has been held that — in the absence of some contractual or statutory obligation — a landowner has a legal right to the free flow of light and air across the adjoining land of his neighbor. Even at common law, the landowner had no legal right, in the absence of an easement or uninterrupted use and enjoyment for a period of 20 years, to unobstructed light and air from the adjoining land. Blumberg v. Weiss, 1941, 129 N.J. Eq. 34, 17 A.2d 823; 1 Am. Jur., Adjoining Landowners, §51. And the English doctrine of "ancient lights" has been unanimously repudiated in this country. 1 Am. Jur., Adjoining Landowners, §49, p. 533; Lynch v. Hill, 1939, 24 Del. Ch. 86, 6 A.2d 614, overruling Clawson v. Primrose, 4 Del. Ch. 643.

There being, then, no legal right to the free flow of light and air from the adjoining land, it is universally held that where a structure serves a useful and beneficial purpose, it does not give rise to a cause of action, either for damages or for an injunction under the maxim *sic utere tuo ut alienum non laedas,* even though it causes injury to another by cutting off the light and air and interfering with the view that would otherwise be available over adjoining land in its natural state, regardless of the fact that the structure may have been erected partly for spite. . . .

We see no reason for departing from this universal rule. If, as contended on behalf of plaintiff, public policy demands that a landowner in the Miami Beach area refrain from constructing buildings on his premises that will cast a shadow on the adjoining premises, an amendment of its comprehensive planning and zoning ordinance, applicable to the public as a whole, is the means by which such purpose should be achieved. (No opinion is expressed here as to the validity of such an ordinance, if one should be enacted pursuant to the requirements of law. Cf. City of Miami Beach v. State ex rel. Fontainebleau Hotel Corp., Fla. App. 1959, 108 So. 2d 614, 619; *certiorari denied,* Fla. 1959, 111 So. 2d 437.) But to change the universal rule — and the custom followed in this state since its inception — that adjoining landowners have an equal right under the law to build to the line of their respective tracts and to such a height as is desired by them (in the absence, of course, of building restrictions or regulations) amounts, in our opinion, to judicial legislation. As stated in Musumeci v. Leonardo, *supra* [77 R.I. 255, 75 A.2d 177], "So use your own as not to injure another's property is, indeed, a sound and salutary principle for the promotion of justice, but it may not and should not be applied so as gratuitously to confer upon an adjacent property owner incorporeal rights incidental to his ownership of land which the law does not sanction."

We have also considered whether the order here reviewed may be sustained upon any other reasoning, conformable to and consistent with the pleadings, regardless of the erroneous reasoning upon which the order was actually based. See McGregor v. Provident Trust Co. of Philadelphia, 119 Fla. 718, 162 So. 323. We have concluded that it cannot.

The record affirmatively shows that no statutory basis for the right sought to be enforced by plaintiff exists. The so-called Shadow Ordinance enacted by the City of Miami Beach at plaintiff's behest was held invalid in City of Miami Beach v. State ex rel. Fontainebleau Hotel Corp., *supra.* It also affirmatively appears that there is no possible basis for holding that plaintiff has an easement for light and air, either express or implied, across defendants' property, nor any prescriptive right thereto — even if it be assumed, arguendo, that the common-law right of prescription as to "ancient lights" is in effect in this state. And from what we have said heretofore in this opinion, it is perhaps superfluous to add that we have no desire to dissent from the unanimous holding in this country repudiating the English doctrine of ancient lights.

NOTES AND QUESTIONS

1. **Coasean economics at work.** In seeking an injunction, the plaintiff claimed that it held an entitlement to sunlight (protected by a property rule); in opposing the injunction so as to build the 14-story tower, the defendant argued for an entitlement to cut off the sunlight to the plaintiff's pool. Under the Coase theorem, in a world of zero transaction costs (and no strategic bargaining), it will not matter whether plaintiff wins or loses. The 14-story tower will get built at whatever distance from the boundary line is the wealth-maximizing outcome. Do you understand why this is so?

2. **Wealth distribution.** If "society" is the client, and wealth maximization is the assured outcome, the law can be indifferent as to where it places the entitlement. But for the individual litigants, whether Eden Roc or Fontainebleau receives the initial entitlement does affect how they slice up the wealth pie. For example, if Eden Roc gains the entitlement, Fontainebleau must either share some of its incremental wealth (from building the tower at 20 feet) with Eden Roc, or abandon its plan.[38] Thus, under this scenario, Eden Roc would suffer no loss and might possibly enjoy a "windfall" gain. Conversely, if Fontainebleau gets the entitlement (the actual outcome in this case), the Fontainebleau tower will necessarily make Eden Roc worse off than before.

3. **How *should* the court decide?** If wealth distribution rather than wealth maximization is the hinge on which a court's decision turns, how should the court decide between two otherwise worthy litigants? One approach is to place the entitlement in the first party to exploit the resource: land, the rays of the sun, whatever. On that approach, Eden Roc wins. An alternative approach is not to take sides (although some might argue that this is also a choice), and to let each party use as much of the zoning envelope as she wishes to. On that approach, Fontainebleau prevails. A third approach is for courts (or the legislature) to prefer some uses — hotel towers over swimming pools, for example, and entitle the landowner whose use is the preferred one. What do you see as the case for each of these approaches?

NOTE ON SPITE FENCES

Should a court ever enjoin a structure, not otherwise unlawful, simply because it was built to spite or harass a neighboring landowner? As a useful corollary to the doctrine of ancient lights, English courts refused to con-

---

38. If Fontainebleau were the least cost avoider, it could not bargain for the privilege of blocking Eden Roc's sunlight and, thus, would not build the tower addition as it had planned.

sider the builder's motives; prior to 1959, the law gave him no other way in which he could unilaterally protect his land against the easement.

One might expect that when the doctrine of ancient lights was rejected in the United States its corollary would also fail. But, on the contrary, some American courts still refuse to examine the builder's motive. For example, Pennsylvania is among the states that have adopted the English position that refuses to enjoin a spite fence. Cohen v. Perrino, 355 Pa. 455, 50 A.2d 348 (1947).

In his well-researched opinion for the Pennsylvania court, Justice Stearne quoted from two decisions that embody the opposing rationales:

> [T]o prohibit him [an adjoining landowner] from causing [injury to his neighbor] in case the structure is neither beneficial nor ornamental, but erected from motives of pure malice, is not protecting a legal right, but is controlling his moral conduct. In this state a man is free to direct his moral conduct as he pleases, in so far as he is not restrained by statute. . . . There is no conflict between law and equity in our practice, and what a man may lawfully do cannot be prohibited as inequitable. It may be immoral, and shock our notion of fairness, but what the law permits equity tolerates. It would be much more inequitable and intolerable to allow a man's neighbors to question his motives every time that he should undertake to erect a structure upon his own premises. . . . [Letts v. Kessler, 54 Ohio St. 73, 81-82, 42 N.E. 765, 766 (1896)]

> . . . Malicious use of property resulting in injury to another is never a "lawful use" but is in every case unlawful. The right to the use of property is therefore a qualified rather than absolute right. When one acting solely from malevolent motives does injury to his neighbor, to call such conduct the exercise of an absolute legal right is a perversion of terms. . . . The use of one's own property for the sole purpose of injuring another is not a right that a good citizen would desire nor one that a bad citizen should have. [Hornsby v. Smith, 191 Ga. 491, 499, 13 S.E.2d 20, 24 (1941)]

If a head count of decisions were taken today, the latter view would predominate; equity, even in the absence of a statute, will usually enjoin as a private nuisance a spite structure serving no useful purpose. Furthermore, several states have supplied a statutory support, e.g., Mass. Ann. Laws c. 49, §21 (Law. Co-op. 1993); Conn. Gen. Stat. Ann. §§52-480, 52-570 (West 1991); N.Y. Real Prop. Acts. Law §843 (McKinney 1979). Rideout v. Knox, 148 Mass. 368, 19 N.E. 390 (1889), is the leading case approving such statutes as a valid exercise of the police power. With his usual aplomb, Justice Holmes wrote for the court (148 Mass. at 372-373):

> Some small limitations of previously existing rights incident to property may be imposed for the sake of preventing a manifest evil; larger ones could not be except by eminent domain . . . The statute is confined to fences and structures in the nature of fences, and to such fences only as unnecessarily exceed six feet in height. It is hard to imagine a more insignificant curtailment

of rights of property. Even the right to build a fence above six feet is not denied, when any convenience of the owner would be served by building higher.

The requirements for injunctive relief under a typical statute are:

(1) malicious erection of a structure on defendant's land that is intended to injure plaintiff's enjoyment of his land;
(2) impairment, in fact, of plaintiff's enjoyment;
(3) a structure otherwise useless to defendant. United Petroleum Corp. v. Atlantic Refining Co., 3 Conn. Cir. Ct. 255, 212 A.2d 589 (1965).

Malice may be inferred solely from the objective facts. See Rapuano v. Ames, 21 Conn. Supp. 110, 145 A.2d 384 (1958).

Three cases illustrate the leaven of good sense that a court must add to the statutory recipe. Sitting in equity, would you have granted an injunction to either plaintiff?

(a) Plaintiff A operated a gasoline station along the southbound lane of a divided highway. Defendant built an Atlantic station to the immediate north and erected a 12' × 25' sign that blocked off plaintiff's advertising from the view of southbound drivers. Plaintiff carried a non-brand-name gasoline, which he sold more cheaply than Atlantic. See United Petroleum Corp. v. Atlantic Refining Co., *supra.*

(b) Plaintiff B owned a building one-quarter mile from the site of the 1964-1965 New York World's Fair. Before the fair began, plaintiff erected a 250'-long red neon advertising sign atop its building. The defendant fair in turn planted a screen of shrubbery that blocked off plaintiff's advertising from the view of fairgoers. See A. & P. Tea Co. v. New York World's Fair, 42 Misc. 2d 855, 249 N.Y.S.2d 256 (Sup. Ct. 1964).

(c) Plaintiff C enjoyed an unobstructed view of Long Island Sound from her residential property. Defendant, plaintiff's southern neighbor, built a six-foot high stockade fence along the common boundary between the two properties, high enough to cut off plaintiff's view completely. See Horan v. Farmer, 1990 WL 275857 (Conn. Super. 1990).

ZILLMAN AND DEENY, LEGAL ASPECTS OF SOLAR ENERGY DEVELOPMENT

25 Ariz. St. L.J. 25, 28-29, 33-35 (1976)

Because approximately one-quarter to one-third of all American energy use is dedicated to heating water and to heating and cooling homes, offices, and factories, the prominent short-term use of solar energy will be to heat water, and to heat and cool buildings. Installation of solar equipment in all new structures and converting (retrofitting) a significant number of existing structures for the use of solar energy can provide a fossil fuel savings sufficient to allay fears of over-dependence on foreign oil for decades to come. The technology is developed for water and space heating, but is not well advanced in the cooling area.

Solar building design has been consistently innovative, creating a diversity of solar energy devices and homes. Nevertheless, there is substantial agreement on the basics of a working solar energy system. Even without actual solar equipment, attention to design and energy conservation can provide substantial savings in heating and cooling costs. As any resident of the southern United States knows, the solar heat input from a southern exposure can be substantial. In the winter this is desirable, but in the summer it is not. By simply constructing an appropriate roof overhang, a significant energy saving occurs. In summer, when the sun is high in the sky, the overhang deflects heat. In winter, when the sun is low on the horizon, heat enters the house without deflection. Similarly, use of curtains, screens, and foliage can admit the sun's rays when desired, trap them for use at night, and exclude them in summer when the sun's heat is a bane rather than a boon. This is solar architecture in its most primitive form — the conscious design of structures to maximize their use of the sun's energy.

Basic solar architecture can save substantial energy. But by no means does it exhaust solar potential. Greater heating efficiency is obtained by using a system which collects solar radiation that falls on a building, stores the heat collected, and circulates it throughout the building when needed. The system begins with the solar collector typically mounted on the building's roof. The most common collecting device has been the flat plate collector. A single collector resembles a shallow rectangular box. A metal receiving surface is painted black for maximum sun absorption and placed within a frame. The frame and metal sheet are covered with glass or plastic to prevent re-radiation, and a heat trap results in which temperatures can approach 200° Fahrenheit. The trapped heat is transferred to air or water circulated just beneath the metallic sheet. When a large number of individual collectors are placed together, the energy absorbed can supply a considerable percentage of the heating needs of a structure. The captured heat is circulated through a closed system to a central storage area. A large rock-filled cylinder often serves this purpose. The rocks will retain the heat for up to several days. As heat is needed, a pump or fan can circulate it throughout the building.

The solar homeowner needs the protection of a negative easement. He must be able to prevent the owner of the servient estate from blocking his access to direct sunlight. An express agreement between landowners can solve the problem.

Another significant aspect of easement law is the distinction between express easements and implied or prescriptive easements. The express easement is a product of agreement between landowners. The prescriptive or implied easement arises by operation of law as either a matter of necessity (one landowner's estate is worthless without the easement) or long usage.

With respect to long usage, a particular difficulty in the United States has been the courts' refusal to recognize implied easement rights to light and air. The English doctrine of "ancient lights" has never been adopted by jurisdictions of this country. While the English doctrine is concerned with access to fresh air and light, rather than direct access to sun rays, it provides an analogy which might be used to protect solar energy devices.

If a court were willing to recognize a prescriptive easement for solar access, it would probably date the prescription from the initial installation of the solar collector. This raises practical problems. The party installing the solar collector would like to have his right to perpetual solar access decreed immediately. Yet he may face a ten-year period before his easement is secure. During this time the initial servient owner or his successor would be free to impede solar access as he wished. Possibly he might find it legally desirable to impede solar access solely for the purpose of preserving his future rights.

In the area of easements by necessity, the law again raises problems for the prospective solar energy user. In classic easement law, a unity of ownership is required to establish an easement by necessity. Such an easement arises, for example, when A owns two parcels of land and conveys one to B, but leaves B no means of egress. B is thus landlocked and his property is far less valuable. In such circumstances, B's easement can be created by necessity.

There are differing views on the degree of necessity required to establish the easement. Some cases hold that "absolute necessity" must be shown where light and air are involved. Others rely on a "reasonable necessity" argument, Bydlon v. United States[69] illustrates the latter category. That case involved air space for airplane travel. In allowing the easement, the court noted changes in technological conditions. Such an argument has obvious relevance to the promotion of solar easements.

Under any set of circumstances it would seem desirable to secure an express or consensual easement. But the newness of solar technology may work against the landowner. His neighbor, who may be quite willing to grant a portion of his land for a footpath or a driveway, may be unsure of the consequences of relinquishing rights to a portion of the airspace over his land. The servient owner may be giving up the right to construct a second story to his residence or to plant trees. His offer of a short-term easement may not be encouraging to the solar energy user contemplating a $10,000 investment. The solar energy user must also consider the types of uses to which he may later put the property. If initially he wishes only to provide sufficient paneling for water heating, he may need to renegotiate

---

69. 175 F. Supp. 891 (U.S. Ct. Claims 1959).

the easement if he later converts to solar space heating and cooling. The solar energy user must also consider how many separate landowners must join in the easement. The construction of a 14-story building two lots over may nullify easement agreements with the immediately adjoining neighbor. The easement's virtue, of course, may be its relative permanency. A properly drafted solar easement can benefit subsequent owners of the solar house and bind subsequent owners of the servient property. While the easement may be lost through abandonment, this seems unlikely. Most probably the person selling a solar house will have to find another solar-inclined purchaser in view of the substantial investment in solar equipment and concomitant increase in resale prices.

Overall, the burdens facing the potential solar energy user seeking an easement may be substantial. But if adjoining property owners are not forbidden by other means (restrictive covenants, zoning) from screening the solar user's property, resort to easements may be necessary. One possible way to avoid the painstaking individual agreement approach would be to create statutory easements. Such easements have been legislated for power companies and cable television.

PRAH v. MARETTI

108 Wis. 2d 223, 321 N.W.2d 182 (1982)

ABRAHAMSON, J. This appeal from a judgment of the circuit court for Waukesha county, Max Raskin, circuit judge, was certified to this court by the court of appeals, sec. (Rule) 809.61, Stats. 1979-80, as presenting an issue of first impression, namely, whether an owner of a solar-heated residence states a claim upon which relief can be granted when he asserts that his neighbor's proposed construction of a residence (which conforms to existing deed restrictions and local ordinances) interferes with his access to an unobstructed path for sunlight across the neighbor's property. This case thus involves a conflict between one landowner (Glenn Prah, the plaintiff) interested in unobstructed access to sunlight across adjoining property as a natural source of energy and an adjoining landowner (Richard D. Maretti, the defendant) interested in the development of his land.

The circuit court concluded that the plaintiff presented no claim upon which relief could be granted and granted summary judgment for the defendant. We reverse the judgment of the circuit court and remand the cause to the circuit court for further proceedings.

I

According to the complaint, the plaintiff is the owner of a residence which was constructed during the years 1978-1979. The complaint alleges that the residence has a solar system which includes collectors on the roof to supply energy for heat and hot water and that after the plaintiff built his solar-heated house, the defendant purchased the lot adjacent to and immediately to the south of the plaintiff's lot and commenced planning construction of a home. The complaint further states that when the plaintiff learned of defendant's plans to build the house he advised the defendant that if the house were built at the proposed location, defendant's house would substantially and adversely affect the integrity of plaintiff's solar system and could cause plaintiff other damage. Nevertheless, the defendant began construction. The complaint further alleges that the plaintiff is entitled to "unrestricted use of the sun and its solar power" and demands judgment for injunctive relief and damages.

After filing his complaint, the plaintiff moved for a temporary injunction to restrain and enjoin construction by the defendant. In ruling on that motion the circuit court heard testimony, received affidavits and viewed the site.

The record made on the motion reveals the following additional facts. Plaintiff's home was the first residence built in the subdivision, and although plaintiff did not build his house in the center of the lot it was built in accordance with applicable restrictions. Plaintiff advised defendant that if the defendant's home were built at the proposed site it would cause a shadowing effect on the solar collectors which would reduce the efficiency of the system and possibly damage the system. To avoid these adverse effects, plaintiff requested defendant to locate his home an additional several feet away from the plaintiff's lot line, the exact number being disputed. Plaintiff and defendant failed to reach an agreement on the location of defendant's home before defendant started construction. The Architectural Control Committee of the subdivision and the Planning Commission of the City of Muskego approved the defendant's plans for his home, including its location on the lot. After such approval, the defendant apparently changed the grade of the property without prior notice to the Architectural Control Committee.[2] The problem with defendant's proposed construction, as far as the plaintiff's interests are concerned, arises from a combination of the grade and the distance of defendant's home from the defendant's lot line.

The circuit court denied plaintiff's motion for injunctive relief, declared it would entertain a motion for summary judgment and thereafter entered judgment in favor of the defendant. . . .

---

2. There appears to be some dispute over the facts that immediately preceded the initiation of construction concerning the granting of building permits, approval of the Architecture Control Committee and subsequent initiation of construction at a grade level not approved by the Committee. The specific dispute over this sequence of events is not relevant to this appeal, but suffice it to say that such facts will become relevant to the question of the reasonableness of the defendant's construction in light of our decision that the plaintiff has stated a claim on the issue of private nuisance.

III

In testing the sufficiency of the complaint the facts pleaded by the plaintiff, and all reasonable inferences therefrom, are accepted as true.

The plaintiff presents three legal theories to support his claim that the defendant's continued construction of a home justifies granting him relief: (1) the construction constitutes a common law private nuisance. . . .

As to the claim of private nuisance the circuit court concluded that the law of private nuisance requires the court to make "a comparative evaluation of the conflicting interests and to weigh the gravity of the harm to the plaintiff against the utility of the defendant's conduct." The circuit court concluded: "A comparative evaluation of the conflicting interests, keeping in mind the omissions and commissions of both Prah and Maretti, indicates that defendant's conduct does not cause the gravity of the harm which the plaintiff himself may well have avoided by proper planning."

We consider first whether the complaint states a claim for relief based on common law private nuisance. This state has long recognized that an owner of land does not have an absolute right or unlimited right to use the land in a way which injures the rights of others. The rights of neighboring landowners are relative; the uses by one must not unreasonably impair the uses or enjoyment of the other. VI-A American Law of Property sec. 28.22, pp. 64-65 (1954). When one landowner's use of his or her property unreasonably interferes with another's enjoyment of his or her property, that use is said to be a private nuisance. Hoene v. Milwaukee, 17 Wis. 2d 209, 214, 116 N.W.2d 112 (1962); Metzger v. Hochrein, 107 Wis. 267, 269, 83 N.W. 308 (1900). See also Prosser, Law of Torts sec. 89, p. 591 (2d ed. 1971).

The private nuisance doctrine has traditionally been employed in this state to balance the conflicting rights of landowners, and this court has recently adopted the analysis of private nuisance set forth in the Restatement (Second) of Torts. CEW Mgmt. Corp. v. First Federal Savings & Loan Association, 88 Wis. 2d 631, 633, 277 N.W.2d 766 (1979). The Restatement defines private nuisance as "a nontrespassory invasion of another's interest in the private use and enjoyment of land." Restatement (Second) of Torts sec. 821D (1977). The phrase "interest in the private use and enjoyment of land" as used in sec. 821D is broadly defined to include any disturbance of the enjoyment of property. The comment in the Restatement describes the landowner's interest protected by private nuisance law as follows:

> The phrase "interest in the use and enjoyment of land" is used in this Restatement in a broad sense. It comprehends not only the interests that a person may have in the actual present use of land for residential, agricultural, commercial, industrial and other purposes, but also his interests in having the present use value of the land unimpaired by changes in its physical condition. Thus the destruction of trees on vacant land is as much an invasion of the owner's interest in its use and enjoyment as is the destruction of crops or flowers that he is growing on the land for his present use. "Interest in use and

enjoyment" also comprehends the pleasure, comfort, and enjoyment that a person normally derives from the occupancy of land. Freedom from discomfort and annoyance while using land is often as important to a person as freedom from physical interruption with his use or freedom from detrimental change in the physical condition of the land itself.

Restatement (Second) of Torts, Sec. 821D, Comment b, p. 101 (1977).

Although the defendant's obstruction of the plaintiff's access to sunlight appears to fall within the Restatement's broad concept of a private nuisance as a nontrespassory invasion of another's interest in the private use and enjoyment of land, the defendant asserts that he has a right to develop his property in compliance with statutes, ordinances and private covenants without regard to the effect of such development upon the plaintiff's access to sunlight. In essence, the defendant is asking this court to hold that the private nuisance doctrine is not applicable in the instant case and that his right to develop his land is a right which is per se superior to his neighbor's interest in access to sunlight. This position is expressed in the maxim "cujus est solum, ejus est usque ad coelum et ad infernos," that is, the owner of land owns up to the sky and down to the center of the earth. The rights of the surface owner are, however, not unlimited. U.S. v. Causby, 328 U.S. 256, 260-261, 66 S. Ct. 1062, 1065, 90 L. Ed. 1206 (1946). See also 114.03, Stats. 1979-80.

The defendant is not completely correct in asserting that the common law did not protect a landowner's access to sunlight across adjoining property. At English common law a landowner could acquire a right to receive sunlight across adjoining land by both express agreement and under the judge-made doctrine of "ancient lights." Under the doctrine of ancient lights if the landowner had received sunlight across adjoining property for a specified period of time,[7] the landowner was entitled to continue to receive unobstructed access to sunlight across the adjoining property. Under the doctrine the landowner acquired a negative prescriptive easement and could prevent the adjoining landowner from obstructing access to light.[8]

Although American courts have not been as receptive to protecting a landowner's access to sunlight as the English courts, American courts have afforded some protection to a landowner's interest in access to sunlight. American courts honor express easements to sunlight. American courts initially enforced the English common law doctrine of ancient lights, but later

---

7. The specified time period of uninterrupted enjoyment required to create a right to receive light across adjoining property varied in English legal history. Thomas, Miller & Robbins, Overcoming Legal Uncertainties About Use of Solar Energy Systems 23 (Am. Bar Foundation 1978).

8. Pfeiffer, Ancient Lights: Legal Protection of Access to Solar Energy, 68 ABAJ 228 (1982). No American common law state recognizes a landowner's right to acquire an easement of light by prescription. Comment, Solar Lights: Guaranteeing a Place in the Sun, 57 Ore. L. Rev. 94, 112 (1977).

every state which considered the doctrine repudiated it as inconsistent with the needs of a developing country. Indeed, for just that reason, this court concluded that an easement to light and air over adjacent property could not be created or acquired by prescription and has been unwilling to rec-

FIGURE 7-5
"Ancient Lights" in Contemporary London

ognize such an easement by implication. Depner v. United States National Bank, 202 Wis. 405, 408, 232 N.W. 851 (1930); Miller v. Hoeschler, 126 Wis. 263, 268-269, 105 N.W. 790 (1905).

Many jurisdictions in this country have protected a landowner from malicious obstruction of access to light (the spite fence cases) under the common law private nuisance doctrine.[9] If an activity is motivated by malice it lacks utility and the harm it causes others outweighs any social values. VI-A Law of Property sec. 28.28, p. 79 (1954). This court was reluctant to protect a landowner's interest in sunlight even against a spite fence, only to be overruled by the legislature. Shortly after this court upheld a landowner's right to erect a useless and unsightly sixteen-foot spite fence four feet from his neighbor's windows, Metzger v. Hochrein, 107 Wis. 267, 83 N.W. 308 (1900), the legislature enacted a law specifically defining a spite fence as an actionable private nuisance.[10] Thus a landowner's interest in sunlight has been protected in this country by common law private nuisance law at least in the narrow context of the modern American rule invalidating spite fences. See, e.g., Sundowner, Inc. v. King, 95 Idaho 367, 509 P.2d 785 (1973); Restatement (Second) of Torts, sec. 829 (1977).

This court's reluctance in the nineteenth and early part of the twentieth century to provide broader protection for a landowner's access to sunlight was premised on three policy considerations. First, the right of landowners to use their property as they wished, as long as they did not cause physical damage to a neighbor, was jealously guarded. Metzger v. Hochrein, 107 Wis. 267, 272, 83 N.W. 308 (1900).

Second, sunlight was valued only for aesthetic enjoyment or as illumination. Since artificial light could be used for illumination, loss of sunlight was at most a personal annoyance which was given little, if any, weight by society.

Third, society had a significant interest in not restricting or impeding land development. Dillman v. Hoffman, 38 Wis. 559, 574 (1875). This court repeatedly emphasized that in the growth period of the nineteenth and early twentieth centuries change is to be expected and is essential to property and that recognition of a right to sunlight would hinder property development. The court expressed this concept as follows:

> As the city grows, large grounds appurtenant to residences must be cut up to supply more residences. . . . The cistern, the outhouse, the cesspool, and the

9. In several of the spite fence cases, courts have recognized the property owner's interest in sunlight. Hornsby v. Smith, 191 Ga. 491, 500, 13 S.E.2d 20 (1941) ("the air and light no matter from which direction they come are God-given, and are essential to the life, comfort, and happiness of everyone"); Burke v. Smith, 69 Mich. 380, 389, 37 N.W. 838 (1888) ("the right to breathe the air and enjoy the sunshine, is a natural one"); Barger v. Barringer, 151 N.C. 433, 437, 66 S.E. 439 (1909) ("light and air are as much a necessity as water, and all are the common heritage of mankind").

10. The legislature specifically overruled Metzger, ch. 81, Laws of 1903; sec. 280.08 Stats. 1925. Cf. Steiger v. Nowakowski, 67 Wis. 2d 355, 277 N.W.2d 104 (1975).

private drain must disappear in deference to the public waterworks and sewer; the terrace and the garden, to the need for more complete occupancy. . . . Strict limitation [on the recognition of easements of light and air over adjacent premises is] in accord with the popular conception upon which real estate has been and is daily being conveyed in Wisconsin and to be essential to easy and rapid development at least of our municipalities.

Miller v. Hoeschler, *supra,* 126 Wis. at 268, 270, 105 N.W. 790; quoted with approval in *Depner, supra,* 202 Wis. at 409, 232 N.W. 851.

Considering these three policies, this court concluded that in the absence of an express agreement granting access to sunlight, a landowner's obstruction of another's access to sunlight was not actionable. Miller v. Hoeschler, *supra,* 126 Wis. at 271, 105 N.W. 790; Depner v. United States National Bank, *supra,* 202 Wis. at 410, 232 N.W. 851. These three policies are no longer fully accepted or applicable. They reflect factual circumstances and social priorities that are now obsolete.

First, society has increasingly regulated the use of land by the landowner for the general welfare. Euclid v. Ambler Realty Co., 272 U.S. 365, 47 S. Ct. 114, 71 L. Ed. 303 (1926); Just v. Marinette, 56 Wis. 2d 7, 201 N.W.2d 761 (1972).

Second, access to sunlight has taken on a new significance in recent years. In this case the plaintiff seeks to protect access to sunlight, not for aesthetic reasons or as a source of illumination but as a source of energy. Access to sunlight as an energy source is of significance both to the landowner who invests in solar collectors and to a society which has an interest in developing alternative sources of energy.[11]

Third, the policy of favoring unhindered private development in an expanding economy is no longer in harmony with the realities of our society. State v. Deetz, 66 Wis. 2d 1, 224 N.W.2d 407 (1974). The need for easy and rapid development is not as great today as it once was, while our perception of the value of sunlight as a source of energy has increased significantly.

Courts should not implement obsolete policies that have lost their vigor over the course of the years. The law of private nuisance is better

---

11. State and federal governments are encouraging the use of the sun as a significant source of energy. In this state the legislature has granted tax benefits to encourage the utilization of solar energy. See Ch. 349, 350, Laws of 1979. See also Ch. 354, Laws of 1981 (eff. May 7, 1982) enabling legislation providing for local ordinances guaranteeing access to sunlight.

The federal government has also recognized the importance of solar energy and currently encourages its utilization by means of tax benefits, direct subsidies and government loans for solar projects. Energy Tax Act of 1978, Nov. 9, 1978, P.L. 95-618, 92 Stat. 3174, relevant portion codified at 26 U.S.C.A. sec. 44(c) (1982 Supp.); Energy Security Act, June 30, 1980, P.L. 96-294, 94 Stat. 611, relevant portion codified at 12 U.S.C.A. sec. 3610 (1980); Small Business Energy Loan Act, July 4, 1978, P.L. 95-315, 92 Stat. 377, relevant portion codified within 15 U.S.C.A. secs. 631, 633, 636, and 639 (1982 Supp.); National Energy Conservation Policy Act, Nov. 9, 1978, P.L. 95-619, 92 Stat. 3206, relevant portion codified at 42 U.S.C.A. secs. 1451, 1703-45 (1982 Supp.); Energy Conservation and Production Act, Aug. 14, 1976, P.L. 94-385, 90 Stat. 1125, relevant portion codified at 42 U.S.C.A. sec. 6881 (1977).

suited to resolve landowners' disputes about property development in the 1980s than is a rigid rule which does not recognize a landowner's interest in access to sunlight. As we said in Ballstadt v. Pagel, 202 Wis. 484, 489, 232 N.W. 862 (1930), "What is regarded in law as constituting a nuisance in modern times would no doubt have been tolerated without question in former times." We read State v. Deetz, 66 Wis. 2d 1, 224 N.W.2d 407 (1974), as an endorsement of the application of common law nuisance to situations involving the conflicting interests of landowners and as rejecting per se exclusions to the nuisance law reasonable use doctrine.

In *Deetz* the court abandoned the rigid common law common enemy rule with respect to surface water and adopted the private nuisance reasonable use rule, namely that the landowner is subject to liability if his or her interference with the flow of surface waters unreasonably invades a neighbor's interest in the use and enjoyment of land. Restatement (Second) of Torts, sec. 822, 829 (1977). This court concluded that the common enemy rule which served society "well in the days of burgeoning national expansion of the mid-nineteenth and early-twentieth centuries" should be abandoned because it was no longer "in harmony with the realities of our society." *Deetz, supra,* 66 Wis. 2d at 14-15, 224 N.W.2d 407. We recognized in *Deetz* that common law rules adapt to changing social values and conditions.

Yet the defendant would have us ignore the flexible private nuisance law as a means of resolving the dispute between the landowners in this case and would have us adopt an approach, already abandoned in *Deetz,* of favoring the unrestricted development of land and of applying a rigid and inflexible rule protecting his right to build on his land and disregarding any interest of the plaintiff in the use and enjoyment of his land. This we refuse to do.[13]

---

13. Defendant's position that a landowner's interest in access to sunlight across adjoining land is not "legally enforceable" and is therefore excluded per se from private nuisance law was adopted in Fontainebleau Hotel Corp. v. Forty-five Twenty-five, Inc., 114 So. 2d 357 (Fla. App. 1959), *cert. den.* 117 So. 2d 842 (Fla. 1960). The Florida district court of appeals permitted construction of a building which cast a shadow on a neighboring hotel's swimming pool. The court asserted that nuisance law protects only those interests "which [are] recognized and protected by law," and that there is no legally recognized or protected right to access to sunlight. A property owner does not, said the Florida court, in the absence of a contract or statute, acquire a presumptive or implied right to the free flow of light and air across adjoining land. The Florida court then concluded that a lawful structure which causes injury to another by cutting off light and air — whether or not erected partly for spite — does not give rise to a cause of action for damages or for an injunction. See also People ex rel. Hoogasian v. Sears, Roebuck & Co., 52 Ill. 2d 301, 287 N.E.2d 677 (1972).

We do not find the reasoning of *Fontainebleau* persuasive. The court leaped from rejecting an easement by prescription (the doctrine of ancient lights) and an easement by implication to the conclusion that there is no right to protection from obstruction of access to sunlight. The court's statement that a landowner has no right to light should be the conclusion, not its initial premise. The court did not explain why an owner's interest in unobstructed sunlight differs from an owner's interest in being free from obtrusive noises or smells or differs from an owner's interest in unobstructed use of water. The recognition of a per se exception to private nuisance law may invite unreasonable behavior.

Private nuisance law, the law traditionally used to adjudicate conflicts between private landowners, has the flexibility to protect both a landowner's right of access to sunlight and another landowner's right to develop land. Private nuisance law is better suited to regulate access to sunlight in modern society and is more in harmony with legislative policy and the prior decisions of this court than is an inflexible doctrine of non-recognition of any interest in access to sunlight across adjoining land.

We therefore hold that private nuisance law, that is, the reasonable use doctrine as set forth in the Restatement, is applicable to the instant case. Recognition of a nuisance claim for unreasonable obstruction of access to sunlight will not prevent land development or unduly hinder the use of adjoining land. It will promote the reasonable use and enjoyment of land in a manner suitable to the 1980s. That obstruction of access to light might be found to constitute a nuisance in certain circumstances does not mean that it will be or must be found to constitute a nuisance under all circumstances. The result in each case depends on whether the conduct complained of is unreasonable.

Accordingly we hold that the plaintiff in this case has stated a claim under which relief can be granted. Nonetheless we do not determine whether the plaintiff in this case is entitled to relief. In order to be entitled to relief the plaintiff must prove the elements required to establish actionable nuisance, and the conduct of the defendant herein must be judged by the reasonable use doctrine.

IV

The defendant asserts that even if we hold that the private nuisance doctrine applies to obstruction of access to sunlight across adjoining land, the circuit court's granting of summary judgment should be affirmed.

Although the memorandum decision of the circuit court in the instant case is unclear, it appears that the circuit court recognized that the common law private nuisance doctrine was applicable but concluded that defendant's conduct was not unreasonable. The circuit court apparently attempted to balance the utility of the defendant's conduct with the gravity of the harm. Sec. 826, Restatement (Second) of Torts (1977). The defendant urges us to accept the circuit court's balance as adequate. We decline to do so.

The circuit court concluded that because the defendant's proposed house was in conformity with zoning regulations, building codes and deed restrictions, the defendant's use of the land was reasonable. This court has concluded that a landowner's compliance with zoning laws does not automatically bar a nuisance claim. Compliance with the law "is not the controlling factor, though it is, of course, entitled to some weight." Bie v. Ingersoll, 27 Wis. 2d 490, 495, 135 N.W.2d 250 (1965). The circuit court also concluded that the plaintiff could have avoided any harm by locating his own house in a better place. Again, plaintiff's ability to avoid the harm is a relevant but not a conclusive factor. See secs. 826, 827, 828, Restatement (Second) of Torts (1977).

Furthermore, our examination of the record leads us to conclude that the record does not furnish an adequate basis for the circuit court to apply the proper legal principles on summary judgment. The application of the reasonable use standard in nuisance cases normally requires a full exposition of all underlying facts and circumstances. Too little is known in this case of such matters as the extent of the harm to the plaintiff, the suitability of solar heat in that neighborhood, the availability of remedies to the plaintiff, and the costs to the defendant of avoiding the harm. Summary judgment is not an appropriate procedural vehicle in this case when the circuit court must weigh evidence which has not been presented at trial. 6 (Pt. 2) Moore's Federal Practice, 56.15[7], pp. 56-638 (1982); 10 Wright and Miller, Federal Practice and Procedure — Civil, secs. 2729, 2731 (1973).

Because the plaintiff has stated a claim of common law private nuisance upon which relief can be granted, the judgment of the circuit court must be reversed. . . .

For the reasons set forth, we reverse the judgment of the circuit court dismissing the complaint and remand the matter to circuit court for further proceedings not inconsistent with this opinion.

The judgment of the circuit court is reversed and the cause remanded for proceedings not inconsistent with this opinion.

CALLOW, J. (dissenting). The majority has adopted the Restatement's reasonable use doctrine to grant an owner of a solar heated home a cause of action against his neighbor who, in acting entirely within the applicable ordinances and statutes, seeks to design and build his home in such a location that it may, at various times during the day, shade the plaintiff's solar collector, thereby impeding the efficiency of his heating system during several months of the year. Because I believe the facts of this case clearly reveal that a cause of action for private nuisance will not lie, I dissent. . . .

While the majority's policy arguments may be directed to a cause of action for public nuisance, we are presented with a private nuisance case which I believe is distinguishable in this regard.[3]

I would submit that any policy decisions in this area are best left for the legislature. "What is 'desirable' or 'advisable' or 'ought to be' is a ques-

---

3. I am amused at the majority's contention that what constitutes a nuisance today would have been accepted without question in earlier times. Slip. op. at 10. This calls to mind the fact that, in early days of travel by horses, the first automobiles were considered nuisances. Later, when automobile travel became developed, the horse became the nuisance. Ellickson, Alternatives to Zoning, Covenants, Nuisance Rules, and Fines as Land Use Controls, 40 U Chi L Rev 681, 731 (1973). This makes me wonder if we are examining the proper nuisance in the case before us. In other words, could it be said that the solar energy user is creating the nuisance when others must conform their homes to accommodate his use? I note that solar panel glare may temporarily blind automobile drivers, reflect into adjacent buildings causing excessive heat, and otherwise irritate neighbors. Certainly in these instances the solar heating system constitutes the nuisance.

tion of policy, not a question of fact. What is 'necessary' or what is 'in the best interest' is not a fact and its determination by the judiciary is an exercise of legislative power when each involves political considerations." In re City of Beloit, 37 Wis. 2d 637, 644, 155 N.W.2d 633 (1968). See generally Holifield v. Setco Industries, Inc., 42 Wis. 2d 750, 758, 168 N.W.2d 177 (1969); Comment, Solar Rights: Guaranteeing a Place in the Sun, 57 Or. L. Rev. 94, 126-127 (1977) (litigation is a slow, costly, and uncertain method of reform). I would concur with these observations of the trial judge: "While temptation lingers for the court to declare by judicial fiat what is right and what should be done, under the facts in this case, such action under our form of constitutional government where the three branches each have their defined jurisdiction and power, would be an intrusion of judicial egoism over legislative passivity."

The legislature has recently acted in this area. Chapter 354, Laws of 1981 (effective May 7, 1982), was enacted to provide the underlying legislation enabling local governments to enact ordinances establishing procedures for guaranteeing access to sunlight. This court's intrusion into an area where legislative action is being taken is unwarranted, and it may undermine a legislative scheme for orderly development not yet fully operational.

Chapter 354, Laws of 1981, sec. 66.032, provides specific conditions for solar access permits. In part that section provides for impermissible interference with solar collectors within specific limitations.

66.032   Solar access permits.

(f) "Impermissible interference" means the blockage of solar energy from a collector surface or proposed collector surface for which a permit has been granted under this section during a collector use period if such blockage is by any structure or vegetation on property, an owner of which was notified under sub. (3)(b). *"Impermissible interference" does not include:*

1. Blockage by a narrow protrusion, including but not limited to a pole or wire, which does not substantially interfere with absorption of solar energy by a solar collector.

2. *Blockage by any structure constructed, under construction or for which a building permit has been applied for before the date the last notice is mailed or delivered under sub. (3)(b).*

3. Blockage by any vegetation planted before the date the last notice is mailed or delivered under sub. (3) (b) unless a municipality by ordinance under sub. (2) defines impermissible interference to include such vegetation.

(Emphasis added.)

Sec. 66.032(3)(b) provides for notice:

(3) Permit applications.

(b) An agency shall determine if an application is satisfactorily completed and shall notify the applicant of its determination. If an applicant receives notice that an application has been satisfactorily completed, *the ap-*

plicant shall deliver by certified mail or by hand a notice to the owner of any property which the applicant proposes to be restricted by the permit under sub. (7). The applicant shall submit to the agency a copy of a signed receipt for every notice delivered under this paragraph. The agency shall supply the notice form. The information on the form may include, without limitation because of enumeration:

1. The name and address of the applicant, and the address of the land upon which the solar collector is or will be located.

2. That an application has been filed by the applicant.

3. That the permit, if granted, may affect the rights of the notified owner to develop his or her property and to plant vegetation.

4. The telephone number, address and office hours of the agency.

5. That *any person may request a hearing* under sub. (4) within 30 days after receipt of the notice, and the address and procedure for filing the request.

(Emphasis added.) This legislative scheme would deal with the type of problem presented in the present case and precludes the need for judicial activism in this area. . . .

I conclude that plaintiff's solar heating system is an unusually sensitive use. In other words, the defendant's proposed construction of his home, under ordinary circumstances, would not interfere with the use and enjoyment of the usual person's property. See W. Prosser, *supra*, sec. 87 at 578-579. "The plaintiff cannot, by devoting his own land to an unusually sensitive use, such as a drive-in motion picture theater easily affected by light, make a nuisance out of conduct of the adjoining defendant which would otherwise be harmless." Id. at 579 (footnote omitted). . . .

I further believe that the majority's conclusion that a cause of action exists in this case thwarts the very foundation of property law. Property law encompasses a system of filing and notice in a place for public records to provide prospective purchasers with any limitations on their use of the property. Such a notice is not alleged by the plaintiff. Only as a result of the majority's decision did Mr. Maretti discover that a legitimate action exists which would require him to defend the design and location of his home against a nuisance suit, notwithstanding the fact that he located and began to build his house within the applicable building, municipal, and deed restrictions.

I believe the facts of the instant controversy present the classic case of the owner of a solar collector who fails to take any action to protect his investment. There is nothing in the record to indicate that Mr. Prah disclosed his situation to Mr. Maretti prior to Maretti's purchase of the lot or attempted to secure protection for his solar collector prior to Maretti's submission of his building plans to the architectural committee. Such inaction should be considered a significant factor in determining whether a cause of action exists.

The majority's failure to recognize the need for notice may perpetuate a vicious cycle. Maretti may feel compelled to sell his lot because of

Prah's solar collector's interference with his plans to build his family home. If so, Maretti will not be obliged to inform prospective purchasers of the problem. Certainly, such information will reduce the value of his land. If the presence of collectors is sufficient notice, it cannot be said that the seller of the lot has a duty to disclose information peculiarly within his knowledge. I do not believe that an adjacent lot owner should be obliged to experience the substantial economic loss resulting from the lot being rendered unbuildable by the contour of the land as it relates to the location and design of the adjoining home using solar collectors.[8]

I am troubled by the majority's apparent retrospective application of its decision. I note that the court in *Deetz* saw the wisdom and fairness in rendering a prospective decision. 66 Wis. 2d at 24, 224 N.W.2d 407. Surely, a decision such as this should be accorded prospective status. Creating the cause of action after the fact results in such unfair surprise and hardship to property owners such as Maretti.

Because I do not believe that the facts of the present case give rise to a cause of action for private nuisance, I dissent.

NOTES AND QUESTIONS

1. **Ancient lights and artificial illumination.** The facts in Tenn v. 889 Associates, Ltd., 500 A.2d 366 (N.H. 1985) were these: Plaintiff owned a six-story office building whose south wall was built to the southerly line of its lot. Defendant owned the lot to the south, on which stood a four-story building on the same lot line. Defendant notified plaintiff of its plans to demolish the existing building and to replace it with a six-story structure, which would block plaintiff's south windows on the two upper floors. When defendant refused to redesign its building with an accommodating setback of several feet — to preserve plaintiff's light and air — plaintiff sought an injunction, plus ancillary damages. In her bill in equity, plaintiff claimed that the proposed structure would be a private nuisance and also that she had gained a prescriptive easement.

At the trial, plaintiff presented testimony that defendant's structure would reduce the value of her building from $700,000 to $300,000. When asked whether she would accept a $300,000 settlement, plaintiff refused that amount as too low. The trial court then dismissed the petition, on the grounds that defendant's building would not be a private nuisance and that there could be no prescriptive right to light, air, and a view.

On appeal, the court refused to adopt the *Fontainebleau* rule limiting

---

8. Mr. Prah could have avoided this litigation by building his own home in the center of his lot instead of only ten feet from the Maretti lot line and/or by purchasing the adjoining lot for his own protection. Mr. Maretti has already moved the proposed location of his home over an additional ten feet to accommodate Mr. Prah's solar collector, and he testified that moving the home any further would interfere with his view of the lake on which the property faces.

a landowner's right to acquire interests in light and air unless they were bargained for.

> If we were so to limit the ability of the common-law to grow, we would in effect be rejecting one of the wise assumptions underlying the traditional law of nuisance: that we cannot anticipate at any one time the variety of predicaments in which protection of property interests or redress for their violation will be justifiable. [T]here is no reason in principle why the law of nuisance should not be applied to claims for the protection of a property owner's interest in light and air. . . .

However, in reviewing the trial evidence, the court concluded that defendant's conduct did not rise to a nuisance, in part because the interference would not exceed "what was normal under the circumstances" in downtown Manchester, and in part because "the utility to the defendant and to the public of a new office building would outweigh the burden to the plaintiff of installing additional lighting and ventilation equipment."

2. **Solar legislation from the Golden State.** The following California law presents a second statutory approach toward "accommodating" neighbors' development rights, where at least one party builds a solar collector. Contrast this law with the Wisconsin statute quoted in Justice Callow's dissent in Prah v. Maretti.

CALIFORNIA PUBLIC RESOURCES CODE

§§25980-25986 (West's Ann. Code 1988)

§25980.   SHORT TITLE; PUBLIC POLICY

This chapter shall be known and may be cited as the Solar Shade Control Act. It is the policy of the state to promote all feasible means of energy conservation and all feasible uses of alternative energy supply sources. In particular, the state encourages the planting and maintenance of trees and shrubs to create shading, moderate outdoor temperatures, and provide various economic and aesthetic benefits. However, there are certain situations in which the need for widespread use of alternative energy devices, such as solar collectors, requires specific and limited controls on trees and shrubs.

§25981.   SOLAR COLLECTOR DEFINED

As used in this chapter, "solar collector" means a fixed device, structure, or part of a device or structure, which is used primarily to transform solar energy into thermal, chemical, or electrical energy. The solar collector shall be used as part of a system which makes use of solar energy for any or all of the following purposes: (1) water heating, (2) space heating or cooling, and (3) power generation.

§25982.   PROHIBITION OF PLACEMENT OR GROWTH OF TREE
          OR SHRUB SUBSEQUENT TO INSTALLATION OF SOLAR
          COLLECTOR ON PROPERTY OF ANOTHER SO AS TO
          CAST SHADOW

After January 1, 1979, no person owning, or in control of a property shall allow a tree or shrub to be placed, or, if placed, to grow on such property, subsequent to the installation of a solar collector on the property of another so as to cast a shadow greater than 10 percent of the collector absorption area upon that solar collector surface on the property of another at any one time between the hours of 10 a.m. and 2 p.m., local standard time; provided, that this section shall not apply to specific trees and shrubs which at the time of installation of a solar collector or during the remainder of that annual solar cycle cast a shadow upon that solar collector. For the purposes of this chapter, the location of a solar collector is required to comply with the local building and setback regulations, and to be set back not less than five feet from the property line, and no less than 10 feet above the ground. A collector may be less than 10 feet in height, only if in addition to the five feet setback, the collector is set back three times the amount lowered.

§25983.   VIOLATIONS; PUBLIC NUISANCE; NOTICE TO ABATE;
          PROSECUTION; PENALTY

Every person who maintains any tree or shrub or permits any tree or shrub to be maintained in violation of Section 25982 upon property owned by such person and every person leasing the property of another who maintains any tree or shrub or permits any tree or shrub to be maintained in violation of Section 25982 after reasonable notice in writing from a district attorney or city attorney or prosecuting attorney, to remove or alter the tree or shrub so that there is no longer a violation of Section 25982, has been served upon such person, is guilty of a public nuisance as defined in Sections 370 and 371 of the Penal Code and in Section 3480 of the Civil Code. For the purposes of this chapter, a violation is hereby deemed an infraction. The complainant shall establish to the satisfaction of the prosecutor that the violation has occurred prior to the prosecutor's duty to issue the abatement notice. For the purpose of this section, "reasonable notice" means 30 days from receipt of such notice. Upon expiration of the 30-day period, the complainant shall file an affidavit with the prosecutor alleging that the nuisance has not been abated if the complainant wishes to proceed with the action. The existence of such violation for each and every day after the service of such notice shall be deemed a separate and distinct offense, and it is hereby made the duty of the district attorney, or the city attorney of any city the charter of which imposes the duty upon the city attorney to prosecute state infractions, to prosecute all persons guilty of violating this section by continuous prosecutions until the violation is corrected. Each and every violation of this section shall be punishable by a fine not to exceed one thousand dollars ($1,000).

§25984. INAPPLICABILITY OF CHAPTER TO CERTAIN TREES

Nothing in this chapter shall apply to trees planted, grown, or harvested on timberland as defined in Section 4526 or on land devoted to the production of commercial agricultural crops. Nothing in this chapter shall apply to the replacement of a tree or shrub which had been growing prior to the installation of a solar collector and which, subsequent to the installation of such solar collector, dies.

§25985. ORDINANCE TO EXEMPT CITY OR UNINCORPORATED AREAS FROM PROVISIONS OF CHAPTER

Any city, or for unincorporated areas, any county, may adopt, by majority vote of the governing body, an ordinance exempting their jurisdiction from the provisions of this chapter. The adoption of such an ordinance shall not be subject to the provisions of the California Environmental Quality Act (commencing with Section 21000).

§25986. PASSIVE OR NATURAL SOLAR SYSTEM WHICH IMPACTS ON ADJACENT ACTIVE SOLAR SYSTEM; ACTION TO EXEMPT FROM PROVISIONS OF CHAPTER

Any person who plans a passive or natural solar heating system or cooling system or heating and cooling system which would impact on an adjacent active solar system may seek equitable relief in a court of competent jurisdiction to exempt such system from the provisions of this chapter. The court may grant such an exemption based on a finding that the passive or natural system would provide a demonstrably greater net energy savings than the active system which would be impacted.

§7.3 Modes of Creating the Servitude

a. Creation by Express Agreement

Most servitudes result from an express arrangement between the benefited party and the owner of the servient estate. At early common law, livery of seisin was regarded as inappropriate for the transfer of an easement;

instead, a sealed writing called a "grant" was used. Paradoxically, the law required a writing for the creation of an easement before one became necessary for a lease or a transfer of a fee. Today, we still speak of the *grant* of an easement — whenever the owner of the servient estate creates this burden on her land. Sometimes, the easement arises not by grant, but by *reservation*. This would happen if B, the owner of adjoining Lots 1 and 2, transferred the fee in Lot 1 to A, but reserved a right of way across Lot 1.[39]

Easements (to say nothing of covenants) may also arise contractually. The common or reciprocal driveway agreement (adjoining owners A and B agree to share the common driveway straddling their lots) and the negative easement (A, the owner of the servient estate, promises her neighbor, B, not to build higher than two stories) are two examples we have already seen. Ordinarily, the parties' rights and duties do not depend on whether a conveyance (grant) or agreement (covenant) documents the servitude.

The formal requirements for creation of an express servitude are the same as those required for creation of an estate in land of like duration.[40] This usually means that a writing is needed.[41] It is good practice for the servitude holder also to file the document in the appropriate land registry so that future holders of the servient estate will have record notice. Where servitudes govern a homes association or condominium, state law may require that a "Declaration of Covenants and Restrictions" be recorded.[42]

TRANSMISSION LINE EASEMENT

FOR AND IN CONSIDERATION of the sum of <u>FOURTEEN DOLLARS and THIRTY-NINE CENTS</u> ($14.39), in hand paid, receipt of which is hereby acknowledged, <u>we, W. WILLIAM PUUSTINEN and LOIS JAYNES PUUSTINEN, husband and wife,</u> have granted, bargained, and sold and by these presents do hereby grant, bargain, sell, and convey unto the UNITED STATES OF AMERICA and its assigns, a permanent easement and right-of-way over, upon, under, and across the following-described land in the County of <u>CLATSOP</u>, in the State of <u>OREGON</u>; to wit: .

That portion of Government Lot 5 in Section 21, Township 8 North, Range 8 West, Willamette Meridian, Clatsop County, Oregon; which lies

---

39. One might also think of an easement by reservation as a legal shortcut to avoid a two-step process whereby B would transfer the unencumbered fee to A, and A would then grant the easement to B. Restatement, Servitudes (T.D. No. 1, 1989).

40. Id at §2.7.

41. Id. at §2.8.

42. Id.

within a strip of land 100 feet in width, the boundaries of said strip lying 50 feet distant on either side of and parallel to the survey line of the St. Johns-Astoria transmission line as now located and staked on the ground over, across, and upon the above property, and particularly described as follows:

Beginning at survey station 1570+28.34, a point on the east line of Section 21, Township 8 North, Range 8 West, Willamette Meridian, said point being S. 0° 09' 52" W. a distance of 810.95 feet from the quarter section corner on the east line of said Section 21, thence N. 79° 43' 04" W. a distance of 2017.31 feet to survey station 1590+45.65 back equals survey station 1590+36.86 ahead; thence continuing N. 79° 43' 04" W. a distance of 2669.77 feet to survey station 1617+06.63 back equals survey station 1617+09.53 ahead; thence continuing N. 79° 43' 04" W. a distance of 647.14 feet to survey station 1623+56.67, a point on the west line of said Section 21, said point being N. 0° 15' 05" W. along said west line a distance of 822.30 feet from the quarter section corner on the west line of said Section 21.

The above-described strip of land has a length of 213 feet and contains 0.50 acre, more or less.

SUBJECT TO:

1. The lien of the 1941 taxes which we, the grantors, agree to pay and against which we undertake and agree to indemnify and hold the grantee harmless.

The aforesaid easement and right-of-way is for the following purposes, namely: the perpetual right to enter and to erect, maintain, repair, rebuild, operate, and patrol one or more electric power transmission lines, and one or more telephone and/or telegraph lines, including the right to erect such poles and other transmission line structures, wires, cables, and the appurtenances necessary thereto; the further right to clear said right-of-way and keep the same clear of brush, timber, inflammable structures, and fire hazards; and the right to remove danger trees, if any, located beyond the limits of said right-of-way.

To HAVE AND TO HOLD the said easement and right-of-way unto the UNITED STATES OF AMERICA and its assigns, forever.

It is further understood and agreed by the undersigned that the payment of such purchase price is accepted as full compensation for all damages incidental to the exercise of any of the rights above described.

We covenant with the UNITED STATES OF AMERICA that we are lawfully seized and possessed of the lands aforesaid; have a good and lawful right and power to sell and convey the same; that the same are free and clear of all encumbrances, except as above noted, and that we will forever warrant and defend the title thereto and quiet possession thereof against the lawful claims of all persons whomsoever.

Dated this 3 day of December, 1940.

_____
W. William Puustinen

WITNESSES: _____
Lois Jaynes Puustinen

_____   _____

_____   _____

NOTES AND QUESTIONS

1. **Transmission line easement: who is bound.** Does this easement bind only the two original parties, or does it bind successors? What is the language that gives you the answer?

2. **Scope.** What is the scope of the transmission line easement? If you represented the landowner, would you try to renegotiate the language that defines the scope of this easement. How? If you represented the power company?

3. **Duration.** How long does it last? Is it perpetual, or time limited?

4. **Problem.** In a western state, A owns two 100-acre parcels that are landlocked within a much larger parcel owned by B. A's family has always farmed the land, but recently they lost their right to receive water from a federal irrigation project and have decided to go into the cattle business. To do so, however, they would need the right to drive cattle between their two parcels.

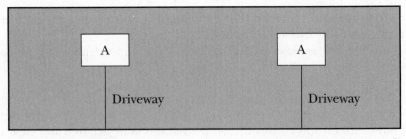

Public road   (shaded area is B's parcel)

A has contacted B, who seems receptive to the idea of selling A the rights he needs. Discuss the key issues involved in drafting the agreement, assuming:

(a)   You are the lawyer for A.   *where, for how long, damages, payment.*

(b)   You are the lawyer for B.

How do A's interests differ from those of B?

not really

b.   Created by Prescription

The adverse use of another's land for the limitations period may establish a prescriptive servitude. Prescription is closely related to adverse possession. In the latter, the adverse possessor acquires title. In prescription, the adverse user gains a servitude. The requirements for a prescriptive servitude under the Restatement of Servitudes[43] are a nonpermissive use that is (1) open or notorious, and (2) continued without effective interruption for the prescriptive period. The Restatement permits the tacking together of periods of prescriptive use.[44]

The periods for prescription and adverse possession are usually the same, to wit, the limitations period for the recovery of land. The prescriptive use need not be exclusive, however, and the prescriptive user often shares the facility with the property's owner. There is no tax-paying requirement for a prescriptive servitude, as some states require for adverse possession,[45] and when the nonpermissive use takes place, courts do not consider, as they sometimes consider for adverse possession, whether the user is (or is not) aware that she is committing a trespass.

not exclusive

Prescriptive servitude cases are a dime-a-dozen. The following is a homely example.

BROCCO v. MILEO

170 A.D.2d 732, 565 N.Y.S.2d (1991)

LEVINE, J.

Plaintiffs and defendants Gerard W. Mileo and Dolores T. Mileo (hereinafter collectively referred to as defendants) are owners of contiguous real

---

43. Id. at §2.16 (T.D. 3, 1993).

44. For tacking to occur, there must be a transfer between the prescriptive users of either the inchoate servitude or the estate benefited by the inchoate servitude. Ibid.

45. See, e.g., Reinsch v. City of Los Angeles, 243 Cal. App. 2d 737, 52 Cal. Rptr. 613 (1966); Hahn v. Curtis, 73 Cal. App. 2d 382, 166 P.2d 611 (1946).

property located in the Town of Ulster, Ulster County. In 1986, plaintiffs commenced the instant action claiming acquisition of either title by adverse possession to an access way over defendants' land or a prescriptive easement over such access way. At an earlier stage of this action, Supreme Court denied defendants' motion for summary judgment dismissing the complaint against them. Defendants appealed and we modified by reversing so much of the order as denied summary judgment with respect to plaintiffs' adverse possession claim (144 A.D.2d 200, 535 N.Y.S.2d 125). We noted in that decision that Supreme Court properly concluded that triable issues existed with regard to plaintiffs' prescriptive easement claim (id., at 201-202, 535 N.Y.S.2d 125).

Subsequently, the parties conducted additional examinations before trial and plaintiffs then moved for summary judgment on their remaining claim. Supreme Court granted that motion and this appeal by defendants ensued.

There should be an affirmance. It is undisputed that defendants purchased their property in 1986 from Robert Marz and Muriel Marz and that plaintiffs acquired title to their property in 1984 from the estate of Zita Herzog, who took title in 1945. William Herzog (hereinafter Herzog), son of Zita Herzog, testified at his examination before trial that he lived on plaintiffs' property from 1945 until 1956 (with the exception of two years when he served in the military) and that he utilized the access way on a daily basis without any interference or obstruction during that period. Additionally, Herzog testified that after he moved from that residence in 1956, he continued to visit the property and to use the access way, again without interference, on almost a daily basis through 1960, and at least once a week thereafter until the property was sold in 1984. Joseph Fiore, Herzog's brother-in-law, testified that he visited plaintiffs' property, also utilizing the access way without interference, either once or twice a week between 1930 and 1984. Both Herzog and Fiore stated that they maintained the access way from 1945 to 1984 by shoveling, filling in potholes and/or cutting brush along the sides. Finally, the affidavit of Dolores Fiore, Herzog's sister, states that the Herzog family used the access way from 1945 for a continuous and uninterrupted period of time in excess of 20 years.

In our view, plaintiffs sufficiently established through the foregoing submissions that the use of the access way by their predecessors was open, notorious and uninterrupted for more than the prescriptive period which, in this case, is 15 years . . . thus giving rise to a presumption that such use was adverse. . . .

Defendants then had the burden of negating that presumption by showing that the use by plaintiffs' predecessors was permissive . . . which they failed to do. In an attempt to meet their burden, defendants submitted, inter alia, an affidavit from their predecessor, Robert Marz, who stated that both he and his grantor gave the Herzogs permission to use the access way. However, any permission which may have been given by Marz after he took title in 1969 is irrelevant, since the easement in question was acquired by plaintiffs' predecessors prior to 1969. Moreover, as we discussed in our earlier decision in this case, Marz's assertion that his grantor gave the Herzogs permission to use the access way is merely hearsay and thus ineffective to defeat plaintiffs' motion. . . . Accordingly, summary judgment was properly granted in plaintiffs' favor. . . .

Although defendants again rely on the absence of a description of the subject easement in the earlier deeds in plaintiffs' claim of title, such reliance is unwarranted since the deed from plaintiffs' grantor, who actually acquired the easement, contains such a description. Finally, defendants' claim that plaintiffs are guilty of laches is entirely without merit.

Order affirmed, with costs.

NOTES AND QUESTIONS

1.   **Why not title by adverse possession?** Plaintiff sued on alternative theories of prescription and title by adverse possession, but the appeals court, in its first review of the case (144 A.D.2d 200, 535 N.Y.S.2d 125), limited plaintiff's recovery to one based on prescription. Without reading the earlier opinion, can you tell why?

Courts are reluctant, where the choice exists, to take away an owner's title to a strip of land rather than to impose a prescriptive servitude. This is because narrowly shaped fee holdings (called "gores") tend not to be readily marketable, except to adjoining owners or as part of a larger parcel.

2.   **A few centuries of history.** The close analogy of prescriptive easements with title by adverse possession is now orthodox legal theory. This equivalence is relatively new; the claim of prescription once rested upon quite a different theory — the fiction of a lost grant.

As early as Bracton, the law had begun to recognize the right to an easement, even though unsupported by a grant from the servient owner. "[I]f there has been any user extending over considerable time, exercised in peace, without any interruption and not by violence or stealth or by virtue of a request . . . the person enjoying the right cannot be ousted of it, at all events without the judgment of the court." (Lib. IV, cap. 37, fol. 220b.)

To establish his prescriptive interest, the claimant had to introduce proof of use from "time immemorial." Seeking to put fixed content into that phrase, the law settled on the year 1189 (the start of Richard I's reign) as the year from which proof of use should begin. In time, the testimonial difficulties of proving use from 1189 onward became unmanageable, and a new test for prescription — similar to the earliest formulation — was introduced. Testimony of usage, continuing for as long as living witnesses could recall, would create a presumption that the use had originated by 1189. But new difficulties for the claimant arose at once, for the presumption of continued user was easily rebutted; to defeat the claim, the servient owner need only show a time interval when use could not have occurred, or when ownership of the dominant and servient estates was merged.

In 1623 the writ of entry became subject to a 20-year statute of limitations, which, as we saw, not only barred the landowner's remedy but also established the occupant's title. Although the statute did not apply to incorporeal interests, courts eventually adopted its 20-year measure as the period of use that would ripen into a prescriptive right. But to regard 20 years as the factual equivalent of use stretching backward for more than four centuries was so transparent a fiction that the courts saw fit to concoct a more plausible fiction and, in doing so, to alter the theoretical basis for prescriptive rights. Hence, a claimant who could prove 20 years or more of uninterrupted use was presumed to have begun his use pursuant to a grant from the servient owner, which grant (instrument) had later disappeared. This, then, was the doctrine of the lost (or mislaid) grant.

If the 1623 statute of limitations had been construed to apply to incorporeal interests, the lost grant fiction would have been unnecessary, since the statute barring the remedy would also have established the prescriptive interest. In making available to the prescriptive claimant the 20-year analogy, the courts certainly lightened the claimant's testimonial load, but it was not an entirely happy accommodation even at that. For the courts could find no consensus as to how the doctrine worked. If the claimant could show the requisite period of uninterrupted use, had he created an irrefutable presumption of a lost grant, or might the owner offer proof that the use initiated under a revocable license or an easement for ten years, or in an openly *hostile* manner? If the claimant attempted to show the requisite period of uninterrupted use, what form of proof would dispute this — a letter from the servient owner demanding that the use cease? A letter from the servient owner privileging the use to continue until the privilege was revoked? For a brief exposure to the operational complexities of the lost grant theory, see Parker & Edgarton v. Foote, 190 Wend. 309 (N.Y. Sup. Ct. of Jud. 1838).

The British attempted statutory reform in 1832, but nearly one century later a commentator wrote that "no branch of English law is in a more unsatisfactory state than the law of prescription." Holdsworth, Historical Introduction of the Land Law 286 (1927). By then, however, the fiction of the lost grant had already given way in American courts to the real life kinship of prescription and adverse possession.

3. **Presumption of adverse use not present in special situations.**
Brocco v. Mileo correctly states the usual presumption of adverse use where an open and notorious use continues for the prescriptive period. There are several fact patterns, however, where this presumption may not govern. If the claimed servient estate is wild, remote, or not actively used by its owner, the claimant's use, absent contrary evidence, is generally seen as permissive. See, e.g., Durbin v. Bonanza Corp., 716 P.2d 1124 (Colo. Ct. App. 1986) (vacant, unenclosed, and unoccupied); Christle v. Scott, 110 Idaho 401, 724

P.2d 137 (1986) (wild and unenclosed). Also, if the claimant and the owner of the claimed servient estate have a "good-neighborly" relationship, an unexplained use may well be viewed as permissive. See, e.g., Wilson v. Cyril Hampel 1985 Trust, 105 Nev. 607, 781 P.2d 769 (1989) (neighbor's use held to be result of neighborly accommodation); Hassinger v. Kline, 91 A.D.2d 988, 457 N.Y.S.2d 847 (1983) (neighborly relation between parties' predecessors created implication that use of road was permissive); Crites v. Koch, 49 Wash. App. 171, 741 P.2d 1005 (1987) (common practice of farmers to park equipment on neighbors' fields was neighborly accommodation). And when the owner of the claimed servient estate has built and still uses the facility, there is no presumption of adverse use. See, e.g., Gerberding v. Schnakenberg, 216 Neb. 200, 343 N.W.2d 62 (1984) (road opened by landowner for his own purposes).

In a few states, the courts presume that an unexplained use is permissive. See, e.g., Carr v. Turner, 575 So. 2d 1066 (Ala. 1991); Caribou Four Corners, Inc. v. Chapple-Hawkes, Inc., 643 P.2d 468 (Wyo. 1982). In these states, the claimant may overcome the presumption by showing that he built and has maintained the facility, see, e.g., Delk v. Hill, 89 N.C. App. 83, 365 S.E.2d 218 (1988), or that the facility offers the sole access to the dominant estate.

4.   **May a negative servitude be acquired by prescription?** Affirmative easements, such as rights of way, drainage ditches, rights to maintain encroaching eaves and foundations, are the usual form of prescriptive servitude. But under the English doctrine of ancient lights, the common law permitted landowners to gain the prescriptive right to prevent a neighbor from building any structure that would block the flow of light and air to windows on the dominant estate. The following excerpts discuss ancient lights.

"Early in its history the common law recognized a landowner's right to the enjoyment of light, air and view unobstructed by buildings on a neighboring estate. Nonetheless, equity would not vindicate the landowner's right unless the deprivation was in such a degree as to render occupation of his home uncomfortable or exercise of his business less beneficial. Under the common law doctrine of 'ancient lights,' the right to light, air and view was acquired by unobstructed enjoyment, first throughout 'immemorial use' and later for a period of twenty years fixed by the statute of limitations." Note, 34 Tul. L. Rev. 599 (1960).

"By the English common law if one opened windows overlooking his neighbor's property, the latter had the right to erect barriers to obstruct the view; and his motives in doing so were wholly immaterial. But there was a reason for this which does not exist [in the United States]. That rule was a necessary corollary to the doctrine of ancient lights, whereby one enjoying the uninterrupted use of a window for a given period . . . acquired an easement in the adjoining land which the owner could neither gainsay nor deny. Hence to open a window overlooking a neighbor's land was regarded as an encroachment, though no action lay therefor. The only remedy was to build a barrier opposite the offending window. The adjoining proprietor not only had the right to erect such barrier; but was obliged to do so to protect the title to his land. This was the only method whereby he could prevent the user into a right." Rumble, Limitations on the Use of Property by Its Owner, 5 Va. L. Rev. 297, 306 (1918).

However well the doctrine of ancient lights may have suited England's one-time agrarian society, its survival to this day is surprising indeed. See, e.g., McGrath v. Munster & Leinster Bank, 94 Ir. L.T.R. 110 (1960) (tenant recovered damages from neighboring landowner whose remodeled building darkened tenant's office).

The Rights of Light Act of 1959 (7 & 8 Eliz. 2, c. 56), although reaffirming the doctrine, made two important concessions to urban life: (1) the prescriptive period was lengthened to 27 years, and (2) the filing of a simple notice became a legally sufficient substitute for an opaque barrier.

A major impetus for the reform law was the difficulty in obtaining planning permission to erect an unsightly screen. Greene, Securing Rights of Light, 112 L.J. 744 (1962).

American courts, reflecting a pro-development stance, have uniformly rejected the doctrine of ancient lights. See, e.g., Fontainebleau Hotel Corp. v. Forty-Five Twenty-Five, Inc., page 641, *supra*. The same attitude led to the courts' refusal to allow landowners to gain a prescriptive negative servitude for lateral support from adjacent lands. Restatement of Servitudes, §2.16 (T.D. No. 3, 1993), at 9. But courts, seeking to insure unbroken sunlight to solar collectors, have begun to invoke nuisance theory against interference by neighboring trees and structures, resulting in even earlier protection than would the doctrine of ancient lights. See, e.g., Prah v. Maretti, page 650, *supra*.

5. **Drafting exercise.** The following is a notice posted each year on the gates to Harvard Yard.

Notice

President and Fellows of Harvard College, a Massachusetts corporation, apprehending that a right of way or other easement may be acquired by custom, use, or otherwise, in or over its land in Cambridge, Massachusetts, on which are located Claverly Hall, College or Senior House and Apley Court, bounded and described as follows: [description omitted] . . . by a passageway extending in a Northerly direction from Mt. Auburn Street by some person or class of persons, hereby gives public notice under General Laws, (Ter. Ed.) Chapter 187, Section 3, of its intention to dispute any such right or easement and to prevent the acquisition of the same.

President and Fellows of Harvard College

What purpose is this designed to serve? Is this the way you would choose to draft it? What alternatives could you suggest?

   6.   **Rockefeller Center.** Upon the advice of their lawyers, the owners of Rockefeller Center close for one day each year the private street called Rockefeller Plaza between the RCA Building and the sunken skating rink. Why do their lawyers so advise?

c.   Servitude Implied from Prior Use

OTERO v. PACHECO

94 N.M. 524, 612 P.2d 1335 (1980)

HERNANDEZ, J.
   Plaintiffs-Appellants sued Defendants-Appellees alleging fraud and unjust enrichment due to plaintiffs' payment of ad valorem taxes which were owed by defendants. They further alleged that the sewer line which serviced both of their homes had backed up on various occasions, causing damage to their home. Defendants answered and counterclaimed, alleging that they had an easement across plaintiffs' property for the maintenance of the sewer line. The trial court, sitting without a jury, entered judgment for the plaintiffs on their claim for payment of taxes owed by defendants, and entered judgment for defendants on their counterclaim. The plaintiffs appeal the judgment entered for defendants.

   The undisputed facts are these. The defendants acquired title to two lots in 1944, lots 4 and 5 of Block 5 of the Indian School Addition in the City of Santa Fe. Lot 5 fronted on Cochiti Street, and lot 4, a corner lot, sided on Taos Street. Defendants' home was constructed partly on lot 5 and partly on lot 4, and originally had a septic tank which was situated on lot 4. In 1950 the City of Santa Fe notified defendants that they had to abandon the use of their septic tank, and connect to the sanitary sewer line which had just been installed along Taos Street.

   Defendants installed a sewer line running from their home across lot 4 to the Taos Street sewer line. There is no evidence that there existed any alternative way to connect to the Taos Street sewer, and there was no sanitary sewer line along Cochiti Street at that time. In 1951 the defendants built another house on the remaining part of lot 4, and connected it to the same sewer line. Defendants in 1953 sold this house to a Mrs. McAfoos. The deed to Mrs. McAfoos did not contain a reservation of an easement. However, defendant Alexandro Pacheco testified that he told Mrs. McAfoos of the sewer line's existence and that it provided service to his home. The title passed from Mrs. McAfoos through several intervening owners and ultimately came to the plaintiffs in 1965. The first owner after Mrs. McAfoos testified that he was never told, and did not know, that the sewer line serviced defendants' home during the approximately eight years that he owned that property. Plaintiff Severo Otero testified that he did not learn until 1974 that the sewer line which serviced his house also serviced that of the defendants.

Plaintiffs raise four points of error, only three of which need be discussed. The essence of the first two is that the trial court erred in deciding that the defendants had an easement across lot 4. The pertinent findings of the trial court, all of which are supported by substantial evidence in the record, are: that the defendants acquired title to both lots 4 and 5 in 1944; that the sewer line was reasonably necessary to the use and enjoyment of lot 5 at the time of the sale of lot 4, and that it continues to be reasonably necessary to the use and enjoyment of lot 5; and "that . . . the . . . sewer line was and now is an improvement of a permanent and substantial character, actually and apparently intended to be preserved as a servitude for the . . . necessary [and] . . . convenient use and enjoyment of the Pacheco lot and residence." The trial court went on to conclude that the defendants had an easement across lot 4 for a sewer line for the benefit of lot 5 and that the plaintiffs took title to lot 4 subject to that easement.

Although the trial court did not characterize the type of easement, it is readily apparent from the findings that the court was speaking of an easement by implied reservation. Whether such an easement is recognized by the appellate courts of this State is a matter of first impression. However, the converse, i.e., an easement by implied grant, was recognized by our Supreme Court in Venegas v. Luby, 49 N.M. 381, 164 P.2d 584 (1945):

> It seems well settled . . . that if the owner of land subjects one part of it to a visible servitude in favor of another and then conveys away the dominant portion while it is enjoying the servitude of the portion retained, and the use is reasonably necessary for the full enjoyment of the part granted, an implied easement arises in favor of the premises conveyed and passes by the conveyance without mention.

The nature of and rationale for these two types of easements was very ably set forth by the Supreme Court of Texas in Mitchell v. Castellaw, 151 Tex. 56, 246 S.W.2d 163 (1952):

> It is universally recognized that where the owner of a single area of land conveys away part of it, the circumstances attending the conveyance may themselves, without aid of language in the deed, and indeed sometimes in spite of such language, cause an easement to arise as between the two parcels thus created — not only in favor of the parcel granted ("implied grant") but also in favor of the one remaining in the ownership of the grantor ("implied reservation"). The basis of the doctrine is that the law reads into the instrument that which the circumstances show both grantor and grantee must have intended, had they given the obvious facts of the transaction proper considera-

tion. And in the case of an implied reservation it is not necessarily a bar to its creation that the grantor's deed, into which the law reads it, actually warrants the servient tract thereby conveyed to be free of incumbrance.

There is a split in authority over the question of the degree of necessity that is required to imply the retention of an easement. According to one view, an easement is implied by reservation only where there is strict necessity. Winthrop v. Wadsworth, 42 So. 2d 541 (S. Ct. Fla. 1949). The other view was set forth by the Supreme Court of Oregon in Jack v. Hunt, 200 Or. 263, 264 P.2d 461 (1953):

> The majority rule makes no distinction between the degree of necessity in the granting or the retaining of an implied easement. In either circumstances the degree of necessity is answered "if necessary to the reasonable enjoyment of the property."

The trial court thought that reasonable necessity was the better view, and so do we. This view is more in harmony with Venegas v. Luby, *supra,* than is strict necessity. However, in *Venegas,* it is clearly indicated that reasonable necessity is not synonymous with mere convenience.

Applying the foregoing to the facts of this case, the trial court was correct in deciding that the defendants had an easement by implied reservation as the result of a reasonable necessity which continues to exist.

The plaintiffs' third point of error is that they were allegedly bona fide purchasers for value of lot 4, and that they took free and clear of any easement of which they had no notice. The general rule is that a bona fide purchaser does not take subject to an easement unless he has actual or constructive knowledge of its existence. Southern Union Gas Co. v. Cantrell, 56 N.M. 184, 241 P.2d 1209 (1952). However, the law charges a person with notice of facts which inquiry would have disclosed where the circumstances are such that a reasonably prudent person would have inquired. Sanchez v. Dale Bellamah Homes of New Mexico, Inc., 76 N.M. 526, 417 P.2d 25 (1966).

> While there is some conflict of authority as to whether existing drains, pipes, and sewers may be properly characterized as apparent, within the rule as to apparent or visible easements the majority of the cases which have considered the question have taken the view that appearance and visibility are not synonymous, and that the fact that the pipe, sewer, or drain may be hidden underground does not negative its character as an apparent condition; at least, where the appliances connected with and leading to it are obvious. 58 A.L.R. 832; Helle v. Markotan, 137 N.E.2d 715 (Ohio Com. Pl. 1955); Frantz v. Collins, 21 Ill. 2d 446, 173 N.E.2d 437 (1961).

The circumstances in this situation were such that a reasonably prudent person would have inquired.

We need not consider plaintiffs' fourth point of error because, even if

we were to decide that it had merit, it would not alter the outcome of
this case.

The judgment is affirmed.

It is so ordered.

LOPEZ, J., concurs.

ANDREWS, J., dissenting.

ANDREWS, Judge (dissenting).

I dissent.

I cannot agree with the majority that the circumstances were such as
to put the Oteros on constructive notice of the existence of the sewer line.

> . . . the purchaser of property may assume that no easements are attached to
> the property purchased which are not of record except those which are open
> and visible, and he cannot otherwise be bound with notice. There should be
> such a connection between the use and the thing as to suggest to the pur-
> chaser that the one estate is servient to the other.

Southern Union Gas Co. v. Cantrell, 56 N.M. 184 at 190, 241 P.2d 1209 at
1213 (1952).

The facts in this case do not support the inference that the Oteros
had constructive notice of the existence of the sewer line. While the appearance of the adjoining Pacheco property was such as to suggest that it
was connected to a sewer line, there is nothing in the record to indicate
that it was in any way apparent that it, *at one time,* had been necessary to lay
such a line under the Oteros' land. The history of the development of the
sewer system in the area is not apparent to the average purchaser, and the
Oteros were justified in assuming that the Pachecos' sewer connections did
not impinge on the property rights of the surrounding landholders.

I would reverse.

NOTES AND QUESTIONS

1. **Prior use.** Essential to the finding of an *implied* servitude from
prior use is the common ownership of the land benefited and burdened by
the prior use and a transfer of either the benefited or burdened parcel.
Might it be possible, however, prior to severance, for A, owner of Lots 1 and
2, to grant an express easement to himself over one of the two lots for the
benefit of the second lot? It is often said that an express easement cannot
arise when the dominant and servient parcels are both owned by the same
party, and therefore any prior use would, at most, result in a "quasi-
easement." But why should this be, and is it true? Consider, for example, a
homes association developer who records a declaration of covenants and

restrictions burdening the yet unsold and undeveloped subdivision. Are the recorded servitudes valid? Or do they gain their validity, that is, their binding nature, only with the first conveyance from the developer?

2. **Reasonable necessity.** The Restatement of Servitudes, §2.12, takes the view that an easement may be implied from prior use wherever continuance of the prior use is "reasonably necessary" to enjoyment of the benefited parcel, without regard to whether the easement arises by grant or reservation. Id. at page 135 (T.D. 1, 1989). The Restatement defines "reasonable necessity" as meaning that "alternative access or utilities cannot be obtained without a substantial expenditure of money or labor." Ibid.

3. **Underground utilities.** It may have seemed surprising that the Oteros were deemed to have notice of the underground utility easement across their lot. The Restatement of Servitudes ignores the notice requirement for underground utilities, and bases its support for the *Otero* result "on the more realistic view that parties buying and selling developed land expect existing utility arrangements to be part of the package." Id. at 137. Earlier the Restatement explained that "refusal to imply a servitude to continue the prior use puts the party whose land carries the utility lines serving the other parcel in a position to exact a much higher price for granting the servitude than would be warranted by the reduction in value to his land." Ibid. But isn't that possibility inherent in every negotiation when entitlements are protected by a property rule?

4. **Inspection of large tracts.** In Heatherdell Farms, Inc. v. Huntley Estates at Greenburg No. 3 Corp., 130 N.Y.S.2d 335 (Sup. Ct. 1954), defendant acquired a wooded 120-acre tract adjoining plaintiff's 25-acre parcel that housed a sanitarium. Plaintiff claimed an implied easement to maintain a septic tank and drainage field 100 feet inside defendant's tract. The tank had a concrete slab top, roughly 12 feet by 10 feet, set flush with the ground, with four or five manhole covers therein. The top and covers were so obscured, however, by tall grass and underbrush that one would not notice them until he had approached within 25 feet. In refusing to find an implied easement, the court wrote (130 N.Y.S.2d at 338):

> It is not reasonable to require a purchaser of large acreage in its natural state to thoroughly inspect every rod or acre or to have it inspected by a title company or its agents. It is a well-known fact that the on-the-ground inspection by an ordinary prudent purchaser of such land consists of looking at it from one or more vantage points with a general locating of the boundaries. Such a purchaser will also generally examine a map or plotting of the acreage, but it is not expected that he will thoroughly inspect the land to search out possible servitudes or encumbrances not ordinarily to be expected on such land.

Suppose that the defendant had chanced upon the concrete slab while inspecting the terrain but had not made further inquiry before purchasing the tract. Would he then be subject to the easement?

d.   Servitude by Necessity

BERKELEY DEVELOPMENT CORP. v. HUTZLER

229 S.E. 732 (W. Va. 1976)

BERRY, C. J. The appellant, Hunter Hutzler, seeks a reversal of a judgment of the Circuit Court of Berkeley County permanently enjoining him from entering on or across the lands of the appellee, Berkeley Development Corporation.

The parties are owners of adjacent tracts of real estate located in Gerrardstown District, Berkeley County, West Virginia. In 1972, the Berkeley Development Corporation acquired its 550 acre tract and began to develop it as a recreational, residential subdivision. By deed dated August 10, 1943, Mr. Hunter Hutzler purchased his 105 acre tract which, subsequent to its acquisition, has been used primarily as a source of timber or pulp wood. Hutzler does not reside on this land.

In 1974, the Berkeley Development Corporation initiated an action in the Circuit Court of Berkeley County to obtain an injunction against Hutzler to prohibit Hutzler from entering on the 550 acre tract and from interfering with the surface of that land. The appellee's complaint recited that Hutzler had entered on the land with equipment to cut trees and grade the surface. By way of defense to the appellee's action, Hutzler contended that he had a prescriptive easement, or, in the alternative, a private way of necessity across an existing road which ran from his land over the plaintiff's land and onto a public road.

At trial, it was stipulated that the tracts of the respective parties shared a common source of title, the two tracts having been originally owned by one Moses S. Grantham. It was further stipulated there were no express easements in any of the conveyances in the line of title of either party.

On behalf of the Berkeley Development Corporation, Mr. Gilbert R. Clarke, the organization's president, testified that prior to purchasing the 550 acres he spent a great deal of time examining the property. He stated that he walked over the common boundary and that he saw a faint trail which he assumed to be a logging trail. He stated that the inspection revealed no indication of any travel on the trail and that there was substantial growth in the way. Mr. Clarke also observed that a small stream which crossed the trail had eroded its banks making passage impossible. It was Mr. Clarke's estimate that the trail had not been used for twelve to fifteen years prior to his inspection.

In advance of its purchase, the appellee had the 550 acre tract and some of the surrounding properties surveyed by a licensed land surveyor, Galtjo Geertsema. Geertsema, called as a witness on behalf of the appellee, described his survey and indicated that he observed the road in question at the time. Geertsema described the road as an old road, averaging approximately ten feet wide and running a thousand feet over the property of the Berkeley Development Corporation, from the point where it crossed the common boundary. The surveyor indicated that he did not observe any evidence of the use of the road although he stated that it was passable.

With reference to alternate ways of ingress and egress, neither Clarke or Geertsema could say with any degree of certainty that there were other roads from the Hutzler property to a public road.

The evidence adduced on behalf of the appellant was that the 105 acre tract had previously been an orchard and for a number of years the roadway in question was used by Hutzler's predecessor in title as a route for hauling fruit to a public road. Walker Brannon, the son of one of the appellee's predecessors in title, testified that the road had been in continuous use to his recollection for more than seventy years. Brannon stated that the road was first used to haul fruit and later to haul timber from the Hutzler property. Brannon indicated that the road followed substantially the same route as it did in 1901 and was in substantially the same condition except for the natural vegetative growth in the roadway. Brannon further testified that there was no other means of access to the Hutzler property except across a precipitous and difficult route which went across the property of others and which was passable only by horse and rider.

The appellant, Hunter Hutzler, testified that prior to his purchase of the tract, he had worked on the orchard and had hauled fruit over the road in question for a number of years. Hutzler indicated that the road had been used for a period of fifty years to his recollection, with the acquiescence of the previous owners of the Berkeley Development tract. In addition, Hutzler had, himself, hauled lumber across the road in the years following his purchase of the orchard tract. Finally, the appellant indicated that the road in question was the only means to get in and out of his property.

Elwood Hutzler, the son of the appellant, confirmed his father's testimony concerning the use of the road, the acquiescence of the previous owner of the adjacent land and the absence of any other way to a public road. In addition Elwood Hutzler stated that he had personally used the road during the previous year.

On the evidence adduced, the circuit court held that the appellant had neither a prescriptive easement nor a way of necessity across the Berkeley Development tract. In accordance with this ruling, the court permanently enjoined Hutzler from entering on or across the appellee's land. Hutzler contends that the trial court erred in holding that he did not have an easement or right-of-way either by prescription or necessity over the land of the appellee. The appellee counters by arguing that the trial court was correct, but if either a prescriptive easement or a way of necessity was established, it was lost by virtue of the fact that the appellee obtained the property in question as a bona fide purchaser for value without notice of the existence of any easement over the land.

The burden of proving an easement rests on the party claiming such right and must be established by clear and convincing proof. [Citations omitted.] It is abundantly clear that the appellant established, by the requisite degree of proof in this case, an easement over the land of the appellee. This conclusion is supported by the evidence presented by both the appellant and the appellee.

First, there is no doubt about the existence of the roadway in question. While the parties have used different terms to characterize this road, the basic facts of its presence and location were confirmed by the statements of all witnesses, including the appellee's president and its surveyor, as well as the appellant and his corroborating witness. In addition, Hutzler, his son and others familiar with the tracts involved, testified, without contradiction, to the continuous use of the road for more than seventy years. Finally, it was virtually stipulated that the private way connected with a public road and the appellee offered nothing to rebut the appellant's unequivocal proof that there was no other reasonable means of ingress and egress to the 105 acre tract. These circumstances patently establish the essential elements of both an easement by prescription and a way of necessity. However, the general rule is that these two easements are distinguished one from the other since they arise by virtue of different and mutually exclusive conditions. Thus, the existence of a prescriptive easement negates the requisite necessity for a way of necessity. Similarly, if a way of necessity exists, its use is not adverse so as to confer a prescriptive right. 25 Am. Jur. 2d Easements and Licenses §§34 & 47 (1966).

In order to establish an easement by prescription, the use of a private way over the land of another must be continuous and uninterrupted for a period of ten years under a bona fide claim of right, adverse to the owner of the land, and with his knowledge and silence. [Citations omitted.] It is apparent from the authorities that, in the absence of a higher right, the evidence of the case at bar pertaining to an easement by prescription clearly establishes the appellant's right to such easement for the use of a private way over the land of the appellant.

Notwithstanding the fact that the record developed below is sufficient to support the finding of a prescriptive easement in favor of the appellant the evidence also establishes a way of necessity. As was noted above, it was essentially stipulated that the tracts owned by the parties were at a prior time a part of a larger tract owned by the same person. Thus, by definition, the parties derived their respective titles from a common source. This fact is essential to demonstrate a way of necessity inasmuch as it cannot exist if the two tracts had never shared common ownership. 2 Thompson, Real Property §363 (1961 Repl. Vol.).

The rationale behind the way of necessity is that the law implies an easement over the servient estate when the grantor owns and conveys a portion of the original lands without expressly providing a means of ingress and egress. This reasoning is reflected in Syllabus point 2 in Gwinn v. Gwinn, 77 W. Va. 281, 87 S.E. 371 (1915): "A way of necessity exists where land granted is completely environed by land of the grantor, or partially by his land and the land of strangers. The law implies from these facts that a private right of way over the grantor's land was granted to the grantee as appurtenant to the estate." In order for a way of necessity to be created or established there must be a reasonable necessity for an easement over the lands of a grantor for the grantee or his successors to have access to a public road and to thereby have full use of the lands conveyed. [Citations omitted.]

A way of necessity having been created by implication for the benefit of the grantee of the dominant estate or his successors, thereafter, it cannot be extinguished so long as the necessity continues to exist. [Citations omitted.]

Applying the applicable principles outlined above to the evidence developed in the trial court, this Court concludes that the appellant has demonstrated the requisite elements of a way of necessity over the land of the appellee. It is not questioned that the parties derived their title to the lands in question from a common source and all the evidence introduced by both the plaintiff and the defendant confirms the fact that there is no reasonable way for the appellant to obtain access to a public way except over the road in question.

It is contended by the appellee that it purchased the 550 acre tract of land without any notice of the existence of an easement over such land, and as a consequence, any easement which the appellant may have had was therefore extinguished. We reject this argument. In the first place, the evidence indicates that the appellee, through its president and its surveyor, was aware of the existence of the roadway in question. The statements of both of these witnesses clearly showed their knowledge that there was a trail or old road on the line where the appellant claimed his easement to be. On this set of facts, it is apparent that the appellee had actual notice of the existence of the easement and there was no extinguishment by virtue of the purchase of the servient estate. Even if it were assumed that the appellee had no notice of the existence of the roadway, it could not prevail. The rule that a bona fide purchaser for value who takes the servient estate without knowledge of an existing easement is relieved of a prescriptive easement does not apply to a way of necessity. A way of necessity exists in favor of a dominant estate whether it is used or not, since, as has been previously stated, the implied easement continues so long as the necessity exists. [Citations omitted.]

Having determined that the record of the trial court below sustains the conclusion that the appellant demonstrated an easement, either by prescription or by necessity, and that the appellee acquired its land with actual notice of the easement, it remains only to determine, as between the two possibilities, which easement is most consonant with the evidence. We are of the opinion that the proof, taken as a whole, more directly supports the implied easement than the prescriptive right. Therefore, we hold that the appellant is entitled to use the roadway across the appellee's land as a way of necessity to and from his 105 acre tract.

The judgment of the Circuit Court of Berkeley County is, therefore, reversed and judgment is entered here for the appellant.

Reversed and judgment entered here.

NOTES AND QUESTIONS

1. **Reasonable enjoyment of the landlocked estate.** The Restatement of Servitudes, §2.15, provides for an implied servitude "necessary to reasonable enjoyment" of the [landlocked] parcel. Suppose, after the decision in *Berkeley Development Corp.*, all of the timber on the Hutzler parcel is removed, and Hutzler now wishes to build an industrial park, which would increase several-fold the volume of traffic across the servient estate. Might this heavier traffic volume be enjoined? Might your answer be different if Hutzler held a prescriptive easement rather than a servitude by necessity?

Although access rights (to a public highway) are the most common form of a servitude by necessity, the conveyance of a profit will include a right of access to the subject of the profit, and the division of property into horizontal estates, such as the surface and mineral right, will include implied servitudes for access from the surface estate to the estate below the ground. Id. at §2.15, T.D. No. 1, at 186 (1989).

2. **Common ownership of the two parcels.** At trial, the parties stipulated that the two tracts were originally owned by one party, Moses Grantham. Proof that there was at one time a unity of ownership of the two parcels is a vital element in establishing a servitude by necessity. Restatement, Servitudes, §2.15, comment c. Why should this be?

3. **Severance must have caused the necessity.** The Restatement also asserts that the servitude can arise only when severance of the two parcels creates the necessity. Id. The Restatement (§2.15, illus. 9) gives the following example:

> O, the owner of two contiguous parcels, conveyed Blackacre to A. At the time of the conveyance, there was an easement appurtenant to Blackacre for access to a public highway across the land of X, a stranger. O's remaining parcel, Whiteacre, abutted on a public highway. When X later extinguished Blackacre's easement by adverse user, the owner of Blackacre had no right to cross Whiteacre to reach the public road. Since the conveyance from O to A did not deprive Blackacre of access to a public way, there was no implied servitude for access.

Compare Finn v. Williams, 376 Ill. 95, 33 N.E.2d 226 (1941). In 1895, Charles Williams owned a 140-acre tract. He sold off a 40-acre parcel to the plaintiff's predecessor. At the time, this parcel had passage across other lands to a public highway. Forty years later this access was lost. Plaintiff thereupon sued to establish a right-of-way by necessity across the 100-acre parcel that Williams had retained. Held: an easement by necessity was implied in the

1895 conveyance. That the grantee had other passage to a highway across strangers' lands was immaterial. When the passage was lost, grantee (and his successors) might avail themselves of the *dormant* easement implied in the deed severing the dominant and servient estates.

Which view do you prefer, that of the Restatement or Finn v. Williams? Might this depend upon your choice between the two theories that undergird the servitude by necessity? See note 5, *infra.*

4. **Historical roots.** One writer traces the doctrine of servitude by necessity at least as far back as the reign of Edward I (1272-1307), citing a contemporary text as stating: "Note that the law is that anyone who grants a thing to someone is understood to grant that without which the thing cannot be or exist." For a leisurely journey through the centuries, see Simonton, Ways by Necessity, 25 Colum. L. Rev. 571 (1925).

5. **Competing theories.** Courts have voiced two quite different theories to explain the servitude by necessity doctrine. One view regards the servitude as a subset of the implied servitude, a carrying out of the parties' presumed intent when the landlocked parcel was first granted or reserved: "And although it is called a way of necessity, yet in strictness the necessity does not create the way, but merely furnishes evidence as to the real intent of the parties. For the law will not presume that it was the intention of the parties, that one should convey land to the other, in such a manner that the grantee could derive no benefit from the conveyance; nor that he should so convey a portion as to deprive himself of the enjoyment of the remainder. The law, under such circumstances, will give effect to the grant according to the presumed intent of the parties." Collins v. Prentice, 15 Conn. 39, 44 (1842).

The second view regards presumed intent as nonessential: "[The foundation of this rule regarding ways of necessity is said to be] a fiction of the law [wherein] there is an implied reservation or grant to meet a special emergency, on grounds of public policy . . . in order that no land should be left inaccessible for purposes of cultivation." Buss v. Dyer, 125 Mass. 287, 291 (1878).

The Restatement of Servitudes elaborates the public policy rationale as avoiding "the costs involved if the property is deprived of rights necessary to make it useable, whether the result is that it remains unused, or that the owner incurs the costs of acquiring rights from land owners who are in a position to demand an extortionate price because of their monopolistic position." Id. at §2.15 (T.D. 1, at 185 (1989)). While recognizing the "force" of both justifications, the Restatement strikes a balance in favor of the parties "presumed intent." Ibid.

6. **Contrary intent.** Suppose in *Berkeley Development Corp.,* that the common owner, Moses Grantham, had barred any passage across the 550 acres that Grantham retained when he sold the 105 acres to Hutzler's predecessor: Would this have changed the result? The Restatement, and most courts, take the position that a servitude would not arise if there was a "clear

indication," from the conveyance or circumstances, that no servitude was intended. Id. at 184, 201-203.

7. **Statutory servitude by necessity.** Statutes in many states give private owners of landlocked parcels the right to acquire a way of necessity over neighboring lands without satisfying the common-law requirement of common ownership. The "condemnee," however, is usually entitled to fair (just) compensation. See, e.g., Okla. Stat. Ann. tit. 27, §6 (West 1991); Franks v. Tyler, 531 P.2d 1067 (Okla. App. 1974). Even if fair compensation is paid to the owner of the servient estate, the statute may yet be vulnerable to the claim that it authorizes the taking of private property for a private purpose. See Estate of Waggoner v. Gleghorn, 378 S.W.2d 47 (Tex. 1964).

e.   Servitude Implied from General Plan

"In modern practice, the developer [of a planned subdivision] normally files a declaration that sets forth the servitudes that will be imposed to implement the general plan. That declaration normally includes a description of the land covered by the plan, a description of the servitudes binding each lot, and a statement that the servitudes run with the land and run to the benefit of every lot in the plan. The declaration becomes effective to create the reciprocal servitudes for the entire development when the first lot is conveyed subject to its terms. . . . This practice has become so common that it justifies the assumption that . . . reciprocal servitudes may be implied if they have not been expressly created." Restatement, Servitudes, §2.14, Comment a. "This doctrine prevents the developer from conveying lots free of the restrictions imposed on the earlier purchasers, and from developing the remaining lots in ways that would violate those restrictions." Id. at Comment b.

NOTES AND QUESTIONS

1. **Existence of a general plan.** Although the presence of a general plan is usually clear, cases may still arise where the subdivider has acted ambiguously, and a court must decide, often years later, whether a common plan was ever intended. The classic, now somewhat dated, case of Sanborn v. McLean, 233 Mich. 227, 206 N.W. 496 (1925), illustrates the issue: There the McLaughlins opened a 91-lot subdivision in which one-family residences were built on every lot. However, only some of the original deeds contained "residential only" restrictions and the argument was made, 30 years later, that the subdividers' failure consistently to include the restrictions showed the lack of a general plan. The Sanborn court rejected the claim and found that a common plan existed from the outset, that the transfer of the first lots subject to the plan created a reciprocal "negative easement" on every other lot, and that current purchasers, including the defendants, had no-

tice of the common plan from the uniform residential character of the subdivision.

Warren v. Detlefsen, 281 Ark. 196, 663 S.W.2d 710 (1984), is a more recent example. Here, a court enjoined the developer from building duplexes on his retained lots by reason of a servitude implied from the presence of single-family restrictions in the deeds to 7 of 9 lots in Unit One, to 13 of 21 lots in Unit Two, and to 12 of 20 lots in Unit 3. Other evidence of the general plan included a master plat map on the wall of the developer's office, and his oral assurances that he would construct only single-family homes. Accord: Citizens for Covenant Compliance v. Anderson, 12 Cal.4th 345, 906 P.2d 1314 (1995) (common plan declaration filed, but not mentioned in deed).

Compare these cases, however, with Steinmann v. Silverman, 14 N.Y.2d 243, 200 N.E.2d 192, 251 N.Y.S.2d 1 (1964). Between 1947 and 1955, O conveyed 20 parcels adjoining Treasure Lake to various persons, including plaintiff. Each deed restricted the plot to a single residence. In 1957, O sold a nearby parcel to defendant, whose deed carried the same restriction. Defendant's parcel already held a house and barn. When defendant began to convert the barn into the second dwelling on the parcel, plaintiff sued to enforce the restriction. The court of appeals (three judges dissenting) overturned the lower court injunction; the court found no common scheme with respect to the covenant.

O had never filed a map in the county clerk's office, although he had prepared a map showing the development of numerous parcels. Evidently O did not show the map to any purchaser. The court stressed that only four of O's deeds referred to a development plan, that the parcels were of varying shapes and sizes and spread out in no discernible pattern, and that (concurring opinion) O retained the privilege to decide as he went along where to fix the lot lines.

2. **Affirmative obligations.** General plan cases usually involve suits to enforce use restrictions. Shalimar Assn. v. D.O.C. Enters., Ltd., 142 Ariz. 36, 688 P.2d 682 (1984), is striking because the defendants, the new owners of a golf course, not only were barred, under the general plan theory, from using the golf course site for any other purpose, but also were required to maintain the golf course for years to come.

The land development consisted of a golf course and adjacent residential lots, but no restrictions were ever recorded against the golf course property itself (sometimes referred to as "Tract A"). The course was actually built, however, and operated for nearly 20 years when the defendants purchased it and proposed a conversion from golf course use that would triple the property's value.

Many factors led to the conclusion that the golf course was an integral part of the general plan. These included:

1. The recorded restrictions for the residential lots referred to "Tract A" as the site of a golf course "which may be constructed."

2. Brochures provided to lot purchasers showed a golf course sur-
    rounded by numbered home lots.
3. Lot sales were made with oral representations that the golf course
    would be maintained as such until the year 2000, with provision
    for an extension of 25 years.
4. The sales materials stated that "all residents of the subdivision will
    have access [to the golf course] by membership."

§7.4   Interpretation and Scope of Servitudes

Servitudes, nowadays, are generally valid unless they offend public policy,
violate a statute or regulation, or infringe a constitutionally protected right.
Restatement, Servitudes, §3.1 (T.D. 2, 1991). Later we shall examine these
limits more closely. And, in doing so, we shall see that not so long ago, this
broad concession to private choice, except for easement-like servitudes,
would have seemed quite remarkable.

Even when it is clear that a valid servitude exists, courts still play an
active role in resolving disputes over the servitude's meaning and scope.
These disputes often involve the location and the duration of the servitude,
and the use rights that the servitude confers. The materials that follow illustrate each of these sets of issues.

a.   Location and Dimensions of the Servitude

UMPHRES v. J. R. MAYER ENTERPRISES, INC.

889 S.W.2d 86 (Mo. Ct. App. 1994)

PUDLOWSKI, J.

This is an appeal from an action in equity seeking an injunction to
restore a roadway, once located over a prescriptive easement, to its original
location. Despite certain wrongful actions taken by owners of the servient
land, the trial court denied a request by the owners of the dominant land
for an injunction to restore the road to its original location and instead
awarded money damages to the owners of the dominant land because their
insignificant injuries did not warrant an injunction which would work great
hardship on the servient landowners. We affirm.

On September 9, 1948, John A. and Alma J. Keller acquired five acres
of a ten acre tract in west St. Louis County owned by Albert and Ida Jacobs.
On August 16, 1950, Sam and Nora Umphres acquired the Kellers' five acre
tract. The five acres are now owned by appellants Nora and James Umphres.

The original 1948 deed from the Jacobs to the Kellers, appellants' predecessors in interest, described an "easement" ten feet wide, running north and south along the eastern line of the five acre tract. The deed was recorded. The land described by the deed as an "easement" was not owned by the Jacobs, the grantors, but rather by Arthur and Hilda Ray, the predecessors in interest of the respondents. No evidence exists whether or not the Jacobs had an interest in the "easement" described in the deed of 1948 over the Rays' land. Nor is there any proof that there ever was a road located within the bounds of the "easement" described in the deed.

An actual gravel road did exist nearby, however, and had been there at least since 1950. Most of the road ran just east of the land described in the 1948 deed. It ran over the Rays' property in 1950 and was used continuously by the appellants Umphres through 1987, for purposes of access to their property. It appears that the deed of 1948 was referring to this existing road, but misdescribed its location.

Mr. J. Randall Mayer, a developer and president of respondent J. R. Mayer Enterprises, Inc., constructed homes on land formerly owned by the Rays as part of a subdivision development. Both the actual road and the "easement" property described in the deed of 1948 ran across three of the lots upon which homes were constructed. These lots, numbered 52, 53, and 54, and the homes constructed on them now belong respectively to respondents Mr. and Mrs. Greco, Mr. and Mrs. Hairisine, and Mr. and Mrs. Cook.

In mid-1987 Mr. Mayer approached appellants, the Umphres, requesting their consent to move the existing roadway farther west, closer to the appellants' property line. Appellants refused. Appellants received a letter dated November 2, 1987 from respondent Mayer Enterprises' attorney that the roadway would be relocated on November 6, 1987, despite appellants' objections. Appellants filed this suit on November 4, 1987, requesting reformation of the deed of 1948 and a temporary restraining order against the repositioning of the road.

On November 4, 1987, Judge Kenneth Weinstock of the Circuit Court of St. Louis County denied the appellants' request for a temporary restraining order. On November 6, as planned, respondent Mayer relocated most of the roadway ten to twelve feet to the west of its original position. The new road lies approximately within the bounds of the "easement" description in the deed of 1948. The new road is also made of gravel and dirt, and is in most ways similar to the old road, except that it makes a slight bend at its northernmost point, is slightly narrower, is intersected by a new subdivision street, and has suffered from lack of maintenance for the last several years. Since the relocation of the road to its present westerly location, the owners of lots 52 through 54 have placed items such as fences, hedges, gardens, and swing sets over land once occupied by the old road.

This cause in equity was heard by Judge Charles B. Blackmar, and he found that appellants held a valid prescriptive easement over the land once

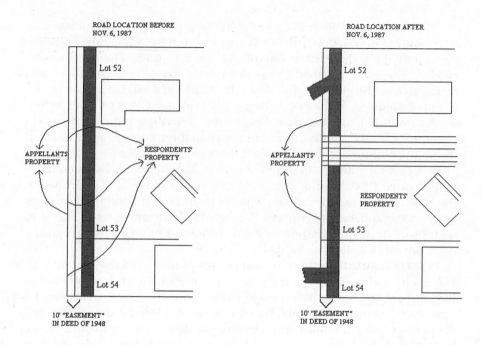

occupied by the old roadway and that the removal of the road abridged appellants' legal rights. Judge Blackmar, however, also found that the appellants' injury was compensable by money damages, and awarded them $7,500.00 to be paid by respondent Mayer Enterprises in lieu of the requested injunction to relocate the road.

The Umphres now appeal this judgment alleging that the trial court erred in determining that injunctive relief was not appropriate. The Umphres stress that injunctive relief is warranted in light of the fact that respondents willfully encroached upon the easement. Respondents deny that the trial court erred in its selection of the remedy. Additionally, respondent J. R. Mayer Enterprises, Inc. cross appeals that the trial court erred in its determination that a prescriptive easement exists over the land once occupied by the old road because such use was permissive at the outset. We will address the cross appeal first. . . . We conclude that a valid prescriptive easement existed over the location once occupied by the old roadway.

Respondents caused a legal injury to appellants by their relocation of the roadway. Once the boundaries of an easement are defined through use, those boundaries cannot be changed without the consent of all parties. Bladdick v. Ozark Ore Co., 381 S.W.2d 760, 765-66 (Mo. 1964). A prescriptive easement is defined solely by its use during the prescriptive period. Curran v. Bowen, 753 S.W.2d 940, 943 (Mo. App. E.D. 1988). Therefore, after the prescriptive period, the boundaries of a prescriptive easement may not be changed without the consent of all parties. Id. It is undisputed that respondents blocked off the old roadway with fences and hedges, altered its shape, and moved it several feet to the west without consent of appellants. Consequently, we agree with the trial court that appellants suffered a legal wrong.

The more pressing issue is whether equitable relief is appropriate to address this wrong. The trial court determined that equitable relief was not warranted here, and instead awarded money damages. We agree with this disposition. Equitable relief is discretionary, extraordinary, and should not be applied when an adequate legal remedy exists. Harris v. Union Elec. Co., 766 S.W.2d 80, 86 (Mo. banc 1989). Nor should equitable relief be granted when the injury is small. RFS, Inc. v. Cohen, 772 S.W.2d 713, 718 (Mo. App. E.D. 1989). To determine appropriate relief in cases involving the use and enjoyment of easements, Missouri courts examine the benefits to the party claiming injunctive relief against the burdens to the other parties. Hubert v. Magidson, 243 S.W.2d 337, 343 (Mo. 1951). We also consider the willfulness of the parties' wrongful actions. Hanna v. Nowell, 330 S.W.2d 595, 603 (Mo. App. 1959).

In this case, the injury to appellants appears to be small. Nothing in the record shows that the route of the old roadway was unique or valuable to the appellants. Nor have appellants averred any loss in value to their estate because of the changes. As the trial court found, the undesirable aspects of the new road stem largely from the lack of maintenance on the road and from minor construction defects, which can be corrected and/or compensated with the awarded sum of $7,500.00. In judge tried equity cases, we afford trial judges considerable deference on conclusions of fact. Here, we find that the weight of the evidence supports the finding that the injury to appellants was due chiefly to lack of maintenance and minor construction defects, and is compensable for $7,500.00.

The hardship to respondents, however, is much more substantial. If a mandatory injunction to move the road were granted, those respondents now living on the subdivided servient land would lose large portions of their yards, fences, plants, gardens, and childrens' play areas.

Appellants rightly point out that much of respondents' hardship was self-imposed. Respondent Mayer Enterprises moved the road, and other respondents made the new uses of the land while this lawsuit was pending. Appellants assert that these affirmative, intentional steps taken by respondents should extinguish any equitable considerations in their favor.

We agree that these intentional actions should weigh against respondents in equitable determination. Hanna v. Nowell, 330 S.W.2d 595, 603 (Mo. App. 1959). However, we do not agree that this factor alone must dictate the outcome of our equitable inquiry. Appellants cite two foreign cases for the proposition that no balancing should take place when a party intentionally and wrongfully makes expensive changes to an easement: LeClerg v. Zaia, 28 Ill. App. 3d 738, 328 N.E.2d 910 (1975), and Ives v. Edison, 124 Mich. 402, 83 N.W. 120 (1900). While we recognize the policy against allowing people to profit by their unjust trespasses which is expressed by these cases, we decline to lay down a blanket rule which would eliminate the traditional balance of the equities test, even under these circumstances. Courts in equity must remain free to consider all equitable considerations and to fashion flexible remedies to meet the needs of justice on a case by case basis. We fear that the blanket rule urged by appellants would overly restrict Missouri courts in equity.

The present action illustrates the case against a blanket rule that any intentional act by a party must bar all equitable considerations in his or her favor. In this case respondent Mayer Enterprises moved the road while this lawsuit was pending. This act, although intentional, was not so malicious that it should force an automatic injunction against the buyers of the lots and homes. Respondent Mayer Enterprises built the new road on a location which more perfectly fit the description in the recorded 1948 deed, under which appellants had originally claimed their interest in this lawsuit. It was substantially similar to and served the same purposes as the old road, and both roads traversed only the servient land. Although ultimately disproved in court, respondents' position was colorable under the terms of the deed of 1948. We agree with the trial court that respondents' actions were not so unclean as to warrant a court to turn its back on all other equitable considerations.

Judgment affirmed.

NOTES AND QUESTIONS

1. **May the servient owner unilaterally relocate the servitude?** Black-letter law, as stated in the *Umphres* opinion, is that the location of an easement cannot be changed without the mutual consent of the parties. The Restatement of Servitudes rejects the common law and allows the holder of the servient estate to make "reasonable changes" in the location or dimensions of an easement "when necessary to permit normal use or development of the servient estate" if the changes:

    (a) do not significantly lessen the utility of the servitude, or
    (b) increase the burdens on the holder of the servitude benefit, or
    (c) frustrate the purpose for which the servitude was created, and
    (d) the holder of the servient estate bears the expenses of making the changes.

Id. at §4.8.

Paradoxically, even though the *Umphres* court pays lip service to the black-letter, it seems to have outdone the Restatement by allowing the servient owner to act unilaterally: in short, while the court protects the appellants' entitlement to the status quo, it does so with a liability, not a property, rule.

Are you persuaded that either the *Umphres* court or the Restatement has it right?

Criticism of the Restatement position appears in Note, The Right of Owners of Servient Estates to Relocate Easements Unilaterally, 109 Harv. L. Rev. 1693 (1996).

2. **May the servitude holder unilaterally relocate the servitude?** One might suppose that any sauce for the goose would also be served for the gander: that the Restatement would allow the servitude holder unilaterally to relocate the easement where this would not increase the burden on the owner of the servient estate and would significantly increase the utility of the servitude.

The Restatement sees the two situations differently and fails to extend §4.8 to benefit the servitude holder. Id. at Comment f. Here, it follows the generally accepted rule barring unilateral moves. See, e.g., Bradley v. Arkansas Louisiana Gas Co., 280 Ark. 492, 659 S.W.2d 180 (1983) (holder of pipeline easement not entitled to relocate line 100 feet south of existing right-of-way).

Do you also see the two situations differently?

3. **Practical location of easements.** In cases where an easement is granted but its exact location is unspecified, practical use fixes the location. See, e.g., Bosley v. Cabot Oil & Gas Corp. 624 F. Supp. 1174 (S.D. W. Va. 1986). Suppose that O grants E an easement across O's land at one location, and without objection from O, E places the right-of-way five feet easterly of where it should be. Should the *Bosley* rule extend to the hypothetical case of an inaccurately placed right-of-way?

b. Duration of Servitude

Except for statutory limitations,[46] the parties creating a servitude usually have complete initial control over the servitude's duration. Thus, they may agree that it will be perpetual, or that it will terminate in X years, when a stated event occurs, when a specified purpose is accomplished, or, as is often done in condominiums and residential subdivisions, when a stated percentage of the benefited owners agree.

Servitudes by necessity last as long as the necessity continues. Restatement of Servitudes, §4.3. Thus, if the dominant estate acquires another permanent means of access, an easement by necessity expires. Servitudes that

---

46. For instance, some states require that historic preservation and conservation servitudes be perpetual. See, e.g., Cal. Civ. Code §815.2(b) (West 1995). For some other examples, see Restatement, Servitudes (T.D. 4, 1994), at 45-46.

are personal to the servitude holder can last no longer than the beneficiary's life.

c.   Scope of Servitude

Some of the most vexing disputes arise over the manner, frequency,
and intensity of the servitude's use. Because the language used to create a
servitude (vis., "30 foot-wide trail," etc.) can often be rather vague, and
because drafters often fail to anticipate technological change or normal
development, years later the present owners of the servitude and the servient estate may be at loggerheads as to what use, exactly, the servitude permits. Not every dispute, thankfully, evokes quite the passion as the one that
follows.

[handwritten: Abuse of Trial by others Brought Closure by Cleland]

SIDES v. CLELAND

436 Pa. Super. 618, 648 A.2d 793 (1994)

OLSZEWSKI, J.:

All of the litigants to this dispute live on Hill Island in the Susquehanna
River. The island houses few permanent residents, is largely recreational,
and has gained a reputation for the occupants' somewhat riotous behavior.[1]
Vacationers and residents alike ride motorcycles and all-terrain vehicles
over the mountainous land. When George and Alice Cleland purchased
their riverfront property in 1983, their tract was undeveloped; the foliage
provided a place for the Cleland family to discover the wonders of nature.
Only one thing prevented the property from remaining in its pristine state:
a recorded plan established a right-of-way over the Clelands' property. It is
the scope of this right-of-way that is at issue in this suit. *[handwritten margin note: ISSUE]*

The plan describes the right-of-way as a "logging trail," but also refers
to it as a "30 foot trail," which is expressly designated for the "common use
of the residents of Hill Island." When the Clelands bought the property,
the trail was covered by forestation and used by no one. This did not last
long, however, as the Clelands, in order to appreciate nature's full beauty,
cleared part of the trail as a footpath. Several years later, in 1990, the Clelands granted one of the plaintiffs, Geary Huntsberger, the right to clear a
path wide enough for vehicles to pass; he wanted to drill a well on his property and found that the trail would provide the most direct route by which

---

1. One of the plaintiffs, Tildon "Butch" Sides, acknowledged that this reputation has
earned the island the cognomen "The Land of Beer and Honey."

he could transport his equipment.[2] What Cleland saw as a favor, however, led to the industrialization of the trail. Although it is still described by many of the islanders as "basically a dirt road," the inhabitants poured shale and other rock debris over the road to prepare it for vehicular use.

The once idyllic condition of the trail traversing the Clelands' property quickly became symbolic of man's excesses: the neighbors and their vacationers drive their motorcycles at dangerous speeds across the Clelands' property. Young children (one was seven years old) ride cycles there. Inhabitants throw beer parties and permit their guests to ride the trail after drinking. All of this was too much for Mr. Cleland. He feared for his family's safety and was annoyed by the use of the trail at all hours of the day and night. He undertook a concerted effort to stop the abuses being wrought upon his land by erecting a fence across the right of way. He did not lock the fence, but erected it to keep the cyclists from travelling at dangerous speeds. He later felled a large tree across the trail and refused to remove it.

Cleland's efforts were not accepted by the neighbors. They claimed that they had a right to use the designated trail for any purpose they saw fit. One of the neighbors (it is unclear from the record exactly who) removed the fence and Geary Huntsberger corralled a group of inhabitants to vindicate their right to use the trail — he wanted to forcibly remove the Clelands' felled tree. Knowing that his vigilantism would not be met without resistance, he asked one of his gang to videotape the confrontation and two of his band to arm themselves with chainsaws. When the group arrived at the Clelands' property, Cleland perched himself in the tree. "Bring on the chainsaws!" Huntsberger cried. The sawyers began to cut around the tree, but after noticing Cleland's resolve, stopped when it was clear that he would not budge.[3] Cleland's resistance, however, did nothing to deter this lawsuit.

Cleland's neighbors, the Sides, and several other Hill Island inhabitants brought this suit in equity. They sought an injunction prohibiting the Clelands from interfering with their use of the trail. The Clelands countersued asking that use of the trail be limited to ingress and egress by abutting property owners and for compensation for damages caused by plaintiffs' trespasses. Mr. Cleland also claimed that he was assaulted by Mr. Huntsberger during the confrontation over the felled tree. After hearing two days of testimony, viewing the videotape, and actually visiting the trail to evaluate its present condition, the Honorable Sebastian Natale found the facts as we

---

2. No one in this case argues that the right-of-way, which essentially runs parallel to the island's beach, is necessary for ingress and egress to other properties from the beach. It appears that using the right-of-way makes it easier for the adjoining property owners to reach their fellow islanders' property without having to navigate the river.

3. The videotape was admitted into evidence at the trial, and we are urged to view it. Much to our chagrin, however, it has not been certified as part of the record on appeal. As a result, we reconstruct the scene from the trial court's findings of fact and evidence at trial, which surely does not capture the confrontation's true drama.

described them and concluded that the trail's current use is unreasonable. He therefore decreed that although Hill Island's residents had a right to use the trail, it would be "restricted to daylight walking [and] vehicles travelling no more than ten miles per hour," and that plaintiffs were enjoined from doing any further damage to the land. Judge Natale also held that Mr. Huntsberger assaulted Mr. Cleland, but that Mr. Cleland suffered no compensable damage.

We begin by noting that where a deed incorporates a plan which makes specific reference to a right of way, an easement is implied over that property. Reed v. Reese, 473 Pa. 321, 374 A.2d 665 (1976); Potis v. Coon, 344 Pa. Super. 443, 496 A.2d 1188 (1985); see also, McAndrews v. Spencer, 447 Pa. 268, 290 A.2d 258 (1972) (easement implied over road which bounded property where recorded plan incorporated road, even though road was never dedicated for public use). There is thus no question, and no one argues to the contrary, that the plan creates a private right in each of Hill Island's residents to use the trail on the Clelands' property. The Clelands' deed specifically refers to the plan which adopts the trail as one for the "common use" of the residents of Hill Island. Appellants, plaintiffs below, complain that Judge Natale erred in enjoining them from further developing the trail and limiting its use to daylight walking and slow moving vehicles. Their biggest gripe is that Judge Natale's restrictions were based on his view of how the trail is used today instead of what the grantor contemplated when the trail was created. We disagree.

Our review of the plan and the deeds in this case leads to the inescapable conclusion that the plan is ambiguous with regard to the trail's contemplated purpose. The plan refers to the trail as a "logging trail," but also refers to it as a "30 foot trail," which is held for the "common use" of the residents. We quite agree that the term "common use" contemplates something more than logging, since the island was developed as a residential and recreational community. We must thus determine why the trail was created in the first place, and reference to the plan alone offers little conclusive help. As was stated in Lease v. Doll, 485 Pa. 615, 403 A.2d 558 (1979), the circumstances attendant to the easement's creation are important when defining the easement's purpose:

> In ascertaining the scope of an easement created by express grant, the intention of the parties to the grant must be advanced. "Such intention [of the parties] is determined by a fair interpretation and construction of the grant and may be shown by the words employed construed with reference to the attending circumstances known to the parties at the time the grant was made." Moreover, when the terms of an express grant of an easement are general, ambiguous, and not defined by reference to the circumstances known to the grantee at the time of the grant, the express easement is to be construed in favor of the grantee, and the easement may be used in any manner that is reasonable.

Id. at 621, 403 A.2d at 562-563 (quoting Merrill v. Mfgrs. Light and Heat Co., 409 Pa. 68, 73, 185 A.2d 573, 575 (1962)) (other citations omitted).

Here, the trial court made reasonable efforts to determine the intent of the parties when the easement was created. It reviewed the maps, heard testimony from the parties with regard to the customary use of the trail, and actually viewed the trail in its current state. Although there was scant evidence with respect to the actual grant of the residents' trail, plaintiffs presented a land surveyor, Charles Cook, who surveyed the property in 1991. He stated that when he surveyed the property, he saw what he considered "just a dirt road" which "looked more like what I would consider a logging trail." N.T. 4/8/92 at 78. Nearly every person who testified, moreover, simply characterized the trail as "basically a dirt road." Geary Huntsberger, the Clelands' grantor and owner of the property when the original plan was filed, claimed that he did not even know that a trail existed until sometime in 1982, two years after the original plan was filed. Thus, we can hardly question the veracity of the Clelands' claim that the trail was undeveloped when they purchased their tract.

This testimony makes it abundantly clear that the "trail" reserved for the common use of Hill Island residents in the 1980 plan is nothing more than "a track made by passage through the wilderness." Webster's New Collegiate Dictionary (9th ed., 1984) (defining "trail"). As such, the grantees — the plaintiffs and Hill Island's residents — are entitled to use the trail in every manner consistent with a wilderness trail: they may walk on it and enjoy the natural setting of the island, they may use it reasonably to carry supplies from one person's tract to another's, or, if they so desire, use it in conjunction with their logging pursuits. It is not, therefore, a highway or a gathering place. Nor is it an amusement park where thrill seekers can drive all-terrain vehicles at potentially dangerous speeds at any time during the day and night. The trial court's prohibitions on plaintiffs' use of the trail — that they do no further damage to the Clelands' land, that they not drive vehicles over ten miles per hour, and that they walk on it only during the daylight hours — implements the intent behind the trail's creation by allowing the residents to use the trail and by preserving so much of its natural state that is consistent with that use. Judge Natale's decree gives plaintiffs everything to which they are entitled (use of the trail) and protects the Clelands' right to insist that the trail will be used reasonably.

Furthermore, we reject plaintiffs' contentions that the trial court focused on the current use of the trail to impose restrictions on its use. The trial court heard testimony from plaintiffs and everyone seemed to agree that the trail was "just a dirt road," and has been a dirt road from time immemorial. Geary Huntsberger testified that the trail, as it exists today, is "pretty well the same as when the first Indian walked down the trail." N.T., 4/8/92, at 110. Thus, when Judge Natale viewed the trail in 1994, he viewed the same trail, with minor exceptions, that was preserved in the

1980 plan. We have no reason to believe that Huntsberger's grantor contemplated preserving the trail for anything other than logging and reasonable recreational uses.[5] Again, Judge Natale's decree is consistent with this
contemplation.

Finally, we disagree with Geary Huntsberger's claim that the evidence
was insufficient to prove that he assaulted Mr. Cleland. An assault occurs
when an actor intends to cause an imminent apprehension of a harmful or
offensive bodily contact. Restatement (Second), of Torts, §21. When a person approaches another with two associates wielding chainsaws, screams
"Bring on the chainsaws!," to which the sawyers respond by dismembering
the tree in which the person sits, a factfinder could reasonably conclude
that an assault has occurred. Frankly, we are at a loss to understand how a
factfinder could arrive at any other conclusion.

Judge Natale's decree is affirmed in all respects.

POPOVICH, J., concurs in the result.

NOTES AND QUESTIONS

1. **Technological change.** The manner, frequency, and intensity of
the use of the servient estate may change to take advantage of new technology and to further the normal development of the dominant estate.
Restatement, Servitudes, §4.10 (T.D. 4, 1994). However, the Restatement
endorses only that change that does not "cause unreasonable damage to
the servient estate or interfere unreasonably with its enjoyment." Ibid. Inevitably, as in *Sides,* courts must often decide where to strike the balance.

Here are some instances of an existing servitude adapted to changed
technology: Hayes v. City of Loveland, 651 P.2d 466 (Colo. Ct. App. 1982)
(replacement of wooden power poles with taller steel structure); Hoffman
v. Capitol Cablevision Sys., 52 A.D.2d 313, 383 N.Y.S.2d 674 (1976) (addition of television cable to telephone-and-electric-line easement); Restatement, Servitudes, §4.10, Illus. 11 (T.D. 4, 1994) (easement for a "horse and
cart way," created in 1889 to provide access to rear of a commercial building, usable by motor vehicles).

Here are some instances where the owner of the servient estate was
able to show that the proposed change would cause unreasonable injury:
Hall v. City of Orlando, 555 So. 2d 963 (Fla. Dist. Ct. App. 1990) (installa-

---

5. We understand that when a grantor reserves a right-of-way for the public that he
envisions certain evolutionary advances which might effect its use. Thus, although we cannot
expect that many Indians rode all-terrain vehicles over the trail, such use might be appropriate
in 1994. Judge Natale's decree acknowledges this and permits vehicular traffic on the trail. He
has merely defined what "reasonable" use of the trail encompasses under the circumstances.
We have absolutely no reason to question the judge's perception.

tion of 54-inch drain pipe that could double flow of water over drainage easement); Stirling v. Dixie Elec. Membership Corp., 344 So. 2d 427 (La. Ct. App. 1977) (holder of easement for electric transmission line with express right to cut and trim shrubs as necessary not entitled to apply herbicide by helicopter so as to kill crops on other parts of the servient estate); Triplett v. Beuckman, 40 Ill. App. 3d 379, 352 N.W.2d 458 (1976) (holder of easement for roadway across bridge not able to replace bridge with causeway that interfered with servient owner's use of lake).

In setting the fulcrum to reflect the proper balancing of interests between the owners of the servitude and the servient estate, how should courts take into account whether the servitude is express, implied, created by necessity, or prescriptive?

2. **Development of the dominant estate.** What is normal or reasonable development of the dominant estate that would allow changed and, quite possibly, greater usage of the servient estate? Suppose that the dominant estate was originally undeveloped acreage in a rural area just beyond the city limits and, years later, is about to become a residential subdivision; see Restatement, Servitudes, §4.10, illus. 14 (T.D. 4, 1994) (normal development). Or suppose that the dominant estate was originally a large suburban residential lot and, years later, is about to become a factory site; id. at illus. 21 (not reasonable development). Or suppose that a new sand-and-gravel business is about to replace a slaughterhouse on the dominant estate; see Birdsey v. Kosienski, 140 Conn. 403, 101 A.2d 274 (1953) (reasonable development).

Once again, how should courts take into account the servitude's method of creation?

3. **Subdivision of the dominant estate.** Suppose that at Time 1, A and B own adjacent two-acre parcels, and that A, the owner of Greenacre, gives to B, the owner of Brownacre, a right of way across Greenacre for a sewerage line that connects to a public sewer. Some years later, B subdivides his acreage into five lots, and runs an intake line from the main trunk that connects with the newly built homes on each lot. Does the original servitude permit this multiple use?

Although the Restatement treats geographical subdivision of the benefited (and the burdened) lands as a discrete matter, it should not surprise you that the initial approach is quite similar — that is, absent contrary intent, multiple use that does not overburden the servient estate is permitted. However, the Restatement requires that the benefit be apportioned, where necessary, to avoid an unreasonable increase in the burden on the servient estate. Restatement, Servitudes, §5.7 (T.D. No. 5, 1995). The Restatement gives the following illustration:

> Blackacre is burdened by an easement for a roadway in favor of Whiteacre. Whiteacre is subdivided into 500 residential lots. If the increase in the burden

on Blackacre from use of the easement by all of the subdivided lots is unreasonable under the rules stated in §4.10,[47] the benefit may be apportioned to some of the lots to reduce the increase in burden to a reasonable level. If the subdivider of Whiteacre does not provide a method for limiting the number of lots benefited, the court may do so if there is a reasonable basis for the apportionment. If there is no reasonable basis for making an apportionment or if the increase in burden cannot realistically be prevented by apportionment, the easement may be terminated. . . .

§7.5   Validity of Servitude Arrangements

a.   Summary of the Traditional Law of Covenants

You have seen that the distinction between an affirmative easement and an affirmative covenant rests on what sort of duty faces the holder of the servient estate. In an affirmative (or negative) easement, the duty is passive, performed by *not* interfering with the servitude's benefit, in short, by doing nothing. By contrast, when the servient estate is subject to an affirmative covenant, the burdened party must take steps to perform its duty, for example, to pay an assessment or to maintain the property.

Many centuries ago, courts would sometimes regard the two forms of servitudes alike. Thus, a convent's covenant to sing in the manor chapel or a landowner's covenant to build a boundary fence was enforceable in the same way as an affirmative easement, that is, as an interest in property, binding against the original covenantor and, where the parties intended it, also against a successor with notice.[48] Had the courts broadened this tack, generations of law students would have been spared the agony (and, who can say, perhaps denied the ecstasy) of learning about affirmative covenants. But this was not to be.

Tenants, especially, often made affirmative covenants. A tenant's assurances to his feudal lord or a lessee's covenant to pay rent are two early

---

47. Section 4.10 reads:

Except where [the parties' intentions would lead] to a different result, the beneficiary of an easement or profit is entitled to make any use of the servient estate that is reasonably necessary for the convenient enjoyment of the servitude for its intended purpose. The manner, frequency, and intention of the beneficiary's use of the servient estate may change over time to take advantage of developments in technology and to accommodate normal development of the dominant estate or enterprise benefited by the servitude. The rules stated in this section are subject to the proviso that the servitude beneficiary is not entitled to cause unreasonable damage to the servient estate or interfere unreasonably with its enjoyment.

48. In his classic work on the English law of easements, Gale referred to the landowner's obligation to build and maintain a fence as a "spurious kind of easement." C. Gale, Easements 465 (8th ed. 1908).

examples. The common law at first treated these promises as personal un-
dertakings, binding on the covenantor (when sued by the covenantee), but
not binding on the covenantor's successor unless he renewed the promise.
Slowly the tradition changed, first as to feudal incidents — which disappeared with the end of feudalism — then as to some of the promises contained in a lease. Where it could be shown that the covenant's burden was
intended to bind assignees, the succeeding tenant was sometimes bound
whether or not he had personally assumed the promise.

By no means, however, was it every affirmative covenant whose burden would "run with the land." In an era when commerce in land was expanding, "dead weight" burdens on land became intolerable.[49] To sort out
covenants that ran, the "real covenants," from those that did not became a
challenge, initially, for the common-law courts, then, several centuries later,
for courts in equity.

The best way to summarize the traditional law of covenants is to start
with a situation where A and B sign an agreement that each will keep her
property in good repair. If A sues B, the cause of action is for contract. But
what if B sells her land to C, and then C refuses to maintain her property.
Then the issue is whether the agreement signed by A and B can bind their
successors, in this case C. The answer is that it can if the agreement runs
at law (creating a covenant at law) or in equity (creating an equitable
servitude).

As the common law of covenants evolved, different substantive tests
emerged depending on the remedy desired by the plaintiff. If he wanted
damages for violation of the covenant, the cause of action was for a *covenant
at law*. If he wanted an injunction to enforce the covenant, the cause of
action was for an *equitable servitude*.

1.   Covenant at law

The requirements that must be met for a covenant to run at law depend on whether the party is trying to enforce the "burden" or the "benefit" of the covenant. At issue here is whether the plaintiff or the defendant
is the successor (as opposed to one of the original covenanting parties).
Take the agreement between A and B to maintain their respective
properties.

Burden Running.   Say that B sells to C, who violates the covenant by refusing to maintain her property, and A wants to sue C for damages.

---

49. For a fair sample of the judicial attitude, albeit expressed several centuries later, see
Keppell v. Bailey, 2 My. & K. 517, 535, 39 Eng. Rep. 1042, 1049 (Ch. 1834): "[I]t must not
therefore be supposed that incidents of a novel kind can be devised and attached to property,
at the fancy or caprice of any owner."

A SIGNS AGREEMENT WITH   B "PROPERTY TO BE MAINTAINED"

π

C NEGLECTS PROPERTY
Δ

Since the defendant is the successor, the issue here is whether the *burden* of the covenant has run, or, to say it differently, whether the covenant burdens a successor who is not one of the original covenanting parties. The answer is that it does if A can prove:

(i) *Intent to bind successors.* Spencer's Case,[50] a late sixteenth-century Lord Coke decision, set the law of covenants on a course we have needed four hundred years to correct. The case involved a tenant's promise to build a brick wall, which the landlord was seeking to enforce against the tenant's assignee. In his opinion, the most famous jurist of his time laid down two rules, one minor, one far-reaching, that became part of the "modern" law of covenants.

The minor rule, one you may quickly forget, related to promises — such as the covenant to build a brick wall — about things not in being (the Latin: "not in esse") when the covenant was made. Lord Coke wrote that for such a covenant to bind an assignee, the covenant must declare, in *haec verba*, that assignees are to be bound.[51] Because the lease in Spencer's Case failed to use the correct verbiage, the promise to build the wall did not bind the assignee who had not agreed to be bound.

This first principle of Spencer's Case had an early following in this country — see, e.g., Lametti v. Anderson, 6 Cow. 302 (N.Y. 1826); Gulf, C. & S.F. Ry. v. Smith, 72 Tex. 122, 9 S.W. 865 (1888) — and even made its way into David Dudley Field's draft code (§695) and the state codes that Field influenced; see, e.g., Cal. Civ. Code §1464 (West 1954). But most courts have either rejected the doctrine or ignored it, and, today, one needs no special words, as to any servitude, to establish an intent to bind an assignee.[52] With respect to some of the more usual covenants in a lease or deed (e.g., covenant to pay rent), we usually presume this intention.

(ii) *Touch and concern.* The second principle of Spencer's Case began as dicta — since the plaintiff had lost already on the issue of intent, but it has clung to the law of covenants almost to the very present. This is the

---

50. 5 Co. Rep. 16a, 77 Eng. Rep. 72 (K.B. 1583).
51. The tenant had covenanted "for him, his executors, and administrators" that "he, his executors, administrators, or assigns" would build the brick wall. By failing to covenant also for his "assigns," the tenant was held not to have bound the assignee "by [the] express words" necessary to satisfy the first principle of Spencer's Case.
52. As a careful drafter, however, you will wish to be clear about your client's intention.

requirement that the covenant "touch or concern" the land. To quote Lord Coke:

> It was resolved that in this case, if the lessee had covenanted for him and his assigns, that they would make a new wall upon some part of the thing demised, that for as much as it is to be done upon the land demised, that it should bind the assignee. . . . But although the covenant be for him and his assigns, yet if the thing to be done be merely collateral to the land, and *doth not touch or concern* the thing demised in any sort, there the assignee shall not be charged.

Although formulated by Lord Coke in a lease dispute, the rule was later extended to fee covenants. To quote the Restatement of Servitudes, "the touch and concern doctrine . . . [provided] courts with a flexible, discretionary power to disallow servitudes . . . they found unwise or pernicious without articulating the policy reasons for their decisions." [53] The case below is a fairly recent example of how courts have used "touch and concern" to defeat servitude enforcement.

EAGLE ENTERPRISES, INC. v. GROSS

39 N.Y.2d 505, 349 N.E.2d 816, 384 N.Y.S.2d 717 (1976)

GABRIELLI, J. In 1951, Orchard Hill Realties, Inc., a subdivider and developer, conveyed certain property in the subdivision of Orchard Hill in Orange County to William and Pauline Baum. The deed to the Baums contained the following provision:

> The party of the first part shall supply to the party of the second part, seasonably, from May 1st to October 1st, of each year, water for domestic use only, from the well located on other property of the party of the first part, and the party of the second part agrees to take said water and to pay the party of the first part, a fee of Thirty-five ($35.00) dollars per year, for said water so supplied.

In addition, the deed also contained the following:

> It is expressly provided that the covenants herein contained shall run with the land . . . and shall bind and shall enure to the benefit of the heirs, distributees, successors, legal representatives and assigns of the respective parties hereto.

Appellant is the successor in interest of Orchard Hill Realties, Inc., and respondent, after a series of intervening conveyances, is the successor

---

53. Restatement, Property (Servitudes) (T.D. 2, 1991), at 20.

in interest of the Baums. The deed conveying title to respondent does not contain the afore-mentioned covenant to purchase water and, in fact, none of the deeds following the original deed to the Baums contained the mutual promises regarding water supply, While some of the deeds in the chain of title from Baum contained a provision that they were made subject to the restrictions in the deed from Orchard Hill Realities to Baum, the deed to respondents contained no such covenants, restrictions or "subject to" clause.

According to the stipulated facts, respondent has refused to accept and pay for water offered by appellant since he has constructed his own well to service what is now a year-round dwelling. Appellant, therefore, instituted this action to collect the fee specified in the covenant (contained only in the original deed to Baum) for the supply of water which, appellant contends, respondent is bound to accept. The action was styled as one "for goods sold and delivered" even though respondent did not utilize any of appellant's water. Two of the lower courts found that the covenant "ran" with the land and, hence, was binding upon respondent as successor to the Baums, but the Appellate Division reversed and held that the covenant could not be enforced against respondent. We must now decide whether the promise of the original grantees to accept and make payment for a seasonal water supply from the well of their grantor is enforceable against subsequent grantees and may be said to "run with the land." We agree with the determination of the Appellate Division and affirm its order.

Regardless of the express recital in a deed that a covenant will run with the land, a promise to do an affirmative act contained in a deed is generally not binding upon subsequent grantees of the promisor unless certain well-defined and long-established legal requisites are satisfied (Nicholson v. 300 Broadway Realty Corp., 7 N.Y.2d 240, 244; Neponsit Prop. Owners' Assn. v. Emigrant Ind. Sav. Bank, 278 N.Y. 248, 254-255; see, also, Morgan Lake Co. v. New York, New Haven & Hartford R. R. Co., 262 N.Y. 234, 239; Miller v. Clary, 210 N.Y. 127; Mygatt v. Coe, 147 N.Y. 456; 13 N.Y. Jur., Covenants and Restrictions, §12, pp. 252-253). In the landmark *Neponsit* case (*supra*), we adopted and clarified the following test, originating in the early English decisions, for the enforceability of affirmative covenants (cf. Spencer's Case, 77 Eng. Rep. 72 [1583]), and reaffirmed the requirements that in order for a covenant to run with the land, it must be shown that:

(1) The original grantee and grantor must have intended that the covenant run with the land.

(2) There must exist "privity of estate" between the party claiming the benefit of the covenant and the right to enforce it and the party upon whom the burden of the covenant is to be imposed.

(3) The covenant must be deemed to "touch and concern" the land with which it runs. (See, also, Nicholson v. 300 Broadway Realty Corp., *supra*; Restatement Property, §§531, 534, 537, 538; 13 N.Y. Jur. Covenants and Restrictions, §8, p. 248.)

Even though the parties to the original deed expressly state in the

instrument that the covenant will run with the land, such a recital is insufficient to render the covenant enforceable against subsequent grantees if
the other requirements for the running of an affirmative covenant are not
met. The rule is settled that "[r]egardless of the intention of the parties, a
covenant will run with the land and will be enforceable against a subsequent
purchaser of the land at the suit of one who claims the benefit of the covenant, only if the covenant complies with certain legal requirements" (*Neponsit, supra,* p. 254; see, also, Morgan Lake Co. v. New York, New Haven &
Hartford R. R. Co., *supra,* p. 238). Thus, although the intention of the original parties here is clear and privity of estate exists, the covenant must still
satisfy the requirement that it "touch and concern" the land.

It is this third prong of the tripartite rule which presents the obstacle
to appellant's position and which was the focus of our decisions in *Neponsit*
and Nicholson v. 300 Broadway Realty Corp. (7 N.Y.2d 240, 244, *supra*).
Neponsit first sought to breathe substance and meaning into the ritualistic
rubric that an affirmative covenant must "touch and concern" the land
in order to be enforceable against subsequent grantees. Observing that it
would be difficult to devise a rule which would operate mechanically to
resolve all situations which might arise, Judge Lehman observed that "the
distinction between covenants which run with land and covenants which
are personal, must depend upon the effect of the covenant on the legal
rights which otherwise would flow from the ownership of land and which
are connected with the land" (*Neponsit, supra,* p. 258). Thus, he posed as
the key question whether "the covenant in purpose and effect substantially
alter[s] these rights" (p. 258). In *Nicholson,* this court reaffirmed the soundness of the reasoning in *Neponsit* as "a more realistic and pragmatic approach" (*supra,* p. 245).

The covenants in issue in *Neponsit* required the owners of property in a
development to pay an annual charge for the maintenance of roads, paths,
parks, beaches, sewers, and other public improvements. The court concluded that the covenant substantially affected the promisor's legal interest
in his property since the latter received an easement in common and a right
of enjoyment in the public improvements for which contribution was received by all the landowners in the subdivision (*supra,* pp. 259-260).

A close examination of the covenant in the case before us leads to the
conclusion that it does not substantially affect the ownership interest of
landowners in the Orchard Hill subdivision. The covenant provides for the
supplying of water for only six months of the year; no claim has been advanced by appellant that the lands in the subdivision would be waterless
without the water it supplies. Indeed, the facts here point to the converse
conclusion since respondent has obtained his own source of water. The
record, based on and consisting of an agreed stipulation of facts, does not
demonstrate that other property owners in the subdivision would be deprived of water from appellant or that the price of water would become
prohibitive for other property owners if respondent terminated appellant's

service. Thus, the agreement for the seasonal supply of water does not seem
to us to relate in any significant degree to the ownership rights of respondent and the other property owners in the subdivision of Orchard Hill. The
landowners in *Neponsit* received an easement in common to utilize public
areas in the subdivision; this interest was in the nature of a property right
attached to their respective properties. The obligation to receive water
from appellant resembles a personal, contractual promise to purchase water rather than a significant interest attaching to respondent's property. It
should be emphasized that the question whether a covenant is so closely
related to the use of the land that it should be deemed to "run" with the
land is one of degree, dependent on the particular circumstances of a case
(*Neponsit, supra,* p. 258). Here, the meager record before us is lacking and
woefully insufficient to establish that the covenant "touches and concerns"
the land, as we have interpreted that requirement.

There is an additional reason why we are reluctant to enforce this
covenant for the seasonal supply of water. The affirmative covenant is disfavored in the law because of the fear that this type of obligation imposes
an "undue restriction on alienation or an onerous burden in perpetuity"
(Nicholson v. 300 Broadway Realty Corp., 7 N.Y.2d 240, 246, *supra*). In *Nicholson,* the covenant to supply heat was not interdicted by this concern because it was conditioned upon the continued existence of the buildings on
both the promisor's and the promisee's properties. Similarly, in *Neponsit,*
the original 1917 deed containing the covenant to pay an annual charge for
the maintenance of public areas expressly provided for its own lapse in
1940. Here, no outside limitation has been placed on the obligation to purchase water from appellant. Thus, the covenant falls prey to the criticism
that it creates a burden in perpetuity, and purports to bind all future owners, regardless of the use to which the land is put. Such a result militates
strongly against its enforcement. On this ground also, we are of the opinion
that the covenant should not be enforced as an exception to the general
rule prohibiting the "running" of affirmative covenants.

Accordingly, the order of the Appellate Division should be affirmed,
with costs.

NOTES AND QUESTIONS

1. **Technical mumbo-jumbo.** "The distinction between covenants
which run with land and covenants which are personal, must depend upon
the effect of the covenant on the legal rights which otherwise would flow
from the ownership of land and which are connected with the land." Eagle
Enterprises v. Gross, *supra,* quoting Neponsit Prop. Owners' Assn. v. Emigrant Industrial Savings Bank, 278 N.Y. at 258.

What *does* that mean? Can you understand why a covenant to purchase
water does not affect the promisor's legal rights, see Eagle Enterprises v.

Gross, when the same court enforced a covenant to supply heat; see Nicholson v. 300 Broadway Realty Corp. 7 N.Y.2d 240, 164 N.E.2d 832, 196 N.Y.S.2d 945 (1959)? Suppose, in *Eagle Enterprises,* that plaintiff had decided it no longer wanted to supply water to the defendant for $35 per year. If the dispute had taken that stance, is it clear that plaintiff would have prevailed?

2.   **The "I know it when I see it" test.** Judge Charles Clark, in a classical work on real covenants, wrote of "touch or concern," in effect, that a layman knows it when he sees it: "Where the parties, as laymen and not as lawyers, would rationally regard the covenant as intimately bound up with the land, aiding the promisee as landowner or hampering the promisor in similar capacity, the requirement should be held fulfilled." Clark, Real Covenants and Other Interests Which "Run with the Land" 99 (2d ed. 1947).

At least one writer saw merit in the waffly contours of "touch or concern": "The 'touch and concern' test, for all its failings, at least has the virtue of vagueness, thus permitting the courts to pour new meaning into the old 'touch and concern' bottle as changing conditions warrant." Rabin, Fundamentals of Modern Real Property Law 484 (3d ed. 1992).

The requirement of "touch or concern" has a further drawback. Suits to enforce (or to terminate) an affirmative covenant often arise years after the covenant is formed, and are likely, as in *Eagle Enterprises,* to involve someone (or ones) other than the original parties. In deciding whether to bind a nonpromisor successor to the servient estate, the court will often speak of "touch or concern." But occasions arise when the covenant ought not to be enforced even against the original covenantor; in that instance, should a court use "touch or concern" to explain its refusal to enforce?

Suppose, for example, that the Baums (the original promisors) still owned the lot in question and Eagle Enterprises had sued them: Did the covenant affect their legal rights as landowners any more or less than it affected those of their successor Gross? If the court hesitated to invoke "touch or concern," on grounds that this litmus works only to determine whether the covenant has run with the land, how might the court decide the case and write its opinion?

This suggests that "touch or concern," besides vagueness, also clouds whether a court would enforce the covenant against the original covenantor, and, if not, whether unenforceability would be for reasons of public policy or of changed conditions (for example, the covenant's purpose can no longer be served).

Recognizing this dilemma, and opting for candor rather than foggery, the Restatement of Servitudes has done away with the "touch or concern" requirement.

> Neither the burden nor the benefit of a covenant is required to touch or concern land in order for the covenant to be valid as a servitude. . . .[54]

54. Id. at §3.2.

3 Requirement
Eng.
U.S.

(i) *Horizontal privity.* Is there "privity of estate" between the party claim-ing the benefit of the covenant and the right to enforce it and the party upon whom the burden of the covenant is to be impressed?[55] In England, the only relationship that sustains privity is if the original covenanting parties are land-lord and tenant.[56] In the United States, courts expanded the doctrine of cove-nants at law to allow covenants to run when the original covenanting parties are grantor and grantee. This allowed courts to uphold covenants imposed by developers of subdivisions on all parcels within the subdivision: this was a cru-cial step in the developing legal infrastructure that created the American sub-urbs. In a few states, courts also held that the horizontal privity requirement was met if the original covenanting parties had an easement running between them, that is, were the owners of the dominant and servient tenements linked by a right of way.[57] The first Restatement of Property included this in the list of relationships that sustains horizontal privity. 5 Restatement of Property §534 (1944). In his treatise on real covenants, Judge Clark termed the require-ment a "barren formality"; Real Covenants and Other Interests Which "Run with the Land" 117 (2d ed. 1947).

If you look again at the opinion in *Eagle Enterprises,* page 703, *supra,* you will see where the court states what was needed for a covenant to run with the land that,

There must exist "privity of estate" between the party claiming the benefit of the covenant and the right to enforce it and the party upon whom the burden of the covenant is to be imposed.

The new Restatement has abolished the horizontal privity requirement; Re-statement, Servitudes (T.D. 1, at §2.4, 1989).

4

(ii) *Vertical privity.* This concerns the issue of whether each of the re-mote parties has the same estate or interest in the land as the original cove-nanting parties had. Restatement of Property §535. In other words, if B had a fee simple, and C had a life estate, the covenant would not run for lack of vertical privity. The important case is when C obtains title through ad-verse possession. Most courts find no vertical privity in this situation, on the theory that C has a "new estate" in the land, which is different from B's estate. (Is this the kind of thinking Felix Cohen, Chapter 1, page 9 *supra,*

55. Note that we break apart horizontal and vertical privity because they are analytically distinct. Courts often confuse the two, see, e.g., *Eagle Enterprises, supra.*

56. See Keppell v. Bailey, 39 Eng. Rep. 1042 (Ch. 1834).

57. See Morse v. Aldrich, 56 Mass. (19 Dick.) 449 (1837); some recent cases follow this view. See, e.g., Moseley v. Bishop, 470 N.E.2d 773 (Ind. App. 1984).

would call transcendental nonsense?) But in the typical case involving a succession of fees, vertical privity presents no problem.

   (iii) *Notice.* Some courts hold that the successor must have notice of the covenant in order to be bound.

Benefit Running.   The alternative is when the remote party is the plaintiff. Say, in the case of the covenant between A and B to restrict to single-family residential use, A sells to D, and B breaches the covenant by building an apartment house.

A SIGNS AGREEMENT WITH   B "PROPERTY TO BE MAINTAINED"

                                    Δ

D
π

The issue here is whether the *benefit* of the covenant has run to D. Not surprisingly, courts were a little less stringent in the requirements they required D to meet, since they were enforcing a covenant against someone who, after all, had bound himself to it.[58] In general, they required only *intent to bind successors,* a relaxed *vertical privity,* and that the covenant *touch and concern land.*

Benefit and Burden Running.   What if neither the plaintiff nor the defendant is one of the original covenanting parties? If both the plaintiff and the defendant are successors, then the covenant will not bind them unless both the burden and the benefit have run. In that case, all five elements of the burden-running test must have been met for the covenant to run.

NOTES AND PROBLEMS

   1.   **Covenants in crop contracts.** Before 1927, when it went bankrupt, the California Associated Raisin Co. (producer of Sun-Maid raisins) signed contracts with raisin growers that prohibited the growers from selling their raisins to anyone but the California Associated Raisin Co. The contracts stipulated that:

> in consideration of the agreements on the part of the buyer herein contained, the Seller agrees that this contract is made for the benefit of, and is beneficial

---

58. See 5 Restatement of Property §548 (1944).

to, the land therein described, and that the obligation of the seller to deliver all of said raisins, dried currants or dried grapes or to pay damages for failure to so deliver, shall be and remain a lien upon said land for the full term of this contract, and such lien may be enforced . . . regardless of the ownership of said land.

In other words, the covenant not to sell raisins to anyone else ran with the land and was not extinguished by selling the land to another. Until the contract term was up (15 years in one such contract, 3 years for another), any owner could only sell her raisins to the California Associated Raisin Co. The penalty for breach by the grower was the liquidated value of each pound of raisins sold to someone else. What language is relevant to the issue of whether this agreement is intended to bind successors? Does the covenant touch and concern land?

2.   **Problem.** A and B are neighbors. They agree to use their lots only for single-family residential use. A sells to C, who starts to build an apartment building. What information and documentation will you need from your client B, who wants to sue for damages? Can he win?

3.   **Problem.** Same facts, except that this time B breaches the covenant, and C wants to sue for damages. Can she win?

4.   **Problem.** This time A and B, still neighbors, covenant, then A sells to C and B sells to D. D breaches the covenant. Can C win?

5.   **Problem.** Same facts, but this time, though A sells to B, D gains title by adverse possession. Can C win?

2.   Covenant Running in Equity (Equitable Servitude)

In England, as has been noted, courts refused to enforce covenants against successive landowners. Instead, they restricted them to the landlord-tenant context. But, in the mid-nineteenth century, English courts were faced with the decision of whether they would enforce against successors agreements made between developers and homeowners to create the distinctive urban structure that still predominates in some London neighborhoods: the square composed of rowhouses all of the same design, around a locked garden to which only the surrounding homeowners had the key. (A notable U.S. example, which preserves the locked garden, is Gramercy Park in New York City.) English courts did enforce these agreements by inventing a new legal form called the *equitable servitude*, which allowed successors to obtain an injunction to enforce covenants against remote parties, Tulk v. Moxhay, 2 Ph. 774, 41 Eng. Rep. 1143 (Ch. 1848), and American courts followed suit shortly after. See, e.g., Trustees of Columbia College v. Lynch, 70 N.Y. 440 (1877). Consider, for example, a covenant between A and B to restrict their land to single-family residential use. If they or a successor finds out about plans to build an apartment house, would they typically want to proceed in law (and get damages) or in equity (and get an injunction)?

FIGURE 7-6

Gramercy Park, with Locked Garden (cf. Tulk v. Moxhay)

Today, equitable servitudes are much more important than covenants at law. On the burden side, to enforce an equitable servitude against a successor — under the pre-Restatement of Servitudes formulation — required proof of only three elements:

(1) *Intent to bind successors.*
(2) The covenant must *touch and concern* land.
(3) The remote party to be bound must have *notice* of the covenant. If the covenant is recorded, which it typically is, this typically fulfills the notice requirement; no actual notice is required.

PROBLEMS

For each of the problems above, can the plaintiff win a suit for an injunction?

b.   The Restatement of Servitudes

The Restatement of Servitudes has drawn a line sharply between the issue of a covenant's initial validity and that of the covenant's enforceability — a distinction often blurred by the "touch or concern" requirement. As to the former issue, according to the Restatement, a servitude is valid unless "the arrangement it purports to implement infringes a constitutionally protected right, contravenes a statute or governmental regulation, or violates public policy, id. at §3.1. In sum, a court must use lay terms to explain why it refuses to enforce a servitude rather than flummery like "touch or concern."

As the following materials indicate, however, whether a servitude offends a constitutionally protected right, contravenes a statute or government regulation, or violates public policy, often poses a troubling question.

1.   Unreasonable Restraints on Alienation

PROCTOR v. FOXMEYER DRUG CO.

884 S.W.2d 853 (Tex. Ct. App. 1994)

LAGARDE, J.

This case presents the issue of whether a corporation, unhappy with an obligation that it voluntarily assumed by an agreement it drafted, may avoid the obligation under the public policy preventing unreasonable restraints on alienation of property. We conclude that it may.

Doak C. Procter, III appeals from a summary judgment declaring that his contractual option to purchase real property from appellee Foxmeyer Drug Company is an unreasonable restraint on alienation. In [his] points of error, Procter complains that (i) as a matter of law the option is not an unreasonable restraint on alienation. We affirm.   *not unreas.*

restraint

FACTS

Appellant was a shareholder and president of Procter Company, the parent company of Jefferson Drug Company ("Jefferson"). Appellee was the parent company of Beaumont Division, Inc. On January 31, 1986, Procter Company, its shareholders (including appellant), and appellee entered into a merger agreement ("agreement") through which appellee acquired Jefferson from Procter Company and simultaneously merged Jefferson with Beaumont Division, Inc. The acquisition price was Jefferson's adjusted December 31, 1985 book value plus almost $3 million dollars. The only real estate Jefferson owned was a warehouse facility located in Beaumont, Texas ("warehouse").

The warehouse and two provisions of the agreement are the subject of this litigation. Paragraph 6.9 of the agreement states as follows:

> Warehouse Facilities. In the event the Surviving Corporation ceases to utilize the warehouse facilities used by Jefferson in conducting its business in Beaumont, Texas, [appellant] shall have the option to purchase from the Surviving Corporation, during the 30-day period following the termination of such use, the warehouse facility (including all fixtures not removed by the Surviving Corporation before the end of the 30-day period) of the Surviving Corporation for a purchase price equal to the book value as set forth on the Final Balance Sheet of such facility and fixtures. Such purchase shall be made without any representations or warranties by the Surviving Corporation and without recourse to the Surviving Corporation.

The agreement defined the Surviving Corporation as the entity resulting from the merger of Jefferson and Beaumont Division, Inc. The undisputed book value of the warehouse on the final December 31, 1985 balance sheet was $79,955.38.

Paragraph 10.7 of the agreement states as follows:

> Benefits of Agreement. All terms and provisions of this Agreement shall be binding upon and inure to the benefit of the parties hereto and their respective successors and assigns. Anything contained herein to the contrary notwithstanding, this Agreement shall not be assignable by either party [sic] hereto without the consent of the other party [sic] hereto.

In May 1987, the Surviving Corporation merged with appellee.

The appraised market value of a fee-simple-absolute interest in the warehouse was $500,000 as of May 3, 1991. On March 10, 1992, appellant notified appellee that he had become aware that appellee had ceased using the warehouse. Complying with the terms of Paragraph 6.9, on March 25, appellant tendered to appellee a cashier's check in the amount of $79,955.38. Appellee refused to accept the tender. The parties agree that the market value of the warehouse on March 25, 1992 was approximately $550,000.

Appellee filed this suit on March 23 seeking a declaratory judgment that the option created in Paragraph 6.9 was an unreasonable restraint on alienation.[2] The trial court denied appellant's motion to transfer venue to Jefferson County, Texas. Appellant also filed a general denial and counterclaims for breach of contract, fraud, and negligent failure to maintain the warehouse; appellant sought specific performance and monetary damages. Neither party pleaded ambiguity.

The trial court granted appellee's motion for summary judgment, expressly stating:

> [Paragraph] 6.9 of the Merger Agreement, which concerns an option unlimited in duration in light of [Paragraph] 10.7 of the Merger Agreement, is unenforceable and void as an unreasonable restraint on alienation. . . .

Further, the trial court ordered that appellant take nothing on his counterclaims. . . .

UNREASONABLE RESTRAINT ON ALIENATION

Although apparently disputed in the trial court, on appeal both parties have presumed that the Donative Transfers provisions of the Restatement (Second) of Property (1981) are relevant. Accordingly, both parties advance arguments relying on the Restatement. Our initial determination, therefore, concerns the Restatement's applicability to a case arising from a commercial, or nondonative, transaction.

As its name implies, the Restatement expressly applies only to donative property transactions:

> This part of the [Restatement (Second)] is concerned with donative transfers of property. Hence, it excludes any treatment of commercial transactions in property, even though some of the property problems dealt with herein may arise in a commercial context as well as in a donative one.

Restatement (second) of Property (Donative Transfers), Introduction, p. 1 (1981). It is undisputed that the agreement creating appellant's option arose

---

2. Although courts generally have tested the legality of options by the rule against perpetuities, commercial transactions might be better analyzed under the restraint on alienation doctrine. Mattern v. Herzog, 367 S.W.2d 312, 319-20 (Tex. 1963). Because neither party has argued the rule against perpetuities, we do not address it.

from an arm's length commercial transaction, not a donative transfer. . . . Public policy should be more lenient when the conveyee consents, through the freedom of contract, to limit his own power to convey in the future as long as the public interest is not harmed. See Mattern v. Herzog, 367 S.W.2d 312, 320 (Tex. 1963).

We conclude that the Restatement expressly limits its applicability in evaluating restraints on alienation. We hold that the provisions in the Restatement (Second) of Property (Donative Transfers) (1981) can conclusively determine the validity — but not the invalidity — of restraints on alienation resulting from nondonative transactions. This approach is consistent with that taken by the only other Texas court to address the adoption of the Restatement. See Randolph, 768 S.W.2d at 739 (concluding that an option was reasonable by adopting and applying section 4.2(3) of the Restatement "in this case").

In his first point of error, appellant asserts that the option created by Paragraph 6.9 is not an unreasonable restraint on alienation as a matter of law. Appellant analogizes his option to a right of first refusal. Appellant points out that a right of first refusal is a preemptive right which requires a property owner to first offer the property to the person holding the right at the stipulated price and terms in the event the owner decides to sell. See Riley v. Campeau Homes (Tex.), Inc., 808 S.W.2d 184, 187 (Tex. App.-Houston [14th Dist.] 1991, *writ dism'd by agr.*). Appellant argues that the unilateral decision of appellee to cease utilizing the warehouse is similar to a decision to sell in the right-of-first-refusal context. In both situations, the option or right holder cannot force the property owner into action. The initial decision to dispose of the property or discontinue its use is made unilaterally by the owner.

Appellant's argument continues by relying on Section 4.4 of the Restatement,[3] which provides that a right of first refusal is not a restraint on alienation if the terms of the right are reasonable regarding both the price to be paid and the time allowed for exercise of the right.[4] See Randolph, 768 S.W.2d at 738 (adopting Section 4.4). Appellant asserts that both the price and time period are reasonable. First, the $79,955.38 option price coincides with the book value of the warehouse at the time of appellee's purchase. Consequently, appellant asserts that the option price is the same price appellee paid Procter Company for the warehouse in 1986 and, as such, appellee cannot now claim the price is unreasonable. Second, appellant argues that the 30-day period to exercise the option is reasonable.

Appellant's argument fails for several reasons. First, the option created by Paragraph 6.9 is not analogous to a right of first refusal. In Texas, a

---

3. Restatement (Second) of Property (Donative Transfers) §4.4 (1981). Future references to "Section" refer to this version of the Restatement unless otherwise noted.

4. In addressing this argument, we assume, without deciding, that Section 4.4 is the law in Texas.

right of first refusal requires the property owner to provide the holder of the right "the opportunity to buy the burdened property on the terms offered by a bona fide purchaser." Riley, 808 S.W.2d at 187. The holder of the right cannot fix the price because the price is determinable only when a willing seller receives an acceptable offer from a bona fide purchaser. Forderhause v. Cherokee Water Co., 623 S.W.2d 435, 439 (Tex. Civ. App.-Texarkana 1981), *rev'd on other grounds,* 641 S.W.2d 522 (Tex. 1982). Thus, appellant's one-price option is much more than a right of first refusal. We conclude that the Restatement's provisions regarding a right of first refusal are inapplicable to the option before us.

Nevertheless, assuming, arguendo, that the option is analogous to a right of first refusal, appellant's reliance on Section 4.4 is misplaced. Appellant attempts to establish the reasonableness of the $79,955.38 option price by equating it to the price appellee paid for the warehouse. The agreement, however, does not refer to specific prices paid for specific assets of Jefferson. The agreement was a negotiated purchase of Jefferson's equity. There is no basis under the terms of the agreement to allocate the total purchase price of Jefferson stock to each of Jefferson's assets that appellee acquired, including the warehouse.

We conclude that $79,955.38 is unreasonable as a matter of law to pay for real estate valued at approximately $550,000. Procter's price does not satisfy the reasonable price requirement under Section 4.4.

Appellant also asserts that summary judgment was improper because appellee failed to conclusively establish that the option was an unreasonable restraint on alienation. In its summary judgment motion, appellee asserted that Section 4.2(3) establishes the unreasonableness of the restraint.[5] On appeal, appellee argues this same theory. As noted above, however, the Restatement is inapplicable for that purpose because it does not consider factors unique to nondonative transactions. Nevertheless, our initial holding is not fatal to appellee's position.

Appellee also relied on several cases that did not apply the Restatement, including one Texas case. See Gray v. Vandver, 623 S.W.2d 172 (Tex. App.-Beaumont 1981, no writ). Specifically, appellee argued that it conclusively established that the option (1) price was fixed, (2) period was unlimited in duration, and (3) operated to restrain alienation. On appeal, appellee continues to assert that these facts establish the option as unreasonable as a matter of law. See id. at 175. Without reference to the Restatement, the trial court's judgment stated that appellant's option was

---

5. Section 4.2(3) lists six factors courts should use to evaluate whether a forfeiture restraint on alienation is reasonable: a. The restraint is limited in duration; b. The restraint is limited to allow a substantial variety of types of transfers to be employed; c. The restraint is limited as to the number of persons to whom transfer is prohibited; d. The restraint is such that it tends to increase the value of the property involved; e. The restraint is imposed upon an interest that is not otherwise readily marketable; or f. The restraint is imposed upon property that is not readily marketable. Restatement (Second) of Property §4.2(3) (1981).

unlimited in duration. We conclude that the trial court decided the case based on appellee's arguments, not on the Restatement.

We must now determine the correctness of the trial court's decision based on appellee's arguments.

FIXED PRICE

It is undisputed that the option price is fixed by the option provision itself. We conclude that the unambiguous language of the agreement and appellee's summary judgment evidence conclusively established the option price as fixed at $79,955.38.

UNLIMITED IN DURATION

Appellee asserts that the option provision in Paragraph 6.9, when read in conjunction with Paragraph 10.7, is unlimited in duration. Appellant points out that the option is contained only in Paragraph 6.9. Relying on Mattern, 367 S.W.2d at 319, appellant argues that we should not construe the option as unlimited in duration because the option itself does not compel such a construction.

When a written instrument is unambiguous, it is the responsibility of the court to give effect to the intent of the parties as expressed therein. See Dallas Bank & Trust Co. v. Frigiking, Inc., 692 S.W.2d 163, 166 (Tex. App.-Dallas 1985, writ ref'd n.r.e.). It is the objective, not subjective, intent of the parties that controls. See id.

Paragraph 6.9 grants a conditional purchase option to appellant and obligates the Surviving Corporation to perform when that condition occurs. Paragraph 10.7 explicitly states that "[a]ll terms and provisions of this [a]greement shall be binding upon and inure to the benefit of the parties hereto and their respective successors and assigns." Clearly, the words of Paragraph 10.7 make no exception for the rights and obligations contained in Paragraph 6.9 but expressly apply to all rights and obligations in the agreement. Thus, the objective intent of the parties as expressed through Paragraph 10.7 was (1) to grant the benefits of the option to appellant's potential successors and assignees and (2) to bind any successors and assignees of the Surviving Corporation to perform under the option. Thus, the option was not appellant's personal right, but was a right inuring to the benefit of his successors or assigns.

The exact meaning of the word "successor" when used in a contract depends largely on the kind and character of the contract, its purposes and circumstances, and the context. Thompson v. North Tex. Nat'l Bank, 37 S.W.2d 735, 739 (Tex. Comm'n. App. 1931, holding approved). "Successor" does not ordinarily mean an assignee, but is normally used in respect to corporate entities, including corporations becoming invested with the rights and assuming the burdens of another corporation by amalgamation, consolidation, or duly authorized legal succession. *Enchanted Estates Community Ass'n, Inc. v. Timberlake Improvement Dist.*, 832 S.W.2d 800, 803 (Tex. App.-Houston [1st Dist.] 1992, no writ).

In our view, "successor" as used in the agreement before us intended the meaning just recited as applied to the corporate parties to the agreement. However, we have found no Texas contract case applying the term "successor" to an individual. In dictum, one Texas court has stated, "[I]n respect to natural persons, [the word 'successor'] is [an] apt and appropriate term to designate one to whom property descends or [the] estate of the decedent." *International Ass'n of Machinists v. Falstaff Brewing Corp.*, 328 S.W.2d 778, 781 (Tex. Civ. App.-Houston 1959, no writ) (citing *In re Murray Realty Co*, 35 F. Supp. 417, 419 (N.D.N.Y. 1940) (citing New York law)). Based on the kind and character of the contract before us, its purposes and circumstances, and its context, we conclude that the term "successor" was also intended to apply to the natural-person parties of the agreement, including appellant.

We further conclude that the term "successor" was intended to designate those to whom property descended through a deceased natural-person party to this agreement. The option in Paragraph 6.9, therefore, extends perpetually to appellant's descendants and is unlimited in duration.

RESTRAINT ON ALIENATION

Finally, appellee asserts that if it "attempts to lease, sell, assign, or otherwise transfer the warehouse to a bona fide purchaser, [appellee] will have ceased to utilize the warehouse in conducting its business and [appellant] can try to compel its sale to him. . . ." Appellant challenges appellee's assertion because "Paragraph 6.9 does not prohibit transfer to anyone."

Prohibited restraints have traditionally been classified as disabling, promissory, or forfeiture restraints. *Mattern*, 367 S.W.2d at 319. These are restraints that either void, impose contractual liability, or subject to termination a grantee's interest in land because of a later attempted conveyance. *Id.* at 319 n. 4 (quoting Restatement (First) of Property §404 (1944)); see also Restatement (Second) of Property §§3.1-3.3 (1981). Options, however, can operate as indirect restraints on alienation even though they do not fit into the usual classifications. See *Mattern*, 367 S.W.2d at 319.

The option provision in Paragraph 6.9 of the agreement is such an alienation restraint.

> In the event the Surviving Corporation ceases to utilize the warehouse facilities used by Jefferson in conducting its business in Beaumont, Texas, [appellant] shall have the option to purchase from the Surviving Corporation. . . .

Although alienation is not expressly prohibited, the unambiguous intent of the quoted provision was to limit the use of the warehouse to the Surviving

Corporation. Thus, utilization by anyone else would trigger the option and, if exercised, subject the Surviving Corporation to either (1) termination of its interest in the warehouse for the fixed price or (2) liability for breaching the option. We conclude that although drafted as a restraint on use, Paragraph 6.9 operates indirectly as a restraint on alienation. Cf. Restatement (Second) of Property (Donative Transfers) §3.4, cmt. b (1981).

UNREASONABLENESS AS A MATTER OF LAW

Our supreme court has written only rarely on restraints on alienation — and rarer still in such cases involving options. In Mattern, however, the supreme court established two guidelines for analyzing options. First, an important factor in analyzing an alienation-restraining option is the reasonableness of the option's time limit. *Mattern,* 367 S.W.2d at 320. Second, a court should not void an option — and, thus, circumvent the parties' freedom of contract — unless the option bears some relationship to the harm the policy against undesirable restraints on alienation was designed to prevent. Id.

The rule preventing unreasonable restraints on alienation rests on the assumption that social welfare requires prohibiting restrictions on property alienation. Restatement (First) of Property, Pt. I, intr. note (1944). The rule serves at least three purposes that support this assumption:

(1) Balances the current property owner's desire to prolong control over his property and a latter owner's desire to be free from the "dead" hand;
(2) Contributes to better utilization of society's wealth by reducing fear from uncertain investments and assisting in assets flowing to those who would put them to their best use; and
(3) Keeps the property available to satisfy the current exigencies of the owner and, thus, stimulate the competitive theory basis of the economy.

Id. Thus, unless appellant's option violates these purposes, we will not interfere with the parties' right to contract. See *Mattern,* 367 S.W.2d at 320.

A fixed-price purchase option of unlimited duration that restricts alienation of real property has been held to be unreasonable and void as a matter of law. See *Gray,* 623 S.W.2d at 174; see also *Gray,* 623 S.W.2d at 175 (Keith, J., concurring). We conclude that appellant's option is an unreasonable restraint on alienation as a matter of law.

Appellant's option violates the second and third stated purposes of the rule against alienation restraints. First, the option hinders the free flow of real property in society because appellee has only two alternatives: use the warehouse or sell it to appellant for a fraction of its worth. The vast disparity between the property's market value and the fixed sales price effectively forecloses alienation forever, see Gray, 623 S.W.2d at 172, thus depriving society of the benefit of having the warehouse put to its best use.

Further, even should appellee attempt to alienate the warehouse, the uncertainty of the investment would prevent a prudent purchaser from paying the market value for the property.

Second, this unlimited, fixed-price option prevents appellee from satisfying its current exigencies. The agreed market price of the warehouse, without the option, is about $550,000, yet appellee could only obtain about $80,000 in a sale to appellant. Thus, appellee is denied the benefit of approximately $470,000 to meet any current exigencies that might arise.

We hold that appellant's fixed-price option, which operates to restrain alienation for an unlimited period, is an unreasonable restraint on alienation and is void as a matter of law. Appellant's first point of error is overruled.

NOTES AND QUESTIONS

1. **Options as servitudes.** Although options did not appear in our listing of servitude forms, pages 623-626, *supra,* do you see why the Restatement treats the purchase option as a servitude? It is helpful to think of the option as a negative servitude in which the property owner (optionor) covenants not to sell the property to a third person without first offering it to the optionee at the option price.

Options, especially rights of first refusal, have wide commercial usage. They often appear in condominium declarations that require the unit owner not to sell or lease his unit without giving the condominium board a chance to match any bona-fide offer from a third party. Although condominium boards rarely exercise their privilege, the option serves as an occupancy control akin to, but far less effective, than the control that cooperative boards retain through their reserved power to approve all apartment transfers.

2. **Restatement of Servitudes.** The *Proctor* court draws its analogy from the Restatement of Donative Transfers, rather than from the Servitudes Restatement, still in tentative draft in 1994 and, quite possibly, not even cited by the attorneys. The latter Restatement would also test direct restraints for their "reasonableness," determined "by weighing the utility of the restraint against the injurious consequences of enforcing the restraint." Id. at §3.4 (T.D. 2, 1991).

The Restatement lists, as instances of direct restraints, absolute prohibitions on some or all types of transfers, prohibitions on transfer without the consent of another, prohibitions on transfers to particular persons, requirements of transfer to particular persons, options to purchase land, and rights of first refusal. Ibid.

Recall *Ernest Pestano,* Chapter 3, where the court tested a leasehold restraint against a standard of "commercial reasonableness." Recall also *Symphony Space,* Chapter 2, where the court tested a commercial option against the Rule of Perpetuities.

3.   **Indirect Restraints on Alienation.** The Restatement applies a more relaxed standard to use or activity restraints that might reduce the value of the burdened property. Such restraints are valid "unless there is no rational justification for the servitude." Id. at §3.5.

4.   **Donative versus commercial restraints.** Recall *Toscano*, Chapter 2, where we first discussed alienation restraints as they arose in a donative transfer.

The Servitudes Restatement suggests that although an indirect restraint arising in a commercial transaction seldom will lack rational justification, a donative transfer is more likely to reflect the donor's or the testator's personal caprice, since she will not have to suffer the financial consequences of the servitude. Ibid.

2.   Unreasonable Restraints on Trade or Competition

DAVIDSON BROS., INC. v. D. KATZ & SONS, INC.

121 N.J. 196, 579 A.2d 288 (1990)

GARIBALDI, J.

This case presents two issues. The first is whether a restrictive covenant in a deed, providing that the property shall not be used as a supermarket or grocery store, is enforceable against the original covenantor's successor, a subsequent purchaser with actual notice of the covenant. The second is whether an alleged rent-free lease of lands by a public entity to a private corporation for use as a supermarket constitutes a gift of public property in violation of the New Jersey Constitution of 1947, article eight, section three, paragraphs two and three.

I

The facts are not in dispute. Prior to September 1980 plaintiff, Davidson Bros., Inc., along with Irisondra, Inc., a related corporation, owned certain premises located at 263-271 George Street and 30 Morris Street in New Brunswick (the "George Street" property). Plaintiff operated a supermarket on that property for approximately seven to eight months. The store operated at a loss allegedly because of competing business from plaintiff's other store, located two miles away (the "Elizabeth Street" property). Consequently, plaintiff and Irisondra conveyed, by separate deeds, the George Street property to defendant D. Katz & Sons, Inc., with a restrictive covenant not to operate a supermarket on the premises. Specifically, each deed contained the following covenant:

> The lands and premises described herein and conveyed hereby are conveyed subject to the restriction that said lands and premises shall not be used as and for a supermarket or grocery store of a supermarket type, however designated,

for a period of forty (40) years from the date of this deed. This restriction shall be a covenant attached to and running with the lands.

The deeds were duly recorded in Middlesex County Clerk's office on September 10, 1980. According to plaintiff's complaint, its operation of both stores resulted in losses in both stores. Plaintiff alleges that after the closure of the George Street store, its Elizabeth Street store increased in sales by twenty percent and became profitable. Plaintiff held a leasehold interest in the Elizabeth Street property, which commenced in 1978 for a period of twenty years, plus two renewal terms of five years.

According to defendants New Brunswick Housing Authority (the "Authority") and City of New Brunswick (the "City"), the closure of the George Street store did not benefit the residents of downtown New Brunswick. Defendants allege that many of the residents who lived two blocks away from the George Street store in multi-family and senior-citizen housing units were forced to take public transportation and taxis to the Elizabeth Street store because there were no other markets in downtown New Brunswick, save for two high-priced convenience stores.

The residents requested the aid of the City and the Authority in attracting a new food retailer to this urban-renewal area. For six years, those efforts were unsuccessful. Finally, in 1986, an executive of C-Town, a division of a supermarket chain, approached representatives of New Brunswick about securing financial help from the City to build a supermarket.

Despite its actual notice of the covenant the Authority, on October 23, 1986, purchased the George Street property from Katz for $450,000, and agreed to lease from Katz at an annual net rent of $19,800.00, the adjacent land at 263-265 George Street for use as a parking lot. The Authority invited proposals for the lease of the property to use as a supermarket. C-Town was the only party to submit a proposal at a public auction. The proposal provided for an aggregate rent of one dollar per year during the five-year lease term with an agreement to make $10,000 in improvements to the exterior of the building and land. The Authority accepted the proposal in 1987. All the defendants in this case had actual notice of the restrictions contained in the deed and of plaintiff's intent to enforce the same. Not only were the deeds recorded but the contract of sale between Katz and the Housing Authority specifically referred to the restrictive covenant and the pending action.

Plaintiff filed this action in the Chancery Division against defendants D. Katz & Sons, Inc., the City of New Brunswick, and C-Town. The first count of the complaint requested a declaratory judgment that the non-competition covenant was binding on all subsequent owners of the George Street property. The second count requested an injunction against defendant City of New Brunswick from leasing the George Street property on any basis that would constitute a gift to a private party in violation of the state constitution. Both counts sought compensatory and punitive damages. That complaint was then amended to include defendant the New Brunswick Housing Authority.

Plaintiff moved for summary judgment, to which defendants responded by submitting three affidavits . . . all alleging the need for a supermarket in the area of George Street.

The trial court denied plaintiff's motion and held, in an unreported opinion, that the covenant was unenforceable, relying on Brewer v. Marshall & Cheeseman, 19 N.J. Eq. 537 (E. & A. 1868). That case held that the burden of a covenant will not run with the land and therefore bind a successor unless the covenant "affects the physical use of the land itself." This view "effectively stifles any possibility of covenants relating to competition," 5 R. Powell & P. Rohan, Powell on Real Property §675[3], 60-108 (rev. ed. 1989). (5 Powell). Although the Brewer decision was an old case, (1868), the trial court was satisfied that it was still controlling and found that the covenant was unenforceable because it did not "touch and concern" the land. Additionally, the trial court noted that the enforcement of non-competition covenants is contrary to a longstanding public policy. However, the trial court observed that the determination of whether the covenant was reasonable and consistent with public policy would require a factual hearing and could not be made in a motion for summary judgment.

The trial court also held that the rent-free lease between the Authority and C-Town did not violate the New Jersey Constitution of 1947, article eight, section three, paragraphs two and three. The court found that the lease was valid inasmuch as it furthered a "public purpose" as defined by a two-part test set forth in Roe v. Kervick, 42 N.J. 191, 207, 199 A.2d 834 (1964).

After the court denied plaintiff's motion for summary judgment, defendants moved for summary judgment, which was granted. Plaintiff appealed, and in an unreported opinion, the Appellate Division affirmed the trial court's judgment. For purposes of its decision the Appellate Division assumed that Brewer was not applicable, that noncompetitive covenants may run with the land in appropriate cases, that a leasehold interest in land is a sufficient interest to enforce a covenant, that two miles between the burdened and benefitted properties does not itself prevent a covenant from being enforced, and that the George Street store would impair the profitability of the Elizabeth Street store. Although the Appellate Division found "some merit" to plaintiff's argument that Brewer v. Marshall, *supra,* 19 N.J. Eq. 537, no longer represented the current law in New Jersey, the court held that the covenant was unenforceable against a subsequent grantee because the benefit did not "touch and concern" plaintiff's Elizabeth Street property. Specifically, the court reasoned that because the covenant restricted such a comparatively small portion of the market area, less than one-half an acre, and did not impair the use of the other 2,000 acres in the market circle from which the Elizabeth store draws its clientele, the covenant did not enhance the value of the retained estate, and therefore, as a matter of law, would not bind a subsequent purchaser. In contrast to the trial court's decision, the Appellate Division's rationale was premised on the failure of the benefit of the covenant to run, not of the burden.

The Appellate Division also affirmed the trial court's judgment that the rent-free lease was constitutionally valid, substantially for the reasons expressed by the trial court.

II

A. GENESIS AND DEVELOPMENT OF COVENANTS REGARDING THE USE OF PROPERTY

Covenants regarding property use have historical roots in the courts of both law and equity. The English common-law courts first dealt with the issue in Spencer's Case, 5 Co. 16a, 77 Eng. Rep. 72 (Q.B. 1583). The court established two criteria for the enforcement of covenants against successors. First, the original covenanting parties must intend that the covenant run with the land. Second, the covenant must "touch and concern" the land. Id. at 16b, 77 Eng. Rep. at 74. . . .

The English common-law courts also developed additional requirements of horizontal privity (succession of estate), vertical privity (a landlord-tenant relationship), and that the covenant have "proper form," in order for the covenant to run with the land. C. Clark, Real Covenants and Other Interests Which Run with the Land 94, 95 (2d ed. 1947) (Real Covenants). Those technical requirements made it difficult, if not impossible, to protect property through the creation of real covenants. Commentary, "Real Covenants in Restraint of Trade — When Do They Run with the Land?," 20 Ala. L. Rev. 114, 115 (1967).

To mitigate and to eliminate many of the formalities and privity rules formulated by the common-law courts, the English chancery courts in Tulk v. Moxhay, 2 Phil. 774, 41 Eng. Rep. 1143 (Ch. 1848), created the doctrine of equitable servitudes. In Tulk, land was conveyed subject to an agreement that it would be kept open and maintained for park use. A subsequent grantee, with notice of the restriction, acquired the park. The court held that it would be unfair for the original covenanter to rid himself of the burden to maintain the park by simply selling the land. In enjoining the new owner from violating the agreement, the court stated:

It is said that, the covenant being one which does not run with the land, this court cannot enforce it, but the question is, not whether the covenant runs with the land, but whether a party shall be permitted to use the land in a manner inconsistent with the contract entered into by his vendor, and with notice of which he purchased. Of course, the price would be affected by the covenant, and nothing could be more inequitable than that the original purchaser should be able to sell the property the next day for a greater price, in consideration of the assignee being allowed to escape from the liability which he had himself undertaken.

[Id. at 777-78, 41 Eng. Rep. 1144]. The court thus enforced the covenant on the basis that the successor had purchased the property with notice of the restriction. Adequate notice obliterated any express requirement of "touch and concern." Reichman, "Toward a Unified Concept of Servitudes," 55 S. Cal. L. Rev. 1177, 1225 (1982); French, "Toward a Modern Law of Servitudes: Reweaving Ancient Strands," 55 S. Cal. L. Rev. 1261, 1276-77 (1982). But see Burger, "A Policy Analysis of Promises Respecting the Use of Land," 55 Minn. L. Rev. 167, 217 (1970) (focusing on language in *Tulk* that refers to "use of land" and "attached to property" as implied recognition of "touch and concern" rule).

Some early commentators theorized that the omission of the technical elements of property law such as the "touch and concern" requirement indicated that Tulk was based on a contractual as opposed to a property theory. C. Clark, *supra*, Real Covenants, at 171-72 nn.3 and 4; 3 H. Tiffany, Real Property §861, at 489 (3d ed. 1939); Ames, "Specific Performance for and against Strangers to Contract," 17 Harv. L. Rev. 174, 177-79 (1904); Stone, "The Equitable Rights and Liabilities of Strangers to the Contract," 18 Colum. L. Rev. 291, 294-95 (1918). Others contend that "touch and concern" is always, at the very least, an implicit element in any analysis regarding enforcement of covenants because "any restrictive easement necessitates some relation between the restriction and the land itself." McLoone, "Equitable Servitudes — A Recent Case and Its Implications for the Enforcement of Covenants Not to Compete," 9 Ariz. L. Rev. 441, 444, 447 n.5 (1968). Still others explain the "touch and concern" omission on the theory that equitable servitudes usually involve negative covenants or promises on how the land should not be used. Thus, because those covenants typically do touch and concern the land, the equity courts did not feel the necessity to state "touch and concern" as a separate requirement. Berger, "Integration of the Law of Easements, Real Covenants and Equitable Servitudes," 43 Wash. & Lee L. Rev., 337, 362 (1986). Whatever the explanation, the law of equitable servitudes did generally continue to diminish or omit the "touch and concern" requirement.

B.   NEW JERSEY'S TREATMENT OF NONCOMPETITIVE COVENANTS
RESTRAINING THE USE OF PROPERTY

Our inquiry of New Jersey law on restrictive property use covenants commences with a re-examination of the rule set forth in Brewer v. Marshall & Cheseman, *supra*, 19 N.J. Eq. at 537, that a covenant will not run with the land unless it affects the physical use of the land. Hence, the burden side of a noncompetition covenant is personal to the covenantor and is, therefore, not enforceable against a purchaser. In Brewer v. Marshall & Cheseman, the court objected to all noncompetition covenants on the basis of public policy and refused to consider them in the context of the doctrine of equitable servitudes. Similarly, in National Union Bank at Dover v. Segur, 39 N.J.L. 173 (Sup. Ct. 1877), the court held that only the benefit of a noncompetition covenant would run with the land, but the burden would be personal to the covenantor. See 5 R. Powell, *supra*, §675[3] at 60-109. Because the burden of a noncompetition covenant is deemed to be personal in these cases, enforcement would be possible only against the original covenantor. As soon as the covenantor sold the property, the burden would cease to exist.

Brewer and *National Union Bank* have been subsequently interpreted as embodying the "unnecessarily strict" position that "while the benefit of [a noncompetition covenant] will run with the land, the burden of the covenant is necessarily personal to the covenantor." 5 Powell, *supra*, §675[3] at 60-109. This blanket prohibition of noncompetition covenants has been ignored in more recent decisions that have allowed the burden of a noncompetition covenant to run, see Renee Cleaners Inc. v. Good Deal Supermarkets of N.J., 89 N.J. Super. 186, 214 A.2d 437 (App. Div. 1965) (enforcing at law covenant not to lease property for dry-cleaning business as against subsequent purchaser of land); Alexander's v. Arnold Constable Corp., 105 N.J. Super. 14, 28, 250 A.2d 792 (Ch. 1969) (enforcing promise entered into by prior holders of land not to operate department store as against current landowner). Nonetheless, *Brewer* may still retain some vitality, as evidenced by the trial court's reliance on it in this case.

The per se prohibition that noncompetition covenants regarding the use of property do not run with the land is not supported by modern real-covenant law, and indeed, appears to have support only in the Restatement of Property section on the running of real covenants, §537 comment f. 5 Powell, *supra*, at §675 [3] at 60-109. Specifically, that approach is rejected in the Restatement's section on equitable servitudes, see Restatement of Property, §539 comment k (1944); see also Whitinsville Plaza, Inc. v. Kotseas, 378 Mass. 85, 95-96, 390 N.E.2d 243, 249 (1979) (overruling similarly strict approach inasmuch as it was "anachronistic" compared to modern judicial analysis of noncompetition covenants, which focuses on effects of covenant).

Commentators also consider the Brewer rule an anachronism and in need of change, as do we. 5 Powell, *supra*, ¶678 at 192. Accordingly, to the extent that Brewer holds that a noncompetition covenant will not run with the land, it is overruled.

Plaintiff also argues that the "touch and concern" test likewise should be eliminated in determining the enforceability of fully negotiated contracts, in favor of a simpler "reasonableness" standard that has been adopted in most jurisdictions. That argument has some support from commentators, see, e.g., Epstein, "Notice and Freedom of Contract in the Law of Servitudes," 55 S. Cal. L. Rev. 1353, 1359-61 (1982) (contending that "touch and concern" complicates the basic analysis and limits the effectiveness of law of servitudes), including a reporter for the Restatement (Third) of Property, see French, "Servitudes Reform and the New Restatement of Property: Creation Doctrines and Structural Simplification," 73 Cornell L. Rev. 928, 939 (1988) (arguing that "touch and concern" rule should be completely eliminated and that the law should instead directly tackle the "running" issue on public-policy grounds).

New Jersey courts, however, continue to focus on the "touch and concern" requirement as the pivotal inquiry in ascertaining whether a covenant runs with the land. Under New Jersey law, a covenant that "exercise[s] [a] direct influence on the occupation, use or enjoyment of the premises" satisfies the "touch and concern" rule. Caullett v. Stanley Stilwell & Sons, Inc., 67 N.J. Super. 111, 116, 170 A.2d 52 (App. Div. 1961). The covenant must touch and concern both the burdened and the benefitted property in order to run with the land. Ibid.; Hayes v. Waverly & Passaic R.R., 51 N.J. Eq. 3, 27 A. 648 (Ch. 1893). Because the law frowns on the placing of restrictions on the freedom of alienation of land, New Jersey courts will enforce a covenant only if it produces a countervailing benefit to justify the burden. Restatement of Property §543, comment c (1944); Reichman, *supra*, 55 S. Cal. L. Rev. at 1229.

Unlike New Jersey, which has continued to rely on the "touch and concern" requirement, most other jurisdictions have omitted "touch and concern" from their analysis and have focused instead on whether the covenant is reasonable.

Even the majority of courts that have retained the "touch and concern" test have found that noncompetition covenants meet the test's requirements.

The "touch and concern" test has, thus, ceased to be, in most jurisdictions, intricate and confounding. Courts have decided as an initial matter that covenants not to compete do touch and concern the land. The courts then have examined explicitly the more important question of whether covenants are reasonable enough to warrant enforcement. The time has come to cut the gordian knot that binds this state's jurisprudence regarding covenants running with the land. Rigid adherence to the "touch and concern" test as a means of determining the enforceability of a restrictive covenant is not warranted. Reasonableness, not esoteric concepts of property law, should be the guiding inquiry into the validity of covenants at law. We do not abandon the "touch and concern" test, but rather hold that the test is but one of the factors a court should consider in determining the reasonableness of the covenant.

A "reasonableness" test allows a court to consider the enforceability of a covenant in view of the realities of today's commercial world and not in the light of out-moded theories developed in a vastly different commercial environment. Originally strict adherence to "touch and concern" rule in the old English common-law cases and in Brewer, was to effectuate the then pervasive public policy of restricting many, if not all, encumbrances of the land. Courts today recognize that it is not unreasonable for parties in commercial-property transactions to protect themselves from competition by executing noncompetition covenants. Businesspersons, either as lessees or purchasers may be hesitant to invest substantial sums if they have no minimal protection from a competitor starting a business in the near vicinity. Hence, rather than limiting trade, in some instances, restrictive covenants may increase business activity.

We recognize that "reasonableness" is necessarily a fact sensitive issue involving an inquiry into present business conditions and other factors specific to the covenant at issue. Nonetheless, as do most of the jurisdictions, we find that it is a better test for governing commercial transactions than are obscure anachronisms that have little meaning in today's commercial world. The pivotal inquiry, therefore, becomes what factors should a court consider in determining whether such a covenant is "reasonable" and hence enforceable. We conclude that the following factors should be considered:

1. The intention of the parties when the covenant was executed, and whether the parties had a viable purpose which did not at the time interfere with existing commercial laws, such as antitrust laws, or public policy.

2. Whether the covenant had an impact on the considerations exchanged when the covenant was originally executed. This may provide a measure of the value to the parties of the covenant at the time.

3. Whether the covenant clearly and expressly sets forth the restrictions.

4. Whether the covenant was in writing, recorded, and if so, whether the subsequent grantee had actual notice of the covenant.

5. Whether the covenant is reasonable concerning area, time or duration. Covenants that extend for perpetuity or beyond the terms of a lease may often be unreasonable. Alexander's v. Arnold Constable, 105 N.J. Super. 14, 27 250 A.2d 792 (Ch. Div. 1969); Cragmere Holding Corp. v. Socony Mobile Oil Co., 65 N.J. Super. 322, 167 A.2d 825 (App. Div. 1961).

6. Whether the covenant imposes an unreasonable restraint on trade or secures a monopoly for the covenantor. This may be the case in areas where there is limited space available to conduct certain business activities and a covenant not to compete burdens all or most available locales to prevent them from competing in such an activity. Doo v. Packwood, 265 Cal. App. 2d 752, 71 Cal. Rptr. 477 (1968); Kettle River R. v. Eastern Ry. Co., 41 Minn. 461, 43 N.W. 469 (1889).

7. Whether the covenant interferes with the public interest. Natural Prods. Co. v. Dolese & Shepard Co., 309 Ill. 230, 140 N.E. 840 (1923).

8. Whether, even if the covenant was reasonable at the time it was executed, "changed circumstances" now make the covenant unreasonable. Welitoff v. Kohl, 105 N.J. Eq. 181, 147 A. 390 (1929).

In applying the "reasonableness" factors, trial courts may find useful the analogous standards we have adopted in determining the validity of employee covenants not to compete after termination of employment. Although enforcement of such a covenant is somewhat restricted because of countervailing policy considerations, we generally enforce an employee non-competition covenant as reasonable if it "simply protects the legitimate interests of the employer, imposes no undue hardship on the employee, and is not injurious to the public." Solari Indus. v. Malady, 55 N.J. 571, 576, 264 A.2d 53 (1970). We also held in Solari that if such a covenant is found to be overbroad, it may be partially enforced to the extent reasonable under the circumstances. Id. at 585, 264 A.2d 53. That approach to the enforcement of restrictive covenants in deeds offers a mechanism for recognizing and balancing the legitimate concerns of the grantor, the successors in interest, and the public.

The concurrence maintains that the initial validity of the covenant is a question of contract law while its subsequent enforceability is one of property law. *Post* at 221, 579 A.2d at 300. The result is that the concurrence uses reasonableness factors in construing the validity of the covenant between the original covenantors, but as to successors-in-interest, claims to adhere strictly to a "touch and concern" test. *Post* at 222, 579 A.2d at 301. Such strict adherence to a "touch and concern" analysis turns a blind eye to whether a covenant has become unreasonable over time. Indeed many past illogical and contorted applications of the "touch and concern" rules have resulted because courts have been pressed to twist the rules of "touch and concern" in order to achieve a result that comports with public policy and a free market. Most jurisdictions acknowledge the reasonableness factors that affect enforcement of a covenant concerning successors-in-interest, instead of engaging in the subterfuge of twisting the touch and concern test to meet the required result. New Jersey should not remain part of the small minority of States that cling to an anachronistic rule of law. *Supra* at 210, 579 A.2d at 295.

There is insufficient evidence in this record to determine whether the covenant is reasonable. Nevertheless, we think it instructive to comment briefly on the application of the "reasonableness" factors to this covenant. We consider first the intent of the parties when the covenant was executed. It is undisputed that when plaintiff conveyed the property to Katz, it intended that the George Street store would not be used as a supermarket or grocery store for a period of forty years to protect his existing business at the Elizabeth Street store from competition. Plaintiff alleges that the purchase price negotiated between it and Katz took into account the value of the restrictive covenant and that Katz paid less for the property because of the restriction. There is no evidence, however, of the purchase price. It is also undisputed that the covenant was expressly set forth in a recorded deed, that the Authority took title to the premises with actual notice of the restrictive covenant, and, indeed, that all the defendants, including C-Town, had actual notice of the covenant.

The parties do not specifically contest the reasonableness of either the duration or area of the covenant. Aspects of the "touch and concern" test also remain useful in evaluating the reasonableness of a covenant, insofar as it aids the courts in differentiating between promises that were intended to bind only the individual parties to a land conveyance and promises affecting the use and value of the land that was intended to be passed on to subsequent parties. Covenants not to compete typically do touch and concern the land. In noncompetition cases, the "burden" factor of the "touch and concern" test is easily satisfied regardless of the definition chosen because the covenant restricts the actual use of the land. Berger, *supra,* 52 Wash. L. Rev. at 872. The Appellate Division properly concluded that the George Street store was burdened. However, we disagree with the Appellate Division's conclusion that in view of the covenant's speculative impact, the covenant did not provide a sufficient "benefit" to the Elizabeth Street property because it burdened only a small portion (George Street store) of the "market circle" (less than one-half acre in a market circle of 2000 acres).

The size of the burdened property relative to the market area is not a probative measure of whether the Elizabeth store was benefitted. Presumably, the use of the Elizabeth Street store as a supermarket would be enhanced if competition were lessened in its market area. If plaintiff's allegations that the profits of the Elizabeth Street store increased after the sale of the George Street store are true, this would be evidence that a benefit was "conveyed" on the Elizabeth Street store. Likewise, information that the area was so densely populated, that the George Street property was the only unique property available for a supermarket, would show that the Elizabeth Street store property was benefitted by the covenant. In this connection the C-Town executive in his deposition noted that the George Street store location "businesswise was promising because there's no other store in town." Such evidence, however, also should be considered in determining the "reasonableness" of the area covered by the covenant and whether the covenant unduly restrained trade.

Defendants' primary contention is that due to the circumstances of the neighborhood and more particularly the circumstances of the people of the neighborhood, plaintiff's covenant interferes with the public's interest. Whether that claim is essentially that the community has changed since the covenant was enacted or that the circumstances were such that when the covenant was enacted, it interfered with the public interest, we are unable to ascertain from the record. "Public interest" and "changed circumstances" arguments are extremely fact-sensitive. The only evidence that addresses those issues, the three affidavits of Mr. Keefe, Mr. Nero and Ms. Scott, are insufficient to support any finding with respect to those arguments.

The fact-sensitive nature of a "reasonableness" analysis make resolution of this dispute through summary judgment inappropriate. We therefore remand the case to the trial court for a thorough analysis of the "reasonableness" factors delineated herein.

The trial court must first determine whether the covenant was reasonable at the time it was enacted. If it was reasonable then, but now adversely affects commercial development and the public welfare of the people of New Brunswick, the trial court may consider whether allowing damages for breach of the covenant is an appropriate remedy. C-Town could then continue to operate but Davidson would get damages for the value of his covenant. On the limited record before us, however, it is impossible to make a determination concerning either reasonableness of the covenant or whether damages, injunctive relief, or any relief is appropriate.

In sum, we reject the trial court's conclusion because it depends largely on the continued vitality of *Brewer,* which we hereby overrule. *Supra* at 201-202, 579 A.2d at 290-291. Likewise, we reject the Appellate Division's reliance on the "touch and concern" test. Instead, the proper test to determine the enforceability of a restricted noncompetition covenant in a commercial land transaction is a test of "reasonableness," an approach adopted by a majority of the jurisdictions. . . .

Judgment reversed and cause remanded for further proceedings consistent with this opinion.

POLLOCK, J., concurring. . . .

My basic difference with the majority is that I believe the critical consideration in determining the validity of this covenant is whether it is reasonable as to scope and duration, a point that has never been at issue in this case. Nor has there ever been any question whether the original parties to the covenant, Davidson Bros., Inc. (Davidson), and D. Katz & Sons, Inc. (Katz) intended that the covenant should run with the land. Likewise, the New Brunswick Housing Authority (the Authority) and C-Town have never disputed that they did not have actual notice of the covenant or that there was privity between them and Katz. Finally, the defendants have not contended that the covenant constitutes an unreasonable restraint on trade or that it has an otherwise unlawful purpose, such as invidious discrimination. Davidson, moreover, makes the uncontradicted assertion that the covenant is a burden to the George Street property and benefits the Elizabeth Street property. Hence, the covenant satisfies the requirement that it touch and concern the benefitted and burdened properties.

The fundamental flaw in the majority's analysis is in positing that an otherwise-valid covenant can become invalid not because it results in an unreasonable restraint on trade, but because invalidation facilitates a goal that the majority deems worthy. Considerations such as "changed circumstances" and "the public interest," when they do not constitute such a restraint, should not affect the enforceability of a covenant. Instead, they should relate to whether the appropriate method of enforcement is an injunction or damages. A court should not declare a noncompetition covenant invalid merely because enforcement would lead to a result with which the court disagrees. This leads me to conclude that the only issue on remand should be whether the appropriate remedy is damages or an injunction.

Enforcement of the restriction by an injunction will deprive the downtown residents of the convenience of shopping at the George Street property. Refusal to enforce the covenant, on the other hand, will deprive Davidson of the benefit of its covenant. Thus, the case presents a tension between two worthy objectives: the continued operation of the supermarket for the benefit of needy citizens, and the enforcement of the covenant. An award of damages to Davidson rather than the grant of an injunction would permit the realization of both objectives. . . .

For me the critical issue is whether the appropriate remedy for enforcing the covenant is damages or an injunction. Ordinarily, as between competing land users, the more efficient remedy for breach of a covenant is an injunction. R. Posner, Economic Analysis of Law 62 (1986) (Posner); R. Epstein, Notice and Freedom of Contract in the Law of Servitudes, 55 S. Cal. L. Rev. 1353-67 (1962); Calabresi and Melamed, Property Rules, Liability Rules, and Inalienability: One View of the Cathedral, 85 Harv. L. Rev. 1089, 1118 (1972) (Calabresi and Melamed). But see Posner, *supra,* at 59; Calabresi and Melamed, *supra,* at 119 (discussing situations in which damages are a more efficient remedy than an injunction). If Katz still owned the George Street property, the efficient remedy, therefore, would be an injunction. The Authority, which took title with knowledge of the covenant, is in no better position than Katz insofar as the binding effect of the covenant is concerned. Although an injunction might be the most efficient form of relief, it would however deprive the residents of access to the George Street store.

The economic efficiency of an injunction, although persuasive, is not dispositive. The right rule of law is not necessarily the one that is most efficient. Saint Barnabas Medical Center v. Essex County, 111 N.J. 67, 88, 543 A.2d 34 (1988) (Pollock, J., concurring); see also R. Coase, The Problem of Social Cost, 3 J. Law & Econ. 1, 19 (1960). In other cases, New Jersey courts have allowed cost considerations other than efficiency to affect the award of a remedy.

Injunctions, moreover, are ordinarily issued in the discretion of the court. Id. at 29, 135 A.2d 204. Hence, "[t]he court of equity has the power of devising its remedy and shaping it so as to fit the changing circumstances of every case and the complex relations of all the parties." Sears, Roebuck & Co. v. Camp, 124 N.J. Eq. 403, 412, 1 A.2d 425 (E. & A. 1938) (quoting Pomeroy, Equity Jurisprudence §109 (5th ed. 1941)). In the exercise of its discretion, a court may deny injunctive relief when damages provide an available adequate remedy at law. See Board of Educ., Borough of Union Beach v. N.J.E.A., 53 N.J. 29, 43, 247 A.2d 867 (1968).

In the past, however, an injunction in cases involving real covenants and equitable servitudes "was granted almost as a matter of course upon a breach of the covenant. The amount of damages, and even the fact that the plaintiff has sustained any pecuniary damages, [was] wholly immaterial."

J. N. Pomeroy, Equity Jurisprudence, §1342 (5th ed. 1941). The roots of that tradition are buried deep in the English common law and are not suited for modern American commercial practices. In brief, the unswerving preference for injunctive relief over damages is an anachronism.   *Davis wins*

At English common law, as between grantors and grantees, covenants running with the land violated the public policy against encumbrances. See Powell, *supra*, §670 n.27 (citing Keppell v. Bailey, 39 Eng. Rep. 1042 (Ch. 1834)). The policy becomes understandable on realizing that England originally did not provide a system for recording encumbrances, such as restrictive covenants. See Berger, A Policy Analysis of Promises Respecting the Use of Land, 55 Minn. L. Rev. 167, 186 (1970). Without a recording system, a subsequent grantee might not receive actual or constructive notice of such a covenant. As the Court points out, "[a]dequate notice obliterated any express requirement of 'touch and concern.'" Ante at 204, 579 A.2d at 292.

For centuries, New Jersey has provided a means for recording restrictive covenants. Hence, the policy considerations that counselled against enforcement of restrictive covenants at English common law do not apply in this state. In the absence of an adequate remedy at law, moreover, the English equity courts filled the gap by providing equitable relief, such as an injunction. *Tulk, supra*, 2 Phil. 774, 41 Eng. Rep. 1143 (discussed by the majority, ante at 204, 579 A.2d at 292.) In this state, unlike in England, covenants between grantor and grantee are readily enforceable. Roehrs v. Lees, 178 N.J. Super. 399, 429 A.2d 388 (App. Div. 1981) (covenant between neighboring property owners arising from a grantor-grantee relationship between original covenanting parties enforceable; matter remanded to trial court to determine whether damages or injunction was appropriate).

Hence, the need for injunctive relief, as distinguished from damages, is less compelling in New Jersey than at English common law, where damages were not always available. I would rely on the rule that a court should not grant an equitable remedy when damages are adequate. *N.J.E.A., supra*, 53 N.J. at 43, 247 A.2d 867.

Here, moreover, the Authority holds a trump card not available to all other property owners burdened by restrictive covenants — the power to condemn. By recourse to that power, the Authority can vitiate the injunction by condemning the covenant and compensating Davidson for its lost benefit. That power does not alter the premise that an injunction is generally the most efficient form of relief. See Calabresi and Melamed, *supra*, at 1118; Posner, *supra*, at 62. It merely emphasizes that the Authority through condemnation can effectively transform injunctive relief into a damages award. Arguably, the most efficient result is to enforce the covenant against the Authority and then remit it to its power of condemnation. This result would recognize the continuing validity of the covenant, compensate Davidson for its benefit, and permit the needy citizens of New Brunswick to enjoy convenient shopping.

Forcing the Authority to institute eminent-domain proceedings conceivably would waste judicial resources and impose undue costs on the parties. A more appropriate result is to award damages to Davidson for breach of the covenant. That would be true, I believe, even against a subsequent grantee that does not possess the power to condemn.

Money damages would compensate Davidson for the wrong done by the opening of the George Street supermarket. Davidson would be "given what plaintiffs are given in many types of cases — relief measured, so far as the court may reasonably do so, in damages." Gilpin v. Jacob Ellis Rea Realties, 47 N.J. Super 26, 34, 135 A.2d 204 (App. Div. 1957). The award of money damages, rather than an injunction, might be the more appropriate form of relief for several reasons. First, a damages award is "particularly applicable to a case, such as this, wherein we are dealing with two commercial properties. . . ." Id. at 35, 135 A.2d 204. Second, the award of damages in a single proceeding would provide more efficient justice than an injunction in the present case, with a condemnation suit to follow. Davidson would be compensated for the loss of the covenant and the needy residents would enjoy more convenient shopping. That solution is both efficient and just.

I can appreciate why New Brunswick residents want a supermarket and why the Authority would come to their aid. Supermarkets may be essential for the salvation of inner cities and their residents. The Authority's motives, however noble, should not vitiate Davidson's right to compensation. The fair result, it seems to me, is for the Authority to compensate Davidson in damages for the breach of its otherwise valid and enforceable covenant.

Justice CLIFFORD joins in this opinion.

NOTES AND QUESTIONS

1. **Evidence at the retrial.** You are the plaintiff's (defendant's) attorney. What forms of evidence would you muster to persuade the court that the noncompetition covenant is reasonable (unreasonable)? That injunctive relief, rather than damages, is the better (poorer) remedy?

2. **The Massachusetts story.** In Norcross v. James, 140 Mass. 188, 2 N.E. 946 (1885), Justice Holmes, writing for the court, described a covenant (in favor of a quarry operator) that barred a fee owner from quarrying on his farm, as seeking to create "an easement of monopoly"; his court denied enforcement. Antagonism to such covenants, treating them as invalid per se, persisted. See Shade v. M. O'Keefe, Inc., 260 Mass. 180, 156 N.E. 867 (1927) (covenant barring fee owner from carrying on grocery business). The opinion in Shell Oil Co. v. Henry Ouellette & Sons, 352 Mass. 725, 731, 227 N.E.2d 509, 513 (1967), first questioned the absolutist view, and the court in Whitinsville Plaza, Inc. v. Kotseas, 390 N.E.2d 243, 250 (Mass. 1979), finally overruled Norcross and Shade, bringing Massachusetts in line with her sister states.

3.   **Leasehold competitive restraints**. Recall *University Club,* Chapter 3. Trade exclusives and their reciprocal, restraints on a tenant's activity, routinely appear in retail leases, especially as part of a shopping center development. Should such restraints be presumed reasonable? Compare Restatement (Second) of Property §13.2, Comment b (1977). Suppose that a major tenant, rather than the landlord, is given the veto power over the sales activities of other tenants in the center? Compare *Gimbel Brothers, Inc.* FTC Dkt. 8885, Consent Order announced Nov. 29, 1973, 39 Fed. Reg. 7164 (1974), Final Order, Jan. 30, 1974 (Gimbels must cease and desist from enforcing, *inter alia,* any agreement giving to Gimbels (a major tenant) the right to limit the brands of merchandise or service that any other retailer in a shopping center may offer).

3.   Interference with Constitutionally or Statutorily Protected Right

RHODES v. PALMETTO PATHWAY HOMES, INC.

400 S.E.2d 484 (S.C. 1991)

FINNEY, J.:

Appellant Palmetto Pathway Homes, Inc., appeals from a circuit court order permanently enjoining it from establishing a group residence for mentally impaired adults on property owned by the appellant and located in a subdivision subject to restrictive covenants. We reverse.

Respondent Frances Fulmer Rhodes owns property in the subdivision where appellant, a non-profit corporation, intended to operate the group residence. Respondent instituted this action for a permanent injunction, alleging that appellant's use of the property as a home for unrelated mentally impaired adults was prohibited by the restrictive covenants. The pertinent portion of the restrictive covenants states:

> E. The property hereby conveyed shall not be used otherwise than for private residence purposes, nor shall more than one residence, with the necessary out-buildings be erected on any one lot, nor shall any apartment house or tenement house be erected thereon; nor shall any one lot be subdivided or its boundary lines changed from the location as shown on said map without in any one of the cases above enumerated the written consent of the grantor endorsed on the deed of conveyance thereof.

The trial court determined that a group residence would violate the restrictive covenants and granted a permanent injunction against the appellant. In his order enjoining establishment of the home, the trial judge stated: "This court cannot override restrictive covenants unless it finds that the restrictive covenants are in violation of our State or General Law." In its findings, the trial court noted, "The defendant is about to engage in a business or commercial enterprise" based upon the fact that the appellant would receive income as a result of housing the residents, pay employees, pay withholding taxes, keep records and prepare profit and loss statements. The trial judge held that "the group housing as described by the Defendant does not meet the definition of a single family house as intended by the restrictive covenants. . ."

First, appellant maintains that the number of handicapped individuals occupying the premises will at no time exceed nine, that the dwelling will be used solely as a residence and no training or treatment will be conducted at the home, and that routine household chores will be performed by the residents with the assistance and round-the-clock supervision of counselors. Second, appellant argues that the functions characterized by the trial court as business activity are incidental to the operation and maintenance of the residence as a home. Finally, appellant contends the right of handicapped individuals to reside in a community setting is protected by public policy and state and federal law, notwithstanding restrictive covenants. We agree.

Courts tend to strictly interpret restrictive covenants and resolve any doubt or ambiguities in a covenant on the presumption of free and unrestricted land use. Edwards v. Surratt, 228 S.C. 512, 90 S.E.2d 906 (1956). The historical disfavor of restrictive covenants by the law emanates from the widely held view that society's best interests are advanced by encouraging the free and unrestricted use of land. See Hamilton v. CCM, Inc., 274 S.C. 152, 263 S.E.2d 378 (1980). Thus, to enforce a restrictive covenant, a party must show that the restriction applies to the property either by the covenant's express language or by a plain unmistakable implication. Hamilton v. CCM, Inc., supra.

This Court finds persuasive the reasoning of other jurisdictions which have held that the incident necessities of operating a group home such as maintaining records, filing accounting reports, managing, supervising, and providing care for individuals in exchange for monetary compensation are collateral to the prime purpose and function of a family housekeeping unit. Hence, these activities do not, in and of themselves, change the character of a residence from private to commercial. Gregory v. State Department of Mental Health Retardation and Hospitals, 495 A.2d 997 (R.I. 1985); J. T. Hobby & Son, Inc. v. Family Homes, 302 N.C. 64, 274 S.E.2d 174, 180 (1981).

We conclude that interpretation of the restrictive covenants in such a way as to prohibit location of a group residence for mentally impaired adults in a community is contrary to public policy as enunciated by both state and federal legislation. See Sea Pines Plantation Co. v. Wells, 294 S.C. 266, 363 S.E.2d 891 (1987) [Restrictive covenants will not be interpreted or given effect if their application would be contrary to public policy]; Craig v. Bossenbery, 134 Mich. App. 543, 351 N.W.2d 596 (1984).

Concern for the mentally handicapped has been embodied in the public policy of South Carolina for many years. The Bill of Rights for Handicapped Persons, as set forth in S.C. Code Ann. §43-33-510 et seq. (1976), demonstrates a commitment to the handicapped. S.C. Code Ann. §6-7-830 (Supp. 1989), which exempts homes for the mentally handicapped from local zoning ordinances, expresses in broad terms the State's public policy that handicapped persons shall not suffer housing discrimination on account of their handicap.

The Fair Housing Amendments Act of 1988 articulates the public policy of the United States as being to encourage and support handicapped persons' right to live in a group home in the community of their choice. 42 U.S.C. §§3602-3608 (Supp. 1990). "This provision is intended to prohibit special restrictive covenants . . . which have the effect of excluding . . . congregate living arrangements for persons with handicaps." H.R. Rep. No. 100-711, 100th Cong. 2d Session, 23 (1988), U.S. Code Cong. & Admin. News 1988, pp. 2173, 2184. Since the need for treatment and maintenance of the mentally handicapped is a legitimate and strong public interest as recognized by state and federal legislation, a refusal to enforce restrictive covenants against otherwise unobtrusive group homes substantially advances that interest by promoting integration of the mentally handicapped into all neighborhoods of the community. Westwood Homeowners Association v. Tenhoff, 155 Ariz. 229, 745 P.2d 976 (Ariz. App. 1987).

The Michigan Appellate Court made a persuasive statement on public policy regarding handicapped individuals in Craig v. Bossenbery, *supra,* declaring:

> The strong public policy supporting group homes overcomes the public policy which favors the right of property owners to create restrictive covenants. We cannot consider the property owners' apparent motive in drafting or retaining a covenant unless we encourage indirect methods to exclude the handicapped where blatant, direct methods would clearly fail.

351 N.W.2d at 601.

We conclude that the location and operation of a group residence for mentally retarded adults in the manner and under the conditions proposed by the appellant would not significantly alter the character of the residential community in which it is situated and would not infringe upon the plain and obvious purpose of the restrictive covenants. Furthermore, this Court finds that enforcement of this restrictive covenant would have the effect of depriving the mentally impaired of rights guaranteed under the Fair Housing Amendments Act. For the foregoing reasons, the ruling of the circuit court is reversed and the injunction is vacated.

Reversed and vacated.

NOTES AND QUESTIONS

1. **Racially restrictive covenants.** Recall Shelley v. Kraemer, 334 U.S. 1 (1948), page 145, *supra,* where the Supreme Court barred state courts, as a denial of equal protection, from injunctively enforcing racially restrictive covenants, and Barrows v. Jackson, 346 U.S. 249 (1953), where the Court also barred the granting of damages for a covenant violation. Note, however, that the Court refused to outlaw such covenants, and left open the avenue of voluntary compliance. Such conduct today would be a discriminatory housing practice under Title VIII of the Civil Rights Act of 1968, 42 U.S.C.A. §§3601-3619 (1994). So, too, would discrimination based on religion, sex, national origin, handicap, or familial status. See Chapter 10.

That racially restrictive covenants are void does not keep them from being an occasional subject of controversy. During 1986 confirmation hearings before he became Chief Justice, William Rehnquist was asked questions about the deed to his Phoenix home, which contained the following provision:

> No lot, nor any part thereof within a period of 99 years . . . shall ever be sold, transferred or leased to, nor shall any lot . . . within said period be inhabited or occupied by any person not of the white or Caucasian race.

N.Y. Times, Aug. 8, 1986, at A8. Additionally, the deed for his Vermont vacation home bore a covenant prohibiting lease or sale to "members of the Hebrew race." Other major political figures have run into similar problems. George Bush was criticized in 1987 because two houses that he purchased in Texas in the fifties were in subdivisions where all of the houses carried covenants disallowing sale and occupancy to "any Negro or person of African descent," or restricting the same to Caucasians. *The Nation,* Nov. 28, 1987, at 616. Even John F. Kennedy purchased a home in 1957 that was covered by a covenant prohibiting resale to members of "the Negro race." Chicago Trib., Jan. 5, 1986, at 5.

Purchasers are often unaware of such covenants, and even when they are, some effort is required to have them removed from deeds. Furthermore, many title companies, fearing civil rights complaints, do not inform buyers of such restrictions. Is it harmful to leave them in, if they have no effect? Some scholars have argued that even if unenforceable, continued repetition of racially restrictive covenants in deeds is objectionable, in that some purchasers may not realize that they are void. N.Y. Times, Aug. 1, 1986, at A9.

2. **Group homes and single-family residential restrictions.** Note that the South Carolina court invoked the 1988 Fair Housing Amendments Act, which extended Title VIII to include discrimination based on handicap, as well as the earlier state law that exempted group homes for the mentally handicapped from the aegis of local zoning. To show a Title VIII violation,

must show

the plaintiff must show either discriminatory intent, Village of Arlington
Heights v. Metropolitan Housing Dev. Corp., 429 U.S. 252 (1977), or dis-
criminatory effect, United States v. City of Black Jack, 508 F.2d 1179 (8th
Cir. 1974), *cert. denied*, 422 U.S. 1042 (1975).

In analyzing whether the enforcement of a restrictive covenant would
have a discriminatory effect (disparate impact), one court cited a House
Report that stated:

> [Section 3604(f)(2)] is intended to prohibit restrictive covenants . . . which
> have the effect of excluding, for example, congregate living arrangements for
> persons with handicaps. . . . Another method of making housing unavailable
> to people with disabilities has been the application or enforcement of other-
> wise neutral rules and regulations on . . . land use in a manner which discrimi-
> nates against people with disabilities. Such determination often results from
> false . . . assumptions about the needs of handicapped people, as well as un-
> founded fears of difficulties about the problems that their tenancies may pose.
> These and similar practices would be prohibited. Martin v. Constance, 843 F.
> Supp. 1321, 1325-26 (E.D. Mo. 1994).

The court also cited §3604(f)(3)(B), which requires "reasonable accommodation" to enable the handicapped to use and enjoy a dwelling, and
that a reasonable accommodation in this instance would be not to seek enforcement of the private restriction.

Might there be any circumstances in which, in the face of Title VIII,
courts might validly enforce single-family residential restrictions whose effect is to bar a group home for the mentally ill or developmentally disabled?
What of a group home for the rehabilitation of substance abusers?

3. **Impairment of contract.** Prior to passage of the 1988 Fair Housing
amendments, an Indiana statute barred enforcement of any restriction that
would permit the residential use of property but prevent its use as a residential facility for developmentally disabled or mentally ill persons. The
state supreme court, failing to see the "societal necessity" to protect these
groups against housing discrimination, held that the statute as to existing
restrictive covenants violated the state constitutional impairment of contract clause. Clem v. Christole, Inc., 582 N.E.2d 780 (Ind. 1991). Faced with
a similar claim in applying a similar state law, a Texas appeals court held
that private contract rights must yield to the state's right to exercise its police power. Deep East Texas Reg. MHMRS v. Kinnear, 877 S.W.2d 550 (Tex.
App. 1994). How would you make the police power case for protective
legislation?

4. **Generalized antidiscrimination laws.** Applying a state law that
barred businesses from engaging in any form of arbitrary discrimination,
the California Supreme Court held that a condominium development, a
housing complex of 629 units, could not limit residency to persons over the
age of 18. O'Connor v. Village Green Owners Assn., 33 Cal. 3d 790 (1983).

4.   Violates Public Policies Affecting Privacy, Personal Autonomy, Expression, and Association

NOBLE v. MURPHY

34 Mass. App. 452, 612 N.E. 2d 266 (1993)

JACOBS, J.

The plaintiffs, as managers of a condominium established under G.L. c. 183A, sought the removal of two pet dogs from a condominium unit owned by John Murphy and Margaret Wilson. They based their action upon a condominium by-law banning all pets from any housing unit or common area of the condominium. They also sought to enforce by-laws providing for the assessment of a $5 per day per violation penalty and payment by the defendants of the "costs and expense of eliminating" violations. The defendants, by answer and counterclaim, questioned the validity of the pet restriction and the enforceability of any fines and assessments based upon it. A judge of the Superior Court allowed the plaintiffs' motion for summary judgment and denied that of the defendants. Murphy and Wilson appealed from a judgment which thereafter was entered ordering them permanently to remove their dogs and to pay to the plaintiffs assessments for penalties, costs, and attorney's fees totalling $15,244.75. We affirm.

The pertinent facts are as follows: Established in 1973, "Weymouthport Condominium — Phase I" is a 271-unit complex managed by a trust of which the plaintiffs are trustees. The trust was formed pursuant to G.L. c. 183A, §8(*i*), to govern the management of the condominium and contained by-laws that incorporated rules and regulations which included a restriction against raising, breeding, or keeping any "animals or reptiles of any kind . . . in any Unit or in the Common Elements . . . ," together with a provision, sometimes referred to as an amortization or no replacement rule, that protected the harboring of pets owned at the time of purchase of a unit. In 1979, the original trust by-laws were amended to provide that "[n]o animals, reptiles or pets of any kind shall be raised, bred, kept or permitted in any Unit or in the Common Elements. . . ." The significant difference was that the pet restriction had ascended from rules and regulations to the by-laws. The amendment was enacted in response to the trustees' concern with pet problems and their understanding that Johnson v. Keith, 368 Mass. 316, 331 N.E.2d 879 (1975), had rendered unenforceable the pet restriction contained in the regulations.[4] The amendment also con-

---

4. A similarly absolute pet restriction was before the Supreme Judicial Court in Johnson v. Keith, *supra*, but the issue of its validity was expressly left unanswered. Id. at 321, 331 N.E.2d 879. The court held that rules and regulations governing use of a condominium unit were unenforceable notwithstanding that they were incorporated by reference into the by-laws of the organization of unit owners of the condominium. It noted that the rules and regulations were not recorded with the by-laws and that they could be amended by other than a two-thirds

tained an amortization provision allowing unit owners and tenants "in occupancy prior to the recording of [the] amendment" to continue to keep
in their unit any household pet owned by them at the time they purchased
or rented their units. Also, the amendment made allowance for unit owners
to have one household pet upon receipt of written permission of the
trustees.

In September of 1983, Murphy and Wilson were notified by the manager of the condominium that a dog which they had acquired since purchasing their unit earlier that year was being kept by them in violation of
the pet restriction amendment. After removing the dog, Murphy and Wilson, in November of 1983, and again in January of 1984, unsuccessfully
sought permission to return it to the unit, the latter request being based
upon Wilson's claimed permanent and total disability. In April, 1985, Murphy and Wilson moved out. After a period of renting out their unit, they
reoccupied it in November, 1987. Upon being notified in May, 1988, that
they were again in violation of the pet restriction, Murphy and Wilson requested and received permission to house their dogs (they had by then
acquired a second dog) temporarily in their unit during weekends until
October 1, 1988. When the dogs were not removed after that date, the
plaintiffs imposed a fine of $5 a day and ultimately brought this action.

1. *Validity of the pet restriction.* The defendants claim the applicable
standard for determining the validity of the pet restriction is that of "unreasonable interference" under G.L. c. 183A, §11(*e*), as inserted by St. 1963,
c. 493, §1, which requires the by-laws of the organization of unit owners to
"at least" contain such use restrictions "not set forth in the master deed, as
are designed to prevent unreasonable interference with the use of [the
owners'] respective units and of the common areas and facilities by the several unit owners." They argue that the question whether the presence of
animals constitutes an unreasonable interference under the circumstances
is one of material fact and therefore not suitable for resolution by summary
judgment. They rely in large part on an affidavit of an expert in animal
behavior who opines that "prohibition of all animals from the condominium units is more restrictive and burdensome than required to meet
the statutory standard of preventing unreasonable interference with use of
other units or the common areas." The affidavit points to animals such as
goldfish and parakeets which "present[ ] no risk of interference of any
kind to use of neighboring units or common areas." The argument misper-
ceives both the thrust of the statute and the basic nature of condominium
ownership.

---

vote of the unit owners, as required for a by-law amendment. The court, in effect, decided that
restrictions relating to the *use of a condominium unit* as distinguished from those relating to *use
of the common areas and facilities* must be contained in either the by-laws or master deed to be
enforceable under G.L. c. 183A. The court noted that "this technicality may be corrected by
appropriate action of the unit owners." Johnson v. Keith, *supra* at 320-321, 331 N.E.2d 879.

Ownership of a condominium unit is a hybrid form of interest in real estate, entitling the owner to both "exclusive ownership and possession of his unit, G.L. c. 183A, §4, and . . . an undivided interest [as tenant in common together with all the other unit owners] in the common areas. . . ." Kaplan v. Boudreaux, 410 Mass. 435, 438, 573 N.E.2d 495 (1991). It affords an opportunity to combine the legal benefits of fee simple ownership[5] with the economic advantages of joint acquisition and operation of various amenities including recreational facilities, contracted caretaking, and security safeguards. Central to the concept of condominium ownership is the principle that each owner, in exchange for the benefits of association with other owners, "must give up a certain degree of freedom of choice which he might otherwise enjoy in separate, privately owned property." Hidden Harbour Estates, Inc. v. Norman, 309 So. 2d 180, 182 (Fla. Dist. Ct. App. 1975). See Franklin v. Spadafora, 388 Mass. 764, 769, 447 N.E.2d 1244 (1983).

General Laws c. 183A, §1(e), permits restrictions on the use of residential units which are "designed to prevent" unreasonable interference by individual unit owners with the other owners' use of their respective units and the common areas and facilities. There is no prohibition against restrictions that, although patently designed to prevent such interference, also incidentally preclude generically similar uses that may not be as likely to encroach on the other owners' use of their units and the common areas and facilities. Close judicial scrutiny and possible invalidation or limitation of fundamentally proper but broadly drawn use restrictions, not expressly prohibited by the enabling statute, would deny to developers and unit owners the "planning flexibility" inherent in c. 183A. See Barclay v. DeVeau, 384 Mass. 676, 682, 429 N.E.2d 323 (1981). In Franklin v. Spadafora, 388 Mass. at 769, 447 N.E.2d 1244, the court upheld a by-law amendment restricting to two the number of condominium units which could be owned by one person or entity and noted that nothing in c. 183A prohibited the type of general restriction at issue even if the court assumed that tenants would not be less responsible than owners. Id. at 768-769 & n.12, 447 N.E.2d 1244. The court stated that, viewed as a compromise between the desires of the majority and the right of an individual owner to use property as he or she desires, "the amendment is a reasonable means of achieving the majority's proper goal." Id. at 769-770, 447 N.E.2d 1244. See Woodvale Condominium Trust v. Scheff, 27 Mass. App. Ct. 530, 534-535, 540 N.E.2d 206 (1989) (a condominium association may prohibit the operation of a family day-care business in a unit notwithstanding that the enterprise's interfering effect on other unit owners is "minor . . . modest[ ] . . . [and] benign . . .").

"The most common standard of review [of condominium use restric-

5. The Uniform Condominium Act approved by the National Conference of Commissioners on Uniform State Laws in 1977 defines "condominium" as meaning "real estate, portions of which are designated for separate ownership and the remainder of which is designated for common ownership solely by the owners of those portions." This Act has been adopted in ten states, but Massachusetts is not among them.

tions] is equitable reasonableness." Goldberg, Community Association Use Restrictions: Applying the Business Judgment Doctrine, 64 Chi. — Kent L. Rev. 653, 655 (1988). Franklin v. Spadafora, 388 Mass. at 770-772, 447 N.E.2d 1244, can be read to favor such a test. Its formulation is commonly attributed to Hidden Harbour Estates, Inc. v. Norman, *supra,* a Florida decision cited in both Franklin v. Spadafora, *supra,* 388 Mass. at 769, 447 N.E.2d 1244, and Woodvale Condominium Trust v. Scheff, 27 Mass. App. Ct. at 533, 540 N.E.2d 206, and in which it is stated that: "the test is reasonableness. If a rule is reasonable the association can adopt it; if not, it cannot. It is not necessary that conduct be so offensive as to constitute a nuisance in order to justify regulation thereof." Hidden Harbour Estates, Inc. v. Norman, 309 So. 2d at 182. This approach recognizes the discretion of the majority of unit owners while at the same time limiting their rule-making authority to those matters "that are reasonably related to the promotion of the health, happiness and peace of mind of the unit owners." Hidden Harbour Estates, Inc. v. Basso, 393 So. 2d 637, 640 (Fla. Dist. Ct. App. 1981). We recognize that a somewhat different standard of review may be implicated where, in contrast to this case, a restriction is promulgated after the owner who is in violation of the rule acquires his unit. See Franklin v. Spadafora, *supra,* 388 Mass. at 772-774, 447 N.E.2d 1244.

When enacting the pet restriction in issue, the trustees expressed concern with "pet problems." The record indicates that they had received several complaints involving dogs and one that concerned a boa constrictor. Unit owners are not required to conduct investigations or cite authority in order reasonably to conclude that the presence of pets within the condominium may interfere with their health, happiness, and peace of mind.[6] It is a subject well within their common knowledge and competence. Also, considerations of efficient and even-handed enforcement support an absolute prohibition of all pets rather than a restriction limited to certain pets. Cf. Wilshire Condominium Assn., Inc. v. Kohlbrand, 368 So. 2d 629, 631 (Fla. Dist. Ct. App. 1979) (citing New York cases in which absolute dog prohibitions have been upheld as a matter of law). Any concern with procrustean effect is met by the provision giving the trustees discretion to permit a unit owner to keep a household pet.

A condominium use restriction appearing in originating documents which predate the purchase of individual units may be subject to even more liberal review than if promulgated after units have been individually acquired. The substance of the pet restriction in issue was part of the originating documents of the Weymouthport condominium. The master deed

---

6. "Attitudes about pet animals are understandably passionate. One person's companion is another's nuisance. It is not necessary to approve or even sympathize with [the trustees'] position to acknowledge that an owner of . . . property may think it best for the property and for the preponderance of current and future [occupants] that there not be pet animals in the [condominium]." Clifford V. Miller, Inc. v. Rent Control Bd. of Cambridge, 31 Mass. App. Ct. 91, 95, 575 N.E.2d 356 (1991).

expressly made unit ownership subject to attached rules and regulations that contained the restriction. The 1979 incorporation of the restriction into the by-laws was undertaken primarily to better accommodate future enforcement. Constructive knowledge of the regulatory scheme of the condominium was chargeable to Murphy and Wilson as of the time they acquired their unit. See Tosney v. Chelmsford Village Condominium Assn., 397 Mass. 683, 688, 493 N.E.2d 488 (1986).

There is sound basis for treating restrictions in the originating documents as being "clothed with a very strong presumption of validity which arises from the fact that each individual unit owner purchases his unit knowing of and accepting the restrictions to be imposed. Such restrictions are very much in the nature of covenants running with the land and they will not be invalidated absent a showing that they are wholly arbitrary in their application, in violation of public policy, or that they abrogate some fundamental constitutional right. . . . Indeed, a use restriction in [the originating documents] may have a certain degree of unreasonableness to it, and yet withstand attack in the courts." Hidden Harbour Estates, Inc. v. Basso, 393 So. 2d at 639-640. See also Natelson, Law of Property Owners Associations, §4.4.4, at 34 n.17 (1989 & Supp. 1991) (questioning the appropriateness of reasonableness review when the regulation in question was enacted prior to its opponents' acquiring ownership and was known by them at the time of acquisition). Also, unit owners, upon purchase, may pay a premium to procure what they regard as a beneficial restrictive scheme. Note, Judicial Review of Condominium Rulemaking, 94 Harv. L. Rev. 647, 653 (1981). Under this formulation, the value of meeting the reasonable expectations of original unit owners and enforcing their right to freely associate by contract with persons of like expectations outweighs the possibility that some owners may purchase into a condominium regime without actual notice and full understanding of its restrictions. Our appellate decisions appear to recognize the validity of this approach. See Tosney v. Chelmsford Village Condominium Assoc., 397 Mass. at 688, 493 N.E.2d 488; Woodvale Condominium Trust v. Scheff, 27 Mass. App. Ct. at 533, 540 N.E.2d 206 (developers may impose reasonable restrictions on condominiums under c. 183A "and persons who contemplate acquisition of a condominium unit can choose whether to buy into those restrictions"). Compare Note, Condominium Rulemaking — Presumptions, Burdens and Abuses: A Call for Substantive Judicial Review in Florida, 34 U. Fla. L. Rev. 219, 227 & n.50 (1982) ("Because most buyers ignore or misunderstand disclosure statements, a presumption of validity based on the unit owners' knowledge of [origination documents] rests on a practical fiction"); Note, Judicial Review of Condominium Rulemaking, 94 Harv. L. Rev. at 650-651. The defendants do not contend that there is any fundamental public policy or constitutional provision guaranteeing the right to raise, breed, or keep pets in a condominium. By insulating properly-enacted and evenly-enforced use restrictions contained in the master deed or original by-laws of a condominium against attack except on constitutional or public policy grounds, already crowded courts and the majority of unit owners who may be presumed to have chosen not to alter or rescind such restrictions will be spared the burden and expense of highly particularized and lengthy litigation.[7]

2. *Enforcement.* Murphy and Wilson received ample and repeated notice of violation and reasonable opportunity to comply with the restriction. The record does reveal a genuine issue of waiver of violation or of arbitrary, capricious, or discriminatory enforcement. That the trustees consistently and reasonably utilized a complaint-driven procedure for enforcement, which incidentally may have focused on pets observed outside the units, rather than on any which might have been kept within, does not give rise to any constitutional issues.

[handwritten note: Ample notice]

3. *Fines and Fees.* The defendants argue that the by-law provision which entitles the plaintiffs to recoup the "cost and expense" of eliminating by-law violations by an offending unit owner does not include attorneys' fees. The expense provision is part of a valid contract between the parties. Barclay v. DeVeau, 11 Mass. App. Ct. 236, 245, 415 N.E.2d 239 (Greaney, J., dissenting), *S.C.,* 384 Mass. 676, 429 N.E.2d 323 (1981). Attorneys' fees generally constitute the most substantial component of the cost of enforcement and, therefore, would appear to be within the context of the word "expense" and the objective intent of the by-laws to shift the financial burden of successful enforcement to the offender. We need not rule on the question, however, since there is no indication in the record that the defendants raised the issue below or objected to the award of attorneys' fees. Edgar v. Edgar, 406 Mass. 628, 629, 549 N.E.2d 1128 (1990). The fines were in accord with the by-laws and were properly assessed by the defendants and included in the judgment.

[handwritten note: Δ must pay attorney fees]

Judgment affirmed.

NOTES AND QUESTIONS

1. **Woman faces fine for kissing her date.** The June 16, 1991, issue of the Los Angeles Times reported that a 51-year-old woman who said that she had only kissed her date good-night received a warning from her con-

---

7. We resist, as unnecessary to our decision, the plaintiffs' suggestion that we adopt the business judgment rule as the measure of the validity of the actions of a unit owners' organization. That rule, when applied, generally is invoked with respect to questions of the propriety of amendments to a preexisting regulatory scheme and essentially imposes fiduciary duties similar to those required of corporate directors. We recognize, however, that several States have adopted this standard and that it receives varying degrees of approval among commentators. See Hyatt, Condominium and Homeowner Association Practice: Community Association Law, §6.02(a)(1), at 212-218 (2d ed. 1988); Goldberg Community Association Use Restrictions: Applying the Business Judgment Doctrine, 64 Chi.-Kent L. Rev. 653; Note, Judicial Review of Condominium Rulemaking, 94 Harv. L. Rev. at 664-667.

dominium association that she would be fined if "kissing and doing bad things for over 1 hour [while parked in circular driveway]" were to happen again. The association apologized a few days later. The violators, it seems, were not the middle-aged grandmother and her date, but a postadolescent young man and woman. But what about restrictions against necking and "doing bad things" in a car parked in your own driveway?

2. **Rule-making power.** Behavioral restrictions usually appear in association rules and regulations promulgated by the governing board. As to rules governing use of the common areas, the Restatement requires only that such rules (if duly enacted) be reasonably related to furthering a legitimate purpose of the association. The Restatement gives as valid examples rules requiring that all dogs in the common area be leashed, and barring vans, trailers, or recreational vehicles from the parking lot. Absent "special facts," the Restatement would regard as invalid a rule that allowed members to reserve exclusive use of the clubhouse but prohibit political gatherings. Restatement, Servitudes, §6.7 (Prelim. Draft 12, 1995).

3. **Other "horror" stories.** For some other instances of warfare between zealous boards and liberty-loving owners, see Notes 4-6, pages 789-790, *infra*.

§7.6   Succession to Benefits and Burdens of Servitudes

a.   Succession to Appurtenant Benefits and Burdens

RESTATEMENT OF THE LAW OF PROPERTY (SERVITUDES)

Council Draft No. 6 (1994)

INTRODUCTORY NOTE

The hallmark of servitudes is that they run with the land, automatically binding and benefiting subsequent owners. Historically, the law governing the running of easement interests was relatively simple: appurtenant easement benefits and burdens passed with the land into the hands of all takers. Only those takers whose title was superior to that of the person who created the easement, or who were bona fide purchasers protected under the recording act, took free of an easement burden.

The law governing the running of covenants was very complex. Traditional treatment of the subject commingled questions of creating running covenants with questions of determining succession to the interests that ran. Different requirements were imposed for the creation of covenants that would run at law and in equity, and the takers bound and benefited were different for benefits than for burdens and for covenants that ran at law and in equity. . . .

This Restatement leaves the rules applicable to easements substantially

unchanged but significantly simplifies the rules governing covenants. . . .
Substantial simplification is accomplished by differentiating covenants on
the basis of their affirmative or restrictive character, rather than on the old
basis of whether they ran at law or in equity, and applying the easement
rules to almost all situations. Under those rules, all subsequent possessors
are bound by and receive the benefit of servitudes appurtenant to the land.

Handwritten: How simplified

Handwritten: Exceptions

The only instances in which a different rule applies is when land burdened or benefited by an affirmative covenant is in the possession of a lessee or an adverse possessor who has not yet acquired title. Unless a lessee
has assumed the obligation to perform the covenant, the lessee is exempted
unless the covenant should reasonably be performed by the person in possession. Adverse possessors are bound to perform all covenants burdening
the land, but until they acquire title to the property, they like lessees are
excluded from the benefit of all covenants except those that consist in direct benefits to the land or can be enjoyed without diminishing the benefit
to the owner of the property or increasing the costs of performance to the
obligor. . . .

Handwritten: lessee

Handwritten: Adv. poss.

The following case, while paying lip-service to the formal requirements for the burden of a covenant to run with the land, as embodied in
the first Restatement of Property (1944), adopts the position taken by the
new Restatement of Servitudes that the *appurtenant* benefits and burdens of
a servitude (except in the case of lessees and those in the midst of taking by
adverse possession) run to all subsequent possessors and owners of the
property to which they are appurtenant. Notice, though, how this court uses
"touch or concern" as surrogate for "appurtenant."

LAKE ARROWHEAD COMMUNITY CLUB, INC. v. LOONEY

112 Wash. 2d 288, 770 P.2d 1046 (1989)

DURHAM, J.

A purchaser at a tax foreclosure sale generally acquires title that
is clear of all prior encumbrances. As an exception to this rule, RCW
84.64.460 protects recorded appurtenant easements from extinguishment.
In Olympia v. Palzer, 107 Wash. 2d 225, 728 P.2d 135 (1986), we first addressed the effect of RCW 84.64.460 on covenants. We held that a restrictive
covenant requiring the owner to maintain his property as a greenbelt for a
planned unit development was akin to a negative easement and, therefore,
survived the tax foreclosure sale. We hold in the present case that a covenant requiring the owner to pay his share of the costs of maintaining the
neighborhood's facilities also survives a tax sale.

Handwritten: easements stick even to foreclosed land

[margin note: Constructive notice]

FACTS

In 1966, the original developers of the Lake Arrowhead housing subdivision executed and recorded with the Mason County Auditor a document entitled "Lake Arrowhead Restrictive Covenants Running With Land." Covenant 21 authorizes the Lake Arrowhead Community Club, Inc. (Club), a nonprofit organization, to charge and assess its members for the operation and maintenance of certain facilities that are provided for the members' use. The Club subsequently enacted bylaws that provide for the imposition of liens if the assessments are not paid. The bylaws are not recorded.

[margin note: All members of Club must chip in for maintenance]

On February 20, 1978, William Looney and his wife purchased property within the Lake Arrowhead development at a tax foreclosure sale. Looney failed to pay the assessments that accrued after the date of his purchase. The Club filed liens against his property but the debt remained unpaid. *[margin note: Servitude survives tax sale]*

The Club filed suit in Mason County Superior Court. In July 1986, the trial court granted summary judgment to the Club, set damages in the amount of $492.58, granted $831 in attorney fees, and authorized the Club to foreclose on its liens if the judgment was not paid within 5 days. The Court of Appeals reversed, holding that the covenant to pay assessments was extinguished by the tax foreclosure sale. *Lake Arrowhead Comm'ty Club, Inc. v. Looney,* 50 Wash. App. 238, 748 P.2d 649 (1988).

[margin note: T. Ct]

[margin note: Ct of Apps]

BACKGROUND

The general rule in Washington is that a purchaser at a tax foreclosure sale takes title to the property free and clear of all previously existing encumbrances. See discussion in *Palzer,* 107 Wash. 2d at 228, 728 P.2d 135. In 1959, however, the Legislature passed a statute establishing an exception to the general rule. The statute provides that easements survive a tax foreclosure sale, as long as they are appurtenant in nature and they are recorded prior to the date of the delinquent taxes:

[margin note: Rule → Exception]

> The general property tax assessed on any tract, lot, or parcel of real property includes all easements appurtenant thereto, provided said easements are a matter of public record in the auditor's office of the county in which said real property is situated. *Any foreclosure of delinquent taxes on any tract, lot or parcel of real property subject to such easement or easements, and any tax deed issued pursuant thereto shall be subject to such easement or easements,* provided such easement or easements were established of record prior to the year for which the tax was foreclosed.

[margin note: STAT]

(Italics ours.) RCW 84.64.460.

In *Palzer,* this court was asked to decide if a restrictive covenant, requiring certain tracts to be maintained as greenbelts for a planned unit development for the general beautification of the entire development, qualified as an "easement" for purposes of RCW 84.64.460. In analyzing this question, the court first noted that restrictive covenants dealing with the use of land or the character or location of buildings historically had been described as negative easements. The court defined a negative easement as "one which curtails the owner of the servient tenement in the exercise of some of his rights in respect of his estate in favor of the owner of the dominant tenement or tenements." (Italics omitted.) *Palzer,* at 230, 728 P.2d 135 (quoting Annot., Easement or Servitude or Restrictive Covenant as Affected by Sale for Taxes, 168 A.L.R. 529, 536 (1947)). We concluded that "restrictive covenants are the same as negative easements because they curtail the rights of the owner of the servient tenement in favor of the owners of all of the dominant tenements." *Palzer,* at 230, 728 P.2d 135.

We also indicated that the objectives of a planned unit development would be served if restrictive covenants were to survive tax foreclosure sales:

> The ability of homeowners in a PUD to enforce restrictive covenants against original and subsequent property owners helps ensure that the community will be able to maintain its planned character and provide the lifestyle sought by its residents in making their homes there.
>
> The restrictive covenants which apply use restrictions on property located in Evergreen Park are meant to benefit all of the homeowners who live there. . . . If these restrictive covenants were extinguished by the tax foreclosure sale, the planned character of Evergreen Park, the expectations of homeowners and statutory authority would be defeated.

(Citation omitted.) *Palzer,* at 230-31, 728 P.2d 135.

Finally, the court noted that other jurisdictions also have held that restrictive covenants are easements and are not extinguished by a tax foreclosure sale. *Palzer,* at 231, 728 P.2d 135 (citing cases from eight jurisdictions). Based on the foregoing analysis, the court determined that the greenbelt covenant survived the tax foreclosure sale.

Not surprisingly, the parties draw different conclusions as to the proper application of *Palzer* to this case. The Club argues that *Palzer* establishes the rule that all restrictive covenants — a term the Club interprets to include the present covenant — survive a tax foreclosure sale. Looney contends that *Palzer* should be interpreted to extinguish only those covenants that can be likened to negative easements. Looney argues that two factors prevent his covenant from being likened to a negative easement: first, a covenant to pay money is an affirmative obligation, and second, it does not directly restrict the use of land.

ANALYSIS

We deal first with Looney's proposed distinction between affirmative and negative covenants. A covenant to contribute one's share of the neighborhood's maintenance expenses generally is characterized as an affirmative covenant. See 5 R. Powell & P. Rohan, Real Property ¶675[2][a] (1988); 6 P. Rohan, Home Owner Associations and Planned Unit Developments Law and Practice §8.03[2] (1988). For the reasons discussed below, however, we conclude that the covenant in question falls within the scope of RCW 84.64.460.

It is important to note that the language of RCW 84.64.460 is not limited to negative easements, but includes also affirmative easements. Just as a negative covenant can be classified as a negative easement for purposes of RCW 84.64.460 under *Palzer,* so too an affirmative covenant can be likened to an affirmative easement.

Any other conclusion would be inconsistent with the tendency in American courts to forego distinctions between the running of affirmative and negative covenants. See Browder, Running Covenants and Public Policy, 77 Mich. L. Rev. 12, 24 (1978), cited in 5 R. Powell & P. Rohan ¶675[1] n.6; 6 P. Rohan §8.03[2][c]. Although historically, American courts were disinclined to allow the running of affirmative covenants, the modern trend is to allow them to run in the same manner as negative covenants. This change of attitude represents an acknowledgment of the social usefulness of affirmative, as well as negative, covenants. 6 P. Rohan §8.03[2]. Indeed, this court long ago allowed the running of an affirmative covenant as if it were a negative covenant. See Rodruck v. Sand Point Maintenance Comm'n, 48 Wash. 2d 565, 295 P.2d 714 (1956).

In *Palzer* we stated that a negative easement is one which "curtails the owner of the servient tenement in the exercise of some of his rights in respect of his estate in favor of the owner of the dominant tenement or tenements." (Italics omitted.) *Palzer,* 107 Wash. 2d at 230, 728 P.2d 135 (quoting Annot., Easement or Servitude or Restrictive Covenant as Affected by Sale for Taxes, 168 A.L.R. 529, 536 (1947)). Along these same lines, the covenant in question qualifies as an *affirmative* easement, at least for purposes of RCW 84.64.460, because it creates additional obligations in respect of the estate of the owner of the servient tenement in favor of the owner of the dominant tenement or tenements.

We next turn to Looney's contention that a covenant must concern the use of land in order to qualify as an easement under the statute. There can be little doubt that easements involve the use of land. See Black's Law Dictionary 457 (5th ed. 1979). Moreover, the statute protects only *appurtenant* easements from extinguishment. Appurtenant easements are those that primarily benefit another piece of land rather than a particular individual. Winsten v. Prichard, 23 Wash. App. 428, 430, 597 P.2d 415 (1979). The analog for covenants are those that run with the land, because such covenants also involve obligations that are intended to benefit property rather than an individual. See below. Therefore, a covenant does not meet the requirements of RCW 84.64.460 unless it is so connected to real estate that it runs with the land.

For a covenant to run with the land, a number of conditions must be met:

> (1) the covenants must have been enforceable between the original parties, such enforceability being a question of contract law except insofar as the covenant must satisfy the statute of frauds; (2) the covenant must "touch and concern" both the land to be benefitted and the land to be burdened; (3) the covenanting parties must have intended to bind their successors in interest; (4) there must be vertical privity of estate, *i.e.,* privity between the original parties to the covenant and the present disputants; and (5) there must be horizontal privity of estate, or privity between the original parties. W. Stoebuck, [Running Covenants: An Analytical Primer, 52 Wash. L. Rev. 861 (1977)].

(Footnotes omitted.) Leighton v. Leonard, 22 Wash. App. 136, 139, 589 P.2d 279 (1978), quoted in Feider v. Feider, 40 Wash. App. 589, 593, 699 P.2d 801 (1985).

For covenants to pay money, the critical issue is the "touch and concern" requirement. 5 R. Powell & P. Rohan ¶675[2][a]. Under Washington law, an obligation to pay assessments for the maintenance of neighborhood property touches and concerns the land. See Rodruck v. Sand Point Maintenance Comm'n, *supra;* Mullendore Theatres, Inc. v. Growth Realty Investors Co., 39 Wash. App. 64, 691 P.2d 970 (1984). The majority of American jurisdictions are in accord. 5 R. Powell & P. Rohan ¶675[2]; 6 P. Rohan §8.03[2][c]; Stoebuck, Running Covenants: An Analytical Primer, 52 Wash. L. Rev. 861, 870 (1977). Accordingly, Looney's covenant satisfies the "touch and concern" requirement.

Horizontal privity also is present in this case. Courts have held generally that this standard is met when one of the original contracting parties was a homeowners' association, even if the association did not have legal title in land at that time. 5 R. Powell & P. Rohan ¶675[2][a]. According to these authorities, even if horizontal privity was lacking in form, "it was present in substance since the association was acting as the agent of all of the property owners." 5 R. Powell & P. Rohan ¶675[2][a]. We find this reasoning persuasive.

Additionally, there can be little doubt that the parties intended the covenant to bind their successors in interest. Covenant 15 provides that "[t]hese covenants are to run with the land and shall be binding on all parties and all persons claiming under them" for a specified number of years in the future.

We cannot determine from the record before us the requirements concerning vertical privity and the covenant's original enforceability. Accordingly, we remand these issues to the trial court for resolution. If these requirements are met, RCW 84.64.460 will protect the covenant from extinguishment, leaving Looney liable for the assessments. . . .

In sum, we hold today that a covenant to pay assessments for the maintenance of neighborhood facilities qualifies as an appurtenant easement under RCW 84.64.460 and, therefore, survives a tax foreclosure sale. The decision of the Court of Appeals is reversed and the case is remanded for additional fact-finding.

CALLOW, C.J. and UTTER, DOLLIVER, PEARSON, ANDERSEN and SMITH, JJ., concur.

This CL Test Proves Aff Cou. + in that → Aff cou. run w/ land even through tax Sale

NOTES AND QUESTIONS

1. **After transfer of the servient estate, is there any further liability in the party who created the servitude?** Consider two cases: In the first case, A, owner of Lot 1, transfers a right-of-way across Lot 1, for the benefit of B's neighboring Lot 2. A then transfers Lot 1 to A', who blocks off the affirmative easement. Although it is clear, where A' has had notice, that the owner of Lot 2 is entitled both to injunctive relief and a damages judgment against A', might the servitude holder also recover damages from A?

In the second case, A, owner of Lot 1, covenants to pay a yearly subdivision assessment to the homeowners' association. A then transfers Lot 1 to A', who refuses to pay the assessment. Although it is clear, where A' has had notice, that the association may collect the fee from A', may it also recover from A, the original obligor?

As to the first case, where A has created an affirmative easement, the outcome is clear. His duties end when he transfers the servient estate. This is no less true even when promissory terms are used to create the easement — the usual mode, for example, for a common-driveway agreement. One simple explanation is that although B has suffered damages, the underlying duty is not money-based; and it can only be performed — that is, not breached — by someone who has a continuing interest in the property. B may protect his rights by in rem relief. Since B may seek a prohibitory injunction as soon as A' blocks off the right of way (or builds so as to block off B's view or competes where competition is barred), it is usually only of secondary importance to B that he may also be able to get a money judgment for damages. A more technical explanation is that neither privity of contract nor privity of estate exists between A and B.

As to the second case, where A by his promise to pay the subdivision assessment has created an affirmative covenant, the outcome is also clear. A's liability for all future payments ends when he transfers title, although he remains liable for any arrearages. The explanation, however, is less clear. You have already seen a possible analogy in the lease, where a tenant's covenant to pay rent, also an affirmative covenant, creates privity of contract between the landlord and the tenant, which does not end even after the tenant has assigned the lease absent a novation. Why shouldn't this principle of contract privity also apply to affirmative covenants between fee holders?

Good Q~1

A~1 -

no privity exist = A don't pay

Neither A's must pay

The direct answer is that we treat fee covenants and leasehold covenants differently. The Restatement, §4.4, provides that unless the original parties intended otherwise, the original promisor to a *fee* servitude, that is, a burden that runs with "ownership" of the property, incurs liability only for those obligations that accrue while he holds the servient estate. In short, if A', the successor, is bound because the servitude runs, A is not. The Restatement explains itself as follows:

> The difference [between the treatment of lease and fee covenants] results from the likely difference in the expectations of parties to leases and parties to covenants among fee owners. In the lease transaction, the duration of the tenant's liability is limited by the duration of the lease term, and the landlord is thought to have relied on the tenant's credit worthiness in determining to enter into the lease. By contrast, servitudes created by fee owners generally have an indeterminate or perpetual duration, and neither party is likely to have expected the other to be liable after transfer of the burdened interest.

Contrast, however, the homeowner's covenant to pay a subdivision assessment with, for example, the developer's covenant to build a recreational complex at a designated site within the subdivision. Although each promise is an affirmative covenant, whose burden would run with the servient estate, the texture of the two promises is quite different. Purchasers might well have relied on the developer's reputation to perform the promise; should he sell out to a second developer who fails to finish the complex, the homeowners might expect recourse against the original covenantor even though he no longer owns the servient estate. In short, if we distinguish between leasehold and fee covenants, we might wish to distinguish further among the varieties of affirmative fee covenants.

2. **Succession by life tenants.** Suppose that A, who has covenanted to pay a subdivision assessment, transfers the property to L for life, remainder to R and her heirs. Under the original Restatement of Property, some confusion existed as to whether L (or R) would succeed to the burden, since the so-called vertical privity requirement meant that unless the present holder of the servient estate held the very estate of the original covenantor, to wit, a fee simple absolute, the burden would not run — at least, at law. The Restatement of Servitudes, wisely, reasons that the life tenant, who is generally seen as the property's owner, should be expected to pay the assessment (and also enjoy any servitude benefits). In some instances, where an assessment results in a capital improvement that also benefits the remaindermen, the two interest holders may, as between themselves, allocate the burden. Id. at §5.3. This reflects the view that the life tenant's liability should not exceed the value of the life estate.

3. **Lessees in possession.** Suppose that A leases his condominium unit to T. What are T's rights and duties as to the servitudes affecting the rented unit?

Here, the Restatement distinguishes between affirmative covenants and all other servitudes — as to the latter, the tenant steps immediately into his landlord's shoes. As to the benefit of an affirmative covenant, the lessee can enforce only those benefits that involve the repair, maintenance, or the performance of some other service to the benefited property, or that can be enjoyed by the tenant "without diminishing their value to the owner of the property and without materially increasing the burden of performance on the [obligor]." Id. at §5.3. On the burden side, however, the tenant is not bound unless (a) he has assumed the obligation, or (b) the performance called for by the servitude should reasonably be performed by the person in possession of the burdened property. Id. A few examples should help clarify these rules:

(a)   the leased unit is burdened by an affirmative easement: the tenant may not interfere with the easement holder's privilege;

(b)   all units may use the community tennis courts: the tenant can enjoy the privilege;

(c)   the condominium association has agreed to remove trash from the unit twice weekly: the tenant may enforce the servitude;

(d)   the condominium rules require the unit owner to place his trash at the curb twice weekly: the tenant would be expected to perform.

(e)   the unit owner has agreed to pay a monthly subdivision fee: unless the tenant has assumed the burden, he is not liable for the fee;

(f)   the condominium association is required to give the unit owner thirty days' notice of any special election: the unit owner, not the tenant, would be entitled to receive the notice.

4.   **Adverse possessors.** Once an individual acquires the servient estate by adverse possession, she takes subject to all servitudes binding the parcel; conversely, she enjoys all benefits appurtenant to the parcel. Restatement, Servitudes, §5.2. Keep in mind, though, that in some instances the occupation may also be adverse to the servitude holder.

The occupant's privileges and duties before his possession ripens into title are less clear-cut as to those servitudes created by affirmative covenants (as to all other servitudes, the party in possession is treated as the owner as soon as possession begins). On the benefit side of affirmative covenants, the Restatement rule for the adverse occupant echoes that for a lessee (Note 3, *supra*.) Id. at §5.5. As to burdens, however, the adverse occupant must begin to perform them as soon as his possession begins. Id. at §5.2.[59]

---

59. The Restatement gives the following illustration:

Able is in adverse possession of Lot 5 in Sand Acres, owned by O. Able has not acquired title to Lot 5 because the statutory period has not elapsed. The declaration of covenants

5.   **Purchasers at foreclosure sales.** Whether the purchaser at a foreclosure sale takes subject to a servitude burden depends entirely on priority rules: Which came first (and satisfied the recording act notice requirements),[60] the servitude or the foreclosed lien? Thus a prior mortgage, which was then foreclosed, would wipe out an easement granted after the mortgage was recorded.

One important exception to the priority regime is the obligation to pay a subdivision assessment. If, for example, the foreclosure sale purchaser acquires a condominium unit, he would be required to pay future assessments, even if the foreclosed mortgage, itself, had priority over the condominium servitudes.

There seems little disagreement that servitude benefits will run to the foreclosure sale purchaser.

b.   Succession to Benefits and Burdens in Gross

The Restatement of Servitudes provides, absent contrary intent, that a benefit in gross may be freely transferred,[61] but that a personal servitude benefit, whether appurtenant or in gross, cannot pass hands.[62] Common-law courts often refused to recognize the transfer of a servitude in gross, although the first Restatement did allow for the transfer of profits and easements, viz. utility easements, that served a commercial purpose. Id. at §489 (1944). Under its default rule, the new Restatement takes the next step as to all in gross benefits. They are seen as independently held property rights, which may be transferred in the same way as other such rights, generally subject to the Statute of Frauds as interests in land, and devolving on the owner's death in the same way as other real property interests. Restatement of Property (Servitudes) §5.8 (T.D. 5, 1995).

---

for Sand Acres requires the payment of assessments for the maintenance of common facilities on lots in Sand Acres, requires all lot owners to keep trees and other vegetation trimmed to protect views from other lots in Sand Acres, and provides that each lot is entitled to one vote in the annual election of the board of directors of the Sand Acres Property Owners Association. Under the rule stated in this section, Able is liable to pay assessments levied on Lot 5 and to keep the trees trimmed on Lot 5. Whether Able is entitled to enforce the covenants requiring payment of assessments with respect to other lots and to enforce the covenant requiring that trees be trimmed to protect the view from Lot 5, or entitled to vote in the election of directors is determined under §5.5.

60. Statutes may give retrospective priority to some kinds of liens, such as tax liens and mechanics liens. In those instances, the retroactivity may displace an earlier servitude.

61. Restatement of Property (Servitudes), §4.6(1)(b) (T.D. 4, 1994).

62. The Restatement treats a benefit as "personal" if the relationship of the parties, consideration paid, nature of the servitude, or other circumstances, indicate that the parties should not reasonably have expected that the servitude benefit would pass to a successor to the original beneficiary. Id. at §4.6 (2).

A burden in gross is, in effect, a contractual duty, which concerns us here only if it creates an appurtenant benefit. For example, a water company may agree to furnish water to a residential subdivision; see, e.g., Eagle Enterprises v. Gross, *supra*. Although the obligor may transfer or delegate its burden, under the law of contracts, this will not discharge any duty or liability of the transferor unless the servitude beneficiary consents. Restatement of Property (Servitudes), §5.8 (T.D. 5, 1995).

c.   Subdivision of the Servient or Dominant Estates

Subdivision of the dominant estate: Suppose that, prior to the subdivision of Brownacre, A, the owner of Greenacre, covenants to limit his use to single-family residential. If the present owner of Greenacre were now to begin construction of a shopping center, any one of the owners of the Brownacre subdivision would be entitled to enforce the covenant. Restatement of Property (Servitudes) §5.7 (T.D. 1995).

Subdivision of the servient estate: Suppose that at Time 1, all lots in an existing subdivision are required to pay an assessment, on a flat fee basis, to the homeowners' association for maintenance of the public areas. Some time later, one of the lots is further subdivided into two parcels of unequal size and value. How should the assessment be handled?

Unless the servitude terms make clear that regardless of lot size, or of when subdivision occurs, each lot must pay the full assessment, the Restatement would apportion the obligation between the two newly created lots on the basis of their value. Id. The Restatement also makes clear that if the original lot were subject to an easement across the entire parcel, the subdivision of the servient estate would carry with it the easement's burden. Hardly surprising!

§7.7   Terminating the Arrangement

a.   By Agreement, Release, or Merger

Agreement. In general, absent statutory limits, pages 777-778 *infra,* the parties who create the servitude have initial control over the servitude's duration. The originating parties may decide that the servitude will be perpetual, or that it will terminate in X years, when a given event occurs, when a specified purpose is accomplished, or, as is common in residential subdivisions, when a stated percentage of the benefited landowners agree.

Release. If the servitude holder agrees to execute a release, the servitude will terminate early. Such a release must satisfy the Statute of Frauds.[63]

Merger. If the servitude holder also acquires the servient estate, this merger of title presumptively terminates the servitude. Professor Powell explained the doctrine of merger in the case of easements. "An easement, by definition, is a right to land which is in the possession of another. This prerequisite situation ceases to exist . . . when the dominant and servient estates of an . . . easement come into the same ownership. . . . [T]he owner of the easement, having become the owner of the servient estate, has, as such owner of the servient estate, right of use greater than those comprised in the easement itself. The lesser is swallowed by the greater and the easement is permanently terminated by this merger." 3 Powell, Real Property ¶425 at 34-264 (Rohan ed., 1979).

Merger operates only when the servitude holder acquires the servient estate in fee. Thus, if the servitude holder acquires a life estate or an estate for years in the servient parcel, the servitude is merely suspended until common ownership ends. Similarly, if less than the entire area of the servient estate is held in common ownership, the agreement is extinguished only as to that area commonly owned.

Although an agreement, release, or merger can relieve the servient owner of his duties to one dominant party, the duties to any other dominant persons remain in force. Thus, if A grants easements of access to B, C, D, and E, and also covenants with all of them not to build a multi-unit dwelling on his property, and subsequently obtains a release from B or purchases B's land, A's duties to C, D, and E are unchanged.

Note that merger may be avoided in some states by a simple declaration, expressed in the deed that creates common ownership, that the servitude is intended to survive merger; in that case, the servitude is revived when common ownership ends. Alternatively, and this should work everywhere, parties can avoid merger by using a second entity to acquire title.

The rules above speak of the usual situation where interests change or terminate much as the parties intend. But courts sometimes face disputes where the servient owner is urging that the arrangement be ended (or modified) even though it remains — by its own terms — still intact. Such cases appear in this section.

In reading this group of cases, notice a shared feature — the heavy stress on facts. By now, it should hardly surprise you that facts do matter,

---

63. Restatement of Servitudes, §7.3 (T.D. #7, 1996), Comment a, states, however, that aside from the problem of the subsequent bona fide purchaser of the dominant estate, failure to comply with the statutes may not be significant because the attempted release will provide evidence of abandonment or estoppel (changed position by owner of servient estate in reliance upon oral release, id. at §7.6).

and that much of a litigator's success lies in her ability to marshall facts clearly and powerfully, stressing that detail that puts a client's case to best advantage. Land use disputes are particularly fact-laden and, of course, what you read in the appellate opinion is only the final distillation.

b.   By Misuse of the Benefit

FRENNING v. DOW [64]

544 A.2d 145 (R.I. 1988)

WEISBERGER, J.

This case comes before us on appeal by the plaintiffs from a judgment entered in the Superior Court extinguishing an easement that had been in existence since 1838 on the ground of excessive use. We vacate the judgment. The facts in the case insofar as pertinent to this appeal are as follows.

The defendants' predecessor in title (Gray) granted to plaintiffs' predecessor (Shaw) an assessment to cross defendants' land "with teams loaded or not, caragies [sic] of any kind, Stock, on Horse back, or on foot, doing as little damage as may be . . . to him his heirs & assigns forever." At the time of the granting of the easement the dominant tenement consisted of 102 acres of land in the town of Little Compton. Since that time, plaintiffs' predecessor and plaintiffs have acquired contiguous parcels of land so that the total holdings of plaintiffs at the time of trial consisted of 257 acres.

The trial justice made the following additional findings of fact:

[A] Plaintiff has used the way to service with farm equipment not just the original parcel but additional contiguous land.

[B] The way has been used for the benefit of another house on an adjoining parcel, recently built.

[C] Plaintiffs' guests have used the way on social occasions, and on one occasion, in 25 automobiles, they entered her property over her right of way from West Main Road and exited over the way here in litigation.

[D] The use of the way by the plaintiff has materially increased, and has burdened defendants' property far more heavily than the right granted.

[E] The use of the way to service some 150 additional acres, to service the house recently built, and to [accommodate] plaintiffs' social guests constitutes an actual trespass for which money damages lie. Brightman v. Chapin, 15 R.I. 166, 1 A. 412.

[F] There is no way here to sever the increased burden (and thus stop

---

64. Under Rhode Island practice, plaintiffs in this opinion refer to the appellants, the holders of the servitude. The defendants-appellants sued to extinguish the easement on the grounds of misuse. — EDS.

the trespass) so as to preserve the original rights and servitude, there being no practical way to monitor and police the user.

[G] Injunctive relief to limit the use to that which was granted would be unenforceable.

As a result of these findings, the trial justice concluded that the easement had been extinguished or forfeited.

The plaintiffs argue in support of their appeal that the additional intensity of use was insufficient to justify a forfeiture or extinguishment of the easement. Generally courts have not favored extinguishing an easement unless injunctive relief would be ineffective to relieve the servient tenement. The cases in support of this proposition are legion and are set forth in an annotation in 16 A.L.R. 2d 609 (1951). The principal case upon which this annotation is based is Penn Bowling Recreation Center, Inc. v. Hot Shoppes, Inc., 86 U.S. App. D.C. 58, 179 F.2d 64 (D.C. Cir. 1949), in which the Court of Appeals for the District of Columbia Circuit set aside a summary judgment extinguishing an easement in circumstances wherein a building had been constructed partly on the dominant parcel and partly upon contiguous land that was not entitled to be benefited by the easement. Moreover the building in question built in part upon land not entitled to the easement consisted of a large bowling alley and restaurant to which the plaintiff had brought fuel oil, food, equipment, and supplies over the right of way, and the plaintiff also used the same right of way to remove trash, garbage, and other material. The court observed:

"Misuse of an easement right is not sufficient to constitute a forfeiture, waiver, or abandonment of such right. The right to an easement is not lost by using it in an unauthorized manner or to an unauthorized extent, unless it is impossible to sever the increased burden so as to preserve to the owner of the dominant tenement that to which he is entitled, and impose upon the servient tenement only the burden which was originally imposed upon it." 179 F.2d at 66.

The court ultimately determined that there was an insufficient basis for the granting of summary judgment of extinguishment, even though it was apparent that difficulties would be encountered in supervising the use of the easement by the dominant and nondominant portion of the plaintiff's premises.

Courts have stated in this type of context that equity abhors a forfeiture. See Parolisi v. Beach Terrace Improvement Association, Inc., 463 A.2d 197, 199 (R.I. 1983); Ball v. Milliken, 31 R.I. 36, 46, 76 A. 789, 794 (1910). Accord National Silk Dyeing Co. v. Grobart, 117 N.J. Eq. 156, 167, 175 A. 91, 96 (1934). However, this only begins the inquiry, since in the foregoing case the court determined that it was the obligation of the owner of the dominant tenement to show that it had altered its mill building so as to limit the enjoyment of the easement to the dominant tenement alone.

We recognize that it is the well-established rule in this jurisdiction that findings of fact of a trial justice will not be disturbed on appeal unless they are clearly wrong or unless the trial justice has overlooked material evidence on a controlling issue. See Bissonnette v. Hanton City Realty Corp., 529 A.2d 139, 141 (R.I. 1987); Fournier v. Fournier, 479 A.2d 708 (R.I. 1984). We also give great deference to the drawing of factual inferences by the trial justice as long as the inferences drawn are logical and flow from the established facts. Pearl Brewing Co. v. McNaboe, 495 A.2d 238 (R.I. 1985); Tanzi v. Fiberglass Swimming Pools, Inc., 414 A.2d 484 (R.I. 1980).

In the case at bar we accept the trial justice's finding of fact as valid and binding; we accept his inferences, save for the ultimate conclusion that this easement must be extinguished because it is impossible to sever the increased burden from that which rightfully adheres to the dominant tenement.

During the past quarter-century, we believe, courts of equity have surmounted problems far greater than that posed by the monitoring of the use of this easement. Without belaboring the point unduly, courts of equity have redistricted legislatures throughout the land. Courts have administered correctional institutions, desegregated school systems, supervised environmental rehabilitation, and undertaken the disposition of complex litigation beyond the wildest dreams of the ancient English chancellors. We are of the opinion that the problems posed by the contiguous acreage owned by the plaintiffs is not beyond the powers of a court of equity to resolve. We may suggest, however, that in accordance with methods established in more complex litigation, it is the burden of the plaintiffs here to propose to the trial justice a plan that may be subject to monitoring by the defendants and ultimate enforcement by the court. We believe that the plaintiffs should be given this opportunity before the easement is totally extinguished.

For the reasons stated, the appeal of the plaintiff is sustained. The judgment of extinguishment of the easement is vacated, and the papers in this case may be remanded to the Superior Court for further proceedings consistent with this opinion.

NOTES AND QUESTIONS

1.   **Counterpoint to** *Frenning v. Dow.* Compare Crimmins v. Gould, 149 Cal. App. 2d 383, 308 P.2d 786 (1957), where the court terminated the easement after a finding that the unauthorized use could not be severed and enjoined. The servitude, which was intended to serve only one parcel, giving that parcel access over a private lane [McCormick Lane] to a public road, was enlarged by the defendant's action to serve 29 residential lots (23 located on a second parcel), and extended to create a thoroughfare between two public roads. In rejecting the defendants' plea for lesser relief than termination, the court wrote:

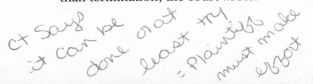

Defendants' contention that lesser relief than a declaration that defendants no longer had any right to use McCormick Lane is without merit. A sign as suggested by defendants to the effect that the lane was restricted to the use of residents of McCormick Lane alone would not protect plaintiff's rights. Nor would an injunction attempting to restrain all persons from using McCormick Lane other than owners or residents fronting on the lane or their invitees be practicable or enforceable. Defendants have extended the lane in a sort of an inverted "Y." The northerly ends of each section of the Y join Watkins Avenue, so that what is equal to two through streets run into McCormick Lane. Such a sign and injunction would not prevent all or any of the residents of parcel 2 as well as the general public from using McCormick Lane. The only practical way of preventing this is to close McCormick Lane at its junction with parcels 1 and 2. This compels the extinguishment of defendants' easement therein. By causing McCormick Lane as extended by defendants . . . , defendants have made it impossible for the portion of McCormick Lane belonging to plaintiff to be used in a limited way. Unless a fence is built across McCormick Lane at its intersection with the southerly line of parcel 1, there is no feasible way of keeping the general public as well as the residents of parcel 2 out of McCormick Lane. . . .

2. **Litigation strategy.** Suppose that you represented the *Crimmins* defendants and believed that the trial court on the known facts would extinguish your clients' right of way. (In short, the outcome would not have surprised you.) What would be your negotiation or litigation strategy to try to prevent total extinguishment? *try it first*

3. **Crafting the injunction.** Back to the *Frenning* decision: How would you, as the servitude holders' attorney, craft a plan that would serve your clients' interest and that the trial court would be likely to endorse? *Have locked gate w/ key*

4. **Forfeiture not favored.** In McCann v. R. W. Dunteman Co., 242 *For Dom ¼* Ill. App. 3d 246, 609 N.E.2d 1076 (1993), the court refused to terminate an easement where defendants had expanded its use from the storage of equipment and sewer pipes into the servicing of an asphalt manufacturing plant. When the trial began, heavy trucks were making on average nearly 500 daily trips over the easement, to benefit not only the original dominant parcel, but four adjoining parcels as well. The court issued an injunction limiting the truck traffic to the original parcel, but would not give any further relief to the plaintiffs who were seeking extinguishment.

c.   By Abandonment

FLANAGAN v. SAN MARCOS SILK CO.

106 Cal. App. 2d 458, 235 P.2d 107 (1951)

GRIFFIN, J. Plaintiffs and respondents brought this action to quiet title to a parcel of land described as Lots 2 and 5 (see Figure 7-7) of Rancho Los

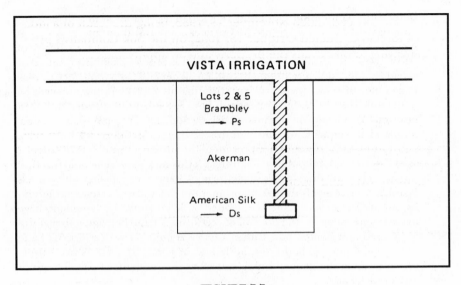

FIGURE 7-7
Map of Easement

Valecitos de San Marcos, located near San Marcos, and it is directed to a claim by these appealing defendants to an easement for the maintenance of a pipe line over a portion of the real property owned by plaintiff. . . .

Plaintiffs concede that defendants' predecessor in interest, American Silk Factors, Inc., a corporation (hereinafter referred to as the Silk Company) owned a large parcel of land south of Lots 2 and 5, which lots were at that time owned by a Mr. and Mrs. Brambley; that by written grant deed, duly recorded in 1927, the Brambleys deeded to the Silk Company a "perpetual easement or right-of-way" for the construction of pipe lines over and across their property which is now owned by plaintiffs. A similar easement was obtained from the Akermans, who owned a parcel of land lying between that owned by the Silk Company and the parcel owned by the Brambleys. The Vista Irrigation District operated a water distributing ditch just north of plaintiffs' property. A pipe line was laid over and across plaintiff's land, across the Akerman property, and across the Silk Company's property to the silk plant, and was the means by which the Silk Company was to obtain its water, operate its silk mills, and grow mulberry trees. The Silk Company's property was not in the irrigation district but in 1927 it obtained an agreement whereby the district would furnish water to it through their pipe line. During the operation of the plant, from 1927 to 1933, there was delivered to it each year in excess of 100 cubic feet. Shortly before 1933 the Silk Company became bankrupt. In February of that year the trustee in bankruptcy executed a trustee's deed and bill of sale to one Poulsen, conveying all property owned by the Silk Company, and specifically conveying the Brambley easement involved in this action. Received in evidence (Exhibit 10) is a

commissioner's deed, dated November 19, 1933, being the result of a judgment of foreclosure dated October 18, 1932, on the Silk Company's property conveying to one Evans the property and all appurtenances thereunto
belonging. By mesne conveyances thereafter a portion of the property originally owned by the Silk Company was transferred to and is now owned by
defendant American Real Silk, Inc., subject to certain liens and trust deeds
held by the other appealing defendants.

The court specifically found and concluded that "The common predecessor in interest of the defendants sometime during the year 1933 abandoned any interest which such predecessor in interest ever had in the
easement in, over and upon a portion of plaintiffs' lands," and ordered
plaintiffs' title quieted accordingly.

The main question on this appeal is the sufficiency of the evidence to
support the finding of abandonment. In this connection the court found
that in 1933 the pipe line in question was broken or blocked at its northerly
end where it had previously been connected to the supply line of the irrigation district, and thereafter no water could or did run through it until
1944; that in 1933 the predecessor in interest of defendants drilled certain
wells upon portions of the property now owned by the defendants and irrigated their premises; that no water was ever carried through the pipe line
here in dispute to any lands of defendants since 1933; that no water has
been available for such delivery to defendants or their predecessors in interest since 1933; that this pipe line has been incapable of conducting water
by reason of severance thereof; that after plaintiffs acquired their property,
they caused the pipe line to be reconnected to the irrigation district system
to supply water to their lands; that prior thereto the line was cut off and
blocked at the south end of the easement; that in 1946, it was broken at a
point on the McCandless property, being a group of lots south of plaintiffs'
property and that these owners connected, with defendants' consent, to
water from a reservoir pumped from wells on defendants' property and
were using that portion of the pipe line as a system wholly separate from
the pipe line here involved. (Thereafter McCandless blocked off both ends
of the pipe line on their property, dug their own well, and continued to use
that portion of the pipe line on their property to carry water to it.) The
evidence supports these particular findings and there is very little conflict
in the evidence in this respect.

It is defendants' position that they acquired their interest and ownership in the property in 1943, in reliance upon the provisions in the several
instruments conveying the easement across plaintiffs' land to them, and
in reliance upon the statements of the seller that such easement was still in
existence for the benefit of the property of defendants; that they had no
knowledge of any purported abandonment at any time, and that they were
innocent purchasers for value; that neither defendants nor their predecessors in interest ever ordered the pipe line disconnected or authorized its
use by plaintiffs and that since no written notice of abandonment of the

easement was ever recorded by defendants or their predecessors in interest, the easement is still in existence.

It is true that plaintiffs purchased their property in April, 1935, and soon thereafter learned about the pipe line and the easement of record across their property.[2] They testified they had no consent of the Silk Company or its successors in interest to connect the pipe line to the irrigation district ditch but since their property was in the district they applied for and received consent from the district to establish a meter and receive water through those pipes. The evidence further shows that on September 28, 1948, defendant American Real Silk Company wrote plaintiffs that it had come to its attention that plaintiffs were using the pipe line belonging to that company and located on the easement in question; that since the company had no present use for it, it would be satisfactory for them to continue using it until such time as the defendant company had a need for it. The source of defendants' claimed title thereto was set forth in the letter. . . .

Defendants contend that although the pipe line in dispute was not being used by defendants to carry water, it was being held by the company as a "stand-by" source of supply to supplement the wells drilled on the property. It is its argument that the evidence shows nothing more than non-use of the easement and pipe line in question since 1932, and that mere "nonuser," without more, is not sufficient evidence of abandonment or intent to abandon. . . . It cites the rule stated in Smith v. Worn, 93 Cal. 206, 213 [28 P. 944], that "The acts of the owner of the dominant tenement in case of nonuser, or to prevent him from obtaining an *easement acquired by grant*, must be of a character so decisive and conclusive as to indicate a clear intent to abandon the easement."

As to this general proposition of law plaintiffs do not quarrel with defendants but strongly maintain that "nonuser," accompanied by an intention, either express or implied, to abandon the easement is sufficient, citing . . . Moon v. Rollins, 36 Cal. 333 [95 Am. Dec. 181], where it is said: ". . . lapse of time does not of itself constitute an abandonment, but that is only a circumstance for the jury to consider in determining the question whether there was an abandonment. . . . It is a question of *intention*, and has been so held over and over again, and *not* a question of time. . . ."

In Home Real Estate Co. v. Los Angeles Pacific Co., 163 Cal. 710 [126 P. 972], the rule is stated that while nonuser alone does not extinguish the easement, a long continued nonuser is some evidence of an intent to abandon, and that an intention with which an act is done is a question of fact to be determined by the trial court from a consideration of the conduct of the parties and the surrounding circumstances, and that where evidence is such that a finding either way might reasonably be made, the conclusion of the

2. Why did plaintiffs learn about the pipeline only after they bought the land? — EDS.

trial court must be upheld under the familiar rule protecting from review on appeal findings based on conflicting evidence.

In the instant case there is no question about the discontinuance of the use of the pipe line in question in the year 1932 or 1933, when the Silk Company went bankrupt. It was not subsequently used by it or its successors in interest. The trial court apparently fixed the year 1933 as the one in which abandonment occurred. Standing alone, this evidence of nonuse may not have been sufficient to support a finding of intent to abandon. . . . It is defendants' argument that any evidence of the conduct of the Silk Company and its successors in interest thereafter was inadmissible and should not be considered for any purpose. The authorities cited by defendants do not support this argument. Since abandonment involves intent, evidence of actions after 1932 by the several successors in interest was relevant as bearing on the question. As pointed out by counsel for plaintiffs, suppose a husband left his wife in 1933 and went to another city and did not return. Evidence as to his subsequent actions would be relevant to determine whether he left her in 1933 with the intent to desert her. . . . Therefore, in connection with the fact of nonuser, there is the additional evidence, as exemplified by pictures in evidence, that the pipe line easement had grown over with thick underbrush, the pipe became exposed, and gulches washed from under it. There is some evidence that it needed repair and that it would soon need replacing due to leaks and deterioration. The grant of easement contained a clause that the grantee and its successors were bound to maintain the pipe line upon plaintiffs' property "as free from leaks as possible." In 17 Am. Jur. 1027, section 142, the rule is stated to be that: "Ordinarily, failure to repair does not constitute an abandonment, but an abandonment may be predicated upon facts showing that the means of enjoyment of an easement have been in a state of disrepair for a long period of time." . . .

The facts here show: (1) Nonuser by defendants and their successors in interest for over 16 years; (2) affirmative acts of these parties in obtaining a new and different source of supply of water by means of digging wells in the year 1934; (3) the sale and grant by defendants' predecessors in interest to a stranger in 1933 of a portion of the Silk Company's original property over which the pipe line passed and lying between the plant and plaintiffs' property without a special reservation of an easement of right-of-way for this particular pipe line contained in the grant; (4) permitting the blocking of a portion of the pipe line for the private use of the McCandless property; (5) the apparent adverse use of a blocked portion of the easement pipe line by plaintiffs since 1944; and (6) failure to maintain the easement line in question free from leaks.

Had the trial court found that there had been no abandonment the finding might be supported by the evidence produced. Defendants bring the case before us upon a finding which is against them as to both the question of abandonment and intent. We cannot say that the finding of the trial court lacks evidentiary support. . . .

Judgment affirmed.

BARNARD, P. J., and MUSSELL, J., concurred.

NOTES AND QUESTIONS

1. **Compare adverse possession.** Consider whether plaintiffs in *Flanagan* might also have won on a theory of adverse possession.

2. **Nonuser sans intent to abandon.** Andrien v. Heffernan, 299 Pa. 284, 149 A. 184 (1930), is as striking a case as one might find for the rule that proof of a nonuser will not by itself destroy an easement. A right of way that had been reserved more than 125 years earlier, that had not been used for at least 40 years, and that was overgrown with trees and shrubbery, was treated as unextinguished and a cloud on title, in a suit for specific performance of a sales contract. Might the *Flanagan* case have been decided differently had plaintiffs been trying to enforce an executory sales contract against a reluctant vendee, whose argument was that the outstanding easement rendered title unmarketable?

3. **Interplay with Statute of Frauds.** California Civ. Proc. Code §1971 (West Supp. 1996) reads: "No estate or interest in real property . . . can be created, granted, assigned, surrendered, or declared, otherwise than by operation of law, or a conveyance or other instrument in writing. . . ." Could the defendants in *Flanagan* have invoked this version of the Statute of Frauds to defeat the claim of abandonment? Why not?

4. **Abandonment of slum properties.** Owner "abandonment" of slum properties has worsened in recent years as these holdings become unprofitable. See generally G. Sternlieb and R. Burchell, Residential Abandonment: The Tenement Landlord Revisited (1974).

In legal terms, what happens when the owner of a building "abandons" it and the underlying land? Does your answer depend on the nature of the operator's interest in the land and building? Compare, for example, someone who owns the land and building in fee simple with someone who runs the building on a 50-year lease. Consider also what happens if the real estate taxes or the mortgage installments remain unpaid.

In short: Can the rules that govern the abandonment of easements also apply to corporeal interests in land and building improvements?

5. **Abandonment of chattels.** A chattel may be abandoned, it is said, when its owner "with the specific intent of desertion and relinquishment casts away or leaves behind his property, or when after a casual and unintentional loss all purpose further to seek and reclaim the lost property is given up." R. Brown, Personal Property 8 (3d ed. 1975). He who first takes possession of abandoned personal property ordinarily becomes its new owner. Eads v. Brazelton, 22 Ark. 499, 79 Am. Dec. 88 (1861).

6.   **Abandonment of bank accounts and other funds.** Statutes in most states provide for the escheat of abandoned or unclaimed bank accounts, life insurance funds, condemnation awards, and the like. See, e.g., N.Y. Aband. Prop. Law §§300-305, 700-706, 1000-1003 (McKinney Supp. 1996).

d.   By Neighborhood Change

TRUSTEES OF COLUMBIA COLLEGE v. THACHER

87 N.Y. 311 (1882)

Appeal from judgment of the General Term of the Superior Court of the city of New York, entered upon an order made June, 1880, which affirmed a judgment in favor of plaintiff, entered upon a decision of the court on trial at Special Term.

The action was brought to enforce the observance of certain covenants in an agreement made on the 25th of July, 1859, between the plaintiffs and Joseph D. Beers, who then owned adjacent portions of the block of land between Fifth and Sixth avenues and Fiftieth and Fifty-first streets, New York, in respect to the mode of improvement and the future occupation of their respective portions.

The case upon a former appeal is reported in 70 N.Y. 440. . . . During the pendency of this action the defendant Thacher became the owner of the said premises, having purchased the same with notice of said agreement and of this action, and he was made a defendant herein by an order of the court, upon his own application. The court found that said

> Thacher permits certain parts of the house upon said premises to be occupied by his tenants for the purpose of trade and business; that is to say, apartments in the first story of said house for the business of a tailor and for that of a milliner, and apartments in the basement of the said house for the business of an insurance agent, of a newspaper dealer, of two express carriers, and of a tobacconist, which trades or businesses were carried on in the said house at the time of the trial. That the several trades or businesses carried on as aforesaid by the defendants Yates and Blaisdell, at the time of the commencement of the action, and by the tenants of the defendant Thacher at the time of trial, were violations of the agreement above set forth, and of the spirit as well as the letter thereof. That since the action was begun an elevated railway has been built in the Sixth avenue, running by the said premises, and a station thereof established at the intersection of Fiftieth street and the Sixth avenue, in front of said premises, and that the said railway and station affect the said premises injuriously, and render them less profitable for the purpose of a dwelling-house, but do not render their use for business purposes indispensable to their practicable and profitable use and occupation. The said railway and station, however, do not injuriously affect all the property fronting on

Fiftieth street and included in the said covenant, but only a comparatively small part thereof.

Further facts appear in the opinion. . . .

DANFORTH, J. The validity and binding obligation of the covenant cannot be questioned by the defendant Thacher. (Trustees of Columbia College v. Lynch, 70 N.Y. 440.) Moreover it appears that he bought with notice, not only of the agreement, but of this action. He, therefore, could not take the property without performing the obligation attached to it, and must be deemed to have taken it at his peril, to the extent of such judgment as might be rendered in the action. . . . We have no doubt that the conclusion of the trial judge was right upon the point presented, and agree with him, that these several trades or occupations were violations, not only of the spirit, but also of the letter of the covenant.

Now having before us a covenant binding the defendant, and his breach of it, if there is nothing more, the usual result must follow, viz.: an injunction to keep within the terms of the agreement. . . . Indeed, this has in substance been recognized in the decision before made by us (70 N.Y. supra). It was then, however, suggested, that another trial might disclose objections not before us, and it is now claimed by the appellant, that there has been such an entire change in the character of the neighborhood of the premises, as to defeat the object and purpose of the agreement, and that it would be inequitable to deprive the defendant of the privilege of conforming his property to that character, so that he could use it to his greater advantage, and in no respect to the detriment of the plaintiff. The agreement before us recites, that the object which the parties to the covenant had in view was "to provide for the better improvement of the lands, and to secure their permanent value." It certainly is not the doctrine of courts of equity, to enforce, by its peculiar mandate, every contract, in all cases, even where specific execution is found to be its legal intention and effect. It gives or withholds such decree according to its discretion, in view of the circumstances of the case, and the plaintiff's prayer for relief is not answered, where, under those circumstances, the relief he seeks would be inequitable. (Peters v. Delaplaine, 49 N.Y. 362; Margraf v. Muir, 57 id. 155; Mathews v. Terwilliger, 3 Barb. 51; Radcliffe v. Warrington, 12 Vesey 331.) If for any reason, therefore, not referable to the defendant, an enforcement of the covenant would defeat either of the ends contemplated by the parties, a court of equity might well refuse to interfere, or if in fact the condition of the property by which the premises are surrounded has been so altered "that the terms and restrictions" of the covenant are no longer applicable to the existing state of things. (1 Story's Eq. Jur. [10th ed.], §750.) And so though the contract was fair and just when made, the interference of the court should be denied, if subsequent events have made performance by the defendant so onerous, that its enforcement would impose great hardship upon him, and cause little or no benefit to the plaintiff. . . .

Value & Purpose of land has been frustrated by Railroad = Release

In the case before us, the plaintiffs rely upon no circumstance of equity, but put their claim to relief upon the covenant and the violation of its conditions by the defendant. They have established, by their complaint and proof, a clear legal cause of action. If damages had been sustained, they must, in any proper action, be allowed. But on the other hand, the defendant has exhibited such change in the condition of the adjacent property, and its character for use, as leaves no ground for equitable interference, if the discretion of the court is to be governed by the principles I have stated, or the cases which those principles have controlled. The general current of business affairs has reached and covered the entire premises fronting on Sixth avenue, both above and below the lot in question. If this was all, however, the plaintiffs would be justified in their claim, for it is apparent from the agreement that such encroachment was anticipated, and that the parties to it intended to secure the property in question from the disturbance which business would necessarily produce. But the trial court has found that since the action was begun, an elevated railway has been built in the Sixth avenue. It runs past the premises, and a station has been established in front of them, at the intersection of Fiftieth street. He finds that "the railway and station affect the premises injuriously and render them less profitable for the purpose of a dwelling-house, but do not render their use of business purposes indispensable to their practicable and profitable use and occupation." The evidence sustains the finding. The premises may still be used for dwellings, but the occupants are not likely to be those whose convenience and wishes were to be promoted by the covenant, persons of less pecuniary ability, and willing to sacrifice some degree of comfort for economy, transient tenants of still another class, whose presence would be more offensive to quiet and orderly people who might reside in the neighborhood. Not only large depreciation in rents when occupied, but also frequent vacancies have followed the construction of the road. Its trains, propelled by steam, run at intervals of a few minutes, until midnight. The station covers from fifteen to twenty feet of the street opposite the defendant's premises. Half the width of the sidewalk is occupied by its elevated platform. From it, persons waiting for the trains, or there for other purposes, can look directly into the windows. Noise from its trains can be heard from one avenue to the other.

It is obvious, without further detail, that the construction of this road and its management have rendered privacy and quiet in the adjacent buildings impossible, and so affected the premises of the defendant, and all those originally owned by him, who, with the plaintiff, entered into the covenant, that neither their better improvement nor permanent value can be promoted by enforcing its observance. Nor are the causes of this depreciation transient. The platform of the railroad station, which renders inspection of the interior of the house easy to all observers; the stairs, which render the road accessible, must remain so long as the road is operated; and the noise and smoke are now, at least, an apparent necessity, conse-

Frustration

quent upon its operation. It is true, the covenant is without exception or limitation, but I think this contingency which has happened was not within the contemplation of the parties. The road was authorized by the legislature, and, by reason of it, there has been imposed upon the property a condition of things which frustrates the scheme devised by the parties, and deprives the property of the benefit which might otherwise accrue from its observance. This new condition has already affected, in various ways and degrees, the uses of property in its neighborhood, and property values. It has made the defendant's property unsuitable for the use to which, by the covenant of his grantor, it was appropriated, and if, in fact of its enactment and the contingencies flowing from it, the covenant can stand anywhere, it surely cannot in a court of equity. The land in question furnishes an ill seat for dwelling-houses, and it cannot be supposed that the parties to the covenant would now select it for a residence, or expect others to prefer it for that purpose. . . .

It is apparent that the original design of the parties has been broken up by acts for which neither the defendant nor his grantors are responsible, that the object of the covenant has been, so far as the defendant is concerned, defeated, and that to enforce it would work oppression, and not equity. Δ Released from Covenant

To avoid this result the judgment appealed from should be reversed; and the complaint dismissed, but as this result is made necessary by reason of events occurring since the commencement of the action, it should be without costs.

All concur.

Judgment reversed, and complaint dismissed.

PETTEY v. FIRST NATIONAL BANK OF GENEVA

225 Ill. App. 3d 539, 588 N.E.2d 412 (1992)

Justice GEIGER delivered the opinion of the court:

The plaintiffs, a group of 130 homeowners whose land is included in a restrictive covenant running with the land, sought injunction and declaratory relief against defendants, including Joseph C. Boyd, Charles J. Groenings, and John A. Groenings, to prevent their proposed development of land in violation of the covenant. The defendants and their cotrustee La Salle National Bank appeal from the bench trial judgment for the plaintiffs. The court declared the covenant to be valid and enforceable and enjoined the defendants' development of Boyd's and Groenings' properties to prevent violation of the provisions of the covenant.

Bench Trial

Boyd argues (1) that his property is explicitly excluded from the legal description contained in the restrictive covenant; (2) that the plaintiffs are barred from relief under the affirmative defense of *laches*. . . . Together, the defendants argue . . . (7) that substantial changes in the area made the restrictive covenant unenforceable; and (8) that the landowners in the area waived enforcement of the covenant. . . .

The following facts were stipulated to at the trial. There is a restrictive covenant dated November 27, 1937, running with the land recorded against approximately 1,000 acres in the City of St. Charles, the Village of Wayne, and St. Charles Township. The covenant begins with a preamble stating that the purpose of the restrictions is to "preserve the present high character of use and occupancy" of the land. The pertinent restrictions provide in part: *purpose*

> 1. No principal residence shall be erected on any one tract of land of less than four (4) acres in extent, any one dimension of which shall be not less than two hundred (200) feet, except that the occupant of such principal residence may erect on such a tract one (1), but not more than one (1), separate additional residence as living quarters for guests or servants.
>
> 3. No principal residence, separate residence for children, guests or servants, incinerator, garage, or other building shall be erected within fifty (50) feet from any property line and within seventy-five feet from the center line of any highway or road.
>
> 4. Said real estate shall be used for residential and farming purposes only; said real estate shall not be used for any commercial purpose whatsoever, nor shall advertising signs or billboards be erected thereon.
>
> 5. No person other than of the Caucasian Race shall be permitted to occupy [*sic*] any portion of said real estate, except as a servant of a Caucasian owner or Caucasian tenant residing thereon.

Boyd owns 8.6 acres, and the Groenings own approximately 70 acres of real estate within the covenant area. Boyd had plans to rezone his property from single-family residential to a planned unit development (PUD) to consist of 12 units. Boyd's proposal would exceed the restriction in the covenant as it allowed two residences per four-acre lot.

Boyd filed his PUD plan with the City of St. Charles on January 14, 1987, and he requested rezoning in accordance with his plan. The St. Charles Plan Commission held a public hearing on the subject, and several plaintiffs appeared and objected to the plan on the basis that it violated the covenant. The City of St. Charles approved the plan and granted the rezoning on November 21, 1988.

On January 26, 1989, the plaintiffs commenced their lawsuit. Before commencement of the suit, Boyd expended over $50,000 installing sewer and water facilities and $70,000 on site plans, landscaping plans and engineering plans. After the St. Charles commission rezoned Boyd's property, the Groenings filed a petition to annex their 70-acre site to St. Charles so that it could be developed with approximately 160 lots ranging from one-fourth to one-half acre.

It was also stipulated that within the area covered by the restrictive covenant, there had been several possible covenant "violations." There are eight homes in Persimmon Woods which sit on tracts of land ranging in size from .71 to 3.75 acres, violating the four-acre lot minimum. Persimmon Woods is located on the one noncontiguous portion of the land affected by the covenant. None of the plaintiffs knew at the time of construction that the Persimmon residences were within the land described in the covenant, and they raised no objections to the residences' construction.

The covenant area also includes two residences which have a structure erected within 50 feet of the property line, in violation of the covenant. One of them is 49.10 feet from the property line. The other lot's structures within 50 feet of the property line were in existence prior to the recording of the covenant.

There are a number of parcels within the covenant which contain principal residences erected on a tract of land which has at least one boundary line less than 200 feet long. The plaintiffs never objected to these violations of the covenant.

There are three possible "use" violations within the covenant area. The first is the 114-acre St. Charles Country Club (Country Club), which together with the Persimmon residences comprise the noncontiguous section of land covered by the covenant. None of the plaintiffs knew at the time of its construction that the club was within the land described in the covenant, and none of them objected to its construction or its operation.

The second possible "use" violation of the covenant is a building known as Dunham Castle, which has been operated as a rental property since 1963. None of the plaintiffs had objected to the operation of Dunham Castle as rental apartments. The third possible "use" violation is by several streets and parcels owned by the City of St. Charles and by the St. Charles Park Foundation used for municipal purposes.

Another possible violation of the covenant is by signs advertising the sale of properties and signs advertising builders, remodelers or decorators. Such signs were placed on properties within the covenant area without objection by any of the plaintiffs.

There was substantial evidence presented by stipulation and expert testimony that development had taken place surrounding the restricted land and that development had occurred in Kane County, the City of St. Charles, and, more specifically, along the southern and eastern boundaries of the covenant property. All of the development which occurred along these boundaries was by residential, single-family dwellings. Most of those dwellings were on lots less than four acres. The residential developments west and north of the covenant boundaries are on lots at least four acres in size.

The evidence also established that (1) when the covenant was signed, there were 22 covered landowners; now there are 260; (2) that the traffic on the roads servicing the covenant area has increased as much as 225%; (3) that various sections of the area have been changed from unincorporated property to incorporated residential subdivisions; (4) that the restrictions make the economic market for the properties smaller and make the properties more difficult to sell; and (5) that if the lots could be sold in smaller parcels, a greater price per acre could be achieved.

We first address the three issues argued in Boyd's appellate brief. Initially, Boyd argues that the court erred in finding that his land falls within the legal description of the covenant. Boyd argues the legal description of the land covered by the covenant can be interpreted as excluding his land. The plaintiffs argue that Boyd's deed to his land specifically states that his property is subject to the restrictive covenant in question and that Boyd's interpretation of the covenant's legal description is not a logical construction of the language.

The court heard extensive testimony from two experts, who testified on behalf of both the plaintiffs and the defendants. The court made an express finding that Boyd's property was subject to the covenant.

The Illinois Supreme Court stated that in the judicial enforcement of restrictive covenants all doubts must be resolved in favor of natural rights and against restrictions thereon. (Watts v. Fritz (1963), 29 Ill. 2d 517, 521, 194 N.E.2d 276.) The court's decision in that regard will only be overturned if the court's findings are against the manifest weight of the evidence. (Rogers v. Jerseyville (1990), 196 Ill. App. 3d 136, 142, 142 Ill. Dec. 573, 552 N.E.2d 1314.) In this case, the court was aware of the standard to use in interpreting restrictive covenants and found that Boyd's property was not excluded by the language of the covenant. Considering the strained interpretation of the language requested by Boyd and the language in Boyd's deed stating that the land is restricted by the covenant, we find that the court's decision on this issue is not against the manifest weight of the evidence. 196 Ill. App. 3d at 142, 142 Ill. Dec. 573, 552 N.E.2d 1314.

Second, Boyd argues that the plaintiffs are barred from injunctive relief, asserting the affirmative defense of *laches*. Boyd argues that he had already spent $120,000 in development costs before the plaintiffs commenced their suit and that, due to the plaintiffs' delay in commencing their suit to enforce the covenant, he was misled and relied on their acquiescence. The plaintiffs argue that Boyd was aware of the covenant's restrictions when he purchased the land and that the plaintiffs timely objected to the development when they attended the zoning hearings and objected to the plan on the basis of the covenant.

Laches is a doctrine which bars a plaintiff relief where, because of the plaintiff's delay in asserting a right, the defendant has been misled or prejudiced. (City of Rochelle v. Suski (1990), 206 Ill. App. 3d 497, 501, 151 Ill. Dec. 478, 564 N.E.2d 933.) However, where the circumstances indicate that the party knowingly violated a restriction or a right and pressed ahead, suggesting a purpose to proceed irrespective of the consequences, *laches* may not be used as an affirmative defense. (Fick v. Burnham (1929), 251 Ill. App. 333, 341.) The application of the equitable doctrine of *laches* is a matter of the trial court's discretion. Ole, Ole, Inc. v. Kozubowski (1989), 187 Ill. App. 3d 277, 286, 134 Ill. Dec. 895, 543 N.E.2d 178.

The record reveals that the plaintiffs objected to the proposed development in a timely fashion and that Boyd knew of the restrictive covenant when he began to develop his land. We do not find that the court erred in finding that the plaintiff was not guilty of *laches. Ole,* 187 Ill. App. 3d at 286-87, 134 Ill. Dec. 895, 543 N.E.2d 178. . . .

Seventh, the defendants argue that the court erred in enforcing the restrictive covenant because the neighborhood has changed significantly since the restrictions were created. It is well settled that even where a general plan is evident in a covenant, its restrictions under the covenant will not be enforced where the character of the neighborhood had changed so much since the restrictions were imposed as to defeat the original purpose of the plan. (Wallace v. Hoffman (1949), 336 Ill. App. 545, 554, 84 N.E.2d 654.) For such a change to relieve or cancel the enforcement of a restriction, it must be so radical and complete as to render the restriction unreasonable, confiscatory, discriminatory, or as practically to destroy the purpose for which the restriction was originally imposed. (Cordogan v. Union National Bank (1978), 64 Ill. App. 3d 248, 254, 21 Ill. Dec. 18, 380 N.E.2d 1194; see also Rogers v. City of Jerseyville (1990), 196 Ill. App. 3d 136, 139-40, 142 Ill. Dec. 573, 552 N.E.2d 1314.) The mere fact that the property in question is worth more without the restrictions is not decisive. Tones Inc. v. La Salle National Bank (1975), 34 Ill. App. 3d 236, 243, 339 N.E.2d 3.

The trial court found that the change in the character and environment of the neighborhood affected by the restrictive covenant was not sufficient to render the restrictive covenant unenforceable. The court further found that the changes in the neighborhood were virtually "nil and *de minimus.*"

As stated in the preamble of the covenant, the restrictions were put in place to preserve the high character of use and occupancy of the subject property. This court ignores the language of the preamble which restricts land ownership to Caucasians as this passage is meaningless and is judicially unenforceable. (See Shelley v. Kraemer (1948), 334 U.S. 1, 92 L. Ed. 1161, 68 S. Ct. 836.) The record included significant evidence that the changes alleged by the defendant in the character of the neighborhood have not transformed it in any manner which would warrant the removal of the lot size restrictions and that the restrictions still support the purpose of the covenant. (See *Cordogan,* 64 Ill. App. 3d at 254, 21 Ill. Dec. 18, 380 N.E.2d 1194.) As the trial court's finding that the covenant was still enforceable was guided by these principles and supported by the record, we will not overturn its findings. See *Rogers,* 196 Ill. App. 3d at 142, 142 Ill. Dec. 573, 552 N.E.2d 1314.

Lastly, the defendants argue that the plaintiffs have waived enforcement of the covenant by acquiescing to prior violations. The defendants specifically refer to the construction of the Country Club, which violates the residential and farming restriction, the Persimmon residences which violate the four-acre minimum restriction, several violations of the 200-foot lot-line restriction, and two homes violating the restriction against structures within 50 feet of a property line. The plaintiffs argue that the past violations are minor, that most occurred without their knowledge, and that acquiesced to violations of one type of restriction do not waive enforcement of all restrictions.

Where there has been acquiescence to prior restrictive covenant violations that go to the very substance of a general plan or of a particular restriction, the plaintiff will be held to have waived any right to enforce it. (Amoco Realty Co. v. Montalbano (1985), 133 Ill. App. 3d 327, 333, 88 Ill. Dec. 369, 478 N.E.2d 860, citing Watts v. Fritz (1963), 29 Ill. 2d 517, 523, 194 N.E.2d 276.) However, acquiescence to minor violations of a restriction will not prohibit the subsequent enforcement of that restriction. (Citizens Utilities Co. v. Centex-Winston Corp. (1989), 185 Ill. App. 3d 610, 614, 133 Ill. Dec. 470, 541 N.E.2d 681.) In determining the extent of prior violations, separate and distinct restrictions which have been violated will not amount to acquiescence of the violation currently at issue. (See Cordogan v. Union National Bank (1978), 64 Ill. App. 3d 248, 255, 21 Ill. Dec. 18, 380 N.E.2d 1194.) The trial court's findings as to the materiality of the past violations of the restrictive covenant will only be overturned on appeal if the findings are against the manifest weight of the evidence. (*Rogers,* 196 Ill. App. 3d at 142, 142 Ill. Dec. 573, 552 N.E.2d 1314.) The trial court's decision will be considered to be against the manifest weight of the evidence if, after a review of the evidence, it is clearly evident that the conclusion opposite to the one reached by the trial court was the proper disposition. 196 Ill. App. 3d at 142, 142 Ill. Dec. 573, 552 N.E.2d 1314.

The court found that the past violations of the lot size restrictions were not substantial or material based on the entire evidence in the case, nor did they defeat the legitimate, enforceable purpose of the covenant provisions. Considering the evidence, including eight demonstrated violations of lot size restrictions, located in a separate, noncontiguous section of the covenanted land, we do not find that the trial court's decision was against the manifest weight of the evidence. See *Amoco,* 133 Ill. App. 3d at 333, 88 Ill. Dec. 369, 478 N.E.2d 860. . . .

For the foregoing reasons, we affirm the judgment of the circuit court of Kane County.

Affirmed.

NOTES AND QUESTIONS

1.   **What became of Tulk v. Moxhay?** The *Thacher* case marks one of the earliest statements of the doctrine of neighborhood change. The *Pettey* case, over a century later, suggests that the doctrine remains actively litigated as landowners chafe from (long-standing) covenants that bar a more profitable use of their land. Indeed, the very neighborhood change that

creates the profit opportunity usually serves as the legal excuse for seeking to grab the opportunity.

As a threshold question, should not the landowner who buys with notice of the restrictions, and who may well have paid less because of them, always lose when he claims that neighborhood change makes the covenant unenforceable? Cf. Tulk v. Moxhay, 41 Eng. Rep. 1143 (Ch. 1848) ("No one purchasing with notice . . . can stand in a different situation from the party from whom he purchased"). Why should courts be party to a windfall gain? Note that some courts refuse to admit into evidence instances of neighborhood change (or violations of deed restrictions) that occurred before the servient holder acquired title; see Wood v. Dozier, 464 So. 2d 1168 (Fla. 1985).

2.   **What next?** By granting the *Pettey* plaintiffs declaratory relief, the court has protected their entitlement with a property rule. Suppose, however, that the defendant Boyd has not given up on his plan for a 12-unit development. He must now try (or, perhaps, he has already tried) to purchase releases. Since 130 homeowners sued to enjoin the Boyd development, how likely is it that Boyd can negotiate to a successful outcome? Does this question suggest to you why the doctrine of neighborhood change, notwithstanding Tulk v. Moxhay, remains viable?

Should it matter, or indeed, should the court even be told, if all but a few of the benefited property owners have no objection to the proposed development (or have agreed to sign releases)? Would the location of the holdouts' property, vis-à-vis the proposed development, make any difference?

3.   **Entitlement protected with a liability rule.** Suppose that, of the 260 landowners covered by the restrictions in *Pettey,* only three refuse to sign releases. In that instance, might the court lift the restrictions from the Boyd property upon payment of damages to the holdout owners? What if the holdouts are unable to prove pecuniary loss, but claim that they will suffer psychic or sentimental injury? Cf. Evangelical Lutheran Church of Ascension of Snyder v. Sahlem, 254 N.Y. 161, 166, 172 N.E. 455, 457 (1930); Wicks v. Pat Pallone Co., 48 Misc. 2d 734, 265 N.Y.S.2d 732 (Sup. Ct. 1965), *rev'd on other grounds,* 29 A.D.2d 626, 285 N.Y.S.2d 1008 (4th Dept. 1967).

4.   **Laches and waiver distinguished.** The defendant in *Pettey* argued, to the court's deaf ear, that plaintiffs were barred from enforcing the restrictions because of laches and waiver. Can you explain the difference between them?

5.   **Interplay between zoning and private restrictions.** The City of St. Charles had already approved Boyd's PUD plan and had rezoned his parcel from residential to PUD. Why doesn't this settle the dispute between Boyd and his neighbors?

The general rule states that a valid restriction is not superseded by the adoption of a zoning except to the extent that the regulation makes compliance with the restriction regulation illegal or against public policy; see Restatement, Servitudes §7.9 (Prelim. Draft 13, 1996). For a review of the cases and a criticism of the courts' failure to state why this should be, see Berger, Conflicts between Zoning Ordinances and Restrictive Covenants, 43 Neb. L. Rev. 449 (1964). Would private restrictions that are created after the zoning ordinance also gain primacy?

6.   **Interpretative issues.** The *Pettey* case raises another much-litigated issue: What is the scope or coverage of a restriction? Wherever any slight ambiguity exists, a landowner hoping to escape the restrictions may have another trump card. Because restrictions under attack tend to be middle-aged, prepared from boiler plate, and not particularly forward-looking, ambiguity is a common trait.

Where ambiguity is in issue, which of the following constructional rules make the most sense to you? (You may choose more than one, or write your own rules.)

(a)   The court should construe any ambiguity against the drafter (usually the subdivider).

(b)   The court should seek to carry out the intent of the drafter.

(c)   The court should seek to reinforce the expectations of those landowners benefiting most directly from the restrictions.

(d)   Since restrictions are a restraint on land use, the court should read generously the uses permitted and narrowly the uses banned.

(e)   The court should construe any ambiguity to allow landowners to build whatever the zoning ordinance allows.

7.   **Anti-apartment covenants.** Homeowners in an affluent Washington, D.C., neighborhood successfully sued a developer who wished to build an apartment building on land that carried a covenant prohibiting such projects. The city had zoned the parcel in question for apartment use, the owner had received a building permit, and had already built a building across the street from the proposed building on land bearing a similar restrictive covenant. In holding for the homeowners, the court found that the neighborhood had been created with a scheme in mind (solely single-family residential), the 76-year old covenant supported that scheme and was still in effect, and that the homeowners had the right to expect that the intended character of their neighborhood would not change. Kenneth Bredemeier, Residents Block Developer's Plans, Wash. Post, Jul. 19, 1986, at E1.

e.   By Legislative Action

Earlier in the text, we examined statutory limits on those defeasible estates that curbed the free use of land. This section deals with statutory limits on servitudes that restrict the use of land. As you read the following materials, consider whether efforts to regulate servitudes present the same

issues for a legislature as would efforts to curb defeasible estates. To help
you crystallize your thoughts, be sure to ask yourself:

(a)   who the winners and the losers are when a servitude (condition)
      is unenforceable;
(b)   the purposes for which servitudes (conditions) are usually
      created;
(c)   whether servitudes (conditions) usually arise from donative or
      commercial transactions;
(d)   to what extent servitudes (conditions) are already subject to
      "regulation" by the courts;
(e)   how the public interest is served by the regulation of servitudes
      (conditions).

MOHAWK CONTAINERS, INC. v. HANCOCK

43 Misc. 2d 716, 252 N.Y.S.2d 148 (Sup. Ct. 1964)

CARDAMONE, J. The plaintiff, Mohawk Containers, Inc., has previously
instituted an action for a declaratory judgment against the defendants to
extinguish certain restrictions on the use of their land, pursuant to the provisions of section 1951 of the Real Property Actions and Proceedings Law.

The plaintiff now moves for an order determining that the restrictions
are of no actual and substantial benefit to the defendants by reason of
changed conditions. The plaintiff further requests judgment that the said
restrictions be completely extinguished upon payment to the defendants
of such damages, if any, which defendants may sustain.

Mohawk Containers, Inc., (hereinafter called Mohawk) is a manufacturer of corrugated boxes, with a plant located in the Village of New Hartford, Oneida County, New York. Its property, industrially zoned, fronts on
Campion Road. The rear of Mohawk's property, which was previously zoned
residential, abuts on a residential area comprised of one-family dwelling
houses located on Colonial Drive, also located in the said Village. The defendants in this action are property owners who reside on Colonial Drive.
In its complaint, Mohawk alleges that it owns, "in fee simple," certain property which is subject to a restrictive covenant that it "shall be used only for
residential purposes . . .," and for "single-family dwellings." On November
14, 1963, the zoning of the premises in question was changed to industrial.
Subsequent to the zoning change, seven of the eleven owners bound by the
restrictions released their rights voluntarily and without financial consideration. One of the owners has remained neutral and the remaining three
property owners affected are the defendants in this action. Each of them
insists that his property will sustain loss in value if the restrictions on the
plaintiff's land are extinguished. In his affidavit, the vice-president of the

plaintiff corporation conceded that "these defendants sincerely believed that they will suffer financial loss if this restriction is released." Mohawk proposes to add an extension to its existing building to accommodate new and necessary equipment. There is a natural boundary line between the plaintiff's residential property (where the proposed addition would be located) and the Colonial Manor residential property, consisting of a natural ridge twenty-five (25) feet high. The Zoning Board of Appeals of the Town of New Hartford at the time that it granted the zoning change, did so subject to eleven conditions designed to protect the residential character of the area. There has been no change in the character of the residential lots comprising the Colonial Manor development. All of the property has been and still is used strictly for residential purposes, the price range of the homes starting at $20,000.00.

Section 1951 of the Real Property Actions and Proceedings Law provides as follows: [65]

> 2. When relief against such a restriction is sought in an action to quiet title or to obtain a declaration with respect to enforceability of the restriction . . . , if the court shall find that the restriction is of no actual and substantial benefit to the persons seeking its enforcement or seeking a declaration or determination of its enforceability, either because the purpose of the restriction has already been accomplished or, by reason of changed conditions or other cause, its purpose is not capable of accomplishment, or for any other reason, it may adjudge that the restriction is not enforceable by injunction . . . and that it shall be completely extinguished upon payment, to the person or persons who would otherwise be entitled to enforce it in the event of a breach at the time of the action, of such damages, if any, as such person or persons will sustain from the extinguishment of the restriction.

This Statute (eff. Sept. 1, 1963) codifies the doctrine of balancing interests (sometimes referred to as the doctrine of relative hardship), long recognized in Evangelical Lutheran Church of the Ascension of Snyder v. Sahlem, 254 N.Y. 161, 172 N.E. 455 (1930). Ordinarily, where the residential area itself has not changed or deteriorated (and such is conceded here) the covenant is enforceable. (Cummins v. Colgate Properties Corp., 2 Misc. 2d 301, 305, 153 N.Y.S.2d 321, 325-326 (1956), *aff'd,* 2 A.D.2d 749, 153 N.Y.S.2d 608 (Second Dep't 1956); Kiernan v. Snowden, 123 N.Y.S.2d 895 (Sup. Ct. Westchester Co. 1953); Bull v. Burton, 227 N.Y. 101, 124 N.E. 111 (1919). Still, the Courts of Equity give or withhold decrees according to their discretion in view of the circumstances of each case. Trustees of Columbia College v. Thacher, 87 N.Y. 311, 316 (1882)). A Court of Equity will not enforce a restrictive covenant when it appears that the injury to the defen-

---

65. For some legislative background on §1951, see N.Y. Law Review Commission, 1958 Report Recommendations and Studies 211-374. — EDS.

dant is not serious or substantial, and when enforcing it would subject the plaintiff to great inconvenience and loss. . . .

While the action instituted by the plaintiff before the Town Zoning Board of Appeals was appropriate, and the action of that Board was proper in the imposition of reasonable conditions upon the plaintiff (Church v. Town of Islip, 8 N.Y.2d 254, 203 N.Y.S.2d 866, 168 N.E.2d 680 (1960)), despite the change of zoning, the defendants still "have the right to insist upon adherence to the covenant." (Lefferts Manor Ass'n v. Fass, 28 Misc. 2d 1005, 1007, 211 N.Y.S.2d 18, 20 (Sup. Ct. Kings County, 1960); Nemet v. Edgemere Garage & Sales Co., 73 N.Y.S.2d 921 (Sup. Ct. Queens Co. 1947)). In the *Nemet* case, the then Justice Froessel, (later a judge of the Court of Appeals) wrote at page 924:

> I do not find in the statute the legislative intention ascribed by the defendants, and if construed as urged by them, Section 35, in my opinion, would, assuming plaintiff had an easement in the street, deprive him of property without due process of law, *and be an unconstitutional exercise of the legislative power. The Board of Standards and Appeals may, within its powers, grant a permit to an owner, but it may not determine rights in real property.* (emphasis supplied)

The outcome of this controversy must be determined then under the equitable principles of law enunciated by Judge Cardozo in Evangelical Lutheran Church of the Ascension of Snyder v. Sahlem, (254 N.Y. 161, 172 N.E. 455, *supra*). Both the plaintiff and defendants have cited this case in their briefs as supporting their respective contentions. Judge Cardozo wrote at page 166 of 254 N.Y., at page 457 of 172 N.E.: "By the settled doctrine of equity, restrictive covenants in respect of land will be enforced by preventive remedies while the violation is still in prospect, *unless the attitude of the complaining owner in standing on his covenant is unconscionable or oppressive.* . . ." (emphasis supplied). The plaintiff concedes that there are no "unconscionable or oppressive" motives on the defendants' part when it admits that "these defendants *sincerely believe* that they will suffer financial loss if this restriction is released." Since the "'parties had the right to determine for themselves in what way and for what purposes their lands should be occupied irrespective of pecuniary gain or loss,'" (Evangelical Lutheran Church v. Sahlem, 254 N.Y. 161, 167, 172 N.E. 455, 457), since the defendants "insist upon adherence to a covenant which is now as valid and binding as at the hour of its making" (Ibid., at 168, 172 N.E. at 457), even though some of the "neighbors are willing to modify the restriction and forego a portion of their rights" (Ibid., at 168, 172 N.E. at 457) and since the defendants believe "that the comfort of (their) dwelling will be imperiled by the change, and so (they chose) to abide by the covenant as framed . . ." (Ibid., at 168, 172 N.E. at 457), the choice is for them only. Further, in this case, as in the *Sahlem* case, "the building is yet a plan, the work on it preliminary . . .", (Ibid., at 169, 172 N.E. at 458). Finally, "In the award of equitable remedies there is often an element of discretion, but . . . 'Discretion . . . "must be regulated upon grounds that will make it judicial".'" (Ibid., at 167, 172 N.E. at 457). Since these defendants are "satisfied with the existing state of things" and refuse to disturb it, they "will be protected in (their) refusal by all the power of the law." (Ibid., at 168, 172 N.E. at 457).

Accordingly, the motion of the plaintiff is denied and the complaint is dismissed.

NOTES AND QUESTIONS

1. **Evidentiary weight.** What weight, if any, should the court in *Mohawk Containers* have given to the following testimony, had plaintiff introduced it:

   (a) Plaintiff occupied the only industrially zoned parcel in the village.

   (b) The village had rezoned to industrial the balance of plaintiff's parcel after conducting a study on the need for industrial expansion within the locality.

   (c) Plaintiff will close down its plant and move elsewhere if it cannot enlarge the present facility. One hundred persons now work at the plant.

   (d) The three homeowners who defended the suit each had asked $50,000 for a release of the tract restrictions.

   (e) The restrictions were filed and the Colonial Drive houses were built after plaintiff had built its plant.

2. **Holdouts redux.** Refer to question 1(d) above. This is a common occurrence — that is, a landowner seeking more for a release than the developer is ready (able) to pay. Where the court believes that a holdup situation is present, should the court treat §1951 as a mandate to award damages and lift the restriction? Even in the absence of a §1951, might the clean-hands doctrine permit equity to lift the restriction where the court believes one party is behaving badly?

3. **A second arrow in the quiver?** Might the village still rescue the situation by condemning the defendants' interest in the plaintiff's property, paying the defendants just compensation, and reselling the interest to the plaintiff? What exactly is the defendants' interest? How would the compensation be fixed? Compare Chapter 6.

4. **Noncovenant servitudes.** Section 1951 applies to restrictions on the use of land created at any time "by covenant, promise or negative easement." In Bardach v. Mayfair-Flushing Corp., 49 Misc. 2d 380, 267 N.Y.S.2d 609 (Sup. Ct.), *aff'd mem.*, 26 A.D.2d 620, 272 N.Y.S.2d 969 (2d Dept. 1966), the court relied on §1951 to declare an easement unenforceable. The easement gave the defendants, tenants of an adjacent apartment house, access to plaintiff's vacant lot for ingress and egress of vehicles and pedestrians,

and for a garden, recreation, and play area. Is it clear that §1951 covers this case?

5. **Interplay with zoning redux.** A Georgia statute provides that no privately held restriction shall be enforceable after 20 years if it conflicts with a zoning law. Ga. Code Ann. §29-301 (Supp. 1996) (exception for interests held by a corporation or a trust for the "public use"). Do you see any problem construing this statute? Compare Note 5, page 776 *supra.*

6. **The British equivalent.** In 1965, a British commission headed by Leslie Searman began a study on restrictive covenants and on January 31, 1967, filed its report. Law Cmnd. No. 11, pursuant to §3(2) of the Law Commissions Act of 1965. The commission would give to the country's Lands Tribunal clear power to modify or discharge a land obligation where two requirements were satisfied, "first, that the restriction was, or unless modified or discharged would be, detrimental to the public interest by impeding the reasonable uses of land for public or private purposes, second, that the persons entitled to the benefit of the restriction could be adequately compensated in money for any disadvantage that they might suffer."

Slightly altered, this proposal has become law: Law of Property Act 1969, §28. How does the English law differ from §1951? Will Britain be nationalizing certain private interests in land? Would you welcome a similar law to your state?

7. **Restrictions on freedom of speech.** Streets, sidewalks, and parks are constitutional public fora, in which the varied forms of speech enjoy strong First Amendment protection. What becomes of that protection when entire sections of the community are closed off to outsiders? Cf. David J. Kennedy, Residential Associations as State Actors: Regulating the Impact of Gated Communities on Nonmembers, 105 Yale L.J. 761, 771-773 (1995); Laguna Publishing Co. v. Golden Rain Foundation, 182 Cal. Rptr. 813 (Ct. App. 1982). More generally, the Kennedy article argues for state action treatment of gated communities because, he asserts, they impose a variety of harms on nonmembers, who are affected by exclusion, discrimination, and a shrinking tax base. Clayton P. Gillette, Courts, Covenants, and Communities, 61 U. Chi. L. Rev. 1375 (1994), views these communities far more sympathetically.

§7.8   Covenants, Contracts, and Community

The proliferation of communities designed around complex systems of covenants[66] raises a variety of important issues. Are the stringent restric-

---

66. Often, in condominiums, developers do not structure the restrictions on use as technical covenants, but rather require each successive homeowner to personally sign onto a contract that binds them to observe the various rules. In subdivisions, typically the restrictions are structured as covenants, not contracts.

tions these communities place on individual landowners justifiable on the grounds that the landowners have freely chosen to buy into a given community? Do these covenants reflect the will of the landowners, or limit it? Are the homeowners' associations more like private contractual arrangements, or more like local governments? The following excerpts raise these questions.

ROBERT ELLICKSON, CITIES AND HOMEOWNERS ASSOCIATIONS

130 U. Pa. L. Rev. 1519, 1519-1520, 1521-1523, 1526-1527 (1982)

. . . Professor Gerald Frug [has] compared the city and the business corporation as possible vehicles for the exercise of decentralized power. In the course of his analysis, Frug asserted that American law is deeply biased against the emergence of powerful cities and, by implication, is less restrictive on corporate power. . . . Frug never directed his attention at a third candidate for the exercise of decentralized power: the private homeowners association. The association, not the business corporation, is the obvious private alternative to the city. Like a city, an association enables households that have clustered their activities in a territorially defined area to enforce rules of conduct, to provide "public goods" (such as open space), and to pursue other common goals they could not achieve without some form of potentially coercive central authority. Although they were relatively exotic as recently as twenty years ago, homeowners associations now outnumber cities. Developers create thousands of new associations each year to govern their subdivisions, condominiums, and planned communities. . . .

This Article compares the legal status of cities and homeowner associations. . . . Although cities are considered "public" and homeowners associations "private," I discern only one important difference between the two forms of organization — the sometimes involuntary nature of membership in a city versus the perfectly voluntary nature of membership in a homeowners association. I assert that this difference explains why cities are more active than associations are in undertaking coercive redistributive programs.

Professor Frank Michelman . . . has offered a characteristically useful one-sentence guide for identifying the existence of "governmental" organization:

> We know perfectly well, granting that there are intermediate hard cases, how to distinguish governmental from non-governmental *powers* and *forms of organization*: governments are distinguished by their acknowledged, lawful authority — not dependent on property ownership — to coerce a territorially defined and imperfectly voluntary membership by acts of regulation, taxation, and condemnation, the exercise of which authority is determined by majoritarian and representative procedures.

. . . The homeowners association, although certainly one of Michelman's "intermediate hard cases," is currently viewed by both ordinary and legal observers as a "private" organization, not a "government." In fact, it is sufficiently "private" that it has rarely been granted any intermediate legal status that a hard case might be thought to deserve, but instead has been treated much like any other private organization. This is so even though the modern homeowners association has virtually all of the indicia that Michelman would have us associate with a government. First, a homeowners association rules a "territorially defined" area, and, in the usual case, obtains its power to do so through no form of property ownership. For example, when the members of a condominium association own the common areas as tenants in common, the association itself owns no real property at all.

Nor does Michelman's list of the tell-tale governmental powers do much to distinguish a homeowners association from a city. An association is typically entitled to undertake acts of both regulation and taxation, as those terms are ordinarily used. Associations, for example, may restrict to whom a member may sell his unit, prohibit certain kinds of conduct (not only in common areas but also within the confines of individual homes), and tightly control the physical alteration of a member's unit. An association's "taxation" takes the form of monthly assessments on members. Assessments can be raised without the unanimous consent of the membership. Payment of an assessment is secured by a lien on a member's unit, making the assessment is almost as hard to evade as a municipal property tax is. To be sure, association powers are not as extensive as those possessed by "public" bodies. The regulations of a homeowners association in sum are likely to be less intrusive and comprehensive than what one finds in a typical municipal code. Cities have far more ways to raise revenue than associations do. Lastly, it would be highly unusual for an association to have the power to condemn a member's unit — the third governmental power Michelman lists. Some homeowners associations do have the power to expel members for misbehavior — a power that comes close to the power of condemnation. But even if they did not, exercise of eminent domain power by a local government is rare; it would be remarkable if the presence of this power were a necessary condition for the use of the adjective "public" in ordinary or legal language.

Nor does one stretch ordinary language out of shape to describe an association as having "majoritarian and representative procedures." Much as city dwellers choose a city council, association members elect a board of directors to manage association affairs.

Only one part of Michelman's description of a government remains: its "imperfectly voluntary membership." Public entities have involuntary members when they were first formed. For example, the statutory procedures for incorporating a new city invariably authorize a majority (perhaps only concurrent or extraordinary majorities) to coerce involuntary minorities to join their organization. By contrast, membership in a private organization is wholly voluntary. A central thesis of this Article is that the presence of *involuntary members* is both a necessary condition for the use of the adjective "public" in ordinary language, and also a powerful explanation for the different legal treatment currently accorded public and private organizations. . . .

The initial members of a homeowners association, by their voluntary acts of joining, unanimously consent to the provisions in the association's original governing documents. . . . The original documents — which today typically include a declaration of covenants, articles of association (or incorporation), and by-laws — are a true social contract. The feature of unanimous ratification distinguishes these documents from and gives them greater legal robustness than non-unanimously adopted public constitutions, not to mention the hypothetical social contracts of Rousseau or Rawls. . . .

RICHARD THOMPSON FORD, THE BOUNDARIES OF RACE: POLITICAL GEOGRAPHY IN LEGAL ANALYSIS

107 U. Pa. L. Rev. 1841, 1883-1885 (1994)

. . . [H]omeowners associations are often not associations in the sense of an expression of "organic life as a center of communal perceptions and common activities," nor, in many cases, are they controlled by homeowners. "The inhabitants, drawn from many different backgrounds, often have little in common, and the developer possesses nearly absolute control over the community."[20]

Nonetheless, such organizations may one day overshadow cities in significance.[21] The proliferation of private governments raises the very tripartite tension between democratic inclusion, individual autonomy, and associational rights that we have examined with respect to local government. Private governments also contribute to the structure of racialized space and follow the same pattern we have seen in the context of municipalities. As the functions of government are privatized, the possibility of collective action in the service of such goals as racial and economic equality wanes. As we have seen, publicly created segregation is often justified by analogy to private rights of association. The mirror image of this process takes place when a private entity exercises traditionally public functions.

Professor Robert Ellickson describes the homeowners association as the obvious "private alternative to the city," and asserts that, although in all

---

20. Uriel Reichman, Residential Private Governments: An Introductory Survey, 43 U. Chi. L. Rev. 253, 286 (1976).

21. See Joel Garrean, The Shadow Governments, Wash. Post, June 14, 1987, at A1, A14.

other relevant respects cities and homeowners associations are identical, the "perfectly voluntary nature of membership in a homeowners association" justifies the public/private split that distinguishes homeowners associations from cities.[24]

Based on his public/private distinction, Professor Ellickson argues that homeowners associations should not be subject to the constitutional scrutiny that attaches to public bodies engaging in "state action," because such scrutiny ignores the contractarian underpinnings of the private associations. With very limited exceptions (such as explicit racial restrictions[25] covered by Title VIII in any case) Ellickson argues that the original rules, or "private constitution," of a homeowners association should be beyond the reach of "external legal norms."

Because Ellickson fails to define voluntariness, we are left to speculate about exactly what arrangements are sufficiently voluntary to justify defining an entity as private rather than public. Perhaps "voluntary" refers to the freedom to move into or to refrain from moving into a home that is part of a homeowners association. But if this is all Ellickson means by voluntary, then city residence is voluntary as well.[28] In theory, one may move into a city or refuse to do so, or move out if conditions of residence change. Hence, there is "no difference at all — no legitimate public/private distinction at all — between cities and homeowners associations."

Moreover, such a "perfect" voluntariness assumes that space is transparent and income disparities irrelevant. It is impossible to determine to what extent the buyer chooses the package of regulations and benefits that constitutes a homeowners association and to what extent she chooses a

---

24. Roberts C. Ellickson, Cities and Homeowners Associations, 130 U. Pa. L. Rev. 1519, 1519-20 (1982).

25. It is significant that Ellickson excludes explicit racial restrictions from the permissible association rules, because Ellickson's assertion that homeowners associations are strictly voluntary and his suggestion that the associations are self-validating and should be judged only according to their own purposes is an argument with a pedigree — it is precisely the argument used to justify racially restrictive covenants. See Shelly v. Kraemer, 334 U.S. 1, 13-14 (1948). Ellickson exorcizes the specter of an explicitly racially restrictive association, but, given income and lifestyle disparities between the races, it is likely that the unfettered associations that Ellickson advocates would be overwhelmingly racially homogeneous.

28. In a reply to Ellickson's article, Professor Frug asks whether Ellickson's voluntariness is post hoc justification for exempting the actions and rules of homeowners associations from public review, or whether Ellickson means to suggest "that we make an inquiry in each case to determine whether the association was in fact originally formed by its residents." Gerald Frug, Cities and Homeowners Associations: A Reply, 130 U. Pa. L. Rev. 1589, 1590 (1982). As Frug points out, such an inquiry would not distinguish homeowners associations from cities, but "some of each from others of each." Id. Additionally, such an inquiry would fail to confront the tautology of community self-determination. See supra p. 1860. The fetishism of origins that characterizes the contractarian notion of association if ill-suited to a spatial context in which the original "contract" affects individuals distant from the agreement in both space and time (nonparties include both those who were not privy to the contract because they were excluded at the time it was made and those who, upon entering the association at a later time, find themselves subject to a contract not of their making). It is this feature that makes the association's rules more like a government than a private contract.

home as a result of uniqueness of location, or topography, or sheer scarcity of housing elsewhere in the vicinity, and purchases *in spite of* a homeowners association. Just as in the case of Tiebout's cities, Ellickson's homeowners associations may survive despite, rather than because of, the wishes of many of the residents.

Furthermore, homeowners associations, no less than cities, define political spaces. The rules of a homeowners association create a political sphere just as do the laws of a city. A homeowners association, like any community with the power to preserve and perpetuate itself, is coercive: it must assert its own interests against the interests both of outsiders and, at times, of some of its own members. . . .

GREGORY ALEXANDER, DILEMMAS OF GROUP AUTONOMY: RESIDENTIAL ASSOCIATIONS AND COMMUNITY

75 Cornell L. Rev. 1, 40-46, 56, 60 (1989)

On the surface, residential associations appear to be straightforward examples of voluntary associations rather than communities. Residential associations are created explicitly by contract. Membership is overtly based on consent, which members express by purchasing their property interest in the development. In this context, the social contract is not a metaphor; the legal documents, which typically include a declaration of covenants, articles of incorporation, and by-laws, all evidence agreement to the rules of the group.

At the same time, however, the contractarian model of residential associations is incomplete. Its focus on the formal mode of creation leads it to ignore the character of social relations within residential groups. As a result, it fails to distinguish between residential groups that are held together only by mutual collaboration and convenience, and those in which individuals choose to live together because of more deeply shared values. . . . More specifically, its contractarian analysis overlooks the *combination* of these aspects in the creation of a residential group. Some empirical work done on the character of social relations within residential associations suggests that this combination exists in modern American residential groups.

Frances Fitzgerald's recent account of Sun City Center details the social experience of members of one residential association, an age-segregated retirement development in Florida. Her study reveals that although some social differentiation does exist in within the group, the population of Sun City Center is strikingly homogeneous in virtually all respects. "They came to Sun City," Fitzgerald observes, "for all of the amenities spelled out in the advertising brochures and for a homogeneity that had little to do with age. In a country where class is rarely discussed, they had found their own niche like homing pigeons." Because of that homogeneity, relationships form easily in Sun City, and the inhabitants feel quite comfortable with each other. They regularly socialize with each other, making isolation from other residents virtually non-existent. They are attracted to each other by their shared values and preferences, and they have created a mode of existence consciously based on that sharing of values and preferences. The effect is that residents of Sun City exhibit a deep sense of belonging there and belonging with each other.

Residential groups like Sun City Center are best understood as a type of constitutive group, that is, a community. The concept of a constitutive group implies an element of involuntariness. What binds the group together is a shared characteristic that is unchosen, or chosen only in a weak sense, such as cultural identity. But it is erroneous to suppose that community contradicts voluntariness. Two crucial insights lay behind the notion of constitutive groups. First, individuals define themselves according to some shared good; second, that good gives to each member of the group a sense of belonging. The experience of belonging can be based on a shared good that individuals have chosen. Consider . . . [the] example of a monastery. Monasteries are residential communities based on shared characteristics that some people suppose individuals have the power to choose, i.e., religious commitment. Members of the monastery interpret their personal identities on the basis of that characteristic, which each defines as a good. The self-identity created by that interpretation virtually impels monks to live in close proximity with each other. In a similar, albeit, weaker, sense, Fitzgerald's account suggests the possibility that the residents of Sun City Center experience the need to live together with other older adults who have made the same life-style choices. Voluntariness and involuntariness are combined in the constitution of such groups.

To be sure, residential associations vary widely in the mixture of communal and contractarian ties that they exhibit. On the surface, many appear to be predominately contractarian aggregations of individuals who exhibit few affective ties with each other. One may react skeptically toward the typical promotional literature that advertises residential associations as "communities" on the basis of shared swimming pools and security patrols. Reliance on these factors alone as evidence of community is, as Thomas Bender states, a "cynical manipulation of symbols of community" that trivializes the very ideal of community. But shared resources, like swimming pools, do affect the social relationships among users, shaping the character of those relationships into one that can be called communitarian. Residents of common unit developments have commented that their arrangements are "more friendly than in a single family home development . . . because we see each other more often at the pool, and we see each other a lot at board meetings, and we've had some problems that we've all had to work out together. I think there's a feeling of togetherness." At the same time, as Constance Perin remarks in her study of culture of condominium ownership, "Feelings of goodwill notwithstanding, condo owners act on the market-driven reciprocity expressly built into their relationship from the start."

Perhaps more than in any other group in modern American society, residential associations overtly blend contractarian and communitarian dimensions of group relationships. Common ownership requires that residents sacrifice individual autonomy for sharing. They choose to be tied together, and, although that choice may initially have been motivated by instrumental reasons, the experience of being tied together creates new, qualitatively different layers in their personal relationships. While at one level sharing in common unit developments is explicitly collaborative, required by the residents' contracts, it generates other levels of sharing that transcend mere collaboration. Describing life within residential associations requires that we identify the multiple layers of the residents' relationships and understand how they can affect each other. . . .

NOTES AND QUESTIONS

1. **Purely voluntary.** Are restrictions imposed by homeowners' associations purely voluntary, in contrast to restrictions imposed by governments?

2. **Contractarian or constitutive?** Are the communities regulated by homeowners' associations contractual or constitutive?

3. **Private residential governments.** Are homeowners' associations private residential governments? If they are, should they be subject to the constitutional and other restrictions imposed on governments?

4. **Homeowners' associations: lax or rigid?** When someone buys a house that is part of a homeowners' association (HOA), she takes on the obligation to abide by all of the covenants that attach to ownership of that lot. Courts are not always sympathetic to claims that subdivision restrictions are unfair, or that the buyer was not aware of them. Seth G. Weissman and Steven J. Silver, The Quiet Revolution, Atlanta J. & Constitution, Feb. 23, 1992, at H14. "Horror stories" of homeowners' associations involve such things as a very strict board tearing down a resident's impermissible ivy, and overzealous patrolling of the community for minor infractions of the regulations. In some situations, small arguments escalate quickly into serious conflicts. Uri Berliner, "Do You Want Horror Stories?," Chi. Trib., Aug. 19, 1989, at Home, p. 15. Proponents contend that most HOAs are too lax rather than too vigilant in enforcing restrictions, and that the rules force people to be good neighbors. Id. Often HOAs significantly reduce the amount of upkeep residents need to perform — for their monthly fee, the grass is mowed or the snow shoveled. Townhouses Wide Scale of Buyers, Chi. Trib., Jul. 12, 1987, at Real Estate, p. 2E. However, some owners, especially those who are older and more affluent, simply feel that the restrictions and responsibilities are not a worthwhile exchange for the amenities

offered in return. Lew Sichelman, Lots to Think about in Purchase, Chi. Trib., Nov. 4, 1989, at Home Guide, p. 13.

5. **Condominium association restrictions.** In an example of how restrictive covenants can be, a California condominium association board set a 35-pound limit on dog weights in the complex, putting certain members with big dogs in violation. The board sued noncomplying members, who refused to get rid of their dogs. One member had to put her dog on a diet after receiving a warning, while others threatened to move out. Associated Press, Residents Barking up a Storm over Paunchy Dogs, Chi. Trib., June 28, 1992, at 18. In another case, a Montgomery County, Maryland, court upheld the right of a condominium association to bar residents from providing day care service in condominium units. The judge found that providing day care, however important and useful that might be, "had no greater claim than the desire of condominium residents for 'the peace and quiet of a relatively traffic-free environment.'" Sandra Evans, Condo Group Can Prohibit Child Care, Wash. Post, June 27, 1987, at G1.

6. **Color Wars.** Homeowners' associations often control the appearance of lots or houses through covenants. People moving into an area governed by these covenants must, for example, mow the lawn with a certain frequency or submit proposed improvements to the house to an architectural board. In one case, a family (the Joneses) who had painted their house purple without first seeking the approval of their homeowners' association's architectural control committee, were sued by the association, who found their choice of color improper. The Joneses refused to repaint the house. Pursuant to a judgment in favor of the association, the family's wages were garnished, and a lien was taken out on their house. Finally, a Washington superior court placed them under court order to repaint, or pay up to $2,000 per day in fines or face possible imprisonment, after which they agreed to submit a new color scheme to the association. The family claimed that the association's requirements were repressive to the point of tyranny, and that since they paid a $1,100 a month mortgage, they ought to be able to choose the color of their house. The association argued that it was simply trying to enforce a covenant to which the Joneses and 440 other families had agreed. Timothy Egan, House of a Different Color Is Shunned, N.Y. Times, June 3, 1993, at A12. Are the Joneses right that this kind of covenant represents an unreasonable restriction on individual property rights? Or are they just trying to reap the benefits of life in a homeowners' association without having to comply with the burdens?

7. **The modern walled city.** In Los Angeles, over 150 communities currently have, or have petitioned the city council for, the right to close off public streets with gates. See Richard Thompson Ford, The Boundaries of Race: Political Geography in Legal Analysis, 107 U. Pa. L. Rev. 1841, 1883 (1994). Said one advocate, "If there's nothing to stop a new development from having security gates, why should there be anything to stop an established neighborhood?" Penelope McMillan, Keepers of the Gates: Are

Neighborhood Barriers Balkanizing Los Angeles?, L.A. Times, Feb. 2, 1992, at B1. Homeowners like the increase in property values, lower traffic speed, and reduced criminal activity that the gates offer. Id. Supporters say that such enclaves provide a feeling of community and comfort against the perceived danger of the outside world; that secure homeowners will then be more likely to go out and help in the "greater community." Critics say that they merely act to reinforce cultural and racial distinctions, allowing the unreasonably fearful to isolate themselves from anyone different than themselves, and further Balkanizing an already highly divided population. Susan Moffat, Both Sides of the Fence; Issue of Gated Public Streets Echoes through Hollywood after Ruling, L.A. Times, Jan. 25, 1993, at B1. Especially in southern California, this has become a very popular approach for communities wishing to protect the character of their neighborhood and safeguard its residents. However, in a recent decision, a California state court held that a community may not use gates to close off access to public streets. Id.

Chapter 8

Land Use and Environmental Planning: Takings Law

In our discussion of landlord-tenant law in Chapter 3, we studied the "revolution in landlord-tenant law" led by a small group of legal services lawyers in the 1960s and 1970s. In this chapter, we will examine a more recent revolution. Like the earlier one, this revolution was led by a small group of lawyers who believed themselves to be acting in the public interest, but this time the activism is on the right, led by a small group of "property rights" advocates. Some key players held responsible jobs in the Reagan and Bush administrations and expressed the antiregulatory fervor of the Reagan years. These advocates' other major institutional base was in advocacy organizations, notably the Pacific Legal Foundation, a conservative public interest law firm in Sacramento, California, and the National Home Builders Association, a trade organization in Washington, D.C. Just as many of the key landlord-tenant cases were litigated by the legal services community, a relatively small group of attorneys show up again and again on the amicus briefs and executive orders of the 1980s.

With our discussion of takings law, we leave the neighborhood of property law crystals and enter deep mud. Courts have long protested that they can offer no crystallized tests for takings cases. Indeed, the law is so murky that the two sides do not even agree on which clause of the Constitution is at issue![1] Leaving aside for the moment the issue of whether law ever functions as an internally consistent set of self-executing rules, takings law surely does not. This murkiness makes takings law a perfect place to focus first-year students' attention on how to construct a persuasive argument. Tak-

---

1. Property rights advocates have argued successfully that takings cases are decided under the just compensation clause of the Fourteenth Amendment of the Constitution, while land use planners argue that takings cases come under the clause forbidding the taking of private property without due process. Property rights advocates won an important round in First English Evangelical Lutheran Church of Glendale v. County of Los Angeles, 482 U.S. 304 (1987). See page 865, *infra*.

ings cases are a good place to study legal argumentation because of the extraordinary virtuosity of some of the leading opinions. We will therefore pay very close attention to the reasoning of individual cases. Our goals are to understand how to construct a persuasive argument, and to understand takings law not as an internally consistent area of doctrine, but as opposing arguments, complete with different senses of which cases are the "leading" cases, what cases mean,[2] and different senses of what is at stake politically.

§8.1   When Is Regulation a Taking? How Do Courts Decide?

Takings law is a fascinating topic because of the brilliant lawyering that has transformed it in the past 15 years. Arguments that began as innovative, dissenting positions now not only command a majority but are often accepted as the way takings law always was. It is important to go back and study the takings revolution by recapturing the initial novelty of the now-conventional arguments, for the virtuosity of the recent legal innovation cannot be appreciated without understanding the settled understandings upset by the Supreme Court's reentry into land use law, after nearly 50 years of leaving the area to state courts.

Our initial discussion of classic cases is followed by a chronological discussion of the U.S. Supreme Court cases since 1978.

a.   Classic Cases

1.   Pennsylvania Coal v. Mahon

PENNSYLVANIA COAL CO. v. MAHON

260 U.S. 393 (1922)

MR. JUSTICE HOLMES delivered the opinion of the Court. This is a bill in equity brought by the defendants in error to prevent the Pennsylvania Coal Company from mining under their property in such way as to remove the supports and cause a subsidence of the surface and of their house. The

---

2. Notice, for example, how often Pennsylvania Coal v. Mahon appears as authority where a court has divided in both the court's and dissenting opinions.

bill sets out a deed executed by the Coal Company in 1878, under which the plaintiffs claim. The deed conveys the surface, but in express terms reserves the right to remove all the coal under the same, and the grantee takes the premises with the risk, and waives all claim for damages that may arise from mining out the coal. But the plaintiffs say that whatever may have been the Coal Company's rights, they were taken away by an Act of Pennsylvania, approved May 27, 1921, P.L. 1198, commonly known there as the Kohler Act. . . .

The statute forbids the mining of anthracite coal in such way as to cause the subsidence of, among other things, any structure used as a human habitation. . . . As applied to this case the statute is admitted to destroy previously existing rights or property and contract. The question is whether the police power can be stretched so far.

Government hardly could go on if to some extent values incident to property could not be diminished without paying for every such change in the general law. As long recognized, some values are enjoyed under an implied limitation and must yield to the police power. But obviously the implied limitation must have its limits, or the contract and due process clauses are gone. One fact for consideration in determining such limits is the extent of the diminution. When it reaches a certain magnitude, in most if not in all cases there must be an exercise of eminent domain and compensation to sustain the act. So the question depends upon the particular facts. The greatest weight is given to the judgment of the legislature, but it always is open to interested parties to contend that the legislature has gone beyond its constitutional power.

This is the case of a single private house. No doubt there is a public interest even in this, as there is in every purchase and sale and in all that happens within the commonwealth. Some existing rights may be modified even in such a case. Rideout v. Knox, 148 Mass. 368. But usually in ordinary private affairs the public interest does not warrant much of this kind of interference. A source of damage to such a house is not a public nuisance even if similar damage is inflicted on others in different places. The damage is not common or public. Wesson v. Washburn Iron Co., 13 Allen, 95, 103. The extent of the public interest is shown by the statute to be limited, since the statute ordinarily does not apply to land when the surface is owned by the owner of the coal. Furthermore, it is not justified as a protection of personal safety. That could be provided for by notice. Indeed the very foundation of this bill is that the defendant gave timely notice of its intent to mine under the house. On the other hand the extent of the taking is great. It purports to abolish what is recognized in Pennsylvania as an estate in land — a very valuable estate — and what is declared by the Court below to be a contract hitherto binding the plaintiffs. If we were called upon to deal with the plaintiffs' position alone, we should think it clear that the statute does not disclose a public interest sufficient to warrant so extensive a destruction of the defendant's constitutionally protected rights.

But the case has been treated as one in which the general validity of the act should be discussed. . . .

It is our opinion that the act cannot be sustained as an exercise of the police power, so far as it affects the mining of coal under streets or cities in places where the right to mine such coal has been reserved. As said in a Pennsylvania case, "For practical purposes, the right to coal consists in the right to mine it." Commonwealth v. Clearview Coal Co., 256 Pa. St. 328, 331. What makes the right to mine coal valuable is that it can be exercised with profit. To make it commercially impracticable to mine certain coal has very nearly the same effect for constitutional purposes as appropriating or destroying it. This we think that we are warranted in assuming that the statute does.

It is true that in Plymouth Coal Co. v. Pennsylvania, 232 U.S. 531, it was held competent for the legislature to require a pillar of coal to be left along the line of adjoining property, that, with the pillar on the other side of the line, would be a barrier sufficient for the safety of the employees of either mine in case the other should be abandoned and allowed to fill with water. But that was a requirement for the safety of employees invited into the mine, and secured an average reciprocity of advantage that has been recognized as a justification of various laws.

The rights of the public in a street purchased or laid out by eminent domain are those that it has paid for. If in any case its representatives have been so short sighted as to acquire only surface rights without the right of support, we see no more authority for supplying the latter without compensation than there was for taking the right of way in the first place and refusing to pay for it because the public wanted it very much. The protection of private property in the Fifth Amendment presupposes that it is wanted for public use, but provides that it shall not be taken for such use without compensation. A similar assumption is made in the decisions upon the Fourteenth Amendment. Hairston v. Danville & Western Ry. Co., 208 U.S. 598, 605. When this seemingly absolute protection is found to be qualified by the police power, the natural tendency of human nature is to extend the qualification more and more until at last private property disappears. But that cannot be accomplished in this way under the Constitution of the United States.

The general rule at least is, that while property may be regulated to a certain extent, if regulation goes too far it will be recognized as a taking. It may be doubted how far exceptional cases, like the blowing up of a house to stop a conflagration, go — and if they go beyond the general rule, whether they do not stand as much upon tradition as upon principle. Bowditch v. Boston, 101 U.S. 16. In general it is not plain that a man's misfortunes or necessities will justify his shifting the damages to his neighbor's shoulders. Spade v. Lynn & Boston R.R. Co., 172 Mass. 488, 489. We are in danger of forgetting that a strong public desire to improve the public condition is not enough to warrant achieving the desire by a shorter cut than the constitutional way of paying for the change. As we already have said, this is a question of degree — and therefore cannot be disposed of by general propositions. But we regard this as going beyond any of the cases decided by this Court. The late decisions upon laws dealing with the congestion of Washington and New York, caused by the war, dealt with laws intended to meet a temporary emergency and providing for compensation determined to be reasonable by an impartial board. They went to the verge of the law but fell far short of the present act. Block v. Hirsh, 256 U.S. 135. Marcus Brown Holding Co. v. Feldman, 256 U.S. 170. Levy Leasing Co. v. Siegel, 258 U.S. 242.

We assume, of course, that the statute was passed upon the conviction that an exigency existed that would warrant it, and we assume that an exigency exists that would warrant the exercise of eminent domain. But the question at bottom is upon whom the loss of the changes desired should fall. So far as private persons or communities have seen fit to take the risk of acquiring only surface rights, we cannot see that the fact that their risk has become a danger warrants the giving to them greater rights than they bought.

Decree reversed.

MR. JUSTICE BRANDEIS, dissenting. . . . Coal in place is land; and the right of the owner to use his land is not absolute. He may not so use it as to create a public nuisance; and uses, once harmless, may, owing to changed conditions, seriously threaten the public welfare. Whenever they do, the legislature has power to prohibit such uses without paying compensation; and the power to prohibit extends alike to the manner, the character and the purpose of the use. Are we justified in declaring that the Legislature of Pennsylvania has, in restricting the right to mine anthracite, exercised this power so arbitrarily as to violate the Fourteenth Amendment?

Every restriction upon the use of property imposed in the exercise of the police power deprives the owner of some right theretofore enjoyed, and is, in that sense, an abridgement by the States of rights in property without making compensation. But restriction imposed to protect the public health, safety or morals from dangers threatened is not a taking. The restriction here in question is merely the prohibition of a noxious use. The property so restricted remains in the possession of its owner. The State does not appropriate it or make any use of it. The State merely prevents the owner from making a use which interferes with paramount rights of the public. Whenever the use prohibited ceases to be noxious, — as it may because of further change in local or social conditions, — the restriction will have to be removed and the owner will again be free to enjoy his property as heretofore.

The restriction upon the use of this property can not, of course, be lawfully imposed, unless its purpose is to protect the public. But the purpose of a restriction does not cease to be public, because incidentally some private persons may thereby receive gratuitously valuable special benefits. Thus, owners of low buildings may obtain, through statutory restrictions upon the height of neighboring structures, benefits equivalent to an easement of light and air. Welch v. Swasey, 214 U.S. 91. Compare Lindsley v. Natural Carbonic Gas Co., 220 U.S. 61; Walls v. Midland Carbon Co., 254 U.S. 300. Furthermore, a restriction, though imposed for a public purpose, will not be lawful, unless the restriction is an appropriate means to the public end. But to keep coal in place is surely an appropriate means of preventing subsidence of the surface; and ordinarily it is the only available means. Restriction upon use does not become inappropriate as a means, merely because it deprives the owner of the only use to which the property can then be profitably put. The liquor and the oleomargarine cases settled that. Mugler v. Kansas, 123 U.S. 623, 668, 669; Powell v. Pennsylvania, 127 U.S. 678, 682. See also Hadacheck v. Los Angeles, 239 U.S. 394; Pierce Oil Corporation v. City of Hope, 248 U.S. 498. Nor is a restriction imposed through exercise of the police power inappropriate as a means, merely because the same end might be effected through exercise of the power of eminent domain, or otherwise at public expense. Every restriction upon the height of buildings might be secured through acquiring by eminent domain the right of each owner to build above the limiting height; but it is settled that the State need not resort to that power. Compare Laurel Hill Cemetery v. San Francisco, 216 U.S. 358; Missouri Pacific Ry. Co. v. Omaha, 235 U.S. 121. If by mining anthracite coal the owner would necessarily unloose poisonous gasses, I suppose no one would doubt the power of the State to prevent the mining, without buying his coal fields. And why may not the State, likewise, without paying compensation, prohibit one from digging so deep or excavating so near the surface, as to expose the community to like dangers? In the latter case, as in the former, carrying on the business would be a public nuisance. . . .

It is said that one fact for consideration in determining whether the limits of the police power have been exceeded is the extent of the resulting diminution in value; and that here the restriction destroys existing rights of property and contract. But values are relative. If we are to consider the value of the coal kept in place by the restriction, we should compare it with the value not of the coal alone, but with the value of the whole property. The rights of an owner against the public are not increased by dividing the interests in his property into surface and subsoil. The sum of the rights in the parts can not be greater than the rights in the whole. The estate of an owner in land is grandiloquently described as extending *ab orco usque ad coelum* [from the center of the earth unto the heavens]. But I suppose that no one would contend that by selling his interest above one hundred feet from the surface could he prevent the State from limiting, by the police power, the height of structures in a city. And why should a sale of underground rights bar the State's power? For aught that appears the value of the coal kept in place by the restriction may be negligible as compared with the value of the whole property, or even as compared with that part of it which is represented by the coal remaining in place and which may be extracted despite the statute. . . . [T]he defendant has failed to adduce any evidence from which it appears that to restrict its mining operations was an unreason-able exercise of the police power. Compare Reinman v. Little Rock, 237 U.S. 171, 180. . . .

May we say that notice would afford adequate protection of the public safety where the legislature and the highest court of the State, with greater knowledge of local conditions, have declared, in effect, that it will not? If public safety is imperiled, surely neither grant, nor contract, can prevail against an exercise of the police power. . . .

[I]t is said that these provisions of the act cannot be sustained as an exercise of the police power where the right to mine such coal has been reserved. The constitution seems to rest on the assumption that in order to justify such exercise of the police power there must be an "average reci-procity of advantage." Reciprocity of advantage is an important considera-tion, and may even be essential, where the State's power is exercised for the purpose of conferring benefits upon the property of a neighborhood, as in drainage projects. . . . But where the police power is exercised, not to confer benefits upon property owners, but to protect the public from detriment and danger, there is, in my opinion, no room for considering reciprocity of advantage. . . .

NOTES AND QUESTIONS

1. *Pennsylvania Coal.* Until this case was decided in 1922, the Su-preme Court had never struck down a statute as an unconstitutional taking of private property.[3] Both the majority and the dissenting opinion are still commonly cited today. This case is important, both for the specific tests it articulates and for its glorious rhetoric. Cull through the opinion and high-light stirring rhetoric for those defending, and those challenging, land use planning programs. (Be careful: Holmes has some rhetoric useful to de-fenders as well as to challengers.)

2. **"This is the case of a single private house."** Note the struggle be-tween Holmes and Brandeis over the public-private distinction. According to Holmes, does the case primarily involve an issue of *public* importance? Does Brandeis agree? A large literature exists on development of the public-private distinction in American law. See, e.g., Morton Horwitz, The History of the Public/Private Distinction, 130 U. Pa. L. Rev. 1423 (1982); Joan C. Williams, The Development of the Public/Private Distinction in American Law, 64 Tex. L. Rev. 225 (1985).

3. **Caveat emptor.** According to Holmes, the "short-sighted" home-owners had ample opportunity to protect themselves. They had, after all, accepted deeds from the coal company that gave the company the right to mine as well as a waiver of all potential claims, including those due to

3. See Susan J. Krueger, Comment, *Keystone Bituminous Coal Association v. DeBenedictis: Towards Redefining Takings Law,* 64 N.Y.U. L. Rev. 877, 885 (1989).

subsidence. In light of this history, do you agree with Holmes that if the homeowners chose not to protect themselves the court should not bail them out? How does Brandeis respond to this argument?

4.   **Diminution in value test.** One reason *Pennsylvania Coal* is so famous is Holmes's formulation of various takings "tests" that have been used in subsequent takings cases. (Recall the old joke that Shakespeare has too many clichés; Holmes in *Pennsylvania Coal* speaks in what subsequently crystallized as the clichés of takings tests.) One of these is the diminution in value test. Note that Holmes never undertakes a financial analysis to assess what percentage of the value of its property the coal company lost as a result of the Kohler statute. Why did he not need to? What was the property interest involved, according to Holmes? How much of its value was lost? How does Brandeis respond to this argument?

5.   **Public/private balancing test.** Holmes's second inquiry is to weigh the *public benefit* involved with the *private loss*. How does this discussion relate to the "this is the case of a single private house" discussion? This balancing of public benefit against private loss is called the balancing test.

6.   **Average reciprocity of advantage test.** In his distinguishing of the *Plymouth Coal* case, Holmes weighs the *private* benefit to the landowner against the detriment to the *landowner*. This is called the average reciprocity of advantage test. Do you think Holmes is successful in distinguishing *Plymouth Coal*? Make sure you understand the difference between the balancing test and the average reciprocity of advantage test. What is Brandeis's response to Holmes on the issue of average reciprocity of advantage?

7.   **Why me?** "But the question at bottom is upon whom the loss of the desired changes should fall." The key argument from the landowner's standpoint is this: Even if the public goal is an important one, why should I pay for it? If the government wants to do this, let it pay for the privilege! What is other language in which Holmes sets forth this argument? How does Brandeis answer it? Whose argument do you find more convincing?

8.   **"Coal in place is land . . . ."** Does the intuitive image of property underlie Holmes's argument? How does Brandeis use the intuitive vision in his argument?

9.   **Nuisance.** How does Justice Brandeis use nuisance law?

10.   **Change.** Is change in the definition of property rights inevitable, according to Brandeis? How, then, does one tell if a change to property rights involves a taking?

11.   **Mugler v. Kansas.** Note the dissent's use of Mugler v. Kansas, 123 U.S. 623 (1887). *Mugler* involved the closing of a brewery pursuant to an early prohibition statute.[4] Said the *Mugler* court:

> The power which the States have of prohibiting such use by individuals of their property as will be prejudicial to the health, the morals, or the safety

---

4. John M. Groen, Exploring the Nuisance Exception, C730 ALI-ABA 282 (1992).

of the public, is not — and, consistently with the existence and the safety of organized society, cannot be — burdened with the condition that the State must compensate such individual owners for pecuniary losses they may sustain, by reason of their not being permitted, by a noxious use of their property, to inflict an injury upon the community. The exercise of the police power by the destruction of property which is itself a public nuisance, or the prohibition of its use in a particular way, whereby its value becomes depreciated, is very different from taking property for public use, or from depriving a person of his property without due process of law. In one case, a nuisance only is abated; in the other, unoffending property is taken away from an innocent owner.

123 U.S. at 669. How does Brandeis use *Mugler?*

12.   **Continuing problem.** Mine subsidence remains a problem in Pennsylvania,[5] as well as in West Virginia, Wyoming, New Mexico, and Colorado. See William E. Schmidt, Wyoming Town Sinking into History as Abandoned Mine Shafts Collapse, N.Y. Times, Apr. 27, 1983, at A18; Michael Hirsh, Paying the Price for Centuries of Growth: Many Homeowners in Pennsylvania Get a Sinking Feeling as Old Shafts Cave-in, L.A. Times, Apr. 13, 1986, at 8. Pennsylvania, the energy capital of the world in the nineteenth century, has by far the largest number of populated acres overlying mines that could collapse. Hirsh, *supra,* at 8. But other areas of the country experience similar problems. One Wyoming resident, the corner of his house sagging, told a reporter that, when it rains, the ground near his driveway disappears like sand through an hourglass. "But that's nothing," he continued, "When I was a kid, I remember coming out of mass one night and seeing the whole street in front of the church gone. It just collapsed into an old coal mine." Schmidt, *supra,* at A18.

13.   **Longwalling.** The problem of subsidence as a result of collapsed mine ceilings has taken on a new urgency in areas permitting "longwall" mining. Longwalling is a controversial and very efficient form of mining that allows coal companies to extract 100 percent of the coal in a given stretch. Large machines remove coal in a 700-foot wide swath, advancing as each section is extracted. As the cutters advance, the hollowed-out earth collapses behind them. Ultimately, a longwall mine will move forward about a mile and a half, causing a massive trough of surface land to drop in, always producing severe subsidence. Companies owning subsidence waivers from property owners claim that they have the right to damage the properties above the mines. However, property owners point out that longwall mining did not exist when the waivers were signed; instead, older methods of mining made subsidence a possibility rather than a certainty. As of 1988, significant longwall mining operations existed in West Virginia, Virginia, Pennsylvania, Alabama, Utah, Illinois, and Kentucky. Elizabeth Ren-

---

5. In Pennsylvania, another antisubsidence statute eventually led to a later Supreme Court case; Keystone Bituminous Coal Assn. v. DeBenedictis, 480 U.S. 470 (1987), see pages 865, *infra.*

shaw, Downstate Mining Method Cuts a Controversial Swath, Chi. Tribune, Nov. 27, 1988, Business, at 1.

A journalist vividly describes the damage he observed in a house under which a longwall mine had passed:

> The whole place tilts. The basement floor is buckled. The walls are cracked. Beams are pulling loose. The bedroom ceiling sags. Pots and pans slide off the stove. The bathroom slants so badly that water runs to the wrong end of the tub and just sits there in a puddle. . . . They do not know if their little natural gas well, which supplies their home with heating and cooking gas, will blow sky-high, as the house next door did. . . .

L. Stuart Ditzen, Lack of Regulations Put Homes at Mining Firm's Mercy, Phil. Inquirer, Aug. 2, 1992, at A4. Say that a state passed a statute forbidding longwalling in populated areas. Would it survive constitutional review under Holmes's majority opinion in *Pennsylvania Coal*?

Pennsylvania Coal firmly established the principle that a governmental action *could* constitute a taking, without giving much guidance as to when such a taking occurs. The coexistence of so many tests added an instability to the law, which it has retained ever since. Shortly, we will examine two Supreme Court decisions (both, like *Pennsylvania Coal*, decided in the 1920s) that established both the basic legitimacy and the constitutional vulnerability of zoning.

The Historical Origins of Police Power

"Government hardly could go on if to some extent values incident to property could not be diminished without paying for every such change. As long recognized, some values are enjoyed under an implied limitation and must yield to the police power." Note how *both* Holmes *and* Brandeis assume that property rights are limited by the police power. Historian William Novak has argued that the police power is part of a legal tradition very different from the notion of government as a threat to individual freedoms. William J. Novak, The Common Law Vision of a Well-Regulated Society; *Salus Populi:* The Roots of Regulation in America, 1787-1873 (Ph.D. diss., 1991); William Novak, Public Economy and the Well-Ordered Market: Law and Economic Regulation in 19th-Century America, 18 Law & Soc. Inquiry 1 (1993). In sharp contrast to the tradition of economic liberalism, which saw government primarily as a potential threat to individual rights, Novak identifies a group of early nineteenth-century theorists with a very different view. Their vision was expressed by two maxims constantly cited in nineteenth-century cases: *salus populi suprema lex est* (the welfare of the people is the supreme law) and *sic utere tuo ut alienum laedus* (use your property so as not to injure others). Novak argues that these two maxims expressed the vision of a well-regulated society, in which citizens were viewed as inherently social creatures whose self-fulfillment lay in their shared common life, and who believed that "Government is instituted for the common good; for the protection of property and prosperity, and happiness of the people; — and not for the profit, honor, or private interest of any man, family or class of men." Id. at 85 (quoting William Sullivan's Political Class Book.) Regulation, Novak asserts, was at the center of this vision: "Only through . . . *regulation* could man's social nature, his tendency to society and the public good, be realized." Id. at 87-88.

While the vision of a well-regulated society differed in many ways from classical republicanism, notable resonances include the shared view, first, that men became fully human only through their shared (political or social) life, and, second, that the role of government was to achieve the common good. The sense of government as a positive role was reflected in the broad definition of the police power Novak found in early nineteenth-century cases. The vision of a well-regulated society defended "'energy in government' necessary to society's preservation, security, improvement, and happiness." Id. at 89. This vision of a positive role for government is reflected in the standard grant of police power necessary to achieve the health, safety, and welfare of the public.

This positive image of government had obvious implications for property rights. Said one such thinker: "The great object of all laws is the general welfare — public utility. *There can be no rights inconsistent with this.*" Id. at 90 (quoting Thomas Cooper). The *sic utere* maxim was viewed as a specific example of "the more general rule, which requires that all the actions of individuals be so directed as to promote the good of the whole." Id. at 26 (quoting Nathaniel Chipman). From this general principle flowed a myriad of restrictions on social and economic life. The right of property was defined as a "social right," which "ought to be regulated and restrained, to extract from it the benefits it can produce, and to counteract the evils it can inflict." Id. at 93 (quoting John Taylor). The following quote, from an early nineteenth-century Massachusetts Supreme Court opinion, summarizes this view of property:

> We think it is a settled principle, growing out of the nature of a well ordered civil society, that every holder of property, however absolute and unqualified may be his title, holds it under the implied liability that his use of it may be regulated, that it shall not be injurious to the rights of the community. All property in this commonwealth . . . is derived directly or indirectly from the government . . . [and is] subject to such reasonable limitations . . . as the legislature . . . may think necessary and expedient.

Id. at 16 (quoting Lemuel Shaw).

2.   *Euclid* (1926) and *Nectow* (1928)

We abuse the land because we regard it as a commodity belonging to us. When we see land as a community to which we belong, we may begin to use it with love and respect.[6]

[Babbitt] serenely believed that the one purpose of real estate was to make money for George F. Babbitt.[7]

European attitudes towards land and its development have long differed from those in the United States. The pro-development attitude built into American law by the early nineteenth century had a profound influence on notions of what rights property ownership entails. The idea that land ownership may not involve the right to develop seems counterintuitive to many Americans. As we noted in Chapter 1, Americans tend to assume that owning land means they can do whatever they want with it, even in a society where they may not be allowed to burn their garbage in their own backyards. Mary Ann Glendon, Rights Talk: The Impoverishment of Political Discourse 9 (1991). See §1.1. Some legal opinions challenge this assumption directly — the 1982 Wisconsin case of Prah v. Maretti (see §7.2.a) comes to mind — but direct challenges to the intuitive image of unlimited ownership are few and far between. Ordinarily, as we have seen, courts simply apply the existing legal doctrines (or change them) without acknowledging the inconsistency between those legal doctrines and the intuitive image of absolute ownership.

Takings law is the exception. In litigation challenging a government action as a violation of constitutional rights, government attorneys often challenge the intuitive image of absoluteness directly and explicitly. In takings cases, more explicitly than anywhere else, courts are called upon to decide what it means to own property as part of the question of whether an owner's rights have been violated. The murkiness of takings law suggests that Americans don't agree on what rights property ownership entails, but we can deepen our appreciation of the patterns of disagreement.

Takings cases need not involve land use regulations. In fact, we have already read one takings case that did not: Allard v. Andrus involved regulation of Native American artifacts. (See §1.1.) Yet land use cases have long been at the center of takings law. Land use planning in the United States began in fits and starts. The first statutes regulated activities akin to private nuisances, such as tanneries, brick-making establishments, and livery stables. A more comprehensive approach emerged gradually in the early twentieth century with the introduction of comprehensive zoning statutes. Instead of regulating individual nuisance-type activities, zoning categorized all land according to the uses to be allowed. Throughout the nineteenth century,

---

6. Aldo Leopold (1886-1948), A Sand County Almanac at viii (1949).
7. Sinclair Lewis, Babbitt 50 (1922).

government had provided both monetary and in-kind subsidies to industry.[8] But the idea of a coordinated approach to planning the use of land was ambitious and relatively new. When *Euclid* was litigated, a number of jurisdictions had adopted zoning ordinances; some had been struck down and some upheld in various state courts.[9]

A central goal behind zoning as it spread through the United States was to segregate residential from commercial and industrial development. See William H. Wilson, Moles and Skylarks, in Introduction to the History of Planning in the United States Today 89, 90, 94-98 (Donald A. Krueckeberg ed., 1983). We tend to take for granted that housing should not be integrated with industrial development, but that assumption is relatively new. In traditional society, not only farmers, but also craftspeople lived at their place of work. Indeed, in the early phases of the Industrial Revolution, the houses of both the owners and the workers were located close to the newly founded factories. Moreover, in cities, workers had to live within walking distance of their place of employment until the advent of streetcars eliminated the need for the tremendous population densities — and mixture of land uses — that characterized, say, the Lower East Side of New York City in the late nineteenth century.[10]

The idea of isolating residential neighborhoods from other types of land uses developed gradually over the course of the nineteenth and twentieth centuries. Cf. Wilson, *supra*. It accompanied Americans' growing horror over conditions in nineteenth-century cities. Nearly 9 million immigrants poured into the country between 1901-1910,[11] many immigrants lived in tenements where conditions were unhealthy and inhumane. The following excerpt provides crucial background for understanding the Supreme Court's *Euclid* decision.

LAWRENCE M. FRIEDMAN, GOVERNMENT AND SLUM
HOUSING: A CENTURY OF FRUSTRATION

29-30 (1968)

. . . By 1900, the City was more crowded, the poor suffered more, and the moral and physical stench from the slums was more offensive than

---

8. Oscar Handlin and Mary Flug Handlin, Commonwealth: A Study of the Role of Government in the American Economy: Massachusetts, 1774-1861, 87-88 (1969).

9. See Joel Kosman, Toward an Inclusionary Jurisprudence: A Reconceptualization of Zoning, 43 Cath. U. L. Rev. 59, 105-106 (1993) (citing pre-1926 decisions invalidating zoning as unconstitutional); id. at 86 (citing decisions upholding its constitutionality).

10. See Richard B. Stott, Workers in the Metropolis 201-202 (1990). The population density of the Lower East Side in the late nineteenth century was higher than it has been any time before or since. A relevant comparison is the population density in Hong Kong in 1986. See Victor Showers, World Facts and Figures 360 (3d ed. 1989) (Hong Kong has over 13,000 people per square mile.)

11. Annual Report of the Immigration and Naturalization Services 29 (1966).

ever to the respectable members of the community. Articulate men of the age were obsessed with fear — fear that the American dream was being destroyed, that the American social system was decaying, that the country was undergoing radical changes for the worse. Prominent New Yorkers could easily hold to these opinions. Political corruption, crime, drunkenness, and juvenile delinquency were, if not more prevalent, more socially visible than before. The gentler classes trembled at the crowds of immigrants pouring into the cities and worried about the lawlessness of strikers, about the concentration of wealth, and about the spread of radicalism — worried, in general, whether America could survive the passing of the symbolic frontier. Whether the problems of the times were as new or as serious as people thought is irrelevant. The sense of crisis was crucial.

In this age of upheaval, the disease of the slums was perceived as a disease of the whole body politic. The sense of the social costs of the slums was dramatically heightened; it affected even stalwart conservatives. Justice Peckham of New York, whose chief claim to fame is his bitter hostility to social legislation as a New York and federal judge, conceded the need for a war on the slums.[3] In his view, the evils of the slums endangered society and called for legal action: fires, disease, "tendencies to immorality and crime where there is a very close packing of human beings of the lower order in intelligence and morals . . . must arouse the attention of the legislator."[4] The sense of social cost set the reform conscience free from the crippling effects of a moralizing attitude toward the poor. The careers of a band of vigorous, reform-minded men and women coincided happily with a point of history in which a heightened sense of the social costs of the slums made tenement house legislation finally possible on a grander scale than before. This took place from 1900 to the present. . . .

Zoning seemed part of an answer to the social problems represented by the slums: It held the promise of clean, safe, well laid-out residential neigh-

---

3. Justice Peckham was noted for his support of the liberty of contract theory and individual property rights, so it does seem surprising that he upheld slum legislation. One author explains,

> The jurisprudence of Peckham was rooted in a philosophical conception of individual liberty and a supporting political conception of the role of government that placed considerable emphasis on the relationship between the judicial and legislative branches of government. In short, the best government was the least government. Trust was placed in the free individual, who, if left unfettered by needless government regulation, would grow more intelligent and more attuned to the moral law, thereby decreasing the need for government. . . .
> If any economic interest was favored by Peckham, it was that of the "rugged individual."

William F. Duker, Mr. Justice Rufus W. Peckham: The Police Power and the Individual in a Changing World, Brigham Young Univ. L. Rev. 47, 49-50 (1980). However, Duker notes that Peckham did recognize limits to the liberty of contract, and upheld traditional uses of the police power and antitrust legislation. Id. at 48-49.

4. J. Peckham, in Health Dep't. v. Rector, etc., of Trinity Church, 145 N.Y. 32, 50 (1895).

borhoods. Zoning prohibited overcrowding by limiting neighborhoods to single-family houses, at times imposing minimum lot requirements and other restrictions to ensure light, air, and the "right" kind of neighbors.

A second crucial context for understanding the *Euclid* decision involves legal, not social history. *Euclid* was decided at the height of the *Lochner* era, the period between 1897 and 1937 when the U.S. Supreme Court struck down as unconstitutional much federal and state legislation designed to protect against the exploitation of industrial workers. The era is named for the famous case of Lochner v. New York, 198 U.S. 45 (1905), in which the Supreme Court invalidated a New York statute that limited bakers to a 60-hour work week. The majority opinion in *Lochner* rejected New York's claim that the maximum-hour restrictions were related to health,[12] and held that the New York law violated the Constitution by precluding bakers from using their freedom of contract to make employment contracts that required them to work more than 60 hours per week. Other Supreme Court decisions during the *Lochner* era invalidated minimum wage legislation and other industrial health and safety legislation.[13] In this context, it is not surprising that the *Lochner* Court initially voted to strike down zoning as unconstitutional. See Alfred McCormack, A Law Clerk's Recollections, 46 Colum. L. Rev. 710, 712 (1946) ("Justice Sutherland . . . was writing an opinion . . . holding the zoning ordinance unconstitutional, when talks with his dissenting brethren (principally Stone, I believe) shook his convictions and led him to request a reargument, after which he changed his mind and the ordinance was upheld"). What is surprising is that the Court changed its mind before the final opinion was written. Id. A focus on the law alone provides no explanation. Does the background provided on the larger political climate help? A study of the *Euclid* case highlights the porous boundary between law and the larger realm of political discourse.

VILLAGE OF EUCLID v. AMBLER REALTY CO.

272 U.S. 365 (1926)

MR. JUSTICE SUTHERLAND delivered the opinion of the Court. The Village of Euclid is an Ohio municipal corporation. It adjoins and practically is a suburb of the City of Cleveland. Its estimated population is between 5000 and 10,000, and its area from twelve to fourteen square miles, the greater part of which is farm lands or unimproved acreage. It lies, roughly, in the form of a parallelogram measuring approximately three

12. Tuberculosis infection.
13. See, e.g., Hammer v. Dagenhart, 247 U.S. 251 (1918) (child labor); Baily v. Drexel Furniture Co., 259 U.S. 20 (1922) (child labor); Adkins v. Children's Hosp., 261 U.S. 525 (1923) (minimum wage for women invalidated); Railroad Retirement Bd. v. Alton R. Co., 295 U.S. 330 (1935) (pension for retired railroad workers); Southern Pac. Co. v. Jensen, 244 U.S. 205 (1917) (workman's compensation).

and one-half miles each way. East and west it is traversed by three principal highways: Euclid Avenue, through the southerly border, St. Clair Avenue, through the central portion, and Lake Shore Boulevard, through the northerly border in close proximity to the shore of Lake Erie. The Nickel Plate railroad lies from 1500 to 1800 feet north of Euclid Avenue, and the Lake Shore railroad 1600 feet farther to the north. The three highways and the two railroads are substantially parallel.

Appellee is the owner of a tract of land containing 68 acres, situated in the westerly end of the village, abutting on Euclid Avenue to the south and the Nickel Plate railroad to the north. Adjoining this tract, both on the east and on the west, there have been laid out restricted residential plats upon which residences have been erected.

On November 13, 1922, an ordinance was adopted by the Village Council, establishing a comprehensive zoning plan for regulating and restricting the location of trades, industries, apartment houses, two-family houses, single-family houses, etc., the lot area to be built upon, the size and height of buildings, etc.

The entire area of the village is divided by the ordinance into six classes of use districts, denominated U-1 to U-6, inclusive; three classes of height districts, denominated H-1 to H-3, inclusive; and four classes of area districts, denominated A-1 to A-4, inclusive. The use districts are classified in respect of the buildings which may be erected within their respective limits, as follows: U-1 is restricted to single-family dwellings, public parks, water towers and reservoirs, suburban and interurban electric railway passenger stations and rights of way, and farming, noncommercial greenhouse nurseries and truck gardening; U-2 is extended to include two-family dwellings; U-3 is further extended to include apartment houses, hotels, churches, schools, public libraries, museums, private clubs, community center buildings, hospitals, sanitariums, public playgrounds and recreation buildings, and a city hall and courthouse; U-4 is further extended to include banks, offices, studios, telephone exchanges, fire and police stations, restaurants, theatres and moving picture shows, retail stores and shops, sales offices, sample rooms, wholesale stores for hardware, drugs and groceries, stations for gasoline and oil (not exceeding 1000 gallons storage) and for ice delivery, skating rinks and dance halls, electric substations, job and newspaper printing, public garages for motor vehicles, stables and wagon sheds (not exceeding five horses, wagons or motor trucks) and distributing stations for central store and commercial enterprises; U-5 is further extended to include billboards and advertising signs (if permitted), warehouses, ice and ice cream manufacturing and cold storage plants, bottling works, milk bottling and central distribution stations, laundries, carpet cleaning, dry cleaning and dyeing establishments, blacksmith, horseshoeing, wagon and motor vehicle repair shops, freight stations, street car barns, stables and wagon sheds (for more than five horses, wagons or motor trucks), and wholesale produce markets and salesrooms; U-6 is further extended to include plants for sewage disposal and for producing gas, garbage and refuse incineration, scrap iron, junk, scrap paper and rag storage, aviation fields, cemeteries, crematories, penal and correctional institutions, insane and feeble minded institutions, storage of oil and gasoline (not to exceed 25,000 gallons), and manufacturing and industrial operations of any kind other than, and any public utility not included in, a class U-1, U-2, U-3, U-4 or U-5 use. There is a seventh class of uses which is prohibited altogether.

Class U-1 is the only district in which buildings are restricted to those enumerated. In the other classes the uses are cumulative; that is to say, uses in class U-2 include those enumerated in the preceding class, U-1; class U-3 includes uses enumerated in the preceding classes, U-2 and U-1; and so on. In addition to the enumerated uses, the ordinance provides for accessory uses, that is, for uses customarily incident to the principal use, such as private garages. Many regulations are provided in respect of such accessory uses.

The height districts are classified as follows: In class H-1, buildings are limited to a height of two and one-half stories or thirty-five feet; in class H-2, to four stories or fifty feet; in class H-3, to eighty feet. To all of these, certain exceptions are made, as in the case of church spires, water tanks, etc.

The classification of area districts is:[2] In A-1 districts, dwellings or apartment houses to accommodate more than one family must have at least 5000 square feet for interior lots and at least 4000 square feet for corner lots; in A-2 districts, the area must be at least 2500 square feet for interior lots, and 2000 square feet for corner lots; in A-3 districts, the limits are 1250 and 1000 square feet, respectively; in A-4 districts, the limits are 900 and 700 square feet, respectively. The ordinance contains, in great variety and detail, provisions in respect of width of lots, front, side and rear yards, and other matters, including restrictions and regulations as to the use of billboards, sign boards and advertising signs. . . .

Appellee's tract of land comes under U-2, U-3 and U-6. The first strip of 620 feet immediately north of Euclid Avenue falls in class U-2, the next 130 feet to the north, in U-3, and the remainder in U-6. . . .

Annexed to the ordinance, and made a part of it, is a zone map, showing the location and limits of various use, height and area districts. . . .

The enforcement of the ordinance is entrusted to the inspector of buildings, under rules and regulations of the board of zoning appeals. Meetings of the board are public, and minutes of its proceedings are kept. It is authorized to adopt rules and regulations to carry into effect provisions of the ordinance. Decisions of the inspector of buildings may be appealed to the board by any person claiming to be adversely affected by any such decision. The board is given power in specific cases of practical difficulty or

---

2. Note that the minimum lot sizes in this early ordinance range *downward* from an approximate one-ninth of an acre. — EDS.

unnecessary hardship to interpret the ordinance in harmony with its general purpose and intent, so that the public health, safety and general welfare may be secure and substantial justice done. Penalties are prescribed for violations, and it is provided that the various provisions are to be regarded as independent and the holding of any provision to be unconstitutional, void or ineffective shall not affect any of the others.

The ordinance is assailed on the grounds that it is in derogation of §1 of the Fourteenth Amendment to the Federal Constitution in that it deprives appellee of liberty and property without due process of law and denies it the equal protection of the law, and that it offends against certain provisions of the Constitution of the State of Ohio. The prayer of the bill is for an injunction restraining the enforcement of the ordinance and all attempts to impose or maintain as to appellee's property any of the restrictions, limitations or conditions. The court below held the ordinance to be unconstitutional and void, and enjoined its enforcement. 297 Fed. 307.

Before proceeding to a consideration of the case, it is necessary to determine the scope of the inquiry. The bill alleges that the tract of land in question is vacant and has been held for years for the purpose of selling and developing it for industrial uses, for which it is especially adapted, being immediately in the path of progressive industrial development; that for such uses it has a market value of about $10,000 per acre, but if the use be limited to residential purposes the market value is not in excess of $2500 per acre; that the first 200 feet of the parcel back from Euclid Avenue, if unrestricted in respect of use, has a value of $150 per front foot, but if limited to residential uses, and ordinary mercantile business be excluded therefrom, its value is not in excess of $50 per front foot. . . .

The record goes no farther than to show, as the lower court found, that the normal, and reasonably to be expected, use and development of that part of appellee's land adjoining Euclid Avenue is for general trade and commercial purposes, particularly retail stores and like establishments, and that the normal, and reasonably to be expected, use and development of the residue of the land is for industrial and trade purposes. Whatever injury is inflicted by the mere existence and threatened enforcement of the ordinance is due to restrictions in respect of these and similar uses; to which perhaps should be added — if not included in the foregoing — restrictions in respect of apartment houses. . . .

We proceed, then, to a consideration of those provisions of the ordinance to which the case as it is made relates, first disposing of a preliminary matter.

A motion was made in the court below to dismiss the bill on the ground that, because complainant [appellee] had made no effort to obtain a building permit or apply to the zoning board of appeals for relief as it might have done under the terms of the ordinance, the suit was premature. The motion was properly overruled. The effect of the allegations of the bill is that the ordinance of its own force operates greatly to reduce the value of appellee's lands and destroy their marketability for industrial, commercial and residential uses; and the attack is directed, not against any specific provision or provisions, but against the ordinance as an entirety. Assuming the premises, the existence and maintenance of the ordinance, in effect, constitutes a present invasion of appellee's property rights and a threat to continue it. Under these circumstances, the equitable jurisdiction is clear. See Terrace v. Thompson, 263 U.S. 197, 215; Pierce v. Society of Sisters, 268 U.S. 510, 535. . . .

Building zone laws are of modern origin. They began in this country about twenty-five years ago. Until recent years, urban life was comparatively simple; but with the great increase and concentration of population, problems have developed, and constantly are developing, which require, and will continue to require, additional restrictions in respect of the use and occupation of private lands in urban communities. Regulations, the wisdom, necessity and validity of which, as applied to existing conditions, are so apparent that they are now uniformly sustained, a century ago, or even half a century ago, probably would have been rejected as arbitrary and oppressive. Such regulations are sustained, under the complex conditions of our day, for reasons analogous to those which justify traffic regulations, which, before the advent of automobiles and rapid transit street railways, would have been condemned as fatally arbitrary and unreasonable. And in this there is no inconsistency, for while the meaning of constitutional guaranties never varies, the scope of their application must expand or contract to meet the new and different conditions which are constantly coming within the field of their operation. In a changing world, it is impossible that it should be otherwise. But although a degree of elasticity is thus imparted, not to the *meaning*, but to the *application* of constitutional principles, statutes and ordinances, which, after giving due weight to the new conditions, are found clearly not to conform to the Constitution, of course, must fall.

The ordinance now under review, and all similar laws and regulations, must find their justification in some aspect of the police power, asserted for the public welfare. The line which in this field separates the legitimate from the illegitimate assumption of power is not capable of precise delimitation. It varies with circumstances and conditions. A regulatory zoning ordinance, which would be clearly valid as applied to the great cities, might be clearly invalid as applied to rural communities. In solving doubts, the maxim sic utere tuo ut alienum non laedas, which lies at the foundation of so much of the common law of nuisances, ordinarily will furnish a fairly helpful clew. And the law of nuisances, likewise, may be consulted, not for the purpose of controlling, but for the helpful aid of its analogies in the process of ascertaining the scope of, the power. Thus the question whether the power exists to forbid the erection of a building of a particular kind or for a particular use like the question whether a particular thing is a nuisance, is to be determined, not by an abstract consideration of the building or of the thing considered apart, but by considering it in connection with the circumstances and the locality. Sturgis v. Bridgeman, L.R. 11 Ch. 852, 865. A nuisance may be merely a right thing in the wrong place — like a pig in the parlor instead of the barnyard.[3] If the validity of the legislative classification for zoning purposes be fairly debatable, the legislative judgment must be allowed to control. Radice v. New York, 264 U.S. 292, 294.

There is no serious difference of opinion in respect of the validity of laws and regulations fixing the height of buildings within reasonable limits, the character of materials and methods of construction, and the adjoining area which must be left open, in order to minimize the danger of fire or collapse, the evils of overcrowding, and the like, and excluding from residential sections offensive trades, industries and structures likely to create nuisances. See Welch v. Swasey, 214 U.S. 91; Hadacheck v. Los Angeles, 29 U.S. 394; Reinman v. Little Rock, 237 U.S. 171; Cusack Co. v. City of Chicago, 242 U.S. 526, 529-530.

Here, however, the exclusion is in general terms of all industrial establishments, and it may thereby happen that not only offensive or dangerous industries will be excluded, but those which are neither offensive nor dangerous will share the same fate. But this is no more than happens in respect of many practice-forbidding laws which this Court has upheld although drawn in general terms so as to include individual cases that may turn out to be innocuous in themselves. Hebe Co. v. Shaw, 248 U.S. 297, 303; Pierce Oil Corp. v. City of Hope, 248 U.S. 498, 500. The inclusion of a reasonable margin to insure effective enforcement, will not put upon a law, otherwise valid, the stamp of invalidity. Such laws may also find their justification in the fact that, in some fields, the bad fades into the good by such insensible degrees that the two are not capable of being readily distinguished and separated in terms of legislation. In the light of these considerations, we are not prepared to say that the end in view was not sufficient to justify the general rule of the ordinance, although some industries of an innocent character might fall within the proscribed class. It can not be said that the ordinance in this respect "passes the bounds of reason and assumes the character of a merely arbitrary fiat." Purity Extract Co. v. Lynch, 226 U.S. 192, 204. Moreover, the restrictive provisions of the ordinance in this particular may be sustained upon the principles applicable to the broader exclusion from residential districts of all business and trade structures, presently to be discussed.

It is said that the Village of Euclid is a mere suburb of the City of Cleveland; that the industrial development of that city has now reached and

---

3. Shades of Dr. Johnson! His biographer, James Boswell, reported this conversation:

Boswell: . . . I talked of the recent expulsion of six students from the University of Oxford, who were methodists, and would not desist from publickly praying and exhorting.

Johnson: Sir, that expulsion was extremely just and proper. What have they to do at an University, who are not willing to be taught, but will presume to teach? . . .

Boswell: But, was it not hard, Sir, to expel them, for I am told they were good beings?

Johnson: I believe they might be good beings; but they were not fit to be in the University of Oxford. A cow is a very good animal in the field; but we turn her out of a garden.

[1 Boswell, The Life of Dr. Johnson 436 (Everyman's ed. 1960)] — EDS.

in some degree extended into the village and, in the obvious course of things, will soon absorb the entire area for industrial enterprises; that the effect of the ordinance is to divert this natural development elsewhere with the consequent loss of increased values to the owners of the lands within the village borders. But the village, though physically a suburb of Cleveland, is politically a separate municipality, with powers of its own and authority to govern itself as it sees fit within the limits of the organic law of its creation and the State and Federal Constitutions. Its governing authorities, presumably representing a majority of its inhabitants and voicing their will, have determined, not that industrial development shall cease at its boundaries, but that the course of such development shall proceed within definitely fixed lines. If it be a proper exercise of the police power to relegate industrial establishments to localities separated from residential sections, it is not easy to find a sufficient reason for denying the power because the effect of its exercise is to divert an industrial flow from the course which it would follow, to the injury of the residential public if left alone, to another course where such injury will be obviated. It is not meant by this, however, to exclude the possibility of cases where the general public interest would so far outweigh the interest of the municipality that the municipality would not be allowed to stand in the way.

We find no difficulty in sustaining restrictions of the kind thus far reviewed. The serious question in the case arises over the provisions of the ordinance excluding from residential districts, apartment houses, business houses, retail stores and shops, and other like establishments. This question involves the validity of what is really the crux of the more recent zoning legislation, namely, the creation and maintenance of residential districts, from which business and trade of every sort, including hotels and apartment houses, are excluded. Upon that question this Court has not thus far spoken. . . .

The matter of zoning has received much attention at the hands of commissions and experts, and the results of their investigations have been set forth in comprehensive reports. These reports, which bear every evidence of painstaking consideration, concur in the view that the segregation of residential, business, and industrial buildings will make it easier to provide fire apparatus suitable for the character and intensity of the development in each section; that it will increase the safety and security of home life; greatly tend to prevent street accidents, especially to children, by reducing the traffic and resulting confusion in residential sections; decrease noise and other conditions which produce or intensify nervous disorders; preserve a more favorable environment in which to rear children, etc. With particular reference to apartment houses, it is pointed out that the development of detached house sections is greatly retarded by the coming of apartment houses, which has sometimes resulted in destroying the entire section for private purposes; that in such sections very often the apartment house is a mere parasite, constructed in order to take advantage of the open spaces and attractive surroundings created by the residential character of

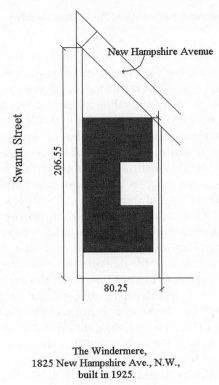

The Windermere,
1825 New Hampshire Ave., N.W.,
built in 1925.

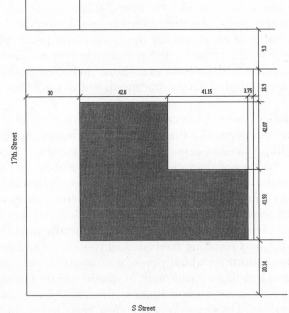

The Shelburne, 1631 S. St., N.W.,
built in 1923.

FIGURE 8-1
Typical Apartment Buildings before *Euclid*, Using High Percentage of Lot

the district. Moreover, the coming of one apartment house is followed by others, interfering by their height and bulk with the free circulation of air and monopolizing the rays of the sun which otherwise would fall upon the smaller homes, and bringing, as their necessary accompaniments, the disturbing noises incident to increased traffic and business, and the occupation, by means of moving and parked automobiles, of larger portions of the streets, thus detracting from their safety and depriving children of the privilege of quiet and open spaces for play, enjoyed by those in more favored localities, — until finally, the residential character of the neighborhood and its desirability as a place of detached residences are utterly destroyed. Under these circumstances, apartment houses, which in a different environment would be not only entirely unobjectionable but highly desirable, come very near to being nuisances.

If these reasons, thus summarized, do not demonstrate the wisdom or sound policy in all respects of those restrictions which we have indicated as pertinent to the inquiry, at least, the reasons are sufficiently cogent to preclude us from saying, as it must be said before the ordinance can be declared unconstitutional, that such provisions are clearly arbitrary and unreasonable, having no substantial relation to the public health, safety, morals or general welfare. . . .

It is true that when, if ever, the provisions set forth in the ordinance in tedious and minute detail, come to be concretely applied to particular premises, including those of the appellee, or to particular conditions, or to be considered in connection with specific complaints, some of them, or even many of them, may be found to be clearly arbitrary and unreasonable. But where the equitable remedy of injunction is sought, as it is here, not upon the ground of a present infringement or denial of a specific right, or of a particular injury in process of actual execution, but upon the broad ground that the mere existence and threatened enforcement of the ordinance, by materially and adversely affecting values and curtailing the opportunities of the market, constitute a present and irreparable injury, the court will not scrutinize its provisions, sentence by sentence, to ascertain by a process of piecemeal dissection whether there may be, here and there, provisions of a minor character, or relating to matters of administration, or not shown to contribute to the injury complained of, which, if attacked separately, might not withstand the test of constitutionality. . . .

. . . What would be the effect of a restraint imposed by one or more of the innumerable provisions of the ordinance, considered apart, upon the value or marketability of the lands is neither disclosed by the bill nor by the evidence, and we are afforded no basis, apart from mere speculation, upon which to rest a conclusion that it or they would have any appreciable effect upon these matters. Under these circumstances, therefore, it is enough for us to determine, as we do, that the ordinance in its general scope and dominant features, so far as its provisions are here involved, is a valid exercise of authority, leaving other provisions to be dealt with as cases arise directly involving them. . . .

Decree reversed.

MR. JUSTICE VAN DEVANTER, MR. JUSTICE MCREYNOLDS and MR. JUSTICE BUTLER, dissent.

NOTES AND QUESTIONS

1.   ***Euclid* as a test case.** *Euclid* is the first of many carefully designed test cases we will see in takings law. Note the village's argument (on page 810) that the realty company's suit was premature. In fact, the landowners had no immediate plans to develop the parcel. So why did they sue? Realty and development interests were the motivating force behind the lawsuit; they were attracted to the case precisely because of the Ambler Realty's lack of interest in immediate development, which meant that the court was precluded from a narrow holding that the Euclid ordinance was unconstitutional *as applied* to the Ambler Realty parcel. This left as the only issue to be decided the question of whether the mere *passage* of a zoning ordinance was an unconstitutional taking of private property, regardless of how the regulations were applied to an individual parcel. The only issue left, in effect, was whether zoning could *ever* be constitutional.

2.   **"The operation of economic laws."** Ambler's attorney, Mr. Newton Baker, drew upon the pro-development tradition in American law, as follows:

> [Zoning], the evidence shows, destroys value without compensation to the owners of lands who have acquired and are holding them for industrial uses. . . .
>
> The property, or value, which is taken away from one set of people, is, by this law, bestowed upon another set of people, imposing an uncompensated loss on the one hand and a gain which is arbitrary and unnatural on the other hand, since its results, not from the operation of economic laws, but from arbitrary considerations of taste enacted into hard and fast legislation. Such legislation also tends to monopolize business and factory sites. . . .
>
> That municipalities have power to regulate . . . in the interest of the public safety, health, morals, and welfare, are propositions long since established: We believe it, however, to be the law that these powers must be reasonably exercised, and that a municipality may not, under the guise of the police power, arbitrarily divert property from its appropriate and most economical uses, or diminish its value, by imposing restrictions which have no other basis than the momentary taste of the public authorities. Nor can police regulations be used to effect the arbitrary desire to have a municipality resist the operation of economic laws and remain rural, exclusive and aesthetic, when its land is needed to be otherwise developed by that larger public good and public welfare, which takes into consideration the extent to which the prosperity of the

country depends upon the economic development of its business and industrial enterprises.

How does Justice Sutherland's opinion answer this argument?

    3.   **Trial court opinion.** The federal district court that held the ordi-
nance unconstitutional recognized a test case when it saw one. "This case,"
said the judge, "is obviously destined to go higher." 297 F. at 308. See Ambler Realty Co. v. Village of Euclid, 297 F. 307 (N.D. Ohio 1924):

> The plain truth is that the true object of the ordinance in question is to place
> all the property in an undeveloped area of 16 square miles in a straitjacket.
> The purpose to be accomplished is really to regulate the mode of living of per-
> sons who may hereafter inhabit it. In the last analysis, the result to be accom-
> plished is to classify the population and segregate them according to their
> income or situation in life. The true reason why some persons live in a man-
> sion and others in a shack, why some live in a single-family dwelling and others
> in a double-family dwelling, why some live in a two-family dwelling and
> others in an apartment, or why some live in a well-kept apartment and others
> in a tenement, is primarily economic. It is a matter of income and wealth, plus
> the labor and difficulty of procuring adequate domestic service. Aside from
> contributing to these results and furthering such class tendencies, the ordi-
> nance has also an aesthetic purpose; that is to say, to make this village develop
> into a city along lines now conceived by the village council to be attractive and
> beautiful. The assertion that this ordinance may tend to prevent congestion,
> and thereby contribute to the health and safety, would be more substantial if
> provision had been or could be made for adequate east and west and north
> and south street highways. Whether these purposes and objects would justify
> the taking of plaintiff's property as and for a public use need not be consid-
> ered. It is sufficient to say that, in our opinion, and as applied to plaintiff's
> property, it may not be done without compensation under the guise of exer-
> cising the police power.

Without a doubt, zoning was felt to promise an escape from the sin and
slums of the city into a healthier and more virtuous life in "nice" residential
neighborhoods. The implicit class bias eventually crystallized into zoning
ordinances that excluded the poor. See Chapter 9. Does this appear to be
part of Justice Sutherland's motivation?

    4.   **Image of property.** What is the court's underlying image of prop-
erty? Does it project property rights as static and absolute? What legal principles does it mobilize to support its image of property?

    5.   **Deference to the legislature.** Is the court deferential to the legis-
lature? (Its deference is ironic, given that this is the *Lochner* Court.)

    6.   **Nuisance law.** The Court uses nuisance law to support its decision
in a variety of ways. Describe them. (Note its characterization of apartment
buildings as near nuisances, page 813, *supra.* Does this reflect the influence
of the slum reform movement?) Note the Court's cite of Reinman v. Little

Rock, 237 U.S. 171 (1915), which has been much cited in recent Supreme Court cases. Said the court in *Reinman:*

> [T]he argument that a livery stable is not a nuisance per se, which is much insisted upon by plaintiffs in error, is beside the question. Granting that it is not a nuisance per se, it is clearly within the police power of the State to regulate the business and to that end to declare that in particular circumstances and in particular localities a livery stable shall be deemed a nuisance in fact and in law, provided this power is not exerted arbitrarily, or with unjust discrimination, so as to infringe upon rights guaranteed by the Fourteenth Amendment. For no question is made, and we think none could reasonably be made, but that the general subject of the regulation of livery stables, with respect to their location and the manner in which they are to be conducted in a thickly populated city, is well within the range of the power of the state to legislate for the health and general welfare of the people.

237 U.S. at 176-177. For what point does the *Euclid* court cite *Reinman?*

7. **Weight of *Euclid*.** Is the *Euclid* decision authority for either of the following principles?

    (a)   The community may limit the height of residential buildings.
    (b)   A zoning ordinance may be valid even if it depresses the worth of land from $10,000 to $2,500 an acre.

8. **"Facial" attacks v. zoning "as applied."** Although the Supreme Court did uphold the community's power to regulate the use of land by creating districts within which various uses would not be allowed, Justice Sutherland carefully refused to rule on the validity of the Euclid ordinance as it applied to the Ambler property. Can you locate this language? It opened the way for the next landmark zoning case.

9. **Prevalence and impact of zoning.** Zoning spread rapidly once it was approved by the U.S. Supreme Court. Zoning appealed to a broad range of constituencies, as evidenced by the fact that the Standard Zoning Enabling Ordinance was promulgated by the U.S. Department of Commerce under Secretary Herbert Hoover. The model act was completed in 1928; three years later every state had authorized some type of zoning. By 1925, over 368 municipalities had zoning; by 1930, 1,000 did. "Today, zoning is virtually universal in the metropolitan areas of the United States, where more than 97% of cities having a population over 5,000 employ it. Of cities with over 25,000 population, only Houston, Texas, has not enacted a zoning ordinance." See Robert Ellickson, Alternatives to Zoning: Covenants, Nuisance Rules and Fines as Land Use Controls, 40 U. Chi. L. Rev. 681, 691 (1973).

10. **"Brandeis" briefs.** Note the court's reliance on the "comprehensive reports" it cites on page 813. Many of these reports were brought to the attention of the court by the amicus brief Alfred Bettman submitted on

behalf of the National Conference on City Planning and other organizations. Reformers developed the "Brandeis brief" during their litigation of the *Lochner*-type cases in the Supreme Court. In fact, the first such brief, was written by Louis Brandeis and his sister-in-law Josephine Goldmark, who was head of the influential National Consumers' League, in Muller v. Oregon 208 U.S. 412 (1908); they presented comprehensive statistics to show that working longer than 10 hours a day in a laundry, factory, etc. was detrimental to the health, safety, and welfare of women. Michael Rustad and Thomas Koenig, The Supreme Court and Junk Social Science: Selective Distortion in Amicus Briefs, 72 N.C. L. Rev. 91, 104 nn.60-61 (1993).

NECTOW v. CITY OF CAMBRIDGE

277 U.S. 183 (1928)

MR. JUSTICE SUTHERLAND delivered the opinion of the Court. A zoning ordinance of the City of Cambridge divides the city into three kinds of districts: residential, business and unrestricted. Each of these districts is subclassified in respect of the kind of buildings which may be erected. The ordinance is an elaborate one, and of the same general character as that considered by this Court in Euclid v. Ambler Co., 272 U.S. 365. In its general scope it is conceded to be constitutional within that decision. The land of plaintiff in error was put in district R-3, in which are permitted only dwellings, hotels, clubs, churches, schools, philanthropic institutions, greenhouses and gardening, with customary incidental accessories. The attack upon the ordinance is that, as specifically applied to plaintiff in error, it deprived him of his property without due process of law in contravention of the Fourteenth Amendment.

The suit was for a mandatory injunction directing the city and its inspector of buildings to pass upon an application of the plaintiff in error for a permit to erect any lawful buildings upon a tract of land without regard to the provisions of the ordinance including such tract within a residential district. The case was referred to a master to make and report findings of fact. After a view of the premises and the surrounding territory, and a hearing, the master made and reported his findings. The case came on to be heard by a justice of the court, who, after confirming the master's report, reported the case for the determination of the full court. Upon consideration, that court sustained the ordinance as applied to plaintiff in error, and dismissed the bill. 260 Mass. 441.

A condensed statement of facts, taken from the master's report, is all that is necessary. When the zoning ordinance was enacted, plaintiff in error was and still is the owner of a tract of land containing 140,000 square feet, of which the locus here in question is a part. The locus contains about 29,000 square feet, with a frontage on Brookline street, lying west, of 304.75

feet, on Henry street, lying north, of 100 feet, on the other land of the
plaintiff in error, lying east, of 264 feet, and on land of the Ford Motor
Company, lying southerly, of 75 feet. The territory lying east and south
is unrestricted. The lands beyond Henry street to the north and beyond
Brookline street to the west are within a restricted residential district. The
effect of the zoning is to separate from the west end of plaintiff in error's
tract a strip 100 feet in width. The Ford Motor Company has a large auto
assembling factory south of the locus; and a soap factory and the tracks of
the Boston & Albany Railroad lie near. Opposite the locus, on Brookline
street, and included in the same district, there are some residences; and
opposite the locus, on Henry street, and in the same district, are other residences. The locus is now vacant, although it was once occupied by a mansion house. Before the passage of the ordinance in question, plaintiff in
error had outstanding a contract for the sale of the greater part of his entire
tract of land for the sum of $63,000. Because of the zoning restrictions, the
purchaser refused to comply with the contract. Under the ordinance, business and industry of all sorts are excluded from the locus, while the remainder of the tract is unrestricted. It further appears that provision has been
made for widening Brookline street, the effect of which, if carried out, will
be to reduce the depth of the locus to 65 feet. After a statement at length
of further facts, the master finds "that no practical use can be made of
the land in question for residential purposes, because among other reasons
herein related, there would not be adequate return on the amount of any
investment for the development of the property." The last finding of the
master is:

> I am satisfied that the districting of the plaintiff's land in a residence
> district would not promote the health, safety, convenience and general wel-
> fare of the inhabitants of that part of the defendant City, taking into account
> the natural development thereof and the character of the district and the re-
> sulting benefit to accrue to the whole City and I so find.

It is made pretty clear that because of the industrial and railroad purposes to which the immediately adjoining lands to the south and east have
been devoted and for which they are zoned, the locus is of comparatively
little value for the limited uses permitted by the ordinance.

We quite agree with the opinion expressed below that a court should
not set aside the determination of public officers in such a matter unless it
is clear that their action "has no foundation in reason and is a mere arbitrary or irrational exercise of power having no substantial relation to the
public health, the public morals, the public safety or the public welfare in
its proper sense." Euclid v. Ambler Co., *supra,* p. 395.

An inspection of a plat of the city upon which the zoning districts are
outlined, taken in connection with the master's findings, shows with reasonable certainty that the inclusion of the locus in question is not indispensable

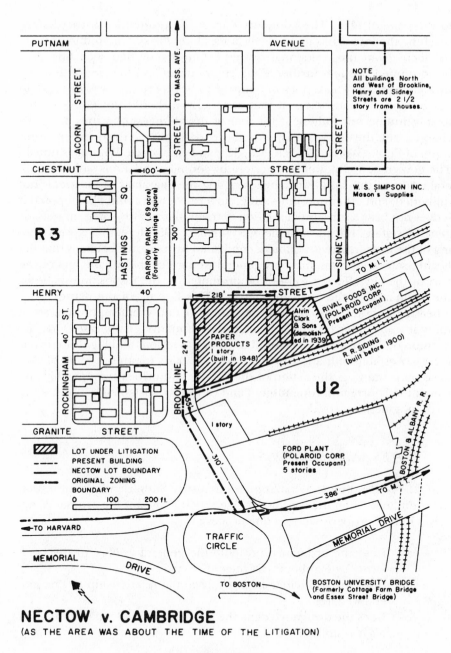

NECTOW v. CAMBRIDGE
(AS THE AREA WAS ABOUT THE TIME OF THE LITIGATION)

FIGURE 8-2
Cambridge Neighborhood of Cambridgeport — *Nectow*

to the general plan. The boundary line of the residential district before reaching the locus runs for some distance along the streets, and to exclude the locus from the residential district requires only that such line shall be continued 100 feet further along Henry street and thence south along Brookline street. There does not appear to be any reason why this should not be done. Nevertheless, if that were all, we should not be warranted in substituting our judgment for that of the zoning authorities primarily charged with the duty and responsibility of determining the question. Zahn v. Bd. of Public Works, 274 U.S. 325, 328, and cases cited. But that is not all. The governmental power to interfere by zoning regulations with the general rights of the land owner by restricting the character of his use, is not unlimited, and other questions aside, such restriction cannot be imposed if it does not bear a substantial relation to the public health, safety, morals, or general welfare. Euclid v. Ambler Co., *supra*, p. 395. Here, the express finding of the master, already quoted, confirmed by the court below, is that the health, safety, convenience and general welfare of the inhabitants of the part of the city affected will not be promoted by the disposition made by the ordinance of the locus in question. This finding of the master, after a hearing and an inspection of the entire area affected, supported, as we think it is, by other findings of fact, is determinative of the case. That the invasion of the property of plaintiff in error was serious and highly injurious is clearly established; and, since a necessary basis for the support of that invasion is wanting, the action of the zoning authorities comes within the ban of the Fourteenth Amendment and cannot be sustained.

Judgment reversed.

NOTES AND QUESTIONS

1. ***Nectow* litmus.** What litmus does Justice Sutherland use for testing the ordinance when the landowner claims that *as applied* the ordinance deprives him of property without due process:

(a) Does the ordinance promote the general welfare of the landowner's neighbors? (Of the entire city?)
(b) Does the ordinance bear a substantial relationship to the general welfare?
(c) Does the ordinance deny the landowner an adequate return on his investment?

2. **Substantive due process.** At the time *Nectow* was decided, it was one of many substantive due process cases in which the Supreme Court struck down challenges to economic regulations such as minimum wage and maximum hour laws. The *Lochner* era ended in 1937 when the Supreme Court upheld minimum wage legislation in West Coast Hotel Co. v. Par-

rish, 300 U.S. 379 (1937). After United States v. Carolene Products, 304 U.S. 144 (1938), the Supreme Court upheld economic regulation as long as such regulation had a rational basis. Laurence H. Tribe, American Constitutional Law 582 (2d ed. 1988). Yet *Nectow* survives. Should it?

Putting aside the semantic difficulty with Justice Sutherland's opinion, be aware that state court reports abound with successful due process attacks on zoning laws as applied. Moreover, you can find cases asserting each of the *Nectow* tests or some recognizable variant thereof. The first and second tests measure the law's soundness, with courts ready to disagree with a legislature's judgment (implicit in any regulation) that the act promotes the general welfare or bears some substantial relation thereto.

Yet an entire generation of law students has grown up learning that courts do (should) not undo social or economic regulation in the name of substantive due process simply because judges question a legislature's wisdom. Is there something about zoning that gives it special vulnerability to substantive due process assaults? In this regard, should an ordinance that requires every employer to pay a minimum wage, which may bankrupt some marginal shopkeepers, have a different (and higher) presumption of validity from an ordinance that limits every parcel along Brookline Street to residential use, which may cause some landowners economic injury?

3.   **What is an adequate return?** Test (c) assumes that the regulation will promote the general welfare but refuses enforcement because of severe hardship to the landowner. Despite the frequency with which courts utter "no adequate return on investment," the concept remains shadowy. On a purely technical level, there are the problems both of procedure and appropriateness of remedy. All zoning laws entitle the landowner to a variance (see Standard State Zoning Enabling Act §7, §9.3) where the restriction visits "unnecessary hardship" because of special conditions. In such a case, the appropriate remedy for the landowner is to seek a variance, an administrative procedure; and, if the zoning board refuses the variance, the landowner may then seek judicial review. At issue on review is the soundness of administrative discretion, not the validity of the ordinance. See generally §9.7. Not every claim of hardship is grist for a variance. As we shall see, the courts do try to distinguish between a hardship that is special to this landowner, because of something about *his* parcel (for example, an irregularly shaped plot), for which variance is the proper remedy, and a hardship that extends to an entire group of landowners (for example, all downtown owners required to provide off-street parking), for which a zoning attack is proper. Clear-cut lines do not always separate the two situations, and courts and zoning boards often blur or ignore the lines, but you as a lawyer should recognize this distinction. From your still-limited vantage, do you believe that the facts in *Nectow* would indicate a variance?

4.   **What is "adequate investment return"?** There is also a technical problem of substance. What is an adequate return on investment? Courts rarely reveal the arithmetic of their decisions concerning this matter, and

the zoning laws give no direct guidance.[14] The adequacy of investment return has two components, the normative yield and the investment base against which one calculates that yield. We know of no case where a court has made explicit what percentage it deemed an adequate rate of return. If you were a landowner's attorney, faced with the courts' inscrutability, what steps would you take to design a normative percentage yield?

No less troublesome than fixing the normative yield is determining the investment base. In each of the following cases, what value should the court use in measuring the adequacy of return?

(a)   X paid $10,000 for her residentially zoned parcel ten years ago. The parcel is currently worth $12,000. Unrestricted, the parcel would sell for $25,000.

(b)   X paid $12,000 for her residentially zoned parcel ten years ago. The parcel is currently worth $10,000. Unrestricted, the parcel would sell for $25,000.

(c)   X paid $25,000 for her parcel six months ago. The zoning then permitted business use. Rezoned for residential use, the parcel would sell for $15,000.

(d)   X paid $10,000 each for two adjoining parcels ten years ago. Each parcel is currently worth $25,000. One parcel is rezoned, reducing its value to $5,000.

5.   **More on adequate investment return.** At the very root of the "no adequate return" test is the philosophical issue we saw earlier: When does a regulation become a "taking"? We know that a law confiscating all land value may sometimes survive attack, cf. Consolidated Rock Products Co. v. City of Los Angeles, 57 Cal. 2d 515, 370 P.2d 342, *appeal dismissed,* 371 U.S. 36 (1962), and that a law causing only moderate harm to the landowner may sometimes fail, cf. Vernon Park Realty v. City of Mount Vernon, 307 N.Y. 493, 121 N.E.2d 517 (1954). With this loose frame of reference, consider the regulation that the Court struck down in the *Nectow* case. Of what purpose was the transitional R-3 zone in which plaintiff's property was placed? Do you find significant the Court's comment that there does not appear to be any reason why the zoning boundary should not be moved 100 feet further west? Does the Court seem to downgrade the purpose of the zone? Or, alternatively, the means taken to achieve the purpose?

Perhaps some principle may be emerging that connects the "legislative soundness" tests with the "no adequate return" test. Try this one out: Where a landowner attacks a zoning law as applied, the hardship he must

14. Statutes in other areas do express a standard. Landmark preservation laws offer a fairly relevant comparison. The owner of a designated landmark may typically obtain relief if his property does not yield a specified return. See, e.g., New York, N.Y., Admin. Code Ann. ch. 8A §§207-1.0q, 207-8.0 (1971) (6 percent of assessed valuation).

prove rises in some proportion to the urgency (or the soundness) of the regulation he attacks, and the burden falls in converse proportion. Could this principle help explain why courts fudge on the arithmetic of adequate return?

6.   **Judicial v. administrative remedy.** If the court seems to be saying that boundaries, particularly in built-up areas, can often be moved a short distance without defeating the plan, should courts leave the boundaries alone and direct the landowner to his administrative remedy? In sustaining the *Nectow* ordinance, the Massachusetts Supreme Court had written:

> If there is to be zoning at all, the dividing line must be drawn some-
> where. There cannot be a twilight zone. If residence districts are to exist, they
> must be bounded. In the nature of things, the location of the precise limits of
> the several districts demands the exercise of judgment and sagacity. There can
> be no standard susceptible of mathematical exactness in its application. Opin-
> ions of the wise and good may well differ as to the place to put the separation
> between different districts . . . . Courts cannot set aside the decisions of public
> officers in such a matter unless compelled to the conclusion that it has no
> foundation in reason and is a mere arbitrary or irrational exercise of power
> having no substantial relation to the public health, the public morals, the pub-
> lic safety or the public welfare in its proper sense. These considerations cannot
> be weighed with exactness. That they demand the placing of the boundary of
> a zone 100 feet one way or the other in land having similar material features
> would be hard to say as a matter of law. . . .

Nectow v. City of Cambridge, 260 Mass. 441, 447, 448, 157 N.E. 618, 620 (1927).

7.   **Who has standing to complain?** Before the *Nectow* decision, X buys a residence on the north side of Henry Street (or the west side of Brookline Street), expecting Nectow's R-3 designation to continue. If the R-3 designation is removed, X's property value will drop. Should this be considered on the issues of (a) X's standing to intervene in the *Nectow* suit; (b) the continuing validity of the R-3 designation? Should a landowner, who enjoys zoning "protection," be able to block any change in a neighbor's zoning status? Consider by analogy a landowner's rights to the continuing enforcement of restrictive covenants (Mohawk Containers, Inc. v. Hancock, §7.7e *supra*). Is the analogy a good one? Is it feasible to develop a compensation and assessment system that will reflect the economic impact of zoning regulation, including zoning changes?

8.   **Changing times.** Look at the map of the *Nectow* site. Why did the planning authorities plan for a 100-foot strip along Brookline Street? The answer lies in pre-zoning urban patterns. The *Nectow* site originally was owned by Alvan Clark, who manufactured an early telescope in the factory he built directly behind his house.[15] In other words, Clark followed the tra-

---

15. See Deborah Jean Warner, Alvan Clark and Sons: Artists in Optics 20 (1968).

ditional pattern in which the factory owner built his factory adjacent to his house (a pattern that can still be seen at the site of the birth of the Industrial Revolution, in Ironbridge, England). Then the zoning authorities came along, with the new idea of segregating residential and industrial uses. They wanted to keep residential uses on the southeast side of Parrow Park, but beyond that the land clearly was destined for industrial use because of the solidly industrial character of the land near the Charles River. Their solution was the 100-foot strip on Brookline Street, presumably on the theory that this strip was suitable for residential use because many of the residential lots in the local area were 100 feet in depth.

9. **Is *Nectow* the last word?** After this decision, may the plaintiff develop his land without restriction? Suppose that the city of Cambridge acted at once to rezone plaintiff's land for business.

3. The Cedar Rust Case: Miller v. Schoene

MILLER v. SCHOENE

276 U.S. 272 (1928)

The Virginia statute presents a comprehensive scheme for the condemnation and destruction of red cedar trees infected by cedar rust. By section 1 it is declared to be unlawful for any person to "own, plant or keep alive and standing" on his premises any red cedar tree which is or may be the source or "host plant" of the communicable plant disease known as cedar rust, and any such tree growing within a certain radius of any apple orchard is declared to be a public nuisance, subject to destruction. Section 2 makes it the duty of the state entomologist, "upon the request in writing of ten or more reputable freeholders of any county or magisterial district, to make a preliminary investigation of the locality to ascertain if any cedar tree or trees are the source of, harbor or constitute the host plant for the said disease and constitute a menace to the health of any apple orchard in said locality, and that said cedar tree or trees exist within a radius of two miles of any apple orchard in said locality." If affirmative findings are so made, he is required to direct the owner in writing to destroy the trees and, in his notice, to furnish a statement of the "fact found to exist whereby it is deemed necessary or proper to destroy" the trees and to call attention to the law under which it is proposed to destroy them. Section 5 authorizes the state entomologist to destroy the trees if the owner, after being notified, fails to do so. Section 7 furnishes a mode of appealing from the order of the entomologist to the circuit court of the county, which is authorized to "hear the objections" and "pass upon all questions involved," the procedure followed in the present case.

As shown by the evidence and as recognized in other cases involving the validity of this statute, cedar rust is an infectious plant disease in the form of a fungoid organism which is destructive of the fruit and foliage of the apple, but without effect on the value of the cedar. Its life cycle has two phases which are passed alternately as a growth on red cedar and on apple trees. It is communicated by spores from one to the other over a radius of at least two miles. It appears not to be communicable between trees of the same species, but only from one species to the other, and other plants seem not to be appreciably affected by it. The only practicable method of controlling the disease and protecting apple trees from its ravages is the destruction of all red cedar trees, subject to the infection, located within two miles of apple orchards.

The red cedar, aside from its ornamental use, has occasional use and value as lumber. It is indigenous to Virginia, is not cultivated or dealt in commercially on any substantial scale, and its value throughout the state is shown to be small as compared with that of the apple orchards of the state. Apple growing is one of the principal agricultural pursuits in Virginia. The apple is used there and exported in large quantities. Many millions of dollars are invested in the orchards, which furnish employment for a large portion of the population, and have induced the development of attendant railroad and cold storage facilities.

On the evidence we may accept the conclusion of the Supreme Court of Appeals that the state was under the necessity of making a choice between the preservation of one class of property and that of the other wherever both existed in dangerous proximity. It would have been none the less a choice if, instead of enacting the present statute, the state, by doing nothing, had permitted serious injury to the apple orchards within its borders to go on unchecked. It will not do to say that the case is merely one of a conflict of two private interests and that the misfortune of apple growers may not be shifted to cedar owners by ordering the destruction of their property; for it is obvious that there may be, and that here there is, a preponderant public concern in the preservation of the one interest over the other. And where the public interest is involved preferment of that interest over the property interest of the individual, to the extent even of its destruction, is one of the distinguishing characteristics of every exercise of the police power which affects property. Mugler v. Kansas, 123 U.S. 623; Hadacheck v. Los Angeles, 239 U.S. 394; Village of Euclid v. Ambler Realty Co., 272 U.S. 365; Reinman v. Little Rock, 237 U.S. 171.

We need not weigh with nicety the question whether the infected cedars constitute a nuisance according to the common law; or whether they may be so declared by statute. See Hadacheck v. Los Angeles, *supra*, 411. For where, as here, the choice is unavoidable, we cannot say that its exercise, controlled by considerations of social policy which are not unreasonable, involves any denial of due process. The injury to property here is no more serious, nor the public interest less, than in Hadacheck v. Los Angeles, *supra,* Reinman v. Little Rock, *supra.* . . .

NOTES AND QUESTIONS

1. **Expectations.** Whose expectations were enforced in Miller v. Schoene? Do courts typically have to choose whose expectations to enforce and whose to override in deciding a takings case?

2. **Choosing between the property of A and the property of B.** Note how the court in *Miller* translates an issue that could be formulated as involving the regulation of the cedar tree owners' property into a choice between the property of A (the cedar tree owners) and the property of B (the apple farmers). Why is this an effective maneuver from a persuasive standpoint for a party arguing in favor of a land use, environmental, or other regulation? Can virtually any situation involving land use or environmental regulation be characterized as involving a choice between the property of A and the property of B? For an effective use of this insight, see Norman Williams Jr. and John M. Taylor, 1 American Land Planning Law: Land Use and the Police Power §2.01 at 72 (1988 revision) (distinguishing land use cases into "developers' cases" and "neighbors' cases").

3. **Precedent.** Does *Miller* apply the legal tests set out in the majority opinion of *Pennsylvania Coal*? Is the holding of *Miller* consistent with the holding of *Pennsylvania Coal*?

4. **The public interest.** What vision of property underlies the notion that property rights can be limited to the extent they conflict with the public interest?

4.   State Takings Law: *Kaiser Development*

KAISER DEVELOPMENT CO. v. CITY AND COUNTY OF HONOLULU

913 F.2d 573 (9th Cir. 1990)

In 1961, Bishop entered into an agreement (the "development agreement") with Kaiser Development Company ("Kaiser") to develop 6,000 acres of land in Honolulu, a portion of which includes a parcel known as Queen's Beach. Kaiser developed most of the property into a new urban community known as Hawaii Kai. Kaiser expected to build a large resort/hotel complex at Queen's Beach, asserting that it considered this project its "crown jewel" and economic reward for having developed the vast Hawaii Kai community. Kaiser spent over $8 million in building the Hawaii Kai infrastructure to accommodate the anticipated resort/hotel development, but made no attempt to develop Queen's Beach until 1971.

The 1960 and 1964 General Plans for the long range development of Honolulu, adopted pursuant to the Honolulu City Charter, designated Queen's Beach as a resort and commercial area. Queen's Beach also was designated as a resort and commercial area in both the 1964 and 1966 Detailed Land Use Maps ("DLUM"), which were adopted for numerous areas of Honolulu to accompany the General Plan.

In 1977, a new General Plan became effective which also listed Queen's Beach as a potential resort site. In 1982, however, a revised General Plan modified the population densities and removed the designation of the area as a future resort site. In 1983, the City enacted the East Honolulu Development Plan (the "Development Plan") which changed the previous DLUM resort designation of Queen's Beach to one of preservation and park uses.

. . . In 1971, Kaiser applied to have its Queen's Beach property rezoned from residential to resort in accordance with the 1964 and 1966 DLUMs, but Kaiser later withdrew the request. In February 1983, Kaiser applied for approval of a residential subdivision at Queen's Beach in conformity with the existing residential zoning. The city denied the application after the passage of the Development Plan later that year. The denial was upheld by the zoning board of appeals. Kaiser made no subsequent attempt to apply for development permits, zoning changes, or variances at Queen's Beach under the new preservation and park zoning.

. . . This zoning allows for a variety of uses. For instance, the zoning permits the land to be used for fish hatcheries and ponds, forests, game preserves, private golf courses, botanical gardens, cemeteries, and camps. . . . This court recognizes that, in some limited circumstances, a city's precondemnation activities can give rise to a takings claim in favor of a property owner. In Richmond Elks Hall Assn. v. Richmond Redevelopment Agency, 561 F.2d 1327 (9th Cir. 1977), for instance, we found that a municipal redevelopment agency's activities effected a compensable taking under the fifth and fourteenth amendments to the United States Constitution. The property had been "rendered unsaleable in the open market; its uses were severely limited by [the] Agency; commercial lenders refused to make loans on the subject property; and [the property owner's] peaceful enjoyment and its right to all rents and profits from the property were substantially impaired." *Id.* at 1331.

Bishop alleges that the district court applied the wrong legal standard in determining whether they had presented sufficient evidence to support their inequitable precondemnation activities claim. The district court found that such a claim requires proof that there is "no economically viable use" for the land. Bishop contends that it need show only that "a public entity acting in furtherance of a public project directly and substantially interfere[d] with property rights and thereby significantly impair[ed] the value of property." *Richmond Elks,* 561 F.2d at 1330; see also Martino v. Santa Clara Valley Water Dist., 703 F.2d 1141, 1147 (9th Cir.), *cert. denied,* 464 U.S. 847 (1983).

We disagree. A cause of action for inequitable precondemnation activities merely states a type of regulatory takings claim. Recent Supreme Court cases unequivocally indicate that the government does not take an individual's property unless it has "'denie[d] [him] economically viable use of his land.'" Nollan v. California Coastal Commn., 483 U.S. 825, 834 (1987) (quoting Agins v. Tiburon, 447 U.S. 255, 260 (1980)). "In the absence of an interference with an owner's legal right to dispose of his land, even a substantial reduction of the attractiveness of the property to potential purchasers does not entitle the owner to compensation under the Fifth Amendment." Kirby Forest Industries, Inc. v. United States, 467 U.S. 1, 15 (1984). . . .

Affirmed.

NOTES AND QUESTIONS

1.   **Commissioned golf course design.** In this case, the governmental authorities had paid $25,000 to the firm of the famous designer Robert Trent Jones to design a golf course on the property at issue. Oral communication, H. Bissell Carey, Robinson and Cole, Hartford. May 1995. Why?

2.   **State court test.** What takings test does this court adopt?

3.   **Temporary restraining orders.** Some have argued that the exclusion of one partner from a co-owned house through a temporary restraining order represents a taking in violation of the Fifth Amendment. For the most part, this argument has not prevailed in court. In one recent case, the Maryland Court of Special Appeals found that a husband ordered to stay away from a house which he co-owned with his wife had not suffered a taking. Cote v. Cote, 599 A.2d 869 (Md. App. 1991). The court reasoned that there was certainly state action and deprivation of a property interest, but that he had not been deprived of all beneficial use of the property (the test in Maryland under Pitsenberger v. Pitsenberger, 410 A.2d 1052 (Md. App. 1980)), in that his wife was living there, and so he did not need to contribute money for another place for her to live while the divorce was pending. The court affirmed its statutory authority to issue such orders especially in cases of possible physical abuse or harassment.

5.   Environmentally Sensitive Land: Just v. Marinette County

As the environmental movement gained momentum after 1970, land use planners increasingly tried to plan development in ways that avoided pollution and preserved natural resources. Probably the key thrust of *federal* environmental policy has been to clean up pollution once it has occurred; in contrast, *state* and *local* authorities have used land use planning to prevent pollution and preserve natural resources. One commentator noted: "The bottom line is that the way we use and misuse land now appears just as dangerous to water quality as the liquid pollution we discharge from sewage and factory pipes or the air pollutants that issue from smokestacks or automobiles." Tom Horton, This Land Is My Land, Mid-Atlantic Country, May 1991, 22, 23.

Many states and localities have enacted land use programs designed to protect environmentally sensitive land. One major source of such programs is the National Flood Insurance Act of 1968, §1340 (codified at 42 U.S.C. §4012 (1982)), which provided federally subsidized insurance to residents in flood-prone areas but also required communities to adopt zoning ordinances minimizing the dangers of development in flood plains. Many states and localities have adopted wetlands protection statutes. A federal district court articulated the rationale behind such legislation in 1992.

> Wetlands, with [their] swamps, marshes, bogs, mud flats and other water-dependent community types, are an ecological treasure. They play a vital role for wildlife by providing nesting and habitat for many species of fish, birds, plants and other wildlife. For the bird community, wetlands foster high species diversity, density, and productivity by providing both food and habitat, in the form of nesting sites, breeding and rearing areas, feeding grounds, and cover from predators. Many endangered species rely on our wetlands for their survival and reproductive success. Without the wetlands, we are all but assured of their extinction.
>
> Beyond the direct impact of wetlands to wildlife, they also serve other equally significant environmental functions. One of the more apparent is their favorable effect on our water quality. By filtering contaminants out of water before they can reach the open water, wetlands serve as nature's own water purifier. By absorbing large amounts of water, wetlands protect us from potential flooding.
>
> As with many of our most precious natural resources, our wetlands are threatened by commercial, agricultural, and industrial development. In the last 200 years, thirty to fifty percent of our nation's wetlands have disappeared. Because wetlands are critical to flood control, water supply, water quality, and, of course, wildlife, their rapid disappearance is setting the stage for what may eventually become a significant environmental catastrophe. The State of Texas alone has lost 8 million acres, nearly half of its original wetlands. With only some 7.6 million acres remaining, wetlands presently constitute a mere 4.4 percent of Texas' acreage. As the wetlands continue to shrink, the threat to our environment escalates.

Sabine River Authority v. U.S. Department of Interior, 951 F.2d 669, 672 (5th Cir. 1992).

In the summer of 1993, severe flooding on the Mississippi produced more than $11 billion worth of damage to buildings and crops. Edward

Walsh, Rivers Leave Zone of Heartbreak, Wash. Post, at A1. "It's economic devastation for the entire area," said Hannibal, Missouri, mayor Richard Schwartz. Edward Walsh, "Flood Summit" Weighs Aid: After Viewing Damage, Clinton Pledges More for Midwest, Wash. Post, July 18, 1993, at A1. Some experts argue that flooding along the Mississippi is getting worse and worse, in significant part because of the destruction of wetlands that previously served to absorb flood waters: Illinois has lost 85 percent of its wetlands; Missouri has lost 87 percent; Iowa has lost 89 percent. Some scientists argue that damming of the river should be accompanied by a system that allows farmlands adjacent to the river to flood during periods of high river flow. William Booth, The Re-Creation: River Ecosystem under Stress, Wash. Post, July 18, 1993, at A1. See Steven L. Dickersin, The Evolving Wetland Program, 44 S.W.L.J. 1473, 1474 (1991) (87 percent of the wetlands losses 1950s-1970s due to conversions to agricultural use).

The following is a key early case, still cited today, in which a court upheld a land use program that involved stringent restrictions on environmentally sensitive land.

JUST v. MARINETTE COUNTY

201 N.W.2d 761 (Wis. 1972)

These two cases [Just v. Marinette, and Marinette v. Just] were consolidated for trial and argued together on appeal. In case number 106, Ronald Just and Kathryn L. Just, his wife (Justs), sought a declaratory judgment stating: (1) The shoreland zoning ordinance of the respondent Marinette County . . . was unconstitutional, (2) their property was not "wetlands" as defined in the ordinance, and (3) the prohibition against the filling of wetlands was unconstitutional. In case number 107, Marinette county sought a forfeiture for the violation of the ordinance in having placed fill on their lands without a permit. The trial court held that the ordinance was valid, the Justs' property was "wetlands," the Justs had violated the ordinance and they were subject to a forfeiture of $100. From the judgments, the Justs appeal.[16]

Marinette [C]ounty's Shoreland Zoning Ordinance Number 24 was adopted September 19, 1967 . . . and follows a unique model ordinance published by the Wisconsin Department of Resource Development. . . . The ordinance was designed to meet standards and criteria for shoreland regulation which the legislature required to be promulgated by the department of natural resources. . . .

_____

16. This is from the West's write-up of the case. See Just v. Marinette County, 201 N.W. 2d at 764. — Eds.

There can be no disagreement over the public purpose sought to be obtained by the ordinance. Its basic purpose is to protect navigable waters and the public rights therein from the degradation and deterioration which results from uncontrolled use and development of shorelands. In the Navigable Waters Protection Act, sec. 144.26, the purpose of the state's shoreland regulation program is stated as . . . The Marinette [C]ounty shoreland zoning ordinance . . . states the uncontrolled use of shorelands and pollution of navigable waters of Marinette [C]ounty adversely affect public health, safety, convenience and general welfare and impair the tax base.

The shoreland zoning ordinance divides the shorelands of Marinette [C]ounty into general purpose districts, general recreation districts, and conservancy districts. A "conservancy" district is required by the statutory minimum standards and is defined in sec. 3.4 of the ordinance to include "all shorelands designated as swamps or marshes on the United States Geological Survey maps which have been designated as the Shoreland Zoning Map of Marinette, Wisconsin or on the detailed Insert Shoreland Zoning Maps." The ordinance provides for permitted uses[17] and conditional uses[18]. . . . One of the conditional uses requiring a permit . . . [for] filling, draining or dredging of wetlands . . . [T]he ordinance requires a conditional-use permit for any filling or grading "Of any area which is within three hundred feet horizontal distance of a navigable water and which has surface drainage toward the water and on which there is: (a) Filling of more than five hundred square feet of any wetland which i[s] contiguous to the water . . . (d) Filling or grading of more than 2,000 square feet on slopes of twelve per cent or less."

In April of 1961, . . . the Justs purchased land in the town of Lake along the south shore of Lake Noquebay, a navigable lake in Marinette [C]ounty. This land had a frontage of 1,266.7 feet on the lake and was purchased partially for personal use and partially for resale. During the years 1964, 1966, and 1967, the Justs made five sales of parcels having frontage and extending back from the lake some 600 feet, leaving the property involved in these suits. This property has a frontage of 366.7 feet and [only three-fourths of the north-half is classified as wetlands under the Act. That area contains vegetation that N.C. Fassett, in his manual of aquatic plants, has classified as "aquatic."] . . . The land slopes generally toward the lake but has a slope less than twelve per cent. No water flows onto the land from the lake, but there is some surface water which collects on land and stands in pools.

---

17. Permitted uses are harvesting of wild crops, sustained yield forestry, utilities, hunting and fishing preserves, nonresidential buildings used solely in conjunction with raising water fowl, hiking and bridle paths, accessory uses, and signs. — EDS.

18. Conditional uses, allowed upon issuance of a permit, are general farming, dams and power plants, relocation of any water course, filling, drainage or dredging, removal of top soil or peat, cranberry bogs, piers, docks, boathouses. — EDS.

The land owned by the Justs is designated as swamps or marshes on the United States Geological Survey Map and is located within 1,000 feet of the normal high-water elevation of the lake. Thus, the property is included in a conservancy district and, by sec. 2.29 of the ordinance, classified as "wetlands." Consequently, in order to place more than 500 square feet of fill on this property, the Justs were required to obtain a conditional-use permit from the zoning administrator of the county and pay a fee of $20 or incur a forfeiture of $10 to $200 for each day of violation.

In February and March of 1968, after the ordinance became effective, Ronald Just, [started to fill], 1,040 square yards of sand onto this property and filled an area approximately 20-feet wide commencing at the southwest corner and extending almost 600 feet north to the northwest corner near the shoreline, then easterly along the shoreline almost to the lot line. He stayed back from the pressure ridge about 20 feet. More than 500 square feet of this fill was upon wetlands located contiguous to the water and which had surface drainage toward the lake. The fill within 300 feet of the lake also was more than 2,000 square feet on a slope less than 12 percent. . . .

Marinette [C]ounty and the state of Wisconsin argue that the restrictions of the conservancy district and wetlands provisions constitute a proper exercise of the police power of the state and do not so severely limit the use or depreciate the value of the land as to constitute a taking without compensation.

To state the issue in more meaningful terms, it is a conflict between the public interest in stopping the despoliation of natural resources, which our citizens until recently have taken as inevitable and for granted, and an owner's asserted right to use his property as he wishes. The protection of public rights may be accomplished by the exercise of the police power unless the damage to the property owner is too great and amounts to a confiscation. The securing or taking of a benefit not presently enjoyed by the public for its use is obtained by the government through its power of eminent domain. The distinction between the exercise of the police power and condemnation has been said to be a matter of degree of damage to the property owner. In the valid exercise of the police power reasonably restricting the use of property, the damage suffered by the owner is said to be incidental. However, where the restriction is so great the landowner ought not to bear such a burden for the public good, the restriction has been held to be a constructive taking even though the actual use or forbidden use has not been transferred to the government so as to be a taking in the traditional sense. Whether a taking has occurred depends upon whether "the restriction practically or substantially renders the land useless for all reasonable purposes." . . . The loss caused the individual must be weighed to determine if it is more than he should bear. As this court stated in *Stefan* [Auto Body v. State Highway Comm., 21 Wis. 2d 363], 369-370, 124 N.W.2d 319, 323, " . . . if the damage is such as to be suffered by many similarly situated and is in the nature of a restriction on the use to which land may be put and ought to be borne by the individual as a member of society for the good of the public safety, health or general welfare, it is said to be a reasonable exercise of the police power, but if the damage is so great to the individual that he ought not to bear it under contemporary standards, then courts are inclined to treat it as a 'taking' of the property or an unreasonable exercise of the police power."

Many years ago, Professor Freund stated in his work on The Police Power, sec. 511, at 546-547, "It may be said that the state takes property by eminent domain because it is useful to the public, and under the police power because it is harmful. . . . From this results the difference between the power of eminent domain and the police power, that the former recognizes a right to compensation, while the latter on principle does not." Thus the necessity for monetary compensation for loss suffered to an owner by police power restriction arises when restrictions are placed on property in order to create a public benefit rather than to prevent a public harm. Rathkopf, The Law of Zoning and Planning, Vol. 1, ch. 6, pp. 6-7.

This case causes us to reexamine the concepts of public benefit in contrast to public harm and the scope of an owner's right to use of his property. In the instant case we have a restriction on the use of a citizen['s] property, not to secure a benefit for the public, but to prevent a harm from the change in the natural character of the citizen['s] property. We start with the premise that lakes and rivers in their natural state are unpolluted and the pollution which now exists is man made. The state of Wisconsin under the trust doctrine has a duty to eradicate the present pollution and to prevent further pollution in its navigable waters. This is not, in a legal sense, a gain or a securing of a benefit by the maintaining of the natural *status quo* of the environment. What makes this case different from most condemnation of police power zoning cases is the interrelationship of the wetlands, the swamps and the natural environment of shorelands to the purity of the water and to such natural resources as navigation, fishing, and scenic beauty. Swamps and wetlands were once considered wasteland, undesirable, and not picturesque. But as the people became more sophisticated, an appreciation was acquired that swamps and wetlands serve a vital role in nature, are part of the balance of nature and are essential to the purity of the water in our lakes and streams. Swamps and wetlands are a necessary part of the ecological creation and now, even to the uninitiated, possess their own beauty in nature.

Is the ownership of a parcel of land so absolute that man can change its nature to suit any of his purposes? The great forests of our state were stripped on the theory man's ownership was unlimited. But in forestry, the land at least was used naturally, only the natural fruit of the land (the trees) were taken. The despoilage was in the failure to look to the future and provide for the reforestation of the land. An owner of land has no absolute and unlimited right to change the essential natural character of his land so as to use it for a purpose for which it was unsuited in its natural state and which injures the rights of others. The exercise of the police power in zoning must be reasonable and we think it is not an unreasonable exercise of that power to prevent harm to public rights by limiting the use of private property to its natural uses.

This is not a case where an owner is prevented from using his land for natural and indigenous uses. The uses consistent with the nature of the land are allowed and other uses recognized and still others permitted by special permit. The shoreland zoning ordinance prevents to some extent the changing of the natural character of the land within 1,000 feet of a navigable lake and 300 feet of navigable river because of such land's inter-relation to the contiguous water. The changing of wetlands and swamps to the damage of the general public by upsetting the natural environment and the natural relationship is not a reasonable use of that land which is protected from police power regulation. Changes and filling to some extent are permitted because the extent of such changes and fillings does not cause harm. We realize no case in Wisconsin has yet dealt with shoreland regulations and there are several cases in other states which seem to hold such regulations unconstitutional; but nothing this court has said or held in prior cases indicate that destroying the natural character of a swamp or a wetland so as to make that location available for human habitation is a reasonable use of that land when the new use, although of a more economical value to the owner, causes a harm to the general public.

Wisconsin has long held that laws and regulations to prevent pollution and to protect the waters of this state from degradation are valid police-power enactments. The active public trust duty of the state of Wisconsin in respect to navigable waters requires the state not only to promote navigation but also to protect and preserve those waters for fishing, recreation, and scenic beauty. To further this duty, the legislature may delegate authority to local units of the government, which the state did by requiring counties to pass shoreland zoning ordinances. . . .

It seems to us that filling a swamp not otherwise commercially usable is not in and of itself an existing use, which is prevented, but rather is the preparation for some future use which is not indigenous to a swamp. Too much stress is laid on the right of an owner to change commercially value-less land when that change does damage to the rights of the public. It is observed that a use of special permits is a means of control and accomplishing the purpose of the zoning ordinance as distinguished from the old concept of providing for variances. The special permit technique is now common practice and has met with judicial approval, and we think it is of some significance in considering whether or not a particular zoning ordinance is reasonable. . . .

The Justs argue their property has been severely depreciated in value. But this depreciation of value is not based on the use of the land in its natural state but on what the land would be worth if it could be filled and used for the location of a dwelling. While loss of value is to be considered in determining whether a restriction is a constructive taking, value based upon changing the character of the land at the expense of harm to public rights is not an essential factor or controlling.

We are not unmindful of the warning in Pennsylvania Coal Co. v. Mahon (1922), 260 U.S. 393, 416:

> . . . We are in danger of forgetting that a strong public desire to improve the public condition is not enough to warrant achieving the desire by a shorter cut than the constitutional way of paying for the change.

. . . The ordinance does not create or improve the public condition but only preserves nature from the despoilage and harm resulting from the unrestricted activities of humans. . . . The judgement is affirmed.

NOTES AND QUESTIONS

1. **Environmental concerns.** The ordinance had two major environmental goals. One was to restrict development near lakes to avoid polluting them.[19] The second was to prevent the destruction of wetlands because of their ecological importance as a habitat for wildlife, for flood control, and for humans to enjoy. Which does the court stress? Why? Wetlands, as the "farmlands" of the aquatic environment, are a productive and valuable ecosystem. They provide food for a variety of species and are critical breeding grounds for birds and fish. Wetlands contribute to society by helping to maintain water quality, controlling erosion, discharging and recharging ground water, and providing fish, timber, wild rice, cranberries, and peat. Hope Babcock, Federal Wetlands Regulatory Policy: Up to Its Ears in Alligators, 8 Pace Envtl. L. Rev. 307 (1991).

2. **The harm/benefit test.** The harm/benefit test, first bruited by Ernest Freund, The Police Power §511, at 546-547 (1904), and further advanced by Allison Dunham, A Legal and Economic Basis for City Planning, 58 Colum. L. Rev. 650 (1958), holds that land use regulations that prevent a harm should be upheld, while regulations that confer a benefit on the public should be invalidated. Land use expert Daniel R. Mandelker notes that the "theory that land use regulation may prevent a harm grows out of fault concepts that have their origins in nuisance law." How does the *Just* court use the harm/benefit test?

19. Shoreside development can produce pollution in two ways. First, septic systems can leak untreated sewage into the lakes. Second, development near rivers and lakes can lead to run-off of phosphates and nutrients that pollutes water and makes it unsuitable for wildlife. James G. Chandler and Michael J. Vechsler, The Great Lakes-St. Lawrence River Basin from an IJC Perspective, 18 Can. U.S.L.J. 261 (1992).

3.   **Another Ahab?** Why did Mr. Just refuse to apply for a permit before filling his land? What image of property appears to have informed his
actions? Consider the following:

> Given the availability of conditional use permits, landowners appear
> to have no great incentive to disobey the law; this may be why, by all accounts,
> very little illegal filling occurs in Marinette County. The Justs, however, were
> not ordinary landowners. The Justs were not just mildly skeptical about govern-
> ment, in the robust but amiable and pragmatic fashion of some rural individ-
> ualists, they were darkly, intensely hostile to the dominant forces in America.
> Confronted by the rules that they perceived as a sinister threat to their portion
> of the American Dream, they fought back with a single-minded tenacity that
> was fueled more by ideological passion than by acquisitive cunning, chasing
> the white whale of regulations all the way to the Supreme Court of Wisconsin.
>   The Justs chose to fill without applying for a permit because they be-
> lieved that the ordinance was unconstitutional: "It was a matter of prin-
> ciple. . . . We intended to break the ordinance, but we didn't intend to break
> the law of the land."

See David P. Bryden, A Phantom Doctrine: The Origins and Effects of *Just
v. Marinette County,* 1978 Am. B. Found. Res. J. 397, 434-437.

4.   **Intuitive image of property.** Does the court share the intuitive image of property? (Compare Brandeis's dissent in *Pennsylvania Coal.*)

5.   **Health, safety, and welfare.** Note that the shorelands zoning ordinance recites that basic police power incantation that it is designed to
protect "the public health, safety, convenience and general welfare."[20]
This influences the way the court formulates the basic issue, as "a conflict
between the public interest in stopping the despoliation of natural resources . . . and an owner's asserted right to use his property as he wishes."
Is the court's formulation resonant of the republican vision that property
should be designed (and, if necessary, redesigned) to achieve the common
good?[21]

6.   **Just v. Marinette's two-factor takings test.** Note that the *Just* court
does not mobilize any of the takings tests Holmes articulated in *Pennsylvania Coal.* It first focuses on the "public interest"; then it assesses the economic impact on the landowner. In the latter analysis, the court does not
use Holmes's diminution in value test. Note the court's lack of interest in
determining exactly what the Justs had paid for the land in question, and
how much they had made from the sale of the five parcels that already had
been sold. Why does the court not need that information? Have the landowners been barred from any existing uses, or have they just been barred

---

20. The ordinance adds that it is also designed to protect the tax base. What does this
mean? Why do you think local legislators added this to the basic police power incantation?

21. How did "common good" get transmuted into "the public interest"? See Joan C.
Williams, Virtue, in Richard Wrightman Fox and James T. Kloppenberg, A Companion to
American Thought (1993).

from future development harmful to the rights of the public? Note that, as in the Prah v. Maretti court, the *Just* court challenges the assumption that the ownership entails the right to (unlimited?) development.

7. **Public trust doctrine.** Does it mean something different to own ecologically sensitive land than it does to own other land?[22] The court builds a case in favor of this proposition in part through its reliance on the public trust doctrine. The doctrine was invented in Illinois Central R.R. v. Illinois, 146 U.S. 387 (1892), in which the Supreme Court set aside the Illinois legislature's (presumably corrupt) grant of lakeshore property to the Illinois Central Railroad.

> It is the settled law of this country that the ownership of and dominion and sovereignty over lands covered by tide waters . . . belong to the respective States within which they are found, with the subsequent right to use or dispose of any portion thereof, when that can be done without substantial impairment of the interest of the public in the waters.

Id. at 435. The Court went on to explain the nature of a state's title to such lands:

> It is a title different in character from that which the State holds in lands intended for sale. . . . It is a title held in trust for the people of the State that they may enjoy the navigation of the waters, carry on commerce over them, and have liberty of fishing therein freed from the obstruction or interference of private parties.

Id. The Court's opinion in *Illinois Central* remains the basic framework for the public trust doctrine in the United States today. However, the doctrine is primarily a product of state law, so there are actually 50 individual doctrines. Each state's enunciation of the public trust doctrine may be determined by examining its case law and any relevant statutory or constitutional provisions. In certain states, particularly California and New Jersey, the doctrine has been extensively used and expanded beyond the limited scope identified in *Illinois Central*. This evolving public trust doctrine parallels those states' expansive attitude towards land use regulation generally.

---

22. See generally Joseph L. Sax, The Public Trust Doctrine in Natural Resource Law: Effective Judicial Intervention, 68 Mich. L. Rev. 471 (1970); Michael L. Wolz, Applications of the Public Trust Doctrine to the Protection and Preservation of Wetlands: Can It Fill the Statutory Gaps?, 6 B.Y.U. J. Pub. L. 475 (1992); Mary Kyle McCurdy, Public Trust Protection for Wetlands, 19 Envtl. L. 683 (1989); Alison Rieser, Ecological Preservation as a Public Trust Right: An Emerging Doctrine in Search of a Theory, 15 Harv. Envtl. L. Rev. 393, 393 (1991) ("[T]he notion that the public has a right to expect certain lands and natural areas to retain their natural characteristics is finding its way into American law. Through interpretation and expansion of the common law public trust doctrine, state courts are identifying governmental duties to redefine existing private property rights where such rights may threaten the ecological value of natural areas.").

In California, any land alienated by the state is subject to a public trust easement that serves to insure the public's right to use the water for such purposes as navigation and fishing. See People v. California Fish Co., 166 Cal. 576, 596, 138 P. 79, 87 (1913) ("The only practicable theory is to hold that all tideland is included, but that the public right of navigation was not intended to be divested . . . and that the buyer of land take title . . . and in subordination to the right of the state to take possession"); see also Marks v. Whitney, 491 P.2d 374 (Cal. 1971) (citing People v. California Fish Co. in construing public easement). Additionally, California has adopted an expansive view as to what is included within the public trust. While the public trust doctrine was traditionally confined to navigation, commerce, and fishing, the California judiciary views the trust as an evolving concept that includes hunting, swimming, boating, and general recreation. The California Supreme Court stated in Marks v. Whitney that "the public uses to which tidelands are subject are sufficiently flexible to encompass changing public needs. In administering the trust the state is not burdened with an outmoded classification favoring one mode of utilization over another." 491 P.2d 374, 381. Similar to the Wisconsin court's opinion in *Just,* the California court appears to endorse the use of the public trust doctrine as a limit on the destruction of the environment. See id. at 380 ("[T]he most important public uses of the tidelands — a use encompassed within the tidelands trust — is the preservation of those lands in their natural state, so that they may serve as ecological units for scientific study, as open space, and environments which provide food and habitat for birds and marine life, and which favorably affect the scenery and climate of the area").

New Jersey has also developed a body of public trust doctrine case law that is more expansive than the traditional framework delineated in *Illinois Central.* In Clifton v. Passaic Valley Water Commn., 539 A.2d 760 (N.J. Super. 1987), the court held that the public trust doctrine extended to the protection of drinking water. Id. at 765 ("While the original purpose of the public trust doctrine was to preserve the use of the public natural water for navigation, commerce and fishing, it is clear that since water is essential for human life, the public trust doctrine applies with equal impact upon the control of our drinking water reserves"). Perhaps most interestingly, the New Jersey Supreme Court has used the public trust doctrine to provide the public with access to private dry sand beaches. Matthews v. Bay Head Improvement Assn., 471 A.2d 355 (N.J. 1984). In *Matthews,* plaintiffs brought a suit against a private nonprofit group that controlled access to the beach through a membership system. The court, in holding that the privately held beach areas were subject to a public right of way, stated that "where use of dry sand is essential or reasonably necessary for enjoyment of the ocean, the [public trust] doctrine warrants the public's use of [privately owned] upland dry sand area subject to an accommodation of the interest of the owner." Id. at 365.

The public trust doctrine provides a useful and flexible tool for arguing in favor of legislation that protects the country's waterways, including wetlands legislation; shoreland preservation acts; and floodplain management statutes. By arguing that preservation of these areas is implicit within the public trust, one can argue that a landowner does not have the right to do something with his property that will adversely affect the environment and thus violate the public trust. Under this line of reasoning, the owner of property falling within the public trust is constrained from any type of development that will generate adverse environmental consequences and thus result in harm to the public.

8.   **Why me?** The *Just* court focuses the landowners' core equitable claim that if the governmental goal is so important, the resulting costs should be fairly spread among all those who benefit, not unfairly concentrated on one hapless victim. (See page 834, *supra*.) Which do you consider the more persuasive argument? A lawyer's first job is to answer that question for herself; her second is to be able to put forth each side's best arguments. Even a lawyer who does not find the "why me?" argument persuasive should recognize its power as the underlying story line of any argument or brief for a landowner in a takings case. The same goes for the *Just* court's arguments about ownership rights in environmentally sensitive land. Even those who do not find such arguments persuasive should recognize their power as the underlying story line in the defense of a land use program designed to protect wetlands, coastal areas, or other environmentally sensitive property.

9.   **Wetlands statutes in other states.** *Just* remains the law in Wisconsin, but courts in some other states have struck down similar wetlands protection programs. One case often linked with *Just* is State v. Johnson, 265 A.2d 711 (Me. 1970), in which a Maine court struck down a statewide wetlands conservation program as unconstitutional. Courts in other states have followed *Just*, see, e.g., Graham v. Estuary Properties, Inc., 399 So. 2d 1374 (Fla. 1981).

b.   The Supreme Court Reenters the Field

For 50 years after *Euclid*, the Supreme Court left land use to state courts. In 1978, the Supreme Court entered the field with a decision upholding the constitutionality of the New York City landmarks law.

1.   *Penn Central* (1978)

Europe has its cathedrals and we have Grand Central Station.[23]

---

23.   Architect Philip Johnson, quoted in Richard F. Babcock and Charles L. Siemon, The Zoning Game Revisited 59 (1985).

PENN CENTRAL TRANSPORTATION CO. v. CITY OF NEW YORK

438 U.S. 104 (1978)[24]

BRENNAN, J., delivered the opinion of the Court, in which STEWART, WHITE, MARSHALL, BLACKMUN, and POWELL, JJ., joined. REHNQUIST, J., filed a dissenting opinion, in which BURGER, C.J., and STEVENS, J., joined.

The question presented is whether a city may, as part of a comprehensive program to preserve historic landmarks and historic districts, place restrictions on the development of individual historic landmarks — in addition to those imposed by applicable zoning ordinances — without effecting a "taking" requiring the payment of "just compensation." . . .

I

. . . The New York City law is typical of many urban landmark laws in that its primary method of achieving its goals is not by acquisitions of historic properties.[6] . . . [T]he major theme of the law is to ensure the owners of any such properties both a "reasonable return" on their investments and maximum latitude to use their parcels for purposes not inconsistent with the preservation goals.

The operation of the law can be briefly summarized. [The Landmark Preservation Commission identifies sites of historic interest and hears objections from interested parties before determining that the site is a landmark. After a final designation is made, restrictions are placed upon the property requiring the owner to keep the exterior of the building in "good repair." Should the owner want to alter the exterior, there are three procedures available for the consideration of his proposal: He can apply for a certificate of no effect, a certificate of appropriateness, or a final procedure that has various mechanisms and considers the economic hardship caused the owner.] . . .

On August 2, 1967, following a public hearing, the Commission designated the Terminal a "landmark" and designated the "city tax block" it occupies a "landmark site." . . . Although appellant Penn Central had opposed the designation before the Commission, it did not seek judicial review of the final designation decision.

On January 22, 1968, appellant Penn Central, to increase its income,

---

24. Amicus curiae briefs were filed by the National Trust for Historic Preservation, The Committee to Save Grand Central Station, and various attorneys general.

6. The consensus is that widespread public ownership of historic properties in urban settings is neither feasible nor wise. Public ownership reduces the tax base, burdens the public budget with costs of acquisitions and maintenance, and results in the preservation of public buildings as museums and similar facilities, rather than as economically productive features of the urban scene. See Paul H. Wilson & H. James Winkler II, The Response of State Legislation to Historic Preservation, 36 Law & Contemp. Prob. 329, 330-331, 339-340 (1971).

entered into a renewable 50-year lease and sublease agreement with appellant UGP Properties, Inc. (UGP). . . . Under the terms of the agreement, UGP was to construct a multistory office building above the Terminal. UGP promised to pay Penn Central $1 million annually during construction and at least $3 million annually thereafter. The rentals would be offset in part by a loss of some $700,000 to $1 million in net rentals presently received from concessionaires displaced by the new building.

Appellants UGP and Penn Central then applied to the Commission for permission to construct an office building atop the Terminal. . . . The Commission denied a certificate of no exterior effect on September 20, 1968 [for both proposals and after] four days of hearings at which over 80 witnesses testified, the Commission denied [them a certificate of appropriateness] as to both proposals.

The Commission's reasons for rejecting certificates respecting Breuer II Revised are summarized in the following statement: "To protect a Landmark, one does not tear it down. To perpetuate its architectural features, one does not strip them off." Record 2255. Breuer I, which would have preserved the existing vertical facades of the present structure, received more sympathetic consideration. . . .

> [We have] no fixed rule against making additions to designated buildings — it all depends on how they are done. . . . But to balance a 55-story office tower above a flamboyant Beaux-Arts facade seems nothing more than an aesthetic joke. Quite simply, the tower would overwhelm the Terminal by sheer mass. The "addition" would be four times as high as the existing structure and would reduce the Landmark itself to the status of a curiosity. . . .

Appellants did not seek judicial review of the denial of either certificate. . . . Further, appellants did not avail themselves of the opportunity to develop and submit other plans for the Commission's consideration and approval. Instead, appellants filed suit in New York Supreme Court, Trial Term, claiming, *inter alia,* that the application of the Landmarks Preservation Law had "taken" their property without just compensation in violation of the Fifth and Fourteenth Amendments and arbitrarily deprived them of their property without due process of law in violation of the Fourteenth Amendment. Appellants sought a declaratory judgment, injunctive relief barring the city from using the Landmarks Law to impede the construction of any structure that might otherwise lawfully be constructed on the Terminal site, and damages for the "temporary taking" that occurred between August 2, 1967, the designation date, and the date when the restrictions arising from the Landmarks Law would be lifted. The trial court granted the injunctive and declaratory relief, but severed the question of damages for a "temporary taking."

Appellees appealed, and the New York Supreme Court, Appellate Division, reversed. 50 App. Div. 2d 265, 377 N.Y.S.2d 20 (1975). The Appellate Division held that the evidence appellants introduced at trial — "Statements of Revenues and Costs," purporting to show a net operating loss for the years 1969 and 1971, which were prepared for the instant litigation — had not satisfied their burden. First, the court rejected the claim that these statements showed that the Terminal was operating at a loss, for in the court's view, appellants had improperly attributed some railroad operating expenses and taxes to their real estate operations, and compounded that error by failing to impute any rental value to the vast space in the Terminal devoted to railroad purposes. Further, the Appellate Division concluded that appellants had failed to establish either that they were unable to increase the Terminal's commercial income by transforming vacant or underutilized space to revenue-producing use, or that the unused development rights over the Terminal could not have been profitably transferred to one or more nearby sites. The Appellate Division concluded that all appellants had succeeded in showing was that they had been deprived of the property's most profitable use, and that this showing did not establish that appellants had been unconstitutionally deprived of their property.

The New York Court of Appeals affirmed.[23]

II

. . . The question of what constitutes a "taking" for purposes of the Fifth Amendment has proved to be a problem of considerable difficulty. While this Court has recognized that the "Fifth Amendment's guarantee . . . [is] designed to bar Government from forcing some people alone to bear public burdens which, in all fairness and justice, should be borne by the public as a whole," Armstrong v. United States, 364 U.S. 40, 49 (1960), this Court, quite simply, has been unable to develop any "set formula" for determining when "justice and fairness" require that economic injuries caused by public action be compensated by the government, rather than remain disproportionately concentrated on a few persons. See Goldblatt v. Hempstead, 369 U.S. 590, 594 (1962). Indeed, we have frequently observed that whether a particular restriction will be rendered invalid by the government's failure to pay for any losses proximately caused by it depends largely "upon the particular circumstances [in that] case." United States v. Central Eureka Mining Co., 357 U.S. 155, 168 (1958). . . .

---

23. The Court of Appeals suggested that in calculating the value of the property upon which appellants were entitled to earn a reasonable return, the "public created" components of the value of the property — i.e., those elements of its value attributable to the "efforts of organized society" or to the "social complex" in which the Terminal is located — had to be excluded. However, since the record upon which the Court of Appeals decided the case did not, as that court recognized, contain a basis for segregating the privately created from the publicly created elements of the value of the Terminal site and since the judgment of the Court of Appeals in any event rests upon bases that support our affirmance, see *infra*, this page, we have no occasion to address the question whether it is permissible or feasible to separate out the "social increments" of the value of property. See John J. Costonis, The Disparity Issue: A Context for the Grand Central Terminal Decision, 91 Harv. L. Rev. 402, 416-417 (1977). [Footnote relocated — EDS.].

In engaging in these essentially ad hoc, factual inquiries, the Court's decisions have identified several factors that have particular significance. The economic impact of the regulation on the claimant and, particularly, the extent to which the regulation has interfered with distinct investment-backed expectations are, of course, relevant considerations. See Goldblatt v. Hempstead, *supra,* at 594. So, too, is the character of the governmental action. A "taking" may more readily be found when the interference with property can be characterized as a physical invasion by government, see, e.g., United States v. Causby, 328 U.S. 256 (1946), than when interference arises from some public program adjusting the benefits and burdens of economic life to promote the common good.

"Government hardly could go on if to some extent values incident to property could not be diminished without paying for every such change in the general law," Pennsylvania Coal Co. v. Mahon, 260 U.S. 393, 413 (1922), and this Court has accordingly recognized, in a wide variety of contexts, that government may execute laws or programs that adversely affect recognized economic values. . . .

. . . [I]n instances in which a state tribunal reasonably concluded that "the health, safety, morals, or general welfare" would be promoted by prohibiting particular contemplated uses of land, this Court has upheld land-use regulations that destroyed or adversely affected recognized real property interests. See Nectow v. Cambridge, 277 U.S. 183, 188 (1928). Zoning laws are, of course, the classic example, see Euclid v. Ambler Realty Co., 272 U.S. 365 (1926) (prohibition of industrial use) . . . which have been viewed as permissible governmental action even when prohibiting the most beneficial use of the property. . . .

Zoning laws generally do not affect existing uses of real property, but "taking" challenges have also been held to be without merit in a wide variety of situations when the challenged governmental actions prohibited a beneficial use to which individual parcels had previously been devoted and thus caused substantial individualized harm. Miller v. Schoene, 276 U.S. 272 (1928), is illustrative. The Court held that the State might properly make "a choice between the preservation of one class of property and that of the other" and since the apple industry was important in the State involved, concluded that the State had not exceeded "its constitutional powers by deciding upon the destruction of one class of property [without compensation] in order to save another which, in the judgment of the legislature, is of greater value to the public." Id., at 279.

. . . Because this Court has recognized, in a number of settings, that States and cities may enact land-use restrictions or controls to enhance the quality of life by preserving the character and desirable aesthetic features of a city . . . appellants do not contest that New York City's objective of preserving structures and areas with special historic, architectural, or cultural significance is an entirely permissible governmental goal. . . .

[A]ppellants, focusing on the character and impact of the New York City law, argue that it effects a "taking" because its operation has significantly diminished the value of the Terminal site. Appellants concede that the decisions sustaining other land-use regulations, which, like the New York City law, are reasonably related to the promotion of the general welfare, uniformly reject the proposition that diminution in property value, standing alone can establish a "taking," see Euclid v. Ambler Realty Co., 272 U.S. 365 (1926) (75% diminution in value caused by zoning law); Hadacheck v. Sebastian, 239 U.S. 394 (1915) (87½% diminution in value). . . .[25]

Stated baldly, appellants' position appears to be that the only means of ensuring that selected owners are not singled out to endure financial hardship for no reason is to hold that any restriction imposed on individual landmarks pursuant to the New York City scheme is a "taking" requiring the payment of "just compensation." Agreement with this argument would, of course, invalidate not just New York City's law, but all comparable landmark legislation in the Nation. We find no merit in it.

It is true, as appellants emphasize, that both historic-district legislation and zoning laws regulate all properties within given physical communities whereas landmark laws apply only to selected parcels. But contrary to appellants' suggestions, landmark laws are not like discriminatory, or "reverse spot," zoning: that is, a land-use decision which arbitrarily singles out a particular parcel for different, less favorable treatment than the neighboring ones. See 2 A. Rathkopf, The Law of Zoning and Planning 26-4, and n. 6 (4th ed. 1978). In contrast to discriminatory zoning, which is the antithesis of land-use control as part of some comprehensive plan, the New York City law embodies a comprehensive plan to preserve structures of historic or aesthetic interest wherever they might be found in the city, and as noted, over 400 landmarks and 31 historic districts have been designated pursuant to this plan.

Equally without merit is the related argument that the decision to designate a structure as a landmark "is inevitably arbitrary or at least subjective, because it is basically a matter of taste," Reply Brief for Appellants 22, thus unavoidably singling out individual landowners for disparate and unfair treatment. The argument has a particularly hollow ring in this case. For appellants not only did not seek judicial review of either the designation or of the denials of the certificates of appropriateness and of no exterior effect, but do not even now suggest that the Commission's decisions concerning the Terminal were in any sense arbitrary or unprincipled. But, in any event, a landmark owner has a right to judicial review of any Commission decision, and, quite simply, there is no basis whatsoever for a conclusion that courts will have any greater difficulty identifying arbitrary or discrimi-

---

25. Historic District Legislation is enacted to preserved landmarks and districts of historical significance such as the French Quarter in New Orleans. It falls under the police power of the state because it effects a legitimate economic and social policy of preserving the country's heritage and areas with unique characteristics. See Maher v. New Orleans, 516 F.2d 1051 (5th Cir. 1975).

natory action in the context of landmark regulation than in the context of classic zoning or indeed in any other context.

Next, appellants observe that New York City's law differs from zoning laws and historic-district ordinances in that the Landmarks Law does not impose identical or similar restrictions on all structures located in particular physical communities. It follows, they argue, that New York City's law is inherently incapable of producing the fair and equitable distribution of benefits and burdens of governmental action which is characteristic of zoning laws and historic-district legislation and which they maintain is a constitutional requirement if "just compensation" is not to be afforded. It is, of course, true that the Landmarks Law has a more severe impact on some landowners than on others, but that in itself does not mean that the law effects a "taking." Legislation designed to promote the general welfare commonly burdens some more than others. The owners of the brickyard in *Hadacheck,* of the cedar trees in Miller v. Schoene, and of the gravel and sand mine in Goldblatt v. Hempstead, were uniquely burdened by the legislation sustained in those cases.[30] Similarly, zoning laws often affect some property owners more severely than others but have not been held to be invalid on that account. For example, the property owner in *Euclid* who wished to use its property for industrial purposes was affected far more severely by the ordinance than its neighbors who wished to use their land for residences.

In any event, appellants' repeated suggestions that they are solely burdened and unbenefited is factually inaccurate. This contention overlooks the fact that the New York City law applies to vast numbers of structures in the city in addition to the Terminal — all the structures contained in the 31 historic districts and over 400 individual landmarks, many of which are close to the Terminal. Unless we are to reject the judgment of the New York City Council that the preservation of landmarks benefits all New York citizens and all structures, both economically and by improving the quality of life in the city as a whole — which we are unwilling to do — we cannot con-

---

30. Appellants attempt to distinguish these cases on the ground that, in each, government was prohibiting a "noxious" use of land and that in the present case, in contrast, appellants' proposed construction above the Terminal would be beneficial. We observe that the uses in issue in *Hadacheck, Miller* and *Goldblatt* were perfectly lawful in themselves. They involved no "blameworthiness, . . . moral wrongdoing or conscious act of dangerous risk-taking which induce[d society] to shift the cost to a [particular] individual." Sax, Takings and the Police Power, 74 Yale L.J. 36, 50 (1964). These cases are better understood as resting not on any supposed "noxious" quality of the prohibited uses but rather on the ground that the restrictions were reasonably related to the implementation of a policy — not unlike historic preservation — expected to produce a widespread public benefit and applicable to all similarly situated property.

Nor, correlatively, can it be asserted that the destruction or fundamental alteration of a historic landmark is not harmful. The suggestion that the beneficial quality of appellants' proposed construction is established by the fact that the construction would have been consistent with applicable zoning laws ignores the development in sensibilities and ideals reflected in landmark legislation like New York City's. . . .

clude that the owners of the Terminal have in no sense been benefited by the Landmarks Law. Doubtless appellants believe they are more burdened than benefited by the law, but that must have been true, too, of the property owners in *Miller, Hadacheck, Euclid,* and *Goldblatt.* . . .

Rejection of appellants' broad arguments is not, however, the end of our inquiry, for all we thus far have established is that the New York City law is not rendered invalid by its failure to provide "just compensation" whenever a landmark owner is restricted in the exploitation of property interests, such as air rights, to a greater extent than provided for under applicable zoning laws. We now must consider whether the interference with appellants' property is of such a magnitude that "there must be an exercise of eminent domain and compensation to sustain [it]." Pennsylvania Coal Co. v. Mahon, 260 U.S., at 413. . . .

Unlike the governmental acts in *Goldblatt, Miller, Causby, Griggs* and *Hadacheck,* the New York City law does not interfere in any way with the present uses of the Terminal. Its designation as a landmark not only permits but contemplates that appellants may continue to use the property precisely as it has been used for the past 65 years: as a railroad terminal containing office space and concessions. So the law does not interfere with what must be regarded as Penn Central's primary expectation concerning the use of the parcel. More importantly, on this record, we must regard the New York city law as permitting Penn Central not only to profit from the Terminal but also to obtain a "reasonable return" on its investment.

Appellants, moreover, exaggerate the effect of the law on their ability to make use of the air rights above the Terminal in two respects. First, it simply cannot be maintained, on this record, that appellants have been prohibited from occupying any portion of the airspace above the Terminal. While the Commission's actions in denying applications to construct an office building in excess of 50 stories above the Terminal may indicate that it will refuse to issue a certificate of appropriateness for any comparably sized structure, nothing the Commission has said or done suggests an intention to prohibit any construction above the Terminal. The Commission's report emphasized that whether any construction would be allowed depended upon whether the proposed addition "would harmonize in scale, material, and character with [the Terminal]." Record 2251. Since appellants have not sought approval for the construction of a smaller structure, we do not know that appellants will be denied any use of any portion of the airspace above the Terminal.[34]

Second, to the extent appellants have been denied the right to build above the Terminal, it is not literally accurate to say that they have been denied all uses of even those pre-existing air rights. [T]hey are made trans-

---

34. Counsel for appellants admitted at oral argument that the Commission has not suggested that it would not, for example, approve a 20-story office tower along the lines of that which was part of the original plan for the Terminal. See Tr. of Oral Arg. 19.

ferable to at least eight parcels in the vicinity of the Terminal. . . . Although appellants and others have argued that New York City's transferable development-rights program is far from ideal, the New York courts here supportably found that, at least in the case of the Terminal, the rights afforded are valuable. While these rights may well not have constituted "just compensation" if a "taking" had occurred, the rights nevertheless undoubtedly mitigate whatever financial burdens the law has imposed on appellants and, for that reason, are to be taken into account in considering the impact of regulation. . . .

On this record, we conclude that the application of New York City's Landmarks Law has not effected a "taking" of appellants' property.[36] . . .

Affirmed.

MR. JUSTICE REHNQUIST, with whom THE CHIEF JUSTICE and MR. JUSTICE STEVENS join, dissenting. . . . The question in this case is whether the cost associated with the city of New York's desire to preserve a limited number of "landmarks" within its borders must be borne by all of its taxpayers or whether it can instead be imposed entirely on the owners of the individual properties. . . .

In August 1967, Grand Central Terminal was designated a landmark over the objections of its owner Penn Central. Immediately upon this designation, Penn Central, like all owners of a landmark site, was placed under an affirmative duty, backed by criminal fines and penalties, to keep "exterior portions" of the landmark "in good repair." Even more burdensome, however, were the strict limitations that were thereupon imposed on Penn Central's use of its property. At the time Grand Central was designated a landmark, Penn Central was in a precarious financial condition. . . .

Appellees do not dispute that valuable property rights have been destroyed. . . . While neighboring landowners are free to use their land and "air rights" in any way consistent with the broad boundaries of New York zoning, Penn Central, absent the permission of appellees, must forever maintain its property in its present state.[5] The property has been thus subjected to a nonconsensual servitude not borne by any neighboring or similar properties. . . .

---

36. We emphasize that our holding today is on the present record, which in turn is based on Penn Central's present ability to use the Terminal for its intended purposes and in a gainful fashion. The city conceded at oral argument that if appellants can demonstrate at some point in the future that circumstances have so changed that the Terminal ceases to be "economically viable," appellants may obtain relief. See Tr. of Oral Arg. 42-43. [Footnote relocated. — EDS.]

5. In particular, Penn Central cannot increase the height of the Terminal. This Court has previously held that the "air rights" over an area of land are "property" for purposes of the Fifth Amendment. See United States v. Causby, 328 U.S. 256 (1946) ("air rights" taken by low-flying airplanes); Griggs v. Allegheny County, 369 U.S. 84 (1962) (same); Portsmouth Harbor Land & Hotel Co. v. United States, 260 U.S. 327 (1992) (firing of projectiles over summer resort can constitute taking). . . .

As early as 1887, the Court recognized that the government can prevent a property owner from using his property to injure others without having to compensate the owner for the value of the forbidden use (citing Mugler v. Kansas, 123 U.S. 623 (1887)). . . .

Thus, there is no "taking" where a city prohibits the operation of a brickyard within a residential area, see Hadacheck v. Sebastian, 239 U.S. 394 (1915), or forbids excavation for sand and gravel below the water line, see Goldblatt v. Hempstead, 369 U.S. 590 (1962). Nor is it relevant, where the government is merely prohibiting a noxious use of property, that the government would seem to be singling out a particular property owner. *Hadacheck, supra,* at 413.[8]

Appellees are not prohibiting a nuisance. The record is clear that the proposed addition to the Grand Central Terminal would be in full compliance with zoning, height limitations, and other health and safety requirements. Instead, appellees are seeking to preserve what they believe to be an outstanding example of beaux arts architecture. Penn Central is prevented from further developing its property basically because too good a job was done in designing and building it. The city of New York, because of its unadorned admiration for the design, has decided that the owners of the building must preserve it unchanged for the benefit of sightseeing New Yorkers and tourists.

Unlike land-use regulations, appellees' actions do not merely prohibit Penn Central from using its property in a narrow set of noxious ways. Instead, appellees have placed an affirmative duty on Penn Central to maintain the Terminal in its present state and in "good repair." Appellants are not free to use their property as they see fit within broad outer boundaries but must strictly adhere to their past use except where appellees conclude that alternative uses would not detract from the landmark. . . .

Even where the government prohibits a noninjurious use, the Court has ruled that a taking does not take place if the prohibition applies over a broad cross section of land and thereby "secure[s] an average reciprocity of advantage." Pennsylvania Coal Co. v. Mahon, 260 U.S., at 415. It is for this reason that zoning does not constitute a "taking." While zoning at times reduces individual property values, the burden is shared relatively evenly and it is reasonable to conclude that on the whole an individual who is harmed by one aspect of the zoning will be benefited by another.

Here, however, a multimillion dollar loss has been imposed on appellants; it is uniquely felt and is not offset by any benefits flowing from the preservation of some 400 other "landmarks" in New York City. Appellees have imposed a substantial cost on less than one-tenth of one percent of

---

8. Each of the cases cited by the Court for the proposition that legislation which severely affects some landowners but not others does not effect a "taking" involved noxious uses of property. See *Hadacheck;* Miller v. Schoene, 276 U.S. 272 (1928); *Goldblatt.* See *ante,* at 125-127, 133.

the buildings in New York City for the general benefit of all its people. It is exactly this imposition of general costs on a few individuals at which the "taking" protection is directed. . . .

As Mr. Justice Holmes pointed out in Pennsylvania Coal Co. v. Mahon, "the question at bottom" in an eminent domain case "is upon whom the loss of the changes desired should fall." 260 U.S., at 416. The benefits that appellees believe will flow from preservation of the Grand Central Terminal will accrue to all the citizens of New York City. There is no reason to believe that appellants will enjoy a substantially greater share of these benefits. If the cost of preserving Grand Central Terminal were spread evenly across the entire population of the city of New York, the burden per person would be in cents per year — a minor cost appellees would surely concede for the benefit accrued. Instead, however, appellees would impose the entire cost of several million dollars per year on Penn Central. But it is precisely this sort of discrimination that the Fifth Amendment prohibits.

Appellees in response would argue that a taking only occurs where a property owner is denied all reasonable value of his property. The Court has frequently held that, even where a destruction of property rights would not otherwise constitute a taking, the inability of the owner to make a reasonable return on his property requires compensation under the Fifth Amendment. . . . But the converse is not true. A taking does not become a noncompensable exercise of police power simply because the government in its grace allows the owner to make some "reasonable" use of his property. . . .

Appellees, apparently recognizing that the constraints imposed on a landmark site constitute a taking for Fifth Amendment purposes, do not leave the property owner empty-handed. As the Court notes, *ante,* at 113-114, the property owner may theoretically "transfer" his previous right to develop the landmark property to adjacent properties if they are under his control. Appellees have coined this system "Transfer Development Rights," or TDR's.

Transferable development rights (TDR) programs are designed to "compensate" property owners whose equitable return on land investment has been lessened by regulatory activity. TDR programs treat development potential as just one of the bundle of rights implicit in fee ownership and sever it from the land allowing it to be transferred without transferring ownership itself. TDR programs establish two types of zones in a particular planning district: (1) conservation zones where development is restricted and (2) transfer zones which can handle increased density and serve as the receiving areas for transferred development potential. Originally, owners of land in both types of zones are allowed to develop their property in accordance with zoning laws, but when the government places a restriction on development (for such purposes as historic preservation, open-space and environmental protection, and urban land control) in the conservation zones, the land in the transfer zones are rezoned to absorb the development potential of the lots that are now prohibited from being developed. For example, if a planning district is divided into 100 lots, each of which is zoned for one residential unit, and the government then steps in and says that the 50 northern lots cannot be developed because they are on environmentally sensitive land which is now a haven for wildlife, then the 50 southern lots will be rezoned to allow two units to be built on each lot instead of one. The land owners of the northern lots will then sell their development rights to the land owners of the southern lots, and they will realize an equitable return on their investments. TDR programs balance the public's needs with the needs of property owners. They serve to protect valuable resources without using the taxpayers' money to compensate owners of restricted land, which would have to be spent if the land was simply "taken." A problem arises in the implementation of TDR programs, however, because development rights are often only allowed to be transferred to property owners in the adjacent receiving areas. TDRs are useless if those owners do not want to further develop their land. In a case like this, should the TDR program be altered to allow persons other than those who own land in the transfer zones to purchase development rights, or should the government be forced to abandon other alternatives and compensate owners of land which has been impermissibly taken? For further discussion of TDRs, see Frank Schnidman et al., Handling the Land Use Case §9.23 (1984 & Supp. 1988); Donald G. Hagman & Julian C. Juergensmeyer, Urban Planning and Land Development Control Law §11.6 (2d ed. 1986).

Of all the terms used in the Taking Clause, "just compensation" has the strictest meaning. The Fifth Amendment does not allow simply an approximate compensation but requires "a full and perfect equivalent for the property taken." . . . Because the record on appeal is relatively slim, I would remand to the Court of Appeals for a determination of whether TDR's constitute a "full and perfect equivalent for the property taken."

II

Over 50 years ago, Mr. Justice Holmes, speaking for the Court, warned that the courts were "in danger of forgetting that a strong public desire to improve the public condition is not enough to warrant achieving the desire by a shorter cut than the constitutional way of paying for the change." Pennsylvania Coal Co. v. Mahon, 260 U.S., at 416. The Court's opinion in this case demonstrates that the danger thus foreseen has not abated. The city of New York is in a precarious financial state, and some may believe that the costs of landmark preservation will be more easily borne by corporations such as Penn Central than the overburdened individual taxpayers of New York. But these concerns do not allow us to ignore past precedents construing the Eminent Domain Clause to the end that the desire to improve the public condition is, indeed, achieved by a shorter cut than the constitutional way of paying for the change.

NOTES AND QUESTIONS

1.   **Designing a statute to be (as) takings-proof (as possible).**[25] How was the New York landmarks statute designed to protect the Commission against takings challenges? (Note the three types of certificates available to landowners.)

2.   **Procedural due process protections.** The New York law was carefully drafted to protect against the charge that a landowner had been denied the opportunity to present its case, in violation of constitutional procedural due process guarantees. The law provided many opportunities for the landowner to be heard. Note that landowner did not seek judicial review either of the landmark designation or of the denial of two of the three types of certificates. What did it do instead? In retrospect, was this a wise litigation strategy? The issue of whether a landowner has properly exhausted all available administrative remedies became increasingly important in subsequent land use takings cases. See page 859, *infra.*

3.   **New York's "reasonable return" test.** The basic takings test under New York State law is that a restriction is invalid unless it leaves the landowner with a "reasonable return." The Supreme Court describes the New York courts' detailed analysis of the books of *Penn Central, supra.* How does this analysis relate to the "reasonable use left" test of Kaiser v. City and County of Honolulu and Just v. Marinette? Are local or federal tax exemptions relevant to a "reasonable return" calculation?

4.   **Social increment of value.** In the New York Court of Appeals' application of the reasonable return test in *Penn Central,* Chief Judge Breitel forwarded an innovative argument on behalf of the landmarks law.[26] 42 N.Y.2d 324, 366 N.E.2d 1271 (1977). He argued that the landmark laws did not deprive the property owners of all reasonable return on their investment, since a portion of that return was attributable to public investments in the area, and only the *privately created* component of property must receive a reasonable return:

> So many of [a building's] attributes are not the result of private effort or investment but of opportunities for the utilization or exploitation which an organized society offers to any private enterprise . . . favored by government and the public. These, too, constitute a background of massive social and governmental investment in the organized community without which the private enterprise could neither exist nor prosper. It is enough, . . . that the privately created ingredient of property receive a reasonable return. It is that privately created and privately managed ingredient which is the property on which the

---

25. As you read the Supreme Court cases *infra,* consider whether New York would be able to design a landmarks statute today with the same level of confidence that the statute was takings-proof.

26. See Charles D. Breitel, A Judicial View of Transferable Development Rights, Land Use L. & Zoning Dig., Feb. 1978, at 5-6.

reasonable return is to be based. All else is society's contribution by the sweat of its brow and the expenditure of its funds. To that extent society is also entitled to its due.

Id. at 328, 1273. The court went on to explain:

Grand Central Terminal is no ordinary landmark. It may be true that no property has economic value in the absence of the society around it, but how much more true it is of a railroad terminal, set amid a metropolitan population, and entirely dependent on a heavy traffic of travelers to make it an economically feasible operation. . . .

Of primary significance, however, is that society as an organized entity . . . has created much of the value of the terminal property. Although recent financial troubles and consequent governmental assistance make the fact more apparent, railroads have always been a franchised and regulated public utility, favored monopolies at public expense, subsidy, and with limited powers of eminent domain, without which their existence and character would not have been possible. . . .

Government has aided the terminal in less direct ways, as well. It is no accident that much of the city's mass transportation system converges on Grand Central. . . .

Absent this heavy public governmental investment in the terminal, the railroads, and connecting transportation, it is indisputable that the terminal property would be worth but a fraction of its current economic value. Plaintiffs may not now frustrate legitimate and important social objectives by complaining, in essence, that government regulation deprives them of a return on so much of the investment made not by private interests but by people of the city and State through their government. Instead, to prevail, plaintiffs must establish that there was no possibility of earning a reasonable return on the privately contributed ingredient of the property's value.

To put the matter another way, the massive and indistinguishable public, governmental and private contributions to a landmark like the Grand Central Terminal are inseparably joint, and for most of its existence, made both the terminal and the railroads of which it was an integral part, a great financial success for generations of stockholders and bondholders. . . . A fair return is to be accorded the owner, but society is to receive its due for its share in the making of a once great railroad.

Id. at 331-333, 1275-1276.

Is this argument still available, or did the Supreme Court rule it out of bounds? This argument dramatically changes the traditional focus in takings cases. The traditional focus assumes that all *increases* in value of a landowner's property automatically belong to the landowner. Because the "up-side" risks associated with landownership are silently allocated to the landowner, takings cases focus exclusively on the issue of where the "down-side" risks associated with landownership should be allocated. The traditional silence about the windfalls involved in landownership — that land increases in value because of governmental actions (for example, a new road is built right past it, or a subway stop opens, or a sewer system is built at the public expense) — can skew the discussion of how to allocate the "down-side risks" associated with downzonings, landmarks statutes, environmental protection programs. The *Penn Central* Court of Appeals decision is a rare instance in which both the windfalls and the wipeouts of landownership are kept simultaneously in focus. See Donald G. Hagman and Dean Misczynski, Windfalls for Wipeouts: Land Value Capture and Compensation (1987).

5. ***Euclid* and *Nectow* issues.** When the Supreme Court opinion finally gets down to applying the law to the facts of the case at hand, it breaks the discussion up into two separate issues. The first is the *Euclid* issue of whether a landmarks statute can *ever* be constitutional. The second is the *Nectow* issue of whether the statute was unconstitutional *as applied* in this case. Trace the basic outlines of each argument. The following questions follow up the somewhat confused majority opinion in greater detail.

6. **Economic impact on the landowner.** Isolate the various places in the majority opinion where the court discusses economic impact on the landowner. Does it use the New York reasonable return test? When it does so, does it undertake the kind of economic analysis undertaken by the Court of Appeals? Does it also use Holmes's diminution in value test? How do the two tests differ? Note that New York courts have continued to use their traditional "reasonable return" takings test, although subsequent Supreme Court cases rarely mention it. (Note, too, Rehnquist's explicit rejection of the test in the dissenting opinion.

7. **Police power language.** Note the Supreme Court's use of the kind of police power language we have already seen in earlier Supreme Court[27] as well as more modern state court cases.[28]

8. **"Ad hoc, factual inquiries."** Probably the most consistently quoted language from this decision is the assertion that takings cases involve "essentially ad hoc, factual inquiries."

9. **Distinct, investment-backed expectations.** In its long summary of takings law (much edited here, and criticized by Justice Rehnquist as inaccurate), the court inserts one test that had never before appeared in a takings case: the claim that a taking occurs when government actions interfere with distinct, investment-backed expectations. Brennan took this test from a law review article by his former law clerk Frank Michelman (now a Harvard Law School professor). Frank Michelman, Property, Utility, and Fairness: Comments on the Ethical Foundations of "Just Compensation" Law, 80 Harv. L. Rev. 1165, 1229-1234 (1967). Note that Brennan never applies the test, although (as we shall see) subsequent Supreme Court decisions attempt to do so. See page 876, *infra*.

---

27. In addition to *Euclid*, the following early Supreme Court opinions also contain strong police power language: Brandeis's *Pennsylvania Coal* dissent, see page 797, *supra;* *Mugler,* see page 800, *supra; Reinman,* page 818, *supra*.

28. State court cases with strong police power language include Just v. Marinette, see page 832, *supra*.

"I feel I should warn you. They've taken down most of Boston and they're putting up something else."

   10.   **Aesthetics as a valid public purpose: "to balance a 55-story office tower above a flamboyant Beaux-Arts facade seems nothing more than a joke."**[29] The seemingly bland statement about "what is not in dispute" that in fact played the important role of stating, for the first time in a Supreme Court case, that aesthetics was a valid public purpose. Until *Penn Central,* the issue had not been fully settled. Note that aesthetics is only one reason for landmarks statutes. Another rationale for landmarks statutes is the preservation of cultural memory. "Very few parcels of land in our largest cities . . . have not had as many as three different structures on them in the last hundred years," wrote an author in 1955, since which time many parcels have no doubt had yet a new structure built. See John Costonis, Icons and Aliens: Law, Aesthetics, and Environmental Change 107 (1989) (quoting Richard Nelson). In contrast to Europe, which has long had stringent

   29. Quote from the New York City Landmarks Commission, quoted in Richard F. Babcock and Charles L. Siemon, The Zoning Game Revisited 64 (1985).

preservation programs, this country's pro-development bias has made the preservation of the built environment difficult. This presents problems of cultural memory, as this cartoon suggests.

11. **Conceptual severance.** How do the railroad and Justice Rehnquist use the "bundle of rights" analysis of property law? Although the "bundle of rights" description initially was invented by legal realists, it increasingly has been used by landowners in what one commentator has called the "conceptual severance" argument. Margaret Jane Radin, The Liberal Conception of Property: Cross Currents in the Jurisprudence of Takings, 88 Colum. L. Rev. 1667, 1676 (1988). This argument harks back to Justice Holmes's argument in *Pennsylvania Coal* that the value of the coal company's property interest had been destroyed completely. But note the difference in context. In *Pennsylvania Coal,* the coal company only owned the coal and the support estate. How does that situation differ from the situation in *Penn Central?* The conceptual severance argument took on increasing importance in subsequent Supreme Court decisions: keep an eye out for it.

12. **Comparing zoning and landmarks statutes.** Consider the court's discussion of whether landmarks statutes are invalid on their face. It focuses on distinguishing between landmarks and zoning statutes. How are they different? How does the court address those differences?

13. **Back to *Pennsylvania Coal.*** Why does the Court argue that the landowner is benefited as well as burdened by the landmarks law? How does Justice Rehnquist respond? Which do you think is the stronger argument?

14. **Why me?** Note that Justice Rehnquist's powerful dissent starts right off with the "why me?" argument. And he never lets go; instead, he uses the powerful "why me?" argument throughout the opinion.

15. **Rehnquist's "nuisance exception."** The conceptual severance argument leaves Rehnquist with the conclusion that property rights have been totally destroyed. He then sets out the famous "nuisance exception." He begins with a long quote from Mugler v. Kansas and then goes on to cite other cases in which the Supreme Court had countenanced dramatic diminutions in value, usually in cases in which residential neighborhoods protested nuisance-like neighboring uses. In one such case, Hadacheck v. Sebastian, 239 U.S. 394 (1915), a court allowed a diminution in value from roughly $800,000 to $60,000, when a local ordinance forbade further excavation at a brickyard after local residents complained of dust, fumes, gases, soot, and steam, which caused occasional "sickness and serious discomfort." In another, Goldblatt v. Hempstead, 369 U.S. 590 (1962), a local ordinance closed down a quarry after complaints from a residential neighborhood. (Compare *Reinman,* also sometimes cited in this context.) These cases fit the pattern of extreme solicitude for residential neighborhoods we have seen in easement and covenant law. See §7.3.e. Also often cited in "nuisance exception" arguments is Miller v. Schoene, 276 U.S. 272 (1928). See page 826, *supra.*

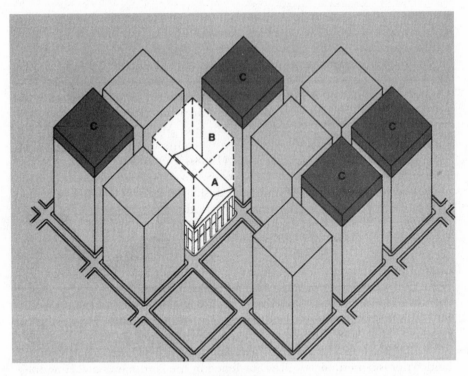

FIGURE 8-3
Transferable Development Rights Allow Taller Buildings to be Built

In their original context, these cases stood for a strong police power defense of land use restrictions. How does Justice Rehnquist use them? (Regardless of whether you agree with Justice Rehnquist, you have to admire his dazzlingly creative use of these cases.)

16.   **Transfer of development rights.** Once he has established that the New York landmarks statute does not fall within the nuisance exception, Rehnquist works the average reciprocity of advantage discussion up into an insistent "why me?" argument, and begins by using the landmarks law's transferable development rights (TDR) program very differently from the way Brennan uses it. How does each opinion use the program?

17.   *United Artists.* One famous case striking down a historic landmarks program was United Artists Theater Circuit, Inc. v. Philadelphia Historical Commn., 595 A.2d 6 (Pa. 1991). In it, the Pennsylvania Supreme Court ruled that a Philadelphia city ordinance that designated a local theater as a historic landmark violated the state constitution and amounted to a taking. The case caused quite a stir in the historic preservation community, which breathed a sigh of relief when the Pennsylvania Supreme Court agreed to a reargument of the case. In a new opinion, 635 A.2d 612 (1993), the highest Pennsylvania court noted that "no other state

has broken with the *Penn Central* decision," and held that no taking had occured. The Pennsylvania court nonetheless struck down the landmark designation on the grounds that the Historical Commission had exceeded its statutory authority.

2.   The Procedural Tango, 1980-1986

The 1980s marked the emergence of an increasingly organized "property rights" movement led by litigators focused on changing takings law. The legal history of this era has not yet been written, but some elements of the "property rights"[30] revolution can be set out.[31]

The Reagan Justice Department under Attorney General Edwin Meese was one institutional base of the movement. Key participants were Roger Marzulla and his former special assistant Mark Pollot. Their crowning achievement was Executive Order 12630, which wrote the antiregulatory takings position into federal government policy.[32] Exec. Order No. 12630, 3 C.F.R. 554 (1989).

A major source of the impetus behind the property rights position came from resistance to environmental legislation of the 1970s and 1980s. As of 1980, the Supreme Court's famous *Carolene Products* footnote, United States v. Carolene Products Co., 304 U.S. 144 (1938), had for over 40 years been interpreted to preclude Supreme Court review of economic legislation — hence it is not surprising that the Supreme Court had not heard a single land use case during that period. But property rights advocates refused to be discouraged by the ever-so-settled state of both takings law, and the Supreme Court's adamant refusal to review economic legislation. Using creative and often audacious arguments that reopened settled understandings — much as the legal services lawyers of the landlord-tenant revolution

---

30. Note the art in the "property rights" slogan: Who, in the United States, is *against* property rights? To call the movement "anti-environmental," or even "antiregulatory," would cast it in a very different light. We will sometimes call the movement "pro-property rights" and sometimes "antiregulatory" to remind students of the two perspectives on this issue.

31. We have focused in the text on litigators, but as of the mid-1980s a grass-roots property rights movement arose as well. One example was the Wise Use Coalition, whose founder Ron Allen has said that his goal is "to eradicate the environmental movement." See Tom Horton, This Land Is My Land, Mid-Atlantic Country, May 1993, 23, 23-24. This position may be extreme, but property rights activists typically feel that the environmental movement has gone too far. The Wise Use Agenda (1989) sets out 25 major goals, including eliminating restrictions on wetlands, opening all public lands to mineral and energy development, and severely limiting the Endangered Species Act.

32. The career paths of these players may interest students. Marzulla was President of the Mountain States Legal Foundation before joining the Justice Department, where he was an Assistant Attorney in charge of the Environment and Natural Resources Division of the United States Justice Department. After he left the government he joined the law firm of Akin, Gump, Strauss, Hauer & Feld to head their environmental department. After Pollott left Justice, he went to the law firm of Keck, Mahin & Cate, in San Francisco, where he also consults for the Pacific Legal Foundation. A third key participant was University of Chicago Law Professor Richard Epstein, a long-time property rights advocate and theorist who has long worked in the area of property law. See, e.g., Richard Epstein, Takings: Private Property and the Power of Eminent Domain (1985).

had done in the 1960s and 1970s — this new group of reformers transformed takings law into a potent tool for challenging the constitutionality
of environmental and other regulation. One reason for the preeminence
of the Pacific Legal Foundation[33] may have been the character of California
land use planning law. Even some preeminent land use planning advocates
have argued that state courts at times have not provided an adequate check
on land use planning in California. Norman Williams noted that "practically anything goes," see Norman Williams, American Land Planning Law
§6.03 (1974); long-time land use lawyers and advocates Richard Babcock
and Charles Siemon described the situation as follows:

> What *can* one say about the California courts other than one has to be a mad-
> man to challenge a government regulation in that bizarre jurisdiction? . . .
> California has always been notorious for being the first jurisdiction to sustain
> extreme municipal regulations. Practitioners in other states have joked about
> why a developer would sue a California community when it would cost a lot
> less and save much time if he simply slit his throat.

Richard Babcock and Charles Siemon, The Zoning Game Revisited 257,
293 (1985) (emphasis in original).

A third impetus behind the takings revolution came from lawyers for
businesspeople who built homes and otherwise developed property. Here
the key institutional base was a Washington, D.C., trade association, the
National Association of Home Builders. Gus Bauman, who worked at the
legal department of the National Homebuilders, filed amicus curiae briefs
in many Supreme Court takings cases before he went to the law firm of
Beveridge & Diamond, where he continued to litigate on behalf of real
estate developers. He currently is also the Chairman of the Montgomery
County Planning Commission.

To discuss the takings revolution without mentioning these activists
gives as distorted a picture as to discuss the landlord-tenant revolution without discussing the legal services movement. The key points in both contexts
are that even settled law can change, that audacious arguments sometimes

---

33. Probably an even more important institutional base than the Reagan Justice Department for the property rights movement was the Pacific Legal Foundation. (There was
considerable cross-fertilization between the Reagan Justice Department and the Pacific Legal
Foundation. For example, Thomas E. Hookano, who wrote a number of takings briefs for the
Pacific Legal Foundation, had joined the Justice Department by the time *Nollan* was argued,
from which he filed a brief urging the Supreme Court to find a taking.) Robert K. Best, Ronald
A. Zumbrun, and Thomas A. Hookano, or some combination of the three, filed briefs for the
Pacific Legal Foundation in virtually every major Supreme Court takings case beginning in
1987. (The two exceptions are *Nollan*, in which Best argued the case for the landowner, and
San Diego in which Zumbrun and Hookano filed a brief for the San Diego Urban League.) The
Pacific Legal Foundation played a central role in identifying and developing suitable test cases
and may have paid the legal fees of some promising plaintiffs. Note that of the eight land use
takings cases the Supreme Court heard between 1980 and 1993, six originated in California.

win, and that good litigators approach the law as a malleable system of persuasion, rather than as a self-executing system of settled rules.[34]

The Supreme Court's performance in this pressure-cooker environment can best be described as baffled. Few, if any, of the justices had had
any substantial experience with land use cases — and, since land use law is
not a staple of the law school diet, few of their clerks probably had much
knowledge of land use law either. Yet the court was under tremendous
pressure to decide both when a taking occurred (with the only guidance
from former Supreme Court opinions being that a regulation was a taking
when it went "too far," *Pennsylvania Coal,* 260 U.S. at 415), and whether the
remedy for a taking was invalidation of the statute (the traditional remedy)
or whether money damages were available for the period when the unconstitutional statute had been in place.

The results of this heady mixture of innovation, determination, creativity, and ignorance was what two experts have called "the procedural
tango." Charles M. Haar and Michael Allan Wolf, Land-Use Planning 902
(4th ed. 1989). Land use professionals watched with increasing amusement
as the Supreme Court took four successive takings cases between 1980 and
1986, only to fail four times to reach the underlying issues of when a taking
occurred and whether monetary compensation is due when a regulation is
struck down as unconstitutional.

These cases retain important precedential value today, because they
establish the principle that a plaintiff forwarding a takings claim must be
dead sure that the case is ripe and ready for review before taking the case
to federal court on a takings claim. These cases indicate the procedural
requirements and the Supreme Court's bafflement in the face of the complex relationships established between developers and planning authorities
by contemporary planning mechanisms. In Agins v. Tiburon, 447 U.S. 255
(1980), the land was downzoned into a Residential Planned Development
and Open Space Zone, which allowed for one to five units per acre; greater
density was available depending on the quality and design of the development.[35] The second case, San Diego Gas & Electric Co. v. San Diego, 450

---

34. When lawyers act as counselors, as when a developer's lawyer gives an opinion in
the context of a real estate transaction, they necessarily (and properly) approach the law more
as a system of settled rules. See Chapter 12.

35. Presumably, in this situation, planning officials may have wanted development
placed in such a way as to allow the public to see the magnificent view the parcel offered. A
footnote in *Agins* notes that the city had begun eminent domain proceedings to acquire the
parcels but had later abandoned the proceedings (reimbursing the landowners for the costs
they incurred). *Agins,* 447 U.S. at 255 n.1.

Agins, today, is commonly cited as the source of the two-part test as to whether a zoning
law effects a taking:

The application of a general zoning law to particular property effects a taking if the
ordinance does not substantially advance legitimate state interests, see *Nectow v. Cam-*

FIGURE 8-4
Ad for Land at Issue in Agins v. Tiburon

U.S. 621 (1981), involved land bought by a power company to build a nuclear power plant and the interaction of planning and zoning. Here the city
had adopted an open-space plan that placed the power company land in
an open-space area, noting that the construction of a power plant would
not necessarily be incompatible with the open-space designation. The town
then tried to buy the land and failed, giving rise to the power company's
$6 million lawsuit for damages. The Supreme Court ultimately held that no
review was possible because the state courts had never determined whether
a taking had occurred — although they had not done so because of a California Supreme Court holding that invalidation of the offending statute
was the proper remedy in a takings context (apparently a final decision if
there ever was one). The third case, Williamson County Regional Planning
Commn. v. Hamilton Bank, 473 U.S. 172 (1985), involved an ordinance
that allowed for cluster development. The Supreme Court acknowledged
that the developer had "passed the *Agins* threshold" by submitting a development plan, but faulted its failure to seek variances waiving compliance
with planning rules, on the theory that such variances may well have been
granted by planning officials. (Indeed they may; for a discussion of variances, see Chapter 9.) The Supreme Court in *Hamilton Bank* also faulted
the developer for failing to sue for damages under established state procedure. Finally, in MacDonald, Sommer & Frates v. County of Yolo, 477 U.S.
340 (1986), the Court once again held that a developer whose initial proposal to develop a cornfield into a subdivision was rejected on the grounds

---

bridge, 277 U.S. 183, 188 (1928), or denies an owner economically viable use of his land,
see *Penn Central Transp. Co. v. New York City,* 438 U.S. 104, 138, n.36 (1978).

447 U.S. at 260.

that it did not provide adequate road or sewer access, water supplies, fire or police protection, had not proceeded far enough in discussions with planning officials. Together, these four cases signalled that a developer must negotiate in good faith with planning officials and pursue all avenues of appeal before filing a takings challenge in federal court.

3.   *Loretto* (1982)

In Loretto v. Teleprompter Manhattan CATV Corp., 458 U.S. 419 (1982), the Court sought to lay down a per se rule that would result in a regulatory taking.

New York law required apartment landlords to permit the installation of cable television facilities in their buildings. The law barred landlords from demanding payment from the CATV company other than a one-time $1 fee. The facilities in question were a one-half inch cable above a building's roof top; directional taps, approximately 4 inches on a side; and two large boxes along the roof cable.

Justice Marshall, writing for the Court's 6 to 3 majority, concluded that a permanent physical occupation authorized by the government is a taking without regard to the public interests it might serve and without regard to how minor the occupation.

> The traditional rule also avoids otherwise difficult line-drawing problems. Few would disagree that if the State required landlords to permit third parties to install swimming pools on the landlords' rooftops for the convenience of the tenants, the requirement would be a taking. If the cable installation here occupied as much space, again, few would disagree that occupation would be a taking. But constitutional protection for the rights of private property cannot be made to depend on the size of the area permanently occupied.

458 U.S. at 436.

On remand, the New York Court of Appeals sent the compensation issue to the Commission on Cable Television, which awarded $1 in compensation, on the grounds that the availability of cable television would usually increase the building's value to tenants.

Loretto was sharply limited by Yee v. Escondito, 503 U.S. 519 (1992). *Escondito* involved a rent control ordinance that applied to mobile homeowners and to owners of mobile home parks. Rents were set at a 1986 level, and unapproved rent increases were prohibited; the ordinance set forth the factors to be considered in rent increases. Mobile homeowners contended that the ordinance in effect gave current tenants a permanent right to occupy their mobile home "pads." An interest in land — the right to occupy it at below-market rent — had been in effect transferred from the park owner to the mobile homeowner. The Court rejected the argument that this constituted a physical invasion of property. The fact that the ordinance transferred wealth from park owners to incumbent mobile homeowners was

FIGURE 8-5
Building at Issue in *Loretto*

not determinative, since many forms of regulation "can be said to transfer wealth from the one who is regulated to another." The Court held that "the government effects a physical taking only where it requires the landowner to submit to the physical occupation of the land." The Court noted that a "different case would be presented" if legislation compelled "a landowner over objection to rent his property or to refrain in perpetuity from terminating a tenancy."

4.   *First English* (1987)

In 1986, Antonin Scalia joined the Court. This brought a justice who would soon become the Court's chief advocate for the property rights movement and the author of several leading decisions that led the Court away from the direction it had taken since *Euclid.* Almost at once, the Court decided First English Evangelical Lutheran Church v. County of Los Angeles, 482 U.S. 304 (1987), in which the Court finally settled the issue it had ducked in the sequence beginning with *Agins:* whether an invalid regulation might entitle the landowner to damages on a theory that the landowner had suffered a temporary taking while the regulation was in effect. Without deciding if a taking had occurred in the instant case, the Court (Rehnquist, C.J.) declared that:

> Where this burden results from governmental action that amount[s] to a taking, the Just Compensation Clause of the Fifth Amendment requires that the government pay the landowner for the value of the use of the land during this period. . . . Invalidation of the ordinance . . . after this period of time, though converting the taking into a "temporary" one, is not a sufficient remedy to meed the demands of the Just Compensation Clause.

482 U.S. at 319.

This holding gave aggrieved landowners a potent legal weapon, since it sweetens the result of a successful claim. Even if the regulation is lifted as soon as a court declares it a taking, the owner can receive damages for the temporary loss.

A persistent issue is the period over which a court should measure the loss. See, e.g., Gregory M. Stein, Pinpointing the Beginning and Ending of a Temporary Regulatory Taking, 70 Wash. L. Rev. 953 (1995); Gregory S. Alexander, Takings, Narratives, and Power, 88 Colum. L. Rev. 1752, 1756-1760 (1998) (discussing alternative definitions of the effective moment).

5.   *Keystone* (1987)

KEYSTONE BITUMINOUS COAL ASSN. v. DEBENEDICTIS

480 U.S. 470 (1987)

Justice STEVENS delivered the opinion of the Court, in which BRENNAN, WHITE, MARSHALL, and BLACKMUN, JJ. joined. REHNQUIST, C.J., filed a dissenting opinion, in which POWELL, O'CONNOR, and SCALIA, JJ. joined.

In Pennsylvania Coal Co. v. Mahon, 260 U.S. 393 (1922), . . . the "particular facts" led the Court to hold that the Pennsylvania Legislature had gone beyond its constitutional powers when it enacted a statute prohibiting the mining of anthracite coal in a manner that would cause the subsidence of land on which certain structures were located.

Now, 65 years later, we address a different set of "particular facts," involving the Pennsylvania Legislature's 1966 conclusion that the Commonwealth's existing mine subsidence legislation had failed to protect the public interest in safety, land conservation, preservation of affected municipalities' tax bases, and land development in the Commonwealth. . . .

Coal mine subsidence . . . can have devastating effects. It often causes substantial damage to . . . the integrity of houses and buildings. Subsidence can also cause the loss of groundwater and surface ponds. In short, it presents the type of environmental concern that has been the focus of so much federal, state, and local regulation in recent decades. . . .[1]

II

In 1982, petitioners[36] [filed a petition contending that §4 and §6 of the Subsidence Act constituted a taking].

[The District Court rejected petitioner's takings claim, distinguishing this case from Pennsylvania Coal v. Mahon. Here, the Subsidence Act served valid public purposes — use of police power for the health, safety, and welfare of the general public. Answering petitioner's claim that a taking occurred because a recognized interest in realty was destroyed, the District Court concluded that under Pennsylvania law] the right to cause damage to the surface may constitute the most valuable "strand" in the bundle of rights was not controlling under our decision in Andrus v. Allard, 444 U.S. 51 (1979). . . . The Court of Appeals affirmed [agreeing that the Act was a legitimate means of protecting health, safety, and welfare. The Court of Appeals disagreed that the support estate itself constituted a bundle of rights, it concluded that the support estate was a segment of a larger bundle of rights that includes the surface estate].

1. Bituminous Mine Subsidence and Land Conservation Act (noting the Subsidence Act was implemented to minimize subsidence and regulate its consequences; §4 prohibits mining that causes subsidence to commercial and noncommercial buildings, human dwellings, and cemeteries, requiring 50% of the coal beneath these structures to be kept in place; §6 authorizes the revocation of a mining permit if removal of coal in §4 areas causes damage and where the operator has not repaired, satisfied a claim, or deposited a sum equivalent to the cost of repairs with the Department of Environmental Resources as security within six months. Although some subsidence eventually occurs over every underground mine, . . . the DER believes that the support provided by its 50% rule will last in almost all cases for the life of the structure being protected. Since 1966, [of the 14,000 structures mined under, there have been subsidence damage claims to only 300].

36. The petitioners were an association of coal mine operators and four corporations engaged in underground mining of bituminous coal in western Pennsylvania. The respondents were the Secretary of the DER, the Chief of the DER's Division of Mine Subsidence, and the Chief of the DER's Section on Mine Subsidence Regulation. — Eds.

III

. . . The holdings and assumptions of the court in *Pennsylvania Coal* provide obvious and necessary reasons for distinguishing *Pennsylvania Coal* from the case before us today. The two factors that the Court considered relevant, have become integral parts of our takings analysis. We have held that land use regulation can effect a taking if it "does not substantially advance legitimate state interests, . . . or denies an owner economically viable use of his land." Agins v. Tiburon, 447 U.S. 255, 260 (1980); see also Penn Central Transp. Co. v. New York City, 438 U.S. 104, 124 (1978). Application of these tests to petitioners' challenge demonstrates that they have not satisfied their burden of showing that the Subsidence Act constitutes a taking. First, unlike the Kohler Act, the character of the governmental action involved here leans heavily against finding a taking. Second, [there is no showing, as there was in *Pennsylvania Coal*,] that the Subsidence Act makes it impossible for petitioners to profitably engage in their business, or that there has been undue interference with their investment-backed expectations.

THE PUBLIC PURPOSE

Unlike the Kohler Act, which was passed upon in *Pennsylvania Coal*, the Subsidence Act does not merely involve a balancing of the private economic interests of coal companies against the private interests of the surface owners. The Pennsylvania Legislature specifically found that important public interests are served by enforcing a policy that is designed to minimize subsidence in certain areas. . . .

Moreover, in *Pennsylvania Coal*, the Court was forced to reject the Commonwealth's safety justification for the Kohler Act because it found that the Commonwealth's interest in safety could as easily have been accomplished through a notice requirement to landowners. The Subsidence Act, by contrast, is designed to accomplish a number of widely varying interests, with reference to which petitioners have not suggested alternative methods through which the Commonwealth could proceed. . . .

Thus, the Subsidence Act differs from the Kohler Act in critical and dispositive respects. With regard to the Kohler Act, the Court believed that the Commonwealth had acted only to ensure against damage to some private landowners' homes. Here, by contrast, the Commonwealth is acting to protect the public interest in health, the environment, and the fiscal integrity of the area. That private individuals erred in taking a risk cannot stop the Commonwealth from exercising its police power to abate activity akin to a public nuisance. The Subsidence Act is a prime example that "circumstances may so change in time . . . as to clothe with such a [public] interest what at other times . . . would be a matter of purely private concern." Block v. Hirsh, 256 U.S. 135, 155 (1921).

Many cases before and since *Pennsylvania Coal* have recognized that the nature of the State's action is critical in takings analysis. . . . [Opinion cites Mugler v. Kansas, Hadacheck v. Sebastian, Reinman v. Little Rock.]

The Court's hesitance to find a taking when the State merely restrains uses of property that are tantamount to public nuisances is consistent with the notion of "reciprocity of advantage" that Justice Holmes referred to in *Pennsylvania Coal.*[20] Under our system of government, one of the State's primary ways of preserving the public weal is restricting the uses individuals can make of their property. While each of us is burdened somewhat by such restrictions, we, in turn, benefit greatly from the restrictions that are placed on others.[21] See Penn Central Transp. Co. v. New York City, 438 U.S. at 144-150 (Rehnquist, J., dissenting). . . . Long ago it was recognized that "all property in this country is held under the implied obligation that the owner's use of it shall not be injurious to the community." Mugler v. Kansas, 123 U.S. at 665; . . . and the Takings Clause did not transform that principle to one that requires compensation whenever the State asserts its power to enforce it.[22] See *Mugler,* 123 U.S. at 664. . . .

DIMINUTION OF VALUE AND INVESTMENT-BACKED EXPECTATIONS

The second factor that distinguishes this case from *Pennsylvania Coal* is the finding in that case that the Kohler Act made mining of "certain coal" commercially impracticable. In this case, by contrast, petitioners have not shown any deprivation significant enough to satisfy the heavy burden placed upon one alleging a regulatory taking. For this reason, their takings claim must fail.

In addressing petitioners' claim we must not disregard the posture in which this case comes before us. The District Court granted summary judgment to respondents only on the facial challenge to the Subsidence Act. . . .Thus, "*the only question before this court is whether the mere enactment of the statutes and regulations constitutes a taking.*" 581 F. Supp. at 513 [emphasis added]. . . .

---

20. The special status of this type of state action can also be understood on the simple theory that since no individual has a right to use his property so as to create a nuisance or otherwise harm others, the State has not "taken" anything when it asserts its power to enjoin the nuisance-like activity. . . .

21. The Takings Clause has never been read to require the States or the courts to calculate whether a specific individual has suffered burdens under this generic rule in excess of the benefits received. Not every individual gets a full dollar return in benefits for the taxes he or she pays; yet, no one suggests that an individual has a right to compensation for the differences between taxes paid and the dollar value of benefits received.

22. Courts have consistently held that a State need not provide compensation when it diminishes or destroys the value of property by stopping illegal activity or abating a public nuisance. It is hard to imagine a different rule that would be consistent with the maxim "*sic utere tuo ut alienum non laedas*" (use your own property in such manner as not to injure that of another). . . .

Petitioners thus face an uphill battle in making a facial attack on the Act as a taking. The hill is made especially steep because petitioners have not claimed, at this stage, that the Act makes it commercially impracticable for them to continue mining their bituminous coal interests in western Pennsylvania. Indeed, petitioners have not even pointed to a single mine that can no longer be mined for profit. The only evidence available on the effect that the Subsidence Act has had on petitioners' mining operations indicates that on 13 mines that the various companies operate, . . . they have been required to leave a bit less than 27 million tons of coal in place to support Sec. 4 areas. The total coal in those 13 mines amounts to over 1.46 billion tons. . . . Thus Sec. 4 requires them to leave less than 2% of their coal in place. . . . But, as we have indicated, nowhere near all of the underground coal is extractable even aside from the Subsidence Act. . . . [T]here is no information in the record as to how much coal is actually left in the ground *solely* because of Sec. 4. We do know, however, that petitioners have never claimed that their mining operations, or even any specific mines, have been unprofitable since the Subsidence Act was passed. . . .

Instead, petitioners have sought to narrowly define certain segments of their property and assert that, when so defined, the Subsidence Act denies them economically viable use. They advance two alternative ways of carving their property in order to reach this conclusion. First, they focus on the specific tons of coal that they must leave in the ground under the Subsidence Act, and argue that the Commonwealth has effectively appropriated this coal since it has no other useful purpose if not mined. Second, they contend that the Commonwealth has taken their separate legal interest in property — the "support estate."

Because our test for regulatory taking requires us to compare the value that has been taken from the property with the value that remains in the property, one of the critical questions is determining how to define the unit of property "whose value is to furnish the denominator of the fraction." In *Penn Central* the Court explained:

> "Taking" jurisprudence does not divide a single parcel into discrete segments and attempt to determine whether rights in a particular segment have been entirely abrogated. In deciding whether a particular governmental action has effected a taking, this Court focuses rather both on the character of the action and on the nature of the interference with rights *in the parcel as a whole* — here the city tax block designated as the "landmark site."

438 U.S. at 130-131. Similarly, in Andrus v. Allard, 444 U.S. 51 (1979), we held that "where an owner possesses a full 'bundle' of property rights, the destruction of one 'strand' of the bundle is not a taking because the aggregate must be viewed in its entirety." Id. at 65-66. Although these verbal formulations do not solve all of the definitional issues that may arise in defining the relevant mass of property, they do provide sufficient guidance to compel us to reject petitioners' arguments.

THE COAL IN PLACE

The parties have stipulated that enforcement of the DER's 50% rule will require petitioners to leave approximately 27 million tons of coal in place. Because they own that coal but cannot mine it, they contend that Pennsylvania has appropriated it for the public purposes described in the Subsidence Act.

. . . This argument fails for the reason explained in *Penn Central* and *Andrus*. The 27 million tons of coal do not constitute a separate segment of property for takings law purposes. Many zoning ordinances place limits on the property owner's right to make profitable use of some segments of his property. A requirement that a building occupy no more specified percentage of the lot on which it is located could be characterized as a taking of the vacant area as readily as the requirement that coal pillars be left in place. Similarly, under petitioners' theory one could always argue that a setback ordinance requiring that no structure be built within a certain distance from the property line constitutes a taking because the footage represents a distinct segment of property for takings law purposes. . . . There is no basis for treating the less than 2% of petitioners' coal as a separate parcel of property.

The record indicates that only about 75% of petitioners' underground coal can be profitably mined in any event, and there is no showing that petitioners' reasonable "investment-backed expectations" have been materially affected by the additional duty to retain the small percentage that must be used to support the structures protected by Sec. 4.[27]

THE SUPPORT ESTATE

Pennsylvania property law is apparently unique in regarding the support estate as a separate interest in land that can be conveyed apart from either the mineral estate or the surface estate. Petitioners therefore argue that even if comparable legislation in another State would not constitute a taking, the Subsidence Act has that consequence because it entirely destroys the value of their unique support estate. It is clear, however, that our takings jurisprudence forecloses reliance on such legalistic distinctions within a bundle of property rights. . . .

The Court of Appeals, which is more familiar with Pennsylvania law than we are, concluded that as a practical matter the support estate is always owned by either the owner of the surface or the owner of the minerals. . . .

---

27. We do not suggest that the State may physically appropriate relatively small amounts of private property for its own use without paying just compensation. The question here is whether there has been any taking at all when no coal has been physically appropriated, and the regulatory program places a burden on the use of only a small fraction of the property that is subjected to regulation. . . .

Thus, in practical terms, the support estate has value only insofar as it protects or enhances the value of the estate with which it is associated. Its value is merely a part of the entire bundle of rights possessed by the owner of either the coal or the surface. Because petitioners retain the right to mine virtually all of the coal in their mineral estates, the burden the Act places on the support estate does not constitute a taking. Petitioners may continue to mine coal profitably even if they may not destroy or damage surface structures at will in the process. . . .

The judgment of the Court of Appeals is affirmed.

Chief Justice REHNQUIST, with whom Justice POWELL, Justice O'CONNOR, and Justice SCALIA join, dissenting.

More than 50 years ago, this Court determined the constitutionality of Pennsylvania's Kohler Act as it affected the property interests of coal mine operators. . . . The Bituminous Mine Subsidence and Land Conservation Act approved today effects an interference with such interests in a strikingly similar manner. The Court finds at last two reasons why this case is different. First, we are told, "the character of the governmental action involved here leans heavily against finding a taking." Ante, at 485. Second, the Court concludes that the Subsidence Act neither "makes it impossible for petitioners to profitably engage in their business," nor involves "undue interference with [petitioners'] investment-backed expectations." Ibid. Neither of these conclusions persuades me that this case is different, and I believe that the Subsidence Act works as a taking of petitioners' property interests. I therefore dissent.

. . . There can be no doubt that the Kohler Act was intended to serve public interests. . . . When considering the protection of the "single private house" owned by the Mahons, the Court noted that "[n]o doubt there is a *public* interest even in this." Id. at 414. . . . The strong public interest in the stability of streets and cities, however, was insufficient to warrant achieving the desire by a shorter cut than the constitutional way of paying for the change." Ibid. Thus, the Court made clear that the mere existence of a public purpose was insufficient to release the government from the compensation requirement. . . .

The Subsidence Act rests on similar public purposes. . . . The legislature determined that the prevention of subsidence would protect surface structures, advance the economic future and well-being of Pennsylvania, and ensure the safety and welfare of the Commonwealth's residents. Ibid. Thus, it is clear that the Court has severely understated the similarity of purpose between the Subsidence Act and the Kohler Act. The public purposes in this case are not sufficient to distinguish it from *Pennsylvania Coal.* . . .

The similarity of the public purpose of the present Act to that in *Pennsylvania Coal* does not resolve the question of whether a taking has occurred; the existence of such a public purpose is merely a necessary prerequisite to

the government's exercise of its taking power. . . . The *nature* of these purposes may be relevant, for we have recognized that a taking does not occur
where the government exercises its unquestioned authority to prevent a
property owner from using his property to injure others without having
to compensate the value of the forbidden use. [See Goldblatt v. Hempstead, Hadacheck v. Sebastian, Mugler v. Kansas; see generally Penn Central
Transp. Co. v. New York City (Rehnquist, J., dissenting).] The Court today
indicates that this "nuisance exception" alone might support its conclusion
that no taking has occurred. . . . This statute is not the type of regulation
that our precedents have held to be within the "nuisance exception" to
takings analysis.

      . . . "The nuisance exception to the taking guarantee," however, "is
not coterminous with the police power itself," *Penn Central Transp., supra,*
at 145 (Rehnquist, J., dissenting), but is a narrow exception allowing the
government to prevent "a misuse or illegal use." Curtin v. Benson, 222 U.S.
78, 86 (1911). . . . [O]ur cases applying the "nuisance" rationale have
involved at least two narrowing principles. First, nuisance regulations exempted from the Fifth Amendment have rested on discrete and narrow purposes. See Goldblatt v. Hempstead, *supra;* Hadacheck v. Sebastian, *supra;*
Mugler v. Kansas, *supra.* The Subsidence Act, however, is much more than
a nuisance statute. The central purposes of the Act, though including
public safety, reflect a concern for preservation of buildings, economic
development, and maintenance of property values to sustain the Commonwealth's tax base. We should hesitate to allow a regulation based on essentially economic concerns to be insulated from the dictates of the Fifth
Amendment by labeling it nuisance regulation.

      Second, and more significantly, our cases have never applied the
nuisance exception to allow complete extinction of the value of a parcel
of property. Though nuisance regulations have been sustained despite a
substantial reduction in value, we have not accepted the proposition that
the State may completely extinguish a property interest or prohibit all
use without providing compensation. . . . [Citing *Mugler, Miller,* and *Penn
Central.*] . . .

      " 'For practical purposes, the right to coal consists in the right to mine
it.' " *Pennsylvania Coal,* 260 U.S. at 414. From the relevant perspective —
that of the property owners — this interest has been destroyed every bit as
much as if the government had proceeded to mine the coal for its own use.
The regulation, then, does not merely inhibit one strand in the bundle . . . ,
but instead destroys completely any interest in a segment of property. In
these circumstances, I think it unnecessary to consider whether petitioners
may operate individual mines or their overall mining operations profitably, for they have been denied all use of 27 million tons of coal. I would
hold that Sec. 4 of the Subsidence Act works a taking of these property
interests. . . .

      In sum, I would hold the Act works to extinguish petitioners' interest in at least 27 million tons of coal by requiring that coal to be left in the ground, and destroys their purchased support estates by returning to them financial liability for subsidence. I respectfully dissent. . . .

NOTES AND QUESTIONS

1. **What made _Keystone_ an awkward case for the majority?** How does Rehnquist use this to his advantage?

2. **The effect of the environmental movement.** One major change between _Pennsylvania Coal_ and _Keystone_ was the rise of the environmental movement. How is this cultural shift reflected in the majority opinion? This is another example of the porous boundary between law and (other forms of?) politics. How does the environmental movement help both the Pennsylvania legislature and Justice Stevens respond to Justice Holmes's characterization of the Kohler Act case as involving "a single private house?"

3. **Andrus v. Allard.** How does the majority opinion use the Andrus v. Allard case? See §1.1.

4. **Nuisance cases.** How does the majority opinion use the so-called nuisance cases (_Mugler, Hadacheck, Reinman,_ Miller v. Schoene, _Goldblatt_)?

5. **Rehnquist's use of nuisance cases.** How does Rehnquist use them?

6. **Takings test.** Which of Holmes's takings tests does the majority opinion apply?

7. **Narrow and broad readings of _Keystone._** What is the narrowest reading you could give _Keystone_ if you were representing a landowner in a takings case? What is the broadest reading?

8. **Economic impact.** How does the majority define the economic impact on the landowner? How does the dissent? Note that the majority adopts the distinct investment-backed expectations test.

9. **Conceptual severance.** What appears to be the status of the conceptual severance argument after _Keystone?_

10. **Limiting regulation power.** How does Rehnquist limit government's ability to regulate even those uses that fall within the nuisance exception?

11. **Nuisance cases.** The following cases are cited frequently throughout the chapter. It will be helpful for you to keep their fact patterns in mind when reading excerpts from their decisions.

In Mugler v. Kansas, 123 U.S. 623 (1887), the plaintiff, an owner of a brewery, challenged the constitutionality of a liquor prohibition statute that substantially devalued his property. The court upheld the statute, finding that no taking is effected by a statute restricting the use of property in an effort to protect the health, morals, or safety of a community.

The power which the States have of prohibiting such use by individuals of their property as will be prejudicial to the health, the morals, or the safety of

the public, is not — and, consistently with the existence and safety of organized society, cannot be — burdened with the condition that the State must
compensate such individual owners for pecuniary losses they may sustain, by
reason of their not being permitted, by a noxious use of their property, to
inflict injury upon the community. The exercise of the police power by the
destruction of property which is itself a public nuisance, or the prohibition of
its use in a particular way, whereby its value becomes depreciated, is very different from taking property for public use, or from depriving a person of his
property without due process of the law. In one case, a nuisance is only abated;
in the other, unoffending property is taken away from an innocent owner.

In Reinman v. City of Little Rock, 237 U.S. 171 (1915), the plaintiff,
an owner of a livery stable, challenged a local ordinance that prohibited the
operation of livery stables in close proximity to populated areas. In upholding the ordinance, the Court validated the government's power to regulate
and restrict otherwise lawful activities that are not a nuisance per se.

> Therefore the argument that a livery stable is not a nuisance per se, which is
> much insisted on by plaintiffs in error, is beside the question. Granting that it
> is not a nuisance per se, it is clearly within the police power of the State to
> regulate the business and to that end to declare that in particular circum-
> stances and in particular localities a livery stable shall be deemed a nuisance
> in fact and in law, provided this power is not exerted arbitrarily, or with unjust
> discrimination, so as to infringe upon rights guaranteed by the Fourteenth
> Amendment. For no question is made, and we think none could be reasonably
> be made, but that the general subject of the regulation of livery stables, with
> respect to their location and the manner in which they are to be conducted
> in a thickly populated city, is well within the range of the power of the State to
> legislate for the health and general welfare of the people.

Goldblatt v. Town of Hempstead, 369 U.S. 590 (1962), is a more recent case in which the owner of a gravel pit challenged the constitutionality
of a town ordinance prohibiting the use of property as a sand or gravel
mine. The Court upheld the ordinance as a valid exercise of legislative authority in regulating to restrict the use of property in a manner harmful to
the general welfare.

> The Town of Hempstead has enacted an ordinance regulating dredging and
> pit excavating on property within its limits. . . . Concededly the ordinance
> completely been devoted. However, such a characterization does not tell us
> whether or not the ordinance is unconstitutional. . . . If this ordinance is oth-
> erwise a valid exercise of the town's police powers, the fact it deprives the prop-
> erty of its beneficial use does not render it unconstitutional. . . . Nor is it of the
> controlling significance . . . that the use prohibited is arguably not a common-
> nuisance, e.g., Reinman v. Little Rock. . . .

Hadacheck v. Sebastian, 239 U.S. 394 (1915), involved a challenge to a Los Angeles city ordinance that prohibited brick making in residential areas. The owner of the property had lawfully operated a brickyard on the premises before the ordinance was passed. The Court ruled that the ordinance effected no taking and was within the charter powers of the city in protecting the public health and safety.

> [Like Reinman v. City of Little Rock,] . . . petitioner . . . asserts that a necessary and lawful occupation that is not a nuisance per se cannot be made so by legislative declaration. There was a like investment in property, encouraged by the then conditions; a like reduction of value and deprivation of property was asserted against the validity of the ordinance there considered; a like assertion of an arbitrary exercise of the power of prohibition. Against all of these contentions, and causing the rejection of them all, was adduced the police power. There was a prohibition of business, lawful in itself, there as here. It was a livery stable there; a brick yard here. They differ in particulars, but they are alike in that which cause and justify prohibition in defined localities — that is, the effect upon the health and comfort of the community. . . . The only limitation upon the police [is] that the power [can] not be exerted arbitrarily or with unjust discrimination. . . .

6.   *Lucas* (1992)

In 1991, Justice Thurgood Marshall resigned after 24 years on the Supreme Court and was replaced by Justice Clarence Thomas. This solidified the property rights/antiregulation block on the Supreme Court and led quickly to Lucas v. South Carolina Coastal Council, 505 U.S. 1003 (1992). As you read *Lucas,* consider whether it overturns any of the state or federal law we have studied up to this point.

Lucas brings the question of environmentally sensitive land into sharp focus. In 1988, South Carolina (pursuant to the federal Coastal Zone Management Act) passed the Beachfront Management Act, which severely limited new construction and reconstruction of damaged buildings near the beach along the state's 180-mile coastline. The legislation, citing concerns about erosion and shifting shorelines, sought to prevent construction in certain high-erosion beach areas that were under water at least once during the previous 40 years. A Closer Look at *Lucas v. South Carolina Coastal Council,* Mich. Law. Wkly., June 28, 1993, at 25. For example, in Hurricane Hazel in 1954, 27 of 29 houses on the southern end of Pawleys Island, 60 miles northeast of Charleston, were destroyed. "The area is an example of a high-risk zone that should never have been developed, and certainly not redeveloped after the storm," according to Prof. Orrin H. Pilkey, a geologist at Duke University and an outspoken opponent of beach development. Peter Applebome, After Hugo, A Storm over Beach Development, N.Y. Times,

Sept. 24, 1989, at 1. One feature of the Beachfront Management Act was to prohibit construction or reconstruction of substantially destroyed[37] houses that are less than 20 feet from the first row of dunes, or 40 times the annual beach erosion rate in the area, whichever is greater. More than 800 structures on the South Carolina coastline are either totally or partially in this so-called dead zone; erosion (in some place occurring at the rate of six inches a year) may well add many others to the list. Id. Particularly after Hurricane Hugo in September 1989, owners of beachfront property objected to this rule. "It would have been nice if they came in here 40 years ago and said 'You all sit back 40 feet, you all sit back 100 feet,'" said one. "That would have been beautiful, but you can't do that today." Applebome, *supra.*

The problem of shifting shorelines is well illustrated by the Isle of Palms, the barrier island where David Lucas, the plaintiff below, owned two beachfront lots. The Lucas lots are now on dry land and surrounded by houses worth hundreds of thousands of dollars. At various times since the late 1940s, the shoreline has at times been 200 feet or more inland from where it is today. Sometimes part of the Lucas lots have been on the beach or even under water. See Cornelia Dean, When a Shoreline Home May Be a Nuisance, N.Y. Times, July 4, 1992, at 6.

LUCAS v. SOUTH CAROLINA COASTAL COUNCIL

505 U.S. 1003 (1992)[38]

Scalia, J., delivered the opinion of the Court, in which Rehnquist, C.J., and White, O'Connor, and Thomas, JJ., joined. Kennedy, J., filed an opinion concurring in the judgment. Blackmun, J., and Stevens, J., filed dissenting opinions. Souter, J., filed a separate statement.

In 1986, petitioner David H. Lucas paid $975,000 for two residential lots on the Isle of Palms in Charleston County, South Carolina, on which he intended to build single-family homes. In 1988, however, the South Carolina Legislature enacted the Beachfront Management Act, S.C. Code §48-39-250 et seq. which had the direct effect of barring petitioner from erecting any permanent habitable structures on his two parcels. A state trial court found that this prohibition rendered Lucas's parcels "valueless." This case requires us to decide whether the Act's dramatic effect on the eco-

---

37. An owner is entitled to reconstruct a house in the dead zone so long as it is at least 33 percent intact after a storm. The law assigns percentages to structural systems within a house — the foundation, the load-bearing walls, and the roof, for example. F. Housley Carr and Michael May, Hugo's $3-billion Punch Puts State Coastal Management Law to the Test, 233 Eng'g-News Rec. 10 (Sept. 28, 1989).

38. Amicus curiae briefs were filed by Sierra Club, South Carolina Wildlife Federation, NCNB Bank of South Carolina, and Pacific Legal Foundation.

nomic value of Lucas's lots accomplished a taking of private property under the Fifth and Fourteenth Amendments requiring the payment of "just
compensation." . . .

I

[The South Carolina Beachfront Management Act] . . . required owners of coastal zone land that qualified as a "critical area" to obtain a permit
from the newly created South Carolina Coastal Council (respondent here)
prior to committing the land to a "use other than the use the critical area
was devoted to on [September 28, 1977]." . . .

Lucas in 1986 purchased the two lots at issue in this litigation, . . . [n]o
portion of the lots . . . qualified as a "critical area" under the 1977 Act;
[therefore] he was not legally obliged to obtain a permit from the Council
in advance of any development activity. . . .

The Beachfront Management Act brought Lucas's plans to an abrupt
end. Under that 1988 legislation, the Council was directed to establish a
"baseline" connecting the landward-most "point[s] of erosion . . . during
the past forty years" in the region of the Isle of Palms that includes Lucas's
lots. §48-39-280(A)(2) (1988). In action not challenged here, the Council
fixed this baseline landward of Lucas's parcels. That was significant, for under the Act construction of occupiable improvements was flatly prohibited
seaward of a line drawn 20 feet landward of, and parallel to, the baseline. . . . The Act provided no exceptions.

Lucas promptly filed suit in the South Carolina Court of Common
Pleas, contending that the Beachfront Management Act's construction bar
effected a taking of his property without just compensation. Lucas did not
take issue with the validity of the Act as a lawful exercise of South Carolina's
police power, but contended that the Act's complete extinguishment of his
property's value entitled him to compensation regardless of whether the
legislature had acted in furtherance of legitimate police power objectives.
[Following a bench trial, the court agreed that when Lucas purchased the
property it was zoned for single-family residential construction with no restrictions but, with the enactment of the Beachfront Management Act, Lucas was "deprived [] of any reasonable economic use of the lots." Id. at 37.]

The Supreme Court of South Carolina reversed. It found dispositive
what it described as Lucas's concession "that the Beachfront Management
Act [was] properly and validly designed to preserve . . . South Carolina's
beaches." 304 S.C. 376, 379, 404 S.E. 2d 895, 896 (1991). Failing an attack on
the validity of the statute as such, the court believed itself bound to accept
the "uncontested . . . findings" of the South Carolina legislature that new
construction in the coastal zone — such as petitioner intended — threatened this public resource. The Court ruled that when a regulation respecting the use of property is designed "to prevent serious public harm,"
(citing, inter alia, Mugler v. Kansas, 123 U.S. 623 (1887)), no compensation

FIGURE 8-6
Damaged Beach House

is owing under the Takings Clause regardless of the regulation's effect on the property's value.

We granted certiorari. [Council suggests that this case is inappropriate for plenary review because . . . the Act was amended to allow issuances of "special permits," rendering Lucas's claims of a permanent deprivation unripe. We disagree because the South Carolina Supreme Court preferred to dispose of Lucas's takings claim on the merits not on ripeness grounds. This does not preclude Lucas from applying for a permit under the amendment but Lucas had no reason to proceed on a "temporary taking" theory because the Act then read the taking as unconditional and permanent. . . .Therefore, we think it would be unfair to force Lucas to pursue the special permit process when he has properly alleged Article III injury-in-fact in this case.]

III

[O]ur decision in *Mahon* offered little insight into when, and under what circumstances, a given regulation would be seen as going "too far" for purposes of the Fifth Amendment. In 70-odd years of succeeding "regulatory takings" jurisprudence, we have generally eschewed any "'set formula'" for determining how far is too far, preferring to "engage in . . . essentially ad hoc, factual inquiries," Penn Central Transportation Co. v. New York City, 438 U.S. 104, 124 (1978) (quoting Goldblatt v. Hempstead, 369 U.S. 590, 594 (1962)). We have, however, described at least two discrete categories of regulatory action as compensable without case-specific inquiry into the public interest advanced in support of the restraint. The first encompasses regulations that compel the property owner to suffer a physical "invasion" of his property . . . [citing *Loretto*].

The second situation in which we have found categorical treatment appropriate is where regulation denies all economically beneficial or productive use of land.[6] See *Agins*, 447 U.S., at 260; see also Nollan v. California Coastal Comm'n, 483 U.S. 825, 834 (1987); Keystone Bituminous Coal Assn. v. DeBenedictis, 480 U.S. 470, 495 (1987); . . . As we have said on numerous occasions, the Fifth Amendment is violated when land-use regulation "does not substantially advance legitimate state interests or *denies an owner economically viable use of his land.*" *Agins, supra,* at 260 [emphasis added].[7]

We have never set forth the justification for this rule. Perhaps it is simply, as Justice Brennan suggested, that total deprivation of beneficial use is, from the landowner's point of view, the equivalent of a physical appropriation. See San Diego Gas & Electric Co. v. San Diego, 450 U.S., at 652

---

6. We will not attempt to respond to all of Justice Blackmun's mistaken citation of case precedent. . . . The cases say, repeatedly and unmistakably, that "'the test to be applied in considering [a] facial [takings] challenge is fairly straightforward. A state regulating the uses that can be made of property effects a taking if it "denies an owner economically viable use of his land."'" *Keystone*, 480 U.S., at 495 (quoting *Hodel*, 452 U.S., at 295-296 (quoting *Agins*, 447 U.S., at 260)).

Justice Blackmun describes that rule (which we do not invent but merely apply today) as "altering the long-settled rules of review" by foisting on the State "the burden of showing [its] regulation is not a taking." Post, at 11, 12. This is of course wrong. Lucas had to do more than simply file a lawsuit to establish his constitutional entitlement; he had to show that the Beachfront Management Act denied him economically beneficial use of his land. Our analysis presumes the unconstitutionality of state land-use regulation only in the sense that any rule-with-exceptions presumes the invalidity of a law that violates it — . . . Justice Blackmun's real quarrel is with the substantive standard of liability we apply in this case, a long-established standard we see no need to repudiate.

7. Regrettably, the rhetorical force of our "deprivation of all economically feasible use" rule is greater than its precision, since the rule does not make clear the "property interest" against which the loss of value is to be measured. Unsurprisingly, this uncertainty regarding the composition of the denominator in our "deprivation" fraction has produced inconsistent pronouncements by the Court. Compare Pennsylvania Coal Co. v. Mahon, 260 U.S. 393, 414 (1922), with Keystone Bituminous Coal Assn. v. DeBenedictis, 480 U.S. 470, 497-502 (1987). The answer to this difficult question may lie in how the owner's reasonable expectations have been shaped by the State's law of property — i.e., whether and to what degree the State's law has accorded legal recognition and protection to the particular interest in land with respect to which the takings claimant alleges a diminution in (or elimination of) value. In any event, we avoid this difficulty in the present case, since the "interest in land" that Lucas has pleaded (a fee simple interest) is an estate with a rich tradition of protection at common law, and since the South Carolina Court of Common Pleas found that the Beachfront Management Act left each of Lucas's beachfront lots without economic value.

(Brennan, J., dissenting). "[F]or what is the land but the profits thereof?" 1 E. Coke, Institutes ch. 1, §1 (1st Am. ed. 1812). Surely, at least, in the extraordinary circumstance when no productive or economically beneficial use of land is permitted, it is less realistic to indulge our usual assumption that the legislature is simply "adjusting the benefits and burdens of economic life," *Penn Central Transportation Co.*, 438 U.S., at 124, in a manner that secures an "average reciprocity of advantage" to everyone concerned. Pennsylvania Coal Co. v. Mahon, 260 U.S., at 415. And the functional basis for permitting the government, by regulation, to affect property values without compensation — that "Government hardly could go on if to some extent values incident to property could not be diminished without paying for every such change in the general law," id., at 413 — does not apply to the relatively rare situations where the government has deprived a landowner of all economically beneficial uses.

On the other side of the balance, affirmatively supporting a compensation requirement, is the fact that regulations that leave the owner of land without economically beneficial or productive options for its use — typically, as here, by requiring land to be left substantially in its natural state — carry with them a heightened risk that private property is being pressed into some form of public service under the guise of mitigating serious public harm. As Justice Brennan explained: "From the government's point of view, the benefits flowing to the public from preservation of open space through regulation may be equally great as from creating a wildlife refuge through formal condemnation or increasing electricity production through a dam project that floods private property." *San Diego Gas & Elec. Co., supra,* at 652 (Brennan, J., dissenting). The many statutes on the books, both state and federal, that provide for the use of eminent domain to impose servitudes on private scenic lands preventing developmental uses, or to acquire such lands altogether, suggest the practical equivalence in this setting of negative regulation and appropriation. . . .

We think, in short, that there are good reasons for our frequently expressed belief that when the owner of real property has been called upon to sacrifice all economically beneficial uses in the name of the common good, that is, to leave his property economically idle, he has suffered a taking.[8]

---

8. Justice Stevens criticizes the "deprivation of all economically beneficial use" rule as "wholly arbitrary," in that "[the] landowner whose property is diminished in value 95% recovers nothing," while the landowner who suffers a complete elimination of value "recovers the land's full value." Post, at 4. This analysis errs in its assumption that the landowner whose deprivation is one step short of complete is not entitled to compensation. Such an owner might not be able to claim the benefit of our categorical formulation, but, as we have acknowledged time and again, "the economic impact of the regulation on the claimant and . . . the extent to which the regulation has interfered with distinct investment-backed expectations" are keenly relevant to takings analysis generally. Penn Central Transportation Co. v. New York City, 438 U.S. 104, 124 (1978). It is true that in at least some cases the landowner with 95% loss will get nothing, while the landowner with total loss will recover in full. But that occasional result is no

The trial court found Lucas's two beachfront lots to have been rendered valueless by respondent's enforcement of the coastal-zone construction ban. Under Lucas's theory of the case, which rested upon our "no economically viable use" statements, that finding entitled him to compensation. Lucas believed it unnecessary to take issue with either the purposes behind the Beachfront Management Act, or the means chosen by the South Carolina Legislature to effectuate those purposes. The South Carolina Supreme Court, however, thought otherwise. In its view, the Beachfront Management Act was no ordinary enactment, but involved an exercise of South Carolina's "police powers" to mitigate the harm to the public interest that petitioner's use of his land might occasion. . . . By neglecting to dispute the findings enumerated in the Act[10] or otherwise to challenge the legislature's purposes, petitioner "concede[d] that the beach/dune area of South Carolina's shores is an extremely valuable public resource; that the erection of new construction, inter alia, contributes to the erosion and destruction of this public resource; and that discouraging new construction in close proximity to the beach/dune area is necessary to prevent a great public harm." . . . In the court's view, these concessions brought petitioner's challenge within a long line of this Court's cases sustaining against Due Process and Takings Clause challenges the State's use of its "police powers" to enjoin a property owner from activities akin to public nuisances. See Mugler

---

more strange than the gross disparity between the landowner whose premises are taken for a highway (who recovers in full) and the landowner whose property is reduced to 5% of its former value by the highway (who recovers nothing). Takings law is full of these "all-or-nothing" situations.

Justice Stevens similarly misinterprets our focus on "developmental uses of property" (the uses proscribed by the Beachfront Management Act) as betraying an "assumption that the only uses of property cognizable under the Constitution are developmental uses." We make no such assumption. Though our prior takings cases evince an abiding concern for the productive use of, and economic investment in, land, there are plainly a number of noneconomic interests in land whose impairment will invite exceedingly close scrutiny under the Takings Clause. See, e.g., Loretto v. Teleprompter Manhattan CATV Corp., 458 U.S. 419, 436 (1982) (interest in excluding strangers from one's land).

10. [The legislature included in its findings for the Act that the coast of South Carolina was important to its people and that the coast serves as a storm barrier, provides as a basis for tourism and revenue due to tourism, provides a natural environment for plant and animals as well as citizens. They further found that the beach/dune system had a unique vegetation that was critical to the preservation of the system and that] "[m]any miles of South Carolina's beaches have been identified as critically eroding. . . . [D]evelopment unwisely has been sited too close to the [beach/dune] system. This type of development has jeopardized the stability of the beach/dune system, accelerated erosion, and endangered adjacent property. It is in both the public and private interests to protect this system from this unwise development. . . . The use of armoring in the form of hard erosion control devices such as seawalls, bulkheads, and rip-rap to protect erosion-threatened structures adjacent to the beach has not proven effective. These armoring devices have given a false sense of security to beachfront property owners. In reality, these hard structures, in many instances, have increased the vulnerability of beachfront property to damage from wind and waves while contributing to the deterioration and loss of the dry sand beach which is so important to the tourism industry. . . . [New construction in areas proximate to the beach/dune system should be discouraged so that the system has space to erode in its natural cycle.]

v. Kansas, 123 U.S. 623 (1887) (law prohibiting manufacture of alcoholic beverages); Hadacheck v. Sebastian, 239 U.S. 394 (1915) (law barring operation of brick mill in residential area); Miller v. Schoene, 276 U.S. 272 (1928) (order to destroy diseased cedar trees to prevent infection of nearby orchards); Goldblatt v. Hempstead, 369 U.S. 590 (1962) (law effectively preventing continued operation of quarry in residential area).

It is correct that many of our prior opinions have suggested that "harmful or noxious uses" of property may be proscribed by government regulation without the requirement of compensation. For a number of reasons, however, we think the South Carolina Supreme Court was too quick to conclude that that principle decides the present case. The "harmful or noxious uses" principle was the Court's early attempt to describe in theoretical terms why government may, consistent with the Takings Clause, affect property values by regulation without incurring an obligation to compensate — a reality we nowadays acknowledge explicitly with respect to the full scope of the State's police power. We made this very point in *Penn Central Transportation Co.*, where . . . we rejected the petitioner's suggestion that *Mugler* and the cases following it were premised on, and thus limited by, some objective conception of "noxiousness":

> "The uses in issue in *Hadacheck, Miller,* and *Goldblatt* were perfectly lawful in themselves. They involved no blameworthiness, . . . moral wrongdoing or conscious act of dangerous risk-taking which induce[d society] to shift the cost to a particular individual." Sax, Takings and the Police Power, 74 Yale L.J. 36, 50 (1964). These cases are better understood as resting not on any supposed "noxious" quality of the prohibited uses but rather on the ground that the restrictions were reasonably related to the implementation of a policy — not unlike historic preservation — expected to produce a widespread public benefit and applicable to all similarly situated property.

438 U.S., at 133-134, n.30. "Harmful or noxious use" analysis was, in other words, simply the progenitor of our more contemporary statements that "land-use regulation does not effect a taking if it 'substantially advances legitimate state interests.' . . . " *Nollan, supra,* at 834 (quoting *Agins, Penn Central, Euclid*).

The transition from our early focus on control of "noxious" uses to our contemporary understanding of the broad realm within which government may regulate without compensation was an easy one, since the distinction between "harm-preventing" and "benefit-conferring" regulation is often in the eye of the beholder. It is quite possible, for example, to describe in either fashion the ecological, economic, and aesthetic concerns that inspired the South Carolina legislature in the present case. One could say that imposing a servitude on Lucas's land is necessary in order to prevent his use of it from "harming" South Carolina's ecological resources; or, instead, in order to achieve the "benefits" of an ecological preserve. . . . Whether one or the other of the competing characterizations will come to one's lips in a particular case depends primarily upon one's evaluation of the worth of competing uses of real estate. See Restatement (Second) of Torts §822, Comment g, p.112 (1979) ("practically all human activities unless carried on in a wilderness interfere to some extent with others or involve some risk of interference"). A given restraint will be seen as mitigating "harm" to the adjacent parcels or securing a "benefit" for them, depending upon the observer's evaluation of the relative importance of the use that the restraint favors. . . . Whether Lucas's construction of single-family residences on his parcels should be described as bringing "harm" to South Carolina's adjacent ecological resources thus depends principally upon whether the describer believes that the State's use interest in nurturing those resources is so important that any competing adjacent use must yield.[12]

When it is understood that "prevention of harmful use" was merely our early formulation of the police power justification necessary to sustain (without compensation) any regulatory diminution in value; and that the distinction between regulation that "prevents harmful use" and that which "confers benefits" is difficult, if not impossible, to discern on an objective, value-free basis; it becomes self-evident that noxious-use logic cannot serve as a touchstone to distinguish regulatory "takings" — which require compensation — from regulatory deprivations that do not require compensation. A fortiori the legislature's recitation of a noxious-use justification cannot be the basis for departing from our categorical rule that total regulatory takings must be compensated. If it were, departure would virtually always be allowed. The South Carolina Supreme Court's approach would essentially nullify *Mahon*'s affirmation of limits to the noncompensable exercise of the police power. Our cases provide no support for this: None of them that employed the logic of "harmful use" prevention to sustain a regulation involved an allegation that the regulation wholly eliminated the value of the claimant's land. See *Keystone Bituminous Coal Assn.*, 480 U.S., at 513-514 (Rehnquist, C.J., dissenting) [citing nuisance cases including Mugler v. Kansas, Reinman v. Little Rock, Hadacheck v. Sebastian, and Goldblatt v. Hempstead].

Where the State seeks to sustain regulation that deprives land of all economically beneficial use, we think it may resist compensation only if the logically antecedent inquiry into the nature of the owner's estate shows that the proscribed use interests were not part of his title to begin with. This accords, we think, with our "takings" jurisprudence, which has traditionally been guided by the understandings of our citizens regarding the content

---

12. In Justice Blackmun's view, even with respect to regulations that deprive an owner of all developmental or economically beneficial land uses, the test for required compensation is whether the legislature has recited a harm-preventing justification for its action. See Post, at 5, 13-17. Since such a justification can be formulated in practically every case, this amounts to a test of whether the legislature has a stupid staff. We think the Takings Clause requires courts to do more than insist upon artful harm-preventing characterizations.

of, and the State's power over, the "bundle of rights" that they acquire when they obtain title to property. It seems to us that the property owner necessarily expects the uses of his property to be restricted, from time to time, by various measures newly enacted by the State in legitimate exercise of its police powers; "as long recognized, some values are enjoyed under an implied limitation and must yield to the police power." Pennsylvania Coal Co. v. Mahon, 260 U.S., at 413. And in the case of personal property, by reason of the State's traditionally high degree of control over commercial dealings, he ought to be aware of the possibility that new regulation might even render his property economically worthless (at least if the property's only economically productive use is sale or manufacture for sale), see Andrus v. Allard, 444 U.S. 51, 66-67 (1979) (prohibition on sale of eagle feathers). In the case of land, however, we think the notion pressed by the Council that title is somehow held subject to the "implied limitation" that the State may subsequently eliminate all economically valuable use is inconsistent with the historical compact recorded in the Takings Clause that has become part of our constitutional culture.

Where "permanent physical occupation" of land is concerned, we have refused to allow the government to decree it anew (without compensation), no matter how weighty the asserted "public interests" involved, Loretto v. Teleprompter Manhattan CATV Corp., 458 U.S., at 426 — though we assuredly would permit the government to assert a permanent easement that was a pre-existing limitation upon the landowner's title. . . .We believe similar treatment must be accorded confiscatory regulations, i.e., regulations that prohibit all economically beneficial use of land: Any limitation so severe cannot be newly legislated or decreed (without compensation), but must inhere in the title itself, in the restrictions that background principles of the State's law of property and nuisance already place upon land ownership. A law or decree with such an effect must, in other words, do no more than duplicate the result that could have been achieved in the courts — by adjacent landowners (or other uniquely affected persons) under the State's law of private nuisance, or by the State under its complementary power to abate nuisances that affect the public generally, or otherwise.[16]

On this analysis, the owner of a lake bed, for example, would not be entitled to compensation when he is denied the requisite permit to engage in a landfilling operation that would have the effect of flooding others' land. Nor the corporate owner of a nuclear generating plant, when it is directed to remove all improvements from its land upon discovery that the

---

16. The principal "otherwise" that we have in mind is litigation absolving the State (or private parties) of liability for the destruction of "real and personal property, in cases of actual necessity, to prevent the spreading of a fire" or to forestall other grave threats to the lives and property of others. Bowditch v. Boston, 101 U.S. 16, 18-19 (1880); see United States v. Pacific Railroad, 120 U.S. 227, 238-239 (1887).

plant sits astride an earthquake fault line. Such regulatory action may well have the effect of eliminating the land's only economically productive use, but it does not proscribe a productive use that was previously permissible under relevant property and nuisance principles. . . .

The "total taking" inquiry we require today will ordinarily entail (as the application of state nuisance law ordinarily entails) analysis of, among other things, the degree of harm to public lands and resources, or adjacent private property, posed by the claimant's proposed activities, see, e.g., Restatement (Second) of Torts §§826, 827, the social value of the claimant's activities and their suitability to the locality in question, see, e.g., id., §§828(a) and (b), 831, and the relative ease with which the alleged harm can be avoided through measures taken by the claimant and the government (or adjacent private landowners) alike, see, e.g., id., §§827(e), 828(c), 830. The fact that a particular use has long been engaged in by similarly situated owners ordinarily imports a lack of any common-law prohibition (though changed circumstances or new knowledge may make what was previously permissible no longer so, see Restatement (Second) of Torts, *supra*, §827, comment (g). So also does the fact that other landowners, similarly situated, are permitted to continue the use denied to the claimant.

It seems unlikely that common-law principles would have prevented the erection of any habitable or productive improvements on petitioner's land; they rarely support prohibition of the "essential use" of land, Curtin v. Benson, 222 U.S. 78, 86 (1911). The question, however, is one of state law to be dealt with on remand. We emphasize that to win its case South Carolina must do more than proffer the legislature's declaration that the uses Lucas desires are inconsistent with the public interest, or the conclusory assertion that they violate a common-law maxim such as sic utere tuo ut alienum non laedas. As we have said, a "State, by ipse dixit, may not transform private property into public property without compensation. . . ." Webb's Fabulous Pharmacies, Inc. v. Beckwith, 449 U.S. 155, 164 (1980). Instead, as it would be required to do if it sought to restrain Lucas in a common-law action for public nuisance, South Carolina must identify background principles of nuisance and property law that prohibit the uses he now intends in the circumstances in which the property is presently found. Only on this showing can the State fairly claim that, in proscribing all such beneficial uses, the Beachfront Management Act is taking nothing.[18]

---

18. Justice Blackmun decries our reliance on background nuisance principles at least in part because he believes those principles to be as manipulable as we find the "harm prevention"/"benefit conferral" dichotomy, see Post, at 20-21. There is no doubt some leeway in a court's interpretation of what existing state law permits — but not remotely as much, we think, as in a legislative crafting of the reasons for its confiscatory regulation. We stress that an affirmative decree eliminating all economically beneficial uses may be defended only if an objectively reasonable application of relevant precedents would exclude those beneficial uses in the circumstances in which the land is presently found.

The judgment is reversed and the cause remanded for proceedings not inconsistent with this opinion.

So ordered.

JUSTICE KENNEDY, concurring in the judgment. [After the suit began, but before it reached us, the Act was modified to allow special permits which petitioner may still apply for — this would dispose of the permanent takings claim. However, the past cannot be undone, in the interim period (1988-1990) the petitioner may have been deprived of the use of his land]. It is well established that temporary takings are as protected as permanent ones. . . . First English Evangelical Lutheran Church of Glendale v. County of Los Angeles, 482 U.S. 304, 318 (1987). . . .

[W]e do not decide if a temporary taking has occurred. . . . [On remand, the court must consider if petitioner had the intent and capacity to develop the property and failed because the State prevented him and whether petitioner complied with all administrative requirements before him.]

The South Carolina Court of Common Pleas found that petitioner's real property has been rendered valueless by the State's regulation. App. Pet. for Cert. 37. The finding appears to presume that the property has no significant market value or resale potential. This is a curious finding, and I share the reservations of some of my colleagues about a finding that a beach front lot loses all value because of a development restriction. Post, at 9-10 (Blackmun, J., dissenting); Post, at 5, n.3 (Stevens, J., dissenting); Post, at 1 (Statement of Souter, J.). While the Supreme Court of South Carolina on remand need not consider the case subject to this constraint, we must accept the finding as entered below. . . . Accepting the finding as entered, it follows that petitioner is entitled to invoke the line of cases discussing regulations that deprive real property of all economic value. See Agins v. Tiburon, 447 U.S. 255, 260 (1980).

The finding of no value must be considered under the Takings Clause by reference to the owner's reasonable, investment-backed expectations. Kaiser Aetna v. United States, 444 U.S. 164, 175 (1979); Penn Central Transportation Co. v. New York City, 438 U.S. 104, 124 (1978); see also W. B. Worthen Co. v. Kavanaugh, 295 U.S. 56 (1935). The Takings Clause, while conferring substantial protection on property owners, does not eliminate the police power of the State to enact limitations on the use of their property. Mugler v. Kansas, 123 U.S. 623, 669 (1887). The rights conferred by the Takings Clause and the police power of the State may coexist without conflict. Property is bought and sold, investments are made, subject to the State's power to regulate. Where a taking is alleged from regulations which deprive the property of all value, the test must be whether the deprivation is contrary to reasonable, investment-backed expectations.

There is an inherent tendency towards circularity in this synthesis, of course; for if the owner's reasonable expectations are shaped by what courts allow as a proper exercise of governmental authority, property tends to become what courts say it is. Some circularity must be tolerated in these matters, however, as it is in other spheres. . . . The definition, moreover, is not circular in its entirety. The expectations protected by the Constitution are based on objective rules and customs that can be understood as reasonable by all parties involved.

In my view, reasonable expectations must be understood in light of the whole of our legal tradition. The common law of nuisance is too narrow a confine for the exercise of regulatory power in a complex and interdependent society. Goldblatt v. Hempstead, 369 U.S. 590, 593 (1962). The State should not be prevented from enacting new regulatory initiatives in response to changing conditions, and courts must consider all reasonable expectations whatever their source. The Takings Clause does not require a static body of state property law; it protects private expectations to ensure private investment. I agree with the Court that nuisance prevention accords with the most common expectations of property owners who face regulation, but I do not believe this can be the sole source of state authority to impose severe restrictions. Coastal property may present such unique concerns for a fragile land system that the State can go further in regulating its development and use than the common law of nuisance might otherwise permit.

The Supreme Court of South Carolina erred, in my view, by reciting the general purposes for which the state regulations were enacted without a determination that they were in accord with the owner's reasonable expectations and therefore sufficient to support a severe restriction on specific parcels of property. . . . The promotion of tourism, for instance, ought not to suffice to deprive specific property of all value without a corresponding duty to compensate. Furthermore, the means as well as the ends of regulation must accord with the owner's reasonable expectations. Here, the State did not act until after the property had been zoned for individual lot development and most other parcels had been improved, throwing the whole burden of the regulation on the remaining lots. This too must be measured in the balance. See Pennsylvania Coal Co. v. Mahon, 260 U.S. 393, 416 (1922).

With these observations, I concur in the judgment of the Court.

JUSTICE BLACKMUN, dissenting.
Today the Court launches a missile to kill a mouse.

I

In 1972 Congress passed the Coastal Zone Management Act and in the 1980 Amendments to the Act, Congress directed States to enhance their coastal programs. . . .[1]

---

1. The country has come to recognize that uncontrolled beachfront development can cause serious damage to life and property. See Brief for Sierra Club, et al. as Amici Curiae 2-5.

South Carolina began implementing the congressional directive by enacting the South Carolina Coastal Zone Management Act of 1977. Under the 1977 Act, any construction activity in what was designated the "critical area" required a permit from the Council, and the construction of any habitable structure was prohibited. The 1977 critical area was relatively narrow and ineffective. . . . In October 1986 the Council appointed [a committee to] investigate beach erosion, they found that the beaches were critically eroding and recommended land-use restrictions. . . . [As a result, the 1988 Act enlarged critical areas to try to combat the problem.] . . .

Petitioner Lucas is a contractor, manager, and part owner of the Wild Dune development on the Isle of Palms. He has lived there since 1978. In December 1986, he purchased two of the last four pieces of vacant property in the development. The area is notoriously unstable. In roughly half of the last 40 years, all or part of petitioner's property was part of the beach or flooded twice daily by the ebb and flow of the tide. Tr. 84. Between 1957 and 1963, petitioner's property was under water. Id., at 79, 81-82. Between 1963 and 1973 the shoreline was 100 to 150 feet onto petitioner's property. Ibid. In 1973 the first line of stable vegetation was about halfway through the property. Id., at 80. Between 1981 and 1983, the Isle of Palms issued 12 emergency orders for sandbagging to protect property in the Wild Dune development. Id., at 99.

The South Carolina Supreme Court found that the Beach Management Act did not take petitioner's property without compensation. The decision rested on two premises that until today were unassailable — that the State has the power to prevent any use of property it finds to be harmful to its citizens, and that a state statute is entitled to a presumption of constitutionality.

The South Carolina Supreme Court correctly found no taking.

II

My disagreement with the Court begins with its decision to review this case [because there has been no final decision regarding the permitted uses of the property and therefore] there is no jurisdiction. [citing *San Diego; Agins*].

The Court admits that the 1990 amendments allowing "special permits" preclude the assertion of a permanent taking, [but the Court contin-

---

Hurricane Hugo's September 1989 attack upon South Carolina's coastline, for example, caused 29 deaths and approximately $6 billion in property damage, much of it the result of uncontrolled beachfront development. See Zalkin, Shifting Sands and Shifting Doctrines: The Supreme Court's Changing Takings Doctrine and South Carolina's Coastal Zone Statute, 79 Cal. L. Rev. 205, 212-213 (1991). The beachfront buildings are not only themselves destroyed in such a storm, "but they are often driven, like battering rams, into adjacent inland homes." Ibid. Moreover, the development often destroys the natural sand dune barriers that provide storm breaks. Ibid.

ues its analysis]. [I]t determines that Lucas's temporary takings claim for July 1, 1988 to June 25, 1990 is ripe. But this claim is not justiciable . . . [because petitioner did not pursue the property administrative remedies available]. . . .

Even if I agreed with the Court that there were no jurisdictional barriers to deciding this case, I still would not try to decide it. The Court creates its new taking jurisprudence based on the trial court's finding that the property had lost all economic value. This finding is almost certainly erroneous. Petitioner still can enjoy other attributes of ownership, such as the right to exclude others, "one of the most essential sticks in the bundle of rights that are commonly characterized as property." Kaiser Aetna v. United States, 444 U.S. 164, 176 (1979). Petitioner can picnic, swim, camp in a tent, or live on the property in a movable trailer. State courts frequently have recognized that land has economic value where the only residual economic uses are recreation or camping. . . . Petitioner also retains the right to alienate the land, which would have value for neighbors and for those prepared to enjoy proximity to the ocean without a house. . . .

I find no evidence in the record supporting the trial court's conclusion that the damage to the lots by virtue of the restrictions was "total." . . . I question the wisdom of deciding an issue based on a factual premise that does not exist in this case, and in the judgment of the Court will exist in the future only in "extraordinary circumstances." Ante, at 12.

Clearly, the Court was eager to decide this case. But eagerness, in the absence of proper jurisdiction, must — and in this case should have been — met with restraint.

III

. . . The Court also alters the long-settled rules of review. The South Carolina Supreme Court's decision to defer to legislative judgments in the absence of a challenge from petitioner comports with one of this Court's oldest maxims: "the existence of facts supporting the legislative judgment is to be presumed." United States v. Carolene Products Co., 304 U.S. 144, 152 (1938). Indeed, we have said the legislature's judgment is "well-nigh conclusive." . . .

Rather than invoking these traditional rules, the Court decides the State has the burden to convince the courts that its legislative judgments are correct. Despite Lucas' complete failure to contest the legislature's findings of serious harm to life and property if a permanent structure is built, the Court decides that the legislative findings are not sufficient to justify the use prohibition. Instead, the Court "emphasizes" the State must do more than merely proffer its legislative judgments to avoid invalidating its law. Ante, at 26. In this case, apparently, the State now has the burden of showing the regulation is not a taking. The Court offers no justification for its sudden hostility toward state legislators, and I doubt that it could.

IV

The Court does not reject the South Carolina Supreme Court's decision simply on the basis of its disbelief and distrust of the legislature's findings. It also takes the opportunity to create a new scheme for regulations that eliminate all economic value. From now on, there is a categorical rule finding these regulations to be a taking unless the use they prohibit is a background common-law nuisance or property principle. . . .

This Court repeatedly has recognized the ability of government, in certain circumstances, to regulate property without compensation no matter how adverse the financial effect on the owner may be [citing *Mugler*] . . .

Mugler was only the beginning in a long line of cases. . . . [The Court discusses *Hadacheck*, Miller v. Schoene, *Goldblatt*]. . . .

In none of the cases did the court suggest that the right of a State to prohibit certain activities without paying compensation turned on the availability of some residual valuable use.[12] Instead, the cases depended on whether the government interest was sufficient to prohibit the activity, given the significant private cost.[13]

These cases rest on the principle that the State has full power to prohibit an owner's use of property if it is harmful to the public. "Since no individual has a right to use his property so as to create a nuisance or otherwise harm others, the State has not taken anything when it asserts its power to enjoin the nuisance-like activity." *Keystone Bituminous Coal*, 480 U.S., at 491, n.20. It would make no sense under this theory to suggest that an owner has a constitutionally protected right to harm others, if only he makes the proper showing of economic loss.[14] See Pennsylvania Coal Co. v. Ma-

---

12. Miller v. Schoene, 276 U.S. 272 (1928), is an example. In the course of demonstrating that apple trees are more valuable than red cedar trees, the Court noted that red cedar has "occasional use and value as lumber." Id., at 279. But the Court did not discuss whether the timber owned by the petitioner in that case was commercially saleable, and nothing in the opinion suggests that the State's right to require uncompensated felling of the trees depended on any such salvage value. To the contrary, it is clear from its unanimous opinion that the *Schoene* Court would have sustained a law requiring the burning of cedar trees if that had been necessary to protect apple trees in which there was a public interest: the Court spoke of preferment of the public interest over the property interest of the individual, "to the extent even of its destruction." Id., at 280.

13. The Court seeks to disavow the holdings and reasoning of *Mugler* and subsequent cases by explaining that they were the Court's early efforts to define the scope of the police power. There is language in the earliest taking cases suggesting that the police power was considered to be the power simply to prevent harms. Subsequently, the Court expanded its understanding of what were government's legitimate interests. But it does not follow that the holding of those early cases — that harmful and noxious uses of property can be forbidden whatever the harm to the property owner and without the payment of compensation — was repudiated. To the contrary, as the Court consciously expanded the scope of the police power beyond preventing harm, it clarified that there was a core of public interests that overrode any private interest. See *Keystone Bituminous Coal*, 480 U.S., at 491, n.20.

14. "Indeed, it would be extraordinary to construe the Constitution to require a government to compensate private landowners because it denied them the right to use property which cannot be used without risking injury and death." *First Lutheran Church*, 210 Cal. 2d., at 1366, 258 Cal. Rptr., at 901-02.

hon, 260 U.S. 393, 418 (1922) (Brandeis, J., dissenting) ("Restriction upon [harmful] use does not become inappropriate as a means, merely because it deprives the owner of the only use to which the property can then be profitably put").

Ultimately even the Court cannot embrace the full implications of its per se rule: it eventually agrees that there cannot be a categorical rule for a taking based on economic value that wholly disregards the public need asserted. Instead, the Court decides that it will permit a State to regulate all economic value only if the State prohibits uses that would not be permitted under "background principles of nuisance and property law." Ante, at 2901.

Until today, the Court explicitly had rejected the contention that the government's power to act without paying compensation turns on whether the prohibited activity is a common-law nuisance. The brewery closed in *Mugler* itself was not a common-law nuisance, and the Court specifically stated that it was the role of legislature to determine what measures would be appropriate for the protection of public health and safety. See 123 U.S., at 661. . . . Instead the Court has relied in the past, as the South Carolina Court has done here, on legislative judgments of what constitutes a harm.[17]

The Court rejects the notion that the State always can prohibit uses it deems a harm to the public without granting compensation because "the distinction between harm preventing 'and benefit-conferring' regulation is often in the eye of the beholder." Ante, at 18. Since the characterization will depend "primarily upon one's evaluation of the worth of competing uses of real estate," ante, at 19, the Court decides a legislative judgment of this kind no longer can provide the desired "objective, value-free basis" for upholding a regulation. Ante, at 20. The Court, however, fails to explain how its proposed common law alternative escapes the same trap.

The threshold inquiry for imposition of the Court's new rule, "deprivation of all economically valuable use," itself cannot be determined objectively. As the Court admits, whether the owner has been deprived of all economic value of his property will depend on how "property" is defined. The "composition of the denominator in our 'deprivation' fraction," ante, at 11, n.7, is the dispositive inquiry. Yet there is no "objective" way to define what that denominator should be. "We have long understood that any land-use regulation can be characterized as the 'total' deprivation of an aptly

---

17. The Court argues that finding no taking when the legislature prohibits a harmful use, such as the Court did in *Mugler* and the South Carolina Supreme Court did in the instant case, would nullify *Pennsylvania Coal*. See ante, at 17. Justice Holmes, the author of *Pennsylvania Coal*, joined Miller v. Schoene, 276 U.S. 272 (1928), six years later. In *Miller*, the Court adopted the exact approach of the South Carolina Court: It found the cedar trees harmful, and their destruction not a taking, whether or not they were a nuisance. Justice Holmes apparently believed that such an approach did not repudiate his earlier opinion. Moreover, this Court already has been over this ground five years ago, and at that point rejected the assertion that *Pennsylvania Coal* was inconsistent with *Mugler, Hadacheck, Miller,* or the others in the string of "noxious use" cases, recognizing instead that the nature of the State's action is critical in takings analysis. *Keystone Bituminous Coal,* 480 U.S., at 490.

defined entitlement. . . . Alternatively, the same regulation can always be characterized as a mere 'partial' withdrawal from full, unencumbered ownership of the landholding affected by the regulation. . . . Michelman, Takings, 1987, 88 Colum. L. Rev. 1600, 1614 (1988).

The Court's decision in *Keystone Bituminous Coal* illustrates this principle perfectly. In *Keystone,* the Court determined that the "support estate" was "merely a part of the entire bundle of rights possessed by the owner." 480 U.S., at 501. Thus, the Court concluded that the support estate's destruction merely eliminated one segment of the total property. Ibid. The dissent, however, characterized the support estate as a distinct property interest that was wholly destroyed. Id., at 519. The Court could agree on no "value-free basis" to resolve this dispute.

Even more perplexing, however, is the Court's reliance on common-law principles of nuisance in its quest for a value-free taking jurisprudence. In determining what is a nuisance at common law, state courts make exactly the decision that the Court finds so troubling when made by the South Carolina General Assembly today: they determine whether the use is harmful. Common-law public and private nuisance law is simply a determination whether a particular use causes harm. See Prosser, Private Action for Public Nuisance, 52 Va. L. Rev. 997, 997 (1966) ("Nuisance is a French word which means nothing more than harm"). There is nothing magical in the reasoning of the judges long dead. They determined a harm in the same way as state judges and legislatures do today. If judges in the 18th and 19th centuries can distinguish a harm from a benefit, why not judges in the 20th century, and if judges can, why not legislators? There simply is no reason to believe that new interpretations of the hoary common law nuisance doctrine will be particularly "objective" or "value-free." [19] . . .

Finally, the Court justifies its new rule that the legislature may not deprive a property owner of the only economically valuable use of his land, even if the legislature finds it to be a harmful use, because such action is not part of the "long-recognized" "understandings of our citizens." Ante, at 2899. . . . It is not clear from the Court's opinion where our "historical compact" or "citizen's understanding" comes from, but it does not appear to be history.

The principle that the State should compensate individuals for property taken for public use was not widely established in America at the time of the Revolution.

> The colonists . . . inherited . . . a concept of property which permitted extensive regulation of the use of that property for the public benefit — regulation

---

19. "There is perhaps no more impenetrable jungle in the entire law than that which surrounds the word 'nuisance.' It has meant all things to all people, and has been applied indiscriminately to everything from an alarming advertisement to a cockroach baked in a pie." It is an area of law that "straddles the legal universe, virtually defies synthesis, and generates case law to suit every taste." W. Rodgers, Environmental Law §2.4, at 48 (1986). The Court itself has noted that "nuisance concepts" are "often vague and indeterminate." . . .

that could even go so far as to deny all productive use of the property to the owner if, as Coke himself stated, the regulation "extends to the public benefit . . . for this is for the public, and every one hath benefit by it."

Even into the 19th century, state governments often felt free to take property for roads and other public projects without paying compensation to the owners.[21] . . . There was an obvious movement toward establishing the just compensation principle during the 19th century, but "there continued to be a strong current in American legal thought that regarded compensation simply as a 'bounty given . . . by the State' out of 'kindness' and not out of justice."

. . . "Until the end of the nineteenth century . . . jurists held that the constitution protected possession only, and not value."[23] . . .

Even when courts began to consider that regulation in some situations could constitute a taking, they continued to uphold bans on particular uses without paying compensation, notwithstanding the economic impact, under the rationale that no one can obtain a vested right to injure or endanger the public. . . .

V

The Court makes sweeping and, in my view, misguided and unsupported changes in our taking doctrine. While it limits these changes to the most narrow subset of government regulation — those that eliminate all economic value from land — these changes go far beyond what is necessary to secure petitioner Lucas' private benefit. One hopes they do not go beyond the narrow confines the Court assigns them to today.

I dissent.

Justice STEVENS, dissenting. Today the Court restricts one judge-made rule and expands another. In my opinion it errs on both counts. . . .

II

[The Court states that it] has adopted a "categorical rule that total regulatory takings must be compensated," ante, at 2899, and then sets itself to the task of identifying the exceptional cases in which a State may be relieved of this categorical obligation. Ante, at 2899.

---

21. In 1796, the Attorney General of South Carolina responded to property holders' demand for compensation when the State took their land to build a road by arguing that "there is not one instance on record, and certainly none within the memory of the oldest man now living, of any demand being made for compensation for the soil or freehold of the lands." Lindsay v. Commissioners, 2 S.C.L. 38, 49 (1796).

23. James Madison, author of the Taking Clause, apparently intended it to apply only to direct, physical takings of property by the Federal Government. . . .

In my opinion, the Court is doubly in error. The categorical rule the Court establishes is an unsound and unwise addition to the law and the Court's formulation of the exception to that rule is too rigid and too narrow.

THE CATEGORICAL RULE

[The categorical rule does not find support in Pennsylvania Coal Co. v. Mahon, 260 U.S. 393 (1922).] To the contrary, Justice Holmes recognized that such absolute rules ill fit the inquiry into "regulatory takings." [Economic injury is merely one factor to be weighed] . . . so the question depends upon the particular facts. Id. at 413. [This new rule also is not supported in decisions following *Mahon*.] We have frequently — and recently — held that, in some circumstances, a law that renders property valueless may nonetheless not constitute a taking [citing *First English, Goldblatt,* Miller v. Schoene, *Mugler,* and other cases]. . . .

In addition to lacking support in past decisions, the Court's new rule is wholly arbitrary. A landowner whose property is diminished in value 95% recovers nothing, while an owner whose property is diminished 100% recovers the land's full value. . . .

Moreover, because of the elastic nature of property rights, the Court's new rule will also prove unsound in practice. In response to the rule, courts may define "property" broadly and only rarely find regulations to effect total takings. This is the approach the Court itself adopts in its revisionist reading of venerable precedents. We are told that — notwithstanding the Court's findings to the contrary in each case — the brewery in *Mugler,* the brickyard in *Hadacheck,* and the gravel pit in *Goldblatt* all could be put to "other uses" and that, therefore, those cases did not involve total regulatory takings.[3]

On the other hand, developers and investors may market specialized estates to take advantage of the Court's new rule. The smaller the estate, the more likely that a regulatory change will effect a total taking. Thus, an investor may, for example, purchase the right to build a multi-family home on a specific lot, with the result that a zoning regulation that allows only

---

3. Of course, the same could easily be said in this case: Lucas may put his land to "other uses" — fishing or camping, for example — or may sell his land to his neighbors as a buffer. In either event, his land is far from "valueless."

This highlights a fundamental weakness in the Court's analysis: its failure to explain why only the impairment of "economically beneficial or productive use," ante, at 10, of property is relevant in takings analysis. I should think that a regulation arbitrarily prohibiting an owner from continuing to use her property for bird-watching or sunbathing might constitute a taking under some circumstances; and, conversely, that such uses are of value to the owner. Yet the Court offers no basis for its assumption that the only uses of property cognizable under the Constitution are developmental uses.

single-family homes would render the investor's property interest "value-less."[4] In short, the categorical rule will likely have one of two effects: Either courts will alter the definition of the "denominator" in the takings "fraction," rendering the Court's categorical rule meaningless, or investors will manipulate the relevant property interests, giving the Court's rule sweeping effect. To my mind, neither of these results is desirable or appropriate, and both are distortions of our takings jurisprudence.

THE NUISANCE EXCEPTION

Like many bright-line rules, the categorical rule established in this case is only "categorical" for a page or two in the U.S. Reports. No sooner does the Court state that "total regulatory takings must be compensated," ante, at 21, than it quickly establishes an exception to that rule. . . .

Under our reasoning in *Mugler*, a state's decision to prohibit or to regulate certain uses of property is not a compensable taking just because the particular uses were previously lawful. Under the Court's opinion today, however, if a state should decide to prohibit the manufacture of asbestos, cigarettes, or concealable firearms, for example, it must be prepared to pay for the adverse economic consequences of its decision. One must wonder if Government will be able to "go on" effectively if it must risk compensation "for every such change in the general law." *Mahon*, 260 U.S., at 413.

The Court's holding today effectively freezes the State's common law, denying the legislature much of its traditional power to revise the law governing the rights and uses of property. . . .

Arresting the development of the common law is not only a departure from our prior decisions; it is also profoundly unwise. The human condition is one of constant learning and evolution — both moral and practical. Legislatures implement that new learning; in doing so they must often revise the definition of property and the rights of property owners. Thus, when the Nation came to understand that slavery was morally wrong and mandated the emancipation of all slaves, it, in effect, redefined "property." On a lesser scale, our ongoing self-education produces similar changes in the rights of property owners: New appreciation of the significance of endangered species, see, e.g., Andrus v. Allard, 444 U.S. 51 (1979); the importance of wetlands, see, e.g., 16 U.S.C. §3801 et seq.; and the vulnerability of coastal lands, see, e.g., 16 U.S.C. §1451 et seq., shapes our evolving understandings of property rights.

---

4. This unfortunate possibility is created by the Court's subtle revision of the "total regulatory takings" dicta. In past decisions, we have stated that a regulation effects a taking if it "denies an owner economically viable use of his land," Agins v. Tiburon, 447 U.S., 225, 260 (1980), indicating that this "total takings" test did not apply to other estates. Today, however, the Court suggests that a regulation may effect a total taking of any real property interest. See ante, at 11, n.7.

Of course, some legislative redefinitions of property will effect a taking and must be compensated — but it certainly cannot be the case that every movement away from common law does so. There is no reason, and less sense, in such an absolute rule. We live in a world in which changes in the economy and the environment occur with increasing frequency and importance. If it was wise a century ago to allow Government "'the largest legislative discretion'" to deal with "'the special exigencies of the moment,'" *Mugler*, 123 U.S., at 669B, it is imperative to do so today. The rule that should govern a decision in a case of this kind should focus on the future, not the past.[5] . . .

The Court's categorical approach rule will, I fear, greatly hamper the efforts of local officials and planners who must deal with increasingly complex problems in land-use and environmental regulation. As this case — in which the claims of an *individual* property owner exceed $1 million — well demonstrates, these officials face both substantial uncertainty because of the ad hoc nature of takings law and unacceptable penalties if they guess incorrectly about that law. . . .

Accordingly, I respectfully dissent.

NOTES AND QUESTIONS

1. **Pressure on the beaches.** Currently, more than half of Americans live within 50 miles of an ocean or the Great Lakes. The director of the Coastal States Organization has estimated that, by the year 2000, that proportion will reach almost 80 percent. As the coastal population increases, it is likely that issues concerning beach development and protection will become more pressing. Robert Lindsey, Crowding the Seashore on Every Coast, N.Y. Times, Aug. 9, 1987, Sec. 4, at 26.

2. **Designing a takings-proof statute.** Recall how the New York landmarks statute was carefully designed to withstand a takings challenge by making available what in essence was a variance provision in the event that a landowner would otherwise be denied a reasonable return. See page 842, *supra,* for information on the landmarks statute; see Chapter 9 *infra* for more information about variances. Did the South Carolina statute have a variance provision when the *Lucas* facts arose? In retrospect, would you

---

5. Even measured in terms of efficiency, the Court's rule is unsound. The Court today effectively establishes a form of insurance against certain changes in land-use regulations. Like other forms of insurance, the Court's rule creates a "moral hazard" and inefficiencies: In the face of uncertainty about changes in the law, developers will overinvest, safe in the knowledge that if the law changes adversely, they will be entitled to compensation. See generally Farber, Economic Analysis and Just Compensation, 12 Int'l Rev. of Law & Econ. 125 (1992).

have recommended including one? (Note that the statute was amended to include a provision for "special permits" after *Lucas* started winding its way up the courts.)

3. **Are the "tango" cases still good law?** Do you think the majority opinion is successful in distinguishing the "procedural tango" cases? What is the precedented value of those cases after *Lucas*? How would you answer this question if you were

   (a) Asked how best to set up a case for takings litigation?
   (b) Asked whether it was worthwhile appealing a takings case to the U.S. Supreme Court when all of the "procedural tango" requirements had not been met?
   (c) Asked whether it was worthwhile litigating a takings case in the state courts without meeting all the procedural tango requirements?

4. **Role of amicus briefs.** In Lucas v. South Carolina Coastal Commn., 505 U.S. 1003 (1992), as in *Nollan,* the Supreme Court opinion relies heavily on amicus curiae briefs. In an omitted section of the Court's opinion, Justice Scalia cites a long list of state court land use cases drawn from the National Home Builders brief.

5. **A new categorical rule.** Note how Justice Scalia crystallizes takings law in Part III of the majority opinion. He articulates a new categorical rule: Do the cases he cites support this rule, in your view? What are Stevens's and Blackmun's criticisms of the new rule?

6. **Conceptual severance.** What is the status of the conceptual severance argument after *Lucas*? Note that, as in *Nollan, infra,* Justice Scalia again places important material in a footnote. Why?

7. **Diminution of value.** Has Lucas's parcel lost all its value, according to the dissent? Whose analysis do you find more convincing: the majority's or Blackmun's? Do the opinions use any other Holmes's taking tests?

8. **Use of the "nuisance" cases.** How does the majority opinion come to terms with the so-called nuisance cases? How do the dissents? Is the argument developed in the majority opinion consistent with Justice Rehnquist's use of the nuisance cases in his *Penn Central* dissent? Note again that the majority opinion's rejection of the harm/benefit test rests on the implicit assumption that some legal tests are "objective." On what basis does Justice Blackmun reject that assumption? With whom do you agree?

9. **Servitude argument.** Note that the majority characterizes South Carolina's actions as imposing a servitude on Lucas's property. Recall that this argument goes back at least to Rehnquist's dissent in *Penn Central, supra.*

10. **Expectations.** Whose expectations does Justice Scalia focus on? Whose expectations does Justice Blackmun focus on? Whose expectations should a court enforce?

11. **Use of the facts.** Turning to Justice Blackmun's opinion, why does he go into the background of the statute in so much greater detail than Justice Scalia does? How does his version of the relevant facts differ from Scalia's?

12. **Presumption of validity.** Does *Lucas* shift *Euclid*'s presumption of legislative validity? If it does, does it do so for all land use cases, or only those that involve regulations that render the land valueless?

13. **Use of history.** How does Blackmun's dissenting opinion use history? Why does it turn to history?

14. **Vision of property.** What vision of property underlies the Scalia, Blackmun, and Stevens opinions?

15. **Beach erosion.** Many coastal communities have been faced in recent years with severe beach loss due to storms, development too near the waterline, and overuse by the public. In Myrtle Beach, South Carolina, for example, hotels were built on the shore as far down as the natural dune line, which increased the rate of erosion. Attempts to curtail this erosion typically include armoring the beaches, forcing new shoreline development back from the water, and "renourishment." Armoring (with jetties or bulkheads) is effective at improving the target beach but causes erosion of the down-current beach, and so is no longer the preferred method. Federal laws and regulations and local ordinances have forced development in certain areas back from the water's edge. Renourishment involves adding new sand from elsewhere to an eroded beach, quieting the eroding forces, and allowing nature to reshape the new beach. This approach has succeeded in some places, but is expensive, and requires close study of the shoreline in the target area to identify and eliminate the causes of erosion at work in that area. Myrtle Beach responded to its erosion problem by raising $4.5 million for beach renourishment and restoration by charging an accommodations tax, and creating a setback for any new development. Sally Lawrence, How to Feed a Beach: Where the Sand Comes From and Where It's Going, Oceans, March-April 1987, at 42.

16. **Follow-up.** In July 1993, South Carolina and David Lucas reached a settlement. South Carolina agreed to pay Lucas $1.5 million: $850,000 to purchase the two lots and $725,000 in interest, attorneys' fees, and court costs. At the time South Carolina announced its intention to resell the properties for development in order to recoup some of the costs of the settlement.

17. **Precondemnation losses.** The 614 Co. v. Minneapolis Community Dev. Agency, 547 N.W.2d 400 (Minn. App. 1996), and its companion, Siegel v. Minneapolis Community Dev. Agency, 1996 WL 229242 (Minn. App. 1996), illustrate the *Lucas* potential (coupled to *First English*) in a quite different setting. The appellate court sustained a cause of action where plaintiffs alleged a temporary deprivation of all economically beneficial or productive use of their land as a result of the agency's announce-

ment of its plans to redevelop the area, a plan that eventually did not proceed. Because of the announcement, one plaintiff could not close an agreement with a major developer to build on its property, and the second plaintiff could not find tenants to replace those who left while the agency's plans were operational. The court held that under *Lucas* if plaintiffs could show that they were precluded from using their property "in an economically viable fashion," they would be entitled to recover.

18. **The Court of Federal Claims.** In 1982, the U.S. Court of Claims was abolished and replaced by two courts: a trial court, now known as the Court of Federal Claims, and an appeals court, the Federal Circuit. Virtually every judge at both the trial and the appellate levels was appointed by the Reagan and Bush administrations; dramatically pro-landowner takings decisions have resulted. Note that these opinions are binding only in the Federal Circuit, which *inter alia* has jurisdiction over damages claims against the United States.

The most famous Federal Circuit cases arise from §404 of the Clean Water Act, which is designed to protect wetlands by prohibiting filling and construction without a permit from the Army Corps of Engineers. These cases show that the Federal Circuit will scrutinize federal regulations more closely than has the Supreme Court, resulting in some controversial decisions. For praise, see Roger J. Marzulla and Nancie G. Marzulla, Regulatory Takings in the United States Claims Court: Adjusting the Burdens that in Fairness and Equity Ought to be Borne by Society as a Whole, 40 Cath. U. L. Rev. 549 (1995) ("The vindication of individual rights against the federal government is the province of this uniquely constituted court. The current docket will afford the Claims Court and the Federal Circuit many additional opportunities to fulfill its duty to adjust those burdens which in fairness ought to be born by society as a whole"). For criticism, see Michael C. Blumm, The End of Environmental Law? Libertarian Property, Natural Law, and the Just Compensation Clause in the Federal Circuit, 25 Envtl. L. 171, 173 (1995) ("the creation of a kind of natural law of property development which has no basis in the text of the Constitution, the intent of the Framers, or the history of Anglo-American property law").

In Florida Rock Indus. v. United States, 18 F.3d 1560 (Fed. Cir. 1994), the court found that a partial diminution in value of a parcel, however small (as opposed to only an economic wipeout), may work a taking in violation of the Just Compensation Clause of the Fifth Amendment: "There remains in such difficult cases as this the difficult task of resolving when a partial loss of economic use of the property has crossed the line from a noncompensable 'mere diminution' to a compensable 'partial taking.'" 18 F.3d at 1570. Further, the court found no meaningful difference between a physical occupation of the land and a regulation that severely limits the economic value of it. This doctrine of "partial takings" accepts as a given a combination of the intuitive vision of property and the "why me" argument. The court asserts that "[m]arketplace decisions should be made under the working assumption that the Government will neither prejudice private citizens, unfairly shifting the burden of a public good onto a few people, nor act arbitrarily . . . to disappoint reasonable investment-backed expectations." 18 F.3d at 1571.

In Loveladies Harbor v. United States, 27 F.3d 1545 (Fed. Cir. 1994), the court worked a conceptual severance — that is, it severed part of the owner's original tract, ignoring it for the purposes of the decision, and considered only the parcel affected by the regulations. The court thus easily discovered a 100 percent diminution in value and therefore a violation of the Just Compensation Clause. This decision brings up the possibility that many more federal environmental regulations would become compensable takings under the Fifth Amendment.

A third example is Bowles v. United States, 31 Fed. Cl. 37 (1994), where a homeowner who owned one building lot received compensation on the following facts. The claimant had acquired his lot in 1980 intending to build a permanent retirement residence, consistent with other uses within the subdivision. When he sought to build years later, he learned that the Clean Water Act required an Army Corps of Engineers permit for the landfill needed to install a septic system, because the Corps considered the property a "wetland." The Corps denied the permit, which the court found diminished the value of the lot no less than 91.8 percent.

As a final note, these decisions are not binding on any other circuit, and at least one has repudiated them. In Clajon Prod. Corp. v. Petera, 70 F.3d 1566 (10th Cir. 1995), the court affirmed the classic state takings law test, ruling that a regulation did not work a taking in violation of the Fifth Amendment, because it "neither deprives Plaintiffs of all economically beneficial use of their land nor fails substantially to advance a legitimate state interest." 70 F.3d at 1574. See also Florida Game and Fresh Water Fish Commn. v. Flotilla, Inc., 636 So. 2d 761 (Fla. Ct. App.) (preservation zone barring development on 48 acres of 173-acre tract in order to protect nesting bald eagles not a taking), review denied, 645 So. 2d 452 (Fla. 1994).

19. **Advocates Interpret Lucas.** Some property rights advocates were bitterly disappointed by Lucas. Can you see why? See Richard A. Epstein, Lucas v. South Carolina Coastal Council: A Tangled Web of Expectations, 45 Stan. L. Rev. 1369, 1369-1372 (1993).

The basic strategy of both land use planning advocates and their opponents appears to be to claim victory in Lucas. Why is this a logical approach from the viewpoint of a litigator? Consider the following diametrically opposed interpretations of Lucas. The first is written by two attorneys for the Washington Legal Foundation. The second is by Glenn Sugameli, an environmental attorney who works for the National Wildlife Federation.

DANIEL J. POPEO AND PAUL D. KAMENAR,[39] IN *LUCAS'S* WAKE,
WHITHER THE LAW OF TAKINGS? THE TIDE HAS FINALLY
TURNED IN FAVOR OF PROPERTY RIGHTS

N.J.L.J., Aug. 3, 1992, at 15

It has been said that a man's home is his castle, and thanks to the
Supreme Court, David Lucas, the owner of two undeveloped beach-front
lots, will not have to content himself with building his out of sand.

In Lucas v. South Carolina Coastal Council, the Court held that a
compensable taking occurs under the Fifth Amendment when the land-use
regulation in question (here, South Carolina's beach erosion set-back line)
deprives the owner of all economically viable use of his property. More importantly, the Court imposed a heavy burden on the state to show, in order
to escape liability, that the prohibited uses of the property fell within traditional common-law nuisance principles.

After disposing of the first two takings cases on this term's docket in
lackluster fashion — Yee v. City of Escondido and PFZ Properties, Inc. v.
Rodriguez — the favorable *Lucas* ruling was good news indeed. Yet many
property-rights advocates remain disappointed and dissatisfied even with
this victory. They fault both its apparent limited application to "total takings" situations and the Court's failure to articulate coherent guiding principles to assist lower courts adjudicating the more common situation of
partial takings. And the fear the government regulators and environmentalists will brush aside the ruling by claiming that many land-use regulatory
schemes leave the property owner with some economic value.

But property-rights advocates need not be so disheartened. A closer
reading of the majority opinion by Justice Antonin Scalia, the concurring
judgment by Justice Anthony Kennedy, and the vigorous dissents by Justice
John Paul Stevens and Harry Blackmun, will give regulators pause if not
heartburn. And *Lucas* should provide renewed hope to property owners
faced with a growing array of confiscatory environmental regulations requiring them to leave their property in its natural state.

Lucas is more a victory than a defeat for two basic reasons. First, although the plaintiff chose to win or lose solely on the test previously articulated in Agins v. Tiburon (1980) — that a taking occurs when the
regulation "does not substantially advance legitimate state interests or denies an owner economically viable use of his land" — the *Lucas* Court, in
fact, left intact an arsenal of other arguments that property owners and
their attorneys can employ to establish a regulatory taking.

---

39. The story notes: "Popeo is chairman and general counsel and Kamenar is executive
legal director of the Washington Legal Foundation, which filed an amicus brief in the Supreme
Court supporting the petitioner in Lucas v. South Carolina Coastal Council."

Second, those arguments can be used to establish a partial, as well as a total, taking. Indeed, the Court's rationale for its new categorical rule — that the regulation is the "equivalent of a physical appropriation"; that requiring private property to be left in its natural state carries with it "the heightened risk that private property is being pressed into some form of public service"; and that the numerous state and federal laws authorizing purchase of scenic easements, wetlands, and the like "suggest the practical equivalence in this setting of negative regulation and appropriation" — provides lawyers with good arguments to establish partial takings. (In our amicus brief in *Lucas,* we argued that this confiscatory character of the government action holds the key to resolving takings disputes, total or otherwise. The government can, on the other hand, easily manipulate the economic-impact argument by leaving the property with some economic value.)

MORE COASTAL RETIREMENT HOMES

As a preliminary observation, we suggest that the total-takings categorical rule that the Court firmly established (which, Justice Harry Blackmun argued, was, in prior opinions, so much dicta) will be invoked much more often than one might initially think. Scores of property owners in South Carolina alone are in the same predicament as David Lucas, not to mention thousands more in other coastal states with similar developmental restrictions.

Numerous wetland cases would also come under this categorical rule, such as Loveladies Harbor Inc. v. United States, now awaiting the decision of the U.S. Court of Appeals for the Federal Circuit. In *Loveladies,* Chief Judge Loren Smith of the U.S. Claims Court ruled that the denial of a fill permit needed to build beach homes on the New Jersey shore failed both prongs of the Agins v. Tiburon test. The denial didn't substantially advance a legitimate state interest, and it destroyed essentially all economically viable use of the property, Judge Smith held.

The categorical rule of *Lucas* will thus benefit hundreds of landowners who have been blocked from building retirement homes on the Eastern Shore of Maryland and on the Florida coast because of wetlands restrictions.

Nor should the regulators delude themselves into thinking they can escape this categorical rule by imposing their own perverse form of the just-compensation clause. Should the government arbitrarily require property owners to compensate it by agreeing, for example, to create one, two, or more acres of wetlands for each one they wish to fill, a property owner could refuse to go along with such extortionist demands. He would then be denied a permit and would be unable to develop his land — in virtually the same position as *Lucas.*

The categorical rule is also sufficient without the qualification offered by Justice Kennedy. In his concurrence, Kennedy suggested that requiring the property owner to prove that the deprivation of all value was "contrary to reasonable, investment-backed expectations." But that test, not adopted by the majority, is clearly suspect. What if Lucas had, for example, unexpectedly sold, given, or devised the property to his children or a homeless person after the restrictive land-use laws were enacted? Surely none of these new owners would have had any investment-backed expectations, reasonable or otherwise. Under Kennedy's scenario, the government could avoid paying compensation by waiting until the current owner dies or otherwise transfers the property.

In Nollan v. California Coastal Commission (1987), the Court rejected this specious argument. Although the Nollans had acquired their property long after the restrictions were put in place, they weren't out of luck, according to the Court; the Nollans had acquired all the rights in the property that the prior owner possessed when it was conveyed.

NUISANCE IN THE COMMON LAW

Probably the most significant part of the *Lucas* decision deals with the so-called nuisance exception to the takings clause. The Court ruled that use of property that causes harm to neighbors or to neighbors' property has never been considered part of the original bundle of rights acquired when the property was obtained. Accordingly, when the state, relying upon common-law principles of what constitutes a nuisance, prevents such noxious use, no compensation is due.

The key, though, is that the state must base its action on common-law principles. "Any limitation so severe cannot be newly legislated or decreed [without compensation]," the Court stated, "but must inhere in the title itself, in the restrictions that background principles of the States' law of property and nuisance already place upon land ownership."

While this part of the ruling will cause lawyers on both sides of the issue to dust off old state law reporters to unearth their respective state's nuisance law, it has other important features as well. First, although the Court technically remanded the case to the South Carolina courts to determine whether building a home can constitute a nuisance under common-law principles, the Court expressed strong doubts that such a showing could be made. Indeed, as explained in our amicus brief, a rich tradition in the common law supports the right to build a home on one's property, and that property interest may even be distinct from or in addition to the right to economically viable use of land — the focus of the Court's attention in *Lucas*.

Justice Kennedy (as well as the two dissenters) objected to the majority's reliance on common-law principles to determine what constitutes a nuisance. He would have greatly expanded the notion to include uses of property that may have remote environmental impacts: "Coastal property may present such unique concerns for a fragile land system that the State can go further in regulating its development and use than the common law of nuisance might otherwise permit."

But such an elastic standard would allow the state to escape takings liability in a variety of cases. The state could require, for example, a wooded lot to remain undeveloped because cutting down the trees would affect a spotted-owl habitat or contribute, however remotely, to the so-called green-house-effect.

Second, and more important, the Court placed the burden on the state to prove at trial that the prohibited use of the property constitutes a nuisance. No longer can regulators hide behind conclusory and fuzzy legislative findings that characterize land-use restrictions as harm-preventing; such findings can be crafted easily, said the Court, unless the "legislature has a stupid staff." Placing the burden on the regulators will also have the salutary effect of curbing the cavalier attitude about private property rights epitomized by one regulator who, in response to a query about the legitimacy of a state's critical-habitat law, blithely replied: "We don't have to justify everything we want to protect" in the name of the environment.

TURNING THE TIDE

In two lengthy footnotes, the Court even left several nuggets that suggest its categorical rule does not foreclose partial-takings claims. The Court reiterated the well-known three-part test articulated in Penn Central Transportation Co. v. New York City (1978), which it described as "keenly relevant" in determining whether a partial taking has occurred. The Court left unclear, however, which situation would require the categorical rule and which ones would demand a balancing test.

For example, if a land-use restriction denies the owner 50 percent of the use of the property, the justices said it was "unclear whether we would analyze the situation as one in which the owner has been deprived of all economically beneficial use of the burdened portion" (in which case the categorical rule would presumably apply) "or whether the owner has suffered a mere diminution in value of the tract as a whole" (in which case, the balancing test of *Penn Central* or some other rule would apply).

Most notably, the Court disclaimed as "extreme" and "insupportable" a rule that would calculate the diminution in value by looking at a claimant's "other holdings in the vicinity," rather than the discrete parcel at issue. The South Carolina Coastal Council thus could not avoid liability, for example, by giving David Lucas a permit to develop only one of his two lots. Even if the council could demonstrate that the fair market value of that permitted lot is more than what Lucas originally paid for both lots, it still could not claim that the second non-permitted lot had not been taken.

Again, the Court implied that whether a regulatory taking occurs should not depend on the fortuity of the property owner or the extent of the owner's holdings.

The court also indicated that such partial takings may be analyzed by looking at how state law has recognized the "particular interest in land" in question. Thus, the Court seems to suggest that restrictions on an owner's mineral rights, water rights, and other discrete interests in land recognized under state law (such as the right to protect one's property from the destructive forces of nature) could amount to a compensable taking without considering the value remaining in the other unrestricted interests.

Indeed, the Court stated that impairment of even "non-economic interests . . . will invite exceedingly close scrutiny under the Takings Clause," citing to Loretto v. Teleprompter. In that 1982 case, the Court laid down its first categorical rule that the government's slightest physical invasion of property, even if the economic value of property is greater due to the invasion, nevertheless constitutes a taking.

While the *Lucas* decision may not be everything hoped for, the tide is clearly turning toward judicial protection of property rights. If the government continues to enact and enforce confiscatory land-use controls, that tide will most surely bring a flood of new litigation.

GLENN P. SUGAMELI,[1] TAKINGS ISSUES IN LIGHT OF *LUCAS v. SOUTH CAROLINA COASTAL COUNCIL:* A DECISION FULL OF SOUND AND FURY SIGNIFYING NOTHING

12 Va. Envtl. L.J. 439 (1993)

THE LIMITED SCOPE AND IMPACT OF LUCAS

On June 29, 1992, the U.S. Supreme Court unanimously rejected the argument by David Lucas and — in amicus briefs — by the mining and timber industries and the American Farm Bureau Federation that there is no nuisance exception to the Fifth Amendment's requirement that private property not be taken without just compensation. . . .

The majority opinion held that land use statutes or regulations that deny *all* economically beneficial or productive use of an *entire* parcel of land generally effect a taking unless they merely repeat restrictions that are inherent in the title to the property. That is, regulations prohibiting those activities that are not permitted by "background principles of the State's

1. Council, Public Lands & Energy Division, National Wildlife Federation, Washington, D.C.; A.B. Princeton University, 1976; J.D., University of Virginia School of Law, 1979.

law of property and nuisance" *never* effect a taking, even if such prohibition deprives a landowner of *all* economic use of the land.[78]

In *Lucas,* the Supreme Court reversed and remanded the South Carolina Supreme Court's decision for a determination of whether the State's 1988 Beachfront Management Act had effected a taking by banning all permanent habitable structures forward of the setback line that lay entirely landward of Lucas's property. Lucas had purchased the property in 1986, two years prior to the Act. The Supreme Court assumed, but did not hold, that the trial court was correct in finding that the statute deprived the plaintiff of all economically viable use of his land. . . .

CONTRADICTIONS AND INCONSISTENCIES: LUCAS AND ITS LIMITED POTENTIAL TO EXTEND THE REACH OF THE TAKINGS CLAUSE

. . . Justice Scalia's attempt to describe a "discrete categor[y] of regulatory action as compensable without case-specific inquiry into the public interest advance in support of the restraint" is analytically flawed. As Donald Ayer has written, "[w]hile stating his holding in terms of a categorical rule, Scalia recognized that this rule must be subject to a substantial exception — indeed one that makes the rule decidedly uncategorical." [90] In particular, the *Lucas* majority recognized that using a "total taking" analysis to determine whether "background principles of nuisance and property law . . . prohibit the uses [a landowner] now intends in the circumstances in which the property is presently found" would "ordinarily entail (as the application of state nuisance law ordinarily entails) analysis of, among other things, the degree of harm to public lands and resources, or adjacent private property, posed by the claimant's proposed activities." . . .

Contrary to Justice Scalia's initial description of the total-taking inquiry, then, courts will, in fact, be required to engage in a "case-specific inquiry into the public interest advanced in support of the restraint." Even in the extraordinary case in which a regulation deprived land of all eco-

---

78. Id. at 2900. Justice Scalia never answered the issue that he described in the first paragraph: "This case *requires us to decide* whether the Act's dramatic effect on the economic value of Lucas's lots accomplished a taking of private property under the Fifth and Fourteenth Amendments requiring the payment of 'just compensation.'" Id. at 2889 (emphasis added). Instead, the case was remanded to the South Carolina Supreme Court for the State to "identify background principles of nuisance and property law that prohibit the uses he now intends in the circumstances in which the property is presently found." Id. at 2901-02.

90. Donald Ayer, Straying from the Right Religion, Legal Times, July 27, 1992, at S39. Donald Ayer was Deputy Attorney General from 1989 to 1990 and Principal Deputy Solicitor General from 1986 to 1988. See also Jed Rubenfeld, Usings, 102 Yale L.J. 1077, 1093 (1993) ("[W]hat began as a ringing endorsement of a per se economic-viability rule . . . ended with a direction to federal judges to decide takings claims by determining how the courts of the relevant state would have decided a hypothetical injunction action against the property owner under the state's common-law nuisance precedents. This result is astonishing.").

nomic use, a fact-specific judicial determination will be necessary to decide whether the affected use is inherent in the title as defined not only by nuisance law but by property law as well.

The majority opinion indeed admits the existence of a separate fact-specific exception in the one area of taking jurisprudence that many had thought was categorical, "permanent physical occupation" of land:

> Where "permanent physical occupation" of land is concerned, we have refused to allow the government to decree it anew (without compensation), no matter how weighty the asserted "public interests" involved, Loretto v. Teleprompter Manhattan CATV Corp., 458 U.S. [419, 426 (1982)] though we assuredly *would* permit the government to assert a permanent easement that was a pre-existing limitation upon the landowner's title.

Ironically, the only categorical rule in the *Lucas* majority opinion is a *negative* one: If a property restriction repeats limitations inherent in the title to property, as defined by property and nuisance law — as well as by emergency circumstances and perhaps by generally applicable criminal laws and other laws that destroy the value of land without being aimed at land — the restriction *never* effects a taking.[97]

Where the majority attempted to articulate the circumstance under which a taking *would occur,* it was not compelling. In dicta, Justice Scalia stated that affirmatively supporting a compensation requirement [is] the fact that regulations that leave the owner of land without economically beneficial or productive options for its use — typically, as here, by requiring land to be left substantially in its natural state — carry with them a heightened risk that private property is being pressed into some form of public service under the guise of mitigating serious public harm.

In fact, however, even land left substantially in its natural state very often has valuable "economically beneficial or productive" options for its use — as grazing land, for example. Furthermore, speculators will purchase land despite current use restrictions, on the chance that changed factual circumstances or relaxed regulation would allow development to occur in the future. In 1986, for example, a five-judge panel of the Federal Circuit in Florida Rock Industries v. United States, 791 F.2d 893 (Fed. Cir. 1986), *cert. denied,* 479 U.S. 1053 (1987), rejected the position that denying an immediately viable use of land would effect a taking. According to the court,

---

97. See David Coursen, *Lucas v. South Carolina Coastal Council:* Indirection in the Evolution of Takings Law, 22 Envtl. L. Rep. (Envtl. L. Inst.) 10,778, 10,788 (Dec. 1992) ("In the guise of articulating one categorical rule — a denial of all use works a taking — the Court has implicitly established another principle that state-imposed limitations on property use always defeat a taking claim. Moreover, while the articulated rule applies in only a narrow range of circumstances, the implicit rule applies in every case. Finally, when the two rules collide, the implicit rule controls: if [the landowner's] property rights are subject to a state property or nuisance-law restriction, his taking claim will be defeated.").

fair market value of the land must include the value to willing speculative buyers: We do not perceive any legal reason why a well-informed "willing buyer" might not bet that the prohibition of rock mining, to protect the overlying wetlands, would some day be lifted. The statute would not have to change, only the perceptions of the army engineers. . . . There is nothing so certain in life as that all certainties become uncertain, and some are replaced by their opposites. One who invests in land on this basis may be a speculator, but he is not on that account a gull. . . . Anyone who buys mineral property is speculating to a large extent, and so is even to some extent one who buys "blue chip" securities.

Regulation in Accord with Background Principles of Property and Nuisance Law: No Taking, Even If Eliminations All Value

Justice Scalia's majority opinion recognizes that it is not a taking to forbid uses barred by "background principles of the State's law of property and nuisance" that are incompatible with, for example, the public trust doctrine or the state law principle that "[a]n owner has no absolute and unlimited right to change the essential natural character of his land so as to use it for a purpose for which it was unsuited in its natural state and which injures the rights of others. . . ."[117]

State courts have also denied takings claims on the authority of the provision in *Lucas* for background state law limitations on state property rights. In Stevens v. City of Cannon Beach, 835 P.2d 940 (Or. App.), *review granted*, 844 P.2d 206 (Or. 1992), the Oregon Court of Appeals rebuffed a claim that denying permits to build a seawall as part of the eventual development of two lots for motel or hotel use constituted a taking. Upholding the trial court's reliance on State ex rel. Thornton v. Hay, 462 P.2d 671 (Or. 1969), the *Stevens* court found "that the denial of the applications took nothing from plaintiffs, because their property interests [had] never included development rights that could interfere with the public's use of the dry sand area." The court reasoned that under *Lucas,* whether the proscribed interests were part of the plaintiffs' title to begin with was to be decided under the state's law of nuisance and property; the *Hay* case was

---

117. Just v. Marinette County, 201 N.W.2d 761, 768 (Wis. 1972) (denying a wetlands takings claim). The *Just* analysis has been followed by other courts in denying wetlands takings claims, including a New Hampshire Supreme Court decision in which Justice Souter joined. See Rowe v. Town of North Hampton, 533 A.2d 1331, 1335 (N.H. 1989) (advancing the notion that the regulation prevents the substantial change of the natural character of [the] land so as to injure the rights of others) (citing *Just,* 201 N.W.2d at 768); Graham v. Estuary Properties, Inc., 399 So. 2d 1374, 1382 (Fla.), *cert. denied,* 454 U.S. 1083 (1981); American Dredging Co. v. State Dep't of Envtl. Protection, 391 A.2d 1265, 1271 (N.J. Super. Ct. Ch. Div. 1978), *aff'd,* 404 A.2d 42 (N.J. Super. Ct. App. Div. 1979).

"an expression of state law that the purportedly taken property interest was not part of plaintiffs' estate to begin with."

BEYOND THE SCOPE OF LUCAS

In his *Lucas* opinion, Justice Scalia repeatedly emphasized the holding's narrow scope, a qualification presumably necessary to garner a bare majority. The opinion makes clear that *Lucas* applies only to denials of *all* economically beneficial uses of *entire* parcels of property, stating that "the 'interest in land' that Lucas has pleaded [to have lost in its entirety is] a fee simple interest," and that "[i]t is true that in at least *some* cases the landowner with 95% loss will get nothing, while the landowner with total loss will recover in full." *Lucas* is limited to "relatively rare situations," "the extraordinary circumstances when *no* productive or economically beneficial use of land is permitted." *Lucas* is thus narrow indeed, for few if any environmental, historic preservation or land use laws prohibit *all* valuable use of an entire parcel.[149] Furthermore, the opinion places on the landowner the burden of proving that the government has deprived him of all "economically beneficial use of his land."

In one illustration of the holding's narrowness, the Supreme Judicial Court of Massachusetts in Steinbergh v. City of Cambridge rejected a takings claim arising from a city ordinance restricting removal of rent-controlled properties from the market for conversion and sale as condominiums, even though the court had in a prior action invalidated the ordinance as exceeding the board's authority. The *Steinbergh* court distinguished *Lucas,* finding that because the plaintiffs continued to collect rents, the ordinance "did not deny all economically beneficial or productive use of the plaintiff's interest in the property." Moreover, the regulation substantially advanced the purpose of rent control and did not interfere with the investment-backed expectations of the plaintiffs, who had acquired the property when the regulation was in effect. . . .

7.   *Nollan* (1987) and *Dolan* (1994)

Nollan v. California Coastal Commission, 483 U.S. 825 (1987), and Dolan v. City of Tigard, 512 U.S. S. Ct. 374 (1994), stand at the crossroads of two important developments in land use planning. The first is environmental planning to preserve coastal areas. Since beach vacations emerged

---

149. Stephen L. Kass & Michael B. Gerrard, *"Lujan," "Lucas,"* and *"Dague"*: A Scalian Trilogy, 208 N.Y.L.J. 3, 27 (July 31, 1992) ("[N]either the majority's nor the dissenters' dicta in *Lucas* is likely to have a significant effect on contemporary land use practice, which already affords 'hardship' relief from zoning and landmarking controls in virtually all jurisdictions (and, in some jurisdictions, from wetlands regulation as well) for property owners denied all economic use of their property").

as a cultural institution in the nineteenth century, development pressure on beach areas has been intense, particularly on the east and west coasts. Early intense development, sometimes directly on sand dunes, led to dramatic erosion of beachfront areas and substantial property loss. Erosion of beaches not only has devastating effects on individual homeowners whose properties are destroyed; it also threatens the tourism industry vital to the economies of many coastal states.[40]

Building houses on beach areas also presents two other kinds of environmental problems. The first is water pollution, which occurs as septic tanks and sewers seep in sandy soils. The second involves the destruction of habitat. Wetlands are the home of one-third of resident, and one-half of migratory, bird species in the United States; in California, only 9 percent of the state's original wetlands still exist. See John G. Mitchell, Our Disappearing Wetlands, 182 Natl. Geographic 13-14 (Oct. 1992).

The second important development reflected in *Nollan* is the growing use of exactions to finance infrastructure necessary to support residential and other development. Traditionally, towns paid for the roads, sewers, water, and other services needed to serve private homes and businesses. However, the funds available to state and local governments decreased after World War II as voters became increasingly unwilling to tolerate tax increases or to vote bond issues to support schools and fund other government services. Towns that were unable to finance the roads, sewers, and so forth for new development gradually began to condition grants of planning approval for new subdivisions on requirements that the subdivision developers provide the services required by the new development. This practice of "exactions" (also called "developers' fees") spread and gradually transmuted into programs where developers were required to contribute funds rather than actually to build the necessary facilities, for example, to contribute to a school fund rather than to build a new school. See, e.g., Home Builders & Contractors Assn. of Palm Beach County v. Board of County Commissioners, 446 So. 2d 140, *rev. denied* 451 So. 2d 848, *appeal dismissed,* 469 U.S. 976 (1984).

State courts generally held that such exactions were legitimate if they had "a reasonable relationship" with the subdivision at issue. The following language provides the leading explanation of the rationale behind this test. See Charles M. Haar and Michael Allan Wolf, Land Use Planning 633 (4th ed. 1989).

> We see no persuasive reason in the face of these urgent needs caused by present and anticipated future population growth on the one hand and the dis-

---

40. See, e.g., Richard Grosso and David J. Russ, Takings Law in Florida: Ramifications of *Lucas* and *Reahard,* 8 J. Land Use & Envtl. L. 431 (1993) (citing *Lucas*); Dennis J. Hwang, Shoreline Setback Regulations and the Takings Analysis, 13 U. Haw. L. Rev. 1 (1991); Elizabeth Cate, Back to Basics: The South Carolina Supreme Court Returns to the *Mugler v. Kansas* Era of Regulatory Takings Doctrine, 12 J. Energy Nat. Resources & Envtl. L. 237 (1992).

appearance of open land on the other to hold that a statute requiring the dedication of land by a subdivider may be justified only upon the ground that the particular subdivider upon whom an exaction has been imposed will, solely by the development of his subdivision, increase the need for recreational facilities to such an extent that additional land for such facilities will be required. . . . [T]he amount and location of land [required to be dedicated for park use] or fees shall bear a reasonable relationship to the use of the facilities by the future inhabitants of the subdivision.

Associated Home Builders of Greater East Bay, Inc. v. City of Walnut Creek, 4 Cal. 3d 633, 484 P.2d 606, 94 Cal. Rptr. 630, *appeal dismissed,* 404 U.S. 878 (1971).[41] This "reasonable relationship" test illustrates both the loose language characteristic of many state land use decisions and the general tendency to uphold a wide range of land use planning programs.

The U.S. Supreme Court federalized this law in *Nollan,* which replaced the state court "reasonable relationship" test with a more stringent text requiring an "essential nexus" between the exaction and the goal planning authorities sought to achieve. *Nollan* involved the exaction by the California Coastal Commission of an easement across the Nollans' beach front, in exchange for allowing the Nollans to tear down a bungalow and replace it with a standard three-bedroom house. The Court held that, although the Commission could have forbidden the Nollans from building their new house altogether under a Coastal Zone Management Act that forbid all new construction, it could not condition its permission to rebuild on the granting of an easement *across* the Nollans' land linking two public beaches because no "essential nexus" existed between the easement and the Commission's stated goal of overcoming the psychological perception (caused by "a wall of residential structures") of an entirely private coastline.

To contrast the bad (beach front easement) from the good, Justice Scalia wrote (surprisingly):

The Commission argues that among these permissible purposes are protecting the public's ability to see the beach, assisting the public in overcoming the "psychological barrier" to using the beach created by a developed shorefront, and preventing congestion on the public beaches. We assume, without deciding, that this is so — in which case . . . if the Commission attached to the permit some condition that would have protected the public's ability to see the beach notwithstanding construction of the new house — for example, a height limitation, a width restriction, or a ban on fences . . . imposition of the condition would also be constitutional. Moreover . . . the condition would be

---

41. In City of College Station v. Turtle Rock Corp., 680 S.W.2d 802 (Tex. 1984), the Texas Supreme Court upheld an ordinance that required developers to grant to the city for parkland one acre of land for each 133 housing units proposed. It said: "College Station's ordinance requires that only a small portion of a developer's subdivision tract be dedicated to serve park needs. It does not render the developer's entire property 'wholly useless' nor does it cause a 'total destruction' of the entire tract's economic value. It is a regulatory response created by the developer's use of the land." Id. at 806.

FIGURE 8-7
Viewing Station, as Proposed by *Nollan* Court

constitutional even if it consisted of the requirement that the Nollans provide a viewing spot on their property for passersby with whose sighting of the ocean their new house would interfere. Although such a requirement, constituting a permanent grant of continuous access to the property, would have to be considered a taking if it were not attached to a development permit, the Commission's assumed power to forbid construction of the house in order to protect the public's view of the beach must surely include the power to condition construction upon some concession by the owner, even a concession of property rights, that serves the same end.

483 U.S. at 835, 836.

An important issue raised by *Nollan* is whether Justice Scalia's majority opinion imposes the heightened standard of review the Supreme Court had abandoned half a century before when it held that economic legislation would be upheld if its means had a rational relationship with its goals. Id. at 845. See also United States v. Carolene Prod. Co., 304 U.S. 144, 154 (1935). Justice Brennan's dissent also included the kind of broad police power language common in state court cases but rarer in federal cases:

> Nonetheless it is important to point out that the Court's insistence on a precise accounting system in this case is insensitive to the fact that increasing intensity of development in many areas calls for farsighted, comprehensive planning that takes into account both the interdependence of land uses and the cumulative impact of development.[13] As one scholar has noted: "Property does not exist in isolation. Particular parcels are tied to one another in complex ways, and property is more accurately described as being inextricably part of a network of relationships that is neither limited to, nor usefully defined by, the property boundaries with which the legal system is accustomed to dealing. Frequently, use of any given parcel of property is at the same time effectively a use of, or a demand upon, property beyond the border of the user." Sax, Takings, Private Property, and Public Rights, 81 Yale L.J. 149, 152 (1971).
>
> State agencies . . . require considerable flexibility in responding to private desires for development in a way that guarantees the preservation of public access to the coast. They should be encouraged to regulate development in the context of the overall balance of competing uses of the shoreline. The Court today does precisely the opposite, overruling an eminently reasonable exercise of an expert state agency's judgment, substituting its own narrow view of how this balance should be struck. Its reasoning is hardly suited to the complex reality of natural resource protection in the 20th century. I can only

---

13. As the California Court of Appeal noted in 1985: "Since 1972, permission has been granted to construct more than 42,000 building units within the land jurisdiction of the Coastal Commission. In addition, pressure for development along the coast is expected to increase since approximately 85 percent of California's population lives within 30 miles of the coast." Grupe v. California Coastal Comm'n, 166 Cal. App. 3d 148, 167, n.12, 212 Cal. Rptr. 578, 589, n.12. See also Coastal Zone Management Act, 16 U.S.C. §1451(c) (increasing demands on coastal zone "have resulted in the loss of living marine resources, wildlife, nutrient-rich areas, permanent and adverse changes to ecological systems, decreasing open space for public use, and shoreline erosion").

hope that today's decision is an aberration, and that a broader vision ultimately prevails.[14]

Id. at 863-864.

Another important aspect of *Nollan* was its use of takings cases involving physical invasion, including *Loretto.*

> In *Loretto* we observed that where governmental action results in "[a] perma-
> nent physical occupation" of the property, by the government itself or by
> others . . . "our cases uniformly have found a taking to the extent of the oc-
> cupation, without regard to whether the action achieves an important public
> benefit or has only economic impact on the owner." We think a "permanent
> physical occupation" has occurred, for purposes of that rule, where individ-
> uals are given a permanent and continuous right to pass to and fro, so that
> the real property may continuously be traversed, even though no particular
> individual is permitted to station himself permanently upon the premises.

483 U.S. at 831-832.

A final element in *Nollan* is the innovative "expectations" argument
developed in Justice Brennan's dissent:

> The Court's demand for this precise fit is based on the assumption that
> private landowners in this case possess a reasonable expectation regarding the
> use of their land that the public has attempted to disrupt. In fact, the situation
> is precisely the reverse: it is private landowners who are the interlopers. The
> public's expectation of access considerably antedates any private development
> on the coast.
>   It is therefore private landowners who threaten the disruption of settled
> public expectations. Where a private landowner has had a reasonable expec-
> tation that his or her property will be used for exclusively private purposes,
> the disruption of this expectation dictates that the government pay if it wishes
> the property to be used for a public purpose. In this case, however, the State
> has sought to protect public expectations of access from disruption by private
> land use. . . .

Id. at 847-848.

Brennan's arguments raise the question of whether the ownership of
environmentally sensitive land entails the same expectations as does ownership of other land. Recall Just v. Marinette, *supra;* another relevant state

---

14. I believe that States should be afforded considerable latitude in regulating private
development, without fear that their regulatory efforts will often be found to constitute a taking. "If . . . regulation denies the private property owner the use and enjoyment of his land and
is found to effect a 'taking,'" however, I believe that compensation is the appropriate remedy
for this constitutional violation. San Diego Gas & Electric Co. v. San Diego, 450 U.S. 621, 656
(1981) (Brennan, J., dissenting). I therefore see my dissent here as completely consistent with
my position in First English Evangelical Lutheran Church of Glendale v. Los Angeles County,
482 U.S. 304 (1987).

case is Thornton v. Hay, 462 P.2d 671 (Or. 1969), in which the Oregon Supreme Court held that local custom gave the public an easement over the dry-sand area of Oregon beaches.[42]

> The dry-sand area in Oregon has been enjoyed by the general public as a recreational adjunct of the wet-sand . . . area since the beginning of the state's political history. The first European settlers on these shores found the aboriginal inhabitants using the [dry-sand area] for their cooking fires. The newcomers continued these customs after statehood. Thus, from the earliest settlement to the present day, the general public has assumed that the dry-sand area was a part of the public beach, and the public has used the dry-sand area for picnics, gathering wood, building warming fires, and generally as a headquarters from which to supervise children or to range out over the [wet-sand area] as the tides advance and recede. In the Cannon Beach vicinity, state and local officers have policed the dry sand, and municipal sanitary crews have attempted to keep the area reasonably free from man-made litter. . . .

462 P.2d at 673. Do *Just* and *Thornton* suggest that owning environmentally sensitive land in Wisconsin or Oregon may entail a different "bundle of rights" than owning ordinary land in those states, or environmentally sensitive land in other states?

Dolan further explores the contours of the "essential nexus" test first articulated in *Nollan*.

DOLAN v. CITY OF TIGARD

512 U.S. 374 (1994)

Chief Justice REHNQUIST delivered the opinion of the Court, in which O'CONNOR, SCALIA, KENNEDY, and THOMAS, JJ., joined. STEVENS, J., filed a dissenting opinion in which BLACKMUN and GINSBERG, JJ., joined. SOUTER, J., filed a dissenting opinion.

Petitioner challenges the decision of the Oregon Supreme Court which held that the city of Tigard could condition the approval of her building permit on the dedication of a portion of her property for flood control and traffic improvements. 317 Ore. 110, 854 P. 2d 437 (1993). We granted certiorari to resolve a question left open by our decision in Nollan v. California Coastal Comm'n, 483 U.S. 825 (1987), of what is the required degree of connection between the exactions imposed by the city and the projected impacts of the proposed development.

---

42. The public ordinarily has an easement over the wet-sand areas (i.e., those areas under water at high tide) under the common law. See, Thornton v. Hay, 462 P.2d 671, 673 (Or. 1969).

I

The State of Oregon enacted a comprehensive land use management program in 1973. Ore. Rev. Stat. §§197.005-197.860 (1991). The program required all Oregon cities and counties to adopt new comprehensive land use plans that were consistent with the state-wide planning goals. §§197.175(1), 197.250. The plans are implemented by land use regulations which are part of an integrated hierarchy of legally binding goals, plans, and regulations. §§197.175, 197.175(2)(b). Pursuant to the State's requirements, the city of Tigard . . . developed a comprehensive plan and codified it in its Community Development Code (CDC). The CDC requires property owners in the area zoned Central Business District to comply with a 15% open space and landscaping requirement. . . . After the completion of a transportation study that identified congestion in the Central Business District as a particular problem, the city adopted a plan for a pedestrian/bicycle pathway intended to encourage alternatives to automobile transportation for short trips. The CDC requires that new development facilitate this plan by dedicating land for pedestrian pathways where provided for in the pedestrian/bicycle pathway plan.

The city also adopted a Master Drainage Plan (Drainage Plan). The Drainage Plan noted that flooding occurred in several areas along Fanno Creek, including areas near petitioner's property. The Drainage Plan also established that the increase in impervious surfaces associated with continued urbanization would exacerbate these flooding problems. To combat these risks, the Drainage Plan suggested . . . ensuring that the floodplain remains free of structures and that it be preserved as greenways to minimize flood damage to structures. The Drainage Plan concluded that the cost of these improvements should be shared based on both direct and indirect benefits, with property owners along the waterways paying more due to the direct benefit that they would receive.

Petitioner Florence Dolan owns a plumbing and electric supply store located on Main Street in the Central Business District. . . . Fanno Creek flows through the southwestern corner of the lot and along its western boundary. The year-round flow of the creek renders the area within the creek's 100-year floodplain virtually unusable for commercial development. The city's comprehensive plan included the Fanno Creek floodplain as part of the city's greenway system.

Petitioner applied to the city for a permit to redevelop the site. Her proposed plans called for nearly doubling the size of the store . . . and paving a 39-space parking lot. . . . In the second phase of the project, petitioner proposed to build an additional structure . . . and to provide more parking. . . .

The City Planning Commission granted petitioner's permit application subject to conditions imposed by the city's CDC. . . . [T]he Commission required that petitioner dedicate the portion of her property lying within the 100-year floodplain for improvement of a storm drainage system along Fanno Creek and that she dedicate an additional 15-foot strip of land adjacent to the floodplain as a pedestrian/bicycle pathway. . . . In accordance with city practice, petitioner could rely on the dedicated property to meet the 15% open space and landscaping requirement mandated by the city's zoning scheme. . . .

Petitioner requested variances from the CDC standards. . . . The Commission denied the request.

The Commission made a series of findings concerning the relationship between the dedicated conditions and the projected impacts of the petitioner's project. First, the Commission noted that "[i]t is reasonable to assume that customers and employees of the future uses of this site could utilize a pedestrian/bicycle pathway adjacent to this development for their transportation and recreational needs." . . . In addition, the Commission found that creation of a convenient, safe pedestrian/bicycle pathway system . . . "could offset some of the traffic demand on [nearby] streets and lessen the increase in traffic congestion." Ibid.

The Commission went on to note that the required floodplain dedication would be reasonably related to petitioner's request to intensify the use of the site given the increase in the impervious surface. . . . [T]he Commission concluded that "the requirement of dedication of the floodplain area on the site is related to the applicant's plan to intensify development on the site." . . .

[Dolan appealed to the Land Use Board of Appeals (LUBA), arguing that the dedication requirements amounted to an unconstitutional taking of private property under the Fifth Amendment. LUBA upheld the dedication requirements. The Oregon Court of Appeals and the Oregon Supreme Court both affirmed. The U.S. Supreme Court reversed.]

II

. . . One of the principal purposes of the Takings Clause is "to bar Government from forcing some people alone to bear public burdens which, in all fairness and justice, should be borne by the public as a whole." Armstrong v. United States, 364 U.S. 40, 49 (1960). Without question, had the city simply required petitioner to dedicate a strip of land along Fanno Creek for public use, rather than conditioning the grant of her permit to redevelop her property on such a dedication, a taking would have occurred. *Nollan, supra,* 483 U.S., at 831. . . .

On the other side of the ledger, the authority of state and local governments to engage in land use planning has been sustained against constitutional challenge as long ago as our decision in Euclid v. Ambler Realty Co., 272 U.S. 365 (1926). . . .

The sort of land use regulations discussed in the cases just cited [*Pennsylvania Coal* and Agins v. Tiburon], however, differ in two relevant particulars from the present case. First, they involved essentially legislative determinations classifying entire areas of the city, whereas here the city made an adjudicative decision to condition petitioner's application for a building permit on an individual parcel. Second, the conditions imposed were not simply a limitation on the use petitioner might make of her own parcel, but a requirement that she deed portions of the property to the city. In *Nollan, supra,* we held that governmental authority to exact such a condition was circumscribed by the Fifth and Fourteenth Amendments. Under the well-settled doctrine of "unconstitutional conditions," the government may not require a person to give up a constitutional right — here the right to receive just compensation when property is taken for a public use — in exchange for a discretionary benefit conferred by the government where the property sought has little or no relationship to the benefit.

Petitioner contends that the city has forced her to choose between the building permit and her right under the Fifth Amendment to just compensation for the public easements. Petitioner does not quarrel with the city's authority to exact some forms of dedication as a condition for the grant of a building permit, but challenges the showing made by the city to justify these exactions. She argues that the city has identified "no special benefits" conferred on her, and has not identified any "special quantifiable burdens" created by her new store that would justify the particular dedications required from her which are not required from the public at large.

III

In evaluating petitioner's claim, we must first determine whether the "essential nexus" exists between the "legitimate state interest" and the permit condition exacted by the city. *Nollan,* 483 U.S., at 837. If we find that a nexus exists, we must then decide the required degree of connection between the exactions and the projected impact of the proposed development. We were not required to reach this question in *Nollan.* . . .

A

We addressed the essential nexus question in *Nollan.* . . . We resolved . . . that the Coastal Commission's regulatory authority was set completely adrift from its constitutional moorings when it claimed that a nexus existed between visual access to the ocean and a permit condition requiring lateral public access along the Nollan's beachfront lot. . . . The absence of a nexus left the Coastal Commission in the position of simply trying to obtain an easement through gimmickry. . . .

No such gimmicks are associated with the permit conditions imposed by the city in this case. Undoubtedly, the prevention of flooding along Fanno Creek and the reduction of traffic congestion in the Central Business District qualify as the type of legitimate public purposes we have upheld. . . .

B

The second part of our analysis requires us to determine whether the degree of the exactions demanded by the city's permit conditions bear the required relationship to the projected impact of petitioner's proposed development. . . . Here the Oregon Supreme Court deferred to what it termed the "city's unchallenged factual findings" supporting the dedication conditions and found them to be reasonably related to the impact of the expansion of petitioner's business. . . .

The question for us is whether these findings are constitutionally sufficient to justify the conditions imposed by the city on petitioner's building permit. . . .

In some states, very generalized statements as to the necessary connection between the required dedication and the proposed development seem to suffice. . . .

Other state courts require a very exacting correspondence, described as the "specific and uniquely attributable" test. . . . [I]f the local government cannot demonstrate that its exaction is directly proportional to the specifically created need, the exaction becomes "a veiled exercise of the power of eminent domain and a confiscation of private property behind the defense of police regulations." . . .

A number of state courts have taken an intermediate position, requiring the municipality to show a "reasonable relationship" between the required dedication and the impact of the proposed development. . . . [A] city may not require a property owner to dedicate private property for some future public use as a condition of obtaining a building permit when such future use is not "occasioned by the construction sought to be permitted."

We think the "reasonable relationship" test adopted by a majority of the state courts is closer to the federal constitutional norm than either of those previously discussed. But we do not adopt it as such, partly because the term "reasonable relationship" seems confusingly similar to the term "rational basis." . . . We think a term such as "rough proportionality" best encapsulates what we hold to be the requirement of the Fifth Amendment. No precise mathematical calculation is required, but the city must make some sort of individualized determination that the required dedication is related both in nature and extent to the impact of the proposed development. . . .

It is axiomatic that increasing the amount of impervious surface will increase the quantity and rate of storm-water flow from petitioner's property. Therefore, keeping the floodplain open and free from development would likely confine the pressures on Fanno Creek created by petitioner's development. . . . The city has never said [however] why a public greenway, as opposed to a private one, was required in the interest of flood control.

The difference to petitioner, of course, is the loss of her ability to exclude others. As we have noted, this right to exclude others is "one of the most essential sticks in the bundle of rights that are commonly characterized as property." *Kaiser Aetna,* 444 U.S., at 176. It is difficult to see why recreational visitors trampling along petitioner's floodplain easement are sufficiently related to the city's legitimate interest in reducing flooding problems along Fanno Creek, and the city has not attempted to make any individualized determination to support this part of its request. . . .

Admittedly, petitioner wants to build a bigger store to attract members of the public to her property. She also wants, however, to be able to control the time and manner in which they enter. . . . [T]he city wants to impose a permanent recreational easement upon petitioner's property that borders Fanno Creek. Petitioner would lose all rights to regulate the time in which the public entered onto the Greenway, regardless of any interference it might pose with her retail store. Her right to exclude would not be regulated, it would be eviscerated.

If petitioner's proposed development had somehow encroached on existing greenway space in the city, it would have been reasonable to require petitioner to provide some alternative greenway space for the public either on her property or elsewhere. . . . But that is not the case here. We conclude that the findings upon which the city relies do not show the required reasonable relationship between the floodplain easement and the petitioner's proposed new building.

With respect to the pedestrian/bicycle pathway, we have no doubt that the city was correct in finding that the larger retail sales facility proposed by petitioner will increase traffic on the streets of the Central Business District. . . . Dedications for streets, sidewalks, and other public ways are generally reasonable exactions to avoid excessive congestion from a proposed property use. But on the record before us, the city has not met its burden of demonstrating that the additional number of vehicle and bicycle trips generated by the petitioner's development reasonably relate to the city's requirement for a dedication of the pedestrian/bicycle pathway easement. The city simply found that the creation of the pathway "could offset some of the traffic demand . . . and lessen the increase in traffic congestion."

. . . No precise mathematical calculation is required, but the city must make some effort to quantify its findings in support of the dedication for the pedestrian/bicycle pathway beyond the conclusory statement that it could offset some of the traffic demand generated.

IV

Cities have long engaged in the commendable task of land use planning, made necessary by increasing urbanization particularly in metropolitan areas such as Portland. The city's goals of reducing flooding hazards and traffic congestion, and providing for public greenways, are laudable, but there are outer limits to how this may be done. . . .

The judgment of the Supreme Court of Oregon is reversed, and the case is remanded for further proceedings consistent with this opinion.

Justice STEVENS, with whom Justice BLACKMUN and Justice GINSBURG join, dissenting.

. . . The Court is correct in concluding that the city may not attach arbitrary conditions to a building permit or to a variance even when it can rightfully deny the application outright. I also agree that state court decisions dealing with ordinances that govern municipal development plans provide useful guidance in a case of this kind. Yet the Court's description of the doctrinal underpinnings of its decision, the phrasing of its fledgling test of "rough proportionality," and the application of that test to this case run contrary to the traditional treatment of these cases and break considerable and unpropitious new ground.

I

[First, the dissent criticizes the majority's reading of the state court opinions from which the majority derived its "rough proportionality" test.]

. . . The Court . . . erect[s] a new constitutional hurdle in the path of these conditions. In addition to showing a rational nexus to a public purpose that would justify an outright denial of the permit, the city must also demonstrate "rough proportionality" between the harm caused by the new land use and the benefit obtained by the condition. . . . The Court also decided for the first time that the city has the burden of establishing the constitutionality of its conditions by making an "individualized determination" that the condition in question satisfies the proportionality requirement. . . .

II

It is not merely state cases, but our own cases as well, that require the analysis to focus on the impact of the city's action on the entire parcel of private property. In *Penn Central* . . . we stated that takings jurisprudence "does not divide a single parcel into discrete segments and attempt to determine whether rights in a particular segment have been entirely abrogated." . . . Andrus v. Allard . . . reaffirmed the nondivisibility principle outlined in *Penn Central,* stating that "[a]t least where an owner possesses a full 'bundle' of property rights, the destruction of one 'strand' of the bundle is not a taking, because the aggregate must be viewed in its entirety." . . . Although limitation of the right to exclude others undoubtedly constitutes a significant infringement upon property ownership . . . , restrictions on that right do not alone constitute a taking, and do not do so in any event unless they "unreasonably impair the value or use" of the property. . . .

The Court's narrow focus on one strand in the property owner's bundle of rights is particularly misguided in a case involving the development of commercial property. . . . The exactions associated with the development of a retail business are . . . a species of business regulation that heretofore warranted a strong presumption of constitutional validity. . . .

IV

The Court has made a serious error by abandoning the traditional presumption of constitutionality and imposing a novel burden of proof on a city implementing an admittedly valid comprehensive land use plan. . . .

The Court has decided to apply its heightened scrutiny to a single strand — the power to exclude — in the bundle of rights that enables a commercial enterprise to flourish in an urban environment. . . .

In our changing world one thing is certain: uncertainty will characterize predictions about the impact of new urban developments on the risks of floods, earthquakes, traffic congestion, or environmental harms. When there is doubt concerning the magnitude of those impacts, the public interest in averting them must outweigh the private interest of the commercial entrepreneur. If the government can demonstrate that the conditions it has imposed in a land-use permit are rational, impartial and conducive to fulfilling the aims of a valid land-use plan, a strong presumption of validity should attach to those conditions. The burden of demonstrating that those conditions have unreasonably impaired the economic value of the proposed improvement belongs squarely on the shoulders of the party challenging the state action's constitutionality. That allocation of burdens has served us well in the past. The Court has stumbled badly today by reversing it.

I respectfully dissent.

Justice SOUTER, dissenting.
[Souter argues that the Court does not actually devise a new level of analysis, but rather has inappropriately applied *Nollan*'s nexus test to the facts of this case.]

. . . I cannot agree that the application of *Nollan* is a sound one here, since it appears that the Court has placed the burden of producing evidence of relationship on the city, despite the usual rule in cases involving the police power that the government is presumed to have acted constitutionally. Having thus assigned the burden, the Court concludes that the City loses based on one word ("could" instead of "would"), and despite the fact that this record shows the connection the Court looks for. Dolan has put forward no evidence that the burden of granting a dedication for the bicycle path is unrelated in kind to the anticipated increase in traffic congestion, nor, if there exists a requirement that the relationship be related in degree, has Dolan shown that the exaction fails any such test. The city, by contrast, calculated the increased traffic flow that would result from Dolan's proposed development to be 435 trips per day, and its Comprehensive Plan, applied here, relied on studies showing the link between alternative modes of transportation, including bicycle paths, and reduced street traffic congestion. . . . *Nollan,* therefore, is satisfied, and on that assumption the city's conditions should not be held to fail a further rough proportionality test or any other. . . .

NOTES AND QUESTIONS

1. **What conditions?** What conditions did the government impose on the landowner?

2. **Relationship of *Nollan* and *Dolan*?** Does *Dolan* impose requirements on governments in addition to those imposed by *Nollan*? What are they? What kinds of evidence will governments have to produce to meet *Dolan*'s requirements?

3. ***Euclid* overruled?** Does *Dolan* shift *Euclid*'s presumption of legislative validity? In all taking cases? In exactions cases?

4. **Visions.** What visions of property underlie each of the opinions?

5. **Takings legislation.** The Omnibus Property Rights Act of 1995 (S. 605) passed the Senate Judiciary Committee in 1995 but did not proceed further. [Nor did a far more limited companion bill passed in the House of Representatives.] This bill, proposed in fulfillment of the property rights section of the 1994 GOP Contract with America, was intended to broaden the rights of businesses and citizens to exact payment from the government for any actions that reduced the value of private property by one-third or more. Opponents of the act had raised concerns that such a bill could have much farther-reaching effects than its sponsors imagined. For example, the government might not be able to ground aircraft for safety violations without paying owners compensation. Telephone interview with Glen Sugameli, National Wildlife Federation (May 29, 1996). Critics also warned that the legislation would undermine local zoning, civil rights, worker safety, human health and public safety, and harm neighboring landowners. H. Jane Lehman, Property Rights Fight Heats Up on Hill, Wash. Post, Feb. 18, 1995, at F1.

Editors for the Washington Post opined that "the cost would be enormous; the government would in many cases be paying people and companies to stop doing things — polluting the air, destroying streams — inimical to the public interest; and the likely effect if not intent would be to shut down a lot of federal regulation." Editorial, Wrong Way on Takings, Wash. Post, Mar. 9, 1995 at A20. However, supporters of property rights say that someone must pay for any regulation; if the government compensates the property owner, then all taxpayers are paying for a public good, as is appropriate, rather than a private owner or business having to suffer the loss for everyone else's benefit. Tom Kenworthy, GOP Plan to Broaden Property Rights Could Cost Public Dearly, Wash. Post, Dec. 13, 1994, at A7.

Many state legislatures have considered property rights acts in the past few years. These typically contain provisions that either exempt private property from the effect of a given regulation if a takings analysis shows that it will reduce that property's value by a certain percentage (the amount required varies from state to state), or require the state to pay the owner for any such diminution. Arizona, Florida, Idaho, Kansas, Louisiana, Montana, North Dakota, Texas, Virginia, and Wyoming have all enacted some form of such legislation. The Legal Intelligencer, Aug. 14, 1995, at S6. See also Note, 108 Harv. L. Rev. 519 (1994), which discusses Utah law that requires state agencies to evaluate their regulations and determine if they could generate a taking.

6.   **Exactions.** In some cities, developers may be required to pay for things as diverse as subway improvements, libraries, museums, low-income housing, day care, fire and police stations, and health clubs. William K. Stevens, Developers Expanding Role in Social Services, N.Y. Times, Nov. 28, 1987 at Sec. 1, p.1. The willingness of developers to provide such services is especially important in those cities, critically short of funds and suffering from cutbacks in federal aid, that are unable to sustain the burden of even basic public services. B. Drummond Ayres Jr., Cities' Fiscal Problems Are Called "Ominous," N.Y. Times, June 30, 1987, at A21. What test must exactions meet under *Nollan*? Under *Dolan*? According to experts, the improvements exactions developers are required to pay may finance amenities that give developments a competitive edge. Is this reflected in the majority's *Nollan* analysis? Should it be? See Blue Jeans Equities West v. City and County of San Francisco, Chapter 9.

Chapter 9

Land Use Planning

Chapter 8 has already introduced a substantial number of land use planning techniques. *Euclid* and *Nectow* provided an example of the most common and basic type of zoning ordinance, which concentrates on dividing land into residential, commercial, and industrial uses, and also regulates building height and bulk. *Agins* and *Hamilton Bank*, two of the procedural tango cases, see Chapter 8 *supra*, involved modern variants of Euclidean zoning, in which the number or density of units allowed per acre depended on the quality of the proposed development plan (as judged by local officials). *San Diego*, another procedural tango case, involved planning to preserve open space. *Penn Central* introduced landmark laws, which aim to preserve the character of specific buildings and historical districts. *Penn Central* also introduced the idea of TDR's, or transferable development rights, in which a landowner required to maintain a landmark (or farm land, or open space) gains the right to sell to another owner the development rights she may not use herself. *Lucas* and *Nollan* both involve planning programs that curbed or conditioned development along coastal areas to preserve their fragile ecology and widen recreational use. *Dolan*, in part, was an effort to offset the perceived harmful impact of commercial development on traffic congestion.

Some of these regulations are called "planning"; some are called "zoning." In theory, zoning regulations are a means to implement a land use plan. (In practice, we shall see, the relationship between planning and zoning is blurrier, but for now that definition will serve.)

§9.1 Theoretical Foundations of Land Use Planning

NORMAN WILLIAMS, PLANNING LAW
AND DEMOCRATIC LIVING

20 Law & Contemp. Prob. 317-318 (1955)

. . . As used here, "planning" means the process of consciously exercising rational control over the development of the physical environment, and of certain aspects of the social environment, in the light of a common scheme of values, goals, and assumptions. Planning is concerned with guiding both public and private action, and may be on a local, metropolitan, or regional basis.

In planning, primary emphasis is on the physical environment; yet the social environment is also involved in many ways. First, intelligent correlation of decisions on the development of the physical environment necessarily involves having consistent assumptions and policies derived from the social environment, as for example on the size and characteristics of the population, even though such matters are left generally to individual decisions. Second, in some instances attempts are made to influence individual decisions on such matters, as for example population migration and the birth rate — although here there is a wide difference of opinion on how far planning should go.[1] Finally, the distinction between the physical and the social environment is really an artificial and untenable one anyway, since the arrangement of the physical environment has a decided impact upon social conditions, and vice versa.

This process of conscious and purposeful control over the development of the physical and social environment in a relatively free society is something rather new in history. Moreover, in such a society the development of techniques to forecast probable future trends, and thus to ascertain and evaluate the range of possibilities within which control may be exercised, is a difficult process at best. The development of effective methods of exercising such control is even more difficult. Any consideration of planning techniques available, while extremely useful, are still rather crude. It is a truism to say that even the best plans must be subject to constant review in the light of changing conditions. Moreover, what techniques are available have generally not been thought out in terms of all their implications for the whole environment. . . .

LISA PEATTIE, REFLECTIONS ON ADVOCACY PLANNING

34 J. Am. Inst. Planners 80, 80-81 (1968)

The concept of "advocacy planning" can only be understood in the context of the management of modern American cities. In ancient cities, planning was primarily a function of individual leaders and of relatively small social groups — families, guilds, religious fraternities, and the like. The "squatter settlements" surrounding cities of the developing countries

---

1. The one point on which there is universal agreement is that the precise outer limits of urban and regional planning are not easy to define. However, we are not concerned here with over-all economic planning in the socialist or collectivist sense.

suggest the degree to which public policy and official planning still control only a relatively limited part of urban life. Our cities are more and more publicly managed environments. Private actions take place within a generally narrowing network of public intervention, public policy, and public planning. . . .

But as a consequence, we have developed a set of bureaucratic management institutions which often seem impersonal and alien to human feelings. "Our technological civilization . . . seems to overtake and overwhelm us as though it were something foreign coming in on us. . . ." People may respond to this sense of being overwhelmed by political apathy and disengagement or they may protest. It is interesting to see how the polemic literature against urban renewal and against fluoridation of drinking water share the angry suspicion that something has been "put over" on ordinary people by the experts. . . .

The shift from politics to expertise changes the rules for exercising power, as well as the structure of effective power. The result may entail a cost in equity, since it can well be argued that those most disadvantaged will be the people at the bottom of the system — those who are, through lack of education and of technical sophistication, particularly ill-prepared to deal with the presentation of issues in a technical framework. Such groups tend to be disadvantaged in the traditional political framework, and still more so when it comes to dealing with those who speak the language of maps, diagrams, and statistical tables. Advocacy planning has its origins initially in the perception that such groups need planners to make their case, to express their interests. Therefore, it represents a search by planners for new kinds of clientele.

Advocate planners take the view that any plan is the embodiment of particular group interests, and therefore they see it as important that any group which has interests at stake in the planning process should have those interests articulated. In effect, they reject both the notion of a single "best" solution and the notion of a general welfare which such a solution might serve. Planning in this view becomes pluralistic and partisan — in a word, overtly political.

NOTES AND QUESTIONS

1. **Two different images of planning.** These two authors present two very different images of planning. How do they differ?

2. **From advocacy planning to local economic development.** One strain of advocacy planning shifts the focus from physical planning to planning and advocacy for jobs and economic development. For contributions by the influential planner Robert Meier, see Robert Meier, Social Justice and Economic Development (1993) and Theories of Local Economic De-

velopment: Perspectives from Across the Disciplines (Richard D. Bingham & Robert Meier eds., 1993).

Houston is the only city in the United States that does not have zoning; the following article by Bernard Siegan is a précis of speeches he gave in the campaign that led to the third defeat of a proposed zoning law, in 1993. (The two earlier defeats were in 1948 and 1962. In those years, according to one author, "It was a simple equation: Zoning equals communism." Paul Weingarten, Unbridled Growth Has Houston Tangling with the Z Word, Atlanta Constitution, Jan. 6, 1991, at M6.) The Houston city council voted in 1991 to draw up a zoning proposal (the one eventually rejected by the voters in 1993) after the construction boom of the 1980s left many people dissatisfied. Developers had built 73 million square feet of office space. Then property prices fell sharply, and homeowners felt unable to take the time-honored solution of moving away from unwanted development. Moreover, many people had become dissatisfied with the system of protecting Houston's more affluent Houston neighborhoods with covenants. Protected residents often felt the covenants were expensive and cumbersome to maintain, and pointed out that the covenants gave the neighborhood no control over what happened outside its borders. Lower-income neighborhoods typically had no covenants, and so were more vulnerable to what many saw as commercial encroachments. One news article cited two examples of dissatisfied homeowners. A retired insurance broker complained that he couldn't grow roses in his garden anymore because two 40-story condominium buildings were built next door, and a 30-story office building was built across the street. (See Figure 9-1.) A homeowner in a modest older neighborhood complained that one neighbor's sign business sent 18-wheeler trucks down his narrow street all night, and that his next-door neighbor had tried to turn his property into a used-car lot. Jacqueline L. Salmon, Wide Open Houston Faces the Unthinkable: Zoning, Wash. Post, June 6, 1992, at E1; Paul Weingarten, Unbridled Growth Has Houston Tangling with Z Word, Atlanta J. & Const., Jan. 6, 1991, at 1-2. This suggests that much of the support for zoning in Houston stemmed from homeowners' desire to protect their expectations over time.

These examples also suggest that one effect of the absence of zoning in Houston was to produce more mixed patterns of land use, particularly in lower-income neighborhoods not protected by covenants. See Weingarten, *supra* (almost half of the city's area, "in general, the poorer neighborhoods," have no zoning or covenants). "Gas stations and burger stands in Houston casually back up to elegant department stores. High-rise condominiums tower over elegant, tree-lined residential communities. Small homes are sandwiched between tire stores and used-car lots." See Jacqueline L. Salmon, *supra*. One effect of zoning may have been to equalize access to purely residential neighborhoods among income groups. The opposite side of the

FIGURE 9-1
Houston Home Surrounded by 40- and 30-Story Buildings

coin, of course, is that zoning often limits homeowners' ability to open up a business in their house. The growing popularity of family day care, where women care for others' children in the women's homes, has raised difficult issues in some communities.

BERNARD H. SIEGAN, NON-ZONING IS THE BEST ZONING

31 Cal. W. L. Rev. 127, 132, 137-138 (1994)

. . . Zoning has been a colossal flop because it is supposed to do things it cannot do. What, for instance, is the "right" mix of homes and apartments? How much industry is "too much?" Where is business to be allowed, and what kinds? Is there some objective measurement available to determine the "best" use of some or all the land, of growth and antigrowth proposals, and whether the land is better suited for open space, mobile homes, industry or the housing of people? Should the land be developed with one, two or four housing units to the acre?

Typically, zoners and planners confront Herculean problems in determining land use. Questions of compatibility, desirability, economic feasibility, property values, existing uses, adjoining and nearby uses, traffic, topography, utilities, schools, future growth, conservation, and environment have to be considered for countless locations covering hundreds of square miles. Yet to determine just economic feasibility for a certain use at any one site for any one period of time would require a professional market survey costing thousands of dollars and taking months to complete.

By now, after seven decades of zoning experience in the United States, it should be clear that there are respectable, distinguished and knowledgeable planners who would disagree in many if not most instances to any or all of the aforementioned alternatives. Planning is unquestionably highly subjective, lacking those standards and measurements that are requisites of a scientific discipline.

IX.   ZONING CAUSES SOCIETAL PROBLEMS

. . . The above practices cause various societal problems, as follows:

First, zoning increases prices. The absence of zoning has enabled Houston to keep rents and housing prices relatively low.[31] Houston's rents have been far less than Dallas' because of the absence of zoning.[32]

Second, zoning wastes land. Zoning usually increases the land area required for building. Bigger lots consume considerably more land for housing and urban purposes, reducing the supply for other uses, such as farming and grazing. The proposed Houston ordinance restricts density over what it would otherwise be, and the operation of the zoning process is likely to restrict it even more.

Third, zoning stifles competition. By limiting development, regulation reduces competition and the creativity, ingenuity, and productivity that go with it. In zoned cities, these talents are often spent in persuading or outmaneuvering the zoning authorities. By contrast, competition thrives in Houston. One result is that Houston is probably the best provider of housing of any major city in the world.

Fourth, zoning eliminates smaller developers. Zoning causes us to lose the talents of small and moderate sized developers. The smaller builders do not have the resources to pay for zoning experts, zoning attorneys, and the cost of keeping the land vacant and unproductive while the zoners mediate. This leaves the market limited to only "the big guys" with the big resources, who, as a result, are often quite satisfied with zoning.

Fifth, zoning promotes politics and graft. Politics in Houston at the present time isn't exactly a minor industry. But with zoning, it will boom.

31. In a report released June, 1994, the accounting firm of Ernst and Young ranked the greater Houston area as the nation's most affordable of seventy metropolitan areas surveyed. It was ranked third most affordable in 1993. The ranking is based on the extent to which housing cost is a percentage of household income. Pat Rosen, Houston Rates Well When Considering Housing Costs, Hous. Post, June 29, 1994, at B1.

32. Bernard H. Siegan, Conserving and Developing the Land, 27 San Diego L. Rev. 299-304 (1990).

The largest political contributors in zoned cities frequently are developers who require approval for their projects.

Zoning transforms city council members into modern alchemists. They are able to change land zoned worthless to land zoned golden simply by passing a law. Allowing either two units to the acre, or three or four units to the acre may make a difference in profits of thousands of dollars for a developer.

Obviously, developers and speculators will seek to secure zoning that will increase the value of their property. This includes hiring the "right" attorneys and experts, and maybe contributing money, either above or under the table, to those well connected. It is said the greatest virtue in a prince is to know his friends. Is there any wonder why there is so much corruption in zoning? When I was seeking a title for a book critical of zoning, one developer suggested the title, "Goodbye Graft."

Finally, zoning curtails development. As a negative device, zoning has curtailed growth and development, reducing construction activity, business, employment and real estate and other tax collections.

There will be less production of commercial, industrial and multi-family real estate, each of which yields substantial taxes, to the financial detriment of the city.

BRADLEY C. KARKKAINEN, ZONING: A REPLY TO THE CRITICS

10 J. Land Use & Envtl. L. 45, 47-54, 61-78 (Fall 1994)

. . . Zoning's proponents traditionally have offered two rationales, neither of which stands up to close scrutiny. First, zoning advocates suggest that zoning is necessary to protect or enhance property values, particularly the values of residential properties (and especially single-family homes). On this analysis, zoning serves principally to protect property owners from the negative externalities of new developments. Without zoning (or some comparable system of land use regulation), residential property owners would face plummeting property values if a development with significant negative externalities — a junkyard or brick factory, for example — moved in next door. Moreover, the mere prospect that such a development could move in would tend to depress the value of residential property. The solution is to divide the municipality into zones so that industries are sited near other industries, commercial enterprises near other commercial enterprises, and residential properties with other residential properties. This rationale has some intuitive appeal, based on the real or imagined horrors of entirely unregulated development.

A significant problem with the property values rationale for zoning, however, is that such a rationale is difficult to support with empirical evidence. It has not been clearly established that zoning results in higher market values for residential property. Another problem with this rationale is that zoning's advocates have not clearly established that zoning is the only means, or even the most effective or efficient means, of controlling externalities.

Second, zoning is defended as a tool of a broader scheme of comprehensive urban planning. However, in many smaller communities that cannot afford their own planning agencies, zoning is often not accompanied by comprehensive planning. Furthermore, critics suggest that in bigger cities that do have planning departments, planners often find zoning a bothersome, time-consuming, and highly technical distraction from what they regard as their more important planning functions, i.e., charting the future of that area. Therefore, it is not clear that zoning has ever been well-integrated with the other tools at a planner's disposal. In particular, with regard to mega-developments that often preoccupy big-city planning departments, traditional zoning appears to play a relatively minor role among the array of available planning tools. Finally, Houston, which has never had a zoning ordinance, does have an active and apparently effective planning department. This suggests that zoning is not a necessary component of successful urban planning.

More recently, some zoning advocates have suggested the prevention of "fiscal freeloading" as a third rationale. According to this view, some new developments place a greater burden on public services than they contribute in new taxes. Zoning is a means by which such developments can be screened out in favor of developments that pay their fair share. This may indeed be one of the ways zoning is used in some exclusive, and exclusionary, suburban communities, but it does not appear to be a major factor in big-city zoning schemes. Moreover, where the fiscal freeloading rationale is employed, it has troublesome normative implications. . . .[It] may become a rationale for excluding lower-income (and often minority) persons from suburban residency and opportunities for economic advancement.

III.   The Critiques

Most of the critiques of zoning fall into four broad categories. . . .

A.   ZONING IS UNFAIR TO SOME PROPERTY OWNERS

Some critics contend that zoning is fundamentally unfair because it grants special privileges to some property owners (typically, current owner/occupants of single-family homes) at the expense of others, including principally those (usually non-resident) owners who wish to develop their property for non-residential purposes. Stated this way, the argument concedes that zoning confers a real benefit to some property owners, e.g., single-family homeowners. . . . This argument rests on the normative judgment that the benefit to homeowners does not justify the harm to would-be developers. A variant of this argument is the utilitarian version, which argues that the wrong is the fact that the harm to would-be developers outweighs the benefit to homeowners. Yet the basic unfairness argument need not go this far. Therefore, under this critique, even if the benefit to homeowners outweighs the harm to would-be developers, zoning is wrong.

. . . Absent a constitutional or positive law norm prohibiting unequal treatment of different classes of property owners, advocates of this position must rely on some deeper moral principle. Yet our legal system recognizes many other kinds of unequal burdens by type of property, such as differential tax treatment. This suggests that under contemporary notions of property, the moral and legal norms implicated here are at best very weak. Ultimately, this type of critique must rest on a highly controversial (and ultimately unsupportable) natural rights notion of property in which property rights are seen as having some nearly-inviolable, pre-political status.

B.   ZONING IS EXCLUSIONARY

This argument, in its attenuated form, has already been alluded to in the prior discussion on fiscal freeloading. In its more general form, the argument is that zoning, because it is prohibitory in nature, is fundamentally a device of exclusion. It is further argued that, in fact, zoning is widely used to exclude racial groups, economic classes, and economic activities that are deemed to be undesirable. These arguments are more commonly directed at suburban zoning because big cities, by their very nature, tend to be less exclusionary, taking all comers. . . .

The idea that some racially discriminatory applications of zoning should somehow taint all zoning is a peculiar one. If zoning is consciously used to achieve racial segregation, then a serious problem exists. But this problem should be addressed by constitutional and statutory equal protection claims, not by scrapping zoning. . . .

More difficult is the claim that zoning is used to exclude persons by economic class, resulting in the side effect of racial exclusion, because racial minorities generally are not as affluent as the white majority. Again, this charge is typically made against suburbs rather than big cities because big cities embrace a greater diversity of income classes. The problem with this claim is that our legal and political culture is at best ambivalent about the principle of equal treatment on the basis of economic status. Even if society were committed to the principle, the appropriate remedy would not be to reject zoning as an institution, but to challenge particular applications of the zoning power based on impermissible categories of economic status. Alternatively, the states or perhaps Congress could enact statutes prohibiting the use of zoning to exclude on the basis of economic status. . . .

D.   ZONING PRODUCES INEFFICIENT LAND USE ALLOCATION DECISIONS

In its purest form, an economic critique of zoning might argue that zoning (or any scheme of land use regulation) is inherently inefficient because it forces landowners to make land use allocation decisions other than those they would make in a free market. According to classical economic theory, free markets efficiently allocate economic resources, and neither legislative-type categorical regulations nor case-by-case decisions by bureaucratic regulators can make such decisions as efficiently as the market. Thus, land use decisions made under a regulatory scheme inevitably result in inefficient distortions of the market.

The classic objection to such a pure laissez-faire approach is that it does not take into account externalities or spillovers from land uses. Internalizing the externalities requires some kind of regulatory scheme. . . .

Most of zoning's critics recognize the need to control negative externalities through some regulatory scheme, but do not make the pure laissez-faire "market distortions" argument. Since any regulatory scheme is arguably subject to the laissez-faire market distortions objections, their objections to zoning principally turn on equity and transactional efficiency arguments. . . .

IV.   ZONING: ANOTHER LOOK

A.   ZONING TO PROTECT THE NEIGHBORHOOD COMMONS

This article contends that both supporters and critics of zoning have misconceived the nature of zoning. Zoning is only partially about protecting individual property owners against the effects of "spillovers" or negative externalities that adversely affect the market values of their property. Specifically, zoning protects a homeowner's consumer surplus in a home and in the surrounding neighborhood, that lies above the market value of that home. This consumer surplus has essentially been overlooked and is fundamental to an understanding of zoning. . . .

Zoning in urban neighborhoods is not merely a system for protecting the market values of individual properties, but rather is a device to protect neighborhood residents' interests in their entirety, including consumer surplus in their homes, as well as their interests in what this article calls the neighborhood commons.

. . . "Home" provides continuity, security, familiarity, and comfort for our most intimate and satisfying life experiences. The intimately bound ideas of home and family strike deep emotional chords in our culture. Since most people feel that these values cannot be reduced to dollars, people tend to be especially sensitive when the use and enjoyment of the home is threatened. In part, this reflects the importance of a homeowner's financial stake, which typically represents a substantial part of that homeowner's net worth. If the only concern were to protect financial investments, however, monetary compensation for any loss of market value would be acceptable. Part of zoning's appeal lies in the fact that it allows homeowners to protect all the value we place in a home, including the consumer surplus that lies above and beyond the market price of the home....

Neighborhoods are not just made up of individual parcels, but include collective resources comprising a neighborhood commons, and the property rights of an urban neighborhood dweller typically consist both in specified rights in an individual dwelling and inchoate rights in a neighborhood commons. This commons consists of open-access (but use-restricted) communally-owned property, such as streets, sidewalks, parks, playgrounds, and libraries. It also includes restricted-access but communally-owned property, such as public schools, public recreational facilities, and public transportation facilities.

It further includes privately-owned "quasi-commons" to which the public generally is granted access, but with privately-imposed restrictions as to use, cost, and duration. These generally include restaurants, nightspots, theaters, groceries, and retail establishments. It will include (risking the appearance of an oxymoron) "private commons," like churches, temples, private schools, political organizations, clubs, and fraternal and civic organizations. These are essentially private associations, but are characterized by some substantial degree of open access to members of the community. Finally, the neighborhood commons will include other tangible qualities such as neighborhood ambiance, aesthetics, the physical environment (including air quality and noise), and relative degrees of anonymity or neighborliness.

These features together make up the "character of a neighborhood. They are what give the neighborhood its distinctive flavor. A purchaser of residential property in an urban neighborhood buys not only a particular parcel of real estate, but also a share in the neighborhood commons. Typically, differences in the neighborhood commons may be as crucial to a decision to purchase as differences in individual parcels.

To some extent, differences in the neighborhood commons will be reflected in the market values of individual parcels. If, for example, other things being equal, neighborhood A has better public schools and more desirable parks than neighborhood B, property in neighborhood A will have a higher market value than similar property in neighborhood B....

This article has argued that, although ultimately we can never be certain, zoning may be welfare-maximizing.... In this idealized model zoning gives current neighborhood residents a kind of "right of prior appropriation" over the neighborhood commons. This right trumps the right of other property owners to use their land in ways that interfere with, or are inconsistent with, current uses of the neighborhood commons. Developments may proceed as long as they are either consistent with current uses of the neighborhood commons, or in ways the neighborhood has agreed in advance (through the political process) to allow. This protects the expectations of neighborhood residents. Moreover, neighborhood residents have the right to change course and to agree to modify the rules to permit developments facially inconsistent with the presumptive prohibitions. But the only compensation that may be offered or accepted for such exceptions is compensation that benefits the community as a whole, i.e., that preserves a healthy and vibrant commons. . . .

§9.2   City Planning: San Francisco as an Example

JANICE C. GRIFFITH AND JOSEPH Z. FLEMING,
SAN FRANCISCO'S DOWNTOWN PLAN —
BLUEPRINT FOR THE 1990s?

---

18 Urb. Law. 1063, 1063-1069 (1986)

I.   INTRODUCTION

On November 29, 1984, San Francisco's City Planning Commission adopted an innovative Downtown Plan (Plan) that incorporates farreaching design, bulk, height, and density controls that a few years ago would have been considered unthinkable.[1] The Plan goes further than this. It also requires the developer to provide a number of amenities that traditionally have not been considered part of a developer's responsibility. San Francisco's downtown developers must provide up-front funding, or, in some cases, ongoing financial support, for mass transit, downtown parks, on-site art works, and child care facilities.

The Plan also focuses on preservation of buildings that represent historical values or present distinctive architecture. Emphasis throughout the Plan is placed upon maximizing and retaining existing urban patterns that conform to San Francisco's physical landscape.

Critics will dismiss the Plan as an antigrowth measure that is bound to cause business to move elsewhere. It deserves, however, to be seriously explored.

---

1. The Downtown Plan [hereinafter referred to as Downtown Plan] was adopted by an ordinance of the City and County of San Francisco effective October 17, 1985. . . .

II.   THE DOWNTOWN PLAN: NEW CONSTRUCTION REQUIREMENTS

A.   DESIGN REVIEW

The Plan seeks to achieve smaller buildings of architectural merit that are tapered to be thinner at the top. The construction is viewed as more aesthetically pleasing that the so-called "benching effect" that has resulted from the construction of a number of rectangular buildings that are all built to the maximum height level and topped by flat roofs. A more practical objective is also sought: tapered buildings which allow more sunlight into the streets and decrease the wind velocity at their bases for the enjoyment of pedestrians in the downtown area.

Design review is done by the zoning administrator and the director of planning . . .

B.   LOWERING OF FLOOR AREA RATIOS TO REDUCE THE SCALE OF DOWNTOWN DEVELOPMENT

By utilizing the concept known as floor area ratios (FARs) the Plan controls the size of buildings by limiting their volume. "Floor area ratio means the ratio of the space (floor area) in a building to the size of the lot."[5] Prior to the advent of the Downtown Plan, FARs in the downtown commercial areas ranged from 14:1 to 7:1. FARs for this area now range from 9:1 to 5:1.

C.   BULK CONTROLS TO TAPER BUILDINGS AT UPPER LEVELS

The Downtown Development Plan applies limits upon the overall bulk of buildings as well as separate bulk controls upon the lower tower and upper tower portions. The emphasis, however, is upon controlling the bulk of the upper tower portion to achieve tapered buildings at the upper levels. San Francisco's planners considered the lowering of bulk in upper towers so desirable that they were willing to provide for an exception to height restrictions to encourage it.[10]

---

5. Downtown Plan, *supra* note 1, at 3. A FAR of 8 to 1, for example, means that 8 square feet of building area may be built for each square foot of lot area.

10. Id. §263.9. Additional height up to 10% of height restrictions shown on Maps 1H, 2H, and 7H of the Zoning Map may be permitted as an extension of the upper tower provided that the volume of the upper tower is reduced. Id. §263.9(a). This additional height is granted, however only if it is determined:

That the upper tower volume is distributed in a way that will add significantly to the sense of slenderness of the building and the visual interest to the termination of the building, and the added height will improve the appearance of the skyline when viewed

D. HEIGHT RESTRICTIONS THAT LOWER MAXIMUM PERMITTED HEIGHTS IN NEARLY ALL DOWNTOWN COMMERCIAL DISTRICTS

The Plan redirects office building expansion to the area south of Market Street by substantially lowering heights in areas north of Market Street where significant groupings of smaller buildings exist. In the Kearny-Market-Mason-Sutter Conservation District, the center of San Francisco's retail center and an area famed for its tourist trade, new construction must be compatible with the existing scale of buildings, three-fourths of which are eighty feet or less.

Two policies account for height and bulk controls: (1) the desire to relate the height of buildings to important city patterns and to the scale of existing development; and (2) the desire to prevent new construction from overwhelming or dominating the downtown area. To retain San Francisco's visual appeal, which is formed in part by its topography of hills and ridges in close proximity to the ocean and bay, the height of new development must be in keeping with the "total pattern of the land and of the skyline."

E. REQUIREMENTS FOR SUNLIGHT ACCESS TO PUBLIC SIDEWALKS AND FOR REDUCTION OF GROUND LEVEL WIND CURRENTS

High-rise buildings can dramatically affect wind accelerations at the street level by intercepting large volumes of moving air. The more exposed the building is to the prevailing wind direction, the greater the potential for wind acceleration. Ground level wind impact is also affected by the shape, area, and uniformity of the upwind facade of the building. Large, uniform facades will cause greater wind velocity at their bases than thinner facades with numerous setbacks.

Buildings and additions to buildings in the downtown area are required to be designed so that they do not cause ground level wind currents to exceed more than 10 percent of the comfort level of eleven miles per hour equivalent wind speed. An exception may be granted if it can be shown that the building cannot be designed to meet this criteria without (1) creating an unattractive building form and (2) unduly restricting the development potential of the building site in question. No exception may be granted, however, that would permit equivalent wind speeds to reach or exceed twenty-six miles per hour for a single hour of the year. . . .

---

from a distance, will not adversely affect light and air to adjacent properties, and will not add significant shadows to public open spaces.

Id. at §263.9(b).

III.   Preservation of Buildings and Districts or Architectural, Historical, and Aesthetic Importance

San Francisco's preservation program is similar to New York City's landmark legislation which was upheld in Penn Central Transportation Co. v. New York City. Its objective is to preserve and continue the use of buildings presenting special architectural, historical, and aesthetic value. The Ordinance states that these buildings contribute to "San Francisco's reputation throughout the United States as a city of outstanding beauty and physical harmony."

Following a survey which systematically evaluated and rated the 1,700 buildings in the downtown commercial area, buildings were placed in five categories: (1) Significant Buildings — Category I; (2) Significant Buildings — Category II; (3) Contributory Buildings — Category III; (4) Contributory Buildings — Category IV; and (5) Unrated Buildings — Category V. Without a permit, alterations or demolition may not be made of Significant or Contributory Buildings or buildings designated Category V that are located in one of the Conservation Districts. The latter districts have been created to preserve a concentration of buildings that together possess a unique historic, architectural, and aesthetic character.[33]

The preservation strategy of retaining the 251 Significant Buildings and the 182 Contributory Buildings is implemented by providing for the transfer of the unused development rights from these buildings.[2] Demolition of a Significant Building or Contributory Building is prohibited unless it is determined that (1) the property retains no substantial market value or reasonable use after taking into account the value of transferable development rights (TDRs) and the costs of rehabilitation to meet building code standards or other laws; or (2) demolition is the only feasible means to eliminate a safety hazard.

An application for alterations will not be granted unless the proposed alterations are consistent with the architectural character of the building.

SHARON SILVA & FRANK VIVIANO, MAKE NO LITTLE PLANS

TWA Ambassador, Jan. 1986, at 52

Critics call it aesthetic fascism; an anti-growth, bureaucratic boondoggle. Others think San Francisco's Downtown Plan will be the blueprint for American cities in the twenty-first century.

---

33. Id. §§1110, 1112. New construction including replacements and additions in Conservation Districts must be compatible in scale and design with the District. *See id. §1113.*

2. For a discussion of transferable development rights, see §8.1(b)(1). — Eds.

. . . By 1966, the 35-year-old [Dean] Macris[3] was assistant commissioner of planning, appointed by Mayor Daley himself to help oversee the first major revision of Daniel Burnham's 57-year-old Chicago Comprehensive Plan, which was as influential in 1909 as San Francisco's plan is today. Like the mid-nineteenth-century visionary Baron Georges Haussmann, who refashioned Paris at the behest of Napoleon III, Burnham conceived an urban ideal and proceeded — often imperiously — to realize it. "Make no little plans," he once told Chicago businessmen. "Let your watchword be order, and your beacon beauty." The Chicago fire of 1871 had made it possible for Burnham to begin his early work on a fairly clean slate, and he filled it with his own notions of beauty — majestic parks and avenues in the French Beaux Arts tradition that he also worked into master plans for Washington, D.C., San Francisco, and Manila.

"The old approach, epitomized by Burnham's grand vision, was an 'end-state' plan, aimed at a point 50 years ahead," says Macris. "What is needed in the modern world is not that kind of fixed vision. Ours are not totalitarian cities that can simply order boulevards built; they are different from the cities of the past — more disorderly, developed under different political conditions. The challenge now is to open up the process to involve the public in solving problems." . . .

Maggie Baylis is one of those "adversely affected" by the modern city's habit of "changing constantly." . . .

"I came to San Francisco in 1938," she says, "and moved to the top of the hill" — Telegraph Hill, which crowns North Beach — "two years later. In those days, it wasn't the chic place it has since become. My neighbors were salesmen, architects, weirdos, eccentric characters like 'the Duchess' — I don't know if she really was one — and a woman who painted birds on the side of her building. Renovation hadn't arrived yet. When they lit the fireplace in the oldest house on the hill, smoke poured out from between the bricks. The community was centered around Speedy's grocery store; all information, whether it be social, political, or plain practical, involved meetings there. I ate out every night in Chinatown, whole meals for 35 cents." . . .

But by the late Sixties and early Seventies, the same pressures that had driven the Baylises from the top of the hill were moving down its slope, says Baylis. "Property values were soaring. There were big demographic changes under way. Singles wanted to live closer to their downtown jobs, and a lot of the Italians were leaving for the suburbs. Cars were becoming a big problem, as commuters began to use us as a parking lot."

Parking was far from North Beach's worst problem, but it emerged as the most visible symbol of the neighborhood's determination to remain livable. "We took a survey and discovered that daytime parking around here

---

3. Macris was the director of San Francisco's Department of City Planning during the development of the San Francisco Downtown Plan. — EDS.

was 103 percent," says Baylis. "Every spot was taken. The 3 percent was across our driveways." The people of North Beach made themselves heard on that issue at City Hall; the result was a system of residential parking stickers that outlawed commuter cars in the area.

Saying "no" was already an established neighborhood tradition in San Francisco, which set many of the local-control precedents now enshrined in the urban environmentalist movement. Twice in the Sixties, neighborhood organizations managed to scuttle major freeway projects. . . .

Enter Dean Macris. Ever since his arrival in San Francisco he had been methodically collecting the components for a new city plan. In 1981, when he took over as planning director, he hired a talented young staff to help him develop the final blueprint. . . .

"The real question for us was not so much downtown itself, as it was the 'ring areas' — the surrounding districts that downtown growth threatens," explains . . . Alton Chinn. Chinn is on the staff of the Chinatown Neighborhood Improvement Resource Center (CNIRC), a non-profit service agency that has spearheaded efforts to safeguard America's largest Asian community from the effects of too much commercial development in their neighborhoods.

"The whole thing boils down to what kind of city you want," says Chinn of the threat to such areas. . . .

From first page to last, the Downtown Plan presumes a world of corporate executives, clerical employees, and service workers. The future, implies the San Francisco plan, belongs to the white-collar economy.

Some call this a betrayal of the city's past, of the blue-collar industries and the port that long gave her energy, of the older San Francisco that, as Alton Chinn puts it, "many of us still love." But Macris calls it realism, and says it reflects trends that are sweeping the entire country. "Big city growth depends on white-collar functions today," he responds. "We're not some isolated economic entity. Everywhere jobs are being created because of white-collar commerce and services. If we are going to have a new job base in this country, we have to accommodate the trend. But the idea is to manage change in our own best interests."

[Says Macris,] "There are always two viewpoints: there are the property owners and builders who favor development, and there are others who live here who want continuity and stability — I won't call them 'anti-growth,' that's an unfair characterization. When both sides say, 'We didn't get all we want, but we reluctantly go along,' I know we've achieved what we set out to: bureaucratic equilibrium. We're at a place where we can move forward with some consensus."

And that place is where America's most dramatic planning instrument, the document that Macris eased through to a 6-5 passage by San Francisco's governing board of supervisors on September 10, 1985, lies today. The mayor of Boston, Raymond Flynn, flew out to San Francisco to witness firsthand the final vote on the Downtown Plan. Like San Francisco, Boston is enjoying an unprecedented boom. Like San Franciscans, Boston residents are voicing "a significant degree of concern," the mayor said. "I'm here to pick up a few pointers."

On the "aye" side were Carol Ruth Silver, who even in tolerant San Francisco is often described as "too liberal," and Wendy Nelder, the fiercely conservative daughter of an ex-police chief. Among the five "nays," three were cast by legislators, both conservative and liberal, whose quarrel centered on the level of the annual limit imposed on downtown growth; some wanted a lower ceiling. In other respects, they tacitly supported the plan.

Walter Shorenstein, who owns or manages some 30 percent of the office structures in the financial district and recently purchased the Bank of America Building (San Francisco's largest structure) for $660 million, the highest price ever paid for a single property, publicly spoke on behalf of development limits, despite his own opposition to the plan's transit fees and height restrictions. "No one wants a Houston-like gridlock here," he conceded, no doubt referring to a huge office complex whose location in the heart of downtown Houston created a bottleneck that literally freezes traffic flow over a four-square-mile area for hours at a time. William Coblentz, an influential attorney who represents many of the city's major developers, offered a fuller endorsement: "It makes sense to me as a planning device," he says, "and I am pleased that it passed." Gordon Chin, executive director of CNIRC, would have liked tougher measures against downtown encroachment into ring neighborhoods. Still, he called the plan "a laudable effort to shape the skyline, to preserve the past, to improve the pedestrian environment for downtown office workers."

If few of the city's key power brokers approved the plan in toto, enough backing emerged for its various components to assure "bureaucratic equilibrium." Mayor Daley would have been proud.

The planner's job "is to channel growth, to prove that cities can be masters of their own destinies," says Edith Netter, APAP secretary-treasurer and assistant planning director for Boston, which is currently drawing up its own design for the future. "The tough part is finding a way to do it that doesn't kill the goose that laid the golden egg, while still ensuring a measure of social and economic justice." . . .

READING THE FINE PRINT

WHAT'S IN THE PLAN?

Mass Transit Fee

When the city's developers build the next generation of skyscrapers, they will contribute, up front, $5 per square foot of new construction to a mass transit fund. This fee, unprecedented in the United States, highlights a facet of the plan that will also make demands on ordinary citizens — a clear bias against the automobile. Although San Francisco's downtown employment is expected to increase by 90,000 workers in the next fifteen years, few additional parking spaces will be created, and some of the present automobile access routes are actually slated for demolition.

"The basic premise," explains land use expert David Prowler, "is that things will get so bad, people will abandon their cars. The question is whether the transit will be there to pick them up — whether the $5 per square foot will be enough if the federal government does go completely out of the transit business."

"Until recently," says Macris of such fees, "providing the infrastructure for growth was thought to be strictly a government responsibility. Federal and state programs helped to a certain degree, but the main weight fell on the cities. The philosophy behind our plan is that if you have a strong market like San Francisco, where people *want* to build and to share fairly in profit, they also have an obligation to share the cost of meeting the problems that growth engenders."

That philosophy is not widely endorsed in the business community, even among developers who support controls on growth. Walter Shorenstein, Downtown's leading landowner, has launched a court challenge to the transit fee, arguing that it will encourage corporations to seek space elsewhere. "Buildings don't pay the fees," he says, "the tenants do. If it's too expensive, they don't locate here."

Art, Open Space, and Child Care

Developers must spend one percent of their total building budget on public artworks, establish an on-site center for the care of children or earmark a $1-per-square-foot contribution to a city child-care fund, and use at least $2 per square foot of new construction to create open spaces — public parks and malls. According to assistant director of city planning George Williams, San Francisco is "the first major city to require that commercial development in a high-density downtown provide usable public open space. The Downtown Plan envisions a central area where almost everyone would be within 900 feet (approximately two blocks) of a publicly accessible space in which to sit, eat a brown-bag lunch, and people-watch."

Housing

Through the use of zoning powers and exemption from height and density requirements, the plan protects some 15,000 low-income residences adjacent to downtown, and encourages new housing in nearby underdeveloped areas. One such exemption is the Santa Fe Southern Pacific Corporation's 200-acre mixed-use Mission Bay community on former railroad warehouse land in the South of Market; with 7,500 housing units, 4.1 million square feet of office space, and 200,000 square feet of retail space, it will be the largest project of its type undertaken in the United States in recent memory.

But the most unusual aspect of Macris's design for sheltering San Franciscans is the Office Housing Production Program (OHPP) — known locally as "OOPS!" — through which developers pay for residential units to accommodate any increase in the work force occasioned by their office construction. The estimated cost of this measure, which has been in effect on a trial basis for four years, is $5.34 per square foot of office space. Since 1981, it has provided the city with $25 million and paid for 3,000 housing units.

Ceiling on Growth

The focal point of the controversy generated by the Downtown Plan was its 950,000-square-foot limit on annual construction of buildings larger than 50,000 square feet. (In recent years, office towers have been going up in a city at the rate of nearly 3 million square feet per year.) San Francisco is alone among U.S. cities in setting such a ceiling, which will be reviewed every three years. Developers and their chamber of commerce allies blanched at the thought of any ceiling; many environmentalists and several members of the city board of supervisors argued strenuously for a much lower limit, or an outright moratorium on new construction. In the end, an elaborate political compromise — forged through years of Chicago-style brokering by the planning director — arrived at the legislated figure, which amounts to roughly one major highrise each year.

After the Supreme Court's *Nollan* decision, see Chapter 8, challenges to the exactions imposed by the San Francisco Downtown Plan were inevitable. The following case is one such challenge.

BLUE JEANS EQUITIES WEST v. CITY & COUNTY OF SAN FRANCISCO

3 Cal. App. 4th 164, 4 Cal. Rptr. 2d 114 (1992)

WHITE, J. In this action we consider whether the heightened scrutiny test alluded to in Nollan v. California Coastal Comm'n (1987), should be applied to San Francisco's Transit Impact Development Fee (TIDF) ordinance. (Ord. No. 224-81, codified at S.F. Admin. Code, §38.1 et seq.) We conclude the *Nollan* analysis is applicable only to "possessory takings," rather than "regulatory takings," and does not apply to the TIDF.

Plaintiff Blue Jeans Equities West is the owner and developer of Levi's Plaza, a five-building office, retail and condominium complex in the north or northeast waterfront section of San Francisco. This area of San Francisco is located away from the financial district, the traditional area of downtown office space. At the time of the project's conception, the main tenant was to be Levi Strauss & Company, which was then located in the financial district of the city. Prior to construction of the complex, a final environmental impact report was prepared by the San Francisco Department of City Planning. Among other things, the report discussed the adverse impact the project would have on transportation.[1]

The permit for Levi's Plaza was approved by the San Francisco Planning Commission's Resolution No. 8142 on January 4, 1979. The resolution contained a condition in its transit mitigation section, designated as paragraph 5(c), which provided: "The owner of the project shall make a good-faith effort to participate in future funding mechanisms to assure adequate transit service to the area of the city in which the project is located."

On May 5, 1981, the San Francisco Board of Supervisors enacted the TIDF ordinance. As our Supreme Court described it: "The ordinance, which became effective the following month, requires developers of downtown buildings containing new office space to pay a TIDF as a condition of issuance of a certificate of completion and occupancy. The TIDF, not to exceed $5 per square foot of new office space, provides revenue for the municipal railway to offset the anticipated costs of the increased peak-period ridership generated by the new office space over the useful life of each office building." (Russ Bldg. Partnership v. City & County of San Francisco 44 Cal. 3d 839, 844-845 (hereafter *Russ II*).) At the time of its enactment, plaintiff had not yet received a certificate of completion for Levi's Plaza.

Plaintiff filed a complaint for declaratory relief against the city, contending the TIDF ordinance is unlawful and invalid as applied to the Levi's Plaza project and the TIDF may not be imposed with respect to plaintiff. While the case was pending, the parties stipulated to the fee calculation and plaintiff deposited the agreed amount, over $3.1 million, in trust, pending the case's outcome.

The trial court entered judgment for defendant, finding that the TIDF ordinance is not an unconstitutional "taking" on its face or as applied to plaintiff, plaintiff acquired no vested right to build or use Levi's Plaza without payment of the TIDF, and defendant is not estopped from requiring plaintiff to pay the TIDF. This appeal followed.

DISCUSSION

In Russ Bldg. Partnership v. City & County of San Francisco (1987) 199 Cal. App. 3d 1496 (hereafter *Russ I*), Division Five of this District held

1. The report states in pertinent part: "Employees arriving by BART, AC Transit, SAM-TRANS, Southern Pacific, and the ferries would have to transfer to another mode (MUNI) to reach the project site. The proportion of vehicle drivers among Levi Strauss employees would tend to increase from about 16% to about 17.5%. Sixteen additional bus runs on Routes 15/42 and 32 would have to be operated during the peak hour to provide adequate capacity to sustain the 17.5% vehicle-driver modal split. This would represent about 4-minute headways on the combined 15 and 42 routes and about 6-minute headways on Route 32."

the San Francisco TIDF ordinance was a valid development fee, which could not be challenged under articles XIII A and XIII B of the California Constitution or the equal protection and due process clauses of the federal and state Constitutions. In essence, the opinion finds the TIDF a fee, rather than a special tax. (Id., at p.1507, 246 Cal. Rptr. 21.)

In *Russ II*, the Supreme Court addressed the question of whether the TIDF ordinance could be applied to projects which, at the time of the enactment of the ordinance, were in the course of construction pursuant to building permits conditioned on the developers' participation "in a downtown assessment district, or similar fair and appropriate mechanism, to provide funds for maintaining and augmenting transportation service. . . ." (*Russ II, supra.*) [2] The high court concluded that the condition encompassed the TIDF, and held that the TIDF could be imposed on the projects without impairing the developers' vested rights. (Ibid.) However, the *Russ II* court expressly declined to address whether the TIDF violated the takings clause of the United States Constitution, as interpreted in *Nollan* (*Russ II, supra.*)

In *Nollan,* the United States Supreme Court held the California Coastal Commission had violated the Fifth Amendment by conditioning a building permit for beachfront property on the owners' dedication of an easement allowing the public to walk on the portion of the property nearest to the ocean. The condition requiring an easement violated the "taking" clause, because it did not serve a governmental purpose related to the permit to rebuild. (*Nollan, supra.*) At least one California court has interpreted the *Nollan* holding as providing "there must be a substantial connection, or 'nexus' between the public burden created by the construction and the necessity for the easement." (Surfside Colony, Ltd. v. California Coastal Com. (1991) 226 Cal. App. 3d 1260, 1267.) This interpretation is based, in part, on footnote 3 of the *Nollan* opinion: "[O]ur opinions do not establish that these standards are the same as those applied to due process or equal protection claims. To the contrary, our verbal formulations in the takings field have generally been quite different. We have required that the regulation 'substantially advance' the 'legitimate state interest' sought to be achieved, [citation], not that 'the State "could rationally have decided" that the measure adopted might achieve the State's objective.' (*Nollan, supra.*)

A threshold issue is whether the *Nollan* nexus test should be applied to the case at bench. Plaintiff takes an affirmative position, while defendant disagrees.

It is settled that any regulation of economic interests which "goes too far" becomes a "taking" under principles of inverse condemnation [citing *Penn Coal, First English*]. However, there is no set formula for determining what constitutes a "taking"; the courts rely instead on ad hoc, factual inquiries into the circumstances of individual cases [citing *Penn Central* and other cases].

---

2. *Russ II* left intact the *Russ I* holding that the TIDF was a valid development fee.

In Agins v. Tiburon (1980), *supra,* the United States Supreme Court stated: "The application of a general zoning law to particular property effects a taking if the ordinance does not substantially advance legitimate state interests or denies an owner economically viable use of his land. The determination that governmental action constitutes a taking is, in essence, a determination that the public at large, rather than a single owner, must bear the burden of an exercise of state power in the public interest." *Nollan* has been construed as refining the first prong of the Agins test "to require that the regulation advance the precise state interest which avowedly motivated it." (Long Beach Equities, Inc. v. County of Ventura (1991) 231 Cal. App. 3d 1016, 1029.)

However, the high court appears to make a distinction between "regulatory takings," i.e., economic regulation, most forms of zoning, and other restrictions on land use, and "possessory takings," where the government, or an authorized third person, physically intrudes upon or appropriates the property. (See Manheim, Tenant Eviction Protection and the Takings Clause, (1989) Wis. L. Rev. 925, 939.)

Nollan specifically points out that "our cases describe the condition for abridgment of property rights through the police power as a 'substantial advanc[ing]' of a legitimate state interest. We are inclined to be particularly careful about the adjective where the actual conveyance of property is made a condition to the lifting of a land-use restriction, since in that context there is heightened risk that the purpose is avoidance of the compensation requirement, rather than the stated police-power objective." (*Nollan, supra,* emphasis in original.) Based on this language, most legal scholars have concluded the *Nollan* strict scrutiny approach is limited to unconstitutional conditions and possessory takings cases. (See, e.g., Manheim, *supra,* Wis. L. Rev. at p.950; Lawrence, Means, Motives, and Takings: The Nexus Test of *Nollan v. California Coastal Commission* (1988) 12 Harv. Envtl. L. Rev. 231, 263; but see Been, "Exit" as a Constraint on Land Use Exactions: Rethinking the Unconstitutional Conditions Doctrine (1991) 91 Colum. L. Rev. 473.)

Case law subsequent to *Nollan* appears to confirm this view. Pennell v. San Jose (1988) 485 U.S. 1, concerns a city rent control ordinance that permits consideration of "hardship to a tenant" when determining whether to approve a rent increase proposed by a landlord. In addressing whether rent control was per se a taking the court stated: "[W]e have 'consistently affirmed that States have broad power to regulate housing conditions in general and the landlord-tenant relationship in particular without paying compensation for all economic injuries that such regulation entails.'" *Pennell* appears to reaffirm the traditional view that as long as governmental regulations do not require a landowner to suffer the physical occupation of a portion of his real estate, the regulations will be analyzed as nonpossessory governmental activity.

More on point, in Commercial Builders v. Sacramento (9th Cir. 1991) 941 F.2d 872, commercial developers challenged a city ordinance that conditioned nonresidential building permits on payment of a fee to offset burdens associated with the influx of low-income workers to work on such developments. The developers argued that pursuant to *Nollan*, an ordinance that imposes an exaction on developers can be upheld only if it can be shown that the development is directly responsible for the social ill that the exaction is designed to alleviate. [T]he Ninth Circuit concluded *Nollan*'s heightened scrutiny test was inapplicable to regulations that do not constitute a physical encroachment on land. (Commercial Builders, *supra*, 941 F.2d at p.874.)

In light of the above-quoted language in *Nollan* and post-*Nollan* case law, we hold that any heightened scrutiny test contained in *Nollan* is limited to possessory rather than regulatory takings cases. . . .

The judgment is affirmed.

NOTES AND QUESTIONS

1. **San Francisco Downtown Plan.** Keep in mind that the original conception of planning was to plan for the physical environment. The San Francisco Downtown Plan clearly goes far beyond this original conception. Reconsider the various elements of the plan. Does it go too far in your view? After you have considered that question, consider what assumptions about ownership inform your viewpoint.

2. *Blue Jeans* **and** *Nollan.* Recall the *Nollan* case discussed in Chapter 8. Does the California court in *Blue Jeans* correctly apply the *Nollan* holding? Some would consider *Blue Jeans* an example of how state courts have evaded the recent Supreme Court cases. Do you?

3. *Blue Jeans* **and** *Dolan.* The Supreme Court had not yet decided *Dolan*, also discussed in Chapter 8, at the time of *Blue Jeans*. If *Dolan* were also in the landowner's precedential mix, would this have changed the *Blue Jeans* outcome? The crafting of the *Blue Jeans* opinion?

4. *Blue Jeans* **and** *Ehrlich.* At issue in Ehrlich v. City of Culver City, 12 Cal. 4th 854, 911 P.2d 429 (1996), was whether *Dolan*, which involved the required dedication of real property, also applied to a monetary exaction. In *Ehrlich*, the city had levied a mitigation fee of $280,000 as its condition for agreeing to rezone property to permit the construction of a 30-unit condominium project. The site, prior to rezoning, had housed a private sports complex (tennis courts, swimming pool, and so on) that its owners had closed down because they could no longer run it profitably. In levying the exaction, the city calculated that it would cost $800,000 to replace the "lost" recreational facilities.

On the first go-round, the California Court of Appeal found a "substantial nexus" (the *Nollan* test) between the proposed condominium project and the $280,000 exaction; 191 Cal. Rptr. 2d 468 (1994). However, the U.S. Supreme Court granted certiorari and summarily vacated the state court judgment, remanding the case for further consideration in light of *Dolan,* which it had just decided; 114 S. Ct. 2731 (1994).

On the remand, the Court of Appeal reaffirmed its earlier ruling in favor of the defendant city (unpublished opinion). On review, the state Supreme Court reversed and held that the city had not met the *Dolan* standard in justifying the exaction.

In returning *Ehrlich* to the state court, the Supreme Court strongly implied that *Dolan*'s "rough proportionality" test also reached monetary exactions, requiring more than a "minimal level of scrutiny." The California court, however, narrowed *Dolan*'s heightened level of scrutiny to a relatively small class of land use cases — "those exhibiting circumstances which increase the risk that the local [agency] will seek to avoid the obligation to pay just compensation." 12 Cal. 4th at 868.

Cutting through this verbiage, the court distinguished between an ordinance or rule of "general applicability," as to which minimal scrutiny would be enough, and the instant case, where the exaction was imposed "neither generally nor ministerially, but on an individual and discretionary basis." (The court's concern here was the potential for extortionate behavior.)

The court then explained why it could not uphold the $280,000 exaction:

> The city argues that its $280,000 recreation fee is warranted as partial compensation for the loss of some $800,000 in recreational improvements that were formerly located on plaintiff's property. But in this case it is error to measure the lost recreational benefits by the lost value of plaintiff's health club. The loss which the city seeks to mitigate by levying the contested recreational fee is not loss of any particular recreational facility, but the loss of property reserved for private recreational use. . . . The city may not constitutionally measure the magnitude of its loss, or of the recreational exaction, by the value of facilities it had no right to appropriate without paying for.

Id. at 882.

In his concurrence, Justice Mosk reasoned that monetary exactions, where generally imposed, were similar to taxes, special assessments, and user fees, which receive substantial judicial deference. Moreover, the Justice argued:

> [In] one fundamental sense, monetary exactions are more like zoning restrictions: like these restrictions they do not involve a physical invasion of property, but merely a diminution in its economic value. As such, development fees may be placed in a class not only with such land use regulations, but also with other sorts of economic regulations that may significantly reduce the profit or value derived from property, yet are not deemed to be takings unless the regulations are arbitrary or confiscatory.

Id. at 891-892. Where does all this leave *Blue Jeans?*

5. **Criticism of design review and standards.** The San Francisco Downtown Plan has drawn sharp criticism from both growth and antigrowth advocates. In addition to curbing growth and ensuring that new development is supported with adequate infrastructure and services, the plan also places a limit on the amount of new building that can take place in San Francisco in any one year. In 1983, when the plan was announced by city planning officials, this growth cap was 950,000 square feet per year. Two years later, a public referendum cut the quota in half. Because the amount of new office space to be constructed is sharply limited, builders must conform not only to local zoning laws, but must also present their designs before a panel of architects and other political appointees. This design review panel evaluates new building permit applications on the basis of architectural quality and economic viability. The results have been mixed. While the plan has helped to preserve the San Francisco skyline by stemming the tide of large office towers, it has failed to alleviate overcrowding in the financial district by shifting development south of Market Street, as the plan had originally intended. This is because the economic concerns central to the approval process have favored development in the already prosperous financial district.

The plan has also drawn the ire of real estate developers, architects, and attorneys who complain that the approval process has shifted the balance of power away from private developers and into the political arena. Paul Goldberg, a noted architecture critic, notes that firms submitting proposals for new buildings have been less willing to take risks in the creative process. The result, says Goldberg, has been "buildings that are unusually tame, even dull." Paul Goldberg, For San Francisco, Cure Is Worse than High-Rise Disease, N.Y. Times, Dec. 5, 1987, at A8.

§9.3   Euclidean Zoning

JAMES H. WICKERSHAM, THE QUIET REVOLUTION CONTINUES: THE EMERGING NEW MODEL FOR STATE GROWTH MANAGEMENT STATUTES

18 Harv. Envtl. L. Rev. 489, 493-496 (1994)

The basic structure of Euclidean zoning has changed little since the 1920s. Zoning ordinances regulate both the type and density of land use by dividing a municipality into zones. A typical zoning code partitions a municipality into residential, commercial, and industrial zones. Uses may then be further subdivided: for example, single-family or multifamily residential; small shops or office complexes; and light or heavy industrial. Finally, requirements for minimum lot sizes, building heights, and building setbacks from lot lines regulate density.

Because the SZEA was drafted before the emergence of federal and state administrative procedure acts, it contains very few procedural requirements at the municipal level. A local, legislatively appointed Board of Adjustment reviews rules on amendments, grievances, special permits, variances, and nonconforming uses, subject to judicial review. Courts give limited deference to special permit and variance decisions, which are usually treated as "quasi-judicial," while giving greater leeway to amendments or rezonings, which are usually treated as "quasi-legislative." Standing in zoning cases is narrowly restricted to include only property owners, abutters, and other immediately affected parties.

B.   THE ROLE OF ZONING IN POSTWAR SUBURBANIZATION

The trend towards suburbanization began in the nineteenth century, long before zoning appeared. The most rapid expansion of suburbia, however, occurred in the latter half of this century. In the postwar era, federal policies spurred the development of interstate highway systems and promoted inexpensive mortgages for suburban homes, encouraging the move to the suburbs. Euclidean zoning has played a major role in the development of recent, distinctive suburban growth patterns. Unlike other health and safety regulations, zoning operates prospectively, affecting only new development. Thus, zoning affected older northern and midwestern cities little, greatly influencing the rapid growth of the southern and far western sunbelt cities.

In suburban communities, the predominant pattern of zoning widely separates residential, business, and industrial uses, rather than permitting the much more fine-grained mixing of uses that is typical of older cities. Suburban zoning has encouraged very low population densities; residential lot size requirements ranging from one to five acres are not uncommon. Zoning has encouraged patterns of "ribbon" or "strip" development along major roads, by setting aside large areas for low-density commercial use.

Low-density suburban development patterns can radically affect the environment. Although each individual house may seem innocuous, the widespread expansion of public services such as sewers and septic systems, road building, clearing, and levelling of lots, can destroy existing ecosystems. Suburban development can also radically transform the visual quality of the landscape. Strip commercial development along major roads gives an impression of an unending landscape of gas stations, shopping centers, and fast food outlets; two or three new houses built in the middle of a field can destroy the visual image of a long established farming community.

Furthermore, Euclidean zoning's low densities and separation of uses have created a dependence on private automobiles as the sole form of transportation in the suburbs. Cost considerations prohibit the development of public transportation systems, such as buses and railroads. Since people no longer live, work, and shop in a single area, each activity requires an additional automobile trip. The reliance on automobiles has resulted in a variety of environment and social problems: air pollution (primarily carbon monoxide and low level ozone, the chief component of smog), road and parking lot construction (destruction of ecosystems), and traffic congestion.

Finally, low-density, large-lot residential zoning exacerbates high housing prices by raising the cost of land and municipal services in relation to each housing unit. Disparities in housing prices between older cities and newer suburbs have reinforced patterns of community segregation by class and race.

KAREN A. FRANCK, THE SOCIAL CONSTRUCTION OF THE PHYSICAL ENVIRONMENT: THE CASE OF GENDER IN WOMEN, HOUSING AND COMMUNITY

60-61, 62, 64, 66 (Willem Van Vliet ed., 1988)

THE SUBURBAN HOUSE AND COMMUNITY

The American suburban house and the larger suburban community support and enforce an age and gender system that divides the activities of men and women and adults and children. . . . [S]uburban settings strengthened and extended these divisions by separating and distancing spaces where the activities of men and women occur. Social divisions became physical divisions and separations. . . .

SEPARATION OF ACTIVITIES AND SPACES

The divisions of activities according to gender centers on the expectations that women will pursue homemaking and childrearing activities and men will pursue wage-earning activities. . . . While women also joined the labor force, society's ideal was that only men would do so and that women's proper place was in the home. At the same time, industrialization eliminated the housework that had been assigned to men and children, without changing much of the work women had to do in the home. . . .

The single-family detached house, located in a setting having more natural amenities than the city, was considered an ideal place to raise children. . . . The design of the house requires each homemaker to take sole responsibility for many homemaking tasks that might otherwise be shared with other homemakers or performed by a commercial service. . . . These tasks are often performed in isolation from other household members as well.

Since the residential units are separated and at some distance from necessary services such as stores, schools, medical care, places for entertainment or athletics, the homemaker is required to spend considerable time transporting herself and others to these different services simply to fulfill her homemaking obligations. . . .

Many of the characteristics of suburbia actually made the tasks of homemaking more difficult than they have been previously and certainly more difficult than they had to be. [One author] suggests that "suburbia as a built environment, at least as presently built, is conducive to and facilitating of only one female role, that of housewife and mother." Yet in many respects the suburban environment does not facilitate even that role. Another difficulty it posed for the homemaker, through exclusionary zoning, was the enforced absence of other types of householders who might be able to assist in homemaking and childrearing, examples being elderly people, single people, or couples without children. . . .

SEPARATION OF SOCIAL RELATIONSHIPS

The opportunities for being intimate may also be decreased by the opposing needs of the wage earner and homemaker. At the end of the working day, the former is likely to want a certain amount of quiet and relaxation while the latter, having been alone or with children all day, may desire adult conversation and more active pastimes. Given such different realms of needs and experiences, wage earner and homemaker may have less understanding of one another's problems than was the case in earlier times when their activities and experiences were regularly observable to one another and were even shared.

By creating physical distance between wage-earning spaces and homemaking ones, suburban settings simply strengthened the experiential differences between wage earner and homemaker and created different arenas for the relationships of each. In addition to distancing husband from wife, suburbia may have distanced the wife from potential friends.

DIFFERENTIAL SUPPORT FOR SELF-IDENTITY

. . . The division of activities, feelings, and space according to gender seems likely to pose problems for any person who does not fit into the stereotype of married, employed man or married, homemaking woman.

The U.S. Department of Commerce, in September 1921, appointed an Advisory Committee on Zoning. Two lawyers, three engineers, two housing consultants, one realtor, one landscape architect, and one "civic investigator" composed its membership. In August 1922, the committee sponsored a model enabling law, which gained immediate and lasting acceptance. By 1925, nineteen states had already adopted the model wholly or in part, and today enabling laws exist in every state. All states allow municipalities to zone, and three quarters of the states now enable countywide zoning. For a comprehensive survey of the enabling laws, see Cunningham,

Land-Use Control — The State and Local Programs, 50 Iowa L. Rev. 367, 268-380 (1965).

A half-century later, the texts of most enabling statutes still show their ancestry, despite enormous changes in zoning theory and practice. This may mean that the committee did its job well, combining a sound intuition about the future with an uncommon skill in drafting. Or, alternatively, this durability may simply reflect legislative inertia — a failure to re-examine first premises and to modify them as needed. Perhaps, as you go through these materials, you will form your own ideas as to which it is.

A STANDARD STATE ZONING ENABLING ACT

U.S. Department of Commerce (1926 rev.)[4]

§1. *Grant of power.* For the purpose of promoting health, safety, morals, or the general welfare[5] of the community, the legislative body of cities and incorporated villages is hereby empowered to regulate and restrict the height, number of stories, and size of buildings and other structures, the percentage of lot that may be occupied, the size of yards, courts, and other open spaces, the density of population,[6] and the location and use of buildings, structures, and land for trade, industry, residence, or other purposes.

§2. *Districts.* For any or all of said purposes, the local legislative body may divide the municipality into districts of such number, shape, and area as may be deemed best suited to carry out the purposes of this act; and within such districts it may regulate and restrict the erection, construction, reconstruction, alteration, repair, or use of buildings, structures, or land. All such regulations shall be uniform for each class or kind of buildings throughout each district[7] but the regulations in one district may differ from those in other districts.

---

4. The general explanatory notes, page 958, *infra*, also derive from the Standard Act.

5. *"General welfare":* The main pillars on which the police power rests are these four, viz., health, safety, morals, and general welfare. It is wise, therefore, to limit the purpose of this enactment to these four. There may be danger in adding others, as "prosperity," "comfort," "convenience," "order," "growth of the city," etc., and nothing is to be gained thereby. . . .

6. *"Density of population":* The power to regulate density of population is comparatively new in zoning practice. It is, however, highly desirable. Many different methods may be employed. For this reason the phrase "density of population": is a better phrase to use than one giving the power to "limit the number of people to the acre," as this is only *one* method of limiting density of population. It may be more desirable to limit the number of families to the acre or the number of families to a given house, etc. The expression "number of people to the acre" is therefore limited in its meaning and describes only one way of reducing congestion of population, while the phrase provision will make possible the creation of one-family residence districts. . . .

7. *"Uniform for each class or kind of buildings throughout each district":* This is important, not so much for legal reasons as because it gives notice to property owners that there shall be no improper discriminations, but that all in the same class shall be treated alike. . . .

§3. *Purpose in view.*[8] Such regulations shall be made in accordance with a comprehensive plan[9] and designed to less congestion in the streets; to secure safety from fire, panic, and other dangers; to promote health and the general welfare; to provide adequate light and air; to prevent the overcrowding of land; to avoid undue concentration of population; to facilitate the adequate provision of transportation, water, sewerage, schools, parks and other public requirements. Such regulations shall be made with reasonable consideration among other things, to the character of the district and its peculiar suitability for particular uses, and with a view to conserving the value of buildings[10] and encouraging the most appropriate use of land throughout such municipality.

§4. *Method of procedure.* The legislative body of such municipality shall provide for the manner in which such regulations and restrictions and the boundaries of such districts shall be determined, established, and enforced, and from time to time amended, supplemented, or changed. However, no such regulation, restriction, or boundary shall become effective until after a public hearing in relation thereto, at which parties in interest and citizens[11] shall have an opportunity to be heard. At least 15 days' notice of the time and place of such hearing shall be published in an official paper, or a paper of general circulation, in such municipality.

§5. *Changes.* Such regulations, restrictions, and boundaries may from time to time be amended, supplemented, changed, modified, or repeated. In case, however, of a protest against such change[12] signed by the owners of

---

8. *"Purposes in view"*: This section should be clearly differentiated from the statement of purpose (under the police power) contained in the first sentence of section 1. *That* defined and limited the powers created by the legislature to the municipality under the police power. *This* section contains practically a direction from the legislative body as to the purposes in view in establishing a zoning ordinance and the manner in which the work of preparing such an ordinance shall be done. It may be said, in brief, to constitute the "atmosphere" under which the zoning is to be done.

9. *"With a comprehensive plan"*: This will prevent haphazard or piecemeal zoning. No zoning should be done without such a comprehensive study. . . .

10. *"Conserving the value of buildings"*: It should be noted that zoning is not intended to enhance the value of buildings but to conserve that value—that is, to prevent depreciation of values such as come in "blighted districts," for instance—but it *is* to encourage the most appropriate use of land.

11. *"And citizens"*: This permits any person to be heard, and not merely property owners whose property interests may be adversely affected by the proposed ordinance. It is right that every citizen should be able to make his voice heard and protest against any ordinance that might be detrimental to the best interest of the city. . . .

12. *"Change"*: This term, as here used, it is believed will be construed by the courts to include "amendments, supplements, modifications, and repeal," in view of the language which it follows. These words might be added after the word "change," but have been omitted for the sake of brevity. On the other hand, there must be stability for zoning ordinances if they are to be of value. For this reason the practice has been rather generally adopted of permitting ordinary routine changes to be adopted by majority vote of the local legislative body but requiring a three-fourths vote in the event of the protest from a substantial proportion of property owners whose interests are affected. This has proved in practice to be a sound procedure and has tended to stabilize the ordinance. . . .

20 percent or more either of the area of the lots included in such proposed change, or of those immediately adjacent in the rear thereof extending-feet therefrom, or of those directly opposite thereto extending-feet from the street frontage of such opposite lots, such amendment shall not become effective except by the favorable vote of three-fourths of all the members of the legislative body of such municipality. The provisions of the previous section changes or amendments.

§6. *Zoning commission.* In order to avail itself of the powers conferred by this act, such legislative body shall appoint a commission, to be known as the zoning commission, to recommend the boundaries of the various origi-nal districts and appropriate regulations to be enforced therein. Such com-mission shall make a preliminary report and hold public hearings thereon before submitting its final report, and such legislative body shall not hold its public hearings or take action until it has received the final report of such commission. Where a city plan commission already exists, it may be appointed as the zoning commission.

§7. *Board of adjustment.* Such local legislative body may provide for the appointment of a board of adjustment, and in the regulations and restric-tions adopted pursuant to the authority of this act may provide that the said board of adjustment may, in appropriate cases and subject to appropriate conditions and safeguards, make special exceptions to the terms of the or-dinance in harmony with its general purpose and intent and in accordance with general or specific rules therein contained. . . .

All meetings of the board shall be open to the public. . . .

Appeals to the board of adjustment may be taken by any person ag-grieved or by any officer, department, board, or bureau of the municipality affected by any decision of the administrative officer. Such appeal shall be taken with a reasonable time, as provided by the rules of the board, by filing with the officer from whom the appeal is taken and with the board of ad-justment a notice of appeal specifying the grounds thereof. The officer from whom the appeal is taken shall forthwith transmit to the board all the papers constituting the record upon which the action appealed from was taken.

The board of adjustment shall fix a reasonable time for the hearing of the appeal, give public notice thereof, as well as due notice to the parties in interest, and decide the same within a reasonable time. Upon the hear-ing any part may appear in person or by agent or by attorney.

The board of adjustment shall have the following powers:

1. To hear and decide appeals where it is alleged there is error in any order, requirement, decision, or determination made by an administrative official in the enforcement of this act or of any ordinance adopted pursuant thereto.

2. To hear and decide special exceptions to the terms of the ordinance upon which such board is required to pass under such ordinance.

3. To authorize upon appeal in specific cases such variance from the terms of the ordinance as will not be contrary to the public interest, where, owing to special conditions, a literal enforcement of the provisions of the ordinance shall be observed and substantial justice done.

In exercising the above-mentioned powers such board may, in conformity with the provisions of this act, reverse or affirm, wholly or partly, or may modify the order, requirement, decision, or determination appealed from and may make such order, requirement, decision, or determination as ought to be made, and to that end shall have all the powers of the officer from whom the appeal is taken. . . .

Any person or persons, jointly or severally, aggrieved by any decision of the board of adjustment, or any taxpayer, or any officer, department, board, or bureau of the municipality, may present to a court of record a petition, duly verified, stetting forth that such decision is illegal, in whole or in part, specifying the grounds of the illegality. Such petition shall be presented to the court within 30 days after the filing of the decision in the office of the board.

Upon the presentation of such petition the court may allow a writ of certiorari directed to the board of adjustment to review such decision of the board of adjustment. . . . The court may reverse or affirm, wholly or partly, or may modify the decision brought up for review.

§8. *Enforcement and remedies.*[13] The local legislative body may provide by ordinance for the enforcement of this act and of any ordinance or regulation made thereunder. A violation of this act or of such ordinance or regulation is hereby declared to be a misdemeanor, and such local legislative body may provide for the punishment thereof by fine or imprisonment or both. It is also empowered to provide civil penalties for such violation.

In case any building or structure is erected, constructed, reconstructed, altered, repaired, converted, or maintained, or any building, structure, or land is used in violation of this act or of any ordinance or other regulation made under authority conferred hereby, the proper local au-

---

13. *"Enforcement and remedies":* This section is vital. Without it the local authorities, as a rule, will be powerless to do more than inflict a fine or penalty for violation of the zoning ordinance. It is obvious that a person desiring undue privileges will be glad to pay a few hundred dollars in fines or penalties if thereby he can obtain a privilege to build in a manner forbidden by law, or use his building in an unlawful manner, when he may profit thereby to the extent of many thousands of dollars. What is necessary is that the authorities shall be able to stop promptly the construction of an unlawful building before it is erected and restrain and prohibit an unlawful use.

[Many communities cannot provide for comprehensive inspection of properties to insure continuing compliance with the zoning laws. As a result, violations may be widespread and enforcement proceedings brought only fitfully. In some places, until someone complains, the violation goes officially unnoticed. At least one state court, however, has condemned the practice of making zoning law enforcement entirely dependent upon citizen complaints. People v. T.S. Klein Corp., 86 Misc. 2d 354, 381 N.Y.S. 2d 787 (City Ct. 1976); cf. also People v. Acme Markets, 37 N.Y.2d 326, 334 N.E.2d 555, 372 N.Y.S.2d 590 (1975). — Eds.]

thorities of the municipality, in addition to other remedies, may institute any appropriate action or proceedings[14] to prevent such unlawful erection, construction, reconstruction, alteration, repair, conversion, maintenance, or use, to restrain, correct, or abate such violation, to prevent the occupancy of said building, structure, or land, or to prevent any illegal act, conduct, business, or use in or about such premises. . . .

EXPLANATORY NOTES IN GENERAL

1. An enabling act is advisable in all cases. A general State enabling act is always advisable, and while the power to zone may, in some States, be derived from constitutional as distinguished from statutory home rule, still it is seldom that the home-rule powers will cover all the necessary provisions for successful zoning.

2. Constitutional amendments not required. No amendment to the State constitution, as a rule, is necessary. Zoning is undertaken under the police power and is well within the powers granted to the legislature by the constitutions of the various States. . . .

14. Note to revised edition, 1926. . . . In this [revision] section 8, dealing with enforcement and remedies, has been revised in order to give the municipality more effective means of obtaining conformance to the zoning ordinance. . . .

JAMES H. WICKERSHAM, THE QUIET REVOLUTION CONTINUES: THE EMERGING NEW MODEL FOR STATE GROWTH MANAGEMENT STATUTES

18 Harv. Envtl. L. Rev. 489, 503 (1994)

III.   PERSISTENT FAILINGS OF EUCLIDEAN ZONING

B.   GOVERNMENTAL FRAGMENTATION AND HOME RULE

1.   Local Inability to Deal with Large Projects

Both the scale and the location of major new development projects tend to frustrate attempts at local control. Not only do small local govern-

---

14. *"Any appropriate action or proceedings":* Under the provisions of this section the local authorities may use any or all the following methods in trying to bring about compliance with the law: They may sue the responsible person for a penalty in a civil suit; they may arrest the offender and put him in jail; they may stop the work in the case of a new building and prevent its going on; they may prevent the occupancy of a building and keep it vacant until such time as the conditions complained of are remedied; they can evict the occupants of a building when the conditions are contrary to law and prevent its reoccupancy until the conditions have been cured.

ments lack the expertise to address the spillover effects of such developments, but their own self-interest may lead them to ignore such problems; most of the benefits may accrue to one city or town (in the form of new jobs and taxes), while the harms (traffic congestion, flooding from filled wetlands, air and water pollution, economic and social dislocations) spill over onto adjoining communities. The development patterns of "edge cities" exacerbate this problem. Since these new commercial cores develop according to their relationship to the highway, not to an existing town center, they frequently overlap the boundaries of two or more municipalities. Thus, only a regional or statewide agency can exercise effective control over large development projects, accurately weighing all their potential benefits and harms.

2.   Local Inability to Protect Critical Resources

A resource that extends over a broad area, whether natural (forests, mountains, lakes and rivers, wetlands, coastal zones) or manmade (historic sites, farmlands), poses the same "tragedy of the commons" problems of degradation of a shared resource as does use of the air and water. Where many actors share the use of a common resource, such as a wetland or forest ecosystem, each is rationally impelled to develop the resource beyond its carrying capacity. This occurs because each individual's short term gain will exceed individual harms, while harms will be spread out among all the users. Voluntary coordination cannot overcome the constant risk of a few holdouts, still seeking their own gain. Where an affected resource overlaps the boundaries of municipal governments, only an effective regional or statewide agency can regulate the private land market in a way that protects the resource from harm.

3.   State Failure to Meet Environmental Goals

Where the states and the federal government have enacted sweeping environmental protection statutes, local control of land use poses a different kind of problem. Some of the most intractable problems in pollution control and resource protection, including air pollution caused by motor vehicles, non-point source water pollution, and destruction of critical habitats for endangered species, are insoluble without effective land use strategies. Yet, although federal and state legislators and policymakers have the legal power to override the principle of local control over land use, in practice they have been unwilling or unable to do so.

Under the Clean Air Act, for example, most urban areas still do not comply with federal standards for low level ozone (smog) and carbon monoxide, despite dramatic reductions in the emission levels of these pollutants by new motor vehicles. The problem is that Americans increasingly own more cars and trucks and drive them further. Increased vehicle use is a direct result of the dispersed land development patterns encouraged by typical suburban zoning. Yet, in the 1970s, when EPA tried to impose controls on transportation and land use as a way of addressing air pollution, the agency encountered bitter opposition and eventually had its powers in this area stripped away by Congress.

Similar problems arise under the Clean Water Act, where the major unaddressed water pollution problem in many areas is the "non-point source" runoff of fertilizers and other pollutants from farms and developments — a problem that requires a land use solution. A third example occurs under the Endangered Species Act, where it has become increasingly clear that many individual species cannot be saved without large-scale preservation of habitat — an approach that some have called "ecological zoning."

In all three cases — air, water, and endangered species — environmental goals cannot be reached unless local control of land use is superseded, or unless such goals are incorporated in an effective manner into the substance of local land use regulation.

C.   THE EXCLUSIONARY EFFECTS OF ZONING

Municipalities often manipulate their zoning powers to exclude unwanted activities and groups of people. With zoning decisions made at the local level, small, homogeneous communities that do not necessarily reflect the more general population in terms of class and race have the opportunity to control entrance into their neighborhoods.

The use of zoning for exclusionary purposes can take on several forms. "Fiscal zoning" seeks to bar uses that produce low taxes and high demand for municipal services, such as dense multifamily housing with many school age children, in favor of uses that will produce high taxes and low demands for services, such as office parks and shopping centers. Proponents of the "NIMBY" ("not in my backyard") syndrome use zoning to bar "LULUs" ("locally undesirable land uses") — projects that are socially necessary but almost universally disliked by their neighbors, such as prisons or waste treatment facilities. In exclusionary zoning, municipalities use large lot requirements and zoning for single-family homes to block affordable housing. This type of exclusionary zoning is often motivated by racial or class bias.

D.   COMPACT DEVELOPMENT AND GROWTH MANAGEMENT REGULATIONS

Greater potential for changing Euclidean zoning exists in the growth management regulations. . . . Growth management regulations are intended to alter the pattern and pace of development. More specifically, their use is aimed at shifting from low-density, monofunctional urban sprawl to compact development with higher densities, a greater mixture of uses, and a sharper transition from urban areas to surrounding greenbelts.

Rather than viewing economic development and growth as inevitably opposed to environmental protection, proponents of growth management argue that these two sets of values can be reconciled. Proponents of growth management maintain that compact development patterns can satisfy the full range of environmental, economic, and social challenges identified earlier in this Note. From an environmental viewpoint, limiting urban sprawl preserves existing open spaces, including undeveloped wetlands, forests, mountains, and cultivated farmland. Preserving this kind of continuous greenbelt strengthens natural ecosystems, offers opportunities for recreation, and maintains the economic viability of farming and other rural industries. Higher densities make public transportation a feasible alternative to automobiles, and a greater mixture of uses can make walking or bicycling a realistic option for short trips. From an economic viewpoint, steering new development to settled areas where transportation and other public services are already available keeps taxes and other costs low, strengthening the competitive position of business. Finally, higher residential densities can reduce housing costs by making housing more available to low- and moderate-income residents.

NOTES AND QUESTIONS

1.   **Density of population.** Would the language in §1 seem to give local government the power to enact the following measures?

(a)   In order to regulate the city's rate of growth, the council fixes an annual quota limiting construction to 500 dwelling units. Cf. Del Oro Hills v City of Oceanside, page 1001, *infra*.

(b)   The council rezones all undeveloped residential acreage to a maximum density of one dwelling unit per four acres. Cf. National Land & Investment Co. v. Kohn, 419 Pa. 504, 215 A.2d 597 (1965).

(c)   The council limits occupancy in residential districts to families — defined as those relative by blood, marriage, or adoption. Cf. Village of Belle Terre v. Boraas, 416 U.S. 1 (1974).

2.   "**In accordance with a comprehensive plan**" (**§3**). By this language, were the drafters of the act expecting each community to have a formal land use plan?

It is more likely that their intent was unformed. City planning was a new development; few communities had either the manpower or the organization to produce such plans. Moreover, there was little agreement — then as now — as to the content of a master plan. Thus the drafters may have hoped that communities would evolve toward master planning, but — in the short run — as zoning laws were written, the "comprehensive plan" requirement implied much less than a master plan.

How *much* less a plan could be before it no longer fulfilled the requirement became a frequently litigated issue. Many of the earliest zoning ordinances had no planning input; the zoning law was, literally, the plan. Faced with the comprehensive plan requirement, courts often examined such a zoning ordinance to see whether it had a rational basis — one that a planning expert, after the fact, could justify. If so, the ordinance survived. For a leading case, see Kozesnik v. Township of Montgomery, 24 N.J. 154, 131 A.2d 1 (1957): ("It may be said for present purposes that 'plan' connotes an integrated product of a rational process and 'comprehensive' requires something beyond a piecemeal approach, both to be revealed by the [zoning] ordinance considered in relation to the physical facts and the purposes authorized by [the zoning act]. . . . Such being the requirements of a comprehensive plan, no reason is perceived why we should infer the Legislature intended by necessary implication that the comprehensive plan be portrayed in some physical form outside the ordinance itself. A plan may be revealed in an end-product — here the zoning ordinance — and no more is required by the statute." *Contra*, Levine v. Town of Oyster Bay, 46 Misc. 2d 106, 259 N.Y.S.2d 247 (Sup. Ct. 1964): ("To say that the Town's 'comprehensive zoning plan' is interchangeable with 'comprehensive plan' is to say that zoning regulations . . . . must be in 'accordance' with themselves. This Court cannot believe that the Legislature intended or contemplated such a meaningless interpretation of these provisions. . . . While a comprehensive plan need not be in writing, it should at least be amenable to statement when proper inquiry is made of those informed in such matters."

3. **The failings of Euclidean zoning.** What are the failings of Euclidean zoning? What strategies would you suggest to overcome them? What institutional and political barriers would you anticipate would make these strategies difficult to carry out?

§9.4   Beyond *Euclid:* Oregon Statewide Planning Act

HENRY R. RICHMOND, LAND USE LAW REFORM SYMPOSIUM: FROM SEA TO SHINING SEA: MANIFEST DESTINY AND THE NATIONAL LAND USE DILEMMA

13 Pace L. Rev. 327, 331-336, 342-350 (1993)

C.   CURRENT DEVELOPMENT PATTERNS: URBAN SPRAWL

By 1990, 78% of all Americans lived in metropolitan regions, however, 46% of that population lived in the suburbs. Shopping facilities, including huge new malls with large parking lots, were built to serve the new suburban residents. As a result, today, there is a higher volume of retail sales in the malls of suburbia than in the downtown areas of many central cities. For example, in California, more retailing occurs in the South Coast Plaza in Orange County than in downtown San Francisco. Similarly, more shoppers frequent the malls of King of Prussia in Chester County, Pennsylvania than shop in downtown Philadelphia. During the 1970s, America's shift from a manufacturing to a service economy created a demand for more office space. Most of that demand was met in the suburbs. This expansion of office space in the suburbs occurred very rapidly, twice as fast as the shift in population. In 1970, 25% of the office space in the United States was located in the suburbs, but by 1990, that figure had risen to 57%.

A number of factors contributed to the transition of office space to suburbia: the availability of cheaper land, lower rents, the option of shipping freight by truck rather than rail, and the availability of skilled workers. This trend was demonstrated in Atlanta where, from 1978 to 1983, the city's share of regional office space slipped from 34% to 26%, while the pace of office construction in Atlanta flourished. The loss was the result of massive construction of new office space in the suburbs. Similarly, from 1960 to 1980, Los Angeles's share of regional office space fell from 60% to 34%. In New York, from 1982 to 1984, Manhattan's share of regional office space fell from 75% to 67%, despite the city's considerable efforts to add new office space.

America's industries also relocated to suburbia. Between 1947 and 1967, America's sixteen largest and oldest central cities lost an average of 34,000 manufacturing jobs each, while their suburbs gained an average of 87,000 jobs. This trend continued through the 1970s as America's industrialized cities lost from 25% (Minneapolis) to 40% (Philadelphia) of the manufacturing jobs that remained.

D.   LAND USE REGULATION TO CONTROL SPRAWL

There exists a twenty to thirty year capacity for accommodating future development within the nation's vastly expanded, Edge City-dominated, freeway-connected, metropolitan regions. However, that growth will come at a very high price economically, environmentally and socially. With the automobile functioning as the nearly exclusive regional transit "system," the sheer size and amount of land encompassed by metropolitan regions generates longer trips, increased fuel consumption, and air pollution. As these vast areas continue to be developed, wetlands will vanish, water supplies will be threatened, and valuable agricultural land will disappear. Taxpayers and utility ratepayers will suffer because as regions expand, the costs of providing public services such as police and fire departments, electricity, sewer systems and water, will increase. Aside from the high costs of servicing sprawling development, the public is also adversely affected by uncontrolled growth because it erodes the local tax base, restricts the accessibility of jobs and housing to less affluent people, and isolates racial minorities and the poor.

II.   OREGON LAND USE PROGRAM: A MODEL FOR NATIONAL REFORM . . .

C.   RESULTS ON THE GROUND

The Oregon program, by taking a balanced and comprehensive approach, has been successful in providing affordable housing, encouraging economic development, preserving the environment, creating a viable and cost effective mass transportation system and preserving agricultural land. Today, each of Oregon's 241 cities has an urban growth boundary, Portland has become a viable urban center, and the supply of affordable housing has been increased significantly. Additionally, some 25 million acres of agricultural and forest land have been rezoned exclusively for farm or forest use, while approximately 750 thousand acres of "Exception" land outside urban growth boundaries has been designed for rural residential development. A review of the concrete results of the Oregon land use initiative illustrates why it has received such broad-based support throughout the state.

1.   Support for Affordable Housing

Oregon's Goal 10, the housing goal, requires all cities and counties to plan for a variety of housing types, including single and multi-family dwellings. In addition, municipalities must create housing plans that accommodate the needs of all residents within the region, regardless of income levels, as far as practicable. In interpreting these requirements, the LCDC held that:

> Goal 10 speaks of the housing needs of Oregon households, (not the residents of the locality). Its meaning is clear: planning for housing must not be parochial. Planning jurisdictions must consider the needs of the relevant region in arriving at a fair allocation of housing types. Goal 10 represents the broader interests of all Oregon households.

By requiring a variety of housing types, Goal 10 seeks to prevent exclusionary zoning practices. In addition, Oregon's regulations prohibit protracted review procedures that might discourage development. Review procedures are required to be "clear and objective" and to not cause "unreasonable cost or delay." Another measure enacted to ensure the availability of affordable housing is the requirement that municipalities must plan for, and provide, adequate infrastructure to promote appropriate housing development in the area.

The supply of affordable housing in Oregon has increased as a result of state and regional laws that require municipalities throughout major metropolitan areas to zone at least 50% of their vacant residential land to provide for the development of housing types other than single-family detached dwellings. These policies have resulted in an increase in the amount of land zoned for multi-family housing and a decrease in the average vacant single-family lot size.

A recent survey conducted jointly by 1000 Friends of Oregon and the Home Builders Association of Metropolitan Portland concluded that Oregon's "land use management goals and efforts to promote affordable housing in the Portland metropolitan area are working." The year-long study showed that housing in the Portland area was more affordable than comparable accommodations in other non-regulated West Coast areas, such as San Diego, Los Angeles, and Seattle. In the Portland area, "slightly more than three-quarters of the region's households can afford to rent a midpriced, two-bedroom apartment, while two-thirds of them can afford to buy a mid-priced, two bedroom house." These findings dispel the myth that land regulations, particularly UGBs, cause inflated land values and result in higher housing costs.

2. Transportation

Pursuant to Goal 12, the transportation goal, municipalities must plan to "provide and encourage a safe, convenient and economic transportation system." The needs of the state, region and locality must be considered in the plan, as well as the use of various transportation systems including mass transit, air, rail, bicycle and pedestrian. To effectuate this goal, Portland has revived the trolley, known as "light rail," to provide mass transportation from the suburbs into the city. The line runs down the center of the freeway and is powered by electricity. The system has been so successful that the voters recently approved a bond issue to finance the development of a second line.

The City of Portland has implemented other measures aimed at dissuading automobile use and encouraging the use of mass transit. To facilitate the movement of those individuals who enter the city by light rail, free bus service is provided within the downtown area. In addition, there is a limit to the number of parking spaces that can be built within city limits. Portland's strategy is to make mass transit more convenient and auto transit less convenient, so as to reduce air pollution, vehicle miles travelled and traffic congestion.

In 1991, Oregon's Land Conservation and Development Commission adopted a precedent-setting, comprehensive administrative rule governing state and local government transportation planning. The new rule addresses numerous topics relating to transportation facility planning, land use, development design and intergovernmental coordination. It requires all metropolitan areas to plan for the development of alternative transportation methods including bicycle and pedestrian, and the reduction of vehicle miles by 20% over the initial thirty year planning period. Local governments can only meet this goal by linking transportation with other land use decisions such as economic development and housing.

3.   Economic Development

Goal 9 requires municipalities to plan in order to "diversify and improve the economy of the state." However, during the early 1980s when the national economy was in a recession, the Land Conservation and Development Commission came under attack with opponents alleging that the land use regulations inhibited, rather than promoted, economic growth. Governor Atiyeh commissioned a task force to examine these allegations. After hearing testimony from over 400 Oregonians, the task force concluded that the economic problems experienced by the state were not the fault of the LCDC.

One of the most hotly debated issues involved the question of whether Oregon's land use program provided enough industrial land to attract industry to the state. In 1982, 1000 Friends of Oregon commissioned a study that compared the supply of industrial land in the state's ten largest urban areas before and after the implementation of Oregon's Land Use Act. The study showed that the quantity of industrial land actually increased 79% after regulation, rising from 15,964 acres to 28,581 acres.

In addition, Oregon's planning process has made easier the development of land designated as "industrial." Prior to S.B. 100, most industrial development required a time-consuming and costly zoning amendment to the county's plan. After the land use statute was enacted, land planned for industrial use was often already zoned for industrial use. The state's planning requirements provide the predictability and efficiency in the development process that land developers value.

4.   Agriculture

Although Oregon's comprehensive land use plan was originally enacted primarily to prevent sprawling development from consuming farmland, Goal 3, dedicated to the preservation and maintenance of agricultural lands, is constantly under attack by realtors and county officials. Currently, these interests are seeking to relax land use regulations that prohibit the development of land outside UGBs alleging that they "strangle legitimate development." Others call for stricter regulation because "farm land . . . faces an uncertain future as urban development continues to apply pressure. . . ."

Some critics argue that the state has failed in its ability to preserve farmland and point to development that occurs either due to the failure of a local government to implement the comprehensive plan properly, or the approval, in the planning process, of "exception" areas when preexisting partitioning and development on otherwise good farm and forest land were found to "precommit" land to nonfarm or nonforest uses. Much of this land is immediately outside of urban growth boundaries. The exception reclassifies the property or area and entitles the owner to develop it, rather than to use it exclusively for agriculture. Local governments are often pressured to misapply state-approved local ordinances to allow development on non-exception land in order to reap the reward of increased land value that residential rezoning brings.

Still, most commentators agree that S.B. 100 has stopped large scale conversion of farmland to development. One study showed that by 1987, 90% of land planned for Exclusive Farm Use (EFU) had been zoned accordingly. In addition, although some EFU land had been redesignated and included within Urban Growth Boundaries, these reclassifications have not been significant.

III.   CONCLUSION

America has learned an important lesson since its expansionist days, when the nation sought to conquer and exploit the "wilderness" with little regard for its impact: the land and its resources are not limitless. As a result, a new form of manifest destiny is sweeping across the country: from Oregon to Vermont, from Maine to Florida, nine states have adopted growth management statutes. These states seek to guide the responsible use of land in order to address a "wide range of "quality of life' issues" including "concerns such as: keeping abreast of infrastructure needs as development occurs; properly balancing development and environmental protection; and promoting economic development, where that is needed, through positive efforts."

Today, the United States is struggling to develop innovative ways of dealing with the effects of over forty years of unguided growth. This concept, that land must be used responsibly, is not new, but has been part of our destiny since the nation's inception. Thomas Jefferson reminded Americans that "while the farmer holds title to the land, actually, it belongs to all the people because civilization itself rests on the soil." If Jefferson were observing the modern scene, he would add to his concern for the farmer the other key interests whose well-being is tied to responsible land use patterns.

Editors' quaere: Take another look at *Dolan*, Chapter 8. Does this seem like a setback for the goals expressed in the Oregon plan?

PHILIPPI v. CITY OF SUBLIMITY

294 Or. 730, 662 P.2d 325 (1983)

ROBERTS, J. Both the City of Sublimity and the Land Use Board of Appeals (LUBA) denied respondents' application for a subdivision development permit for their property zoned single family residential (SFR) in the zoning ordinance and designated "single family" in the Sublimity Comprehensive Plan. This denial was based upon, inter alia, an "agricultural retention policy" set out in the city's acknowledged comprehensive plan. The Court of Appeals held that such a policy cannot be employed to defeat development of residentially zoned property within an acknowledged urban growth boundary (UGB) and reversed. 59 Or. App. 295, 650 P.2d 1038 (1982). We accepted review to determine whether Sublimity may delay development of properties within the UGB which are designated "single-family" in the comprehensive plan and zoned SFR, based upon an expressed comprehensive plan policy in favor of preserving agricultural land until needed for urban purposes.

The City of Sublimity's comprehensive plan, with its concomitant zoning and subdivision ordinances, was acknowledged by the Land Conservation and Development Commission (LCDC) in April, 1980. ORS 197.251. This acknowledged package demarcates the city's UGB and designates a particular zoning classification for all properties within that boundary. There are various zone classes, but all of them are urban in nature; there is none akin to a "agricultural" zone.

Respondents' property, the parcel here at issue, is within the UGB at the extreme northeast edge of the city. It is abutted on several sides on properties in residential use and is itself zoned SFR [Single Family Residence]. The parcel is presently undeveloped and was until recently in active agricultural production. In early 1981, respondent applied for a permit to develop the parcel, which comprises roughly ten acres, into a 34-lot residential subdivision. Although such a use is compatible with the parcel's SFR zone, the city after a public hearing denied respondent's request and adopted findings in justification of the denial. See Philippi v. City of Sublimity, 4 Or. LUBA 291, 293-294 (1981). These findings indicate that the city's decision was, in part, based upon an "agricultural retention policy" set out in its comprehensive plan, which policy favors preservation of productive farm land within the UGB until such time as it is needed for urban purposes.[1]

---

1. Sublimity's "agricultural retention policy" finds its expression in several locations in the city's comprehensive plan, a document written largely in essay format. Specifically, in Chap-

Respondents petitioned LUBA for review of the decision challenging both the sufficiency of the evidence upon which the city based its findings and the propriety of imposing on respondents' subdivision request the agricultural retention policy. LUBA remanded the dispute back to the city for reconsideration and the adoption of more complete findings. Id. In so ruling, however, LUBA rejected respondents' contention that it was improper for the city to apply an agricultural retention policy to bar or delay development of residentially zoned property within the UGB. Id., at 299-300.

Respondents appealed to the Court of Appeals and cited as error only the latter aspect of LUBA's decision; the city did not cross-appeal. On the narrow issue thus presented, the court reasoned:

> Only those general policies contained in the comprehensive plan that are consistent with the plan designation and zoning classification may be used at the subdivision approval stage to regulate the development of urbanizable land. It must be conclusively presumed that general policies stated in the comprehensive plan have been considered and found inapplicable by the time property is zoned for a use that is inconsistent with the general policy. That is to say, the general policy to preserve land presently in agricultural use for that use must have been considered and found inapplicable when it was zoned for single-family residential use. It may be that there are other impediments to approval of this subdivision that are properly governed by specific requirements contained in the subdivision ordinance, or that other general policies can be validly applied in such a way as to require modification of the proposed development or to postpone it. But that is not the question here. 59 Or. App. at 301, 650 P.2d 1038.

And concluded: "We hold only that a general policy in a comprehensive plan favoring retention of agricultural land within an acknowledged UGB may not be applied to preclude development on land designated and zoned for residential use." Id. at 302, 650 P.2d 1038. The court then reversed and remanded the case to LUBA.

Analysis here must be prefaced with the recognition that a local government's comprehensive plan holds the preeminent position in its land use powers and responsibilities. Zoning and subdivision ordinances, and

---

ter IV, entitled "Natural Resources," it states: "Agriculture is of major importance to the Sublimity area. The lands surrounding the City are currently in agricultural use as pastures and for grains and grass seeds, and are classified as either Class II or III soils. The City recognizes this resource and seeks to preserve this land in its natural open state as a means of maintaining the rural atmosphere for which the town is named. . . . The most striking aspect of Sublimity's residential land is the open feeling one derives from the rural character of the community. The citizens of Sublimity are well aware of the rural character of the City, and do not desire future development to alter it. . . . It is a foregone conclusion, though, that eventually urbanization pressures will necessitate the conversion of these agricultural uses to urban uses. The city is cognizant of this fact, but desires urbanization to occur in an orderly fashion. The following policies have been adopted, concerning open space: Discourage the premature and wasteful conversion of valuable agricultural land to city uses. . . ."

local land use decisions, are intended to be the means by which the plan is effectuated and, to such an extent, they are subservient to the plan. Baker v. City of Milwaukee, 271 Or. 500, 533 P.2d 772 (1975); see ORS 92.044(6) and ORS 197.175(2)(d). Accordingly, a particular zoning designation does not of itself entitle the landowner to a particular corresponding use irrespective of whether applicable provisions of the plan may mandate otherwise. The question thus presented is whether the challenged "agricultural retention policy" is applicable to the subject parcel and whether it permits the city to delay the parcel's development.

It is clear that the challenged policy was intended by the plan drafters to apply to properties within the UGB regardless of their particular zone designation. Recalling that there is no zone designation in the plan akin to "agricultural," the policy statements in the plan, set out in note 1, *supra*, unambiguously contemplate that properties currently in agricultural production within the UGB, however zoned, should be kept in such a use until the land is needed for the use for which it is zoned. For instance, the plan provides at 11: "Land which is inside the City Limits and the urban growth boundary that is in agricultural use shall remain in agricultural use until it is needed for urbanization and can be provided with urban facilities."

A plan policy to retain agriculturally productive land in that use until such time as it is needed for the zoned use is not inconsistent with the concept of zoning designations. A zoning ordinance may be but is not necessarily, a mere catalog of existing uses; nor does a zoning ordinance necessarily give an automatic license to a landowner to develop his or her property to a use permitted by its particular zone class. The comprehensive plan here involved sets forth a legislative decision as to which future property uses will or will not be in the public interest, and in what order. Where the comprehensive plan permits uses more intensive than a parcel's present use, the question of when and under what conditions the parcel may be permitted to be further developed can be made to turn on policies or factors within the zoning ordinance itself or the plan, provided they are applicable, clearly set out, and consistent with the zoning designation. Sublimity points out that the entire city is presently zoned that the ultimate end use designation.

We disagree with respondents' contention that Sublimity's "agricultural retention policy" is necessarily so inconsistent and inimical to a SFR zone that it cannot, as a matter of law, be employed to delay development of properties so zoned. With regard to respondents' parcel, the policy does not stand as an absolute bar to residential development — it merely delays such development until either the parcel cannot be realistically or productively framed or there is a need in Sublimity for more residential lots. Moreover, retaining the parcel as agricultural does not, as a practical matter, affect respondent's ability to develop it for residential use some time in the future. Therefore, assuming that respondents' parcel is capable of agricultural production and that there is no present need in Sublimity for more residential lots, we conclude that Sublimity may employ its "agricultural retention policy" to defer the residential development of respondents' parcel at this time.

Contrary to respondents' position, this result is not inconsistent with the statewide land use planning scheme. Their argument on this point evinces a misconception as to the legal significance of an acknowledged UGB. LCDC's Statewide Planning Goal 14, the "Urbanization" Goal, specifies the consideration relevant to conversion or rural land to urban. In pertinent part it provides:

> GOAL: To provide for an orderly and efficient transition from rural to urban use.
> Urban growth boundaries shall be established to identify and separate urbanizable land from rural land.
> Establishment and change of the boundaries shall be based upon consideration of the following factors:
> (1) Demonstrated need to accommodate long-range urban population growth requirements consistent with LCDC goals;
> (2) Need for housing, employment opportunities, and livability;
> (3) Orderly and economic provision for public facilities and services;
> (4) Maximum efficiency of land uses within and on the fringe of the existing urban area;
> (5) Environmental, energy, economic and social consequences;
> (6) Retention of agricultural land as defined, with Class I being the highest priority for retention and Class IV the lowest priority; and,
> (7) Compatibility of the proposed urban uses with nearby agricultural activities. . . .
> Land within the boundaries separating urbanizable land from rural land shall be considered available over time for urban uses. Conversion of urbanizable land to urban uses shall be based on consideration of:
> (1) Orderly, economic provision for public facilities and services;
> (2) Availability of sufficient land for the various uses to insure choices in the market place;
> (3) LCDC goals; and
> (4) Encouragement of development within urban areas before conversion of urbanizable areas.

Under Goal 14, then, a city's UGB stands as the dividing line between "rural" and "urbanizable" land. The first seven factors govern the establishment of the line; the latter four govern the conversion of urbanizable land within an acknowledged UGB to urban uses. The import of this goal is that once LCDC has acknowledged an UGB, the lands within the boundary are no longer "rural," have been committed to urbanization and must be "considered available over time for urban uses." Since respondents' parcel is within Sublimity's acknowledged UGB, it must be deemed non-rural and urbanizable.

This is not to say, however, that a policy favoring retention of agricultural uses within an acknowledged UGB is improper or inconsistent with Goal 14. The dichotomy established by Goal 14 is between urban/ urbanizable and rural, not between urban and agricultural. LCDC's definitions of these terms demonstrate that agricultural and rural are not synonymous and that an agricultural retention policy within an UGB is not a contradiction in terms:

> URBAN LAND: Urban areas are those places which must have an incorporated city. Such area may include lands adjacent to and outside the incorporated city and may also: (a) Have concentrations of persons who generally reside and work in the area; and (b) Have supporting public facilities and services.
> URBANIZABLE LAND: Urbanizable land are those lands within the urban growth boundary and which are identified and: (a) Determined to be necessary and suitable for future urban uses; (b) Can be served by urban services and facilities; and (c) Are needed for the expansion of an urban area.
> RURAL LAND: Rural lands are those which are outside the urban growth boundary and are: (a) Non-urban agricultural, forest or open spaced lands or, (b) Other lands suitable for sparse settlement, small farms or acreage homesites with no or hardly any public services, and which are not suitable, necessary or intended for urban use. OAR 660-15-000.

When a city which anticipates some future growth establishes an UGB, it must generally include within the boundary properties that are not currently "urban" to serve as a buffer zone into which the city's growth may expand. These lands may be sparsely developed, agricultural, forest, or vacant. Their inclusion in to the UGB makes the "urbanizable" but not ipso facto urban. Although inclusion within the UGB and within an urban zone classification necessarily is a determination that such properties will ultimately be developed as urban, the city may, as contemplated by the last four factors of Goal 14, establish policies governing the conversion of these urbanizable properties into urban uses. We see nothing improper or inconsistent with Goal 14 in Sublimity's decision to preserve the status quo with regard to agricultural land within its UGB until such time as the land is needed for urban purposes.

Reversed and remanded in accordance with LUBA's order.

NOTES AND QUESTIONS

1. **First English and Sublimity.** Under *First English*, damages are required for a temporary taking, see §8.1 (b). Is the *Sublimity* decision in conformity with *First English*, which had not yet been decided in 1983?

2. **Lucas and Sublimity.** *Lucas* seems to place some curb on land use regulation where "background principles of nuisance and property law" would not have proscribed the use, see §8.1 (b). Is the *Sublimity* outcome consistent with *Lucas*, which had not yet been decided in 1983?

3. **The agricultural "crisis."** Farmland crisis theorists argue that prime farmland is disappearing in the United States, as the demand for farm products grows. To support this claim, they cite a study that shows a loss of three million acres of farmland yearly, one-third being prime land located on the urban fringe. Apart from growing export demand, domestic needs are rising about 1 percent every year.

State and local governments are taking many steps to stanch this loss. Beside agricultural zoning (at least ten states), limiting land use either to farming or very low density residential, states have enacted preferential assessment programs ("current use" rather than "highest and best use" valuation), public purchase of development rights measures, and inheritance and estate tax reforms, among other techniques. See, Teri E. Popp, A Survey of Governmental Response to the Farmland Crisis: States' Application of Agricultural Zoning, 11 U. Ark. Little Rock L.J. 515 (1988/1989).

§9.5 Exclusionary Zoning

MISS PORTER'S SCHOOL, INC. v. FARMINGTON

151 Conn. 425, 198 A.2d 707 (1964)

MURPHY, J. The defendant Edmond Cadoux petitioned the Farmington town plan and zoning commission for a change of zone from R 12, a residence zone, to RA, a restricted apartment zone, to permit the erection of a fifteen-unit garden apartment on 2.1 acres of land owned by the defendant Catherine C. Rourke on Garden Street. After a public hearing at which some nearby property owners and other residents of the town opposed the petition, the commission granted the change of zone. The plaintiffs appealed to the Court of Common Pleas, which sustained the action of the commission, whereupon this appeal followed. Although the appellants do not include two of the original plaintiffs, who were found not to be aggrieved persons, we shall refer to the appellants as the plaintiffs.

The Farmington zoning regulations provide: "Restricted Apartment zones may be designated on the zoning map, and may also be established in any other zone by petition in accordance with the following procedure, and subject to the following limitations." Farmington Zoning Regs., art. 2, §5 (1961). One of these limitations is: "No development plan shall be approved which is inconsistent with the public welfare, or which impairs the integrity of this ordinance, or which does not fully safeguard the appropriate use of the land in the immediate neighborhood. No R A zone will be designated or approved unless there is clear evidence of safe and satisfactory means of providing water supply and sewerage disposal." Farmington

Zoning Regs., art. 2, §5(3) (1961). The regulations governing the designation of a restricted apartment zone contained many other limitations and requirements as to use, area, yards and courts, spaces between structures, building coverage, and building and dwelling size as well as special requirements for parking areas, access ways and sidewalks, and recreation and open space. The plaintiffs make no claim that the apartment plans submitted to the commission do not conform to the requirements of the regulations. Their claim is that the change of zone constitutes spot zoning, is detrimental to the neighborhood and does not conform to the comprehensive plan or benefit the entire community.

Restricted apartment zones may be created by the commission on its own motion or on the petition of interested persons. Farmington Zoning Regs., art. 2, §5 (1961). As the regulations provide for their establishment, they come within the comprehensive plan and are not violative of it. Corsino v. Grover, 148 Conn. 299, 313, 170 A.2d 267; Couch v. Zoning Commission, 141 Conn. 349, 355, 106 A.2d 173.

A two-family house in a run-down condition now stands on the Rourke property. An R 12 zone permits two-family dwellings and all the uses allowed in the higher residential zones, including the keeping of not more than four roomers or boarders per family. Also permitted are hospitals, nursing homes and charitable and philanthropic institutions except correctional institutions and institutions for the mentally ill. Farmington Zoning Regs., art. 2, §3 (1961). The tenor of the opposition expressed at the public hearing was mainly to the effect that the approval of the petition would open the door to a procession of similar petitions, which, if granted, would cause the character of the village to change. The principal of the named plaintiff stated the objection of its executive committee to be that apartments are inimical to the idea of a country boarding school. The zoning map does not show any area presently designated as a restricted apartment zone.

This type of zone is similar in character to those involved in DeMeo v. Zoning Commission, 148 Conn. 68, 167 A.2d 454, and Zandri v. Zoning Commission, 150 Conn. 646, 192 A.2d 876, and much that was said in those cases is applicable here. The standards for restricted apartment zones in Farmington are specifically prescribed in the regulations. Petitions, before they are submitted to the commission, have to satisfy the town planner that all of the requirements and safeguards for a restricted apartment zone have been met. The present petition complied with those standards.

The commission gave as its reasons for granting the petition that "[i]t constitutes an improvement of the property over its present condition; and represents the highest and best use of the property." On the surface, these reasons are not particularly persuasive. The function of the court in reviewing the commission's action on appeal would have been materially aided had the commission included in the minutes of its executive session the results of its observations of the character of the neighborhood, the types of buildings in it, and the uses to which the buildings and land are being put. At the public hearing, the petitioners called to the attention of the commission the fact that Garden Street was not an exclusively residential area, since there was a greenhouse across the street from the Rourke property, a barber shop and other business establishments were between the Rourke property and Farmington Avenue to the north, and, to the south, there were a cemetery, the gymnasium of the named plaintiff, and a building containing several small apartments for its employees. In their brief, the petitioners state that there were also a laundry and a cow barn nearby. The commission's brief describes the area as being of mixed use, consisting of one- and two-family houses as well as "high density residential, institutional, and business uses." The brief also points out that a business zone on Farmington Avenue is approximately 500 feet away. In argument, the plaintiffs made no attempt to dispute these statements in their opponents' briefs. We assume that the conditions recited were known to the commission when it acted on the petition and that it considered them in arriving at its conclusion. Another factor which was before the commission for consideration was the voluntary statement of one resident, who, at the public hearing, opposed the change of zone because of his fear that the garden apartments would be the beginning of a change in the character of the village. He stated, however, that a building he owns on Garden Street and the land he owns on both sides of the street would actually be more valuable if the petition was granted.

As was pointed out in Zandri v. Zoning Commission, *supra*, 649 of 150 Conn. p. 878 of 192 A.2d a change of a small area from one residential classification to another residential classification does not, if permitted by the regulations, in and of itself constitute spot zoning. The expanding population of Farmington and the desirability of apartments to accommodate it were called to the attention of the commission, as well as the fact that the property was close to transportation facilities and shopping areas. The change of zone was in accordance with the comprehensive plan and its logical development. Allin v. Zoning Commission, 150 Conn. 129, 133, 186 A.2d 802.

There is no error.

In this opinion the other judges concurred.

NOTES AND QUESTIONS

1. **Development pressure.** When this case was decided, Farmington was under heavy development pressure from New York City.

2. **Motivation.** Why did Miss Porter's oppose the proposed development?

3. **Employee housing.** Did Miss Porter's have some provision for housing for its own employees? Why was this thought to be different?

VICKERS v. GLOUCESTER TOWNSHIP

37 N.J. 232, 181 A.2d 129 (1962)

PROCTOR, J. On September 3, 1957 the township adopted an ordinance entitled "An Ordinance to Regulate and Control Trailers, Trailer Coaches, Camp Cars and Trailer Camps in the Township of Gloucester." (Trailer Ordinance.) The effect of this ordinance and the zoning ordinance was to repeal a 1947 trailer ordinance barring trailer camps in the entire township and to ban such camps in the residence, business and agricultural districts, but permit them in the industrial district. At present there are no trailer camps in the township.

[T]he result of the ordinances was to prohibit trailer camps throughout the township. Plaintiff on May 5, 1960, filed a . . . complaint in lieu of prerogative writ demanding a judgment declaring the ordinances invalid and inapplicable to the use of his property as a trailer camp. In its answer the township contended it had the power to enact the ordinances under its zoning powers and general police powers.

The parties agree the only issues on this appeal are: (1) In the circumstances, could the township through its zoning power totally exclude trailer camps from the municipality? and, (2) Were the procedural requirements of N.J.S.A. 40:55-35 met in the adoption of the zoning ordinance amendment?

As to the first issue, the township contends the zoning ordinance as amended represents a valid exercise of the municipality's power to "develop itself as an orderly and well integrated community," and that trailer camps with their accompanying disadvantages can only interfere with its planned growth. The plaintiff argues the township, although it can regulate the operation of trailer camps, cannot absolutely prohibit them, that such an attempt is invalid since it "goes beyond the essential objects of zoning." He asserts "There is everything to indicate that Gloucester Township is not the type of community where the absolute prohibition of mobile home parks is warranted."

The role of the judiciary in reviewing zoning ordinances adopted pursuant to the statutory grant of power is narrow. The court cannot pass upon the wisdom or unwisdom of an ordinance, but may act only if the presumption in favor of the validity of the ordinance is overcome by an affirmative showing that it is unreasonable or arbitrary. Kozesnik v. Township of Montgomery, 24 N.J. 154, 167 (1957); see Cunningham, "Control of Land Use in New Jersey," 14 Rutgers L. Rev. 37, 48 (1959). By these standards which control judicial review, the plaintiff to prevail must show beyond debate that the township in adopting the challenged amendment transgressed the standards of R.S. 40:55-32. In other words, if the amendment presented a debatable issue we cannot nullify the township's decision that its welfare would be advanced by the action it took.

We conclude that the Township of Glocester had the power to prohibit trailers from all residential districts, even though those districts include rural areas which will remain undeveloped for the reasonably foreseeable future. We said, at p. 494 of 29 N.J., at p.488 of 150 A.2d: "Zoning must subserve the long-range needs of the future as well as the immediate needs of the present and the reasonably foreseeable future. It is, in short, an implementing tool of sound planning."

[The court also holds that the relevant procedural requirements were met.] The judgment of the Appellate Division is reversed and the judgment of the Law Division is reinstated.

HALL, J. dissenting. The majority decides that this particular municipality may constitutionally say, through exercise of the zoning power, that its residents may not live in trailers — or in mobile homes, to use a more descriptive term. I am convinced such a conclusion in this case is manifestly wrong. Of even greater concern is the judicial process by which it is reached and the breadth of the rationale. The import of the holding gives almost boundless freedom to developing municipalities to erect exclusionary walls on their boundaries, according to local whim or selfish desire, and to use the zoning power for aims beyond its legitimate purposes. Prohibition of mobile home parks, although an important issue in itself, becomes, in this larger aspect, somewhat a symbol.

The instant case, both in its physical setting and in the issues raised, is typical of land use controversies now current in so many New Jersey municipalities on the outer ring of the built up urban and suburban areas. These are municipalities with relatively few people and a lot of open space, but in the throes, or soon to be reached by the inevitable tide, of industrial and commercial decentralization and mass population migration from the already densely settled central cores. They are not small, homogeneous communities with permanent character already established, like the settled suburbs surrounding the cities in which planning and zoning may properly be geared around things as they are and as they will pretty much continue to be. On the contrary these areas are sprawling, heterogeneous governmental units, mostly townships, each really amounting to a region of considerable size in itself. Their present rural, semi-rural or mixed nature is about to change substantially and they are soon to become melded into the whole metropolitan area. Their political boundaries are artificial and hence of relatively little significance beyond defining one unit of local government. Their existing conglomeration of land uses is sectionally distributed — large or small scale agriculture, residences in separated communities and on good sized plots or acreage in the open country, business establishments in the populated sectors and along through highways, and perhaps a spot or two of industry much sought after to aid municipal tax revenues. Many differing land uses, both present and future, are and can be made comfortably compatible by reason of the distances involved and the varying characteristics of geographical sections. Present municipal services are not more extensive than necessary to serve a population scattered over a large territory. Increased facilities, especially schools, required to accommodate a sudden population growth of large proportions must be provided almost solely at local expense, which in New Jersey means from additional taxation on real estate within the municipal boundaries. And it is elementary knowledge that small homes with children to be educated in local schools cannot pay their own way tax-wise.

Such municipalities, above all others, vitally need and may legally exercise comprehensive planning and implementing zoning techniques to avoid present haphazard development which can only bring future grief. They are entitled to aim thereby for a sound and balanced area . . . . They do not have to permit an Oklahoma land rush or a Western boom town.

And this gets to the nub of what this, and similar cases, are really all about, i.e., the outer limit of the zoning power to be enjoyed by these municipalities most in need of comprehensive authority. What action is not legitimately encompassed by that power and what is the proper role of courts in reviewing its exercise?

The inquiry involves important fundamentals. In the broad sense the considerations are well posed in Williams, "Planning Law and Democratic Living," 20 Law and Contemporary Problems 317 (1955):

> The main premises of American constitutional law represent a codification and institutionalization of the primary values of a democratic society — equality of opportunity and equality of treatment, freedom of thought and considerable freedom of action, and fairness. Under the American system, a more or less independent mechanism of judicial review is established to provide an independent check on whether specific governmental decisions conform to these standards. . . .
>
> . . . An intelligent application of constitutional law to the measures used in planning the environment will therefore force a searching inquiry into basic problems — and thus become in fact an excellent vehicle for getting at what is really involved in planning decisions. If such searching inquiries are to be undertaken, this means that no major problem in planning law can really be understood except by an analysis thereof in relation to the whole background of the changing physical, economic and social environment. In short, what is needed in planning law is a super-Brandeis-brief approach. . . .

In my opinion legitimate use of the zoning power by such municipalities does not encompass the right to erect barricades on their boundaries through exclusion or too tight restriction of uses where the real purpose is to prevent feared disruption with a so-called chosen way of life. Nor does it encompass provisions designed to let in as new residents only certain kinds of people,[4] or those who can afford to live in favored kinds of housing, or

___

4. That this kind of motivation was not entirely absent in the barring of mobile homes from Gloucester Township is indicated by the statement at oral argument of the township's

to keep down tax bills of present property owners. When one of the above is the true situation deeper considerations intrinsic in a free society gain the ascendancy and courts must not be hesitant to strike down purely selfish and undemocratic enactments. I am not suggesting that every such municipality must endure a plague of locusts or suffer transition to a metropolis over night. I suggest only that regulation rather than prohibition is the appropriate technique for attaining a balanced and attractive community. The opportunity to live in the open spaces in decent housing one can afford and in the manner one desires is a vital one in a democracy.

. . . Trailer living is a perfectly respectable, healthy and useful kind of housing, adopted by choice by several million people in this country today. Municipalities and courts can no longer refuse to recognize its proper and significant place in today's society and should stop acting on the basis of old wives' tales.

NOTES AND QUESTIONS

1. **The *Vickers* dissent.** Justice Hall's dissent is probably the most famous zoning opinion between *Euclid* and *Mount Laurel*, and deservedly so. It was this opinion that first spelled out the problems of exclusionary zoning to the judiciary; and 13 years later the New Jersey court came around with *Mount Laurel I*, see *infra* page 980.

2. **Judicial review.** What, in your view, is the proper role of the courts in this context? What criteria do you use to make that decision?

3. **Mobile homes as poor people's housing.** Mobile homes represent one of the most affordable and efficient forms of home ownership. At one-fourth the cost of the average single-family dwelling, mobile homes are a particularly appealing housing option for older Americans and those who are relatively poor. Werner Z. Hirsch and Joel G. Hirsch, "Legal-Economic Analysis of Rent Controls in a Mobile Home Context: Placement Values and Vacancy Decontrol," 35 UCLA L. Rev. 399, 401-403 (1988). Communities that permit mobile homes are better able to provide a wider range of housing options for their residents. In fact, in many areas that lack affordable rental housing, mobile homes represent the only viable option for low-income families who otherwise must choose between housing priced beyond their means or living in substandard conditions. Rural residents, in particular, experience a disproportionate degree of substandard housing

---

counsel, during the course of discussion of the local reasons for the action, that people who lived in trailers were shifting population without roots and did not make good citizens. Aside from the fact that such characterizations are today without true foundation, the statement is an example of frequently found resentment and distrust by present residents of newcomers, including renters, who vote on school budgets and the election of local officials with the power over municipal appropriations, but who do not pay real estate taxes directly or in sufficient amount to cover the cost of local services rendered to them.

conditions because their communities do not have resources to construct, rehabilitate or repair affordable housing. Craig Anthony Arnold, "Ignoring the Rural Underclass: The Biases of Federal Housing Policy," 2 Stan. L. & Poly. Rev. 191 (1990). At least one court has recognized, as did Justice Hall in his dissent in *Vickers*, that mobile homes are a legitimate housing option and that municipalities have a duty to provide for a wide range of housing needs. Geiger v. Zoning Hearing Board of North Whitehall, 510 Pa. 231, 507 A.2d 361 (1986) (holding that mobile homes have status equal to that of other single-family dwellings, therefore, zoning ordinances cannot exclude them from residential districts absent a relationship to public health, safety, or welfare considerations).

Mount Laurel Township lies within ten miles of Philadelphia and seven miles of Camden, New Jersey. Its area is 22 square miles; its 1970 population exceeded 11,000, more than twice the 1960 population. Individual plaintiffs, current and former Mount Laurel residents, were unable to acquire decent housing within the township at prices they could afford. They blamed a congeries of zoning controls that, in the aggregate, made the construction of low-rent housing impossible. The controls included:

(a)   minimum lot size requirements (9,375 square feet in one zone, 20,000 square feet in the other zone);

(b)   residential areas zoned for only one type of housing, i.e., single-family detached dwellings; no area zoned for multifamily, row houses, or mobile home parks;

(c)   minimum floor area of 1,100 square feet for one-story houses and 1,300 square feet for all other houses;

(d)   planned unit developments allowing apartments by agreement only — units for the relatively affluent, and sharply limited as to numbers of bedrooms;

(e)   30 percent of township area set aside for industrial uses — far more than a 100-year supply.

SOUTHERN BURLINGTON COUNTY NAACP v.
TOWNSHIP OF MOUNT LAUREL (*MT. LAUREL I*)

---

67 N.J. 151, 336 A.2d 713 (1975)

HALL, J. This case attacks the system of land use regulation by defendant Township of Mount Laurel on the ground that low and moderate income families are thereby unlawfully excluded from the municipality. The trial court so found, 119 N.J. Super. 164 (Law Div. 1972), and declared the township zoning ordinance totally invalid. . . .

Plaintiffs represent the minority group poor (black and Hispanic)[3] seeking such quarters. But they are not the only category of persons barred from so many municipalities by reason of restrictive land use regulations. We have reference to young and elderly couples, single persons and large, growing families not in the poverty class, but who still cannot afford the only kinds of housing realistically permitted in most places—relatively high-priced, single-family detached dwellings on sizeable lots and, in some municipalities, expensive apartments. We will, therefore, consider the case from the wider viewpoint that the effect of Mount Laurel's land use regulation has been to prevent various categories of persons from living in the township because of the limited extent of their income and resources. In this connection, we accept the representation of the municipality's counsel at oral argument that the regulatory scheme was not adopted with any desire or intent to exclude prospective residents on the obviously illegal bases of race, origin or believed social incompatibility.

As already intimated, the issue here is not confined to Mount Laurel. The same question arises with respect to any number of other municipalities of sizeable land area outside the central cities and older build-up suburbs of our North and South Jersey metropolitan areas (and surrounding some of the smaller cities outside those areas as well) which, like Mount Laurel, have substantially shed rural characteristics and have undergone great population increase since World War II, or are now in the process of doing so, but still are not completely developed and remain in the path of inevitable future residential, commercial and industrial demand and growth. Most such municipalities, with but relatively insignificant variation in details, present generally comparable physical situations, courses of municipal policies, practices, enactments and results and human, governmental and legal problems arising therefrom. It is in the context of communities now of this type or which become so in the future, rather than with central cities or older built-up suburbs or areas still rural and likely to continue to be for some time yet, that we deal with the question raised. . . .

I. THE FACTS

The record thoroughly substantiates the findings of the trial court that over the years Mount Laurel "has acted affirmatively to control devel-

---

3. Plaintiffs fall into four categories: (1) present residents of the township residing in dilapidated or substandard housing; (2) former residents who were forced to move elsewhere because of the absence of suitable housing; (3) nonresidents living in central city substandard housing in the region who desire to secure decent housing and accompanying advantages within their means elsewhere; (4) three organizations representing the housing and other interests of racial minorities. The township originally challenged plaintiffs' standing to bring this action. The trial court properly held (119 N.J. Super. at 166) that the resident plaintiffs had adequate standing to ground the entire action and found it unnecessary to pass on that of the other plaintiffs. The issue has not been raised on appeal. We merely add that both categories of nonresident individuals likewise have standing. N.J.S.A. 40:55-47.1; cf Walker v. Borough of Stanhope, 23 N.J. 657 (1957). No opinion is expressed as to the standing of the organizations.

opment and to attract a selective type of growth" (119 N.J. Super. at 168) and that "through its zoning ordinances has exhibited economic discrimination in that the poor have been deprived of adequate housing and the opportunity to secure the construction of subsidized housing, and has used federal, state, county and local finances and resources[9] solely for the betterment of middle and upper-income persons." (119 N.J. Super. at 178.)

There cannot be the slightest doubt that the reason for this course of conduct has been to keep down local taxes on *property* (Mount Laurel is not a high tax municipality) and that the policy was carried out without regard for non-fiscal considerations with respect to *people*, either within or without its boundaries. . . .

This pattern of land use regulation has been adopted for the same purpose in developing municipality after developing municipality. Almost every one acts solely in its own selfish and parochial interest and in effect builds a wall around itself to keep out those people or entities not adding favorably to the tax base, despite the location of the municipality or the demand for varied kinds of housing. There has been no effective intermunicipal or area planning or land use regulation. . . .

II.   THE LEGAL ISSUE

The legal question before us, as earlier indicated, is whether a developing municipality like Mount Laurel may validly, by a system of land use regulation, make it physically and economically impossible to provide low and moderate income housing in the municipality for the various categories of persons who need and want it and thereby, as Mount Laurel has, exclude such people from living within its confines because of the limited extent of their income and resources. Necessarily implicated are the broader questions of the right of such municipalities to limit the kinds of available housing and of any obligation to make possible a variety and choice of types of living accommodations.

We conclude that every such municipality must, by its land use regulations, presumptively make realistically possible and appropriate variety and choice of housing. More specifically, presumptively it cannot foreclose the opportunity of the classes of people mentioned for low and moderate income housing and in its regulations must affirmatively afford that opportunity, at least to the extent of the municipality's fair share of the present and prospective regional need therefor. The obligations must be met unless the particular municipality can sustain the heavy burden of demonstrating

---

9. Such "finances and resources" have reference to monies spent by various agencies on highways within the municipality, loans and grants for water and sewer systems and for planning, federal guarantees of mortgages on new home construction, and the like.

peculiar circumstances which dictate that it should not be required to do so.[10]

We reach this conclusion under the state law and so do not find it necessary to consider federal constitutional grounds urged by plaintiffs. . . .

Land use regulation is encompassed within the state's police power. . . .

It is elementary theory that all police power enactments, no matter at what level of government, must conform to the basic state constitutional requirements of substantive due process and equal protection of the laws. The are inherent in Art. I, par. 1 of our Constitution,[11] the requirements of which may be more demanding than those of the federal Constitution. Robinson v. Cahill, 62 N.J. 473, 482, 490-492 (1973); Washington National Insurance Co. v. Board of Review, 1 N.J. 545, 553-554 (1949). It is required that, affirmatively, a zoning regulation, like any police power enactment, must promote public health, safety, morals or the general welfare. (The last term seems broad enough to encompass the others.)

This brings us to the relation of housing to the concept of general welfare just discussed and the result in terms of land use regulation which that relationship mandates. There cannot be the slightest doubt that shelter, along with food, are the most basic human needs. See Robinson v. Cahill, *supra* (62 N.J. at 483). "The question of whether a citizenry has adequate and sufficient housing is certainly one of the prime considerations in assessing the general health and welfare of the body." New Jersey Mortgage Finance Agency v. McCrane, 56 N.J. 414, 420 (1970). Cf. DeSimone v. Greater Englewood Housing Corp. No. 1, 56 N.J. 428, 442 (1970). The same thought is implicit in the legislative findings of an extreme, long-time need in this state for decent low and moderate income housing, set forth in the numerous statutes providing for various agencies and methods at the both state and local levels designed to aid in alleviation of the need.

It is plain beyond dispute that proper provision for adequate housing of all categories of people is certainly an absolute essential in promotion of the general welfare required in all local and land use regulation. Further the universal and constant need for such housing is so important and of such broad public interest that the general welfare which developing municipalities like Mount Laurel must consider extends beyond their boundaries and cannot be parochially confined to the claimed good of the particular municipality. It has to follow that, broadly speaking, the presumptive obligation arises for each such municipality affirmatively to plan and

10. While, as the trial court found, Mount Laurel's actions were deliberate, we are of the view that the identical conclusion follows even when municipal conduct is not shown to be intentional, but the effect is substantially the same as if it were.

11. The paragraph reads: "All persons are by nature free and independent, and have certain natural and unalienable rights, among which are those of enjoying and defending life and liberty, or acquiring, possessing, and protecting property, and of pursuing and obtaining safety and happiness."

provide, by its land use regulations, the reasonable opportunity for an appropriate variety and choice of housing, including, of course, low and moderate cost housing, to meet the needs, desires and resources of all categories of people who may desire to live within its boundaries. Negatively it may not adopt regulations or policies which thwart or preclude that opportunity.

We have spoken of this obligation of such municipalities as "presumptive." The term has two aspects, procedural and substantive. Procedurally, we think the basic importance of appropriate housing for all dictates that, when it is shown that a developing municipality in its land use regulations has not made realistically possible a variety and choice of housing, including adequate provision to afford the opportunity for low and moderate income housing or has expressly prescribed requirements or restrictions which preclude or substantially hinder it, a facial showing of violation of substantive due process of equal protection under the state constitution has been made out and the burden, and it is a heavy one, shifts to the municipality to establish a valid basis for its action or non-action. Robinson v. Cahil, *supra*, 62 N.J. at 491-492, and cases cited therein. The substantive aspect of "presumptive" relates to the specifics, on the one hand, or what municipal land use regulation provisions, or the absence thereof, will evidence invalidity and shift the burden of proof and, on the other hand, of what bases and considerations will carry the municipality's burden and sustain what is has done or failed to do. Both kinds of specifics may well vary between municipalities according to peculiar circumstances. . . .

Without further elaboration at this point, our opinion is that Mount Laurel's zoning ordinance is presumptively contrary to the general welfare and outside the intended scope of the zoning power in the particulars mentioned. A facial showing of invalidity is thus established, shifting to the municipality the burden of establishing valid superseding reasons for its action and non-action.[19] We now examine the reasons it advances.

[The court rejects as insufficient the chief reasons given by Mount Laurel for its zoning controls: the need for fiscal balance; the absence of sewer and water facilities.]

By way of summary, what we have said comes down to this. As a developing municipality, Mount Laurel must, by its land use regulations, make realistically possible the opportunity for an appropriate variety and choice of housing for all categories of people who may desire to live there, of course including those of low and moderate income . . . In other words, such municipalities must zone primarily for the living welfare of people and not for the benefit of the local tax rate.[20]

19. The township has not been deprived of the opportunity to present its defense on this thesis, since the case was very thoroughly tried out with voluminous evidence on all aspects of both sides.

20. This case does not properly present the question of whether a developing municipality may time its growth and, if so, how. See, e.g., Golden v. Planning Board of the Town of

We have earlier stated that a developing municipality's obligation to afford the opportunity for decent and adequate low and moderate income housing extends at least to ". . . that municipality's fair share of the present and prospective regional need therefor." Some comment on that conclusion is in order at this point. Frequently it might be sounder to have more of such housing, like some specialized land uses, in one municipality in a region than in another, because of greater availability of suitable land, location of employment, accessibility of public transportation or some other significant reason. But, under present New Jersey legislation, zoning must be on an individual municipal basis, rather than regionally. So long as that situation persists under the present tax structure, or in the absence of some kind of binding agreement among all the municipalities of a region, we feel that every municipality therein must bear its fair share of the regional burden.

[Justice Pashman wrote an extended concurring opinion urging that the court "go farther and faster" in implementing its principles. Justice Mountain wrote a brief concurring opinion resting his decision on a *statutory* reading of "general welfare" appearing in the zoning enabling law.]

NOTES AND QUESTIONS

1.   **The sunny side of *Mount Laurel.*** Researchers at Rutgers University performed an extensive study of the application of the *Mt. Laurel* doctrine. Martha Lamar, Alan Mallach, John Payne, Mount Laurel at Work: Affordable Housing in New Jersey, 1983-1988, 41 Rutgers L. Rev. 1197, 1258 (1989). In addition to the direct benefits resulting from the houses built pursuant to the doctrine's guidelines, the reseachers also found secondary benefits from the program: with the erection and presence of the Mount Laurel housing in various suburbs, "stereotypes about affordable housing [began] to soften," even in some areas which had vigorously opposed any such housing. Id. at 1259. In the study authors concluded that "Mount Laurel can work, it does work, and it sets a model for an effective partnership between public and private forces that can be made to work elsewhere." Id. at 1277. Furthermore, Mount Laurel has "left an imprint on almost every institution, every city and town, in New Jersey," put fair housing on the

---

Ramapo, 30 N.Y.2d 359, 285 N.E.2d 291 (1972), *appeal dismissed,* 409 U.S. 1003 (1972); Construction Industry Association of Sonoma County v. City of Petaluma, 375 F. Supp. 574 (N.D. Cal. 1974), *appeal pending* (citation of these cases is not intended to indicate either agreement or disagreement with their conclusions). We now say only that, assuming some type of timed growth is permissible, it cannot be utilized as an exclusionary device or to stop all further development and must include early provision for low and moderate income housing.

public agenda in New Jersey, and affected housing policies in other states. David W. Chen, Slouching Toward Mount Laurel, N.Y. Times, Mar. 31, 1996, at NJ1.

2. **The dark side of** *Mount Laurel.* The vision of the Mount Laurel court cases has met a number of political, social, and financial setbacks. First, Governor Kean and the legislature took the side of the suburbs in opposing any such plan. Under the Kean administration,[5] municipalities were allowed to pay other municipalities to shoulder up to half of their Mount Laurel housing obligation, which many of them have done, with the result that many cities, where the poor were already concentrated, took on the responsibility of providing affordable housing in exchange for badly needed funds. Robert Hanley, Housing the Poor in Suburbia: A Failed Vision in Jersey, N.Y. Times, Jun. 1, 1987, at B1. Another problem, and one noted in the Rutgers survey, is that certain minority groups, especially blacks, are dramatically underrepresented in Mount Laurel housing: Many developments have no black residents at all, while others are 1 to 3 percent black. Reasons suggested for this are a failure of developers to reach out to inner cities, and the fact that since most units are for sale, not rent, purchase requires significant financial resources. Martha Lamar, Alan Mallach, John Payne, Mount Laurel at Work: Affordable Housing in New Jersey, 1983-1988, 41 Rutgers L. Rev. 1197, 1256 (1989).

3. **Judge of character.** New Jersey Chief Justice Robert N. Wilentz retired from the bench on June 14, 1996, shortly before his death. During his tenure, the court, which was noted for its "intellectual rigor and creativity," rendered thoughtful opinions "on some of the most divisive and difficult issues of the day." Legal experts attribute his success as chief justice to his recognition of the political realities of issues, pushing for "strong regulatory and administrative machinery" to enforce court decisions. Jennifer Preston, Chief Justice of New Jersey Resigns after 17 Years on the High Court, N.Y. Times, Jun. 14, 1996, at B1. His legacy included *Mount Laurel* II, *infra,* Matter of Baby M (banning surrogate mother contracts in New Jersey), State v. Kelley (recognizing battered woman's syndrome as a defense to homicide), Abbott v. Burke (holding the current (1990) state school funding formula unconstitutional because it didn't provide for poorest school districts), and Doe v. Poritz (upholding Megan's Law requiring community notification when a convicted sex offender moves into a neighborhood). Rulings Shaped by a Vision of Change, N.Y. Times, Jun. 14, 1996, at B6.

4. **"The Magna Carta of suburban low- and moderate-income housing."** *Mt. Laurel I* is probably the leading exclusionary zoning case and has spawned a tremendous amount of commentary. Other states whose courts

---

5. Thomas Kean was the Republican governor of New Jersey from 1981 to 1989.

have decried exclusionary zoning include Pennsylvania: National Land & Investment Co. v. Kohn, 419 Pa. 504, 215 A.2d 597 (1965); New York: Berenson v. Town of New Castle, 38 N.Y.2d 102, 341 N.E.2d 236 (1975); California: Associated Home Builders v. City of Livermore, 18 Cal. 3d 582, 557 P.2d 473, 135 Cal. Rptr. 41 (1976); Washington, Save a Valuable Environment v. City of Bothell, 89 Wash. 2d 862, 576 P.2d 401 (1987); New Hampshire: Britton v. Town of Chester, 134 N.H. 434, 595 A.2d 492 (1991). See also James A. Kushner, Land Use Litigation and Low Income Housing: Mandating Regional Fair Share Plans, 9 Clearinghouse Rev. 10 (1975) (*Mt. Laurel* the "Magna Carta of low and moderate income housing").

5.   **A right to housing?** Does *Mt. Laurel I* grant a right to housing? Note that no right to housing exists under the federal constitution. See Lindsey v. Normet 405 U.S. 56, 74 (1972): "We do not denigrate the importance of decent, safe and sanitary housing. But the Constitution does not provide judicial remedies for every social and economic ill. We are unable to perceive in that document any constitutional guarantee of access to dwellings of a particular quality."

6.   **Legal basis.** What is the legal basis for the court's opinion? Is the court's opinion based on state or federal constitutional law? Why? Note that discrimination on the basis of poverty has never been illegal under the federal constitution. Is it illegal in New Jersey? How broadly can *Mt. Laurel I* be read?

The court in *Mount Laurel* cites Robinson v. Cahill, 62 N.J. 473, 303 A.2d 273 (1973), to assert that the due process and equal protection requirements of New Jersey's constitution are more demanding than those imposed by the Constitution of the United States. In *Robinson*, the New Jersey Supreme Court addressed the constitutionality of the existing system of financing the state's public schools. The court found the system, which relied on local taxes to fund 67 percent of the costs related to public schools, to be unconstitutional because it led to great disparities among the state's school districts in funds allocated to education, leaving students in poorer districts with inferior educational opportunities. The court felt that these disparities were in direct conflict with a state constitutional provision that requires the state to "provide for the maintenance and support of a thorough and efficient system of free public schools for the instruction of all the children in this State between the ages of five and eighteen years," and ordered the state to establish a new statutory scheme.

7.   **Developing municipalities.** What is the obligation of a developing municipality under *Mt. Laurel I*? Why do you suppose this was limited to developing municipalities?

8.   **Fair share.** Why does the court feel the need to require each municipality to shoulder its "fair share" of regional need? The court stated that the fair share allocation of individual jurisdictions would depend on a variety of factors, including the amount of housing needed and environmental

conditions. According to one group of commentators, "The greatest problem facing the three *Mt. Laurel* judges [assigned to handle post-*Mt. Laurel II, infra,* cases] was determining a methodology for calculating the specific numerical size of each municipality's fair share obligation." Martha Lamar, Alan Mallach, John M. Payne, *Mt. Laurel* at Work: Affordable Housing in New Jersey, 1983-1988, 41 Rutgers L. Rev. 1197 (1989).

How much housing does Mt. Laurel have to accommodate, according to the court? How is the amount to be calculated?

9.   **Remedies.** What remedies does this case offer? For whom?

10.   **Case history between *Mt. Laurel I* and *Mt. Laurel II.*** The years after *Mt. Laurel I* saw ongoing litigation that focused on defining fair share and pinpointing what kinds of municipalities had the responsibility to accommodate low- and moderate-income housing. See Oakwood at Madison, Inc. v. Township of Madison, 72 N.J. 481, 371 A.2d 1192 (1977) (ordering defendant to submit to trial court revised ordinance which creates opportunity for fair and reasonable share of "least cost" regional housing needs but refusing to require numerical specification of such fair and reasonable share); Home Builders League of South Jersey v. Township of Berlin, 81 N.J. 127, 405 A.2d 381 (1979) (holding that zoning ordinance's minimum floor area requirements were unrelated to legitimate zoning purposes and were, therefore, invalid exercise of municipal police power). A number of municipalities argued that they were not developing municipalities, and therefore were not required to accommodate low- and moderate-income housing. See, e.g., Glenview Dev. Co. v. Franklin Township, 164 N.J. Super. 563, 397 A.2d 384 (1978) (thinly populated, rural township, distant from urban centers, exempt); Pascack Assn., Ltd. v. Township of Washington, 74 N.J. 470, 379 A.2d 6 (1977) ("fully developed, single-family residential" township exempt). The N.J. Supreme Court became increasingly frustrated by what it perceived as foot-dragging by Mt. Laurel and other New Jersey municipalities. Mt. Laurel's revised ordinance is a case in point. It rezoned only 20 acres out of the town's 22.4 square miles: 13 swampy acres were zoned for townhouse garden apartments; a small, low-lying swampy parcel was zoned for single-family houses; and a third zone allowed for a planned unit development, in which housing restrictions would be relaxed. The New York Times reported in 1983:

> Despite the order's potential for broad social and economic change, Mount Laurel's landscape remains dominated by horse farms, orchards, farms, woods and back-country roads, even though it is a 15-minute drive east of Philadelphia. None of the 515 new housing units that the Planning Board in 1976 thought would satisfy the court's dictate were ever built. . . .
>
> Mount Laurel's response to the 1975 holding — the action that drew the court's wrath in the ruling Thursday — was to rezone three widely scattered plots for low-income housing. Together, the three parcels contain 33 of the 14,176 predominantly rural acres in the town. . . .

The 33 acres set aside years ago remain as they did then. One plot of 13 acres is a field on the fringe of an apple orchard. . . .

Another plot has 13 acres of idle land at the rear of the Moorestown Shopping Mall. Another Philadelphia company, the Binswanger Management Corporation, which plans and manages office buildings, owns it. Binswanger has never proposed construction of housing on the site, . . . although Binswanger attempted to win approval for an industrial part on adjacent land it owns. . . .

The third designated low-income housing plot, with seven acres, has for years been a farm for Christmas trees owned by Alfred DiPietro, an engineer for RCA, who lives in Guam. His nephews run the farm.

Mr. Godfrey, the owner of the country store and a friend of Mr. DiPietro, said, "Until he gets a fortune for the land, he'll never sell it for any housing."

Robert Hanley, After 7 Years, Town Remains under Fire for Its Zoning Code, N.Y. Times, Jan. 22, 1983, at 31.

Finally, in 1983, the N.J. Supreme Court issued the opinion known as *Mt. Laurel II,* which "put some steel into the [Mt. Laurel] doctrine." 92 N.J. at 200, 456 A.2d at 410. What does the court see at stake in the perceived failure of *Mt. Laurel I?* How does it attempt to solve the problem?

SOUTHERN BURLINGTON COUNTY NAACP v. TOWNSHIP OF MOUNT LAUREL (*MOUNT LAUREL II*)

92 N.J. 158, 456 A.2d 390 (1983)[6]

WILENTZ., C.J. This is the return, eight years later, of Southern Burlington County N.A.A.C.P. v. Township of Mount Laurel, 67 N.J. 151, 336 A.2d 713 (1975) (*Mount Laurel I*). We set forth in that case, for the first time, the doctrine requiring that municipalities' land use regulations provide a realistic opportunity for low and moderate income housing. The doctrine has become famous. The *Mount Laurel* case itself threatens to become infamous. After all this time, ten years after the trial court's initial order invalidating its zoning ordinance, Mount Laurel remains afflicted with a blatantly exclusionary ordinance. Papered over with studies, rationalized by hired experts, the ordinance at its core is true to nothing but Mount Laurel's determination to exclude the poor. Mount Laurel is not alone; we

---

6. One of the longest-ever reported opinions, *Mt. Laurel II* runs for 120 pages in the Atlantic Reporter.

believe that there is widespread non-compliance with the constitutional mandate of our original opinion in this case.

To the best of our ability, we shall not allow it to continue. . . .

[W]hile we have always preferred legislative to judicial action in this field, we shall continue — until the Legislature acts — to do our best to uphold the constitutional obligation that underlies the *Mount Laurel* doctrine. That is our duty. We may not build houses, but we do enforce the Constitution.

We note that there has been some legislative initiative in this field. We look forward to more. The new Municipal Land Use Law explicitly recognizes the obligation of municipalities to zone with regional consequences in mind, N.J.S.A. 40:55D-28(d); it also recognizes the work of the Division of State and Regional Planning in the Department of Community Affairs (DCA), in creating the State Development Guide Plan (1980) (SDGP), which plays an important part in our decisions today. Our deference to these legislative and executive initiatives can be regarded as a clear signal of our readiness to defer further to more substantial actions.

The judicial role, however, which could decrease as a result of legislative and executive action, necessarily will expand to the extent that we remain virtually alone in this field. In the absence of adequate legislative and executive help, we must give meaning to the constitutional doctrine in the cases before us through our own devices; even if they are relatively less suitable. That is the basic explanation of our decisions today. . . .

The initial question in every *Mount Laurel* case is whether the municipality is subject to the *Mount Laurel* obligation. In its initial formulation in *Mount Laurel I*, this Court described the characteristics of *Mount Laurel*, implying that any municipality with similar characteristics would have the obligation announced in that opinion. *Mount Laurel I*, 67 N.J. at 160, 336 A.2d 713. Those municipalities are referred to as "developing municipalities." . . .

Lacking any official guidance, however, as to the state's plans for its own future, its own determination of where development should occur and where it should not, and what kind of development, this Court fashioned its own remedial planning guide in the form of a definition of "developing." It was obvious to anyone who studied the matter that such definition of the *Mount Laurel* responsibility furnished no guarantee that if lower income housing resulted, it would be built where it should be built, i.e., where a comprehensive plan for the State of New Jersey might indicate such development was desirable. We proceeded in spite of this drawback since, given the constitutional requirement and the lack of any assurance that such a statewide plan would be forthcoming, there appeared no justification for delay.

We now have a satisfactory alternative. The State Development Guide Plan (May 1980) promulgated pursuant to N.J.S.A. 13:1B-15.52, provides a statewide blueprint for future development. Its remedial use in Mount Laurel disputes will ensure that the imposition of fair share obligations will coincide with the State's regional planning goals and objectives. . . .

The SDGP divides the state into six basic areas: growth, limited growth, agriculture, conservation, pinelands and coastal zones (the pinelands and coastal zones actually being the product of other protective legislation). . . . By clearly setting forth the state's policy as to where growth should be encouraged and discouraged, these maps effectively serve as a blueprint for the implementation of the Mount Laurel doctrine. Pursuant to the concept map, development (including residential development) is targeted for areas characterized as "growth." The Mount Laurel obligation should, as a matter of sound judicial discretion reflecting public policy, be consistent with the state's plan for its future development. . . .

As noted before, *all* municipalities' land use regulations will be required to provide a realistic opportunity for the construction of their fair share of the region's present lower income housing need generated by present dilapidated or overcrowded lower income units, including their own. Municipalities located in "growth areas" may, of course, have an obligation to meet the present need of the region that goes far beyond that generated in the municipality itself; there may be some municipalities, however, in growth areas where the portion of the region's present need generated by that municipality far exceeds the municipality's fair share. The portion of the region's present need that must be addressed by municipalities in growth areas will depend, then, on conventional fair share analysis, some municipality's fair share being more than the present need generated within the municipality and in some cases less. In non-growth areas, however (limited growth, conservation, and agricultural), no municipality will have to provide for more than the present need generated within the municipality, for to require more than that would be to induce growth in that municipality in conflict with the SDGP. . . .

There are two basic types of affirmative measures that a municipality can use to make the opportunity for lower income housing realistic: (1) encouraging or requiring the use of available state or federal housing subsidies, and (2) providing incentives for or requiring private developers to set aside a portion of their developments for lower income housing. Which, if either, of these devices will be necessary in any particular municipality to assure compliance with the constitutional mandate will be initially up to the municipality itself. Where necessary, the trial court overseeing compliance may require their use. We note again that least-cost housing will not ordinarily satisfy a municipality's fair share obligation to provide low and moderate income housing unless and until it has attempted the inclusionary devices outlined below or otherwise has proven the futility of the attempt. . . .

There are several inclusionary zoning techniques that municipalities must use if they cannot otherwise assure the construction of their fair share of lower income housing. Although we will discuss some of them here, we in no way intend our list to be exhaustive; municipalities and trial courts are encouraged to create other devices and methods for meeting fair share obligations.

The most commonly used inclusionary zoning techniques are incentive zoning and mandatory set-asides. The former involves offering economic incentives to a developer through the relaxation of various restrictions of an ordinance (typically density limits) in exchange for the construction of certain amounts of low and moderate income units. The latter, a mandatory set-aside, is basically a requirement that developers include a minimum amount of lower income housing in their projects. . . .

In addition to the mechanisms we have just described, municipalities and trial courts must consider such other affirmative devices as zoning substantial areas for mobile homes and for other types of low cost housing and establishing maximum square footage zones, i.e., zones where developers cannot build units with *more* than a certain footage or build anything other than lower income housing or housing that includes a specified portion of lower income housing. In some cases, a realistic opportunity to provide the municipality's fair share may require over-zoning, i.e., zoning to allow for *more* than the fair share if it is likely, as it usually is, that not all of the property made available for lower income housing will actually result in such housing.

Although several of the defendants concede that simply removing restrictions and exactions is unlikely to result in the construction of lower income housing, they maintain that requiring the municipality to use affirmative measures is beyond the scope of the courts' authority. We disagree. . . .

The specific contentions are that inclusionary measures amount to a taking without just compensation and an impermissible socio-economic use of the zoning power, one not substantially related to the use of land. Reliance is placed to some extent on Board of Supervisors v. DeGroff Enterprises, Inc., 214 Va. 235, 198 S.E.2d 600 (1973), to that effect. We disagree with that decision. We now resolve the matter that we left open in *Madison*, 72 N.J. at 518-19. We hold that where the Mount Laurel obligation cannot be satisfied by removal of restrictive barriers, inclusionary devices such as density bonuses and mandatory set-asides keyed to the construction of lower income housing, are constitutional and within the zoning power of a municipality. . . .

Townships such as Mount Laurel that now ban mobile homes do so in reliance upon Vickers v. Gloucester, 37 N.J. 232 (1962), in which this Court upheld such bans. *Vickers,* however, explicitly recognized that changed circumstances could require a different result. Id. at 250. We find that such changed circumstances now exist. As the court found below, mobile homes have since 1962 become "structurally sound [and] attractive in appearance." 161 N.J. Super. at 357. Further, since 1974, the safety and soundness of mobile homes have been regulated by the National Mobile Home Construction and Safety Standards Act, 42 U.S.C. 5401 (1974). *Vickers*, therefore, is overruled; absolute bans of mobile homes are no longer permissible on the grounds stated in that case. . . .

Lest we be misunderstood, we do *not* hold that every municipality must allow the use of mobile homes as an affirmative device to meet its Mount Laurel obligation, or that any ordinance that totally excludes mobile homes is per se invalid. Insofar as the Mount Laurel doctrine is concerned, whether mobile homes must be permitted as an affirmative device will depend upon the overall effectiveness of the municipality's attempts to comply: if compliance can be just as effectively assured without allowing mobile homes, Mount Laurel does not command them; if not, then assuming a suitable site is available, they must be allowed. . . .

There may be municipalities where special conditions such as extremely high land costs make it impossible for the fair share obligation to be met even after all excessive restrictions and exactions, i.e., those not essential for safety and health, have been removed and all affirmative measures have been attempted. In such cases, *and only in such cases,* the Mount Laurel obligation can be met by supplementing whatever lower income housing can be built with enough "least cost" housing to satisfy the fair share. Least cost housing does not, however, mean the most inexpensive housing that developers will build on their own; it does not mean $50,000-plus single family homes and very expensive apartments. Least cost housing means the least expensive housing that builders can provide after removal by a municipality of *all* excessive restrictions and exactions and after thorough use by a municipality of all affirmative devices that might lower costs. Presumably, such housing, though unaffordable by those in the lower income brackets, will be inexpensive enough to provide shelter for families who could not afford housing in the conventional suburban housing market. At the very minimum, provision of least cost housing will make certain that municipalities in "growth" areas of this state do not "grow" only for the well-to-do. . . .

We hold that where a developer succeeds in Mount Laurel litigation and proposes a project providing a substantial amount of lower income housing, a builder's remedy should be granted unless the municipality establishes that because of environmental or other substantial planning concerns, the plaintiff's proposed project is clearly contrary to sound land use planning. We emphasize that the builder's remedy should not be denied solely because the municipality prefers some other location for lower income housing, even if it is in fact a better site. Nor is it essential that considerable funds be invested or that the litigation be intensive. . . .

Trial courts should guard the public interest carefully to be sure that plaintiff-developers do not abuse the Mount Laurel doctrine. Where builder's remedies are awarded, the remedy should be carefully conditioned to assure that in fact the plaintiff-developer constructs a substantial amount of lower income housing. Various devices can be used for that purpose, including prohibiting construction of more than a certain percentage of the non-lower income housing until a certain amount of the lower income housing is completed. . . .

The provision of decent housing for the poor is not a function of this Court. Our only role is to see to it that zoning does not prevent it, but rather provides a realistic opportunity for its construction as required by New Jersey's Constitution. The actual construction of that housing will continue to depend, in a much larger degree, on the economy, on private enterprise, and on the actions of the other branches of government at the national, state and local level. We intend here only to make sure that if the poor remain locked into urban slums, it will not be because we failed to enforce the Constitution.

NOTES AND QUESTIONS

1. **Relationship with the legislature.** Is the court's role in the *Mt. Laurel* litigation a proper role of a court? How does the court attempt to address and resolve this issue?

2. **Fair share.** How, if at all, does *Mt. Laurel II* change the definition of fair share?

3. **Developing municipalities.** Why does the court abandon the notion of developing municipalities? What does it put in its place? Note that some influential commentators argued that the SDGD was not suited for the purposes to which *Mt. Laurel II* put it. See Anthony De Palma, New Jersey Housing Woes Are All Over the Map, N.Y. Times, Apr. 17, 1983, §4, p. 6:

> George Sternlieb, Director of the Center for Urban Policy Research at Rutgers University, has called the entire document "poorly done." The administration of Governor Kean, openly opposed to the mandate because of what the Governor has called "overly aggressive judicial action," has refused to endorse it on the ground the plan is not sufficient as a statewide zoning map.
>
> "It's a good plan for the purpose for which it was written — to help with new infrastructure projects," said W. Cary Edwards, the Governor's chief counsel. "It simply is not a very accurate tool for the purposes the court wants it used."

4. **Managing *Mt. Laurel* litigation.** What steps does the court take to manage the *Mt. Laurel* litigation? Why were they important, in the court's view, to achieving its goals?

5. **Remedies.** Why does the court spend so much time on delineating the remedies available to *Mt. Laurel* plaintiffs? What remedies does the court make available?

6. **Subsequent case history.** *Mt. Laurel II* led to intense negotiations within the legislature. A compromise was reached in the Fair Housing Act of 1985. The Act established an administrative agency, the Council on Af-

fordable Housing (COAH) to determine "fair share" obligations and set up a process whereby COAH could certify municipalities that submitted acceptable plans. Municipalities need not go through COAH, but have substantial incentive to do so, for they are guaranteed protection from further exclusionary zoning lawsuits for six years after they are certified. The Act also provided $15 million of funding for affordable housing or rehabilitation. A key, and controversial, provision of the Act allowed towns to meet one-half of their fair share obligation by paying for the construction of low- and moderate-income housing in another town in the same region. (The COAH divided the state into six regions.) It was expected that such transfers would result in suburban communities arranging for substantial proportions of their fair share of *Mt. Laurel* housing to be constructed in older urban areas. Does this transfer mechanism undercut the goals of *Mt. Laurel?* Does it fulfill the constitutional mandate set out in the *Mt. Laurel* opinions?

7.   **Is *Mt. Laurel* a success?** Predictably, controversy exists over whether the *Mt. Laurel* litigation has been successful. Some commentators have attacked *Mt. Laurel* as ineffective. See David G. Anderson, Urban Blight Meets Municipal Manifest Destiny: Zoning at the Ballot Box, the Regional Welfare, and Transferable Development Rights, 85 Nw. U. L. Rev. 519, 540 (1991) (asserting that exclusionary zoning persists in New Jersey despite *Mt. Laurel* rulings); Robert Hanley, Housing the Poor in Suburbia: A Failed Vision in Jersey, N.Y. Times, June 1, 1987, at B1 (arguing that "vision" of suburbs taking wealthy and poor alike "has gone largely unfulfilled"). As of early 1996, 75 communities were still battling developers in court and another 80 were either procrastinating or ignoring their "fair share" obligation. N.Y. Times, Apr. 14, 1996, at Sec. 9, p.11. In Mount Laurel, where it all began, about 150 low-cost units have been built or are under way, out of a "fair share" of 839; in 1970, blacks made up 3.3 percent of the population of 11,000; by 1990, that figure had risen to 6 percent out of 30,270 residents. Statewide, the minority population continues to cluster in about a third of the 1900 census tracts, mainly cities and older suburbs, and New Jersey schools are the fourth most segregated in the nation. David W. Chen, Slouching Toward Mount Laurel, N.Y. Times, Mar. 31, 1996, at Sec. 13 NJ, p. 1.

On the other hand, some change can be seen. In 1995, 12 percent of the 24,000 housing permits issued in the state were for affordable housing, compared with 2 percent of the 55,000 permits issued in 1985. N.Y. Times, Apr. 14, 1996, *supra.* And an earlier study concluded:

> The most basic conclusion to be drawn from the data is that the *Mt. Laurel* doctrine can be successfully implemented. Almost 23,000 units have been planned, including more than 14,000 units that have been completed or are far enough along in the development process that they are likely to be occupied within the next few years. This is far and away the principal source of affordable housing being constructed for lower-income households in New Jersey, as the number of federally-subsidized housing units constructed dropped to 350 last year and is expected to continue declining.

Martha Lamar, Alan Mallach, and John M. Payne, Mount Laurel at Work: Affordable Housing in New Jersey, 1983-1988, 41 Rutgers L. Rev. 1197, 1258 (1989). The study found that most *Mt. Laurel* housing results from "set-asides," in which the developer of new housing sets aside a certain number of units for low- and moderate-income people. The study also found that most of the *Mt. Laurel* units were for sale, not for rent, and that the units were about evenly split between units for low-income, and those for moderate-income, people. See id. at 1214 (Table III).

NOTE ON INCLUSIONARY ZONING

Note the heavy reliance in *Mt. Laurel II* on inclusionary zoning. This practice, which requires developers of residential housing units to commit themselves before rezoning or site plan approval to build a minimum percentage of units as low and moderate incoming housing, has been frequently debated.

In Board of Supervisors of Fairfax County v. DeGroff Enterprises, 214 Va. 235, 198 S.E.2d 600 (1973), the Supreme Court of Virginia struck down inclusionary zoning after evaluating an amendment of the Fairfax County Zoning Ordinance. Key language follows:

> [E]very planned development of a PDH district shall provide dwellings units for families of low and moderate income. An applicant for PDH zoning . . . shall provide . . . low income dwelling units which shall be not less . . . than six per cent (6%) of the total number of dwelling units in the development. The applicant shall also provide . . . the number of moderate income dwelling units which, when added to the number of low income dwelling units, shall not be less . . . than fifteen per cent (15%) of the total number of dwelling units in the development.

The court invalidated the amendment, holding that the state legislators intended to "permit localities to enact only traditional zoning ordinances directed to physical characteristics and having the purpose neither to include nor exclude any particular socio-economic group."

Legislators in other jurisdictions pressed on undaunted by this judicial warning. See, for example, Cal. Govt. Code §65915 (West Supp. 1987):

> (a) When a developer of housing agrees to construct at least (1) 25 percent of the total units of a housing development for persons and families of low or moderate income . . . or (2) 10 percent of the total units of a housing development for lower-income households . . . or (3) 50 percent of the total dwelling units of a housing development for qualifying residents . . . a city, county, or city and county shall either (1) grant a density bonus or (2) provide other incentives of equivalent financial value. . . .
>
> (c) For the purposes of this chapter, "density bonus" means a density increase of at least 25 percent of the otherwise maximum allowable residential

density under the applicable zoning ordinance and land use element of the general plan. . . .

In May 1977, Newton, Massachusetts, a middle-class suburb of Boston, adopted the following modification to the city ordinances:

Whenever a request under this Section for permission of the Board of Aldermen seeks to increase the density of residential development for apartment houses, apartment hotels, garden apartments, or attached dwellings to a level greater than that permissible without said permit, the Board of Aldermen shall require as a condition of any such grant of permission, the provision, within the development, of low income family and/or elderly housing units amounting to ten percent (10%) of the development's total number of dwelling units.

Iodice v. City of Newton, 397 Mass. 329, 491 N.E.2d 618, 620 (1986) (quoting §24-29(b) of Newton revised ordinances). This set-aside program was enacted pursuant to Mass. Gen. L. ch. 40A §9 (West 1979), enacted in 1975, which reads in pertinent part,

Zoning ordinances or by-laws may also provide for special permits authorizing increases in the permissible density of a population or intensity of a particular use in a proposed development; provided that the petitioner or applicant shall, as a condition for the grant of said permit, provide . . . housing for persons of low or moderate income . . . .

[T]he Supreme Judicial Court heard challenges to the Newton "ten-percent program." In Middlesex & Boston St. Ry. v. Alderman of Newton, 371 Mass. 849, 359 N.E.2d 1279 (1977), the court invalidated a conditional permit based on a pre-1975 city set-aside program. . . .

[I]n In the Matter of Egg Harbor Associates, 94 N.J. 358, 464 A.2d 1115 (1983) the [New Jersey Supreme Court] turned down a challenge to ten percent low-income and ten percent moderate-income set-asides required of a residential community developer in the Atlantic City area.

Charles M. Haar and Michael Allan Wolf, Land-Use Planning 431-433 (1989).

The Supreme Court decision in Nollan v. California Coastal Commn., 483 U.S. 825 (1987), *supra* Chapter 8, raises questions as to whether challenges to such programs can still be so readily dismissed. Critics claim that the programs are poorly targeted and economically insufficient. Professor Robert C. Ellickson argues:

. . . Inclusionary zoning can also constitute a double tax on new housing construction — first, through the burden of its exactions; and second, through the "undesirable" social environment it may force on new housing projects. In the sorts of housing markets in which inclusionary zoning has been practiced, this double tax is likely to push up housing prices across the board, often to the net injury of the moderate-income households inclusionary zoning was supposed to help. The irony of inclusionary zoning is thus that, in the places where it has proven most likely to be adopted, its net effects are apt to be the opposite of the ones advertised.

Robert C. Ellickson, The Irony of "Inclusionary Zoning," 54 S. Cal. L. Rev. 1167, 1215-1216 (1981).

Robert A. Williams and Alan Mallach provide more positive assessments of inclusionary zoning. Williams, in On the Inclination of Developers to Help the Poor, Lincoln Institute of Land Policy, Policy Analysis Series No. 211 (1985), advocates linking lower income housing programs with nonresidential real estate development:

> . . . First, such a strategy avoids the weakness inherent in most mandatory set aside programs that rely only upon one sector of the real estate development economy. . . . [S]tructural imperfections in one sector of the market will not necessarily destroy the total effectiveness of a program. . . .
>
> Second, such a strategy assures that all forms of real estate development "pay their way" with respect to the housing externalities created by a particular project. . . .
>
> Finally . . . a non-residentially linked lower income housing provision program assures that municipalities cannot avoid lower income housing obligations without also sacrificing all other forms of real estate development within their borders. Mandating such a strategy as an affirmative measure assures that office, commercial and industrial development in a municipality will also be accompanied by lower income housing construction. The historical craving by municipalities for these types of favorable tax ratables indicates that few municipalities would willingly sacrifice promoting all forms of nonresidential real estate development as the cost for continuing in their attempts to exclude the poor. . . .

Id. at 24.

Alan Mallach, The Fallacy of Laissez-Faire: Land Use Deregulation, Housing Affordability, and the Poor, 30 Wash. U.J. Urb. & Contemp. L. 35 (1986), questions Ellickson's theory concerning increased costs due to inclusionary zoning and emphasizes the importance of programs which encourage the development of low-income housing:

> Ellickson argues that in many cases, the landowner will end up bearing much of the cost in the form of a reduction in land value on his property. Where Ellickson errs, however, is in suggesting that such an outcome is necessarily unfair or unreasonable. Indeed, it generally is recognized that government can and does affect land values in the interest of public policy. . . .
>
> Beyond that, there is the underlying issue that value both is created and removed by public action and rarely by the landowner. The degree to which many commentators are upset by the unfairness of the distribution of the costs of inclusionary housing programs appears to be vastly out of proportion to the dimensions of the issue. Indeed, from an economic standpoint, the imposi-

tion of an inclusionary requirement readily can be compared either to the downzoning of land, . . . or to the imposition of an exaction.

Id. at 65.

§9.6   Growth Controls

Communities can be spurred to pass growth controls for a variety of reasons. Sometimes the move reflects citizens fed up with local roads overloaded with traffic. Sometimes it reflects the knowledge that development rarely pays its own way, but instead imposes costs on the existing community in order to pay for extensions to sewer, water and other services. Sometimes it simply reflects the desire to preserve an existing way of life — a desire that may or may not contain exclusionary motives.

Florida's growth management plan illustrates many of the issues surrounding growth control ordinances. In 1985, the Florida legislature passed the Omnibus Growth Management Act. The Act required that each local community create a blueprint or "comprehensive plan" for its growth by mapping out future roads, neighborhoods, commercial and industrial centers, sewers, parks, and schools. The Act further required planners to ensure that adequate infrastructure (parks, roads, sewers and other services) is available "concurrent" with the impact of new development. Possible sanctions for non-compliance or untimely compliance with the Act included the withholding of state funds from revenue sharing, grants, and other programs.

Hailed as landmark legislation, the results of the Act have been hotly debated. The Act spawned over 450 local growth management plans, but although the Act was designed to control growth, local governments have approved enough residential development to sustain a six-fold increase in population by the year 2010. See Christina Binkley, Florida Land-Use Laws: How Florida's Land-Use Law Has Failed, Wall St. J., Mar. 22, 1995, at F1 (explaining that the Act "hasn't worked"); John Maines, County May Lift Moratorium on East Broward Development, Sun Sentinel (Fla.), May 17, 1994, at 1B (calling the Act "[t]he flop"); but see James F. Murley, Regulation Creates Value Squaring off on Property Rights, Florida Trend, Mar. 1, 1995, at 63 (arguing that growth management should not be abandoned in favor of "property rights" rhetoric because growth control ordinances, by preserving and improving quality of life, actually increase property values).

Experts offer a number of explanations for the Act's failures. First of all, local governments lack the money to develop blueprints, hold hearings, and provide the infrastructure necessary to sustain development. A 1 percent sales tax increased was passed in 1987 to finance the costs of comprehensive plans, but it was repealed six months later. See Binkley, *supra*.

The lack of adequate schools coupled with a burgeoning population in Florida present further problems for the Act. The Growth Management Act did not originally require the presence of schools as part of the infrastructure required to accompany development growth (although a recent revision to the Act would enable counties to stop development until schools and other facilities are in place), and impact fees have not provided nearly enough revenue to build the schools needed to keep up with the population growth. See Leon F. Bouvier, No More Growth in Florida? A Dilemma of Too Many People, Orlando Sentinel, Oct. 24, 1994, at A9 ("Florida can expect another 70,000 school students every year. An additional $280 million will have to be allocated for the state's school system every year. This means hiring 3,500 more teachers every year and building a new school every four days."); John Gittelsohn and Melinda Donnelly, Planners Doing Homework on School Crowding, Sun Sentinel, Apr. 4, 1993, at 1B ("Until last month, the planning council had never used school crowding as a reason to reject more homes. . . . It wasn't until last month that school district staff sent a lengthy memo warning that unfettered growth has plunged the system into crisis."); Vital Role of Schools is Recognized by County Planners' Land-Use Votes, Sun Sentinel, Mar. 28, 1993, at 4G (arguing that "schools are infrastructure too, and should be a key part of development decision-making").

Experts also claim that developer activities have greatly impeded the ability of local governments to effectively implement their own growth management ordinances. Developers wield enormous economic power and may obtain exemptions from or amendments to comprehensive plans through the promise of increased tax revenues — or the threat of legal action. The Florida Supreme Court has facilitated the ability of developers whose plans are rejected by local authorities by permitting builders to obtain judicial review of these decisions. See Board of Cty. Commrs. v. Snyder, 627 So. 2d 469, 474 (Fla. 1993) (holding that board's procedure in denying developer's application was quasi-judicial in nature and therefore developer could properly seek judicial review of decision); see also Lee County v. Sunbelt Equities, II, Ltd., 619 So. 2d 996, 1001-1002 (Fla. Dist. 1993) (holding that "site-specific, owner-initated rezoning requests" are quasi-judicial, rather than legislative, in character and therefore "any party adversely affected by a rezoning decision is entitled to some form of direct appellate review"). Florida courts have also held that developers are not bound by the 30-day statute of limitations established by the Act. See Parker v. Leon Cty., 627 So. 2d 476 (Fla. 1993) (holding that although Act provides for 30-day time limit for any "aggrieved or adversely affected party" to file complaint with local government as condition precedent to filing suit, that provision did not apply to developers seeking judicial review of application decisions, only to private citizens seeking to prevent the local government from taking action on development order that is not consistent with comprehensive plan).

At the same time, Florida courts have limited the developer's cause of action against local government. In *Parker*, 627 So. 2d at 476, the court laid out a burden-shifting scheme for a developer's challenge to a local government's decision to deny a rezoning request: (1) the developer must show that the proposal is consistent with the comprehensive plan and complies with the procedural requirements of the zoning ordinance; and (2) the burden then shifts to the government board to show that its decision to maintain the status quo served a legitimate public purpose. The court explained: "In effect, the landowners' traditional remedies will be subsumed within this rule, and the board will now have the burden of showing that the refusal to rezone the property is not arbitrary, discriminatory, or unreasonable. If the board carries its burden, the application should be denied." Id.

Compounding the problem of developer suits is the difficulty of *enforcement*. Local governments may be reluctant to take on the financial burden of formulating and implementing a comprehensive plan. See Santa Rosa Cty. v. Administrative Commn., 643 So. 2d 618, 624 (Fla. Dist. 1994) (dismissing county's constitutional challenge to Growth Management Act on standing grounds). The state may intervene to prevent a local government from violating its own zoning ordinances only when a citizen first files a suit. See Binkley, *supra*. Furthermore, when the state gets involved, it has not always zealously policed compliance with the Act. See Caliente Partnership v. Johnston, 604 So. 2d 886, 887 (Fla. Dist. 1992) ("In the present cases [the state] has expressed its intent to find the amendment not in compliance. However, . . . the notice came two days late."); Florida League of Cities v. Administrative Commn., 586 So. 2d 397, 400 (Fla. Dist. 1991) (setting aside sanctions against Town of Pembroke, Village of Virginia Gardens, and Indian Creek Village for noncompliance with Act pending administrative hearings because state did not provide local governments with proper "clear point of entry" into adminstrative process); see also Cabinet to Allow Farmland Rezoning, Sun Sentinel (Fla.), Nov., 24, 1993, at 8A (state will not punish St. Lucie County for rezoning 164 acres of farmland to residential use, even though allowing residential development violates urban sprawl standard under 1985 Growth Management Act).

The following is a recent case involving a challenge to a growth control ordinance.

DEL ORO HILLS v. CITY OF OCEANSIDE

31 Cal. App. 4th 1060, 37 Cal. Rptr. 2d 677 (1995)

HUFFMAN, Acting Presiding J. The initial questions posed by this appeal as to the validity of a residential growth control initiative . . . commonly known as Proposition A (Prop. A) . . . were answered by this court in our opinion filed July 19, 1994 . . . We [held] that Prop. A was facially and as applied in conflict with the City's general plan and with state planning and zoning law. We thus found that initiative measure invalid from its adoption date.

This appeal by Del Oro Hills, a partnership (Del Oro), of summary adjudication and judgment entered against it in its companion and consolidated action against the City, raises additional questions as to the viability of its claims for damages in light of the constitutional prohibition against governmental regulatory takings without just compensation. . . .

Although we found in our [initial] opinion [in this case] that Prop. A could not stand because it was in conflict with the City's general plan and statutory provisions, we do not find that conclusion mandates a finding here that Prop. A also violates constitutional rights so as to constitute a per se taking of private property. Instead, we conclude that Del Oro has failed to show Prop. A promotes no legitimate state purpose and would thus be facially invalid under takings standards. In addition, Del Oro has failed to show any valid "as-applied" challenge to Prop. A because it did not exhaust administrative remedies to obtain a final determination on a specific development plan. . . . We affirm.

FACTUAL AND PROCEDURAL BACKGROUND

Building Industry Assn. v. Superior Court (1989) 211 Cal. App. 3d 277 [259 Cal. Rptr. 325] [hereafter Building Industry I or the prior opinion]. . . .

1.   History of Prop. A

"Our [Building Industry I] opinion contains the following summary of the adoption and content of Prop. A, alternatively referred to as Chapter 32A:

> " 'Ch. 32A, adopted by the Oceanside electorate in April 1987, declares one of its purposes is "to augment the policies of the City as recorded in the General Plan and City ordinances relating to the regulation of residential development," and "[i]n order to accomplish this purpose, the City must be able to control the rate, distribution, quality and economic level of proposed development on a year to year basis." Ch. 32A adopts a "Residential Development Control System" (RDCS) which, with what may be significant exceptions, adopts a maximum number of dwelling units to be constructed each year, called annual allotments. The allotments are 1,000 for 1987 and 800 for each year thereafter until December 31, 1999, with power granted to the City Council to modify the annual allotment by an amount no greater than 10 percent more or less for any given year and a requirement the annual allotment for a next succeeding year be adjusted higher or lower in order to redress any excess or deficit in the preceding year. Excepted from the RDCS are the following: " '(a) Projects of not more than four residential dwellings, limited to only one such project per developer per calendar year.

" ' " (b) Fourplexes or less numbered multiple dwellings on a single existing lot.

" ' " (c) Single family residential units on a single existing lot.

" ' " (d) Rehabilitation or remodeling of an existing dwelling, or conversion of apartments to condominiums, so long as no additional dwelling units are created.

" ' " (e) Units within the legally designated redevelopment project area.

" ' " (f) Those specific Units which are formally dedicated for occupancy by low income persons or senior citizens pursuant to the provisions of applicable federal, state, or local laws or programs provided these types of units are spread equitably throughout the city and not concentrated in one neighborhood. For the purposes of this section, a project is funded or subsidized pursuant to applicable federal, state or local laws or programs if it receives a loan, grant or continuing financial subsidy for the purpose of developing low-income or senior citizen housing units. This section does not exempt low income or senior citizen projects built with density bonuses or other development considerations under any program.

" ' " (g) Single family dwelling unit projects with lots an average of which are 10,000 square feet or better, which can achieve a minimum of 70% or better, of the maximum awardable points using the Residential Development Evaluation System are exempt." . . .

"Under Prop. A, projects are reviewed by a 'Residential Development Evaluation Board' (the Board) made up of members of the City's planning commission, who evaluate proposed projects for their impact upon public facilities and services (the 'A' criteria) and site and architectural quality (the 'B' criteria). A project which does not receive a score of 51 percent on the 'A' criteria and 70 percent on the 'B' criteria is eliminated from consideration for an annual allocation. The Board's recommendations are forwarded to the city council, which makes the annual allocations."

FACTUAL . . . BACKGROUND

The facts on which this action was based were as follows: Del Oro is a partnership which acquired a 300-acre parcel of property in the City and obtained City approval of a master tentative subdivision map on the property. The planning commission resolution of approval for this master tentative map states, among other things:

"1. That the Tentative Map is for financing and land management purposes. The approval of the map does not grant any development rights because under the Del Oro Hills Specific Plan, further public hearings on Development Plans and/or Tentative Maps will be required prior to development."

The project buildout was proposed to be over a five-year period. Del Oro then obtained approval of a specific plan and planned residential development master plan for its development, a proposed complex of a series of smaller residential neighborhoods or villages. The villages were not themselves building sites, as each of them would be sold to another developer for building after Del Oro prepared the infrastructure for the property.

Before the developer could build its village as purchased from Del Oro, it needed to obtain additional approvals for a final master tentative tract map, tentative and final subdivision tract maps and development plans, all relevant grading permits and landscape plans, and building permits.

In December 1985, Del Oro and the City entered into improvement agreements and Del Oro recorded its master final subdivision map in February 1986. Del Oro then obtained construction financing and bonds for its improvement plans to commence the grading and subdivision improvements called for in the subdivision map and other City approvals. Del Oro contracted with a construction company to grade and install storm drains, sewer, water, utilities, and street improvements in the development area. Del Oro entered into contracts to sell several of its villages, conditioned on completion of subdivision improvements before close of escrow. Some of these contracts were pending when Prop. A was proposed and adopted.

A month after Prop. A passed, Del Oro's attorney wrote a letter to the city attorney requesting an exemption from the effects of Prop. A on Del Oro's property, on the theory it had an implied-in-fact development agreement with the City. This request was denied. Del Oro alleges that when Prop. A was proposed, from that point on, it became practically impossible to market its property. A number of escrows were cancelled and, under business necessity and with its lender's approval, Del Oro later sold four of the villages to one of its constituent partners, Robinhood Homes, Inc. The price, $7.5 million, was $1.5 million below a tentative agreement that was reached to sell the property before Prop. A came on the scene. Other buyers closed their escrows for some of the villages in the latter part of 1987, but Del Oro had to make some $700,000 in concessions to keep the escrows going after Prop. A passed.[4]

Building permits had been issued for 371 of the planned 1,200 units before Prop. A was adopted. Within three and one-half years after Prop. A was adopted, the developers of Del Oro's villages received allocations or exceptions under Prop. A for all of the units necessary to complete the twelve hundred-unit project. Del Oro never applied to build under the low-income exception. Del Oro sold all of its villages within a two-year time frame.

Before Prop. A was adopted, an unrelated developer based in the City, Rancho Del Oro (Rancho), entered into a development agreement with the City to develop 4,840 residential units over a 10-year period. (§65864 et seq., covering development agreements.) Because of this development agreement, the City exempted Rancho from the effect of Prop. A. Del Oro had no such formal development agreement, although it claimed an implied agreement of the sort existed.

---

4. These two sets of losses form the main basis of Del Oro's damages claims.

In its complaint, Del Oro sought declaratory and injunctive relief that Prop. A was invalid, and an award of monetary damages on theories of (1) unconstitutional taking of its property, in violation of federal civil rights (42 U.S.C. §1983), (2) denial of equal protection due to the City's exemption from Prop. A of Rancho, an allegedly similarly situated developer, (3) breach of an implied-in-fact agreement with the City not to interfere with the timing of its development or wrongful denial of a vested rights exemption from Prop. A. . . .

DISCUSSION

[The key issues here are whether under] the applicable tests, does an invalid regulation create damage per se, or is something more required to show a taking, such as loss of all economically beneficial use that was substantially caused by the governmental entity's activities? Also, how does Del Oro's status as essentially a wholesaler of land, rather than an on-site developer, affect its claim that Prop. A applied directly to it and caused it loss? Was exhaustion of remedies required as to such a plaintiff, regarding facial or as-applied claims of unconstitutionality? Finally, is this case suitable for summary disposition as having an adequately developed record? With all these issues in mind, we first address the takings claim and then the alternative damages theories: Equal protection and vested or implied contract rights.

I.   "TAKINGS" CLAIMS: INVERSE CONDEMNATION

Does the invalidity of Prop. A due to its impermissible conflicts with state planning and zoning law and the City's general plan . . . mean that Prop. A does not substantially advance legitimate state interests, and its enactment accomplished some kind of per se taking of Del Oro's property interests? . . .

"The general rule, at least, is that while property may be regulated to a certain extent, if regulation goes too far it will be recognized as a taking." [citing Pennsylvania Coal Co. v. Mahon] . . . In Agins v. Tiburon, the United States Supreme Court outlined the following two-pronged test for regulatory takings: "The application of a general zoning law to particular property effects a taking if the ordinance does not substantially advance legitimate state interests, or denies an owner economically viable use of his land. The determination that governmental action constitutes a taking is, in essence, a determination that the public at large, rather than a single owner, must bear the burden of an exercise of state power in the public interest. Although no precise rule determines when property has been taken, the question necessarily requires a weighing of private and public interests."

In Nollan, supra, the Supreme Court relied on the Agins test but stated it in the conjunctive: "We have long recognized that land-use regulation

does not effect a taking if it 'substantially advance[s] legitimate state interests' and does not 'den[y] an owner economically viable use of his land,'
[citing *Agins*]." The court further refined the first part of the Agins test to
explain that there must be a nexus between the conditions that the government sought to impose on the development before it could proceed and
the governmental interest that the regulation seeks to further. The regulation must substantially advance the state interest said to justify it; a finding
that the regulation has a "rational basis" is not enough.[8]

In Dolan v. City of Tigard (1994), the Supreme Court reiterated the
Agins test but stated it in the negative and the conjunctive: "A land use
regulation does not effect a taking if it 'substantially advance[s] legitimate
state interests' and does not 'den[y] an owner economically viable use of
his land. . . .'[9] In all of these formulations, the focus of both parts of the test
is on whether property has been taken without just compensation, not on
whether a regulation is in the abstract an invalid one; the inquiry must be
what effect the regulation has on affected property owners.

In general, growth control ordinances are routinely upheld by federal
and state courts as valid exercises of a municipality's police power. (Associated Home Builders etc., Inc. v. City of Livermore (1976) 18 Cal. 3d 582,
602 [135 Cal. Rptr. 41, 557 P.2d 473]; Construction Ind. Ass'n, Sonoma
Co. v. City of Petaluma (9th Cir. 1975) 522 F.2d 897; Long Beach Equities,
Inc. v. County of Ventura (1991) 231 Cal. App. 3d 1016, 1030 [282 Cal. Rptr.
877].) Such regulations are normally upheld if they bear a "substantial
relationship to the public welfare" and inflict no irreparable injury on landowners. (Id. at p.1030.) A substantial diminution in value of property is not
irreparable injury in this context.

Moreover, because Prop. A was a growth control regulation, it is entitled to some deference in constitutional analysis, regardless of its statutory
or general plan infirmities. Thus, "the type of taking alleged is also an often
critical factor. It is well settled that a '"taking" may more readily be found
when the interference with property can be characterized as a physical in-

---

8. The Ninth Circuit Court of Appeals, as well as the California Court of Appeal for the
First District, Division Three, has rejected the argument that the Nollan "substantial advancement" test applies to regulatory, as opposed to possessory, takings. (Commercial Builders v.
Sacramento (9th Cir. 1991) 941 F.2d 872, 874 ; Blue Jeans Equities West v. City and County of
San Francisco (1992) 3 Cal. App. 4th 164, 171 [4 Cal. Rptr. 2d 114].) However, we need not
decide this issue because we do not deal with a particular imposed permit condition, but rather
with an overall growth control scheme; in addition, as we shall show, only facial challenges to
the regulation are properly presented here.

9. See discussion in First English Evangelical Lutheran Church v. County of Los Angeles
(1989) 210 Cal. App. 3d 1353, 1365-1367 [258 Cal. Rptr. 893] (First English II) (on remand
from United States Supreme Court, sub nom. First English Evangelical Lutheran Church v.
County of Los Angeles (1987) 482 U.S. 304 of the question of whether the two elements of the
Agins test are "either/or" in nature or if establishment of one part of the test will suffice to
show a taking; the court did not have to decide that issue as the ordinance under discussion
survived either test. (210 Cal. App. 3d at p. 1367.)

vasion by government, than when interference arises from some public program adjusting the benefits and burdens of economic life to promote the common good [citing *Keystone*].'

In this case, the City's version of such an ordinance was fatally flawed because of its conflict with related statutory provisions and the applicable general plan. In our *Building Industry II* opinion, however, we were not presented with and did not decide any constitutional challenges to Prop. A; the matter was presented as requiring resolution of conflicting legislative provisions, and Prop. A lost. To decide if this invalidity is of constitutional dimension so as to support takings claims, we must look at the nature of the challenges Del Oro brought against the measure.

B.   FACIAL VERSUS AS-APPLIED CHALLENGES: THE RULES

[T]he distinction between facial challenges to regulation and "as-applied" challenges has several aspects. Neither type of challenge, however, can avoid analysis of both prongs of the Agins test. Generally, a facial challenge presents an issue of law and case-specific factual inquiry is not required. Thus, in Gilbert v. City of Cambridge (1st Cir. 1991) 932 F.2d 51, 55-56, it is explained that a plaintiff may challenge a regulation as unconstitutional on its face by demonstrating that the mere enactment of the law constituted a taking without just compensation, i.e., by denying the owner economically viable use of the land. In Lucas v. South Carolina Coastal Council (1992), *supra,* the court described two categories of regulatory action which were compensable without case-specific inquiry into the public interest said to support the regulation. These were (1) where the property owner suffers physical invasion of the property, and (2) where the regulation denies all economically beneficial or productive use of the land.

However, an ordinance is safe from a facial challenge if it preserves, through a permit procedure or otherwise, some economically viable use of the property. In such a case, administrative remedies must be pursued if available because the challenge is actually an "as-applied" one. In short, there is also a third category of regulatory takings, where some restrictions burden the property, but the owner is left with some possibility of a beneficial or productive use, so that a case-specific inquiry may be needed to determine if a taking has occurred [citing *Lucas*].

In Hensler v. City of Glendale (1994) 8 Cal. 4th 1, 8, fn. 2, 9-13 [32 Cal. Rptr. 2d 244, 876 P.2d 1043], the Supreme Court took a strict approach to requiring exhaustion of administrative remedies as a prerequisite to challenging a land use ordinance as an uncompensated taking of property. The court held that in challenging a regulatory taking, an owner must afford the governmental entity the opportunity to rescind the regulation or exempt the property from the restriction, by means of a facial challenge through a declaratory relief action, the seeking of a variance if available, and then the exhaustion of other administrative and judicial remedies.

C.   APPLICATION OF RULES: NO "AS-APPLIED" CHALLENGE

To attack regulation as applied, the plaintiff must show a meaningful application for approval of the project was denied, as was any subsequent application for a variance or other permit. "Informal or tentative development proposals are insufficient to meet these tests." Here, Del Oro made a letter request, referring to an earlier claim, that it be exempted entirely from the scope of Prop. A; that request was denied.

Analysis of the exhaustion of remedies issue is complicated by Del Oro's status as an intermediary type of developer. It was not to be the ultimate developer of housing on the land, and was thus not in the usual position of a developer seeking building permits. It could, however, have sought approval of tentative subdivision maps and allocations or other specific ruling under Prop. A; it did not. Under the settled rules for property owners, it is evident that Del Oro has failed to perfect an "as-applied" challenge because it did not apply for permits or allocations to develop the property or seek a variance of some type, other than complete exemption. We are reluctant to create a new category of wholesaler of land or intermediary who is exempt from the requirement of exhaustion of administrative and judicial remedies, based solely on Del Oro's timing argument that it lost profits due to the growth control restrictions which allegedly impeded a timely sale of its property. Del Oro's as-applied claim must be deemed barred for lack of exhaustion of administrative remedies. (Hensler v. City of Glendale, *supra*, 8 Cal. 4th at pp. 12-19, 32 Cal. Rptr. 2d 244, 876 P.2d 1043.)

However, to the extent this is a facial challenge to the constitutionality of Prop. A, through the medium of the cause of action for violation of federal civil rights (42 U.S.C. §1983), there is no bar of exhaustion of administrative remedies. Del Oro attacks here the "whole regime" Prop. A imposed on properties in the City, and claims that the ordinance in its entirety does not substantially advance legitimate state interests "no matter how it is applied." . . .

D.   FACIAL CHALLENGE COGNIZABLE: THEORY

Having determined Del Oro's facial attack on Prop. A is cognizable, we outline its theory and first point out what is not in dispute. Prop. A does not affect the nature of the use of Del Oro's property, as Del Oro admits that its property remains zoned and specifically planned as it was in 1986, before Prop. A was introduced. Instead, Prop. A allegedly interfered only with the timing of development. Del Oro contends, "Prop. A threw a 'monkey-wrench' into the timing of a time-crucial cycle from which Del Oro could not extricate itself. Because Prop. A rendered it impossible to market all the Villages on time in a conventional market, Del Oro was forced to sell its Villages at about $2 Million less than if Prop. A had not come along, and further because of Prop. A, Del Oro was 'over a barrel' and had to make additional concessions to its buyers which lost Del Oro hundreds of thousands of dollars."

However, Del Oro does not dispute that it sold all its property within its own time frame and it or its buyers received permits to develop all the property for residential use within five years of the 1987 adoption of Prop. A. Del Oro's damages claims are thus based upon its lost profits, which it blames on Prop. A's interference with its projected timing of its land development deals. It argues, "In the bundle of rights which constituted Del Oro's property, the only 'stick' which had any value or meaning to Del Oro in mid-1987 was the right to sell its property. Only a sale, and a quick one at that, would save Del Oro and its principals from financial ruin. Oceanside drastically impaired that right with Prop. A." Del Oro theorizes, "reasonable profit expectations, backed by investment, are protected against governmental destruction by the Fifth Amendment just compensation clause."

E.   WAS THERE ANY TAKING DUE TO THE MERE ENACTMENT
     OF PROP. A?

There are several problems with Del Oro's attempt to show that, as a matter of law, a taking of property occurred here. First, we cannot accept Del Oro's theory that satisfaction of one element of the Agins test (i.e., that there was an invalid regulation) is enough to establish a taking as a matter of law. In *Nollan, Lucas,* and *Dolan,* the United States Supreme Court's analysis of the taking issue inextricably interlinked both the regulation's validity and the question of whether any economically beneficial use of the property remained in light of the regulation. In light of later authority, Agins did not establish an "either/or" type of test.

Next, it is well established that "[m]ere fluctuations in value during the process of governmental decisionmaking, absent extraordinary delay, are 'incidents of ownership. They cannot be considered as a "taking" in the constitutional sense'" [citing *Agins* and discussing whether precondemnation activities by a city constitute a taking]. Similarly, although the Supreme Court in First Lutheran Church v. Los Angeles County, *supra,* 482 U.S. at 319-320 held that property owners must be compensated for takings that occurred during the effective period of a regulation that was later struck down as violative of the Fifth Amendment ("temporary takings"), a determination must first be made that the regulation accomplished a taking. (See *First English II, supra,* 210 Cal. App. 3d 1353 [there was no taking so no remedy in damages].)

On a similar point, Del Oro claims it is entitled to at least nominal damages for a per se constitutional violation of its property rights. However, as we have suggested above, the statutory and other infirmities found in Prop. A do not convert it into an unconstitutional taking of property on the undisputed facts here. An invalid regulation is not necessarily an unconstitutional one. (. . . see Keystone Bituminous Coal Assn. v. DeBenedictis, *supra*, 480 U.S. at pp.488-489, fn. 18: "[A] taking may more readily be found when the interference with property can be characterized as a physical invasion by government, than when interference arises from some public program adjusting the benefits and burdens of economic life to promote the common good.") The only available remedy for Del Oro is invalidation of the ordinance, as has already been adjudicated in our [prior] opinion.

This record shows that Del Oro was essentially engaged in speculation in land development. Although it complains Prop. A was solely responsible for its inability to sell some of its 13 villages for as much as it sought, or exactly when it sought, market forces cannot be ignored in analyzing causation of loss or damage here. The courts have been unsympathetic to such claims of lost value of property. Even though the meaning of the concept of deprivation of substantially all economically viable use of property is somewhat elusive, ". . . the general rule is that 'the existence of permissible uses determines whether a development restriction denies a property holder the economically viable use of its property.' [¶] The denial of the highest and best use does not constitute an unconstitutional taking of the property. Even where there is a very substantial diminution in the value of land, there is no taking. The burden of proof is on the applicant, who faces an uphill battle." In any case, the undisputed facts showed that this property was eventually sold and used for the same purpose which had been planned all along, i.e., residential development. It should also be recalled that Del Oro does not now seek compensation for exactions, i.e., the cost of improvements the City required it to make at the property. Del Oro cannot show any facial invalidity of the ordinance due to any deprivation of all economically beneficial use of the property [citing *Lucas*].

In conclusion, this record is adequate to resolve the facial challenges to Prop. A and the takings issues as a matter of law. Accordingly, the trial court did not err in granting summary adjudication and judgment on the takings claim.

II. EQUAL PROTECTION

Del Oro's claims of entitlement to damages due to violation of its right of equal protection may be disposed of summarily. Del Oro argues that there is no rational basis to distinguish between Rancho, a developer which entered into a development agreement with the City, and itself, as a developer without such an agreement but which also made substantial expenditures in constructing subdivision improvements on its property. Del Oro's theory is that whatever rights Rancho's development agreement provided it, the agreement did not protect it against timing controls such as were imposed by Prop. A, and thus should not have been used to distinguish between the two developers for purposes of applying Prop. A (¶65866, governing development agreements).

"Absent the allegation of the invasion of fundamental rights or the existence of a suspect classification, there is no violation of equal protection unless the classification bears no rational relationship to a legitimate state interest. This is true even if some discrimination is alleged." (Long Beach Equities, Inc. v. County of Ventura, *supra*, 231 Cal. App. 3d at p.1041.) In our view, the existence of the development agreement provides a rational basis to distinguish between these two developers for purposes of determining whether any vested rights to development had accrued before Prop. A went into effect. The purpose of Rancho's development agreement was to protect it from changes made by subsequent land use regulations regarding uses and densities. Certainly, those were the main focus of Prop. A, even though timing controls were used to promote those purposes. No triable issues remain as to any damages claimed by Del Oro for denial of equal protection under these circumstances.

III.   VESTED RIGHTS / IMPLIED CONTRACT THEORIES

Finally, Del Oro claims it should be considered to have an implied-in-fact development agreement with the City, due to its construction of subdivision improvements on its property pursuant to agreement with the City, such that vested rights arose.[15] Damages are sought for the denial of a vested rights exemption from the effects of Prop. A. In finding these claims unmeritorious, the trial court relied on the authority of Avco Community Developers, Inc. v. South Coast Regional Com. (1976) 17 Cal. 3d 785, 800 [132 Cal. Rptr. 386, 553 P.2d 546], for the proposition that the City cannot contract away its police power. The main issue in analyzing a vested rights question is whether any further approvals are contemplated before development rights vest. A promise such as that implied by a building permit is necessary before vested rights may accrue. In this case, the master tentative subdivision map approved by the City was not a final discretionary approval. The planning commission resolution states that the tentative map is made for financing and land management purposes, and further public hearings were required to be held on development plans and/or tentative maps before any development rights matured under the tentative map.

In the alternative, Del Oro pleads that equitable estoppel should prevent application of Prop. A to its project. It contends there were implied promises by City officials that the proposed use would not be prohibited by regulations, and Del Oro reasonably relied on these promises to its detriment, by constructing the improvements on the property. We fail to see how

15. Although the City contends that Del Oro's claims were not ripe for decision by the trial court, Del Oro's first amended complaint alleges that it sought an exemption under Prop. A which was denied. Also, a claim for damages for the denial of a vested rights exemption was pled in the complaint. To this extent, these damages claims were properly before the court (in contrast to the takings claims where Del Oro failed to pursue any administrative remedies so as to create a ripe takings claim and where Del Oro did not pursue its takings claim for the "exactions," i.e., the improvements at the site).

any reasonable reliance on implied promises was possible in light of the express statement in the planning commission's resolution approving the master tentative subdivision map to the effect that the approval did not grant any development rights because further public hearings on development plans and/or tentative maps would be required. There was no express representation by the government that this property would be exempt from future regulations governing the timing of development. Summary adjudication and judgment as to this claim were proper.

The judgment is affirmed.

NOTES AND QUESTIONS

1. **Prior case.** This is the second stage of developers' challenges to the Oceanside ordinance. In the first, the developers persuaded the court to strike down the ordinance on the grounds that it violated the city's general plan, and conflicted with state statutes. Building Industry of San Diego v. City of Oceanside, 27 Cal. App. 4th 744, 33 Cal. Rptr. 2d 137 (1994) (hereinafter "BIA").

Recall that, in many states, zoning does not have to conform to a relevant land use plan, despite the enabling law requirement that zoning be "in accordance with a comprehensive plan." However, California law requires that a city or county's zoning ordinance must be consistent with that entity's general plan, such that "the various land uses authorized by ordinance are compatible with objectives, policies, general land uses, and programs specified in such a plan." Cal. Govt. Code §65860 (West. Ann. 1996); Lesher Communications, Inc. v. City of Walnut Creek, 52 Cal. 3d 531, 547 (1990).

In the *Oceanside* case, the developers convinced the court that the growth control measure would jeopardize the city's ability to provide its fair share of low- and moderate-income housing. 33 Cal. Rptr. 2d at 142. The city proved it had met its regional share for all new residential housing units and, even with the limits of Prop. A, would continue to meet its total regional share for the period up to the year 2000, id. at 150. Yet, in the court's view, the city had not shown that it would meet its near-term share of affordable (low- and moderate-income) housing. After Prop. A went into effect, a drastic reduction of more affordable units, such as condos and townhouses, occurred, as compared to more expensive detached homes. The city also failed to show that any of the Prop. A exceptions would lead to more low-income housing.

Do growth controls necessarily hurt low-income people? How would you design growth controls to avoid this result?

2. **Statutory versus constitutional theories.** Given that the developers had won on their statutory claims, why did they file the lawsuit that resulted in this opinion? Note in this context that the Pacific Legal Foundation took part in the challenges to the Oceanside ordinance.

3. **Constitutionality of growth control ordinances.** As the court notes,

growth control ordinances typically have been upheld. The two most famous opinions are the *Petaluma* case mentioned by the court, Construction Industry Assn. v. City of Petaluma, 522 F.2d 897 (9th Cir.), *cert. denied,* 424 U.S. 934 (1975), and Golden v. Planning Board of Ramapo, 30 N.Y.2d 369, 285 N.E.2d 291, 334 N.Y.S.2d 138, *appeal dismissed,* 409 U.S. 1003 (1972). *Del Oro* indicates that the recent spate of Supreme Court case law on takings does not change at least California courts' willingness to uphold growth controls against constitutional challenges.

4. **Standard Zoning Enabling Act.** Reexamine §§1 and 3 of the Standard Zoning Enabling Act, pages 954-955, *supra.* Are growth control ordinances with the act's scope?

5. **The argument for growth control.**

[T]here are at least five well-considered motivations for regulating the timing of urban development. These derive from the specific nature of modern community-building activities and community requirements:

1. *The need to economize on the costs of municipal facilities and services.* These costs are strongly affected by the sequence in which the different areas of a municipality are developed. This matter involves the efficient provision of police and fire protection, schools, bus lines, streets and highways, utilities, and other important facilities. The sequence of building operations determines, for example, whether linear facilities such as pipes and streets will have to be extended gradually to serve areas built in careful phase with efficient facility growth.

The order in which the parts of a large community are built affects both the initial expense of facilities and their costs of maintenance and operation. Large-scale builders like the Levitts place great emphasis in their construction operations on careful scheduling for the most economical possible sequence of development, section by section. . . .

2. *The need to retain municipal control over the eventual character of development.* For example, the desired over-all future town pattern may require intensive development served by public sewer and water lines in an extensive valley at present remote from any utilities lines. If there is no control over the timing of building, however, the area in question may be the early subject of a substantial amount of low-intensity construction served by individual wells and separate sewage disposal fields. The existence of this type of development may later make it impossible to convert the valley to the more intensive character required by the evolving municipal pattern, even though important community-wide reasons exist for doing so. In similar fashion, an important future industrial area may become so cut-up by scattered small-scale factories as to preclude its eventual development as a planned, coordinated industrial district when the time is ripe.

3. *The need to maintain a desirable degree of balance among various uses of land.* For example, it is essential to the economic stability of certain municipalities which contain large areas of low-value homes that the service costs be offset by tax income from commercial and industrial ratables. In such places it is essential that new residential construction be timed in proper relation with business and industrial expansion.

Another sort of balance involves the subtle relationship of areas of varied character. The village of Hastings-on-Hudson in New York has a policy exercised through the zoning ordinance which regulates the timing of apartment construction in relation to the rate of one-family home building in accordance with a 15 to 85 ratio. Thus, for instance, whenever 85 new one-family dwellings have been built, the village may issue permits enabling 15 dwelling-units in apartment buildings. This regulation is intended to maintain what is locally felt to be desirable predominance of one-family dwellings in a commuter village, but at the same time to make possible a necessary though smaller supply of rental apartments. The device makes the timing of one element conditional on the timing of another related element.

4. *The need to achieve greater detail and specificity in development regulation.* The growing awareness of this need is evidenced by the trends in zoning towards increased use of special permit devices subject to detailed requirements and conditions and by the popularity of "designed-district" provisions.

In Great Britain a desire for greater sensitivity of controls led to the present system of development permissions instituted after country-wide public acquisition of "development rights." Local authorities may grant or withhold permission to build, according to the needs of a development plan. At least in the negative sense — that is, being able to prevent development unless it accords with a municipally determined time schedule — the British regulations illustrate an application of control over timing to enable specific conformity with a detailed municipal plan. Under the British controls, for example, on a specific site in a developing area, permission for a store building may be denied on one day if the planning authority considers the construction premature, and at a later date permission may be granted.

There is, of course, a direct but generally unrecognized counterpart to this in the United States. Commonly, a municipality, petitioned to rezone a residential tract for a regional shopping center, refuses to do so when requested, but later decides the propitious moment has arrived and enacts the necessary amendment. . . .

5. *The need to maintain a high quality of community services and facilities.* This requires during periods of rapid building expansion that adequate intervals of time be assured for the assimilate of residential, business or industrial additions to the community.

When newcomers are added faster than municipal facilities and services can be increased, the resulting overloads in existing capacities cause a decline in the quality of services. Uncontrolled, this deterioration can result in seriously substandard levels of water supply, sewage and waste disposal, public school education, and public recreation. Moreover, if the rate of sudden and unanticipated shopping or industrial expansion outstrips the pace of highway improvement, residential streets may be flooded by excessive traffic seeking to by-pass congestion. (It is possible that adequate time for *social* integration of incoming families represents a sixth legitimate basis for regulating community growth.) . . .

Henry Fagin, Regulating the Timing of Urban Development, 20 Law & Contemp. Prob. 298, 300-302 (1955).

6. **Alternatives.** Permit quotas, as in *Oceanside* or *Petaluma,* are only one growth control mechanism. Another approach is a complete morato-

rium on all building (typically for a limited time). See, e.g., Sun Ridge Dev., Inc. v. City of Cheyenne, 787 P.2d 583 (Wyo. 1990) (construction moratorium until developer complied with drainage regulations); Gilbert v. State, 218 Cal. App. 3d 234, 266 Cal. Rptr. 891 (1990) (moratorium on issuance of water permits pending adequate water supply). How does the *First English* decision, making "temporary takings" compensable, affect such moratoria?

A third approach involves refusal to extend services to accommodate new development. See, e.g., Wilson v. Hidden Valley Municipal Water Dist., 236 Cal. App. 2d 271, 63 Cal. Rptr. 889 (1967) (court will not override water district refusal to enlarge supply to service nonfarm activity); Board of County Commrs. v. Denver Board of Water Commrs., 718 P.2d 235 (Colo. 1986) (municipal water service cannot be forced to supply water to new developments); Allstate Ins. Co. v. City of Boca Raton, 387 So. 2d 478 (Fla. Ct. App. 1980) (city need not supply water and sewer services to extramunicipal properties).

Yet another approach is the levying of exactions on new developments to cover the cost of the services, including schools and parks, which the new homes will require. See, e.g., Russ Building Partnership v. City & County of San Francisco, 199 Cal. App. 3d 1496, 246 Cal. Rptr. 21 (1987) (exaction to cover increased public transit costs); Coulter v. City of Rawlins, 662 P.2d 888 (Wyo. 1983) (exaction to cover sewer and water lines extension); Banberry Dev. Corp. v. South Jordan City, 631 P.2d 899 (Utah 1981) (exaction to cover water connection and park improvement).

The market may also provide incentives for developers to provide physical facilities, finance social services, and even preserve the environment.

> For decades real estate developers have played a catalytic, often decisive part in creating the economic character, social profile and sometimes even the government of much of metropolitan America.
>
> Now they are assuming a larger and more diversified public role than ever before. Not only are they taking over an increasing share of government's function by providing such physical facilities as roads and sewers. They are also providing social services, financing schools, libraries and cultural facilities, preserving and restoring the environment and helping to pay for low-income housing. In doing so, they are helping to alter institutional realtionships in city and suburb alike.
>
> This new thrust, both developers and those who study their work say, is partly driven by local governments' growing insistence that developers carry more of the public load that their developments create in transportation, housing and other services. But equally important, say the experts, are new competitive pressures, particularly in suburban and exurban areas offering lucrative opportunities for development, that are forcing builders to pay more attention to the quality of life in and around their developments.

William K. Stevens, Developers Expanding Role in Social Services, N.Y. Times, Nov. 28, 1987, at p.1.

§9.7   Zoning Flexibility — The Variance Procedure

One of zoning's key tenets has been district-wide, uniform classification: All parcels within a zoning district should suffer the same use and bulk restrictions. Yet zoners readily understood that universal classification might cause particular hardship to some landowners whose parcels, by reason of size, shape, location, or topography, were unsuited for the development prescribed for their district. To meet the hardship case, zoners adopted the variance procedure — an administrative appeal that allows a relaxing of the use or bulk restrictions if the landowner can satisfy statutory criteria. The materials that follow, despite their age, still capture the storm and fury of an everyday zoning board hearing. One could be going on in your hometown at this very moment.

NEW YORK TOWN LAW

§267(5) (1965)

. . . Where there are practical difficulties or unnecessary hardships in the way of carrying out the strict letter of such ordinances, the board of appeals shall have the power in passing upon appeals, to vary or modify the application of any of the regulations or provisions of such ordinance relating to the use, construction or alteration of buildings or structures, or the use of land, so that the spirit of the ordinance shall be observed, public safety and welfare secured and substantial justice done.

TOWN OF HEMPSTEAD, BUILDING ZONE ORDINANCE

Art. 5[7]

B   RESIDENCE DISTRICTS

§B-1.0. In a B Residence District the following regulations shall apply:
A building may be erected, altered or used, and a lot or premises may be used for any of the following purposes and for no other:

§B-1.1.   SINGLE FAMILY DETACHED DWELLING.

§B-1.2. Club, Fraternity House or Lodge, when authorized as a special exception by the Board of Appeals.

---

7. The following is adapted from the Record on Appeal, Matter of Clark v. Board of Zoning Appeals, 301 N.Y. 86, 92 N.E.2d 903 (1950), *infra.*

§B-1.3. A regularly organized institution of learning approved by the State Board of Regents; religious use; or philanthropic use when authorized as a special exception by the Board of Appeals.

§B-1.4. Hospital, Sanitarium, Telephone Exchange or Golf Course when authorized as a special exception by the Board of Appeals.

§B-1.5. Agriculture or Nursery, provided there is no display for commercial purposes or advertisement on the premises; Municipal Recreational Use; Railway Passenger Station.

§B-1.6. Accessory use on the same lot with and customarily incidental to any of the above permitted uses, including a private garage. This shall be understood to include the professional office or studio of a doctor, dentist, masseur, teacher, artist, architect, engineer, musician, or lawyer, or rooms used for home occupations such as dressmaking, millinery or similar handicrafts; PROVIDED the office, studio or occupational room is located in the dwelling in which the practitioner resides and PROVIDED further, no goods are publicly displayed on the premises. Such accessory use, exclusive of a private garage, shall not include the erection or maintenance hereafter of any structures other than one erected on the ground and not exceeding two hundred fifty (250) cubic feet content unless authorized as a special exception by the Board of Appeals.

APPEAL TO THE BOARD OF ZONING APPEALS

IN THE MATTER OF APPEAL OF **RICHARD W. BARNES**
1 2 BEDELL AVENUE, P.O. ADDRESS HEMPSTEAD, N.Y.
TO THE **BOARD OF ZONING APPEALS TOWN OF HEMPSTEAD**

The undersigned hereby appeals from the decision of the Building Inspector of the Town of Hempstead in denying application to construct private dwelling and funeral home.

"B" zone.

N/W cor. Westminster Rd & Regent P1, West Hempstead

GROUND OF APPEAL: Practical difficulties and unnecessary hardships. Appeal made under Sec. 267 of the Town Law.

RICHARD W. BARNES
(Owner-Agent-Lessee)
August 18, 1948

EXCERPTS FROM TRANSCRIPT OF HEARING BEFORE THE BOARD OF ZONING APPEALS

RICHARD W. BARNES, construct private dwelling & funeral home, N/W cor. Westminster Road (Rockaway Ave.) & Regent Place, West Hempstead. Present in favor: NATHANIEL KAHN, attorney for the applicant

Various other witnesses

Present opposed: ARTHUR W. RENANDER, attorney for the opposition
Various other witnesses . . .

RICHARD W. BARNES, appearing in favor of this application, after being duly sworn, was questioned by Mr. Kahn and testified as follows:

Q.   You are the applicant in this matter?
A.   Yes.
Q.   You are the owner of a parcel on the northwest corner of Westminster Road and Regent Place?
A.   Yes.
Q.   How long have you owned this piece of ground?
A.   Three years.
Q.   What is the frontage on Westminster Road?
A.   100 feet on Westminster Road.
Q.   And the depth?
A.   110 feet.
Q.   How much did you pay for the plot?
A. $5500.00
Q.   How is that property zoned at the present time?
A.   "B" zone.
Q.   What is immediately adjacent to it on the north?
A.   A residence and doctor's office.
Q.   That is Dr. McKenna's residence and office?
A.   Yes.
Q.   What is immediately adjacent to it on the south across Regent Place?
A.   The same type, a residence and doctor's office.
Q.   What is back of it, that is to the west?
A.   Vacant property.
Q.   What is across Westminster Road on the east side of the road?
A.   At the present time it is a parking space owned by St. Thomas, the Apostle.
Q.   Adjacent to the parking space is the church and rectory?
A.   That is right.
Q.   Do you know whether there are any plans at the present time for the building of a Parochial School there?
A.   Yes, there are plans for the building of a school.
Q.   Do I understand that you propose to build if the variance is granted, a combined home for yourself and your family and a funeral home?
A.   Yes.
Q.   You are now in business and have a funeral home in a store around the corner on Hempstead Turnpike?
A.   Yes . . .
Q.   I show you another photograph and ask you if this is a fair view looking north along Westminster Road showing where your parcel is located, and the gas station and doctor's office on the west side?

A.   That is right . . .

Q.   Have you consulted with Mr. Mazzara, a builder, with respect to building the premises for you and the blue prints that have been submitted
have been prepared by him or by an architect for him at your request?

A.   That is right.

Q.   Did you also have drawings made of the structure you propose to erect?

A.   I did.

Q.   And is this the drawing of the building you propose to erect?

A.   Yes.

Mr. Renander: No objections.

Drawing received in evidence and marked, "Applicant's Exhibit 5." . . .

Reverend Joseph A. Smith, 24 Westminster Road, was called by
Mr. Kahn, and testified as follows:

Q.   You are the Pastor, are you not, of the St. Thomas Apostle's Parish?

A.   I am.

Q.   Your church is located where?

A.   Westminster Rd. at Argyle Rd. in West Hempstead.

Q.   Adjacent to your Church and out of it is your Rectory?

A.   Yes.

Q.   What lies beyond that on the south?

A.   At the present time a parking lot.

Q.   Have any plans been made with respect to erecting a Parochial School
on that property?

A.   Plans have been completed but work, of course, hasn't started.

Q.   That is the status of it, that plans have been completed and you are just
waiting?

A.   Waiting for money to build the school.

Q.   Where is this proposed school with respect to Mr. Barnes' property?

A.   Directly opposite Mr. Barnes' property is the proposed site of the
school.

Q.   You have known Mr. Barnes for how long?

A.   Twenty-five years.

Q.   Have you any objection to the granting of a variance here so that
Mr. Barnes can build his residence and funeral home across from your
property?

A.   I have no objection whatever . . .

Q.   How long, Father, have you been in West Hempstead as a Pastor?

A.   Seventeen years.

Q.   And before that you were in Hempstead?

A.   Some years ago I was in Hempstead, and in between I was in Brooklyn.

Q.   During the seventeen years that you have been in West Hempstead,
you have seen the community grow?

A.   I have.

Q. Are you familiar with the type of structure that Mr. Barnes wishes to build?

A. Yes, Mr. Barnes has shown it to me and I have studied it very carefully.

Q. Do you believe that the granting of this variance to Mr. Barnes and the erection by him of the home which he seeks to build for himself, combined with a funeral home, will in any way hurt the community?

A. I don't think it will hurt the community in any sense, and even in the smallest way . . .

Q. Now, Father, does Mr. Barnes conduct a good number of his funerals each year for people who are members of your parish?

Q. I suppose about two-thirds of his funerals, the funeral is conducted from your church?

A. That is right.

Q. So that such traffic conditions as may arise in connection with those funerals arise now with his funeral parlor around the corner on Hempstead Turnpike?

A. That is right. In coming to the church, the same conditions will be there.

Q. Would the granting of this variance and the building by Mr. Barnes of his funeral home and residence on Westminster Road in your opinion, in any way create any greater hazard to the children of the community than now exists?

A. I do not think so.

CROSS-EXAMINATION BY MR. RENANDER:

Mr. Renander: I do not wish to appear disrespectful and this questioning is not in that line. It is for laying the foundation for something which I wish to bring out later.

Q. You have testified as to the effect of this on the community, I ask you whether or not you believe a public dance hall conducted on the premises in question would be objectionable to the community?

A. I don't see any comparison.

Q. What about a shooting gallery?

A. I don't see any comparison and they are not relative at all.

Q. Or a theatre, a motion picture theatre?

A. I still say they are not relative, and I see no comparison between what you are trying to say and what we are trying to make our opinion.

Q. A freak show or a wax museum?

A. I still don't see any comparison, I think, on the other hand, it is disrespectful to speak of a funeral home in relation to such of those things you have mentioned.

Mr. Renander: I am glad you brought that up because in the City of New York and practically every large city in the country, a funeral home is placed in the same classification, and is prohibited in all retail districts.

Mr. Kahn: I object to any statement of counsel with respect to the pro-
              visions of any other district.

Mr. Renander: That is the experience of zoning experts . . .

[LOUIS H. MCMAHAN, a real estate and insurance broker, testifies that
the Barnes parcel cannot yield a reasonable return if used only for the purposes allowed under the Zoning Ordinance. His only explanation for this
conclusion is that no one is "going to put up a beautiful home" which is
one block north of the business zone and which faces a parking field and a
church.]

FRANK E. WRIGHT, 7 Hempstead Turnpike, West Hempstead, after being duly sworn, was questioned by Mr. Kahn and testified as follows:

Q. What is your occupation or business?
A. Real Estate.
Q. How long have you been in the real estate business?
A. About twenty-nine years.
Q. Where is your place of business located?
A. 7 Hempstead Turnpike, West Hempstead.
Mr. Renander: I will concede his qualifications.

BY MR. KAHN:

Q. How long have you been in West Hempstead?
A. Since 1932.
Q. In your business in West Hempstead, have you had occasion to buy and
    sell or to assist in the purchase or sale of numerous homes in the Ca-
    thedral Gardens area?
A. I have.
Q. Are you familiar with the proposed application for a variance here?
A. Yes.
Q. Do you know Mr. Barnes?
A. Yes.
Q. You are familiar with the land on which he requests permission to build
    this combined home and funeral parlor?
A. I am.
Q. In your opinion would the granting of this variance in any way affect
    the community of Cathedral Gardens?
A. I do not think so.
Q. Why?
A. I think the type of building he is putting up and living in the house
    itself, and also the location that he is putting it up, I don't think it will
    hurt the community at all.
Q. You have been interested in Community welfare in that community for
    a number of years?
A. Quite a few.

CROSS-EXAMINATION BY MR. RENANDER:

Q. You testify that you have sold a number of homes in the Cathedral Gardens area?

A. I have.

Q. You testified that you do not believe that the graving of this variance for use of this premises as a funeral parlor has any derogatory effect as to the property in the area in general.

A. In general, that is right.

Q. Would you still testify that the location of the funeral parlor and the maintenance of the funeral parlor will affect any property in the area?

A. That is a big question. It would take me a little time to explain why.

Q. Will it affect the value? You know the Susan Clark property and you are familiar with the back porch, aren't you?

A. No, I am not.

Q. If I told you the porch was on the southeast corner, would you say no?

A. I have never taken notice of that. I don't know.

Q. If you were the owner of that property and were sitting on that porch having your tea in the afternoon, and you saw ambulances drive up to this site, discharging cadavas [*sic*].

Mr. Kahn: I object.

Mr. Wright: Let me answer it.

Mr. Michaelis: Wait a minute. Do you press your objection?

Mr. Kahn: I do.

Mr. Renander: I withdraw my question.

Q. The property of Susan Clark, would it affect that, would it affect the value of her property?

A. In some ways it would if it was the location, at the location it is in, I don't believe it would harm the valuation very much and you have funeral services at the church now, and they can see it from the house, can't they? And they see them drive in Westminster Road and see them drive away. If they hold services across the street I can't see much difference. And also Mr. Barnes is making his home and the way this has been explained to me, they drive in and you don't see them any more. The hearses do not stand in the street . . .

Mr. Renander: I have been a resident of Cathedral Gardens since 1930, one of the first members of the Civic Association, and I am still a resident there and I have been asked here because the attorney for the Civic Association is away on his vacation and to present this matter to the best of my ability, and I wish to offer in evidence the petitions, No. 1 through 13 inclusive, containing the verified objections of 240 residents in the area.

Mr. Kahn: I object to those petitions on two grounds, first because a great many of the signers live nowhere near the proposed building. Secondly because to my knowledge and perhaps I am equally, with counsel, aware of civic affairs in the West Hempstead community, to my knowledge these petitions were obtained under false and misleading circumstances, and unless counsel or somebody else who has obtained these petitions, comes in here and testifies, and I am given an opportunity to question them as to the contents pursued in obtaining these signatures, I must object to them. My information, and not only is it my information, but I know it as a fact, that these petitions were circulated together with other petitions in which the community was very vitally interested, and I represented this community, and that was in connection with the erection of an incinerator in West Hempstead.

Mr. Kane: You mean this is a tie-in?

Mr. Kahn: Yes, and they came back to me and I had some of these very petitions brought to me at the same time that they went around to get signatures to oppose an incinerator in West Hempstead. They tied this in and I certainly object to it.

Mr. Renander: I object. This is a public hearing.

BY MR. MICHAELIS [MEMBER OF THE BOARD OF ZONING APPEALS]:

Q. Do the petitions indicate the addresses of the signers?

A. Yes.

Mr. Renander: I wish counsel would state after being sworn, and specifically state further the charges. I have six important witnesses here that I would like to bring up and prove that there has been no fraud.

Mr. Michaelis: Let me see the petitions.

Mr. Michaelis: We will take them for what they are worth. The objection is overruled.

Mr. Kahn: Exception.

Petitions received in evidence and marked, "Objector's Exhibit 'A.'" . . .

ARTHUR W. RENANDER, after being duly sworn, testified as follows:

I have been a resident in Cathedral Gardens at the same place where I now reside since 1930. I have been a member of the Cathedral Gardens Civic Association since that time. I am familiar with the premises which are the subject of this application. I am familiar with the properties immediately adjoining on the east, west, north and south. I am familiar with the nature of the improvement in all of the properties in the area generally. I know that there are approximately 238 private dwellings in the Cathedral Gardens area. The petitions which I have presented to this Board contain the names of 240 people, all of them property owners in this area of 238 homes. This does not represent all of the owners, because some of them were away on vacation and there are two signatures for some properties, because the properties sometimes are in a man and wife's name. The opposition represents, on the one family dwellings, approximately 90% of the owners. I was present at a meeting of the Cathedral Gardens Civic Association on October 16th, 1947, at which time the question of whether or not the Association would approve of the proposed variance which is before the Board today, was discussed, and thereafter, and a standing vote was taken with the result that 177 votes, all members of the Cathedral Gardens area were opposed to the granting of the variance and four were not. . . .

Mr. Renander: I wish to offer in evidence a copy of the minutes of that meeting.

Minutes of the meeting shown to Mr. Kahn.

Mr. Kahn: I object. I don't think you have to testify. I will concede that this probably took place, but I object to it being admitted in evidence as having any force in this application. The strange thing is that all of those 177 people, including the counsel, didn't even know that the property which is the subject of this application is in a different zone from theirs. I think the main thing they were concerned about was that this would affect zoning in their section of the community which is zoned "A," and I think if all of those people had been apprised of the true situation, they would not vote that way, and if all of the people who secured the petitions knew the true situation, they would not have signed the petitions.

Mr. Renander: Counsel, I am surprised. The man in the different zone is entitled to the benefits of the adjoining zone, you know that is the law.

. . . [Query? — EDS.]

NATHAN H. CHERWIN, 1 Westminster Road, West Hempstead, after being duly sworn, was questioned by Mr. Renander and testified as follows:

Q. You own the property on the southwest corner of Regent Place and Westminster Road?

A. Yes.

Q. Are you opposed to this application?
A. I am.
Q. Do you believe that the granting of this variance will have an adverse effect of the value of your property?
A. I do.

CROSS-EXAMINATION BY MR. KAHN:

Q. Don't you conduct your practice in your residence?
A. I do.
Q. You also live there?
A. I do.
Q. On the other side of Mr. Barnes' property does Dr. McKenna reside and conduct a practice?
A. Yes.
Q. Do you have office hours in your practice?
A. I do.
Q. What are the hours?
A. 1 to 2 and 7 to 8.
Q. Do patients come to your office during those hours?
A. Yes, and others.
Q. And they come by automobile?
A. Sometimes.
Q. Park their cars along Westminster Road?
A. No, they park on Regent Place, wherever they get a place to park. . . .
Q. Can you see the funerals coming from Mr. Barnes to the church?
A. I have never watched. I suppose I could see them.
Q. Are you aesthetically affected by deaths?
A. I am accustomed to death.
Mr. Renander: I object to the line of questioning.
Mr. Michaelis: Objection overruled.
Dr. Cherwin: I have children in my house who are not in the same position that I am. A physician's children do not have to know the same things a physician knows, and I have female occupants of my house that are affected. . . .

EDWARD J. PHILLIPS, 2 Regent Place, West Hempstead, after being duly sworn, was questioned by Mr. Renander and testified as follows:

Q. How long have you lived on Regent Place?
A. 19½ years.
Q. And what number are you on Regent Place?
A. I am immediately adjoining Dr. Cherwin to the west.
Q. In other words, you would be the nearest house on the south side of Regent Place except for Dr. Cherwin, to the site which is the subject of this application?

A.   Yes.

Q.   Are you opposed to having a funeral parlor?

A.   Yes.

Q.   Will you give any additional reasons you may have to the Chairman of the Board?

A.   When I purchased the house in the year 1929 we came there as a residential district. We bought the property knowing that the south, the abutting property to the rear would eventually become business but there was a zoning restriction that there was a certain amount of space that would have to come from my boundary line to the building on the Turnpike.

Mr. Michaelis: Counsel, out of burning curiosity all morning, what happened to the deed restrictions?

Mr. Renander: They all expired.

Mr. Philips: That is my reason when I bought it, I bought it for a sum that if I wanted to buy in the business section, I could have bought on the Turnpike anywhere along from Franklin Square to Hempstead for the amount I paid for the house.

CROSS-EXAMINATION BY MR. KAHN:

Q.   I suppose you are sorry that you did not buy a little property on the Turnpike in 1929?

A.   I am not a speculator.

Q.   From your rear porch or from your rear yard you can look out to Hempstead Turnpike?

A.   Yes.

Q.   And at the present time there are no stores there?

A.   No.

Q.   You can see Mr. Barnes' property very clearly?

A.   Yes.

Q.   If there were any cadavers brought into this property you could see them right now?

A.   I could see them if my eyesight was a little better.

Q.   And all you would see would be a car driving past Regent Place?

A.   Yes, that is all. . . .

Mr. Michaelis: Do you have any re-direct or do you go into argument?

Mr. Kahn: I have no re-direct and frankly, since this isn't a jury matter, I see no necessity for going into argument. If counsel wants to make some argument, I might feel called upon to answer what he says.

Mr. Renander: I wish to bring up two or three matters to explain some of the cross-examination.

Mr. Michaelis: Do you want to submit a written memorandum?

Mr. Renander: Not necessarily, it will only take me about two minutes.

Mr. Michaelis: We will allow each of you five minutes, and we will hear you first, Mr. Renander. Bear in mind that we sit here and we are a veteran of almost ten thousand variances. . . .

Mr. Renander: I contend that no hardship has been proved on the part of the applicant, because the applicant acquired the premises while they were zoned for the present existing zoning, and there is no proof that the property can't be used for the purpose for which it is zoned. I call your general attention to the fact that irregardless of whether or not, and I am sure if Father Smith sponsors it, the type and personnel would be of the highest, but nevertheless, even when pork is worth a great deal, a pig may not be a nuisance unless you have him in your parlor, I say a funeral parlor in itself would not be objectionable in a proper place, but it would be objectionable in a very highly restricted residential area. I further contend that no proof of hardship being present, petitioner and this Board have no right to grant a nonconforming use which is wholly foreign to the spirit of the Ordinance. This Ordinance directly and explicitly says that it cannot be used for anything but a residential purpose and if this Board had the power, where there is no hardship to grant this variance, we would be giving to the Board the legislative power which it does not have and there is a long string of cases on that. I perhaps will be called to task with my questioning of Father Smith in relation to the things he would object to, but I wish to explain that. I also called attention to the decision in 244 N.Y. 280 which says explicitly that the power of the Board of Appeals is confined to variation in specific cases where there is some unusual emergency and some unusual hardship. I have had, perhaps, the privilege or the experience to practice before the various Boards of Appeals in Westchester and Nassau and New York City, the five Boroughs of New York City. I consider myself fairly familiar with the zoning laws and the reasons for them, and I also helped write the text some years ago on city improvements and city development, and in the course of my experience I have read a great number of treatises on zoning and what I wanted to press home here is the use of the building to be erected, the very use of the premises for undertaking establishment and funeral parlor, not only in the City of New York but in dozens of the major cities, is not permitted in either retail districts or in restricted retail districts and they class it with the kind of a nuisance that I have mentioned before. They say it is in the same classification, and there are twelve of them, of freak shows, or wax museums, theatre or motion picture, undertaking establishment, public dance hall, shooting gallery, skee ball or similar games. That is the experience of a great many other communities. It is not binding on your Board and I realize it when I bring it up, but I am bringing it out to show that this particular matter between denominations, as a matter of fact, I am here because the parishioners of St. Thomas have asked me to be here and it is their names on these petitions which is about 50-50 are nonparishioners, that has brought this thing on. Nobody has any axes to grind in this matter. Perhaps we are over vehement in our objection, perhaps not zealous enough but I want to leave this to your Board and respectfully ask that the application be denied, because this community has existed for twenty odd years without any nonconforming uses and it would like to continue to do so.

Mr. Kahn: Mr. Chairman, gentlemen, this is rather an unusual case in that if you were to take the position of the objectors seriously and by that I mean not only the witnesses and their experts, but also their counsel, this Board had better resign and disband itself because if you are going to have no nonconforming uses and you are going to have objection as we have here to every and any nonconforming use regardless of the merits, and that is what every one of the objectors testified, that they just don't want nonconforming uses in Cathedral Gardens regardless of the merits of the case. They concede that everything Father Smith sponsors will be good and run in a proper manner but they don't want nonconforming uses. If nobody wanted nonconforming uses and were all to take that seriously there would be no occasion for having a Board of Zoning Appeals. I believe that the Town Fathers, in providing for the ordinances for a Board of Zoning Appeals, were well aware that instances might arise, where although numbers of residents might not want a nonconforming use, there might be a particular hardship to one individual, and therefore this Board was created to handle that case and I am not going to belabor you by telling you what the law is. All of you men know it a lot better than I do, but it seems to me very simply that we have a piece of property which is unique in its general set up and surroundings and that hasn't been disputed in any way. The objectors can't show us another piece of property here in Cathedral Gardens which has the same situation as Mr. Barnes. He is suffering a hardship. It is testified to by Mr. McMahan who is certainly a qualified expert, his qualifications conceded by counsel. . . . They can look out into Westminster Road and bought their homes in back of the business property and it is not a hardship to Dr. McKenna because he is not here to oppose. It is not a hardship on the people who own the property immediately west of Mr. Barnes because they are not here to oppose it and Father Smith, who is directly across the street on the east, and [not] only is he not opposed, but he is highly in favor of it. . . . If I did not believe that this was a good thing for the community I would not be here and I know this and this Board well knows and counsel knows that if Father Smith, who has been the leading citizen of West Hempstead for seventeen years did not believe this was a good thing for the community he would not advocate it. I honestly and sincerely believe that the granting of this variance will bring an improvement, that what he hopes to build will be an improvement in the community, it will not hurt anybody in West Hempstead and it will give him an opportunity to utilize his property. I respectfully ask that the application be granted.

It was regularly moved, seconded and carried that the public hearing be closed. It was regularly moved, and seconded that the Board reserve decision. Motion carried, all voting "aye."

OBJECTORS' EXHIBIT A

TO THE BOARD OF ZONING APPEALS OF THE TOWN OF HEMPSTEAD:

WHEREAS, Richard W. Barnes petitioned the Board of Zoning Appeals of the Town of Hempstead for a variance to permit the erection of a funeral home on the northwest corner of Westminster Road and Regent Place, in West Hempstead, County of Nassau, State of New York; and

WHEREAS, the said property is presently zoned for residential purposes; and

WHEREAS, the immediate adjacent property and surrounding area is zoned for residential purposes and is fully developed, consisting of single one family homes;

NOW THEREFORE, we, the understanding property owners hereby respectfully petition the Board to deny such application for a variance upon the following grounds:

1. To grant this application will adversely affect the value of real property in our community.

2. Our community is residential in nature and to permit a part of such area to be used for business purposes, and particularly for undertaking

and embalming, would violate the spirit of the zoning ordinances, impair public safety and welfare, and would do substantial injustice not only to the owners of properties immediately adjacent to the proposed site, but to the owners in the entire neighborhood.

3. The vehicular traffic which is necessarily a part of a funeral parlor will add to the already heavy traffic on Westminster Road and create a hazard to pedestrians and particularly to our children who are obliged, in most instances, to cross Westminster Road going to and returning from school.

DECISION OF THE BOARD OF ZONING APPEALS

AFFIDAVIT OF WALTER G. MICHAELIS, MEMBER OF THE BOARD OF ZONING APPEALS, ANNEXED TO ANSWER

SUPREME COURT, NASSAU COUNTY

STATE OF NEW YORK, COUNTY OF NAUSSAU, SS.:

WALTER G. MICHAELIS, being duly sworn, deposes and says that he is one of the respondents herein and a member of the Board of Zoning Appeals of the Town of Hempstead. That prior to the hearing upon the application of the petitioner herein a committee of the Board inspected the premises in this proceeding, as well as the surrounding neighborhood.

Hempstead Turnpike, running east and west and located approximately 250 feet south of the applicant's premises, is a six lane state highway. The property to the north of said state highway for 100 feet is zoned for business, and at either side of the intersection of Westminster Road and Hempstead Turnpike to the north of said state highway are located gasoline stations which are indicated in Applicant's Exhibits 1 and 3. Immediately west and across the street from the applicant's property there exists a Catholic church with a large public parking ground immediately adjacent to said church, which faces the applicant's property as described in Applicant's Exhibit 2. Adjoining the applicant's property to the north and south are the homes of two doctors who carry on their medical practice in their residences. There has been testimony to the effect that the erection of a school is contemplated on the unimproved site now occupied by the public parking field. The committee of the Board further considered the fact that the surrounding area was almost completely improved and its character fixed and not subject to change.

The committee of the Board, including your deponent, after viewing the premises of the applicant and the surrounding area, and considering the testimony adduced at the hearing, was of the opinion that the applicant's position, because of this exceptional environment, was unique and that his property did suffer hardship and that a variance would not damage nor depreciate the value of the existing surrounding property.

/s/ WALTER G. MICHAELIS.

(Sworn to by Walter G. Michaelis, Oct. 6, 1948.)

CLARK v. BOARD OF ZONING APPEALS OF TOWN OF HEMPSTEAD

90 N.Y.S.2d 507 (Sup. Ct. 1948)

FROESSEL, J. This is a proceeding to review and annul the determination of the Board of Zoning Appeals of the Town of Hempstead, which granted a variance of the Building Zone Ordinance of said Town so as to permit the erection in a "B" Residence District of a two-story brick veneer building to be used as a private dwelling and funeral home. The premises in question are located on the northwest corner of Westminster Road and Regent Place, West Hempstead, Naussau County, and the respondent intervenor has been the owner thereof since 1945. . . .

The intervenor owner of the property in question, which is virtually on the edge of the residential area, claims that his land, situated as it is, and flanked by properties used as hereinbefore indicated, was unique, its uniqueness was not a general condition of the neighborhood, which is almost completely improved, that his said land cannot yield a reasonable return if restricted to a conforming use, that a case or hardship was presented, and that a variance would not damage or depreciate the value of existing surrounding property, nor alter the essential character of the locality.

A full and complete hearing was had and several of the six petitioners appeared and testified in opposition to the granting of the application. The petitioners were represented by experienced counsel. The members of the Board of Appeals, following the hearing, inspected the premises as well as the surrounding neighborhood, before the application was granted. I have read with care the record of the hearing, and am constrained to conclude that there is evidence to support the determination of the Board. It cannot be said upon the record before me that the Board's action was arbitrary, oppressive, capricious, nor an abuse of discretion.

Under all the circumstances, and notwithstanding the fact that a different result might well have been arrived at, this Court has no right to interfere, and to substitute its judgment for that of the administrative officers charged with the duty of making the determination [citations omitted]. The rule has been stated as follows in Matter of Foy Productions, Ltd. v. Graves (253 App. Div. 475, 478, *aff'd*, 278 N.Y. 498):

> And it has now become academic under our law that if there is evidence to constitute a reasonable basis for the determination of the Commissioner, if his determination is not arbitrary nor capricious, if the verdict of a jury reaching the same conclusion would not be set aside as against the weight of evidence, the court is not at liberty to disturb his finding. . . .

In the light of the foregoing, as well as the presumption that exists in favor of the determination by the Board (Werner v. Walsh, 212 App. Div.

635, 640, 209 N.Y.S. 454, *aff'd,* 240 N.Y. 689), I have no alternative but to deny that application to annul its determination.

Settle order.

Order of Affirmance [8]
ORDER ON APPEAL FROM FINAL ORDER

At a Term of the Appellate Division of the Supreme Court of the State of New York held in and for the Second Judicial Department at the Borough of Brooklyn on the 6th day of June, 1949.

Present: HON. GERALD NOLAN, Presiding Justice.

HON. JOHN B. JOHNSTON,

HON. FRANK F. ADEL,

HON. CHARLES W.U. SNEED,

HON. JOHN MACCRATE, Justices.

In the matter of the application of SUSAN H. CLARK, et al., Appellants, To review a determination AGAINST

BOARD OF ZONING APPEALS OF THE TOWN OF HEMPSTEAD, et al., Respondents, and RICHARD W. BARNES, Intervenor-Respondent.

The above named Susan H. Clark, Nathan H. Cherwin, Walter E. Swansen, Ruth Swansen, Miriam R. Phillips, John E. Hahn, Dorothy Hahn, Michael Liebl and Mabel Liebl, the petitioners in this proceeding having appealed to the Appellate Division of the Supreme Court from a final order of the Supreme Court entered in the office of the Clerk of the County of Nassau on the 16th day of November, 1948, denying petitioners' application to annul a determination of the Board of Zoning Appeals of the Town of Hempstead in granting a variance of the building zone ordinance of said town so as to permit the erection of a funeral home in a residential zoned area; dismissing the petition and affirming the determination of said Board of Zoning Appeals, herein, and the said appeal having been argued by Mr. Irving H. Schafer of Counsel for appellants, and argued by Mr. George R. Brennan, Town Attorney, of Counsel for respondents, and argued by Mr. Nathaniel A. Kahn of Counsel for intervenor-respondent, and due deliberation having been had thereon; and upon the opinion and decision slip of the court herein, heretofore filed:

It is Ordered that the final order so appealed from be and the same hereby is unanimously affirmed, with one joint bill of $50, costs and disbursements to respondents and intervenor-respondent.

Enter:

JOHN J. CALLAHAN, Clerk.

---

8. Record on Appeal at 134-135. Opinion reported at 275 A.D. 939, 89 N.Y.S. 2d 916, leave to appeal and motion for reargument denied, 275 A.D. 1001, 91 N.Y.S. 2d 838 (1949).

MATTER OF CLARK v. BOARD OF ZONING APPEALS

301 N.Y. 86, 92 N.E. 2d 903, motion for reargument denied, *301 N.Y. 681, 95 N.E. 2d 44 (1950),* cert. denied, *340 U.S. 933 (1951)*

DESMOND, J. This proceeding was brought, under article 78 of the Civil Practice Act, to review a determination by respondent board of zoning appeals of the town of Hempstead, Nassau County, by which determination the board had granted to intervenor-respondent Barnes, a variance of the town zoning ordinance, so as to permit Barnes to erect, on a lot owned by him in a "B Residence District," a building to be used as a combined residence and funeral home. Petitioners-appellants are a few of the more than two hundred nearby residents who objected, before the board, to the application for the variance. Petitioners were defeated in the courts below, but we granted them leave to come here.

We hold that the board's action in authorizing this variance was without legal basis. The premises of intervener-respondent, as to which the variance was granted, is a vacant lot, 100 feet wide, on the west side of Westminster Road, in a section of the town of Hempstead known as Cathedral Gardens. When intervener-respondent bought that lot, in 1945, it was and for some years had been, in a "B Residence District" under the town building zone ordinance. In such B residence zones, the permitted uses, under the ordinance, are: single residences, clubhouses, schools, churches, professional offices in dwellings, and some others. A funeral home, or undertaker's establishment, is not such a lawful use. Nevertheless, intervener Barnes purchased the lot, then applied for a variance. We could end this opinion at this point by saying that one who thus knowingly acquires land for a prohibited use, cannot thereafter have a variance on the ground of "special hardship" (Matter of Henry Steers, Inc., v. Rembaugh, 259 App. Div. 908, 909, *aff'd,* 284 N.Y. 621). But beyond that, we hold that the proof here made out, under applicable rules of law, no case for a variance.

At the hearing before the zoning board of appeals, intervener called witnesses to show that, about 260 feet south of his property, Westminster Road, on which his lot fronts, intersects the wide, much-traveled Hempstead Turnpike, that the lands along the turnpike are zoned for business, that on the corner lots at that Westminster-Hempstead intersection there are two gas stations, that the parcels nearest to intervener's, on the west side of Westminster Road, are both used for physicians' homes and offices, and that, just opposite to Barnes' lot on Westminster Road, the frontage, for 600 feet north from the gas stations, is owned by a church corporation, on it being a church, rectory, and (erected after the hearing) a parish school. All of these are, of course, specifically permitted uses, under the zoning ordinance, and there are no unauthorized uses anywhere in the vicinity. A real estate broker called by intervener testified, before the board, that intervener's parcel could not yield a reasonable profit if used only for purposes allowed under the ordinance. However, it is clear that the only basis for that conclusion was the witness' opinion that no one would be likely to buy that lot as the site for a fine residence, and it was not claimed that any effort had been made to sell the premises for any of the authorized uses. There was dispute, in the testimony heard by the board, as to whether the presence of a funeral parlor would depreciate values in the neighborhood. It was brought out, also, at the hearing, that intervener was then conducting his funeral establishment in a store around the corner on Hempstead Turnpike, but wished to move his business onto Westminster Road.

The proof just above summarized was insufficient for a variance. Section 267 of the Town Law empowers boards of appeals to vary the application of town zoning ordinances (subd. 5) "Where there are practical difficulties or unnecessary hardships in the way of carrying out the strict letter of such ordinances." But, as was recently held in Matter of Hickox v. Griffin (298 N.Y. 365, 370-371). "There must at least be proof that a particular property suffers a singular disadvantage through the operation of a zoning regulation before a variance therof can be allowed on the ground of 'unnecessary hardship.'" Most frequently cited for that proposition is Matter of Otto v. Steinhilber (282 N.Y. 71, 76) where it is written that, before the board may vote a variance, there must be shown, among other things, "that the plight of the owner is due to unique circumstances and not to the general conditions in the neighborhood which may reflect the unreasonableness of the zoning ordinance itself." The board, being an administrative and not a legislative body, may not review or amend the legislatively enacted rules as to uses, or amend the ordinance under the guise of a variance (Dowsey v. Village of Kensington, 257 N.Y. 221, 227), or determine that the ordinance itself is arbitrary or unreasonable (Matter of Otto v. Steinhilber, *supra*). If there be a hardship, which, like the alleged hardship here, is common to the whole neighborhood, the remedy is to seek a change in the zoning ordinance itself (Arverne Bay Constr. Co. v. Thatcher, 278 N.Y. 222, 233; Matter of Levy v. Board of Standards & Appeals, 267 N.Y. 347). Nothing less than a showing of hardship special and peculiar to the applicant's property will empower the board to allow a variance [cases cited]. The substance of all these holdings is that no administrative body may destroy the general scheme of a zoning law by granting special exemption from hardships common to all.

The orders below should be reversed and the determination of the zoning board of appeals annulled, with costs in all courts.

DYE, J. (dissenting). I vote for affirmance. To reverse the action of the board of zoning appeals and annul its determination is to say that the granting of the variance was arbitrary and capricious and constituted an abuse of discretion. This we may not do on the record before us. It is axiomatic and no longer open to doubt that there is evidence to constitute a reasonable basis for the determination the court has no right to interfere and substitute its judgment for that of the administrative board charged with the duty of making a determination. . . .

LOUGHRAN, C.J., LEWIS, and FULD JJ., concur with DESMOND, J., DYE, J., dissents in opinion in which CONWAY, J. concurs; FROESSEL, J., taking no part.

Orders reversed, etc.

NOTES AND QUESTIONS

1. **Statutory Update.** When *Clark* was litigated, in the early 1950s, N.Y. Town L. §267(5) was a first-generation variance statute that spoke, as nearly all did, solely in terms of "practical difficulties or unnecessary hardships." Not until 1991 did the state legislature modernize the section (it is now §267-b), to reflect some lessons learned over the half-century of experience with the sketchy law that the new statute replaced.

The most significant changes are (1) to provide separately for use variances and area variances, and (2) to detail carefully what is needed to obtain a variance. In the case of a use variance (as in *Clark*), the applicant must show "unnecessary hardship," which exists only when:

(a)   for each and every permitted use the applicant cannot realize a reasonable return, and that the lack of return is substantial;

(b)   the alleged hardship relating to the property in question is unique, and does not apply to a substantial portion of the district or neighborhood;

(c)   the requested use variance, if granted, will not alter the essential character of the neighborhood; and

(d)   the alleged hardship has not been self-created.

In granting a use variance, the board shall approve the minimum variance necessary to redress the unnecessary hardship.

Which, if any, of these criteria would the applicant in *Clark* have satisfied?

2. **Lack of reasonable return.** By far the stiffest requirement for the granting of a use variance is a showing that the applicant cannot realize a reasonable return from each of the permitted uses. (Such a showing, absent a variance, would almost certainly be deemed a taking.) A New York court rejected a real estate expert's conclusionary opinion that the permitted uses were not economically feasible and insisted that the expert opinion be based on an analysis that included: the purchase price of the property, the present value of the property, the amount of real estate taxes, the amount of mortgages and liens, the asking price for the property when it was offered for sale, the cost of demolishing the old structure on the property and of

erecting a new building, the cost of obtaining area variances, and the pro-jected income from the proposed use. Miltope Corp. v. Zoning Board of Appeals, 184 A.D.2d 565, 584 N.Y.S.2d 865 (2d Dept. 1992).

3. **Self-created hardship.** The landowner acquires the property that is already subject to the restrictions from which relief is sought. Self-created hardship? See First Natl. Bank of Downsville v. City of Albany Board of Zon-ing Appeals, 216 A.D.2d 680, 628 N.Y.S.2d 199 (3d Dept. 1995) (held: "yes," where bank acquired mortgaged properties after default and had accepted borrower's word that the premises complied with zoning law prior to mak-ing the loan); La Dirot v. Smith, 169 A.D.2d 896, 564 N.Y.S.2d 620 (3d Dept. 1991) (held: "no," where zoning official erroneously assured landowner that dog kennel a permitted use, and landowner then spent $250,000 be-fore problem surfaced). What if the landowner acquires the property not through purchase, but by inheritance?

4. **Area or bulk variances.** Borrowing from the ALI Model Land De-velopment Code, which would create separate standards for granting bulk and use variances, as well as a body of case law that tended to lower the hardship threshold for non-use variances, the revised Town Law has a sepa-rate subsection for "area" variances. The statute defines "area variance" as a land use not allowed by the "dimensional or physical requirements" of the applicable zoning: examples might include variances of the front-yard, side-yard, or rear-yard set-back requirements, or of the minimum frontage or lot size requirements. Typically, the landowner seeking an area variance bases her appeal on the property's irregular physical dimensions or unusual topography.

To obtain an area variance, the landowner need not show an inability to earn a reasonable return. The factors to be considered include:

    (a)   whether an undesirable change will be produced in the charac-ter of the neighborhood or a detriment to nearby properties will be created;

    (b)   whether the benefit sought by the applicant can be achieved by some other method, feasible for the applicant to pursue;

    (c)   whether the alleged difficulty was self-created; even if present, this "shall not necessarily preclude the granting of the area variance."

As with use variances, the zoning board is directed to grant the "mini-mum [area] variance that it shall deem necessary and adequate." Id. at §§265, 267-b(3).

5. **The zoning bazaar.** A generation of empiricists have examined the variance process, often with damning findings as to a zoning board's pliability, cowardice before neighborhood pressure, and evasion of legal rules. Examples include: Note, Zoning Variances and Exceptions: The Phil-adelphia Experience, 103 U. Pa. L. Rev. 516 (1955); Dukeminier and Sta-

pleton, The Zoning Board of Adjustment: A Case Study in Misrule, 50 Ky. L.J. 273 (1962) (Lexington, Ky.-Fayette County); Note, Syracuse Board of Zoning Appeals — An Appraisal, 16 Syracuse L. Rev. 632 (1965); Note, Zoning Variances in New York City, 3 Colum. J.L. & Soc. Prob. 120 (1967); Citizens Research Council of Michigan, Detroit Board of Zoning Appeals (1969) (variance approval rate more than 80 percent); Contemporary Studies Project, Rural Land Use in Iowa: An Empirical Analysis of County Board of Adjustment Practices, 68 Iowa L. Rev. 1083 (1983). But see Johannessen, Zoning Variances: Unnecessarily an Evil, 41 Land Use L. & Zoning Dig., No. 7, at 3 (1989).

Compare the current N.Y. Town L. variance standards, *supra,* with those that preceded them. Are the more-detailed standards likelier to reduce the number of variances granted, or simply lead to better "lawyering" in behalf of the variance applicant?

6. **Other modes for gaining zoning flexibility.**

a. *The special exception.* Although often confused with the variance, the special exception serves zoning theory quite differently. Exceptions have nothing to do with individual hardship. Instead, they serve to shift from the legislature to an agency the authority to decide when various designated land uses can coexist with their surroundings. For example, the ordinance might designate, as a conditional use, medical offices in a residential zone. In this instance, an offices developer would apply to (let us say) the planning commission for zoning approval. We call this a special exception, or conditional use. If there were no exception device, the zoning law might face a set of unhappy choices: to allow the use as of right within the zone, to bar the use entirely from the zone, to create many more zoning categories, or to district the community with far greater detail. The exception, therefore, offers the community a sensible mean between rigid exclusion and carte blance inclusion without forcing the ordinance into *ex ante* decisions as to which parcels within a zoning district are best suited for the conditional use. The special exception is also more attractive to the landowner than is rigid exclusion. If medical offices were barred entirely from a residential zone, the landowner must either seek a zoning change or pursue a (possibly illegal) variance.

Part of the confusion between the variance and special exception derives from their similarity in administration. In many communities, the same agency, the zoning board of appeals, handles both procedures (although in other communities, the planning board — not the board of appeals — deals with exceptions). Part of the confusion also stems from the common failure of ordinances to fix guidelines for reviewing the exception application, with agencies tending to apply (or misapply) variance criteria to the exception request.

In reviewing the exception application, the agency may look at a host of variables such as traffic flow, building design, impact on adjacent owners, landscaping, off-street parking, etc., in deciding whether, and on what terms, to issue the permit. The underlying premise, however, is that the use should be approved if it meets "reasonable" (custom-tailored) conditions. See, e.g., Schultz v. Pritts, 432 A.2d 1319 (Md. 1981).

Recall *Nollan* and *Dolan*, §8.1.b.6 for their discussion of constitution-ally invalid conditions.

b. *Cluster zoning.* Cluster development breaks with the pattern of each house to its own minimum-sized lot. Without adding to the area's overall housing density, the cluster subdivision usually contains many "undersized" lots; land spared from development may then retain its natural setting or become available for community facilities. See Figure 9-2. Apart from these advantages, the cluster concept invites considerable variety in both tract design and housing types, reduces street and utility infrastructure costs, and, for the individual lot-owner, may even make grass-cutting and gardening a less onerous chore. As townhouse and condominium ownership continue to gain in popularity, cluster development is a useful device for creating these arrangements. N.Y. Town L. §278 (McKinney Supp. 1996) enables cluster zoning. It provides in part:

> 2. Authorization; purposes.
> (a) The town board may, by local law or ordinance, authorize the plan-ning board to approve a cluster development simultaneously with the ap-proval of a plat . . . subject to the conditions set forth in this section. . . .
> (b) The purpose of a cluster development shall be to enable and en-courage flexibility of design and development of land in such a manner as to preserve the natural and scenic qualities of open lands.
> 3. Conditions.
> (b) A cluster development shall result in a permitted number of build-ing lots or dwelling units which shall in no case exceed the number which could be permitted, in the planning board's judgment, if the land were sub-divided into lots conforming to the minimum lot size and density require-ments of the zoning ordinance applicable to the district or districts in which such land is situated and conforming to all other applicable requirements. . . .

c. *The "floating zone" — planned unit development (PUDs).* In the decades since *Euclid,* the scale of land development has grown enormously: huge subdivisions instead of the custom-built house; regional shopping centers instead of the commercial block; industrial parks instead of the factory building. Increased scale has also brought diversity within the development: a multiplicity of housing types; homes plus convenience shopping, parks, and schools; the entry of office buildings and motels into a shopping center. It is no surprise that the Euclidean "one lot at a time" approach, which biases against many mixtures of land use because it cannot readily distin-guish harmful mixtures from beneficial ones, does not serve present-day, large-scale planning realities as well as zoning should.

The arrival of zoning for planned unit developments (PUDs) has helped significantly to loosen the Euclidean bind. PUDs may be residential,

The same number of families can be accommodated in the cluster development below as in the conventional subdivision above.

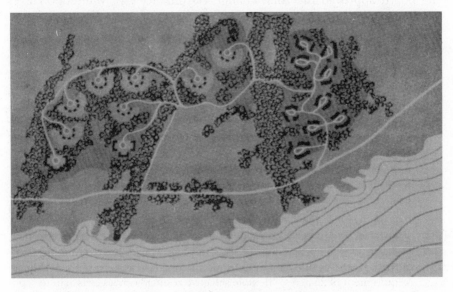

Source: Outdoor Recreation Resources Review Commission, Outdoor Recreation for America 151 (1962).

FIGURE 9-2
Cluster Zoning

nonresidential, or mixtures thereof; invariably PUDs occupy relatively large plots (20 acres or more); and, significantly, PUD districts often do not appear on the zoning map until after a landowner assembles acreage and applies to the governing body for permission to develop the parcel. It is this aspect of PUD that gives rise to the concept of "floating zone" and has occasionally lifted a judicial eyebrow.

Eves v. Zoning Board of Adjustment of Lower Gwynedd Township, 401 Pa. 211, 164 A.2d 7 (1960), gave PUD theory an initial jolt. The influential Pennsylvania Supreme Court found a PUD ordinance doubly wanting: The state enabling law did not enable it; worse still, it violated the "comprehensive plan" requirement.

At issue in *Eves* was the "F-1" zone, a limited industrial district that the town board could map anywhere in Lower Gwynedd, upon application of a landowner who satisfied various statutory criteria: a parcel 25 acres or larger; a "single architectural scheme"; a ceiling on lot coverage; prescribed building setbacks; satisfactory parking, landscaping, and buffering. In April 1958, the board authorized F-1 zoning (Ordinance 28). In September 1958, an industrial concern sought F-1 approval for its 103-acre tract within an A-residential zone. Despite 300 protesting residents at the public hearing, the board approved the zone change (Ordinance 34), whereupon Eves sued to invalidate the two ordinances.

On the "comprehensive plan" issue, the court's opinion reads:

> The adoption of a procedure whereby it is decided which areas of land will eventually be zoned "F-1" Limited Industrial Districts on a case by case basis patently admits that at the point of enactment of Ordinance 28 there was no orderly plan of particular land use for the community. Final determination under such a scheme would expressly await solicitation by individual landowners, thus making the planned land use of the community dependent upon its development. In other words, the development itself would become the plan, which is manifestly the antithesis of zoning "in accordance with a comprehensive plan."
>
> Several secondary evils of such a scheme are cogently advanced by counsel for the appellants. It would produce situations in which the personal predilections of the supervisors or the affluence or political power of the applicant would have a greater part in determining rezoning applications than the suitability of the land for a particular use from an overall community point of view. Further, while it may not be readily apparent with a minimum acreage requirement of 25 acres, "flexible selective zoning" carries evils akin to "spot zoning," for in theory it allows piecemeal placement of relatively small acreage areas in differently zoned districts. Finally, because of the absence of a simultaneous delineation of the boundaries of the new "F-1" district, no notice of the true nature of his vicinity or its limitations is afforded the property owner or the prospective property owner. While it is undoubtedly true that a property owner has no vested interest in an existing zoning map and, accordingly, is always subject to the possibility of a rezoning without notice, the zoning ordinance and its accompanying zoning maps should nevertheless at any given

time reflect the current planned use of the community's land so as to afford as much notice as possible.

The *Eves* setback launched a torrent of academic criticism. Planners and builders were together on this one as well, and other communities, undaunted by *Eves,* ventured PUD zoning. In Donahue v. Zoning Bd. of Adjustment, 412 Pa. 332, 194 A.2d 610 (1963), the Pennsylvania Supreme Court seemed to retreat on the *Eves* front. Five years later, the court had still another chance to consider the PUD problem. This time, in Cheney v. Village 2 at New Hope, Inc., 429 Pa. 626, 241 A.2d 81 (1968), it upheld the PUD concept, in a case where the Borough rezoned a large farm tract from low-density residential to PUD, after which developer gained approval for its higher-density mixed residential use community. The court's opinion described a New Hope PUD district as one within which there may be: single-family attached or detached dwellings; apartments; accessory private garages; public or private parks and recreation areas including golf courses, swimming pools, ski slopes, etc. (so long as these facilities do not produce noise, glare, odor, air pollution, etc., detrimental to existing or prospective adjacent structures); a municipal building; a school; churches; art galleries; professional offices; certain types of signs; a theatre (but not a drive-in); motels and hotels; and a restaurant. The ordinance then set certain overall density requirements, not exceeding ten residential units per acre, nor more than two bedrooms per unit. The PUD district may have a maximum of 80 percent of the land devoted to residential uses, a maximum of 20 percent for the permitted commercial uses and enclosed recreational facilities, and must have a minimum of 20 percent for open spaces.

How would you feel, as a property owner living in a low-density residential neighborhood, to have a PUD drop from the sky onto the neighboring farm? And doesn't PUD zoning, a three-step process (step one: creating the classification; step two: identifying a PUD parcel; step three: approving a PUD proposal) encourage the peddling of political influence?

§9.8 Nonconforming Uses

CITY OF AKRON v. CHAPMAN

160 Ohio St. 382, 116 N.E.2d 697 (1953)

LAMNECK, J.

There is no claim of nuisance in this case. The sole issue is whether the city may terminate the lawful nonconforming use (junk business), which was in existence at the time of the passage of the zoning ordinance, after the use has been permitted to continue for an extended period.

The zoning ordinance passed in 1922 contains the following provision:

> A building, existing at the time of the passage of this ordinance, which does not conform to the regulations of the use district in which it is located may remain for a reasonable period and the existing use of such building may be continued or extended to any portion of such building which portion was arranged or designed for such use at the time of the passage of this ordinance, but a nonconforming use shall not be otherwise extended. *A nonconforming use shall be discontinued and removed when, in the opinion of the council, such use has been permitted to exist or continue for a reasonable time.* (Emphasis ours.)

The defendant contends:

1. The council of a municipality is prohibited by the Fourteenth Amendment to the United States Constitution and by Section 2, Article I of the Constitution of this state, from enacting a zoning ordinance which outlaws an existing lawful business, unless compensation is paid therefor.

2. If a council has that power, the enactment of the ordinance . . . directed to him individually, is discriminatory and in violation of the same constitutional provisions.

. . . It has been uniformly held that the enactment of a comprehensive zoning ordinance, which has a substantial relationship to the public health, safety, morals and the general welfare and which is not unreasonable or arbitrary, is proper exercise of the police power.

. . . Most comprehensive zoning ordinances apply to prospective use only, and contain no provisions making them retroactive to cover an existing structure or to terminate an existing use.

This court has consistently approved the constitutionality of comprehensive zoning ordinances containing provisions regulating prospective use. . . .

In the instant case, the 1950 ordinance does not order the defendant to raze the buildings now existing on his premises. We know of no zoning ordinance in this state intended to accomplish such a result unless the existing structures are a nuisance affecting the public health, safety, morals or general welfare or unless the city exercises its power of eminent domain. . . . Zoning ordinances contemplate the gradual elimination of nonconforming uses within a zoned area, and, where an ordinance accomplishes such a result without depriving a property owner of a vested property right, it is generally held to be constitutional.

Thus the denial of the right to resume a nonconforming use after a period of nonuse has been upheld, as well as the denial of the right to extend or enlarge an existing nonconforming use. The denial of the right to substitute new buildings for those devoted to an existing nonconforming use and to add or extend such buildings has also been upheld.

But in the instant case no such situation exists. We are asked by the plaintiff herein to uphold the provision of a municipal ordinance, which in effect denies the owner of property the right to continue to conduct a lawful business thereon, which use was in existence at the time of the passage of the ordinance and has continued without expansion or interruption ever since. If we do this on the ground that the provision is a proper exercise of the police power, then the right to continue to conduct other lawful businesses, similarly established and conducted on zoned property, may likewise be denied by legislative fiat under the guise of a proper exercise of the police power. . . .

We have examined the cases . . . in support of [plaintiff's] contention that the exercise of the power to terminate a lawful nonconforming use in existence at the time of the passage of a comprehensive zoning ordinance, where such use has continued for an extended period thereafter, is a proper exercise of the police power. Although some of these citations support the plaintiff's position, we are of the opinion that they are in conflict with the great weight of authority on the subject and not consistent with past pronouncements of this court.

What is property? It has been defined as not merely the ownership and possession of lands or chattels but the unrestricted right of their use, enjoyment and disposal. Anything which destroys any of these elements of property, to that extent destroys the property itself. The substantial value of property lies in its use. If the right of use is denied, the value of the property is annihilated and ownership is rendered a barren right.

The right to continue to use one's property in a lawful business and in a manner which does not constitute a nuisance and which was lawful at the time it was acquired is within [constitutional] protection. . . .

The effect of the provisions of the 1922 ordinance and the 1950 ordinance, complained of in this case, is to deprive the defendant of a continued lawful use of his property and is in violation of the due process clauses of the state and federal Constitutions. . . .

Judgment reversed.

NOTES AND QUESTIONS

1. **Reasonableness of amortization period.** Typically, the right to continue a nonconforming use may not terminate until a reasonable time has passed, thereby providing the landowner a reasonable return on his investment. "Amortization" in this context refers to the termination within a set time period of an existing vested property right in order to comply with zoning regulations. Amortization periods are designed to insulate zoning ordinances from takings challenges (like the landowner challenge in *Akron*).

In Naegele Outdoor Advertising, Inc. v. City of Durham, 803 F. Supp.

1068, 1077 (M.D.N.C. 1992), *aff'd*, 19 F.3d 11 (4th Cir.), *cert. denied*, 115 S. Ct. 317 (1994), the court explained the amortization principle as applied to nonconforming uses:

> The inclusion of an amortization period in a zoning ordinance allows the property owner, if he cannot make his use of the property conform to the ordinance, to recover all or part of the value of the property before the use is forbidden at the end of the period. . . . Amortization periods have been used in lieu of eminent domain proceedings, which require the payment of compensation, . . . and instead of forbidding a non-conforming use as of the date of enactment, which could effect a taking. . . .
>
> The presence of an amortization period does not establish the validity of the ordinance as a matter of law, nor does the absence of such a provision render such an ordinance an unconstitutional taking. . . . For an amortization to be reasonable it must give the property owner a reasonable opportunity to recoup or minimize the loss of use of his property by the end of the amortization period.

In *Naegele,* an outdoor advertising company sued the city of Durham to overturn a Durham ordinance prohibiting all commercial, off-premises advertising signs after the expiration of a five and one-half year amortization period. The court noted that the advertising company earned almost two million dollars during the amortization period and for the two years it was in litigation with the city, id. at 1077, and concluded that the ordinance did not effect an unconstitutional taking of private property without just compensation. Id. at 1080.

Although most state courts in reviewing amortization periods have upheld their validity, the Supreme Court of Pennsylvania in Pennsylvania Northwestern Distributors, Inc. v. Zoning Hearing Bd. of Moon Township, 584 A.2d 1382, 1373 (Pa. 1991), held that the amortization and discontinuance of a nonconforming use is per se confiscatory and violative of the state's constitution. The court reasoned:

> The effect of the amortization provision herein is to deprive appellant of the lawful use of its property in that the ordinance forces appellant to cease using its property as an adult book store within 90 days. Appellee argues that appellant is free to relocate to one of the few sites in the Township of Moon that complies with the place restrictions of the ordinance, or to change its use to sell some other commodity, in an attempt to convince this court that the ordinance has not effectuated a "taking" of appellant's property without just compensation. . . . If government desires to interfere with the owner's use, where the use is lawful and is not a nuisance nor is it abandoned, it must compensate the owner for the resulting loss. A gradual phasing out of nonconforming uses which occurs when an ordinance only restricts future uses differs in significant measure from an amortization provision which restricts future uses and extinguishes a lawful nonconforming use on the timetable which is not of the property owner's choosing.

Id. at 1376; see also Hoffman v. Kinealy, 389 S.W.2d 745, 746 (Mo. 1965) (holding that amortization of nonconforming uses constituted taking of property without just compensation).

2. **The "natural expansion" doctrine.** Courts sometimes construe a zoning ordinance providing for the continuation of nonconforming uses broadly to allow some reasonable expansion of their scope. Some courts even hold that a property owner has a constitutional right to expand a lawful nonconforming use in accordance with normal business expansion, as long as nonconforming use does not imperil the health, safety, and welfare of the community. See B & B Shoe Prods. Co. v. Zoning Hearing Bd., 368 A.2d 1332 (Pa. 1977). For example, one court upheld a town's decision to allow a nonconforming restaurant that had been operating on a seasonal basis to shift to year-round operation. McAleer v. Board of Appeals of Barnstable, 280 N.E.2d 166 (Mass. 1972). But see Warner Co. v. Zoning Hearing Bd. of Tredyffrin Township, 612 A.2d 578, 582-83 (Pa. Comm. Ct. 1992) (holding that doctrine of natural expansion did not prevent town from enacting reasonable setback requirements on quarrying activity, despite prior use of site as quarry); Town of Belleville v. Parillo's, Inc. 416 A.2d 388 (N.J. 1980) (holding that transformation of restaurant into night club that attracted a larger and younger clientele was impermissible alteration of nonconforming use).

3. **Abandonment.** Typically, zoning ordinances will provide that if a nonconforming use is abandoned, subsequent uses must conform to zoning regulations. Applying the common law definition of abandonment, most courts hold that a municipality must prove both a period of non-use and the landowner's intent to abandon the old use. See Dusdal v. City of Warren, 196 N.W.2d 227 (Mich. 1972).

A "discontinuation ordinance" may provide that a landowner forfeits the right to continue a nonconforming use if the use is discontinued for a set period (typically a year). In that case, the municipality need not show intent to abandon, only discontinuation for the statutory period. See Smith v. Board of Adjustment, 460 N.W.2d 854 (Iowa 1990). But see Ansley House, Inc. v. City of Atlanta, 397 S.E.2d 419 (Ga. 1990) (holding that developer's activities showing intent not to abandon nonconforming use tolled running of one-year discontinuation ordinance). How are the concerns about landowner expectations in the context of nonconforming uses similar to those concerns in the context of adverse possession?

4. **Destruction.** If a nonconforming structure burns down or is otherwise destroyed, should its owner be able to rebuild it? Typically, a zoning ordinance will provide that if a certain percentage of the nonconforming structure is destroyed, the landowner may not repair or rebuild. For example, in Stanton v. Town of Pawleys Island, 455 S.E.22 171, 173 (S.C. 1995), the South Carolina Supreme Court held that a damaged beach front house could be repaired pursuant to a city ordinance allowing repair as long as the prior nonconforming use was not more than 50 percent de-

stroyed. In *Stanton,* the lower level of the house was 100 percent destroyed, but the entire house was not 50 percent destroyed. The court held that "the building inspector and Zoning Board erred . . . in severing the lower level of the Stantons' house from the entire structure and assessing the percentage of the destruction based upon only the lower level and not the entire house. Since it is uncontroverted that, as a whole, the house was not more than 50% destroyed, it is a prior nonconforming use . . . and may be repaired." Id. at 173.

5. **Ongoing developments and vested rights.** In H.R.D.E., Inc. v. Zoning Officer of the City of Romney, 430 S.E.2d 341 (W. Va. 1993), the City of Romney, West Virginia, passed a zoning ordinance under which it denied a permit for an apartment house for elderly and physically disabled individuals. H.R.D.E. was a nonprofit corporation that obtained the support of the mayor and city council of Romney for construction of the four-story apartment project in 1984. It bought two parcels of land for $30,000 and spent $7,145 for culverts, for storm sewers, for the access road and another $1,000 on surveys before it lost funding for the project in 1985. H.R.D.E. resumed preparations in 1987, paying $45,000 for an architect and $7,000 on soil samplings and analysis. In 1989, Romney began considering a zoning ordinance, and the mayor sent a letter to H.R.D.E. indicating that the zoning law would not interfere with completion of the project. When H.R.D.E. filed an application for a building permit, the application was denied on the basis of the zoning ordinance.

H.R.D.E. argued that its apartment project was a nonconforming use even though it had not yet begun construction. Typically, neither planned (as opposed to actual) uses nor preliminary site improvements will count as nonconforming uses. However, whether a developer's actions were sufficient to vest a nonconforming use is a question of fact that must be decided on a case-by-case basis. The court listed a series of relevant factors: (1) the ratio of expenditure to the total cost of the project; (2) the good faith of the landowner; (3) whether notice of the proposed zoning change was given prior to the expenditures; (4) whether the expenditures could apply to other uses of the property; and (5) whether the acts go beyond "mere contemplated use or preparation." H.R.D.E., Inc. v. Zoning Officer of the City of Romney, 430 S.E.2d 341 (W. Va. 1993); see also Heath Township v. Sall, 502 N.W.2d 627, 634 n.17 (Mich. 1993) ("Important factors to be considered are whether the developer obtained a permit, what and when the developer knew and what further construction was necessary to complete the project").

Chapter 10

Discrimination

STATEMENT OF CONGRESSMAN FLYNT

112 Cong. Rec. 17,333 (Aug. 3, 1966)

MR. FLYNT (D. Ga.). Mr. Chairman, title IV of H.R. 14765 should be stricken from the pending bill. It has no place in the laws of a democratic, representative government.

This proposal strikes at the very heart of a free enterprise system in which the fee simple ownership of real property is a vital part.

The right of private ownership of property in fee simple has been a privilege and right of the American people. Until this legislation was proposed, we had believed that as long as a property owner paid the taxes on his property, and as long as he did not use it for illegal or immoral purposes, that he could do what he pleased with it, occupy it or leave it unoccupied, and rent it or sell it as he saw fit and to whom he saw fit.

If a member of any group, a majority or a minority group, wants to buy or rent a particular piece of property, he has always had that right, provided the owner would be equally willing to sell it or rent it to him. A contract for the purchase and sale of real property has historically required a meeting of the minds between a willing buyer and a willing seller. The only exceptions to this rule have been when the right of eminent domain has been exercised and when property has been sold under court order.

If the language of title IV of H.R. 14765 is enacted into law, it could set off a chain reaction which could eventually result in legislation, Executive orders, or judicial decrees that a property owner could be required to sell or rent property even though he might prefer to retain it and even to occupy it personally.

The right of private ownership of property is an integral part of a free enterprise system. If the Congress of the United States undertakes to destroy the basic rights and concepts of private ownership of property, then it will, at the same time, begin to wipe out the free enterprise system in this country and on this planet.

Human rights cannot exist without property rights, and a healthy respect for both. Any attempt to destroy or weaken the right of private ownership of property is an attempt to destroy a system of private capital, and to substitute a totalitarian form of government in its place, whether it is called socialism, state socialism, or communism.

The statement above appears in the House Debates on Title IV of the proposed Civil Rights Act of 1966, which would have created a federal fair housing law. Two years later, Congress finally passed a similar statute, Title VIII of the Civil Rights Act of 1968, to bar discrimination on the basis of race, color, religion, or national origin. Congress has since amended Title VIII, in 1974, to include sex as a protected category, and in 1988, to add handicap and familial status. In addition to the federal law, there are also many state and local laws directed against housing discrimination, which in some cases go beyond Title VIII to include "marital status"[1] and "sexual orientation"[2] within the law's ambit.

It is clear that Congressman Flynt's exaggerated rhetoric is historically unsound; for example, eminent domain is, after all, one form of forced sale. Also, Title VIII has not brought down the Republic or "wipe[d] out the free enterprise system . . . on this planet." On the other hand, fair housing laws have not managed to wipe out racism in the sale or rental of housing, or to end discrimination against gays, or unmarried couples, or persons with mental and physical disabilities, or families with children, even when these groups enjoy the law's protection.

Attitudes, such as those implicit in the Congressman's statement, have a long half-life, and create real tension between landlords and prospective tenants, and within residential neighborhoods. In the materials that follow, we will look at these tensions in several areas: as they affect race, marital status and sexual orientation, physical and mental disability, and children.

First, a look at some crucial provisions of Title VIII.

TITLE VIII, CIVIL RIGHTS ACT OF 1968

42 U.S.C. §§3601-3619 (1996)

§3601.   DECLARATION OF POLICY

It is the policy of the United States to provide, within constitutional limitations, for fair housing throughout the United States.

---

1. See, e.g., Anchorage (Alaska) Municipal Code §5.20.020; Cal. Govt. Code §12955 (West 1996).

2. See, e.g., Conn. Gen. Stat. Ann. §46a-81e(a) (West 1996); Wis. Stat. Ann. §106.04 (West 1996).

§3602. Definitions

As used in this subchapter —

(a) "Secretary" means the Secretary of Housing and Urban Development.

(b) "Dwelling" means any building, structure, or portion thereof which is occupied as, or designed or intended for occupancy as, a residence by one or more families, and any vacant land which is offered for sale or lease for the construction or location thereon of any such building, structure, or portion thereof.

(c) "Family" includes a single individual.

(d) "Person" includes one or more individuals, corporations, partnerships, associations, labor organizations, legal representatives, mutual companies, joint-stock companies, trusts, unincorporated organizations, trustees, trustees in cases under Title II, receivers, and fiduciaries.

(e) "To rent" includes to lease, to sublease, to let and otherwise to grant for a consideration the right to occupy premises not owned by the occupant.

(f) "Discriminatory housing practice" means an act that is unlawful under section 3604, 3605, 3606, or 3617 of this title.

(g) "State" means any of the several States, the District of Columbia, the Commonwealth of Puerto Rico, or any of the territories and possessions of the United States. . . .

. . . §3603(b) Exemptions

Nothing in section 3604 of this title (other than subsection (c)) shall apply to —

(1) any single-family house sold or rented by an owner: *Provided,* That such private individual owner does not own more than three such single-family houses at any one time: *Provided further,* That in the case of the sale of any such single-family house by a private individual owner not residing in such house at the time of such sale or who was not the most recent resident of such house prior to such sale, the exemption granted by this subsection shall apply only with respect to one such sale within any twenty-four month period: *Provided further,* That such bona fide private individual owner does not own any interest in, nor is there owned or reserved on his behalf, under any express or voluntary agreement, title to or any right to all or a portion of the proceeds from the sale or rental of, more than three such single-family houses at any one time: *Provided further,* That after December 31, 1969, the sale or rental of any such single-family house shall be excepted from the application of this title only if such house is sold or rented (A) without the use in any manner of the sales or rental facilities or the sales or rental services of any real estate broker, agent, or salesman, or of such facilities or services of any person

in the business of selling or renting dwellings, or of any employee or agent of any such broker, agent, salesman, or person and (B) without the publication, posting or mailing, after notice, of any advertisement or written notice in violation of secton 3604(c) of this title; but nothing in this proviso shall prohibit the use of attorneys, escrow agents, abstractors, title companies, and other such professional assistance as necessary to perfect or transfer the title, or

(2) rooms or units in dwellings containing living quarters occupied or intended to be occupied by no more than four families living independently of each other, if the owner actually maintains and occupies one of such living quarters as his residence.

(c) For the purposes of subsection (b), a person shall be deemed to be in the business of selling or renting dwellings if —

(1) he has, within the preceding twelve months, participated as principal in three or more transactions involving the sale or rental of any dwelling or any interest therein, or

(2) he has, within the preceding twelve months, participated as agent, other than in the sale of his own personal residence in providing sales or rental facilities or sales or rental services in two or more transactions involving the sale or rental of any dwelling or any interest therein, or

(3) he is the owner of any dwelling designed or intended for occupancy by, or occupied by, five or more families.

§3604.   Discrimination in the Sale or Rental of Housing and other Prohibited Practices

As made applicable by section 3603 and except as exempted by sections 3603(b) and 3607, it shall be unlawful —

(a) To refuse to sell or rent after the making of a bona fide offer, or to refuse to negotiate for the sale or rental of, or otherwise make unavailable or deny, a dwelling to any person because of race, color, religion, sex, familial status, or national origin.

(b) To discriminate against any person in the terms, conditions, or privileges of sale or rental of a dwelling, or in the provision of services or facilities in connection therewith, because of race, color, religion, sex, familial status, or national origin.

(c) To make, print, or publish, or cause to be made, printed, or published any notice, statement, or advertisement, with respect to the sale or rental of a dwelling that indicates any preference, limitation, or discrimination based on race, color, religion, sex, handicap, familial status, or national origin, or an intention to make any such preference, limitation, or discrimination.

(d) To represent to any person because of race, color, religion, sex, handicap, familial status, or national origin that any dwelling is not available for inspection, sale, or rental when such dwelling is in fact so available.

(e) For profit, to induce or attempt to induce any person to sell or rent any dwelling by representations regarding the entry or prospective entry into the neighborhood of a person or persons of a particular race, color, religion, sex, handicap, familial status, or national origin.

(f) (1) To discriminate in the sale or rental, or to otherwise make unavailable or deny, a dwelling to any buyer or renter because of a handicap of —

(A) that buyer or renter,

(B) a person residing in or intending to reside in that dwelling after it is so sold, rented, or made available; or

(C) any person associated with that buyer or renter.

(2) To discriminate against any person in the terms, conditions, or privileges of sale or rental of a dwelling, or in the provision of services or facilities in connection with such dwelling, because of a handicap of —

(A) that person; or

(B) a person residing in or intending to reside in that dwelling after it is so sold, rented, or made available; or

(C) any person associated with that person. . . .

§3605. Discrimination in Residential Real Estate-Related Transactions

(a) In general. It shall be unlawful for any person or other entity whose business includes engaging in residential real estate-related transactions to discriminate against any person in making available such a transaction, or in the terms or conditions of such a transaction, because of race, color, religion, sex, handicap, familial status, or national origin.

(b) "Residential real estate-related transaction" defined. As used in this section, the term "residential real estate-related transaction" means any of the following:

(1) The making or purchasing of loans or providing other financial assistance —

(A) for purchasing, constructing, improving, repairing, or maintaining a dwelling; or

(B) secured by residential real estate.

(2) The selling, brokering, or appraising of residential real property.

(c) Appraisal exemption. Nothing in this subchapter prohibits a person engaged in the business of furnishing appraisals of real property to take into consideration factors other than race, color, religion, national origin, sex, handicap, or familial status.

§3606.   DISCRIMINATION IN THE PROVISION
OF BROKERAGE SERVICES

After December 31, 1968, it shall be unlawful to deny any person access to or membership or participation in any multiple-listing service, real estate brokers' organization or other service, organization, or facility relating to the business of selling or renting dwellings, or to discriminate against him in the terms or conditions of such access, membership, or participation, on account of race, color, religion, sex, handicap, familial status, or national origin.

§3607.   EXEMPTION

Nothing in this title shall prohibit a religious organization, association, or society, or any nonprofit institution or organizaton operated, supervised or controlled by or in conjuncton with a religious organization, association, or society, from limiting the sale, rental or occupancy of dwellings which it owns or operates for other than a commercial purpose to persons of the same religion, or from giving preference to such persons, unless membership in such religion is restricted on account of race, color, or national origin. Nor shall anything in this title prohibit a private club not in fact open to the public, which as an incident to its primary purpose or purposes provides lodgings which it owns or operates for other than a commercial purpose, from limiting the rental or occupancy of such lodgings to its members or from giving preference to its members. . . .

§3617.   INTERFERENCE, COERCION, OR INTIMIDATION

It shall be unlawful to coerce, intimidate, threaten, or interfere with any person in the exercise or enjoyment of, or on account of his having exercised or enjoyed, or on account of his having aided or encouraged any other person in the exercise or enjoyment of, any right granted or protected by section 3603, 3604, 3605, or 3606 of this title.

The remaining provisions of Title VIII serve various purposes. 42 U.S.C. §§3608(e)(5) and (d) impose on HUD and all executive departments and agencies the obligation "affirmatively to further" the purposes and policies of Title VIII in the administration of their housing and urban development programs. There are three methods of enforcement of the prohibitions of §§3604-3606 and 3617: by complaint to HUD, by a private party's filing suit in federal or state court, and by "pattern or practice," "general public importance," and other kinds of suits that the Department of Justice may file. These are authorized in §§3610-3612, 3613, and 3614, respectively. See Schwemm, Housing Discrimination: Law and Litigation, ch. 23-26.

§10.1   Racial Discrimination

Congress, more than one century before the passage of Title VIII, enacted the Civil Rights Act of 1861, which plays an important role (along with Title VIII) in cases involving racial discrimination. The following are excerpts:

> *Be it enacted by the Senate and House of Representatives of the United States of America in Congress assembled,* That all persons born in the United States and not subject to any foreign power, . . . are hereby declared to be citizens of the United States; and such citizens, of every race and color, without regard to any previous condition of slavery or involuntary servitude . . . shall have the same right, in every State and Territory in the United States, to make and enforce contracts, to sue, be parties, and give evidence, to inherit, purchase, lease, sell, hold, and convey real and personal property, and to full and equal benefit of all laws and proceedings for the security of person and property, as is enjoyed by white citizens, and shall be subject to like punishment, pains, and penalties, and to none other, any law, statute, ordinance, regulation, or custom, to the contrary notwithstanding.

The crucial section of the Civil Rights Act is §1982, which gives all citizens the same rights as white citizens. In 1968, shortly after Title VIII became law, the Supreme Court considered the scope of §1982 in Jones v. Alfred H. Mayer Co., 392 U.S. 409 (1968). Defendant builder had refused to sell plaintiffs a newly constructed subdivision home for the sole reason, according to the complaint, that one of the plaintiffs was a Negro. Plaintiffs sought injunctive and other relief under section 1982. In a landmark judgment, the Court held that the section bars *all* racial discrimination, private as well as public, in the sale or rental of property, and that the statute, so construed, was a valid exercise of the congressional power to enforce the Thirteenth Amendment.

Justice Stewart, writing for the Court, contrasted the two "fair housing" statutes:

> At the outset, it is important to make clear precisely what this case does *not* involve. Whatever else it may be, 42 U.S.C.A. §1982 is not a comprehensive open housing law. In sharp contrast to the Fair Housing Title (Title VIII) of the Civil Rights Act of 1968, Pub. L. 90-284, 82 Stat. 73, the statute in this case deals only with racial discrimination and does not address itself to discrimination on grounds of religion or national origin. It does not deal specifically with discrimination in the provision of services or facilities in connection with the sale or rental of a dwelling. It does not prohibit advertising or other representations that indicate discriminatory preferences. It does not refer explicitly to discrimination in financing arrangements or in the provisions of brokerage services. It does not empower a federal administrative agency to assist aggrieved parties. It makes no provision for intervention by the Attorney

General. And, although it can be enforced by injunction it contains no provision expressly authorizing a federal court to order the payment of damages.
[392 U.S. at 413-414.]

An important issue when plaintiffs claim a pattern or practice of discrimination is whether Title VIII requires proof of *intent to discriminate* (see
discussion of Metropolitan Housing Dev. Corp. v. Village of Arlington
Heights, in note 1 below), or whether proof of a significant *discriminatory
effect* suffices. Because the Supreme Court has never addressed this issue,
litigants are bound by the decisions of the circuit in which they are litigating. The case and notes that follow set out various tests for proving discriminatory intent and discriminatory effects.

HANSON v. THE VETERANS ADMINISTRATION

800 F.2d 1381 (5th Cir. 1986)

W. Eugene Davis, J.:
Plaintiffs appeal the dismissal of their claims against the Veterans
Administration (VA) alleging racial discriminaton in its appraisal practices.
We affirm.

I.   Background

The VA is authorized by the Veteran's Benefits Act, 38 U.S.C.A. §§101-
5228 (West 1979), to operate a Home Loan Guaranty Program that allows
veterans to obtain home loans under favorable terms including little or
no down payment. Under the program, the VA induces qualified private
lenders to loan eligible veterans 100% of a home's purchase price by guaranteeing up to 60% of the loan or $27,500, whichever is less.[1] 38 U.S.C.A.
§1810(c) (West Supp. 1986).

Before guaranteeing a loan, the VA hires a fee appraiser to appraise
the home being purchased and determine its "reasonable value." The
reasonable value is calculated by the "market approach" method; the fee
appraiser locates three homes which were sold recently and which are as
similar as possible to the property being appraised. The sales price of these
three "comparables" is used as a starting point to appraise the subject
property; the appraiser may adjust the sales price of the comparable property either up or down depending on the perceived differences between
the comparables and the home being appraised. In using this appraisal

---

1. For the time period relevant to this suit, the maximum amount the VA was authorized
to guarantee was $17,500. See Act of October 18, 1978, Pub.L. No. 95-476, §105(a), 92 Stat.
1499 (1978) (substituting $25,000 for $17,500 as the ceiling for VA loan guarantees). The
$25,000 ceiling was later increased to $27,500. *See* 38 U.S.C.A. §1810(c) (West Supp. 1986).

method, the fee appraiser does not take into consideration a sales price that has been agreed to on the home being appraised.

The appraised value submitted by the fee appraiser is then reviewed by a VA review appraiser who can adopt, modify or reject the estimate. 38 C.F.R. §4340(b) (1985). When he completes his review, the review appraiser issues a Certificate of Reasonable Value (CRV) which acts as a ceiling above which the VA may not guarantee any loan. 38 U.S.C.A. §1810(b)(5) (West 1979). Additionally, the veteran must certify that he paid in cash "from his own resources" any difference between the cost of his home and its reasonable value. 38 C.F.R. §4336(a)(3) (1985). The veteran, however, can request an increase in the CRV amount by submitting additional comparables.

Each appellant was party to a different agreement for the sale of property in which a VA guaranteed home loan was sought. The properties at issue in all of the agreements are located in the MacGregor subdivision, a predominantly black, middle class neighborhood, in Houston, Texas. In each instance, the VA's appraisal estimate and CRV value were below the price prospective purchasers had agreed to pay for the property. These "underappraisals," as they are referred to in the industry, caused many of the prospective purchasers to reduce their offers or look elsewhere for a home where a 100% VA loan was available.[4]

Appellants filed suit against the VA seeking an injunction and damages on the ground that the value of their property was discriminatorily adjusted downward by the VA fee appraisers because MacGregor was a racially mixed neighborhood. As support, appellants offered statistical evidence comparing the percentage of VA underappraisals in MacGregor with that of South Hampton, a white neighborhood allegedly similar to MacGregor. The evidence purported to show that MacGregor had a significantly higher percentage of underappraisals than South Hampton; appellants argued that the underappraisals resulted from the application of racially discriminatory appraisal practices by the VA in violation of the Fair Housing Act of 1968, 42 U.S.C.A. §§3601-3612 (West 1977), the Civil Rights Act of 1866, 42 U.S.C.A. §§1981 & 1982 (West 1981), the Fifth Amendment, and the Thirteenth Amendment.

After a bench trial, the district court dismissed the suit on multiple grounds including a lack of standing, prescription, failure to state a claim and failure to establish discriminatory intent or effect.

---

4. Amy and William Hanson contracted to sell their house at 4406 Roseneath for $59,000, but the property was appraised by the VA at $55,000. Judge Bonnie Fitch agreed to sell her home at 5019 Ventura for $55,000, but the VA appraised her property at $49,350 "as is" and $52,750 if she repaired its cracked slab. Judge Robert Anderson agreed to buy the house at 4114 Fernwood for $54,000, but the property was appraised at $41,500. Donald and Annie Hill agreed to purchase a home at 5324 Calhoun for $75,000, but the property was appraised at $72,750. Professor Otis King contracted to buy the property at 4304 Roseneath for $46,950, but the home was appraised at $40,000. Unable to fulfill this contract, he later agreed to buy the home at 4106 South MacGregor Way for $55,000. The VA issued a CRV on this property for $51,000.

II.   STANDING

A

As a threshold matter, we must consider appellant's standing to bring this suit. The requirement that a litigant have standing to institute litigation in federal court has evolved from Article III of the Constitution [which] limits the jurisdiction of federal courts to actual "Cases and Controversies;" ...

Applying the Article III standard, we are persuaded that at least one plaintiff, Professor Otis King, has standing. King contracted to buy the house at 4304 Roseneath for $46,950. He was unable to purchase the house because the VA issued a CRV for $40,000 thereby limiting the amount of the loan they would guarantee, and he was unable to raise $6,950 from his own resources for a down payment. King later agreed to purchase the house at 4106 South MacGregor Way for $55,000. The VA appraised this home and issued a CRV for $51,000. King was able to pay a $4,000 down payment and bought the house. King alleges that racially discriminatory appraisal practices resulted in the VA's underappraisals of these homes which prevented him from acquiring the Roseneath home. . . . Because Professor King has standing to bring this action, we need not consider the standing of the remaining appellants.

III.   FAILURE TO STATE A CLAIM

The district court held that appellants failed to state a claim for relief under section 804(a) of the Fair Housing Act which makes it unlawful "(a) to refuse to sell or rent after the making of a bona fide offer or to refuse to negotiate for the sale or rental of, or otherwise make unavailable or deny, a dwelling to any person because of race, color, religion, sex or national origin." 42 U.S.C. §3604(a) (1977). The district court held that because the plaintiffs did not complain of discrimination in the sale or rental of housing their complaint failed to state a claim under the Act.

The authorities do not support the district court's conclusion. Courts have consistently given an expansive interpretation to the Fair Housing Act; to state a claim uner the Act, it is enough to show that race was a consideration and played some role in a real estate transaction. Moore v. Townsend, 525 F.2d 482 (7th Cir. 1975).

In United States v. Mitchell, 580 F.2d 789 (5th Cir. 1978), the district court found that the defendant, which owned an apartment complex, steered black tenants to a particular section of the complex and that this effectively denied the black tenants access to equal housing opportunities. We affirmed the conclusion of the district court that these acts by the defendant made unavailable or denied "a dwelling to any person because of race." We held that "steering evidences an intent to influence the choice of the renter on an impermissible racial basis. The government need only establish that race was a consideration and played some role in the real estate transaction." 580 F.2d at 791 (citations omitted).

We conclude that section 804(a) does address the claim asserted by appellants. Discriminatory appraisal may effectively prevent blacks from purchasing or selling a home for its fair market value. This interferes with the exercise of rights granted by the Fair Housing Act.

IV.   THE MERITS

A finding of intentional racial discrimination is necessary for recovery against a defendant under the Civil Rights Act and the Fifth Amendment. Firefighters Local Union No. 1784 v. Stotts, 467 U.S. 561, 567, n.16, 104 S. Ct. 2576, 2590 n.16, 81 L. Ed. 2d 483 (1984) (§1981); Washington v. Davis, 426 U.S. 229, 96 S. Ct. 2040, 48 L. Ed. 2d 597 (1976) (Fifth Amendment); Save our Cemeteries, Inc. v. Archdiocese of New Orleans, Inc., 568 F.2d 1074, 1078 (5th Cir. 1978), *cert. denied*, 439 U.S. 836, 99 S. Ct. 120, 58 L. Ed. 2d 133 (1978) (§1982). However, a violation of section 804 of the Fair Housing Act may be established not only by proof of discriminatory intent, but also by a showing of a significant discriminatory effect. Woods-Drake v. Lundy, 667 F.2d 1198, 1202 (5th Cir. 1982); United States v. Mitchell, 580 F.2d 789, 791-92 (5h Cir. 1978). See also Arthur v. City of Toledo, Ohio, 782 F.2d 565, 574 (6th Cir. 1986) (and cases cited therein).

The district court found that appellants failed to prove discriminatory intent or effect. The question for decision narrows to whether the subsidiary findings of fact essential to this ultimate determination are clearly erroneous. Irby v. Sullivan, 737 F.2d 1418, 1424 (5th Cir. 1984).

We take note of the Supreme Court's recent instruction that:

> If the district court's account of the evidence is plausible in light of the record viewed in its entirety, the court of appeals may not reverse it even though convinced that had it been sitting as the trier of fact it would have weighed the evidence differently. Where there are two permissible views of the evidence, the factfinder's choice between them cannot be clearly erroneous.

Anderson v. City of Bessemer City, North Carolina, 470 U.S. 564, 573-74, 105 S. Ct. 1504, 1512, 84 L. Ed. 2d 518 (1985). We conclude, after careful examinaton of the record, that the district court's findings are not clearly erroneous.

A.   DISCRIMINATORY INTENT

Appellants first assert that the district court did not recognize the significance of their evidence in reaching its conclusion that the VA appraisals and CRV's at issue conformed to the established "market approach" method of appraisal without discriminatory intent.

Appellants introduced proof that a widely used appraisal text, *The Appraisal of Real Estate,* instructed appraisers until 1977 that the value of the property being appraised should be adjusted downward if the ethnic composition of the neighborhood to which it belonged was not homogeneous. The "principal of conformity" categorized different ethnic groups according to their detrimental effect upon property values after their "infiltration" into the neighborhood.

Although this principle was no longer taught after 1977, appellants produced evidence that the VA had never issued guidelines instructing its appraisers not to use this racially biased practice and argued that the VA's appraisers, who had learned the "principal of conformity," continued to apply it. They contend that this is borne out by evidence that several VA appraisal reports concerning MacGregor property referred to "economic depreciation," "changes in the neighborhood" and "lack of pride of ownership," all of which their experts testified indicated racial considerations.

In response to this evidence, five Houston appraisers examined the appraisals in evidence and testified that these phrases did not have racial connotations. They also testified that the appraisal values appeared reasonable and that they were not aware of any Houston appraiser who used racial consideration in their appraisals, emphasizing that such consideration would be unethical. Additionally, the VA appraisal forms require the appraiser to certify that he did not take race into account in the appraisal.

We are persuaded that the district court was entitled to accept the testimony of the VA's experts over that of appellants' experts. The district court's decision "to credit the testimony of one of two or more witnesses, each of whom has told a coherent and facially plausible story that is not contradicted by extrinsic evidence, . . . if not internally inconsistent, can virtually never be clear error." *Anderson,* 470 U.S. at 575, 105 S. Ct. at 1513.

Appellants also contend that the district court failed to properly appreciate the significance of the evidence that the VA appraisals of MacGregor property were riddled with errors, such as understating the size of a home or overstating its age. They argue that these numerous errors — all of which tended to justify a lower appraisal — considered collectively, create an inference of racial bias. The district court did not err in characterizing these as "independent instances of human error" which did not prove discriminatory intent. This finding is supported by testimony of several Houston appraisers that correction of some of the errors would not necessarily entitle the property owner to a higher appraisal.

B.   DISCRIMINATORY EFFECT

Appellants argue that the discriminatory effect of the VA appraisals is established by their statistical evidence. The statistical evidence they presented is based on a comparison of facts surrounding sales of homes in MacGregor and South Hampton subdivisions in which VA financing was sought. Appellants obtained the addresses of the homes being sold, the sales prices agreed to by the parties and the VA appraised value of the homes. Based on this information, appellants' expert, Dr. Barton Smith, made computations which, he testified, revealed that the VA appraisals discriminated against prospective buyers and sellers of MacGregor homes.

Dividing the samples into two time periods, 1970-1977 and 1978-1982, Smith found that 80% and 86%, respectively, of the MacGregor homes were underappraised. The 80% figure was based on twenty-four samples and the 86% figure was based on thirteen; Smith found a 2% chance that this many underappraisals would occur on a random basis. Smith concluded that the four sample sales in South Hampton used for 1970-1977 was too small to be reliable, but based on seven sales in the 1978-1982 period he found that 29% of the VA appraisals in South Hampton were underappraisals.

Smith also calculated that for the periods 1970-1975 and 1976-1980, respectively, the rate of appreciation of the home values in MacGregor was 6.8% and 15.7% while the average appreciation rate for Houston was 11.2% and 13.9%. He testified that this was unusual because MacGregor was no longer experiencing the effects of the racial transition which ended in approximately 1970. He concluded that the homes in MacGregor should have appreciated at a greater rate than the market generally because MacGregor was recovering from deflationary forces such as panic selling that occurred during racial transition.

Additionally, Smith performed a regression analysis on sixteen properties located in MacGregor using data compiled by the Society of Real Estate Appraisers (SREA). This analysis predicted the value of the homes assuming the market took racial factors into account (race included) and their values assuming the market excluded these factors from consideration (race excluded). He then compared these predicted values to the VA appraised values and concluded that on the average, the VA appraised value of these homes was below both predicted values. Because the VA appraisal values were below even the race included values, Smith concluded that VA appraisers were double counting the racial factors.

Based on these statistical studies, Smith determined that home prices in MacGregor were artificially being held below their true market price and expressed confidence that this resulted from the VA appraisers' improper consideraton of racial factors in the neighborhood when appraising the homes. Smith further testified that the VA underappraisals could effectively place a "lid" on the entire MacGregor market. If the appraisal caused the home to be sold at a price below its true market value, its later use as a comparable for another piece of property would result in a lower appraisal, and a lower sales price, of that home. Since VA financing accounts for 45% of the institutional lending in MacGregor, the sale of one house below its true market value could have a substantial impact on the entire neighborhood.

Despite this evidence, the record supports the district court's decision to reject "the various hypotheses and conclusions offered by the plaintiffs' expert witnesses." The VA's expert, Dr. Cooke, examined the statistics offered by Smith and determined that they were inconclusive. Cooke testified that Smith failed to adequately control the data. No comparative data from other parts of Houston or comparative data on the appraisal behavior of other loans, such as FHA loans, was used as a control for the MacGregor data. In addition, Cooke found that the only comparative data available for use by Smith, South Hampton sales with VA appraisals, was derived from too few samples — a total of eleven sales from 1970-1982 — to be reliable. Smith himself admitted that the lack of comparative data concerning other types of loans created a problem with his "lid" theory.

Cooke asserted that Smith had failed to consider important non-racial variables, such as crime rate and school quality, in his regression analysis although an earlier study Smith had done, using the same SREA data, found these variables to be contributing factors in the decrease of home prices. Cooke testified that the regression analysis or "hedonic model" used by Smith presumes that the effect of the omitted non-racial variables on home value is purely random. The district court was entitled to conclude that these omitted variables are important to home value and that their impact would not be purely random. If the variables of crime rate and school quality are not random in their impact on home value, Smith's analysis was skewed and this gave the district court adequate grounds to reject Smith's conclusion based on this study.

Cooke also testified that Smith's race excluded value has minimal importance in explaining how the market reacts because Smith improperly computed this value by merely removing the coefficient assigned to race from his race included value rather than recomputing the entire regression without the race variable. Cooke testified that if done properly, the race excluded value would probably not be much higher than the race included value, indicating that race is not as important a factor in the lower property values as Smith's figures suggest. Cooke also determined that some of the variables used in the regression analysis had been given incorrect values. Correcting these mistakes, Cooke reproduced the regression and determined that the new race included predicted value was statistically insignificant from the VA appraisal value, suggesting that there was no double counting of racial factors by the VA appraisers.

Cooke also recalculated the appreciation rate of homes in MacGregor and produced lower rates than Smith. Cooke testified that his lower rates weakened Smith's "lid" theory by indicating that the ceiling on prices may not be as binding as Smith's numbers suggested. He also disputed Smith's assertion that the VA underappraisals acted as a "lid" on MacGregor property values, pointing out that the data indicated that only eleven of the MacGregor underappraisals had been used as comparables from 1966-1982.

Based on all of this evidence, the district court was entitled to conclude that appellants failed to show that the VA appraisals resulted in a racially-based negative impact on home value in the MacGregor area.

Having concluded that the district judge was not clearly erroneous in finding appellants' evidence insufficient to establish discriminatory intent or effect, we need not review the other reasons offered by the district court for dismissing appellants' claims on the merits. The judgment of the district court is Affirmed.

NOTES AND QUESTIONS

1.   **"Discriminatory effect."** Metropolitan Housing Dev. Corp. v. Village of Arlington Heights, 558 F.2d 1283 (7th Cir. 1977), *cert. denied,* 434 U.S. 1025 (1978), helped to establish the "discriminatory effect" standard. Plaintiffs sued to compel the village defendant to rezone the plaintiffs' property to permit the construction of 190 federally subsidized housing units for lower income families. The Village Board of Trustees had earlier refused to rezone, basing its refusal upon a desire to protect property values and to preserve the zoning plan integrity. When Arlington Heights made that decision, only 27 (!) of the Village's 64,000 residents, compared to 18 percent of the residents in the entire Chicago metropolitan area, were black. If the project were built, as many as 40 percent of the area families eligible for the subsidized units would have been black.

Plaintiffs, who included the prospective nonprofit developer and a black worker (who was employed locally and eligible for a unit in the project) based their suit upon the Equal Protection Clause and the two federal "fair housing" statutes. The trial court dismissed the suit after finding that the Village's refusal to rezone was motivated by factors unrelated to racial discrimination. 373 F. Supp. 208 (N.D. Ill. 1974). The court of appeals reversed, however, on the ground that the zoning decision had a discriminatory impact; in that context, the Village's refusal could not be upheld absent a compelling interest in support of the decision. Since the Village had failed to supply a compelling justification, its action violated the Equal Protection Clause. 517 F.2d 409 (7th Cir. 1974).

The Supreme Court reversed, holding that a showing of discriminatory intent would be required to establish an Equal Protection violation. The opinion said, in part:

> [A] plaintiff . . . [need not] prove that the challenged action rested solely on racially discriminatory purposes. Rarely can it be said that a legislature or administrative body operating under a broad mandate made a decision motivated solely by a single concern, or even that a particular purpose was the "dominant" or "primary" one. . . . In fact, it is because legislators and administrators are properly concerned with balancing numerous competing considerations that courts refrain from reviewing the merits of their decisions, absent a showing of arbitrariness or irrationality. But racial discrimination is not just another competing consideration. When there is a proof that a discriminatory purpose . . . has been a motivating factor in the decision, this judicial deference is no longer justified.

Determining . . . whether invidious discriminatory purpose was a motivating factor demands a sensitive inquiry into such circumstantial and direct evidence of intent as may be available. The impact of the official action — whether it "bears more heavily on one race than another," Washington v. Davis, *supra,* may provide an important starting point. Sometimes a clear pattern, unexplainable on grounds other than race, emerges from the effect of the state action even when the governing legislation appears neutral on its face. . . . The evidentiary inquiry is then relatively easy. . . . But such cases are rare. Absent a pattern as stark as that in Gomillion or Yick Wo,[3] impact alone is not determinative, and the court must look to other evidence.

. . . The specific sequence of events leading up to the challenged decision also may shed some light on the decisionmaker's purposes. . . . For example, if the property involved here always had been zoned R-5 but suddenly was changed to R-3 when the town learned of MHDC's plans to erect integrated housing, we would have a far different case. Departures from the normal procedural sequence also might afford evidence that improper purposes are playing a role. Substantive departures too may be relevant, particularly if the factors usually considered important . . . by the decisionmaker strongly favor a decision contrary to the one reached.

. . . The legislative or administrative history may be highly relevant, especially where there are contemporary statements by members of the decisionmaking body, minutes of its meetings, or reports. In some extraordinary instances the members might be called to the stand at trial to testify concerning the purpose of the official action, although even then such testimony frequently will be barred on privilege. . . .

The Court noted that this discussion of "subjects of proper inquiry" was not exhaustive. In an important footnote, it also discussed the common situation where discriminatory motives were mixed with nondiscrminatory ones.

Proof that the decision by the Village was motivated in part by a racially discriminatory purpose would not necessarily have required invalidation of the challenged decision. Such proof would, however, have shifted to the Village the burden of establishing that the same decision would have resulted even had the impermissible purpose not been considered. If this were established, the complaining party . . . no longer fairly could attribute the injury complained of to a discriminatory purpose. . . .

429 U.S. at 270-271 (n. 21).

The Court then remanded the case for a determinaton of whether the Village's conduct, in the absence of discriminatory intent, violated Title VIII. 429 U.S. 252 (1977). Upon remand, the Seventh Circuit decided

3. In Gomillion v. Lightfoot, 364 U.S. 339 (1960), a racial gerrymandering case, an "uncouth twenty-eight-sided figure" excluded most blacks and had almost no white voters; in Yick Wo v. Hopkins, 118 U.S. 356 (1886), an administrative board refused licenses to all Chinese candidates and granted them to nearly all Caucasian ones. — EDS.

that a Title VIII violation could take place, *under some circumstances,* by a showing of discriminatory effect without a showing of discriminatory intent. The court refused, however, to rule that every action that produces discriminatory effects causes Title VIII illegality.

In applying this malleable rule to the case at bar, the Seventh Circuit examined four "critical" factors:

(a)   how strong the plaintiff's showing of discriminatory effect is;

(b)   whether there is some evidence of discriminatory intent, though less than needed to show a constitutional violation;

(c)   what the defendant's interest is in taking the action complained of;

(d)   the nature of the relief plaintiff seeks: in this case, plaintiff was seeking to build interracial housing itself rather than trying to compel defendant to do so. In discussing this factor, the court wrote that "to require a defendant to appropriate money, utilize his land for a particular purpose, or take other affirmative steps toward integrated housing is a massive judicial intrusion on private authority." [558 F.2d 1283, 1293]

This examination led the Seventh Circuit to return the suit to the district court to determine whether any parcel existed in Arlington Heights that was both already properly zoned and suitable for subsidized low-cost housing. The Village would have the burden of identifying such a site and, should the Village falter, plaintiffs would be entitled to the relief sought.

The plaintiffs and defendant then compromised their dispute. A suitable parcel was located, lying just beyond the Village boundaries. The Village agreed to annex the parcel and to permit the development to proceed on that site. The plaintiffs in turn agreed to undertake the project and (to the extent federal law permitted) to give residents of Arlington Heights (99.6 percent white) priority in occupying the units. Over the objections of nearby landowners, the district court approved the settlement. 469 F. Supp. 836 (N.D. Ill. 1979), *aff'd,* 616 F.2d 1006 (7th Cir. 1980).

2. **Refusal to rezone.** *Arlington Heights* made clear that a town's refusal to rezone, so as to permit subsidized housing, might violate Title VIII. Huntington Branch, NAACP v. Town of Huntington, 844 F.2d 926 (2d Cir.), *aff'd in part,* 488 U.S. 15 (1988) (per curiam), reached a similar result, and set out a somewhat more relaxed test for "discriminatory effect" than that of the Seventh Circuit in *Arlington Heights.*

The Huntington zoning law limited privately owned, multifamily housing to the town's urban renewal area where over half of the residents were minority. The plaintiff, wishing to build a racially integrated, subsidized low-income, 162-unit project on a 14.8 parcel zoned R-40 (single family, one acre), sought to have the parcel rezoned. Ninety-eight percent of the persons living within a one-mile radius of the site were white. Two thousand attended a protest meeting opposing the project, and shortly after, the town board rejected the proposed zoning change. The board explained that "the location [was] not an appropriate location [for the project] due to lack of transportation, traffic hazard and disruption of the existing residential patterns in the area. . . . "

In reviewing the Town's action, the Second Circuit stated that "discriminatory effect . . . arises in two contexts: adverse impact on a particular minority group and harm to the community generally by the perpetuation of segregation." The court found that the town's refusal had caused both injuries. Minorities disproportionately were eligible for the subsidies needed to live in the proposed project. And the refusal to permit this project except in an urban renewal area would significantly reinforce the town's segregation.

The prima facie showing of discriminatory effect shifted the burden to the town to give "bona fide and legitimate justifications for its action [here, inaction] with no less discriminatory alternatives available." The town's reasons, including one first advanced at the appeal — the need to encourage private development in the urban renewal area — failed to impress the court.

In its per curiam affirmance, the Supreme Court wrote:

> Since appellants conceded the application of the disparate-impact test for evaluating the zoning ordinance under Title VIII, we do not reach the question whether that test is the appropriate one. Without endorsing the precise analysis of the Court of Appeals, we are satisfied on this record that disparate impact was shown, and that the . . . justification proffered to rebut the prima facie case was inadequate.

488 U.S. at 18.

3.   **Episodic versus systemic discrimination.** Much of the reported Title VIII litigation has been of the "wholesale" variety, where a defendant's pattern of discrimination, as in *Hanson*, has been the target. Some prejudiced real estate professionals, bent on bias, yield to no one in their ingenuity to subvert the law. Here are some, both episodic and systemic, that courts have examined under Title VIII:

(a)   Using a credit check as a ruse, rental agents routinely denied apartments to black applicants. United States v. Reddock, 467 F.2d 897 (5th Cir. 1972).

(b)   Subdivider refused to sell lots to black buyers unless they dealt with an "approved" builder. Williams v. Matthews Co., 499 F.2d 819 (8th Cir. 1974), *cert. denied,* 419 U.S. 1021 (1974).

(c)   Building and loan association "red-lined" neighborhoods in which minority group families were concentrated and refused to make loans in those areas. Laufman v. Oakley Bldg. & Loan Co., 408 F. Supp. 489 (D. Ohio 1976).

(d)   Real estate salesman told black couple that they would not be happy living in the house or in the part of subdivision in which they were interested and suggested to the couple that they contact a brokerage firm owned by blacks and specializing in the sale of homes to black purchasers. Bradley v. John M. Brabham Agency, Inc., 463 F. Supp. 27 (D.S.C. 1978).

(e)   Building manager refused to rent apartment to black woman on grounds of "affordability," even before he determined her salary. Hamilton v. Svatik, 779 F.2d 383 (7th Cir. 1985).

(f)   Property insurers charged higher premiums for policies in areas with large or growing numbers of minority residents. NAACP v. American Family Mut. Ins. Co., 978 F.2d 287 (7th Cir. 1992); *cert. denied,* 508 U.S. 907 (1993).

(g)   Advertisements for residential apartments repeatedly used only white models. Ragin v. Harry Macklowe Real Estate Co., 6 F.3d 898 (2d Cir. 1993).

4.   **Use of quotas to promote racial integration.** Starrett City, in Brooklyn, New York, consists of 46 high-rise buildings with nearly 6,000 apartments. Opened in 1973, the project, through the use of various marketing and preferential measures, sought to maintain a racial blending that would be 64 percent white, 22 percent black, and 8 percent Hispanic. In setting this course, the owners stated that they were not motivated by racial animus but were concerned that "white flight" and the "tipping" phenomenon would otherwise create a predominantly minority community.

In a suit brought by the Justice Department, the court agreed that a Title VIII violation had been shown, where the owners' practices meant that rental opportunities for blacks and Hispanics were far fewer "than would be expected if race and national origin were not taken into account." United States v. Starrett City Assoc., 840 F.2d 1096 (2d Cir.), *cert. denied,* 488 U.S. 946 (1988). In dissent, Judge Newman wrote:

> Though the terms of the statute literally encompass the defendants' actions, the statute was never intended to apply to such actions. This statute was intended to bar perpetuation of segregation. To apply it to bar maintenance of integration is precisely contrary to the congressional policy "to provide, within constitutional limitations, for fair housing throughout the United States."

Id. at 1105.

In your view, what should be national policy? To curb the use of any race-conscious rental policies that impose artificial burdens on minorities in their quest for housing? Not to undo integration efforts even if current conditions make integration feasible only by imposing some extra delay on minority applicants for housing?

5.   **The Yonkers saga.** United States v. Yonkers Bd. of Educ., 624 F. Supp. 1276 (S.D.N.Y. 185), *aff'd* 837 F.2d 1181 (2d Cir. 1987), *cert. denied,*

486 U.S. 1055 (1988), illustrates both the reach of Title VIII and the limits of a judicial decree. In 1980, the United States Department of Justice, on behalf of the NAACP, sued the City of Yonkers and two city agencies for practicing racial discrimination in public housing and schooling. In 1985, the district court ordered the city to build or otherwise provide new units of both low- and moderate-income housing, and shortly after the court of appeals affirmance, the city signed a consent decree setting a timetable for 200 public housing and 800 subsidized, moderate-income units. That, however, did not end the matter, nor did it result in prompt compliance.

Almost at once, the City Council refused to amend the zoning law needed to implement the decree, and the court heavily fined the city and the council members who opposed the amendment. (The U.S. Supreme Court later stayed the fines against the council members.) Then the city ran into location, developer, and financing problems. Widespread disagreement over site selection ensued, with the court threatening to fix the sites itself. Contractors were reluctant to plunge into the political maelstrom, and the contractor chosen by the city had trouble getting a bank loan.

Construction on the first of the 200 low-income units began only in mid-1991, and the first tenants did not receive their keys until mid-1992, a dozen years after the lawsuit began. Progress on the 800 moderate-income units remains almost at a standstill, despite the efforts of a special master whom the court named to oversee this phase of the decree; N.Y. Times, Sept. 18, 1994, §9, p.1 (44-unit development, last of seven public housing projects built under court order, opened for occupancy).

What lessons do you draw from this recital?

6. **Racial steering.** Title VIII extends to the practice of racial steering, whereby brokers and rental agents "steer" potential homebuyers and tenants to or away from particular areas or apartment buildings. Often the statements or means used are quite subtle: truthful informational statements with racial content; failure to show homes in a particular location absent a specific request; failure to show additional homes to a black prospect upon learning that the first home shown was no longer on the market. See, e.g., Zuch v. Hussey, 394 F. Supp. 1028 (E.D. Mich. 1975), *aff'd and remanded,* 547 F.2d 1168 (6th Cir. 1977); Heights Community Congress v. Hilltop Realty, Inc., 774 F.2d 135, 140 (6th Cir. 1985).

7. **Blockbusting.** Title VIII, §3604(e), expressly deals with blockbusting, the practice of inducing the panic sale of homes in a racially changing neighborhood — almost always formerly all-white neighborhoods. Here, too, brokers often use subtle techniques. A good example appears in Heights Community Congress v. Hilltop Realty, Inc., *supra,* where the agent sent a postcard to residents announcing that a neighborhood home had been listed with him and inviting calls from any "friend or relative who would like to live near you." One month later, the agent sent a second mail-

ing that stated that the listed home had been sold, and represented: "In selling this property, we came into contact with other families who wish to buy in your neighborhood. Are you interested in selling your property?" Against the backdrop of a racially transitional neighborhood, the trial court found a Title VIII violation. The appeals court reversed, but it agreed that, where panic had already set in (not shown here), a racially neutral form of solicitation might be a prima facie instance of blockbusting. Id. at 143.

8. **The persistence of racial discrimination in housing.** Notwithstanding the two federal statutes and a spate of state and local fair housing laws, racial discrimination in housing remains a common practice. Study after study have confirmed the persistence of this discrimination. A 1991 study by the Urban Institute and Syracuse University, prepared for HUD, conducted 3,800 fair housing audits (paired tests) in 25 metropolitan areas during 1989 and produced these findings:

a. *Stage One — Housing Availability:* For 8 percent of the sales audits for both blacks and Hispanics and for 12 percent (Hispanic) and 15 percent (black) of the rental audits, minorities inquiring about advertised units were unable to meet sales or rental agents or were told nothing was available, even though units were made available to comparable white Anglos. A much larger share of minority auditors, roughly one-third, faced somewhat less restrictive information barriers as to housing availability; here, while they were shown units, they were told of fewer available units than were white checkers.

b. *Stage Two — Contributions to Completing a Transaction:* Where minority auditors were given access to available housing, more than 40 percent both of minority renters and buyers received unfavorable treatment, as to the terms and conditions offered, the assistance given homebuyers in obtaining financing, or the level of "sales effort" invested in the transaction.

c. *Stage Three — Steering:* The study found that 21 percent of both black and Hispanic homebuyers were subject to steering. In these cases, the houses shown or urged on minority buyers were in neighborhoods that were lower percent white (by at least 5 percentage points), lower per capita income (by at least $2,500), or lower median house value (by at least $5,000).

The gross overall incidence of unfavorable treatment, reported by the Study, was:

46 percent for black renters;
43 percent for Hispanic renters;
56 percent for black homebuyers; and
45 percent for Hispanic homebuyers.

9. **"American apartheid."** An influential recent study of the 30 largest black populations in the United States documented the persistence of

"a chocolate city with vanilla suburbs" and tied those patterns to the making of the urban underclass. Douglas S. Massey & Nancy A. Denton, American Apartheid: Segregation and the Making of the Underclass 61 (1993). "Despite the legal banning of discrimination and the apparent easing of white racial hostility, blacks and whites [are] still very unlikely to share a neighborhood within most metropolitan areas." Id. at 66. The authors document a pattern of "hypersegregation," id. at 74-78, in which one-third of all blacks in the United States live under conditions of intense racial segregation. African American residents of poor inner-city neighborhoods experience isolation much more severe than any ever documented for any European ethnic group. In fact, they are so isolated that inner-city blacks in areas studied are very unlikely to have significant social contact with whites unless they work in the larger white economy. Among the 30 largest black urban areas, only one relatively unusual city (Greensboro, North Carolina) displayed a consistent trend towards integration; in some cities, the trend towards residential segregation actually increased in the period from 1970 to 1980. Id. at 66.

10.   **Enforcement: The Fair Housing Amendments of 1988.** Originally, Title VIII provided for no effective public enforcement for individual victims of housing discrimination. Administrative complaints could be handled in most cases only by referring the case to the Justice Department, where the typical complaint could be resolved only by voluntary conciliation. The Attorney General was entitled to file cases involving a pattern and practice of discrimination, but for much of the 1980s few resources were devoted to fair housing suits. Moreover, private enforcement was almost nonexistent outside of a few metropolitan areas, due to the severe statutory and judicial limits placed on damages and attorneys' fees. The Fair Housing Amendments of 1988 went a long way towards addressing criticism that Title VIII lacked effective enforcement mechanisms. The amendments provided for a private cause of action in the federal courts: The limits on damages and attorneys' fees that made private suits rare have been eliminated. Changes were also made to the administrative procedures required before plaintiffs are eligible to file suit. Early data also suggest that many (60 percent) complainants are proceeding to federal court litigation. James A. Kushner, Enforcement and Review of the Fair Housing Amendments Act of 1988, 3 Housing Policy Debate 537 (1992).

11.   **The threshold question.** Typically, law students are expected to concentrate on the law, that is, the statutes and cases that define legal rights and duties and the remedies to enforce those relationships. Occasionally, law students are reminded that the "customary law," that is, the de facto rights and duties that individuals actually enjoy and suffer, may deviate considerably from the formal legal doctrine. The above sources, and possibly your own experience, establish such deviation in the case of housing opportunity.

Carry your thoughts one level deeper. Why, in your opinion, does racially based housing discrimination remain so widespread?

§10.2   Discrimination Based on Marital Status and Sexual Orientation

Federal law does not reach discrimination based on marital status and sexual orientation, but a few states or local communities have such laws, whose enforcement raises troubling issues. Consider the following case.

STATE BY COOPER v. FRENCH

460 N.W.2d 2 (Minn. 1990)

YETKA, J.

Appellant was found guilty of discrimination by an administrative law judge to whom a complaint filed with the Department of Human Rights was referred for hearing. Appellant had refused to rent his property to one Susan Parsons because she planned to live there with her fiancé. A trial de novo before the district court was denied, and the court of appeals affirmed the action of the administrative law judge. French was ordered to pay $368.50 in compensatory damages to Parsons, $400 for mental anguish and suffering, and $300 civil penalties. We reverse the administrative law judge and the court of appeals.

A summary of the facts are as follows:

French owned and occupied a two-bedroom house ("subject property") in Marshall, Minnesota, until moving to a house he purchased in the country. While attempting to sell the subject property, French rented it to both single individuals and married couples. From January to March 1988, French advertised the subject property as being available for rent. On February 22, 1988, French agreed to rent the property to Parsons and accepted a $250 check as a security deposit.

Shortly thereafter, French decided that Parsons had a romantic relationship with her fiancé, Wesley Jenson, and that the two would likely engage in sexual relations outside of marriage on the subject property. On February 24, 1988, French told Parsons that he had changed his mind and would not rent the property to her because unmarried adults of the opposite sex living together were inconsistent with his religious beliefs. French is a member of the Evangelical Free Church in Marshall, and his beliefs include that an unmarried couple living together or having sexual relations outside of marriage is sinful. Despite being questioned by French, neither Parsons nor Jenson told French whether they were planning to have sexual relations on the subject property. The record is in dispute as to whether appellant had knowledge of Parsons' intended sexual activity with her fiancé, but Parsons did not deny such an intent when queried by French. Even if they would not have had sexual relations on the property, French believes that living together constitutes the "appearance of evil" and would not have rented to them on that basis. French admits that if Parsons had been married to Jenson, he would not have objected renting to them.

Parsons filed a charge of discrimination against French with respondent department alleging that French committed marital status discrimination in violation of the Minnesota Human Rights Act (MHRA) when he refused to rent the subject property to her because she planned to live there with her fiancé. Following an investigation, the department issued a complaint against French.

An administrative law judge granted the department partial summary judgment on the issue of liability, ruling that French violated the act's (Minn. Stat. §363.03, subd. 2(1)(a) (1986)) prohibition of marital status discrimination by refusing to rent the subject property to Parsons because she was single and living with her fiancé and rejected French's defenses. Following a hearing on damages, the judge found French liable to Parsons for $363.50 in compensatory damages and $400.00 in mental anguish and suffering. In addition, the judge assessed a civil penalty of $300 to be paid to the State of Minnesota by French, but declined to award punitive damages. French's motion for a trial de novo in district court was denied.

After issuing French a writ of certiorari, a court of appeals panel affirmed that French discriminated against Parsons because of her marital status in violation of the Human Rights Act and that neither the free exercise of religion nor any of French's other arguments provided a defense. We granted French's petition for further review.

On an appeal from summary judgment, we ask two questions: (1) whether there are any genuine issues of material fact and (2) whether the lower courts erred in their application of the law.

Initially, the department must establish a prima facie case of discrimination. State ex rel. McClure v. Sports & Health Club, Inc., 370 N.W.2d 844, 849 (Minn. 1985), *appeal dismissed,* 478 U.S. 1015, 106 S. Ct. 3315, 92 L. Ed. 2d 730 (1986). We must examine whether appellant's refusal to rent to Parsons constituted a prima facie violation of the Human Rights Act's prohibition of marital status discrimination. The act provides in relevant part:

It is an unfair discriminatory practice:

> (1) For an owner, lessee . . .
>   (a) to refuse to sell, rent, or lease . . . any real property because of race, color, creed, religion, national orgin, sex, marital status, status with regard to public assistance, disability, or familial status.

Minn. Stat. §363.03, subd. 2. As applied to this case, French was the owner and lessee of the subject property, and Parsons attempted to rent the property from him.

I.   THE DEFINITION OF "MARITAL STATUS"

The administrative law judge (ALJ) found that appellant refused to rent to Parsons because she "was single *and planned to cohabit*[1] *with another person of the opposite sex.*" The version of the MHRA in effect at the time the alleged discrimination occurred and when the charge was filed did not contain a definition of the term "marital status."[2] *See* Minn. Stat. §363.01 (1987 Supp.).

It is well settled that, in the interpretation of ambiguous statutes, this court is required to discover and effectuate legislative intent. The term "marital status" is ambiguous because it is susceptible to more than one meaning, namely, a meaning which includes cohabiting couples and one which does not. In order to show that construing "marital status" to include unmarried cohabiting couples is inconsistent with public policy, legislative intent, and previous decisions of this court, it is necessary to examine the history of the MHRA and our cases interpreting it.

The MHRA was amended in 1973 to add the prohibition against discrimination on the basis of "marital status." Act of May 24, 1973, ch. 729, §3, 1973 Minn. Laws 2158, 2162 (codified at Minn. Stat. §363.03, subd. 2 (1988)). This court, in construing the term "marital status" has consistently looked to the legislature's policy of discouraging the practice of fornication and protecting the institution of marriage. See Kraft, Inc. v. State ex rel. Wilson, 284 N.W.2d 386, 388 (Minn. 1979) (8-0 decision). *Kraft* presented the question of whether an employer's anti-nepotism policy constituted marital status discrimination within the meaning of the MHRA. Id. at 387-88. In answering this question in the affirmative, Chief Justice Sheran stated:

> Endorsing a narrow definition of marital status and uncritically upholding an employment policy such as respondent's *could discourage similarly situated employees from marrying.* In a locale where a predominant employer enforced such a policy, economic pressures might lead two similarly situated individuals to forsake the marital union and *live together in violation of Minn. Stat. §609.34*

---

1. "Cohabit" means to live together in a sexual relationship when not legally married. The American Heritage Dictionary of the English Language 259 (1980) (New College Distionary).

2. In 1988, the legislature amended the MHRA for the purpose of "clarifying the definition of marital status discrimination." Act of Apr. 26, 1988, ch. 660 §1, 1988 Minn. Laws 917, 918 (codified at Minn. Stat. §363.01, subd. 40 (1988)). This definition, however, does not apply in the instant case because it did not become effective until August 1, 1988. *See* Minn. Stat. §645.02 (1988); see also Minn. Stat. §645.21 (1988) (presumption against retroactive effect).

[fornication statute.] Such an employment policy would thus undermine the *preferred status enjoyed by the institution of marriage.*

In view of these considerations, we hold the employment policy of respondent presumptively invalid under Minn. Stat. §363.03, subd. 1.

Kraft, 284 N.W.2d at 388 (emphasis added) (footnote omitted). The *Kraft* court unanimously concluded that the fornication statute was a valid expression of Minnesota public policy. Moreover, the *Kraft* court did not ignore the destructive practical effect of a contrary ruling simply because there was no direct evidence of fornication. It is easy to see that, but for these important public policies, the *Kraft* decision would have been different. . . .

Respondent makes the surprising suggestion that the fornication statute no longer expresses this state's public policy because "it has fallen into a complete disuse." Not only is such a notion of implied repeal unprecedented, it is factually mistaken. See State v. Ford, 397 N.W.2d 875 (Minn. 1986). In *Ford,* an educator was charged with fornication in connection with consensual sex acts with 16-year-old students. Id. at 876-77. Although the educator entered into a plea bargain agreement pursuant to which he pleaded guilty to different charges, there was no suggestion by anyone that the fornication statute was a nullity.

The *Kraft* approach of defining the scope of the term "marital status" in light of legislative intent was followed in Cybyske v. Independent School Dist. No. 196, 347 N.W.2d 256 (Minn. 1984) (5-2 decision). In *Cybyske,* however, this court declined to extend the definition of "marital status" discrimination to encompass distinctions by an employer based on the conduct of a prospective employee's spouse. See id. at 261. In reaching this conclusion, this court stated:

> The legislature did not intend to proscribe a particular political posture, whether of an employee or of the employee's spouse, in the Human Rights Act. *Nor do we think the term marital status should be construed to include what the legislature excluded.* Here the alleged immediate reason for the discrimination is not directed at the institution of marriage itself.

Id. (emphasis added). Read together, *Kraft, Cybyske,* and *Sports & Health Club* stand for the proposition that, *absent express legislative guidance,* the term "marital status" will not be construed in a manner inconsistent with this state's policy against fornication and in favor of the institution of marriage.

The legislative response to the *Cybyske* decision also demonstrates that the legislature did not intend to expand the definition of "marital status" in order to penalize landlords for refusing to rent to unmarried, cohabiting couples. Minn. Stat. §363.01, subd. 40 (1988) defines "marital status" as follows:

> "Marital status" means whether *a person* is single, married, remarried, divorced, separated, or a surviving spouse *and, in employment cases,* includes protection against discrimination on the basis of the identity, situation, actions, or beliefs of a spouse or former spouse.

(Emphasis added.) The plain language of this new definition shows that, in non-employment cases, the legislature intended to address only the status of an *individual*, not an individual's relationship with a spouse, fiancé, fiancée, or other domestic partner. The extremely broad language following the phrase "and, in employment cases" constitutes legislative recognition that employment cases are fundamentally different from housing cases such as the case at bar.

The legislative history of this subdivision indicates that the legislature did not intend to extend the protection of the MHRA to unmarried, cohabiting couples in the area of housing. In a legislative hearing on a bill for an act to clarify the definition of "marital status," State Human Rights Commissioner Cooper explained the bill as being a response to the *Cybyske* case. *See* Hearing on H.F. 2054, H. Civil Law Subcomm. of Jud. Comm., 75th Minn. Leg., Feb. 26, 1988 (audio tape). Representative Quist, objecting to the broad language of the bill, referred to a hypothetical scenario in which a landlord would be forced to rent to a person whose spouse was a polygamist. Id. Representative Quist indicated that employment and housing were different situations and that the bill's language was much too broad, at least as to housing. Id. Commissioner Cooper stated that he would reconsider the impact of the bill in the housing area and report back to the subcommittee. Id. At the next hearing on the bill, an amendment to the bill was offered that confined the extremely broad language to employment cases only. Hearing on H.F. 2054, H. Civil Law Subcomm. of Jud. Comm., 75th Minn. Leg., Feb. 26, 1988 (audio tape). The amendment limiting the broad definition of "marital status" to employment cases was ultimately enacted into law. Finally, it is worth noting that subsequent attempts to expand the definition of marital status also failed. For example, at one point, the proposed definition included "single, married, divorced, widowed, separated, *or other like status.* . . . See 4 Journal of the House of Representatives 8696 (75th Minn. Leg., Mar. 14, 1988). This "or other like status" did not survive in the final bill.

It is obvious that the legislature did not intend to extend the protection of the MHRA to include unmarried, cohabiting couples in housing cases. It is the duty of this court to follow *Cybyske* and decline to construe the term "marital status" "to include what the legislature excluded." See *Cybyske,* 347 N.W.2d at 261. . . .

Respondent cites *Sports & Health Club* in support of its argument that French gave up his constitutional rights "by entering the public marketplace." As outlined above, employment cases are distinguishable from housing cases. In addition, the *Sports & Health Club* court made it clear that the discrimination in that case was "pernicious" because it was practiced by a Minnesota business corporation engaged in business for profit and the discrimination was irrelevant to "the main decision of competence to perform the work." *Sports & Health Club,* 370 N.W.2d at 853.

It is one thing to prohibit an entity which has availed itself of the privilege of doing business for profit in the corporate form from denying Minnesota residents the basic right to earn a living. An employer is entitled to less control over what an employee does away from the place of employment, but, here, French was renting his former residence while it was for sale in a depressed real estate market. It is unreasonably cynical to say that his choice is simple: that he need not rent at all. Economic necessity may require him to seek rental income and this may be as critical to him as the need for wage income underlying the *Sports & Health Club* decision.[4] On the other hand, what burden is imposed on Parsons to enable her to rent, but not live with her fiancé on the premises?

It is simply astonishing to me that the argument is made that the legislature intended to protect fornication and promote a lifestyle which corrodes the institutions which have sustained our civilizaton, namely, marriage and family life. If the legislature intended to protect cohabiting couples and other types of domestic partners, it would have said so. The legislative history of this statute indicates that an attempt to do this was defeated by a substantial majority of the Minnesota House of Representatives. It is not the role of this court, especially in light of the foregoing analysis, to read such protections into the MHRA.

II.   MINNESOTA CONSTITUTION

Although, in arguments to this court, appellant emphasized the United States Constitution, the issue of protection of religious liberty under the Minnesota Constitution was properly preserved for appeal. In light of the unforeseeable changes in established first amendment law set forth in recent decisions of the United States Supreme Court, justice demands that we analyze the present case in light of the protections found in the Minnesota Constitution.

The people of the State of Minnesota have always cherished religious liberty. The Preamble to the Constitution of the State of Minnesota provides:

> We, the people of the state of Minnesota, grateful to God for our civil *and religious liberty,* and desiring to perpetuate its blessings and secure the same to ourselves and our posterity, do ordain and establish this Constitution.

---

4. The administrative law judge found that French had a net income of $3,851 in 1986, $5,481 in 1987, and $6,470 in 1988.

(Emphasis added.) The Minnesota Constitution, unlike the United States Constitution, treats religious liberty as more important than the formation of government. See Preamble, U.S. Const. ("[I]n order to form a more perfect union. . . .").

The pertinent language in the Minnesota Constitution addressing religious liberty is as follows:

> The right of every man to worship God according to the dictates of his own conscience shall never be infringed . . . *nor shall any control of or interference with the rights of conscience be permitted,* or any preference be given by law to any religious establishment or mode of worship; but the liberty of conscience hereby secured shall not be so construed as to excuse acts of licentiousness or justify practices inconsistent with the peace or safety of the state. . . .

Minn. Const. art. I, §16 (emphasis added). The plain language of this section commands this court to weigh the competing interests at stake whenever rights of conscience are burdened. Under this section, the state may interfere with the rights of conscience only if it can show that the religious practice in question is "licentious" or "inconsistent with the peace or safety of the state." In the present case, the state has simply failed to make such a showing. Moreover, the state contends that it has a compelling interest in protecting licentious practices which is sufficient to override French's religious freedom.

The broad protection of religious liberty required by the Minnesota Constitution is not surprising given the background of the people who adopted this constitution. This special history, shared by the people who adopted the Minnesota Constitution, was eloquently described by the Wisconsin Supreme Court as follows:

> The early settlers of Wisconsin came chiefly from New England and the Middle States. They represented the best religious, intellectual, and moral culture, and the business enterprise and sagacity, of the people of the states from whence they came. They found here a territory possessing all the elements essential to the development of a great state. They were intensely desirous that the future state should be settled and developed as rapidly as possible. They chose from their number wise, sagacious, Christian men, imbued with the sentiments common to all, to frame their constitution. The convention assembled at a time when immigration had become very large and was constantly increasing. The immigrants came from nearly all the countries of Europe, but most largely from Germany and Ireland. As a class, they were industrious, intelligent, honest, and thrifty — just the material for the development of a new state. Besides, they brought with them, collectively, much wealth. They were also religious and sectarian. Among them were Catholics, Jews, and adherents of many Protestant sects. These immigrants were cordially welcomed, and it is manifest the convention framed the constitution with reference to attracting them to Wisconsin. Many, perhaps most, of these immigrants came from countries in which a state religion was maintained and enforced, while some of

them were non-conformists and had suffered under the disabilities resulting from their rejection of the established religion. . . . Such were the circumstances surrounding the convention which framed the constitution. In the light of them, *and with a lively appreciation by its members of the horrors of sectarian intolerance and the priceless value of perfect religious and sectarian freedom and equality, is it unreasonable to say that sectarian instruction was thus excluded . . . ?*

State ex rel. Weiss v. District Bd. of School Dist. No. Eight, 76 Wis. 177, 197-98, 44 N.W. 967, 974-75 (1890) (emphasis added).

In view of the above considerations and the history our state shares with the State of Wisconsin, we are compelled to conclude that French must be granted an exemption from the MHRA unless the state can demonstrate compelling and overriding state interest, not only in the state's general statutory purpose, but in refusing to grant an exemption to French.

In short, we interpret the Minnesota Constitution as requiring a more stringent burden on the state; it grants far more protection of religious freedom than the broad language of the United States Constitution. Pursuant to this analysis, we conclude that the state has failed to sustain its burden in demonstrating a sufficiently compelling interest. . . .

How can there be a compelling state interest in promoting fornication when there is a state statute on the books prohibiting it? See Minn. Stat. §609.34 (1988). Moreover, if the state has a duty to enforce a statute in the least restrictive way to accommodate religious beliefs, surely it is less restrictive to require Parsons to abide by the law prohibiting fornication than to compel French to cooperate in breaking it. Rather than grant French an exemption from the MHRA, the state would rather grant everyone an exemption from the fornication statute. Such a result is absurd. . . .

There are certain moral values and institutions that have served western civilization well for eons. See Maynard v. Hill, 125 U.S. 190, 211, 8 S. Ct. 723, 729-30, 31 L. Ed. 654 (1888) (characterizing marriage as "the foundation of family and society, without which there would be neither civilization nor progress"), *cited with approval in* Zablocki v. Redhail, 434 U.S. 374, 384, 98 S. Ct. 673, 680, 54 L. Ed. 2d 618 (1978). This generation does not have a monopoly on either knowledge or wisdom. Before abandoning fundamental values and institutions, we must pause and take stock of our present social order: millions of drug abusers; rampant child abuse; a rising underclass without marketable job skills; children roaming the streets; children with only one parent or no parent at all; and children growing up with no one to guide them in developing any set of values. How can we expect anything else when the state itself contributes, by arguments of this kind, to further erosion of fundamental institutions that have formed the foundation of our civilization for centuries?

Since our decision is based entirely on interpretation of our state statutes and on the Minnesota Constitution, we need not address respondent's arguments as to the application of the United States Constitution, and we decline to do so. We find that, on statutory grounds and on the grounds of the Minnesota Constitution, French was within his rights in refusing to rent to Parsons.

In summary, because the state should not be able to force a person to break one statute to obey another, because there is a less restrictive means to reconcile the statutes in queston, and because of the state's paramount need under our constitution to protect religious freedom, we reverse the decision of the court of appeals.

SIMONETT, J. (concurring as to Part I).

I join Part I of the court's opinion. Because the issue of statutory construction is dispositive here, I do not reach the constitutional questions.

POPOVICH, C.J. (dissenting).

I respectfully dissent. Precedent establishes the refusal to rent real property to an unmarried woman because she would be living with her fiance is a prima facie violation of the Minnesota Human Rights Act's (MHRA) prohibition of marital status discrimination. I believe the majority misconstrues legislative history, public policy and the facts presented to reach a result contrary to this court's interpretation of the MHRA. . . .

The conduct at issue here, the refusal to rent to an unmarried woman becaue she was single and living with a person of the opposite sex, constitutes marital discrimination and a prima facie violation of the Minnesota Human Rights Act. . . .

Despite being questioned by French, neither Parsons nor Jenson told French whether they were planning to have sexual relations on the subject property. Thus, when he refused to rent to Parsons, French had no knowledge of Parsons' actual or intended sexual activity. French, as owner and lessor, admits that had Parsons been married when she sought to rent the property, he would not have objected to renting to her. There is no "dispute," as the majority claims, regarding whether French had knowledge of Parsons' intended sexual activity with her fiance. The administrative law judge did *not* find that Parsons was going to live with her fiancee in a sexual relationship, and could not make such a finding on this record. The administrative law judge's findings of fact include, "Parsons . . . intended to *reside* on the property with her fiancee. . . . [*French*] *informed her* that *he could not rent* the property to her because cohabitation by two unmarried adults of the opposite sex was not in accord with *his religious beliefs.*" (Emphasis added.) "Cohabitation" was the reason French gave for refusing to rent to Parsons. Use of the word "cohabitation" does not necessarily assume a sexual relationship, and it is often used interchangeably with "living together." See Webster's New International Dictonary 520 (2nd ed.) and Webster's New Collegiate Dictionary 218 (1976). Thus, French's conduct in refusing to rent to Parsons because she was *single* and living with a person of the opposite sex constituted marital discrimination, a prima facie violation of the Minnesota Human Rights Act. . . .

Once a prima facie discrimination case is established, a presumption of discrimination arises and the burden shifts to appellant to prove his conduct was motivated by a legitimate nondiscriminatory defense. Sigurdson v. Isanti County, 386 N.W.2d 715, 720 (Minn. 1986); *Sports & Health Club,* 370 N.W.2d at 849. The remaining question is whether there was a "legitimate nondiscriminatory" defense for French's violation. French asserts two defenses: free exercise of religion and due process/equal protection.

Is appellant's first amendment right to free exercise of religion violated by enforcement of this provision of the Human Rights Act against him? . . .

Our leading case establishes a four-part test for analyzing a request for an exemption from a statute based on the free exercise of religion under both the federal and state constitutions:

1.   whether the objector's religious belief is sincerely held;
2.   whether the state regulation burdens the exercise of this religious belief;
3.   whether the state interest in this regulation is overriding or compelling; and
4.   whether the state regulation uses the least restrictive means.

Sports & Health Club, 370 N.W.2d at 851. An individual claiming an exemption must prove the first two parts, but the state can successfully defend its statute by proving the third and fourth requirements. L. Tribe, American Constitutional Law §14-12, at 1242 (2d ed. 1988). The majority's attempt to interpret the Minnesota Constitution's Freedom of Conscience provision more broadly is not supported by a single decision of this court.

1.   SINCERELY HELD RELIGIOUS BELIEFS

The first requirement is the individual must have a sincerely held religious belief with regard to the contested matter. . . . According to French, he believes "sex outside of marriage is sinful [and] living together . . . constitutes the 'appearance of evil' to which I am also opposed." The sincerity of these beliefs is undisputed, and French has satisfied this requirement.

2.   BURDEN ON RELIGIOUS BELIEF

Second, an individual claiming an exemption must show the applicable government regulation burdens this sincerely held religious belief. . . . While the Act imposes a burden on French's sincerely held religious belief that living together is sinful, such a burden is greatly lessened because it occurred only when French voluntarily entered into the rental marketplace — by crossing over the line drawn by the legislature — and thus subjecting himself to potentially burdensome regulations such as the Act's prohibition of marital status discrimination.

3.   STATE'S OVERRIDING OR COMPELLING INTEREST

If the state shows it has a compelling or overriding interest for the burdensome regulation it can prevent a religious-based exemption from that regulation. . . .

Providing equal access to housing in Minnesota by eliminating pernicious discrimination, including marital status discrimination, is an overriding compelling state interest. The majority outlines numerous situations where the *state, not private individuals,* treats people differently because of their marital status. The facts of this case involve one individual discriminating against another individual because of marital status. Housing is a basic human need regardless of a person's personal characteristics, and the legislature has properly determined that it should be available without regard to "race, color, creed, religion, national origin, sex, marital status, status with regard to public assistance, disability, or familial status." Minn. Stat. §363.03, subd. 2(1)(a). "[A] court cannot lightly dispute a determination by the political branches that the . . . interests at stake are compelling." Finzer v. Barry, 798 F.2d 1450, 1459 (D.C. Cir. 1986), *aff'd sub nom.* Boos v. Barry, 485 U.S. 312, 108 S. Ct. 1157, 99 L. Ed. 2d 333 (1988). An individual's marital or familial status, just like the other prohibited classifications, is irrelevant to holding a job or renting a house, because it "bears no relation to the individual's ability to participate in and contribute to society." Mathews v. Lucas, 427 U.S. 495, 505, 96 S. Ct. 2755, 2762, 49 L. Ed. 2d 651 (1976). . . .

4.   LEAST RESTRICTIVE MEANS

The last requirement is that the state regulation use the least restrictive means of achieving the state's goals. Although the government has a compelling interest that justifies a burden on religious activity, the state must also show the regulation is no more burdensome than necessary to promote the secular interest. . . . Courts have found some alternatives to be less restrictive and less burdensome on an individual's free exercise rights.

French contends a less restrictive means is for the state simply to not enforce the Act's prohibition of marital status discrimination. That is not a less restrictive means; it would be a complete abrogation of the state's goal of preventing invidious discrimination. . . . The legislature, in Minn. Stat. §363.02, subd. 2(1)(b), has already drawn a line that grants an exemption from the Human Rights Act to small-scale landlords renting out a room in the home in which they live. The majority ignores our *Sports & Health Club* holding and the fact the legislature has already drawn a line for granting religiously based exemptions in the case of small-scale landlords. The majority's arguments properly should be left to the legislature. If the legislature wishes to redraw this line so as to exclude individuals like French from the Human Rights Act, it is perfectly free to do so. But until the legislature changes the statute it should be enforced as written, since it is within the permissible parameters of constitutional principles. Appellant's request for an exemption from the Human Rights Act would substantially hinder the fulfillment of the state's goal of preventing invidious discrimination. No alternative means appear available. . . .

IV

Discriminating against unmarried individuals living with members of the opposite sex is neither the cause or the solution to societal woes. The majority's decision rejects the reasoned precedents of this court. Unless the legislature acts differently or until those cases are overruled, we are obliged to follow clear, established precedent in this state.

WAHL, J.
I join the dissent of Chief Justice Popovich.

KEITH, J.
I join the dissent of Chief Justice Popovich.

NOTES AND QUESTIONS

1. **Another view.** Compare Foreman v. Anchorage Equal Rights Commn., 779 P.2d 1199 (Alaska 1989). Anchorage Municipal Law made it unlawful for the owner of rental property to refuse to lease to a person because of marital status. The Foremans, who owned several rental properties in the Anchorage area, refused to rent a single-bedroom apartment to an unmarried woman, for herself, her child, and the child's father. The Alaska court upheld the Commission's determination of unlawful discrimination.

In its opinion, the court alluded to an earlier law reform that repealed the criminal fornication statute. Further contrasting the Minnesota case, the Alaskan landlords did not make a religious freedom argument. From our brief factual statement, do you see any other distinguishing feature of the Alaskan case?

In an extended footnote, the court reviewed authority (as of 1989) from six states and the District of Columbia, which seemed about evenly split as to the scope of "marital status."

2. **Alaska redux.** In Swanner v. Anchorage Equal Rights Commn., 868 P.2d 301 (Alaska 1994), the Alaska court had to face the free exercise

issue head on. Here, landlord refused to rent to unmarried complainants who intended to live together. Landlord based his refusal on his Christian religious belief that considered cohabitation outside of marriage immoral.

In affirming the agency's decision in favor of complainants, the court ruled that the governmental interest in abolishing improper discrimination in housing outweighed landlord's interest in reaffirming his religious beliefs. The court wrote:

> It is important to note that any burden placed on Swanner's religion by the state and municipal interest in eliminating discrimination in housing falls on his conduct and not his beliefs. . . . Swanner has made no showing of a religious belief which requires that he engage in the property-rental business. Additionally, the economic burden, or "Hobson's choice," of which he complains, is caused by his choice to enter into a commercial activity that is regulated by anti-discrimination laws. Swanner is voluntarily engaging in property management. . . . Voluntary commercial activity does not receive the same status accorded to directly religious activity. . . .

As one might expect, the court's decision drew a vigorous dissent. In small part, the dissent reads:

> My research has not revealed a single instance in which the government's interest in eliminating marital status discrimination has been accorded substantial weight when balanced against other state interests, let alone fundamental constitutional rights. I find nothing to suggest that marital status discrimination is so invidious as to outweigh the fundamental right to free exercise of religion.

3. **And on to California.** The dissenting vitriol is even stronger in Smith v. Fair Employment & Housing Commn., 51 Cal. Rptr. 2d 700, 913 P.2d 909 (Cal. 1996), where a divided court upheld the agency's finding of discrimination, when the owner (of two duplexes) refused for religious reasons to rent to an unmarried heterosexual couple.

Besides her constitutional claim, the landlord also relied upon the 1993 (federal) Religious Freedom Restoration Act (RFSA), 42 U.S.C. §§2000bb et seq. Congress's intent was to overturn the holding in Employment Division v. Smith, 494 U.S. 872 (1990), by restoring the "compelling interest test" whenever the free exercise of religion is substantially burdened by laws which, on their face, are neutral toward religion. The dissenters argued that the state had not met RFSA's compelling interest standard.

4. **Where do you stand?** Recognizing that good argument exists on either side of the divide, where do you stand? Do these cases present different issues than, let us say, whether (1) a Mormon commercial landlord would be acting reasonably in refusing to approve a leasehold assignment to a liquor store; (2) a Roman Catholic shopping center owner should be

able to bar "pro choice" leafletters from using his mall in a state that follows *PruneYard*, §1.4.d, *supra?*

5. **Sexual orientation.** "Sexual orientation" as a protected category appears far less often than does marital status, although the Supreme Court struck down a Colorado referendum that would have barred local communities, as well as the state, from extending this protection. Romer v. Evans, 116 S. Ct. 1620 (1996). Where a state or local law extends to sexual orientation, should a landlord's free exercise claim be viewed any differently for a refusal to rent to a homosexual couple than for a refusal to rent to an unmarried heterosexual couple? Why? Why not?

Where state or local law covers marital status but not sexual orientation, how persuasive is the claim, as an issue of statutory interpretation, that homosexual partners in a long-term relationship are protected parties?

Braschi v. Stahl Assoc., 1987 WL 343445 (N.Y. Sup.) (unreported), posed, in a non-fair housing rental context, whether homosexual partners, who view themselves as married to each other, should enjoy the same rights as legally married persons do. At issue, under New York law, was whether the surviving partner in a gay relationship could succeed to the decedent's rent-controlled lease. In holding that the right of succession existed, the court wrote:

> Braschi and Blanchard as evidenced by the affidavits were together in a meaningful, close and loving relationship. They were economically, socially and physically a couple like any traditional couple except their relationship could not be legally consummated. The mere non-existence of a legal piece of paper should not erase the time, love and commitment given by Braschi and Blanchard to each other. They must be considered as a nontraditional family with all the protection that follows from such a finding.

On Sept. 21, 1996, at 12:50 A.M.(!), President Clinton signed the G.O.P.-sponsored Defense of Marriage Act. This measure allows each state to decide whether it will give legal recognition to same-sex marriages formalized in a sister state; L.A. Times, Sept. 22, 1996, part A, p.22.

§10.3   Discrimination Based on Physical or Mental Disability

Congress in 1990 passed the Americans with Disabilities Act, 42 U.S.C.A. §12101 et seq. (West), which extended sweeping protections in all realms of American life to the 43 million persons said to suffer one or more physical or mental disabilities at the time. The measure was intended to provide "clear and comprehensive national mandate for the elimination of discrimination against [disabled] individuals" and "clear, strong, consistent, enforceable standards addressing [such] discrimination."

Although the statute mentions housing as an area of persistent discrimination against the disabled, ADA's substance deals mostly with employment, or with access to public facilities, places of public accommodation, and commercial properties. But two years earlier, in its amendments to Title VIII, Congress anticipated ADA when it made unlawful housing discrimination based on "handicap," defined as "a physical or mental impairment which substantially limits one or more of such person's major life activities," 42 U.S.C.A. §3602(h)(1) (West 1994).

In describing what unlawful discrimination could include, the law is unusually detailed. Section 3604(f)(3) provides:

> (3) For purposes of this subsection, discrimination includes —
>
> (A) a refusal to permit, at the expense of the handicapped person, reasonable modifications of existing premises occupied by such person if such modifications may be necessary to afford such person full enjoyment of the premises except that, in the case of a rental, the landlord may where it is reasonable to do so condition permission for a modification on the renter agreeing to restore the interior of the premises to the condition that existed before the modification, reasonable wear and tear excepted.
>
> (B) a refusal to make reasonable accommodations in rules, policies, practices, or services, when such accommodations may be necessary to afford such person equal opportunity to use and enjoy a dwelling; or
>
> (C) in connection with the design and construction of covered multi-family dwellings[4] for first occupancy after the date that is 30 months after September 13, 1988, a failure to design and construct those dwellings in such a manner that —
>
> (i) the public use and common use portions of such dwellings are readily accessible to and usable by handicapped persons;
>
> (ii) all the doors designed to allow passage into and within all premises within such dwellings are sufficiently wide to allow passage by handicapped persons in wheelchairs; and
>
> (iii) all premises within such dwellings contain the following features of adaptive design;
>
> (I) an accessible route into and through the dwelling;
>
> (II) light switches, electrical outlets, thermostats, and other environmental controls in accessible locations;
>
> (III) reinforcements in bathroom walls to allow later installation of grab bars; and
>
> (IV) usable kitchens and bathrooms such that an individual in a wheelchair can maneuver about the space. . . .
>
> (5) . . . (B) A State or unit of general local government may review and approve newly constructed covered multifamily dwellings for the purpose of

---

4. The term "covered multifamily dwellings" means (a) buildings consisting of four or more units if such buildings have one or more elevators, and (b) ground floor units in other buildings consisting of four or more units.

making determinations as to whether the design and construction requirements of paragraph (3)(C) are met.

In their first decade, these amendments have become the most heavily
litigated part of Title VIII. Disputes fall into three general categories. The
first, which we have already seen, §7.5(d)*supra,* involves private restrictions
that would prevent a group facility from locating within a residential neighborhood. The second involves zoning laws that would do the same. The
third involves the reasonable accommodation required of a landlord to afford a disabled person equal opportunity to use and enjoy a dwelling.

The next two cases illustrate the second and third kinds of dispute.

ASSOCIATION FOR ADVANCEMENT OF THE MENTALLY HANDICAPPED, INC. v. CITY OF ELIZABETH

876 F. Supp. 614 (D.N.J. 1994)

HAROLD A. ACKERMAN, J.

This matter comes before the court today upon a motion by plaintiffs
for partial summary judgment pursuant to Federal Rule of Civil Procedure
56. For the reasons detailed below, plaintiff's motion is granted.

I.   INTRODUCTION

This case involves the following question: Does a municipal ordinance, and the state statute upon which the ordinance is based, that sets
up three barriers to the provisioning of community residences for people
with developmental disabilities violate the Fair Housing Amendments Act
of 1988. Let me begin by setting forth the relevant parties.

Plaintiff Association for Advancement of the Mentally Handicapped,
Inc. ("AAMH") is a nonprofit corporation that provides social support
services, including assistance obtaining housing, employment, education,
financial management and medical assistance, to its developmentally disabled members. AAMH also manages and holds an ownership interest in
plaintiff Creative Property Management of N.J., Inc.

Plaintiff Creative Property Management of N.J., Inc. ("CPM") is a
nonprofit corporation which purchases and holds real estate for use and
occupancy by developmentally disabled persons.

Plaintiffs Annie Sims and James Williams are members of AAMH living semi-independently in Elizabeth with support and services provided by
AAMH. Both are developmentally disabled.

The defendants in the case are the City of Elizabeth, the City Council
of the City of Elizabeth, and William Rapp, who is the director of construction for the city of Elizabeth.

II. FACTUAL AND PROCEDURAL BACKGROUND

The following constitutes the undisputed facts of record in this case:

In December of 1990, SERV Centers of New Jersey, Inc., ("SERV") entered into a contract with the New Jersey Department of Human Services ("DHS") pursuant to which SERV would provide a transitional community residence for emotionally disturbed children discharged from Elizabeth General Hospital. SERV then located a suitable house under construction on Livingston Road in Elizabeth. The Elizabeth Construction and Zoning Department informed SERV that a community residence for the developmentally disabled was a permitted use at this location. Consequently, SERV contracted to buy the house.

In September of 1991, members of the community in which the SERV house was located learned of SERV's intended use for the house. On September 15, they voiced their concerns about the house at a meeting with Elizabeth City Councilman Robert Jaspen. In particular, people were concerned that their children might not be safe if the SERV residence housed emotionally disturbed children.

Upon being informed of the situation by Councilman Jaspen, then Elizabeth Mayor Thomas Dunn called a meeting with his department heads to discuss the situation. At the meeting Mayor Dunn "strongly suggested" to Elizabeth Director of Construction, William Rapp that he take every legal step to stop the renovation of the SERV house until an investigation of the situation could be completed. Director Rapp stated that he had sufficient legal reasons to issue a stop work order and it was thereafter issued. Mayor Dunn later stated, referring to this meeting,

> there was a general attitude initiated by myself, . . . , that, 'Well, we better damn well stop what's going on up there in view of the fact that [SERV] didn't communicate with the city through proper channels.'

Deposition of Thomas Dunn, Joint Appendix of Plaintiffs at 52a-53a [hereinafter "Dunn Dep."]

Mayor Dunn also contacted Mr. Steven Ramsland, the President of SERV. Mr. Ramsland informed the Mayor that the SERV house would be occupied by eight severely emotionally disturbed teenagers. Mayor Dunn later stated that he told Mr. Ramsland of his "disgust and of [his] determination to use every legal and proper maneuver available to [the mayor] to stop SERV's invasion of Elizabeth." Dunn Dep. at 30a-31a. When later explaining this comment, the Mayor stated that he thought it to be "illegal," "when a highly residential neighborhood was to be changed in character without any communication to the Mayor and Chief Executive of the City, nor to the City Council." Id.

On September 18, 1991, Mayor Dunn sent a telegram to the State Commissioner of DHS requesting that funding for the SERV house be withdrawn. On September 19, 1991, Mayor Dunn spoke to a group of — by the Mayor's estimation — 600 to 700 residents of Elizabeth who were concerned about the SERV situation. Referring to SERV, the Mayor told the crowd,

> The law may seem, to the enemy, to be on its side. If so, the law must be changed. Regardless of words in the law, right is on our side.

Dunn Dep. at 39a. The Mayor later explained what he meant by this statement. The Mayor stated that Mr. Ramsland, the president of SERV, told him that neither the mayor nor the city council need be consulted prior to the establishment of a residence like the SERV house. The Mayor concluded that if Mr. Ramsland's statement of the law was correct, then the law was wrong and should be changed.

On October 7, 1991, at a special meeting, the Elizabeth Planning Board adopted a resolution recommending that the Elizabeth City Council amend the city's zoning code. The city zoning code was subsequently amended by Ordinance No. 2426 which required conditional use permits for community residences housing more than six developmentally disabled persons. Ordinance No. 2426 further provided, among other things, that a conditional use permit would be automatically denied in two situations:

1) If the proposed residence is located within 1,500 feet of an existing residence for developmentally disabled; or
2) if existing community residences or community shelters within the township exceed 50 persons or 0.5% of the township population, whichever is greater.

The ordinance drew its authority from the New Jersey Municipal Land Use Law ("MLUL"). N.J.S.A. 40:55D-66.1 et seq. The MLUL generally permits community residences for the developmentally disabled, however, in the case of community residences housing more than six persons, it authorizes municipalities to enact zoning ordinances that require conditional use permits. Requirements for the issuance of these conditional use permits must be "reasonably related to the health, safety and welfare of the residents of the district." N.J.S.A. 40:55D-66.1. The statute also provides that a conditional use permit may be denied if (a) the residence will be located within 1,500 feet of an existing residence or community shelter for victims of domestic violence, or (b) the number of persons, other than resident staff, residing at existing such residences or shelters within the municipality exceeds the greater of 50 persons or 0.5% of the municipal population. Id.

On December 23, 1991, the Elizabeth City Council passed Ordinance No. 2434 which added a third situation in which a conditional use permit would be automatically denied: if the proposed community residence is within 1,500 feet of a school or day care center.

At this point the plaintiffs in this case entered the picture. In December of 1991, CPM purchased a condominium unit in a complex in Elizabeth known as Joelle Manor.[1] AAMH offered the unit to plaintiffs Annie Sims and James Williams. CPM subsequently applied to the city for a certificate of occupancy. In a letter to AAMH's attorney in response to the application, defendant William Rapp stated that the proposed use of the condominium — housing developmentally disabled persons — would violate "the requirement of not being 'located with 1500 feet of a community residence' . . . since the AAMH has indicated . . . that it has 'ownership interest as to seven of twelve units contained in the building.' " Letter of William Rapp, January 17, 1992, Joint Appendix of Plaintiffs at 165a-166a. On January 22, 1992, Rapp denied the certificate of occupancy.

On February 13, 1992, AAMH and CPM filed this action against defendants alleging housing discrimination against developmentally disabled persons based on various federal and state grounds. On February 24, 1993, Annie Sims and James Williams filed a separate civil action against the same defendants and also alleged that defendants' actions violated both federal and state law. These cases were consolidated in April of 1992.

After the commencement of this suit, on June 23, 1993, the City of Elizabeth enacted Ordinance No. 2607 which revised the requirements for the granting of conditional use permits for community residents with more than six residents. However, the ordinance retains the three restrictions which are the subject of this motion. The ordinance continues to provide for the automatic denial of a conditional use permit if

(1)   the proposed location of a community residence for more than six residents is within 1,500 feet of an existing residence or shelter for victims of domestic violence;

(2)   the total number of persons residing in community residences or shelters in the City exceed fifty persons or five-tenths of one percent of the population of the City of Elizabeth, whichever is greater; or

(3)   the proposed location of a community residence for more than six residents is within 1,500 feet of a school or day care center.

City of Elizabeth, N.J., Ordinance No. 2607 (June 23, 1993).

In this motion for partial summary judgment plaintiffs ask the court to declare these three provisions the City ordinance and the portion of the MLUL upon which the ordinance is based to be violative of the Federal Housing Amendments Act of 1988, 42 U.S.C. §3601 *et seq.*[2] Plaintiffs also

---

1. At the time of the purchase, CPM owned seven other units in the complex. On average, five of the units were used to house ten developmentally disabled persons. The other two units housed AAMH staff and served as a location from which counseling, supervision and support were provided.

2. In this motion, plaintiffs also request that the court declare the Elizabeth Ordinance invalid based on the New Jersey Law Against Discrimination (N.J.S.A. 10:5-1 et seq.) and the Due Process and Equal Protection Clauses of the United States and the New Jersey Constitutions. However, because I am declaring the ordinance and the relevant portion of the New Jersey Statute invalid under the FHAA, I will not address these claims. See Jean v. Nelson, 472 U.S. 846, 854, (1985) ("[a court] ought not to pass on questions of constitutionality . . . unless such adjudication is unavoidable") (citations omitted).

seek an order permanently enjoining the defendants from enforcing the portions of the city ordinance which the court invalidates. . . .

III.   DISCUSSION

A.   THE FAIR HOUSING AMENDMENTS ACT OF 1988

The Fair Housing Amendments Act of 1988 (the "FHAA"), 42 U.S.C. §3601 et seq., extended the protection of the federal fair housing law to persons with disabilities. The FHAA prohibits discrimination on the basis of a physical or mental handicap. 42 U.S.C. §3604(f)(1). . . .

The FHAA states that "any law of a State, a political subdivision, or other such jurisdiction that purports to require or permit any action that would be a discriminatory housing practice under this subchapter shall to that extent be invalid." 42 U.S.C. §3615.

The FHAA's legislative history indicates that Section 3604(f) was intended to reach a wide array of discriminatory housing practices, including licensing laws which purport to advance the health and safety of the community. The legislative history states:

> [§3604(f)] would also apply to state or local land use and health and safety laws, regulations, practices and decisions which discriminate against individuals with handicaps. While state and local governments have authority to protect safety and health, and to regulate use of land, that authority has sometimes been used to restrict the ability of individuals with handicaps to live in communities. This has been accomplished by such means as the enactment or imposition of health, safety or land-use requirements on congregate living arrangements among non-related persons with disabilities. Since these requirements are not imposed on families and groups of similar size of other unrelated people, these requirements have the effect of discriminating against persons with disabilities.
>
> The Committee intends that the prohibitions against discrimination against those with handicaps apply to zoning decisions and practices. The Act is intended to prohibit the application of special requirements through land-use regulations, restrictive covenants, and conditional or special use permits that have the effect of limiting the ability of such individuals to live in the residence of their choice.

United States v. Schuylkill Township, Pa., 1990 WL 180980 *4-5 (E.D. Pa. November 16, 1990) (quoting H.R. Rep. No. 100-711, 100th Cong., 2d Sess. 24, *reprinted in* 1988 U.S. Code Cong. & Admin. News at 2173, 2185).

Despite the broad reach of the FHAA, however, not all zoning ordinances which impact on the handicapped are per se invalid. "Rather Congress has indicated the FHAA is intended to allow reasonable government limitations so long as they are imposed on all groups and do not effectively discriminate on the basis of a handicap." Id.

A violation of the FHAA can be established by demonstrating that the challenged statute or ordinance discriminates against the handicapped on its face and serves no legitimate government interest.[3] Horizon House v. Township of Upper Southhampton, 804 F. Supp. 683, 693 (E.D. Pa. 1992), *aff'd mem.*, 995 F.2d 217 (3d Cir. 1993); Potomac Group Home v. Montgomery County, Md., 823 F. Supp. 1285, 1295 (D. Md. 1993). In addition, whether the motives of the drafters of a facially discriminating ordinance are benign or evil is irrelevant to a determination of the lawfulness of the ordinance. The court must focus on the explicit terms of the ordinance. *Horizon House,* 804 F. Supp. at 694 (citing International Union, United Auto, etc. v. Johnson Controls, Inc., 499 U.S. 187, 199 (1991) in which the Supreme Court stated in a Title VII case that "the absence of a malevolent motive does not convert a facially discriminatory policy into a neutral policy with a discriminatory effect. Whether an employment practice involves disparate treatment through explicit facial discrimination does not depend on why the employer discriminates but rather on the explicit terms of the discrimination.").

If the statute or ordinance is discriminatory on its face, then the burden is on the defendant to justify the discriminatory classification. See Resident Advisory Board v. Rizzo, 564 F.2d 126, 149 (3d Cir. 1977) (hereinafter "*Rizzo*"); *Horizon House,* 804 F. Supp. at 693; *Potomac Group Home,* 823 F. Supp. at 1295. "[A] justification must serve, in theory and in practice, a legitimate, bona fide interest of the Title VIII defendant, and the defendant must show that no alternative course of action could be adopted that would enable that interest to be served with less discriminatory impact." *Rizzo,* 564 F.2d at 149.

Before analyzing the validity of the Elizabeth Ordinance and the authorizing New Jersey Statute under the FHAA, it should be noted that the ordinance and the statute clearly apply to the same persons Congress sought to protect by enacting the FHAA.

Under the FHAA, a person is considered handicapped if he or she has a physical or mental impairment which substantially limits one or more major life activities, has a record of having such an impairment, or is regarded as having such an impairment. 42 U.S.C. §3602(h). See also, *Horizon House,* 804 F. Supp. at 694 (stating that FHAA had broad definition of handicap); *Borough of Audobon,* N.J., 797 F. Supp. at 358 (holding that persons suffering

---

3. A prima facie case under the FHAA will also be established if the plaintiff can show either "discriminatory treatment or discriminatory effect alone, without proof of discriminatory intent." Doe v. City of Butler, Pa., 892 F.2d 315, 323 (3d Cir. 1989) (citations omitted); Horizon House v. Township of Upper Southhampton, 804 F. Supp. 683, 693 (E.D. Pa. 1992), *aff'd mem.*, 995 F.2d 217 (3d Cir. 1993); Oxford House, Inc. v. Township of Cherry Hill, 799 F. Supp. 450, 460 (D.N.J. 1992); United States v. Borough of Audobon, N.J., 797 F. Supp. 353, 359 (D.N.J. 1991), *aff'd mem.*, 968 F.2d 14 (3d Cir. 1993). However, these two alternative theories need not be addressed because both the ordinance and the state statute clearly discriminate on their face.

or recovering from alcoholism and/or drug addiction are "handicapped" within the meaning of the FHAA).

The Elizabeth Ordinance derives its definition of developmentally disabled from the authorizing New Jersey statutes. The authorizing statute defines developmentally disabled as those persons who meet five criteria — one of which is a substantial limitation in three or more major life activities.[4] The FHAA's definition of handicapped encompasses the Elizabeth ordinance's and the New Jersey Statute's definition of developmentally disabled. Therefore, the FHAA applies to the ordinance and the statute.

B.   THE ELIZABETH ORDINANCE

"An ordinance that uses discriminatory classifications is unlawful in all but rare circumstances." *Horizon House,* 804 F. Supp. at 693.

The City of Elizabeth ordinance uses a discriminatory classification on its face. The ordinance states, in part,

> Community residences for the developmentally disabled . . . shall be a permitted use in all residential zones of a municipality, and the requirements therefor shall be the same as for single family dwelling units located within such zones, provided, however, community residence [sic] for the developmentally disabled . . . , as authorized by N.J.S.A. 40:55D-66.1 and 40:55D-66.2, housing more than six (6) persons excluding resident staff, shall be permitted as a conditional use in all residential zones provided the following conditions are met or maintained: [the conditions that follow are the three delineated, *supra,* at pp. 618-619 which are at issue in this case].

City of Elizabeth, N.J., Ordinance No. 2607 (June 23, 1993).

The ordinance discriminates on its face by imposing conditions on the establishment of community residences for the developmentally disabled housing more than six persons that are not imposed on residences

---

4. Under these statutes, "developmentally disabled" means a severe, chronic disability of a person which:

a. is attributable to a mental or physical impairment or combination of mental or physical impairments;
b. is manifest before age 22;
c. is likely to continue indefinitely;
d. results in substantial functional limitations in three or more of the following areas of major life activity, that is, self-care, receptive and expressive language, learning, mobility, self-direction and capacity for independent living or economic self-sufficiency; and
e. reflects the need for a combination and sequence of special interdisciplinary or generic care, treatment or other services which are of lifelong or extended duration and are individually planned and coordinated.

N.J.S.A. 30:11B-2. Developmental disabilities include, but are not limited to, severe disabilities attributable to mental retardation, autism, cerebral palsy, epilepsy, spina bifida and other neurological impairments where the above criteria are met. Id.

housing more than six persons who are not developmentally disabled.[6] This clearly restricts the housing choices of people based on their handicaps. . . . Therefore, the ordinance is facially discriminatory and will only be upheld if it serves a legitimate government purpose.

The defendants appear to put forward two rationales for the ordinance.

First, the defendants argued at oral argument and in their brief in opposition to this motion that because developmentally disabled persons may pose a risk of danger to the community, the City has a right to be notified and to have input into the types of residences the city will "host." See, e.g., Defendants' Brief in Opposition to Plaintiffs' Motion for Partial Summary Judgment at 4. ("[B]oth the State Statute and the Ordinances enacted pursuant to its authority represent valid exercises of the police power, designed as they are to prevent any threat of danger to the community. . . . [therefore], as a matter of basic fairness, the host community is entitled to know about the kinds of residents whom they will host.").

Second, an examination of the record before the court indicates that another rationale for the ordinance may have been that because, in the defendants' view, community residences of this sort change the character of a residential neighborhood, communication with the mayor and the city council should be required before a community residence is established. See, e.g., Dunn Dep. at 31a (Mayor Dunn stated in a deposition that he thought it to be "illegal" "when a highly residential neighborhood was to be changed in character without any communication to the Mayor and Chief Executive of the City, nor to the City Council.")

I will first address defendants' argument concerning the threat of harm created by the presence of developmentally disabled persons in the community.

This argument fails because there is no evidence in the record that indicates that developmentally disabled persons, as defined by the New Jersey statutes, would pose any danger to the community. The defendants have not exceeded the "mere scintilla" standard; there is no evidence in the record upon which a factfinder could reasonably conclude that developmentally disabled persons would pose a risk of danger to other members of the community. See *Petruzzi's IGA,* 998 F.2d at 1330. Courts have held that unsubstantiated, generalized fears are not a valid basis for discriminating against the handicapped. See, e.g., City of Cleburne, Tex. v. Cleburne Liv-

---

6. That the ordinance also applies to community shelters for victims of domestic violence does not detract from its facial invalidity. See *Horizon House,* 804 F. Supp. at 694 ("the fact that the 1,000 foot spacing requirement may also incidentally catch in its net some group homes that serve individuals without handicaps does not vitiate the facial invalidity of the rule which clearly restics the housing choices of people based on their handicaps. . . ."); *Potomac Group Home,* 823 F. Supp. at 1296 n.9 ("Defendants contend that the regulation is not discriminatory because it also applies to group homes for disadvantaged youths. There is no merit to this argument. The parties agree that the vast majority of group homes to which the regulation applies provide housing for the disabled.").

ing Center, 473 U.S. 432, 448 (1985) (unsubstantiated fears of residents rejected as a basis for differential treatment of home for mentally retarded persons in an Equal Protection case); *Horizon House,* 804 F. Supp. at 695-97 ("no evidence in the record to support the perception that group homes are a 'burden' on the neighborhood"; invalidating ordinance requiring 1000 foot spacing requirement between group homes).

Not only is there no evidence in the record to support defendants' claim that developmentally disabled persons may pose a risk of harm, there is evidence in the record that the New Jersey Department of Human Services ("DHS") takes affirmative steps to ensure that no person who could be considered dangerous is placed in a community residence. Claire Mahon, the Assistant Director for Community Services of the Division of Developmental Disabilities in the DHS, explained in her certification that DHS staff "review each person with a developmental disability being considered for placement in a community residence, . . . , to ensure that no person who could be considered a danger to the community is released from the hospital or placed in a community residence." See Certification of Claire Mahon at ¶6, Supplemental Joint Appendix of Plaintiffs.

In addition, even if there were an evidentiary basis in the record to support defendants' claim that some developmentally disabled persons may pose a risk of harm to the community, defendants would still have failed to meet their burden in justifying the ordinance. This is because, while protecting members of the community from harm is clearly a legitimate government purpose, the conditions in the ordinance do not serve that interest, "in theory and in practice." See *Rizzo,* 564 F.2d at 149.

There is no evidence in the record which indicates that automatically denying conditional use permits to community residences housing six or more developmentally disabled persons which are sought to be established within 1,500 feet of an existing residence or within 1,500 feet of a school or day care center furthers the City's interest in protecting its citizens from potential danger. Likewise, there is no evidence in the record which indicates that automatically denying a conditional use permit when the total number of persons residing in such residences or shelters in the City exceeds fifty persons or five-tenths of one percent of the population of the City of Elizabeth, whichever is greater, furthers the City's interest in protecting its citizens from potential danger.

These conditions do not seem to be related in any way to the City's professed objective of ensuring that potentially dangerous persons are not housed in community residences for the developmentally disabled. Defendants argue that because developmentally disabled persons may be dangerous, the City should be notified and have input before a community residence is established. However, the ordinance is not one which provides for some type of screening process by the City — which may or may not be valid under the FHAA. The ordinance merely provides for the automatic denial of a conditional use permit if one of the three conditions are met.

This in no way serves the interest put forward by defendants to justify the ordinance.

Therefore, the defendants did not meet their burden of justifying the ordinance based on this rationale.

Defendants' second ratonale is that the ordinance protects the residential character of neighborhoods surrounding community residences. The City has a legitimate interest in protecting the residential character of the surrounding neighborhood. See Oxford House, Inc. v. Township of Cherry Hill, 799 F. Supp. 450, 462 (D.N.J. 1992).

However, this rationale suffers from a defect similar to that suffered by their first rationale. Namely, the record is devoid of any evidence upon which a factfinder could reasonably conclude that community residences housing more than six developmentally disabled persons would detract from a neighborhood's residential character. Defendants have not exceeded the "mere scintilla" standard. See *Anderson,* 477 U.S. at 252 ("The mere existence of a scintilla of evidence in support of the [nonmovant's] position will be insufficient; there must be evidence on which the jury could reasonably find for the [nonmovant].").

There is no evidence in the record which suggests that the presence of the developmentally disabled persons that currently live in Elizabeth in the CPM-owned condominium complex detracts from the residential character of the neighborhood. Furthermore, even if there were evidence in the record which indicated that community residences detracted from the residential character of the neighborhood, the defendants have not put forward any evidence that the three requirements for automatic denial in the ordinance "serve, in theory and in practice," that interest, and that there is "no alternative course of action could be adopted that would enable that interest to be served with less discriminatory impact." See *Rizzo,* 564 F.2d at 149.

Therefore, the defendants also have not met their burden of justifying the ordinance based on this rationale.

In summary, the defendants have not exceeded the "mere scintilla" standard. There is no evidence in the record upon which a factfinder could reasonably conclude that the three, alternative requirements for automatic denial of a conditional use permit in the Elizabeth Ordinance, "serve, in theory and in practice, a legitimate, bona fide interest" of the City of Elizabeth. Therefore, the three conditions in the Elizabeth Ordinance at issue in this case violate the FHAA and plaintiffs' motion for partial summary judgment on this ground is granted. . . .

NOTES AND QUESTIONS

1. **Equal protection challenge.** As the opinion notes, the Supreme Court had decided prior to the 1988 amendments that a city law that re-

quired a special use permit for the operation of a proposed group home (for the mentally retarded) was as applied a deprivation of equal protection when the city refused to issue the permit. City of Cleburne, Texas v. Cleburne Living Center, 473 U.S. 432 (1985).

In that case, the Court of Appeals for the Fifth Circuit had determined that mental retardation was a quasi-suspect classification, requiring heightened scrutiny that the city's action could not withstand. 726 F.2d 191 (1984). The Supreme Court rejected the Fifth Circuit's rationale but affirmed the result on grounds that the record revealed *no rational basis* for believing that the proposed group home posed any special threat to the city's legitimate interests.

In his separate concurrence and partial dissent, Justice Marshall wrote:

> The Court appears to act out of a belief that the ordinance might be "rational" as applied to some subgroup of the retarded under some circumstances, such as those utterly without the capacity to live in a community, and that the ordinance should not be invalidated *in toto* if it is capable of ever being validly applied. But the issue is not "whether the city may never insist on a special use permit for the mentally retarded in an R-3 zone." The issue is whether the city may require a permit pursuant to a blunderbuss ordinance drafted many years ago to exclude all the "feeble-minded," or whether the city must enact a new ordinance carefully tailored to the exclusion of some well-defined subgroup of retarded people in circumstances in which exclusion might reasonably further legitimate city purposes. By leaving the sweeping exclusion of the "feeble-minded" to be applied to other groups of the retarded, the Court has created peculiar problems for the future. The Court does not define the relevant characteristics of respondents or their proposed home that make it unlawful to require them to seek a special permit. Nor does the Court delineate any principle that defines to which, if any, set of retarded people the ordinance *might* validly be applied. . . . As a consequence, the Court's as-applied remedy relegates future retarded applicants to the standardless discretion of low-level officials who have already shown an all too willing readiness to be captured by the "vague, undifferentiated fears," of ignorant or frightened residents.

473 U.S., at 474.

Two questions: (1) Are there any reasons, in the light of the Court's holding in *City of Cleburne*, to couple an Equal Protection with a Title VIII claim? (2) In your opinion, would the City of Elizabeth's action have met the rational basis test? More broadly, does Title VIII provide greater (or less) protection to disabled persons than does Equal Protection?

2.   **Occupancy limits.** In a decision that strengthens the fair housing hand, City of Edmonds v. Oxford House, Inc., 115 S. Ct. 1776 (1995), the Court refused to immunize a local ordinance that would have barred the opening of a group home for recovering substance abusers.

In the summer of 1990, Oxford House opened a group home in a single-family neighborhood for 10 to 12 adults recovering from alcoholism and drug addiction. Upon learning of the home, the city issued a criminal citation charging a zoning violation of the rule that limited who might live in single-family dwelling units. The code defined a family as "an individual or two or more persons related by genetics, adoption, or marriage, or a group of five or fewer persons who are not related by genetics, adoption, or marriage." Although it conceded that the group home residents were "handicapped persons" within the Fair Housing Act, the city tried to bring itself within the FHA exemption for "any reasonable local, State, or Federal restrictions regarding the maximum number of occupants permitted to occupy a dwelling."

The Court held that an occupancy cap directed against overcrowding of a dwelling fell within the exemption, but that rules designed to preserve the family character of a neighborhood did not. Because the five-person cap applied only to unrelated persons — for example, ten siblings, their parents and grandparents could lawfully live in the Edmonds' single-family zone — the ordinance was subject to review as to whether it discriminated against the handicapped.

3. **Condemnation of site for proposed treatment facility.** In Kessler Inst. for Rehabilitation, Inc. v. Mayor & Council of the Borough of Essex Fells, 876 F. Supp. 641 (D.N.J. 1994), the owner and operator of health care facilities for disabled persons owned a 12.5-acre tract, on which it proposed to build a transitional residence. Learning of the proposal, the borough authorized condemnation of the site for use as park land, recreational use, and the protection of a critical environmental area. The institute, joined by several individual plaintiffs, sued to enjoin the borough's action, alleging both statutory (ADA and Title VIII) and constitutional violations. In a complex holding, involving, *inter alia,* issues of standing, ripeness, and abstention, the court ruled that individual plaintiffs had stated an Equal Protection claim, and that both the institute and at least one individual had stated a fair housing claim. As to the latter claim, the court wrote:

> Plaintiffs allege that Defendants' stated purpose for their action, to acquire Kessler's property for a public park, is merely a pretext. Plaintiffs allege that Defendants' actual motive is to prevent disabled persons and the health care professionals who treat them from coming to Essex Fells because of their disabilities or associations with disabled persons. . . . In the complaint, Plaintiffs have alleged all elements necessary to support a claim under the FHA.

876 F. Supp. at 664.

Suppose at trial, the borough admits it would prefer that the facility be built elsewhere, but also shows that the 12.5-acre tract would make an excellent park site. How should this case be decided under Title VIII? Under Equal Protection?

4. **NIMBY persists.** Years after passage of the 1988 amendments, the "not-in-my-back-yard" animus toward group homes continues. The May 10,

1996, issue of the *Chicago Sun-Times* tells of the town of Liberty, Illinois, and its effort to use zoning to block three group homes that would house 24 developmentally disabled clients. The town attorney informed residents that statewide he knew of 16 settled cases arising from discrimination claims against local communities; the communities had lost all but two and had paid damages ranging upwards to $240,000.

Almost every week seems to bring another reported decision of some town's effort to "zone out" a group facility intended to benefit disabled residents. Below is a sampler of these efforts:

(a) Oxford House operated a group home for 10 to 12 adults recovering from alcoholism and drug addiction in a neighborhood zoned for one-family residences. The city issued criminal citations to the owner of the house charging a zoning code violation. In remanding the enforcement suit to the lower courts to decide whether the city's actions violated Title VIII, the Supreme Court (Ginsburg, J.) held that the code's "family" definition to include a "group of five or fewer [unrelated] persons" was not an exempt maximum occupancy restriction. City of Edmonds v. Oxford House, Inc., 115 S. Ct. 1776 (1995). See Note 3, *supra*. On remand, the appeals court refused to find a Title VIII violation, noting that the zoning code allowed group homes for as many as eight handicapped residents, a higher maximum than for other unrelated groups of persons. 64 U.S.L.W. 2536 (8th Cir. 1996).

(b) Developer agreed to purchase a nine-acre parcel to construct a group home for 24 elderly handicapped persons. The city planning commission refused to rezone the property from R-1 to R-3, a multifamily district, nor would the city issue a conditional use permit for a nursing home that would also have allowed the project. The courts found no evidence of the city's failure to make a reasonable accommodation. Erdman v. City of Fort Atkinson, 84 F.3d 960 (7th Cir. 1996).

(c) Plaintiff operated a group home for up to 8 elderly people with disabilities, in most cases Alzheimer's disease or related forms of dementia. It sought permission to increase the number of residents to 15, which the county denied on grounds of inadequate parking and the possible incompatibility of off-street loading areas with the neighboring homes. (Because of the neighbors' protest, the county viewed the matter as "politically sensitive.") In granting the county summary judgment, the court held that plaintiff had shown neither intentional discrimination against persons with disabilities nor a failure to make reasonable accommodation. Bryant Woods Inn, Inc. v. Howard County, 911 F. Supp. 918 (D. Md. 1996).

(d) Owner of an adult foster care home for elderly handicapped persons sought to relocate in an R-1A zone, but the city refused to issue a building permit to renovate the new structure, nor would the city rezone. Finding discriminatory animus and the city's failure to make reasonable accommodation, the court granted an injunction, required city to pay damages (the plaintiff's lost revenues), and imposed a $20,000 civil penalty. Smith & Lee Assoc., Inc. v. City of Taylor, 872 F. Supp. 423 (E.D. Mich. 1995).

BRONK v. INEICHEN

54 F.3d 425 (7th Cir. 1995)

CUMMINGS, J.

After a brief but contentious tenancy, plaintiffs Alisha Bronk and Monica Jay vacated their Madison, Wisconsin, apartment and brought suit against their former landlord, Bernhard Ineichen. Plaintiffs, two profoundly deaf women, alleged that defendant Ineichen had discriminated against them in violation of the federal Fair Housing Act, 42 U.S.C. §3601 et seq., as amended by the Fair Housing Amendments Act of 1988 ("FHAA"); [1] Wisconsin state discrimination law, Sec. 101.22 Wis. Stat. Ann.; [2] and the Madison housing discrimination ordinance, Sec. 3.23(4), [3] by refusing to allow them to keep a dog in their rented townhouse. A jury found otherwise, returning a special verdict of no liability against Ineichen. Plaintiffs subse-

---

1. The Fair Housing Act reads as follows, in pertinent part:

[I]t shall be unlawful — . . .

(f)(1) To discriminate in the sale or rental, or otherwise to make unavailable or deny, a dwelling to any buyer or renter because of a handicap of —

(A) that buyer or renter . . . [or]

(2) To discriminate against any person in the terms, conditions, or privileges of sale or rental of a dwelling, or in the provision of services or facilities in connection with such dwelling, because of a handicap of —

(A) that person. . . .

(3) for purposes of this subsecton, discrimination includes — . . .

(B) a refusal to make reasonable accommodations in rules, policies, practices, or services, when such accommodations may be necessary to afford such person equal opportunity to use and enjoy a dwelling. . . .

42 U.S.C. §3604.

2. The Wisconsin state statute provides that:

If an individual's vision, hearing or mobility is impaired, it is discrimination for a person to refuse to rent or sell housing to the individual, cause the eviction of the individual from housing, require extra compensation from an individual as a condition of continued residence in housing or engage in the harassment of the individual because he or she keeps an animal that is specially trained to lead or assist the individual with impaired vision, hearing or mobility if all of the following apply:

a. Upon request, the individual shows to the lessor, seller or representative of the condominium association credentials issued by a school recognized by the department as accredited to train animals for individuals with impaired vision, hearing or mobility. . . .

101.22(2r)(bm) Wis. Stats. (1994).

3. The Madison Equal Opportunities Ordinance, Sec. 3.23(4)(h), forbids landlords:

to charge a higher price or to assess an extra charge, or otherwise to deny or withhold from any eyesight impaired, hearing impaired,or mobility impaired person such housing because that person owns a guide or service animal. Provided that:

1. The tenant may be charged for any damages caused by the animal . . .

2. The landlord is not required to make modifications to the premises. . . .

4. The animal's owner may be required to provide current proof that the animal has successfully passed a course of training at a bona fide school for training such animals.

Sec. 3.23(4)(h), reprinted in Pl. App. at 13.

quently moved for judgment as a matter of law or for a new trial, and now challenge on appeal the district judge's denial of these motions and certain of her evidentiary rulings. While the record demonstrates ample evidence to support the determination of no liability, we are concerned that the tendered jury instructions may have confused jury members by unnecessarily conflating local, state, and federal law. We therefore reverse and remand for a new trial.

FACTS

Plaintiffs' history of conflict with the defendant dates back to the day they signed the townhouse lease in the summer of 1992. Frequent and varied disputes soon ensued, but the sorest of all subjects was a dog named Pierre. Bronk asked Ineichen when she signed the lease whether he would permit her and Jay to have a "hearing" dog,[4] but Ineichen refused to modify his no-pets policy. Shortly after plaintiffs took possession of the townhouse, Bronk's brother Keith arrived for a visit with Pierre and another dog, Debbie. Pierre, whom Keith allegedly had trained as a hearing dog, was to remain with plaintiffs. On discovering Pierre in the townhouse, Ineichen put his foot down; he quickly evicted Pierre, who went to Bronk's parents' home in Kenosha, Wisconsin.

Over the next few months, plaintiffs argued Pierre's case with Ineichen. There is some dispute as to how much of the dialogue Ineichen, a Swiss immigrant, actually comprehended (according to his testimony, not much), but the conversations involved repeated attempts to explain the distinction between mere house pets and hearing dogs. Bronk testified, for example, that she offered to show Ineichen a certificate proving Pierre's abilities but that Ineichen showed no interest. For his part, Ineichen threatened in writing to raise Plaintiffs' rent and charge them an additional security deposit if they brought Pierre back to the townhouse, accused them of making trouble, and hinted that he would prefer them to find new living arrangements.

In November 1992, Bronk and Jay filed a complaint with the Madison Equal Opportunities Commission ("MEEOC") alleging that Ineichen had discriminated against them on the basis of both their gender and their disability. After a cursory investigation the MEEOC found probable cause to believe that Ineichen had discriminated against Bronk and Jay based on their disability (but no probable cause to support the sex discrimination claim) and sought to enjoin Ineichen from enforcing his no-pets policy against them. Ineichen reluctantly conceded and did not resist the injunction, which subsequently was issued on December 23, 1992. Relations be-

---

4. A "hearing" dog is trained to assist deaf individuals in their daily activities. The skills of such dogs can vary; Pierre allegedly was trained to alert his owners to the ringing of the doorbell, telephone or smoke alarm, and to carry notes. Pl. Br. at 3.

tween landlord and tenants never recovered, however, and in March 1993, after both women lost their jobs in Madison, Bronk and Jay relocated to Kenosha. Thereafter they brought the instant suit for damages in federal court.

At trial, defense counsel for Ineichen conceded his client's sour disposition as well as his unyielding refusal to allow Pierre in the townhouse. Nevertheless, he argued, Ineichen's obduracy did not violate plaintiffs' rights or any of the applicable statutes for the simple reasons that Pierre was not a hearing dog and plaintiffs did not have a legitimate need for him. The defense tendered evidence that Pierre had received no training beyond that purportedly provided by Keith Bronk, an amateur with no demonstrated experience in training hearing dogs; that contrary to Bronk's deposition testimony, no facility had ever certified Pierre as a hearing dog; and that the various affidavits produced by plaintiffs which set forth Pierre's assistive functions were contradictory as to what he could actually do. Maria Merrill, the women's former roommate, testified that in a brief encounter with Pierre before he was shipped off to Kenosha she did not see any evidence he was trained. An expert witness for the defense testified that intensive, professional schooling and isolation from other animals (both of which Pierre concededly lacked) were prerequisites for a hearing dog. The defense also attempted to undermine plaintiffs' claim that they needed Pierre's assistance and suffered without it. Under cross examination, plaintiffs acknowledged that they had lived together on several previous occasions in other apartments, and had never before demanded or had access to a hearing dog.

At the close of the evidence, the district judge instructed the jury regarding the claims against Ineichen. Although the plaintiffs had asserted violations of state and municipal equal protection ordinances as well as federal law, the jury did not render separate verdicts on each claim. Instead, they received a two-question special verdict form on liability that asked only whether Ineichen had discriminated against plaintiffs by failing to reasonably accommodate their disability. After deliberation, the jury returned with an answer of "no" as to both plaintiffs.

ANALYSIS

Plaintiffs raise several challenges to both the trial procedures and its result. Initially they contend that Ineichen's absolute refusal to allow Pierre in the townhouse required the district judge to issue judgment in their favor on the federal claim despite the adverse jury verdict. Acknowledging that judgment as a matter of law is appropriate "only when there can be but one conclusion from the evidence" and inferences reasonably drawn therefrom, McNabola v. Chicago Transit Authority, 10 F.3d 501, 515 (7th Cir. 1993), plaintiffs contend that evidence supported the sole conclusion that Ineichen would have rejected their request to have Pierre live with them under any circumstances. That, they contend, should have ended the jury's inquiry.

The proper focus of this trial, however, was not simply the motivation behind Ineichen's actions, but the import of these actions: regardless of his cantankerous or even malevolent attitude, did Ineichen violate the FHAA? The amended statute under which plaintiffs claim a violation bars discrimination "against any person in the terms, conditions, or privileges of . . . rental . . . of a dwelling . . . because of a handicap of . . . that . . . renter," and defines discrimination as, among other things, "a refusal to make reasonable accommodations in rules, policies, practices, or services, when such accommodations may be necessary to afford such person equal opportunity to use and enjoy a dwelling." 42 U.S.C. §3604(f)(2). Two adjectives, "reasonable" and "necessary," figure prominently in this definition, modifying both the term "accommodations" and Ineichen's obligations under the law.

The statute is worded as a broad mandate to eliminate discrimination against and equalize housing opportunities for disabled individuals. The House Report on the FHAA identifies a "clear pronouncement of a national commitment to end the unnecessary exclusion of persons with handicaps from the American mainstream," H.R. Rep. No. 711, 100th Cong., 2d Sess. 18, U.S. Code Cong. & Admin. News 1988, pp.2173, 2179, and adds that "the right to be free from housing discrimination is essential to the goal of independent living." Id. Implicit nonetheless in the text of the FHAA is the understanding that while reasonable accommodations to achieve necessary ends are required, some accommodations may not be reasonable under the circumstances and some may not be necessary to the laudable goal of inclusion. The requirement of reasonable accommodation does not entail an obligation to do everything humanly possible to accommodate a disabled person; cost (to the defendant) and benefit (to the plaintiff) merit consideration as well.[5] United States v. Village of Palatine, 37 F.3d 1230, 1234 (7th Cir. 1994) ("determining whether a requested accommodation is reasonable requires, among other things, balancing the needs of the parties involved."); see also Vande Zande v. State of Wisconsin Dep't of Administration, 44 F.3d 538 (7th Cir. 1995) (employer not required under Americans with Disabilities Act to make unreasonable accommodations, in the sense of cost exceeding benefit). Similarly, the concept of necessity requires at a minimum the showing that the desired accommodation will affirmatively enhance a disabled plaintiff's quality of life by ameliorating the effects of the disability.

Were it acknowledged by the parties in this case that Pierre was a hearing dog providing needed assistance to the plaintiffs, this case might be

---

5. As such, plaintiffs' reliance on cases involving housing discrimination on the basis of race are inapposite. The concept of reasonable accommodation has meaning only when an accommodation is required; in race discrimination cases, it is not accommodation but equal treatment that is mandated, and the notion that a defendant could explain away facially discriminatory behavior as reasonable under a cost-benefit analysis is ludicrous.

susceptible to determination as a matter of law. Balanced against a landlord's economic or aesthetic concerns as expressed in a no-pets policy, a deaf individual's need for the accommodation afforded by a hearing dog is, we think, *per se* reasonable within the meaning of the statute.[6] Pierre's skill level, however, was hotly contested, and there was ample evidence to support a jury determinaton in favor of the defendant. Other than their own protestations and self-serving affidavits which were undermined at trial, plaintiffs offered no evidence that Pierre had ever had any discernible skills. The defendant, on the other hand, introduced evidence that Pierre was not a hearing dog — the testimony of plaintiffs' former roommate and the defense expert — and impeached plaintiffs on a number of aspects of their testimony including the claim that Pierre had been certified at a training center. Given this level of uncertainty and conflicting evidence about Pierre's training level, it was well within the province of a rational jury to conclude that Pierre's utility to plaintiffs was as simple house pet and weapon against cranky landlord, not necessarily in that order. If Pierre was not necessary as a hearing dog, then his presence in the townhouse was not necessarily a reasonable accommodation.

Deference to the jury's conclusions in this matter, however, is not absolute if there is a possibility that jurors were influenced by improper considerations or by a misunderstanding of the applicable law. This brings us to plaintiffs' request for a new trial, the second and sounder basis for their appeal. Regardless of whether there was enough evidence to sustain a jury verdict of no liability against the defendant, plaintiffs allege that the verdict actually reached in this case was fatally tainted by improper jury instructions. . . .

As noted above, the district court in this case instructed the jury as if there were just one cause of action rather than three. Thus, after deciding that the appropriate question for the jury was whether or not Ineichen "discriminated against [the plaintiffs] by failing to reasonably accommodate [their] disability," the district judge combined requirements of local, state, and federal law in instructing the jury regarding the import of these terms:

> It is discrimination for a landlord to refuse to make reasonable accommodations in rules, policies, practices, or services when such accommodations may be necessary to afford a tenant equal opportunity to use and enjoy a dwelling.

---

6. In reaching this conclusion we are guided by the regulations instituting the provisions of the FHAA. 24 C.F.R. §100.204(b), promulgated by the Department of Housing and Urban Development ("HUD"), gives two examples of reasonable accommodation: the first is that of a blind applicant for rental housing who wishes to keep her seeing eye dog in a building with a no-pets policy. Clearly, the situation of a deaf resident who wishes to keep a hearing dog is analogous. With respect to the present situation, however, the example begs the question of whether Pierre was a hearing dog, in which case he falls directly within the scope of the regulations; or was merely a house pet, in which case the regulations have no explicit application to him.

Additionally, it is discrimination to refuse to rent to, or engage in the harassment of, an individual with impaired hearing because the individual keeps an animal that is specially trained to assist that individual.

It is not discriminatory or unreasonable for a landlord to require a tenant wishing to keep a hearing dog to show the landlord training credentials from a school. Also, it is not discriminatory or unreasonable for the landlord to request the tenant to accept liability for sanitation with respect to the dog and liability for damages to the premises caused by the dog. However, a landlord cannot require an additional security deposit for a hearing dog that has credentials issued by an accredited training school.

Tr. of Jury Instructions 4-5.

These instructions are a muddle. They begin with a clear statement of federal law, the reasonable accommodation requirement, which finds its echo in both the Wisconsin statute and the Madison ordinance. Fair enough: but the federal standard stops there, without providing further guidance as to what accommodations are considered reasonable. As we stated above, this determination properly belongs to the jury, which is free to consider all of the evidence — the defendant's costs, the plaintiffs' benefits, the credibility of parties' assertions as to each — in reaching a decision. Just as judgment as a matter of law in favor of plaintiffs would unfairly deprive the jury of its appropriate factfinding mission in this case, so too would judgment as a matter of law against them.

Unfortunately, the instructions took matters out of the jury's hands. Instead of allowing jurors to evaluate Ineichen's behavior in order to determine its legal significance, the district court fleshed out the concept of "reasonable accommodation" with standards borrowed from state and local law. The jury instructions thus implied that as a matter of law it was reasonable for Ineichen to demand Pierre's training credentials from a school, or to make Pierre's residence contingent on plaintiffs' accepting responsibility for damages caused by their dog.[7] A jury could logically infer from this that without school training, a dog cannot be a reasonable accommodation.

The federal statute, however, does not say any of these things, and there is no basis for imputing them into a text that is silent on the subject. While it is true that reasonable accommodation must have some meaning in the context of this case, we have already spelled out that meaning. The accommodation must facilitate a disabled individual's ability to function, and it must survive a cost-benefit balancing that takes both parties' needs into account. On one side of the equation is the degree to which Pierre aids the plaintiffs in coping with their disability. Professional credentials may be part of that sum; they are not its *sine qua non*. Plaintiffs must have been allowed to argue that by dint of Keith Bronk's efforts, Pierre accumulated enough skills so that he could actually aid in the daily functions of a

---

7. Ineichen did neither of these things, but the jury may well have applied the instruction's "rule" regarding reasonable conduct to the facts of this case.

deaf person. An instruction that elevates specific levels of training to *per se* reasonable status instead of allowing the jury to evaluate Pierre's abilities and assign its own weight to his lack of schooling essentially forecloses that argument. . . .

CONCLUSION

Judgment against plaintiffs is vacated, and a new trial is ordered. The parties will bear their own costs; on remand, Circuit Rule 36 will apply.

NOTES AND QUESTIONS

1. **What is "reasonable accommodation?"** As the lead case illustrates, whether a landlord has made reasonable accommodation is often a vexing issue, and one that is especially fact-based once we move beyond the statutory or regulatory detail. Consider some of the contexts seen in the reported decisions:

   (a) Tenant, an amputee, uses a leg prosthesis. For years, he used an adjoining lot, also owned by his landlord, to park his car; however, the rent for the parking space was separate from the rent for the apartment. Landlord refused to renew the parking lease, explaining that tenant had been uncooperative and rude and abusive to other parties using the lot. In its ruling for the landlord (reversing the trial court), the appeals court held that because of the tenant's abusive conduct, to accommodate tenant would impose an undue hardship on landlord. Rakuz v. Spunt, 39 Mass. App. 171, 654 N.E.2d 67 (1995).

   (b) Tenant suffers from multiple sclerosis. In 1990, she moved into a two-bedroom co-op apartment. Two years later she acquired an automobile. Because of her difficulty in finding curbside parking, even with a city-issued "handicapped" sticker, tenant sought an immediate parking spot within the apartment complex. No available spaces (66 spaces for 302 apartments) existed, however, and over her objection, the co-op board put tenant on the waiting list. The appeals court upheld a trial court finding that tenant should be accommodated under the statute, since three parking spaces were reserved for building workers who could park in a commercial garage. Shapiro v. Cadman Towers, Inc., 51 F.3d 328 (2d Cir. 1995).

   (c) Tenant, who has lived in her fourth-floor apartment since 1983, became largely confined to a wheelchair in 1992. Tenant made a showing that the elevator often suffered mechanical problems or broke down completely, forcing her, on such occasions to remain in her apartment or miss appointments. Landlord offered tenant a first-floor apartment in the same building or an upper-floor apartment in a second building having two elevators, but he refused to spend $65,000 to install a new (and, presumably, more reliable) elevator. The court ruled against the tenant. Congdon v. Strine, 854 F. Supp. 355 (E.D. Pa. 1994).

(d)   Tenant, a wheelchair-bound arthritic, whose mobility worsened after she moved into her fourth floor apartment, asked to be relocated to an apartment on a lower floor. Because the building had no elevator, tenant's daughter had to drag the wheelchair up and down three flights of stairs whenever tenant wished to leave the building. Landlord refused to accommodate her, even though more suitable units were available. The trial court denied summary judgment in favor of landlord. Roseborough v. Cottonwood Apartments, 1996 U.S. Dist. LEXIS 7687 (N.D. Ill. 1996).

(e)   Tenant, a 79-year-old man with symptoms both of mental disability and hearing impairment, faced eviction based on his abusive and threatening behavior. The court held that eviction could not proceed absent a showing that no reasonable accommodation would end or acceptably minimize any risk tenant posed to other residents. Roe v. Housing Auth. of the City of Boulder, 909 F. Supp. 814 (D. Colo. 1995).

2.   **Range of disabilities.** A related issue, germane to the question of "reasonable accommodation," are the disabilities for which accommodation must be attempted. The range is as broad as the human condition and may include chronic alcoholism ("what of the tenant who during a bender becomes loud and abusive?"); manic-depression ("what of the tenant who, during periods of depression, holes up and forgets to pay her rent?"); HIV-infection; drug abuse.

§10.4   Discrimination Based on Familial Status

Title VIII, and many state and local laws, bar discrimination based on familial status, a rather obscure phrase that usually translates into "adults only," or, as defined by Title VIII, discrimination against "one or more individuals (who have not attained the age of 18 years) being domiciled with a parent or [legal custodian] . . . and any person who is pregnant."

Adult communities may qualify for an exemption where the housing is intended for, and solely occupied by, persons 62 years of age or older, or intended and operated for occupancy by at least one person 55 years of age or older per unit. Regulations also permit communities to satisfy the exemption with an 80 percent occupancy factors (of persons 55 years of age or older) where significant services designed to meet the physical or social needs of older persons are present.

It may seem surprising, but age-based discrimination within the general rental market is widespread; single mothers of young children, especially, often are refused housing or otherwise disadvantaged. Sometimes, as the following case illustrates, the violation may be quite devious.

UNITED STATES v. BADGETT

976 F.2d 1176 (8th Cir. 1992)

Beam, J.

This appeal comes to us from a Fair Housing Act case filed in the district court for the Eastern District of Arkansas. The district court found a housing policy requiring single occupancy for one-bedroom apartments to be facially neutral and therefore not to be a violation of the Fair Housing Act, as amended in 1989. We reverse and remand for further proceedings consistent with this opinion.

I. BACKGROUND

Georgetown apartments, ("Georgetown"), is a 156-unit apartment complex located in Little Rock, Arkansas. J. Rogers Badgett, Sr., ("Badgett") is the sole owner of Georgetown Apartments, and Jean Brittain, ("Brittain") was employed by Badgett as a Georgetown leasing agent.[1] Until March of 1989, Georgetown was an all-adult complex that had an explicit policy which excluded families with children. Georgetown also has a long-standing policy of limiting occupancy of one-bedroom apartments to one person. Appellees admitted during discovery that they also have a policy limiting occupancy of two- and three-bedroom apartments to two people.

The applicable Little Rock Code requires that every dwelling have at least 150 square feet of floor space for the first occupant and at least 100 square feet of additional space for each additional occupant. Every room to be used for sleeping must have at least 70 square feet of space for the first occupant, and at least 50 square feet for each additional occupant. Little Rock Code §8-406(a) and (b), Appellant's Appendix at 23. Total living space in a one-bedroom apartment at Georgetown is 636 square feet. It is undisputed that the living space in a one-bedroom apartment is well in ex-

---

1. For the sake of clarity, Georgetown, Badgett and Brittain will be referred to collectively as Appellees.

cess of the legally required minimum for two persons under the Little Rock municipal code.

On May 15, 1989, Ms. Donna Mayeaux, ("Mayeaux"), and her five-year-old daughter, Lauren, went to Georgetown to inquire about renting a one-bedroom apartment. Brittain refused to show Mayeaux a one-bedroom apartment on the grounds that Georgetown did not rent one-bedroom apartments to more than one person. Brittain mentioned the two-bedroom apartments, but told Mayeaux the complex had no playground equipment, and no other children of the same age, so her daughter would have no playmates. Brittain admitted in court that such information would have discouraged her from renting at Georgetown, had she been in Mayeaux's position. Mayeaux and her daughter left without looking at an apartment.

Mayeaux filed a complaint with the Department of Housing and Urban Development ("HUD") alleging that Appellees discriminated against her on the basis of her family status. The Secretary of HUD filed a charge with a HUD administrative law judge. Badgett removed to federal court under 42 U.S.C. §3612(a) and on April 16, 1990, the United States filed a complaint in the Eastern District of Arkansas pursuant to 42 U.S.C. §3612(o).

The complaint alleged that Appellees illegally discouraged Mayeaux from renting any apartment at Georgetown on the basis of her familial status, and refused to rent Mayeaux a one-bedroom apartment because of an unreasonable occupancy standard, in violation of 42 U.S.C. §3604(a)-(d). The complaint sought monetary damages, and an injunction prohibiting Appellees from further discrimination. Trial was held on August 28, 1991. At the conclusion of the trial, the court ruled from the bench in favor of Appellees. Judgment was filed on August 29, 1991. The government appeals this decision.

II.   DISCUSSION

The district court held that the occupancy standard at issue, which limited occupancy of one-bedroom apartments to one person, did not violate the Fair Housing Act because the requirement was facially neutral. In doing so, the district court applied an incorrect analysis. HUD has adopted the three-part test set forth in McDonnell Douglas Corp. v. Green, 411 U.S. 792, 93 S.Ct. 1817, 36 L.Ed.2d 668 (1973) for evaluating claims of discrimination under the Fair Housing Act. See, HUD v. Blackwell, 908 F.2d 864 (11th Cir. 1990); Pinchback v. Armistead Homes Corp., 689 F. Supp. 541 (D. Md. 1988), aff'd in part, vacated in part, 907 F.2d 1447 (4th Cir. 1990), cert. denied, 111 S. Ct. 515 (1990). The McDonnell Douglas test recognizes that direct proof of unlawful discrimination is rarely available. Therefore, after a plaintiff makes a prima facie case, a presumption of illegality arises and respondent has the burden of articulating a legitimate, non-discriminatory justification for the challenged policy. This scheme is routinely used in housing and employment discrimination cases. The test is:

> First, the plaintiff has the burden of proving a prima facie case of discrimination by a preponderance of the evidence. Second, if the plaintiff sufficiently establishes a prima facie case, the burden shifts to the defendant to articulate some legitimate undiscriminatory [sic] reason for its action. Third, if the defendant satisfies this burden, the plaintiff has the opportunity to prove by a preponderance that the legitimate reasons asserted by the defendant are in fact mere pretext.

Pollitt v. Bramel, 669 F. Supp. 172, 175 (S.D. Ohio 1987), (citations omitted). The district court failed to apply the *McDonnell Douglas* standard, and therefore erred as a matter of law.

The elements of a prima facie case of discrimination will vary from case to case, depending on the allegations and the circumstances. HUD has a rule of thumb that an occupancy policy of two persons per bedroom is presumptively reasonable. Memorandum for Regional Counsel: Fair Housing Enforcement Policy, Intervenor's Brief, Appendix B at 2 (hereinafter "HUD Memorandum"); but see, United States v. Lepore, No. 1:CV-90-1956, slip op., 1991 WL 330890 (M.D. Pa. Dec. 23, 1991) (Appellant's Appendix at 35) (finding that a two-person occupancy restriction discriminated on the basis of familial status, and therefore violated the Fair Housing Act) (hereinafter *"Lepore"*). HUD's general rule does not mean that a single occupancy requirement is always invalid, but it does render such a requirement suspect; particularly when the single occupancy requirement is accompanied by other factors enumerated in the HUD Memorandum.

Some of the factors identified in the HUD Memorandum are applicable to Georgetown. Georgetown previously marketed itself as an "adults only" complex. In addition, Georgetown has "taken other steps to discourage families with children from living in its housing," HUD Memorandum at 4, through Brittain's representations of the disadvantages of living in the complex. The mere fact that the one person/one bedroom requirement was "applied to everybody, whether they be married [sic] or whether they be couples [sic] seeking to live together without benefit of marriage or whether they be a child [sic]," Transcript of Court's Findings, Addendum to Appellant's Brief at 3, is not sufficient to demonstrate compliance with the Fair Housing Act. If the result of this policy is a disparate impact on a protected class, facial neutrality will not save the restriction from violating the Act. McDonnell Douglas Corp. v. Green, 411 U.S. 792 (1973); See also, FEHC v. Merribrook Apartments, FEHC Decision #89-19 (Calif. Fair Empl. & Hous. Comm'n, Nov. 11, 1988) (one person per bedroom restriction used to maintain a no children policy).

The district court stated: "if Congress really intended that you could not have a restriction on one bedroom apartments, they would have said it." Transcript of Court's Findings, Addendum to Appellant's Brief at page 3. The issue in this case, however, is not whether Congress intended that there be *no* restrictons on one-bedroom apartments, but whether the particular restrictions at issue in this case violate the Act. The Act specifically provides that:

> [n]othing in this subchapter limits the applicability of any reasonable local, State, or Federal restriction regarding the maximum number of occupants permitted to occupy a dwelling.

42 U.S.C. §3607(b)(1). The restrictions at issue in this case are not governmentally imposed, and are far in excess of restrictions imposed by the applicable municipal code. HUD, the agency charged with enforcing the statute, has stated:

> In this regard, it must be noted that, in connection with a complaint alleging discrimination on the basis of familial status, the Department will carefully examine any such *non-governmental* restriction to determine whether it operates unreasonably to limit or exclude families with children.

24 C.F.R. Chapter I, Subchapter A, Appendix I at 693 (1991) (emphasis added). Rather than authorizing *any* facially neutral occupancy standard, the Fair Housing Act requires that a court examine the totality of the circumstances to determine whether the facially neutral standard results in discrimination against a protected class. *Lepore,* slip op. at 12; See also, Village of Arlington Heights v. Metropolitan Housing Dev. Corp., 429 U.S. 252, 266 (1977).

The district court placed significant emphasis on the fact that Brittain did not refuse to rent Mayeaux a two-bedroom apartment. There are three problems with this reliance. First, the issue is not whether any housing was made available to Mayeaux, but whether she was denied the housing she desired on impermissible grounds. HUD v. Riverbend Club Apartments, No. 04-89-0676-1 (Oct. 15, 1991), Intervenor's Brief, Appendix A at 9, n. 9. Second, there is a significant increase in cost between a one-bedroom and a two-bedroom apartment. Third, Brittain volunteered discouraging information which makes it understandable that Mayeaux did not wish to view a two-bedroom apartment.[3] These representations qualify as "other steps [taken] to discourage families with children from living in its housing." HUD Memorandum at 4. A prima facie case of discrimination was clearly presented, and thus the burden shifts to Appellees to provide a non-discriminatory explanation for the restriction.

---

3. Furthermore, Appellees admitted that occupancy of the two-bedroom and three-bedroom apartments is restricted to two persons. As a result of this policy, no family which consisted of two parents and a child, or a single parent and two children could rent any apartment at Georgetown. While there is no allegation that these policies were adopted in response to the 1989 amendments to the Fair Housing Act, these policies prevent the majority of families with children from living at Georgetown, and therefore violate the Act.

The only explanation offered by Appellees is the limited availability of parking. We find, as a matter of law, that no reasonable fact-finder could accept this proffered justification as anything other than a pretext. Mayeaux's five year old daughter could not possibly affect the availability of parking spaces. While parking may indeed be at a premium at Georgetown, the occupancy restriction is not a reasonable means of dealing with the problem. See *Lepore,* slip op. at 26-28. There is nothing in the restriction to prevent a resident of a one-bedroom apartment from having more than one car, and the restriction does not take into account the fact that infants will not require parking spaces. Appellees have never attempted any alternative method of allocating parking.

We therefore find that the occupancy restrictions imposed by Georgetown violate sections 3604(a)-(d) of the Fair Housing Act. Based on this conclusion, we remand this matter to the district court and direct that the district court enjoin Georgetown from discriminating on the basis of familial status, and that it determine the affirmative steps that may be necessary to notify the public that Georgetown will be operated in a manner that comports with the Fair Housing Act. On remand, the district court should also determine any other appropriate remedy to be awarded Mayeaux.

III.   CONCLUSION

For the reasons stated above, we reverse the judgment of the district court and remand for further proceedings consistent with this opinion.

NOTES AND QUESTIONS

1. **"Per room" occupancy limits as a discriminatory vehicle.** Compare the *Badgett* policy (one person, one bedroom) with that in United States v. Tropic Seas, Inc., 887 F. Supp. 1347 (D. Hawaii 1995), which limited occupancy to two persons in studio and one-bedroom apartments. The government was able to show that this occupancy limit would exclude 92 to 95 percent of all families with children but only 19 to 21 percent of families without children in the relevant area. This showing, coupled with evidence that the apartment complex had not so long before restricted children under age 14 (as well as a possibly damaging admission), established a Title VIII violation.

Suppose that the government in *Tropic Seas* could only show the disparate impact of the respondent's policy on families with children. Is that enough? As the landlord's attorney, what arguments would you make to try to overcome a prima facie case of disparate impact?

2. **Zoning and apartments.** No zoning that we know of, except that permitting adult or retirement communities, would openly seek to keep residential areas child-free. But in many suburban communities, zoning's

treatment of rental apartments can significantly limit the school-age population. This results from the "not as of right" status many local laws give to multiple dwellings, requiring the developer to obtain a special exception permit before he is able to build. As part of the special exception process, the town and developer might bargain over the project's physical design and layout; this can lead to restrictions on the number of multibedroom units and, ultimately, on the number of large families who will live there. Has there been a prima facie Title VIII violation when plaintiffs can show a town's "preference" for smaller-unit apartments?

3. **The roots of prejudice.** What is it about children and teenagers that landlords so object to? Is it "prejudice" if the objections are often well-founded? Should legitimate prejudice ever be deemed unlawful discrimination? Consider the following: The owner of a 10-unit apartment building would like to refuse to rent a one-bedroom unit to a divorced mother of a teenaged son. All of the other building tenants are either childless or have grown children. The owner has had several prior bad experiences with teenaged occupants who were often noisy and disruptive, or whose friends were. Why shouldn't the owner be able to adopt a generic exclusionary policy? Might age-based discrimination sometimes be used to mask racial or gender-based discrimination?

Chapter 11

Commodification: Wealth and the Marketplace

You may recall Andrus v. Allard with which we opened this text. At issue was whether Congress, in order to protect our national bird, might ban the sale of eagle feathers. The court's analysis assumed that were it not for the statute, there would be no legal or moral objection to traffic in wild creatures, dead or alive. Yet, even as to this limited proposition, persons who believe in the sanctity of all life would disagree.

In this chapter, we will explore whether whatever has possible commercial value can be the object of commerce. The answer, obviously, is no: For example, even if you were willing to sell your vote in the next election, the law would not let you do so. What if this were wartime: Could you pay someone to replace you in the draft? The answer, again obviously, would be no, yet during the Civil War, well-to-do conscripts were allowed to avoid military service if they could "bribe" someone, usually a poor immigrant, to serve in their stead.

More so than anything we have considered so far, the limits of commodification touch deeply held moral views. This exploration will force us to examine our most basic beliefs as we try to articulate what those are and why we hold them.

We begin by talking about whether people should be the object of property. The Thirteenth Amendment ended slavery, but an individual's right to sell his body or bodily organs, or to sell the fruit of her womb, or to lease the womb itself, are problems that the legal system must struggle with even as you read.

§11.1 Slavery

Why does the judge in the next case feel so awkward about his decision? Does he seem to feel caught between two strains in the liberal tradition?

1111

STATE v. MANN
_____

13 N.C. (2 Dev.) 263 (1829)

The defendant was indicted for an assault and battery upon Lydia, the slave of one Elizabeth Jones. On the trial it appeared that the defendant had hired the slave for a year; that during the term the slave had committed some small offense, for which the defendant undertook to chastise her; that while in the act of so doing the slave ran off, whereupon the defendant called upon her to stop, which being refused, he shot at and wounded her.

His Honor, Judge DANIEL, charged the jury that if they believed the punishment inflicted by the defendant was cruel and unwarrantable, and disproportionate to the offense committed by the slave, that in law the defendant was guilty, as he had only a special property in the slave. A verdict was returned for the State, and the defendant appealed.

No counsel for the defendant.

The Attorney-General, for the State.

RUFFIN, J. A Judge cannot but lament when such cases as the present are brought into judgment. It is impossible that the reasons on which they go can be appreciated, but where institutions similar to our own exist and are thoroughly understood. The struggle, too, in the Judge's own breast between the feelings of the man and the duty of the magistrate is a severe one, presenting strong temptation to put aside such questions if it be possible. It is useless, however, to complain of things inherent in our political state. And it is criminal in a Court to avoid any responsibility which the laws impose. With whatever reluctance, therefore, it is done, the Court is compelled to express an opinion upon the extent of the dominion of the master over the slave in North Carolina.

The indictment charges a battery on Lydia, a slave of Elizabeth Jones. Upon the face of the indictment, the case is the same as S. v. Hall, 9 N.C., 582. No fault is found with the rule then adopted; nor would be, it were now open. But it is not open; for the question, as it relates to a battery on a slave by a stranger, is considered as settled by that case. But the evidence makes this a different case. Here the slave had been hired by the defendant, and was in his possession; and the battery was committed during the period of hiring. With the liabilities of the hirer to the general owner for an injury permanently impairing the value of the slave no rule now laid down is intended to interfere. That is left upon the general doctrine of bailment. The inquiry here is whether a cruel and unreasonable battery on a slave by the hirer is indictable. The Judge below instructed the jury that it is.

He seems to have put it on the ground that the defendant had but a special property. Our laws uniformly treat the master or other person having the possession and command of the slave as entitled to the same extent of authority. The object is the same — the services of the slave; and the same powers must be confided. In a criminal proceeding, and indeed in

reference to all other persons but the general owner, the hirer and possessor of a slave, in relation to both rights and duties, is, for the time being,
the owner. This opinion would, perhaps, dispose of this particular case; because the indictment, which charges a battery upon the slave of Elizabeth
Jones, is not supported by proof of a battery upon defendant's own slave;
since different justifications may be applicable to the two cases. But upon
the general question whether the owner is answerable *criminaliter* for a battery upon his own slave, or other exercise of authority or force not forbidden by statute, the Court entertains but little doubt. That he is so liable has
never yet been decided; nor, as far as is known, been hitherto contended.
There have been no prosecutions of the sort. The established habits and
uniform practice of the country in this respect is the best evidence of the
portion of power deemed by the whole community requisite to the preservation of the master's dominion. If we thought differently we could not set
our notions in array against the judgment of everybody else, and say that
this or that authority may be safely lopped off. This had indeed been as-
similated at the bar to the other domestic relations; and arguments drawn
from the well-established principles which confer and restrain the authority of the parent over the child, the tutor over the pupil, the master over
the apprentice, have been pressed on us. The Court does not recognize
their application. There is no likeness between the cases. They are in opposition to each other, and there is an impassable gulf between them. The
difference is that which exists between freedom and slavery — and a greater
cannot be imagined. In the one, the end in view is the happiness of the
youth, born to equal rights with that governor, on whom the duty devolves
of training the young to usefulness in a station which he is afterwards to
assume among freemen. To such an end, and with such a subject, moral
and intellectual instruction seem the natural means; and for the most part
they are found to suffice. Moderate force is superadded only to make the
other effectual. If that fails it is better to leave the party to his own head-
strong passions and the ultimate correction of the law than to allow it to be
immoderately inflicted by a private person. With slavery it is far otherwise.
The end is the profit of the master, his security and public safety; the subject, one doomed in his own person and his posterity, to live without knowledge and without the capacity to make anything his own, and to toil that
another may reap the fruits. What moral considerations shall be addressed
to such a being to convince him what, it is impossible but that the most
stupid must feel and know can never be true — that he is thus to labor upon
a principle of natural duty, or for the sake of his own personal happiness,
such services can only be expected from one who has no will of his own;
who surrenders his will in implicit obedience to that of another. Such obedience is the consequence only of uncontrolled authority over the body.
There is nothing else which can operate to produce the effect. The power
of the master must be absolute to render the submission of the slave perfect. I most freely confess my sense of the harshness of this proposition; I

feel it as deeply as any man can; and as a principle of moral right every person in his retirement must repudiate it. But in the actual condition of things it must be so. There is no remedy. This discipline belongs to the state of slavery. They cannot be disunited without abrogating at once the rights of the master and absolving the slave from his subjection. It constitutes the curse of slavery to both the bond and free portion of our population. But it is inherent in the relation of master and slave. . . .

I repeat that I would gladly have avoided this ungrateful question. But being brought to it the Court is compelled to declare that while slavery exists amongst us in its present state, or until it shall seem it to the legislature to interpose express enactments to the contrary, it will be the imperative duty of the Judges to recognize the full dominion of the owner over the slave, except where the exercise of it is forbidden by statute. And this we do upon the ground that this dominion is essential to the value of slaves as property, to the security of the master, and the public tranquility, greatly dependent upon their subordination; and, in fine, as most effectually securing the general protection and comfort of the slaves themselves.

Reversed and judgment entered for defendant.

NOTES AND QUESTIONS

1.   **Understanding the facts.** Why did Lydia run away? What did Mann do then?

2.   **Holding.** What did the court hold?

3.   **Reasoning.** Why? Were the reasons the court gave addressed to the equities in the case at hand, or to general societal considerations?

4.   **Internal conflict.** Why did the judge feel a struggle "between the feelings of man and the duty of the magistrate"?

PATRICIA J. WILLIAMS, ON BEING THE OBJECT OF PROPERTY

14 Signs: Journal of Women in Culture and Society 5, 5-6 (1988)

. . . I have been picking through the ruins for my roots.

What I know of my mother's side of the family begins with my great-great-grandmother. Her name was Sophie and she lived in Tennessee. In 1850, she was about twelve years old. I know that she was purchased when she was eleven by a white lawyer named Austin Miller and was immediately impregnated by him. She gave birth to my great-grandmother Mary, who was taken away from her to be raised as a house servant. I know nothing more of Sophie (she was, after all, a black single mother — in today's terms — suffering the anonymity of yet another statistical teenage pregnancy). While I don't remember what I was told about Austin Miller before I decided to go to law school, I do remember that just before my first day of class, my mother said, in a voice full of secretive reassurance, "The Millers were lawyers, so you have it in your blood."

When my mother told me that I had nothing to fear in law school, that law was "in my blood," she meant it in a very complex sense. First and foremost, she meant it defiantly; she meant that no one should make me feel inferior because someone else's father was a judge. She wanted me to reclaim that part of my heritage from which I had been disinherited, and she wanted me to use it as a source of strength and self-confidence. At the same time, she was asking me to claim a part of myself that was the dispossessor of another part of myself; she was asking me to deny that disenfranchised little black girl of myself that felt powerless, vulnerable and, moreover, rightly felt so.

In somewhat the same vein, Mother was asking me not to look to her as a role model. She was devaluing that part of herself that was not Harvard and refocusing my vision to that part of herself that was hard-edged, proficient, and Western. She hid the lonely, black, defiled-female part of herself and pushed me forward as the projection of a competent self, a cool rather than despairing self, a masculine rather than a feminine self.

I took this secret of my blood into the Harvard milieu with both the pride and the shame with which my mother had passed it along to me. I found myself in the situation described by Marguerite Duras, in her novel *The Lover:* "We're united in a fundamental shame at having to live. It's here we are at the heart of our common fate, the fact that [we] are our mother's children, the children of a candid creature murdered by society. We're on the side of society which has reduced her to despair. Because of what's been done to our mother, so amiable, so trusting, we hate life, we hate ourselves."

Reclaiming that from which one has been disinherited is a good thing. Self-possession in the full sense of that expression is the companion to self-knowledge. Yet claiming for myself a heritage the weft of whose genesis is my own disinheritance is a profoundly troubling paradox. . . .

Others have analyzed whiteness as a property right. One of the simplest, and most dramatic, illustrations of this was a test by a black professional who was surprised with the low appraisal rate of his house. He removed all of his family pictures, and replaced them with pictures of his secretary's family, who was white, when the appraiser came the secretary and her son were present, the difference in the appraisal was substantial (from low $70,000s to $125,000). "Black Tax," or Hidden Cost of Skin Color, National Public Radio, May 22, 1992 (Morning Edition). See also Plessy v. Ferguson, 163 U.S. 537 (1896), the case that upheld the constitutionality of segregation in the South; in particular the attorney's argument that "the reputation of being white [is] property. Indeed, is it not the most valuable sort of property, being the master-key that unlocks the golden door of opportunity?"; Brief for Plaintiff in Error at 9, *Plessy* (No. 210).

CHERYL T. HARRIS, WHITENESS AS PROPERTY

106 Harv. L. Rev. 1709, 1710, 1713-1714 (1993)

In the 1930s, some years after my mother's family became part of the great river of Black migration that flowed north, my Mississippi-born grandmother was confronted with the harsh matter of economic survival for herself and her two daughters. Having separated from my grandfather, who himself was trapped on the fringes of economic marginality, she took one long hard look at her choices and presented herself for employment at a major retail store in Chicago's central business district. This decision would have been unremarkable for a white woman in similar circumstances, but for my grandmother, it was an act of both great daring and self-denial, for in so doing she was presenting herself as a white woman. In the parlance of racist America, she was "passing."

Her fair skin, straight hair, and aquiline features had not spared her from the life of sharecropping into which she had been born in anywhere/ nowhere, Mississippi — the outskirts of Yazoo City. But in the burgeoning landscape of urban America, anonymity was possible for a Black person with "white" features. She was transgressing boundaries, crossing borders, spinning on margins, traveling between dualities of Manichean space, rigidly bifurcated into light/dark, good/bad, white/Black. No longer immediately identifiable as "Lula's daughter," she could thus enter the white world, albeit on a false passport, not merely passing, but trespassing.

Every day my grandmother rose from her bed in her house in a Black enclave on the south side of Chicago, sent her children off to a Black school, boarded a bus full of Black passengers, and rode to work. No one at her job ever asked if she was Black; the question was unthinkable. By virtue of the employment practices of the "fine establishment" in which she worked, she could not have been. Catering to the upper-middle class, understated tastes required that Blacks not be allowed.

She quietly went about her clerical tasks, not once revealing her true identity. She listened to the women with whom she worked discuss their worries — their children's illnesses, their husbands' disappointments, their boyfriends' infidelities — all of the mundane yet critical things that made up their lives. She came to know them but they did not know her, for my grandmother occupied a completely different place. That place — where white supremacy and economic domination meet — was unknown turf to her white co-workers. They remained oblivious to the worlds within worlds that existed just beyond the edge of their awareness and yet were present in their very midst.

Each evening, my grandmother, tired and worn, retraced her steps home, laid aside her mask, and reentered herself. Day in and day out, she made herself invisible, then visible again, for a price too inconsequential to do more than barely sustain her family and at a cost too precious to conceive. She left the job some years later, finding the strain too much to bear. . . .

My grandmother's story illustrates the valorization of whiteness as treasured property in a society structured on racial caste. . . . Even though the law is neither uniform nor explicit in all instances, in protecting settled expectations based on white privilege, American law has recognized a property interest in whiteness that, although unacknowledged, now forms the background against which legal disputes are framed, argued, and adjudicated. . . .

Slavery produced a peculiar, mixed category of property and humanity — a hybrid possessing inherent instabilities that were reflected in its treatment and ratification by the law. The dual and contradictory character of slaves as property and persons was exemplified in the Representation Clause of the Constitution. Representation in the House of Representatives was apportioned on the basis of population computed by counting all persons and "three-fifths of all other persons" — slaves. Gouverneur Morris's remarks before the Constitutional Convention posed the essential question: "Upon what principle is it that slaves shall be computed in the representation? Are they men? Then make them Citizens & let them vote? Are they property? Why then is no other property included?" . . .

Because the "presumption of freedom [arose] from color [white]" and the "black color of the race [raised] the presumption of slavery," whiteness became a shield from slavery, a highly volatile and unstable form of property. In the form adopted in the United States, slavery made human beings market-alienable and in so doing, subjected human life and personhood — that which is most valuable — to the ultimate devaluation. Because whites could not be enslaved or held as slaves, the racial line between white and Black was extremely critical; it became a line of protection and demarcation from the potential threat of commodification, and it determined the allocation of the benefits and burdens of this form of property. White identity and whiteness were sources of privilege and protection; their absence meant being the object of property. . . .

THOMAS L. HASKELL, CAPITALISM AND THE ORIGINS OF THE HUMANITARIAN SENSIBILITY, PART 1

90 Am. Hist. Rev. 339 (1985)

An unprecedented wave of humanitarian reform sentiment swept through the societies of Western Europe, England, and North America in the hundred years following 1750. Among the movements spawned by this new sensibility, the most spectacular was that to abolish slavery. Although its morality was often questioned before 1750, slavery was routinely defended and hardly ever condemned outright, even by the most scrupulous moralists. . . .

Now let us proceed to a more elaborate exercise designed to show how inescapable conventions are in the allocation of moral responsibility, and how the conventions themselves change in time. Let us call this the "case of the starving stranger." As I sit at my desk writing this essay, and as you, the reader, now sit reading it, both of us are aware that some people in Phnom Penh, Bombay, Rangoon, the Sahel, and elsewhere will die next week of starvation. They are strangers; all we know about them is that they will die. We also know that it would be possible for any one of us to sell a car or a house, buy an airline ticket, fly to Bombay or wherever, seek out at least one of those starving strangers, and save his life, or at the very least extend it. We could be there tomorrow, and we really could save him. Now to admit that we have it in our power to prevent this person's death by starvation is to admit that our inaction — our preference for sitting here, reading and writing about moral responsibility, going on with our daily routine — is a necessary condition for the stranger's death. But for our refusal to go to his aid, he would live.

This means that we are causally involved in his death. Our refusal to give aid is one of the many conditions that, all together, make up what John Stuart Mill called the cause "philosophically speaking" of this event. Now to say that we are causally involved is, of course, not to say that our failure to act is "the cause" of his death: it is only one among many conditions, and not every condition is properly regarded as "the cause." But the troubling fact remains that *but for* our inaction this evil event would not occur.

Why do we not go to his aid? It is not for lack of ethical maxims teaching us that it is good to help strangers. Presumably we all subscribe to the Golden Rule, and certainly if we were starving we would hope that some stranger would care enough to drop his daily routine and come to our aid. Yet we sit here. We do not do for him what we would have him do for us. Are we hypocrites? Are we engaged in self-deception? Do we in any sense *intend* his death?

I think not — unless, of course, we wish to stretch the meaning of intention way beyond customary usage, so that it indiscriminately lumps together premeditated murder with a failure to avail ourselves of an opportunity to do good. There is much more to say about the way we arrive at judgments of both causation and intention, but for my purposes it is enough to observe that the limits of moral responsibility have to be drawn somewhere and that the "somewhere" will always fall far short of much pain and suffering that we could do something to alleviate. What is crucially important to see is that we never include within our circle of responsibility all those events in which we are causally involved. We always set limits that fall short of our power to intervene. Whatever limits we do set can therefore always be challenged and made to look arbitrary or "selective" by insistent questioning — for they are finally nothing more than conventions. Good reasons can be given for preferring some conventions to others, but there is no escaping convention itself and even a degree of arbitrariness in our choice of which to accept. The necessity for being selective is built into the nature of the problem. Even the person who tries to extend his limits to encompass all those events in which he is causally involved will, in his futile efforts to save all the starving strangers in the world, have to choose whether to go first to Bombay or Calcutta and whether to begin with person X or person Y. These choices will appear no less arbitrary (at least to the stranger not chosen) than the convention that permits you and me to exclude this predictable consequence of our inaction from the category of intention, and to sit here with only a pinprick of guilt as we contemplate our involvement in the stranger's death. . . .

These preconditions drawn from the case of the starving stranger help clarify both the way in which revolutions in moral sensibility ought to be conceived and the way in which they are to be explained. First, we ought to construe major alterations of sensibility such as the rise of abolitionism as the result of shifts in the conventional boundaries of moral responsibility. Thus, what emerged in the century after 1750 was not, in the first instance at least, either a new configuration of class interests or a novel set of values geared to the hegemony of a rising class. Instead, the principal novelty was an expansion of the conventional limits of moral responsibility that prompted people whose values may have remained as traditional (and as unrelated to class) as the Golden Rule to behave in ways that were unprecedented and not necessarily well suited to their material interests. What happened was that the conventional limits of moral responsibility observed by an influential minority in society expanded to encompass evils that previously had fallen outside anyone's operative sphere of responsibility. The evils in question are of course the miseries of the slave, which had always been recognized but which before the eighteenth century had possessed the same cognitive and moral status that the misery of the starving stranger in Ethiopia has for us today. . . .

The final excerpt, by Anthony T. Kronman and Richard Posner, asks whether contracts for self-enslavement should be enforced. Do the writers ultimately conclude that such contracts should not be enforced? On what grounds? Given the American consensus on this issue, is it even necessary to state and defend a rationale? How does the Kronman and Posner analysis reflect the underlying imagery of autonomous persons with rights making choices? The rhetoric of "paternalism" is part and parcel of this vision. How?

ANTHONY T. KRONMAN & RICHARD POSNER, THE ECONOMICS OF CONTRACT LAW

253-254, 256-260 (1979)

NOTE ON PATERNALISM

The law of contracts recognizes many important limitations on what is often, and unhelpfully, called "freedom of contract." For example, two parties cannot create a binding contract to commit a crime (or a tort on a third party); nor can they by contractual arrangement alter established rules of evidence or certain substantive rules of law such as the formal requisites of negotiability in the law of commercial paper. A minor who contracts to do something is generally not bound by a promise extracted at gunpoint. Contracts in restraint of trade, oral contracts for the sale of land, penal clauses, promises unsupported by consideration, contracts for the sale of children (or, for that matter, adults) and a host of other promises are likewise unenforceable.

The limitations that the law imposes on an individual's freedom of contract assume different forms and are justified in different ways. For example, the unenforceability of an oral promise to sell land is a result of the *manner* in which the promise is expressed, and is most often justified in terms of the "cautionary" and "evidentiary" functions of the Statute of Frauds. . . .[1] In contrast, the invalidity of a promise given under duress (or motivated by a fraudulent misrepresentation) is a consequence of the *circumstances* in which the promise is in some sense involuntary. . . . In the case of a promise to commit a burglary it is the *content* of the promise, rather than its form or accompanying circumstances, that cause it to be unenforceable, and the reason for not enforcing a promise of this sort is that it is injurious to third parties.

At first glance, the existence of legal limitations on freedom of contract may appear to contradict a fundamental assumption of the positive economic analysis of law. However, although economic analysis does rest upon a strong conception of individual autonomy, not all limitations on an individual's freedom of contract are inconsistent with this conception. For example, the rule that certain contracts must be in writing to be enforceable, while in one sense limiting an individual's freedom of contract, is intended to reduce the risk normally associated with oral transactions and to protect the interests of third parties. If we assume that these advantages are especially great in the cases to which the Statute of Frauds applies, it is reasonable to view the Statute as an efficiency-promoting device whose con-

---

1. The Statute of Frauds requires certain contracts to be written, not oral, in order to avoid fraud in specific situations. See U.C.C. §2-201 (1990).

straints reduce the cost of contracting and thus facilitate rather than retard the voluntary transfer of entitlements. Consequently, although the Statute of Frauds limits freedom of contract, it imposes constraints which would in all likelihood be acceptable even to those whose freedom the Statute restricts if they were to deliberate about the matter in a rational and disinterested fashion.

However, while many limitations on freedom of contract may be consistent with even the strongest conception of individual autonomy, at least one class of limitations is not. These are limitations which may be called paternalistic. As we use the term, a limitation on an individual's freedom of contract is paternalistic if the sole justification for imposing it is to promote or protect the individual's own welfare (or happiness or good). If a particular limitation is imposed in order to reduce the costs of the bargaining process (for example, by insuring its procedural propriety), or to protect the interests of third parties, it can be justified on nonpaternalistic economic grounds.

Arguably, a number of the limitations the law imposes on an individual's freedom of contract are paternalistic in nature. For example, it has been suggested that the doctrine of unconscionability is often used in a paternalistic fashion, to protect poor and uneducated consumers from the consequences of their own bad bargains. . . .

It would be impossible, in a brief note, to consider every constraint on freedom of contract which *is* arguably paternalistic, and we limit our discussion here to three: the contractual incapacity of minors, the invalidity of contracts of self-enslavement, and the unenforceability of penal clauses. . . .

II.   CONTRACTS OF SELF-ENSLAVEMENT

Our legal system does not permit individuals to sell themselves into slavery, or to pledge their personal liberty as collateral for a loan. Of course, even if contracts of self-enslavement were enforceable, few individuals in our society would make them. But what is the justification for disallowing even the rare individual who wishes to enslave himself, or to pledge his freedom as security, from doing so?[3]

The simplest answer would be that slavery — whether self-imposed or not — is immoral and must therefore be suppressed. When stated in this general form, the argument against self-enslavement is not (at least not nec-

---

3. John Stuart Mill argues that contracts of self-enslavement are prohibited because the would-be slave "defeats, in his own case, the very purpose which is the justification of allowing him to dispose of himself. He is no longer free; but is thenceforth in a position which has no longer the presumption in its favor, that would be afforded by his voluntarily remaining in it. The principle of freedom cannot require that he should be free not to be free. It is not freedom to be allowed to alienate his freedom." Utilitarianism, Liberty, and Representative Government 213 (A. D. Lindsay ed., 1951). Mill's argument is criticized by Gerald Dworkin in his essay Paternalism in Morality and the Law 107, 118 (Richard A. Wasserstrom ed., 1971).

essarily) either utilitarian or paternalistic. For example, suppose one believes that slavery is immoral because it violates a divine command to treat all human beings as equals. On this view, the justification for prohibiting self-enslavement has nothing to do with the welfare of the would-be slave himself or even society as a whole: the prohibition is justified because it is required in order to satisfy an obligation owed to God. But since our principal concern is the conflict between paternalism and economic theory, we shall limit our discussion to paternalistic and utilitarian defenses of the prohibition on self-enslavement.

One intriguing explanation of the unenforceability of contracts of self-enslavement is offered by Tullock:

> The individual who would be willing to pledge himself in order to obtain additional capital the following year may this year think that it would be unwise. He knows that next year he would be likely to take a course of action which considered from the distant perspective of the present, seems undesirable. Under the circumstances, he would like to bind himself today not to make such a mortgage agreement in the future. . . . The situation is the same as that of a compulsive drunkard who hires private detectives to forcibly prevent him from taking a drink. When considered calmly, most of us would agree that we should not take the risk of enslavement and also that we might make a fatal mistake some time in the future. Thus, a prohibition on contracts containing clauses involving enslavement is similar to voting for prohibition because we feel that we are too subject to temptation.

Tullock's general argument could be used to justify any conceivable limitation on freedom of contract. If the argument is convincing in the case of contracts of enslavement, it is only because we believe that the disadvantages of being a slave are so great that no one in his "right mind" would risk enslavement. The following line of reasoning lends some support to this view: Although human beings pursue many different ends in life, the achievement of any end — whatever it might be — can never constitute a good for the individual who achieves it unless it is accompanied by a sense of self-worth or self-respect. A feeling of self-respect is possible only if the individual in question regards the ends guiding his conduct as his own, as ends which he himself has chosen to pursue. A slave has few opportunities to pursue ends of his own choosing. In this respect, slavery may be distinguished, at least in degree, from other forms of domination — for example, that of an employer over his employee. A slave will therefore find it especially difficult to sustain a sense of self-respect, without which life has little meaning. Hence a person in his right mind would never choose enslavement.

Although this argument gives some content to Tullock's explanation of the unenforceability of contracts of enslavement, it is not entirely convincing. Tullock himself suggests an example which substantially weakens the argument from self-respect. Suppose that in return for promising to be a slave, a father receives food to feed his starving children (or enough money to finance their education). By sacrificing his own interest, the father advances the interest of his children in a way he might otherwise be unable to do. In this very act of sacrifice, the father may well attain his highest and most cherished good and provide the foundation for a lasting sense of self-respect.

A second justification for the unenforceability of contracts of enslavement attempts to avoid the paternalism of Tullock's approach by invoking the interest of third parties. According to this view, a contract of enslavement ought to be invalidated, even if it is in the best interest of the promisor, because the institution of slavery is offensive to most people in our society and its legal legitimation would cause them moral anguish. Private parties should not be permitted to enforce a contract which imposes these substantial (psychic) costs on others for the same reason that two people should not be allowed to make an enforceable contract to commit a tort on a third.[6]

This kind of argument is frequently made in order to justify the imposition of limitations on individual conduct in a way which avoids the embarrassments of paternalism. The problem with the argument is that it obliterates the line between what is sometimes called "self-regarding" and "other-regarding"[7] conduct and can therefore be used to justify virtually any limitation on individual freedom.

To be persuasive, an argument which rests upon an appeal to the interests of third parties must show, in any particular case, that the interests in question are sufficiently important to justify the limitation. In the case of slavery, there are two different ways in which this might be done. First, one might offer empirical evidence to show that most Americans are, as a matter of fact, deeply opposed to slavery and would be profoundly disturbed if contracts of enslavement were made legally enforceable. Even assuming that most Americans do feel this way about voluntary slavery (as distinct from enslavement by force), this first approach suffers from one important defect, at least in the eyes of many modern critics of slavery: it ties the illegitimacy of slavery to the shifting tides of public opinion.

This defect might prompt one to adopt a second, nonempirical approach, according to which slavery is outlawed because it offends a conception of liberty and personal dignity which is embodied in the central provisions of our Constitution and to which we are committed as a people. On this second view, every American has an interest in the maintenance of this conception and the institutions which reflect it, a permanent moral interest that is unaffected by the vagaries of public opinion.

---

6. Compare the discussion of "moralities" in Guido Calabresi & Douglas Melamed, Property Rules, Liability Rules, and Inalienability: One View of the Cathedral, 85 Harv. L. Rev. 1089, 1111-1112 (1972).

7. John Stuart Mill, supra n.3, at 176-179; James Fitzjames Stephen, Liberty, Equality, Fraternity 28 (R. White ed., 1967).

It follows, from this second view, that voluntary enslavement is bound to have a deleterious effect on third parties even if public opinion vigorously approves such arrangements. Of course, it is now necessary to assume that the third parties whose moral well-being is threatened by contracts of enslavement may not themselves know what is in their own best interest. As a result, the most attractive feature of the appeal to third parties — its avoidance of paternalism — is lost. A proponent of this view must show that no person in his right mind would abandon the moral ideal embodied in the Constitution and that any expression of opinion to the contrary must be assumed not to reflect the person's true interests (just as Tullock's drunk is not asserting his true interests when he passionately insists that nothing could be better for him than a stiff drink). How this could be shown convincingly is unclear. One might argue, perhaps, that slavery means the loss of self-respect and that the loss of self-respect by some inevitably undermines the self-respect of others. But this argument is merely a more complicated version of the one outlined earlier and is subject to the same criticisms. It is subject to the further objection that it assumes the interdependence of different individuals' feelings of self-respect, something which is far from obvious. Why should my sense of self-worth be conditioned upon others' having a similar attitude toward themselves?

There is one other explanation for the unenforceability of contracts of enslavement that is worth noting. If people are extremely reluctant to enter into contracts of this sort, we may assume that almost every promise to become the slave of another has been given under duress or under the influence of misrepresentation (for example, a promise by the other party that he will not enforce the contract). If this is the case, then it is plausible to regard the rule prohibiting contracts of enslavement as a cost-saving presumption which achieves the same results as the more traditional, but also more cumbersome, ideas of fraud and duress. That it is an irrebuttable presumption is to be explained by the fact that the instances in which it is false are so few as not to justify the judicial costs that would be required to scrutinize each contract of enslavement more closely. Although this argument has considerable appeal, many opponents of self-enslavement are likely to find it unsatisfactory, merely because it rests on nothing loftier than the idea of administrative convenience. A deeper objection is that the argument rests on the same unproven assumption as Tullock's — that there are no strong (and morally respectable) reasons for people to enslave themselves.

NOTES AND QUESTIONS

1. **Contracts of self-enslavement.** Should contracts to sell oneself into slavery be banned, according to Kronman and Posner? Why? Do you find this a convincing explanation?

2.   **Contracts of indenture.** An indenture contract binds one person into the service of another for a specified term. Students of American history will recall that such contracts, often in exchange for passage to the new world, helped to settle the colonies. At the end of the indenture period, typically four or five years, the worker would gain his employment freedom and, in some instances, land of his own.

Could an employer enforce such a contract today? How do you explain the difference between an indenture contract and that of a professional athlete who signs a five-year contract (perhaps, his remaining professional lifetime) to play for one team? Is it only the compensation level?

3.   **Universal commodification.** The Kronman and Posner approach has been called the "universal commodification" position. See Margaret Jane Radin, Justice and the Market Domain, in Market and Justice — NOMOS XXXI, 165 (John W. Chapman and J. Rolland Pennock eds., 1989). "Under universal commodification, all things desired or valued — from personal attributes to good government — are goods or commodities. . . . All human attributes are conceived of as possessions bearing a value characterizable in money terms, and all human interactions are conceived as exchanges in terms of gains from trade. . . . Thus, in the universal commodification methodology, the only exceptions to the rule of laissez-faire are situations in which laissez-faire cannot arrive at an efficient result. These are the situations called market failure. . . . For one who is willing to conceive of everything (corneas for transplant, sexuality, babies for adoption) in market rhetoric, the only explanation for why some things might be held out of the market is market failure. . . ." Id. at 167-168.

§11.2   Adoption: Should There Be a Market for Babies?

In another famous article, Judge Posner advocates allocating babies through a market system. Elisabeth Landes and Richard Posner, The Economics of the Baby Shortage, 7 J. Legal Stud. 323 (1978). The following article enters the ensuing debate in a measured and rigorous way. The issue is an important one because approximately 11 percent of the American population is infertile.[1] As you read the excerpt, list arguments for and against a market

---

1. A higher percentage of students reading this book are likely to experience fertility problems because of the tendency among American professionals to defer childbearing to establish careers before taking on the demands of childrearing. Elizabeth Kastor, Older First-Time Mothers Find Lots to Brood Over, Wash. Post, Jan. 16, 1995, A1. Some of the social and legal consequences of this pattern were discussed in Chapter 5. However, infertility appears to be on the increase even among young women; some observers have suggested a link to environmental degradation.

for babies, and assess how the various arguments track the themes we developed in the beginning of this chapter.

Infertility and adoption [2] are commonplace in contemporary America. No doubt some of the students in your class are adoptees. How does the excerpt's discussion make you feel, if you were adopted? If you were not, how do you imagine it would make an adopted person feel?

In an excerpt relevant both to baby- and organ-selling, Margaret Jane Radin argues that changing property rules can change "the texture of the human world." [3] How would a market for adoption change the "texture of the human world" for adopted children, adoptive parents, and for biological children and parents?

Do you think baby-selling contracts should be enforced?

J. ROBERT S. PRICHARD, A MARKET FOR BABIES?

34 U. Toronto L.J., 341-347, 350, 350-357 (1984)

The market is perhaps the most commonly used mechanism for allocating scarce resources. As an allocative mechanism it has many attractive features which permit it to predominate over other systems such as bureaucracies, regulatory agencies, lotteries, juries, queues, and the like. But despite its predominance, the market is far from universal in its use. As a result, an important aspect of economic analysis is to examine the characteristics of situations in which the market is not used as the primary allocative device in order to illuminate the limits and implications of the market as an allocative mechanism.

This essay addresses that task in the context of family law. In particular, I examine the reasons why we are reluctant to use a market mechanism in place of existing bureaucratic procedures for the adoption of newborn babies. The purpose of the essay is to understand the limits of the market rather than to promote its use. However, I pursue the topic by first detailing the affirmative case for a market in babies and then examining its deficiencies. . . .

In proceeding in this way I run the risk of being misunderstood as

2. Many adoptive parents turn to adoption because they are infertile, but this is by no means the universal rule. Others adopt because they prefer adoption to biological parenthood for a variety of emotional and physical reasons and, sometimes, in the belief that the planet already has too many people.

3. Her analysis stems in part from a feminist desire to critique the discussions of rape by Posner and others. Margaret Jane Radin, 100 Harv. L. Rev. 1849, 1884 (1987). Again, someone in your law school class, if not your section, probably has been raped. (Recent statistics from a government-funded study indicate that 1 of every 8 adult women in America has been raped at least once. Cynthia Grant Bowman, Street Harassment and the Informal Ghettoization of Women, 106 Harv. L. Rev. 517, 580 (1993).) How does the property analysis of rape change the "texture of the universe" for rape victims (or, for that matter for all women)?

advocating a market mechanism for allocating newborn babies. The oppo-site is true. My primary motivation in writing this essay has been a desire to reconcile my intuitive opposition to such a system (opposition which I as-sume is widely, if not universally, shared) with the analytical methods of economic analysis of law. Indeed, the purpose runs deeper, extending to the vitality of economic analysis of law. For if economic analysis is to remain a vital and creative role within legal scholarship, its limits must be explored as vigorously as its strengths.

THE PRESENT SITUATION

The results of the existing regulatory system governing the allocation and adoption of newborn children are in many respects tragic. At present in Canada and the United States many people unable to have children natu-rally want to adopt, but there are far too few newborn children to meet the demand, leaving many couples deprived of the privileges and joys of child rearing. In addition, the existing regulatory procedures allocating these scarce newborns subject childless couples to very substantial costs. . . .

The evidence of the tragedy can also be found in increasing evidence of black market activity in the sale of babies. News reports from Vancouver, Toronto, and the United States are unanimous in reporting increasing black market activity characterized by very high prices for newborns (as much as $40,000) but continued interest on the part of childless couples. However, these reports also suggest that most of the economic rewards derived from these transactions are being gathered by the physicians and the lawyers in-volved in arranging them and not by the mothers who bear the children.

The reasons for the shortage are simple. The supply of newborns has decreased dramatically primarily as a result of the increased availability of contraceptive devices and legal abortions. . . . The consequences of this very substantial undersupply of adoptable babies are varied. The primary effect is that many couples who desire children are left childless. While ac-curate statistical information is not available, it has been estimated that up to six percent of couples who desire children are unable to have them naturally. Given the existing short supply of babies, the magnitude of the social tragedy from the perspective of childless couples is readily apparent. The other consequences are somewhat less obvious. Childless couples are tempted to use fertility drugs and other fertility increasing treatments which necessarily increase the risk of children being born with various kinds of infirmities. Couples are also tempted to have children naturally even in circumstances where genetic counselling indicates they should not, since the alternative of adoption is so unavailable. On the supply side, there is no incentive for mothers to give up their newborns since at present those who do so are not remunerated in any way for their children. As a result the decision that the child is unwanted is often delayed for a year or two until the opportunities for and desirability of adoption are substantially decreased. Furthermore, the pregnant woman who plans to give up her child is under no economic incentive to care for her child while it is in utero since no reward is paid for producing a well cared for child. Thus, injury-reducing abstinence such as forgoing smoking and drinking is not economically encouraged by the present system.

In Ontario the present scheme of regulation is created by the Child Welfare Act. This statute creates a virtual monopoly in the adoption business for certain licensed agencies, although it does permit individually licensed adoptions under restrictive conditions. Under the statute, the Children's Aid Societies which are the primary agencies charged with adoption regulation must screen and approve prospective adopting couples. Once a couple is approved, they join a queue formed at a central registry in each geographic district in the province. When a newborn becomes available, three couples who might be appropriate parents for the child are selected administratively. Then the social worker assigned to each couple engages in an advocacy process within the agency to determine which of the three couples should succeed. As a general rule, there is an attempt to match the education backgrounds and economic circumstances of the couples and the natural[4] mother. In addition, subject to the best interests of the child, an attempt is made to respect the desires of the natural mother as to the type of home environment she wishes for her child.

In addition to creating this regulatory scheme, section 67 of the Child Welfare Act provides that 'no person, whether before or after the birth of a child, shall make, give or receive or agree to make, give or receive a payment or reward for or in consideration of or in relation to' an adoption or a proposed adoption. As a result, market transactions in babies are strictly prohibited.

Similar administrative and regulatory schemes are in place across Canada.[5] Their details vary substantially but their essential characteristic — administrative allocation — remains constant. A clear alternative would be a market-oriented system in which babies would be allocated to couples based on the prices the couples were prepared to pay. In the section which follows, the possible advantages of such a mechanism are set out.

THE MARKET MECHANISM

At first blush the market mechanism might seem to be considerably more attractive than the existing regulatory scheme in that it appears to be able to make most people better off. The reasons are numerous.

First, one would anticipate an increase in the quantity of babies sup-

---

4. An alternative term is "biological parent." What different cultural messages do the two terms send? — EDS.

5. And the United States. — EDS.

plied in order to meet the demand, thus eliminating the present queue
and satisfying the desires of virtually all the childless couples left unsatisfied
by the present system and shortage. Women would engage in the production of children for adoption, responding to the financial incentives of the
market-place.

Second, one would anticipate that the market would lead to the realization of comparative productive advantages in that the supply of newborns would be undertaken by those best able to produce, satisfying the
needs of those unable to have children and providing a realistic alternative
for those for whom childbirth is possible but genetically unwise. Furthermore, one might anticipate some substitution of producers with relatively
low opportunity costs for those with high opportunity costs. That is, persons
for whom pregnancy comes only at the cost of substantial disruption of
their other activities (for example, employment) might well decline to carry
a child, opting to purchase a baby from a substitute carrier whose opportunity costs would be lower. This effect would be limited, of course, by the
extent to which mothers derived positive utility (and paid maternity leaves)
from carrying their own children and by the extent to which parents preferred natural to purchased children.

Third, one would anticipate that the market would generate information about the pedigrees of newborns which would permit the matching
of couples' desires and the newborn's attributes. One would anticipate that
there would be an incentive to disclose the quality of the newborns and
that information certification procedures and agencies would develop to
enhance the information market.

Fourth, one would expect the newborns to be of a higher quality than
the existing newborns available for adoption. The promise of remuneration
for prospective mothers would lead to an incentive for the appropriate care
of children in utero since a warranty of such behavior would attract a positive reward in the market-place. In addition, one would anticipate that prospective mothers would exercise greater care in the selection of their sexual
mates since the quality of the mate would also influence the price to be
obtained upon birth.

Fifth, one would expect an extremely competitive market structure.
There would be extremely low entry barriers, a very large number of producers, both actual and potential, slight economies of scale, and enormous
difficulties in cartelization. While there might be some brand name identification over time, one would not anticipate that this would lead to significant barriers to entry.

Sixth, the market process would provide an incentive for parents to
correct errors in judgment and shortcomings in contraceptive devices since
they would be in a position to sell the child for a positive reward rather than
simply give it away. This should reduce the number of foster children since
the market for newborns would create an incentive to make the disposal at
the time of birth. At the same time, however, reducing the cost of errors in

judgment and inadequate contraceptive techniques and devices might lead to a corresponding decrease in the care exercised by sexually active friends and couples.

Seventh, one would expect the market to produce the children at a relatively low cost and certainly a cost much below the existing black market prices. The market would be free from the costs of hiding transactions from law enforcement officials, from substantial legal penalties, and from fraudulent practices and the like which at present permeate the black market. Furthermore, one would anticipate that the suppliers of the children would get a substantial portion of the economic return and that lawyers and physicians would be in a less strong position to take advantage of their clients and patients. With respect to price, one would anticipate that it would approximate the opportunity cost of a woman's time during pregnancy. It should be stressed that this need not by any means equal the amount of compensation that a person would earn in other market activities for the full nine months since pregnancy is far from totally disabling. Therefore, it would not be surprising if a price as low as $3000 to $5000 per child were common in some segments of the market.

Eighth, the market could develop various efficiency enhancing mechanisms. In particular, one might anticipate that a futures market would develop in which children in utero could be traded, permitting the reallocation of the risks inherent in childbirth so as to better reflect the various tastes for risks of different participants in the market. Furthermore, one might imagine that market intermediaries might form so as to hold portfolios of children in utero, thus diversifying and reducing the nonsystematic risk.

Ninth, on the distributive side, the market would be likely to display qualities considerably more attractive than the existing system. One would expect that the producers would be persons with relatively low opportunity costs who at present have very limited opportunities for income earning activities. This would present a new source of productive activity at a reasonable level of reward. Furthermore, one could anticipate that this would result in some shift of wealth away from the purchasers of babies to the producers, who would presumably be from less advantaged circumstances. In addition, the distributive effects of devoting some of the economic returns to the mothers and taking it away from those at present able to exploit the illegality of the black market would surely be attractive. In sum, quite a robust case for the market can be made. It would appear to work well. It would satisfy a lot of unsatisfied people, have attractive distributive results, and increase the degree of individual freedom and choice in the adoption process as the monopolistic regulatory powers at present enjoyed by the Children's Aid Societies would be eliminated.

Despite these attractions, and despite the inadequacies of the present system, most would find the prospect of a market for babies to be grotesque.

Indeed, the mere description has a ring of parody to it as the incongruity of market notions and babies jars the reader. Somewhere within most of us there is at least an intuitive reaction that there is something indecent about the prospect of a market for babies. The prospect of prices, contracts, advertising, credit, discounts, specials, and all the other attributes of consumer transactions seems disquieting. But when asked for an explanation for this reaction, can one do better than simply assert its unacceptability? In what follows, I consider a number of possible objections.

There are three categories of objections to relying on a market mechanism. The first might be termed market failure concerns. Here the argument meets the proposal on its own terms, not objecting to the market in principle but stressing that the market would not work well in this particular context. The second category of objections concedes that the market would work essentially as I have suggested, but that, as a market mechanism, it would possess one or more objectionable characteristics which cause us to reject the mechanism as a whole. The third category of objects attacks the entire proposal, not just its market aspects, arguing that it fails in its essential conception.

MARKET FAILURE OBJECTIONS

The first line of reaction to the proposal for a baby market is to meet it on its own terms. That is, a critic might ask whether or not this is a situation in which the market would in fact produce optimal results even if the other categories of objections canvassed below are found unpersuasive. A number of doubts might be raised.

[The author raises five doubts: (1) "Good" babies may drive out the "bad," as adoptive parents eschew infants with birth defects and other infirmities, adding to the number of unwanted children; (2) Information failures may arise, as natural parents conceal facts, such as possible genetic flaws, that would lower the market price if known; (3) Higher total population could result, causing an externality that market decisions would fail to recognize; (4) Genetic breeding might occur, to meet a demand for custom-bred babies; (5) Markets in used children might result from parents tempted to "trade in" an unsatisfactory child and "trade up" to a newborn.]

OBJECTIONS IN PRINCIPLE

DISTRIBUTIVE CONCERNS

[The author finds unpersuasive the next criticisms: (1) some couples, after paying for a child, would be so impoverished as to be unable to provide high-quality care; (2) the rich would get all the good babies.]

COST OF COSTING

Another principled objection to the market focuses on one of its inevitable aspects: the creation of prices. The concern is that a market for babies would generate negative secondary consequences as a result of the fact that a market mechanism by definition generates explicit prices. In particular, the pricing of babies might violate two principles, each of which we hold dear. The first is that life is infinitely valuable — "a pearl beyond price." With prices of $3000 per baby, the reality of the limited price of life (at least at the point of creation) and the ideal of the infinitely valuable would contrast starkly. The second principle is that all lives are equally valuable. With higher prices for white than non-white children, and higher prices for healthy than sick children, and other similar forms of price differentials, the reality and the ideal would again clash.

The concern here is real but difficult to evaluate. It is but one example of a much more general problem of public policy. Whenever life is at stake the difficulties of pricing and of costing must be faced. Thus, whether it is the standard of care in tort law, the design of a Pinto, highway design, or medical research one cannot avoid implicitly or explicitly dealing with the price of life. Perhaps it is the degree of explicitness that would be inherent in this scheme that gives rise to the vigour of the opposition. It may also be that the differences in prices would correspond with differences which we strive particularly hard to overcome by means of other social policies. That is, to the extent that differences in price fell along racial grounds, to adopt a policy of a market for babies would be directly contradictory to the wide range of social policies designed to minimize discrimination on racial grounds.

COMMODIFICATION

While related to the previous concern regarding the costs of costing, the concern here is that trading in certain commodities degrades the commodities themselves. That is, certain things should be above the hustle and bustle of the market-place so as to preserve their dignity, leading to the conclusion that trading in such commodities is inherently bad. That is, by creating a market one would commodify something — life — which should not be treated as a commodity. Put even more strongly, the concern is that the special value we attribute to children depends in part on the fact they cannot be traded. Thus, trafficking in lives becomes presumptively bad. There is a dynamic dimension to this concern as well, since trading activity would alter our views regarding the nature of the commodity at stake, reducing over time our aversion to engaging in this form of trade.

Again, the difficulty in evaluating this concern is that it is hard to know which goods fall within this category of goods that should not be commodified. Trading in babies is not directly analogous to slavery. Is it more closely analogous to long-term contracts for services? If so, why do we not have the same sense of concern about the multi-year contracts of professional athletes as we do about a market for babies?

In addition, in the midst of whatever reactions one has along this line or some of the earlier lines of objection, it is important they not be treated in isolation from some of the compensating effects of the market proposal. That is, unless these concerns are made absolutes they must be considered in the context of a probably substantial reduction in the number of abortions performed and of the very substantial increase in happiness for previously childless couples. How these compensating effects should be weighed in the balance is unclear, but absent the most extreme forms of rejection of the utilitarian calculus some consideration must be given to them.

OPPRESSION

Put bluntly, the proposal for a market for babies smacks of slavery. More broadly, the concern is that such a scheme would oppressively and involuntarily relegate poor women to an occupation which we do not wish to promote (or to be seen to promote) and which would deprive the participants of their dignity. This concern may be similar to concerns about prostitution, wet nurses, and markets for blood. However, it is not entirely clear what makes this matter oppressive when other lines of poorly paid work are seen to be less so. If the concern is simply that wages will be low, regulatory intervention is possible. If the concern is that this type of production takes advantage of the women's low opportunity cost, the response must be to recognize the truth of that proposition but to ask how this differs from any other situation of employing someone with a low opportunity cost. If it is a concern for the nature of the work, what is it about child-bearing that makes it somehow dishonourable when done for money but most honourable when done for other reasons? Why does paying for childbirth or engaging in child-bearing for the sake of money convert a dignified activity into a despised one? The answer must lie in one of the other concerns, for example, commodification rather than in oppression per se. That is, we may object to the commodification of sex (prostitution), blood donation, or mothers' milk production (wet nurses) not only because of the low opportunity cost, but because of the combining of low opportunity cost with an opportunity to engage in market activity in an area where commodification itself is objectionable.

At the same time it is not entirely clear exactly what the focus of the concern is in this respect. Some would argue that it is women who are being oppressed, but others might argue that it is the newborns who are being oppressed. One way to test this proposition might be to ask whether the concern would be the same if the market were in test tube babies, so as to relieve any concern about a class of women being oppressed. If the concern remains, it seems that it must be broader than merely the oppression of women.

THE ABSENCE OF A RELATIONSHIP BETWEEN WILLINGNESS TO PAY AND QUALITY OF PARENT

Another line of attack on the proposal would be to point out that while willingness to pay for a commodity may be the best measure of desire, people may desire children for the wrong reasons. That is, someone may wish to acquire a child for the purpose of beating or otherwise abusing it, rather than loving it or caring for it. This is no doubt true, but again does it go the heart of the problem? Presumably the same perverted desires motivate people to give birth naturally. We do not in Canadian society require an ex ante check on the reasons for having natural children, and thus one must question why ex ante review of suitability for parenting should be required under the market scheme. However, even if some ex ante scheme is desired (as it is under the existing regulatory mechanism), it is, of course, not inconsistent with having a market scheme of allocation. That is, it would be quite simple to require anyone wishing to make a bid in the baby market first to obtain a parenting certificate from some regulatory agency. This license would be granted or denied on the basis of whether or not one met the minimum necessary qualifications for parenting. There would be no limit on the number of certificates granted. If this step were adopted, it is difficult to see how the divergences of willingness to pay and quality of parent would be any more extreme under the market for babies proposal than under the existing regulatory mechanism.

Misconception Objections

The first category of objections focused on market failure and the second on principled objections to the use of the market in the context. The third category, while related to the second, attacks the proposal as being wrong in its very conception of the problem. This objection can be stated in three ways.

THE IMPROPER OBJECTIVE

[The present system under attack has, as its prime function, taking care of a limited number of unwanted newborns, not meeting the desires of childless couples for children.]

THE SECOND BEST ARGUMENT

[There are better ways than a market mechanism to increase the supply of babies: these include banning abortion or barring the use of contraceptives.]

JONATHAN SWIFT'S 'MODEST PROPOSAL'

[The writer builds, then debunks, an analogy between the market for babies proposal and Swift's satirical solution to the problem of starvation in Ireland — the killing of babies.]

CONCLUSION

I end where I started, focusing on the limits of markets by asking whether these objections to a market for babies are persuasive. To the extent that they are, they may help define the limits of markets in other situations requiring an allocative device.

The need for a coherent appreciation of the limits of market-based allocative mechanisms is enhanced at a time when we are being inundated by signs of the increased commercialization of activities closely related to a market for babies. Campus newspapers advertisements seek sperm donors: "Semen will be used for artificial insemination for couples who cannot have children due to male infertility. Men of all backgrounds are needed and in particular of Chinese, Japanese, Black and East Indian backgrounds. Donors . . . will be paid for their involvement." A couple having a child but wanting a new car are reported to have traded in their baby for a used Corvette. News reports tell of surrogate mothers who charge a fee for carrying a child for a couple who are not otherwise able to produce their own child but who desire the injection of at least the husband's genes: "[Through] Surrogate Parenting Associates, Inc. . . . an infertile couple and their surrogate can be matched for a fee of between $15,000 and $20,000 which covers payment to the surrogate as well as medical, incidental, and legal fees." Speculation is common that the near future holds promise of commercial banks for sperm, body parts, and other life-creating products.

In many of these situations, a market mechanism may offer the promise of increased supply. For example, kidneys, livers, hearts, and other body parts would no doubt be far more available — at a price — if financial rewards could be paid to the donors. But despite this promise of supply, the predominant reaction is to resist and to look to alternatives. This common pattern of resistance surely reflects concerns of the kind identified in this essay. At the same time, I believe that these concerns should be understood as to some extent contingent upon cultural and social values that themselves change over time. Transitions in these values can and do occur, responding to a complex shifting social consensus.

We may well be in just such a period of transition to a society in which the objections to the baby market will lose much of their force. Such a transition was experienced in the late nineteenth century with respect to life insurance, which was thought for a time to represent a form of trafficking in and valuing of lives. Whether or not the same transition is about to occur with respect to the market for babies, semen, surrogate mothers, body parts, and the like may well depend in part on the strength, coherence, and nature of the objections to the market for babies proposal and the extent to which we can identify them and commit ourselves to the preservation of the values which inform them.

PATRICIA J. WILLIAMS, SPARE PARTS, FAMILY VALUES, OLD CHILDREN, CHEAP

28 New Eng. L. Rev. 913, 914-920 (1994)

. . . Last week I was reading an article by that great literary mogul of the University of Chicago's School of Law and Economics, Judge Richard Posner and his associate Elizabeth Landes. In their short opus, "The Economics of the Baby Shortage,"[1] newborn human beings are divided up into white and black and then taken for a spin around a monopoly board theme park where the white babies are put on demand curves and the black babies are dropped off the edge of supply sides. "Were baby prices quoted as prices of soybean futures are quoted," they say, "a racial ranking of these prices would be evident, with white baby prices higher than nonwhite baby prices." The trail of the demand curve leads straight into the arms of the highest bidder; the chasm of oversupply has a heap of surplus at the bottom of its pit. In this house of horrors, the surplus (or "second quality") black babies will continue to replicate themselves like mushrooms, unless the wise, invisible, strong arm of the market intervenes to allow the wisdom of pure purchasing power to effect some clearing away of the underbrush. In a passage that some have insisted is all about maximizing the kindness of strangers, Landes and Posner argue that "[b]y obtaining exclusive control over the supply of both 'first quality' adoptive children and 'second quality' children residing in foster care but available for adoption, agencies are able to internalize the substitution possibilities between them. Agencies can charge a higher price for the children they place for adoption, thus increasing not only their revenues from adoptions but also the demand for chil-

1. Elizabeth M. Landes & Richard A. Posner, The Economics of the Baby Market, 7 J. Legal Stud. 323 (1978).

dren who would otherwise be placed or remain in foster care at the agency's expense. Conversely, if agency revenues derive primarily from foster care, the agencies can manipulate the relative price of adopting 'first-quality' children over 'second quality' children to reduce the net flow of children out of foster care." The conclusion that these authors make, in a not surprising rhetorical turn, is that the current "black market" for adoptive children must be replaced with what they call a "free baby market."

When this article first appeared almost twenty years ago, it created a storm of controversy. Since Judge Posner has reaffirmed its premises many times, most recently in his book, *Sex and Reason*, the article has remained a major bone of contention in his constellation of publications. . . .

[M]y purpose in resurrecting this piece as a reference for this essay is to examine: (1) the degree to which it is a reflection of what goes on in the world of not just adoption but reproduction in general; (2) the degree to which market valuation of bodies, even when for ostensibly notable purposes, embodies what is most wrong with community as well as family in America; and (3) the possibility that a shift in focus could help us imagine a more stable, less demeaning, and more inclusive sense of community. . . .

When I decided to adopt a child, I was unprepared for the reality that adoption is already a pretty straightforward market. I was unprepared for the "choices" with which I was presented, as to age, race, color, and health of prospective children. I was unprepared for the fact that I too would be shopped for, by birth mothers as well as social workers, looked over for my age, marital and economic status, and race. All that was missing was to have my tires kicked.

"Describe yourself," said the application form. Oh lord, I remember thinking, this is worse than a dating service. What's appealing about me, and to whom? Responsible non-smoker omnivore seeks . . . what? Little persons for lifetime of bicycle rides, good education, and peanut butter sandwiches? Forty and fading fast so I thought I'd better get a move on? "You can't tell them you're forty," advised a friend of mine. "No one will ever pick you." OK, I sighed. "Very well rounded," I wrote. . . .

"What age, what sex," asked the social worker. "Doesn't matter," I said, "though I'd like to miss out on as little as possible."

"If you're willing to take a boy, you'll get younger," she replied. "There's a run on girls." . . .

"What color?" asked the form. You've got to be kidding. I looked quizzically at the social worker. "Some families like to match," she said. You mean, like color-coordinated? You mean like the Louisiana codes? Like ebony, sepia, quadroon, mahogany? Like matching the color of a brown paper bag? Like red, like Indian, like exotic, like straight haired, like light skinned? Like 1840, is that what this means? Like 1940, sighed my mother, when I mentioned this to her. (And is this what the next generation will be sighing about, so sadly like that, in 2040? . . .)

"I don't care," I wrote.

And with that magical stroke of the pen, the door to a whole world of plentiful, newborn, brown-skinned little boys with little brown toes and big brown eyes and round brown noses and fat brown cheeks opened up to me from behind the curtain marked, "Doesn't Care." . . .

My son, because he is a stylish little character, arrived at my home in a limousine. (Credit for this must also be shared with the social worker, who was a pretty jazzy sort herself.) I had a big party and a naming ceremony and invited everyone I knew. I was so happy that I guess I missed that price tag hanging from his little blue-knit beanie. A few weeks later I got a call from the agency: "Which fee schedule are you going to choose?"

"What's this?" I asked the adoption agent, flipping madly through Landes and Posner for guidance: "Prospective adoptive parents would presumably be willing to pay more for a child whose health and genealogy were warranted in a legally enforceable instrument than they are willing to pay under the present system where the entire risk of any deviation from expected quality falls on them."

"Are you going with the standard or the special?" came the reply. There followed a description of a system in which adoptive parents paid a certain percentage of their salaries to the agency, which fee went to administrative costs, hospital expenses for the birth mother, and counseling. Inasmuch as it was tied exclusively to income, in a graduated scale, it clearly met the definition of a fee for services rendered. This, it was explained to me, was the Standard Price List.

"And the special?" I asked. After an embarrassed pause, I was told that that referred to "older, black, and other handicapped children," and that those fees were exactly half of those on the standard scale. Suddenly, what had been a price system based on services rendered became clearly, sickening, irretrievably, a price system for "goods," a sale for chattel, linked not to services but to the imagined quality of the "things" exchanged. Although it is true that, as the agency asserted, this system was devised to provide "economic incentives" for the adoption of "less requested" children, it is perhaps more than true, in our shopping mall world, that it had all the earmarks of a two-for-one sale. . . .

A friend of mine who has given birth to two children assures me that biological parents where no money was exchanged feel exactly the same way — exhilarated, disbelieving, unworthy of the list with which they are suddenly charged. I am sure that it is true — I too feel great amazement at my own motherhood. But my point is that the ideology of the marketplace devalues such emotions, either by identifying them as externalities in and of themselves, or by using them to infuse, even impassion, certain price structures, uncritically crystallizing into a dollars and cents equivalent what we might be better off trying to understand as "priceless" relation.

How will my son's price at birth relate to what value doctors put on his various parts if he ever has an accident and shows up at a hospital? Will he be valued more as a series of parts in the marketplace of bodies or more as a whole, as a precious social being with not just a will but a soul? Will his fate be decided by a fellow human being who cares for him or will his "outcome" be negotiated by some formulaic economic tracing policy based on his having health insurance or a job? Will his idiosyncratic, non-market value be visible in the subconscious, well-intentioned decision of a nice suburban doctor who has never known, spoken, lived, or worked with a black person in a status position of anything close to equality? Will "ethics" be able to consider this complicated stuff or will we decide the whole topic is too risky, too angrifying, so that forced neutrality and pretend-we-don't-see-ness will rule the day? Who will rule the fate of this most precious bit of "living property" as Harriet Beecher Stowe called that status of blacks?

"[T]he precarious difference between persons and things appears . . . as the difference between consuming and being consumed . . . the competition for personhood in the market is the choice between eating and being eaten." How will our children, figured as the tidy "consumption preferences" of unsocial actors, be able to value themselves?

I was unable to choose a fee schedule. I was unable to conspire in putting a price on my child's head. . . .

The "Baby M" case, the first surrogate mother case to receive widespread attention, involved a contract between Mrs. Whitehead, the surrogate mother, and Dr. Stern and his wife, the intended parents of the infant Ms. Whitehead agreed to carry in her womb. (Dr. Stern would provide the sperm.) At the birth of Baby M, Mrs. Whitehead decided that she wanted to keep the infant, and the Sterns sued to enforce the contract. The New Jersey Supreme Court refused to do so. Although the case presents complex issues far beyond what we can discuss here, the following excerpt from the opinion presents arguments relevant in the market-for-babies context.

IN THE MATTER OF BABY M, A PSEUDONYM FOR AN ACTUAL PERSON

109 N.J. 396, 537 A. 2d 1227 (1988)

B.   PUBLIC POLICY CONSIDERATIONS . . .

The surrogacy contract's invalidity, resulting from its direct conflict with the above statutory provisions, is further underlined when its goals and means are measured against New Jersey's public policy. . . . This is the sale of a child, or, at the very least, the sale of a mother's right to her child, the only mitigating factor being that one of the purchasers is the father. Almost every evil that prompted the prohibition on the payment of money in connection with adoptions exists here. . . . With surrogacy, the "problem," if one views it as such, consisting of the purchase of a woman's procreative capacity, at the risk of her life, is caused by and originates with the offer of money. . . . In the scheme contemplated by the surrogacy contract in this case, a middle man, propelled by profit, promotes the sale. Whatever idealism may have motivated any of the participants, the profit motive predominates, permeates, and ultimately governs the transaction. The demand for children is great and the supply small. The availability of contraception, abortion, and the greater willingness of single mothers to bring up their children has led to a shortage of babies offered for adoption. See [Nancy C.] Baker, Baby Selling: The Scandal of Black Market Adoption, [(Vanguard Press)]; Adoption and Foster Care, 1975: Hearings on Baby Selling before the Subcomm. on Children and Youth of the Senate Comm. on Labor and Public Welfare, 94th Cong., 1st Sess. 6 (1975) (Statement of Joseph H. Reid, Executive Director, Child Welfare League of America, Inc.). The situation is ripe for the entry of the middleman who will bring some equilibrium into the market by increasing the supply through the use of money.

Intimated, but disputed, is the assertion that surrogacy will be used for the benefit of the rich at the expense of the poor. See, e.g., Radin, "Market Inalienability," 100 Harv. L. Rev. 1849, 1930 (1987). In response it is noted that the Sterns are not rich and the Whiteheads not poor. Nevertheless, it is clear to us that it is unlikely that surrogate mothers will be as proportionately numerous among those women in the top twenty percent income bracket as among those in the bottom twenty percent. Ibid. Put differently, we doubt that infertile couples in the low-income bracket will find upper income surrogates.

In any event, even in this case one should not pretend that disparate wealth does not play a part simply because the contrast is not the dramatic "rich versus poor." At the time of trial, the Whiteheads' net assets were probably negative — Mrs. Whitehead's own sister was foreclosing on a second mortgage. Their income derived from Mr. Whitehead's labors. Mrs. Whitehead is a homemaker, having previously held part-time jobs. The Sterns are both professionals, she a medical doctor, he a biochemist. Their combined income when both were working was about $89,500 a year and their assets sufficient to pay for the surrogacy contract arrangements.

The point is made that Mrs. Whitehead agreed to the surrogacy arrangement, supposedly fully understanding the consequences. Putting aside the issue of how compelling her need for money may have been, and how significant her understanding of the consequences, we suggest that her consent is irrelevant. There are, in a civilized society, some things that money cannot buy. In America, we decided long ago that merely because conduct purchased by money was "voluntary" did not mean that it was good or beyond regulation and prohibition. West Coast Hotel Co. v. Parrish, 300 U.S. 379 (1937). Employers can no longer buy labor at the lowest price they can bargain for, even though that labor is "voluntary," 29 U.S.C. §206 (1982), or buy women's labor for less money than paid to men for the same job, 29 U.S.C. §206(d), or purchase the agreement of children to perform oppressive labor, 29 U.S.C. §212, or purchase the agreement of workers to subject themselves to unsafe or unhealthful working conditions, 29 U.S.C. §§651-678. (Occupational Safety and Health Act of 1970). There are, in short, values that society deems more important than granting to wealth whatever it can buy, be it labor, love, or life. Whether this principle recommends prohibition of surrogacy, which presumably sometimes results in great satisfaction to all of the parties, is not for us to say. We note here only that, under existing law, the fact that Mrs. Whitehead "agreed" to the arrangement is not dispositive.

The long-term effects of surrogacy contracts are not known, but feared — the impact on the child who learns her life was bought, that she is the offspring of someone who gave birth to her only to obtain money; the impact on the natural mother as the full weight of her isolation is felt along with the full reality of the sale of her body and her child; the impact on the natural father and adoptive mother once they realize the consequences of their conduct. Literature in related areas suggests that these are substantial considerations, although, given the newness of surrogacy, there is little information. See N. Baker, Baby Selling: The Scandal of Black Market Adoption, *supra;* Adoption and Foster Care, 1975: Hearings on Baby Selling before the Subcomm. on Children and Youth of the Senate Comm. on Labor and Public Welfare, 94th Cong., 1st Sess (1975). . . .

MARGARET JANE RADIN, MARKET INALIENABILITY

100 Harv. L.Rev. 1849, 1879-1887 (1987)

. . . **2. Injury to Personhood.**   In some cases market discourse itself might be antagonistic to interests of personhood. Recall that Posner conceives of rape in terms of a marriage and sex market. Posner concludes that "the prevention of rape is essential to protect the marriage market . . . and more generally to secure property rights in women's persons."[108] Calabresi and Melamed also use market rhetoric to discuss rape. In keeping with their view that "property rules" are prima facie more efficient than "liability rules" for all entitlements, they argue that people should hold a "property

_____

108. Richard Posner, Economic Analysis of Law 202 (2d ed. 1977). In the passage in which this sentence appears, Posner examines the argument that rape should not be punished criminally if there is "no market substitute for rape" because the rapist "derives extra pleasure from the coercive character of his act." (Presumably, the "market substitutes" would be marriage, dating, and prostitution.) Posner finds the argument "weak" — and is thus able to conclude that rape should be punished criminally — for three reasons: protecting the marriage market and property rights in women's persons, avoiding "wasteful expenditures" on protecting women and on overcoming the protections, and "the fact that the rapist cannot find a consensual substitute does not mean that he values the rape more than the victim disvalues it." Id.

rule" entitlement in their own bodily integrity. Further, they explain criminal punishment by the need for an "indefinable kicker," an extra cost to the rapist "which represents society's need to keep all property rules from being changed at will into liability rules." Unlike Posner's view, Calabresi and Melamed's can be understood as pluralist,[6] but like Posner's their view conceives of rape in market rhetoric. Bodily integrity is an owned object with a price.

What is wrong with this rhetoric? The risk-of-error argument discussed above is one answer. Unsophisticated practitioners of cost-benefit analysis might tend to undervalue the "costs" of rape to the victims. But this answer does not exhaust the problem. Rather, for all but the deepest enthusiast, market rhetoric seems intuitively out of place here, so inappropriate that it is either silly or somehow insulting to the value being discussed.

One basis for this intuition is that market rhetoric conceives of bodily integrity as a fungible object.[115] A fungible object is replaceable with money or other objects; in fact, possessing a fungible object is the same as possessing money. A fungible object can pass in and out of the person's possession without effect on the person as long as its market equivalent is given in exchange. To speak of personal attributes as fungible objects — alienable "goods" — is intuitively wrong. Thinking of rape in market rhetoric implicitly conceives of as fungible something that we know to be personal, in fact conceives of as fungible property something we know to be too personal even to be personal property. Bodily integrity is an attribute and not an object. We feel discomfort or even insult, and we fear degradation or even loss of the value involved, when bodily integrity is conceived of as a fungible object. . . .

Market rhetoric, if adopted by everyone, and in many contexts, would indeed transform the texture of the human world. This rhetoric leads us to view politics as just rent seeking, reproductive capacity as just a scarce good for which there is high demand, and the repugnance of slavery as just a cost. To accept these views is to accept the conception of human flourishing they imply, one that is inferior to the conception we can accept as properly ours. An inferior conception of human flourishing disables us from conceptualizing the world rightly. Market rhetoric, the rhetoric of alienability of all "goods," is also the rhetoric of alienation of ourselves from what we can be as persons.

---

6. By "pluralist," Radin refers to an approach that takes into account nonefficiency motives such as justice. — Eds.

115. In Radin, Property and Personhood, 34 Stan. L. Rev. 957 (1982), I suggest that property may be divided into fungible and personal categories for purposes of moral evaluation. Property is personal in a philosophical sense when it has become identified with a person, with her self-constitution and self-development in the context of her environment. Personal property cannot be taken away and replaced with money or other things without harm to the person — to her identity and existence. In a sense, personal property becomes a personal attribute. On the other hand, property is fungible when there is no such personal attachment. See id. at 959-61, 978-79, 986-89.

NOTES AND QUESTIONS

1. **Intuitions.** Why does market rhetoric seem to many people "silly or somehow insulting" in certain contexts? Note Radin's reliance on intuitions, with no attempt to examine the cultural context in which those intuitions take shape. Why are these "intuitions" so hard to state and defend explicitly? Does the difficulty stem from the fact that an explicit statement of the intuitions would sound like religion, or ethics, or something other than law?

2. **Texture of the world.** Would allowing surrogacy contracts "change the texture of the human world"? Is the difference other than semantic between the mother's sale of her infant and the mother's rental of her womb to the infant's natural father?

3. **Prostitution.** Most (but not all, vis. Holland) Western societies have criminalized prostitution, a state of affairs that most (but not all, vis. Nevada) Americans take for granted. If it is criminal for a woman to "rent" her body to a John for 30 minutes, why should it not also be criminal for a woman to "rent" her womb for nine months? Or criminal for the other party to the rental contract? Alternatively, why criminalize prostitution?

The arguments for the criminal treatment of prostitution include concern for the spread of venereal disease (and now AIDS); the immorality of "unloving" sex; the potential for commodified sex to erode the value of marriage; the compulsion for impoverished women to "sell themselves"; the association of prostitution with crime and drugs. Can you think of any others?

Respect for a woman's personhood is a claim that is made on both sides of the criminalization debate. As to that issue, which side has the stronger claim?

Although prostitution is a bilateral crime, the prostitute is twice as likely as her patron to be arrested: in 1992, 25,000 men and 49,500 women throughout the United States.

§11.3   Sale of Bodily Organs

HENRY B. HANSMANN, THE ECONOMICS AND ETHICS OF MARKETS FOR HUMAN ORGANS

14 J. Health Pol., Poly. & L. 57 (1989)

I.   INTRODUCTION

The important recent advances in the technology for transplanting human organs have led to a large increase in the demand for suitable organs. As a consequence, demand now considerably exceeds supply. This situation gives rise to two problems of policy. First, can we and should we increase the overall supply of organs? Second, how should we allocate the existing scarce supply among the many individuals who would benefit from a transplant? In the United States, markets are the conventional mechanism for dealing with both these issues for most goods and services. At present, however, federal law, and the law of many states as well, prohibits the commercial sale of organs and thus rules out market solutions to problems of organ supply and distribution.

In this essay I analyze the advantages and disadvantages of markets for human organs, explore the ways in which such markets might be organized and regulated, and assess the wisdom of the statutes that outlaw such markets. The subject, which is complicated in any event, is rendered even more difficult because it is heavily fraught with strong moral sentiments. To many individuals, the notion of employing markets in such a setting is deeply disturbing. I shall take these moral concerns seriously here. In particular, I shall ask whether it is possible to design compensation schemes that are not strongly antithetical to our ethical intuitions. But beyond this, I shall also explore why it is that these intuitions, at least initially, often run so strongly counter to the notion of paying compensation for transplantable organs.

Whatever our initial sentiments, we have an obligation as a society to inquire seriously into these issues, difficult as they may be. Each year many thousands of lives are lost for lack of transplantable organs, and hundreds or millions of dollars are spent on the existing transplant system — and these figures are likely to increase significantly in the future. We cannot afford to reject any approach that would increase the supply of organs, or improve the efficiency with which organs are allocated and transplanted, without the most thoughtful consideration. Moreover, careful analysis here also promises to illuminate other areas where prohibition of commercial sales is currently a topic of serious debate, such as adoption and surrogate motherhood.

II.   THE CURRENT LEGAL REGIME

Historically, the common law did not provide anyone with a clear property right in a human corpse, and thus did not give anyone the authority to transfer a cadaver or any of its parts for any purpose by gift or sale. When transplants first became feasible, therefore, there was no legal mechanism whereby individuals could designate that, upon death, their organs could be used for transplants. To rectify this situation, the Uniform Anatomical Gift Act was promulgated in 1968. This Act, which was adopted in some form in every state by 1973, explicitly gives individuals the right to designate prior to death whether their bodies or organs are to be donated for transplants. In case a decedent's wishes are not known, the Act provides that the next of kin has the right to designate whether or not organs are to be donated.

The Uniform Anatomical Gift Act deals expressly only with donations of organs; it is silent on the subject of sales. According to the chairman of the committee that drafted the Act, it was intended neither to encourage nor to discourage remuneration: "It is possible, of course, that abuses may occur if payment could customarily be demanded, but every payment is not necessarily unethical. . . . Until the matter of payment becomes a problem of some dimensions, the matter should be left to the decency of intelligent human beings."

In the 1960s, prior to the adoption of the Uniform Anatomical Gift Act, some states had adopted statutes explicitly prohibiting the sale of human bodies and organs. Most of these states repealed such statutes when they adopted the Uniform Act. It is unclear whether these repeals were simply the result of a program of repealing all relevant statutes predating the Uniform Act, or whether they reflected a judgment that the prohibitions on sales were either overridden by the Act or, conversely, made redundant by it. Delaware, in any event, was evidently not of the latter view, since it added an explicit prohibition on sales to its version of the Act.

The status of the sale of organs for transplantation therefore remained uncertain for another decade, until the adoption by Congress of the National Organ Transplant Act (NOTA) in 1984. NOTA was essentially an effort to enhance the system of voluntary provision of transplantable organs contemplated by the Uniform Anatomical Gift Act. Its principal provisions established federal financial support for local nonprofit organ procurement organizations and for a national organ procurement and transplantation network to assist in matching organ donors and recipients. NOTA also, however, effectively outlawed commercial markets in transplantable organs by making it a federal crime "for any person to knowingly acquire, receive, or otherwise transfer any human organ for valuable consideration for use in human transplantation if the transfer affects interstate commerce." Several states have subsequently supplemented this enactment with separate statutes of their own outlawing the sale or purchase of human organs. As a consequence, any effort to establish a market for organs would today require the repeal or amendment of legislation at both the federal and state levels.

Neither the federal nor the state legislation outlawing markets for organs was accompanied by careful policy analysis justifying the ban. NOTA did, however, establish a federal Task Force on Organ Procurement and Transplantation to inquire further into the policy issues raised by transplants. Yet, when the Task Force submitted its report in 1986, it reaffirmed NOTA's ban on the commercialization of organ transplantation without further analysis, simply offering the conclusory observation that "society's moral values militate against regarding the body as a commodity" and suggesting that such a ban is appropriate to "encourage altruism." The task force also proceeded to encourage individual states to adopt their own prohibitions on the commercial sale of organs because NOTA, limited as it is to sales affecting interstate commerce, might not be entirely effective in suppressing such sales. . . .

III.   Markets for Procuring Organs

Some organs can be obtained from living donors. This is true, in particular, of kidneys, since most individuals can lose one of their two kidneys without serious impairment of their health. It appears that, in banning commercial sale of organs, the authors of NOTA and of the similar state statutes were focusing particularly on sales by living donors, and especially on one notorious effort by a former Virginia doctor, whose license had previously been revoked for fraud, to establish a company to solicit living individuals (including indigents from the third world) to sell one of their kidneys for transplantation in transactions to be brokered by the company for a profit. Most transplantable organs, however, are "harvested" (as current terminology would have it) from cadavers, and indeed many organs, including livers, hearts, and lungs, can only be obtained from persons who are deceased. I shall therefore focus first on markets for cadaveric organs, and then later turn to the issues raised by sales of organs from living donors. . . .

B.   MARKETS FOR ORGANS FROM LIVING DONORS

In theory, it would be much simpler to employ compensation in procuring organs — in particular, kidneys — from living donors than it would be in procuring cadaveric organs. In the past, payment has routinely been made to living donors for replenishable body products such as blood, sperm, skin, and hair. Strong controversy has arisen, however, over proposals to extend payment to kidneys. In fact, as observed earlier, the existing legal bans on organ sales seem primarily to have been inspired by such proposals.

Before assessing the objections that have offered to purchasing organs from living donors, let us first consider the potential advantages. . . .

1.   Some Advantages

The chief advantage of using living donors for kidneys is that they offer a source of supply that could easily satisfy 100 percent of foreseeable demand for transplants. . . .Widespread acquisition of kidneys from living donors therefore holds the promise of saving many lives, and of avoiding the substantial public expense and private agony of hemodialysis, which (aside from death) is the current alternative to a transplant.

Further, a large pool of living donors could lead to an important increase in the *quality* as well as the quantity of kidneys for transplant. The long-run success rate of kidney transplants has been closely correlated with the closeness of the match of tissue types between donor and recipient, and there is evidence that this correlation continues to hold even with the use of the new immunosuppressive drug cyclosporin. . . . Moreover, transplants from living donors eliminate the critical problems of timing that affect transplants of cadaveric organs, which require that a recipient be located and prepared, and the transplant undertaken, within hours of the (often unexpected) death of the donor.

2.   Protecting the Poor and Improvident

From a large fraction of the population, selling a single kidney might be a reasonable decision at prices in a range that demand could support. Donation is evidently not highly hazardous to the donor's health: the increased risk of death to a healthy 35-year-old from giving up a single kidney, it has been estimated, is about the same as that involved in driving a car 16 miles every workday. Many individuals willingly (and, most of us would probably conclude, reasonably) incur risks on this order to achieve savings in personal expenses or to obtain higher wages. Moreover, the fact that living individuals commonly donate kidneys to their relatives also suggests that such transactions are efficient in the economic sense — that is, that the organ is worth more to the recipient than it is to the donor — and thus that there will commonly be a price that will make both donor and recipient better off even in the absence of true altruism.

It is commonly argued that the poor would be the principal sellers in a market for organs, and that therefore such a market would unacceptably exploit the poor for the benefit of the rich. The classical objection to this argument is, of course, that it is a perverse kind of paternalism that prohibits a class of transactions simply because the poor are likely to be the principal sellers, since the result of the prohibition is to leave the poor worse off by their own rights: any individual who would agree to sell would evidently rather have the money than have the slightly greater chance of avoiding death or illness that would result from keeping the kidney. Thus, if society is not willing to give the poor sufficient assets so that they are not inclined to sell a kidney, then society should not refuse to let them sell one of the few assets they have. And, after all, society does not prevent the poor from accepting, in return for money, jobs such as coal mining and meatpacking that carry substantial risks of injury or death. Why should kidneys be different?

One might well conclude that kidneys are not in fact different, and that concerns about exploitation of the poor are misplaced here. But there are at least two reasons why selling kidneys might be thought distinguishable from selling one's labor to a meatpacking plant.

[The writer discusses (1) the irreversibility of the kidney sale, unless the seller were later to become a recipient; by contrast, one can quit the meat-packing job at any time; and (2) the poor man's anguish if he refuses to sell his kidney knowing that to do so could benefit his family.]

In any event, a market for kidneys from living donors would need to be regulated in some fashion to guard against improvident transactions. Presumably one would not want a situation in which any unscrupulous doctor could induce any drunk to come in off the streets at any time and yield up a kidney on the spot for $50. Many forms of regulation would be possible. A rather heavily regulated regime, for example, might require that only federally licensed agencies can purchase kidneys (and perhaps require as well that the agencies be nonprofit); that there be a six-month waiting period between the time that the agreement of sale is entered into and the time the kidney is removed, at any time during which the transaction can be rescinded; that sellers must be at least 25 years of age, be examined by a physician and a social worker, and be approved by a consultative panel unconnected to the purchasing agency; and that the price not be below a mandated minimum sum. The question, then, is whether a commercial market for kidneys, *even with* an appropriate degree of regulation, would so harm the poor and improvident that such a market would be socially unacceptable. As a further way to test one's sensibilities here, consider a system under which the poor would be specifically prohibited from selling their organs — for example, by prohibiting purchases from individuals whose average income for the past three years was not at least 80 percent of median family income in the U.S. (thus cutting persons in the lower 40 percent of the income distribution out of the market).

Moreover, in considering distributive issues it is important to recognize that the poor and improvident are quite disproportionately represented among those who suffer from kidney failure. If commercial purchase of kidneys from living donors would substantially increase the supply available for transplantation, these groups would therefore gain much of the benefit. The net result might therefore be quite progressive.

In sum, although the issues are difficult, it is not at all obvious that concern for the poor and improvident is a sufficient, or perhaps even a substantial, reason to reject purchases from living donors.

3.   Commodification

It is frequently said — as in the statement from the federal Task Force Report quoted above — that the commercial sale of human organs, and particularly organs from living donors, should be prohibited because it would tend to "commodify" them. It is difficult, however, to find a clear statement of precisely what is meant by commodification, or why it is undesirable.[28]

---

28. One of the most recent efforts to give content to the notion of commodification appears in Margaret Jane Radin, Market Inalienability, 100 Harv. L. Rev. 1879 (1987). Her analysis, which still leaves the general concept rather vague, becomes most substantive when she discusses the considerations that determine which transactions (at least at this stage

Normative Categories. The underlying problem here, perhaps, is at least in part that as a society we tend to put most transactions into one or the other of two rather distinct normative categories, which we might label "market transactions" and "non-market transactions." (Surely our culture in fact provides for many normative categories that differ on a number of dimensions; the simple two-category model suggested here is offered only to be suggestive.) In market transactions, a good or service is exchanged for cash or other valuable consideration under circumstances in which both parties to the transaction enter into it in the expectation that they will be personally better off after the transaction than before. In non-market transactions, on the other hand, an individual's willingness to enter into the transaction is governed not by calculation of immediate personal gain, but rather by a variety of other-regarding social mores and norms that the individual feels obliged to observe. Transactions involving the acquisition and care of automobiles tend to be put in the first category; transactions involving the acquisition and care of children tend to be put in the second category. For those transactions that are in the first category, social mores not only permit, but in fact encourage, individuals to be strongly self-seeking. Thus, if one sells one's used car to a stranger for less than its full market value, one is likely to be subjected to some social shaming for being a chump rather than praised for being an altruist. For those that are in the second category, on the other hand, narrow calculations of personal advantage are considered inappropriate. Thus if one tires of one's child it is not deemed acceptable, much less praiseworthy, to stop giving it food or to sell it to the highest bidder. . . .

This inflexibility in our normative categories may help explain the reflexively negative moral response that commonly greets proposals for marketing human organs. There are a number of reasons why individuals might commonly be inclined to feel that giving up a body part to another individual belongs in the category of non-market transactions, to be governed largely by norms of altruism: There have previously been no markets here to which individuals might become accustomed. To those who have not thought closely about the nature of the risks involved, yielding up a vital organ such as a kidney while still alive may seem like the kind of life-threatening sacrifice, such as attempting to rescue a drowning person in heavy seas, that cannot easily be made the subject of market transactions and that have therefore always been governed primarily by other-regarding

---

of social development) are inappropriate for commodification — i.e., for commercial sales — and which are not. (Id. at 1909-14.) These considerations are: (1) improvident sales may make the seller worse off by her own estimation; (2) certain things become "different" (and presumably inferior) things if they are bought and sold; (3) market transactions will tend to drive out non-market (and particularly altruistic) transactions, which for some goods have special value. Unfortunately, Radin offers very little analysis of considerations (2) and (3) — which, as she notes, are closely related.

norms. For the past fifteen years, for good reasons or ill, our society has sought to delegitimate markets and encourage norms of altruism in the seemingly analogous area of blood donation. And for twenty-five years we have also been trying to encourage norms of altruism in the area of organ donation itself.

But initial resistance to shifting normative categories should not in itself be a sufficient reason for avoiding change. Transactions can be and have been recategorized when technological changes have made market mechanisms advantageous. For example, we are now quite accustomed to having proprietary institutions market nursing care for the elderly and matchmaking ("dating services") for the young. Or, to take another example closer to the subject at hand, after several decades' experience our society has accepted a thriving market in human sperm brokered by proprietary firms. It would be easy to characterize such a market as deeply offensive to fundamental values involving paternity, sexual relations, responsibility for and identity with one's biological offspring, and the need to make children feel that their relationship with their parents transcends that of mere commodities — and evidently there was in fact substantial ethical resistance to this market when it was first introduced. Yet over time we have chosen not to so characterize such transactions, but rather to draw the symbolic lines between our normative categories elsewhere so that market transactions in human sperm are not perceived as undermining non-market norms in those areas where such norms continue to play a strong functional role.

On the other hand, it is costly to make people upset their received normative categories and there is no point in doing so unless substantial benefits will result. Moreover, there may be some circumstances in which it is unusually difficult to acculturate individuals to distinguish between different categories of transactions for normative purposes. For example, transplants of kidneys are least likely to be rejected by the recipient's body when there is a close match between the tissue types of the donor and the recipient. This means that transplants of kidneys from living donors within the same family are often the most successful. Most intra-family transactions are and must remain non-market transactions rather than market ones, however, and thus we are socialized to think that the calculus of the market is inappropriate among family members. Introducing market considerations into one very significant type of intra-family transaction — that involving transfers of kidneys — might therefore strain the whole moral fabric of the families involved. You cannot extract a high price from your brother for one of your kidneys and then expect him to willingly provide you with extensive moral support for free while you go through your divorce.

Moreover, it may not even be possible to employ market transactions just for kidney transplants *outside* the family without putting severe strains on intra-family relationships. For example, an individual might feel deeply resentful if subjected to moral pressure to donate a kidney to a family member without compensation when a substantial payment would be forthcoming if the organ were transplanted outside the family.[31] In short, it may be very difficult here to draw lines — whether between transfers of kidneys within the family and other types of intra-family transfers, or between intra-family and inter-family transfers of kidneys.

It follows that, if most kidneys from living donors had to come from family members, it might be best not to try to develop market transactions for kidneys even among strangers. The rapid development of immunosuppressive drugs, however, has made transplants among unrelated individuals increasingly feasible. As this development reduces the need for intra-family donations, the costs of using market transactions among living kidney donors — in the form of moral strain on family relationships in general, and perhaps also in the form of reduced intra-family kidney donations — may decline (indeed, may already have declined) to the point where they no longer need be considered important.

In any event it is understandable that, whatever the ultimate merits of a market for human organs, the initial reaction to a proposal for such a market is likely to be one of strong moral opposition. NOTA's proscription of market transactions in organs presumably reflects precisely this type of reaction. Ironically, but perhaps expectably, this ban has been enacted just at the time when such a policy is probably becoming anachronistic, not only for cadaveric organs but perhaps for organs from living donors as well. Before markets for organs were feasible, there was little incentive to outlaw them. And now that such markets *do* seem feasible, the idea of having them offends the norms that developed in their absence. . . .

NATIONAL ORGAN TRANSPLANT ACT (NOTA)

42 U.S.C.S. §274e (1993)

§274(e)   PROHIBITION OF ORGAN PURCHASES

(A)   PROHIBITION

It shall be unlawful for any person to knowingly acquire, receive, or otherwise transfer any human organ for valuable consideration for use in human transplantation if the transfer affects interstate commerce.

---

31. An analogous problem arises for daughters or sons who have a particular skill — for example, as a doctor or lawyer — that is in demand by other members of the family, who apply pressure for the contribution of professional time that could be charged for on the market.

(B)   PENALTIES

Any person who violates subsection (a) of this section shall be fined not more than $50,000 or imprisoned not more than five years, or both.

(C)   DEFINITIONS

For purposes of subsection (a) of this section:

(1) The term "human organ" means the human (including fetal) kidney, liver, heart, lung, pancreas, bone marrow, cornea, eye, bone, and skin or any subpart thereof and any other human organ (or any subpart thereof, including that derived from a fetus) specified by the Secretary of Health and Human Services regulation.

(2) The term "valuable consideration" does not include the reasonable payments associated with the removal, transportation, implantation, processing, preservation, quality control, and storage of human organ or the expenses of travel, housing, and lost wages incurred by the donor of a human organ in connection with the donation of the organ.

(3) The term "interstate commerce" has the meaning prescribed for it by section 321(b) of Title 21.

(Pub. L. 98-507, Title III, §301, Oct. 19, 1984, 98 Stat. 2346; Pub. L. 100-607, Title IV, §407, Nov. 4, 1988, 102 Stat. 3116.)

"I hold the organ donors record."

NOTES AND QUESTIONS

1.   **Advantages of a market.** What are Hansmann's efficiency and distributional arguments in favor of a market for human organs?

2.   **Disadvantages.** How does Hansmann respond to those who have opposed a market for organs?

3.   **Consent.** Hansmann considers in much greater depth the issue of voluntariness or consent addressed by the *Baby M* court. Do you find his argument convincing?

4.   **Commodification, pro and con.** Hansmann provides a forceful response to Radin's anti-commodification argument. Which side do you find more convincing?

5.   **Organ sales are common.** Sales of human organs are legal in many countries. There has been a considerable amount of reporting on various practices and abuses. Britain forbade the selling of organs from live donors in 1989; particularly influential was the testimony of a Turk who stated he had been lured to Britain with a job offer and sent to a hospital where an IV was inserted for what he believed was a health check; he awoke in pain, to discover that one of his kidneys had been removed. See Alastair Percival, Turkish Housewife Who Swapped Her Kidney for Furniture, Press Association Newsfile, April 4, 1990; Trading Flesh Around the Globe, Time, June 17, 1991, at 61. A 1991 story reported the going rate for a kidney in India is $1,500, for a cornea $4,000 and for a patch of skin $50. Trading Flesh, *supra*. Stories include those of Mohammad Ageel, a poor tailor who sold a kidney for $2,600, who said he needed the money "for the marriage of two daughters and paying off of debts." Trading Flesh, *supra*. Varantha Muthulakshmy, a 31-year-old housemaid and mother of two, was interviewed as she sat waiting to sell her kidney: "I can't bear this debt anymore; I can't bear to go home. . . . If I can sell my kidney for 27,500 rupees ($1,100), I'll pay the debt and save the rest for my eldest daughter's wedding dowry." For Poor Indians, Sale of Kidney Can Be Price of Survival; Organ Trade Raises Ethical Questions, Atlanta Const., Nov. 28, 1991. Other stories report organ sales to pay for college educations, Time, *supra*, for children's operations, Percival, *supra*, for a divorcee to support her five-year-old son and buy apartment furniture, id. Middlemen in India, where law prohibits organ transplants from unrelated donors, are reported to make large profits. David L. James, Body Parts for Sale: Poor of India Take Drastic Measures for Promises of Wealth, The Ottawa Citizen, Feb. 22, 1992, at J4. "It is a dirty business," said Mother Teresa from her premises in Calcutta. "The rich are eating the poor." Id.

How would you use this media coverage if you were arguing in favor of a ban on sales of organs? How would you respond if you were arguing in favor of a market for organs?

6.   **Sales of blood.** Sales of blood are legal in the United States. Today the commercial blood industry pays donors at about $10 per pint. The sale of blood is common among the very poor; many "skid row" areas have

blood banks. Recent cuts in welfare benefits have been followed by a rise in blood sales to blood banks. See Jason DeParle, Off the Rolls — A Special Report: The Sorrows, and Surprises, after a Welfare Plan Ends, N.Y. Times, Apr. 14, 1992, at A1.

7.   **Death and the market.** In July 1990, *The New York Times* reported on the proposal of Milwaukee County Board of Supervisors member Anthony Zielinski to sell the organs of dead AFDC[7] recipients to reduce the county's burial expenses. "If they can't help society when they're alive, maybe they can help it when they're dead," he commented. The report notes: "A flood of subsequent criticism that the plan would rob welfare recipients of dignity even in death persuaded him to drop the idea and apologize." AP, Furor over Call to Sell Organs of Poor People, N.Y. Times, July 21, 1990, at 9. Compare Whaley v. Tuscola County, 58 F.3d 1111 (6th Cir. 1995), holding that the next-of-kin have a constitutionally protected property interest in the dead body of a relative, in a suit by the next-of-kin to bar the county pathologist from removing decedent corneas or eyeballs and their use (through an eye bank) for transplant purposes.

MOORE v. REGENTS OF THE UNIVERSITY OF CALIFORNIA

51 Cal. 3d 120, 793 P.2d 479 (1990)
cert. denied, *499 U.S. 936 (1991)*

§I

. . . The plaintiff is John Moore (Moore), who underwent treatment for hairy-cell leukemia at the Medical Center of the University of California at Los Angeles (UCLA Medical Center). The five defendants are: (1) Dr. David W. Golde (Golde), a physician who attended Moore at UCLA Medical center; (2) the Regents of the University of California (Regents), who own and operate the university; (3) Shirley G. Quan (Quan), a researcher employed by the Regents; (4) Genetics Institute, Inc. (Genetics Institute); and (5) Sandoz pharmaceutical corporations and related entities (collectively Sandoz).

Moore first visited UCLA Medial Center on October 5, 1976, shortly after he learned that he had hairy-cell leukemia. After hospitalizing Moore and "withdraw[ing] extensive amounts of blood, bone marrow aspirate, and other bodily substances," Golde confirmed that diagnosis. At this time all defendants, including Golde, were aware that "certain blood products and scientific efforts" and access to a patient whose blood contained

---

7. Aid for Families with Dependent Children (AFDC) is the formal name for the government program that provides income for families with dependent children, commonly called "welfare."

these substances would provide "competitive, commercial and scientific advantages."

On October 8, 1976, Golde recommended that Moore's spleen be removed. Golde informed Moore "that he had reason to fear for his life, and that the proposed splenectomy operation . . . was necessary to slow down the progress of his disease." Based upon Golde's representations, Moore signed a written consent form authorizing the splenectomy.

Before the operation, Golde and Quan "formed the intent and made arrangements to obtain portions of [Moore's] spleen following its removal" and to take them to a separate research unit. . . . Those research activities "were not intended to have . . . any relation to [Moore's] medical . . . care." However neither Golde nor Quan informed Moore of their plans to conduct this research or requested his permission. . . .

Moore returned to the UCLA Medical Center several times between November 1976 and September 1983. He did so at Golde's direction and based upon representation "that such visits were necessary and required for his health and well-being, and based upon the trust inherent in and by virtue of the physician-patient relationship. . . ." On each of these visits Golde withdrew additional samples of "blood, blood serum, skin, bone marrow aspirate, and sperm." On each occasion Moore travelled to the UCLA Medical Center from his home in Seattle because he had been told that the procedures were to be performed only there and only under Golde's direction.

[The court quoted the plaintiff's complaint as follows:] "In fact, throughout the period of time that [Moore] was under [Golde's] care and treatment . . . The defendants were actively involved in a number of activities which they concealed from [Moore]. . . ." Specifically, defendants were conducting research on Moore's cells and planned to "benefit financially and competitively . . . by virtue of [Golde's] on-going physician-patient relationship. . . ."

Sometime before August 1979, Golde established a cell line from Moore's T-lymphocytes. On January 30, 1981, the Regents applied for a patent on the cell line, listing Golde and Quan as inventors. "[B]y virtue of an established policy . . . , [the] Regents, Golde, and Quan would share in any royalties or profits . . . arising out of [the] patent." The patent issued on March 20, 1984, naming Golde and Quan as the inventors of the cell line and the Regents as the assignee of the patent. (U.S. Patent No. 4,438,032 (Mar. 20, 1984).)

The Regents' patent also covers various methods for using the cell line to produce lymphokines. Moore admits in his complaint that "the true clinical potential of each of the lymphokines . . . [is] difficult to produce, [but] . . . competing commercial firms in these relevant fields have published reports in biotechnology industry periodicals predicting a potential market of approximately 3.01 billion dollars by the year 1990 for a whole range of [lymphokine products]. . . ."

With the Regents' assistance, Golde negotiated agreements for commercial development of the cell line and products to be derived from it. Under an agreement with Genetics Institute, Golde "became a paid consultant" and "acquired the rights to $75,000 shares of common stock." Genetics Institute also agreed to pay Golde and the Regents "at least $330,000 over three years, including a pro-rata share of [Golde's] salary and fringe benefits, in exchange for . . . exclusive access to the material and research performed" on the cell line and products derived from it. On June 4, 1982, Sandoz "was added to the agreement," and compensation payable to Golde and the Regents was increased by $100,000. [T]hroughout this period, . . . Quan spent as much as 70 [percent] of her time working . . . on research" related to the cell line. . . .

§III. Discussion

A. Breach of Fiduciary Duty and Lack of Informed Consent

Moore repeatedly alleges that Golde failed to disclose the extent of his research and economic interest in Moore's cells before obtaining consent to the medical procedures by which the cells were extracted. These allegations, in our view, state a cause of action against Golde for invading a legally protected interest of his patient. This cause of action can properly be characterized either as the breach of a fiduciary duty to disclose facts material to the patient's consent or, alternatively, as the performance of medical procedures without first having obtained the patient's informed consent.

Our analysis begins with three well-established principles. First, "a person of adult years and in sound mind has the right, in the exercise of control over his own body, to determine whether or not to submit to lawful medical treatment." Cobbs v. Grant, 502 P.2d 1 (Cal. 1972). Second, "the patient's consent to treatment, to be effective, must be an informed consent." Id. at 9. Third, in soliciting the patient's consent, a physician has a fiduciary duty to disclose all information material to the patient's decision. Id. . . .

[A] reasonable patient would want to know whether a physician has an economic interest that might affect the physician's professional judgment. As the Court of Appeal has said, "[c]ertainly a sick patient deserves to be free of any reasonable suspicion that his doctor's judgment is influenced by a profit motive." Magan Medical Clinic v. Cal. State Bd. of Medical Examiners, 57 Cal. Rptr. 256, 262, (Ct. App. 1967). . . .

[A] physician who treats a patient in whom he also has a research interest has potentially conflicting loyalties. This is because medical treatment decisions are made on the basis of proportionality — weighing the benefits to the patient against the risks to the patient. As another court has said, "the determination as to whether the burdens of treatment are worth enduring for any individual patient depends upon the facts unique to each case," and "the patient's interest and desire are the key ingredients of the decision-making process." A physician who adds his own research interests to this balance may be tempted to order a scientifically useful procedure or test that offers marginal, or no, benefits to the patient. The possibility that an interest extraneous to the patient's health has affected the physician's judgment is something that a reasonable patient would want to know in deciding whether to consent to a proposed course of treatment. It is material to the patient's decision and, thus, a prerequisite to informed consent. . . .

Accordingly, we hold that a physician who is seeking a patient's consent for a medical procedure must, in order to satisfy his fiduciary duty and to obtain the patient's informed consent, disclose personal interest unrelated to the patient's health, whether research or economic, that may affect his medical judgement. . . .

B. CONVERSION

Moore also attempts to characterize the invasion of his rights as a conversion — a tort that protects against interference with possessory and ownership interests in personal property. He theorizes that he continued to own his cells following their removal from his body, at least for the purpose of directing their use, and that he never consented to their use in potentially lucrative medical research. Thus, to complete Moore's argument, defendant's unauthorized use of his cells constitutes a conversion. As a result of the alleged conversion, Moore claims a proprietary interest in each of the products that any of the defendants might ever create from his cells or the patented cell line. . . .

1. Moore's Claim under Existing Law

. . . Since Moore clearly did not expect to retain possession of his cells following their removal, to sue for their conversion he must have retained an ownership interest in them. . . .

Moore relies, as did the Court of Appeal, primarily on decisions addressing privacy rights. One line of cases involves unwanted publicity. These opinions hold that every person has a proprietary interest in his own likeness and that unauthorized, business use of a likeness is redressible as a tort. Moore . . . argues that "[i]f the courts have found a sufficient proprietary interest in one's persona, how could one not have a right in one's own genetic material, something far more profoundly the essence of one's human uniqueness than a name or a face?" However, . . . the goal and result of defendant's effort has been to manufacture lymphokines. Lymphokines, unlike a name or a face, have the same molecular structure in every human system. Moreover, the particular genetic material which is responsible for the natural production of lymphokines, and which defendants use to manufacture lymphokines in the laboratory, is also the same in every person; it is no more unique to Moore than the number of vertebrae in the spine or the chemical formula of hemoglobin. [Moore also uses the privacy cases holding that patients have the right to refuse medical treatment because each person has a right to determine what shall be done with his or her own body. However, we can protect privacy and personal dignity by requiring disclosure under fiduciary duty and informed consent doctrines, rather than] accepting the extremely problematic conclusion that interference with those interests amounts to a conversion of personal property. . . .

The next consideration that makes Moore's claim of ownership problematic is California statutory law, which drastically limits a patient's control over excised cells. . . . By restricting how excised cells may be used and requiring their eventual destruction, the statute eliminates so many of the rights ordinarily attached to property that one cannot simply assume that what is left amounts to "property" or "ownership" for purposes of conversion law. . . .

Finally, the subject matter of the Regents' patent — the patent cell line and the product derived from it — cannot be Moore's property. This is because the patent cell line is both factually and legally distinct from the cells taken from Moore's body. Federal law permits the patenting of the organisms that represent the product of "human ingenuity," but not naturally occurring organisms. Diamond v. Chakrabarty, 447 U.S. 303, 309-310 (1980). Human cell lines are patentable because "[l]ong-term adoption and growth of human tissues and cells in culture is difficult — often considered an art . . . ," and the probability of success is low. It is the inventive effect that patent law rewards, not the discovery of naturally occurring raw materials. Thus, Moore's allegations that he owned the cell line and that products derived from it are inconsistent with the patent, which constitutes an authoritative determination that the cell line is the product of invention. . . .

2.   Should Conversion Liability be Extended?

. . . Of the relevant policy considerations, two are of overriding importance. The first is protection of a competent patient's right to make autonomous medical decisions. . . . This policy weighs in favor of providing a remedy to patients when physicians act with undisclosed motives that may affect their professional judgment. The second important policy consideration is that we not threaten with disabling civil liability innocent parties who are engaged in socially useful activities, such as researchers who have no reason to believe that their use of a particular cell sample is, or may be against a donor's wishes. . . .

Research on human cells plays a critical role in medical research. This is so because researchers are increasingly able to isolate naturally occurring medically useful biological substances and to produce useful quantities of such substances through genetic engineering. These efforts are beginning to bear fruit. Products developed through biotechnology that have already been approved for marketing in this country include treatments and tests for leukemia, cancer, diabetes, dwarfism, hepatitis-B, kidney transplant rejection, emphysema, osteoporosis, ulcers, anemia, infertility and gynecological tumor, to name but a few. . . .

To expand liability by extending conversion law into this area would have a broad impact. The House Committee on Science and Technology of the United States Congress found that "49 percent of the researchers at the medical institutions surveyed used human tissues or cells in their research." Many receive grants from the National Institute of Health for this work. In addition, "there are nearly 350 commercial biotechnology firms in the United States actively engaged in biotechnology research and commercial product development and approximately 25 to 30 percent appear to be engaged in research to develop a human therapeutic or diagnostic reagent. . . . Most, but not all, of the human therapeutic products are derived from human tissues and cells, or human cell lines or cloned genes." . . .

If the scientific uses of human cells are to be held liable for failing to investigate the consensual pedigree of their raw materials, we believe that Legislature should make the decision. Complex policy choices affecting all society are involved, and "[l]egislatures, in making such policy decisions, have the ability to gather empirical evidence, solicit the advice of experts and hold hearings at which all interested parties present evidence and express their views. . . ." Foley v. Interactive Data Corp., 765 P.2d 373, 397 n.31 (Cal. 1988). . . .

For these reasons, we hold that the allegations of Moore's third amended complaint state a cause of action for breach of fiduciary duty or lack of informed consent, but not conversion.

ARMAND ARABIAN, J., concurring. . . . Plaintiff has asked us to recognize and enforce a right to sell one's own body tissue for profit. He entreats us to regard the human vessel — the single most venerated and protected subject in any civilized society — as equal with the basest commercial commodity. He urges us to commingle the sacred with the profane. He asks much. . . .

I share Justice Mosk's sense of outrage [at defendants' conduct], but I cannot follow its path. His eloquent paean to the human spirit illuminates the problem, not the solution. Does it uplift or degrade the "unique human persona" to treat human tissue as a fungible article of commerce? Would it advance or impede the human condition, spiritually or scientifically, by delivering the majestic force of the law behind plaintiff's claim? I do not know the answers to these troubling questions, nor am I willing — like Justice

Mosk — to treat them simply as issue of "tort" law, susceptible of judicial resolution.

Where then shall a complete resolution be found? Clearly the Legislature, as the majority opinion suggests, is the proper deliberative forum. . . .

ALLEN BROUSSARD, J., concurring and dissenting. . . .

[T]he majority's fear that the availability of a conversion remedy will restrict access to existing cell line is unrealistic. In the vast majority of instances the tissues and cells in existing repositories will not represent a potential source of liability because they will have come from patients who consented to their organ's use for scientific purposes under circumstances in which such consent was not tainted by a failure to disclose the known valuable nature of the cells. . . .

Furthermore, even in the rare instance — like the present case — in which a conversion action might be successfully pursued, the potential liability is not likely "to destroy the economic incentive to conduct important medical research," as the majority asserts. If, as the majority suggests, the great bulk of the value of a cell line patent and derivative products is attributable to the efforts of medical research and drug companies, rather than to the "raw materials" taken from a patient, the patient's damages will be correspondingly limited, and innocent medical researchers and drug manufacturers will retain the considerable economic benefits resulting from their own work. . . .

Justice Arabian's concurring opinion suggests that the majority's conclusion is informed by the precept that it is immoral to sell human body parts for profit. But the majority's rejection of plaintiff's conversion cause of action does not mean that body parts may not be bought or sold for research or commercial purposes or that no private individual or entity may benefit economically from the fortuitous value of plaintiff's diseased cells. Far from elevating these biological materials above the marketplace, the majority's holding simply bars plaintiff, the source of the cells, from obtaining the benefit of the cells' value, but permits defendants, who allegedly obtained the cells from plaintiff by improper means, to retain and exploit the full economic value of their ill-gotten gains free of their ordinary common law liability for conversion. . . .

STANLEY MOSK, J., dissenting. . . .[T]he concept of property is often said to refer to a "bundle of rights" that may be exercised with respect to that object — principally the rights to possess the property, to use the property, to exclude others from property, and to dispose of the property by sale or by gift. . . . But the same bundle of rights does not attach to all forms of property. For a variety of policy reasons, the law limits or even forbids the exercise of certain rights over certain forms of property. For example, both law and contract may limit the right of an owner of real property to use his parcel as he sees fit. Owners of various forms of personal property may likewise be subject to restrictions of time, place and manner of their use. Limitations on the disposition of real property, while less common, may also be imposed. Finally, some types of personal property may be sold but not given away,[9] while others may be given away but not sold,[10] and still others may neither be given away nor sold.[11]

In each of the foregoing instances, the limitation or prohibition diminishes the bundle of rights that would otherwise attach to the property, yet what remains is still deemed in law to be a predictable property interest. . . . [Moore] at least had the right to do with his own tissue whatever the defendants did with it: i.e., he could have contracted with researchers and pharmaceutical companies to develop and exploit the vast commercial potential of his tissue and its product. Defendants certainly believe that their right to do the foregoing . . . is a significant property right. . . . The Court of Appeal summed up the point by observing the "Defendants' position that plaintiff cannot own his tissue, but that they can, is fraught with irony." It is also legally untenable. . . .

To be sure, the patent granted defendants the exclusive right to make, use, or sell the invention for a period of 17 years. But Moore does not assert any such right for himself. Rather, he seeks to show that he is entitled, in fairness and equity, to some share in the profits that defendants have made and will make from their commercial exploitation of the Mo cell line. I do not question that the cell line is primarily the product of defendant's inventive effort. Yet likewise no one can question Moore's crucial contribution to the invention — an invention named, ironically, after him: but for the cells of Moore's body taken by defendants, there would have been no Mo cell line. . . .

[E]very individual has a legally predictable property interest in his own body and its products. First, our society acknowledges a profound ethical imperative to respect the human body as the physical and temporal expression of the unique human persona. One manifestation of that respect is our prohibition against direct abuse of the body by torture or other form of cruel or unusual punishment. Another is our prohibition against indirect abuse of the body by its economic exploitation for the sole benefit of another person. The most abhorrent form of such exploitation, of course, was the institution of slavery. Lesser forms, such as indentured servitude or even debtor's prison, have also disappeared. Yet their specter haunts the laboratories and board rooms of today's biotechnological research-industrial complex. It arises wherever scientist or industrialists claim, as defendants claim

---

9. A person contemplating bankruptcy may sell his property at its "reasonably equivalent value," but he may not make a gift of the same property. (See 11 U.S.C. § 548(a).)

10. A sportsman may give away wild fish or game that he has caught or killed pursuant to his license, but he may not sell it. (Fish & Game Code §§3039, 7121.) The transfer of human organs and blood is a special case that I discuss below.

11. E.g., a license to practice a profession, or a prescription drug in the hands of the person for whom it is prescribed.

here, the right to appropriate and exploit a patient's tissue for their sole economic benefit — the right, in other words to freely mine or harvest valuable physical properties of the patient's body: " . . . Such research tends to treat the human body as a commodity — a means to a profitable end. The dignity and sanctity with which we regard the human whole, body as well as mind and soul, are absent when we allow researchers to further their own interest without the patient's participation by using a patient's cells as the basis for a marketable product." Danforth, Cells, Sales, & Royalties: The Patient's Right to a Profit, 6 Yale L. & Pol'y Rev. 179, 190 (1988).

A second policy consideration adds notions of equity to those of ethics. Our society values fundamental fairness in dealings between its members, and condemns the unjust enrichment of any member at the expense of another. This is particularly true when, as here, the parties are not in equal bargaining positions. We are repeatedly told that the commercial products of the biotechnological revolution "hold the promise of tremendous profit." In the case at bar, for example, the complaint alleges that the market for the kinds of proteins produced by the Mo cell line was predicted to exceed $3 billion by 1990. These profits are currently shared exclusively between the biotechnology industry and the universities that support that industry. . . .

There is, however, a third party to the biotechnology enterprise — the patient who is the source of the blood or tissue for which all these profits are derived. While he may be a silent partner, his contribution to the venture is absolutely crucial: . . . but for the cells of Moore's body taken by defendants there would have been no Mo cell line at all. Yet defendants deny that Moore is entitled to any share whatever in the proceeds of this cell line. This is both inequitable and immoral. . . .

NOTES AND QUESTIONS

1. **Role-playing.** It seems clear that the case would have been decided differently if Dr. Golde had informed Moore of his plans to produce and patent the cell line at issue. Suppose that you are Dr. Golde and one of your classmates is Moore, about to undergo surgery. What do you say to your "patient" in seeking his "informed consent?" Do you advise him to have an attorney at his bedside?

2. **Rationales.** What were the bases of the majority opinion? Each of the other opinions?

3. **Visions of property.** What visions of property are reflected in the various opinions? In the context, compare *Moore* with the *Vanna White* case, §1.4.6 *supra.*

4. **"Judge" Hansmann.** If Professor Hansmann were Judge Hansmann sitting on the California Supreme Court, which of the four opinions would he most likely have written?

5.   **Commodification of the human embryo.** What began as a divorce action turned into a custody battle over seven "frozen embryos" stored in a Knoxville fertility clinic. Davis v. Davis, 842 S.W.2d 588 (Tenn. 1992).

Prior to their divorce action, the parties had created the embryos through in vitro fertilization, intending at some time to use one or more of them. At the time of the decision, however, both parties had remarried. Mary Sue Davis (now Mary Sue Stowe) no longer wished to use the embryos herself, but wanted to donate them to a childless couple. Junior Davis, furiously opposed to such donation, wanted the embryos destroyed. The lower court, Solomonically perhaps, awarded the former spouses "joint custody" of the embryos.

In affirming the judgment, the state supreme court further explained what "joint custody" in this matter would entail:

> Balanced against Junior Davis's interest in avoiding parenthood is Mary Sue Davis's interest in donating the preembryos to another couple for implantation. Refusal to permit donation of the preembryos would impose on her the burden of knowing that the lengthy IVF procedures she underwent were futile, and that the preembryos to which she contributed genetic material would never become children. While this is not an insubstantial emotional burden, we can only conclude that Mary Sue Davis's interest in donation is not as significant as the interest Junior Davis has in avoiding parenthood. If she were allowed to donate these preembryos, he would face a lifetime of either wondering about his parental status or knowing about his parental status and having no control over it. . . . The case would be closer if Mary Sue Davis were seeking to use the preembryos herself, but only if she could not achieve parenthood by any other reasonable means. . . .
>
> In summary, we hold that disputes involving the disposition of preembryos produced by in vitro fertilization should be resolved, first, by looking to the preferences of the progenitors. If their wishes cannot be ascertained, or if there is dispute, then their prior agreement concerning disposition should be carried out. If no prior agreement exists [there was none here], then the relative interests of the parties in using or not using the preembryos must be weighed. Ordinarily, the party wishing to avoid procreation should prevail, assuming that the other party has a reasonable possibility of achieving parenthood by means other than use of the preembryos in question. . . . If the party seeking control of the preembryos intends merely to donate them to another couple, the objecting party obviously has the greater interest and should prevail.

842 S.W.2d at 604.

The court rejected the view that the embryos were either "persons" (quaere: is this why the court refers to them as preembryos?) or "property."

> It follows that any interest that Mary Sue Davis and Junior Davis have in the preembryos in this case is not a true property interest. However, they do have an interest in the nature of ownership, to the extent that they have decision-

> making authority concerning disposition of the preembryos, within the scope
> of policy set by law.

842 S.W.2d at 597.

Suppose (we realize this is unlikely) the former spouses had agreed to sell the preembryos. Would (should) the state interfere with that decision?

§11.4　Native American Artifacts

Unlike Anglo-American law, where most wealth became commodified by the early modern period, Native American property never fully entered the market place. In the following case before the Chilkat Indian Tribal Court, two attitudes clash: one that assumes commodification, the other that does not.

In reading the following opinion, some background information is helpful. The Tlingits are a tribal nation of the Chilkat Indians. Two hundred years ago, they were a rich and powerful people, controlling Indian trade routes along the Alaskan coast. Today, the Tlingit nation is concentrated in the poor rural Alaskan village of Klukwan. Over the years, many of its members have left the village in search of work and settled in other areas of the country.

The Tlingit nation is organized into matrilineal groups. Birthright runs through the mother's line; however, tribal leadership is dominated by males. For this reason, brothers of the matrilineal line are the dominant figures of authority and are referred to as "uncles." Each group maintains a house in which sacred family items reflecting Tlingit culture are stored and cared for. Each house is considered an integral part of a larger community hall. Members of the Whale House Group are descendants of Mildred Hotch Sparks. Mildred's brother, Victor Hotch, was the uncle and caretaker (hitsaati) of the Whale house for 40 years. When Victor died, leadership of the house passed to his brother Clarence Hotch. Both Clarence and Mildred wanted to sell the artifacts. Bill Thomas is the nephew of Clarence Hotch and a member of the Whale House Group. He, too, wanted to sell. Victor's son, Joe Hotch, was born into the Bear Clan and opposed the sale of the artifacts.

Michael Johnson is a Seattle art dealer who began a campaign to acquire the artifacts in the mid-1970s. Sometime in the early 1970s, he visited Klukwan and was allowed to see the Whale House artifacts. He immediately began to put pressure on tribal elders to sell the artifacts. He dealt mainly with Victor Hotch, offering large sums of money and promising to find an art dealer who would donate the works to a well-known and reputable museum so that they could be seen and appreciated by a large number of people. His first offer was $100,000 — a huge sum of money for a poor community. Victor Hotch was tempted by these offers, and on at least two occasions, had promised Michael Johnson that he would sell the artifacts. Each time, however, he rescinded and told Michael Johnson that the items could not be sold without the approval of the entire Whale House clan. Undaunted, Michael Johnson stepped up his offers, and began dealing with other family and tribal members in an effort to buy the artifacts.

Mildred Hotch Sparks, Clarence Hotch, and Bill Thomas were all in favor of the sale of the Whale House totems and screen. In addition, other Whale House members began to appear and make claims to the right to sell the artifacts. Estelle Johnson (no relation to Michael Johnson) surfaced and entered into sales negotiations with Michael Johnson. With so many family members in favor of the sale, Michael Johnson almost acquired the artifacts in the mid-1970s. By 1976, he had gotten a first option to buy the artifacts from Victor and Mildred, pending the approval of the rest of the clan. Martha Willard, another Whale house clan member, resisted. Johnson proceeded to write to Willard a series of letters in which he offered sums ranging from $100,000 to $500,000. She continued to resist. In the meantime, in 1976, the Frog House, another Tlingit clan, sold its screen and totems to a Canadian art dealer who promptly whisked them across the Canadian border. Other members of the Tlingit community were outraged. A tribal meeting was held and the Tlingits resolved to bar further sale of any Tlingit artifacts.

Negotiations to sell the artifacts collapsed and Estelle Johnson then sued Joe Hotch and others for interfering with her efforts to sell the artifacts. Michael Johnson paid her litigation fees. Her case was dismissed; but, Michael Johnson kept in touch with the family. He continued to write letters and make phone calls, reminding the family of his "contract" with them and urging them to sell so that the artifacts might be preserved and appreciated by a large number of people. In 1984, after years of relentless pressure, Michael Johnson got the phone call he had been waiting for. Members of the Whale house family, including Clarence Hotch, had agreed to sell the artifacts. The plan was simple. Michael Johnson would show up with heavy equipment and contracts in hand and simply haul the artifacts away. Johnson was to find a buyer willing to donate the items to the Museum of Natural History in New York City. Whale House members would receive upwards of $1 million. On an April evening in 1984, the items were loaded onto pick-up trucks and driven out of the village to the nearby town of Haines. There, they were stored in a van. One week later, the van was loaded onto a ferry and arrived in Seattle. Michael Johnson stored the artifacts in a Seattle warehouse until a buyer could be located and the sales transaction completed. He quickly found a buyer and anticipated a commission of more than $100,000. The artifacts were, of course, discovered missing. Martha Willard called the Alaska state troopers. Outraged members sued for recovery of the items. An injunction barring their sale was issued and the screen and totems remained in the Seattle warehouse for ten years until the dispute was resolved.

It is worth noting that Mildred Sparks did not live in Klukwan. Like many tribal members, she had left the village years earlier and lived and worked in a nearby town. Estelle Johnson had long since moved out of the village and lived in Arizona. The sale divided families and shattered tribal unity. Those favoring the sale justified their position in terms of both the monetary benefits involved and the careful attention and preservation the items would receive in a major museum. Opponents argued that the items were an extension of their culture and history. Beyond that, they argued, the items were a personification of their ancestors and were venerated objects for worship purposes. Finally, opponents argued that the items were community property belonging to the Tlingit nation as a whole and could not be sold by the unilateral action of any one person or clan.

Michael Johnson and the Tlingit defendants then began a campaign to keep the case out of tribal court. With the backing of the Alaska attorney general, they argued that the case could only be heard in federal court since the tribal court had no jurisdiction over individuals who were not tribal members. The case came before a federal district court in Anchorage. In an unprecedented move, the district court judge removed it and sent it to the village tribal court. The tribal court convened in 1993 and decided in favor of the plaintiffs, ordering the artifacts returned to the village. On October 3, 1994, the artifacts arrived in nearby Haines, Alaska. The objects were placed in a storage shed to protect them from damp conditions at the Whale House which would cause further deterioration. Village members celebrated their return; however most members of the Whale House group did not participate in the festivities. A new caretaker has been appointed and tribal members are planning to repair the leaky conditions at the house so that the objects can be restored there.

CHILKAT INDIAN VILLAGE IRA v. JOHNSON

No. 90-01 (Chilkat Tribal Court, Nov. 3, 1993)

BOWEN, Tribal Court Judge. This case involves the 1984 removal of four house posts and a rain screen, known as the "Whale House artifacts," from the Chilkat Indian Village in Klukwan, Alaska. The Chilkat Indian Village . . . filed this action in this court on January 8, 1990, against Michael R. Johnson, his corporation, and the individuals comprising the "Whale House Group."

The complaint sets forth two causes of action. First, the village alleges that defendants attempted to convert tribal trust property to their exclusive use and benefit. Second, the village alleges that defendants violated a tribal ordinance which prohibits removal of such property from the village without prior notification of an approval by the Chilkat Village counsel, which is the tribe's governing body. The village seeks declaratory and injunctive relief, as well as money damages. . . .

The law applicable in this tribal court action is tribal law which is comprised of both written and unwritten custom law of the village. The written manifestations of applicable tribal law include the Ordinance of May 12, 1976 (Artifacts Ordinance) which reads as follows:

> No person shall enter onto the property of the Chilkat Indian Village for the purpose of buying, trading for, soliciting the purchase of, or otherwise seeking to arrange a removal of artifacts, clan crests, or other traditional Indian art work owned or held by members of the Chilkat Indian Village or kept within the boundaries of the real property owned by the Chilkat Indian Village Council, without first requesting and obtaining permission to do so from the Chilkat Indian Village Council.

> No traditional Indian artifacts, clan crests, or other Indian art works of any kind may be removed from the Chilkat Indian Village without prior notification of and approval by, the Chilkat Indian Village Council.

There is no dispute about the basic facts surrounding the physical removal of the artifacts from the Whale House in Klukwan during April 1984. Rather, the issues to be decided are: (1) whether the Whale House rain screen and four house posts constitute "artifacts, clan crest, or other Indian art works" within the meaning of the relevant tribal ordinance; (2) whether the tribe has the power to enforce the ordinance against the defendants, including the non-Indian art dealer, Michael Johnson, and his corporation: (3) whether any or all of the defendants violated the ordinance. . . .

Plaintiff must establish its claims by a preponderance of the evidence. The same standard applies to defendants' counterclaims. The following discussion is a chronological account of the testimony and documentary evidence presented at trial which is relevant to the above issues. . . .

Discussion

[The opinion includes extensive discussion of Michael Johnson's attempts, going back to the mid-1970s, to purchase artifacts, and of the artifacts' status as "clan trust property," with "great spiritual significance to the Ganexteidi Clan." Representative excerpts follow:]

[Joe Hotch] recalled the two unsuccessful attempts in the mid-1970s to remove the artifacts from the Whale House in Klukwan. He recalled that in 1976 Estelle DeHaven Johnson, a Tlingit who was the granddaughter of "Chief Shortridge" of the Whale House, attempted to remove the artifacts with the backing of art dealer Michael Johnson. The attempt was thwarted when villagers (Victor Hotch in particular by some accounts) placed one or more skiffs (small vessels) in front of the door to the Whale House. Joe Hotch (and others) recalled that following the first unsuccessful removal attempt, Michael Johnson financed a federal court action to determine ownership of the artifacts. . . . That second attempt was unsuccessful when the village siren was sounded, trees were felled blocking exits of the village, and members of the tribe acted together to prevent [the artifacts'] removal. . . .

Joe Hotch testified that he had taken it upon himself to earlier write to Michael and Sharon Johnson to express his objection to Mr. Johnson's offers of large sums to entice the sale of the Whale House and other artifacts. Mr. Hotch's May 27, 1975 letter to Michael and Sharon Johnson (who then resided in Seattle, Washington) reads in pertinent part as follows.

> I find it imperative to present my objection to your technique and tremendous dollar offers you present to gain possession of our artifacts here in Klukwan. These artifacts are a part of our Tlingit needs to retain, as they represent our past and our future within the art itself; for this reason they have been handed down generation after generation. . . .
>
> A Tlingit selling its tribal artifacts is degrading its entire Clan, much more the Tlingit nation. . . . We have gone on record year after year to protect our tribal artifacts. I'm sure our . . . president Dick Hotch made you aware of this by telephone previously, however I'm doing likewise, being that this affects many tribes in our Tlingit nation. I'm sending copies to the newspapers listed below. . . .

Joe Hotch testified that he was saddened when around this same time (during the mid-1970s) Michael Johnson was ultimately successful in persuading Joe's brother Dick Hotch to sell a bear mask, which was lost to their Bear Clan forever. Joe Hotch testified that Michael Johnson furnished Dick Hotch with a replica of the bear mask which was intended to fool the community into thinking that the replica was the original. According to Mr. Hotch, that folly proved fruitless and the replica was recognized as such.

This testimony by Joe Hotch laid the foundation for discussion of what is referred to simply as the Ordinance of May 12, 1976, quoted above, which prohibits removal from the village (without prior council approval) of "artifacts, clan crests, or other Indian art works," which defendants are accused of violating. . . .

Noted Tlingit writer and scholar Andrew Hope III provided the court with useful testimony covering details of Tlingit social structure, and the meaning of "clan crest objects." Mr. Hope explained that such objects, which include the artifacts here at issue, have gone through a ceremonial process, such as a potlatch in which the objects are dedicated. The spirits of ancestors are honored, and those spirits are warmed and like to be around clan crests such as the Whale House artifacts, according to the Tlingit belief.

On the subject of ownership and sale of crest objects, Andy Hope expressed his view that such objects, which can include songs and stories, cannot be "owned"; there is no way to put a price on spirits, and certainly no *hitsati*, i.e., caretaker of a tribal house, has the right to unilaterally dispose of clan crest objects. Mr. Hope offered his view that the artifacts should remain in the village, and that the spirits will feel better upon the return of the artifacts to the Tlingit community in Klukwan. . . .

Mr. Thomas recited the basic facts involving the actual removal of the artifacts in late April 1984, about which there is virtually no dispute. Clarence Hotch came to Bill's house in Klukwan and told him the time had come to act to remove the artifacts. Bill called his brother Clifford, who brought a truck from his residence in Haines. Buzzy and Vincent Hotch also assisted, according to Bill Thomas. Clarence opened the door to the Whale House, they removed the artifacts (except the worm dish, which was too fragile and old to even be carried), loaded them onto three trucks, and transported the artifacts to the Haines motel where Michael Johnson was staying, so that he could inspect the property. After being stored in the garage of Defendant Evans Willard for a few days, Michael Johnson and Bill Thomas arranged for and effected transportation of the artifacts to Seattle by ferry. . . .

CONCLUSIONS

I.   THE WHALE HOUSE RAIN SCREEN AND HOUSE POSTS AS
     ARTIFACTS, CLAN CRESTS, AND INDIAN ART WITHIN THE
     MEANING OF THE ORDINANCE

The artifacts consist of four elaborately carved wooden posts (made of spruce and over nine feet high) and a wooden partition (made of thin cedar boards) called a rain screen. George Emmons wrote that they are "unquestionably the finest example of native art, either Tlingit or Tsimshian, in Alaska, in boldness of conception — although highly conventionalized in form — in execution of detail, and in arrangement of detail." The record indicates that if the artifacts were sold on the open market they would likely reap a price of several million dollars.

The artifacts were created around 1830. A prominent leader in Klukwan, Xetsuwu, resolved to build a new house (Whale House) in order to unify certain existing house groups of the Ganexteidi Clan. He commissioned the house post from a famous carver who resided in the Stikine River area, near what is currently referred to as Old Wrangell, Alaska. The name of that artist remained unknown until 1987, when a written account was discovered which identified his name as Kadjisdu. The artist, who made detailed sketches while being told about the clan's stories during the canoe trip to Klukwan, is said to have resided in Klukwan for one year while carving the posts. By some accounts he was paid 10 slaves, 50 dressed moose skins, and several blankets.

The four posts represented the four groups that were brought together to form the new Whale House. The posts and rain screen tell stories of the clan; not just of the Whale House. The artifacts and the Whale House itself were created and dedicated in the traditional manner. The Ganex-teidi hired Eagles to construct the original house. The Eagles were then repaid in a traditional "payback party," and the property was brought out in a potlatch and dedicated as clan property. . . .

Defendant art dealer Michael Johnson has . . . been obsessed with the artifacts' acquisition, and his actions in this respect have caused tremendous conflicts and ill will at Klukwan. While the Tlingit defendants cooperated with him to remove the artifacts in 1984, the evidence brought out at trial leads this court to conclude that they seem to regret their 1984 actions in concert with Michael Johnson. Their spokesman Bill Thomas expressed such regret, and all of the Tlingit defendants now want the artifacts returned to Klukwan, and want nothing more to do with Michael Johnson and his attempts to sell the artifacts.

This court concludes that, inexorably, the Whale House property at issue constitutes "artifacts, clan crest, or other Indian art works" within the meaning of the tribe's 1976 Ordinance prohibiting removal of such property without first obtaining the consent of the council at Klukwan.

II.   POWER OF THE VILLAGE TO ENACT THE ORDINANCE AND ENFORCE IT AGAINST THE DEFENDANTS

Defendants have challenged the tribe's authority to enact and apply its 1976 Ordinance. The assertion directly raises two issues going to the heart of this dispute. First, does the Chilkat Indian Village have the power to enact this legislation? If so, may it lawfully apply the ordinance to some or all of the defendants? Answers to these dual questions require a two-tiered analysis.

[The court concludes that the Village has the power to enact the legislation, and that it can lawfully be applied to all the defendants.]

. . . The trial evidence convincingly demonstrated the continuing importance of the artifacts to the tribe. As such, this court concludes that the removal of the artifacts from Klukwan has a direct effect on and posed a distinct threat to the political integrity, health, and welfare of the tribe. This court heard extensive, credible testimony about the significance of the artifacts to the welfare of the Ganexteidi Clan as well as the entire tribe. All members of the village continue to rely on the artifacts for essential ceremonial purposes. The artifacts embody the clan's history. Just as earlier attempts to remove the artifacts caused injury to the tribe through friction and clashes among tribal houses and clans, a fortiori the 1984 removal in violation of the tribes's 1976 Ordinance had a direct effect on the health and welfare of the tribe. This court finds that . . . the tribe retains inherent power to exercise authority over the conduct of Michael Johnson, who conspired with the Tlingit defendants to remove the artifacts from the village in violation of the 1976 Ordinance.

III.   VIOLATION OF THE ORDINANCE BY DEFENDANTS

There is abundant evidence in the trial record establishing that all of the defendants, including Michael Johnson, violated the 1976 Ordinance. The Tlingit defendants did not counter any of the evidence regarding their role with Michael Johnson, as well as the actual removal. Neither did Michael Johnson, who elected to not attend the trial, offer any such evidence. This court finds that the Tlingit defendants violated the tribe's 1976 Ordinance.

If any defendant can be singled out as the architect of the removal it is Michael Johnson. . . . Defendant Michael Johnson conducted an obsessive campaign to acquire the artifacts. He dealt with any and all people in the village who might assist him to remove the artifacts. Acting through his corporation, he played village members off against each other, while making inconsistent representations to them. The evidence at trial uniformly established that Michael Johnson conspired with the Tlingit defendants to remove the artifacts, and that he aided and abetted the actual physical removal of the artifacts. This court finds that Michael Johnson and his corporation violated the tribe's 1976 Ordinance. . . .

RELIEF AND ORDER

In fashioning the appropriate relief in this tribal court case, this court first recognizes that the artifacts are currently stored in a Seattle warehouse pursuant to an injunction of the federal district court. . . . Therefore, plaintiff, as the prevailing party in this action, is directed to make appropriate application to the district court to enforce necessary aspects of this court's order; principally for a modification allowing for the return of the artifacts to the Whale House at Klukwan. . . .

ORDER

Under these circumstances, and upon due deliberation under tribal law, this court orders the following: The artifacts are to be returned to the Whale House in Klukwan. Plaintiff shall make appropriate application to the federal district court to accomplish this as soon as possible. Michael Johnson (and his corporation) are to pay for all expenses required to return the artifacts to the Whale House at Klukwan. Additionally, defendants Michael Johnson and his corporation are responsible to plaintiff, as the prevailing party, for costs and fees in this tribal court action. Plaintiff is ordered to submit a bill of costs and a statement of its attorneys' fees within 30 days of receipt of this decision. Michael Johnson (and other defendants) shall have 30 days after served of said bill and statement to file an objection. No other actual or punitive damages are awarded.

FIGURE 11-1
Klukwan Whale House Artifacts Returned — 1994

NOTES AND QUESTIONS

1.   **Common property revisited.** Recall Demsetz's argument about the undesirability of common property, §1.4.a *supra.* What purposes does common property in *Chilkat* appear to serve?

2.   **Personhood property?** Are the artifacts "personhood property" according to Margaret Jane Radin's formulation? What elements of the situation does that language appear to capture? What elements does it fail to capture?

3.   **Elgin marbles.** The Elgin marbles are a fifth-century B.C. group of classical Greek sculptures, including parts of the Parthenon's friezes and pediments. Lord Elgin, the British Ambassador to Turkey, purchased these

marbles in 1812 (at the time Greece was under Turkish rule) and resold them to the British government in 1816. They are now on display in London's British museum.

The Greek government has sought, unsuccessfully, for more than 50 years to recover these marbles. In 1983, the actress Melina Mercouri, then the Greek Minister of Culture, asserted that the marbles belonged in Greece; The Economist, May 20, 1983, p.20 (U.S. ed., p.18). To return the marbles would set a "precedent that would lead to the emptying of museums around the world," has been the British reply; L.A. Times, Apr. 27, 1994, p.1.

What of Native American artifacts that through conquest, discovery, or purchase have made their way into museums throughout the country? Should they be returned?

Chapter 12

Introducing the Real Estate Transaction

Few areas of legal practice have clung to their parochial ways as tightly as real estate. One could write, not so long ago, that the lawyer from Illinois would find much of Indiana practice unfamiliar; indeed, if she practiced in Chicago, she might even be unfamiliar with the usages in many downstate rural counties. This variation from one state to another — and, in large, diverse states, from one locale to another — has made it difficult to generalize about the basic elements of the real estate transaction: the documents; the forms of title protection; the role of brokers, lawyers, and insurers.

Although some differences remain, so that a lawyer handling an out-of-state transaction may wish (or be forced) to hire local counsel, the standardization of both real estate law and practice has begun to move quite swiftly. This is especially so as to home purchases — an activity that general practitioners are likely to experience wherever homebuyers regularly use lawyers. Several factors account for the new regime: the growth of the secondary market and the securitization of home mortgages; the vast expansion of interstate lending; the dominant role of title insurance; the intrusion of Congress into state finance law; and the outfall of the consumer and environmental protection movements.

In this chapter, we will trace the steps that a home purchaser would take to acquire the property with the help of various intermediaries: lawyers, lenders, title assurers, brokers, escrowees. The sequence, however, extends to most real estate purchases, although the complexity of each step may multiply as we move from the one-family house to the 40-story office building. These steps would include:

1. the formation of the contract;
2. the executory interval;
3. the closing;
4. the post-transfer period.

This is the sequence that we shall follow also as we open the gateway to a field whose full understanding will require much beyond this course.

§12.1   The Formation of the Contract

On a Sunday afternoon, in response to a full-page newspaper ad, the Smiths visit a tract development where they immediately fall for a three-bedroom Georgian Colonial, which the broker assures them is a steal at $120,000. If the broker is typically earnest, he is likely to urge the Smiths to leave a deposit check and sign a binder before they depart. If the Smiths are typically inexperienced, they will do as they are asked. On the spur of the moment, without a lawyer at their side, the Smiths may legally commit themselves to the largest financial undertaking they will ever make, outside of marriage itself.

The first step in a real estate transaction is the formation of a binding contract of sale between seller and buyer. This contract, or a note or memorandum thereof, must be in writing to satisfy the Statute of Frauds. However, even a relatively short, simple document, four or five paragraphs long, may be enough in many places to cement the parties to the transaction. The "binder" that the Smiths signed may contain no more than the parties' names, the property address, the sales price, mortgage terms, and the closing of title date; yet it might suffice to create a right of action in either the seller or buyers should the other party later change his or her mind.

The legal "minimum" for a binding contract of sale is an issue often before the courts. M. Friedman, Contracts and Conveyances of Real Property §1.3, Binders, Memoranda, and Incomplete Contract of Sale (5th ed. 1991).

Courts handle these cases in terms familiar from contracts courses: "preliminary negotiations, indefiniteness, significance of formal contract to follow," and so on. Rather than rework familiar, if unsettled, ground, it seems more useful for you to examine a "finished" contract of sale form. We can assume that the Smiths signed a "binder" of this completeness.

We have selected a standard form — that is, mostly boilerplate — that is widely used throughout California. Note the prefatory warning. Usually, the selling broker will complete the blanks, a practice that courts have been reluctant to call an unauthorized practice of law. See, e.g., Chicago Bar Assn. v. Quinlan & Tyson, Inc., 34 Ill. 2d 116, 214 N.E.2d 771 (1966); cf. Florida Bar v. Irizarry, 268 So. 2d 377, 379 (Fla. 1972) ("where the broker has no interest in the transaction except as broker, he may not complete standard conveyancing forms such as deeds, mortgages, notes, assignments and satisfactions" (but broker may prepare the contract of sale)).

As you study the California form, try to think through the significance of its many provisions.

Real Estate Purchase Contract and Receipt for Deposit

THIS IS MORE THAN A RECEIPT FOR MONEY. IT IS INTENDED TO BE A LEGALLY BINDING CONTRACT. READ IT CAREFULLY. CALIFORNIA ASSOCIATION OF RE-ALTORS® (CAR) STANDARD FORM

DATE:_____ , 19_____ AT _____

_____ , California, RECEIVED FROM_____

_____ ("Buyer")

THE SUM OF_____

Dollars $_____

BY   ☐ Cash,   ☐ Cashier's check,   ☐ Personal check, or ☐ _____

_____

PAYABLE TO_____

TO BE HELD UNCASHED UNTIL ACCEPTANCE of this offer as a

Buyer and Seller acknowledge receipt of copy of this page, which constitutes Page 1 of _____ Pages.

Buyer's Initials (_____) (_____) Seller's Initials (_____) (_____)

THIS STANDARDIZED DOCUMENT FOR USE IN SIMPLE TRANSACTIONS HAS BEEN APPROVED BY THE CALIFORNIA ASSOCIATION OF REALTORS® IN FORM ONLY. NO REPRESENTATION IS MADE AS TO THE APPROVAL OF THE FORM OF ANY SUPPLEMENTS NOT CURRENTLY PUBLISHED BY THE CALIFORNIA ASSOCIATION OF REALTORS® OR THE LEGAL VALIDITY OR ADEQUACY OF ANY PROVISION IN ANY SPECIFIC TRANSACTION. IT SHOULD NOT BE USED IN COMPLEX TRANSACTIONS OR WITH EXTENSIVE RIDERS OR ADDITIONS.

A real estate broker is the person qualified to advise on real estate transactions. If you desire legal or tax advice, consult an appropriate professional.

OFFICE USE ONLY

Reviewed by Broker or Designee _____

Date _____

☐

Property   Address: _____ _____ , 19__

deposit to be applied toward the
PURCHASE PRICE OF _____
Dollars $_____
FOR PURCHASE OF PROPERTY SITUATED IN_____
_____ ,   COUNTY OF_____ , California,
DESCRIBED AS _____("Property").
1. **FINANCING:** The obtaining of the loan(s) shown below is a contingency of this agreement.

   A. DEPOSIT, upon acceptance, to be deposited into_____
     _____ $ _____

   B. INCREASED DEPOSIT, within _____ calendar days after
     acceptance, to be desposited into_____
                                            $ _____

   C. BALANCE OF DOWN PAYMENT to be deposited into_____
     _____ on or before _____ $ _____

   D. Buyer to apply, qualify for, and obtain a NEW FIRST LOAN in
     the amount of .... $ _____
     payable monthly at approximately $_____
     including interest at origination not to exceed _____%,
     ☐ fixed rate, ☐ other _____ ,
     all due _____ years after origination. Buyer's loan points
     not to exceed _____ . Seller agrees to pay a
     maximum of _____ VA discount points. Additional financing terms _____
     _____ .

   E. Buyer to ☐ assume, ☐ take title subject to, an EXISTING FIRST
     LOAN with an approximate balance of .... $ _____
     payable to _____ monthly at $_____
     including interest at current rate of_____% ☐ fixed rate,
     ☐ other _____ . Buyer's fees not to exceed
     _____ . Additional financing terms _____
     _____ .

   F. Buyer to execute a NOTE SECURED BY a ☐ first, ☐ second, or
     ☐ third DEED OF TRUST in the amount of .... $ _____

     Buyer and Seller acknowledge receipt of copy of this page, which constitutes Page 2
of _____ Pages.
     Buyer's Initials (_____) (_____)   Seller's initials (_____) (_____)

OFFICE USE ONLY

Reviewed by Broker or Designee _____

Date _____

☐
Property   Address: _____   _____ , 19__

payable to SELLER monthly at $_____(☐ or more), including interest at_____% all due _____ years after origination (or ☐ upon sale or transfer of the Property). A late charge of _____ shall be due on any installment not paid within _____ calendar days after due date. ☐ Deed of Trust to contain a request for notice of default and/or sale for benefit of Seller. Buyer ☐ will, ☐ will not execute a request for notice of delinquency. Additional financing terms _____ .

If the Property contains 1-4 dwelling units, Buyer and Seller shall execute a Seller Financing Disclosure Statement (Civil code §§2956-2967), if applicable, as provided by arranger of credit, as soon as practicable prior to execution of security documents. (CAR FORM SFD-14, SELLER FINANCING DISCLOSURE STATEMENT, OR SIMILAR FORM, SHALL SATISFY THIS REQUIREMENT.)

G. Buyer to apply, qualify for, and obtain a NEW SECOND LOAN in the amount of .... $ _____ payable monthly at approximately $ _____ including interest at origination not to exceed _____% ☐ fixed rate, ☐ other _____ , all due _____ years after origination. Buyer's loan points not to exceed _____ . Additional financing terms _____ .

H. Buyer to ☐ assume, ☐ take title subject to, an EXISTING SECOND LOAN with an approximate balance of .... $ _____ payable to _____ monthly at $_____ including interest at current rate of _____% ☐ fixed rate, ☐ other _____ . Buyer's fees not to exceed

_____ .

Additional financing terms _____ .

I. If Buyer assumes or takes title subject to an existing loan, Seller shall provide to Buyer, as soon as practicable, copies of applicable notes and deeds of trust. A loan may contain a number of features which affect the loan. Buyer is allowed _____ calendar days after receipt of such copies to provide written notice to Seller of any

Buyer and Seller acknowledge receipt of copy of this page, which constitutes Page 3 of _____ Pages.

Buyer's Initials (_____) (_____) Seller's initials (_____) (_____)

OFFICE USE ONLY

Reviewed by Broker or Designee _____

Date _____

☐

Property Address: _____ _____ , 19___

items disapproved. READ PARAGRAPH 19 FOR IMPORTANT TERMS. Difference(s) in existing loan balance(s) shall be adjusted in ☐ Cash, ☐ Other _____ .
Disposition of impound account _____ .

J. Buyer shall act diligently and in good faith to obtain all applicable financing. For loan(s) above requiring an application, Buyer shall submit to lender a completed written application within _____ calendar days after acceptance of the offer and shall provide to Seller or Seller's agent, written notice of compliance within that same period.

K. ADDITIONAL FINANCING TERMS: _____
_____
_____
_____
_____

L. TOTAL PURCHASE PRICE............................. $ _____

2. **OCCUPANCY:** Buyer ☐ does, ☐ does not intend to occupy Property as Buyer's primary residence.

3. **SUPPLEMENTS:** The following ATTACHED supplements are incorporated: _____
_____ .

4. **ESCROW:** Buyer and Seller shall deliver signed escrow instructions to _____ , the escrow holder, within _____ calendar days after acceptance of the offer which shall provide for closing ☐ on_____ 19___ , or ☐ within _____ calendar days after acceptance. Escrow fee to be paid as follows: __
_____ .

5. **POSSESSION AND KEYS:** Possession and occupancy shall be delivered to Buyer ☐ on date of recordation at _____ AM/PM, or ☐ not later than _____ calendar days after date of recordation at _____ AM/PM, or ☐ _____ . Seller and Buyer shall execute CAR FORM IOA-14, INTERIM OCCUPANCY AGREEMENT, OR RLAS-11, RESIDENTIAL LEASE AGREEMENT AFTER SALE, OR SIMILAR FORM(S), IF APPLICABLE. When possession is avail-

Buyer and Seller acknowledge receipt of copy of this page, which constitutes Page 4 of _____ Pages.
Buyer's Initials (_____) (_____)   Seller's initials (_____) (_____)

OFFICE USE ONLY

Reviewed by Broker or Designee _____

Date _____

☐
Property   Address: _____   _____ , 19___

able to Buyer, Seller shall provide keys and/or means to operate all Property locks, mailbox, security systems/alarms, and Association facilities.

6. TITLE AND VESTING: Buyer shall be provided a current preliminary report at _____ expense. Title shall be free of liens, encumbrances, easements, restrictions, rights, and conditions of record or known to Seller, with the following exceptions: (a) Current county consolidated property tax bill charges, (b) covenants, conditions, restrictions, and public utility easements of record, and (c) _____ . However, Buyer is allowed _____ calendar days after receipt of the preliminary report to provide written notice to Seller of any of the preceding items disapproved. READ PARAGRAPH 19 FOR IMPORTANT TERMS. Unless otherwise designated in Buyer's escrow instructions, title shall vest as follows: _____ . **(The manner of taking title may have significant legal and tax consequences. Therefore, give this matter serious consideration.)** Buyer shall be provided at _____ expense a California Land Title Association policy issued by _____ Company, showing titlevested in Buyer as above. Upon request, the designated title insurance company can provide information about other types of title insurance coverage.

7. PRORATIONS:

(a) County consolidated property tax bill charges, interest, rents, Association regular dues/assessments, premiums on insurance acceptable to Buyer, as applicable, and _____ _____ shall be paid current by Seller and prorated between Buyer and Seller as of
☐ date of recordation of the deed; or
☐ _____ ;
except as shown in paragraphs 7(b) or 7(c) below.

(b) Bonds or assessments of Special Assessment Districts which are now a lien, shall be
☐ paid current by Seller as of the date shown in paragraph 7(a); payments that are not yet due shall be assumed by Buyer; or

---

Buyer and Seller acknowledge receipt of copy of this page, which constitutes Page 5 of _____ Pages.
Buyer's Initials (_____) (_____)   Seller's initials (_____) (_____)

OFFICE USE ONLY

Reviewed by Broker or Designee _____

Date _____

☐

Property   Address: _____   _____ , 19__

☐ paid in full by Seller, if prepayable, including payments that are not yet due; or

☐ _____ .

(c) Association Special Assessments which are now a lien, shall be
☐ paid current by Seller as of the date shown in paragraph 7(a); payments that are not yet due shall be assumed by Buyer; or
☐ paid in full by Seller, if prepayable, including payments that are not yet due; or

☐ _____ .

(d) County transfer tax or transfer fee shall be paid by _____
_____ . City transfer tax or transfer fee shall be paid by _____ .
Association transfer fee shall be paid by _____ .

(e) **PROPERTY WILL BE REASSESSED UPON CHANGE OF OWNERSHIP. THIS WILL AFFECT THE TAXES TO BE PAID.** A supplemental tax bill will be issued, which shall be paid as follows: (1) for periods after close of escrow, by Buyer (or by final acquiring party if part of an exchange), and (2) for periods prior to close of escrow, by Seller. TAX BILLS ISSUED AFTER CLOSE OF ESCROW SHALL BE HANDLED DIRECTLY BE-TWEEN BUYER AND SELLER.

8. **CONDOMINIUM/ P.U.D.:** If the Property is in a condominium/ planned unit development: (a) the Property has _____ assigned parking space(s); (b) the current regular Association dues/assess-ments are $_____ ☐ monthly, or ☐ _____ ; (c) Seller shall, as soon as practicable, prior to close of escrow, (1) disclose in writing to Buyer any known pending special assessments, claims, or litigation, and (2) provide to Buyer copies of covenants, conditions, and restrictions, articles of incorporation, by-laws, other governing documents, most current financial statement distributed pursuant to Civil Code §1365, statement regarding limited enforceability of age restrictions, if applicable, current Association statement show-ing amount of any unpaid assessments (Civil Code §1368), any other documents required by law, and _____ .
READ PARAGRAPH 7 FOR PRORATIONS AND TRANSFER

Buyer and Seller acknowledge receipt of copy of this page, which constitutes Page 6 of _____ Pages.
Buyer's Initials (_____) (_____)   Seller's initials (_____) (_____)

OFFICE USE ONLY
Reviewed by Broker or Designee _____
Date _____

☐
Property   Address: _____   _____ , 19___

FEES. Buyer is allowed _____ calendar days after receipt to provide written notice to Seller of any items disapproved. READ PARAGRAPH 19 FOR IMPORTANT TERMS.

9. **HOME PROTECTION PLAN:** Buyer and Seller have been informed that home protection plans are available. These plans may provide additional protection and benefit to Seller or Buyer. CAR and the Broker(s) in this transaction do not endorse or approve any particular company or program:

   (a) ☐ A Buyer's Home Protection Plan with the following optional coverage _____ , at a cost not to exceed $_____ , to be paid by ☐ Buyer, ☐ Seller, and to be issued by _____ _____ Company, **OR**

   (b) ☐ Buyer and Seller elect not to purchase a Home Protection Plan.

10. **PERSONAL PROPERTY:** The following items of personal property, free of liens and without warranty of condition, are included:

   _____

   _____ .

11. **FIXTURES:** All permanently installed fixtures and fittings that are attached to the Property or for which special openings have been made are included, free of liens, in the purchase price, including electrical, light, plumbing and heating fixtures, solar systems, built-in appliances, screens, awnings, shutters, window coverings, attached floor coverings, TV antennas/satellite dishes and related equipment, air cooler or conditioner, pool and spa equipment, security systems and/or alarms (if owned by Seller), garage door openers and controls, attached fireplace equipment, mailbox, all existing landscaping including trees and shrubs, and _____ , except _____ .

12. **TRANSFER DISCLOSURE:** Unless exempt, Seller shall provide to Buyer a Real Estate Transfer Disclosure Statement (TDS) (Civil Code §§1102 et seq.): (a) ☐ Buyer has received and read a TDS, or (b) ☐ Seller shall provide a TDS within_____ calendar days after acceptance of the offer, after which Buyer shall have three (3) days

Buyer and Seller acknowledge receipt of copy of this page, which constitutes Page 7 of _____ Pages.
   Buyer's Initials (_____) (_____) Seller's initials (_____) (_____)

OFFICE USE ONLY

Reviewed by Broker or Designee _____

Date _____

☐

Property Address: _____ _____ , 19__

after delivery to Buyer in person, or five (5) days after delivery by deposit in the mail, to terminate this Agreement by delivering written notice of termination to Seller or Seller's Agent. (CAR FORM TDS-14, OR EQUIVALENT FORM, SHALL SATISFY THIS REQUIREMENT.)

13. **SELLER REPRESENTATION:** Seller represents that Seller has no knowledge of any notice of violations of City, County, State, or Federal building, zoning, fire, or health laws, codes, statutes, ordinances, regulations, or rules filed or issued against the Property. If Seller receives notice of violations prior to close of escrow, Seller shall immediately notify Buyer in writing. Buyer is allowed _____ calendar days after receipt of notice to provide written notice to Seller of any items disapproved. READ PARAGRAPH 19 FOR IMPORTANT TERMS.

14. **SMOKE DETECTOR(S):** State law requires that residences be equipped with operable smoke detector(s). Local law may have additional requirements. Unless exempt, Seller shall deliver to Buyer a written statement of compliance in accordance with applicable state and local law prior to close of escrow. (CAR FORM SDC-11, SMOKE DETECTOR STATEMENT OF COMPLIANCE, OR SIMILAR FORM, SHALL SATISFY THIS REQUIREMENT.)

15. **RETROFIT:** Compliance with any minimum mandatory government retrofit standards, including proof of compliance, shall be paid for by ☐ Buyer, ☐ Seller.

16. **FLOOD HAZARD DISCLOSURE:** If the Property is situated in a Special Flood Hazard Area designated by the Federal Emergency Management Agency, Seller shall, within _____ calendar days after acceptance of the offer, disclose this fact in writing to Buyer. Flood insurance may be required by lender. (CAR FORM GFD-14, GEOLOGIC, SEISMIC AND FLOOD HAZARD DISCLOSURE, OR SIMILAR FORM, SHALL SATISFY THIS REQUIREMENT.) Buyer is allowed _____ calendar days from receipt of the disclosure to make further inquiries at appropriate governmental agencies, lenders, insurance agents, or other appropriate entities. Buyer shall provide written notice to Seller of any items disapproved within this latter time period. READ PARAGRAPH 19 FOR IMPORTANT TERMS.

Buyer and Seller acknowledge receipt of copy of this page, which constitutes Page 8 of _____ Pages.

Buyer's Initials (_____) (_____)   Seller's initials (_____) (_____)

OFFICE USE ONLY

Reviewed by Broker or Designee _____

Date _____

☐

Property   Address: _____   _____ , 19__

17. **GEOLOGIC/SEISMIC HAZARD DISCLOSURE:** If the Property is situated in a Special Studies Zone (SSZ) or Seismic Hazard Zone (SHZ) designated under Public Resources Code §§2621-2625 or 2690-2699.6, or in a locally designated geologic hazard zone(s) or area(s) where disclosure is required by local ordinance, Seller shall, within _____ calendar days after acceptance of the offer, disclose in writing to Buyer this fact(s) and any other information required by law. Construction or development of any structure may be restricted. Disclosure of SSZs and SHZs is required only where the maps, or information contained in the maps, are "reasonably available." (CAR FORM GFD-14, GEOLOGIC, SEISMIC AND FLOOD HAZARD DISCLOSURE, OR SIMILAR FORM, SHALL SATISFY THIS REQUIREMENT.) Buyer is allowed _____ calendar days after receipt of the disclosure(s) to make further inquiries at appropriate government agencies, lenders, insurance agents, or other appropriate entities concerning use of the Property under local building, zoning, fire, health, and safety codes as may be applicable under the Special Studies Zone Act, Seismic Hazards Mapping Act, and local geologic ordinance(s). Buyer shall provide written notice to Seller of any items disapproved within this latter time period. READ PARAGRAPH 19 FOR IMPORTANT TERMS.

18. **ADDITIONAL TERMS AND CONDITIONS:**
ONLY THE FOLLOWING PARAGRAPHS 'A' THROUGH 'E' *WHEN INITIALLED* **BY** *BOTH BUYER AND SELLER* **ARE INCORPORATED IN THIS AGREEMENT.**

Buyer's Initials   Seller's Initials

_____/_____   _____/_____   **A. PHYSICAL AND GEOLOGIC INSPECTION:** Buyer shall have the right, at Buyer's expense, to select an inspector(s), to make "Inspections" (including tests, surveys, and other studies) of the Property, including but not limited to structural, plumbing, sewer/septic, well, heating, air conditioning, electrical, and mechanical systems, built-in appliances, roof, soil, foundation, pool/spa and related equipment, possible environmental hazards (such as asbestos, formaldehyde, radon gas, lead-based paint, fuel or chemical storage tanks, hazardous waste, and other substances, materials or products), geologic conditions, location of

Buyer and Seller acknowledge receipt of copy of this page, which constitutes Page 9 of _____ Pages.
Buyer's Initials (_____) (_____)   Seller's initials (_____) (_____)

OFFICE USE ONLY

Reviewed by Broker or Designee _____

Date _____

☐
Property   Address: _____   _____, 19__

property lines, size/square footage of the real property and improvements, and water/utility use restrictions. Seller shall make the Property available for all Inspections. Buyer shall keep the Property free and clear of liens, shall indemnify and hold Seller harmless from all liability, claims, demands, damages, and costs, and shall repair all damages arising from the Inspections. Buyer shall provide Seller, at no cost, copies of all reports concerning the Property obtained by Buyer. Buyer shall provide written notice to Seller of any items disapproved: (1) within _____ calendar days after acceptance of the offer, FOR INSPECTIONS OTHER THAN GEOLOGIC, and/or (2) within _____ calendar days after acceptance of the offer, FOR GEOLOGIC INSPECTIONS. READ PARAGRAPH 19 FOR IMPORTANT TERMS. (A BOOKLET TITLED "ENVIRONMENTAL HAZARDS: GUIDE FOR HOMEOWNERS AND BUYERS" IS PUBLISHED BY THE DEPARTMENT OF HEALTH SERVICES AND THE DEPARTMENT OF REAL ESTATE.)

Buyer's Initials   Seller's Initials

_____/_____ _____/_____ **B. CONDITION OF PROPERTY:** Seller warrants that on the date possession is made available to Buyer: (1) built-in appliances and plumbing, heating/air conditioning, electrical, water, sewer/septic, and pool/spa systems, if any, shall be operative; (2) the roof shall be free of known leaks; (3) all broken or cracked glass shall have been replaced; (4) all other items, including landscaping, grounds, and pool/spa, if any, shall be maintained in the same condition as on the date of acceptance of the offer; (5)

_____

_____ .

Buyer's Initials   Seller's Initials

_____/_____ _____/_____ **C. PEST CONTROL:** (1) Within _____ calendar days after acceptance of the offer, Seller shall furnish Buyer at the expense of ☐ Buyer, ☐ Seller, a current written report of inspection by _____ , a registered Structural Pest Control Company, of the main building, ☐ detached garage(s) or carport(s), if any, and ☐ the following other structures on the Property:_____

_____ .

Buyer and Seller acknowledge receipt of copy of this page, which constitutes Page 10 of _____ Pages.
Buyer's Initials (_____) (_____)   Seller's initials (_____) (_____)

OFFICE USE ONLY
Reviewed by Broker or Designee _____
Date _____

☐

Property   Address: _____ _____ , 19__

(2) If requested by Buyer or Seller, the report shall separately identify each recommendation for corrective work as follows:
"Section 1": Infestation or infection which is evident. "Section 2": Conditions that are present which are deemed likely to lead to infestation or infection.

(3) If no infestation or infection by wood destroying pests or organisms is found, the report shall include a written Certification as provided in Business and Professions Code §8519(a) that on the inspection date "no evidence of active infestation or infection was found."

(4) Work recommended to correct conditions described in "Section 1" shall be at the expense of ☐ Buyer, ☐ Seller.

(5) Work recommended to correct conditions described in "Section 2," **if requested by Buyer,** shall be at the expense of ☐ Buyer, ☐ Seller.

(6) If inspection of inaccessible areas is recommended in the report, Buyer has the option to accept and approve the report, or within _____ calendar days after receipt of the report to request in writing further inspection be made. BUYER'S FAILURE TO NOTIFY SELLER IN WRITING OF SUCH REQUEST SHALL CONCLUSIVELY BE CONSIDERED APPROVAL OF THE REPORT. If further inspection recommends "Section 1" and/or "Section 2" corrective work, such work shall be at the expense of the respective party designated in subparagraph (4) and/or (5). If no infestation or infection is found, the cost of inspection, entry, and closing of the inaccessible areas shall be at the expense of Buyer.

(7) Inspections, corrective work, and certification under this paragraph shall not include roof covering(s). Read paragraph 18A concerning inspection of roof covering(s).

(8) Work shall be performed with good workmanship and materials of comparable quality and shall include repair of leaking shower stalls and pans, and replacement of tiles and other materials removed for repair. It is understood that exact restoration of appearance or cosmetic items following all such work is not included.

(9) Work to be performed at Seller's expense may be performed by Seller or through others, provided that (a) all required permits and

Buyer and Seller acknowledge receipt of copy of this page, which constitutes Page 11 of _____ Pages.
Buyer's Initials (_____) (_____)   Seller's initials (_____) (_____)

☐
Property   Address: _____   _____ , 19__

final inspections are obtained, and (b) upon completion of repairs a written Certification is issued by a registered Structural Pest Control Company showing that the inspected property "is now free of evidence of active infestation or infection."

(10) Funds for work agreed to be performed after close of escrow shall be held in escrow and disbursed upon receipt of a written Certification as provided in Business and Professions Code §8519(b) that the inspected property "is now free of evidence of active infestation or infection."

(11) Other _____ .

Buyer's Initials   Seller's Initials

_____/_____ _____/_____ **D. LIQUIDATED DAMAGES: Buyer and Seller agree that if Buyer fails to complete this purchase by reason of any default of Buyer: (1) Seller shall be released from obligation to sell the Property to Buyer; (2) Seller shall retain, as liquidated damages for breach of contract, the deposit actually paid (Buyer and Seller shall execute CAR FORM RID-11, RECEIPT FOR INCREASED DEPOSIT/LIQUIDATED DAMAGES, or a similar liquidated damages provision, for any increased deposits). However, the amount retained shall be no more than 3% of the purchase price if Property is a dwelling with no more than four units, one of which Buyer intends to occupy as Buyer's residence. Any excess shall be promptly returned to Buyer; (3) Seller retains the right to proceed against Buyer for specific performance or any other claim or remedy Seller may have in law or equity, other than breach of contract damages. (Funds deposited in trust accounts or in escrow are not released automatically in the event of a dispute. Release of funds requires written agreement of the parties, judicial decision, or arbitration.)**

E. ARBITRATION OF DISPUTES: Any dispute or claim in law or equity arising out of this contract or any resulting transaction shall be decided by neutral binding arbitration in accordance with the rules of the American Arbitration Association, and not by court action except as provided by California law for judicial review of arbitration proceedings. Judgment upon the award rendered by

Buyer and Seller acknowledge receipt of copy of this page, which constitutes Page 12 of _____ Pages.

Buyer's Initials (_____) (_____) Seller's initials (_____) (_____)

OFFICE USE ONLY

Reviewed by Broker or Designee _____

Date _____

☐

Property Address: _____ _____, 19__

the arbitrator(s) may be entered in any court having jurisdiction thereof. The parties shall have the right to discovery in accordance with Code of Civil Procedure §1283.05. The following matters are excluded from arbitration hereunder: (a) a judicial or non-judicial foreclosure or other action or proceeding to enforce a deed of trust, mortgage, or installment land sale contract as defined in Civil Code §2985, (b) an unlawful detainer action, (c) the filing or enforcement of a mechanic's lien, (d) any matter which is within the jurisdiction of a probate or small claims court, or (e) an action for bodily injury or wrongful death, or for latent or patent defects to which Code of Civil Procedure §337.1 or §337.15 applies. The filing of a judicial action to enable the recording of a notice of pending action, for order of attachment, receivership, injunction, or other provisional remedies, shall not constitute a waiver of the right to arbitrate under this provision.

Any dispute or claim by or against broker(s) and/or associate licensee(s) participating in this transaction shall be submitted to arbitration consistent with the provision above only if the broker(s) and/or associate licensee(s) making the claim or against whom the claim is made shall have agreed to submit it to arbitration consistent with this provision.

"NOTICE: BY INITIALLING IN THE SPACE BELOW YOU ARE AGREEING TO HAVE ANY DISPUTE ARISING OUT OF THE MATTERS INCLUDED IN THE 'ARBITRATION OF DISPUTES' PROVISION DECIDED BY NEUTRAL ARBITRATION AS PROVIDED BY CALIFORNIA LAW AND YOU ARE GIVING UP ANY RIGHTS YOU MIGHT POSSESS TO HAVE THE DISPUTE LITIGATED IN A COURT OR JURY TRIAL. BY INITIALLING IN THE SPACE BELOW YOU ARE GIVING UP YOUR JUDICIAL RIGHTS TO DISCOVERY AND APPEAL, UNLESS THOSE RIGHTS ARE SPECIFICALLY INCLUDED IN THE 'ARBITRATION OF DISPUTES' PROVISION. IF YOU REFUSE TO SUBMIT TO ARBITRATION AFTER AGREEING TO THIS PROVISION, YOU MAY BE COMPELLED TO ARBITRATE UNDER THE AUTHORITY OF THE CALIFORNIA

Buyer and Seller acknowledge receipt of copy of this page, which constitutes Page 13 of _____ Pages.

Buyer's Initials (_____) (_____)   Seller's initials (_____) (_____)

OFFICE USE ONLY

Reviewed by Broker or Designee _____

Date _____

☐

Property   Address: _____   _____, 19__

CODE OF CIVIL PROCEDURE. YOUR AGREEMENT TO THIS ARBITRATION PROVISION IS VOLUNTARY."

"WE HAVE READ AND UNDERSTAND THE FOREGOING AND AGREE TO SUBMIT DISPUTES ARISING OUT OF THE MATTERS INCLUDED IN THE 'ARBITRATION OF DISPUTES' PROVISION TO NEUTRAL ARBITRATION."

Buyer's Initials   Seller's Initials

_____/_____   _____/_____

19. **BUYER DISAPPROVAL:** If Buyer gives written notice of disapproval of items under paragraphs 1(I), 6, 8, 13, 16, 17 OR 18(A), Seller shall respond in writing within _____ calendar days after receipt of such notice. If Seller is unwilling or unable to correct items reasonably disapproved by Buyer, then Buyer may cancel this Agreement by giving written notice of cancellation to Seller within _____ calendar days (after receipt of Seller's response, or after expiration of the time for Seller's response, whichever occurs first), in which case Buyer's deposit shall be returned to Buyer. BUYER'S FAILURE TO GIVE WRITTEN NOTICE OF DISAPPROVAL OF ITEMS OR CANCELLATION OF THIS AGREEMENT WITHIN THE SPECIFIED TIME PERIODS SHALL CONCLUSIVELY BE DEEMED BUYER'S ELECTION TO PROCEED WITH THE TRANSACTION WITHOUT CORRECTION OF ANY REMAINING DISAPPROVED ITEMS WHICH SELLER HAS NOT AGREED TO CORRECT. Buyer and Seller may agree in writing to extend these time periods.

20. **TAX WITHHOLDING:** (a) Under the Foreign Investment in Real Property Tax Act (FIRPTA), IRC §1445, every Buyer of U.S. real property must, unless an exemption applies, deduct and withhold from Seller's proceeds 10% of the gross sales price. The primary FIRPTA exemptions are: No withholding is required if (i) Seller provides Buyer an affidavit under penalty of perjury, that Seller is not a "foreign person," or (ii) Seller provides Buyer a "qualifying statement" issued by the Internal Revenue Service, or (iii) Buyer purchases real property for use as a residence and the purchase price is $300,000 or less and Buyer or a member of Buyer's family has definite plans to reside at the Property for at least 50% of the

Buyer and Seller acknowledge receipt of copy of this page, which constitutes Page 14 of _____ Pages.
Buyer's Initials (_____) (_____)   Seller's initials (_____) (_____)

OFFICE USE ONLY

Reviewed by Broker or Designee _____

Date _____

☐

Property   Address: _____   _____ , 19__

number of days it is in use during each of the first two 12-month periods after transfer. (b) In addition, under California Revenue and Taxation Code §§18805 and 26131, every Buyer must, unless an exemption applies, deduct and withhold from the Seller's proceeds 3⅓% of the gross sales price if the Seller has a last known address outside of California, or if the Seller's proceeds will be paid to a financial intermediary of the Seller. The primary exemptions are: No withholding is required if (i) the Property is Seller's principal residence, under specified conditions, or (ii) the Property is selling for $100,000 or less, or (iii) the Franchise Tax Board issues a certificate authorizing a lower amount or no withholding, or (iv) the Seller signs an affidavit stating that the Seller is a California resident or a corporation qualified to do business in California. (c) Seller and Buyer agree to execute and deliver as directed any instrument, affidavit, or statement reasonably necessary to carry out those statutes and regulations promulgated thereunder. (CAR FORM AS-14, SELLER'S AFFIDAVIT OF NON-FOREIGN STATUS AND/OR CALIFORNIA RESIDENCY, OR CAR FORM AB-11, BUYER'S AFFIDAVIT, OR SIMILAR FORMS, IF APPLICABLE, SHALL SATISFY THESE REQUIREMENTS.)

21. **MULTIPLE LISTING SERVICE:** If Broker is a Participant of a Board/Association multiple listing service ("MLS"), Broker is authorized to report the sale, price, terms, and financing for publication, dissemination, information, and use of the Board/Association, authorized members, MLS Participants, and Subscribers.

22. **OTHER TERMS AND CONDITIONS:** _____

_____

_____

_____

_____ .

23. **ATTORNEY'S FEES:** In any action, proceeding or arbitration arising out of this agreement, the prevailing party shall be entitled to reasonable attorney's fees and costs.

24. **AGENCY CONFIRMATION:** The following agency relationship(s) are hereby confirmed for this transaction:

Buyer and Seller acknowledge receipt of copy of this page, which constitutes Page 15 of _____ Pages.
    Buyer's Initials (_____) (_____)   Seller's initials (_____) (_____)

OFFICE USE ONLY

Reviewed by Broker or Designee _____

Date _____

☐

Property   Address: _____   _____ , 19__

Listing Agent: _____ is the agent of (check one):
(Print Firm Name)

☐ the Seller exclusively; or   ☐ both the Buyer and Seller.

Selling Agent: _____ (if not same as Listing
(Print Firm Name)

Agent) is the agent of (check one):

☐ the Buyer exclusively; or   ☐ the Seller exclusively; or

☐ both the Buyer and Seller.

25. **ENTIRE CONTRACT:** Time is of the essence. All prior agreements between the parties are incorporated in this agreement which constitutes the entire contract. Its terms are intended by the parties as a final expression of their agreement with respect to such terms as are included herein and may not be contradicted by evidence of any prior agreement or contemporaneous oral agreement. The parties further intend that this agreement constitutes the complete and exclusive statement of its terms and that no extrinsic evidence whatsoever may be introduced in any judicial or arbitration proceeding, if any, involving this agreement. The captions in this agreement are for convenience of reference only and are not intended as part of this agreement. **This agreement may not be amended, modified, altered or changed in any respect whatsoever except by a further agreement in writing executed by Buyer and Seller.**

26. **OFFER:** This is an offer to purchase the Property. Unless acceptance is signed by Seller and a signed copy delivered in person, by mail, or facsimile, and **personally received** by Buyer or by _____

_____ ,

who is authorized to receive it, by _____ 19__ at AM/PM, this offer shall be deemed revoked and the deposit shall be returned. Buyer has read and acknowledges receipt of a copy of this offer. This agreement and any supplement, addendum or modification or modification relating hereto, including any photocopy or facsimile thereof, may be executed in two or more counterparts, all of which shall constitute one and the same writing.

Buyer and Seller acknowledge receipt of copy of this page, which constitutes Page 16 of _____ Pages.

Buyer's Initials (_____) (_____)   Seller's initials (_____) (_____)

OFFICE USE ONLY

Reviewed by Broker or Designee _____

Date _____

☐

Property   Address: _____   _____ , 19__

REAL ESTATE BROKER _____

By _____
Address _____
_____

Telephone_____ Fax _____

BUYER _____

BUYER _____
Address _____
_____

Telephone _____ Fax _____

ACCEPTANCE

The undersigned Seller accepts and agrees to sell the Property on the above terms and conditions and agrees to the above confirmation of agency relationships (☐ subject to attached counter offer). Seller agrees to pay compensation for services as follows:

_____ to_____ ,
Broker, and

_____ to _____ ,
Broker,

payable: (a) on recordation of the deed or other evidence of title, or (b) if completion of sale is prevented by default of Seller, upon Seller's default, or (c) if completion of sale is prevented by default of Buyer, only if and when Seller collects damages from Buyer, by suit or otherwise, and then in an amount not less than one-half of the damages recovered, but not to exceed the above compensation, after first deducting title and escrow expenses and the expenses of collection, if any. Seller hereby irrevocably assigns to Broker(s) such compensation from Seller's proceeds in escrow. In any action, proceeding, or arbitration between Broker(s) and Seller arising out of this agreement, the prevailing party shall be entitled to reasonable attorney's fees and costs. The undersigned has read and acknowl-

Buyer and Seller acknowledge receipt of copy of this page, which constitutes Page 17 of _____ Pages.

Buyer's Initials (_____) (_____)   Seller's initials (_____) (_____)

OFFICE USE ONLY

Reviewed by Broker or Designee _____

Date _____

☐
Property   Address: _____ _____ , 19__

edges receipt of a copy of this agreement and authorizes Broker(s) to deliver a signed copy to Buyer.

Date _____ Telephone _____ Fax _____

Address_____

_____

SELLER_____ _____

SELLER_____

Real Estate Broker(s) agree to the foregoing.

Broker_____
By_____
Date_____
Broker_____
By_____
Date_____

OFFICE USE ONLY

Reviewed by Broker or Designee _____

Date _____

Page 18 of _____ Pages.

NOTES AND QUESTIONS

1. **Boilerplate comparison.** Try to locate a standard contract-of-sale form used in the vicinity of your law school. Compare it with the California form. What are their similarities? Differences?

2. **Plain English.** Standard forms, in their avoidance of legalese, have in many places become more user-friendly. In reading over the California contract form, notice where it would seem that the drafters chose language that most laypersons could readily understand. Is there still contract language that you, and by extension the untrained layperson, would have difficulty with?

3. **"Miranda" warnings.** California homebuyers are unlikely to use a lawyer at any stage of the transaction. The real estate broker fills in the contract form (for buyers' signature) and helps arrange the financing; a title insurance company prepares the preliminary title report and issues the title policy; and an impartial escrow company (see paragraph 4) deals with any issues that arise during the executory interval and handles the closing. In the face of the various caveats sprinkled throughout the form, does it surprise you that California homebuyers rarely seek a lawyer's counsel?

4. **Practical exercise.** Try to complete the California form, as if you were the broker, on the basis of the following assumptions: Purchase price, $120,000; New first loan, $90,000. What other information would you need to prepare this form for the buyer's signature?

5. **Buyer's deposit.** Is a buyer's deposit legally required to "cement" the deal? What is the standard deposit amount, do you suppose? To whom should the deposit be payable? Who should hold the deposit during the executory interval? Read the form carefully: What happens to the deposit if a closing does not take place?

6. **Consumer protection.** The California form has evolved, as have parallel forms elsewhere, to give homebuyers several protections that neither the law nor most earlier forms would have provided. In this context, examine closely the following paragraphs: 12. Transfer Disclosure; 13. Seller Representation; 14. Smoke Detectors; 16. Flood Hazard Disclosure; 17. Geologic/Seismic Hazard Disclosure; 18A. Physical and Geologic Inspection; 18B. Condition of Property; 18C. Pest Control. Consider the possible risks to the buyer if the contract does not contain these provisions.

7. **"Buyer disapproval."** Paragraph 19 allows the buyer to reasonably disapprove of various items and to cancel the contract if the seller fails to respond satisfactorily. Who decides whether the buyer's approval is reasonable or the seller's response is satisfactory?

8. **Seller's remedies.** Paragraph 18D, as your reading will show, is more than a "liquidated damages" provision; it sets forth a panoply of seller remedies should the buyer default. Other than paragraph 19, which allows the buyer to cancel the contract in certain instances, is the form clear as to any other remedies the buyer might have should the seller default?

9. **Agency relationships.** A fast-changing area of practice (and, to a lesser extent, legal doctrine) involves the broker-client relationship. Until quite recently, standard doctrine presumed that the broker was acting as the seller's agent, even though the broker and the buyer might have had a much closer relationship. This often led to tortured fiduciary situations, where the broker, while nominally the seller's agent, would seek the best possible deal for the buyer. Where the contract is silent, the doctrinal presumption generally survives, but notice how the California form reflects a growing practice, the advent of the broker with exclusive loyalty to the buyer or, somewhat trickier, an admittedly dual loyalty to the seller and buyer.

10. **Who buys where?** United States metropolitan areas show especially high levels of racial and economic segregation in housing. According to a landmark study, blacks have less mobility than other minorities in moving to majority-white areas; even the poorest Hispanics and Asian Americans experience less segregation in many large U.S. cities than the most affluent blacks. This is true for white communities of all economic levels, except that very affluent white communities have a higher percentage of blacks than working class and middle-income white areas. Alex M. Johnson Jr., How Race and Poverty Intersect to Prevent Integration: Destabilizing Race as a Vehicle to Integrate Neighborhoods, 143 U. Pa. L. Rev. 1595, 1638-1639 (1995). Why would there be more black residents in high-income white neighborhoods than in those of other economic levels?

Discrimination against homebuyers, discussed in greater depth in Chapter 10, takes a variety of different forms. It is a pervasive phenomenon. The expected incidence of discrimination was 56 percent for black homebuyers, and 45 percent for hispanic homebuyers, according to a 1991 study prepared for HUD. See §10.1. Another study reported that black home seekers were 12 percent more likely than whites to be steered to neighborhoods with a lower proportion of whites, 11 percent more likely to be shown communities with lower-income residents, and 17 percent more likely to see areas with lower home values. Michael H. Schill and Susan M. Wachter, Housing Market Constraints and Spacial Stratification by Income and Race, 6 Housing Pol. Debate 141, 153 (1995).

§12.2   The Executory Interval

Very rarely does someone agree to buy and also take title to real property all at once. Ordinarily some weeks elapse between the two events. During this interval both parties to the transaction are busy. The buyers must arrange their financing, be certain that the sellers' title and the property's condition meet the contract standard, and prepare to take possession. For their part, the sellers must prepare the title documents and the closing adjustments, give evidence of title, and prepare to turn over possession. Buildings under construction must be completed. Sometimes problems will arise about the state of sellers' title, the condition of the premises, or the quality or pace of construction, and the parties must try to iron out their differences. Deals sometimes fall apart between the contract signing and the formal closing.

We call this period of some weeks the *executory interval. Legal* title to the real estate remains in the sellers; it will not pass to the buyers until the formal closing. But the contract gives buyers some interest in the real estate; and under a doctrine known as equitable conversion, courts have said that the buyers hold *equitable* title to the premises. By dint of equitable conversion, the buyers are able to seek and obtain specific performance of the sales contract if the sellers do not perform. Cf. Stone, Equitable Conversion by Contract, 13 Colum. L. Rev. 369, 386 (1913).

a.   Damages to the Premises during the Executory Interval

The doctrine of equitable conversion generates a series of knotty legal problems that the sales contract may fail to address. One quite vexing problem has been the risk of loss if the premises are damaged or destroyed before the formal closing. Suppose, for example, that a house burns down and insurance does not cover the entire value: Must buyers perform the contract anyway? If so, must buyers pay the full contract price or may they get an abatement to reflect the uninsured loss? Who gets the insurance proceeds? Does it matter whether buyers are at fault for the damage or not?

Consider how the following case handles some of these questions.

HOLSCHER v. JAMES

124 Idaho 443, 860 P.2d 646 (1993)

SILAK, J.

Curtis and Brenda James signed an agreement to purchase a cabin and five acres of land from Ernest and Abbielena Holscher. Before the closing date, the Jameses insured the cabin by entering into an insurance binder[1] with State Farm General Insurance Co. through one of its agents. The Jameses then took possession of the premises. Thereafter, but also

---

1. An insurance binder is a contract for insurance in the form of "[a] written memorandum of the important terms of contract of insurance which gives temporary protection to insured pending investigation of risk by insurance company or until a formal policy is issued." Black's Law Dictionary 169 (6th ed. 1990).

prior to closing, the cabin was destroyed by fire. The parties disputed who should bear the loss of the cabin. The district court entered judgment in favor of the Holschers, concluding that State Farm was obligated to pay the insurance proceeds to the Jameses pursuant to the insurance binder, and that equitable principles required the Jameses to pay the Holschers the value of the cabin. As set forth below, we reverse that portion of the district court's judgment which held the Jameses liable for the loss of the cabin, and we affirm the judgment against State Farm, although on different grounds, concluding that the Holschers are entitled to recover directly against State Farm as third-party beneficiaries of the James/State Farm insurance binder.

FACTS AND PROCEDURAL BACKGROUND

On March 29, 1989, the Jameses and Holschers entered into a purchase agreement whereby the Jameses agreed to purchase from the Holschers a cabin and five acres. Under the terms of the purchase agreement, the Jameses deposited $500 as earnest money towards the purchase price of $50,000. The purchase agreement specified May 1, 1989, as the closing date for the transaction. Paragraph 13 of the purchase agreement also provided that "[s]hould the premises be materially damaged by fire or other causes, prior to closing this sale, this agreement shall be voidable at the option of the Buyer."

On April 5, 1989, the Jameses entered into an insurance binder with State Farm to insure the cabin. The insurance binder provided $50,000 coverage on the cabin and $35,000 coverage on the contents of the cabin. A section of the binder form entitled "other int[erests]" provided for the listing of parties other than the named insured who, by virtue of some interest in the covered property, would have a beneficial interest in the insurance. In this section of the binder, the State Farm agent listed the name and address of Ernest Holscher. The binder stated that its effective date was April 5, 1989, and the Jameses made their first premium payment that same day. The amount of the premium was calculated to pay for coverage beginning on April 5th. The Holschers did not themselves purchase any insurance coverage for the cabin.

Also on April 5, 1989, pursuant to the purchase agreement, the Jameses took possession of the property and began moving their personal belongings into the cabin. On April 11, the Jameses moved more of their belongings into the cabin. At about 5 p.m. or 6 p.m. on the 11th, the cabin caught fire and was destroyed. The district court found that the fire was not the fault of either party, and the parties do not dispute that finding. Prior to May 1, the date set for closing, the Jameses notified the Holschers that, because the cabin had been destroyed, they were exercising their option under paragraph 13 to void the purchase agreement.

The Holschers subsequently sued the Jameses and State Farm seeking to recover the value of the cabin. At trial, two issues were submitted to the jury for determination: (1) whether the Holschers were intended beneficiaries of the insurance binder between the Jameses and State Farm, and (2) the fair market value of the cabin at the time it was destroyed. The jury returned a verdict finding that the Holschers were not intended beneficiaries of the insurance binder, and that the fair market value of the cabin was $36,125. The district court entered judgment on the jury's verdict in favor of State Farm, concluding that the Holschers were not third-party beneficiaries, and therefore that they had no claim under the James/State Farm insurance binder.

Two equitable issues were tried to the court: (1) whether the purchase agreement should be reformed, based on mutual mistake, to provide that the Jameses bore the risk of loss prior to closing, and (2) whether the doctrine of equitable conversion applied to shift the pre-closing risk of loss to the Jameses. The district court concluded that reformation of the purchase agreement was inapplicable in this case based on its finding that there was no mutual mistake regarding allocation of the risk of loss or the obligation to insure the property prior to closing because the parties never even considered, much less reached an agreement upon, those issues. The district court did not determine the second issue, whether equitable conversion applied to shift the risk of loss to the Jameses.

However, the district court entered judgment in favor of the Holschers based on two other conclusions: (1) that State Farm was liable to the Jameses for the value of the cabin, and (2) that the Jameses were liable to the Holschers for the value of the cabin. The court concluded that State Farm was liable to the Jameses by applying the doctrine of equitable conversion to determine that the Jameses had an insurable interest in the cabin, and therefore, under the insurance binder, they were entitled to the insurance proceeds after the cabin was destroyed. The court reached its second conclusion, that the Jameses were liable to the Holschers for the value of the cabin, based on its construction of paragraph 13 of the purchase agreement. The court construed paragraph 13 to mean that if the premises were materially damaged prior to closing, the Jameses were entitled to seek equitable rescission of the contract from the court. From this the district court reasoned that the Jameses could not avail themselves of the equitable remedy of rescission unless they restored the Holschers to their pre-contract position. Based on its two conclusions, the district court ordered State Farm to pay the Jameses the proceeds of the insurance on the cabin, and then ordered that the Jameses pay the insurance proceeds to the Holschers before they could void the purchase agreement.

Issues on Appeal

The appeal and cross-appeal of the parties require us to address three issues: (1) whether the district court erred in its application of the doctrines of equitable conversion and equitable rescission; (2) whether the district court erred in entering judgment on the jury's finding that the Holschers were not third-party beneficiaries of the James/State Farm insurance binder; and (3) whether the Holschers should be awarded attorney fees against State Farm under I.C. §41-1839. We address each of these issues in turn.

ANALYSIS

I.   APPLICABILITY OF EQUITABLE CONVERSION AND
     EQUITABLE RESCISSION

The parties raise three issues regarding the application of equitable conversion and rescission. The Holschers assert that the district court erred by not applying equitable conversion to conclude that the risk of loss was on the Jameses at the time of the fire. State Farm asserts that the district court erred because it did apply equitable conversion to conclude that the Joneses had an equitable, and thus insurable, interest in the cabin at the time of the fire. Finally, the Jameses claim that the district court erred by applying the doctrine of equitable rescission to conclude that they were liable to the Holschers for the value of the cabin.

A.   Whether the District Court Should Have Applied Equitable
     Conversion to Conclude that the Jameses Bore the Risk of
     Loss Prior to Closing

This Court has explained the doctrine of equitable conversion as follows:

> The doctrine of equitable conversion is a fiction resting upon the fundamental rule of equity that equity regards that as done which ought to be done. Under the doctrine, an equitable conversion takes place when a contract for the sale of real property becomes binding on the parties. The purchaser is then treated in equity as having an interest in realty, and the vendor an interest in personalty, that is, the right to receive the purchase money.

First Security Bank of Idaho v. Rogers, 91 Idaho 654, 657, 429 P.2d 386, 389 (1967). Thus, when equitable conversion applies, the contract purchaser is deemed the equitable owner of the realty, and assumes the risk of loss on the property. Rector v. Alcorn, 241 N.W.2d 196, 200 (Iowa 1976). The Holschers assert that the district court should have applied equitable conversion to place the risk of loss of the cabin on the Jameses, as purchasers and equitable owners of the property. For the following reasons, we disagree.

The doctrine of equitable conversion applies only if "nothing in the contract states otherwise." Rush v. Anestos, 104 Idaho 630, 634, 661 P.2d 1229, 1233 (1983); *Rector*, 241 N.W.2d at 200. Thus, equitable conversion does not apply if the effect would be to shift the risk of loss to a buyer contrary to the terms of the parties' agreement. Id. In this case, paragraph 13 of the parties' purchase agreement provided: "Should the premises be materially damaged by fire or other causes, prior to closing this sale, this agreement shall be voidable at the option of the Buyer." We construe this provision as placing the risk of loss prior to closing on the Holschers. In a factually similar case, Georgia's Supreme Court held that when a provision in a purchase agreement allows the buyer to cancel the agreement if the premises are destroyed prior to closing, the effect of that provision is to allocate to the seller the risk of loss prior to closing. Phillips v. Bacon, 245 Ga. 814, 267 S.E.2d 249 (1980). See also Bishop Ryan High School v. Lindberg, 370 N.W.2d 726 (N.D. 1985); Rector, 241 N.W.2d at 201. The same reasoning applies here. Paragraph 13 absolved the Jameses from assuming the risk of any material damage to the property prior to closing, leaving that risk upon the Holschers. It would be inconsistent and illogical to say that the Jameses had the right to void the purchase agreement if the premises were materially damaged prior to closing, but also hold them responsible to pay for any pre-closing damages to the property. Such a construction would essentially take away the very right conferred upon the Jameses by paragraph 13. Because we construe paragraph 13 of the parties' purchase agreement as placing the pre-closing risk of loss on the Holschers, we hold that the district court did not err in refusing to apply the doctrine of equitable conversion to shift the pre-closing risk of loss to the Jameses.

B.   Whether the District Court Erred by Applying Equitable Conversion to Conclude that the Jameses had an Insurable Interest in the Cabin Prior to Closing

State Farm challenges the district court's conclusion that it was liable to the Jameses under the insurance binder, contending that the Jameses lacked an insurable interest in the cabin at the time of the loss, and I.C. §41-1806 prohibits any person from enforcing a contract of insurance against an insurer unless that person has an insurable interest in the insured property. By applying the doctrine of equitable conversion, the district court concluded that the Jameses had equitable ownership of, and thus an insurable interest in, the cabin at the time of the loss. The arguable lack of an insurable interest in the Jameses is not conclusive, however, under I.C. §41-1806, for it is the Holschers, not the Jameses, who are seeking to enforce the insurance contract against State Farm. The Holschers assert coverage in their own right as intended third-party beneficiaries of the insurance binder, not as derivative beneficiaries of the Jameses' rights under the binder. State Farm has not asserted that the Holschers lacked an insurable interest in the property at the time of the loss. Because the Jameses are not seeking to enforce the insurance contract against State Farm, we need not decide whether they had an insurable interest in the cabin at the time of the loss.

C.   Whether the District Court Erred in Applying Equitable Rescission to Conclude that the Jameses were Liable for the Value of the Cabin

The district court construed paragraph 13 of the purchase agreement as giving the Jameses the right to seek equitable rescission of the contract from the court in the event that the premises were materially damaged prior to closing. Based on this determination, the district court concluded that the Jameses could not "equitably rescind" the purchase agreement unless they restored the Holschers to their pre-contract position. The legal meaning and effect of contract terms are questions of law which we review freely. Barr Development, Inc. v. Utah Mortg. Loan Corp., 106 Idaho 46, 47, 675 P.2d 25, 26 (1983).

Paragraph 13 gave the Jameses the right under the contract to void the contract at their option if the premises were materially damaged prior to closing. They did not need to apply to the court and prove the elements essential to a decree of equitable rescission before they could void the contract. Once the premises were materially damaged, the Jameses' right to void the contract was "at law," under the terms of the contract. They could simply refuse to close. A right provided by contract is, by definition, legal and not equitable. Equitable remedies are not dependent upon contractual authorization, but apply precisely because there is no adequate remedy at law under the contract's terms, and because sufficient grounds to invoke equity, such as mutual mistake, fraud, or impossibility, are present. We hold that under paragraph 13 of the parties' purchase agreement the Jameses had the legal right to void the contract once the premises were materially damaged, and their choice to exercise that right was not dependent on their satisfaction of the elements required for the application of equitable rescission. Accordingly, the district court erred in concluding that the Jameses were obliged to restore the value of the cabin to the Holschers.

II.   THIRD-PARTY BENEFICIARY STATUS OF THE HOLSCHERS UNDER THE JAMES/STATE FARM INSURANCE BINDER

. . . Because the insurance binder listed the Holschers as having a beneficial interest in the insurance with April 5, 1989, as the effective date of coverage, and because the binder contained no words limiting the coverage either to the Holschers' mortgagee interest in the property or to their post-closing losses, we hold that the insurance binder unambiguously provided the Holschers with a beneficial interest in the insurance to cover whatever insurable interest they had in the property as of April 5, 1989. We will not read into the binder a time or nature-of-interest limitation which State Farm did not deem important enough to write into the binder. We hold as a matter of law that the Holschers were third-party beneficiaries under the insurance binder, and that this beneficial interest was limited only to the extent of their insurable interest in the cabin under I.C. §41-1806. . . .

III.   ATTORNEY FEES AGAINST STATE FARM UNDER I.C. §41-1839

. . . In view of our decision that the Holschers should have prevailed on their claim against State Farm, we hold that the Holschers should be awarded reasonable attorney fees against State Farm, both at the trial level, Associates Discount Corp. of Idaho v. Yosemite Ins. Co., 96 Idaho 249, 257, 526 P.2d 854, 862 (1973), and on appeal, Stephens v. New Hampshire Ins. Co., 92 Idaho 537, 542, 447 P.2d 14, 19 (1968).

CONCLUSION

We hold that the parties' purchase agreement placed the pre-closing risk of loss on the Holschers, and allowed the Jameses to void the agreement at their option once the premises were materially damaged prior to closing. Accordingly, we reverse the district court's judgment holding the Jameses liable to the Holschers. We further hold that the Holschers were intended third-party beneficiaries of the insurance binder between the Jameses and State Farm, and therefore the Holschers are entitled to judgment against State Farm for the proceeds of that insurance. The Holschers are also entitled to an award of reasonable attorney fees against State Farm.

NOTES AND QUESTIONS

1. **Contrary authority.** Several courts have rejected the doctrine of equitable conversion and have placed the risk of loss on the vendor, regardless of possession. See, e.g., Skelly Oil Co. v. Ashmore, 365 S.W.2d 582 (Mo. 1963); Lampesis v. Travelers Ins. Co, 101 N.H. 323, 143 A.2d 104 (1958).

2. **California form.** Review the California form, *supra*. How does it deal (or does it deal) with possible damage to or destruction of the premises during the executory interval?

3. **Uniform Vendor and Purchaser Risk Act.** Twelve states (California among them) have adopted the Uniform Vendor and Purchaser Risk Act, which readjusts the common-law rights and duties, except where the contract expressly provides otherwise. The act's key points are as follows:

   (a)   If the sellers retain possession, and damage occurs without fault of the buyers, the sellers may not enforce the contract, and the buyers may recover their deposit.

   (b)   If the buyers are in possession, and damage occurs without fault of the sellers, the buyers are not relieved of their duty to complete the contract.

(c)   The above rules also apply if all or part of the premises are taken by eminent domain.

New York has embellished the uniform act where the sellers have kept possession and only an *immaterial* part of the premises is damaged by fire or taken by eminent domain. Here the sellers may continue to enforce the contract provided they accept appropriate abatement of the purchase price. N.Y. Gen. Oblig. Law §5-1311 (McKinney 1996).

4.   **Counseling advice.** Your client has just agreed to buy a $120,000 house. She wishes to know whether she should obtain fire insurance during the executory interval, and, if so, how much. How do you advise her? Suppose that your client has just agreed to sell the $120,000 house and asks whether she should retain coverage during the executory interval: How do you advise her?

5.   **Equitable conversion in other contexts.** The doctrine of equitable conversion may surface in various nondamage contexts as well.

(a) During the executory interval, the seller's creditor dockets a judgment that creates a statutory lien against the seller's real property. Does the purchaser take title free of the judgment creditor's lien? Cf. Mueller v. Novelty Dye Works, 273 Wis. 501, 78 N.W.2d 881 (1956) (Held: creditor must look to the sales proceeds, not the land, to satisfy judgment against the seller); *accord,* Texas American Bank/Levelland v. Resendez, 706 S.W.2d 343 (Tex. App. 1986).

(b) During the executory interval, the property is downzoned (28 to 12 condominium units per acre), making the venture less profitable to the contract purchaser. Absent contract protection against such change, must the purchaser perform? Cf. J. C. Penney Co. v. Koff, 345 So. 2d 732 (Fla. App. 1977) (Held: equitable conversion applies; purchaser assumes the risk of detrimental governmental action during the executory period).

(c) Seller dies during the executory interval. Pursuant to her will, real property goes to X, personalty goes to Y. Who is entitled to the sales proceeds? Cf. In re Estate of McDonough, 113 Ill. App. 2d 437, 251 N.E.2d 405 (1969) (Held: seller's interest in real estate equitably converted to personalty on date of contract and devisee (X) not entitled to the balance due on the contract). If purchaser dies during the executory interval, her interest descends as realty to the heirs or devisees, while the purchase price must be paid from the personalty assets of the estate, thus reducing the amount passing to the legatees or next-of-kin. Cf. Timberlake v. Heflin, 180 W. Va. 644, 379 S.E.2d 149 (1989).

b.   Financing the Acquisition

Buyers of improved real estate seldom pay the entire purchase price in cash. Few persons have the ready cash that even a modest transaction requires. Besides, most buyers — even when they have all the cash needed — would prefer to keep it in more liquid form than real estate. Moreover, as to income-producing property, an investor can lever his investment return into a higher yield by reducing his cash or equity position.[1]

In the sales contract, therefore, the parties must agree not only on the purchase price but also on the buyers' plan for financing some of the purchase price. To give us numbers for discussing this situation, suppose that the buyers have agreed to pay $120,000 for a house, toward which they can make a $30,000 down payment.

In at least two cases, our buyers would not have to search for a $90,000 loan to complete the purchase. There may already be a $90,000 mortgage on the property, which, if the lender gives its consent (or the loan documents permit this as of right), the buyers can take over at the closing. Alternatively, the sellers may agree to finance some or all of the purchase price themselves, by taking back a (junior) mortgage for whatever amount is needed to make up the difference between the $90,000 and whatever other financing can be had.[2]

Whether the buyers gain their financing from the seller or a third-party lender, they will want to know not only the size of the loan but also the loan's repayment terms. Years ago Professor Charles Haar coined the phrase "credit trio" to describe the chief variables of a mortgage loan, to which we would add a fourth member. Our credit "quartet" consists of loan-to-ratio, length of loan, rate of interest, and rate of amortization. We discuss each in the next section.

---

1. To illustrate leverage, let us start with an investor who buys a $10 million apartment house that throws off $1.5 million after expenses. On an all-cash purchase, he will earn a 15 percent cash yield on his investment. Suppose instead that he borrows to make the purchase: first $5 million, then $9 million. If the mortgages bear 9 percent interest, and if the annual debt service (that is, the combined amount of interest and principal reduction) is sufficient to pay off the mortgages in 25 years, the cash flow and cash yield appear below:

(a) $5,000,000 mortgage ($5,000,000 cash down payment)
      Cash flow before debt service $1,500,000
      Less debt service   505,000

      Cash flow after debt service   995,000
      Cash yield on $5,000,000 down payment   (19.99%)

(b) $9,000,000 mortgage ($1,000,000 cash down payment)
      Cash flow before debt service $1,500,000
      Less debt service   909,000

      Cash flow after debt service   591,000
      Cash yield on $1,000,000 down payment   (59.1%)

If we were to continue to project cash yield based on ever-shrinking down payments, the investment return, drawn on a hyperbolic curve, would approach infinity.

2. For example, if the property is subject to a $70,000 mortgage that the buyers are able to take over, the sellers might agree to take back a $20,000 purchase money, second mortgage.

NOTES

1. **Who gets loans.** Surveys conducted under the Home Mortgage Disclosure Act (HMDA) show that only 15 percent of whites or Asians are turned down for mortgages, while Hispanics are rejected 25 percent, and blacks 34 percent of the time. Furthermore, a Boston Federal Reserve Bank study showed that even controlling for "financial, employment, and neighborhood factors," there was still a significant gap attributable to race, for both nonminority and minority-owned institutions. In Boston, the study found that, controlling for other factors, blacks were 60 percent more likely to be turned down for mortgages than whites. Vern McKinley, Community Reinvestment Act: Insuring Credit Adequacy or Enforcing Credit Allocation?, 1994 Regulation, No. 4, 25, at 27, 32.

2. **Redlining.** Redlining is the practice by lenders of systematically denying mortgages in certain geographic areas for reasons not attributable to economic factors such as loan loss. A. Brooke Overby, The Community Reinvestment Act Reconsidered, 143 U. Pa. L. Rev. 1431, 1451 (1995). The Community Reinvestment Act (CRA) (1977) encourages financial institutions to reinvest deposit funds to meet the credit needs of the community in which they are located. For fuller discussion of redlining, see pages 1249-1255, *infra.*

1.   Loan-to-Value Ratio

The loan-to-value ratio states, as a percentage, the relationship between the amount of money borrowed and the real estate's (appraised) value; for example, $90,000 borrowed on a $120,000 property results in a 75 percent loan. In making a mortgage loan, regulated lenders must comply with any maximum loan-to-value ratio that federal and state laws have fixed for each group of lenders. Often the loan-to-value ceiling will also depend on the class or age of property given as security. Also, federally insured or guaranteed mortgages carry their own loan-to-value ratios, which either Congress or an agency sets.

Value, the ratio's denominator, need not be identical to the property's cost, although often the two will coincide. Statutes use different adjectives to qualify value — for example, "appraised value," "reasonable value," "estimated replacement cost" — and the phrasing used may reflect significant policy choices, when it affects the potential size of the minimum down payment. Moreover, lenders may themselves appraise "generously" or "conservatively" to reflect their eagerness to make a loan; the inexactitude of the appraisal art readily allows this. Nor are lenders required to give a maximum loan; as a matter of policy, either to discourage borrowing or to strengthen their security, lenders may insist on larger down payments than the law requires.

2.   Length of Mortgage

Back in the 1930s, in an effort to stimulate a depressed housing market, Congress provided for 90 percent loans on federally insured home purchases. For the buyer of a $15,000 house, this meant only a $1,500 down
payment, an unrivaled prospect at the time. But two factors affect one's
ability to purchase real estate. If buyers must borrow $13,500 to finance
their purchase, they have more debt to repay and greater carrying costs
than if they need borrow only $10,000.

Since Congress did not want to undo the good effects of increased
loan-to-value ceilings, it met the carrying cost problem by stretching out the
life of the loan. As Table 12-1 shows, a $96,000 loan repayable at 9 percent
interest in equal monthly installments over 30 years costs the borrower little
more monthly than does a $60,000 loan repayable over 10 years. The prin-
ciple of stretch-out, which was a fairly radical idea in the mid-1930s, now
enjoys wide acceptance. Again, state or federal laws govern the maximum
duration of most real estate loans.

An extended maturity is not all to the borrowers' advantage. The
longer they repay the loan, the larger will be their total interest charges. A
$96,000 20-year loan, at 9 percent interest, costs $111,360 in interest; the
interest on a 30-year loan rises to $182,208! Some might boggle at this sum.
Given, however, the migratory habits of American households, 30-year mortgages rarely go to term. Most mortgages are paid off long before maturity,
often when the property is sold to a refinancing buyer. Moreover, the differences are less startling when present value discounting is applied to the
absolute amounts. And the deductibility of home mortgage interest payments for taxpayers itemizing their expenses further shrinks the "actual"
outlays.

Extended maturities cause a further concern. Since the loan balance
drops more slowly as the mortgage is stretched out, this increases the peril
for borrowers and lenders alike that the value of the property may not cover
the unpaid debt if a default happens somewhere down the line.

TABLE 12-1
Monthly Debt Service Related to Length
of Mortgage and Loan-to-Value Ratio
(in dollars) ($120,000 value)
(9 percent interest)

Loan-to-Value Ratio	Loan	10 years	20 years	30 years
50 percent	$60,000	$760.05	$539.83	$482.77
80 percent	$96,000	$1216.08	$863.73	$772.44
90 percent	$108,000	$1368.09	$971.70	$868.99

(i)   "Due-On" Clauses

> If all or any part of the Property or any interest in it is sold or transferred . . .
> without Lender's prior written consent, Lender may, at its option, require im-
> mediate payment in full of all sums secured by this Security Instrument.

This "due-on" clause has become a standard mortgage provision. It
allows lenders, in the event the mortgaged property is transferred in any
way, to demand repayment of the loan, even when the loan has not matured. At one time, some courts refused to enforce "due-on" clauses unless the lender could show that a change in ownership would threaten
the security.[3] This would prevent the lender from using a fortuitous sale
to demand a higher interest rate, if rates had risen after the loan was
made. In short: Where the transferee was creditworthy, the lender could
not refuse to approve a mortgage takeover at the original, lower interest
rate.

Believing (correctly) that restrictions on a lender's ability to accelerate fixed-interest loans during periods of rising interest rates would impair
the solvency of the mortgage lending industry, Congress passed the Garn-
St. Germain Depository Institutions Act of 1982, Pub. L. 97-320, 96 Stat.
1469.[4] This measure covers nearly all lenders, individual and institutional,
and all properties, residential and commercial. The law's effect with some
enumerated exceptions[5] is to curb state power over "due-on" clauses, making such clauses operative entirely at the lender's discretion.

---

3. The legal basis for this refusal was that such clauses were an unreasonable restraint
on alienation; see, e.g., Lemon v. Nicolai, 33 Mich. App. 646, 190 N.W.2d 549 (1971) ("due-on
sale" clause enforceable only when lender shows "waste or impairment or loss of security"). At
least five state legislatures also restricted the enforceability of "due-on" provisions.

4. A "Due-on-Sale Task Force," assembled by the Federal Home Loan Bank Board, concluded that if all states refused to enforce "due on" clauses, except where transfer would impair
the security, federal and state savings and loan associations would suffer annual losses exceeding $1 billion. Barad and Layden, Due-on-Sale Law as Preempted by the Garn-St. Germain Act,
12 Real Estate L.J. 138, 140 (1983).

In addition to forestalling a possible financial bath for mortgage lenders, Congress listed
other evils it hoped the new law would prevent: inflated home prices; higher mortgage origination fees; higher interest rates on newly issued mortgages; the advantaging of existing homeowners to the disadvantage of homebuyers; and the encouragement of riskier lending practices.

5. The exemptions, which apply only to residential real property containing fewer than
five dwelling units (including a dwelling unit in a cooperative housing corporation) and residential manufactured homes, include the creation of junior liens; a transfer by devise, descent,
or operation of law on the death of a joint tenant or tenant by the entirety; transfers to a relative
resulting from the borrower's death; intervivos transfers to the borrower's spouse or children;
and transfers resulting from a dissolution of marriage.

There are, in addition, three states, Michigan, New Mexico, and Utah that, under the
statute's "opt-out" proviso, have retained their autonomy over some loans.

NOTES AND QUESTIONS

1.   **Bargaining strategy.** Have you any suggestions for the borrower who would like to "lock in" a current low interest rate in the event he wishes to sell the property in a few years?

2.   **"Due-on further encumbrance" clauses.** Garn-St. Germain, with an exception for smaller residential properties, also curbs state power to prevent lenders from calling the loan if the borrower created a subordinate lien. Since the lender would suffer no loss in priority, can you think of any reasons for a senior lender's uneasiness over a secondary loan?

(ii)   Mortgage Prepayment

Suppose that two years after financing the purchase of their home, the borrowers win the state lottery and decide to use some of the prize money to pay off their mortgage: Are they privileged to do so? Or to take a more likely scenario: Interest rates have declined sharply and the borrowers would like to refinance at the current lower rates.

As the materials that follow make clear, the right to prepay is not automatic. Unless the mortgage papers provide otherwise, the lender may stand on the original bargain and insist that payments continue, as provided for, until maturity. But it is common for mortgages expressly to include the right to prepay, either absolutely and without penalty, or — quite usual with commercial mortgages — only with restrictions and the payment of some premium by the borrowers.

McCAUSLAND v. BANKERS LIFE INSURANCE CO.

110 Wash. 2d 716, 757 P.2d 941 (1988)

ANDERSEN, J.

FACTS OF CASE

This declaratory judgment case raises issues concerning the validity of due-on-sale clauses and prepayment restrictions in commercial real estate financing transactions.

In 1984, appellant Bankers Life Insurance Company (lender), loaned $700,000 to Brent and Colleen McCausland (borrowers) at 13.25% interest for a term of 15 years. This commercial loan provided permanent financing for a retail shopping center owned by the borrowers. The borrowers gave the lender a promissory note and deed of trust. The note provided that no prepayment of principal could be made during the first seven years of the loan. During the 8th through the 10th year, principal prepayment was permitted if accompanied by a 5% fee. After the 10th year, the note could be prepaid without restriction.

Both the note and deed of trust contained due-on-sale and due-on-encumbrance clauses permitting the lender to declare the entire note payable upon transfer or encumbrance of the property. The lender also had the right to declare the remaining unpaid principal and accrued interest due and payable at the end of the tenth year of the loan's term.

In 1986, 2 years after the loan was made, the borrowers inquired about the possibility of prepaying the note. No sale was involved; the borrowers simply wanted to refinance the loan. Relying on the prepayment restriction, the lender refused prepayment unless the borrowers would agree to pay an additional $115,000, which the lender asserted would be the loss occasioned to it by such a prepayment.

The borrowers then filed this declaratory judgment action seeking a declaration that the prepayment restrictions were invalid. Both parties moved for summary judgment. Relying on Terry v. Born, 24 Wash. App. 652, 604 P.2d 504 (1979), the trial court concluded that the prepayment restrictions were an unreasonable restraint on alienation and granted borrowers' motion for summary judgment, but denied their request for attorneys' fees and costs.

The lender then moved to alter or amend the judgment on the basis that the trial court's ruling conflicted with federal law prohibiting state restrictions on due-on-sale clauses. That motion was denied. The lender sought and was granted direct review by this court. The borrowers cross-appealed the denial of attorneys' fees.

Three issues are determinative of this appeal.

ISSUES

ISSUE ONE

Under the Garn-St. Germain Depository Institutions Act of 1982, a federal enactment, are due-on-sale clauses in real estate loan transactions now enforceable in Washington?

ISSUE TWO

Does a 7-year prepayment restriction in a commercial real estate loan constitute an unreasonable restraint on alienation?

ISSUE THREE

Do *both* a due-on-sale clause and a prepayment restriction in a commercial loan transaction combine together to unreasonably restrain alienation?

DECISION

ISSUE ONE

Conclusion

The Garn-St. Germain Depository Institutions Act of 1982 preempts prior state law so that due-on-sale clauses are now enforceable in Washington.

In this declaratory judgment action, we are asked to decide whether the combination of a due-on-sale clause with a prepayment restriction in a commercial loan agreement causes an unreasonable restraint on alienation so that we should declare the prepayment prohibition unenforceable. In order to analyze the combination of a due-on-sale clause and a prepayment clause, and their effect on alienation, it is helpful to first separately consider the history and purpose of each clause.

Prior to the federal legislation in question, state courts were divided on the issue of whether due-on-sale (DOS) clauses were reasonable restraints on alienation.[1] In this jurisdiction, DOS clauses were held to be unreasonable restraints on alienation unless the lender could show that the enforcement of the clause was necessary to protect the lender's security.[2] However, the federal Garn-St. Germain Depository Institutions Act of 1982 (Garn Act)[3] now preempts state laws that restrict the enforcement of due-on-sale clauses in real property loan cases, thereby making such clauses generally enforceable.[4] We have heretofore recognized that Congress intended to preempt state efforts to regulate the enforcement of DOS provisions in real estate loans.[5] This intent has been made eminently clear:

> The purpose of this permanent preemption of state prohibitions on the exercise of due-on-sale clauses by all lenders, whether federally- or state-chartered, is to reaffirm the authority of Federal savings and loan associations to enforce due-on-sale clauses, and to confer on other lenders generally comparable authority with respect to the exercise of such clauses. This part applies

---

1. See Bellingham First Fed. Sav. & Loan Ass'n v. Garrison, 87 Wash. 2d 437, 440, 553 P.2d 1090 (1976) collecting authorities on both sides of this issue.
2. *Bellingham*, at 441, 553 P.2d 1090; Riste v. Eastern Wash. Bible Camp, Inc. 25 Wash. App. 299, 301, 605 P.2d 1294 (1980).
3. The pertinent provisions of the Garn-St. Germain Depository Institutions Act of 1982, 12 U.S.C. §1701j-3, at 841 (1983) provide:

   (b)(1) Notwithstanding any provision of the constitution or laws (including the judicial decisions) of any State to the contrary, a lender may . . . enter into or enforce a contract concerning a due-on-sale clause with respect to a real property loan.

4. See G. Nelson & D. Whitman, Real Estate Finance Law §5.24 (2d ed. 1985).
5. Perry v. Island Sav. & Loan Ass'n, 101 Wash. 2d 795, 802, 684 P.2d 1281 (1984).

to all real property loans, and all lenders making such loans, as those terms are defined in §591.2 of this part.

12 C.F.R. §591.1(b) (1987).

There are cogent reasons supporting a uniform national policy enforcing due-on-sale clauses. As the United States Supreme Court has pointed out,

> the [savings and loan associations'] practice of borrowing short and lending long . . . combined with rising interest rates, has increased the cost of funds to these institutions and reduced their income. Exercising due-on-sale clauses enables savings and loans to alleviate this problem by replacing long-term, low-yield loans with loans at the prevailing interest rates and thereby to avoid increasing interest rates across the board.

Fidelity Fed. Sav. & Loan Ass'n v. de la Cuesta, 458 U.S. 141, 168-69 (1982). As a recent scholarly treatise further explains,

> the enforcement of due-on-sale clauses tends to reduce the discrimination that otherwise exists in favor of those buyers who are fortunate enough to find a low interest loan to assume against those who are forced to obtain new mortgage financing. Indeed, because existing low interest loans have been paid down to some extent, and because of inflation in the value of real estate, those who are able to assume an existing loan generally will be those who can come up with a significant amount of cash, whereas those who are not so fortunate in this regard will be forced to obtain new financing at higher market interest rates. Thus, to the extent that due-on-sale clauses are not enforced, an inordinate interest rate advantage may be afforded to higher net worth buyers over those who are less fortunate.

G. Nelson & D. Whitman, Real Estate Finance Law §5.21, at 318-19 (2d ed. 1985).

Thus, to the extent DOS clauses are not enforced, buyers unable to assume existing low interest mortgages have to pay artificially inflated interest rates to counterbalance lenders' older below market interest loans. In any event, it is no longer the prerogative of any state to restrict the enforceability of due-on-sale clauses. While the Garn Act did establish a window period phasing in the full enforceability of the Act[6] all contracts entered into after October 15, 1982 are subject to the Act's mandate of enforceability.[7] Since the date of the loan in the case before us was May 2, 1984, the Garn Act preempts prior state law.

---

6. 12 U.S.C. §1701j-3(c)(1) (1983).
7. *Perry*, 101 Wash. 2d at 810, 684 P.2d 1281. See also G. Nelson & D. Whitman, §5.4.

ISSUE TWO

Conclusions

A 7-year prepayment prohibition in a commercial real estate loan agreement does not constitute an unreasonable restraint on alienation.

Recognizing, as we do, that the Garn Act has preempted prior Washington law regarding due-on-sale clauses, the issue becomes to what extent the Garn Act preempts regulation of other real estate financing provisions, specifically, prepayment restrictions? Where Congress has not completely displaced state regulation in a specific area, state law is nullified to the extent it actually conflicts with federal law or when state law stands as an obstacle to the accomplishment and execution of the full purposes and objectives of Congress.[8]

The Garn Act clearly intended to preempt prior Washington case law restricting lenders' rights to use due-on-sale clauses, since that prior law directly conflicts with federal law and would stand as an obstacle to the congressional purpose of making such clauses uniformly enforceable. There is no indication in the Garn Act, however, evidencing an intent by Congress to preempt real estate loan provisions other than due-on-sale clauses. As one recent treatise explains, "[t]he Act preempts state law only with respect to due-on-sale clauses that 'authoriz[e] a lender, at its option, to declare due and payable sums secured by a lender's security instrument if all or any part of the property, or an interest therein, securing the real property loan is sold or transferred without the lender's prior written consent.'" G. Nelson & D. Whitman, §5.24, at 336, citing 12 U.S.C.A. §1701j-3(a)(1).

We must, therefore, decide whether, under Washington law, a 7-year prepayment restriction violates the public policy of this state because it imposes an unreasonable restraint on alienation. Unreasonable restraints on alienation of real property are, of course, invalid; reasonable restraints on alienation, on the other hand, are valid if justified by the legitimate interests of the parties.[9]

A prepayment penalty or restriction is generally used by a lender to preclude borrowers from refinancing loans in times of declining interest rates.[10] The prepayment restriction usually arises (as it did in this case) in the context of an effort to refinance, although it could arise if a seller wished to prepay a loan in order to convey title free of the security interest.

Absent a specific provision in a note, there is no common law right to pay off a debt prior to its maturity.[11] Washington law has long followed the

---

8. Fidelity Fed. Sav. & Loan Ass'n v. de la Cuesta, 458 U.S. 141, 153 (1982).

9. Magney v. Lincoln Mut. Sav. Bank, 34 Wash. App. 45, 51, 659 P.2d 537, *review denied,* 99 Wash. 2d 1023 (1983); *Bellingham,* 87 Wash. 2d at 439, 553 P.2d 1090.

10. G. Nelson & D. Whitman, §6.1 at 423.

11. G. Nelson & D. Whitman, §6.1; Williams v. Fassler, 110 Cal. App. 3d 7, 167 Cal. Rptr. 545 (1980).

common law principle that a lender is not obligated to accept prepayment of a loan which was set for a specific period.[12]

In an analogous situation, the Oregon Supreme Court held that a mortgage note provision which prohibited a complete payoff for 11 years was not an unreasonable restraint upon alienation.[13] That court reasoned that the only restraint on the borrowers was their inability to refinance and pay off the encumbrance. "There is an expense attached to loaning money on real property, and it is an entirely legitimate aim of purveyors of credit to loan it for a length of time and at a rate of interest which guarantee a certain net return on the management of the money."[14]

There are basically two types of prepayment clauses commonly found in real estate loans.[15] One type, an option clause, involves a specific penalty for the privilege of prepaying. The other, which is involved here, is a non-option clause that arises when the contract constitutes a locked-in loan that prevents all prepayment rights for a set period of time. As a California court recently explained, "[w]hen the trustor requests permission to repay the loan, or a part of it, before it becomes due, the lender can negotiate the charge he will accept in return for consenting to the prepayment."[16] That court, finding that the lender had a justifiable interest in motivating an intended long-term debtor to refrain from early prepayment of principal, held that prepayment is a privilege and the lender may extract a payment for the exercise of such privilege.[17] The court also noted that, in the absence of statute, a debtor has no more right to pay off the obligation prior to its maturity date than it does to pay it off after its maturity date.[18]

The borrowers argue, however, that an absolute restriction on prepayment for 7 years is unnecessarily restrictive and that some penalty provision could effectively protect the lender's interests. Conceivably a prepayment fee or formula could achieve that result while leaving a borrower greater flexibility to refinance. However, this court does not deem it appropriate to forbid prepayment restrictions on public policy grounds in order to protect commercial borrowers who, in most cases, are well able to bargain on their own with lenders who have a potential economic advantage. Our imposition of any such prohibition could well have serious consequences on the availability of commercial loans in Washington and on the salability of Washington loans on the secondary mortgage market.

If there is a need for regulations to be imposed in commercial loans regarding the amount of prepayment penalties that can be demanded, that

---

12. Pedersen v. Fisher, 139 Wash. 28, 245 P. 30 (1926); Cook v. Washington Mut. Sav. Bank, 143 Wash. 145, 152, 254 P. 834 (1927).

13. Hartford Life Ins. Co. v. Randall, 283 Or. 297, 583 P.2d 1126 (1978).

14. *Hartford*, at 300-01, 583 P.2d 1126.

15. *Williams*, 110 Cal. App. 3d at 10-11, 167 Cal. Rptr. 545.

16. *Williams*, at 10, 167 Cal. Rptr. 545.

17. *Williams*, at 10-11, 167 Cal. Rptr. 545. See also G. Nelson & D. Whitman, §6.1, at 422.

18. *Williams*, at 10, 167 Cal. Rptr. 545. See also G. Nelson & D. Whitman, §6.1, at 421-22.

subject is more appropriately addressed to the legislature. As another California court observed in that regard,

> the control of charges, if it be desirable, is better accomplished by statute . . . than by *ad hoc* decisions of the courts. . . . [I]nstitutions which lend vast sums of money should be informed, not by judgments after the facts on a case-to-case basis, but by laws or regulations which are in existence in advance of the undertaking to execute loans, of the validity or invalidity of terms that are commonly used.

Lazzareschi Inv. Co. v. San Francisco Fed. Sav. & Loan Ass'n, 22 Cal. App. 3d 303, 311, 99 Cal. Rptr. 417 (1971).[19] We agree.

Some kind of prepayment provision is obviously of great importance to commercial lenders who rely on the fixed interest due on their long term loans. The commercial borrowers in this case were on notice that they were restricted from retiring their loan prior to maturity unless they could reach an understanding with the lender on the matter. There is no allegation of fraud or overreaching in this case and the provisions in question were clearly set forth in both the loan papers and the commitment letter signed by borrowers.

Accordingly, we decline to hold that prepayment restrictions in commercial loans of the nature involved here violate public policy by unreasonably restraining alienation of real property. Such prohibitions do not preclude borrowers from selling their property although it may preclude them from refinancing their loan.

ISSUE THREE

Conclusion

We also conclude that the combination of a due-on-sale clause with a prepayment prohibition clause does not violate public policy by unreasonably restraining alienation.

Having examined the nature of both due-on-sale clauses and prepayment restrictions, the issue is then presented as to how these two provisions operate together in one loan instrument, and whether such a combination unreasonably restrains the alienation of real estate.

The most important consideration in this regard is that these two clauses do not operate simultaneously. As the lender here concedes, if it elects upon sale or encumbrance to accelerate the debt, it may *not* demand any prepayment penalty. This is correct, because payment after acceleration is not prepayment. As this court long ago explained,

---

19. Although legislation has limited prepayment restrictions and penalties in some jurisdictions, such legislation has been limited to loans secured by *residential* property and has not attempted to regulate prepayment clauses in nonresidential loan transactions. G. Nelson & D. Whitman, Real Estate Finance Law §6.4 (2d ed. 1985).

[o]f course, if the indebtedness is payable on or before some specified date, or the creditor has the right to so elect, and exercising such right elects an earlier date, then the date of his election becomes the maturity date, on or after which effective tender may be made by the debtor of principal and *interest up to date of tender.*

(Italics ours.) Pedersen v. Fisher, 139 Wash. 28, 33, 245 P. 30 (1926). Contemporary commentators agree that this is sound policy.[20] If a lender elects to accelerate the debt upon sale because interest rates have increased, the lender should not also be allowed to collect a prepayment fee. The function of the prepayment fee or prohibition is to protect lenders from borrower refinancing in times of falling interest rates and should not be used to penalize borrowers who refuse to accept lender's increased interest rates at resale in times of rising rates.[21] It is only fair that the lender be prohibited from demanding prepayment fees upon acceleration of the debt since, in that instance, it is the lender who is insisting on prepayment.

The two provisions, rather than working contemporaneously, are used as economic complements to one another. While the *due-on-sale clause* enables a lender to require early payment of lower than market interest rate loans, the *prepayment penalty* is used to discourage refinancing by the borrower when market interest rates fall below the rate on the borrower's existing loan.[22] The two provisions, therefore, are used by lenders to achieve different goals. Both are at least arguably necessary to protect a lender's long term loan portfolio.

The trial court in this case, in concluding that the prepayment prohibition combined with the due-on-sale clause unreasonably restrained alienation, relied primarily on the Court of Appeals decision in Terry v. Born, 24 Wash. App. 652, 604 P.2d 504 (1979). Such reliance is misplaced. In *Terry,* the real estate contract prohibited any assignment or conveyance and also flatly prohibited prepayment. It also provided for forfeiture in case of assignment. A complete, direct restraint on alienation is distinguishable from a due-on-sale clause which only requires payment of the loan upon sale. Additionally, *Terry* relied on the decision in Bellingham First Fed. Sav. & Loan Ass'n v. Garrison, 87 Wash. 2d 437, 553 P.2d 1090 (1976), which made due-on-sale clauses largely unenforceable in Washington. Since the enactment of the Garn Act by Congress, *Bellingham* no longer declares state law regarding DOS clauses. More recently, in discussing *Terry,* we pointed out that a due-on-sale clause is not even similar to the prohibition on assignment clause found in the contract the Court of Appeals had before it in *Terry.* Morris v. Woodside, 101 Wash. 2d 812, 818, 682 P.2d 905 (1984). As we there observed, "[t]his due-on-sale clause does not prohibit conveyance, assignment or prepayment." *Morris,* at 818, 682 P.2d 905. The *Terry* court

20. G. Nelson & D. Whitman, §6.5.
21. See Cohen, Judicial Treatment of the Due-on-Sale Clause: The Case for Adopting Standards of Reasonableness and Unconscionability, 27 Stan. L. Rev. 1109, 1130 (1975).
22. G. Nelson & D. Whitman, §6.1, at 423.

recognized that by prohibiting prepayment, the lender has an additional interest in receiving installment payments over a fixed period of time. *Terry,* 24 Wash. App. at 655, 604 P.2d 504.

To allow the trial court's decision in this case to stand would allow all borrowers to refinance their loans (which many would doubtless do if market interest rates fell below their loan rates) with no prepayment penalty. The converse of this, however, is not true. Lenders could not require borrowers to refinance their loans if market interest rates became higher than the loan interest rates.

We do not perceive it to be sound judicial policy to require lenders to choose between due-on-sale clauses and prepayment restrictions since they serve different interests. The clauses in question provide a means of allocating risks in a period of fluctuating interest rates. By enforcing them, the court is carrying out the parties' own allocation of the commercial risks involved. Prohibiting prepayment restrictions, but allowing for prepayment penalties through the use of prescribed fees or formulas, is a device better suited to determination by negotiation between the parties or, if necessary, for the Legislature which has the power to hold public hearings before enacting legislation.

The borrower has cross-appealed the issue of the trial court's refusal to award attorneys' fees and the lender has argued that such cross appeal was not timely. Because we reverse the trial court's decision, neither of these issues need be addressed. No attorneys' fees are awarded.

Reversed.

NOTES AND QUESTIONS

1. **FNMA/FHLMC Uniform Multistate Fixed Rate Mortgage Note.** Examine this note, page 1228, *infra,* which is widely used for home mortgages. How does it handle prepayment?

2. **Does acceleration after borrowers' default trigger a prepayment penalty?** In Eyde Bros. Dev. Co. v. Equitable Life Assurance Society, 697 F. Supp. 1431 (W.D. Mich. 1988), it was held that a mortgagee was not entitled to recover a prepayment penalty if it had accelerated the due date of the debt because of default by the borrower. In reaching this decision, the opinion quotes with approval as follows from Matter of LHD Realty Corp., 726 F.2d 327, 330-331 (7th Circuit 1984):

> [R]easonable prepayment premiums are enforceable. . . .
> There are, however, some limitations upon the right to receive a prepayment premium. For one, the lender loses its right to a premium when it elects to accelerate the debt. . . . [T]his is so because acceleration, by definition, advances the maturity date of the debt so that payment thereafter is not prepayment but instead is payment made after maturity.

697 F. Supp. at 1436.

In *Eyde Bros.,* the court indicated that the parties have avoided the usual limitation by clearly expressing the intent to do so in their agreement. Also, in "appropriate" cases, a prepayment penalty would be enforced, even if the lender had accelerated the debt. But the instant case was held not appropriate for enforcing a prepayment penalty, even though the mortgagor had intentionally defaulted in an effort to avoid paying the penalty.

3. **An historical explanation.** On the evolution of mortgage prepayment law, see Alexander, Mortgage Prepayment: The Trial of Common Sense, 72 Cornell L. Rev. 288 (1987). Alexander stresses that a dominant theme in the history of mortgage prepayment law has been tension between equitable principles of property law and rigid application of contract law. Rigorous application of contract formalism, that prohibited prepayment without consent of the creditor, emerged during the early nineteenth century, with twentieth century courts and legislatures often reversing this approach by easing the harshness of its application.

Creditors' interests in mortgages, Alexander concludes, have become largely commercial investments, with a majority of mortgages becoming commercial paper securitized in the secondary mortgage market. Alexander believes that residential mortgage debtors should have similar flexibility to mortgagees in marketing their debt obligations to third persons. He suggests that this flexibility be encouraged by a rule that if a creditor refuses prepayment, the debtor has a nonwaivable right to have the mortgage released from the property upon adequate substitute security being provided. Substitute security could be a guarantee from a highly rated credit institution that payment would be made of the underlying debt, and the credit institution might even assume the debt. The original mortgagor, of course, would normally pay the credit institution for guaranteeing or assuming the debt. The suggested security substitution proposal would not prevent prepayment penalties from being included in mortgage debt agreements. However, Alexander argues, the prospect of debts being transferred without prepayment becoming necessary would tend to reduce prepayment benefits to lenders and hold down amounts charged for the privilege of prepaying. Alexander is of the opinion that residential homeowner mortgagors are particularly deserving of more favorable treatment in relation to prepayment of their mortgage debt obligations.

4. **Problem.** Your brother Roger is trying to borrow money to buy a house in a period of high interest rates. He has finally located a company willing to give him the current market rate of 14.5 percent, with a five-year "balloon," that is, after five years, the entire amount of the loan becomes due and he will have to refinance (get another loan in place of the existing one). Roger is eager to sign the note, whose relevant paragraphs are printed below. He asks you whether there is anything in the boilerplate that he should be concerned about. Is there? (Hints: Interest rates may fluctuate within a five-year period from 9 percent to 16 or 17 percent; compare this note to the FNMA/FHLMC note at page 1228, *infra.*)

MORTGAGE NOTE

(FAMILY HOME)
US $ _____   _____ , New Jersey
                                              City

                                  _____ , 19_____

        FOR VALUE RECEIVED, the undersigned ("Borrower") promise(s)
to pay _____ ,
or order, the principal sum of _____ Dollars,
with interest on the unpaid principal balance from the date of this Note,
until paid, at the rate of _____ percent per annum.
Principal and interest shall be payable at _____ ,
or such other place as the Note holder may designate, in consecutive
monthly installments of _____ Dollars
(US $ _____), on the first day of each month begin-
ning _____ , 19_____ . Such monthly installments
shall continue until the entire indebtedness evidenced by this Note is fully
paid, except that any remaining indebtedness, if not sooner paid, shall be
due and payable on _____ .
        If any monthly installment under this Note is not paid when due and
remains unpaid after a date specified by a notice to Borrower, the entire
principal amount outstanding and accrued interest thereon shall at once
become due and payable at the option of the Note holder. The date specified shall not be less than thirty days from the date such notice is mailed.
The Note holder may exercise this option to accelerate during any default
by Borrower regardless of any prior forbearance. If suit is brought to collect
this Note, the Note holder shall be entitled to collect all reasonable costs and
expenses of suit, including, but not limited to, reasonable attorney's fees.
        Borrower shall pay to the Note holder a later charge of four (4%)
percent of any monthly installment not received by the Note holder within
fifteen (15) days after the installment is due.
        Presentment, notice of dishonor, and protest are hereby waived by all
makers, sureties, guarantors and endorsers hereof. This Note shall be the
joint and several obligation of all makers, sureties, guarantors and endorsers, and shall be binding upon them and their successors and assigns.
        Any notice to Borrower provided for in this Note shall be given by
mailing such notice by certified mail addressed to Borrower at the Property
Address stated below, or to such other address as Borrower may designate
by notice to the Note holder. Any notice to the Note holder shall be given
by mailing such notice by certified mail, return receipt requested, to the
Note holder at the address stated in the first paragraph of this Note, or at
such other address as may have been designated by notice to Borrower.
        The indebtedness evidenced by this Note is secured by a Mortgage,
dated even date herewith.

3.　Rate of Interest

Because interest payments are the largest item of housing expense for most homeowners and landlords, interest rate levels have much to do with the ability of consumers to afford decent shelter and with the willingness of both consumers and suppliers to engage in new shelter investment. Unusually high interest rate levels signal a sharp decline in the volume of housing starts and existing home sales; the volume seldom revives until the next downturn in rates. A family earning $50,000 yearly would nearly exhaust its housing budget on interest costs alone if its shelter (whether owned or rented) were financed by a $90,000, 12 percent mortgage — not a fanciful illustration at all, since in many areas even modest apartments can no longer be built for much less than $100,000, and home mortgage interest rates have soared to 14 percent and beyond as recently as the early 1980s.

Interest rate levels also are major influences on the market for all kinds of nonresidential real estate and affect the prices at which such properties may be sold, the viability of many new development projects, and where refinancing of an existing mortgage is needed, the ability to do so and remain profitable.

(i)　Adjustable Rate Mortgages (ARMs)

When borrowers arrange their mortgage financing, they often may choose between a fixed rate or an adjustable rate mortgage. One appeal of the adjustable rate mortgage (ARM) is an initial rate that is often much lower than the fixed rate would be, perhaps as much as 2 percent yearly. But, as ARM denotes, the interest rate fluctuates (both upward and downward) over the life of the loan in response to inflationary or market swings as measured by some statistical index: Examples are the weekly average yield on U.S. Treasury securities, adjusted to a constant maturity of one year; the Federal Reserve discount rate; and one of the widely used prime rates. As a safeguard to borrowers, there is usually a cap on how much ARM interest rates may move upward in any adjustment interval, for example in any one year, and in the aggregate, for example, not more than 5 percent. Borrowers are most likely to be attracted to ARMs when interest rates are relatively high but are expected to trend downward.

Competition among lenders has led to a variety of ARMs. In addition to different indexes and caps, other variations include the convertible ARM, giving borrowers the option of converting to a fixed rate loan after a specified period of time; and the negative amortization ARM, enabling borrowers to add interest increases onto the principal balance, thereby stabilizing the amount of installment payments.

How the adjustable rate mortgage works: Suppose that R borrows $90,000 on an ARM, which calls for an initial interest rate of 6 percent, a 25-year maturity, and annual debt service (based on monthly payments) of $6966. Three years later, interest rates have risen to 7 percent and an ARM adjustment is required. What is the ARM adjustment? Under present theory, it might take one of three forms:

   (1) Maturity remains constant; debt service rises to reflect increased interest rate. At the end of three years, R will have reduced the mortgage balance from $90,000 to $84,892. The interest rate having risen to 7 percent, the debt service must be adjusted upward so as to pay off the unpaid balance, at the higher rate, in the remaining 22 years. The revised annual debt-service increase: $7,581, or $631.73 monthly.

   (2) Debt service remains constant; maturity extended. This formula would seek to avoid entirely the risk of default that might follow higher debt-service payments. To maintain the level of debt service, while adjusting for higher interest rates, the mortgage term must be extended. After three years, when R's mortgage balance is $84,892, the annual debt service of $6,966 — adjusted for a 7 percent interest rate — will require nearly 28 more years in which to amortize that balance. Thus the original ARM maturity must be extended nearly 6 years.

   (3) Combination of debt service increase and maturity extension. This formula would seek to reduce the risk of default that might follow higher debt-service payments while avoiding extreme extensions of the mortgage term. The parties might agree, for example, that any maturity extension would not exceed a fixed duration, viz., 25 years; and that the borrower would pay higher debt service to complete the adjustment. In the illustration above, R would be obliged after three years to pay an adjusted annual debt service of $7,207, to reflect an extended remaining maturity from 22 to 25 years. The annual debt service increase: only $241.

   One key variable is the index to which interest rates are geared. For the borrowers' protection, the index used should not be one that the lender can manipulate. Thus, an index based on changes in the dividend rate on deposits would clearly be unsuitable. Short-term rates — for example, the rate on prime commercial paper — change too frequently and swing too widely to be a useful index. The Consumer Price Index measures *current* inflation whereas interest rates reflect *anticipated* inflation; therefore, the CPI does not seem entirely suitable, either.

(ii)   Limitations on the Lender's Return: Usury

   In setting their interest rate, lenders have had to consider — in addition to profitability, risk, and market demand — one other constraint: the legal ceiling, set either by state law or, in the case of federally insured or guaranteed loans, by Congress. A loan exceeding the legal ceiling is usurious, and where a borrower can show usury, sanctions ranging from a loss of the excess interest to a loss of the entire interest and principal may await the lender. The earliest usury laws, which appear in the Bible, forbade the taking of any interest (cf. Leviticus 25:36 and Deuteronomy 23:20). Centuries later, Aristotle argued that money, as an inorganic object, cannot breed new coins; therefore he who demands payment for the lending of money causes money to beget money and thus defies the laws of nature. During the Middle Ages, the church treated the exaction of any interest as a mortal sin punishable by excommunication. But as the Western world turned to capitalism, and as credit became essential for economic growth, laws fixing interest ceilings replaced the absolute bar against interest. One might still ask, however, why interest — of all charges made for goods and services — continues to be one of the most consistently regulated.

State usury statutes vary widely, as to rates, penalties, covered transactions, defenses, exemptions, statutes of limitations, and so on. In addition, the courts have added an enormous body of usury doctrine in sorting out the illegal from the legal loan.

Thus, purchase money mortgages — those mortgages that the seller "takes back" from the buyer to help finance the purchase price — are generally not subject to usury limits. See, e.g., Mandelino v. Fribourg, 23 N.Y.2d 145, 242 N.E.2d 823, 295 N.Y.S.2d 654 (1968). At least 30 states have enacted a corporate borrower exception, which would remove any ceiling from loans made to a corporation. See, e.g., N.J. Stat. Ann. §31:1-16 (West 1996). In some of these states, however, the exception does not apply to a corporation whose principal asset is a one- or two-family dwelling if the corporation was formed so recently as to suggest evasion. See, e.g., N.Y. Gen. Oblig. Law. §5-521(2) (McKinney 1996).

State usury controls, however, have become far less important in the wake of quite recent federal legislation. A 1980 law gave a federal agency (the now-defunct Federal Home Loan Bank Board) power to adopt regulations preempting state usury laws with respect to federally related *first* mortgages made after March 31, 1980. Federally related mortgages embrace virtually all residential loans issued by institution lenders. The agency exercised its power, although it did not have the further power to substitute a federal rate ceiling for the preempted state limits. Thus, except for certain federally originated or insured loans — for example, FHA insured mortgages regulated by the Department of Housing and Urban Development (HUD) — and for junior mortgages, residential lending has become virtually interest-unregulated.

4. Amortization Method

The fourth member of the credit quartet, amortization method, describes the rate at which the borrowers repay the loan balance. Debt service payments have two components: interest and principal reduction or amortization. Most real estate mortgages are *self-amortizing,* that is, each installment contains enough principal reduction to lower the loan balance to zero when the borrowers pay their final installment. Mortgages that are not self-amortizing, that is, not self-liquidating by regular debt service installments, are said to have a *balloon.* One finds balloon mortgages on investment properties and sometimes as second mortgages on homes. While a balloon mortgage could be written to require interest payments only, more often the rate of amortization simply falls below that needed to achieve self-liquidation. For the property owners, the balloon arrangement has the key advantage of improving their cash flow during the loan period (because debt service is reduced); but they must be ready, when the mortgage matures, either to find cash to satisfy the balloon or to obtain a new or extended mortgage.

Self-amortizing loans come in two forms: *level payment* and *constant amortization*. The former signifies that each installment (usually monthly) of debt service remains constant throughout the mortgage term. Given this objective, the calculation of the (monthly) installment derives from a formula with three variables: original principal balance, the length of the loan, and the rate of interest. Tables that aid in the computation are readily available, for example, from banks and mortgage brokers. Table 12-2 enables you to calculate the monthly debt service needed to self-amortize various amounts of debt at varying interest rates and maturities.

Problem: Compute the level payments required monthly to amortize a $60,000, 15-year mortgage at 11 percent interest; an $80,000, 25-year mortgage at 9 percent; a $35,000, 40-year mortgage at 13 percent.

You should be aware of the changing relationship between interest and principal in the level payment mortgage; with each installment the interest component gets smaller while the amortization grows. Take, for example, a $50,000, 12 percent, 30-year mortgage, carrying monthly debt service of $514.50. Each installment of debt service goes first toward the payment of interest on the unpaid loan; whatever sum remains goes then into principal reduction. Allocation of interest and principal for the first three months and the final months appears in Table 12-3.

Notice, also, how slowly amortization proceeds via the level payment mortgage. Table 12-4 shows the percent of unpaid debt remaining at five-year intervals on this illustrative loan.

The usual alternative to a *level payment* self-amortizing mortgage is the so-called *constant amortization* (declining payment) loan, which one sees more often in investment situations. This method of amortization requires

TABLE 12-2
Monthly Level Payments to Amortize $1000.
Various Amortization Periods and Interest Rates (in dollars)

Interest Rate (percent)	Term in Years						
	10	15	20	25	30	35	40
7.0	11.61	8.99	7.75	7.07	6.65	6.39	6.21
8.0	12.13	9.56	8.36	7.72	7.34	7.10	6.95
9.0	12.67	10.14	9.00	8.39	8.05	7.84	7.71
10.0	13.21	10.75	9.65	9.09	8.78	8.60	8.49
11.0	13.77	11.37	10.32	9.80	9.52	9.37	9.28
12.0	14.35	12.00	11.01	10.53	10.29	10.16	10.08
13.0	14.93	12.65	11.72	11.28	11.06	10.95	10.90

TABLE 12-3

Month	Installment	Interest	Principal	Principal Balance After Monthly Payment
1	$514.50	$500.00	$ 14.50	$49,985.50
2	514.50	499.86	14.64	49,970.86
3	514.50	499.71	14.79	49,956.07
—	—	—	—	—
—	—	—	—	—
—	—	—	—	—
360	514.50	5.00	509.50	0

TABLE 12-4

Year	Principal Balance	% Original Balance
5	$48,830	97.66
10	46,710	93.42
15	42,855	85.71
20	35,845	71.69
25	23,120	46.24
30	0	0

TABLE 12-5

Month	Installment	Interest	Principal	Principal Balance After Monthly Payment
1	$638.89	$500.00	$138.89	$49,861.11
2	637.50	498.61	138.89	49,722.22
3	636.11	497.22	138.89	49,583.33
—	—	—	—	—
—	—	—	—	—
—	—	—	—	—
360	140.28	1.39	138.89	0

equal amounts of principal reduction in each installment. Again using the example of a $50,000, 12 percent, 30-year mortgage, the schedule of debt service appears in Table 12-5. Over the 30 years, if the illustrative mortgages go to term, the level payment mortgage will be far more costly. Why is that? Yet the greatly reduced cost of the level payment mortgage in the loan's early years makes it a far more popular borrowing device in financing the sale of housing.

c.   Forms of Security Devices

1.   The Mortgage

We have already used the word "mortgage" repeatedly and have generally done so as a layman would — to describe a loan on real property. The lawyer knows better. A mortgage is not the loan itself, but a security interest in property given to an obligee (usually a lender) to secure the loan or, occasionally, some other obligation. Such other obligation might be the promise of the obligor to act as surety for the debts of a third person; in that instance the mortgage would be called a collateral security mortgage. The party who holds a mortgage is called the *mortgagee;* the party whose property is subject to a mortgage is called the *mortgagor.* Very often neither the mortgagee nor the mortgagor will be the original mortgaging parties, since the mortgage will have been sold or assigned or the mortgaged property will have been transferred. The mortgages dealt with in this text are mostly mortgages on real estate, not mortgages on personality, which are called chattel mortgages. Real estate mortgages may be either fee mortgages or leasehold mortgages; the common law treatment of leaseholds as "chattels real" causes some blurring of the distinction between real and chattel mortgages.

What is the effect on a real estate mortgage of improvements made on the property after the mortgage becomes effective? What if a building is built or a new elevator or furnace installed in an existing building, do the improvements become part of the mortgage security? Assuming no exemption of future improvements in the mortgage, they are added to the security of the mortgage if considered fixtures and thereby treated as additions to the real property. However, a troublesome problem can arise as to mortgage priority if before an item became a fixture it was covered by a chattel mortgage. The Uniform Commercial Code deals with this problem and under some circumstances the chattel mortgage will have priority over the real estate mortgage as to the fixture. Further problems may also arise because of uncertainty over what is and is not a fixture.

Where a mortgage is given to secure a loan, the loan usually is evidenced by the obligor's note or bond, which accompanies the mortgage. Although the terms often are used interchangeably, technically a bond is a sealed instrument and a note is an unsealed instrument; until the 1966 repeal of the federal excise tax on corporate bonds mooted the difference, a corporate mortgagor could avoid the tax by issuing a note instead of a bond. For an instance in which the archaic difference may still matter, see N.J.S.A. 2A:50-3 (1977); 79-83 Thirteenth Ave., Ltd. v. De Marco, 44 N.J. 525, 210 A.2d 401 (1965).

What does the mortgagee get when it receives a mortgage? The answer to that question has varied greatly over the course of centuries, but today, for most practical purposes, the mortgagee receives a lien[6] on the

---

6. Even in states where conveyancing practice still uses language in the mortgage instrument that signifies the transfer of legal title to the mortgagee, all that he gets is a lien interest. At an earlier time, American courts differentiated between the interest of a mortgagee holding title and the interest of a mortgagee having a lien only; today, most of the differences have disappeared. There remains, however, one. In a few states, known as title states, the mortgagee has the continuing right to possession, as he does in England. In one or two other states, known as "hybrid" or "intermediate" theory states, the mortgagee is entitled automatically to possession immediately upon default. Everywhere else, the mortgagee must petition the court for the

mortgagor's property as of the time that the mortgage is recorded. (Between the mortgaging parties, the lien is effective when the mortgage is executed and delivered, but since most disputes over priority involve third parties, the critical date is that of recordation.) In an earlier era, the mortgagee obtained title to the mortgagor's property subject to divestment if the debt were paid on the due or law day. Often this arrangement meant hardship for the mortgagor, for a late tender of payment, late even by so little as one day, would not bring a return of title unless the mortgagee volunteered to give it. In time, chancery intervened in behalf of defaulting mortgagors by letting them "redeem" the property from the mortgagee if they tendered payment within a reasonable period after the law day. This equitable right of redemption[7] grew into an implied term of every mortgage bargain, enforceable by a bill in equity.[8]

Now the mortgagee faced hardship — the hardship of uncertainty — for he could not be sure, after default, when his title would indefeasibly vest. A late tendering mortgagor might yet persuade chancery that the tender was not unreasonably delayed. Taking the initiative, mortgagees began to petition the courts to cut off, or foreclose, the mortgagor's equity of redemption. In this way, the procedural remedy of foreclosure was born. The decree of foreclosure, which was issued some months after the law date and upon notice to the defaulting mortgagor, vested the mortgagee's title to the real estate security; prior to the decree redemption was possible, but after the decree, it was not.

If, when foreclosure occurred, the real estate was worth more than the mortgage debt, still another source of hardship remained for the mortgagor. Since foreclosure vested title in the mortgagee, he stood to benefit, while the mortgagor stood to lose, from any surplus in property value. No restitution was necessary. By the early 1800s, state legislatures began to respond to the evident harshness of this situation; mortgagees who applied

---

right to possession — via a court appointed receiver — to protect the security from waste or dissipation of the rents; usually the petition is received and granted as part of a foreclosure proceeding.

7. Be sure not to confuse the equitable right of redemption, which the mortgagor holds until the default hardens into foreclosure, with the statutory right to redeem. The latter operates only after the equity of redemption is extinguished and entitles the mortgagor, in states where the right exists, to buy back the real estate from the purchaser at the foreclosure sale.

8. Redemption will normally be ordered by an equity court if the mortgagor alleges ability to pay whatever is due. The court then determines the precise amount due and sets a date, usually some months in the future, when the mortgagor must pay or, in most states, be foreclosed. Payment within the prescribed time discharges the mortgage. If the mortgagor defaults, others with interests in the land, including secured junior lenders, also may redeem to protect their interests from foreclosure.

The courts will not uphold or enforce any provision in the mortgage that attempts, through waiver by the mortgagor or otherwise, to eliminate or reduce the mortgagor's equitable right of redemption. This prohibition on "clogging the equitable right of redemption" has been rigorously adhered to since the seventeenth century. For consideration of the modern significance of the clogging principle, see Licht, The Clog on the Equity of Redemption and Its Effect on Modern Real Estate Finance, 60 St. John's L. Rev. 452 (1986). On clogging the equity of redemption also see Restatement of the Law, Property-Security (Mortgages) (Tentative Draft No. 1, 1991), §3.1 and the helpful Comment following that section.

for a foreclosure decree were ordered to sell the property at a public sale and to pay over to the mortgagor (and to any junior lienors) the surplus moneys from the sale, i.e., the money not needed to satisfy the claims of the foreclosing mortgagee. (Sometimes, of course, the sales price fails to satisfy the debt, and this may give rise to further claim for a deficiency judgment.) In a substantial majority of states, *foreclosure by judicial sale* has become the exclusive or generally used process, and it is available everywhere. The process that it supplanted, which for obvious reasons became known as *strict foreclosure,* survives in only a few states as a permitted remedy.[9]

One other form of foreclosure deserves mention, for it does not depend upon judicial decree. Where the mortgage instrument gives the mortgagee the power, and state law does not prevent its exercise, a sale arranged for by the mortgagee may be held to transfer the interest of the defaulted mortgagor. A *mortgage with power of sale* grew out of the efforts of English lawyers to avoid Chancery; by the mid-1800s, statutes confirmed the practice, and today, in England, the practice prevails. It exists in over half the states and is gaining popularity.[10] In England the sale may be held privately, the mortgagor being deemed protected sufficiently by the requirement that the sale must be "bona fide to a stranger and at a reasonable price." In the United States the sale is public and statutes carefully regulate the conduct of the sale and the method of giving notice.

The purchaser in theory obtains the same rights in the property he would enjoy had he purchased at a judicial sale, since the mortgagee is selling the title as it existed when the mortgage containing the power of sale was given. Nevertheless, the costlier, slower, and more cumbersome judicial sale is frequently preferred because it creates a permanent court record of the events leading to the transfer of the mortgagor's interest, while the purchaser at a nonjudicial sale may have only the recitals in his deed to establish the regularity of his title.

State law varies as to whether a mortgagee may bid at any sale that he conducts pursuant to the power of sale. Generally he will be permitted to do so if the mortgage gives him the privilege or if the sale is actually conducted by a public officer. What arguments do you see for and against letting the mortgagee participate in the bidding?

If the sale results in surplus moneys, the foreclosing mortgagee will usually bring a bill of interpleader joining the mortgagor and junior lienors so that their rights to the surplus may be decided judicially.

---

9. Strict foreclosure, while not permitted in the original foreclosure proceeding, may sometimes be used to correct an error in the original proceeding. Take this example: X, who holds a first mortgage, obtains a foreclosure decree and bids in (i.e., purchases) the property at the public sale. Then X discovers that service on Y, who held a second mortgage or a subordinate judgment lien against the property, was omitted in the foreclosure action, so that his lien survives the decree. Rather than reinstitute the sale, X may be able to apply for a decree of strict foreclosure — upon notice to Y, of course — that would cut off Y's interest in the real estate and relegate Y to a claim against the mortgage proceeds. Whether the decree is granted or not would probably depend on the showing of the relationship between the value of the property and the sales price and on the circumstances of Y's non-service.

10. Jones and Ivens, Power of Sale Foreclosure in Tennessee: A Section 1983 Trap, 51 Tenn. L. Rev. 279, 293 (1984).

Multistate Fixed Rate Note*

.... , 19.........   .... ,
                                                                    [City]

.........NEW JERSEY............
          [State]

....
                                  [Property Address]

1. BORROWER'S PROMISE TO PAY

In return for a loan that I have received, I promise to pay U.S. $.. (this amount is called "principal"), plus interest, to the order of the Lender. The Lender is ....BERKELEY FEDERAL SAVINGS BANK...........................

I understand that the Lender may transfer this Note. The Lender or anyone who takes this Note by transfer and who is entitled to receive payments under this Note is called the "Note Holder."

2. INTEREST

Interest will be charged on unpaid principal until the full amount of principal has been paid. I will pay interest at a yearly rate of ....%.

The interest rate required by this Section 2 is the rate I will pay both before and after any default described in Section 6(B) of this Note.

3. PAYMENTS

(A) Time and Place of Payments

I will pay principal and interest by making payments every month.

I will make my monthly payments on the .....FIRST...... day of each month beginning on ...., 19......... I will make these payments every month until I have paid all of the principal and interest and any other charges described below that I may owe under

---

this Note. My monthly payments will be applied to interest before principal. If, on ...., ..., I still owe amounts under this Note, I will pay those amounts in full on that date, which is called the "maturity date."

I will make my monthly payments at ....21 BLEEKER STREET..........
......MILLBURN........NEW JERSEY..07041........ or at a different place if required by the Note Holder.

(B) Amount of Monthly Payments

My monthly payment will be in the amount of U.S. $..............
....

4. BORROWER'S RIGHT TO PREPAY

I have the right to make payments of principal at any time before they are due. A payment of principal only is known as a "prepayment." When I make a prepayment, I will tell the Note Holder in writing that I am doing so.

I may make a full prepayment or partial prepayments without paying any prepayment charge. The Note Holder will use all of my prepayments to reduce the amount of principal that I owe under this Note. If I make a partial prepayment, there will be no changes in the due date or in the amount of my monthly payment unless the Note Holder agrees in writing to those changes.

5. LOAN CHARGES

If a law, which applies to this loan and which sets maximum loan charges, is finally interpreted so that the interest or other loan charges collected or to be collected in connection with this loan exceed the permitted limits, then: (i) any such loan charge shall be reduced by the amount necessary to reduce the charge to the permitted limit; and (ii) any sums already collected from me which exceeded permitted limits will be refunded to me. The Note Holder may choose to make this refund by reducing the principal I owe under this Note or by making a direct payment to me. If a refund reduces principal, the reduction will be treated as a partial prepayment.

6. BORROWER'S FAILURE TO PAY AS REQUIRED

(A) Late Charge for Overdue Payments

If the Note Holder has not received the full amount of any monthly payment by the end of ....15... calendar days after the date it is due, I will pay a late charge to the Note Holder. The amount of the charge will be ....5.......% of my overdue payment of principal and interest. I will pay this late charge promptly but only once on each late payment.

(B) Default

If I do not pay the full amount of each monthly payment on the date it is due, I will be in default.

(C) Notice of Default

If I am in default, the Note Holder may send me a written notice telling me that if I do not pay the overdue amount by a certain date, the Note Holder may require me to pay immediately the full amount of principal which has not been paid and all the interest that I owe on that amount. That date must be at least 30 days after the date on which the notice is delivered or mailed to me.

(D) No Waiver By Note Holder

Even if, at a time when I am in default, the Note Holder does not require me to pay immediately in full as described above, the Note Holder will still have the right to do so if I am in default at a later time.

(E) Payment of Note Holder's Costs and Expenses

If the Note Holder has required me to pay immediately in full as described above, the Note Holder will have the right to be paid back by me for all of its costs and expenses in enforcing this Note to the extent not prohibited by applicable law. Those expenses include, for example, reasonable attorneys' fees.

7. GIVING OF NOTICES

Unless applicable law requires a different method, any notice that must be given to me under this Note will be given by delivering it or by mailing it by first class mail to me at the Property Address above or at a different address if I give the Note Holder a notice of my different address.

Any notice that must be given to the Note Holder under this Note will be given by mailing it by first class mail to the Note Holder at the address stated in Section 3(A) above or at a different address if I am given a notice of that different address.

8. OBLIGATIONS OF PERSONS UNDER THIS NOTE

If more than one person signs this Note, each person is fully and personally obligated to keep all of the promises made in this Note, including the promise to pay the full amount owed. Any person who is a guarantor, surety or endorser of this Note is also obligated to do these things. Any person who takes over these obligations, including the obligations of a guarantor, surety or endorser of this Note, is also obligated to keep all of the promises made in this Note. The Note Holder may enforce its rights under this Note against each person individually or against all of us together. This means that any one of us may be required to pay all of the amounts owed under this Note.

9. WAIVERS

I and any other person who has obligations under this Note waive the rights of presentment and notice of dishonor. "Presentment" means the right to require the Note Holder to demand payment of amounts due. "Notice of dishonor" means the right to require the Note Holder to give notice to other persons that amounts due have not been paid.

10. UNIFORM SECURED NOTE

This Note is a uniform instrument with limited variations in some jurisdictions. In addition to the protections given to the Note Holder under this Note, a Mortgage, Deed of Trust or Security Deed (the "Security Instrument"), dated the same date as this Note, protects the Note Holder from possible losses which might result if I do not keep the promises which I make in this Note. That Security Instrument describes how and under what conditions I may be required to make immediate payment in full of all amounts I owe under this Note. Some of those conditions are described as follows:

Transfer of the Property or a Beneficial Interest in Borrower. If all or any part of the Property or any interest in it is sold or transferred (or if a beneficial interest in Borrower is sold or transferred and Borrower is not a natural person) without Lender's prior written consent, Lender may, at its option, require immediate payment in full of all sums secured by this Security Instrument. However, this option shall not be exercised by Lender if exercise is prohibited by federal law as of the date of this Security Instrument.

If Lender exercises this option, Lender shall give Borrower notice of acceleration. The notice shall provide a period of not less than 30 days from the date the notice is delivered or mailed within which Borrower must pay all sums secured by this Security Instrument. If Borrower fails to pay these sums prior to the expiration of this period, Lender may invoke any remedies permitted by this Security Instrument without further notice or demand on Borrower.

WITNESS THE HAND(S) AND SEAL(S) OF THE UNDERSIGNED.

....(SEAL)
Witness: -Borrower

....(SEAL)
Witness: -Borrower

                                                   ....(Seal)
                                                                            -Borrower

[Sign Original Only]

Mortgage
New Jersey—Single
Family*

This instrument was prepared by:
_____[Space Above This Line For Recording Data]_____

MORTGAGE

THIS MORTGAGE ("Security Instrument") is given on ....

.... ,

19........ . The mortgagor is ....

....

("Borrower"). This Security Instrument is given to...**BERKELEY FEDERAL**

SAVINGS BANK ...... , which is organized and existing under the laws of

THE UNITED STATES OF AMERICA...... , and whose principal office and mail-

ing address is......**21 BLEEKER STREET, MILLBURN, NEW JERSEY 07041**......

("Lender"). Borrower owes Lender the principal sum of ....

.... Dollars (U.S. $...................). This debt is evidenced

by Borrower's note dated the same date as this Security Instrument

("Note"), which provides for monthly payments, with the full debt, if not

paid earlier, due and payable on ....
This Security Instrument secures to Lender: (a) the repayment of the
debt evidenced by the Note, with interest, and all renewals, extensions
and modifications of the Note; (b) the payment of all other sums, with
interest, advanced under paragraph 7 to protect the security of this
Security Instrument; and (c) the performance of Borrower's covenants

* **NEW JERSEY**—Single Family—**Fannie Mae/Freddie Mac UNIFORM INSTRU-
MENT**   **Form 3031   9/90**

and agreements under this Security Instrument and the Note. This Security Instrument and the Note secured hereby are subject to modification (including changes in the interest rate, the due date, and other terms and conditions), as defined in New Jersey Laws 1985, ch. 353, §1 *et seq., and* upon such modification, shall have the benefit of the lien priority provisions of that law. The maximum principal amount secured by this Security Instrument is $............... . For these purposes, Borrower does hereby mortgage, grant and convey to Lender the following described property located in .... County, New Jersey:

which has the address of .... ,
                                                              [Street]
.... , New Jersey .... ("Property Address");
            [City]   [Zip Code]

TOGETHER WITH all the improvements now or hereafter erected on the property, and all easements, appurtenances, and fixtures now or hereafter a part of the property. All replacements and additions shall also be covered by this Security Instrument. All of the foregoing is referred to in this Security Instrument as the "Property."

BORROWER COVENANTS that Borrower is lawfully seised of the estate hereby conveyed and has the right to mortgage, grant and convey the Property and that the Property is unencumbered, except for encumbrances of record. Borrower warrants and will defend generally the title to the Property against all claims and demands, subject to any encumbrances of record.

THIS SECURITY INSTRUMENT combines uniform covenants for national use and non-uniform covenants with limited variations by jurisdiction to constitute a uniform security instrument covering real property.

UNIFORM COVENANTS.   Borrower and Lender covenant and agree as follows:

1. Payment of Principal and Interest; Prepayment and Late Charges.   Borrower shall promptly pay when due the principal of and interest on the debt evidenced by the Note and any prepayment and late charges due under the Note.

2. Funds for Taxes and Insurance. Subject to applicable law or to a written waiver by Lender, Borrower shall pay to Lender on the day monthly payments are due under the Note, until the Note is paid in full, a sum ("Funds") for: (a) yearly taxes and assessments which may attain priority over this Security Instrument as a lien on the Property; (b) yearly leasehold payments or ground rents on the Property, if any; (c) yearly hazard or property insurance premiums; (d) yearly flood insurance premiums, if any; (e) yearly mortgage insurance premiums, if any; and (f) any sums payable by Borrower to Lender, in accordance with the provisions of paragraph 8, in lieu of the payment of mortgage insurance premiums. These items are called "Escrow Items." Lender may, at any time, collect and hold Funds in an amount not to exceed the maximum amount a lender for a federally related mortgage loan may require for Borrower's escrow account under the federal Real Estate Settlement Procedures Act of 1974 as amended from time to time, 12 U.S.C. § 2601 *et seq.* ("RESPA"), unless another law that applies to the Funds sets a lesser amount. If so, Lender may, at any time, collect and hold Funds in an amount not to exceed the lesser amount. Lender may estimate the amount of Funds due on the basis of current data and reasonable estimates of expenditures of future Escrow Items or otherwise in accordance with applicable law.

The Funds shall be held in an institution whose deposits are insured by a federal agency, instrumentality, or entity (including Lender, if Lender is such an institution) or in any Federal Home Loan Bank. Lender shall apply the Funds to pay the Escrow Items. Lender may not charge Borrower for holding and applying the Funds, annually analyzing the escrow account, or verifying the Escrow Items, unless Lender pays Borrower interest on the Funds and applicable law permits Lender to make such a charge. However, Lender may require Borrower to pay a one-time charge for an independent real estate tax reporting service used by Lender in connection with this loan, unless applicable law provides otherwise. Unless an agreement is made or applicable law requires interest to be paid, Lender shall not be required to pay Borrower any interest or earnings on the Funds. Borrower and Lender may agree in writing, however, that interest shall be paid on the Funds. Lender shall give to Borrower, without charge, an annual accounting of the Funds, showing credits and debits to the Funds and the purpose for which each debit to the Funds was made. The Funds are pledged as additional security for all sums secured by this Security Instrument.

If the Funds held by Lender exceed the amounts permitted to be held by applicable law, Lender shall account to Borrower for the excess Funds in accordance with the requirements of applicable law. If the amount of the Funds held by Lender at any time is not sufficient to pay the Escrow

Items when due, Lender may so notify Borrower in writing, and, in such case Borrower shall pay to Lender the amount necessary to make up the deficiency. Borrower shall make up the deficiency in no more than twelve monthly payments, at Lender's sole discretion.

Upon payment in full of all sums secured by this Security Instrument, Lender shall promptly refund to Borrower any Funds held by Lender. If, under paragraph 21, Lender shall acquire or sell the Property, Lender, prior to the acquisition or sale of the Property, shall apply any Funds held by Lender at the time of acquisition or sale as a credit against the sums secured by this Security Instrument.

3. Application of Payments.   Unless applicable law provides otherwise, all payments received by Lender under paragraphs 1 and 2 shall be applied: first, to any prepayment charges due under the Note; second, to amounts payable under paragraph 2; third, to interest due; fourth, to principal due; and last, to any late charges due under the Note.

4. Charges; Liens.   Borrower shall pay all taxes, assessments, charges, fines and impositions attributable to the Property which may attain priority over this Security Instrument, and leasehold payments or ground rents, if any. Borrower shall pay these obligations in the manner provided in paragraph 2, or if not paid in that manner, Borrower shall pay them on time directly to the person owed payment. Borrower shall promptly furnish to Lender all notices of amounts to be paid under this paragraph. If Borrower makes these payments directly, Borrower shall promptly furnish to Lender receipts evidencing the payments.

Borrower shall promptly discharge any lien which has priority over this Security Instrument unless Borrower: (a) agrees in writing to the payment of the obligation secured by the lien in a manner acceptable to Lender; (b) contests in good faith the lien by, or defends against enforcement of the lien in, legal proceedings which in the Lender's opinion operate to prevent the enforcement of the lien; or (c) secures from the holder of the lien an agreement satisfactory to Lender subordinating the lien to this Security Instrument. If Lender determines that any part of the Property is subject to a lien which may attain priority over this Security Instrument, Lender may give Borrower a notice identifying the lien. Borrower shall satisfy the lien or take one or more of the actions set forth above within 10 days of the giving of notice.

5. Hazard or Property Insurance.   Borrower shall keep the improvements now existing or hereafter erected on the Property insured against loss by fire, hazards included within the term "extended coverage" and any other hazards, including floods or flooding, for which Lender requires insurance. This insurance shall be maintained in the amounts and for the periods that Lender requires. The insurance carrier providing the insurance shall be chosen by Borrower subject to Lender's approval which shall not be unreasonably withheld. If Borrower fails to maintain coverage described above, Lender may, at Lender's option, obtain coverage to protect Lender's rights in the Property in accordance with paragraph 7.

All insurance policies and renewals shall be acceptable to Lender and shall include a standard mortgage clause. Lender shall have the right to hold the policies and renewals. If Lender requires, Borrower shall promptly give to Lender all receipts of paid premiums and renewal notices. In the event of loss, Borrower shall give prompt notice to the insurance carrier and Lender. Lender may make proof of loss if not made promptly by Borrower.

Unless Lender and Borrower otherwise agree in writing, insurance proceeds shall be applied to restoration or repair of the Property damaged, if the restoration or repair is economically feasible and Lender's security is not lessened. If the restoration or repair is not economically feasible or Lender's security would be lessened, the insurance proceeds shall be applied to the sums secured by this Security Instrument, whether or not then due, with any excess paid to Borrower. If Borrower abandons the Property, or does not answer within 30 days a notice from Lender that the insurance carrier has offered to settle a claim, then Lender may collect the insurance proceeds. Lender may use the proceeds to repair or restore the Property or to pay sums secured by this Security Instrument, whether or not then due. The 30-day period will begin when the notice is given.

Unless Lender and Borrower otherwise agree in writing, any application of proceeds to principal shall not extend or postpone the due date of the monthly payments referred to in paragraphs 1 and 2 or change the amount of the payments. If under paragraph 21 the Property is acquired by Lender, Borrower's right to any insurance policies and proceeds resulting from damage to the Property prior to the acquisition shall pass to Lender to the extent of the sums secured by this Security Instrument immediately prior to the acquisition.

6. Occupancy, Preservation, Maintenance and Protection of the Property; Borrower's Loan Application; Leaseholds. Borrower shall occupy, establish, and use the Property as Borrower's principal residence within sixty days after the execution of this Security Instrument and shall continue to occupy the Property as Borrower's principal residence for at least one year after the date of occupancy, unless Lender otherwise agrees in writing, which consent shall not be unreasonably withheld, or unless extenuating circumstances exist which are beyond Borrower's control. Borrower shall not destroy, damage or impair the Property, allow the Property to deteriorate, or commit waste on the Property. Borrower shall be in default if any forfeiture action or proceeding, whether civil or criminal, is begun that in Lender's good faith judgment could result in forfeiture of the Property or otherwise materially impair the lien created by this Security Instrument or Lender's security interest. Borrower may cure such a default and reinstate, as provided in paragraph 18, by causing the action or proceeding to be dismissed with a ruling that, in Lender's good faith determination, precludes forfeiture of the Borrower's interest in the Property or other material impairment of the lien created by this Security Instrument or Lender's security interest. Borrower shall also be in default if Borrower, during the loan application process, gave materially false or inaccurate information or statements to Lender (or failed to provide Lender with any material information) in connection with the loan evidenced by the Note, including, but not limited to, representations concerning Borrower's occupancy of the Property as a principal residence. If this Security Instrument is on a leasehold, Borrower shall comply with all the provisions of the lease. If Borrower acquires fee title to the Property, the leasehold and the fee title shall not merge unless Lender agrees to the merger in writing.

7. Protection of Lender's Rights in the Property.   If Borrower fails to perform the convenants and agreements contained in this Security Instrument, or there is a legal proceeding that may significantly affect Lender's rights in the Property (such as a proceeding in bankruptcy, probate, for condemnation or forfeiture or to enforce laws or regulations), then Lender may do and pay for whatever is necessary to protect the value of the Property and Lender's rights in the Property. Lender's actions may include paying any sums secured by a lien which has priority over this Security Instrument, appearing in court, paying reasonable attorneys' fees and entering on the Property to make repairs. Although Lender may take action under this paragraph 7, Lender does not have to do so.

Any amounts disbursed by Lender under this paragraph 7 shall become additional debt of Borrower secured by this Security Instrument. Unless Borrower and Lender agree to other terms of payment, these amounts shall bear interest from the date of disbursement at the Note rate and shall be payable, with interest, upon notice from Lender to Borrower requesting payment.

8. Mortgage Insurance.   If Lender required mortgage insurance as a condition of making the loan secured by this Security Instrument, Borrower shall pay the premiums required to maintain the mortgage insurance in effect. If, for any reason, the mortgage insurance coverage required by Lender lapses or ceases to be in effect, Borrower shall pay the premiums required to obtain coverage substantially equivalent to the mortgage insurance previously in effect, at a cost substantially equivalent to the cost to Borrower of the mortgage insurance previously in effect, from an alternate mortgage insurer approved by Lender. If substantially equivalent mortgage insurance coverage is not available, Borrower shall pay to Lender each month a sum equal to one-twelfth of the yearly mortgage insurance premium being paid by Borrower when the insurance coverage lapsed or ceased to be in effect. Lender will accept, use and retain these payments as a loss reserve in lieu of mortgage insurance. Loss reserve payments may no longer be required, at the option of Lender, if mortgage insurance coverage (in the amount and for the period that Lender requires) provided by an insurer approved by Lender again becomes available and is obtained. Borrower shall pay the premiums required to maintain mortgage insurance in effect, or to provide a loss reserve, until the requirement for mortgage insurance ends in accordance with any written agreement between Borrower and Lender or applicable law.

9. Inspection.   Lender or its agent may make reasonable entries upon and inspections of the Property. Lender shall give Borrower notice at the time of or prior to an inspection specifying reasonable cause for the inspection.

10. Condemnation.   The proceeds of any award or claim for damages, direct or consequential, in connection with any condemnation or other taking of any part of the Property, or for conveyance in lieu of condemnation, are hereby assigned and shall be paid to Lender.

In the event of a total taking of the Property, the proceeds shall be applied to the sums secured by this Security Instrument, whether or not then due, with any excess paid to Borrower. In the event of a partial taking of the Property in which the fair market value of the Property immediately before the taking is equal to or greater than the amount of the sums secured by this Security Instrument immediately before the taking, unless Borrower and Lender otherwise agree in writing, the sums secured by this Security Instrument shall be reduced by the amount of the proceeds multiplied by the following fraction: (a) the total amount of the sums secured immediately before the taking, divided by (b) the fair market value of the Property immediately before the taking. Any balance shall be paid to Borrower. In the event of a partial taking of the Property in which the fair market value of the Property immediately before the taking is less than the amount of the sums secured immediately before the taking, unless Borrower and Lender otherwise agree in writing or unless applicable law otherwise provides, the proceeds shall be applied to the sums secured by this Security Instrument whether or not the sums are then due.

If the Property is abandoned by Borrower, or if, after notice by Lender to Borrower that the condemnor offers to make an award or settle a claim for damages, Borrower fails to respond to Lender within 30 days after the date the notice is given, Lender is authorized to collect and apply the proceeds, at its option, either to restoration or repair of the Property or to the sums secured by this Security Instrument, whether or not then due.

Unless Lender and Borrower otherwise agree in writing, any application of proceeds to principal shall not extend or postpone the due date of the monthly payments referred to in paragraphs 1 and 2 or change the amount of such payments.

11. Borrower Not Released; Forbearance By Lender Not a Waiver. Extension of the time for payment or modification of amortization of the sums secured by this Security Instrument granted by Lender to any successor in interest of Borrower shall not operate to release the liability of the original Borrower or Borrower's successors in interest. Lender shall not be required to commence proceedings against any successor in interest or refuse to extend time for payment or otherwise modify amortization of the sums secured by this Security Instrument by reason of any demand made by the original Borrower or Borrower's successors in interest. Any forbearance by Lender in exercising any right or remedy shall not be a waiver of or preclude the exercise of any right or remedy.

12. Successors and Assigns Bound; Joint and Several Liability; Co-signers. The covenants and agreements of this Security Instrument shall bind and benefit the successors and assigns of Lender and Borrower, subject to the provisions of paragraph 17. Borrower's covenants and agreements shall be joint and several. Any Borrower who co-signs this Security Instrument but does not execute the Note: (a) is co-signing this Security Instrument only to mortgage, grant and convey that Borrower's interest in the Property under the terms of this Security Instrument; (b) is not personally obligated to pay the sums secured by this Security Instrument; and (c) agrees that Lender and any other Borrower may agree to extend, modify, forbear or make any accommodations with regard to the terms of this Security Instrument or the Note without that Borrower's consent.

13. Loan Charges. If the loan secured by this Security Instrument is subject to a law which sets maximum loan charges, and that law is finally interpreted so that the interest or other loan charges collected or to be collected in connection with the loan exceed the permitted limits, then: (a) any such loan charge shall be reduced by the amount necessary to reduce the charge to the permitted limit; and (b) any sums already collected from Borrower which exceeded permitted limits will be refunded to Borrower. Lender may choose to make this refund by reducing the principal owed under the Note or by making a direct payment to Borrower. If a refund reduces principal, the reduction will be treated as a partial prepayment without any prepayment charge under the Note.

14. Notices. Any notice to Borrower provided for in this Security Instrument shall be given by delivering it or by mailing it by first class mail unless applicable law requires use of another method. The notice shall be directed to the Property Address or any other address Borrower designates by notice to Lender. Any notice to Lender shall be given by first class mail to Lender's address stated herein or any other address

Lender designates by notice to Borrower. Any notice provided for in this Security Instrument shall be deemed to have been given to Borrower or Lender when given as provided in this paragraph.

15. Governing Law; Severability.   This Security Instrument shall be governed by federal law and the law of the jurisdiction in which the Property is located. In the event that any provision or clause of this Security Instrument or the Note conflicts with applicable law, such conflict shall not affect other provisions of this Security Instrument or the Note which can be given effect without the conflicting provision. To this end the provisions of this Security Instrument and the Note are declared to be severable.

16. Borrower's Copy.   Borrower shall be given one conformed copy of the Note and of this Security Instrument.

17. Transfer of the Property or a Beneficial Interest in Borrower. If all or any part of the Property or any interest in it is sold or transferred (or if a beneficial interest in Borrower is sold or transferred and Borrower is not a natural person) without Lender's prior written consent, Lender may, at its option, require immediate payment in full of all sums secured by this Security Instrument. However, this option shall not be exercised by Lender if exercise is prohibited by federal law as of the date of this Security Instrument.

If Lender exercises this option, Lender shall give Borrower notice of acceleration. The notice shall provide a period of not less than 30 days from the date the notice is delivered or mailed within which Borrower must pay all sums secured by this Security Instrument. If Borrower fails to pay these sums prior to the expiration of this period, Lender may invoke any remedies permitted by this Security Instrument without further notice or demand on Borrower.

18. Borrower's Right to Reinstate.   If Borrower meets certain conditions, Borrower shall have the right to have enforcement of this Security Instrument discontinued at any time prior to the earlier of: (a) 5 days (or such other period as applicable law may specify for reinstatement) before sale of the Property pursuant to any power of sale contained in this Security Instrument; or (b) entry of a judgment enforcing this Security Instrument. Those conditions are that Borrower: (a) pays Lender all sums which then would be due under this Security Instrument and the Note as if no acceleration had occurred; (b) cures any default of any other covenants or agreements; (c) pays all expenses incurred in enforcing this Security Instrument, including, but not limited to, reasonable attorneys' fees; and (d) takes such action as Lender may reasonably require to assure that the lien of this Security Instrument, Lender's rights in the Property and Borrower's obligation to pay the sums secured by this Security Instrument shall continue unchanged. Upon reinstatement by Borrower, this Security Instrument and the obligations secured hereby shall remain fully effective as if no acceleration had occurred. However, this right to reinstate shall not apply in the case of acceleration under paragraph 17.

19. Sale of Note; Change of Loan Servicer.   The Note or a partial interest in the Note (together with this Security Instrument) may be sold one or more times without prior notice to Borrower. A sale may result in a change in the entity (known as the "Loan Servicer") that collects monthly payments due under the Note and this Security Instrument. There also may be one or more changes of the Loan Servicer unrelated to a sale of the Note. If there is a change of the Loan Servicer, Borrower will be given written notice of the change in accordance with paragraph 14 above and applicable law. The notice will state the name and address of the new Loan Servicer and the address to which payments should be made. The notice will also contain any other information required by applicable law.

20. Hazardous Substances.   Borrower shall not cause or permit the presence, use, disposal, storage, or release of any Hazardous Substances on or in the Property. Borrower shall not do, nor allow anyone else to do, anything affecting the Property that is in violation of any Environmental Law. The preceding two sentences shall not apply to the presence, use, or storage on the Property of small quantities of Hazardous Substances that are generally recognized to be appropriate to normal residential uses and to maintenance of the Property.

Borrower shall promptly give Lender written notice of any investigation, claim, demand, lawsuit or other action by any governmental or regulatory agency or private party involving the Property and any Hazardous Substance or Environmental Law of which Borrower has actual knowledge. If Borrower learns, or is notified by any governmental or regulatory authority, that any removal or other remediation of any Hazardous Substance affecting the Property is necessary, Borrower shall promptly take all necessary remedial actions in accordance with Environmental Law.

As used in this paragraph 20, "Hazardous Substances" are those substances defined as toxic or hazardous substances by Environmental Law and the following substances: gasoline, kerosene, other flammable or toxic petroleum products, toxic pesticides and herbicides, volatile solvents, materials containing asbestos or formaldehyde, and radioactive materials. As used in this paragraph 20, "Environmental Law" means federal laws and laws of the jurisdiction where the Property is located that relate to health, safety or environmental protection.

NON-UNIFORM COVENANTS. Borrower and Lender further covenant and agree as follows:

21. Acceleration; Remedies. Lender shall give notice to Borrower prior to acceleration following Borrower's breach of any covenant or agreement in this Security Instrument (but not prior to acceleration under paragraph 17 unless applicable law provides otherwise). The

notice shall specify: (a) the default; (b) the action required to cure the default; (c) a date, not less than 30 days from the date the notice is given to Borrower, by which the default must be cured; and (d) that failure to cure the default on or before the date specified in the notice may result in acceleration of the sums secured by this Security Instrument, foreclosure by judicial proceeding and sale of the Property. The notice shall further inform Borrower of the right to reinstate after acceleration and the right to assert in the foreclosure proceeding the non-existence of a default or any other defense of Borrower to acceleration and foreclosure. If the default is not cured on or before the date specified in the notice, Lender at its option may require immediate payment in full of all sums secured by this Security Instrument without further demand and may foreclose this Security Instrument by judicial proceeding. Lender shall be entitled to collect all expenses incurred in pursuing the remedies provided in this paragraph 21, including, but not limited to, attorneys' fees and costs of title evidence permitted by Rules of Court.

22. Release.   Upon payment of all sums secured by this Security Instrument, Lender shall cancel this Security Instrument without charge to Borrower. Borrower shall pay any recordation costs.

23. No Claim of Credit for Taxes.   Borrower will not make deduction from or claim credit on the principal or interest secured by this Security Instrument by reason of any governmental taxes, assessments or charges. Borrower will not claim any deduction from the taxable value of the Property by reason of this Security Instrument.

24. Riders to this Security Instrument.   If one or more riders are executed by Borrower and recorded together with this Security Instrument, the covenants and agreements of each such rider shall be incorporated into and shall amend and supplement the covenants and agreements of this Security Instrument as if the rider(s) were a part of this Security Instrument. [Check applicable box(es)]

☐ Adjustable Rate Rider	☐ Condominium Rider	☐ 1–4 Family Rider
☐ Graduated Payment Rider	☐ Planned Unit Development Rider	☐ Biweekly Payment Rider
☐ Balloon Rider	☐ Rate Improvement Rider	☐ Second Home Rider
☐ Other(s) [specify]		

BY SIGNING BELOW, Borrower accepts and agrees to the terms and covenants contained in this Security Instrument and in any rider(s) executed by Borrower and recorded with it.

Signed, sealed and delivered in the presence of:

....(Seal)
                                                                            —Borrower

....(Seal)
                                                                            —Borrower

_____[Space Below This Line For Acknowledgment]_____

STATE OF NEW JERSEY, ... County ss:

On this .... day of ...., 19........, before me, the
subscriber, personally appeared ....
.... who, I am satisfied, ...
the person(s) named in and who executed the within instrument, and
thereupon .... acknowledged that .... signed,
sealed and delivered the same as .... act and deed, for the
purposes therein expressed.

....
                                    Notary Public

This instrument was prepared by:

Receipt of a true copy of this instrument, provided without charge, is
hereby acknowledged.
Witness:

....(Seal)
                                                                            —Borrower

....(Seal)
                                                                            —Borrower

2.   The Trust Deed Mortgage (Deed of Trust)

Many states, both in lien and title, recognize a device called a *trust deed* mortgage, which creates a three-party mortgage transaction. When the loan is made, the borrower deeds the real estate security to a trustee, usually an institution specializing in that role.[11] While the mortgage remains current, the trustee has few duties; mortgage payments go directly to the lender who is the trust beneficiary. At maturity, or whenever the loan is repaid, the trustee reconveys the property to its rightful owner. But if a default occurs, the trustee must arrange a public sale of the mortgagor's interest — much as would a mortgagee with power of sale.[12] The trustee will usually conduct the sale and deed the property to the highest bidder. The trustee may not, however, acquire the property himself.[13]

Assignment of the mortgage leaves the trust intact. The original lender transfers the note or other evidence of obligation. The assignee then becomes the trust beneficiary.

While the differences between the straight mortgage and the trust deed mortgage may have once been significant,[14] that no longer is so. Courts and legislatures recognize the functional identity between the two mortgage forms, and, in a lien state, for example, the rights and powers of the trustor-mortgagor do not end because he parts with legal title. Thus, the mortgagor retains the right to possession until a default occurs and there has been a public sale or appointment of receiver. The mortgagor may also sell, lease, or further mortgage the real estate, subject, of course, to the trust. Which of the two forms the lender uses depends mainly upon the custom within the state.

---

11. It would be fairly unusual for the lender also to act as the trustee. Where such identity exists, courts have required, in the event of the obligor's default, that the trustee-lender sue to foreclose the debtor's interest rather than proceed under the power of sale. Spruill v. Ballard, 61 App. D.C. 112, 58 F.2d 517 (1932).

12. The trust beneficiary notifies the trustee that the default has occurred and directs him to arrange the public sale. After receiving the foreclosure request, the trustee owes the mortgagor no affirmative duty to investigate whether, in fact, there has been a default. Spires v. Edgar, 513 S.W.2d 372 (Mo. 1974).

13. Casa Monte Co. v. Ward, 342 S.W.2d 812 (Tex. Civ. App. 1961); Lee v. Lee, 236 Miss. 260, 109 So. 2d 870 (1959) (trustee's wife may not purchase); Whitlow v. Mountain Trust Bank, 215 Va. 149, 207 S.E.2d 837 (1974) (corporation in which trustee interested may not purchase).

14. For a good discussion of these differences, see Bank of Italy National Trust & Savings Assn. v. Bentley, 217 Cal. 644, 20 P.2d 940 (1933).

Deed of Trust*

DEED OF TRUST

THIS DEED OF TRUST ("Security Instrument") is made on ....
.... ,
19........ . The trustor is ....
....
("Borrower"). The trustee is .... ,
("Trustee"). The beneficiary is .... ,
which is organized and existing under the laws of ....
.... , and whose address is ....
....
("Lender"). Borrower owes Lender the principal sum of ....
.... Dollars (U.S. $....................). This debt is evidenced
by Borrower's note dated the same date as this Security Instrument
("Note"), which provides for monthly payments, with the full debt, if not
paid earlier, due and payable on ....
This Security Instrument secures to Lender: (a) the repayment of the
debt evidenced by the Note, with interest, and all renewals, extensions
and modifications of the Note; (b) the payment of all other sums, with
interest, advanced under paragraph 7 to protect the security of this
Security Instrument; and (c) the performance of Borrower's covenants
and agreements under this Security Instrument and the Note. For this
purpose, Borrower irrevocably grants and conveys to Trustee, in trust,
with power of sale, the following described property located in ....
.... County, California:

which has the address of .... ,
                                                    [Street]

.... , California .... ("Property Address");
            [City]   [Zip Code]

TOGETHER WITH all the improvements now or hereafter erected on the property, and all easements, appurtenances, and fixtures now or hereafter a part of the property. All replacements and additions shall also be covered by this Security Instrument. All of the foregoing is referred to in this Security Instrument as the "Property."

BORROWER COVENANTS that Borrower is lawfully seised of the estate hereby conveyed and has the right to grant and convey the Property and that the Property is unencumbered, except for encumbrances of record. Borrower warrants and will defend generally the title to the Property against all claims and demands, subject to any encumbrances of record.

THIS SECURITY INSTRUMENT combines uniform covenants for national use and non-uniform covenants with limited variations by jurisdiction to constitute a uniform security instrument covering real property.

UNIFORM COVENANTS.

[The Uniform Covenants are the same as those in the Mortgage (New Jersey)—Single Family (Fannie Mae/Freddie Mac Uniform Instrument) (see page 1232, *supra*).]

NON-UNIFORM COVENANTS.   Borrower and Lender covenant and agree as follows:

21. Acceleration; Remedies. Lender shall give notice to Borrower prior to acceleration following Borrower's breach of any covenant or agreement in this Security Instrument (but not prior to acceleration under paragraph 17 unless applicable law provides otherwise). The notice shall specify: (a) the default; (b) the action required to cure the default; (c) a date, not less than 30 days from the date the notice is given to Borrower, by which the default must be cured; and (d) that failure to cure the default on or before the date specified in the notice may result in acceleration of the sums secured by this Security Instrument and sale of the Property. The notice shall further inform Borrower of the right to reinstate after acceleration and the right to bring a court action to assert the non-existence of a default or any other defense of Borrower to acceleration and sale. If the default is not cured on or before the date specified in the notice, Lender at its option may require immediate payment in full of all sums secured by this Security Instrument without further demand and may invoke the power of sale

and any other remedies permitted by applicable law. Lender shall be entitled to collect all expenses incurred in pursuing the remedies provided in this paragraph 21, including, but not limited to, reasonable attorneys' fees and costs of title evidence.

If Lender invokes the power of sale, Lender shall execute or cause Trustee to execute a written notice of the occurrence of an event of default and of Lender's election to cause the Property to be sold. Trustee shall cause this notice to be recorded in each county in which any part of the Property is located. Lender or Trustee shall mail copies of the notice as prescribed by applicable law to Borrower and to the other persons prescribed by applicable law. Trustee shall give public notice of sale to the persons and in the manner prescribed by applicable law. After the time required by applicable law, Trustee, without demand on Borrower, shall sell the Property at public auction to the highest bidder at the time and place and under the terms designated in the notice of sale in one or more parcels and in any order Trustee determines. Trustee may postpone sale of all or any parcel of the Property by public announcement at the time and place of any previously scheduled sale. Lender or its designee may purchase the Property at any sale.

Trustee shall deliver to the purchaser Trustee's deed conveying the Property without any covenant or warranty, expressed or implied. The recitals in the Trustee's deed shall be prima facie evidence of the truth of the statements made therein. Trustee shall apply the proceeds of the sale in the following order: (a) to all expenses of the sale, including, but not limited to, reasonable Trustee's and attorneys' fees; (b) to all sums secured by this Security Instrument; and (c) any excess to the person or persons legally entitled to it.

22. Reconveyance.   Upon payment of all sums secured by this Security Instrument, Lender shall request Trustee to reconvey the Property and shall surrender this Security Instrument and all notes evidencing debt secured by this Security Instrument to Trustee. Trustee shall reconvey the Property without warranty and without charge to the person or persons legally entitled to it. Such person or persons shall pay any recordation costs.

23. Substitute Trustee.   Lender, at its option, may from time to time appoint a successor trustee to any Trustee appointed hereunder by an instrument executed and acknowledged by Lender and recorded in the office of the Recorder of the county in which the Property is located. The instrument shall contain the name of the original Lender, Trustee and Borrower, the book and page where this Security Instrument is recorded and the name and address of the successor trustee. Without conveyance of the Property, the successor trustee shall succeed to all the title, powers and duties conferred upon the Trustee herein and by applicable law. This procedure for substitution of trustee shall govern to the exclusion of all other provisions for substitution.

24. Request for Notices.   Borrower requests that copies of the notices of default and sale be sent to Borrower's address which is the Property Address.

25. Statement of Obligation Fee.   Lender may collect a fee not to exceed the maximum amount permitted by law for furnishing the statement of obligation as provided by Section 2943 of the Civil Code of California.

26. Riders to this Security Instrument.   If one or more riders are executed by Borrower and recorded together with this Security Instrument, the covenants and agreements of each such rider shall be incorporated into and shall amend and supplement the covenants and agreements of this Security Instrument as if the rider(s) were a part of this Security Instrument. [Check applicable box(es)]

☐ Adjustable Rate Rider   ☐ Condominium Rider   ☐ 1–4 Family Rider

☐ Graduated Payment Rider   ☐ Planned Unit Development Rider   ☐ Biweekly Payment Rider

☐ Balloon Rider   ☐ Rate Improvement Rider   ☐ Second Home Rider

☐ Other(s) [specify]

BY SIGNING BELOW, Borrower accepts and agrees to the terms and covenants contained in this Security Instrument and in any rider(s) executed by Borrower and recorded with it.

Witnesses:

....(Seal)
                                                                  —Borrower

          Social Security Number...

....(Seal)
                                                                  —Borrower

          Social Security Number...

_____[Space Below This Line For Acknowledgment]_____

NOTES AND QUESTIONS

1.   **Amortization method.** Examine the mortgage note form. Does it call for level payment or constant amortization debt service? Does it call for self-amortization?

2.   **Principal acceleration.** Examine the mortgage note form. Under what circumstances may the lender accelerate the principal, that is, declare the debt all due and payable?

3.   **Allocation of debt service installments.** Examine the mortgage note form. Suppose that the scheduled installment is $500, but that the borrowers are able to make only a $400 monthly payment. How is the payment allocated?

4.   **Borrowers' mortgage obligations.** Examine the mortgage note form. List each of the borrowers' obligations to the lender.

5.   **Lender's mortgage obligations.** Examine the mortgage note form. List each of the lender's obligations to the borrowers.

6.   **Escrow funds.** Lenders usually require the borrowers to make (monthly) payments into an escrow account so that the lender will be able to cover the property's real estate taxes and hazard insurance premiums as these items become due. Can you explain why the lender is concerned that moneys be on hand to make the tax and premium payments in timely fashion? Some states now require the lender to place funds into interest-bearing accounts for the mortgagor's benefit. Cf., e.g., N.Y. Gen. Oblig. Law §5-601 (McKinney 1996). (Federal law now limits escrow account accumulations.)

7.   **Foreclosure.** Compare carefully paragraph 21 in both the mortgage and deed of trust forms. What are their differences? Be aware that the procedural differences between judicial foreclosure (mortgage) and power of sale foreclosure (deed of trust) are not inherent in the choice of security instrument. For example, the trust deed trustee may have the choice, in many states, to proceed either by judicial or power of sale foreclosure. Note, also, that not all states permit power of sale foreclosure.

d.   Racial Geography: Redlining

MARCIA DUNCAN, EDWIN T. HOOD AND JAMES L. NEET,
REDLINING PRACTICES, RACIAL RESEGREGATION AND
URBAN DECAY: NEIGHBORHOOD HOUSING SERVICES
AS A VIABLE ALTERNATIVE

7 Urb. Law. 510, 513-514, 517-518 (1975)

One of the more common instances of discrimination in mortgage lending is the almost universal practice of redlining. In its narrowest sense, the term "redlining" simply denotes the practice of denying mortgage financing on property located within certain geographical areas of a city. These areas are generally the older, rundown sections of the city — the ghetto and adjacent areas, and sections undergoing racial transition. Typically a lending institution simply delineates an area as being too risky for investment. This initial "disinvestment decision" by local lenders, often acting individually, results in an inability on the part of residents or potential residents of the area to secure conventional mortgage loans for the purchase or repair of neighborhood homes. Although the outright denial of mortgage money to sections of a city is not as blatant a practice as it once was, the same effects are achieved by subtle though often well-intentioned means. Some common techniques include: the charging of higher prices and the imposition of more stringent terms for loans in rundown, minority, or racially transitional neighborhoods; a shortening of the length of time for loan repayment; refusing to lend on homes past a certain age, or the setting of a minimum dollar amount for mortgages; underappraising homes in transitional neighborhoods, and, especially if F.H.A. insured mortgages are involved, the charging of discount "points" in such areas. Through the use of such techniques, redlining becomes a subtle practice which is difficult to detect and even harder to prove. . . .

As the process of neighborhood deterioration gains impetus, local financial institutions begin to implement some of the more subtle redlining practices in order to discourage loan applications in the area. Again, the motives for such practices may be primarily economic. Since the underlying basis of long-term financing is stability over an equivalent period of years, areas in transition are suspect to potential lenders. Therefore, conventional lenders must be lured into such areas by more favorable terms — relatively short-term mortgages and higher rate of return. Over time, and further deterioration of the neighborhood, these subtle practices commonly evolve into a final decision by local lenders to disinvest the area as "too risky" for conventional loans. . . .

NOTES AND QUESTIONS

1. **Statutory Counterattack.** Among statutes directed against redlining, or financial discrimination as it also is known, are the federal government's Home Mortgage Disclosure Act of 1975 and Connecticut's Home Mortgage Disclosure Act, enacted in 1977. These statutes in part provide:

12 U.S.C.A. (1989)

§2801. *Congressional Findings and Declaration of Purpose*
(a) The Congress finds that some depository institutions have sometimes contributed to the decline of certain geographic areas by their failure

pursuant to their chartering responsibilities to provide adequate home financing to qualified applicants on reasonable terms and conditions.

(b) The purpose of this chapter is to provide the citizens and public officials of the United States with sufficient information to enable them to determine whether depository institutions are filling their obligations to serve the housing needs of the communities and neighborhoods in which they are located and to assist public officials in their determination of the distribution of public sector investments in a manner designed to improve the private investment environment.

(c) Nothing in this chapter is intended to, nor shall it be construed to, encourage unsound lending practices or the allocation of credit.

§2802.   Definitions

For purposes of this chapter —

(1) the term "mortgage loan" means a loan which is secured by residential real property or a home improvement loan;

(2) the term "depository institution" —

(A) means —

(i) any bank (as defined in section 1813(a)(1) of this title) [includes most all banks];

(ii) any savings association (as defined in section 1813(b)(1) of this title [includes most all savings banks and S&Ls]; and

(iii) any credit union,

which makes federally related mortgage loans as determined by the Board; and

(B) includes any other lending institution (as defined in paragraph (4) other than any institution described in subparagraph (A);

(3)   the term "completed application" means an application in which the creditor has received the information that is regularly obtained in evaluating applications for the amount and type of credit requested;

(4)   the term "other lending institutions" means any person engaged for profit in the business of mortgage lending;

(5)   the term "Board" means the Board of Governors of the Federal Reserve System; . . .

§2803.   Maintenance of records and public disclosure

(a) Duty of depository institutions; nature and content of information:

(1) Each depository institution which has a home office or branch office located within a primary metropolitan statistical area, metropolitan statistical area, or consolidated metropolitan statistical area that is not comprised of designated primary metropolitan statistical areas, as defined by the Department of Commerce shall compile and make available, in accordance with regulations of the Board, to the public for inspection and copying at the home office, and at least one branch office within each primary metropolitan statistical area, metropolitan statistical area, or consolidated metropolitan statistical area that is not comprised of designated primary statistical areas in which the depository institution has an office the number and total dollar amount of mortgage loans which were (A) originated (or for which the institution received completed applications), or (B) purchased by that institution during each fiscal year (beginning with

the last full fiscal year of that institution which immediately preceded the effective date of this chapter).

(2) The information required to be maintained and made available under paragraph (1) shall also be itemized in order to clearly and conspicuously disclose the following:

(A) The number and dollar amount for each item referred to in paragraph (1), by census tracts for mortgage loans secured by property located within any county with a population of more than 30,000, within that primary metropolitan statistical area, metropolitan statistical area, or consolidated metropolitan statistical area that is not comprised of designated primary metropolitan statistical areas, otherwise by county, for mortgage loans secured by property located within any other county within that primary metropolitan statistical area, metropolitan statistical area, or consolidated metropolitan statistical area that is not comprised of designated primary metropolitan statistical areas.

(B) The number and dollar amount for each item referred to in paragraph (1) for all such mortgage loans which are secured by property located outside that primary metropolitan statistical area, metropolitan statistical area, or consolidated metropolitan statistical area that is not comprised of designated primary metropolitan statistical areas.

For the purpose of this paragraph, a depository institution which maintains offices in more than one primary metropolitan statistical area, metropolitan statistical area, or consolidated metropolitan statistical area that is not comprised of designated primary metropolitan statistical areas shall be required to make the information required by this paragraph available at any such office only to the extent that such information relates to mortgage loans which were originated or purchased (or for which completed applications were received) by an office of that depository institution located in the primary metropolitan statistical area, metropolitan statistical area, or consolidated metropolitan statistical area that is not comprised of designated primary metropolitan statistical areas in which the office making such information available is located. For purposes of this paragraph, other lending institutions shall be deemed to have a home office or branch office within a primary metropolitan statistical area, metropolitan statistical area, or consolidated metropolitan statistical area that is not comprised of designated primary metropolitan statistical areas if such institutions have originated or purchased or received completed applications for at least 5 mortgage loans in such area in the preceding calendar year.

(b) Itemization of loan data. Any item of information relating to mortgage loans required to be maintained under subsection (a) of this section shall be further itemized in order to disclose for each such item —

(1) the number and dollar amount of mortgage loans which are insured under Title II of the National Housing Act [12 U.S.C.A. §1707 et seq.] or under Title V of the Housing Act of 1949 [42 U.S.C.A. §1471 et seq.] or which are guaranteed under chapter 37 of Title 38;

(2) the number and dollar amount of mortgage loans made to mortgagors who did not, at the time of execution of the mortgage, intend to reside in the property securing the mortgage loan;

(3) the number and dollar amount of home improvement loans; and

(4) the number and dollar amount of mortgage loans and completed applications involving mortgagors or mortgage applicants grouped according to census tract, income level, racial characteristics, and gender.

(c) Period of maintenance. Any information required to be compiled and made available under this section shall be maintained and made available for a period of five years after the close of the first year during which such information is required to be maintained and made available. . . .

Conn. Gen. Stat. Ann. (West 1987)

§36-444.   Definitions (Supp. 1991)
As used in this chapter —

(1) "Financial institution" means any state bank and trust company, savings bank, savings and loan association or credit union organized under the laws of this state which makes mortgage loans or home improvement loans; . . .

§36-445.   Discrimination in making of mortgage or home improvement loans
No financial institution shall discriminate, on a basis that is arbitrary or unsupported by a reasonable analysis of the lending risks associated with the applicant for a given loan or the condition of the property to secure it, in the granting, withholding, extending, modifying, renewing or in the fixing of the rates, terms, conditions or provisions of any mortgage loan or home improvement loan on one to four family owner-occupied residential real property located in the municipality in which such financial institution has a home or branch office, or in any municipality contiguous to such municipality, solely because such property is located in a specific neighborhood or geographical area, provided it shall not be a violation of this section if the mortgage loan or home improvement loan is made pursuant to a specific public or private program, the purpose of which is to increase the availability of mortgage loans or home improvement loans within a specific neighborhood or geographical area in which such investment capital has generally been denied.

§36-449.   Violations by financial institutions. Rights of loan applicant
Any applicant who has been discriminated against as a result of a violation of section 36-445 and the regulations pursuant to this chapter may bring an action in a court of competent jurisdiction. Upon finding that a financial institution is in violation of this chapter, the court may award damages, reasonable attorneys' fees and court costs. No class action shall be permitted pursuant to the provisions of this section. Any applicant alleging a violation under this section shall do so in his own individual complaint and each case resulting from such complaints shall be heard on its own merits unless consolidation of such cases is greed to by each defendant affected thereby.

§36-451.   Commissioner's duties. Penalty for violation of chapter
If the commissioner finds that a financial institution is violating the provisions of this chapter, he shall order the institution to cease its unlawful prac-

tices. A financial institution which continues to violate the provisions of this chapter after having been ordered by the commissioner to cease such practices shall be liable to a penalty of five thousand dollars for each offense to be recovered with costs by the state in any court of competent jurisdiction in a civil action prosecuted by the attorney general. The penalty provided by this section shall be in addition to and not in lieu of any other provision of law applicable upon a financial institution's failure to comply with an order of the commissioner.

Would you expect that either of these statutes would significantly curtail redlining? Why or why not?

2. **What is good policy?** Do you think redlining should be eliminated; and if it should, how can this effectively be accomplished? Should institutional lenders that obtain customer savings from ghetto communities be required to loan these moneys within the communities from which they are obtained? Should an institutional lender that operates over an entire metropolitan area be required to make riskier or less profitable real estate mortgage loans in older, rundown sections of the central city than it makes in other parts of the metropolitan area? If so, should there be any exceptions (East New York in Brooklyn, for instance)? And, if so, should government subsidize the losses or reduced profits from loans in these rundown sections or should they be absorbed by the lender's owners or other customers?

3. **Community Reinvestment Act.** Another federal statute pertaining to redlining is the Community Reinvestment Act of 1977, 12 U.S.C.A. §2901-2906 (1989 and Supp. 1991). This Act and regulations issued pursuant to it avoid mandating loans and other credit allocations by private lending institutions but seek indirectly to increase lending by these institutions in low- and moderate-income neighborhoods through requiring that each institution state in writing the communities it intends to serve and the types of credit it intends to make available in these communities. These statements are made available to the public, including community activist groups concerned with credit allocation in their areas, for exerting credit extension pressure on the lenders. The federal regulatory agencies also may consider an institution's record in meeting local community credit needs when acting on applications by the institution for such new developments as opening added branch offices, relocating offices, or merging with another institution. One analysis of the Community Reinvestment Act's impact concludes that the effect of the Act has been modest, although it has strengthened somewhat community activist groups in seeking more financial resources for their neighborhoods, and also has had some influence in making banks and other lending institutions conscious of their credit-providing responsibilities to low- and moderate-income communities. Robert C. Art, Social Responsibility in Bank Credit Decisions: The Community Reinvestment Act One Decade Later, 18 Pacific L.J. 1071 (1987); see also A. Brooke Overby, the Community Reinvestment Act Reconsidered, 143 U. Pa.

L. Rev. 1431 (1995); Michael H. Schill and Susan M. Wachter, Housing Market Constraints and Spacial Stratification by Income and Race, 6 Housing Poly. Debate 141, 156-157 (1995) (Because neighborhood risk factors often correlate strongly with race, using them to make lending decisions can still result in discrimination.)

4. **Federal preemption.** A number of states have enacted anti-redlining laws but many of these state efforts have been preempted by federal laws. Conference of Fed. Savs. & Loan Assns. v. Stein, 604 F.2d 1256 (9th Cir. 1979), *aff'd,* 445 U.S. 921 (1980). See also Lechner, National Banks and State Anti-Redlining Laws: Has Congress Preempted the Field?, 99 Banking L.J. 388 (1982). Examples of current state redlining statutes are the Connecticut Act appearing above and Cal. Code Ann., Health and Safety §§35800-35833 (West Supp. 1992).

e. Examining the Seller's Title

In the absence of contrary language in the sales contract, the seller of real property implicitly covenants to deliver a "marketable title" on the day of closing. The meaning of "marketable title" occupies a 300-page annotation in American Law Reports (57 A.L.R. 1253 (1928)) and 129 pages in the earliest commercial land transactions casebook (M. Handler, Cases on Vendor and Purchaser (1933)). Very generally, a marketable title consists of a fee simple absolute in the subject premises, free of encumbrances such as leases, liens (mortgage, tax, etc.), marital rights, easements, private use restrictions, or encroachments. In point of fact, few parcels *are* any longer strictly marketable, and as a study of the California sales contract would show, the parties invariably restate the basic obligation (paragraph 6, Title and Vesting, page 1181, *supra*). Thus, we might more accurately speak of the seller's duty to furnish the buyers with a "contract title."

Under the doctrine of merger, the seller's promise of contract title expires with the formal closing. If the buyers want seller to covenant title beyond the closing, they must either get new assurances in the deed (page 1275, *infra*), or provide in the contract for the survival of seller's promises after title has passed. Often, the seller will refuse to agree to this. In any case, most buyers will want to learn, before they pay over the purchase price, whether they are getting the very title they have bargained for. Therefore, two key events during the executory interval are the seller's proof of title and the buyers' examination thereof.

1. Methods of Title Examination

In the United States there are three major forms of title search and examination, each dominated by a different skill group or combination of skill groups.[15] In the first, lawyers in private practice make both searches and examinations and provide their clients with title opinions, usually in writing. These opinions ordinarily state who has title, indicate whether or not title is marketable, and describe any defects.

Under the second form of search and examination, lawyers in private practice do the examining and provide their clients with opinions but do not search the public records. Searching is done by professional abstracters who prepare written summaries of the titles to individual land parcels as disclosed by the public records. These summaries, or abstracts as they are called, are histories of the titles to particular parcels. An abstract has a series of entries, normally arranged chronologically, each entry a synopsis of or excerpt from a recorded document or other public record relevant to the land title in question. To the extent that the abstract is an accurate and complete reflection of the public records, it will have an entry for every step in the public record history of the title; every deed, mortgage, will, judicial decree, or other instrument or event bearing on the title and appearing in the public records will be referred to in a separate abstract entry. By carefully examining these entries a competent lawyer can determine the nature of the record title, including its current marketability. The companies that prepare abstracts are staffed by specialists in title searching, although few abstracters are lawyers. Many title insurance companies originally started as abstract companies, and some of the insurers still prepare and sell abstracts.

The third major form of title search and examination is one in which both search and examination functions are performed by a title insurance company as preliminary steps to issuance of title insurance policies. When a policy is ordered, company employees assemble and evaluate data requisite to insurability. Those employees who search rarely are lawyers; those who examine often are.

In counties where there is not enough title work to justify title company search and examination staffs, some companies, on request, will issue policies based on opinions of expert title lawyers in private practice. Thus title insurance is fairly frequent even under lawyer or lawyer-abstracter forms of title search and examination.

In recent years, the practice has increased of title insurance company agents, who are not company employees, making searches and examination for title companies and then issuing title insurance policies for the companies if the agents conclude that the titles are acceptable for insurance purposes. Many of these agents are lawyers in private practice, but many are nonlawyer abstracters or title searchers. The use of agents in this

---

15. For the results of a bar association survey of forms of title search and examination in different sections of the country, see Dansby, Survey of Lawyers' Current Role in the Title Insurance Process, 3 Prob. and Prop. 43 (Sept./Oct. 1989). The Dansby article also includes a state by state listing of a majority of states as to prevalence of title insurance and how extensively private lawyers are utilized in title searches and examination.

manner is an effort by the title insurers to expand market and reduce costs. Another not uncommon practice in some communities is for lawyers or title insurance companies to contract with outside title searchers to make title searches for them but not examinations. These searchers are independent contractors and most are nonlawyers. Many law firms also assign their employed paralegals to title searching work.

In New England and many rural and small-town communities in the United States, other than in the Far West, title searches and examinations are still largely monopolized by law firms and abstracters. However, where title insurance companies have moved into both title insurance searching and examination by their own employees, there has been considerable displacement of private practitioners of law in performing one or both of these functions. In some communities, especially most major metropolitan centers, this displacement is almost complete, and the title work of lawyers in private practice is restricted to clearing defective titles and negotiating with title insurers to limit the scope of coverage exceptions and otherwise expand coverage. The shift away from title work has had important implications for the private practice of law, as at one time such work was a major source of income to lawyers in all parts of the United States. This loss of title searching and examination illustrates the vulnerability of lawyers in private practice to competition from specialized, high volume businesses and professions. Other occupations that have been particularly effective in cutting in on the work of private law firms include collection agencies, banks in their probate and trust work, and accountants dealing with tax matters.

2.   Recording Acts

Fundamental to title protection in the United States are the recording acts, statutes in effect in every state. The term "recording acts" has a variety of meanings, but here it is used in a narrow sense common to discussions of real property law. It means only those statutes that provide for land conveyancing records to be maintained by recorders of deeds (or equivalent public officials) and that establish priorities among successive purchasers of land interests. Under some circumstances these acts reverse the common law rule that priority among successive purchasers of land interests from the same grantor is dependent on priority in time of execution. Although they differ in detail, all the recording acts provide for (1) centralized filing of documents creating or transferring land interests, (2) maintenance of systems of public records, consisting primarily of copies of the filed documents, and (3) priorities for those interests appearing in the public records against those that do not.

Public land records provided for by the recording acts are generally maintained in the office of a designated public official of the county where the lands are located. In many states this official bears the title of county recorder of deeds. Most of the records maintained in recorders' offices are open for public inspection and are the principal source of land title data sought by professional searchers. But records kept pursuant to the recording acts are not the only sources of information about land titles; and, on theories of notice or priority irrespective of notice, interests not apparent from an examination of these records may be outstanding and superior to any others. Such interests may be ascertainable from other public records, including court and tax records, and from an examination of the premises. Title examinations frequently involve inspection of these other sources, but some outstanding land interests still may not be uncovered, nor may any reasonable kind of search prove successful. The existence of such interests is an off-record risk that usually cannot be eliminated, although through title insurance or other means the risk may be passed on to someone else. However, known title defects, including interests with priority under the recording acts, frequently can be eliminated by such means as purchase of outstanding claims, passage of time and operation of limitations or curative acts, and suits to quiet title. Professional title searchers and examiners who negligently fail to locate title defects or report on them may be liable in tort or contract.

American recording acts were highly developed by the close of the colonial period.[16] In their early evolution they were probably influenced by English legislation, by the statute of enrollments and registry acts for the counties of Middlesex and York, and by English judicial decisions that purchasers with notice of unregistered conveyances were not protected by the registration statutes. But a general system of recording never developed in England as it did in the United States, and original title instruments kept in private hands have been the main sources relied on in title examinations of English lands. Registration somewhat similar to that provided for by the American Torrens system has, however, largely replaced this so-called title deeds system in England.

It is conventional to classify American recording acts into three main groups, emphasizing the varied significance of notice and the act of recording. The three types are often referred to as race, notice, and race-notice statutes. Under the race type statute, a purchaser who records has priority over any interest then unrecorded, whether or not the purchaser had notice of the unrecorded interest when he took. In other words, the race to the recorder's office determines who prevails. Under a notice type statute, a purchaser takes priority over all prior unrecorded interests of which he had no notice when he took. Once such a purchaser takes title, it is advisable for him to record in order to protect himself from subsequent purchasers, but he need not record to be protected against prior but unrecorded interests of which he had no notice. Race-notice type statutes are

16. On the history of the recording acts, see 4 American Law of Property §§17.4 and 17.5 (Casner ed. 1952); and 6A Powell on Real Property §904[1] (1991).

similar to notice statutes, except that for a purchaser under a race-notice statute to prevail over a prior unrecorded interest of which he had no notice when he took, he must record before the prior unrecorded interest holder does. Thus, under a race-notice statute, the subsequent uninformed purchaser is not accorded automatic protection against a prior unrecorded but recordable interest, as is the case under the notice statute. The term race-notice is applied to statutes so designated because under them both the race and the notice are material to determination of priority.

Only two states, Louisiana and North Carolina, have race statutes applicable to conveyances generally; several other states have them for mortgages. Of the remaining states, about half have notice statutes and half have race-notice statutes.[17] Arizona, Illinois, and Massachusetts are among the notice states; and California, Michigan, and New York among the race-notices ones.

Filing for record under the recording acts is not essential to validity of an unrecorded but recordable instrument. Such an instrument is valid between the parties and is effective as against subsequent takers not protected by the recording acts. When recording act priorities do not apply, then priority among successive conflicting interests in the same land parcel normally is determined by the common law preference for the interest senior in time of execution.

Public records kept pursuant to the recording acts also have evidentiary value in judicial proceedings. In many states the recorded copies of instruments are primary evidence, with no requirement that the original be produced or accounted for. In other states contents of an instrument may be proven from the recorded copy, but only after accounting for the original.

The recording acts, with their stress on readily accessible public land records and priorities for interests appearing in these records, have been largely responsible for creating enough certainty in American land titles to meet the needs of a highly developed industrial society extensively based on private property rights. But there are serious weaknesses in the recording acts that have resulted in more title uncertainty than is necessary and high costs of title protection to minimize the risks inherent in the system. Weaknesses in the recording acts include: the extensive and complex searches that must be made, both on and off record, to determine the apparent state of a title; inefficiently maintained and indexed public records; the risk of outstanding title interests that cannot be ascertained from any reasonable search; and limited effectiveness of recording due to possible errors by recorders and chain of title restrictions on search obligations.

---

17. For a state by state listing of recording acts and their classification as race, race notice, or notice enactments, see Baxter Dunway, The Law of Distressed Real Estate, App. 27C (1992).

What was no doubt a very good system in earlier days when title histories were short and searches comparatively easy is now a cumbersome and expensive procedure, particularly in highly urbanized communities. Following are representative recording acts, including examples of race, notice, and race-notice statutes.

WASHINGTON REVISED CODE ANNOTATED

(West 1996)

§65.08.070.   *Real property conveyances to be recorded.* A conveyance of real property, when acknowledged by the person executing the same (the acknowledgment being certified as required by law), may be recorded in the office of the recording officer of the county where the property is situated. Every such conveyance not so recorded is void as against any subsequent purchaser or mortgagee in good faith and for a valuable consideration from the same vendor, his heirs or devisees, of the same real property or any portion thereof whose conveyance is first duly recorded. An instrument is deemed recorded the minute it is filed for record.

FLORIDA STATUTES ANNOTATED

(West 1996)

§695.01   *Conveyances to be recorded.* (1) No conveyance, transfer or mortgage of real property, or of any interest therein, not any lease for a term of 1 year or longer, shall be good and effectual in law or equity against creditors or subsequent purchasers for a valuable consideration and without notice, unless the same be recorded according to law; nor shall any such instrument made or executed by virtue of any power of attorney be good or effectual in law or in equity against creditors or subsequent purchasers for a valuable consideration and without notice unless the power of attorney be recorded before the accruing of the right of such creditor or subsequent purchaser.

ARKANSAS STATUTES ANNOTATED

(1995)

§18-40-102.   *Lien attaches when recorded.* Every mortgage of real estate shall be a lien on the mortgaged property from the time it is filed in the recorder's office for record, and not before. The filing shall be notice to all persons of the existence of the mortgage.

INDIANA CODE ANNOTATED

(Burns 1980, Supp. 1996)

§32-1-2-11.   *Conveyances and leases — recorded deed required.* No conveyance of any real estate in fee simple or for life or of any future estate, and no lease for more than three [3] years from the making thereof, shall be valid and effectual against any person other than the grantor, his heirs and devisees, and persons having notice thereof, unless it is made by a deed recorded within the time and in the manner provided in this chapter.

§32-1-2-16.   *Recording required — effect.* Every conveyance or mortgage of lands or of any interest therein, and every lease for more than three [3] years shall be recorded in the recorder's office of the county where such lands shall be situated; and every conveyance, mortgage or lease shall take priority according to the time of the filing thereof, and such conveyance, mortgage or lease shall be fraudulent and void as against any subsequent purchaser, lessee or mortgagee in good faith and for a valuable consideration, having his deed, mortgage or lease first recorded.

NOTES AND QUESTIONS

1.   **Race, notice, or race-notice?** Without reference to interpretive judicial opinions, it is not always possible to determine with accuracy whether a particular recording act falls in the race, notice, or race-notice group. But from the statutory language appearing above, how do you think each of the enactments is classified?

2.   **Recordation problems.** To test your understanding of how race, notice, and race-notice systems differ from one another, work through the following priority disputes (A versus B) under each form of statute:

   (a)   X, the fee owner, to A, a mortgagee. A does not record. X to B, B having no notice of the X-A mortgage. B records the deed. A records the mortgage.

   (b)   X, the fee owner, to A, a mortgagee. A does not record. X to B, B having notice of the X-A mortgage. B records the deed. A records the mortgage.

   (c)   X, the fee owner, to A, a mortgagee. A does not record. X to B, B having no notice of the X-A mortgage. B does not record the deed. A records the mortgage. B records the deed.

3.   **What is "notice"?** We have already met the doctrine of notice in this course, fleetingly, when we discussed servitudes and the burden of servitudes on successor owners of the servient estate (§§7.3.c, 7.5.a, *supra*). *Actual* notice means that a party has direct information about the earlier transaction. This may come from an examination of the records, or from off-record sources brought directly to the party's attention. *Constructive* notice leads us to impute notice to a party who has means of knowledge that the party is duty-bound to use but fails to. *Record* notice is a form of constructive notice; this is the notice that one would gain of outstanding interests from a proper examination of the records. A second form of constructive notice might be called *inspection* notice. Parties who acquire an interest in real property are expected to inspect the premises carefully before they close. Facts that such an inspection would disclose — whether inspection is actually made or not — will be imputed to a party seeking recording act priority over an earlier interest holder. For example, if X acquires a lease from O but fails to record it, O's subsequent mortgagee Y still takes subject to X's lease if X has occupied the premises. X's possession places Y on constructive notice.

This discussion of notice, especially constructive notice, might be greatly expanded. What constitutes a "proper" examination of the records depends on the chain of title that an examiner must analyze. Courts disagree as to what this chain should consist of. See Note 3, page 1271, *infra*. Similar disagreement underlies the inspection of the premises requirement. Moreover, the doctrine of constructive notice requires a questioning attitude in the party making the examination or inspection. If a well-worn path leads from the highway to the pond behind the lot, there need not also be a billboard warning "This is an easement" to serve notice of a possible outstanding interest. In this connection, recall the (extreme) facts that led to constructive notice in Otero v. Pacheco, §7.3.a, *supra* (implied servitude). Suppose, also, that the property is a large office building. What kind of inspection or written inquiry would satisfy a subsequent purchaser's or mortgagee's duties under the recording acts? Cf., Martinique Realty Corp. v. Hull, 46 N.J. Super. 599, 166 A.2d 803 (App. Div. 1960).

4.   **What is the crucial notice date?** The concept of notice is critical to all but race systems. The relevant date for notice is when the party seeking recording act protection (that is, the grantee, mortgagee, etc.) obtains delivery of the title instrument (that is, the deed, mortgage, etc.) Notice of an earlier transaction, received prior to the delivery date, disables the party from claiming a superior interest. Notice received after that date is nondisabling even when — under a race-notice setup — the party has not recorded the title instrument.

5.   **Purchasers and creditors.** For subsequent takers to be entitled to priority under the recording acts against prior unrecorded interest holders, they must have paid for their land interest; and payment must have been substantial in relation to the value of the interest acquired. Donees as sub-

sequent takers are not protected by the recording acts;[18] and in some states certain classes of creditors are not protected even though they have acquired interests in particular land parcels.[19] However, a number of statutes expressly include creditors, or at least designated kinds of creditors,[20] and universally mortgagees are included as protected subsequent takers.

Whether someone has qualified for recording act protection, where the statute requires that the party be a good faith purchaser for valuable consideration, is sometimes controversial, as seen in the following case.

HORTON v. KYBURZ

53 Cal. 2d 59, 346 P.2d 399 (1959)

SCHAUER, J. In this action to have defendant declared the constructive trustee for plaintiff of an undivided one half interest in real property, plaintiff appeals from a judgment which decrees that he has no interest in such property. Plaintiff alleged and the trial court found facts sufficient to raise a constructive trust under the view of Notten v. Mensing (1935), 3 Cal. 2d 469, 473-477 [1-6], 45 P.2d 198, and Ryan v. Welte (1948), 87 Cal. App. 2d 897, 901-903 [4-6], 198 P.2d 357; i.e., plaintiff's father and step-mother orally agreed that all their property would go to the survivor for life and that the survivor would will such property one half to plaintiff and one half to those relatives of the step-mother whom she chose; in reliance on the oral agreement the spouses put their property in joint tenancy and plaintiff's father forebore to make any testamentary or other disposition of his property to members of his own family which would have been effective in the event the step-mother survived him, which she did; the step-mother took the subject realty as surviving joint tenant, conveyed it to herself and defendant, her relative, as joint tenants, and on her death defendant took as surviving joint tenant. But defendant alleged and the trial court found

---

18. Colorado is an exception to this. In Colorado donees are protected by the recording acts. Colo. Rev. Stat. §38-35-109 (West 1990), as interpreted in Eastwood v. Shedd, 166 Colo. 136, 442 P.2d 423 (1968).

19. Judgment creditors, for example, are not protected as subsequent takers under some recording acts. They have been held to lose out to prior grantees from judgment debtors, even though the prior grantees' deeds were unrecorded when the judgment liens became effective. Johnson v. Casper, 75 Idaho 256, 270 P.2d 1012 (1954); and Kartchner v. State Tax Commn., 4 Utah 2d 382, 294 P.2d 790 (1956).

20. Illustrative of a broad creditor protection statute is Ky. Rev. Stat. §382.270 (1970): "No deed or deed of trust or mortgage conveying a legal or equitable title to real or personal property shall be valid against a purchaser for a valuable consideration, without notice thereof, or against creditors, until such deed or mortgage is acknowledged or proved according to law and lodged for record. As used in this section 'creditors' includes all creditors irrespective of whether or not they have acquired a lien by legal or equitable proceedings or by voluntary conveyance."

that he gave "good and valuable consideration" for the conveyance and took as a bona fide purchaser.

Plaintiff urges that as a matter of law defendant is not a bona fide purchaser because (1) there is no evidence that he gave consideration adequate to cut off plaintiff's equity, because (2) the evidence establishes that defendant took with constructive notice of plaintiff's equity, and because (3) there was no agreement between defendant and plaintiff's step-mother that defendant would receive *all* the subject property on her death but rather defendant alleged and the trial court found that defendant gave "good and valuable consideration" for the agreement of plaintiff's step-mother to convey "a joint tenancy interest" which plaintiff asserts, is only a one-half interest. Plaintiff also contends that the trial court erred (4) in admitting, over objection, evidence of assertedly "self-serving" oral declarations of plaintiff's deceased step-mother, (5) in admitting, over objection, the will of plaintiff's step-mother, which states that she devises her entire estate to defendant, and (6) in rejecting evidence of the value of the subject realty shortly before the institution of this action, offered on the issue of adequacy of the consideration given by defendant.

We have concluded that plaintiff's contentions, considered (as they must be) on the basis of facts found by the trial court from conflicting evidence, do not impel reversal.

Plaintiff is the son of Robert and Annie Horton, who were divorced prior to 1916. In 1916 Robert married Elizabeth. They remained married until Robert's death in 1931. There was no issue of their marriage. Robert throughout his life had a close and affectionate relationship with plaintiff, and plaintiff often visited Robert and Elizabeth in their home.

In 1930 Robert and Elizabeth purchased and took up residence on the subject property, a ranch of 223 acres. During their marriage they had orally agreed that all property owned by either of them would go to the survivor for life and the survivor on his or her death would will such property one half to plaintiff and one half to those relatives of Elizabeth whom she might select.[2] In reliance on their oral agreement they put all their property, including the subject ranch, in joint tenancy and Robert made no will or other disposition of his property to any members of his own family in the event Elizabeth should survive him. On February 18, 1930, he made

---

2. The evidence of this oral agreement is as follows: Plaintiff testified that on January 18, 1931, the day following his father's death, plaintiff and his wife, at Elizabeth's request, called at the home of plaintiff's aunt and uncle (Robert's brother) where Elizabeth was visiting. There Elizabeth told plaintiff, in the presence of his wife, aunt, and uncle, that "The reason I wanted to see you was, your father and I had an agreement that if he died first, I was to have the use of all the property until I died; and then it was to be divided to — his half was to go to you, and I could leave my half to anyone I wished, on my side of the family. . . . Now, it won't do you any good to start any trouble, because all the property is in joint tenancy, and that is the way it is going to be." Plaintiff's wife, uncle, and aunt gave substantially similar testimony. Also plaintiff, his wife, and his aunt each testified that Robert, prior to his death, had made statements to the effect that "I am going to give this ranch to Vincent [plaintiff] when I die."

a will which would have devised the entire ranch to plaintiff if Elizabeth had predeceased Robert.

Defendant is Elizabeth's grandnephew. She took defendant into her home in 1932, when he was four years old, and their relationship was similar to that of mother and son.

From the time of Robert's death until 1949 Elizabeth leased the ranch for grazing purposes for $125 a year. In 1948 Elizabeth sold 63 acres of the ranch to the United States government for $50 an acre.

On February 15, 1954, without plaintiff's knowledge Elizabeth conveyed the ranch to defendant and herself as joint tenants. She caused this deed to be recorded on February 19, 1954. The trial court found

> That said conveyance . . . was made for good and valuable consideration in that prior to 1954 ["About the end of '49" and "Quite a few times" thereafter, according to defendant's testimony] said Elizabeth A. Horton informed defendant, Norvin R. Kyburz, that if said Norvin R. Kyburz would maintain and improve said real property during the lifetime of said Elizabeth A. Horton that she would convey to him a joint tenancy interest in said real property; that for more than seven (7) years prior to the death of said Elizabeth A. Horton on October 11, 1956, said Norvin R. Kyburz did improve and maintain said property.[4] . . . That at no time prior to the filing of the plaintiff's complaint herein did . . . defendant, have any knowledge that said plaintiff claimed any right, title or interest in and to said real property. . . . That defendant . . . is a bona fide purchaser of said real property . . . and to enforce against said defendant the oral agreement made and entered into between [Robert and Elizabeth] . . . would be harsh, oppressive, and unjust.

Sufficiency of Consideration paid by Defendant to Elizabeth. Plaintiff urges that because "This entire proceeding is one in equity and involving equitable considerations" defendant, to establish his position as bona fide purchaser, must show not merely that he gave value for the conveyance but

---

4. Defendant testified that before 1949 he had done some work in maintaining and repairing the ranch property and other property of Elizabeth; that "About the end of '49 [when defendant was 21 years of age] she said if I would continue helping her with her maintaining her places and the ranch, she would leave them to me"; that thereafter Elizabeth repeated the substance of this statement "Quite a few times" and defendant from time to time worked on Elizabeth's property and contributed some of his money to its improvement and maintenance; that in 1954 "She told me as long as I was putting part of my money in on the ranch that she would protect me too, that she would give me a joint tenancy deed and that is when she went to Judge Mundt."

Judge Albert H. Mundt testified that in 1954, while he was engaged in the private practice of law, Elizabeth asked him to draw a joint tenancy deed of the ranch to herself and defendant; that "I suggested to her that it would not be in her best interest to do so in that it was taking control of the property from her and putting it at least partially in control of her nephew. She informed me at that time that she not only wanted to do so but was obligated to do so because she had agreed with him previously that if he would assist her and maintain that property and other properties that she would convey the property to him in joint tenancy and upon her death he would get all of it. And she told me that he had complied with his agreement and that he had done certain work the nature and extent of which I do not recall."

that he gave "adequate consideration" in the sense that such adequacy is necessary to obtain specific performance of a contract. To uphold this contention would appear to contravene rules of contract and real property law long established in this state. When the Legislature in 1872 enacted as code law the familiar rule (Civ. Code, §3391) that "Specific performance cannot be enforced against a party to a contract . . . 1. If he has not received an *adequate* consideration for the contract . . ." (italics added) it also dealt with subjects pertinent to the present action by enacting the following rules:

"No implied or resulting trust can prejudice the rights of a purchaser . . . of real property for value and without notice of the trust." (Civ. Code, §856.)

"Any benefit conferred, or agreed to be conferred, upon the promisor, by any other person, to which the promisor is not lawful entitled, or any prejudice suffered, or agreed to be suffered, by such person, other than such as he is at the time of consent lawfully bound to suffer, as an inducement to the promisor, is a good consideration for a promise." (Civ. Code, §1605.) The term "good consideration" in section 1605 is equivalent to the term "valuable consideration." (Aden v. City of Vallejo (1903), 139 Cal. 165, 168, 72 P. 905, rejecting the earlier view, expressed in Clark v. Troy (1862), 20 Cal. 219, 224, that "A good consideration is such as that of blood, or of natural affection. A valuable consideration is such as money or the like.") The Clark case refused to accept the contention, similar to that advanced by the present plaintiff, that the expression "valuable consideration" in the former Conveyancing Act did not mean "only that amount of money, or its equivalent, which would support a contract at common law — that is, one dime or one cent" but rather meant "such a consideration as would support an executory contract in a Court of Equity" (at page 222 of 20 Cal.), and held that "The inadequacy of price is a circumstance proper to be considered in determining the question of good faith, but it will not the less fall within the legal definition of a valuable consideration, however disproportionate it may be to the value of the land" (at page 224 of 20 Cal.).

This remained the rule under the 1872 enactment of section 1107 of the Civil Code, which provides that "Every grant of an estate in real property is conclusive against the grantor, also against everyone subsequently claiming under him, except a purchaser . . . who in good faith and for a valuable consideration acquires a title . . . by an instrument that is first duly recorded." (See Civ. Code, §5; Cain v. Richmond (1932), 126 Cal. App. 254, 260, 14 P.2d 546; cf. United States v. Certain Parcels of Land (U.S. Dist. Ct., S.D. Cal., C.D. 1949), 85 F. Supp. 986, 1006, footnote 17.)

It has been pointed out that "The recording laws were not enacted to protect those whose ignorance of the title is deliberate and intentional, nor does a mere nominal consideration satisfy the requirement that a valuable consideration must be paid. Their purpose is to protect those who honestly believe that they are acquiring a good title, and who invest some substantial sum in reliance on that belief." (Beach v. Faust (1935), 2 Cal. 2d 290, 292, 40 P.2d 822.) But here there is evidence that defendant gave more than "mere nominal consideration." He testified that he and Elizabeth did the following work on the ranch:

> Well, we fixed the fences. We put in the northeast fence which was about a little over a quarter of a mile, and I built the northwest fence. It is about a quarter of a mile, about ready to fall down, and a couple of cross fences. We had three wells drilled. We paid fifty percent apiece . . . on the wells. Put an aluminum roof on the barn and jacked it up and poured a foundation on the north end of it and pillars through the middle and through the south end. We ran water to the corral and across the road; put in pressure pumps and separator house. We knocked the front of it off and rebuilt that, reroofed it; put a foundation in the front of it and put a cement floor in it. We built a three-car garage out of aluminum; and the clearing of the land and the reservoir around the hill; and the seeding of the south side; and there is about an acre of permanent pasture besides the brush clearing and burning and stuff that we had done before that.

Defendant paid for half the roofing and half the cost of bulldozers to clear part of the land. He bought the seed, pump, and sprinkler pipe for the permanent pasture. The clearing of brush and repair of fences were done prior to 1949. The wells were drilled in 1954 and 1955. The record is silent as to just when the rest of the work was done, but it can be inferred that it was after 1949 because from the time of Robert's death until 1949 Elizabeth "leased [the ranch] out for cattle grazing," and after 1949 defendant "started running stock on it."

Plaintiff argues that defendant could have done little work on the ranch after the making of the 1949 agreement because from September, 1949, until September, 1953, he was in the armed services and thereafter he worked full time at various jobs. These circumstances were for the appraisal of the trier of fact; they do not show as a matter of law that defendant's contribution to the maintenance and improvement of the realty was barely nominal. Plaintiff further argues that work of defendant done after the 1954 conveyance by Elizabeth to herself and defendant as joint tenants could not have been consideration for such conveyance since defendant was co-owner of the property. But the consideration for which Elizabeth bargained and which defendant gave was *continued* help in maintaining the property, not help merely until Elizabeth should convey a legal interest in the property to defendant.

Also pertinent to the subject of consideration is plaintiff's attack on the trial court's refusal to admit evidence that in 1956, shortly after Elizabeth's death and shortly before the institution of this action, defendant agreed to sell the ranch (then reduced to 160 acres) for $950 an acre. The trial court took the position that evidence of value in 1956 was not relevant. It appears that evidence of the value of the property in 1956, when defendant received full legal title as surviving joint tenant, would be relevant to the question of "inadequacy of price [which] is a circumstance proper to be considered in determining the question of good faith" necessary to constitute defendant a bona fide purchaser (Clark v. Troy (1862), supra, 20 Cal. 219, 224), but that exclusion of the evidence was not prejudicial because had it been received it would have required interpretation by other evidence to connect it controllingly with value in 1954 (when Elizabeth executed the joint tenancy deed to herself and defendant). Furthermore, insofar as relates to the reasonableness of the original oral offer made by Elizabeth to defendant in 1949, the value in 1956 would be entitled to little, if any, weight. It will be recalled that there was evidence that in 1949 Elizabeth ceased to rent the ranch (then comprising 223 acres) for $125 a year and sold 63 acres of it to the United States government for $50 an acre. This 63 acres apparently had some connection, not adequately explained, with construction of Folsom Dam. The finding of the trial court, as hereinabove mentioned, is that "prior to 1954 said Elizabeth . . . informed defendant . . . that if [defendant] . . . would maintain and improve said real property during the lifetime of said Elizabeth A. Horton that she would convey to him a joint tenancy interest in said real property; that for more than seven (7) years prior to the death of said Elizabeth A. Horton on October 11, 1956, said Norvin R. Kyburz did improve and maintain said property."

Concerning the value of the ranch the following may also be mentioned: In the course of a colloquy as to admissibility of evidence of its value in 1956, defendant's counsel remarked, "the court may well take judicial notice of the fact that in this particular area that we are concerned here with that there has been a vast increase in property values owing to Folsom dam being erected or construction there and in the past six or seven years." The court replied, "Yes, what I had in mind when I was inquiring of Mr. Paras [plaintiff's counsel], value — " and Mr. Paras interjected a comment on the consideration allegedly given by defendant. From the foregoing colloquy it is not apparent whether the court felt that it could take judicial notice of the rising value of the ranch for its bearing on defendant's good faith, but it does at least appear that the matter was brought to its attention.

Plaintiff cites Bank of Ukiah v. Gibson (1895), 109 Cal. 197, 200, 41 P. 1008, for the proposition that a mere promise of the purchaser is not value within the rule which protects a bona fide purchaser. The proposition is generally sound (Davis v. Ward (1895), 109 Cal. 186, 189-190, 41 P. 1010; Rest. Trusts 2d (1959), §302) but it does not necessarily control the factual situation here. At the time of plaintiff's attack on the conveyance, the contract was fully executed; any implied promise of the purchaser-defendant to render services and assist in maintaining the ranch had been performed; at least some services had been rendered which were accepted by Elizabeth as full performance.

Evidence Assertedly Establishing that Defendant was Put on Notice of Plaintiff's Claim. Plaintiff urges that the following testimony of defendant shows that defendant had constructive notice of plaintiff's interest, i.e., that defendant had "actual notice of circumstances sufficient to put a prudent man upon inquiry as to a particular fact" and "by prosecuting such inquiry, he might have learned such fact" (Civ. Code. §19):

Q.　Norvin, during the time that you lived with your aunt [great aunt Elizabeth], did your aunt ever say anything to you about . . . plaintiff Vincent Horton getting any of her property?

A.　No sir.

Q.　Did you ever have any conversation with her concerning the possibility of his coming in on any of the property?

A.　Between '55 and '56 she brought it up one day that if anything happened to her that she didn't want my mother or her sister to come in on the will or anything. And I brought it up about did she think that Vincent would ever try to come in.

Q.　I see. You asked her if she thought that Vincent would ever come in?

A.　Yes, sir.

Q.　What was her answer?

A.　She didn't think he would. . . .

Q.　May I ask why you asked that question?

A.　Because Vincent was the only one on the other side that I thought would have anything to say about it or — well, that is the only one we ever saw.

Q.　Can you tell me what made you think that he might have anything to say about it?

A.　No, I don't — he was the only one I could think of.

Q.　Just occurred to you to ask that question about Vincent, is that correct?

A.　Well, it came up that spur of the moment. It was over —

Q.　You brought it up?

A.　I brought it up about Vincent but she started about the other party.

Q.　Was this after 1953 when you had this conversation?

A.　'53? It was '49.

Q.　This conversation concerning Vincent was in '49?

A.　Oh, '55 and '56.

Q.　'55 and '56?

A.　Yes, sir.

Q.　I see. It was after your father had died?

A.　He died in '53.

Q.　You indicated that he died in '53 and this conversation took place afterwards?

A.　'55, yes sir.

Q.　And is that the only conversation you ever had with your aunt concerning Vincent Horton?

A.　Yes.

The foregoing conversation held after Elizabeth had executed and caused recordation of the joint tenancy deed to herself and defendant in

1954, and after defendant had furnished some consideration for the conveyance, does not as a matter of law show that defendant was put on notice of plaintiff's equitable claim. It shows that defendant was concerned with the possibility that plaintiff might assert some claim but neither the conversation alone nor the conversation coupled with the rather small and indefinite, but valuable consideration which defendant gave for the ranch shows that defendant deliberately remained ignorant of a state of facts as to which he should have been put on notice.

Plaintiff's Claim that Defendant was at Most a Bona Fide Purchaser of a One Half Interest in the Ranch. Defendant alleged and the trial court found that prior to 1954 Elizabeth agreed that if defendant would maintain and improve the ranch "she would convey to him a joint tenancy interest in said real property." Since "A joint interest is one owned by two or more persons in equal shares . . ." (Civ. Code, §683) plaintiff argues that under the agreement between Elizabeth and defendant Elizabeth undertook to convey and defendant gave consideration for only a one half interest in the ranch; plaintiff says that Elizabeth did not agree not to sever the joint tenancy and urges that the joint tenancy deed did not convey to defendant the one half interest which Elizabeth had orally agreed with Robert was to go to plaintiff.

Judge Mundt, however, testified that when (in 1954) Elizabeth asked him to prepare the joint tenancy deed she said that she had agreed with defendant "that she would convey the property to him in joint tenancy and upon her death he would get all of it" and defendant testified that Elizabeth said "if I would continue helping her with her maintaining her places and the ranch, she would leave them to me." The foregoing testimony supports the view the defendant gave consideration for Elizabeth's promise not merely to put the ranch in joint tenancy with defendant but also to leave it in joint tenancy so that the right of survivorship would operate. The trial court stated that "I think everyone has been telling the truth in this case. . . . I believe all the folks in the case." It is apparent that the case was tried on the theory that defendant claimed as bona fide purchaser of the entire interest in the ranch, and that if the trial court had specifically found concerning the present contention of plaintiff its finding would have been adverse to plaintiff and in accord with the above quoted testimony of Judge Mundt and defendant. Therefore, under familiar rules of appellate review, we must reject plaintiff's argument that the judgment decreeing that defendant is the owner of the ranch and plaintiff has no interest in it is not supported by the allegation and finding that Elizabeth agreed to convey to defendant a joint tenancy interest. . . .

While on the record it may seem to some of us that, were we triers of fact, we might have reached findings differing in some respects from those declared by the trial judge, we recognize that we did not see and hear the witnesses and, hence, on conflicting evidence have neither right nor power to disagree with the trier of fact.

For the reasons above stated the judgment is affirmed.

NOTES AND QUESTIONS

1.   **Protection of donees.** Why should not donees or those paying nominal consideration be protected as subsequent takers? Is there sufficient merit to the valuable consideration requirement to justify its retention? Can it be justified as bolstering the notice requirement on the theory that in many situations the meager consideration paid indicates that the transferees involved must have had notice of a possibly defective title?

2.   **Protection of mortgagee who obtains a mortgage to secure a preexisting debt.** There is considerable authority to the effect that a mortgagee is not a taker for value under the recording acts if he accepts a mortgage to secure a preexisting debt. Brown v. Mifflin, 220 Ark. 166, 246 S.W.2d 567 (1952), and Salem v. Salem, 245 Iowa 62, 60 N.W.2d 772 (1953). But there are cases holding that he does qualify as a taker for value if at the time he accepts the mortgage he gives up some significant legal right. Thus extending time for payment or forbearance from suit may be such a relinquishment of a right. Tripler v. MacDonald Lumber Co., 173 Cal. 144, 159 P. 591 (1916), and Manufacturers & Traders Trust Co., v. First Natl. Bank in Fort Lauderdale, 113 So. 2d 869 (Fla. Dist. Ct. App. 1959).

3.   **Notice from recording.** The recording of an instrument does not necessarily mean that constructive notice of its contents will be held to exist. Even though an instrument is recordable and filed for record by someone entitled to protection of the recording act, it is possible under some circumstances that the instrument will not be given recording effect. It may, for instance, be outside the chain of title of some persons who may acquire an interest in the parcel involved, and recording is generally not constructive notice to such persons. See, e.g., Kiser v. Clinchfield Coal Corp., 200 Va. 517, 106 S.E.2d 601 (1959); Cross, The Record "Chain of Title Hypocrisy," 57 Colum. L. Rev. 787 (1957). Although an instrument may have been filed for record, a public official may have been negligent and as a result the instrument was never placed of record or indexed, or it may have been inaccurately transcribed onto the records or inaccurately indexed. In some states these circumstances prevent an instrument from having recording effect. See, e.g., Howard Sav. Bank v. Brunson, 244 N.J. Super. 571, 582 A.2d 1305 (1990) (mortgage misindexed; subsequent parties not on notice).

§12.3   The Closing

If the buyer obtains financing, if the seller tenders contract title, if the premises have not burned down, and if nothing else has gone amiss, the parties will close title — and legal ownership will pass from seller to buyer. Title closings lack the ceremony of earlier centuries, when the parties, with their witnesses, went together on or within sight of the land, and the grantor (called the "feoffor") delivered to the grantee (called the "feoffee") a twig, clod, key, or other symbol in the name of the whole. Oral, rather than written, words of conveyance usually attended the transfer: the feoffor spoke the Latin for "I give to him and his heirs," to transfer a fee simple absolute, or appropriate other words to transfer other freehold estates. While the parties could also use a writing, and sometimes did when fairly complex interests were involved, the requirement of a written instrument to convey freehold estates awaited the English Statute of Frauds in 1677. Even then, this ceremony, *livery of seisin,* theoretically remained essential to transfer freehold estates until its abolition by the Real Property Act of 1845.

In fact, a competing system for the transfer of title grew up in chancery. It depended exclusively on the use of written documents. Codified by the Statute of Uses in 1535, this system relied upon so-called bargain and sale contracts, or "contracts to stand seized" — contracts made for consideration that chancery would execute. (To this day, the phrase "bargain and sale" marks certain deed forms.) In addition, common-law conveyances, with the same ingenuity that led to fine and common recovery, page 121 *supra,* invented the system of "lease and release," which also avoided livery of seisin. Since only transfers of present freehold estates required the ceremony, the owner would execute two instruments outside the ritual: first, a lease (usually in the form of a bargain-and-sale deed of an estate for one year); second, a release to the lessee of the owner's reversionary interest. This fiction also gave way by the mid-nineteenth century.

The modern American closing is mostly a humdrum paper-shuffle, with occasional breaks for a signature, explanation, and writing of checks. The venue may be the recorder's office, or the offices of a lawyer, escrow agent, or title company. A handshake wishing the buyers good luck as they assume the burdens of ownership will usually seal the event.

a. The Deed

Modern statutes of frauds require a written instrument, signed by the grantor or his duly authorized agent, for the transfer of a freehold interest in land. This instrument, the deed, still retains much of the litany that seventeenth-century conveyancers would have found familiar; but stripped of its legalese veneer, the deed's essential parts are:

1. grantor's name,
2. grantee's name,
3. description of the property,
4. indication of the legal interest (e.g., fee simple absolute),
5. words denoting intent to transfer an interest, and
6. grantor's signature.

Any scrap of writing that contains these vitals would satisfy the Statute of Frauds. But as you examine the form below, you will notice, besides the mumbo-jumbo, other elements as well.

WARRANTY DEED

This indenture, made the _____ day of _____, nineteen hundred and _____, between _____, party of the first part, and _____, party of the second part,

Witnesseth, that the party of the first part, in consideration of Ten Dollars and other valuable consideration paid by the party of the second part, does hereby grant and release unto the party of the second part, the heirs or successors and assigns of the party of the second part forever.   *A? & B*

All that certain plot, piece or parcel of land, with the buildings and improvements thereon erected, situate, lying and being in the _____.

Together with all right, title and interest, if any, of the party of the first part of, in and to any streets and roads abutting the above-described premises to the center lines thereof; Together with the appurtenances and all the estate and rights of the party of the first part in and to said premises; To Have and To Hold the premises herein granted unto the party of the second part, the heirs or successors and assigns of the party of the second part forever.

And the party of the first part, in compliance with Section 13 of the Lien Law, covenants that the party of the first part will receive the consideration for this conveyance and will hold the right to receive such consideration as a trust fund to be applied first for the purpose of paying the costs of the improvement and will apply the same first to the payment of the cost of the improvement before using any part of the total of the same for any other purpose.

And the party of the first part covenants as follows: that said party of the first part is seized of the said premises in fee simple, and has good right to convey the same; that the party of the second part shall quietly enjoy the said premises; that the said premises are free from incumbrances, except as aforesaid; that the party of the first part will execute or procure any further necessary assurance of the title to said premises; and that said party of the first part will forever warrant the title to said premises.

The word "party" shall be construed as if it read "parties" whenever the sense of this indenture so requires.

In witness whereof, the party of the first part has duly executed this deed the day and year first above written.

In presence of _____

State of New York
County of _____ } ss.

On the _____ day of _____, 19_____, before me personally came _____, to be known to be the individual _____ described in and who executed the foregoing instrument, and acknowledged that _____ executed the same.

State of New York
County of _____ } ss.

On the _____ day of _____, 19_____, before me personally came _____, to me known, who, being by me duly sworn, did depose and say that _____ he resides at No. _____; that _____ he is the _____ of _____, the corporation described in and which executed the foregoing instrument; that _____ he knows the seal of said corporation; that the seal affixed to said instrument is such corporate seal; that it was so affixed by order of the board of directors of said corporation, and that _____ he signed h_____ name thereto by like order.

State of New York
County of _____ } ss.

On the _____ day of _____, 19_____, before me personally came _____, the subscribing witness to the foregoing instrument, with whom I am personally acquainted, who, being by me duly sworn, did depose and say that _____ he resides at No. _____; that _____ he knows _____ to be the individual described in and who executed the foregoing instrument; that _____ he, said subscribing witness, was present and saw _____ execute the same; and that _____ he, said witness, at the same time subscribed h_____ name as witness thereto.

NOTES AND QUESTIONS

1. **Recital of consideration.** Deed forms rarely lack a paragraph denoting consideration. As between the parties, however, consideration is not needed for a valid legal transfer. Consider, for example, that one may make a gift of real property. The recital avoids the implication that the grantor intended to create a resulting trust, under which the grantee holds property as trustee for the benefit of the grantor.

2. **Acknowledgment clause.** The party signing the deed acknowledges the authenticity of his signature before a notary public, or other person having the authority to take acknowledgments. Generally, the transfer is good even without the acknowledgment, but recording acts require either acknowledgment or some equivalent (for example, attestation by witnesses) before the instrument may be accepted for recordation. Why this requirement?

3.   Types of deed: quitclaim and warranty.

It oversimplifies to classify instruments into two categories, *warranty deeds* in which seller-grantor has responsibility for after-discovered title flaws and *quitclaims* in which he does not. Each term is used to describe a number of different sorts of instruments, and the classification into quitclaim or warranty deed has significance for legal issues other than title liability. Thus a warranty deed serves to pass title from grantor to grantee where grantor acquires that title *after* the delivery of the deed, while a mere quitclaim supposedly does not. Yet courts, in the after-acquired property situation, have strained to thrust particular instruments into the former category, so that an instrument entitled *quitclaim deed* (as against mere *quitclaim*) has been held to carry after-acquired property. 18 Baylor L. Rev. 618 (1966). . . .

A warranty deed is one which contains one or more of six "covenants for title." These covenants split into two triads, the first of which consists of the covenants of *seisin, right to convey,* and *against encumbrances.* The first two generally guarantee that grantor owns what he purports to grant, and the last that the estate is free of liens, mortgages, easements, etc. except as otherwise noted in the deed. The first two are generally regarded as indistinguishable (but see the detailed discussion of all the covenants for title in Aigler, Smith, and Tefft, Cases on Property 737-749 (1960), and in the cases they blur into the last.

This first group represents guarantees against title flaws extant at the date of the conveyance and thus differ in form from the second triad in which grantor promises in the future to defend and hold grantee harmless against hostile claimants or encumbrances. Of this latter triad, the covenants of *quiet enjoyment* and *warranty* are again indistinguishable, and the last, that of *further assurances,* is little used in the United States.

You will notice that the first triad is phrased in present tense and the second is phrased in future tense. This has resulted in controversy over whether the first group can run with the land so as to benefit subsequent grantees. Since these covenants are broken, if at all, upon delivery of the deed, they become mere choses in action, which do not run. However, some courts have found that the chose in action passed to a subgrantee by implicit assignment when the subgrantee received his deed. The future-phrased covenants do run with the land. (Query: How can a covenant for title run with the land to a subgrantee when the original grantor didn't own the land for the covenant to run with?) . . .

The protection afforded by the warranties is not generous; the warrantor's liability generally is limited to the consideration he received for the land. McCormick, Damages §185 (1932). You can see how negligible a recovery this would produce for an evicted buyer of California land who sues against a remote grantor-warrantor. Convenantee may also recover his expenses in reasonable though unsuccessful defense of the title. [Berger and Johnstone, Land Transfer and Finance 676-678 (4th ed. 1993)]

4.   **Grantee's signature.** Ordinarily the grantee does not sign the deed. However, if the grantee is taking over an existing mortgage and in-

tends to assume it — i.e., to become personally liable for the underlying debt — statutes generally require that the assumption be in writing. See, e.g., Cal. Civ. Code §1624(7) (West 1996); N.Y. Gen. Oblig. Law §5-705 (McKinney 1996).

5. **Delivery and acceptance.** The operative event for the transfer of legal title — i.e., the instant when grantee becomes the new owner — comes not when grantor signs the deed, or when he acknowledges his signature, but when grantor *delivers* the deed to grantee or his agent and grantee accepts the conveyance. We usually infer acceptance from the grantee's parting with the purchase price, his taking the deed without comment, his recording of the deed, or his entry into the premises and bestowing ownership upon them; but sometimes in the donative situation we may have to look harder to see whether the grantee-donee has acceded to the gift. (Be aware that ownership of real property may carry more burdens than benefits.) The subject of delivery, especially of gifts, creates more troublesome problems. The sampling below will introduce you to problem areas:

(a)   X signed a deed conveying property to his nephew, N. X and N lived together on the property, where the deed was kept. Both had access to the deed. X told others that he had deeded the property to N, but X continued to operate the property and to enjoy its benefits as he had before. Has there been a valid conveyance? Cf. Berrigan v. Berrigan, 413 Ill. 204, 108 N.E.2d 438 (1952). Compare Noble v. Fickes, 230 Ill. 594, 82 N.E. 950 (1907).

(b)   Y was indebted to his mother. He signed a deed conveying land to her and gave the instrument to his brother with oral instructions: "Give this to Mother if I predecease her." Y died fifteen years later, predeceasing his mother. Y's widow claims that delivery was conditioned upon Y's predecease of his mother, that this made the transfer testamentary, and that, as a testamentary transfer, the deed failed to satisfy the formal requirements of the statute of wills. Y's mother argues that Y made a present gift of a future interest, and that delivery occurred when Y placed the deed in third-party hands. Inter vivos gift or testamentary transfer? Cf. Atchison v. Atchison, 198 Okla. 98, 175 P.2d 309 (1946).

(c)   S and B enter into a contract of sale. The contract names an escrow agent to whom S will give the deed with the understanding that the agent will record the deed when B pays him the purchase price. The agent absconds with the purchase price after recording the deed. Does B have title? See generally Annot., 15 A.L.R.2d 870 (1951); cf. also Doherty v. Elskamp, 58 Misc. 2d 653, 296 N.Y.S.2d 127 (Civ. Ct. 1968), *aff'd*, 58 Misc. 2d 654, 298 N.Y.S.2d 743 (App. T. 1969).

4.   **Escrow agents.** In some areas escrow agents commonly handle the details of a real estate transaction:

> Brown, in The Lawyer's Prescription, 30 Unauth. Prac. News 1, 7 n.3 (1964), estimates that over 90 percent of home sales in southern California take place without a lawyer directly representing either buyer or seller. Closings there are handled by independent escrow agents.
>
> Escrows are possible as closing devices since buyer and seller each satisfy their contract obligations by providing appropriate pieces of paper for the other: in the seller's case, principally a deed and some sort of title assurance; in the buyer's, a certified check for the price (and where appropriate a mortgage to the bank which lends him the money to buy the property). Under escrow arrangements, after the contract of sale is executed, the parties enter an escrow agreement, which provides that the parties are to deposit the required pieces of paper with the escrow agent. If all the paper comes in within a specified time, the escrow is closed; the escrow agent then files for record the appropriate documents and gives each party the instruments to which he is entitled. If the transaction is not timely closed, papers are returned to the depositors who can then decide who sues whom for what.
>
> Escrow provides a convenient device for handling the procurement and deposit of the parties' papers at times convenient to them individually, as well as an efficient institution for handling other closing mechanics. For example, escrow agents may request a title search; obtain reports; draft deeds or other documents; obtain rent statements; pay off authorized demands; adjust taxes, rents and insurance between the parties; compute interest on loans; and acquire insurance for title, fire, or other liability. California Real Estate Transactions 507 (State Bar of California 1967).
>
> There is a rule of law which gives escrow a further advantage over the ordinary transaction of contract of sale followed by lawyer's office closing three weeks hence. In such a transaction if seller dies during the interim, buyer, to enforce his rights, has to get entangled with the administration of decedent seller's estate, whereas if a deed is deposited in escrow, even if the seller dies before the escrow is closed, the escrow can proceed to normal closing. (However, hypercautious local practice may require buyer's attorney to clear the transaction with the court of probate.)
>
> Past litigation involving escrow agents raises such questions as which party bears the loss for various sorts of escrow agent default; whether a written escrow agreement satisfies the statute of frauds so as to make binding a contract of sale not otherwise evidenced; and whether to define the parties' obligations according to the contract of sale, when the escrow agreement calls for party actions different from those specified in the contract. See Aran, Escrows in California Real Estate Transactions 503 (State Bar of California 1967). [Alexrod, Berger, and Johnstone, Land Transfer and Finance 66-67 (2d ed. 1978).]

b.   The Closing Adjustments

Reexamine paragraph 7 ("Prorations") of the California contract of sale form, page 1181, *supra.* To test your ability to calculate the adjustments to the purchase price that fairly must be made at the closing, consider in the following problem: first, whether seller or buyers should receive a credit; and second, what the size of the credit should be. In doing so, keep as your guiding principle that the benefits and burdens of ownership should inure to the party having legal title, unless the parties have agreed differently.

Problem: S and B have entered into a contract of sale. The contract price is $120,000. B has agreed to pay $30,000 in cash. For the balance, B will take over an existing mortgage of $90,000. The mortgage bears interest at 9 percent per annum payable monthly in advance. S made the payment due April 1. The property has one tenant, who pays her monthly rental of $1,200 in advance. She has paid the April rental. The real estate taxes are payable quarterly in advance. Taxes of $1,800 for the April-June quarter are unpaid. There is a full tank of oil in the basement for which S has paid $800. The closing occurs on April 10. Compute the mortgage interest, rent, real estate taxes, and fuel adjustments. (The convention is to treat B's ownership as beginning on April 11.)

c.   Title Insurance

In most parts of the United States, including nearly all metropolitan areas, title insurance is a major form of title protection. It is an American innovation and little such insurance is written outside the United States.[21] The first American title insurance company was formed in 1876, and by World War II some title insurance was being written on lands in most all parts of the United States, with well-established companies in nearly all big cities. But the great expansion of this kind of coverage has come mostly since the mid-1940s, a period marked by extensive real estate activity, a tremendous volume of new subdivisions, and a vast number of new conveyances and mortgages. Title insurance has grown in both absolute and relative terms, for it has gradually cut in on other forms of title protection, particularly title search and examination by lawyers in private practice. In a number of big cities private practitioners of law have been eliminated from both title search and examination; and in some areas, notably in the Far West, this has happened in many middle and small-sized cities as well. In these communities the title work of the private bar is reduced largely to occasional efforts at curing title defects that title companies will not insure or negotiating with title insurers to waive minor defects. But in all of New England and in much of the Midwest and South outside large metropolitan centers, private law firms still do a great deal of title examination work, and in some communities they do title searching as well.

---

21. A modest amount of title insurance is now being written on lands in Canada, England, several Caribbean countries, and Mexico. Insurers of much of this coverage are U.S. title companies or their subsidiaries. Roller, Title Insurance — An International Perspective, 62 Title News No. 3, 7 (1983). See also Payne, Second Thoughts on the Future of Title Insurance in England, 124 Solic. J. 699 (1980).

There are several major types of title insurance operations. In one the title company determines whether or not to insure, based on the title opinion of a lawyer in private practice, whose opinion is forwarded to the company for decision on insuring. The lawyer or an abstracter does the search, and the lawyer examines the title data and gives the opinion. In another, title company employees do the search and examination and then determine whether or not to insure, in many places using a company title plant for the search. A title plant consists principally of duplicate copies of public records pertaining to all land parcels in a particular county, arranged and indexed to enable accurate and speedy searching of titles for individual parcels. Most highly developed plants are in counties with large populations. In a third type of operation, non-employee agents of the company, lawyers or nonlawyers, make the search and examination and determine whether or not the company will insure. In some instances, the searching is farmed out to independent contractors, who report back to the agents. The agents are authorized to issue company policies, usually without further clearance from the company. Within limits, some agents may even settle claims. The agent format has become much more common in recent years.

The phenomenal growth of title insurance is attributable to a series of factors. For one thing, the big national lenders, especially the life insurance companies, like the relatively standardized coverage given by mortgagees' policies wherever written. This makes it easier for these large volume operators to determine the acceptability of mortgages originated for them or that they purchase in the secondary market. They also like the risk insurance feature. Demand for title insurance by national lenders is probably the single most significant reason for expansion in this type of title protection since World War II. Another reason for title insurance growth is that in many large metropolitan areas public records pertaining to land have become so voluminous and difficult to search that only specialists with a large volume of title work can operate efficiently. And only the mass volume operator can afford a comprehensive title plant, an essential to maximum efficiency in many big counties. Still another reason why title insurance has expanded so is that, being businesses, title companies have vigorously and successfully promoted their services, whereas their lawyer and Torrens competitors have been ineffective at such promotion, until recently lawyers in private practice even being prohibited from advertising.

Title insurance differs from most other kinds of insurance in that it does not insure against future risks but only against those existing at the time coverage is obtained. Further, it is issued only after a careful title search and examination and excludes any risks of substance disclosed by this process. As a result, loss ratios are low, with principal risks being negligence in search and examination and relatively rare defects not apparent from customary public record searches. Only one premium is paid for title insurance, and this includes a charge for search and examination if made by the title company. It is common, at the time land is sold, for a title company to issue two separate policies of insurance for which separate premiums are paid: one policy to the mortgagee and the other to the purchasing owner. Owners' policies do not cover grantees from the insured; if a buyer wishes coverage, a new policy must be ordered and paid for, even though the seller was covered. Mortgagees' policies usually cover assignees. In addition to fee owners and mortgagees, long-term lessees and holders of valuable oil and gas rights frequently obtain title insurance coverage.

Title insurance protects the insured from loss as the result of title deficiencies not excepted by the policy. Most policies contain a number of exceptions: any material defects uncovered by the insurer in its search of the particular title, and certain risks that, in standard printed clauses, the insurer excludes in all coverage of the kind in question. For an added premium, there are companies that will provide extended coverage by eliminating some of their standard exceptions. State insurance regulations in some states control the kinds of extended coverage permitted.

Most title policies insure the title against both record and off-record claims, subject, of course, to stated exceptions. Coverage of off-record risks is desired by many knowledgeable insureds because of the difficulty, often the impossibility, of ascertaining that such risks exist. However, one type of policy, sometimes referred to as a title guarantee, insures only the record title. The policy states, in essence, that the insured has good record title, subject to any listed exceptions, and then obligates the company to pay any losses incurred by the insured should the record title be otherwise. It provides not only protection against negligence in search and examination of the public records, but guarantees that the record title is as represented, thus protecting against non-negligent search and examination errors. This limited form of policy was extensively written at an earlier stage in the evolution of title insurance.

Many insurers insist that at the time of policy issuance, an owner insure for the full value of the fee and a mortgagee for the full amount of the mortgage. Additional coverage is not required by the policy if subsequently the value of the property goes up, although if this happens, the owner may deem it wise to increase the face amount of the policy, which normally can be done by paying an added premium. If the owner substantially improves the property after he insures, some policies make him a coinsurer, providing he does not adequately increase the amount of coverage. As a coinsurer, he must bear some of the risk of loss.

In addition to protecting against title deficiencies, title insurance policies commonly provide certain benefits in case of litigation. These benefits usually include a commitment by the insurer, at its cost, to defend the insured in litigation over the title based on any claim not excepted by the policy. Failure of the insurer to defend can result in it being obligated to pay defense counsel retained by the insured.

As is true of other kinds of insurance, the scope of title insurance coverage is determined in large part by standard provisions in the insurers' policies. All companies use printed policy forms and their terms are often borrowed from state or national trade association approved documents.

Of special importance have been the title policy forms developed and approved by the American Land Title Association, a national association of commercial title insurance companies, abstracters, and title lawyers, including counsel for large lending institutions. This association's forms, particularly its standard mortgagee's policies, have been widely adopted by title insurers. They are periodically revised. See Figure 12-1.

FIGURE 12-1
American Land Title Association Owner's Policy

AMERICAN LAND TITLE ASSOCIATION OWNER'S POLICY (continued)

Schedules A and B appear at the end of the owner's policy. Schedule A, not included herein, lists such information about the particular transaction as name of the insured, description of the property, legal interest being insured, policy number and date, and insurance premium and other charges. Schedule B appears below.

EXCLUSIONS FROM COVERAGE

The following matters are expressly excluded from the coverage of this policy and the Company will not pay loss or damage, costs, attorneys' fees or expenses which arise by reason of:

1. (a) Any law, ordinance or governmental regulation (including but not limited to building and zoning laws, ordinances, or regulations) restricting, regulating, prohibiting or relating to (i) the occupancy, use, or enjoyment of the land; (ii) the character, dimensions or location of any improvement now or hereafter erected on the land; (iii) a separation in ownership or a change in the dimensions or area of the land or any parcel of which the land is or was a part; or (iv) environmental protection, or the effect of any violation of these laws, ordinances or governmental regulations, except to the extent that a notice of the enforcement thereof or a notice of a defect, lien or encumbrance resulting from a violation or alleged violation affecting the land has been recorded in the public records at Date of Policy.

    (b) Any governmental police power not excluded by (a) above, except to the extent that a notice of the exercise thereof or a notice of a defect, lien or encumbrance resulting from a violation or alleged violation affecting the land has been recorded in the public records at Date of Policy.

2. Rights of eminent domain unless notice of the exercise thereof has been recorded in the public records at Date of Policy, but not excluding from coverage any taking which has occurred prior to Date of Policy which would be binding on the rights of a purchaser for value without knowledge.

3. Defects, liens, encumbrances, adverse claims or other matters:

    (a) created, suffered, assumed or agreed to by the insured claimant;

    (b) not known to the Company, not recorded in the public records at Date of Policy, but known to the insured claimant and not disclosed in writing to the Company by the insured claimant prior to the date the insured claimant became an insured under this policy;

    (c) resulting in no loss or damage to the insured claimant;

    (d) attaching or created subsequent to Date of Policy; or

(e) resulting in loss or damage which would not have been sustained if the insured claimant had paid value for the estate or interest insured by this policy.

4. Any claim, which arises out of the transaction vesting in the insured the estate or interest insured by this policy, by reason of the operation of federal bankruptcy, state insolvency, or similar creditors' rights laws.

CONDITIONS AND STIPULATIONS

1.   DEFINITION OF TERMS

The following terms when used in this policy mean:

(a) "insured": the insured named in Schedule A, and, subject to any rights or defenses the Company would have had against the named insured, those who succeed to the interest of the named insured by operation of law as distinguished from purchase including, but not limited to, heirs, distributees, devisees, survivors, personal representatives, next of kin, or corporate or fiduciary successors.

(b) "insured claimant": an insured claiming loss or damage.

(c) "knowledge" or "known": actual knowledge, not constructive knowledge or notice which may be imputed to an insured by reason of the public records as defined in this policy or any other records which impart constructive notice of matters affecting the land.

(d) "land": the land described or referred to in Schedule A, and improvements affixed thereto which by law constitute real property. The term "land" does not include any property beyond the lines of the area described or referred to in Schedule A, nor any right, title, interest, estate or easement in abutting streets, roads, avenues, alleys, lanes, ways or waterways, but nothing herein shall modify or limit the extent to which a right of access to and from the land is insured by this policy.

(e) "mortgage": mortgage, deed of trust, trust deed, or other security instrument.

(f) "public records": records established under state statutes at Date of Policy for the purpose of imparting constructive notice of matters relating to real property to purchasers for value and without knowledge. With respect to Section 1(a)(iv) of the Exclusions From Coverage, "public records" shall also include environmental protection liens filed in the records of the clerk of the United States district court for the district in which the land is located.

(g) "unmarketability of the title": an alleged or apparent matter affecting the title to the land, not excluded or excepted from coverage, which would entitle a purchaser of the estate or interest described in Schedule A to be released from the obligation to purchase by virtue of a contractual condition requiring the delivery of marketable title.

2.   CONTINUATION OF INSURANCE AFTER CONVEYANCE OF TITLE

The coverage of this policy shall continue in force as Date of Policy in favor of an insured only so long as the insured retains an estate or interest in the land, or holds an indebtedness secured by a purchase money mortgage given by a purchaser from the insured, or only so long as the insured shall have liability by reason of covenants of warranty made by the insured in any transfer or conveyance of the estate or interest. This policy shall not continue in force in favor of any purchaser from the insured of either (i) an estate or interest in the land, or (ii) an indebtedness secured by a purchase money mortgage given to the insured.

3.   NOTICE OF CLAIM TO BE GIVEN BY INSURED CLAIMANT

The insured shall notify the Company promptly in writing (i) in case of any litigation as set forth in Section 4(a) below, (ii) in case knowledge shall come to an insured hereunder of any claim of title or interest which is adverse to the title to the estate or interest, as insured, and which might cause loss or damage for which the Company may be liable by virtue of this policy, or (iii) if title to the estate or interest, as insured, is rejected as unmarketable. If prompt notice shall not be given to the Company, then as to the insured all liability of the Company shall terminate with regard to the matter or matters for which prompt notice is required; provided, however, that failure to notify the Company shall in no case prejudice the rights of any insured under this policy unless the Company shall be prejudiced by the failure and then only to the extent of the prejudice.

4.   DEFENSE AND PROSECUTION OF ACTIONS; DUTY OF INSURED CLAIMANT TO COOPERATE

(a) Upon written request by the insured and subject to the options contained in Section 6 of these Conditions and Stipulations, the Company, at its own cost and without unreasonable delay, shall provide for the defense of an insured in litigation in which any third party asserts a claim adverse to the title or interest as insured, but only as to those stated causes of action alleging a defect, lien or encumbrance or other matter insured against by this policy. The Company shall have the right to select counsel of its choice (subject to the right of the insured to object for reasonable cause) to represent the insured as to those stated causes of action and shall not be liable for and will not pay the fees of any other counsel. The Company will not pay any fees, costs or expenses incurred by the insured in the defense of those causes of action which allege matters not insured against by this policy.

(b) The Company shall have the right, at its own cost, to institute and prosecute any action or proceeding or to do any other act which in its opinion may be necessary or desirable to establish the title to the estate or interest, as insured, or to prevent or reduce loss or damage to the insured. The Company may take any appropriate action under the terms of this policy, whether or not it shall be liable hereunder, and shall not thereby concede liability or waive any provision of this policy. If the Company shall exercise its rights under this paragraph, it shall do so diligently.

(c) Whenever the Company shall have brought an action or interposed a defense as required or permitted by the provisions of this policy, the Company may pursue any litigation to final determination by a court of competent jurisdiction and expressly reserves the right, in its sole discretion, to appeal from any adverse judgment or order.

(d) In all cases where this policy permits or requires the Company to prosecute or provide for the defense of any action or proceeding, the insured shall secure to the Company the right to so prosecute or provide defense in the action or proceeding, and all appeals therein, and permit the Company to use, at its option, the name of the insured for this purpose. Whenever requested by the Company, the insured, at the Company's expense, shall give the Company all reasonable aid (i) in any action or proceeding, securing evidence, obtaining witnesses, prosecuting or defending the action or proceeding, or effecting settlement, and (ii) in any other lawful act which in the opinion of the Company may be necessary or desirable to establish the title to the estate or interest as insured. If the Company is prejudiced by the failure of the insured to furnish the required cooperation, the Company's obligations to the insured under the policy shall terminate, including any liability or obligation to defend, prosecute, or continue any litigation, with regard to the matter or matters requiring such cooperation.

5.   PROOF OF LOSS OR DAMAGE

In addition to and after the notices required under Section 3 of these Conditions and Stipulations have been provided the Company, a proof of loss or damage signed and sworn to by the insured claimant shall be furnished to the Company within 90 days after the insured claimant shall ascertain the facts giving rise to the loss or damage. The proof of loss or damage shall describe the defect in, or lien or encumbrance on the title, or other matter insured against by this policy which constitutes the basis of loss or damage and shall state, to the extent possible, the basis of calculating the amount of the loss or damage. If the Company is prejudiced by the failure of the insured claimant to provide the required proof of loss or damage, the Company's obligations to the insured under the policy shall terminate, including any liability or obligation to defend, prosecute, or continue any litigation, with regard to the matter or matters requiring such proof of loss or damage.

In addition, the insured claimant may reasonably be required to submit to examination under oath by any authorized representative of the Company and shall produce for examination, inspection and copying, at such reasonable times and places as may be designated by any authorized representative of the Company, all records, books, ledgers, checks, correspondence and memoranda, whether bearing a date before or after Date of Policy, which reasonably pertain to the loss or damage. Further, if requested by any authorized representative of the Company, the insured claimant shall grant its permission, in writing, for any authorized representative of the Company to examine, inspect and copy all records, books, ledgers, checks, correspondence and memoranda in the custody or control of a third party, which reasonably pertain to the loss or damage. All information designated as confidential by the insured claimant provided to the Company pursuant to this Section shall not be disclosed to others unless, in the reasonable judgment of the Company, it is necessary in the administration of the claim. Failure of the insured claimant to submit for examination under oath, produce other reasonably requested information or grant permission to secure reasonably necessary information from third parties as required in this paragraph shall terminate any liability of the Company under this policy as to that claim.

6.   OPTIONS TO PAY OR OTHERWISE SETTLE CLAIMS;
     TERMINATION OF LIABILITY

In case of a claim under this policy, the Company shall have the following additional options:

(a)   To Pay or Tender Payment of the Amount of Insurance.

To pay or tender payment of the amount of insurance under this policy together with any costs, attorneys' fees and expenses incurred by the insured claimant, which were authorized by the Company, up to the time of payment or tender of payment and which the Company is obligated to pay.

Upon the exercise by the Company of this option, all liability and obligations to the insured under this policy, other than to make the payment required, shall terminate, including any liability or obligation to defend, prosecute, or continue any litigation, and the policy shall be surrendered to the Company for cancellation.

(b)   To Pay or Otherwise Settle With Parties Other than the Insured or With the Insured Claimant.

(i) to pay or otherwise settle with other parties for or in the name of an insured claimant any claim insured against under this policy, together with any costs, attorneys' fees and expenses incurred by the insured claimant which were authorized by the Company up to the time of payment and which the Company is obligated to pay; or

(ii) to pay or otherwise settle with the insured claimant the loss or damage provided for under this policy, together with any costs, attorneys' fees and expenses incurred by the insured claimant which were authorized by the Company up to the time of payment and which the Company is obligated to pay.

Upon the exercise by the Company of either of the options provided for in paragraphs (b)(i) or (ii), the Company's obligations to the insured under this policy for the claimed loss or damage, other than the payments required to be made, shall terminate, including any liability or obligation to defend, prosecute or continue any litigation.

7.   DETERMINATION, EXTENT OF LIABILITY AND COINSURANCE

This policy is a contract of indemnity against actual monetary loss or damage sustained or incurred by the insured claimant who has suffered loss or damage by reason of matters insured against by this policy and only to the extent herein described.

(a) The liability of the Company under this policy shall not exceed the least of:

(i) the Amount of Insurance stated in Schedule A; or,

(ii) the difference between the value of the insured estate or interest as insured and the value of the insured estate or interest subject to the defect, lien or encumbrance insured against by this policy.

(b) In the event the Amount of Insurance stated in Schedule A at the Date of Policy is less than 80 percent of the value of the insured estate or interest or the full consideration paid for the land, whichever is less, or if subsequent to the Date of Policy an improvement is erected on the land which increases the value of the insured estate or interest by at least 20 percent over the Amount of Insurance stated in Schedule A, then this Policy is subject to the following:

(i) where no subsequent improvement has been made, as to any partial loss, the Company shall only pay the loss pro rata in the proportion that the amount of insurance at Date of Policy bears to the total value of the insured estate or interest at Date of Policy; or

(ii) where a subsequent improvement has been made, as to any partial loss, the Company shall only pay the loss pro rata in the proportion that 120 percent of the Amount of Insurance stated in Schedule A bears to the sum of the Amount of Insurance stated in Schedule A and the amount expended for the improvement.

The provisions of this paragraph shall not apply to costs, attorneys' fees and expenses for which the Company is liable under this policy, and shall only apply to that portion of any loss which exceeds, in the aggregate, 10 percent of the Amount of Insurance stated in Schedule A.

(c) The Company will pay only those costs, attorneys' fees and expenses incurred in accordance with Section 4 of these Conditions and Stipulations.

8. APPORTIONMENT

If the land described in Schedule A consists of two or more parcels which are not used as a single site, and a loss is established affecting one or more of the parcels but not all, the loss shall be computed and settled on a pro rata basis as if the amount of insurance under this policy was divided pro rata as to the value on Date of Policy of each separate parcel to the whole, exclusive of any improvements made subsequent to Date of Policy, unless a liability or value has otherwise been agreed upon as to each parcel by the Company and the insured at the time of the issuance of this policy and shown by an express statement or by an endorsement attached to this policy.

9. LIMITATION OF LIABILITY

(a) If the Company establishes the title, or removes the alleged defect, lien or encumbrance, or cures the lack of a right of access to or from the land, or cures the claim of unmarketability of title, all as insured, in a reasonably diligent manner by any method, including litigation and the completion of any appeals therefrom, it shall have fully performed its obligations with respect to that matter and shall not be liable for any loss or damage caused thereby.

(b) In the event of any litigation, including litigation by the Company or with the Company's consent, the Company shall have no liability for loss or damages until there has been a final determination by a court of competent jurisdiction, and disposition of all appeals therefrom, adverse to the title as insured.

(c) The Company shall not be liable for loss or damage to any insured for liability voluntarily assumed by the insured in settling any claim or suit without the prior written consent of the Company.

10.   REDUCTION OF INSURANCE; REDUCTION OR
      TERMINATION OF LIABILITY

All payments under this policy, except payments made for costs, attorneys' fees and expenses, shall reduce the amount of the insurance
pro tanto.

11.   LIABILITY NONCUMULATIVE

It is expressly understood that the amount of insurance under this
policy shall be reduced by any amount the Company may pay under any
policy insuring a mortgage to which exception is taken in Schedule B or to
which the insured has agreed, assumed, or taken subject, or which is hereafter executed by an insured and which is a charge or lien on the estate or
interest described or referred to in Schedule A, and the amount so paid
shall be deemed a payment under this policy to the insured owner.

12.   PAYMENT OF LOSS

(a) No payment shall be made without producing this policy for endorsement of the payment unless the policy has been lost or destroyed, in
which case proof of loss or destruction shall be furnished to the satisfaction
of the Company.

(b) When liability and the extent of loss or damage has been definitely
fixed in accordance with these Conditions and Stipulations, the loss or
damage shall be payable within 30 days thereafter.

13.   SUBROGATION UPON PAYMENT OR SETTLEMENT

(a)   The Company's Right of Subrogation.

Whenever the Company shall have settled and paid a claim under this
policy, all right of subrogation shall vest in the Company unaffected by any
act of the insured claimant.

The Company shall be subrogated to and be entitled to all rights and
remedies which the insured claimant would have had against any person or
property in respect to the claim had this policy not been issued. If requested
by the Company, the insured claimant shall transfer to the Company all
rights and remedies against any person or property necessary in order to
perfect this right of subrogation. The insured claimant shall permit the
Company to sue, compromise or settle in the name of the insured claimant
and to use the name of the insured claimant in any transaction or litigation
involving these rights or remedies.

If a payment on account of a claim does not fully cover the loss of the insured claimant, the Company shall be subrogated to these rights and remedies in the proportion which the Company's payment bears to the whole amount of the loss.

If loss should result from any act of the insured claimant, as stated above, that act shall not void this policy, but the Company, in that event, shall be required to pay only that part of any losses insured against by this policy which shall exceed the amount, if any, lost to the Company by reason of the impairment by the insured claimant of the Company's right of subrogation.

(b)   The Company's Rights Against Non-Insured Obligors.

The Company's right of subrogation against non-insured obligors shall exist and shall include, without limitation, the rights of the insured to indemnities, guaranties, other policies of insurance or bonds, notwithstanding any terms or conditions contained in those instruments which provide for subrogation rights by reason of this policy.

14.   ARBITRATION

Unless prohibited by applicable law, either the Company or the insured may demand arbitration pursuant to the Title Insurance Arbitration Rulers of the American Arbitration Association. Arbitrable matters may include, but are not limited to, any controversy or claim between the Company and the insured arising out of or relating to this policy, any service of the Company in connection with its issuance or the breach of a policy provision or other obligation. All arbitrable matters when the Amount of Insurance is $1,000,000 or less shall be arbitrated at the option of either the Company or the insured. All arbitrable matters when the Amount of Insurance is in excess of $1,000,000 shall be arbitrated only when agreed to by both the Company and the insured. Arbitration pursuant to this policy and under the Rules in effect on the date the demand for arbitration is made or, at the option of the insured, the Rules in effect at Date of Policy shall be binding upon the parties. The award may include attorneys' fees only if the laws of the state in which the land is located permit a court to award attorneys' fees to a prevailing party. Judgment upon the award rendered by the Arbitrator(s) may be entered in any court having jurisdiction thereof.

The law of the situs of the land shall apply to an arbitration under the Title Insurance Arbitration Rules.

A copy of the Rules may be obtained from the Company upon request.

15.   LIABILITY LIMITED TO THIS POLICY;
      POLICY ENTIRE CONTRACT

(a) This policy together with all endorsements, if any, attached hereto by the Company is the entire policy and contract between the insured and the Company. In interpreting any provision of this policy, this policy shall be construed as a whole.

(b) Any claim of loss or damage, whether or not based on negligence, and which arises out of the status of the title to the estate or interest covered hereby or by any action asserting such claim, shall be restricted to this policy.

(c) No amendment of or endorsement to this policy can be made except by a writing endorsed hereon or attached hereto signed by either the President, a Vice President, the Secretary, an Assistant Secretary, or validating officer or authorized signatory of the Company.

16.   SEVERABILITY

In the event any provision of this policy is held invalid or unenforceable under applicable law, the policy shall be deemed not to include that provision and all other provisions shall remain in full force and effect.

17.   NOTICES, WHERE SENT

All notices required to be given the Company and any statement in writing required to be furnished the Company shall include the number of this policy and shall be addressed to the Company at the issuing office or to:

Chicago Title Insurance Company
Claims Department
111 West Washington Street
Chicago, Illinois 60602

SCHEDULE B

Policy Number: _____
Owners

Policy Number: _____
Loan

This policy does not insure against loss or damage (and the Company will not pay costs, attorneys' fees or expenses) which arise by reason of:

The mortgage, if any, referred to in Schedule A.

(This exception does NOT apply to Loan Policies.)

Standard Exceptions:

(a) Rights of present tenants, lessees or parties in possession.

(b) Any liability for mechanics' or materialmen's liens.

(c) Discrepancies, conflicts in boundary lines, shortage in area, encroachments, and any facts which an accurate survey and inspection of the premises would disclose.

(d) Taxes or special assessments which are not shown as existing liens by the public records.

Additional Title Exceptions are as follows:

1. Taxes to the City/Town of _____ on the List of _____ and subsequent lists, however this policy insures that said taxes are current and the next payment is not yet due and payable.

Deletions of Standard Exceptions:

LOAN POLICY: Standard Exceptions _____ are hereby omitted from the LOAN POLICY

OWNER'S POLICY: Standard Exceptions _____ are hereby omitted from the OWNER'S POLICY

Affirmative insurance language contained in Schedule B does NOT apply to the Owner's Policy unless otherwise specified.

Countersigned   NOTE: The following endorsements appearing after Schedule B are an integral part of this policy.

_____
Authorized Signatory

NOTES AND QUESTIONS

1.   **Scope of coverage.** These questions will test your reading of the policy and suggest potential problems for the buyer's lawyer.

a. X has purchased a 50-acre parcel, intending to develop it for a shopping center. After he acquires title, which is insured under the standard policy form, X discovers that tract restrictions bar the sale of alcoholic beverages. How would you determine whether X has a claim against the insurer? Suppose, instead, that X learns that only 40 acres are zoned for commercial development: any recourse against the insurer? Suppose, instead, that X orders a survey that shows that the parcel contains only 48.5 acres: any recourse under this policy?

b. Y acquires an apartment house for $1 million. Her title is insured for the purchase price. Two years later, Y signs a contract to sell the property for $1.2 million, but her buyer rejects Y's title as partly defective. The records contain a forged deed of an undivided one-half interest in the property, reducing Y's valid interest by 50 percent. What recourse, if any, does Y have under this policy? Suppose that Y had signed to resell the property for $900,000?

c. Z buys a lakeside cottage, which the seller's daughter and her family have used for several summers. During this period, Z has rented the cottage next door. Z obtains a title policy at the closing. A few months later, Z learns that the seller's daughter holds an unrecorded lease for the cottage, good for three summers more. The lease bears the fair market rental. What recourse, if any, does Z have against his insurer? The policy does not mention the lease.

2.   **Extended coverage.** Experienced real estate lawyers know that the standard owner's policy need not be the final contract between the title company and the insured. Exceptions may be bargained away, and there exist an inventory of extended protections, which usually involve a further premium. Examples include:

a. Zoning rider [in part]:

> The following use or uses are allowed . . . subject to compliance with any conditions, restrictions, or requirements contained in the zoning ordinances and amendments thereto. . . .

b. Comprehensive endorsement [in part]:

> The Company hereby insures against loss . . . by reason of any . . . damage to existing improvements, including lawns, shrubbery or trees which are located or encroach upon that portion of the land subject to any easement shown in Schedule B, which damage results from the exercise of the right to use or maintain such easement for the purposes for which the same was granted or reserved. . . .

c. Nonimputation endorsement [in part]:

The Company hereby assures notwithstanding the terms of the Conditions and Stipulations or schedule of Exclusions from Coverage to the contrary, that in the event of loss or damage insured against under the terms of the policy, the Company will not deny its liability thereunder to said insured on the grounds that said insured had knowledge of any matter solely by reason of notice thereof imputed to it . . . by operation of law.

LICK MILL CREEK APARTMENTS v. CHICAGO TITLE INSURANCE CO.

283 Cal. Rptr. 231 (Cal. App. 1991)

AGLIANO, J.

Plaintiffs Lick Mill Creek Apartments and Prometheus Development Company, Inc. appeal from a judgment of dismissal entered after the trial court sustained, without leave to amend, the demurrer of defendants Chicago Title Insurance Company and First American Title Insurance Company to plaintiffs' first amended complaint. The trial court determined, based on undisputed facts alleged in the complaint, that title insurance policies issued by defendants did not provide coverage for the costs of removing hazardous substances from plaintiffs' property. For the reasons stated below, we conclude the trial court's ruling was correct and affirm the judgment.

SCOPE OF REVIEW

"A general demurrer presents the same question to the appellate court as to the trial court, namely, whether the plaintiff has alleged sufficient facts to justify any relief, notwithstanding superfluous allegations or claims for unjustified relief. '[T]he allegations of the complaint must be liberally construed with a view to attaining substantial justice among the parties. (Code Civ. Proc., §452.)' Pleading defects which do not affect substantial rights of the parties should be disregarded. In evaluating a demurrer, we assume the truth of all material facts properly pleaded in the complaint unless they are contradicted by facts judicially noticed but no such credit is given to pleaded contentions or legal conclusions. Specific factual allegations modify and limit inconsistent general statements." (B & P Development Corp. v. City of Saratoga (1986) 185 Cal. App. 3d 949, 952-953, 230 Cal. Rptr. 192.)

THE FIRST AMENDED COMPLAINT

The first amended complaint alleges the following material facts:
The real property which is the subject of this case comprises approxi-

mately 30 acres of land near the Guadalupe River in Santa Clara County. Prior to 1979, various corporations operated warehouses and/or chemical processing plants on the property. Incident to this use of the property, the companies maintained underground tanks, pumps, and pipelines for the storage, handling, and disposal of various hazardous substances. These hazardous substances eventually contaminated the soil, subsoil, and groundwater.

In 1979, Kimball Small Investments 103 (KSI) purchased the property. Between 1979 and 1981, the California Department of Health Services ordered KSI to remedy the toxic contamination of the property. KSI, however, did not comply with this order.

In early October 1986, plaintiffs acquired lot 1 of the property from KSI. In connection with this acquisition, plaintiffs purchased title insurance from Chicago Title Insurance Company (Chicago Title). The insurance policy issued was of the type known as an American Land Title Insurance Association (ALTA) policy (policy 1). Prior to issuing this policy, Chicago Title commissioned a survey and inspection of the property by Carroll Resources Engineering & Management (Carroll Resources).

Plaintiffs subsequently purchased lots 2 and 3 from KSI and secured two additional ALTA policies (policies 2 and 3) from Chicago Title and First American Title Insurance Company (First American). The entire site was surveyed and inspected. During its survey and inspection, Carroll Resources noted the presence of certain pipes, tanks, pumps, and other improvements on the property. At the time each of the policies was issued, the Department of Health Services, the Regional Water Quality Control Board, and the Santa Clara County Environmental Health Department maintained records disclosing the presence of hazardous substances on the subject property.

Following their purchase of the property, plaintiffs incurred costs for removal and clean-up of the hazardous substances in order "to mitigate plaintiffs' damages and avoid costs of compliance with government mandate." Then, claiming their expenses were a substitute, i.e., a payment made under threat of compulsion of law, for restitution to the State Hazardous Substance Account (Health & Saf. Code, §25300, et seq.) and "response costs" as defined under the Comprehensive Environmental Response, Compensation, and Liability Act (CERCLA) (42 U.S.C., §9601, et seq.), plaintiffs sought indemnity from defendants for the sums expended in their clean-up efforts. Defendants, however, denied coverage.

DISCUSSION

I.   THE NATURE OF TITLE INSURANCE

"Title insurance is an exclusively American invention. It involves the issuance of an insurance policy promising that if the state of the title is other than as represented on the face of the policy, and if the insured suffers loss as a result of the difference, the insurer will reimburse the insured for that loss and any related legal expenses, up to the face amount of the policy." (Burke, Law of Title Insurance (1986), §1.1, p.2.)

Pursuant to Insurance Code section 12340.1,

> "[/t]itle insurance" means insuring, guaranteeing, or indemnifying owners of real or personal property or the holders of liens or encumbrances thereon or others interested therein against loss or damage suffered by reason of:
>
> (a)   Liens or encumbrances on, or defects in title to said property;
>
> (b)   Invalidity or unenforceability of any liens or encumbrances thereon; or
>
> (c)   Incorrectness of searches relating to the title to real or personal property.

Thus, under both the traditional concept and the statutory definition, title insurance covers matters affecting title.

Essentially two types of title insurance policies are available to owners of real property interests in California: California Land Title Association Standard Coverage (CLTA) policies and American Land Title Association (ALTA) policies. CLTA insures primarily against defects in title which are discoverable through an examination of the public record. (Hosack, California Title Insurance Practice (C.E.B. 1980), pp.38-41, §3.7) Thus, a CLTA policy insures against loss incurred if the insured interest is not vested as shown in the policy; loss from defects in or liens or encumbrances on the title; unmarketability of title; and loss due to lack of access to an open street or highway under certain circumstances. (Ibid.) A CLTA policy also covers a limited number of off-record risks. (Ibid.) The ALTA policy, such as those purchased by plaintiffs here, provides greater coverage than the CLTA policy. (Id. at p.35, §3.2.) Generally, it additionally insures against "off-record defects, liens, encumbrances, easements, and encroachments; rights of parties in possession or rights discoverable by inquiry of parties in possession, and not shown on the public records; water rights, mining claims, and patent reservations; and discrepancies or conflicts in boundary lines and shortages in areas that are not reflected in the public records." (Id. at p.36, §3.3.) Since an ALTA policy covers many off-record defects in title, the insurer will typically survey the property to be insured. (See Contini v. Western Title Insurance Company (1974) 40 Cal. App. 3d 536, 543-544, 115 Cal. Rptr. 257.)[1]

---

1. Some title companies also offer an environmental protection lien endorsement (ALTA Form 8.1). (Hosack, California Title Insurance Practice (1987 Supp.) p. 35, §3.9.) It provides coverage against any recorded environmental protection liens which have not been excluded from coverage. (Ibid.) The endorsement also lists state statutes which could create a lien in the future. (Ibid.)

II.   CONSTRUCTION OF LANGUAGE IN INSURANCE POLICIES

The insuring clauses of an insurance policy define and limit coverage. (Glavinich v. Commonwealth Land Title Ins. Co. (1984) 163 Cal. App. 3d 263, 270, 209 Cal. Rptr. 266.) Where a reviewing court is required to interpret an insurance policy without extrinsic evidence, the question is one of law. (Aerojet-General Corp. v. Superior Court (1989) 211 Cal. App. 3d 216, 224, 257 Cal. Rptr. 621.) Any ambiguity arising from policy language should be resolved in favor of the insured. (Insurance Co. of North America v. Sam Harris Constr. Co. (1978) 22 Cal. 3d 409, 412-413, 149 Cal. Rptr. 292, 583 P.2d 1335.) However, this rule of construction applies only when the policy language is unclear. (Gray v. Zurich Insurance Co. (1966) 65 Cal. 2d 263, 271, 54 Cal. Rptr. 104, 419 P.2d 168.) " 'A policy provision is ambiguous when it is capable of two or more constructions, both of which are reasonable.' " (Delgado v. Heritage Life Ins. Co. (1984) 157 Cal. App. 3d 262, 271, 203 Cal. Rptr. 672.) Whether language in a contract is ambiguous is a question of law. (Id. at p. 270, 203 Cal. Rptr. 672.)

Here the insuring clauses of policies 1, 2, and 3 are identical and provide the following: "SUBJECT TO THE EXCLUSIONS FROM COVERAGE, THE EXCEPTIONS CONTAINED IN SCHEDULE B AND THE PROVISIONS OF THE CONDITIONS AND STIPULATIONS HEREOF [the insurer] insures, as of Date of Policy shown in Schedule A, against loss or damage, not exceeding the amount of insurance stated in Schedule A, and costs, attorneys' fees and expenses which the Company may become obligated to pay hereunder, sustained or incurred by the insured by reason of:

"(1) Title to the estate or interest described in Schedule A being vested otherwise than as stated therein;

"(2) Any defect in or lien or encumbrance on such title;

"(3) Lack of a right of access to and from the land; or

"(4) Unmarketability of such title."

III.   MARKETABILITY OF TITLE

Plaintiffs first contend the policies in the instant case expressly insured that title to the subject property was marketable and since the presence of hazardous substances on the property impaired its marketability, defendants were obliged to pay cleanup costs. Plaintiffs' position, however, is dependent upon their view that California courts have adopted a definition of marketable title that encompasses the property's market value. Our review of relevant authority establishes no support for this position.

In Mertens v. Berendsen (1931) 213 Cal. 111, 112, 1 P.2d 440, the plaintiff attempted to rescind a real estate purchase contract, claiming that the property encroached upon the street and rendered the title defective. (Id. at p.113, 1 P.2d 440.) In considering this issue, the court defined marketability of title as follows:

Such a title must be free from reasonable doubt, and such that a reasonably prudent person, with full knowledge of the facts and their legal bearings, willing and anxious to perform his contract, would, in the exercise of that prudence which business men ordinarily bring to bear upon such transactions, be willing to accept and ought to accept. It must be so far free from defects as to enable the holder, not only to retain the land, but possess it in peace, and, if he wishes to sell it, to be reasonably sure that no flaw or doubt will arise to disturb its market value. But a mere suspicion against the title or a speculative possibility that a defect in it might appear in the future cannot be said to render a title unmarketable. It is not required to be free from mere shadows or possibilities, but from probabilities. Moral, not mathematical, certainty that the title is good is all that is required.

(Ibid., quoting from Kenefick v. Schumaker, 64 Ind. App. 552, 116 N.E. 319, 323.) Plaintiffs focus on the court's reference to the market value of the property. What plaintiffs ignore, however, is the fact that the court made this reference only in the context of examining an alleged defect in title. *Mertens* does not stand for the proposition that a defect in the physical condition of the land itself renders the title unmarketable. . . .

Other jurisdictions have also recognized the distinction. In Chicago Title Ins. Co. v. Kumar (1987) 24 Mass. App. Ct. 53, 506 N.E.2d 154, 156, the defendant had purchased property on which hazardous substances were discovered. The defendant sought payment for cleanup costs from its title insurer. (*Ibid.*) The insurer sought a declaration as to its obligations under the policy. The defendant owner filed a counterclaim, seeking a declaration that the presence of hazardous substances constituted a defect in title and the state's statutory power to impose a lien to secure payment of clean-up costs rendered his title unmarketable. (*Ibid.*) Relying on Hocking v. Title Ins. & Trust Co., *supra,* 37 Cal. 2d 644, 651, 234 P.2d 625, the court found in favor of the insurer, stating "the defendant confuses economic lack of marketability, which relates to physical conditions affecting the use of the property, with title marketability, which relates to defects affecting legally recognized rights and incidents of ownership. . . . The presence of hazardous material may affect the market value of the defendant's land, but, on the present record [since no lien had been recorded], it does not affect the title to the land." (Id. 506 N.E.2d at p. 157.)

Plaintiffs attempt to distinguish *Kumar* on the ground that here they purchased ALTA policies while the defendant in *Kumar* purchased a CLTA policy.[2] They point out an ALTA policy which required a physical inspection and survey of the property would have insured against off-record risks and potential liens not covered by a CLTA policy. While an ALTA policy provides greater coverage than a CLTA policy, it does not follow that an ALTA policy extends coverage to matters not affecting title. We must still examine the

---

2. Plaintiffs did not purchase an environmental protection endorsement (ALTA Form 8.1 policy).

policy language for a determination of coverage. Here the policy insures against "unmarketability of title." The definition of this term is not dependent upon the type of title insurance policy in which it appears.

We find no ambiguity in the insuring clause: defendants are obligated to insure plaintiffs against unmarketability of title on the subject property. Because marketability of title and the market value of the land itself are separate and distinct, plaintiffs cannot claim coverage for the property's physical condition under this clause of the insurance policies.

IV.   ENCUMBRANCE ON TITLE

The policies in question insure plaintiffs against "any defect in or lien or encumbrance" on title. Although no lien had been recorded or asserted at the time the title insurance policies were issued, plaintiffs contend the presence of hazardous substances on the property constituted an encumbrance on title.

Encumbrances are defined by statute as "taxes, assessments, and all liens upon real property." (Civ. Code, §1114.) Where a property is contaminated with hazardous substances, a subsequent owner of the property may be held fully responsible for the financial costs of cleaning up the contamination. (42 U.S.C. §9607, subd. (a); Health & Saf. Code, §§25323.5 and 25363.) A lien may also be imposed on the property to cover such cleanup costs. (42 U.S.C., §9607, subd. (*l*).) Plaintiffs reason that because any transfer of contaminated land carries with it the responsibility for cleanup costs, liability for such costs constitutes an "encumbrance on title" and is covered. We disagree.

In United States v. Allied Chemical Corp. (1984) 587 F. Supp. 1205, the plaintiff alleged a breach of warranty that property conveyed was free of encumbrance where hazardous substances were present on the property at the time it was conveyed. The court dismissed the plaintiff's cause of action, stating:

> Plaintiff argues that the term "encumbrance" is broad enough to include the presence of hazardous substances. However, the only authorities cited have interpreted "encumbrance" to include only liens, easements, restrictive covenants and other such interests in or rights to the land held by third persons. (See Evans v. Faught, 231 Cal. App. 2d 698, 706 [42 Cal. Rptr. 133]....) Plaintiff has given no authority establishing its broad argument that any physical condition, including the presence of hazardous substances, is an "encumbrance" if "not visible or known" at the time of conveyance. The court declines to interpret "encumbrance" as broadly as plaintiff urges. The court finds that, under current law, the term "encumbrance" does not extend to the presence of hazardous substances alleged in this case.

(Id. at p.1206.) (Accord Cameron v. Martin Marietta Corp. (E.D.N.C. 1990) 729 F. Supp. 1529, 1532.)

In Chicago Title Ins. Co. v. Kumar, *supra*, 506 N.E.2d 154, the court also held that the presence of hazardous substances on the land at the time title was conveyed did not constitute an encumbrance. "The mere possibility that the Commonwealth may attach a future lien . . . , as a result of the release of hazardous material (existing but unknown at the time a title insurance policy is issued) when the Commonwealth has neither expended moneys on the property requiring reimbursement nor recorded the necessary statement of claim, is insufficient to create a 'defect in or lien or encumbrance on . . . title.'" (Id. at p.156.) . . .

V.   EXCLUSIONS IN POLICIES 1 AND 3

Plaintiffs contend the governmental regulation and police power exclusions included in policies 1 and 3 are inapplicable.[3] We need not decide this question, since we have found no coverage under the identical insuring clauses of each policy.

Plaintiffs also contend they had a reasonable expectation that cleanup costs would be covered by the policies, because policies 1 and 3 did not include environmental exclusions as did policy 2.[4]

Where there is ambiguity in the language of an insurance policy, a court will interpret coverage so as to protect the objectively reasonable expectations of the insured. (AIU Ins. Co. v. Superior Court (1990) 51 Cal. 3d 807, 822, 274 Cal. Rptr. 820, 799 P.2d 1253.)

As previously discussed, the language of the insuring clauses of all three policies unambiguously provides coverage only for defects relating to title. These clauses make no reference to the physical condition of the land. Moreover, this interpretation is fully supported by relevant authority. Un-

---

3. Policies 1 and 3 contain exclusions from coverage as follows: "Any law, ordinance or governmental regulation (including but not limited to building and zoning ordinances) restricting or regulating or prohibiting the occupancy, use or enjoyment of the land, or regulating the character, dimensions or location of any improvement now or hereafter erected on the land, or prohibiting a separation in ownership or a reduction in the dimensions or area of the land, or the effect of any violation of any such law, ordinance or governmental regulation." The police power exclusion states as follows: "Rights of eminent domain or governmental rights of police power unless notice of the exercise of such rights appears in the public records at Date of Policy."

4. Policy 2 stated in relevant part:

The following matters are expressly excluded from the coverage of this policy: . . .

(b) Any law, ordinance or governmental regulation relating to environmental protection. . . .

(d) The effect of any violation of the matters excluded under (a), (b) or (c) above, unless notice of a defect, lien or encumbrance resulting from a violation has been recorded at Date of Policy in those records in which under state statutes, deeds, mortgages, lis pendens, liens or other title encumbrances must be recorded in order to impart constructive notice to purchasers of the land for value and without knowledge; provided, however, that without limitation, such records shall not be construed to include records in any of the offices of federal, state or local environmental protection, zoning, building, health or public safety authorities.

der these circumstances, we fail to see how a specific exclusion in one policy leads to a reasonable expectation of coverage in the insuring clauses of other policies.

DISPOSITION

The judgment is affirmed.

NOTES AND QUESTIONS

1.   **The insured's recovery.** Suppose that an insured were to prevail in her claim under the policy: What is the potential recovery?

Consider the facts in White v. Western Title Ins. Co., 40 Cal. 3d 870, 221 Cal. Rptr. 509, 710 P.2d 309 (1985). In 1978 plaintiffs purchased 84 acres of ranchland whose title the defendant had insured. Schedule B excluded from coverage "easements, liens or encumbrances, or claims thereof, which are not shown by the public records," as well as "water rights, claims or title to water." Six months after closing, plaintiffs learned of a recorded "easement deed for waterline and well sites," which had not been specifically listed in Schedule B. Plaintiffs sued insurer for breach of contract, negligence, and breach of the implied covenants of good faith and fair dealing, claiming that their property was less valuable because of the potential loss of ground water. The court affirmed a jury award of $8,400 for breach of contract and negligence and an additional $20,000 for breach of the covenants of good faith and fair dealing.

As to the contractual liability, the court stated that "any ambiguity or uncertainty in an insurance policy is to be resolved against the insurer. . . . Coverage clauses are interpreted broadly so as to afford the greatest possible protection to the insured. . . . [E]xclusionary clauses are interpreted narrowly against the insurer." Applying this dogma, the court rejected the defendant's view that the reference in Schedule B to "water rights" was controlling: Instead, the court drew the negative inference (that coverage was intended) from the "easement . . . not shown by the public record" language in the same Schedule. The court rested negligence liability on the insured's failure to list the water easement in the preliminary title report — "the failure of a title company to note an encumbrance of record is prima facie negligent." The insurer's breach of good faith and fair dealing stemmed from its handling of the claim. In an earlier California case, a court awarded plaintiff $200,000 for emotional distress when the insurer failed to report an easement and then refused for three years to pay for the loss; Jarchow v. Transamerica Title Insurance Co., 48 Cal. App. 3d 917, 122 Cal. Rptr. 470 (1975).

Other courts have refused to find negligence on facts similar to those in the White case; see, e.g., Somerset Sav. Bank v. Chicago Title Ins. Co., 420

Mass. 422, 649 N.E.2d 1123 (1995) ("[a]s a general rule" a title insurer's liability "is limited to the policy, and it will not be liable for negligence in searching the record"); *accord* Brown's Tie & Lumber Co. v. Chicago Title Co. of Idaho, 115 Idaho 56, 764 P.2d 423 (1988).

    2.   **Insurer's obligation to defend.** Read carefully section 4 of the title policy: "Defense and Prosecution of Actions." This is of significant value to the insured, and the insurer cannot escape the obligation by asserting that an unmeritorious claim has been made against the title. Note, however, that section 6 of the policy does give the company another option.

§12.4   After the Closing

a.   The Condition of the Premises: Caveat Emptor

    As recently as the 1950s there was a reasonably coherent body of law dealing with seller's responsibilities to buyer as to structures on the sold premises. The law was "caveat emptor": the warning to the buyer was generally, "Guard yourself at all times," and particularly, "Look before you sign," "Don't assume, ask," and "Get it in writing."

    One could find in the authorities a whole series of propositions that made up the "caveat emptor" system. They were all derived from the general bodies of contract and tort law, and as you read below a selection from the more important of the rules you will find nothing startling. To be sure, you ought to doubt whether there ever was a time and place where every proposition listed was rigidly applied to defeat every disappointed buyer, and you ought to recognize that some of the propositions have been weakened in recent years in their general applicability, whatever may be true about land sales. Nevertheless, here are propositions that defeated many a buyer in many a case.

NOTE: CAVEAT EMPTOR AS A SYSTEM OF PROPOSITIONS

    1.   *Promissory obligations of the seller: seller has contractual quality responsibilities only to the extent that he makes express warranties in contract of sale or deed.*

    (a) There are no implied warranties of quality in the sale of real estate.

    (b) Seller's oral promises preceding the contract of sale are unavailing to buyer because of the parol evidence rule.

    (c) Seller's oral promises preceding the contract of sale are made unenforceable by the statute of frauds.

    (d) Seller's oral promises between contract of sale and deed are unavailing to buyer because they are not supported by consideration.

    (e) Express warranties in the contract of sale but not contained in the deed are unavailing to buyer because of the doctrine of merger. (This is a variant of the parol evidence rule.)

(f) An express quality warranty in the deed inures only to the grantee and does not run with the land.

(g) The remedy for breach of an express quality warranty is damages, not rescission.

(h) Breach of an express quality warranty does not subject the warrantor to liability for consequential damages, particularly personal injury damages.

2. *Duties of the seller not to misrepresent.* Here is a sampling of propositions from the tort law of misrepresentation: innocent, negligent, and intentional:

(a) *Nondisclosure:* (1) Seller has no duty to disclose any quality defect detectable by inspection. (2) Seller has no duty to disclose a concealed defect unless buyer proves that the defect is actually known to seller. (3) Seller has no duty to disclose a concealed defect known to him unless he knows that buyer is unaware of the defect and that the buyer would regard the defect as material.

(b) *Intentional misrepresentation:* (1) Seller's words are an unenforceable oral promise, rather than a duty-laden representation of fact. (2) Seller's quality affirmation is a mere opinion. (3) Buyer's inspection shows he does not rely on the representation. (4) Buyer's opportunity to inspect shows that he has no right to rely on the representation.

(c) *Agency problems:* (1) A real estate broker is not authorized to make quality representations to prospective purchasers. (2) Seller who authorizes a broker to make quality representations is not liable for intentional misrepresentations made by the agent.

(d) *Regulatory statutes:* Statutory duties imposed on seller by building codes or like regulatory statutes do not run to buyer.

(e) *Remedies:* (1) Buyer's remedy for misrepresentation is restricted to rescission. (2) A buyer who, after discovering a defect, keeps up mortgage payments while deciding on a course of action, has waived the tort. (3) The statute of limitations runs from the date of the tort, not the date of its discovery.

When it came to purchase of new homes from builder-vendors, all the rules that denied buyer protection unless he had it in writing got their bite from the fact that the instrumentation of the transaction was in the hands of the seller. In one of the last significant cases that reaffirmed the one-time nationwide rule that there were no implied warranties in the sale of a new home, Steiber v. Palumbo, 219 Or. 479, 347 P.2d 978 (1959), the court noted that the transaction's documents did not contain any mention at all of the structure being sold.

Caveat emptor has recently been nationally undercut in a common law process that is still under development. This legal change also should come as no surprise to persons who have studied recent products law and recent landlord-tenant decisions.

You must note that we are dealing systematically only with private remedies for disappointing housing, and not with building codes, criminal statutes, conditional public subsidy programs, antitrust laws, and myriad other institutional and governmental constraints on the housing seller. The prophylaxis of a tightly administered building code might be enormously more protective to buyers than the opportunity to engage in expensive, time-consuming, nerve-frazzling, common law litigation — even if successful. And it may be that a vigorous, innovative, competitive housing supply industry would be the best protection of all.

STAMBOVSKY v. ACKLEY[22]

---

169 A.D.2d 254, 572 N.Y.S.2d 672 (1991)

RUBIN, J.

Plaintiff, to his horror, discovered that the house he had recently contracted to purchase was widely reputed to be possessed by poltergeists, reportedly seen by defendant seller and members of her family on numerous occasions over the last nine years. Plaintiff promptly commenced this action seeking rescission of the contract of sale. Supreme Court reluctantly dismissed the complaint, holding that plaintiff has no remedy at law in this jurisdiction.

The unusual facts of this case, as disclosed by the record, clearly warrant a grant of equitable relief to the buyer who, as a resident of New York City, cannot be expected to have any familiarity with the folklore of the Village of Nyack. Not being a "local," plaintiff could not readily learn that the home he had contracted to purchase is haunted. Whether the source of the spectral apparitions seen by defendant seller are parapsychic or psychogenic, having reported their presence in both a national publication ("Readers' Digest") and the local press (in 1977 and 1982, respectively), defendant is estopped to deny their existence and, as a matter of law, the house is haunted. More to the point, however, no divination is required to conclude that it is defendant's promotional efforts in publicizing her close encounters with these spirits which fostered the home's reputation in the community. In 1989, the house was included in a five-home walking tour of Nyack and described in a November 27th newspaper article as "a riverfront Victorian (with ghost)." The impact of the reputation thus created goes to the very essence of the bargain between the parties, greatly impairing both the value of the property and its potential for resale. The extent of this

---

22. Note that this case was litigated in 1991 not 1691.

impairment may be presumed for the purpose of reviewing the disposition of this motion to dismiss the cause of action for rescission (Harris v. City of New York, 147 A.D.2d 186, 188-189, 542 N.Y.S.2d 550) and represents merely an issue of fact for resolution at trial.

While I agree with Supreme Court that the real estate broker, as agent for the seller, is under no duty to disclose to a potential buyer the phantasmal reputation of the premises and that, in his pursuit of a legal remedy for fraudulent misrepresentation against the seller, plaintiff hasn't a ghost of a chance. I am nevertheless moved by the spirit of equity to allow the buyer to seek rescission of the contract of sale and recovery of his downpayment. New York law fails to recognize any remedy for damages incurred as a result of the seller's mere silence, applying instead the strict rule of caveat emptor. Therefore, the theoretical basis for granting relief, even under the extraordinary facts of this case, is elusive if not ephemeral.

"Pity me not but lend thy serious hearing to what I shall unfold" (William Shakespeare, Hamlet, Act I, Scene V [Ghost]).

From the perspective of a person in the position of plaintiff herein, a very practical problem arises with respect to the discovery of a paranormal phenomenon: "Who you gonna call?" as the title song to the movie "Ghostbusters" asks. Applying the strict rule of caveat emptor to a contract involving a house possessed by poltergeists conjures up visions of a psychic or medium routinely accompanying the structural engineer and Terminix man on an inspection of every home subject to a contract of sale. It portends that the prudent attorney will establish an escrow account lest the subject of the transaction come back to haunt him and his client — or pray that his malpractice insurance coverage extends to supernatural disasters. In the interest of avoiding such untenable consequences, the notion that a haunting is a condition which can and should be ascertained upon reasonable inspection of the premises is a hobgoblin which should be exorcised from the body of legal precedent and laid quietly to rest.

It has been suggested by a leading authority that the ancient rule which holds that mere non-disclosure does not constitute actionable misrepresentation "finds proper application in cases where the fact undisclosed is patent, or the plaintiff has equal opportunities for obtaining information which he may be expected to utilize, or the defendant has no reason to think that he is acting under any misapprehension" (Prosser, Law of Torts §106, at 696 [4th ed., 1971]). However, with respect to transactions in real estate, New York adheres to the doctrine of caveat emptor and imposes no duty upon the vendor to disclose any information concerning the premises (London v. Courduff, 141 A.D.2d 803, 529 N.Y.S.2d 874) unless there is a confidential or fiduciary relationship between the parties (Moser v. Spizzirro, 31 A.D.2d 537, 295 N.Y.S.2d 188, aff'd., 25 N.Y.2d 941, 305 N.Y.S.2d 153, 252 N.E.2d 632; IBM Credit Fin. Corp. v. Mazda Motor Mfg. (USA) Corp., 152 A.D.2d 451, 542 N.Y.S.2d 649) or some conduct on the part of the seller which constitutes "active concealment" (see, 17 East 80th

Realty Corp. v. 68th Associates, — A.D.2d —, 569 N.Y.S.2d 647 [dummy ventilation system constructed by seller]; Haberman v. Greenspan, 82 Misc. 2d 263, 368 N.Y.S.2d 717 [foundation cracks covered by seller]). Normally, some affirmative misrepresentation (e.g., Tahini Invs., Ltd. v. Bobrowsky, 99 A.D.2d 489, 470 N.Y.S.2d 431 [industrial waste on land allegedly used only as farm]); Jansen v. Kelly, 11 A.D.2d 587, 200 N.Y.S.2d 561 [land containing valuable minerals allegedly acquired for use as campsite] or partial disclosure (Junius Constr. Corp. v. Cohen, 257 N.Y. 393, 178 N.E. 672 [existence of third unopened street concealed]; Noved Realty Corp. v. A.A.P. Co., 250 App. Div. 1, 293 N.Y.S. 336 [escrow agreements securing lien concealed] is required to impose upon the seller a duty to communicate undisclosed conditions affecting the premises (contra, Young v. Keith, 112 A.D.2d 625, 492 N.Y.S.2d 489 [defective water and sewer systems concealed]).

Caveat emptor is not so all-encompassing a doctrine of common law as to render every act of non-disclosure immune from redress, whether legal or equitable. "In regard to the necessity of giving information which has not been asked, the rule differs somewhat at law and in equity, and while the law courts would permit no recovery of *damages* against a vendor, because of mere concealment of facts *under certain circumstances,* yet if the vendee refused to complete the contract because of the concealment of a material fact on the part of the other, equity would refuse to compel him so to do, because equity only compels the specific performance of a contract which is fair and open, and in regard to which all material matters known to each have been communicated to the other" (Rothmiller v. Stein, 143 N.Y. 581, 591-592, 38 N.E. 718 [emphasis added]). Even as a principle of law, long before exceptions were embodied in statute law (see, e.g., UCC 2-312, 313, 314, 315; 3-417[2][e]), the doctrine was held inapplicable to contagion among animals, adulteration of food, and insolvency of a maker of a promissory note and of a tenant substituted for another under a lease (see, Rothmiller v. Stein, *supra,* at 592-593, 38 N.E. 718 and cases cited therein). Common law is not moribund. *Ex facto jus oritur* (law arises out of facts). Where fairness and common sense dictate that an exception should be created, the evolution of the law should not be stifled by rigid application of a legal maxim.

The doctrine of caveat emptor requires that a buyer act prudently to assess the fitness and value of his purchase and operates to bar the purchaser who fails to exercise due care from seeking the equitable remedy of rescission (see, e.g., Rodas v. Manitaras, 159 A.D.2d 341, 552 N.Y.S.2d 618). For the purposes of the instant motion to dismiss the action pursuant to CPLR 3211(a)(7), plaintiff is entitled to every favorable inference which may reasonably be drawn from the pleadings (Arrington v. New York Times Co., 55 N.Y.2d 433, 442, 449 N.Y.S.2d 941, 434 N.E.2d 1319; Rovello v. Orofino Realty Co., 40 N.Y.2d 633, 634, 389 N.Y.S.2d 314, 357 N.E.2d 970), specifically, in this instance, that he met his obligation to conduct an in-

spection of the premises and a search of available public records with respect to title. It should be apparent, however, that the most meticulous
inspection and the search would not reveal the presence of poltergeists at
the premises or unearth the property's ghoulish reputation in the community. Therefore, there is no sound policy reason to deny plaintiff relief for
failing to discover a state of affairs which the most prudent purchaser would
not be expected to even contemplate (see, Da Silva v. Musso, 53 N.Y.2d 543,
551, 444 N.Y.S.2d 50, 428 N.E.2d 382).

The case law in this jurisdiction dealing with the duty of a vendor of
real property to disclose information to the buyer is distinguishable from
the matter under review. The most salient distinction is that existing cases
invariably deal with the physical condition of the premises (e.g., London v.
Courduff, *supra* [use as a landfill]; Perin v. Mardine Realty Co., 5 A.D.2d
685, 168 N.Y.S.2d 647 *aff'd* 6 N.Y.2d 920, 190 N.Y.S.2d 995, 161 N.E.2d 210
[sewer line crossing adjoining property without owner's consent]), defects
in title (e.g., Sands v. Kissane, 282 App. Div. 140, 121 N.Y.S.2d 634 [remain-
derman]), liens against the property (e.g., Noved Realty Corp. v. A.A.P.
Co., supra), expenses or income (e.g., Rodas v. Manitaras, supra [gross re-
ceipts]) and other factors affecting its operation. No case has been brought
to this court's attention in which the property value was impaired as a result
of the reputation created by information disseminated to the public by the
seller (or, for that matter, as a result of possession by poltergeists).

Where a condition which has been created by the seller materially
impairs the value of the contract and is peculiarly within the knowledge of
the seller or unlikely to be discovered by a prudent purchaser exercising
due care with respect to the subject transaction, nondisclosure constitutes
a basis for rescission as a matter of equity. Any other outcome places upon
the buyer not merely the obligation to exercise care in his purchase but
rather to be omniscient with respect to any fact which may affect the bargain. No practical purpose is served by imposing such a burden upon a
purchaser. To the contrary, it encourages predatory business practice and
offends the principle that equity will suffer no wrong to be without a
remedy.

Defendant's contention that the contract of sale, particularly the
merger or "as is" clause, bars recovery of the buyer's deposit is unavailing.
Even an express disclaimer will not be given effect where the facts are peculiarly within the knowledge of the party invoking it (Danann Realty Corp.
v. Harris, 5 N.Y.2d 317, 322, 184 N.Y.S.2d 599, 157 N.E.2d 597; Tahini Invs.,
Ltd. v. Bobrowsky, supra). Moreover, a fair reading of the merger clause
reveals that it expressly disclaims only representations made with respect to
the physical condition of the premises and merely makes general reference
to representations concerning "any other matter or things affecting or relating to the aforesaid premises." As broad as this language may be, a reasonable interpretation is that its effect is limited to tangible or physical
matters and does not extend to paranormal phenomena. Finally, if the lan-

guage of the contract is to be construed as broadly as defendant urges to encompass the presence of poltergeists in the house, it cannot be said that she has delivered the premises "vacant" in accordance with her obligation under the provisions of the contract rider.

To the extent New York law may be said to require something more than "mere concealment" to apply even the equitable remedy of rescission, the case of Junius Construction Corporation v. Cohen, 257 N.Y. 393, 178 N.E. 672, supra, while not precisely on point, provides some guidance. In that case, the seller disclosed that an official map indicated two as yet unopened streets which were planned for construction at the edges of the parcel. What was not disclosed was that the same map indicated a third street which, if opened, would divide the plot in half. The court held that, while the seller was under no duty to mention the planned streets at all, having undertaken to disclose two of them, he was obliged to reveal the third (see also, Rosenschein v. McNally, 17 A.D.2d 834, 233 N.Y.S.2d 254).

In the case at bar, defendant seller deliberately fostered the public belief that her home was possessed. Having undertaken to inform the public at large, to whom she has no legal relationship, about the supernatural occurrences on her property, she may be said to owe no less a duty to her contract vendee. It has been remarked that the occasional modern cases which permit a seller to take unfair advantage of a buyer's ignorance so long as he is not actively misled are "singularly unappetizing" (Prosser, Law of Torts §106, at 696 [4th ed. 1971]). Where, as here, the seller not only takes unfair advantage of the buyer's ignorance but has created and perpetuated a condition about which he is unlikely to even inquire, enforcement of the contract (in whole or in part) is offensive to the court's sense of equity. Application of the remedy of rescission, within the bounds of the narrow exception to the doctrine of caveat emptor set forth herein, is entirely appropriate to relieve the unwitting purchaser from the consequences of a most unnatural bargain.

Accordingly, the judgment of the Supreme Court, New York County (Edward H. Lehner, J.), entered April 9, 1990, which dismissed the complaint pursuant to CPLR 3211(a)(7), should be modified, on the law and the facts and in the exercise of discretion, and the first cause of action seeking rescission of the contract reinstated, without costs.

Judgment, Supreme Court, New York County (Edward H. Lehner, J.), entered on April 9, 1990, modified, on the law and the facts and in the exercise of discretion, and the first cause of action seeking rescission of the contract reinstated, without costs.

All concur except MILONAS, J.P. and SMITH, J., who dissent in an opinion by SMITH, J.

SMITH, Justice (dissenting).

I would affirm the dismissal of the complaint by the motion court.

Plaintiff seeks to rescind his contract to purchase defendant Ackley's residential property and recover his down payment. Plaintiff alleges that

Ackley and her real estate broker, defendant Ellis Realty, made material misrepresentations of the property in that they failed to disclose that Ackley believed that the house was haunted by poltergeists. Moreover, Ackley shared this belief with her community and the general public through articles published in Readers' Digest (1977) and the local newspaper (1982). In November 1989, approximately two months after the parties entered into the contract of sale but subsequent to the scheduled October 2, 1989, closing, the house was included in a five-house walking tour and again described in the local newspaper as being haunted.

Prior to closing, plaintiff learned of this reputation and unsuccessfully sought to rescind the $650,000 contract of sale and obtain return of his $32,500 down payment without resort to litigation. The plaintiff then commenced this action for that relief and alleged that he would not have entered into the contract had he been so advised and that as a result of the alleged poltergeist activity, the market value and resaleability of the property was greatly diminished. Defendant Ackley has counter-claimed for specific performance.

"It is settled law in New York that the seller of real property is under no duty to speak when the parties deal at arm's length. The mere silence of the seller, without some act or conduct which deceived the purchaser, does not amount to a concealment that is actionable as a fraud (see Perin v. Mardine Realty Co., Inc., 5 A.D.2d 685, 168 N.Y.S.2d 647, aff'd., 6 N.Y.2d 920, 190 N.Y.S.2d 995, 161 N.E.2d 210; Moser v. Spizzirro, 31 A.D.2d 537, 295 N.Y.S.2d 188, aff'd., 25 N.Y.2d 941, 305 N.Y.S.2d 153, 252 N.E.2d 632). The buyer has the duty to satisfy himself as to the quality of his bargain pursuant to the doctrine of caveat emptor, which in New York State still applies to real estate transactions." London v. Courduff, 141 A.D.2d 803, 804, 529 N.Y.S.2d 874, app. dism'd., 73 N.Y.2d 809, 537 N.Y.S.2d 494, 534 N.E.2d 332.

The parties herein were represented by counsel and dealt at arm's length. This is evidenced by the contract of sale which, inter alia, contained various riders and a specific provision that all prior understandings and agreements between the parties were merged into the contract, that the contract completely expressed their full agreement and that neither had relied upon any statement by anyone else not set forth in the contract. There is no allegation that defendants, by some specific act, other than the failure to speak, deceived the plaintiff. Nevertheless, a cause of action may be sufficiently stated where there is a confidential or fiduciary relationship creating a duty to disclose and there was a failure to disclose a material fact, calculated to induce a false belief. County of Westchester v. Welton Becket Assoc., 102 A.D.2d 34, 50-51, 478 N.Y.S.2d 305, aff'd., 66 N.Y.2d 642, 495 N.Y.S.2d 364, 485 N.E.2d 1029. However, plaintiff herein has not alleged and there is no basis for concluding that a confidential or fiduciary relationship existed between these parties to an arm's length transaction such as to give rise to a duty to disclose. In addition, there is no allegation that defendants thwarted plaintiff's efforts to fulfill his responsibilities fixed by the doctrine of caveat emptor. See London v. Courduff, supra, 141 A.D.2d at 804, 529 N.Y.S.2d 874.

Finally, if the doctrine of caveat emptor is to be discarded, it should be for a reason more substantive than a poltergeist. The existence of a poltergeist is no more binding upon the defendants than it is upon this court.

Based upon the foregoing, the motion court properly dismissed the complaint.

b.   Implied Warranty

In the sale of new homes in most American states, the doctrine of caveat emptor has been largely replaced and buyers are protected by implied warranties of fitness and habitability. This is a relatively new doctrine in the United States for the sale of homes, first appearing in the late 1950s and steadily spreading ever since; its rate of adoption has been particularly rapid for a new real property concept that is largely the creation of judicial case law. Implied warranty doctrine as it relates to housing sales is still evolving and there is a question as to how far it will be extended — whether it will become widely applicable to used home purchases, for example — and what defenses to implied warranty claims will be available to builder-vendors.

RICHARDS v. POWERCRAFT HOMES, INC.

139 Ariz. 242, 678 P.2d 427 (1984)

GORDON, Vice C. J. Each of the several individually named plaintiffs purchased homes in the Indian Hills subdivision near Casa Grande, Arizona at varying times during 1975, 1976, and 1977. The houses had been built by defendant Powercraft Homes beginning in 1974. Plaintiffs Woodward, Fillion, Schaar, and Grant purchased their homes directly from Powercraft while plaintiffs Richards, Farina, and White bought repossessed homes from Farmers Home Administration. After occupying the houses, each plaintiff discovered numerous defects. The defects included, inter alia, faulty water pipes, improperly leveled yards that resulted in pooling and flooding with any rain, cracking of the interior and exterior walls, separation of the floors from the walls, separation of sidewalks, driveways, and carports from the houses, and doors and windows which were stuck closed or which could not be locked because of misalignment. Powercraft was notified of many of these defects and attempted some repairs. The repairs in most cases provided only temporary or partial relief from the problems.

In the spring of 1978, each of the plaintiffs filed a complaint with the

Arizona Registrar of Contractors. The Registrar found that Powercraft had failed to follow certain plans and specifications in the building of each home and that it had failed to properly compact the soil beneath each house before building commenced. Powercraft's contractor's license was revoked on December 6, 1978.

Plaintiffs filed suit against Powercraft on August 17, 1979 alleging violation of the Consumer Fraud Act, A.R.S. §44-1521 et seq., and breach of the implied warranty that houses be habitable and constructed in a workmanlike manner. A jury awarded the plaintiffs $210,000 in compensatory and punitive damages. Powercraft appealed; the Court of Appeals affirmed in part and reversed in part. Richards v. Powercraft Homes, Inc., 139 Ariz. 264, 678 P.2d 449 (App. 1983). The Court of Appeals ordered the consumer fraud count dismissed, the punitive damage award vacated, and the verdicts in favor of plaintiffs Richards, Farina, and White set aside. The plaintiffs petitioned this Court to review the Court of Appeal's opinion. We have jurisdiction pursuant to Ariz. Const. art. 6, §5(3) and Ariz. R. Civ. App. P.23. While we approve the Court of Appeal's decision regarding the consumer fraud claim and the punitive damages, we vacate that portion of the Court of Appeal's decision regarding the verdicts of plaintiffs Richards, Farina, and White. The jury verdict in favor of those three plaintiffs against defendant Powercraft for the breach of the implied warranty of habitability is reinstated for the reasons set forth below.

In setting aside the verdicts in favor of Richards, Farina, and White, the Court of Appeals held that "there must be privity to maintain an action for breach of the implied warranty of workmanship and habitability," *Richards,* supra, 139 Ariz. at 266-267, 678 P.2d at 451-452. One basis cited for that holding was this Court's decision in Flory v. Silvercrest Industries, Inc., 129 Ariz. 574, 633 P.2d 383 (1981). In *Flory,* we held that warranties implied pursuant to A.R.S. §44-2331 (the Arizona version of U.C.C. §2-314(2)) require privity. We specifically stated:

> It is important to note that what we have said herein regarding the requirement of privity to recover for breach of warranty under the Uniform Commercial Code is limited to those actions.

Id. at 579, 633 P.2d at 388. In the instant case, the warranty at issue is not implied pursuant to A.R.S. §44-2331.[1] Rather, it is imposed by law. In Columbia Western Corp. v. Vela, 122 Ariz. 28, 592 P.2d 1294 (App. 1979), builder-vendors of new homes were held to impliedly warrant that construction has been done in a workmanlike manner and that the structure is

---

1. Article 2 of the Uniform Commercial Code, A.R.S. §44-2301 et seq., applies only to the sale of "goods" as that word is defined in §§44-2305 and -2307. Sales of realty, and structures affixed thereto, are not within the purview of that definition. Anderson, 1 Uniform Commercial Code, §2-105:32 at 572 (3d ed. 1981).

habitable. The issue before us now is whether this implied warranty extends to subsequent buyers of the homes.[2]

The courts of several states have confronted this issue. Many of those courts have refused to extend the implied warranty of habitability to remote purchasers or to those not in privity with the builder-vendor. See, e.g., H.B. Bolas Enterprises, Inc. v. Zarlengo, 156 Colo. 530, 400 P.2d 447 (1965); Coburn v. Lenox Homes, Inc., 173 Conn. 567, 378 A.2d 599 (1977); Strathmore Riverside Villas Condominium Assn., Inc. v. Paver Development Corp., 369 So. 2d 971 (Fla. App. 1979); Oliver v. City Builders, Inc., 303 So. 2d 466 (Miss. 1974); John H. Armbruster & Co. v. Hayden Company-Builder Developer, Inc., 622 S.W.2d 704 (Mo. App. 1981); Herz v. Thornwood Acres "D," Inc., 86 Misc. 2d 53, 381 N.Y.S.2d 761 (Justice Ct. 1976), aff'd, 91 Misc. 2d 130, 397 N.Y.S.2d 358 (App. Term. 1977); Brown v. Fowler, 279 N.W.2d 907 (S.D. 1979). Others, however, have rejected the imposition of a privity requirement and have allowed remote purchasers to maintain a cause of action against a builder-vendor for breach of the implied warranty of habitability. See, e.g., Blagg v. Fred Hunt Co. Inc., 272 Ark. 185, 612 S.W.2d 321 (1981); Redarowicz v. Ohlendorf, 92 Ill. 2d 171, 65 Ill. Dec. 411, 441 N.E.2d 324 (1982); Barnes v. Mac Brown & Co., Inc., 264 Ind. 227, 342 N.E.2d 619 (1976); Hermes v. Staiano, 181 N.J. Super. 424, 437 A.2d 925 (Law Div. 1981); McMillan v. Brune-Harpenau-Torbeck Builders, Inc., 8 Ohio St. 3d 3, 455 N.E.2d 1276 (1983); Elden v. Simmons, 631 P.2d 739 (Okl. 1981); Terlinde v. Neely, 275 S.C. 395, 271 S.E.2d 768 (1980); Gupta v. Ritter Homes, Inc., 646 S.W.2d 168 (Tex. 1983); Moxley v. Laramie Builders, Inc., 600 P.2d 733 (Wyo. 1979). We find the latter group of cases to be more in line with the public policy of this state and hold that privity is not required to maintain an action for breach of the implied warranty of workmanship and habitability.

We agree with the persuasive comments of the Wyoming Supreme Court in *Moxley*, supra, that:

> [t]he purpose of a warranty is to protect innocent purchasers and hold builders accountable for their work. With that object in mind, any reasoning which would arbitrarily interpose a first buyer as an obstruction to someone equally deserving of recovery is incomprehensible.

600 P.2d at 736. In addition, such reasoning might encourage sham first sales to insulate builders from liability.

Since *Columbia Western*, an original homebuyer in this state has been able to rely on the builder-vendor's implied warranty. The same policy considerations that led to that decision — that house-building is frequently undertaken on a large scale, that builders hold themselves out as skilled

---

2. This issue is considered in a recent article, Comment, Implied Warranties in New Homes and Their Extension to Subsequent Purchasers in Arizona, 1983 Ariz. St. L.J. 113 (1983).

in the profession, that modern construction is complex and regulated by many governmental codes, and that homebuyers are generally not skilled or knowledgeable in construction, plumbing, or electrical requirements and practices — are equally applicable to subsequent homebuyers. Also, we note that the character of our society is such that people and families are increasingly mobile. Home builders should anticipate that the houses they construct will eventually, and perhaps frequently, change ownership. The effect of latent defects will be just as catastrophic on a subsequent owner as on an original buyer and the builder will be just as unable to justify improper or substandard work. Because the builder-vendor is in a better position than a subsequent owner to prevent occurrence of major problems, the costs of poor workmanship should be his to bear.

The implied warranty of habitability and proper workmanship is not unlimited. It does not force the builder-vendor to "act as an insurer for subsequent vendees" as the Court of Appeals feared, *Richards,* supra, 139 Ariz. at 267, 678 P.2d at 452. It is limited to latent defects which become manifest after the subsequent owner's purchase and which were not discoverable had a reasonable inspection of the structure been made prior to purchase. We adopt the standard set forth by the Indiana Supreme Court in *Barnes,* supra.

> The standard to be applied in determining whether or not there has been a breach of warranty is one of reasonableness in light of surrounding circumstances. The age of a home, its maintenance, the use to which it has been put, are but a few factors entering into this factual determination at trial.

264 Ind. at 229, 342 N.E.2d at 621. The burden is on the subsequent owner to show that the defect had its origin and cause in the builder-vendor and that the suit was brought within the appropriate statute of limitations. Defenses are, of course, available. The builder-vendor can demonstrate that the defects are not attributable to him, that they are the result of age or ordinary wear and tear, or that previous owners have made substantial changes.

In the present case, the plaintiffs met their burden and proved that the defect had its origin and cause in Powercraft. There was no indication that the original owners substantially changed the structure of the homes. The cracking of the exterior and interior walls, the separation of the floors from the walls, and the separation of the sidewalks, driveways, and carports from the homes were due to improper compacting done by Powercraft prior to building the houses coupled with an apparent systematic lack of reinforcement in the floors, walls, ceilings, and roofs of the houses. Such improper compaction and lack of structural reinforcement could not have been determined from a reasonable inspection prior to purchase. Each of the plaintiffs moved into their homes before the end of 1977. The defects became manifest only after extraordinarily heavy rains in early 1978. Therefore, all the plaintiffs, whether or not in privity with Powercraft, are entitled to the jury verdicts rendered in their favor.

The decision of the Court of Appeals that the consumer fraud count be dismissed and that the punitive damage award be vacated is approved; the decision of the Court of Appeals that the verdicts in favor of plaintiffs Richards, Farina, and White be set aside is vacated; the verdicts in favor of plaintiffs are affirmed in all other respects. The case is remanded for further proceedings not inconsistent with this opinion.

NOTES AND QUESTIONS

1. **Contract privity.** Warranties normally are indicative of a contract relationship in which there is privity between obligor and obligee. Is the court in *Richards* justified in disregarding established contract doctrine by extending implied warranty protection to remote purchasers with whom the obligor is not in contractual privity? Should common law logic be violated in this way? Would not tortious responsibility of the builder-vendor or negligence adequately further the public policy of the state that the *Richards* opinion favors? Note that it is reasonably foreseeable that a high percentage of new homes will be resold in the relatively near future and, of course, that subsequent buyers will be adversely affected by defects resulting from negligent construction by the builder-vendor.

2. **Statutory warranty.** In 1988, a statute was passed in New York providing for implied warranties that new homes sold are free of latent defects. New York Gen. Bus. §§777-777a (McKinney Supp. 1992). The statute limits the time span of the warranties but gives subsequent purchasers remedies for warranty breach. In part, the New York act states:

§777

6. "Owner" means the first person to whom the home is sold and, during the unexpired portion of the warranty period, each successor in title to the home and any mortgagee in possession. Owner does not include the builder of the home or any firm under common control of the builder.

§777-a

. . . a housing merchant implied warranty is implied in the contract or agreement for the sale of a new home and shall survive the passing of title. A housing merchant implied warranty shall mean that:

a. one year from and after the warranty date the home will be free from defects due to a failure to have been constructed in a skillful manner;

b. two years from and after the warranty date the plumbing, electrical, heating, cooling and ventilation systems of the home will be free from defects due to a failure by the builder to have installed such systems in a skillful manner; and

c. six years from and after the warranty date the home will be free from material defects.

2. Unless the contract or agreement by its terms clearly evidences a different intention of the seller, a housing merchant implied warranty does not extend to:

a. any defect that does not constitute (i) defective workmanship by the builder or by an agent, employee or subcontractor of the builder, (ii) defective materials supplied by the builder or by an agent, employee or subcontractor of the builder, or (iii) defective design provided by a design professional retained exclusively by the builder; . . . or

b. any patent defect which an examination ought in the circumstances to have revealed, when the buyer before taking title or accepting construction as complete has examined the home as fully as the buyer desired, or has refused to examine the home. . . .

4. An action for damages or other relief caused by the breach of a housing merchant implied warranty may be commenced prior to the expiration of one year after the applicable warranty period, as described in subdivision one of this section, or within four years after the warranty date, whichever is later. . . . The measure of damages shall be the reasonable cost of repair or replacement and property damage to the home proximately caused by the breach of warranty, not to exceed the replacement cost of the home exclusive of the value of the land, unless the court finds that, under the circumstances, the diminution in value of the home caused by the defect is a more equitable measure of damages.

On the New York statute, see Note, New York's Implied Merchant Warranty for the Sale of New Homes: A Reasonable Extension to Reach Initial Owners?, 1990 Colum. Bus. L. Rev. 373; and Note, The New York Housing Merchant Warranty Statute: Analysis and Proposals, 75 Cornell L. Rev. 754 (1990).

Examples of other statutes providing for statutorily created implied warranties by builders protecting home purchasers are Minn. Stat. Ann. §§327A.01 and .02 (West 1996); and N.J. Stat. Ann. §§46:38B-2 and 4 (West 1996).

3. **Construction lender liability.** Construction lenders run a risk of being held liable under implied warranties of quality if the lenders are co-joint venturers with builders or owners and share ownership or profits and losses. There is some authority holding construction lenders who are not co-joint venturers liable in negligence for defectively built homes. The lead case for such lender liability, with little subsequent support, is Connor v. Great Western Sav. & Loan Assn., 60 Cal. 2d 850, 73 Cal. Rptr. 369, 447 P.2d 609 (1968). In the *Connor* case, the majority took the position that

since the developers' lender had sufficient power over the construction process through control over loan funds, it had a duty to exercise reasonable care to prevent the construction and sale of seriously defective homes to home buyers. The *Connor* case was a 4-3 decision and there were strong dissents. For an extended discussion of the case and its impact, see 7 Powell on Real Property §938.10 (1991). Shortly after the *Connor* case was decided, the California legislature passed a statute limiting lender liability, Cal. Civ. Code §3434 (West 1970):

> A lender who makes a loan of money, the proceeds of which are used or may be used by the borrower to finance the design, manufacture, construction, repair, modification or improvement of real or personal property for sale or lease to others, shall not be held liable to third persons for any loss or damage occasioned by any defect in the real or personal property so designed, manufactured, constructed, repaired, modified or improved or for any loss or damage resulting from the failure of the borrower to use due care in the design, manufacture, construction, repair, modification or improvement of such real or personal property, unless such loss or damage is a result of an act of the lender outside the scope of the activities of a lender of money or unless the lender has been a party to misrepresentations with respect to such real or personal property.

4.   **Waiver and disclaimer.** Can implied warranties be waived by disclaimer clauses in agreements between home buyers and builder-vendors? Some courts have said yes if the waiver language is clear and free from doubt. G-W-L, Inc. v. Robichaux, 643 S.W.2d 392 (Tex. 1982), held that the following language constituted an effective waiver: "no . . . warranties, express or implied, in addition to said written instruments." It "could not be clearer," the Texas Supreme Court said, and added, "The parties to a contract have an obligation to protect themselves by reading what they sign." 643 S.W.2d at 393. But another court has insisted that for a valid disclaimer the buyer actually must have known of the waiver when the contract was entered into, and boilerplate clauses, however worded, are ineffective for that purpose. Crowder v. Vandendeale, 564 S.W.2d 879, 881 (Mo. 1978). Also, many courts will strictly construe disclaimer clauses against the builder-vendor. E.g., Petersen v. Hubschman Constr. Co., Inc., 76 Ill. 2d 31, 43, 389 N.E.2d 1154, 1159 (1979). In Nastri v. Wood Bros. Homes, Inc., 142 Ariz. 439, 690 P.2d 158 (Ariz. App. 1984), a disclaimer clause in an original purchaser's agreement with builder was held not to preclude an implied warranty action against the builder by a subsequent purchaser for latent construction defects. The *Nastri* court considered the attempted disclaimer void as to an innocent subsequent purchaser. There obviously is a strong but not universal tendency for courts to take a proconsumer approach to disclaimer clauses in home sale agreements, home buyers being considered consumers acquiring what are to them very expensive items, so meriting special protection.

5.   **"As is" provision.** If an agreement for sale of an interest in commercial real property includes an "as is" clause, in effect a form of disclaimer, does this eliminate seller responsibility for physical defects in the property? In PBS Coals, Inc. v. Burnham Coal Co., 558 A.2d 562 (Pa. Super. 1989), the transferee of coal mining properties asserted that the cost of correcting polluted water drainage from the mine site should be borne by the transferor. Neither buyer nor seller was aware of the pollution situation when the transfer agreement was entered into. The sale agreement provided that the transferee would accept the properties "as is." The court held that the as is clause put the buyer on notice that there may be liabilities attendant to the purchase and that the as is language prevented any implied warranties from attaching. "While the harshness of placing the risk of loss in such a situation on an inexperienced consumer has sometimes been avoided by the courts, the facts of this case do not present us with a basis of relieving PBS [the transferee] of the burden here. The individuals who signed this agreement are seasoned businessmen who can safely be presumed to be familiar with terms of common usage in business transactions." 558 A.2d at 564. Would it have made a difference to the Pennsylvania court if the seller was aware of the condition at the time the contract was entered into but the buyer was not?

The result in *PBS Coals* has been questioned, the argument being advanced that environmental protection issues are so important that a broader range of criteria other than the commercial nature of a transaction should be considered in determining whether or not as is clauses shift responsibility for environmental risks. See Note, An "As Is" Provision in a Commercial Property Contract: Should It Be Left As Is When Assessing Liability for Environmental Torts?, 51 U. Pitt. L. Rev. 995 (1990).

6.   **Abnormally dangerous activity.** In T&E Industries v. Safety Light Corp., 123 N.J. 371, 587 A.2d 1249 (1991), it was held that a purchaser of a radium-contaminated industrial site could recover clean-up costs, and maintenance costs until clean up, from a remote predecessor in title that had polluted the site. Plaintiff was unaware of the pollution or pollution risk at the time of purchase. The current property owner, it was held, could successfully assert an action based on strict liability for abnormally dangerous activity. The doctrine of caveat emptor would not apply to bar recovery. And by merely signing an "as is" contract, a purchaser ignorant of the abnormally dangerous condition would not assume risks from that condition, the court said.

7.   **Other defenses.** In addition to disclaimer clauses, other defenses that may be successfully raised against a home buyer's assertion of implied warranty breaches include statutes of limitations, limited express warranties, reasonable care shown in construction, and proof that defects are so minor as not to be covered by the warranty. These defenses are discussed in Note, Implied Warranties in New Home Sales — Is the Seller Defenseless?, 35 S.C.L. Rev. 469 (1984).

c.   Express Warranty

Many contracts for the sale of real property contain express warranties as to the quality of the premises being sold. However, ambiguity in warranty terms often leads to conflict and litigation, even when the contract is in writing. Recovery on asserted oral warranties may be especially difficult, as the oral statements relied upon may be considered merely expressions of opinion, not promises; and if promises, they may be unenforceable under the Statute of Frauds.

GARRIFFA v. TAYLOR

675 P.2d 1284 (Wyo. 1984)

CARDINE, J. This is an appeal from an action to recover damages for breach of an express warranty. Judgment was entered in favor of plaintiffs-appellees in the amount of $1,650, the cost of installing a septic tank, plus court costs, for a total judgment of $1,692.75.

We will reverse.

FACTS

The appellants sold a house to the appellees. Approximately nineteen months after appellees had moved into the house, they replaced the septic tank and sent the bill for the cost of replacement to appellants with a request for payment. Appellants refused payment and this suit was initiated.

Appellants had lived in the house for five years prior to the time of sale. Prior to that time, appellant, Marla Garriffa, had lived in the house for ten years with her parents, the previous owners. The house was at least forty years old. The preprinted real estate listing form had a category entitled sewerage. Above this the real estate agent had typed "Septic." These forms are prepared from information provided by the sellers. While the appellees were looking at the property, Mrs. Taylor asked Mrs. Garriffa where the septic tank was located. Mrs. Garriffa indicated that the tank was located north of the house. Mrs. Taylor also asked Mrs. Garriffa if the tank had been pumped; Mrs. Garriffa replied that they had not pumped the tank but that they had used chemicals to keep the system working properly. Appellees testified that there were some problems with the sewerage system several months after they moved into the house, but nothing was done.

Nineteen months after taking possession and occupying the house, the appellees contacted a septic tank sales and service company to pump the tank. When they dug into the area north of the house, they did not find a septic tank. However, they found two pipes running out of the house. At the end of the pipes appellees testified that there was an accumulation of rocks, dirt, and debris. The appellees then employed a contractor who installed a new septic tank. Appellees did not notify appellants concerning any of this until after the installation of the septic tank. They then forwarded them the bill, which appellants refused to pay. Appellees contend that there was an express warranty by the appellants that the property had a septic sewer system and that this warranty was breached because no septic system existed. Therefore, they contend that appellants are liable for the cost of installing the septic tank.

Appellants raised several issues for review, however, we need only address one to dispose of this case — whether or not there was an express promise or warranty enforceable against the appellants regarding the existence and durability of a septic system.

Contracts for the sale and purchase of land may include an express warranty on the sellers' part as to the physical quality or condition of the property.

> . . . It has been held that such an express warranty of quality is governed by the common law principles applicable to warranties of quality in the sale of goods. . . . 77 Am. Jur. 2d Vendor and Purchaser §336.

An express warranty is created by any affirmation of fact made by the seller to the buyer which relates to the goods and becomes a part of the basis of the bargain. 67 Am. Jur. 2d Sales §442. The primary question is whether there were any affirmations of fact or promises which amounted to an express warranty or whether the representations were merely opinions. General Supply and Equipment Co., Inc. v. Phillips, Tex. Civ. App., 490 S.W.2d 913 (1972). The standard generally used is that:

> . . . [W]hen a seller asserts a fact of which the buyer is ignorant, and the buyer relies on the assertion, the seller makes an express warranty; but, when the seller merely states his opinion or his judgment upon a matter of which the seller has no special knowledge, . . . then the seller's statement does not constitute an express warranty. . . . Lovington Cattle Feeders, Inc. v. Abbott Lab., 97 N.M. 564, 642, P.2d 167, 170 (1982). See also, Scovil v. Chilcoat, Okl., 424 P.2d 87 (1967).

In order for an express warranty to exist, there must be some positive and unequivocal statement concerning the thing sold which is relied upon by the buyer and which is understood to be an assertion concerning the items sold and not an opinion. Maupin v. Nutrena Mills, Inc., Okl., 385 P.2d 504 (1963). A representation which expresses the seller's opinion, belief, judgment, or estimate does not constitute an express warranty. Scheirman v. Coulter, Okl., 624 P.2d 70 (1980). It is important to consider whether the seller asserts a fact about which the buyer is ignorant or whether he merely states an opinion or judgment upon a matter of which the seller has no special knowledge and upon which the buyer might be expected to have an opinion or to exercise his own judgment. Carpenter v. Alberto Culver Co., 28 Mich. App. 399, 184 N.W.2d 547 (1970). All the circumstances surrounding a sale are to be considered in determining whether there was an express warranty or merely an expression of opinion. Lovington Cattle Feeders, Inc. v. Abbott Lab, supra; Price Brothers Co. v. Philadelphia Gear Corp. 649 F.2d 416 (6th Cir. 1981), *cert. denied,* 454 U.S. 1099.

The question of whether an express warranty exists is for the trier of fact. Scheirman v. Coulter, supra. In the absence of special findings of facts, the reviewing court must consider that the judgment carries with it every finding of fact which is supported by the evidence. Hendrickson v. Heinze, Wyo., 541 P.2d 1133, 1135 (1975). However, where nonconflicting evidence admits of only one conclusion, a contrary conclusion cannot stand. Wyoming Farm Bureau Mutual Ins. Co. v. May, Wyo., 434 P.2d 507 (1967).

In this case there is not a conflict in evidence; therefore, we must look at the undisputed facts in relation to the requirements necessary for an express warranty. There was uncontradicted testimony by the real estate agent that the phrase, "Septic" on the real estate listing agreement is interpreted as meaning that it does not have city sewer, "[i]t has some sort of a septic system." There was also testimony by appellee that appellant had stated that there was a septic system located north of the house and that they had not had any difficulty with the system. There was no testimony presented that they had had problems with the system, knew of any present difficulties, or that they had information which they did not disclose. Appellee testified concerning the septic system:

"Q. (*By Mr. Tate*) You said on your direct examination you didn't look at the system when you bought it; is that correct?
"A.   We looked at what we could see.
"Q.   You can't look at a sewage system when you buy an old house.
"A.   That's true.
"Q.   It would be pretty impractical.
"A.   That's right.
"Q.   And if the Garriffas never dug that system up, they really wouldn't know what was under there themselves either.
"A.   They wouldn't know what was under the ground, no."

We do not find that these statements were sufficient to form an express warranty concerning the septic sewerage system. The house was at least forty years old. Appellants stated that they had never had any problem with the septic system and that the tank had not been pumped. There was no testimony contradicting these statements. The statements were very general. They related to appellants' experience in the house. Appellants were not dealers of septic systems, nor were they people who had a special knowledge about these matters. Guess v. Lorenz, Mo. App., 612 S.W.2d 831

(1981). Representations of fact which are capable of determination are warranties, but the mere expression of an opinion is not. Young & Cooper, Inc. v. Vestring, 214 Kan. 311, 521 P.2d 281 (1974).

We find that these statements merely expressed the sellers' opinions and beliefs concerning the septic system and did not constitute an express warranty. If both parties are free from fault, there is no compelling reason to require the seller, instead of the purchaser, to bear the loss. Cook v. Salishan Properties, Inc., 279 Or. 333, 569 P.2d 1033 (1977). Appellees purchased a forty-year-old house not connected to the city sewer. Sewage was moved from the house by a septic system installed forty years earlier. What kind of system was installed forty years earlier we do not know. We do know that these systems do not last forever. When, more than a year after purchase of the house, this system did not function as expected, appellees, without demand or notice to appellants, employed a contractor of their choice and installed a new septic tank. They now ask that appellants be required to pay for that new septic tank. That was not their bargain. Because appellants' statements did not constitute an express warranty, we will reverse with instructions to the trial court to enter a judgment in accordance with this opinion.

P.B.R. ENTERPRISES v. PERREN

243 Ga. 280, 253 S.E.2d 765 (1979)

PER CURIAM. In this case the appellees, as purchasers of a house and grantors of a subordinate deed to secure debt, sued the appellants, sellers-grantees. The complaint alleged substantially that the house had been still under construction and that the defendants had orally agreed, at the time of closing and both prior and subsequent thereto, to make the necessary repairs and changes and to complete the construction; that, unknown to the plaintiffs at that time, there were certain latent, structural defects in the construction of the house, of which the defendants failed to advise the plaintiffs; that the defendants orally agreed that no payment would be due them under their deed to secure debt until the orally promised repairs and work were performed; that the defendants have failed to comply with the plaintiffs' demands for completion of the work; that the defendants have commended advertising for a foreclosure of their second mortgage, which would result in the plaintiffs' loss of their home, their equity therein, their good credit rating, and their adequate remedy at law; that the plaintiffs had had to make numerous emergency repairs to the house because of the defendants' failure to do the promised work; that the defendants had made wilful misrepresentations of material facts as to the structural soundness of the house and had failed to abide by a one-year warranty allegedly granted to the plaintiffs. The prayers for relief were for a temporary injunction against the impending foreclosure; money damages for the cost of repairing the alleged structural defects; a set-off of the sun due under the mortgage (in the original amount of the principal) against the amount for the repairs; and punitive damages, interest and costs.

The trial judge, after a hearing, overruled the defendants' motions for directed verdict and to dismiss, and granted the temporary injunction, contingent upon the plaintiffs' payment into the registry of the court of the sum due under the defendants' mortgage and the monthly installments thereon until further order of the court. The defendants appeal. *Held:*

1. Subject to certain exceptions, the doctrine of caveat emptor applies to the sale of realty, there are no implied warranties as to the physical condition of the property sold, the purchaser buys at his own risk, and the purchaser cannot have an abatement of the purchase price on account of the seller's misrepresentations unless he exercised ordinary diligence to discover the falsity of the representations. Collier v. Sinkoe, 135 Ga. App. 732(2, 3), 218 S.E.2d 910 (1975) and cits.

2. The plaintiffs relied on three alleged oral contracts with the defendant sellers, i.e., that there was a one-year warranty on the house, that the sellers would repair all defects in the house, and that the sellers would forbear to foreclose their second mortgage until such promised repairs and completion of construction were made. As far as the record discloses, none of these promises was reduced to writing in the sales contract, the warranty deed, the deed to secure debt, or elsewhere. "Both this court and the Court of Appeals have followed the general rule that antecedent sales contracts covering the purchase and sale of real property merge in a subsequent deed involving the same property. Thus, where in a contract for sale of land the parties execute a preliminary sales contract and subsequently reduce that contract to a finality evidenced by a deed to secure debt, the terms of the preliminary contract, where not otherwise reserved, are merged into the deed, and those terms, conditions or recitals contained in the preliminary sales contract which are not included in the deed are considered as eliminated, abandoned or discarded." Jordan v. Flynt, 240 Ga. 359, 362, 240 S.E.2d 858, 861 (1977). Thus, the oral promises of a one-year warranty and a forbearance to foreclose, which were included in neither the sales contract not in either of the deeds, were unenforceable.

3. As to the promise for effecting completions and repairs on the house after the delivery of possession of the property and the warranty deed, such promises generally may be found to have survived the closing and not merged in the deed. Cullens v. Woodruff, 137 Ga. App. 262(1), 223 S.E.2d 293 (1976) and cits. Again, however, in order for such promise to survive the closing and not merge in the deed, it must have been included in the sales contract, which it was not in the case sub judice. The plaintiffs did not seek rescission based on the vendor's misrepresentations, and "no remedy is generally available for any breach by the vendor of any promise

contained in the contract but *omitted in the deed.*" Walton v. Petty, 107 Ga. App. 753, 756, 131 S.E.2d 655 (1963).

4. The complaint did allege, however, that, unknown to the plaintiffs at the time of closing and prior and subsequent thereto, there were certain latent structural defects in the construction of the house, of which the defendants failed to advise the plaintiffs. In Wilhite v. Mays, 140 Ga. App. 816, 813(3), 232 S.E.2d 141, 143 (1976),[1] the Court of Appeals held that "in cases of passive concealment by the seller of defective realty, we find there to be an exception to the rule of caveat emptor, which exception is applicable to the instant case. That exception places upon the seller a duty to disclose in situations where he or she has special knowledge not apparent to the buyer and is aware that the buyer is acting under a misapprehension as to facts which would be important to the buyer and would probably affect its decision. Prosser, Law of Torts 697-698 (4th ed. 1971); Keeton, Fraud — Concealment and Non-Disclosure, 15 Tex. L. Rev. 1, 37-39 (1936). See Rothstein v. Janss Inv. Corp., 45 Cal. App. 2d 64, 113 P.2d 465 (1941) (improperly filled ground); Kaze v. Compton, 283 S.W.2d 204 (Ky. 1955) (drain under house causing yard to flood); Williams v. Benson, 3 Mich. App. 9, 141 N.W.2d 650 (1966) (termites); Brooks v. Ervin Construction Co., 253 N.C. 214, 116 S.E.2d 454 (1960) (house located on improperly filled ground)." Although some of the alleged defects were made known to the purchasers by the vendors' oral promises to repair, and other defects may have been discoverable by the purchasers' exercise of reasonable diligence to investigate and inspect, there remains the possibility that others of the defects come within the exception created or recognized by the Court of Appeals and approved by this court in Wilhite v. Mays, supra.

5. However, we hold that the trial court erred in granting the temporary injunction. "This state has long recognized the equitable maxim that '[h]e who would have equity must do equity, and give effect to all equitable rights in the other party respecting the subject-matter of the suit.' Code Ann. §37-104. Pursuant to this basic principle of equity, this court has held that 'a borrower who has executed a deed to secure debt is not entitled to an injunction against a sale of the property under a power in the deed, unless he first pays or tenders to the creditor the amount admittedly due." Wright v. Intercounty Properties, 238 Ga. 492, 233 S.E.2d 160 (1977). *Accord,* Mickel v. Pickett, 241 Ga. 528(9), 247 S.E.2d 82 (1978). In this case, the plaintiffs made no tender of the amount due. The fact that the trial judge, as a condition for the grant of the temporary injunction, required payment into the registry of the court of the installments due under the defendants' mortgage and the monthly installments due thereon until further order of the court does not constitute tender to the defendants.

Judgment reversed.

---

1. *Affirmed,* Wilhite v. Mays, 239 Ga. 31, 235 S.E.2d 532 (1977).

NOTES AND QUESTIONS

1. **Opinion or warranty?** In a case involving representations by sellers that filled-in land being sold was fit for buyer's proposed restaurant building, the court in Stanford v. Owens, 46 N.C. App. 388, 265 S.E.2d 617 (1980), held the statements to be opinions not rising to the level of affirmations of fact or promise so required for an express warranty. In so holding, the court, at 265 S.E.2d 621, quotes as follows from an earlier North Carolina case:

> Assertions concerning the value of property which is the subject of a contract of sale, or in regard to its qualities and characteristics, are the usual and ordinary means adopted by sellers to obtain a high price, and are always understood as affording to buyers no ground for omitting to make inquiries for the purpose of ascertaining the real condition of the property. Affirmations concerning the value of land or its adaptation to a particular mode of culture or the capacity of the soil to produce crops or support cattle are, after all, only expressions of opinion or estimates founded on judgment, about which honest men might well differ materially.

2. **"Oral" warranty.** In a suit involving warranties, in which the party charged had not signed the contract, it was held that conveyance of the parcel by defendant followed by plaintiff taking possession constituted sufficient performance under the doctrines of full or part performance to bar the defendant from raising the Statute of Frauds as a defense. Scribner v. O'Brien, Inc., 169 Conn. 389, 403, 363 A.2d 160, 168 (1975).

3. **HOW program.** Since 1973, a substantial percentage of new home construction in the United States has been by builders participating in the Home Owners Warranty Program (HOW) sponsored and administered by the National Association of Home Builders. Under the HOW program participating builders must provide certain express warranties to buyers as to quality of work and materials. The warranties are backed by insurance paid for by the builders but the cost presumably is passed on to the buyers. A conciliation and arbitration scheme for buyers' complaints against builders is also part of the program. On the HOW program, see Reid, HOW to Insure Quality, 45 Mortgage Banking 41 (June 1985); and Note, The Home Owners Warranty Program: An Initial Analysis, 28 Stan. L. Rev. 357 (1976).

4. **Federal warranty requirement.** Federal agencies that insure or guarantee mortgage loans are directed by Congress to require warranties of quality by builders or sellers of new homes financed by these insured or guaranteed mortgage loans. 12 U.S.C. §1701j-1 (1988), applicable to HUD; and 38 U.S.C. §1805 (1988), applicable to the Veterans Administration. The warranty requirements in the two statutes are very similar. The HUD statute provides in part:

> *§1701j-1 (a)* The Secretary of Housing and Urban Development is authorized and directed to require that, in connection with any property upon which

there is located a dwelling designed principally for not more than a four-family residence and which is approved for mortgage insurance prior to the beginning of construction, the seller or builder, and such other person as may be required by the said Secretary to become warrantor, shall deliver to the purchaser or owner of such property a warranty that the dwelling is constructed in substantial conformity with the plans and specifications . . . on which the Secretary of Housing and Urban Development based his valuation of the dwelling: . . . Provided further, that such warranty shall be in addition to, and not in derogation of, all other rights and privileges which such purchaser or owner may have under any other law or instrument. . . .

5.   **Universal protection?** Should there be a requirement that all sales contracts for new housing being sold to persons who intend to live in the housing include government specified warranties of quality? If not, why not?

d.   Mortgage Default

1.   Foreclosure

WILLIAM C. PRATHER, FORECLOSURE OF THE SECURITY INTEREST

1957 Univ. Ill. L.F. 420, 427-430

METHODS OF FORECLOSURE

After a default by the borrower, the lender or his successor in interest must seek to realize upon the real property security by selling or acquiring ownership of the land, at the same time extinguishing any equitable rights belonging to the borrower. The process is called foreclosure, which in its dictionary definition means "to shut out; exclude or bar."

In the early days of English mortgage law there was no necessity for foreclosure. The courts enforced the mortgage in accordance with its written terms, and a failure of the borrower to pay his debt when due simply extinguished all of his rights in the land. Because of the gradual development of a borrower's equitable right to redeem the land at a later date, however, foreclosure became necessary to extinguish the right.

Methods of foreclosure vary greatly from state to state. In some states foreclosure is quick and cheap; in others it is a long and expensive process.

Foreclosure procedures available for use must be sought under the laws of the state where the property is situated. While the diversity of state foreclosure laws is formidable, the most prevalent methods in use are foreclosure by sale in judicial proceedings, and foreclosure by exercise of a power of sale contained in the mortgage. . . . Although in some states one method is exclusive, in many states the mortgagee may elect which method he will pursue, including an election to proceed on the note alone, on the mortgage, or on both concurrently.

Strict Foreclosure. In jurisdictions which permit its use, strict foreclosure usually is one of several remedies, although ordinarily it is confined to cases where (1) the mortgagor is insolvent, (2) the mortgaged premises are not of sufficient value to pay the debt, and (3) there are no outside creditors or encumbrancers. The process begins with a complaint or a petition to foreclose. The complaint is brought against not only the owner but all persons who may have the right to redeem, including a spouse, tenants, and junior lien holders, if any. After summons either by personal delivery, or by publication and mailing of notice where personal summons is not possible, the defendants are given the opportunity to introduce defenses such as invalidity of the mortgage, prior payment, or failure of consideration.

After hearing any defenses, the court will determine if there has been a default and if the mortgagee has the right to foreclose. A decree or judgment is then entered, setting out the amount due to the lender, and specifying a period, ordinarily from two to six months, in which the borrower may redeem by payment of the amount due. The decree provides also that if the property shall not have been redeemed within the period specified, the borrower and all persons claiming under him shall be forever barred and foreclosed. As of the time the specified period expires, the mortgagee becomes the sole owner of the property. No sale of the premises is involved.

Some courts have called strict foreclosure a harsh remedy since it transfers the property to the mortgagee without a sale, the value appearing not to be taken into account.

Foreclosure by Sale in Judicial Proceedings. Under this method, the procedure is identical with that of strict foreclosure until the point that judgment or decree is about to be entered. At this time, the procedure becomes different, due to the widespread belief that if the land is sold at a public sale it might bring more than the mortgage debt, leaving something for the borrower. Although judicial sale predominates in most parts of the country, it later will be shown that in practical operation the theory seldom works out in accordance with the original purpose.

At the time of entering the decree, the court determines the amount due to the mortgagee. The decree provides that a specified period of notice shall be given to the public that the property is to be sold at public auction. The notice, usually by newspaper publication, must include a description of the property, the time, place, and terms of the sale, and the officer designated to conduct the sale. The officer usually is a master in chancery, a sheriff, or other officer appointed or authorized by the court.

The mortgagee customarily is permitted to bid at the auction, and in practice, the mortgagee almost invariably is the only or the highest bidder. If such bids are confined to the unpaid amount of the mortgage, the mortgagee may avoid parting with any cash. The bid price is merely applied to the mortgage debt.

Upon receiving a report of the auction, the court will determine the equity and propriety of the sale, and if it approves, the officer is ordered to execute either a deed to the purchaser or, as in Illinois, a certificate of sale. If the state law does not provide statutorily for a further period in which the borrower may redeem, the purchaser at this point becomes the sole and absolute owner of the land.

Foreclosure by Exercise of Power of Sale. In a great many states, a mortgage may be foreclosed without recourse to the courts, and the usual method is that of foreclosure by exercise of a power of sale contained in the security instrument. Power of sale mortgages are used primarily because they afford a less expensive as well as a more convenient and expeditious mode of foreclosure, and the mortgagor is not required to pay the greater expenses of a regular foreclosure action.

Foreclosure by power of sale specifically must be authorized in the mortgage instrument. Such clauses spell out what shall be considered a default, and, in the event of such default, confer power on the mortgagee (or trustee in the case of a trust deed) to sell the property after public notice at public auction.

Ordinarily personal notice of the proposed sale to the borrower is necessary, but certain states permit notice by advertisement. In order to be able to bid in at his own sale, the mortgagee or trustee must have expressly provided such authorization in the mortgage instrument, otherwise he is barred from the bidding. A deed is issued by the mortgagee as conductor of the sale to the highest bidder. Almost invariably this is the mortgagee himself. Again, while the equity of redemption is cut off by the process, statutory redemption may or may not be allowed, depending upon state statutory provisions. While the purchaser at the sale obtains immediate possession in states having no period of redemption, in states allowing a redemption period the majority allow the mortgagor to remain in possession, although the statute or the mortgage may contain different stipulations as to rents. To exercise the power of sale there is no need for the mortgagee to make entry. . . .

2.　Deficiency Judgments

A real estate mortgage transaction involves the transfer of an interest in land by the mortgagor to the mortgagee as security for payment of a debt. The mortgagor has promised to pay the debt and has in addition provided the mortgagee with security to back up that promise. If the mortgagor defaults, the mortgagee generally can resort to the security through foreclosure, and if this fails to produce enough to pay the amount due, the mortgagee usually can obtain a deficiency judgment against the mortgagor for the balance still owed. Of course, if foreclosure produces more than what the mortgagor owes, the mortgagor is entitled to the excess. In case of default by the mortgagor, a mortgagee commonly may, but seldom will, sue on the debt without seeking resort to the security.

In some states deficiency judgments have been highly controversial and restrictions have been placed on mortgagees obtaining such judgments. These restrictions, many of them originating in the depression of the 1930s, reflect popular feeling that mortgage debtors who lose their homes or farms or other lands, especially in adverse economic times, have lost enough and should not be subject to further liability on the underlying debts. It is also felt that foreclosure sales frequently do not bring fair market prices, being forced sales often in depressed periods; hence their prices should not be the basis for determining deficiencies. Deficiency judgment restrictions are mostly statutory and take different forms, such as no deficiency judgment if a certain type of mortgage is foreclosed — a purchase money or nonjudicial power of sale mortgage, for example; or the deficiency may only be sought in a foreclosure proceeding; or the deficiency must be based on a separate determination of fair or reasonable value of the foreclosed property rather than on the foreclosure sale price. Antideficiency legislation varies considerably among the states, and many states have no serious deterrents to a mortgagee securing a deficiency judgment, plus accrued interest and foreclosure expenses, whenever a foreclosure sale price is insufficient to pay off the mortgage debt.

NEW YORK REAL PROPERTY ACTIONS AND PROCEEDINGS LAW

§1371 (McKinney 1996)

1. If a person who is liable to the plaintiff for the payment of the debt secured by the mortgage is made a defendant in the action, and has appeared or has been personally served with the summons, the final judgment may award payment by him of the whole residue, or so much thereof as the court may determine to be just and equitable, of the debt remaining unsatisfied, after a sale of the mortgaged property and the application of the proceeds, pursuant to the directions contained in such judgment, the amount thereof to be determined by the court as herein provided.

2. Simultaneously with the making of a motion for an order confirming the sale, provided such motion is made within ninety days after the date of the consummation of the sale by the delivery of the proper deed of conveyance to the purchaser, the party to whom such residue shall be owing may make a motion in the action for leave to enter a deficiency judgment upon notice to the party against whom such judgment is sought or the attorney who shall have appeared for such party in such action. Such notice shall be served personally or in such other manner as the court may direct. Upon such motion the court, whether or not the respondent appears, shall determine, upon affidavit or otherwise as it shall direct, the fair and reasonable market value of the mortgaged premises as of the date such premises were bid in at auction or such nearest earlier date as there shall have been

any market value thereof and shall make an order directing the entry of a deficiency judgment. Such deficiency judgment shall be for an amount equal to the sum of the amount owing by the party liable as determined by the judgment with interest, plus the amount owing on all prior liens and encumbrances with interest, plus costs and disbursements of the action including the referee's fee and disbursements, less the market value as determined by the court or the sale price of the property whichever shall be the higher.

3. If no motion for a deficiency judgment shall be made as herein prescribed the proceeds of the sale regardless of amount shall be deemed to be in full satisfaction of the mortgage debt and no right to recover any deficiency in any action or proceeding shall exist. . . .

NOTES AND QUESTIONS

1. **An historical note.** The New York statute both confirms the mortgagee's right to a deficiency and limits the deficiency to the difference between the amount of claim and the "fair and reasonable market value," not to the difference between the amount of claim and the foreclosure sale price. In practically every state the mortgagee may obtain a judgment for a deficiency — usually without benefit of statute. Through the years, however, courts and legislatures have devised methods to protect the debtor from being victimized by superficial bidding at the sale. There are, of course, provisions for the giving of notice, the time, place, manner and terms of conducting the sale. A court of equity may refuse to confirm a sale or may set it aside upon evidence of chilled bidding or upon a showing of inadequacy so gross as to "shock the conscience or raise a presumption of fraud or unfairness." See Ballentyne v. Smith, 205 U.S. 285 (1907). Where foreclosure is by power of sale, the mortgagee is not permitted to buy unless the mortgagor has given his consent or, under some statutes, a public officer conducts the sale. Nearly half the states allow the mortgagor (and junior lienors) to redeem from the foreclosure sale upon payment of the sale price plus specified interest; these *statutory rights to redeem,* dating back to the panic of 1837, were intended to dissuade a perfunctory bid on the theory that too low a price would invite redemption. (Since the redemption period may run six months or longer, redemption may cause the very lackluster interest on the part of potential bidders it was expected to prevent.)

The depression of the 1930s gave new impetus to the effort to protect mortgage debtors, for even in normal times the result of a forced sale does not usually reflect the "reasonable" market value of the property. Some states, like New York, abandoned the sale price as the presumptive measure of fair value and forced the mortgagee who was seeking the deficiency judgment to prove "fair and reasonable market value." Fine in theory, except during the 1930s no market existed. Wrestling with this conundrum, some lower courts went back to pre-depression values, until the New York Court of Appeals held that the statute intended to set up a new "equitable standard" in lieu of market value, in which market transactions, if any, were only one item. See Heiman v. Bishop, 272 N.Y. 83, 4 N.E.2d 944 (1936). The values found on the new test were said to approximate tax assessments. See Friedman, Personal Liability on Mortgage Debts in New York, 51 Yale L.J. 382, 396 (1942).

If property is sold at foreclosure for less than fair market value, the mortgagor, under the New York statute, is not entitled to be reimbursed for the difference between the fair market value and the mortgage debt. Evergreen Bank v. D & P Justin's, Inc., 152 A.D.2d 898, 544 N.Y.S.2d 244 (1989).

2. **Military personnel.** Military personnel are entitled to benefits of The Soldiers' and Sailors' Civil Relief Act of 1940, 50 U.S.C.A. app. §§501-591 (1990). This law tolls the statute of limitations during military service, permits a mortgagor to reopen foreclosure after release from duty on proof of a meritorious defense, and authorizes a court to stay foreclosure or execution on a money judgment. Service personnel must be able to show, however, that military service has "materially affected" their ability to meet their debts or defend actions brought against them. On the Act, see Nelson and Whitman, Real Estate Finance Law §§8.9-8.11 (2d ed. 1985); and Switzer, Mortgage Defaults and the Soldiers' and Sailors' Civil Relief Act: Assigning the Burden of Proof When Applying the Material Effect Test, 18 Real Est. L.J. 171 (1989).

3. **Strict foreclosure.** Deficiency judgments are possible with strict foreclosure, as is illustrated by a Connecticut statute providing for a judicial valuation and deficiency judgment on motion after the time for redemption has expired. Conn. Gen. Stat. Ann. §49-14 (West Supp. 1991).

MID KANSAS FEDERAL S&L v. DYNAMIC DEVELOPMENT CORP.

167 Ariz. 122, 804 P.2d 1310 (1991)

OPINION

FELDMAN, Vice C. J.

A construction lender held notes secured by first and second deeds of trust on a residential developer's property. The lender acquired title to the property at a trustee's sale on the second trust deed and thereafter brought an action against the developer for the balance due on the first notes. The court of appeals held that the lender was precluded from doing so under A.R.S. §33-814(G) [1] and the rationale of our decision in Baker v. Gardner, 160 Ariz. 98, 770 P.2d 766 (1989).

---

1. Then codified as §33-814(E).

We must determine whether the anti-deficiency statutes apply to a residential developer and whether a lender may recover the balance owing on the first notes after it has acquired title to the property at the foreclosure sale of its second deed of trust. Rule 23, Ariz. R. Civ. App. P., 17B A.R.S. We have jurisdiction under Ariz. Const. art. 6, §5(3) and A.R.S. §12-120.24.

Facts and Procedural History

A.   FACTUAL BACKGROUND

Dynamic Development Corporation (Dynamic) is a developer that builds and sells residential and commercial property. In May 1985, Dynamic secured financing from Mid Kansas Federal Savings and Loan Association (Mid Kansas) for the construction of ten "spec" homes on lots Dynamic owned in a Prescott subdivision. The total loan, amounting to $803,250, was disbursed in the form of ten separate loans, each evidenced by a separate note and secured by a separate deed of trust on a single unimproved lot. Unable to complete construction with the amounts financed under the first notes, Dynamic obtained an additional $150,000 loan from Mid Kansas in January of 1986. This loan was evidenced by a single promissory note and a blanket deed of trust on the seven lots remaining unsold.

The first and second notes came due in the summer of 1986. Two more lots were sold and released from the liens. In the fall of 1986, Mid Kansas notified Dynamic that the five remaining properties would be sold at a trustee's sale if the total debt on the first and second notes was not paid. Dynamic was unable to pay the total balance due, but did sell one more lot prior to the trustee's sale and applied the proceeds to the second note.

Mid Kansas noticed a trustee's sale on the four remaining properties, each of which was by then improved by a substantially finished residence. At the time of the trustee's sale, Dynamic owed Mid Kansas approximately $102,000 on the second note and $425,000 on the four first notes. Originally, the sales on the first deeds were scheduled for the day after the sale on the second deed. On January 20, 1987, the second-position blanket deed of trust was foreclosed by the sale of the four parcels. Mid Kansas purchased the property with a credit bid of the balance owed on the second note. The four first-position sales were postponed and ultimately never held. Having thus acquired title to the property, Mid Kansas now seeks to waive the security of the first liens and sue for the balance due on the first notes.

B.   PROCEDURAL BACKGROUND

Mid Kansas's amended complaint stated causes of action for recovery of the balance due under each of the four promissory notes. Mid Kansas moved for partial summary judgment on the four debt claims. The trial court granted the motion and entered judgment for Mid Kansas pursuant to Rule 54(b), Ariz. R. Civ. P., 16 A.R.S.

The court found that Dynamic was in default on the four construction notes in the principal amount of $425,250 plus interest at thirteen percent. The court rejected Dynamic's claim that Mid Kansas had "artificially created a deficiency and now seeks a deficiency judgment against the maker of the notes." The court determined that

> under the holding of Southwest Savings and Loan v. Ludi, 122 Ariz. 226 {594 P.2d 92 (1979)}, Plaintiff can maintain an action on these notes notwithstanding there was a Trustee's Sale instituted by Plaintiff on a separate deed of trust involving the {same} subject properties.

On appeal, Dynamic argued that Mid Kansas was prohibited from recovering on the promissory notes by the Arizona anti-deficiency statute, A.R.S. §33-814(G). After the release of our opinion in *Baker,* Dynamic filed a supplemental brief asserting that *Ludi* could no longer be read to permit a residential mortgage holder to waive its security and sue on the note. See Southwest Sav. & Loan Ass'n v. Ludi, 122 Ariz. 226, 594 P.2d 92 (1979). Dynamic argued that *Baker* prohibited any attempt to waive the security and sue on the note as a disguised action for deficiency. Therefore, Mid Kansas could not both foreclose the second deed by power of sale and elect to sue Dynamic on the first notes covering the same property.

The court of appeals reversed and remanded the case for entry of judgment for Dynamic. Mid Kansas Fed. Sav. & Loan Ass'n v. Dynamic Dev. Corp., 163 Ariz. 233, 787 P.2d 132 (Ct. App. 1989). The court held that under *Baker,* Mid Kansas' attempt to waive the security and sue on the debt was an action for a deficiency, barred after a trustee's sale under §33-814(G). Judge Brooks concurred in the result, but argued that the case should have been decided according to the principles of merger and extinguishment, rather than under the anti-deficiency statute, because he was "not persuaded that a residential developer may claim the statutory protection against deficiency judgments afforded to homeowners under Baker v. Gardner." Id. at 239, 787 P.2d at 138 (Brooks, J., concurring).

Mid Kansas petitioned for review in this court, presenting the following issues for our consideration:

1. Whether commercial developers of residential property who borrow for business purposes are entitled to the benefit of Arizona's consumer anti-deficiency statutes, A.R.S. §§33-729(A) and 33-814(G).
2. Whether Arizona's anti-deficiency statutes apply when the encumbered properties are not actually used as residences.
3. Whether a lender's election to waive its security and sue upon a construction loan note secured by a deed of trust constitutes an action for a deficiency prohibited by Arizona's anti-deficiency statutes, A.R.S. §§33-729(A) and 33-814(G).

Discussion

A.　THE APPLICABILITY OF THE ANTI-DEFICIENCY STATUTES

Arizona has two anti-deficiency statutes. A.R.S. §33-729(A) applies to purchase money mortgages and purchase money deeds of trust foreclosed judicially pursuant to the authority of A.R.S. §33-807(A). A.R.S. §33-814(G) applies to deeds of trust that are foreclosed by trustee's sale, regardless of whether they represent purchase money obligations. Both sections prohibit a deficiency judgment after sale of a parcel of "property of two and one-half acres or less which is limited to and utilized for either a single one-family or single two-family dwelling." A.R.S. §§33-729(A), 33-814(G).

Arizona also has an election of remedies statute within the general law applicable to mortgages. Under A.R.S. §33-722, a mortgagee can foreclose and seek a deficiency judgment or can sue on the note and then execute on the resultant judgment but cannot bring both actions simultaneously. See Washburn, The Judicial and Legislative Response to Price Inadequacy in Mortgage Foreclosure Sales, 53 S. Cal. L. Rev. 843, 928 (1980). The election statute is intended to protect the debtor from multiple suits and at the same time grant the creditor the benefit of the security.

The election statute alters the traditional common law rule that a holder of a note secured by a mortgage has the right to sue on the note alone, to foreclose on the property, or to pursue both remedies at once (although there may be only one recovery on the debt). See Paramount Ins., Inc. v. Rayson & Smitley, 86 Nev. 644, 472 P.2d 530, 533 (1970).[2] However, the reach of the statute, as applied to most mortgages, is quite limited. In Smith v. Mangels, 73 Ariz. 203, 207, 240 P.2d 168, 170 (1952), this court held the election statute does not preclude a subsequent foreclosure action after judgment on the debt, as is the case in some other states. See, e.g., Neb. Rev. Stat. §§25-2140 and 25-2143 (1989); N.Y. Real Prop. Acts. Law §1301 (McKinney 1979); S.D. Codified Laws Ann. §§21-47-5, and 21-47-6 (1987).

In *Baker*, we held the election statute was limited by the subsequently enacted purchase money mortgage anti-deficiency statute, A.R.S. §33-729(A), which barred the lender from waiving the security and suing on the debt. 160 Ariz. at 104, 770 P.2d at 772. In so holding, we joined the courts

---

2. Under the statutory scheme, the provisions within the law of mortgages (chapter 6 of A.R.S. Title 33) are not applicable to deeds of trust unless the deed of trust is judicially foreclosed as a mortgage pursuant to A.R.S. §33-807(A). See A.R.S. §33-805. The election statute is within chapter 6. Therefore, the election statute is not applicable to deeds of trust foreclosed by trustee's sale, and there is no analogous statute within the law applicable to deeds of trust. Dynamic does not contend that the lender lost its common law right to elect among its remedies. See generally Universal Inv. Co. v. Sahara Motor Inn, Inc., 127 Ariz. 213, 215, 619 P.2d 485, 487 (Ct. App. 1980) (deed of trust statute does not mandate foreclosure by trustee's sale, but allows option to foreclose as mortgage or bring action on debt).

of California and North Carolina in finding that such an election is inconsistent with the anti-deficiency statutes, which limit the lender to recovery from the land itself. Id.

Baker held that the lender should not be allowed to circumvent the anti-deficiency statute by electing to sue the debtor on the note, thereby realizing any difference between the value of the real property and the amount owed on the debt. As our supplemental opinion pointed out, *Baker*'s holding applies whenever the anti-deficiency statutes apply and therefore is not always limited to the purchase money situation. 160 Ariz. at 106-07, 770 P.2d at 774-75. Assuming that the deed of trust falls within one of the anti-deficiency statutes, an action for a deficiency is prohibited after a trustee's sale on any deed of trust and after judicial foreclosure on purchase money deeds of trust. See A.R.S. §§33-814(G) and 33-729(A). If a lender holds a non-purchase money deed of trust, he *may* recover a deficiency *if* he does so through an action for judicial foreclosure because A.R.S. §33-729(A) applies only to purchase money liens. In this latter case, of course, the debtor receives the protections of judicial foreclosure, including a statutory redemption right.[3]

Read together, therefore, the statutes enact the following scheme: when the holder of a non-purchase money deed of trust of the type described in A.R.S. 33-814(G) forecloses by non-judicial sale, the statute protects the borrower from a deficiency judgment. The lender therefore may not waive the security and sue on the note. *Baker,* 160 Ariz. at 106, 770 P.2d at 774. The holder may, however, seek to foreclose the deed of trust as if it were a mortgage, as allowed by §33-814(E); if he does so, the debtor is allowed redemption rights under §33-726 and 12-1281 through 12-1289 and is thus protected from low credit bids, but the holder may recover a deficiency judgment — the difference between the balance of the debt and the sale price — unless the note is a purchase money obligation. In the latter case, the borrower is protected by the mortgage anti-deficiency statute, A.R.S. §33-729(A), which applies only to purchase money obligations. *Baker,* 160 Ariz. at 106, 770 P.2d at 774.

---

3. In Arizona, the debtor has no right of statutory redemption after the deed of trust is foreclosed by trustee's sale. A.R.S. §33-811(B). This is also the rule in California, where deficiency judgments are prohibited after foreclosure by trustee's sale. The following comments regarding the California statute inform our discussion of A.R.S. §33-814(G):

> The [statute's] purpose . . . was to put nonjudicial enforcement of a deed of trust on a par with judicial foreclosure and sale. . . . [Prior to its enactment] . . . [c]reditors preferred private sale because it avoided a statutory period of redemption. By exercising the power instead of foreclosing judicially, the creditor could obtain a deficiency judgment as well as the enhanced proceeds of a redemption-free sale. This procedure allowed the creditor to bid in the property himself at an unfairly low price — or offer that opportunity to someone else — secure in the knowledge that any deficiency would be recoverable in a personal judgment against the principal. Comment, Exonerating the Surety: Implications of the California Antideficiency Scheme, 57 Cal. L. Rev. 218, 232 (1969).

Thus, if under *Baker* and the facts of this case Dynamic is protected by an anti-deficiency statute, Mid Kansas could not elect to waive its security and sue on the first notes after having already chosen to proceed by trustee's sale under the second deed of trust.

B. PERSONS AND PROPERTIES INCLUDED WITHIN THE STATUTORY DEFINITIONS

Mid Kansas argues that neither Dynamic, as a developer, nor the property under construction is protected by an anti-deficiency statute. Neither of the statutes is limited to individual homeowners rather than residential developers. Rather, the statutes apparently protect any mortgagor, provided the subject property is a single one- or two-family residential dwelling on two and one-half acres or less.[4]

As we noted in *Baker,* both anti-deficiency statutes were enacted in 1971, along with several other laws designed to protect consumers. 160 Ariz. at 101, 770 P.2d at 769. As with virtually all anti-deficiency statutes, the Arizona provisions were designed to temper the effects of economic recession on mortgagors by precluding "artificial deficiencies resulting from forced sales." Id. (quoting Boyd and Balentine, Arizona's Consumer Legislation: Winning the Battle But . . . , 14 Ariz. L. Rev. 627, 654 (1972)). Anti-deficiency statutes put the burden on the lender or seller to fairly value the property when extending the loan, recognizing that consumers often are not equipped to make such estimations. See generally Spangler v. Memel, 7 Cal. 3d 603, 102 Cal. Rptr. 807, 812-13, 498 P.2d 1055, 1060-61 (1972); Leipziger, Deficiency Judgments in California: The Supreme Court Tries Again, 22 U.C.L.A. Rev. 753, 759-61 (1975). Indeed, the articulated purpose behind A.R.S. §33-729(A) (and presumably behind its deed of trust counterpart, as we held in *Baker*) was to protect "homeowners" from deficiency judgments. See *Baker,* 160 Ariz. at 101, 770 P.2d at 769.

However, absent express limiting language in the statute or explicit evidence of legislative intent, we cannot hold that the statute excludes residential developers. Where the language of a statute is plain and unambiguous, courts must generally follow the text as written. *Mid Kansas,* 163 Ariz.

---

4. The statutes read as follows (relevant portions emphasized):

A.R.S. §33-729(A):

> [I]f a mortgage is given to secure the payment of the balance of the purchase price, or to secure a loan to pay all or part of the purchase price, of *a parcel of real property of two and one-half acres or less which is limited to and utilized for either a single one-family or single two-family dwelling* . . . [there shall be no deficiency judgment] . . .

A.R.S. §33-814(G):

> If *trust property of two and one-half acres or less which is limited to and utilized for either a single one-family or single two-family dwelling* is sold pursuant to the trustee's power of sale, no action may be maintained to recover any difference between the amount obtained by sale and the amount of the indebtedness and any interest, costs and expenses.

at 238, 787 P.2d at 137 (citing State Farm Mut. Ins. Co. v. Agency Rent-A-Car, Inc., 139 Ariz. 201, 203, 677 P.2d 1309, 1311 (Ct. App. 1983); cf. Ritchie v. Grand Canyon Scenic Rides, 165 Ariz. 460, 799 P.2d 801 (1990) (rule inapplicable where it would produce absurd result)). While we can infer that the legislature's primary intent was to protect individual homeowners rather than commercial developers, neither the statutory text nor legislative history evinces an intent to *exclude* any other type of mortgagor.[5] Indeed, the North Carolina Supreme Court decided to apply a similar anti-deficiency statute to a commercial borrower, finding that the statute expressed no intent to exclude commercial transactions and therefore that the court could not read in such an intent. Barnaby v. Boardman, 313 N.C. 565, 330 S.E.2d 600, 603 (1985). Therefore, we hold that so long as the subject properties fit within the statutory definition, the identity of the mortgagor as either a homeowner or developer is irrelevant.

In contrast to the lack of legislative limitation as to the type of mortgagor protected, there is specific textual expression as to the type of property protected. Both statutes require that the property be (1) two and one-half acres or less, (2) limited to and utilized for a dwelling that is (3) single one-family or single two-family in nature. In applying a statute, we have long held that its words are to be given their ordinary meaning, unless the legislature has offered its own definition of the words or it appears from the context that a special meaning was intended. State Tax Comm'n v. Peck, 106 Ariz. 394, 395, 476 P.2d 849, 850 (1970).

A.R.S. §33-814(G) calls for the property to be "limited to" a single one- or two-family dwelling. The word "dwelling" is susceptible to several interpretations, depending on the context of its use. See 28 C.J.S. Dwelling (1941 and 1990 Supp.). However, the principal element in all such definitions is the "purpose or use of a building for human abode," meaning that the structure is wholly or partially occupied by persons lodging therein at night or *intended* for such use. Id.; see also Smith v. Second Church of Christ, Scientist, 87 Ariz. 400, 405, 351 P.2d 1104, 1107 (1960) (defining "dwelling" as "a building suitable for residential purposes").

The anti-deficiency statutes require not only that the property be limited to dwelling purposes, but also that it be "utilized for" such purposes. In Northern Arizona Properties v. Pinetop Properties Group, the court of appeals held that an investment condominium, which was occasionally occupied by the owners and occasionally rented out to third persons, fell within the statutory definition. 151 Ariz. 9, 725 P.2d 501 (Ct. App. 1986). In deciding that the statute applied to a dwelling used for investment purposes and not as the mortgagor's principal residence, the court employed the

---

5. We take notice of the fact that the legislature has included such a limitation in other statutory provisions. For example, A.R.S. §33-806.01(D), which deals with a trustee's right to transfer his interest in trust property, applies only to trust property that is limited to and utilized for dwelling units and that is *not* used for commercial purposes.

definition of "dwelling" in Webster's Ninth New Collegiate Dictionary and in several housing codes as "a shelter . . . in which people live." Hence, although the condominium was held as an investment, it was also used (utilized) as a dwelling. Id. at 12, 725 P.2d at 504.

In contrast to the *Northern Arizona Properties* case, the property in question here had never been used as a dwelling, and was in fact not yet susceptible of being used as a dwelling. There is a difference between property intended for eventual use as a dwelling and property utilized as a dwelling. We hold that commercial residential properties held by the mortgagor for construction and eventual *resale* as dwellings are not within the definition of properties "limited to" and "*utilized* for" single-family dwellings. The property is not utilized as a dwelling when it is unfinished, has never been lived in, and is being held for sale to its first occupant by an owner who has no intent to ever occupy the property. Cf. *Northern Arizona Properties* (mortgagors intended to occupy property occasionally and rent it out).

Therefore, we hold that by its terms, the anti-deficiency statute does not apply to Dynamic in this case and A.R.S. §33-814(G) does not preclude Mid Kansas from waiving its security and bringing a debt action on the notes.[6]

C.   THE DOCTRINE OF MERGER AND EXTINGUISHMENT

Because we hold that the anti-deficiency statute does not apply, we must reach the merger and extinguishment issue that is the basis of the concurring opinion in the court of appeals. Dynamic listed that issue for our consideration under Rule 23(c), Ariz. R. Civ. App. P., 17B A.R.S., as an issue not decided by the court of appeals but that would need to be addressed if the court of appeals' opinion were reversed.[7]

1.   Merger of Estates

As Dynamic has noted, the facts in this case provide the basis for two merger arguments. The first is the theory of merger of estates. Generally, when one person obtains both a greater and a lesser interest in the same

---

6. Because we conclude that Dynamic is not protected by the anti-deficiency statute, we do not reach the issue of whether Mid Kansas's action on the first notes would have constituted an action for deficiency under *Baker* or an action on an "independent obligation" under *Ludi.* In *Ludi,* as in *Baker,* two notes were secured by the same real estate. However, unlike *Baker,* the second note in *Ludi* was given to obtain a home improvement loan and therefore was "independent from" the first note, given to secure a purchase money deed of trust. *Ludi,* 122 Ariz. at 228, 594 P.2d at 94. We note that, in any case, *Ludi* is not in direct conflict with *Baker* because the lender in *Ludi* used a judicial proceeding to foreclose its first deed of trust before bringing an action on the second, non-purchase money obligation. Id. at 227, 594 P.2d at 93.

7. In its response, Dynamic characterizes this issue as one involving unjust enrichment and election of remedies. The doctrine takes into consideration a little of both, but is more properly characterized as merger and extinguishment.

property, and no intermediate interest exists in another person, a merger occurs and the lesser interest is extinguished. 3 R. Powell, The Law of Real Property §459 (1990 Rev.). Thus, merger may occur when a mortgagee's interest and the fee title are owned by the same person. Id. The potential for merger arises whenever a mortgagee acquires the mortgagor's equity of redemption. However, even if a merger would otherwise occur at law, contrary intent or equitable considerations may preclude this result under appropriate circumstances. 2 L. Jones, The Law of Mortgages §1080 (8th ed. 1928). This court has long recognized these general rules of merger of estates. Bowman v. Cook, 101 Ariz. 366, 419 P.2d 723 (1966); Hathaway v. Neal, 31 Ariz. 155, 251 P. 173 (1926).

We assume, therefore, no one arguing to the contrary, that when Mid Kansas acquired title on the foreclosure of its *second* lien, its rights under *that* lien were merged in the title. See *Bowman*, 101 Ariz. at 367, 419 P.2d at 724. The question before us, however, is somewhat different. Today we must consider if Mid Kansas's rights under the *first* lien were affected when it acquired title by foreclosure on its *second* lien.

2. Merger of Rights

Where the same mortgagee holds both a first and second mortgage on the mortgagor's land, and becomes the purchaser at the foreclosure sale of one of the mortgages, the question of merger of *rights* — often called extinguishment — arises. The merger of rights doctrine addresses the narrow question of whether the mortgagor's personal liability on the senior debt has been discharged. Wright v. Anderson, 62 S.D. 444, 253 N.W. 484, 487 (1934). The primary issue in the doctrine of merger of rights is whether the lender would be unjustly enriched if he were permitted to enforce the debt. See generally Burkhart, Freeing Mortgages of Merger, 40 Vand. L. Rev. 283, 382 (1987).

Although the mortgagee's purchase of the property at the foreclosure of the senior mortgage will not extinguish the debt secured by a junior mortgage, the reverse is true where the junior mortgage is foreclosed. If one holding both junior and senior mortgages forecloses the junior and purchases the property at the foreclosure sale, the long-standing rule is that, absent a contrary agreement, the mortgagor's personal liability for the debt secured by the first mortgage is extinguished. G. Nelson & D. Whitman, Real Estate Finance Law §6.16, at 467 (2d ed. 1985). The rule has been followed for generations. . . .

The basis of the merger of rights doctrine is that the purchaser at a foreclosure sale of a junior lien takes subject to all senior liens. *Ren-Cen Club*, 377 N.W.2d at 434; *Wright*, 253 N.W. at 487; see also Burkhart, supra, 40 Vand. L. Rev. at 377. Although the purchaser does not become personally liable on the senior debt (as does an assuming grantee), the purchaser must pay it to avoid the risk of losing his newly acquired land to foreclosure by the senior lienholder. Therefore, the land becomes the primary fund for the senior debt, and the purchaser is presumed to have deducted the amount of the senior liens from the amount he bids for the land. *Tri-County Bank,* 449 N.W.2d at 541.[8] As the court in *Wright* explained, when the same mortgagee holds both the junior and senior mortgages on the land and buys at the foreclosure sale of the junior mortgage:

> The mortgagor . . . has an equitable right to have the land pay the mortgage before his personal liability is called upon and the purchaser will not be permitted to retain the land . . . and enforce the same against the mortgagor personally.

253 N.W. at 487. Similarly, the court in *Ren-Cen Club* noted that

> [t]he indebtedness will be presumed to have been discharged so soon as the holder of it becomes invested with title to the land upon which it is charged, on the principle that a party may not sue himself at law or in equity. The purchaser is presumed to have bought the land at its value, less the amount of indebtedness secured thereon, and equity will not permit him to hold the land and still collect the debt from the mortgagor.

377 N.W.2d at 435 (quoting Belleville Savings Bank v. Reis, 136 Ill. 242, 26 N.E. 646, 647 (1891) (citations omitted)).

Thus, the merger of rights doctrine holds that the senior lien is merged into — or extinguished by — the title acquired by the lienholder when he acquires the mortgagor's equity of redemption under a sale on the junior lien. Of course, this rule comes into play only when the equity of redemption is extinguished. See *Wright,* 253 N.W. at 487; 2 Jones, supra, §1080, at 514. Although the deed of trust is a relatively new instrument that postdates cases such as *Wright* and *Belleville,* we find the doctrine of merger and extinguishment even more compelling under a modern deed of trust statute, which cuts off the borrower's equity of redemption at the time of the trustee's sale. See A.R.S. §33-811(B). In Patton v. First Federal Savings & Loan Ass'n, we commented on the unique features of the deed of trust that required a strict construction in favor of the borrower:

> Compared to mortgage requirements, the Deed of Trust procedures authorized by statute make it far easier for lenders to forfeit the borrower's interest in the real estate securing a loan, and also abrogate the right of redemption after sale guaranteed under a mortgage foreclosure. . . . [U]nder a Deed of Trust, the trustee holds a power of sale permitting him to sell the property out of court with no necessity of judicial action. The Deed of Trust statutes thus strip borrowers of many of the protections available under a mortgage. There-

---

8. In a transfer "subject to" the senior mortgage, the essence of the transaction is that "the transferee agrees, as between her and her transferor, that the debt is to be satisfied out of the land." Nelson & Whitman, supra, §5.3, at 271.

fore, lenders must strictly comply with the Deed of Trust statutes, and the statutes and Deeds of Trust must be strictly construed in favor of the borrower.

118 Ariz. 473, 477, 578 P.2d 152, 156 (1978).

As we have previously noted, even where a merger would otherwise occur at law, an express agreement between the parties that no merger shall occur often precludes such a finding by the court. Nelson & Whitman, supra, §6.16, at 467 (citing Toston v. Utah Mortgage Loan Co., 115 F.2d 560 (C.C.A. Idaho 1940); Continental Title & Trust Co. v. Devlin, 209 Pa. 380, 58 A. 843 (1904); Van Woerden v. Union Improvement Co., 156 Wash. 555, 287 P. 870 (1930)). Of course, where the mortgagee acquires title to the property through an involuntary conveyance, such as foreclosure, the parties obviously will not have formed a mutual intent concerning the continued enforceability of the debt. Burkhart, supra, 40 Vand. L. Rev. at 377.

However, such an intent may be implied under circumstances that would make a finding of merger inequitable to the parties. The dissent in *Wright*, for instance, argued that where the mortgagee paid the full value of the property without deducting the amount of the prior lien, the rule of merger should not apply. 253 N.W. at 489 (Polley, J., dissenting). This argument was adopted by a recent decision that allowed a bank to retain its claim for the unsecured deficiency remaining on the first mortgage even though the bank purchased the property at the foreclosure sale on the second mortgage. In re Richardson, 48 B.R. 141 (Bkrtcy. E.D. Tenn. 1985). The court found that the bank had not tried to take unfair advantage of the debtor because its bid had reflected the value of the property and the bank had, in addition, credited the debtors with the amount beyond the bid it received on reselling the property. Id. at 142. A different result would obtain where the mortgagee is permitted to keep land that is worth as much as the two mortgage debts and also allowed to collect on the senior debt. In the latter situation, the mortgagee would be unjustly enriched, and the merger doctrine is appropriately applied to destroy the senior debt. Nelson & Whitman, supra, §6.16, at 467-68.

The facts in this case clearly illustrate and require application of the doctrine of merger and extinguishment; they also demonstrate that no equitable exception is appropriate here. Mid Kansas held the four first deeds of trust and the second blanket deed of trust on the four lots. Mid Kansas purchased all four pieces of property with a credit bid of the amount due on the second lien, $101,986.67. Mid Kansas thus acquired free and clear title to improved property apparently worth between $555,750 and $608,000.[9] Even accepting the lower figure, it is apparent that the sum of

9. The value of the properties, as listed on the IRS Statements of Acquisition or Abandonment of Secured Property filed by Mid Kansas, totalled $555,750. Mid Kansas submitted appraisals to the trial court estimating the value of the lots, if completed in accordance with the plans and specifications, at $608,000. Ironically, the IRS statements filed by Mid Kansas stated that the "borrower was not personally liable for repayment of the debt," although Mid Kansas attributes this to "clerical error" and has since "corrected" the forms.

the junior and senior liens ($527,236.67 — exclusive of interest and costs) on the property at the relevant time — the date of the foreclosure sale — was probably less than the value of the property. Mid Kansas obviously tendered a credit bid that was discounted by the amount of the senior liens. Therefore, Mid Kansas would be unjustly enriched were we to allow it to acquire, for $100,000, property worth over $500,000 and also sue Dynamic for another $400,000 under the first notes. Mid Kansas does not contend that the property it acquired was worth less than the total owed on the first and second liens.

On these facts, we hold that the doctrine of merger and extinguishment applies. . . .

CONCLUSION

The anti-deficiency statute, A.R.S. §33-814(G), does not apply to Dynamic in this case because the homes under construction were not utilized for single-family dwellings. We vacate the court of appeals' opinion and reverse the trial court's judgment. The case is remanded to the trial court for proceedings consistent with this opinion. On remand, the parties will have the opportunity to present evidence as to the value of the property at the time of the foreclosure sale. If the facts are as they appear on this record, equity will require no exception to the doctrine of merger and extinguishment. If Dynamic prevails, it will be eligible for its attorney's fees subject to Rule 21, Ariz. R. Civ. App. P., 17B A.R.S.

NOTES AND QUESTIONS

1. **The argument against mortgagor protection.** An argument against such mortgagor protection laws as antideficiency and postforeclosure statutes is that these laws appreciably increase the cost of mortgage money to home buyers. See, for example, Meador, The Effects of Mortgage Laws on Home Mortgage Rates, 34 J. Econ. & Bus. 143 (1982). A subsequent study, however, concludes that from its data this cost increase is so limited as not to be statistically significant. Schill, An Economic Analysis of Mortgagor Protection Laws, 77 Va. L. Rev. 489, 500-515 (1991). Professor Schill advances the further argument in support of antideficiency and postforeclosure redemption laws that these laws function as a desired and desirable form of insurance for mortgagors. He concludes: "Mortgagors, especially those who live in states with volatile economies, may place a high value on mortgagor protections, such as an entitlement to be free from personal liability, the ability to remain in possession of the property during the foreclosure and redemption periods, or the ability to repurchase their homes within a certain period after the foreclosure sale." Id. at 500. He goes on to assert that mortgagor protection laws may also advance economic efficiency by reducing homebuying risks and increasing optimal levels of housing con-

sumption. However, he adds, these laws should be narrowed to cover only those in need of protection — homebuyers and perhaps small businesses.

Referring to some of the more restrictive antideficiency legislation, the Powell treatise states: "[This legislation] is a recognition of the modern shift from viewing the mortgage as a personal relationship predicated upon acquaintance and the believed solvency of the borrower, to seeing it as an investment device largely handled by corporations. It is to be hoped that more states will enact similar statutes." 3 Powell on Real Property §473 (1991). Do you agree that more states should enact legislation restricting mortgagees' rights to deficiency judgments?

2. **The argument for mortgagor protection.** For arguments strongly opposing unlimited deficiency liability of home mortgage borrowers following foreclosure and also proposing a statutory limit on such liability of 5 percent of the amount of debt owing at the time of foreclosure, see Mixon, Deficiency Judgments Following Home Mortgage Foreclosure: An Anachronism That Increases Personal Tragedy, Impedes Regional Economic Recovery, and Means Little to Lenders, 22 Texas Tech L. Rev. 1 (1991). Professor Mixon is especially concerned with the deficiency laws of Texas, but much of what he has to say is relevant to other states as well. He, of course, favors section 511(b) of the Uniform Land Security Interest Act providing that after foreclosure of a mortgage on property bought for individual use as a personal residence "there is no liability for a deficiency, notwithstanding any agreement." See Mixon and Shepard, Antideficiency Relief for Foreclosed Homeowners: ULSIA Section 511(b), 27 Wake Forest L. Rev. 455 (1992).

3. **The nonrecourse mortgage loan.** Many loans for large amounts on income-producing properties, such as office buildings, often are nonrecourse. If a mortgage loan is nonrecourse, this means that the lender, in case of default, can obtain recovery of amounts due only from the security and may not sue the mortgagor on the underlying debt or seek a deficiency judgment against the mortgagor if the full amount due is not recovered in a foreclosure. In a nonrecourse mortgage loan, the lender is relying on income from the property rather than other income and assets of the borrower as the source of payment on the loan. The mortgage note may signify a nonrecourse loan by such language as "the borrower is not personally liable on this loan," or "in case of default, the lender shall have recourse only against the property secured by the mortgage."

3.   Postforeclosure Redemption Rights

In about half the states, statutes provide for redemption after foreclosure for a period, varying among the states, from six months to two years. These postforeclosure rights are often referred to as statutory redemption and are to be distinguished from preforeclosure equity of redemption rights. Those entitled to redeem after foreclosure include junior lienors as well as mortgagors and their successors. In most states the mortgagor has the right to possession during the period in which redemption is permitted. The amount that must be paid to redeem is usually the foreclosure sale price plus the expenses of foreclosure. Priorities exist for the right to redeem if more than one person has redemption rights, the mortgagor normally having the highest priority.

If a mortgagor or his successor redeems, junior liens are often considered to be revived. If a junior lienor redeems, he acquires the rights of the foreclosure sale purchaser and this interest can become a full title if no one with superior redemption rights redeems by the close of the redemption period. However, as illustrated by First Vermont Bank & Trust Co. v. Kalomiris, 138 Vt. 491, 418 A.2d 43 (1980), this is not true everywhere, and it may be necessary for the redeeming junior lienor to foreclose separately the mortgagor's interest in order to terminate all rights of the mortgagor.

The usual arguments in favor of postforeclosure redemption rights are that they tend to encourage higher prices for property when sold at foreclosure sale and to act as a corrective when foreclosure sale prices are inadequate in relation to real value. Also, these statutes can be of major benefit to mortgagors in temporary financial difficulties, such as farmers in a bad crop year. Among arguments against such statutes are that they increase the cost of the foreclosure process, including expensive delays to purchasers at foreclosure sale in obtaining possession and marketable title, and that postforeclosure redemption rights are unnecessary because infrequently exercised.[23]

---

23. A recent empirical study of postforeclosure redemption rights in two Iowa counties indicates that postforeclosure redemptions may occur more frequently than generally supposed and hence that price inadequacy in foreclosure sales may rather commonly exist. See Bauer, Statutory Redemption Reconsidered: The Operation of Iowa's Redemption Statute in Two Iowa Counties Between 1881 and 1980, 70 Iowa L. Rev. 343 (1985).

Table of Cases

Index